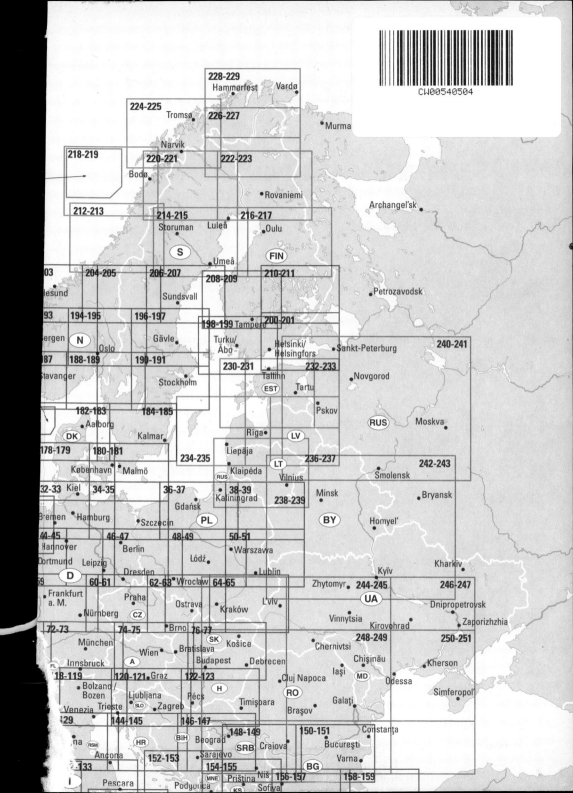

CW00540504

228-229
Hammerfest • Vardø

224-225
Tromsø

226-227

Murma

218-219

Narvik

220-221

222-223

Bodø

• Rovaniemi

Archangel'sk

212-213

214-215
Storuman

216-217
Luleå

• Oulu

S

• Umeå

FIN

03

204-205

206-207

208-209

210-211

Petrozavodsk

lesund

Sundsvall

93

194-195

196-197

198-199 Tampere

200-201

240-241

ergen

N

Gävle •

Oslo

Turku/
Åbo

Helsínki/
Helsingfors

• Sankt-Peterburg

187

188-189

190-191

230-231

232-233

Novgorod

tavanger

Stockholm

Tallinn

• Tartu

EST

182-183
Aalborg

184-185

Rīga •

LV

Pskov

RUS

Moskva

DK

Kalmar •

178-179

180-181

Liepāja

234-235

236-237

242-243

København •

Malmö

RUS Klaipėda

Smolensk

32-33 Kiel

34-35

36-37

38-39
Kaliningrad

Vilnius

LT

Minsk

Bryansk

Bremen • Hamburg

Gdańsk

238-239

BY

• Szczecin

PL

Homyel'

44-45
Hannover

46-47
Berlin

48-49

50-51
• Warszawa

Dortmund Leipzig

Lódź

Kharkiv

D

Dresden

Wrocław 64-65

Lublin

Kyïv

59

60-61

62-63

Zhytomyr

244-245

246-247

• Frankfurt
a. M.

Praha

Ostrava

L'vIv

UA

Dnipropetrovsk

• Nürnberg

CZ

Kraków

Vinnytsia

Kirovohrad

Zaporizhzhia

72-73

74-75

Brno 76-77

248-249

250-251

München

SK Košice

Chernivtsi

Chişinău

Kherson

FL Innsbruck

A

Wien •

Bratislava

Debrecen

Iaşi

MD

Odessa

18-119

120-121 Graz

122-123

Cluj Napoca

• Bolzano /
Bozen

Ljubljana

Pécs

H

RO

Simferopol'

Venezia Trieste

SLO Zagreb

Timişoara

Galaţi

29

144-145

146-147

Braşov

Constanţa

na RSM

HR

BiH Beograd

148-149

150-151

Bucureşti

Ancona

SRB Craiova

Varna •

133

152-153

154-155

Sarajevo

BG

Pescara

Podgorica

MNE Priština Niš

156-157

158-159

KS Sofiya

2nd edition December 2008

© Istituto Geografico De Agostini, Novara and
© Automobile Association Developments Limited

Original edition January 2004

Enabled by [OS Ordnance Survey] This product includes mapping data licensed from Ordnance Survey® with the permission of the Controller of Her Majesty's Stationery Office.
© Crown copyright 2008
All rights reserved. Licence number 100021153

This atlas includes Northern Ireland mapping. This material is based upon Crown Copyright and is reproduced with the permission of Land and Property Services under delegated authority from the Controller of Her Majesty's Stationery Office, © Crown copyright and database rights LA59. Permit. No. 80047

© Ordnance Survey Ireland/Government of Ireland Copyright Permit No. MP000108

Published by Istituto Geografico De Agostini, Novara and Automobile Association Developments Limited whose registered office is Fanum House, Basing View, Basingstoke, Hampshire RG21 4EA, UK. Registered number 1878835

ISBN: 978 0 7495 5644 0

A CIP catalogue record for this book is available from The British Library.

Printed in Italy by DEAPRINTING-Novara 2008

The contents of this atlas are believed to be correct at the time of the latest revision. However, the publishers cannot be held responsible for loss occasioned to any person acting or refraining from action as a result of any material in this atlas, nor for any errors, omissions or changes in such material. This does not affect your statutory rights.

DRIVER'S ATLAS
ATLANTE STRADALE
ATLAS DE CARRETERAS
ATLAS ROUTIER
STRASSENATLAS

EUROPE
EUROPA

CONTENTS • SOMMARIO • SUMARIO
SOMMAIRE • INHALTSVERZEICHNIS

Legend - Legenda - Leyenda Légende - Zeichenerklärung	2-3
Road network - Rete stradale Red de carreteras - Réseau routier Straßennetz	4-7
Road distances - Distanze stradali Distancias kilométricas - Distances routières Straßenentfernungen	8-9
Road atlas - Atlante stradale Atlas de carreteras - Atlas routier Straßenatlas	10-251
Index of names - Indice dei nomi Índice de topónimos - Index des noms Namenverzeichnis	252-360

GB

I

GB	I	
Toll-free motorway, dual carriageway	Autostrada senza pedaggio a doppia	
Toll-free motorway, single carriageway	Autostrada senza pedaggio a singola carreggiata	
Toll motorway, dual carriageway	Autostrada a pedaggio a doppia carreggiata	
Toll motorway, single carriageway	Autostrada a pedaggio a singola carreggiata	
Interchange; restricted interchange; service area	Svincolo; svincolo con limitazione; area di servizio	
Motorway under construction (opening year)	Autostrada in costruzione (anno di apertura)	2010
Motorway in tunnel	Autostrada in galleria	
Number of motorway; european road; national road; regional or local road	Numero di autostrada; itinerario europeo; strada nazionale; strada regionale o locale	A11 E50 N13 D951
National road, dual carriageway	Strada nazionale a doppia carreggiata	
National road, single carriageway	Strada nazionale a singola carreggiata	
Regional road, dual carriageway	Strada regionale a doppia carreggiata	
Regional road, single carriageway	Strada regionale a singola carreggiata	
Local road, dual carriageway	Strada locale a doppia carreggiata	
Local road, single carriageway	Strada locale a singola carreggiata	
Secondary road	Strada secondaria	
Road under construction (opening year)	Strada in costruzione (anno di apertura)	2010
Road in tunnel	Strada in galleria	
Motorway distances in kilometres (miles in United Kingdom and Ireland)	Distanze in chilometri (miglia nel Regno Unito e Irlanda) sulle autostrade	63
Road distances in kilometres (miles in United Kingdom and Ireland)	Distanze in chilometri (miglia nel Regno Unito e Irlanda) sulle strade	23
Gradient 14% and over; gradient 6%–13%	Pendenza maggiore del 14%; pendenza dal 6% al 13%	
Panoramic routes	Percorsi panoramici	
Pass with height and winter closure	Passo di montagna, quota e periodo di chiusura invernale	Col d'Izoard 2360 10-6
Toll point	Barriera di pedaggio	
Railway and tunnel	Ferrovia e tunnel ferroviario	
Ferry route (with car transportation) and destination	Linea di traghetto (con trasporto auto) e destinazione	Bastia
Transport of cars by rail	Trasporto auto per ferrovia	
National park, natural reserve	Parco nazionale, riserva naturale	
International boundaries	Confini internazionali	
Disputed boundary; internal boundary	Confine in contestazione; confine interno	
International airport	Aeroporto internazionale	⊕
Religious building; Castle, fortress	Edificio religioso; Castello, fortezza	
Isolated monument	Monumento isolato	
Ruins, archaeological area; wall	Rovine, area archeologica; vallo, muraglia	
Cave; natural curiosity	Grotta; curiosità naturale	
Panoramic view	Punto panoramico	
Other curiosities (botanical garden, zoo, amusement park etc.)	Altre curiosità (giardino botanico, zoo, parco divertimenti ecc.)	★
Town or place of great tourist interest	Città o luogo di grande interesse turistico	**LONDON**
Interesting town or place	Città o luogo interessante	**RAVENNA**
Other tourist town or place	Altra città o luogo turistico	MONTPELLIER
Ski resort, mountain tourist resort	Stazione sciistica o di turismo montano	**Zermatt**

E	F	D
Autopista de doble vía sin peaje	Autoroute sans péage à chaussées séparées	Zweibahnige Autobahn ohne Gebühr
Autopista de una vía sin peaje	Autoroute sans péage à chaussée unique	Einbahnige Autobahn ohne Gebühr
Autopista de doble vía de peaje	Autoroute à péage à chaussées séparées	Zweibahnige Autobahn mit Gebühr
Autopista de una vía de peaje	Autoroute à péage à chaussée unique	Einbahnige Autobahn mit Gebühr
Acceso; acceso parcial; estación de servicio	Échangeur; échangeur partiel; aire de service	Anschlussstelle; Autobahnein- und/oder -ausfahrt; Tankstelle
Autopista en construcción (año de apertura)	Autoroute en construction (année d'ouverture)	Autobahn in Bau (Fertigstellungsjahr)
Túnel en autopista	Tunnel autoroutier	Autobahntunnel
Número de autopista; carretera europea; carretera nacional; carretera regional o local	Numéro d'autoroute; route européenne; route nationale; route régionale ou locale	Straßennummer: Autobahn; Europastraße; Nationalstraße; Regional- oder Lokalstraße
Carretera nacional de doble vía	Route nationale à chaussées séparées	Zweibahnige Nationalstraße
Carretera nacional de vía unica	Route nationale à chaussée unique	Einbahnige Nationalstraße
Carretera regional de doble vía	Route régionale à chaussées séparées	Zweibahnige Regionalstraße
Carretera regional de vía unica	Route régionale à chaussée unique	Einbahnige Regionalstraße
Carretera local de doble vía	Route locale à chaussées séparées	Zweibahnige Lokalstraße
Carretera local de vía unica	Route locale à chaussée unique	Einbahnige Lokalstraße
Carretera secundaria	Route secondaire	Nebenstraße
Carretera en construcción (año de apertura)	Route en construction (année d'ouverture)	Straße in Bau (Fertigstellungsjahr)
Túnel en carretera	Tunnel routier	Straßentunnel
Distancias en kilómetros (millas en Gran Bretaña e Irlanda) en autopista	Distances autoroutières en kilomètres (miles en Royaume-Uni et Irlande)	Autobahnentfernungen in Kilometern (Meilen in Großbritannien und Irland)
Distancias en kilómetros (millas en Gran Bretaña e Irlanda) en carretera	Distances routières en kilomètres (miles en Royaume-Uni et Irlande)	Straßenentfernungen in Kilometern (Meilen in Großbritannien und Irland)
Pendientes superiores al 14%; pendientes entre 6%–13%	Pente 14% et outre; pente 6%–13%	Steigungen über 14%; Steigungen 6%–13%
Rutas panorámicas	Routes panoramiques	Aussichtsstraßen
Puerto de montaña con altura y cierre invernal	Col avec altitude et fermeture en hiver	Pass mit Höhe und Wintersperre
Peaje	Barrière de péage	Gebührenstelle
Ferrocarril y túnel	Chemin de fer et tunnel	Eisenbahn und Tunnel
Línea marítima (con transporte de coches) y destino	Ligne de navigation (bac pour voitures) et destination	Schiffahrtslinie (Autofähre) und Ziel
Transporte de coches por ferrocarril	Transport de voitures par chemin de fer	Autoverladung per Bahn
Parque nacional, reserva natural	Parc national, réserve naturelle	Nationalpark, Naturschutzgebiet
Límites internacionales	Frontières internationales	Staatsgrenzen
Frontera en disputa; límite interno	Frontière en contestation; frontière intérieure	Strittige Grenze; Verwaltungsgrenze
Aeropuerto internacional	Aéroport international	Internationaler Flughafen
Edificio religioso; Castillo, fortaleza	Édifice religieux; Château, château-fort	Religiösgebäude; Schloss, Festung
Monumento aislado	Monument isolé	Alleinstehendes Denkmal
Ruinas, zona arqueológica; muralla	Ruines, site archéologique; vallum, muraille	Ruinen, archäologisches Ausgrabungsgebiet; Wall, Mauer
Cueva; paraje de interés natural	Grotte; curiosité naturelle	Höhle; Natursehenswürdigkeit
Vista panorámica	Vue panoramique	Rundblick
Otras curiosidades (jardín botánico, zoo, parque de atracciones etc.)	Autres curiosités (jardin botanique, zoo, parc d'attractions etc.)	Andere Sehenswürdigkeiten (Botanischer Garten, Zoo, Freizeitpark usw.)
Ciudad o lugar de gran interés turístico	Localité ou site de grand intérêt touristique	Ortschaft oder Platz von großem touristischen Interesse
Ciudad o lugar interesante	Localité ou site remarquable	Sehenswerte Ortschaft oder Platz
Otra ciudad o lugar turístico	Autre localité ou site touristique	Andere touristischen Ortschaft oder Platz
Estación de esquí, localidad turística de montaña	Station de ski, localité touristique de montagne	Skistation, Touristenort in den Bergen

LEGEND - SEGNI CONVENZIONALI - LEYENDA - LÉGENDE - ZEICHENERKLÄRUNG

Nations with toll motorway and toll-controlled link roads
requiring a pre-paid permit or "vignette"
Paesi con autostrade e collegamenti stradali a pedaggio
mediante pre-pagamento di un contrassegno o "vignetta"
Pays con autopistas y carreteras de peaje mediante prepago
de un sello acreditativo o "viñeta"
Pays avec autoroutes et liaisons routières à péage
par système de vignette
Länder mit gebührenpflichtigen Autobahnen und
Straßenverbindungen (Vignettenpflicht)

Main toll roads, tunnels, bridges etc.
Principali strade, gallerie, ponti ecc. a pedaggio
Principales carreteras, túneles, puentes etc. de peaje
Principales routes, tunnels, ponts etc. à péage
Wichtigste gebührenpflichtige Straßen, Tunnels, Brücken usw.

Toll-free motorway and road with motorway characteristics
Autostrade e superstrade senza pedaggio
Autopistas y autovías sin peaje
Autoroutes et routes de type autoroutier sans péage
Gebührenfreie Autobahnen und autobahnähnliche Straßen

Toll motorway and toll-controlled link road
Autostrade e collegamenti stradali a pedaggio
Autopistas y carreteras de peaje
Autoroutes et liaisons routières à péage
Gebührenpflichtige Autobahnen und Straßenverbindungen

Other roads
Altre strade
Otras carreteras
Autres routes
Sonstige Straßen

Road number
Numero di strada
Número de carretera
Numéro de route
Straßennummer
E15
M1

Distances in kilometres
Distanze in chilometri
Distancias en kilómetros
Distances en kilomètres
Distanzen in Kilometern
169

Standard Time Zones from Greenwich time (GMT/UTC)
Fusi orari rispetto al tempo medio di Greenwich
Husos Horarios a partir de la hora de Greenwich
Fuseaux horaires à partir de l'heure de Greenwich
Das weltzeitsystem von Greenwich
0 +1 +2 +3

Distances in Great Britain and Ireland are expressed in miles.
Nel Regno Unito e in Irlanda le distanze sono espresse in miglia.
Las distancias en Gran Bretaña e Irlanda son expresas en millas.
Les distances en Grande-Bretagne et Irlande sont exprimées en miles.
Entfernungsangaben in Großbritannien und Irland sind in Meilen wiedergegeben.

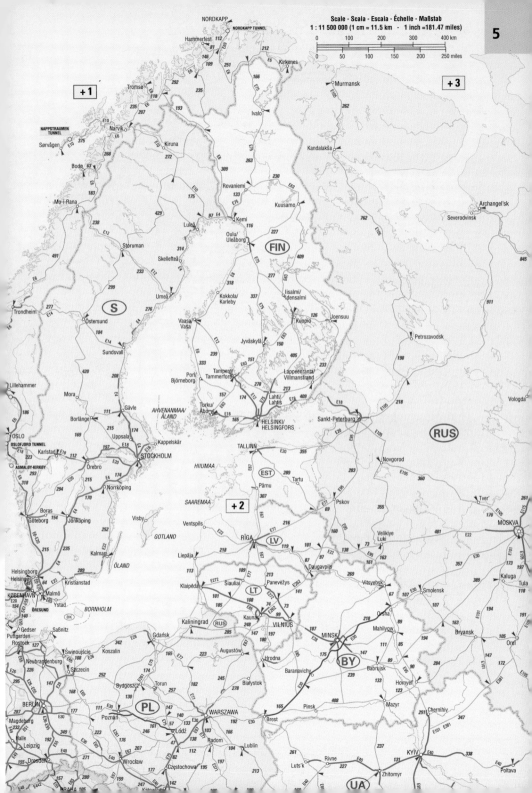

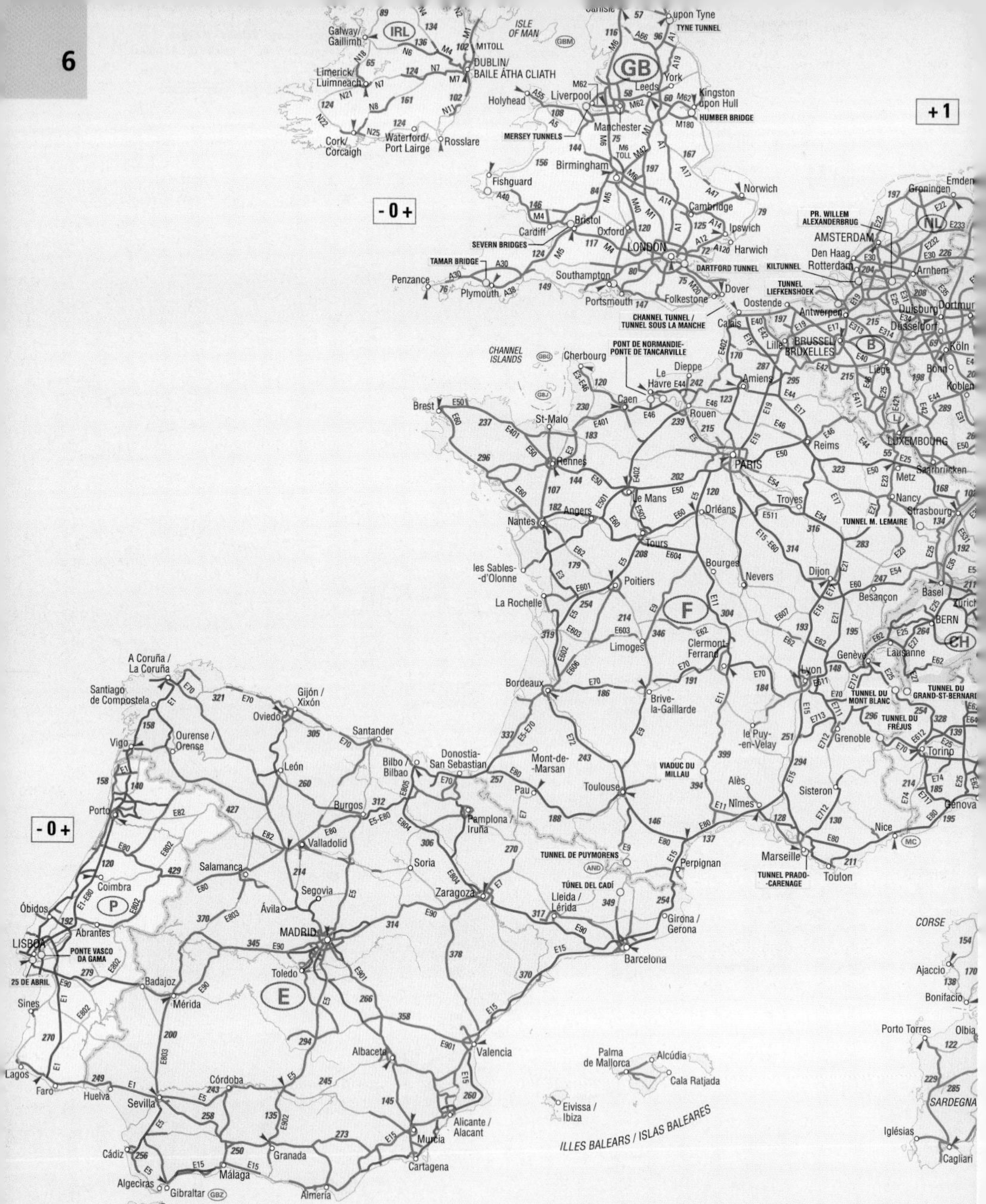
IRL
Galway/
Gaillimh
Limerick/
Luimneach
Cork/
Corcaigh
Waterford/
Port Lairge
Rosslare
DUBLIN/
BAILE ÁTHA CLIATH
ISLE
OF MAN
GBM
GB
upon Tyne
TYNE TUNNEL
York
Leeds
Kingston
upon Hull
HUMBER BRIDGE
Holyhead
Liverpool
Manchester
MERSEY TUNNELS
Birmingham
Norwich
Fishguard
Cambridge
Ipswich
Harwich
Cardiff
Bristol
Oxford
SEVERN BRIDGES
LONDON
DARTFORD TUNNEL
TAMAR BRIDGE
Penzance
Plymouth
Southampton
Portsmouth
Folkestone
Dover
CHANNEL TUNNEL /
TUNNEL SOUS LA MANCHE
-0+
+1
Groningen
Emden
NL
PR. WILLEM
ALEXANDERBRUG
AMSTERDAM
Den Haag
Rotterdam
KILTUNNEL
Arnhem
TUNNEL
LIEFKENSHOEK
Oostende
Antwerpen
Duisburg
Dortmund
Düsseldorf
Calais
Lille
BRUSSEL
BRUXELLES
B
Liège
Köln
Bonn
Koblenz
CHANNEL
ISLANDS
GBG
GBJ
Cherbourg
PONT DE NORMANDIE-
PONTE DE TANCARVILLE
Le
Havre
Dieppe
Amiens
Brest
Caen
Rouen
St-Malo
LUXEMBOURG
L
Reims
PARIS
Saarbrücken
Metz
Rennes
Le Mans
Orléans
Troyes
Nancy
Strasbourg
TUNNEL M. LEMAIRE
Nantes
Angers
Tours
Bourges
Nevers
Dijon
Besançon
Basel
Zürich
BERN
CH
les Sables-
-d'Olonne
Poitiers
La Rochelle
F
Limoges
Clermont-
Ferrand
Genève
Lausanne
Lyon
TUNNEL DU
MONT BLANC
TUNNEL DU
GRAND-ST-BERNARD
TUNNEL DU
FRÉJUS
Bordeaux
Brive-
la-Gaillarde
le Puy-
en-Velay
Grenoble
Torino
A Coruña /
La Coruña
Santiago
de Compostela
Gijón /
Xixón
Oviedo
Santander
Ourense /
Orense
Vigo
León
Bilbo /
Bilbao
Donostia-
San Sebastian
Mont-de-
-Marsan
Pau
Toulouse
VIADUC DU
MILLAU
Alès
Nîmes
Sisteron
Genova
Porto
Burgos
Pamplona /
Iruña
Nice
MC
-0+
Valladolid
Soria
TUNNEL DE PUYMORENS
AND
Perpignan
Marseille
TUNNEL PRADO-
-CARENAGE
Toulon
Coimbra
Salamanca
Segovia
Zaragoza
TÚNEL DEL CADÍ
Lleida /
Lérida
P
Óbidos
Ávila
Girona /
Gerona
CORSE
Abrantes
LISBOA
PONTE VASCO
DA GAMA
MADRID
Barcelona
25 DE ABRIL
Toledo
Ajaccio
Bonifacio
Badajoz
Mérida
E
Sines
Porto Torres
Olbia
Valencia
Albacete
Palma
de Mallorca
Alcúdia
Cala Ratjada
Lagos
Faro
Huelva
Sevilla
Córdoba
SARDEGNA
Eivissa /
Ibiza
Alicante /
Alacant
Murcia
Iglésias
Cádiz
Granada
Cartagena
ILLES BALEARS / ISLAS BALEARES
Cagliari
Algeciras
Gibraltar
GBZ
Málaga
Almería
Ceuta
Melilla

Frankfurt am Main-Ljubljana = 803 km

	Amsterdam	Athina	Barcelona	Belfast	Beograd	Berlin	Bern	Birmingham	Bordeaux	Bratislava	Brussel/Bruxelles	Bucureşti	Budapest	Dublin	Edinburgh	Frankfurt am Main	Genève	Göteborg	Hamburg	Helsinki/Helsingfors	İstanbul	København	Köln	Kyïv	Lisboa	Ljubljana	London	Luxembourg	Madrid
Athina	2885																												
Barcelona	1549	2224																											
Belfast	1213	3025	2229																										
Beograd	1779	1044	1981	2712																									
Berlin	655	2362	1863	1768	1257																								
Bern	835	1674	944	1687	1363	922																							
Birmingham	372	2730	1691	525	2290	1297	1166																						
Bordeaux	1081	2365	552	1702	2007	1634	852	1161																					
Bratislava	1225	1618	1866	2226	571	671	938	1704	1854																				
Brussel/Bruxelles	206	2783	1344	1032	1673	763	637	514	883	1181																			
Bucureşti	2181	1106	2597	3209	619	1646	1893	2692	2613	977	2136																		
Budapest	1398	1429	1897	2390	377	864	1111	1873	2020	194	1353	826																	
Dublin	641	3027	1944	164	2587	1594	1466	304	1483	2015	814	2989	2181																
Edinburgh	1190	3243	2160	250	2802	1810	1571	460	1698	2231	1030	3205	2396	416															
Frankfurt am Main	445	2396	1323	1434	1281	550	423	917	1150	788	400	1744	961	1207	1429														
Genève	908	1635	778	1653	1331	1119	165	1136	687	1088	706	1946	1261	1426	1648	573													
Göteborg	1178	2924	2602	1381	1810	535	1684	905	2252	1248	1307	2258	1440	1056	1050	1270	1837												
Hamburg	463	2776	1763	1592	1547	294	910	1074	1489	985	591	1961	1178	1364	697	487	1059	503											
Helsinki/Helsingfors	1839	3347	3203	1520	2226	1046	2195	1599	2728	1631	1870	2070	1760	1535	1448	1781	2348	636	1014										
İstanbul	2747	1092	2913	3680	935	2179	2294	3212	2929	1509	2605	681	1320	3452	3675	2213	2261	2778	2493	3208									
København	920	2767	2220	2053	1664	390	1378	1535	1927	1100	1048	2110	1292	1686	2048	955	1528	316	355	827	2630								
Köln	265	2578	1342	1251	1464	575	585	734	1062	972	208	1928	1145	1024	1258	192	735	1141	425	1696	2396	882							
Kyïv	2111	1994	3093	3224	1322	1378	2190	2707	2988	1251	2123	888	1123	2996	3219	1874	2340	2037	1675	1338	1569	1883	1935						
Lisboa	2244	3399	1237	2869	3188	2797	2074	2352	1198	3067	2082	3804	3103	2641	2864	2340	1915	3442	2670	3899	4119	3117	2250	4187					
Ljubljana	1241	1572	1455	2223	530	999	836	1170	1471	435	1153	1146	443	1996	2218	803	802	1490	1202	2119	1462	1346	987	1565	2628				
London	442	2910	1450	708	2039	1090	947	193	989	1521	320	2495	1687	480	645	720	905	743	898	1723	2964	1538	539	2369	2153	1496			
Luxembourg	363	2355	1149	1246	1469	762	431	728	946	1010	213	2086	1183	1018	1233	240	500	1432	610	1928	2483	1130	188	2072	2102	956	529		
Madrid	1773	3369	614	2397	2573	2343	1535	1879	706	2458	1591	3206	2489	2169	2392	1849	1374	2901	2134	3425	3556	2631	1735	3598	619	2046	1509	1615	
	661	3415	1794	406	2374	1425	1282	138	1333	1865	664	2837	2031	214	339	1064	1240	1053	1242	1501	3309	1677	876	2706	2497	1838	323	888	2068
	1236	2306	505	1906	1526	1541	623	1388	647	1419	1034	2141	1441	1678	1881	1003	422	2243	1442	2797	2500	1965	1025	2542	1662	999	1172	832	1096
	1077	656	977	1128	1033	350	1391	985	919	876	642	942	1700	1891	662	318	1525	1112	2442	1990	1574	823	2037	2134	499	1178	669	1568	
	1742	2448	2878	2856	1513	1124	1938	2338	2714	1178	1850	1341	1125	2628	2833	1620	2205	1654	1408	783	1997	1510	1662	567	3927	1593	2163	1817	3574
	2449	2864	3584	3559	2084	1830	2644	3042	3420	1885	2556	1809	1854	3331	3539	2326	2933	1503	2114	1089	2471	1694	2368	871	4489	2300	2874	2523	4277
	827	1990	1370	3426	947	585	437	1297	1278	466	739	1564	639	1588	1792	390	591	1083	789	2058	1909	1242	573	1718	2452	407	1074	521	1961
	1852	592	1555	2704	1161	1693	1132	2166	1698	1376	1628	1240	1399	2477	2666	1444	1085	2664	1908	3174	1414	2370	1000	2492	2712	935	1953	1442	2146
	1532	3221	2790	823	2109	834	1981	902	2514	1547	1618	2557	1739	838	753	1567	2134	298	802	700	3077	613	1446	2336	3686	1789	1026	1714	3217
	508	2895	1039	1128	1800	1068	565	610	583	1324	312	2396	1489	900	1113	573	529	1626	887	2718	2778	1365	488	2428	1736	1240	470	373	1290
	2087	3242	1076	2712	2986	2637	1916	2195	1000	2889	1893	3602	2902	2484	2696	2153	1758	3249	2450	3752	3971	2908	2072	3997	300	2459	1824	1930	531
	887	1946	1709	1952	900	341	769	1435	1601	328	902	1304	522	1725	1923	510	965	912	645	1865	1860	764	693	1362	2687	664	1222	731	2219
	1618	2807	2825	2849	1917	996	1971	2257	2704	1333	1784	1760	1408	2621	2763	1527	2137	779	1273	309	2402	1276	1537	1029	3803	1748	2050	1799	3396
	1654	895	1354	2516	985	1493	932	1968	1503	1175	1457	1433	1198	2288	2468	1243	884	2466	1710	2977	1603	2181	1405	2294	2514	755	1755	1244	1945
	2180	3190	3388	3507	2241	1558	2546	2831	3279	1809	2360	2116	1842	3339	3339	2127	2712	827	1488	380	2748	1018	2157	1196	4164	2223	2619	2375	4225
	1727	1121	1990	3102	303	1523	1372	2246	2007	849	1737	824	577	2535	2704	1290	1350	2079	1691	2568	1173	1881	1554	1601	3160	539	2006	1478	2603
	2236	3340	998	2863	2957	2838	1922	2343	1183	2842	2057	3573	2935	2636	2858	2345	1759	3469	2662	3980	4073	3119	2255	3991	403	2430	1974	2228	510
	2139	654	2402	3136	424	1668	1783	2619	2418	998	2143	598	800	2908	3115	1702	1750	2210	2098	2648	781	2062	1961	1530	3567	951	2413	1890	2993
	2159	735	2358	3092	380	1624	1739	2615	2375	954	2099	372	756	2864	3071	1714	1707	2166	2054	2604	582	2018	1917	1310	3523	907	2369	1846	2949
	1580	3246	2935	1354	2155	879	2029	1433	2562	1593	1704	2603	1785	1369	1292	1615	2182	470	848	166	3123	661	1530	1338	3733	1835	1557	1762	3259
	1920	3347	3127	3175	2226	1310	2284	2608	3017	1631	2097	2070	1760	2947	3036	1829	2450	470	1085	0	3208	661	1595	1338	4105	2119	2380	2076	3749
	2333	516	2507	3088	619	1862	1978	2854	2613	1193	2338	696	1001	3109	3310	1953	1945	2434	2293	2848	646	2286	2156	1608	3499	1145	2608	2085	3188
	2103	735	1805	3244	566	1888	1748	2702	2383	1211	2058	886	1014	3016	3210	1842	1715	2484	2182	2963	1053	2336	2045	1755	3572	915	2497	1979	2957
	3004	4692	4371	2199	3914	2663	3619	3772	4153	3264	3330	4280	3460	2479	2199	3205	3772	1914	2710	1361	4074	2247	3121	2719	5324	3530	3567	3352	4855
	1897	2565	351	2501	2322	2202	1283	1983	803	2206	1681	2937	2285	2273	2482	1663	1123	2908	2151	3449	3299	2630	1721	3341	894	1795	1629	1492	342
	1636	2550	2776	2841	1487	1018	1948	2263	2654	1077	1756	1401	1121	2613	2727	1518	2114	1639	1280	596	2044	1491	1555	738	3821	1492	2023	1803	3325
	1202	2097	2342	2317	1158	584	1519	1799	2225	643	1309	1240	788	2089	2293	1084	1685	1115	868	970	2119	967	1121	774	3387	1057	1594	1320	2910
	1148	1664	1789	2162	614	676	861	1644	1777	77	1104	1022	240	1938	2154	711	1011	1318	936	1697	1576	1166	895	1328	2990	378	1444	933	2381
	1326	1435	1586	2326	405	1101	968	1843	1603	417	1328	1014	347	2098	2302	943	936	1592	1279	2131	1358	1444	1145	1403	2751	135	1594	1074	2194

Ferry routes; average crossing time
Traghetti; tempi medi di percorrenza
Carroferrils; tiempo medio de travesía
Lignes de navigation; temps moyen de traversée
Schiffahrtslinien; mittlere Fahrzeit der Überfahrt

Newcastle upon Tyne (GB) - Stavanger (N) 17h 30m
Belfast (NIR) - Stranraer (GB) 2h 30m
Dublin (IRL) - Liverpool (GB) 6h 10m
Kingston upon Hull (GB) - Rotterdam (NL) 9h 50m
Harwich (GB) - Esbjerg (DK) 17h 10m
Folkestone (GB) - Calais (F) 0h 40m (Channel Tunnel)
Stockholm (S) - Tallinn (EST) 11h 30m
Stockholm (S) - Turku (FIN) 8h 30m
Tallinn (EST) - Helsinki (FIN) 2h 20m
Rostock (D) - Trelleborg (S) 4h 20m
Rostock (D) - Gedser (DK) 1h 30m
Puttgarden (D) - Rødbyhavn (DK) 0h 40m
Ancona (I) - Zadar (HR) 4h 50m
Ancona (I) - Durrës (AL) 15h 10m
Bari (I) - Durrës (AL) 9h 0m
Brindisi (I) - Vlorë (AL) 6h 0m
Brindisi (I) - Igoumenitsa (GR) 10h 15m
Brindisi (I) - Pátra (GR) 15h 30m

Distances (in kilometres) are calculated by the shortest or quickest route
and should be considered to be approximate.
The calculation does not include any part of the journey taken by car ferry or by rail
(in these cases distances are in red).

Le distanze sono calcolate sui percorsi più veloci o più brevi e sono da ritenersi indicative.
Nel conteggio chilometrico non sono incluse le eventuali tratte marittime o su ferrovia
(in questi casi le distanze sono in rosso).

Las distancias están calculadas según los itinerarios más cortos o rápidos y son aproximadas.
En el cálculo kilométrico no están incluidas las eventuales rutas marítimas o ferroviarias
(en estos casos, las distancias están marcadas en rojo).

Les distances sont calculées sur les itinéraires les plus brefs ou rapides et ne sont donc qu'approximatives.
Dans le comptage kilométrique ne sont pas comprises les éventuelles traversées maritimes ou ferroviaires
(dans ces cases, les distances sont marquées en rouge).

Die Entfernungen sind auf den küfrzesten oder schnellsten Routen berechnet und sind als approximativ zu halten.
In der kilometrischen Berechnung sind die eventuellen See- oder Bahnverbindungen nicht inbegriffen
(in diesen Fällen sind die Entfernungen in rot dargestellt).

Manchester	Marseille	Milano	Minsk	Moskva	München	Napoli	Oslo	Paris	Porto	Praha	Riga	Roma	Sankt-Peterburg	Sarajevo	Sevilla	Skopje	Sofiya	Stockholm	Tallinn	Thessaloniki	Tiranë	Tromsø	Valencia	Vilnius	Warszawa	Wien	Zagreb
1510																											
1515	520																										
2469	2660	2048																									
3180	3372	2755	704																								
1411	1030	558	1524	2231																							
2290	1099	779	2534	3240	1109																						
804	2566	2229	1946	1568	1382	2960																					
737	774	849	2144	2861	830	1611	1937																				
2313	1514	1981	3724	4430	2316	2559	3506	1589																			
1560	1389	937	1149	1855	375	1483	1211	1031	2533																		
2387	2575	2147	472	931	1548	2707	844	2136	3601	1260																	
2092	898	578	2333	3090	908	220	2763	1417	2358	1281	2456																
2950	3151	2723	891	701	2227	3164	892	2644	4235	1816	562	2963															
2344	1534	1034	1713	2426	958	891	2328	1779	3030	1046	1980	778	2392														
2462	1485	1952	3853	4559	2346	2530	3690	1771	650	2717	3802	2329	4441	3000													
2751	1946	1446	1934	2356	1370	603	2509	2191	3406	1324	2187	791	2632	456	3377												
2707	1902	1402	1713	2202	1326	823	2465	2147	3363	1281	2155	1011	2455	601	3333	255											
1335	2631	2276	783	1089	1892	3008	535	2012	3586	1257	309	2811	357	2374	3814	2555	2511										
2717	2856	2352	783	1089	1899	3015	535	2378	4064	1865	309	2817	357	2568	4216	2648	2604	0									
2946	2141	1416	1997	2500	1565	788	2730	2385	3631	1519	2381	976	2740	686	3572	228	284	2779	2848								
2835	1910	929	1939	2616	1334	406	2780	2246	3395	1422	2417	494	2768	385	3342	288	514	2874	2829	393							
1502	4221	3867	2442	4297	3482	4598	1616	3585	5176	2817	1904	4401	1502	3941	5319	4331	4210	1595	1595	4447	4477						
2112	849	1316	3217	4012	1710	1895	3205	1375	879	2048	3210	1694	3728	2328	644	2743	2712	3283	3521	2936	2174	4843					
2361	2552	1947	181	863	1424	2432	1131	2030	3674	1095	291	2231	713	1692	3843	1911	1756	596	596	2104	2111	3221					
1931	2123	1513	541	1247	990	1998	1410	1596	3245	666	661	1838	1148	1259	3413	1476	1433	1460	970	1774	1659	3041	2792	435			
1788	1342	842	1255	1962	389	1299	1624	1247	2812	285	1371	1098	1886	816	2765	1043	999	1663	1700	1237	1225	3266	2129	1154	730		
1932	1130	632	1472	2203	554	706	1891	1391	2621	645	1730	593	2205	400	2562	815	771	1937	2131	1008	862	3612	1941	1519	1039	359	

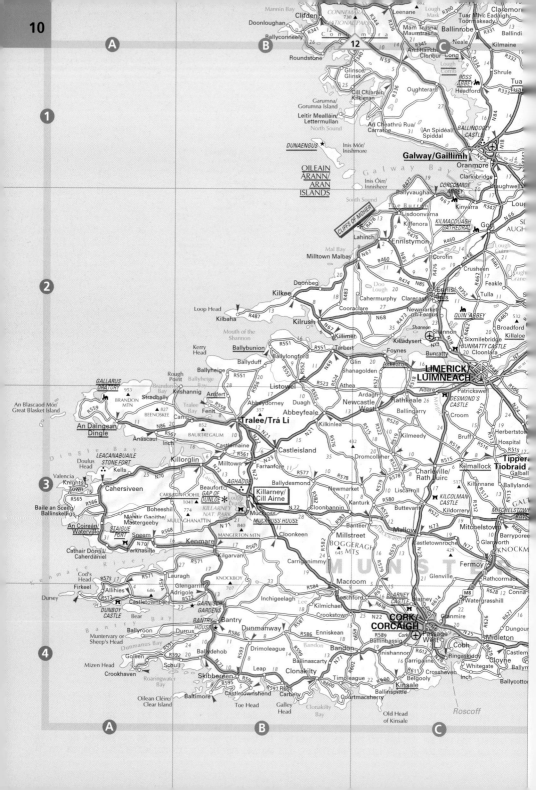

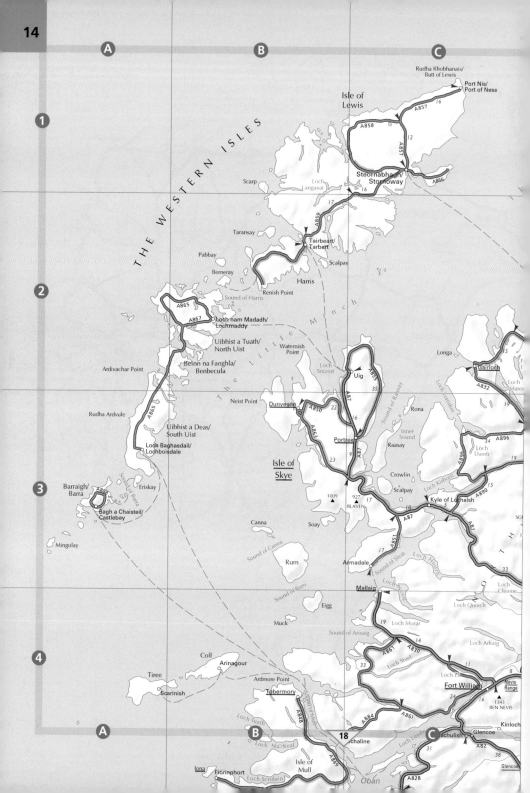

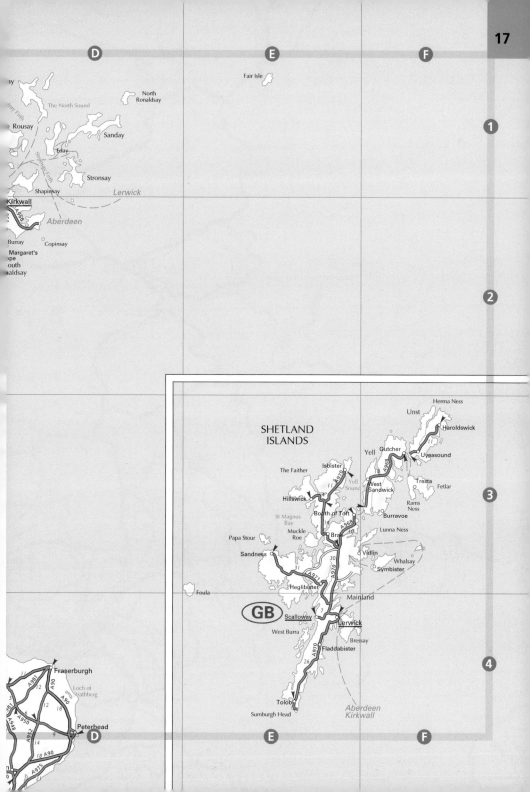

D   E   F

Fair Isle

North
Ronaldsay

The North Sound

Rousay

Sanday

Eday

Stronsay

Shapinsay

Lerwick

Kirkwall

Aberdeen

Burray   Copinsay

Margaret's
ope
outh
aldsay

1

2

SHETLAND
ISLANDS

Herma Ness

Unst

Haroldswick

Yell   Gutcher

Uyeasound

The Faither   Isbister

West
Sandwick

Tresta   Fetlar

Hillswick

Yell
Sound

Rams
Ness

3

Booth of Toft

Burravoe

St Magnus
Bay

Brae

A968

Lunna Ness

Papa Stour

Muckle
Roe

Sandness

Vidlin

Whalsay

Symbister

Foula

30

A971

31

Heglibister

A970

Mainland

GB

Scalloway

Lerwick

West Burra

Bressay

Fraserburgh

A981

A90

Loch of
Strathbeg

A970

Fladdabister

26

A950

A90

4

Tolob

Sumburgh Head

Aberdeen
Kirkwall

Peterhead

A975

A90

D   E   F

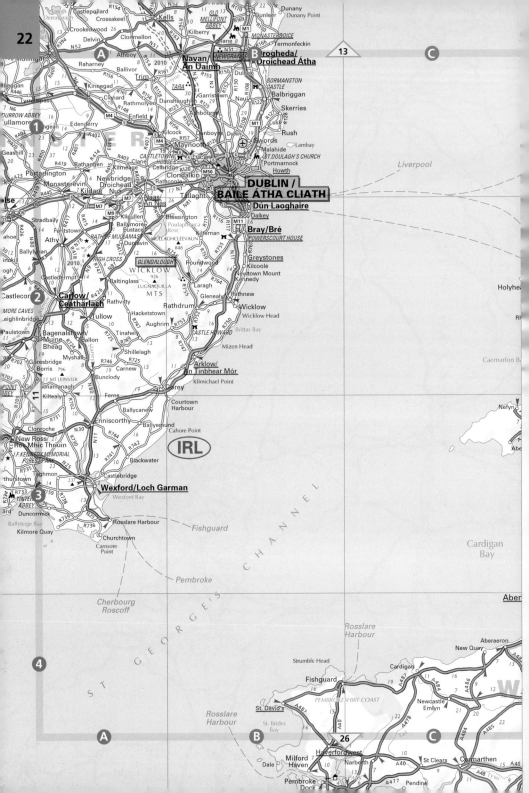

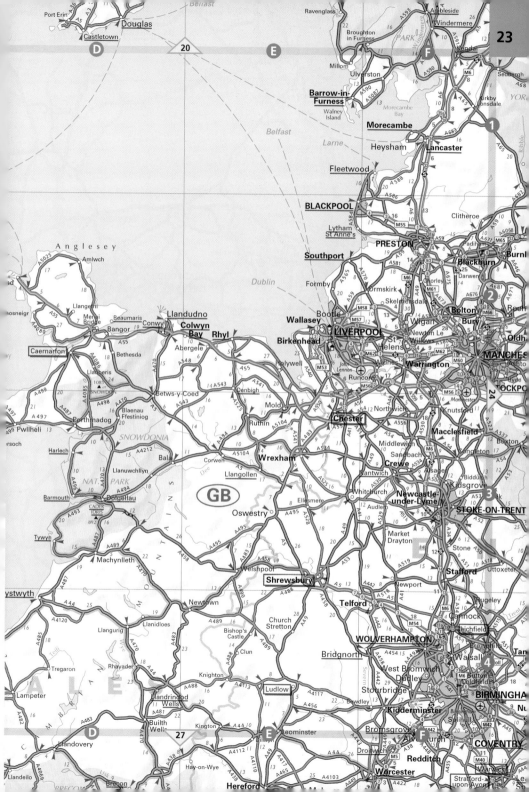

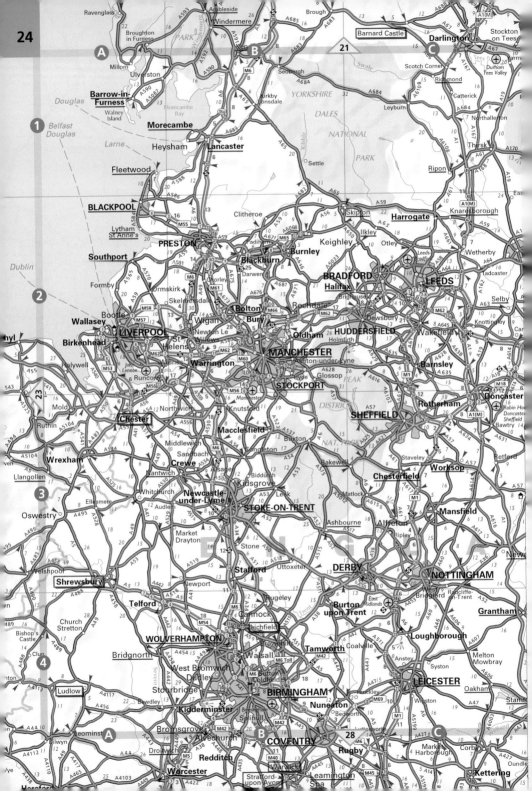

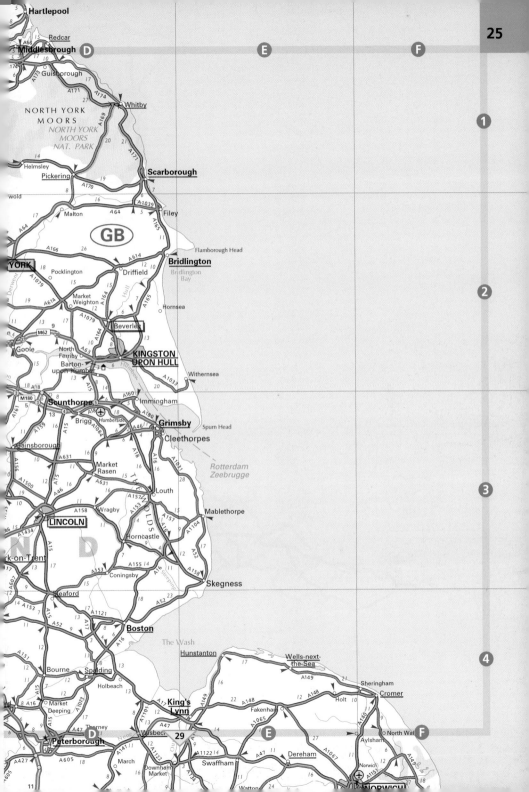

A   B   C

1

2

3

4

SŁOWIŃSKI PARK NARODOWY

Białogóra Karwia Jastrzębia NADMORSKI PARK KRAJOBRAZOWY
Wierzchucino 213 Władysławowo
Łeba Ulinia Krokowa 213 Swarzewo
Choczewo Mierzyno Puck Celbowo Zatoka Pucka

Jezioro Gardno Jezioro Łebsko
Kluki Stęknica Żelazna Wielka Piaśnica
Rowy Smołdzino Wicko Zamostne Bolszewo Reda

Ustka Objazda Gabino Żelkowo Główczyce Nowa Wieś Lęborska Godętowo Wejherowo Rumia

Jarosławiec Wicie Lubuczewo Damno Lębork TRÓJMIEJSKI PARK KRAJOBRAZOWY GDYNIA
Drozdowo Postomino Słupsk Mianowice Osowo Lęborskie Kolęczkowo Sopot
Darłówko Kanin Rędzikowo Lupawa Oskowo Lębno Chwaszczyno
Dąbki Darłowo Staniewice Warszkowo Dębnica Kaszubska Czarna Dąbrówka Sierakowice Przodkowo Miszewo Rębiechowo
Łazy Bukowo Morskie Małechowo Sławno Korzybie Budowo Kartuzy Kolbudy Górne Egiertowo
Mielno Jezioro Jamno Ostrowiec Barcino Suchorze Unichowo Jasień Kłukowa Huta Żukowo A1
Niemica Krąg Kępice Kołczygłowy Pomysk Wielki Sulęczyno WIEŻYCA Sobowidz
Koszalin Sianów Laski Borzysław Łubno Bytów Nowa Karczma Trzepowo Godziszewo
Biesiekierz Mostowo Jacinki Mzdowo Tuchomie Półczno Korne Kościerzyna Skarszewy
Niedalino Radew Polanów Dretyń Udorpie Lipusz Swarożyn
Białogard Rosnowo Głodowo Piaszczyna Studzienice Dziemiany Wdzydze Starogard Gdański
Byszyno Wełdkowo Bobolice Miastko Lipnica Wiele WDZYDZKI PARK KRAJOBRAZ. Bytonia Zblewo Pelplin
Tychowo Drzewiany Upiłka ZABORSKI PARK KRAJOBRAZOWY Borzechowo Lubichowo
Stare Dębno Wierzchowo Biały Bór Koczała Zielona Chocina Osowo Leśne Ocypel
Kołacz Grzmiąca Brzezie Konarzyny Swornegacie Męcikał Czarna Woda Wda Skórcz
Barwice Gwda Wielka Przechlewo Brusy PL Osieczna Luby Osiek
Szczecinek Rzeczenica Rytel PARK NAR. BORY TUCHOLSKIE Czersk B O R Y
Jelenino Czarne Człuchów Charzykowy Chojnice Legbąd Śliwice TUCHOLSKI PARK KRAJOBR. Tleń Osie Warlubie
Łubowo Lotyń Barkowo Silno Tuchola TUCHOLSKI PARK KRAJOBR. Lniano Ostrowite Dolna Grupa
Czaplinek Borne Sulinowo Okonek Debrzno Zamarte Kamień Krajeński Pamiętowo Laskowice
Złocieniec Machliny Ledyczek Lipka Lutowo Gostycyn Bisław
Podgaje Radawnica Obodowo Świecie
Iłowiec Jastrowie Górzna Sępólno Krajeńskie Mąkowarsko Tuszyny Chełmno
Sośnica Byszki Złotów Sypniewo Więcbork Łowinek Sztlno
Kłębowiec Szwecja Rudna Wierzchucin Królewski Koronowo Pruszcz Papowo Bisku...
Bronikowo Płytnica Krajenka Zbrachlin Dobrcz Bielczyny
Wałcz Skórka Łobżenica Mrocza Tryszczyn Unisław Wybcz
Tuczno Gostomia Wysoka Kosztowo Sadki Ostromecko Łubianka Łysomice
Businowo Piła Wyrzysk Nakło nad Notecią BYDGOSZCZ Brzoza
Szydłowo Śmiłowo Paterek Solec Kujawski TORUŃ
Czop Trzcianka Ujście Studzienki Smogulec Rynarzewo Szubin
Siedlisko Szamocin Kcynia Łabiszyn Inowrocław
Czarnków Chodzież Margonin Gołańcz Morakowo Barcin Gniewkowo Aleksandrów Kujaw...
Sarbia Budzyń Pawłowo Żońskie Złotniki Kujawskie Murczyn
Lubasz Przybychowo Damasławek Znin 48 Pakość Tupadły
Krucz Wągrowiec Janowiec Wielkopolski Biskupin Kruszwica
Klempicz Połajewo Rogóźno Mieścisko Rogowo Dąbrowa
Rzecin Piotrowo Ludomy SIERAKOWSKI PARK KRAJOBR.
Wronki Dąbrówka Leśna Skoki

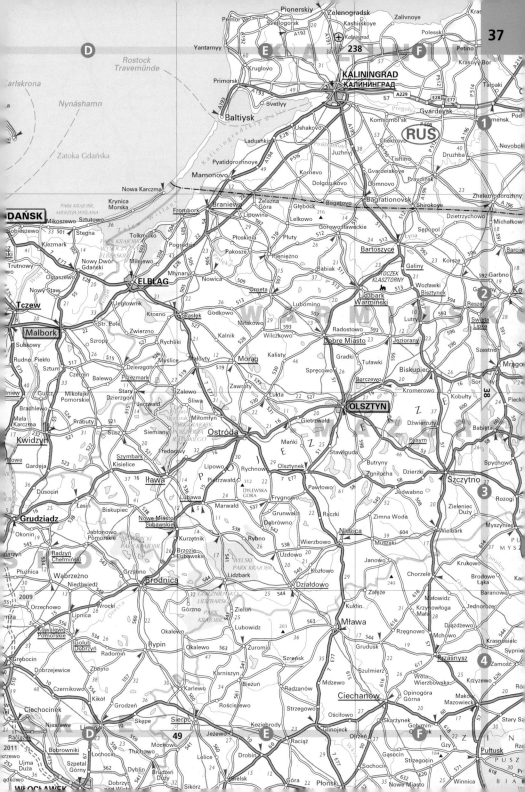

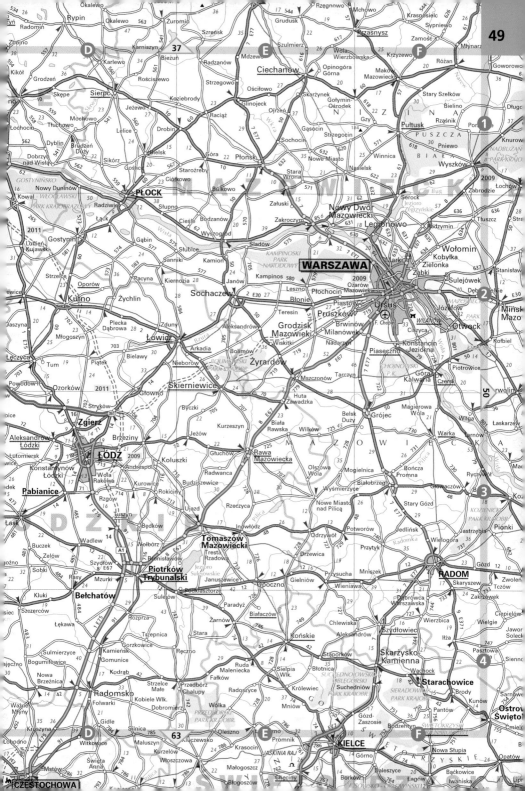

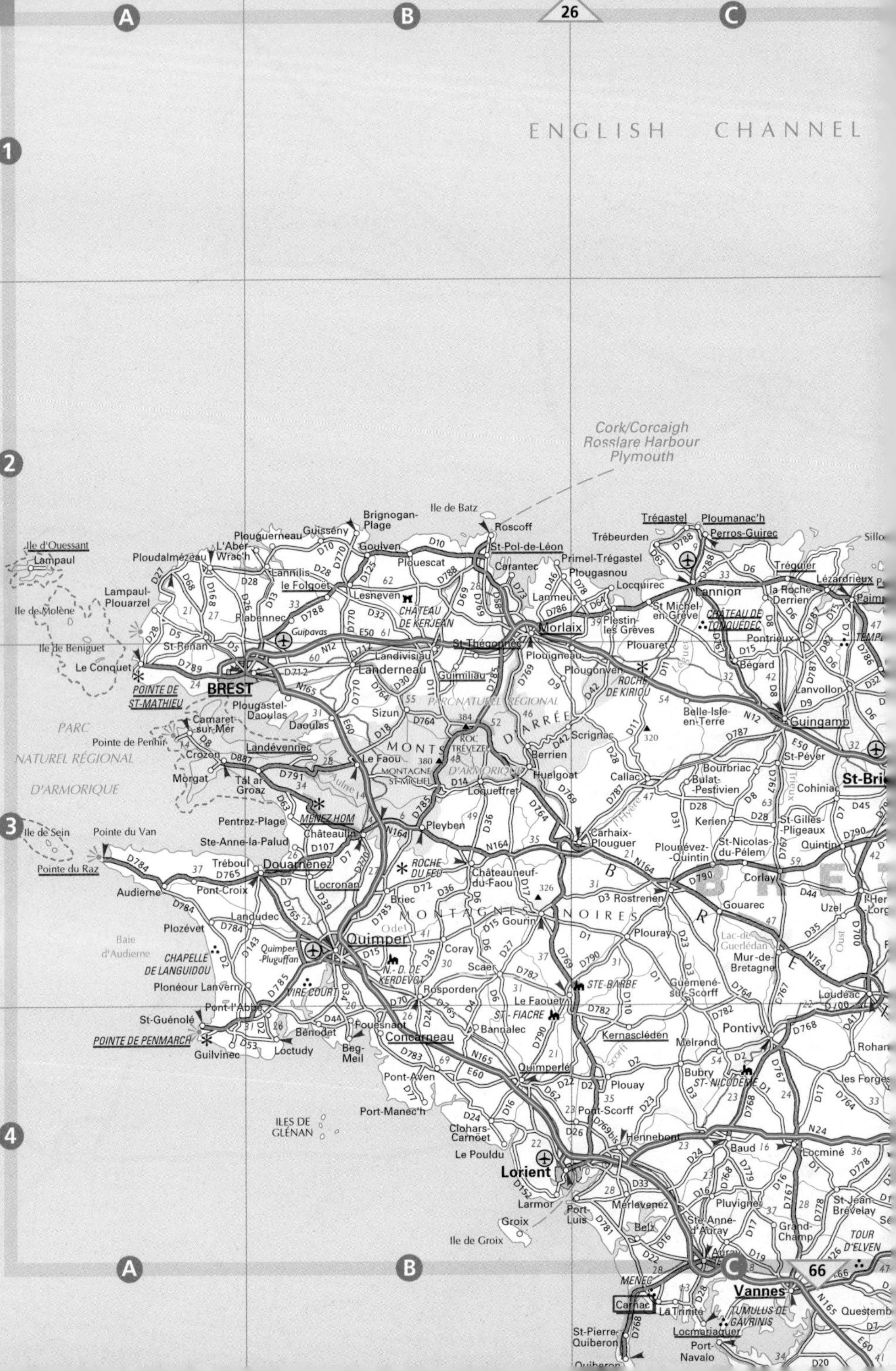

A   B   26   C

ENGLISH CHANNEL

1

2

Cork/Corcaigh
Rosslare Harbour
Plymouth

Île d'Ouessant
Lampaul

Île de Molène

Île de Beniguet

Le Conquet

POINTE DE
ST-MATHIEU

PARC

NATUREL RÉGIONAL

D'ARMORIQUE

Ploudalmézeau
L'Aber-Wrac'h
Lannilis
le Folgoët
Plabennec
Guipavas
St-Renan

BREST

Plougastel-Daoulas
Daoulas

Camaret-sur-Mer
Pointe de Penhir
Crozon
Landévennec
Morgat
Tál ar Groaz
D'887

Plouguerneau
Guissény
Brignogan-Plage
Goulven
Plouescat
Lesneven

CHÂTEAU DE KERJEAN

Landivisiau
Landerneau
Sizun

Guimiliau

MONTS

Le Faou

Île de Batz
Roscoff
St-Pol-de-Léon
Carantec
Primel-Trégastel
Plougasnou
Locquirec
Lanmeur

Morlaix

St-Thégonnec
Plounéour

D'ARRÉE

ROC TRÉVEZEL
MONTAGNE
D'ARMORIQUE
ST-MICHEL
Berrien
Huelgoat
Loqueffret

Trégastel
Ploumanac'h
Perros-Guirec
Trébeurden
St-Michel-en-Grève
Plestin-les-Grèves
Plouaret

Tréguier
Lézardrieux
la Roche-Derrien

CHÂTEAU DE
TONQUÉDEC

Lannion

ROCHE DE KIRIOU

Pontrieux
Bégard
Balle-Isle-en-Terre

Lanvollon

Guingamp

St-Péver
St-Brieuc

Bourbriac
Bulat-Pestivien
Callac
Kerien
Carhaix-Plouguer
Plounévez-Quintin
St-Nicolas-du-Pélem
Corlay
Cohiniac

St-Gilles-Pligeaux
Quintin

Gouarec
Uzel
Mur-de-Bretagne

3

Île de Sein
Pointe du Van
Pointe du Raz
Audierne
Plozévet

Baie d'Audierne

CHAPELLE DE LANGUIDOU

Ploneour-Lanvern
St-Guénolé

POINTE DE PENMARCH

Guilvinec

Tréboul
Douarnenez
Locronan
Pont-Croix
Landudec

Quimper
Plûguffan

VIRE-COURT

Pont-l'Abbé
Loctudy
Bénodet
Beg-Meil

MENEZ HOM
Châteaulin
Ste-Anne-la-Palud
Pentrez-Plage

ROCHE DU FEU
Pleyben
Briec

MONTAGNES NOIRES

Coray
Scaer
Rosporden

N.-D. DE KERDEVOT

Fouesnant
Concarneau
Bannalec

Pont-Aven

Port-Manec'h

Gourin
Plouray

STE-BARBE
Le Faouet
ST-FIACRE

Kernascléden

Le Pouldu

Clohars-Carnoët

ÎLES DE GLÉNAN

Lorient

Larmor
Port-Louis
Groix
Île de Groix

Châteauneuf-du-Faou
Rostrenen

Lac de Guerlédan
Loudéac
Pontivy

Plouay
Quimperlé
Plouay
Pont-Scorff
Hennebont

Baud
Locminé

Guémené-sur-Scorff

Melrand
Bubry
ST-NICUDEM

Loudéac

Rohan
les Forges

Merlevenez
Belz
Ste-Anne-d'Auray
Pluvigner
St-Jean-Brévelay
Grand-Champ

TOUR D'ELVEN

4

A   B   66   C

MENEC

Carnac
La Trinité
Locmariaquer
Port-Navalo

St-Pierre-Quiberon

Vannes
TUMULUS DE GAVRINIS
Questembert

D | 27 | E | F

1

Rosslare Harbour
Jersey
Guernsey

Poole
Portsmouth

MANCHE

Alderney /
Aurigny

Cap de
la Hague

St-Germain-
des-Vaux

Cherbourg
Poole
Portsmouth
Weymouth

Auderville

Beaumont

Nez de
Jobourg

Cap de
Levy

St-Pierre-
Eglise

Pointe de Barfleur

GBG
Guernsey/
Guernesey

Vauville

Cherbourg

Maupertus

Barfleur

St Peter Port

Herm

Martinvast

le Vast

Guettehou

Cherbourg
Poole
Portsmouth
Weymouth

Les Pieux

Maupertus-
sur-Mer

St-Vaast-
la-Hougue

Sark/Sercq

Surtainville

Bricquebec

Valognes

Quineville

Montebourg

CHANNEL ISLANDS /
ILES NORMANDES

Carteret

Barneville-
Carteret

Ste-Mère-Eglise

Jersey

Cap de Carteret

St-Sauveur-
le-Vicomte

Ste-Marie-du-Mont

Portbail

Grandcamp-Maisy

Jersey

Isigny-
sur-Mer

Vierville

2

St Helier

La Haye-
du-Puits

St-Jores

Carentan

Côte du

Port-en-

GBJ

Pirou-Plage

Lessay

MEMORIAL
DU OMAHA BEACH

Weymouth
Poole
Portsmouth

Périers

le Mesnil
Vigot

Bayeux

ABB DE MONDAYE
Balleroy

Golfe de St-Malo

Agon-
Coutainville

Moon-
sur-Elle

St-Lô

ILES
CHAUSEY

Coutances

Torigni-
sur-Vire

Villers-Bo

Hauteville
Plage

Tessy-
sur-Vire

Aunay-
sur-Odon

Côte d'Émeraude

Bréhal

ABB DE
HAMBYE

Condé-su
Noireau

Cap Fréhel

Granville

Gavray

Gouvets

Vassy

St-Quay-
Portrieux

Sables-d'Or-
les-Pins

Pointe du
Grouin

Jullouville

Percy

Villedieu-
les-Poêles

Vire

3

Étables-sur-Mer

Erquy

St-Cast-le-Guildo

Rothéneuf

St-Jean-
le-Thomas

Sartilly

St-Sever

Flers

Binic

Le Val-André

Cancale

Sartilly

St-Pois

Hillion

St-Malo

Baie du Mont St-Michel

Le Mont-
St-Michel

Avranches

Brécey

Juvigny-
le-Tertre

Sourdeval

Lamballe

St-Lunaire

Dinard

MONT-DOL

Pontaubault

Mortain

Domfront

CHÂT. DE
HUNAUDAYE

Plancoët

Dol-de-
Bretagne

Ducey

St-Hilaire-
du-Harcouët

Barenton

Bagnoles-
de-l'Orne

Moncontour

Jugon-
les-Lacs

Corseul

Dinan

Pontorson

St-James

Louvigné-
du-Desert

Landivy

Le Teilleul

La Ferté-
Macé

Collinée

le Gouray

Evran

Combourg

Liffré

St-Brice-
en-Coglès

Gorron

Lassay

Plémet

Broons

St-Jouan-
de-l'Isle

Bécherel

Hédé

Sens-
de-Bretagne

Domfront

Ernée

Ambrières

Merdrignac

St-Méen

Montauban

Gévezé

St-Aubin-
d'Aubigné

Fougères

la Tannière

Gorron

Couterne

Ménéac

Gaël

Bédée

Montfort

Mordelles

St-Aubin-
du-Cormier

Dompierre-
du-Chemin

Mayenne

La Trinité-
Porhoet

Mauron

le Coquet

RENNES

Châteaubourg

La Croixille

Chaillan

4

Ploërmel

CHÂT. DE
TRECESSON

Plélan-le-Grand

Pont-Réan

Val-d'Izé

Vitré

Caro

Bel-Air

Châteaugiron

FORÊT DES ROCHERS

Montsûrs

CHÂT DU
ROCHER

Evron

Guer

Maure

le Ballon

Laval

67

Argentré

Ste-
Suzanne

Malestroit

Pipriac

Guipry

Janzé

La Guerche-de-
Bretagne

Cuillé

Retiers

Laubrières

Quelaines-
St-Gault

GROTTE DE
ROCHEFORT

St-Denis-
d'Orques

Rochefort-
en-Terre

La Gacilly

Bain-de-
Bretagne

Rougé

Martigné-
Ferchaud

Craon

Cossé-le-
Vivien

Thorigné-en-Chav

Redon

Grand-
Fougeray

Teillay

St-Aignan

Meslay

D | E | F

A   28   B   C

Newhaven

E N G L I S H   C H A N N E L   /   M A N C H E

Portsmouth

Baie de la Seine

Côte du Calvados

LE HAVRE

Pointe de Barfleur

St-Pierre-église
Barfleur
Quettehou
St-Vaast-la-Hougue
Quinéville
Utebourg
Ste-Mère-Eglise
Ste-Marie-du-Mont
Grandcamp-Maisy
Vierville
Isigny-sur-Mer
St-Laurent
Port-en-Bessin
Arromanches-les-Bains
Courseulles-sur-Mer
St-Aubin-sur-Mer
Luc-sur-Mer
Riva-Bella
Cabourg
Ouistreham
MÉMORIAL DU OMAHA BEACH
Moon-sur-Elle
Bayeux
CHÂTEAU DE FONTAINE-HENRY
ABB. DE MONDAYE
Balleroy
St-Lô
Torigni-Vire
Caumont
Tessy-sur-Vire
Villers-Bocage
Aunay-sur-Odon
Laize-la-Ville
Moult
Airan
CAEN
Troarn
Dozulé
Cambremer
Crèvecoeur-en-Auge
St-Pierre-sur-Dives
Livarot
Orbec
Thiberville
Bernay
Beaumont-le-Roger
Neubourg
Broglie
Beaumesnil
Courteilles
Landepéreuse
La Neuve-Lyre
Conches-en-Ouche
Damville

Veulettes-sur-Mer
St-Valery-en-Caux
Varengeville-sur-Mer
Veules-les-Roses
MANOIR D'ANG
St-Pierre-en-Port
Yport
Fécamp
Cany-Barville
Fontaine-le-Dun
Bacqueville-en-Caux
Cap d'Antifer
FALAISE D'AVAL
Etretat
Goderville
Fauville
Yerville
Cauville
Octeville
Montivilliers
Bolbec
Lillebonne
Caudebec-en-Caux
Barentin
Duclair
St-Wandrille
Cap de la Hève
Harfleur
Tancarville
Honfleur
Villerville
Trouville
Deauville
Villers
Houlgate
Dives-sur-Mer
Pont-l'Evêque
Beuzeville
Pont-Audemer
Cormeilles
Lieurey
Bourgtheroulde
Infreville
Elbeuf
ABB. DE BONPORT
Louviers
CHÂT. DU CHAMP DUBATAILLE
Bourg-Achard
Jumièges
Bosguet
PARC ZOO
Sotteville-lès-Rouen
ROU
Boc

Côte Fleurie
Lisieux
Brionne
Evreux
Pacy-sur-Eure
St-André
Ivry-la-Bataille
Nonancourt
Dreux

Vire
Vassy
Condé-sur-Noireau
Clécy
Falaise
Vimoutiers
Trun
Gacé
Rugles
L'Aigle
Breteuil
Verneuil-sur-Avre
Brézolles
Blévy

Thury-Harcourt
Flers
ROCHE D'OETRE
Taillebois
Putanges-Pont-Ecrepin
Briouze
Fromental
Argentan
Exmes
HARAS DU PIN
Le Pin-au-Haras
Nonant-le-Pin
Ste-Gauburge-Ste-Colombe
Merlerault
Moulins-la-Marche
Courtomer
Bazoches-sur-Hoëne
La Ferté-Vidame
Senonches
Digny
Châteauneuf-en-Thymerais
Courville
Chartres

Sourdeval
St-Barthélemy
Mortain
Barenton
Domfront
La Ferté-Macé
Bagnoles-de-l'Orne
Rânes
Mortrée
Sées
La Ferté-Bernard

Le Teilleul
Gorron
Ambrières
Couterne
Couptrain
Lassay
Pré-en-Pail
Carrouges
MONT DES AVALOIRS
PARC NAT. RÉGIONAL
RÉGIONS
NORMANDIE-MAINE
Mortagne-au-Perche
Longny-au-Perche
La Loupe
Mayenne
Villaines-la-Juhel
Alençon
Bais
Rémalard
MANOIR DE COURBOYER
Bellême
Nogent-le-Rotrou
Champrond-en-Gâtine
Thivars
Chassant
Illiers-Combray
Luigny

Montsûrs
Evron
Sillé-le-Guillaume
Fresnay-sur-Sarthe
Mamers
Courgains
St-Cosme-en-Vairais
Beaumont-sur-Sarthe
Bonnétable
Villaines-la-Gonais
Authon-du-Perche
La Bazoche-Gouet
Brou
le-Gault-St-Denis
Argentré
CHÂT. DU ROCHER
La Hutte
Assé-le-Boisne
Ste-Suzanne
St-Denis-d'Orques
Conlie
Ballon
Tuffé
Connerré
Vibraye
Montmirail
Chapelle-Royale
Bonneval
Cormainville

Vaiges
GROTTE DE ROCHEFORT
Thorigné-en-Charnie
Brûlon
Loué
Vaiges
CHÂT. DE VERDELLES
LE MANS
ABB. DE SOLESMES
Tharigné-sur-Dué
Bouloire
St-Calais
Vancé
Montplaisir
Savigny-sur-Braye
Cloyes-sur-le-Loir
Châteaudun

Meslay
Grez-en-Bouère
Bierné
Daon
Ste-Jaille-Yvon
Château-Gontier-Champigne
Sablé-sur-Sarthe
La Suze
ABB. DE L'EPAU
Arnage
Mulsanne
Parigné
CHÂT. DU PLESSIS-BOURRÉ
La Flèche
Durtal
Malicorne
St-Quentin-lès-Béru
Eeommoy
Le Grand-Lucé
CHÂT. DE COURTANVAUX
Mayet
Pontvallain
St-Vincent-du-Lorouër
Vaas
Bouloire
Arville
Mondoubleau
Epuisay
D106
Fréteval
Prénouvelon
Ouzouer-le-Marché
Gaubert

A   67   B   C

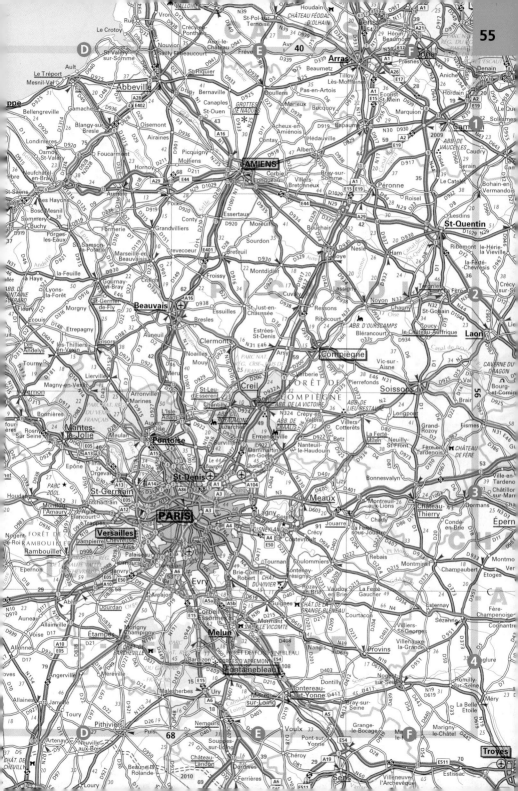

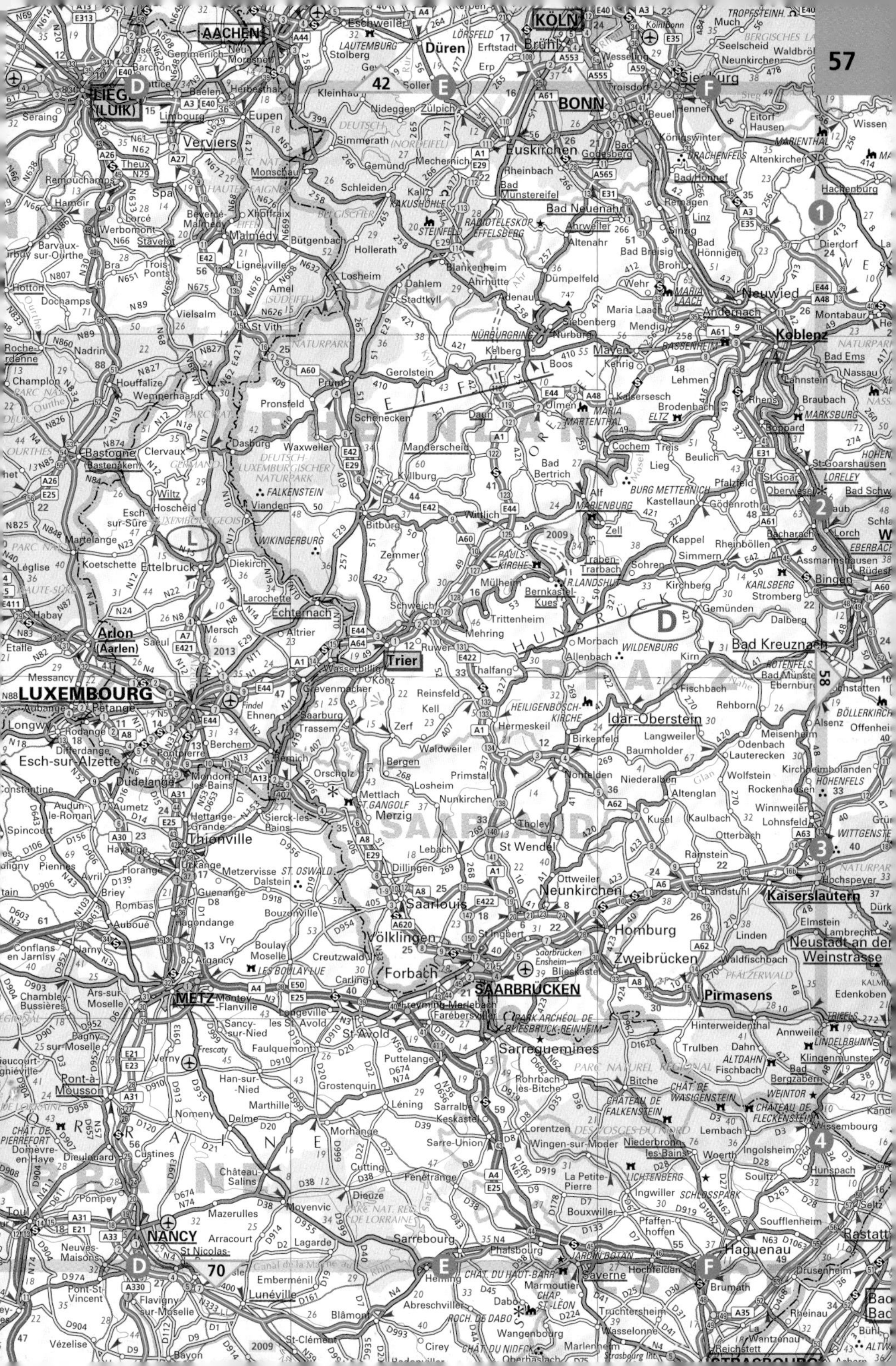

AACHEN
KÖLN
Düren
BONN
LIEG (LUIK)
Verviers
Eupen
Koblenz
Neuwied
Andernach
Mayen
Bastogne
Clervaux
Wiltz
Vianden
Diekirch
Ettelbruck
Bitburg
Gerolstein
Prüm
Wittlich
Cochem
Boppard
Bacharach
Bingen
Bad Kreuznach
LUXEMBOURG
Esch-sur-Alzette
Arlon (Aarlen)
Echternach
Trier
Saarburg
Merzig
Idar-Oberstein
Birkenfeld
Thionville
Saarlouis
Völklingen
Forbach
SAARBRÜCKEN
Neunkirchen
Homburg
Zweibrücken
Kaiserslautern
Neustadt an der Weinstrasse
Pirmasens
METZ
Sarreguemines
Bitche
Haguenau
NANCY
Lunéville
Sarrebourg
Phalsbourg
Saverne
STRASBOURG

OPOLE PL CZĘSTOCHOWA KATOWICE KRAKÓW OSTRAVA BIELSKO-BIAŁA

Radomsko Wieluń Jędrzejów Olesno Kluczbork Lubliniec Tarnowskie Góry BYTOM ZABRZE CHORZÓW GLIWICE SOSNOWIEC Mysłowice Jaworzno TYCHY Chrzanów Olkusz DĄBROWA GÓRNICZA Będzin Zawiercie Myszków Kłobuck

Racibórz RYBNIK Żory Oświęcim Pszczyna Wodzisław Śląski

Havířov Český Těšín Cieszyn Trinec Żywiec Wadowice Andrychów Kalwaria Zebrzydowska Sucha Beskidzka Myślenice

Frýdek-Místek Nový Jičín Valašské Meziříčí Rožnov pod Radhoštěm Bystřička

SK Žilina Martin Ružomberok Liptovský Mikuláš Zakopane Nowy Targ Rabka Mszana Dolna

Čadca Turzovka Nové Mesto Kysucké Bytča Vrútky Jablunkov

1 2 3 4
D E 49 F
D E 76 F

Świdnik • Dorohucza • Chełm • Turka • Solovychi

Piaski • Wola Idzikowska • Rejowiec Fabryczny • Rejowiec • Dubienka

Piotrków • Łopiennik • Krupe • Siennica Różana • Sielec • Busno • Horodło • **Volodymyr-Volyns'kyi / Володимир-Волинський**

Bychawa • Krasnystaw • Ustyluh • M8 • Loka

Stara Wieś • Gorzków-Osada • Wojsławice • Teresin • Teratyn • Strzyżów • **Novovolyns'k / Нововолинськ** ①

Wysokie • Żółkiewka-Osada • Kraśniczyn • Uchanie • Hrubieszów • Zhovtneve

Tarnawka • Stryjów • Skierbieszów • Grabowiec • Ivanychi • Pavlivka

Batorz • Tarnawa Duża • Turobin • Chomęciska Małe • **Zamość** • Miączyn • Terebin • Zakhidny Buh

Modliborzyce • Gródki • Bodaczów • Łabunie • Kotlice • Przewale • Dołhobyczów • Variazh • Sokal'

Janów Lubelski • Szczebrzeszyn • Lipsko • Wółka Łabuńska • Witków • **Chervonohrad / Червоноград**

Frampol • Panasówka • Zwierzyniec • Tarnawatka • Wożuczyn • Łaszczów • Nowosiółki • 267

Kąty • Zarzecze • Biłgoraj • Tomaszów Lubelski • Ulhówek • Belz • Hirnyk • Radekhiv

Ulanów • Nowy Majdan • Józefów • Bełżec • Uhniv • ②

Rudnik • Aleksandrów • Narol • Sosnivka

Krzeszów • **PL** • Tarnogród • Wola Obszańska • Płazów • Hrebenne • Richky • Velyki Mosty

Nowa Sarzyna • Naklik • Dąbrówka • Cewków • Dachnów • Cieszanów • Rava-Rus'ka • **UA**

Leżajsk • Oleszyce • Lubaczów • Radruż • Maheriv • Dobrosyn • Kamianka-Buz'ka

Sokołów Małopolski • Sieniawa • Mołodycz • Budomierz • Nemyriv • Zhovkva • Bus'

Tryńcza • Zapałów • Wiązownica • Sople • Laszki • Buczyna • Krakovets • Starychi • Kulykiv • Zapytiv • 244

Przeworsk • Jarosław • Kidałowice • Duńkowice • Yavoriv • Novoiavorivs'ke • Ivano-Frankove • **L'VIV / Львів** • Vynnyky

Kańczuga • Radymno • Rokietnica • Mosty'ska • Horodok • Sknyliv • Krasn

Pruchnik • Hyżne • Błażowa • Bachórz • Babice • Żurawica • Medyka • Sudova Vyshnia • Vel. Liubin' • Kurovychi

Dynów • Szklary • Krasiczyn • **Przemyśl** • Rudky • Schirets' • Komarno • 473 ③

Nozdrzec • Bircza • Nyzhankovychi • Peremozhne • Vel. Horozhanka • Vybranivka • Khodorkivtsi

Grabownica Starzeńska • Mrzygłód • Kuźmina • Huwniki • Dobromyl' • Kolodruby • Mykolaïv • Novyi Rozdil

Sanok • Zaluż • Khyriv • **Sambir / Самбір** • Dubliany • Rozdil • Khodoriv

Zagórz • Uherce Mineralne • Kroscienko • Staryi Sambir • Medenychi • Zhydachiv

Lesko • Ustrzyki Dolne • Strilky • **Drohobych / Дрогобич** • E50 • Zhuravno

Szczawne • Hoczew • Myczków • Czarna Górna • **Boryslav / Борислав** • Truskavets' / Трускавець • **Stryi / Стрий** • Sivka-Voinyliv

Komańcza • Sakowczyk • Limna • Turka • Morshyn • 394

Cisna • Dołżyca • Stuposiany • Boryma • Bolekhiv • Kalush / Калуш • 62

Wetlina • Ustrzyki Górne • Wołosate • Verch. Syn'ovydne • Skole • Broshniv-Osada • Rozhniativ ④

Zubne • Nová Sedlica • Zboj • Uzhok • Dolyna • Krasne

Snina • Ulič • Ruská Volová • Uzhots'kyi Pereval • Vyhoda • Bohorc

Ubľa • Velykyi Berezny • Matkiv • Tuchol'ka • Perehins'ke

Liuta • Roztoka • Klymets'

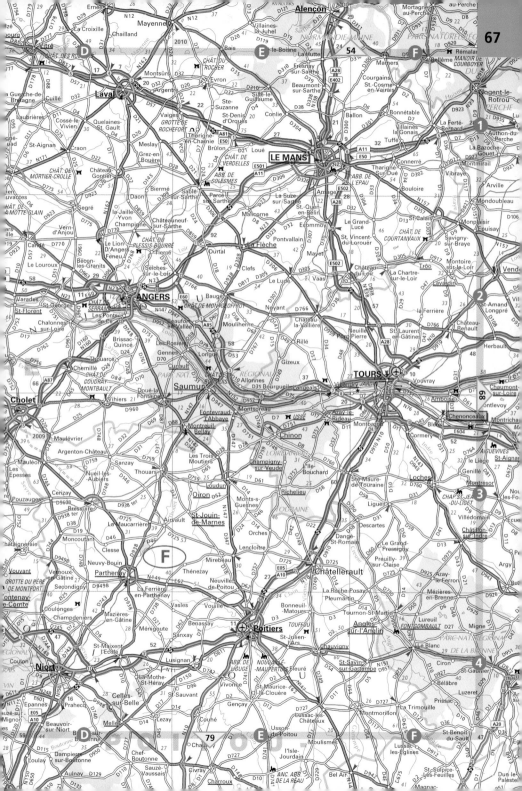

A B C

R I A S

1

2010
Cabo Prior
Cabo Prioriño
Vixía Herbeira
Punta Candelaria
Cedeira
SAN ANDRÉS
Valdoviño
AC862
Me do Boi
CASTILLO DE MOECHE
Ferrol
NVI
Xubia
Neda
San Sadurniño
CAST. DE NARAIO
Murgados
Ares
Fene
MONASTERIO DE CAAVEIRO 34
Cabo San Adrián
Malpica de Bergantiños
La Coruña
A CORUÑA/
LA CORUÑA
Pontedeume
Miño
Mera
Cabañas
CAST. DE ANDRADE
Illas Sisargas
Punta del Roncudo
Pontecedo
AC422
Arteixo
Oleiros
Sada
Bergondo
As Pontes de García Rodríguez
Puentes de García Rodríguez
Cabo Vilán
Camariñas
Baio
CASTRO DE BORNEIRO
AC55
Cambre
Guisamo
Betanzos
Monfero
Embalse de Eume
C640
Muxía
CEREIXO
DOLMEN DE DÓMBATE
San Roque
Carballo
Laracha
Carral
Coirós
Curtis
Irixoa
Pedreira
Cabo Touriñán
Vimianzo
Zás
Cerceda
N550
Lanzá
Lourdes
Guitiriz
1

2

Laxe
AC552
AC2904
Silva
AC413
Mesón do Vento
C542
Oroso
Teixeiro
SOBRADO DOS MONXES
Baamonde
A6
Fisterra
Finisterre
AC445
Cee
Cercubión
Ézaro
Ponte Oliveras
Brandomil
AC400
Santa Comba
Bembibre
Trazo
Ordes
STA. MARÍA DE MEZONZO
Ru
Sobrado
Friol
Rabade
Begonte
LU934
Cabo Fisterra
AC400
Pino do Val
A Baña
Portomouro
Sigüeiro
Pastor
Toques
Guntin
Lugo
El Picato 660
2009
Carnota
Dutes
Embalse Barrié de la Maza
Negreira
AC550
Santiago de Compostela
STA. MARÍA DE CONXO
O Pino
Arzúa
Melide
Palas de Rei
Nadi
Muros
Punta Carreiros
Porto do Son
Noia
Noya
AC543
Padrón
N634
Santiago
N547
Fontedias
Ramallosa
Ponte Ulla
Cruces
N547
Portomarín
CASTRO DE BARONA
Pobra do Caramiñal
Puebla del Caramiñal
Oleiros
Boiro
Rianxo
VRG1.1
Catoira
AP53
Teo
Pontecesures
MAZO DE OCA
Silleda
Agolada
Monterroso
Antas de Ulla
Narón
Cabo Corrubedo
Santa Uxía de Ribeira
Vilanova de Arousa
PO549
A Estrada
N640
Cuntis
N640
Lalín
Rodeiro
CRG2.1
Chantada
MONASTERIO DE RIBAS DO MIÑO
Escairón
Bóved
Punta de Couso
Illa de Arousa
Cambados
VRGA4.1
Caldas de Reis
A Lagoa/
Campo Lameiro
Forcarei
Souteto
Dozón Castro
STA. MARÍA DA REAL
A Barrela
LU5709
Saff
Illa de Sálvora
PARQUE NACIONAL
A Toxa
PO550
CONVENTO
PO308 Boiro
Cerdedo
Beariz
Pinor
Cea
Embalse dos Peares
Pantón
3

Illa de Ons
DAS ILLAS
Sanxenxo
Combarro
Maria
Pontevedra
Ponte-Caldelas
Avión
O Carballiño
Maside
MONASTERIO DE SAN CLODIO
Os Peares
Monforte de Lemos
ATLÁNTICAS
Illas Cíes
Cangas
Moaña
Redondela
Berducido
Leiro
Punxín
Cambeo
Sober
Cabo Silleiro
Panxón
Nigrán
VIGO
AG57
Areas
Mondariz-Balneario
Mondariz
Ribadavia
Cartelle
OURENSE/
ORENSE
MONASTERIO DE SANTO ESTEVO
Castro Caldelas
Puerto de Alto da Cerdeira 890
Baiona
Ramallosa
O Porriño
Pontearas
Cañiza
Cortegada
Ramirás
Esgos
Maceda
A Pobra de Trives
Arrabal
Oia
Vilameán
Salvaterra de Miño
Melgaço
Padrenda
Celanova
A Merca
Allariz
Xunqueira de Ambía
Paredes
Embalse de Chandrexa
MANZANEDA
A Guarda
La Guardia
MTE. DE STA. TEGRA
PO552
Vila Nova de Cerveira
Extremo
São Gregório
Lobios
Muiños
Verea
OU531
Sandiás
Vilar de Barrio
SERRA DE QUEI
PAR. NAT. DO INVERNADEIRO
Villarino de Conso
Moledo
Vila Praia de Ancora
Afife
Paredes de Coura
A3
Portela
SERRA DA PENEDA
P
PARQUE NAT.
Entrimo
Bande
OU301
Xinzo de Limia
Ginzo de Limia
Trasmiras
Laza
Campobecerros
4

Viana do Castelo
IP9
Ponte de Lima
Deão
Balugães
IC1
SERRA DO XURÉS
Randín
Baltar
Cualedro
Vérin
A Gudiña
N525
A Me
PARQUE NATURAL DO LITORAL NORTE
A28
Esposende
Castelo do Neiva
Vila Verde
Caldelas
N. S. D'ABADIA
DA PENEDA-GERÊS
Paradela
Montalegre
Ríos
Vilardevós
A
B
84
C
Ofir
Barcelos
N205
N103
Venda Nova
Boticas
Oimbra
Estela
A11
IP9
Rio Mau
Jesús do Monte
Louredo
Barragem do Alto Rabagão
N311
Chaves
Tronco
Vila Verde da Raia
Póvoa de Varzim
Braga
IC14
A11
Póvoa de Lanhoso
N. SENHORA DA AZINHEIRA
E801

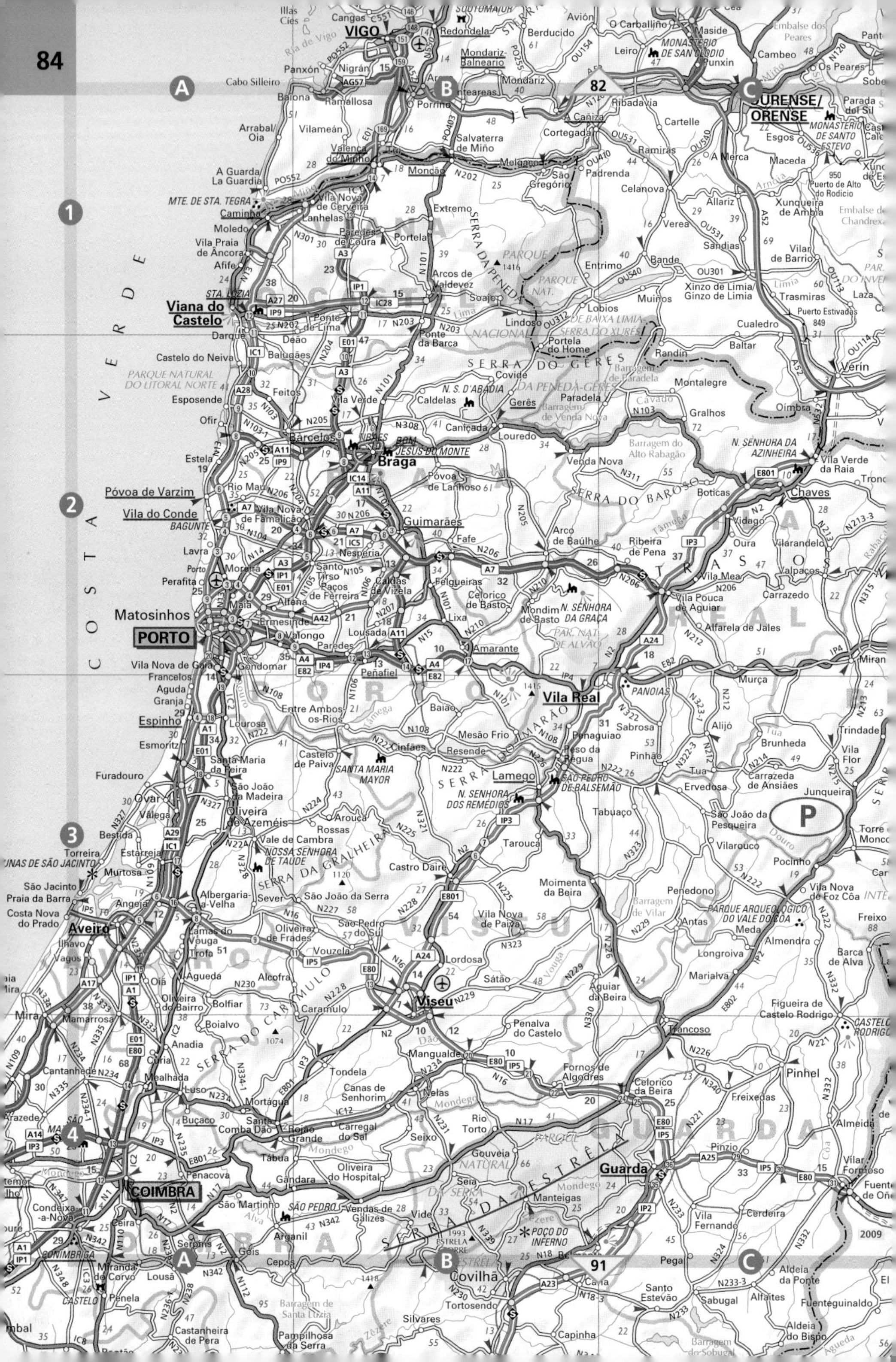

A　　　　　　B　　　　　　C

V E R D E

o Vidio
Cudillero
El Pito
Cabo de Peñas
Salinas
Lluanco/Luanco
l Barón
AS236
Candás
4MO
Avilés
GIJÓN/
XIXÓN
Noñeda
A8
Nubledo
A66
Posada
Tazones
Punta de Tazones
S.M. DE NARANCO
Grau/
Grado
Lugones
Villaviciosa
Lastres
OVIEDO
El Pino
Pola de Siero
Colunga
La Isla
Punta de Carreros
Trubia
VALDEDIOS
Cabranes
Ribadesella
CUEVA DE TITO BUSTILLO
Santolaya
Llangréu/Langreo
Nava
MIRADOR DEL FITO
Arriondas
S. Antolín
Caranga
Mieres
Infiesto
SAN PEDRO
Cangas
de Onís
Posada
Cabo Prieto
Llanes
BUFÓN DE
ARENILLAS
Riosa
Sotrondio
San Martín del
Rey Aurelio
Pola de Laviana
COVADONGA
FIFA DEL BUXU
SIERRA DE CUERA
LA FRANCA
CUEVA
DEL PINDAL
La Rola
(Lena)
STA. CRISTINA
DE LENA
Cabañaquinta
Campo de Caso/
Caso
Sarnes
PARQUE NACIONAL
Covadonga
Arenas
Onguera
San Vicente
de la Barquera
Punta del
Dichoso
Suances
Campomanes
PAR. NAT.
DE REDES
PARQUE NACIONAL
DE LOS PICOS DE EUROPA
Panes
CUEVAS DE ALTAMIRA
Comillas
Santillana
N611
Pino
Felechosa
PAR. NAT.
DE PONGA
Covadonga
Cares
Cabezón
de la Sal
Puerto de
Pajares
PICOS DE EUROPA
Posada
de Valdeón
La Hermida
STA. MARÍA
DE LEBEÑA
Embalse de
Palombera
Las Caldas
de Besaya
Torrelavega
Villamanín
de la Tercia
Cármenes
Puerto San Isidro
Oseja de
Sajambre
Fuente Dé
Puente Viesgo
Sta. María
de Cayón
Mirantes
Puebla
de Lillo
CA185
Potes
STO. TORIBIO
DE LIÉBANA
Sarceda
Valle de
Cabuérniga
Los Corrales
de Buelna
La Pola
de Gordón
Valporquero de Torío
Vegacervera
Embalse de Porma
Burón
Portilla de la Reina
Espinama
PAR. NAT.
CUEVAS EL CASTILLO
PASIEGA LAS CHIMENEAS
Robles de
Valcueva
Matallana
de Torío
Riaño
Pesaguero
Puerto de
Piedrasluengas
Embalse de
la Cohilla
Molledo
Bárcena de
Pie de Concha
Vega
de Pas
La Robla
Bonar
La Vecilla
DE PICOS
DE EUROPA
Boca de
Huérgano
PAR. NAT.
DE F. CARRIONAS Y F. COBRE-
MONTAÑA PALENTINA
Puerto de
Palombera
Espinilla
Corconte
Puerto del
Escudo
Cuadros
Garrafe de Torío
Prioro
Besande
Triollo
Areños
Branosera
Reinosa
Cervatos
HIJEDO
Embalse del Ebro
Soncillo
S. Andrés del
Rabanedo
Villaquilambre
Sabero
Puerto
Monteviejo
Cervera de
Pisuerga
Salinas
de Pisuerga
Puerto Pozazal
Embalse de
Camporredondo
León
Gradefes
Cistierna
Puente
Almuhey
Guardo
Santibáñez
Embalse de
Requejada
Mataporquera
Puerto de
Carrales
Onzonilla
S. MIGUEL
DE ESCALADA
Valdepolo
Villalba
de Guardo
Congosto
de Valdavia
CANTORAL
de la Peña
SANAT
EUFEMIA
Embalse de
Aguilar
STA. MARÍA
LA REAL
Aguilar de Campoo
Rebolledo
de la Torre
Polientes
Escalada
Valdenoceda
Mansilla de
las Mulas
Villamartín
de Don Sancho
Vecilla de
Valderaduey
La Puebla
de Valdavia
Fuencaliente
de Lucio
Humada
Tubilla
del Agua
Santas
Martas
El Burgo
Ranero
Cea
N. S. DEL VALLE
Saldaña
Villaeles
de Valdavia
Herrera de
Pisuerga
Sotresgudo
Basconcillos
del Tozo
Úrbel del
Castillo
Villamañán
Bercianos del
Real Camino
Terradillos de
los Templarios
Villanuño de
Valdavia
Bahíllo
Ventosa
de Pisuerga
Osorno
la Mayor
Portillo
del Fresno
Montorio
Cernégu
Valencia
de Don Juan
Matallana
de Torío
Gordaliza
del Pino
Sahagún
Melgar
de Arriba
Calzadilla
de la Cueza
Carrión de
los Condes
Villadiego
Quintanilla
Sobresierra
La Matanza
Ledigos
Villalcázar
de Sirga
Melgar
de Fernamental
Santibáñez
Zarzaguda
Villanueva
del Campo
Villada
Cervatos
de la Cueza
Villasadino
Olmillos
de Sasamón
Quintanaortuño
Valderas
Santervás
de Campos
Paredes
de Nava
Frechilla
Fuentes de
Nava
Villoldo
Castrojeriz
Estepar
BURGOS
Rubena
Villanueva
del Campo
SAN
FRANCISCO
Villalón
de Campos
Villarramiel
Monzón
de Campos
Astudillo
Villaquejida
Mayorga
Becilla de
Valderaduey
Cisneros
LAS HUELGAS
MIRAFLORES
Valdunquillo
Villamartín
de Campos
Villafruela
PEDRO DE CARDEÑA
Ibeas de
Juarros
Villanueva
de la Condesa
Torremormojón
Sarracín
Villalpando
Villafrechós
Medina de
Rioseco
Montealegre
PALENCIA
Magaz de
Pisuerga
Torquemada
Santa María
del Campo
Cogollos
Hontoria
la Cantera
Madrid
del Mte
NUESTRA SEÑORA
DE LA ANUNCIADA
Ampudia
Venta de
Baños
Cuevas de
San Clemente
Villaldefrádes
Castromonte
Villalba de
los Alcores
Dueñas
Baños
de Cerrato
Baltanás
Antigüedad
Covarrubias
Quintani
la Vie
La Mudarra
MONASTERIO
DE STA. ESPINA
Cigales
Quintanilla
del Puente
93
Villahoz
Lerma
BU114
Hortigü

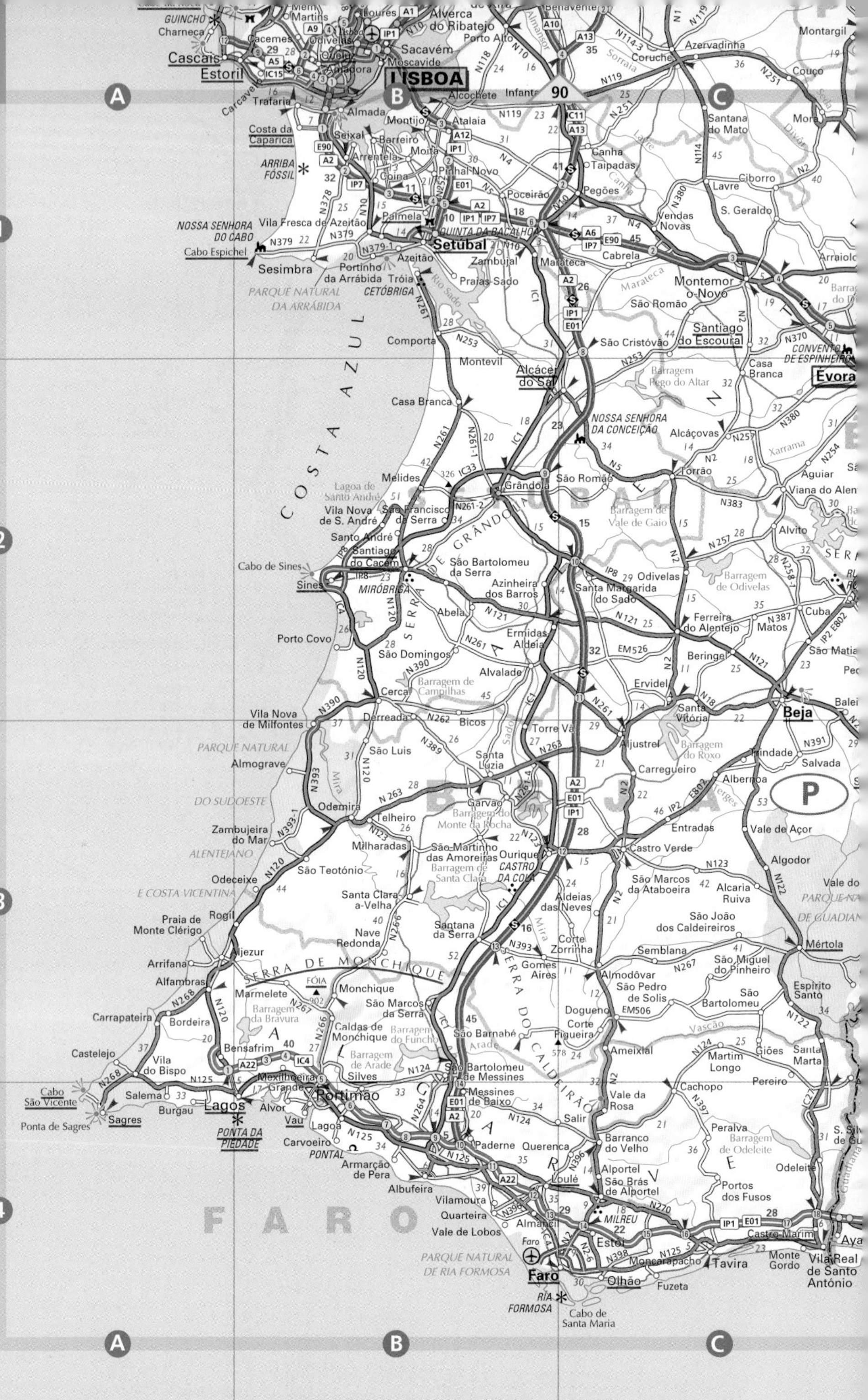

A   B   90   C

Guincho
Charneca
Cascais
Estoril
Trafaria
Almada
Seixal
Arrentela
Costa da Caparica
ARRIBA FÓSSIL
NOSSA SENHORA DO CABO
Cabo Espichel
Sesimbra
Portinho da Arrábida
PARQUE NATURAL DA ARRÁBIDA

LISBOA
Alcochete
Montijo   Atalaia
Barreiro   Moita
Pinhal Novo
Poceirão
Palmela
Vila Fresca de Azeitão
QUINTA DA BACALHOA
Setúbal
Azeitão
Zambujal
Praias Sado
CETÓBRIGA
Tróia

COSTA AZUL

Comporta
Montevil
Alcácer do Sal
Casa Branca
Melides
Lagoa de Santo André
Vila Nova de S. André
São Francisco da Serra
Santo André
Santiago do Cacém
Cabo de Sines
Sines
MIRÓBRIGA
Porto Covo
São Domingos
Cercal
Derreada
Vila Nova de Milfontes
PARQUE NATURAL DO SUDOESTE ALENTEJANO E COSTA VICENTINA
Almograve
São Luis
Santa Luzia
Odemira
Telheiro
Zambujeira do Mar
Milharadas
São Teotónio
Odeceixe
Santa Clara-a-Velha
Rogil
Praia de Monte Clérigo
Nave Redonda
Arrifana
Aljezur
Alfambras
SERRA DE MONCHIQUE
Marmelete
FÓIA
Monchique
Carrapateira
Bordeira
Barragem da Bravura
São Marcos da Serra
Castelejo
Bensafrim
Caldas de Monchique
Barragem do Funcho
Vila do Bispo
Salema
Mexilhoeira Grande
Silves
Barragem de Arade
Cabo São Vicente
Sagres
Burgau
Lagos
PONTA DA PIEDADE
Alvor
Portimão
Vau
Lagoa
Carvoeiro
PONTAL
Armação de Pera
Albufeira
Vilamoura
Quarteira
Vale de Lobos

FARO

PARQUE NATURAL DE RIA FORMOSA
Faro
RIA FORMOSA
Cabo de Santa Maria
Olhão
Fuzeta

Alverca do Ribatejo
Sacavém
Porto Alto
Infantado
Coruche
Azevadinha
Montargil
Couço
Santana do Mato
Lavre
S. Geraldo
Pegões
Vendas Novas
Canha
Taipadas
Cabrela
Matateca
São Romão
Montemor o Novo
São Cristóvão
Santiago do Escoural
CONVENTO DE ESPINHEIRO
Évora
NOSSA SENHORA DA CONCEIÇÃO
Alcáçovas
Torrão
Aguiar
Viana do Alen
Alvito
São Romão
Grândola
Barragem de Vale de Gaio
Azinheira dos Barros
Santa Margarida do Sado
Abela
Ermidas Aldeia
Alvalade
São Bartolomeu da Serra
Odivelas
Ferreira do Alentejo
Beringel
Cuba
São Matia
Barragem de Odivelas
Barragem de Campilhas
Bicos
Torre Vã
Santa Vitória
Ervidel
Aljustre
Beja
Barragem do Roxo
Carregueiro
Albernoa
Trindade
Salvada
Garvão
Barragem do Monte da Rocha
Ourique
CASTRO DA COLA
Entradas
Vale de Açor
Castro Verde
Algodor
São Marcos da Ataboeira
Alcaria Ruiva
Vale do PARQUE NATURAL DE GUADIANA
Aldeias das Neves
São João dos Caldeireiros
Semblana
Mértola
Santana da Serra
Corte Zorrinha
Gomes Aires
Almodôvar
São Pedro de Solis
Corte Figueira
EM506
Doueno
São Bartolomeu
Espírito Santo
Ameixial
Martim Longo
Gióes
Santa Marta
Pereiro
Cachopo
Peralva
Barragem de Odeleite
São Bartolomeu de Messines
São Marcos da Serra
Messines de Baixo
Salir
Querença
Paderne
Boliqueime
Almançil
Barranco do Velho
S. Brás de Alportel
São Brás de Alportel
Alportel
Portos dos Fusos
Odeleite
Vale da Rosa
MILREU
Estói
Moncarapacho
Tavira
Castro Marim
Monte Gordo
Vila Real de Santo António

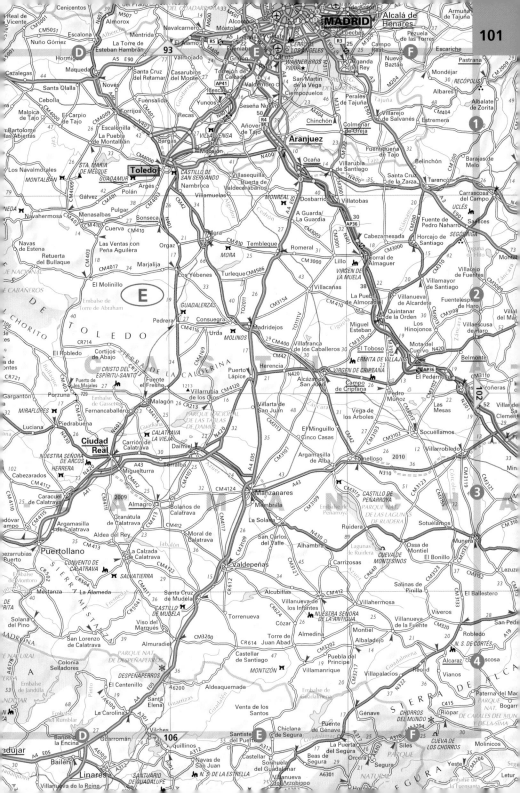

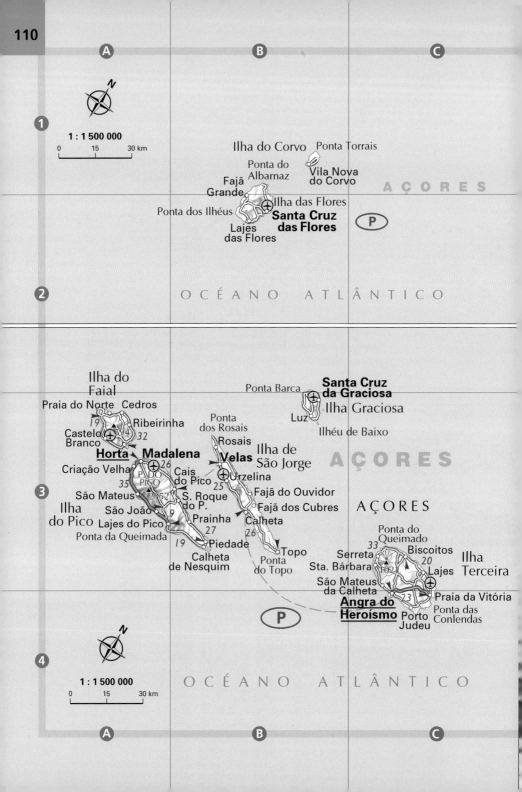

N

1 : 1 500 000

0   15   30 km

Ilha do Corvo   Ponta Torrais

Ponta do
Albarnaz   Vila Nova
do Corvo

Fajã
Grande   A Ç O R E S

Ponta dos Ilhéus   Ilha das Flores
**Santa Cruz
das Flores**   P

Lajes
das Flores

O C É A N O   A T L Â N T I C O

Ilha do
Faial   Ponta Barca   **Santa Cruz
da Graciosa**

Praia do Norte Cedros   Luz   Ilha Graciosa
Castelo   Ribeirinha   Ponta
Branco   dos Rosais   Ilhéu de Baixo

19   32   Rosais

Horta Madalena   **Velas**   Ilha de
São Jorge   A Ç O R E S

Criação Velha   Cais   Urzelina
PICO   do Pico   25   Fajã do Ouvidor   AÇORES

35   Fajã dos Cubres
São Mateus   S. Roque
do P.   Ponta do
Ilha   São João   9   Prainha   Calheta   Queimado   Biscoitos
do Pico   Lajes do Pico   27   Serreta   33   20   Ilha
Ponta da Queimada   19   Piedade   26   Sta. Bárbara   Lajes   Terceira
Calheta   Ponta   Topo   São Mateus   Praia da Vitória
de Nesquim   do Topo   da Calheta   23   Ponta das
**Angra do
Heroísmo** Porto   Conlendas
Judeu

P

O C É A N O   A T L Â N T I C O

1 : 1 500 000

0   15   30 km

D   E   F

Mosteiros   Lagoa Azul

ER1-1
29

Ponta da Agulha

Capelas

**Ponta
Delgada**   EN3-1a   35   Ribeira Grande

ER8

16   17   Maia

ER6

Lagoa   29   Fenais da Ajuda

Vila Franca   EN1-1a   EN1-1a   39   Pta.
do Campo   Furnas   da Ribeira

Povoação   39   Nordeste

Pta. da
Madrugada

**Ilha de
São Miguel**

O C É A N O

A T L Â N T I C O

A Ç O R E S

Ⓟ

A Ç O R E S

**Ilha de
Santa Maria**

Anjos   Baia do São Lourenço

Almagreira

**Vila
do Porto**   Maia

Ponta do Castelo

N

1 : 1 500 000

0   15   30 km

O C É A N O   A T L Â N T I C O

M A D E I R A

**Ilha da
Madeira**

Ponta do Pargo   Porto Moniz   *PARQUE NATURAL
DA MADEIRA*   **Ilha do
Porto Santo**

18   São Vicente

R101   43   Ponta do São Jorge

Calheta   RUIVO   Santana   Ponta   Camacha

Serra de Água   1862   Vila Baleira

R104   31   Faial   Ilhéu de
Ribeira Brava   21   Baixo

28   R103   Machico

Funchal   Caniço   26   Santa   Ponta de São Lourenço
Cruz

Ⓟ

N

1 : 1 500 000

0   15   30 km

Ilhéu do Chão

Ilhas Desertas

*RISERVA
NATURAL DAS
ILHAS DESERTAS*   Ilhéu Deserta Grande

Ilhéu do Bugio

D   E   F

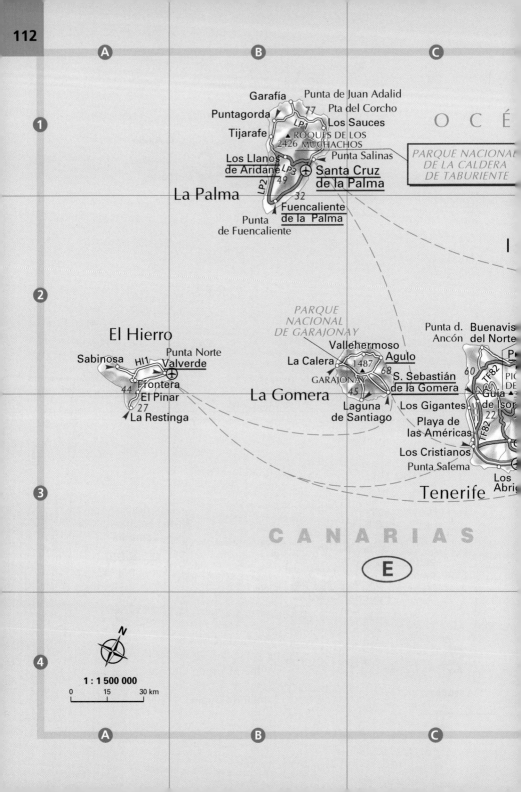

A   B   C

1

Garafía   Punta de Juan Adalid
Puntagorda   Pta del Corcho
                              77   Los Sauces
Tijarafe   LP1   ROQUES DE LOS
              2426   MUCHACHOS
Los Llanos   Punta Salinas
de Aridane   LP3
              LP2   49   Santa Cruz
La Palma   de la Palma

O C É

PARQUE NACIONAL
DE LA CALDERA
DE TABURIENTE

I

32
Fuencaliente
de la Palma
Punta
de Fuencaliente

2

PARQUE
NACIONAL
DE GARAJONAY

Punta d. Buenavis
Ancón del Norte

El Hierro

Vallehermoso   Agulo
La Calera   1487
              GARAJONAY   68   S. Sebastián
              45   de la Gomera

Sabinosa   HI1   Punta Norte
              Valverde
44   Frontera
El Pinar
27   La Restinga

La Gomera

Laguna
de Santiago   Los Gigantes

P

60   TF82   PICO
                    DE

Guía
de Isor
22

Playa de
las Américas   TF82

3

Los Cristianos
Punta Salema

Los
Abri

Tenerife

C A N A R I A S

E

4

N

1 : 1 500 000
0   15   30 km

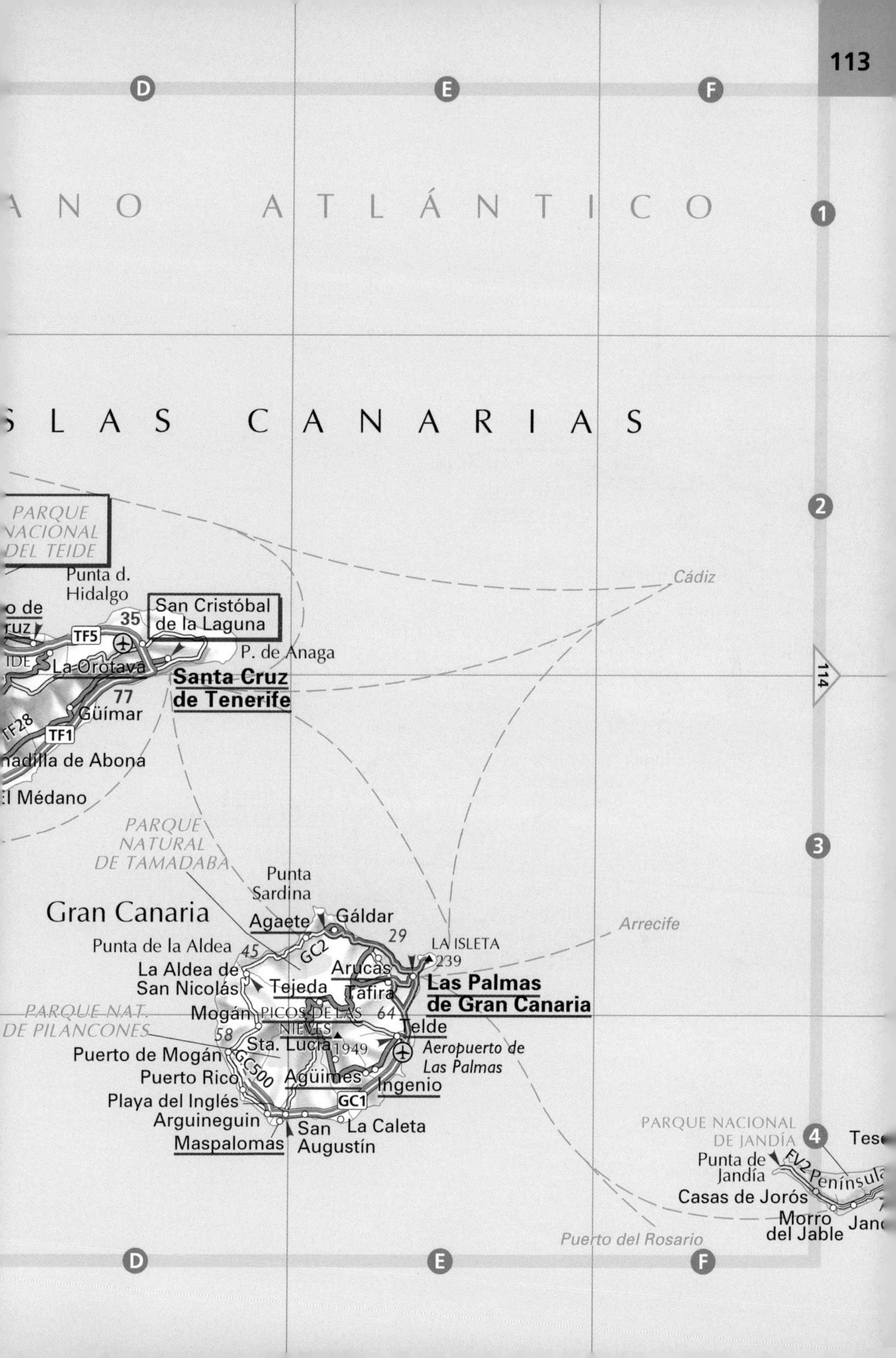

D E F

1

ᴀNO ATLÁNTICO

Cádiz

2

SLAS CANARIAS

PARQUE
NACIONAL
DEL TEIDE

Punta d.
Hidalgo

o de
ruz

San Cristóbal
de la Laguna

35

TF5 ✈

IDE

La Orotava

P. de Anaga

**Santa Cruz
de Tenerife**

114

77

Güímar

TF28

TF1

adilla de Abona

El Médano

PARQUE
NATURAL
DE TAMADABA

3

Punta
Sardina

Gran Canaria

Agaete

Gáldar

29

LA ISLETA
239

Arrecife

Punta de la Aldea

45

GC2

Arucas

**Las Palmas
de Gran Canaria**

La Aldea de
San Nicolás

Tejeda

Tafira

PARQUE NAT.
DE PILANCONES

Mogán

PICOS DE LAS
NIEVES

64

Telde

58

Sta. Lucia

1949

Aeropuerto de
Las Palmas

Puerto de Mogán

GC500

Aguimes

Ingenio

Puerto Rico

PARQUE NACIONAL
DE JANDÍA

4

Playa del Inglés

GC1

Tes

Arguineguin

San

La Caleta

Punta de
Jandía

FV2

Península

Maspalomas

Augustín

Casas de Jorós

Morro
del Jable

Jand

Puerto del Rosario

D E F

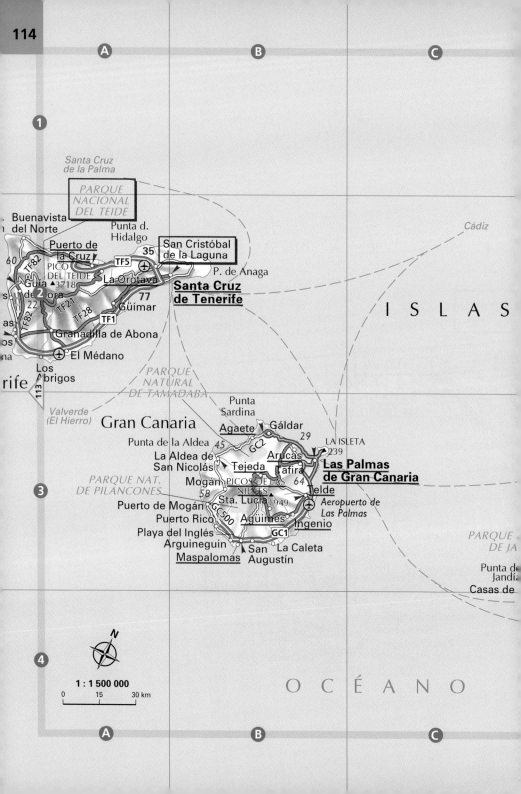

A   **B**   **C**

1

Santa Cruz de la Palma

PARQUE NACIONAL DEL TEIDE

Cádiz

Buenavista del Norte

Punta d. Hidalgo

Puerto de la Cruz   **35**

TF5

San Cristóbal de la Laguna

60

TF82

PICO DEL TEIDE ▲3718

La Orotava

P. de Anaga

Santa Cruz de Tenerife

Güia   ora

2

22

TF21

TF82

TF28

77

Güímar

TF1

Granadilla de Abona

as

os

na

El Médano

Los Abrigos

I S L A S

rife

113

Valverde (El Hierro)

PARQUE NATURAL DE TAMADABA

Gran Canaria

Punta Sardina

Agaete   Gáldar

LA ISLETA ▲239

29

Punta de la Aldea   **45**

GC2

La Aldea de San Nicolás

Arucas

Las Palmas de Gran Canaria

Tejeda   Tafira

3

PARQUE NAT. DE PILANCONES

Mogán

PICOS DE LAS NIEVES

64

Puerto de Mogán

58

Sta. Lucía ▲1949

Telde

Aeropuerto de Las Palmas

Puerto Rico

GC500

Agüimes

PARQUE DE JA

Playa del Inglés

Ingenio

GC1

Arguineguin

San

La Caleta

Maspalomas

Augustín

Punta de Jandía

Casas de

4

N

1 : 1 500 000

0   15   30 km

O C É A N O

A   **B**   **C**

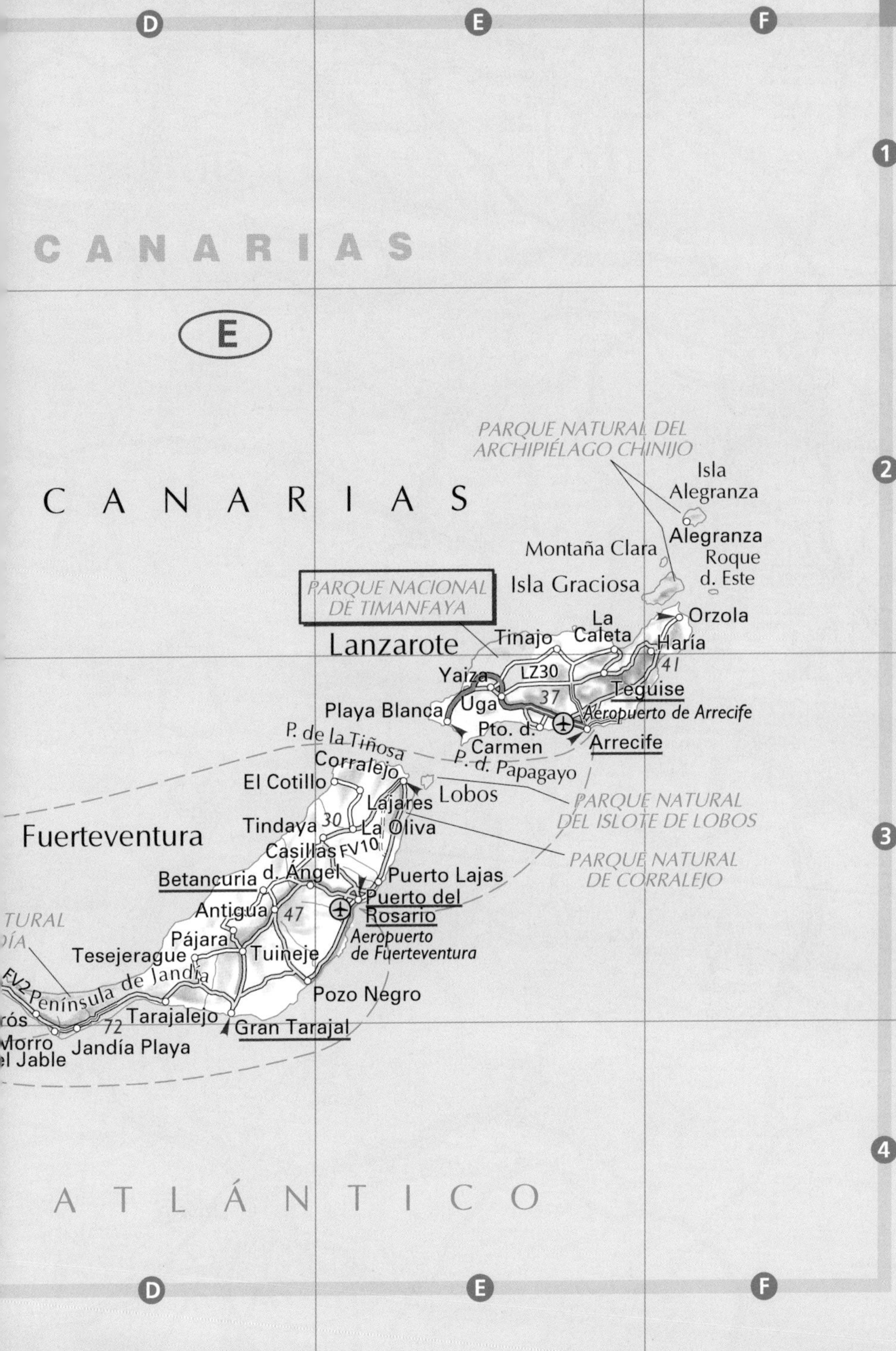

CANARIAS

E

CANARIAS

PARQUE NATURAL DEL
ARCHIPIÉLAGO CHINIJO

Isla
Alegranza

Montaña Clara
Isla Graciosa

Alegranza
Roque
d. Este

PARQUE NACIONAL
DE TIMANFAYA

Tinajo
La
Caleta

Orzola

Lanzarote

Haría

Yaiza

LZ30

Teguise

41

Uga

37

Playa Blanca

Pto. d.
Carmen

Aeropuerto de Arrecife

Arrecife

P. de la Tiñosa

Corralejo

P. d. Papagayo

El Cotillo

Lobos

Lajares

PARQUE NATURAL
DEL ISLOTE DE LOBOS

Tindaya

30

La Oliva

Fuerteventura

Casillas
d. Ángel

FV10

PARQUE NATURAL
DE CORRALEJO

Betancuria

Puerto Lajas

Antigua

47

Puerto del
Rosario

TURAL
ÍA

Pájara

Aeropuerto
de Fuerteventura

Tesejerague

Tuineje

FV2 Península de Jandía

Pozo Negro

rós

72

Tarajalejo

Gran Tarajal

Morro
el Jable

Jandía Playa

ATLÁNTICO

73
129
144
120
D
E
F
1
2
3
4
A
SLO
HR
KITZBÜHELER ALPEN
HOHE TAUERN
NATIONALPARK HOHE TAUERN
NIEDERE TAUERN
FRIULI
VENEZIA GIULIA
TRIGLAVSKI NARODNI PARK
KRAS
Jochberg
Saalbach
Bischofshofen
Eben im Pongau
Filzmoos
Öblarn
Thurn Pass 1274
Maishofen
Hinterthal
Mühlbach
Altenmarkt
Ramsau
Bramberg
Neukirchen
Zell am See
Bruck an der Grossglocknerstrasse
Dienten
St Johann im Pongau
Wagrain
Radstadt
Schladming
Donnersbachwald
Uttendorf
Taxenbach
Lend
Schwarzach
Mittersill
Felben
Kaprun
Wald
Krimml
Fellern
Fusch
Rauris
Grossarl
Obertauern
Hochgolling 2863
Sölk Pass 1790
St Nikolai
Radstädter-Tauern Pass
Tweng
Fiegler
Oberwölzstadt
Kesselfall
Luggau
Wörth
Tauerntunnel
Felber-Tauern-Tunnel
Einzinger Boden
Ferleiten
Bad Hofgastein
Hüttschlag
Mauterndorf
Seethal
Seebach
Schöder
Niederwölz
Grossvenediger
Bucheben
Badgastein
Rotgülden
Mooshām
St Michael i. Lungau
Tamsweg
Predlitz
Murau
Stadl a. d. Mur
St Lambrecht
Grossglockner
Prägraten
Kolm-Saigurn
Böckstein
Katschberg Tunnel
Katschberg
Hinterbichl
Virgen
Weirenstein
Matrei in Osttirol
Kals
Heiligenblut
Rennweg
Döllach
Mallnitz
Wasserfall Groppensteine
Turrach
Metnitz
Erlsbach
St. Veit
Huben
Obervellach
Malta
Leoben
Innerkrems
Oberhof
St. Jakob
Kienberg
Stampfen
Mörtschach
Gmünd
Flattnitz
St. Salvator
Ainet
Winklern
Stall
Polinik
Turracher Höhe
Torf
Strassburg
Lahnberg
Schlaiten
Lienz
Iselsberg
Seeboden
Klein Glödnitz
Dom
Bruck
Möllbrücke
Millstatt
Patergassen
Weitensfeld
Gurk
Thal
Amlach
Kreuzeckgruppe
Teurnia
Spittal an der Drau
Bad Kleinkirchheim
Sillian
Tessenberg
Mittewald
Oberdrauburg
Greifenburg
Steinfeld
Döbriach
Radenthein
Gnesau
St Veit
San Candido/Innichen
Sesto/Sexten
St Lorenzen
Lienzer Dolomiten
Karnische Dolomitenstrasse
Techendorf
Stockenboi
Feld
Afritz
Feldkirchen
Kötschach-Mauthen
Weissensee
Paternion
Laas
Dellach
Weissbriach
Weissenbach
Annenheim
Sattendorf
Krumpendorf
Misurina
Comelico Superiore
Reisach
Kirchbach
Hermagor
Ossiach
Pörtschach
Sappada
Plöcken Pass/Pso. di Monte Croce Carnico
Wasserleonberg
Villach
Warmbad Villach
Velden
Cortina d'Ampezzo
Auronzo di Cadore
Santo Stefano di Cadore
Forni Avoltri
Paluzza
Nassfeld Pass 1530
Arnoldstein
Faak
Rosegg
Viktring
Lozzo di Cadore
Comeglians
Paularo
Pontebba
Tarvisio
Ratece
Fürnitz
St. Jakob im Rosental
Sankt Margareten
San Vito di Cadore
Pieve di Cadore
Passo della Mauria 1298
Arta Terme
Podkoren
Wurzenpass
Kranjska Gora
Ferlach
Forni di Sopra
Ampezzo
Villa Santina
Cave del Predil
Passo del Predil 1156
Mojstrana
Jesenice
Karavanški Predor
Loiblpass
Tai di Cadore
Forni di Sotto
Tolmezzo
Chiusaforte
Predel
prelaz Vršič 1611
Podljubelj
Zoldo
Passo Cibiana 1536
Passo di Sant' Osvaldo 827
Parco Nat. D. Dolomiti Friulane
Pozzis
Log
Trenta
Triglav 2864
Vintgar
Bled
Vrba
Tržič
Jezersko
Carnia
Passo di Nevea 1190
Soča
Tramonti di Sopra
Venzone
Lesce
Radovljica
Longarone
Cimolais
Gemona del Friuli
Bovec
Bohinjska Bela
Goln
Žaga
Bohinjsko jezero
Ljubno
Naklo
Ponte nelle Alpi
Bárcis
Trnovo ob Soči
Kobarid
Ribčev Laz
Bohinjska Bistrica
Kropa
Rudno
Tarcento
Železniki
Kranj
Maniago
Lago di S Croce
Montereale Valcellina
Tolmin
Podbrdo
Sorica
Selca
Piancavallo
Spilimbergo
San Daniele del Friuli
S. Pietro al Natisone
Drenchia
Kneža
Škofja Loka
Tricesimo
Most na Soči
Bača
Cerkno
Gorenja vas
Vajont
Aviano
Dignano
Reka
Polcenigo
Cansiglio
Cividale del Friuli
Kanal
Želin
Trebija
Brode
Medvode
Vittório Véneto
S. Giorgio della Richinvelda
Campoformido
Udine
Cepovan
Spodnja Idrija
Žiri
Ljubljana
Cordenons
Deskle
Lokve
Idrija
Brezovica
Pordenone
Sacile
Codróipo
Mortegliano
Plave
Horjul
Conegliano
San Vito al Tagliamento
Nova Gorica
Gorizia
Šempeter
Šempas
Golak 1495
Rovte
Vrhnika
Logatec
Azzano Decimo
Palmanova
Godovič
Črni Vrh
Sesto al Reghena
Varmo
Gradisca d'Isonzo
Vrtojba
Ajdovščina
Kalce
Rakitna
Fontanelle
Cervignano del Friuli
Redipuglia
Branik
Vipava
Motta di Livenza
San Giórgio di Nogaro
Monfalcone
Štanjel
Dutovlje
Planina
Oderzo
Portogruaro
Latisana
Ronchi dei Legionari
Postojnska Jama
Postojna
Rakek
Cerknica
Ponte di Piave
Cessalto
Concordia Sagittaria
Marano Lagunare
Ausa Corno
Aquileia
Sistiana
Razdrto
Grahovo
Santo Stino di Livenza
Lignano Sabbiadoro
Lignano Pineta
Duino
Monrupino
Sežana
Cerkniško jezero
Otok
San Biagio di Callalta
Golfo di Panzano
Castello di Miramare
Opicina
Lipica
Senožeče
Pivka
Roncade
San Donà di Piave
San Giorgio di Livenza
Bibione
Grado
Golfo di Trieste
Trieste
Škocjanske Jame
Parje
Caorle
Eraclea
Caposile
Eraclea Mare
Múggia
Ankaran
Kozina
Ribnica
Knežak
Torcello
Jesolo
Durrës
Koper/Capodistria
Škofije
Bač
Prem
Ilirska Bistrica
Snežnik 1796
Burano
Lido di Jésolo
Izola/Isola d'Istria
Marco Polo
Murano
Cavallino
Piran/Pirano
Portorož
Jagodje
Hrastovlje
Obrov
Podgrad
Malcontenta
Venézia
Lido di Venézia
Lucija
Šmarje
Grašišće
Rakitovec
Starod
Pasjak
Rupa
Kérkyra
Igoumenítsa
Pátra
Savudrija
Sečovlje
Sočerga
Slavnik
Čičarija
Sapjane
Umag/Umago
Gradin
Požane
Alberoni
Kršete
Buje/Buie
Grožnjan/Grisignana
Buzet
Klana
Livade
Istarske Toplice
Hum
Učka Tunnel
Viškovo
Matulji
Pallestrina
Novigrad/Cittanova
Vižinada/Visinada
Motovun/Montona
Karojba
Opatija
Rijeka
Vranja
Boljun
Učka
Lovran
Park Prirode Učka
Sottomarina
Poreč/Parenzo
Pazin
Mošćenice
Mošćenička Draga
Rosolina Mare
Baderna
Gračišće
Pićan
Brseč
Riječki zaljev
Vrsar/Orsera
Kršan
Albarella
Žminj
Limski kanal
Plomin
Brestova
Porozina

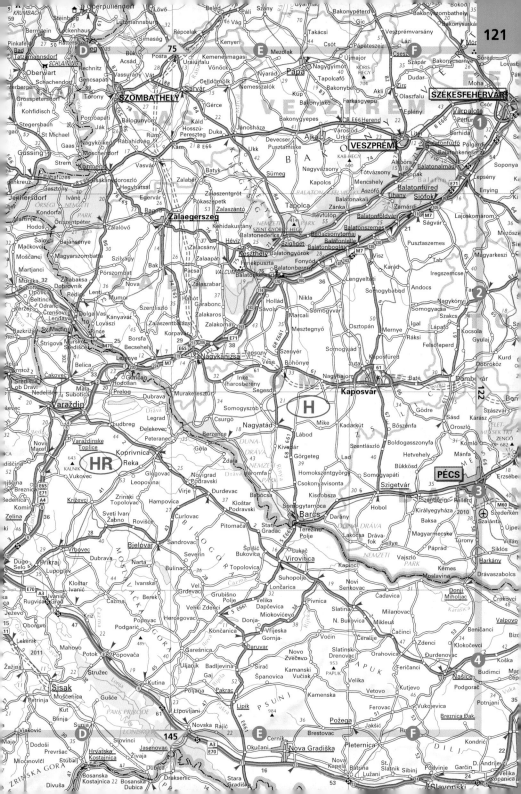

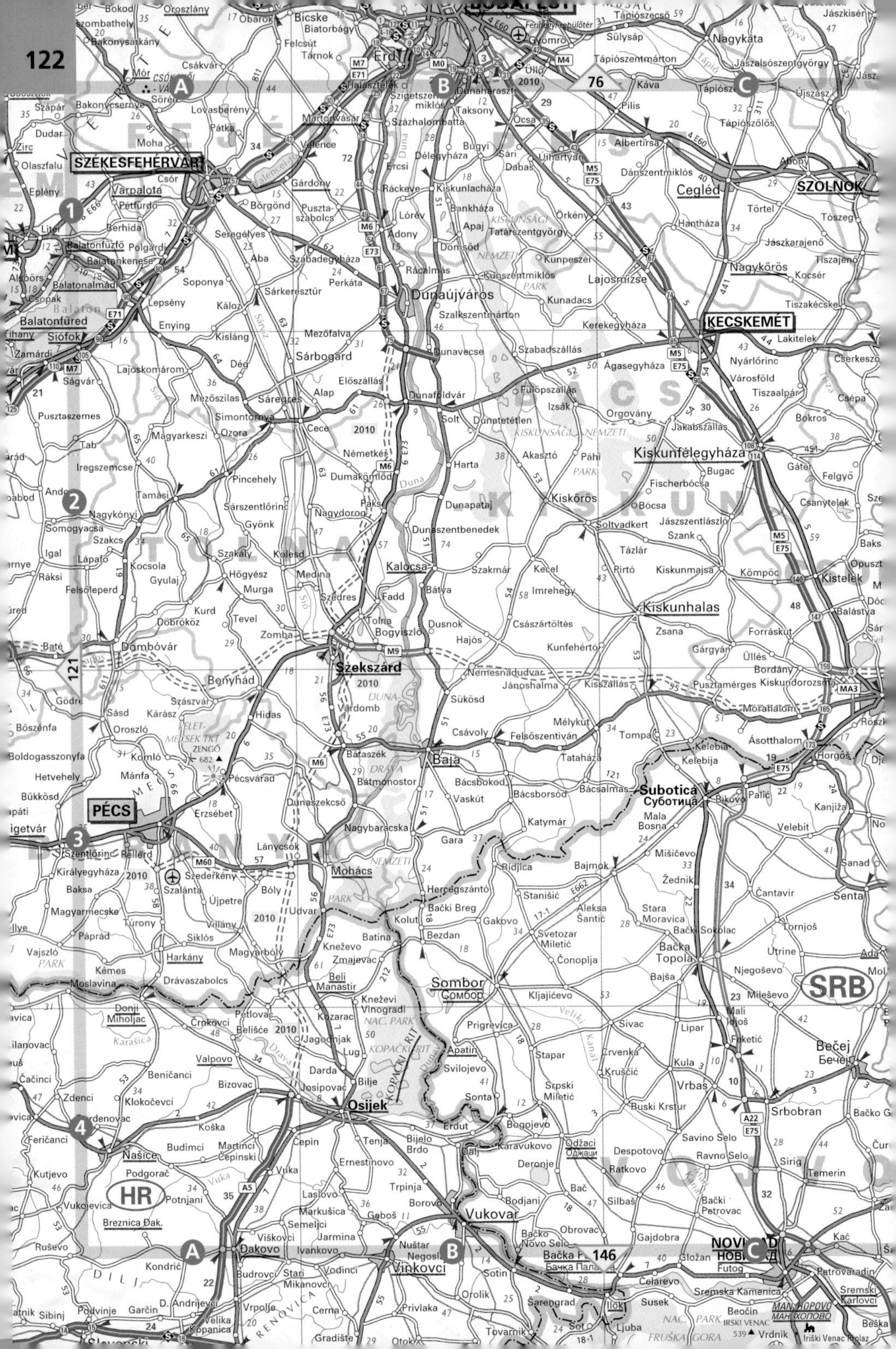

BUDAPEST
Ferihegyi repülőtér
Tápiószecső
Jászkisér
Bokod
Oroszlány
Óbarok
Bicske
Biatorbágy
Gyömrő
Sülysáp
Nagykáta
Bakonysárkány
Felcsút
Tárnok
Érd
Üllő
Tápiószentmárton
Jászalsószentgyörgy
Csákvár
Mór
Halásztelek
Szigetszentmiklós
Dunaharaszti
Káva
Tápiószele
Újszász
Szápár
Bakonycsernye
Söréd
Lovasberény
Martonvásár
Százhalombatta
Taksony
Ócsa
Pilis
Tápiószőlős
Zirc
Dudar
Pátka
Moha
Velence
Bugyi
Sári
Újhartyán
Albertirsa
Abony
Olaszfalu
SZÉKESFEHÉRVÁR
Ercsi
Délegyháza
Dabas
Dánszentmiklós
Eplény
Csór
Várpalota
Gárdony
Ráckeve
Kiskunlacháza
Cegléd
SZOLNOK
Pétfürdő
Börgönd
Pusztaszabolcs
Bankháza
Örkény
Törtel
Berhida
Lórév
Apaj
Tatárszentgyörgy
Hantháza
Tószeg
Litér
Balatonfűzfő
Polgárdi
Seregélyes
Adony
Dömsöd
Jászkarajenő
Balatonkenese
Aba
Szabadegyháza
Kunpeszér
Nagykőrös
Tiszajenő
Alsóörs
Balatonalmádi
Soponya
Perkáta
Rácalmás
Kunszentmiklós
Lajosmizse
Kocsér
Csopak
Sárkeresztúr
Dunaújváros
Kunadacs
Tiszakécske
Balaton
Lepsény
Káloz
Szalkszentmárton
Balatonfüred
Enying
Kerekegyháza
KECSKEMÉT
Tihany
Siófok
Kisláng
Mezőfalva
Dunavecse
Szabadszállás
Lakitelek
Zamárdi
Sárbogárd
Ágasegyháza
Nyárlőrinc
Cserkeszőlő
Lajoskomárom
Dég
Ságvár
Előszállás
Dunaföldvár
Fülöpszállás
Városföld
Mezőszilas
Sáregres
Alap
Izsák
Orgovány
Tiszaalpár
Csépa
Simontornya
Solt
Dunatetétlen
Jakabszállás
Bokros
Pusztaszemes
Cece
Ozora
Magyarkeszi
KISKUNSÁGI NEMZETI PARK
Tab
Németkér
Harta
Akasztó
Páhi
Kiskunfélegyháza
Gátér
Iregszemcse
Dunakömlőd
Felgyő
Pincehely
Bugac
Andocs
Tamási
Dunapataj
Fischerbócsa
Csanytelek
Sárszentlőrinc
Paks
Kiskőrös
Nagykónyi
Bócsa
Somogyacsa
Nagydorog
Gyönk
Dunaszentbenedek
Soltvadkert
Jászszentlászló
Szakcs
Szank
Igal
Lápafő
Tázlár
Szakály
Kölesd
Kalocsa
Szakmár
Kecel
Pirtó
Kiskunmajsa
Kömpöc
Kistelek
Ráksi
Kocsola
Hőgyész
Medina
Imrehegy
Gyulaj
Murga
Felsőleperd
Szedres
Fadd
Bátya
Kiskunhalas
Balástya
Kurd
Dombóvár
Tevel
Dusnok
Császártöltés
Dobrököz
Tolna
Zsana
Forráskút
Zomba
Bogyiszló
Hajós
Kunfehértó
Gárgyán
Üllés
Baté
Szekszárd
Nemesnádudvar
Bordány
Bonyhád
Jánoshalma
Kisszállás
Pusztamérges
Kiskundorozsma
Sükösd
Gödre
Szászvár
Várdomb
Mórahalom
Sásd
Kárász
Hidas
Mélykút
Bőszénfa
Oroszló
Csávoly
Felsőszentiván
Tompa
Ásotthalom
Röszke
Boldogasszonyfa
Komló
ZENGŐ
682
Bátaszék
Baja
Tataháza
Kelebia
Kelebija
Horgoš
Hetvehely
Mánfa
Pécsvárad
Bátmonostor
Bácsbokod
Bácsborsód
Bácsalmás
Subotica
Суботица
Bikovo
Palić
Bükkösd
Dunaszekcső
Vaskút
Kanjiža
PÉCS
Erzsébet
Mala Bosna
Szigetvár
Nagybaracska
Katymár
Velebit
Szentlőrinc
Pellérd
Lánycsók
Gara
Mišićevo
Királyegyháza
Szederkény
Mohács
Ridjica
Bajmok
Sanad
Baksa
Szalánta
Bóly
Hercegszántó
Stanišić
Žednik
Senta
Magyarmecske
Újpetre
Udvar
Bački Breg
Aleksa Šantić
Stara Moravica
Čantavir
Túrony
Villány
Kolut
Gakovo
Svetozar Miletić
Bački Sokolac
Tornjoš
Páprád
Siklós
Batina
Bezdan
Čonoplja
Bačka Topola
Vajszló
Harkány
Magyarbóly
Kneževo
Zmajevac
Utrine
Kémes
Beli Manastir
Njegoševo
Moslavina
Drávaszabolcs
Sombor
Сомбор
Kljajićevo
Bajša
SRB
Donji Miholjac
Kneževi Vinogradi
Mileševo
Petlovac
Kozarac
Mali Idjoš
Črnkovci
Belišće
Jagodnjak
Prigrevica
Sivac
Lipar
Bečej
Бечеј
Valpovo
Lug
Apatin
Stapar
Crvenka
Feketić
Beničanci
Darda
Svilojevo
Kruščić
Kula
Bizovac
Bilje
Srpski Miletić
Vrbas
Zdenci
Klokočevci
Josipovac
Sonta
Srbobran
Koška
Osijek
Bogojevo
Ruski Krstur
Bačko Gradište
Budimci
Martinci Čepinski
Čepin
Tenja
Erdut
Bijelo Brdo
Karavukovo
Odžaci
Оџаци
Despotovo
Savino Selo
Našice
Dalj
Deronje
Ravno Selo
Sirig
Kutjevo
Podgorač
Vuka
Ernestinovo
Ratkovo
Temerin
HR
Potnjani
Trpinja
Bač
Vukojevica
Laslovo
Borovo
Bodjani
Silbaš
Bački Petrovac
Markušica
Gaboš
Vukovar
Breznica Đak.
Semeljci
Obrovac
Gajdobra
Kać
Ruševo
Viškovci
Jarmina
Bačko Novo Selo
Nuštar
Negoslavci
Novi Sad
Нови Сад
Kondrić
Đakovo
Ivankovo
Vinkovci
Bačka Palanka
Бачка Паланка
Gložan
Futog
Petrovaradin
Budrovci
Stari Mikanovci
Vođinci
Sotin
Čelarevo
Sremski Karlovci
D. Andrijevci
Orolik
Sremska Kamenica
Podvinje
Garčin
Vrpolje
Cerna
Privlaka
Šarengrad
Ilok
Susek
Beočin
Manđelos
Sibinj
Velika Kopanica
Tovarnik
Sot
Ljuba
FRUŠKA GORA
NAC. PARK
Vrdnik
Irški Venac
Beška
Slavonski
Gradište
Otok
FEJÉR
PEST
BÁCS KISKUN
TOLNA
BARANYA
VOJVODINA
DUNA
DRÁVA
Sió
Sárvíz
Vuka
Karašica
Veliki Kanal
KOPAČKI RIT
NAC. PARK
2010
76
121
146
M0
M1
M3
M4
M5
M6
M7
M9
M60
MA3
A5
A22
E60
E66
E71
E73
E75
E662

Valence
Privas
Montélimar
Orange
Avignon
NÎMES
Arles
Carpentras
Cavaillon
Salon-de-Provence
Aix-en-Provence
MARSEILLE
Aubagne
La Ciotat
TOULON
Hyères
Manosque
Sisteron
Apt
Nyons
Die
Alès
Uzès
Bagnols-sur-Cèze
Pont-St-Esprit
Tarascon
Beaucaire
Martigues
Istres
Aigues-Mortes
Stes-Maries-de-la-Mer
Forcalquier
Crest
Aubenas
Les Baux-de-Provence
St-Rémy-de-Provence
PONT DU GARD
CHÂTEAU D'IF
LES CALANQUES
DU LUBERON
MONTS DE VAUCLUSE
CHAÎNE DES ALPILLES
DU VERCORS
DU LION
Oran
Alger
Tūnis
Annaba
Bejaïa
Skikda
Propriano
Ajaccio
Porto Tórres
Porto-Vecchio
Bastia
L'Ile Rousse
Calvi
Porquerolles
Ile de Porquerolles
81
126
D
E
F
1
2
3
4

81 116

F

1

2

3

4

A B C

Cities and towns:

La Grande Moucherolle, Laffrey, Alpe du Grand Serre, Les Deux-Alpes, Oisans, La Grave, Col du Lautaret, Bardonecchia, Bussoleno, Condove, SACRA DI SAN MICHELE, Avigliana, Rivoli

Monestier-de-Clermont, La Mure, Col de Ornon, La Bérarde, Le Monêtier-les-Bains, Sauze d'Oulx, Fenestrelle, FORTE, Cesana Torinese, Perosa Argentina, Orbassano, Piossasco

Clelles, Valbonnais, MASSIF DES, MT PELVOUX, Ailefroide, La Salle-les-Alpes, Chantemerle, Briançon, Clavière, Montgenèvre, Sestriere, Perrero, Villar Perosa, Prali, Pinerolo

Châtillon-en-Diois, St-Firmin, La Chapelle-en-Valgaudemar, Vallouise, L'Argentière-la-Bessée, La Roche-de-Rame, Arvieux, Aiguilles, Abriès, Château-Ville-Vieille, L'Echalp, Bobbio Pellice, Torre Pellice, Cavour, Villafranca Piemonte

Lus-la-Croix-Haute, St-Julien-en-Beauchêne, Col du Festre, St-Bonnet-en-Champsaur, Orcières, St-Clément-sur-Durance, Mt Dauphin, Guillestre, St-Véran, Crissolo, BELVEDERE DU CIRQUE, M VISO, Paesana, Bagnolo Piemonte, Barge, ABB. DI STAFFARDA, Moretta

Aspres-sur-Buëch, Veynes, Gap, La Bâtie-Neuve, Chorges, Embrun, Savines-le-Lac, Lac de Serre-Ponçon, Vars, Col de Vars, Casteldelfino, Saluzzo

Rosans, Serres, Tallard, St-Vincent-les-Forts, GRAND BÉRARD, St-Paul, Col de Larche / Colle della Maddalena, Argentera, Sampeyre, Frassino, Verzuolo, Busca

St-Auban-sur-l'Ouvèze, Laragne-Montéglin, Monêtier-Allemont, La Motte-du-Caire, Seyne, Le Lauzet-Ubaye, Jausiers, Barcelonnette, Larche, S. Damiano Macra, Dronero, Caraglio, Cuneo

Séderon, Curel, Noyers-sur-Jabron, Sisteron, Selonnet, Col de Maure, Uvernet-Fours, Col d'Allos, Acceglio, Stroppo, Monterosso Grana, Vinadio

MONTAGNE DE LURE, St-Etienne-les-Orgues, Château-Arnoux, Peyruis, Authon, Barles, Le Vernet, Allos, MT PELAT, Col de la Cayolle, St-Etienne-de-Tinée, Isola, SANTUARIO DI SANT'ANNA, Demonte, Borgo San Dalmazzo, Valdieri, TERME DI VALDIERI

Banon, PRIEURÉ GANAGOBIE, Mézel, La Javie, Beauvezer, CHEVAL BLANC, St-Martin-d'Entraunes, Auron, Col de la Lombarde, ARGENTERA, Col de Tende

Forcalquier, Reillanne, Brillanne, Digne-les-Bains, la Colle St-Michel, St-André-les-Alpes, Valberg, Beuil, St-Sauveur-sur-Tinée, Le Boréon, St-Martin-Vésubie, Tende

Voix, Oraison, Brás-d'Asse, Barrême, GORGES DE DALUIS, Abeliéra, Roquebillière, Col de Turini, NOTRE-DES-FONS

Manosque, Valensole, Senez, St-Julien-du-Verdon, Annot, Puget-Théniers, Lantosque, Peira-Cava, Saorge, Breil-sur-Roya

Ste-Tulle, Gréoux-les-Bains, Riez, Moustiers-Ste-Marie, Col des Lecques, Entrevaux, Le Moulin du Pali, Villars-sur-Var, Levens, Col de Braus, Sospel, Dolceacqua

Vinon-sur-Verdon, Montmeyan, Castellane, N.D. DE MIRACLES, St-Aubane, Roquestéron, Carros, Contes, L'Escarène, Menton, Ventimiglia

Rians, Varages, Tavernes, La Palud-sur-Verdon, Le Logis-du-Pin, Gréolières, Vence, St-Paul, NICE, Monte-Carlo, Monaco (MC)

Vauvenargues, Sillans-la-Cascade, Aups, Ampus, Comps-sur-Artuby, La Bastide, St-Vallier-de-Thiey, Le Bar, Mougins, Antibes, Cap d'Antibes, Beaulieu-sur-Mer, Cap-Ferrat

St-Maximin-la-Ste-Baume, Trets, Auriol, Barjols, Cotignac, Salernes, Draguignan, Montferrat, Fayence, la Colle Noire, Mandelieu, Grasse, Cannes, Golfe Juan

Aubagne, Brignoles, Lorgues, Les Arcs, Vidauban, Le Muy, Les Adrets, Puget-sur-Argens, Fréjus, Miramar, Le Trayas, Agay, Théoule, La Napoule Plage

Nans-les-Pins, La Roque-Brussanne, Le Luc, La Garde-Freinet, ABB. DU THORONET, NOTRE-DAME-DE-LA-ROCHETTE, St-Aygulf, St-Raphaël, Anthéor

Signes, Besse-sur-Issole, Puget-Ville, Cogolin, Grimaud, Port-Grimaud, St-Tropez, Ste-Maxime, Beauvallon, Val d'Esquières, L'Île Rousse, Ajaccio, Calvi, Bastia

Le Beausset, MT CAUME, Cuers, Solliès-Pont, MASSIF DES MAURES, Bormes-les-Mimosas, La Croix Valmer, Cavalaire-sur-Mer, Cap Camarat

Bandol, La Seyne, TOULON, Carqueiranne, Hyères, Cap Cépet, La Capte, Le Lavandou, Cap Bénat

N.-D. DU MAI, Cap Sicié, Giens, Porquerolles, Île de Porquerolles, Île du Levant, Port-Cros, Île de Port-Cros

Ajaccio, Porto Tórres, Bastia, ÎLES D'HYÈRES, PARC NATIONAL DE PORT-CROS

CÔTE D'AZUR

PROVENCE

A B C

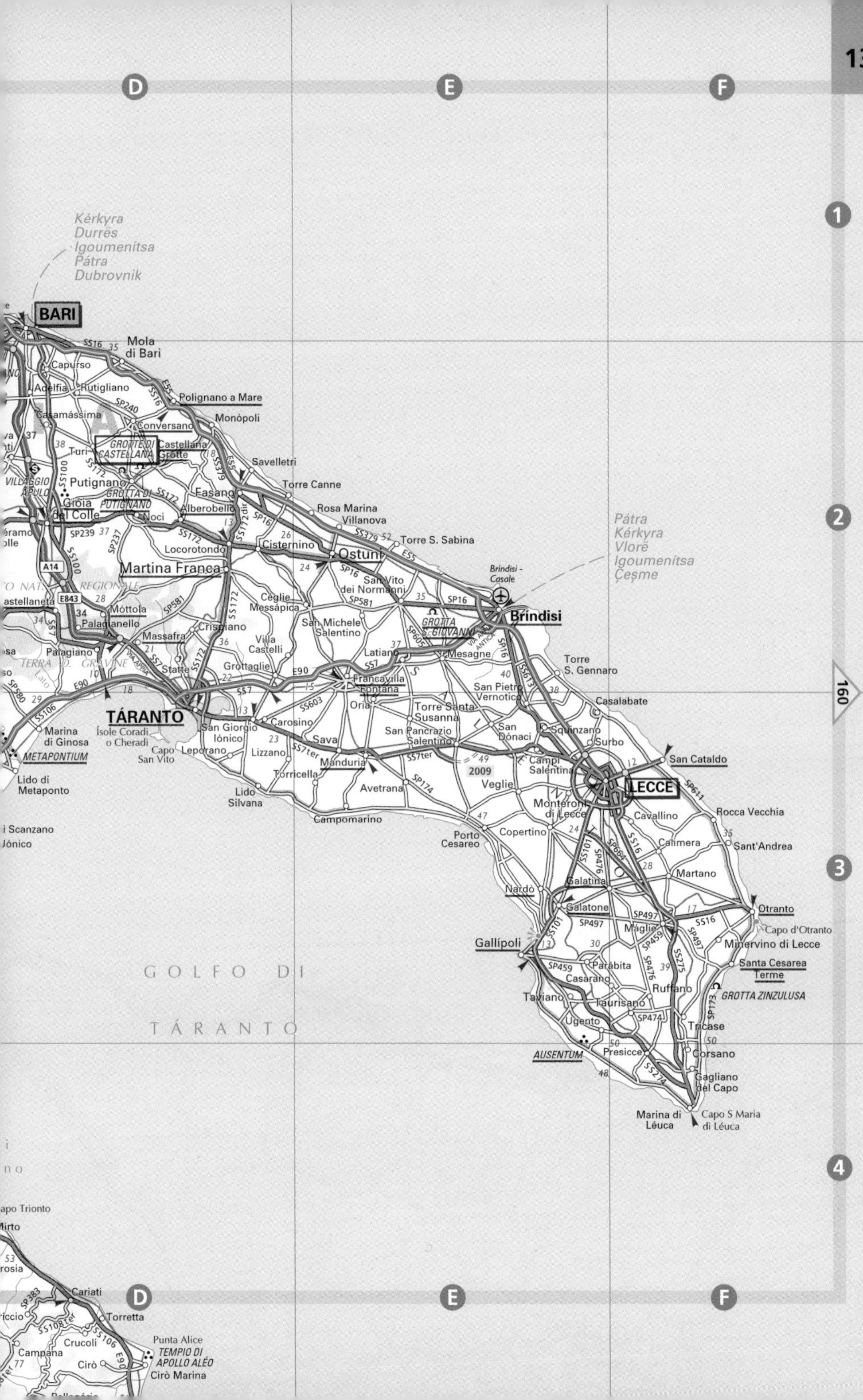

D E F

1

Kérkyra
Durrës
Igoumenítsa
Pátra
Dubrovnik

BARI
SS16 35
Mola
di Bari
Capurso
Adelfia Rutigliano
Casamássima Conversano
Polignano a Mare
SP240 Monópoli
Turi SS100 Castellana
GROTTE DI Grotte
CASTELLANA
VILLAGGIO Putignano Savelletri
APULO GROTTA DI Fasano Torre Canne
Gioia PUTIGNANO Alberobello Rosa Marina
del Colle Noci Villanova
SP239 37 Locorotondo
Martina Franca SS172 Cisternino SP16 Ostuni Torre S. Sabina
A14 E843 28 Ceglie San Vito
castellaneta 34 Messápica dei Normanni
Móttola Crispiano San Michele SP581 GROTTA
Palagianello Massafra Salentino Latiano S.GIOVANNI
TERRA DI GRAVINE Statte Villa Mesagne **Brindisi**
Castelli Grottaglie San Pietro
Francavilla Torre Santa Vernotico
TÁRANTO Fontana Susanna Casalabate
Carosino Oria Torre Squinzano
Marina Ísole Coradi San Giorgio San Pancrazio San Surbo
di Ginosa o Cheradi Iónico Lizzano Sava Salentino Dónaci San Cataldo
METAPONTIUM Capo Leporano Campi **LECCE**
San Vito Manduria Salentina
Lido di Tórricella Avetrana Veglie Montéroni Cavallino Rocca Vecchia
Metaponto Lido SP174 di Lecce Calimera Sant'Andrea
Silvana Campomarino 2009 Copertino Martano
i Scanzano Porto Galatina Otranto
Jónico Cesareo Capo d'Otranto
Nardó Galatone SP497 Máglie Minervino di Lecce
Gallípoli SP497 Parabita Santa Cesarea
Casarano Ruffano Terme
GOLFO DI Taviano Taurisano GROTTA ZINZULUSA
Ugento Tricase
TÁRANTO AUSENTUM Presicce Corsano
Gagliano
del Capo
Marina di Capo S Maria
Léuca di Léuca

2

Pátra
Kérkyra
Vlorë
Igoumenítsa
Çeşme

Brindisi -
Casale

160

3

4

apo Trionto
Mirto
rosia
Cariati
Torretta
Crucoli
Campana Ciró
Punta Alice
TEMPIO DI
APOLLO ALÉO
Ciró Marina

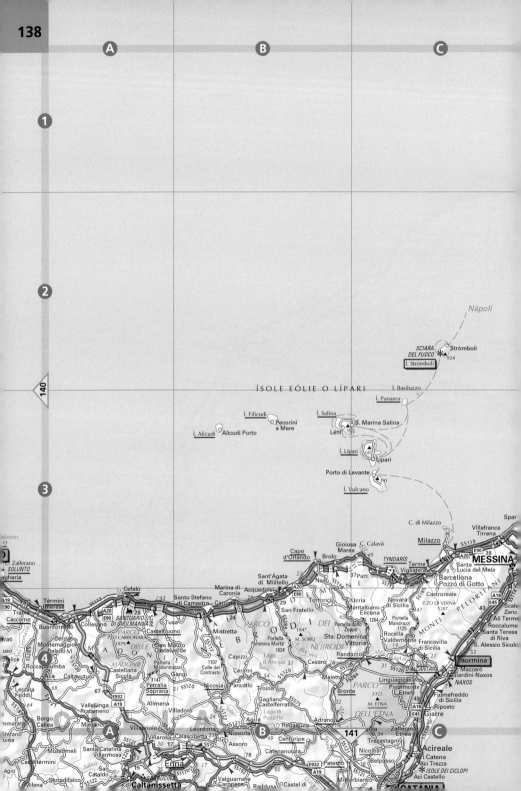

A   B   C

1

2

Nápoli

SCIARA
DEL FUOCO ✳ · Strómboli
924
Í. Strómboli

ÍSOLE EÓLIE O LÍPARI   Í. Basiluzzo

Í. Panarea

Í. Filicudi   Í. Salina
Pecorini   S. Marina Salina
a Mare   962
Í. Alicudi   Alicudi Porto   Léni

Í. Lípari   60
Lípari

Porto di Levante   941
Í. Vulcano

3

C. di Milazzo   Spar
Villafranca
Tirrena
Milazzo
Gioiosa C. Calavà   SS113
Capo Marea   TYNDARÍS   E90   38   MESSINA
d'Orlando Brolo   Terme   Santa
SS113   Vigliatore   18   Lucia del Mela
Sant'Ágata   Naso   Barcellona
di Militello A20 E90   Pozzo di Gotto
Marina di   Patti   A18   E45
Cefalù   Caronia   Acquedolci   SS116   Scale
Términi   SS113   Santo Stefano   San Fratello   Ucria   Novara   P.ZO DI VERNA   43   Zanc
Imerese   di Camastra   Caronia   Montalbano   di Sicilia   1287   Roccalume
Trabia   Castelbuono   Mistretta   Elicona   Santa Teresa
Cáccamo   Portella   Portella   Mandrazzi   di Riva
Buonfornello   Collesano   Femmina Morta   Rocella   1125   S. Alessio Siculo
Cerda   P.ZO CARBONARA   1524   Sta. Domenica   Valdemonte   Francavilla
Montemaggiore   1979   San Mauro   Vittoria   di Sicilia   21
Belsito N   Castelverde   Capizzi   Lago   Randazzo   Taormina
Roccapalumba   Portella   d'Ancipa   Mazzarò
Alia   Caltavuturo   Madonnuzza   Gangi   Cesarò   28   SS120   Giardini-Naxos
Castellana   Petralia   Maletto   NAXOS
Lercara   Sicula   Soprana   SS120   Linguaglossa
Friddi   Nicosia   Troina   Bronte   3323   Piedimonte   Fiumefreddo
67   Pancallo   M. ETNA   Etneo   di Sicilia
Vallelunga   A19   Alimena   Gagliano   Riposto
Borgo   Pratameno   Villadoro   Castelferrato   Giarre
Callea   Lago di   DELL'ETNA   E45
Mariano   Pozzillo   Adrano
Villapriolo   Leonforte   Regalbuto   141   Zafferana
Mussomeli   Villarosa Calascibetta   Nissoria   Centuripe   Etnea   Acireale
Santa Caterina   Assoro   Catenanuova   Nicolosi   Aci Catena
Villarmosa   Paternò   Belpasso   Aci Trezza
Caltavuturo   Enna   Valguarnera   A19   ISOLE DEI CICLOPI
San   SS122   Caropepe   Misterbianco   Aci Castello
Serradifalco   Castel di   Radusa   CATANIA

A   B   C

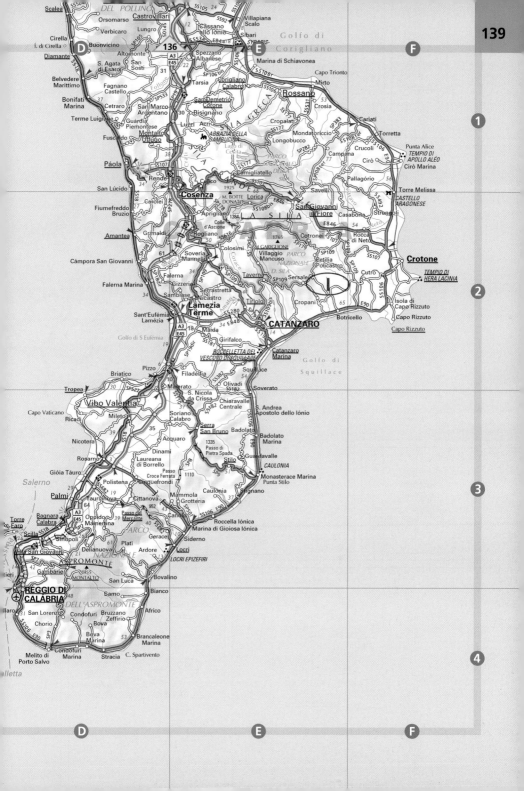

Sardegna
Corse
Costa Smeralda
SASSARI
Nuoro
Olbia
Alghero
Porto Tórres
Castelsardo
Tempio Pausània
Santa Teresa Gallura
La Maddalena
Palau
Arzachena
Porto Cervo
Porto Rotondo
Golfo Aranci
Capo Figari
Ìsola Tavolara
Ìsola Molara
Capo Coda Cavallo
San Teodoro
Budoni
Posada
La Caletta
Siniscola
Capo Comino
Cala Liberotto
Orosei
Dorgali
Cala Gonone
Golfo di Orosei
Oliena
Orgosolo
Ottana
Macomer
Bosa
Ozieri
Ittiri
Thiesi
Bonorva
Pattada
Buddusò
Alà dei Sardi
Òschiri
Monti
Telti
Calangianus
Luras
Aggius
Perfugas
Valledoria
Sorso
Sènnori
Òsilo
Ploaghe
Stintino
Ìsola Asinara
Capo del Falcone
Golfo dell' Asinara
Capo Càccia
Rada di Alghero
Fertilia
Olmedo
Capo Marárgiu
Tresnuraghes
Cùglieri
Santa Caterina di Pittinuri
Abbasanta
Ghilarza
Bonifacio
Porto Vecchio
Sartène
Propriano
Figari
Bocche di Bonifacio
Marseille
Porto Tórres
Toulon
Ajaccio
Génova
Piombino
Livorno
Civitavécchia
Árbatax

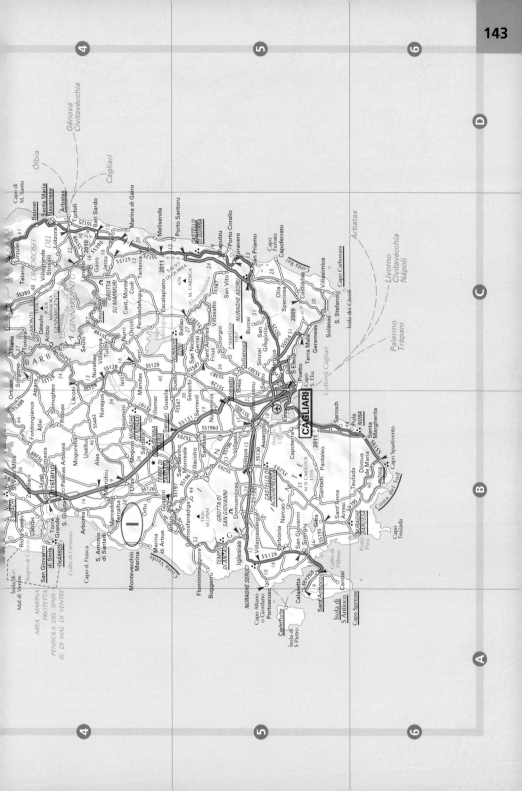

D   E   F

1

2

Illichivs'k
Sinop
Trabzon
Samsun
Zonguldak

Yalıköy

Karacaköy   Ormanlı

Karaburun   Pa

Çamkonak

Karamandere   361   Kara   Terkoz   KILYOS   Kefken

Vurusu Gölü   Ağaçlı   Kumköy   Çayağzı   Sahilköy   Şile   Ağva/Yeşilçay   Kandıra

75   Akalan   Yassıören   016   Rumelifeneri   Bozhane   Yeşilvadi   Akçakese   74   Akçova   Kocakaymaz   Kayma

Kabakca   Subaşı   020   Arnavutköy   Kemerburgaz   Sarıyer   Beykoz   70   Teke   Türas   605

Çatalca   Boyalık   İSTANBUL   Yenıköy   Alemdağ   Ömerli   Oruçoğlu   Kargalı   Akmeşe

E80   O-3   Cemke   Sarıgazi   Ömerli Barajı   Karayakuplu   Sapakpınar   Uzuntarla

82   Esenyurt   Küçükçekmece   Üsküdar   Samandıra   Tepecik   KOCAELİ (İZMİT)   41.07   40   Kurtköy

Silivri   Büyükçekmece   Bakırköy   Kartal   Tepeören   Mollafeneri   Gölcük   Suadiye

Gürpınar   Yeşilköy   Maltepe   100   89   Hereke   Körfez   Değirmendere

Kavaklı   Avcılar   Atatürk   Büyükada   Pendik   Gebze   Tavşancil   Yenıköy   Bahçecik

Kızıl Adalar   Tuzla   Darıca   39

İzmir
Çanakkale

İmralı Adası

Altınova   28   130   Karamürsel   1314

DENİZİ   Yalova   Çiftlikköy   Yalakdere   Sarısu   Pamuko

Şencöy   Çınarcık   575   Candarlı   Şehvarmaz   Mekece   65

Arnavutköy   Termal   20   Yenıköy   Bayındır   595   Ebeylı

TR   Hayriye   921   Orhangazi   150   Boyalıca   İznik   30   Sevler

Armutlu   Fıstıklı   Kapaklı   Karacaali   18   İznik Gölü   NIKAIA   Osmane

Gemlik   Sölöz   Narlıca   44

Zeytinbağı   Mudanya   Umurbey   Bayırköy   Köprühisar   160   Vezlhan

Kurşunlu   Ericek   Yenişehir   Pelitözu

D   165   APAMEA   E   O-33   46   F

Bayramdere   HISARTEPE DASCYLIUM   Koyunhis   Boğazköy   Koyunköy   Bilecik

Yenice   PLAKIA   Yunuseli   Demirtaş   Gürsün   Turan

Gölecik   Görükle   14   29   1004

Yemikaraağaç   MILETOPOLIS   Hasanağa   BURSA

Pellg i Drinit

Ligeni Ulzës · Ligeni Ullzes · ZALL-GJOKAJ NAT. PARK · Fushë Muhurr · Peshkopi · SVETI JOVAN BIGORSKI СВ. ЈОВАН БИГОРСКИ · Maqellarë · Mavrovsko Ezero · DOBRA VODA

Fushë-Kuqe · Laç · Lis · Selishtë · Mavrovo Маврово · NACIONALNI PARK MAVROVO · Zajas · Tuin

Patog · Burrel · MI KRESHTES · 154 · Dolno · Jance · Gari · Izvor · Kičevo · Čelopeci

Kep i Rodonit · Shetaj · Krujë · Shtamës 1228 · Klos · Bulqizë · Zerqan · Osbar · Dzepišta · Kosovrasti · Presek Prolaz 903 · Belica · Cer · Golem

Kep i Palit · Katundi i Ri · Fushë-Krujë · QAFE SHTAME NAT. PARK · Rinas · DAJTI NAT. PARK · MAL I LOPES 2020 · MAL I DAJTIT 1612 · Qafae e Stilles 1522 · 1828 · Klenjë · Lukovo · STOGOVO СТОГОВО · Pesočani · Globočica Ezero · Belčišta · MK · Sopot

Durrës · Vorë · Kamëz · Shijak · Lalm · Shëngjergj · Zabzun · Botun · Ohrid · Mešeišta · 1999 · Bukovo Prolaz

Trieste Ancona Bari · Gji i Durrësit · Ndroq · TIRANË · Petrelë · Vakumonë · CERMENICA · Doréz · MAL I SHEBENIK 2263 · Veleshta · Struga Струга · Kösel

Kavajë · Kërrabë · Labinot Fushë · Librazhd · Čafasan · Lin · Ohrid Охрид · NACIONALNI PARK GALIČICA · Carev Dvor · Resen · E65

Kep i Lagit · Shëmhill · Elbasan · Babjen · Prenjas · Ohridsko ezero Охридско Езеро · Peštani · KURBI

Luzi Madhi · Rogozhinë · Vidhas · Peqin · Gjinar · MAL I SHPATIT 1840 · Stravaj · Ligeni i Ohrit · Otešavo

Čermë · Cërrik · Shtërmen · Drizë · MI SHPATIT · GURI UZI 2076 · Podgradec · SVETI NAUM · Goricë · Presponsko ezero

Divjakë · Gji i Karavastasë · Ballshi · Mollas · Ligeni Banjes · Gramsh · Cërravë · Veliterne · Podgorie · Dol

DIVJAKA PINES NATIONAL PARK · Kryekuq · Lushnjë · Selitë · Mashan · Koklë · Moglicë · Zvarisht · Sovjan · Zemblak · Krista

ARDENICÉS · Kolonjë · Poshnjë · Kucovë · TOMORRI MOUNTAIN NATIONAL PARK · VALAMARE 2376 · Malig · PRESPA NATIONAL PARK

Grykë · Ura Vajgurore · Roskovec · Berat · MI TOMORRIT · Devoll · Voskopojë · Bilisht

APOLLONIA · Fier · Patosi · Zhitom i Madh · Vertop 2416 · Gjerbës · VALAMARE · Korçë · BREDHI I DRENOVES NATIONAL PARK · Ieropigi

Levan · HEKAL · Ballsh · Terpan · Poliçan · Koritë · Vithkuq · 1196 · Dardhë · LOFKA · Komnina

Novoselë · Mifol · BYLLIS · 903 · Corovodë · OSTROVICA 2352 · Nestori

Vijosë · MALLAKASTRA · Gllavë · Buz · Çepan · AL · 1879 · Péfkos

Vlorë · Panaje · Selenicë · Vlahinë · Krahës · Ballaban · Osum · BREDHI I HOTOVES NAT. PARK · Mollas · OROS GRAMMOS 2253 · Poly

Kep i Gjuhëzës · Peshkëpija · AMANTIA · Sevaster · Sinanaj · Tepelenë · Frashër · Erseke · Plikáti · Lykorrachi · Barmash

Pasha Liman · Kote · Vajzë · 2122 · MI GRABES · Vijosë · Kosine · TREMISHT · 1075 · Leskovik · Amáranos · Pyrsógianni · Foúrka

Orikum · Lepenicë · Rexhin · Gusmar · Tepelenë · Përmet · 61 · Barmash · SMÓLIKAS 2631

Dukat · Brataj · Shushicë · Kuç · ANTIGONEA · Hoshtevë · Vithkuq · Poliçan · Çarshovë · Konitsa · FARANGI VIKOU

Dhërmi · Himarë · 1842 · Goleim · Palokastër · 2486 · Libohovë · OROS TYMF 2480 · Monodéndri

Palermo · Ftterë · Piqeras · Gjirokastër · Melissopetra · Pogoniani · Kefalóvryso · Kalpáki · E90

Borsh · Lukovë · Delvina · Jergucati · Ktismata · Delviniáki · Doliana · Kakavi · Asfáka · Zitsa · E853

Vlorë Venezia Ancona Brindisi Bari · Kep Kefali · PHÖNIX · Finiq · Sarandë · BUTRINT NAT. PARK · Koklëi · Aetópetra · Soulópoulo · Klimátia · Pérama

N. Ereíkousa · N. Othonoi · N. Mathráki · N. Otthonoi · Róda · Sidári · Avliótes · Karousádes · Ypsos · Nisáki · Butrint · Shkalle · Konispol · Agios Nikólaos · Filiátes · Vrosina · Grammenó · Ioánnina

Akr. Ag. Aikateríni · Kassiópi · Gouviá · BUTHROTUM · Sagiáda · Keramítsa · Kourénta · Mázia

Palaiokastrítsa · Liapádes · Kontokáli · Kérkyra · Péleka · Ágios Górdios · Mpestiá · Moraítika · Igoumenitsa · 166 · Ménina · Petoúsi · Dodóni · Pérdika

Kérkyra · Ag. Matthaíos · Lefkími · Argyrádes · Kávos · Platariá · Syvóta · Karvounári · Paramythiá · Dérviziana

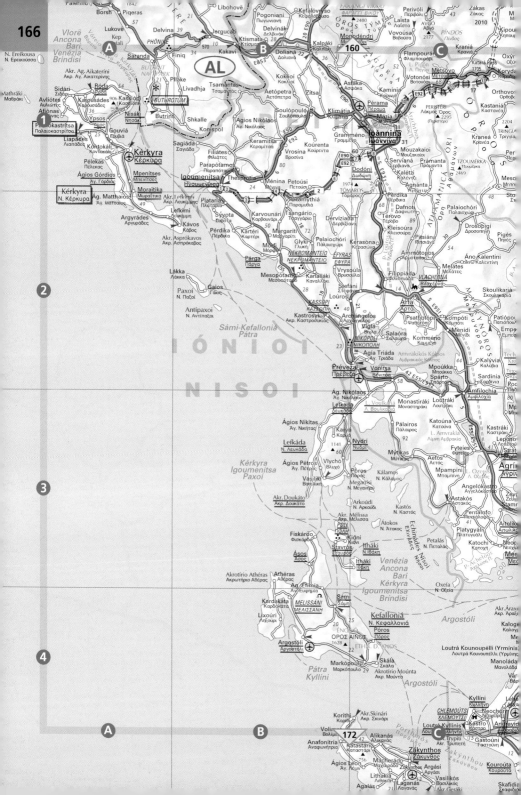

D · E · F

1

2

3

4

Panaiá · Elafí · Kraniá Elassónas · Elassóna · Rapsáni · Stómio · Stómio

Desáti · Kefalóvrysо · Tsaritsáni · Ampeláki · Kókkino Neró

Ánoixi · Sykiá · Doméniko · Rodiá · TEMPI · Akrotírio Dermatás

Vlacháva · Koniskós · Tyrnavos · Ampelónas · Sykoúri · Agiókampos

METÉORA · Kalampáka · Verdikoússa · Mesochóri · Dámasi · **LÁRISA** · Dímitra · Mavrovoúni · Sklithro

Rizoma · Lióprasо · Neochóri · Grizáno · Koutsóchero · Nikaía · Platýkampos · Keramídi

Tríkala · Farkadóna · Mavrovoúni · Chálki · Kalamáki · Makrinítsa · Chorefto

Megalochóri · Palamás · Psychikó · Ag. Anárgyroi · Rizómylos · **Vólos** · Tsagkaráda

Xiloparóïko · Agnantero · Ypéreia · Sófo · Velestíno · Portariá · Kalamáki

Mouzáki · Mataránga · Chalkiádes · Rígaio · Aerinó · Sésklo · Miliés · Neochóri

Kardítsa · Stavrós · Vamvakoú · **PAGASAE** · Agriá · Kalá Nerá

Mitrópoli · Gefýra · Farsala · Fýlaki · Mikrothíves · Néa Anchíalos · Argalastí

Neochóri · Safádes · Néo Monastíri · Narthaki · Almyrós · Milína

Kastaniá · Kédros · Domókos · Anthótopos · Anávra · Soúrpi · Platanias

Amárantos · Karyés · **GR** · Vrýtaina · Tríkeri · Skiáthos

Prasiá · Loutrá Smokóvou · Órоs Óthrys · Pigádi · Artemísio · Geronoúni

Mavromáta · Rentína · Trílofo · Divri · Pelagía · Istiaía · Vasilikà

Voúlpi · Gούrа · Makrakómi · Stylída · Ráches · Loutrá Aidipsoú · Oreoí

Kerasochóri · Platýstomo · Leianokládi · Ag. Marína · Giáltra · Iliá

Fragkísta · Ag. Geórgios · **Lamía** · Ilaía · Rovlés · Límni

Karpenísi · Tymfristós · Spercheiáda · Loutrá Ypátis · **THERMOPYLES** · Gregolímano

Mikró Chorió · Gardíki · Iráklеia · Mólos · Kaménа Voúrla · Arkitsa · M. GALAT.

Agios Vlásios · Mégа Chorió · Pávliani · Thermopýles · Ag. Konstantínos · Skála

Domnítsa · Grammeni Oxyá · Kalloskopí · Regkínio · Zéli · Theológos

Panaitóliko · Arachóva · Amfíkleia · Káto Fithóta · Atalánti · Kolála · Lárymna

Aráchova · Eptálofos · Eláteia · Martíno · Martino

Ag. Dimítrios · Lefkadíti · Léfkadión · Exarchos · Pávlos · Kástro · PTÓ

Thérmo · Pentagioí · Dávleia · **ORCHOMENÓS** · AKRAIFIA

Límnitsa · **ÁMFISSA** · **DELFOÍ** · Chairóneia · Orchomenós · GLA

Lidoriki · Delfoí · Aráchova · Distomo · **Livadeiá** · Ifnio

Paleópyrgos · Malandrinо · Antíkyra · Kyriáki · Agia Anna · Vágia

Rígani · Amygdaliá · Galaxidi · Kyriáki · Thespiés · Aliartos

Náfpaktos · Marathiás · Ag. Andrómachi · Pródromos · Thisvi · **Thíva**

Antírrio · Glyfáda · Akr. Psaromyta · Pláka · Ag. Ioánnis · Plataiés

Psathópyrgos · **Río** · Ag. Nikolaos · Póo · Germenó · **AIGÓSTHENA**

PÁTRA · Áno Kastrítsi · Diakoftó · Derveni · Káto Alepochóri · Mégara

Vrachnéïka · **Aígio** · Paralía Platánou · Xylókastro · **GERÁNEIA**

Kagkádi · Chalándritsa · Zachloroú · **MÉGA SPÍLAIO** · Kiáto · Agioi Theódoroi

Santoméri · Káto Vlasía · Petsáko · Trikala · **Kórinthos** · Isthmía

Káto Velítses · Kalávryta · Mána · **SYKIÓNA** · **AR. KORÍNTHOS**

Kéntro · Tripótama · Gkoúra · Kefaláni · **NEMÉA** · Chiliomódi · Sofikó

Efyra · **AG. LAVRA** · Kaliánoi · Sofikó · Korfos

D · Lámpeia · **ORCHOMENÓS** · Leóntio · **MYKÍNES** · Dimainia

Koúmanis · Valtesíniko · Kandíla · Limnes · Néa Epídavros

Láaas · Platanos · Daphní · Levídi · **MANTINEIA** · **Árgos** · Palaiá Epídavros

Yenifoça
Aslan Burun
İstanbul
Çanakkale
Kara Burun
Mytilíní-Lésvos

PHOKAIA
Foça
TAŞKULE
Bozalan
Menemen
Kaklıç
Çamaltı

Hasseki
Karaburun
Parlak
1212
AK DAĞ
505
Küçükbahçe
Uzon Adası
Mordoğan
İn
1

Agiásmata
Αγιάσματα
Kampiá
Καμπιά
Mármaro
Μάρμαρο
Oinoússes
Ν. Οινούσσες
Balıklıova
Çeşmealtı
KLAZOMENAI
Urla
Güzelbahçe
1042

Melaniós
Μελανιός
1297
Kardámyla
Καρδάμυλα
27
Lagkáda
Λαγκάδα
Vrontádos
Βροντάδος
300

Volissós
Βολισσός
34
Chíos
Χίος
TR
İlıca
Urla
40
Bedemler

Chíos
Ν. ΧΙΟΣ
NEA MONÍ
Ν. ΜΟΝΗ
Kallimasiá
Καλλιμασιά
Thymianá
Θυμιανά
Çeşme
Uzunkuyu
30
O-32
58
Orhanlı

Pasá Limáni
Πασά Λιμάνι
Véssa
Βέσσα
Armólia
Αρμόλια
Kalamotí
Καλαμωτή
Alaçatı
28
Seferihisar
Sığacık
TEOS

Mestá
Μεστά
Pyrgío
Πυργίο
Kómi
Κώμη
Empereiós
Εμπορειός
Sığacık Körfezi
Doğanbey
MYONNE

Akr. Másticho
Ακρ. Μάστιχο
Sámos
Karlóvasi
Koraka Burun
Doğanbey Burun
Ükn

Rafína
Mýkonos
Peiraiás
Ancona
Brindisi
Chíos
Peiraiás
Náxos
Adámas-Milos
2

Ag. Konstantínos
Αγ. Κωνσταντίνος
Avláki
Αμλάκι
Kokk
62
1151

Karlóvasi
Νέο Καρλόβασι
34
Pýrgos
Πύργος
39

Marathókampos
Μαραθόκαμπος
1455
Sámos
Ν. Σάμος
170

Akr. Fanári
Ακρ. Φανάρι
Ag. Kyriakí
Αγ. Κυριακή
Spatha
Σπαθα
Sámos
Ν. Σάμος
IRAÍO
ΗΡΑΙΟ
Ιρέ

Thessaloníki

Ikaría
Ν. Ικαρία
Thérma
Θέρμα
Foúrnoi
Ν. Φούρνοι
Ag. Mínas
Αγ. Μηνάς

Évdilos
Εύδηλος
Ag. Kýrikos
Αγ. Κήρυκος
Foúrnoi
Φούρνοι

Náxos
Armenistís
Αρμενιστής
Christós
Χριστός
Thýmaina
Ν. Θύμαινα

Ámalo
Άμαλο
984
Mýkonos
Náxos

Akr. Pápas
Ακρ. Πάπας

Pátmos
Ν. Πάτμος

Tínos
Ν. Τήνος
Kómi
Κώμη
Falatádos
Φαλατάδος
Kámpos
Κάμπος
Leipsoí
Ν. Λειψοί

Stérnia
Ιστέρνια
27
Kiónia
Κιόνια
EXÓMVOURGO
ΕΞΩΜΒΟΥΡΓΟ
Chíos
Skála
Σκάλα
Pátmos
Πάτμος
3

Áno Sýros
Áno Meriá
Άνω Μεριά
Dragonísi
Δραγονήσι
Partheni
Παρθένι

Ermoúpoli
Ερμούπολη
Mýkonos
Ν. Μύκονος
Ag. Stéfanos
Αγ. Στέφανος
Mýkonos
Μύκονος
Platýs Gialós
Πλατύς Γιαλός
Kálymnos
Astypálaia
Kos
Léros
Ν. Λέρος
Xirókam

Varí Βάρη
Ríneia
Ν. Ρήνεια
DILOS
ΔΗΛΟΣ
Dílos
Ν. Δήλος

Thessaloníki
Náxos
Peiraiás

érifos'
Milos
L Á D E S
Κ Λ Α Δ Ε Σ
Ág. Kýrikos-Ikaría
Évdilos-Ikaría
Sámos
Skála-Pátmos
Akr. Stavroí
Ακρ. Σταυροί
Apóllon
Απόλλων
Leipsoí

Sýros
Tínos
Ν. Πόρος
Kórthos
Κόρθος
Náxos
Νάξος
Donoúsa
Δονούσα
Levitha
Ν. Λεβίθα
Kálymnos

Peiraiás
Kamáres
Καμάρες
Néousa
Νάουσα
Filóti
Φλώτι
Moutsoúna
Μουτσούνα
Kínaros
Ν. Κίναρος

Páros
Πάρος
Kóstos
Κώστος
Léfkes
Λεύκες
Galanádo
Γαλανάδο
26
Apeirathos
Απείραθος
4

Poúnta
Πούντα
745
Marpissa
Μάρπισσα
19
Áno Sagkri
Άνω Σαγκρί
Náxos
Ν. Νάξος

Antíparos
Αντίπαρος
Dryós
Δρυός
Pyrgáki
Πυργάκι
Koufonísi
Κουφονήσι
Aigiáli
Αιγιάλη

Antíparos
Ν. Αντίπαρος
Akr. Petalída
Ακρ. Πεταλίδα
Alykí
Αλυκή
Kéros
Ν. Κέρος
CHOZOVIÓTISSA
Παναγία Χαζοβιώτισσα
Amorgós
Ν. Αμοργός

alós
αλός
Iráklia
Ηράκλεια
Schoinoússa
Ν. Σχοινούσσα
Katápola
Κατάπολα
Amorgós
Αμοργός
MÍNOA
ΜΙΝΩΑ

Ágios Nikólaos-Kríti
Karavostásis
Iráklia
Ν. Ηράκλεια
Arkesíni
Αρκεσίνη
Astypálaia
Vathý
Βαθύ
Astypálaia
Ν. Αστυπάλαια
Kálymnos
Kos

Síkinos
Σίκινος
Íos
Ν. Ίος
Ν. Ίος
175

Folégandros
Síkinos
Ν. Σίκινος
552
713
Magkanári
Μαγκανάρι
Ánydros
Ν. Ανύδρου
Astypálaia
Análipsi
Ανάληψη

Folégandros
Ν. Φολέγανδρος
Akr. Achládes
Ακρ. Αχλάδες
Astypálaia
Αστυπάλαια
Ofidoúsa
Ν. Οφιδούσα

GR

ATTIKI

ΑΘΗΝΑ ATHINA
ΠΕΙΡΑΙΑΣ PEIRAIAS

Elefsina Ελευσίνα
Glyfada Γλυφάδα
Mégara Μέγαρα
Kórinthos Κόρινθος
Korinthos
Isthmia Ίσθμια
Loutró Elénis Λουτρό Ελένης
Ag. Theódoroi Άγ. Θεόδωροι
Salamína Σαλαμίνα
Salamína Ν. Σαλαμίνα
Selínia Σελίνια
Vouliagméni Βουλιαγμένη
Lagonísi Λαγονήσι
Anávyssos Ανάβυσσος

Akratas Ακράτας
Xylókastro Ξυλόκαστρο
Kiáto Κιάτο
Loutráki Λουτράκι
Sykióna Σικυώνα
Perachóra Περαχώρα
Sparta Σπάρτα
Mégara Νέα Πέραμος
Kinéta Κινέτα
Karakiani Καρακιανή
Mándra Μάνδρα
Nea Iosia Νέα Ιωσία
Aspropyrgos Ασπρόπυργος
Achárnes Αχαρνές
Pallíni Παλλήνι
Spáta Σπάτα
Markó Μαρκό
Koropí Κορωπί

ARONIKOS KOLPOS ΣΑΡΩΝΙΚΟΣ ΚΟΛΠΟΣ
SARONIKOS

Aígina Αίγινα
AFAÍA ΑΦΑΙΑ
Agia Marína Αγ. Μαρίνα
Pérdika Πέρδικα
Méthana Μέθανα
Póros Πόρος
N. Póros Ν. Πόρος
Galatás Γαλατάς
Ág. Geórgios Άγ. Γεώργιος
Akr. Spáthi Ακρ. Σπάθι

Kalávryta Καλάβρυτα
MEGA SPILAIO ΜΕΓΑ ΣΠΗΛΑΙΟ
AG. LAVRA ΑΓ. ΛΑΥΡΑ
Trikala Τρίκαλα
Mana Manna Μάνα Μάννα
Kefalári Κεφαλάρι
Kalianói Καλιάνοι
STYMFALIA ΣΤΥΜΦΑΛΙΑ
Kastánia Καστάνια
Láfka Λάφκα
Kandila Κανδήλα
Leóntio Λεόντιο
NEMEA ΝΕΜΕΑ
Nemées Νεμέες
MYKINES ΜΥΚΗΝΕΣ
MYKINES
IRAIO ΗΡΑΙΟ
Chiliomódi Χιλιομόδι
Sofikó Σοφικό
Kórfos Κόρφος
Angelokastro Αγγελόκαστρο
Néa Epídavros Νέα Επίδαυρος
Palaia Epídavros Παλαιά Επίδαυρος
AR. EPIDAVROS ΑΡΧ. ΕΠΙΔΑΥΡΟΣ
Ágios Nikólaos Άγιος Νικόλαος
Kaiméni Chóra Καϊμένη Χώρα
Dryópi Δρυόπη
Kalloni Καλλονή
Ýdra Ύδρα
N. Ýdra Ν. Ύδρα

ORCHOMENOS ΟΡΧΟΜΕΝΟΣ
MANTINEIA ΜΑΝΤΙΝΕΙΑ
Levídi Λεβίδι
Kápsas Κάψας
Kapsás
Nestáni Νεστάνι
Argos Άργος
TIRYNTHA ΤΙΡΥΝΘΑ
ARCH. TIRYNTHOS ΑΡΧ. ΤΙΡΥΝΘΟΣ
Midéa Μιδέα
Náfplio Ναύπλιο
Ligourió Λιγουριό
Kántia Κάντια
Tracheia Τραχεία
TROIZINA ΤΡΟΙΖΗΝΑ
Thermisía Θερμησία
Troizína Τροιζήνα

Vytina Βυτίνα
Davia Δάβια
Loukás Λουκάς
LERNI ΛΕΡΝΗ
LERNA ΛΕΡΝΑ
Kivéri Κιβέρι
Myloi Μύλοι
Achladókampos Αχλαδόκαμπος
Parthéni Παρθένι
Tolo Τολό
ASINI ΑΣΙΝΗ
Asíni Ασίνη
Parália Irion Παραλία Ιρίου
Didyma Δίδυμα
Koiláda Κοιλάδα
Kranídi Κρανίδι
Ermióni Ερμιόνη
Dokós Ν. Δοκός

Tripoli Τρίπολη
Makri Μάκρη
Stenó Στενό
Kato Doliana Κάτω Δολιανά
Palaio Astros Παλαιό Άστρος
Astros Άστρος
TEGEA ΤΕΓΕΑ
Vlachokerasiá Βλαχοκερασιά
Ag. Andréas Αγ. Ανδρέας
Plátanos Πλάτανος
Pórto Cheli Πόρτο Χέλι
Akr. Kóras Ακρ. Κόρακας
Kósta Κόστα
Spétses Σπέτσες
N. Spétses Ν. Σπέτσες

Karytaina Καρύταινα
GORTYS ΓΟΡΤΥΣ
Káto Aséa Κάτω Ασέα
Megalopoli Μεγαλόπολη
Leontári Λεοντάρι
Kollínes Κολλίνες
Karyés Καρυές
Ag. Pétros Αγ. Πέτρος
Tyrós Τυρός
Sampatiki Σαμπατική
Palaiochóri Παλαιοχώρι
Leonídio Λεωνίδιο

Paros Πάρος
Ermoúpoli-Sýros
Adámas-Mílos
Chios
Ródos
Skála-Pátmos
Soúda-Kríti
Irákleio-Kríti
Réthymno-Kríti
Sámos
Astypálaia

Lemesos-Cyprus
Hefa-Yisrael'
Kuşadasi-Türkiye
Çeşme-Türkiye
Mytilíni-Lésvos

Peiraías

Arfará Αρφαρά
Poliani Πολιανή
Dyrráchio Δυρράχιο
Artemisía Αρτεμισία
Thouria Θουρία
Trýpi Τρύπη
Sellasía Σελλασία
Sparti Σπάρτη
Spárti Σπάρτη
Mystrás Μυστράς
Amykles Αμύκλες
Xirokámpi Ξηροκάμπι
Chrýsafa Χρύσαφα
Kosmás Κοσμάς
Peletá Πελετά
Gkoritsá Γκόριτσα
PYRGOS GERAKIOU ΠΥΡΓΟΣ ΓΕΡΑΚΙΟΥ
Kremasti Κρεμαστή
Rhichéa Ρειχέα
Velopoúla Ν. Βελοπούλα

Kalamáta Καλαμάτα
Almyró Αλμυρό
Kámpos Κάμπος
Avía Αβία
Kardamýli Καρδαμύλη
Ag. Nikólaos Αγ. Νικόλαος
Kastánia Καστανιά
Plátsa Πλάτσα
Lagkáda Λαγκάδα
Liméni Λιμένι
Agéranos Αγέρανος
Gkeráki Γκεράκι
Agios Dimitrios Άγιος Δημήτριος
Skoúra Σκούρα
Arna Άρνα
Vlachiótis Βλαχιώτης
Skála Σκάλα
Molaoi Μολάοι
Sykéa Συκέα
Gérakas Γέρακας
Akrotírio Iérax Ακρωτήριο Ιέραξ

Messiniakós Kólpos Μεσσηνιακός Κόλπος
Akr. Livada Ακρ. Λιβάδα
Gýtheio Γύθειο
Gýtheio Γύθειο
Mavrovoúni Μαυροβούνι
Karyoúpoli Καρυούπολη
Asopós Ασωπός
Elaía Ελαία
Plýtra Πλύτρα
Papadiánika Παπαδιάνικα
Daimonía Δαιμονιά
Monemvasia Μονεμβασιά
Ágios Apóstoli Αγ. Απόστολοι
Kastaniá Καστανιά
Neápoli Νεάπολη
Velanidia Βελανιδιά

SPÍLAIA DIROÚ ΣΠΗΛΑΙΑ ΔΙΡΟΥ
Mézapos Μέζαπος
Kótronas Κότρωνας
Kokkála Κοκκάλα
Koíta Κοίτα
Gerolimenas Γερολιμένας
Areópoli Αρεόπολη
Pórto Kágio Πόρτο Κάγιο
Akrotírio Taínaro Ακρωτήριο Ταίναρο
MANI ΜΑΝΗ

Lakonikós Kólpos Λακωνικός Κόλπος
Elafónisos Ελαφόνησος
N. Elafónisos
Pantánassa Παντάνασσα
Akrotírio Xylís Ακρ. Ξυλής
Akrotírio Maléas Ακρ. Μαλέας

Kalamáta Kastélli-Kríti
Potamós Kastélli-Kríti

Akr. Spathi Ακρ. Σπαθί
Karavás Καραβάς
Agia Pelagia Αγ. Πελαγία
Potamós Ποταμός
Kýthira Ν. Κύθηρα
Mylopótamos Μυλοπόταμος
Livádi Λιβάδι
Avlémonas Αυλέμονας
Kýthira Κύθηρα
Karsáli Καψάλι

Falkonéra Ν. Φαλκονέρα

168
174
167

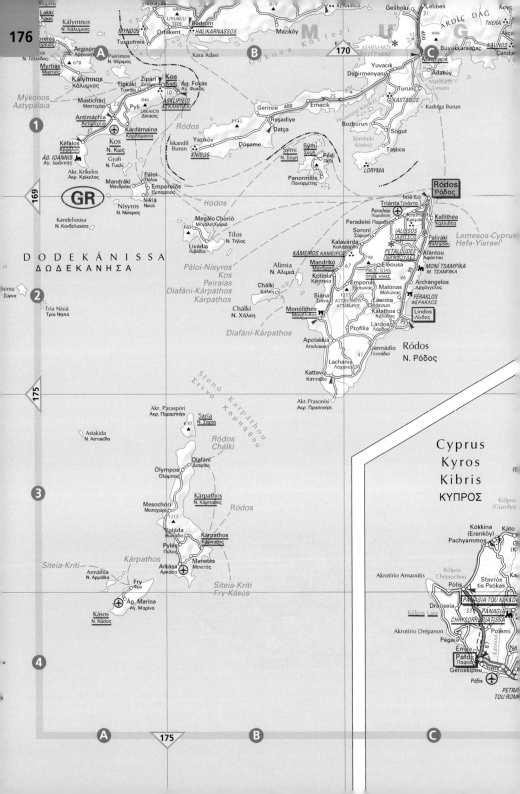

RINGKØBING

A B 182 C

1

Sønderby Ulfborg Karup Frederiks Houlbjerg Hadsten Odum
Ørnhøj Avlum Simmelkær Vildbjerg Ilskov Vinderslev Ans Fårvang Hinnerup Hammel
Kryle Hee Spjald Skibbild Favrholt Herning Ikast Bording Silkeborg Gjern Låsby Galten
Ringkøbing Røgind Videbæk 2009 Isenvad Virklund Them Seis Framlev Å
Hvide Sande Lem Finderup Kibæk Arnborg Fasterholt Hjøllund Skanderborg Hørning Malling
Ringkøbing Fjord Faster Brande Nørre Snede Nim Lund Gedved Ødder Ørting
Skjern Borris Sønder Felding Thyregod 2009 Uldum Horsens Hov Gylling
Bjerregård Hemmet Tarm Høven Blåhøj Give Tørring Horsens Fjord
Nymindegab Lyne Ølgod Sønder Omme Filskov Lindved Jelling Vejle
Henne Strand Nørre Nebel Ovtrup Grindsted LEGOLAND Billund Vandel Bredsten Daugård Overby Endelave By
Vittarp Hindsig Tistrup Ansager Hejnsvig Billund Hedensted Vesterby Hosby Juelsminde
Vejers Strand Oksbøl Starup Agerbæk Hovborg Ødsted Stouby Trelde
Blåvands Huk Billum Varde Ärre Bække Egtved Daugård Bjerre
Blåvand Kravnsø Hjerting Nørre Vejrup Holsted Gravens Fredericia Vester Egense
NATIONALPARK VADEHAVET Esbjerg Tjæreborg Vejen Kolding Bogense Uggersiev Søndersø
Harwich Nordby Bramming Tønderskov Middelfart Nørre Aaby Korup
Fanø Store Darum Foldingbro Vamdrup Jels Brandsø Aarup Morud LANGESØ
Sønderho Ribe Obbekær Rødding Sommersted Christiansfeld Hjorte Bågø Vissenbjerg Bellinge
Mandø Seem Gram Vojens Fjelstrup Årø Assens Glamsbjerg Nørre Broby
NATIONALPARK VADEHAVET Egebæk GRAM SLOT Haderslev Starup Arøsund Ebberup Nørre Lyndelse
Juvre Frifelt Hønning Bevtoft Oversø Hoptrup Halk Faaborg
Lakolk Brøns Toftlund Rangstrup Helnæs Faldsled Millinge Korinth
Rømø Skærbæk Døstrup Hellevad Løjt Kirkeby Barsø Bøjden Horne Ærø
Havneby Ballum Bredebro Tvsen Rødekro BRUNDLUND Aabenraa Nordborg Havnbjerg Vester Åby Tåsinge
List Hjerpsted TØNDERG Visby Abild Søvang Broderup Als Gudrup Augustenborg Ærøskøbing
TØNDERG SCHACKENBORG Højer Bredevad Tingley Rens Kliplev Gråsten Fynshav Skarø
Westerland Kampen Tønder Sæd 2009 Feldsted Ballebro Søby Avernakø
Sylt Morsum Neukirchen Helbol Sønderborg Mommark Skovby
Rantum NORD- Føhr Klanxbüll Süderlügum Padborg Glücksburg Skelde Tranderup
Hörnum Süderende Niebüll Klixbüll Lück Flensburg Langballig Nieby
Amrum Dagebüll Risum Lindholm Wallsbüll Steinberg Gelting Kronsgaard
Wittdün Wyk Langenhorn Hörup Langballig Sörup Oersberg Kappeln
FRIESISCHE Bredstedt Goldelund Wanderup Tarp Süderbrarup Schönhagen
Langeness Hattstedt Haselund Böklund Lindaunis Kopperby Schönhagen
Hooge Tammensiel England Silberstedt Schleswig Eckernförde Strande
NATIONALPARK Pellworm Süden Treia HATTHABU Damp 2000 Laboe Schönberge
SCHLESWIG- INSELN Husum Busdorf Jagel Schönberg
HOLSTEINISCHES Nordstrand Ülvesbüll Dörpstedt Kropp Owschlag Gettorf Friedrichshort
WATTENMEER Westerhever Osterhever Friedrichstadt Lunden Erfde Holtsee KIEL Helkendorf
Garding Tönning Alt Duvenstedt Fockbek Rendsburg Jevenstedt Westensee Selent
St Peter-Ording Schalkholz Tellingstedt Hamdorf Preetz
Helgoland Wesselburen Heide Schenefeld HOLSTEINISCHE SCHW...
Büsum Albersdorf Hanerau-Hademarschen 32 Bordesholm Ascheberg Plön
NATIONAL PARK Trischen Meldorf Hohenwestedt Neumünster Wankendorf
HAMBURGISCHES Friedrichskoog Gökels Bornhöved
WATTENMEER Hochdonn Schenefeld NATURPARK
NATIONALPARK Michaelisdonn Burg Marne HOLSTEINISCHE SCHW...
NIEDERSÄCHSISCHES Sankt- Kaiser-
Scharhörn Wilhelm

2

3

4

A B C

Deutsche Bucht

A B 187 C

1

FÆRØERNE
FØROYAR

Kalsoy Kunoy Viðoy
Tjørnuvík Eiði 882 Gjóv Viðareiði
790 Eysturoy Oyndarfjørður Fugloy
Streymoy Fluglafjørður 18
▲ Vestmanna Hvalvík Leirvík
722 Eysturoy 22 Klaksvík
Mykines Vágar 40 18 18 Svinoy
Sørvágur 20 20 Borðoy
20 Toftir

Tórshavn Seyðisfjörður
Bergen
Hanstholm
Thurso

Nólsoy

Kirkjubøur

Skopun Kristiansand
Sandoy Haugesund
Sandur 17 479 Skálavík Egersund
Skúvoy Bergen
Tórshavn
Seyðisfjörður

FR

2

Hvalba 10
Fámjin 610 Tvøroyri
22 Suðuroy
Vágur 15
Sumba

NATIONALPARK Lild
THY Vigsø Strand
Hanstholm Bugt Ræhr Frøstrup 569 Torup
Klitmøller 557 Nors Korsø Strand
181 Østerild Øslos
Vangså 26 Fjerritslev 179
Nørre Vorupør 126 Skinnerup 11 58 Aggersund
Sjørring 15 Amtoft Løgstør
Stenbjerg 539 Snedsted Thisted Feggeklit Limfjorden
571 14 Sønder 587 Ranum
Lyngby Vilsund Dråby Solbjerg Fur 40 533
Agger Bedsted Koldby 19 Tødsø Trend Stranby
VesterHvig Hurup Karby 25 Vils Nykøbing Selde
Thyborøn 181 527 545 Ør. Hvidbjerg Mors Harre Roslev Hvalpsur
545 Gedsted
Harboøre 16 Hvidbjerg Sundsøre Ulbjerg
Hove Nissum Tambohuse SPØTTRUP HESSEL Løvns
Ferring Bredning Rødding Sønder Bredning
513 565 Oddesund Balling Skive 579 22
Lemvig 18 Lihme 591 KRABBESHOLM
Fjaltring 181 Rom By 513 Humlum Venø Bygt 189 189 LYNDERUPG
28 Struer Vinderup STUBBERGÅRD Højslev Stby 29
Torsminde 37 Bækmarksbro 521 506 Sevel 21 186 KALKGRUBER
NATURRESERVAT Vemb 509 Linde Skave Bjergby Sjørup 26 ★ Mønsted
Fjand Gårde Bur Storå Haderup Grønhøj Birgittelyst
Husby Idom Holstebro 25 Rønka
Vedersø Klit 537 Tvis 185 467 Karup 186 Frederiks
Ulfborg Avlum 34 Kjellerup
Sønderby 16/28 Ørnhøj Simmelkær Karup 40 Vinderslev
Kryle Vildbjerg Sunds Ilskov 37 Engesv
Søndervig Hee Spjald 467 Skibbild 18 Favrholt Bording Silke
Ringkøbing Røgind 15 Videbæk 28 15 Herning Ikast 195 13
Hvide Sande Lem Finderup Kibæk 2009 Lind 15 185 Isenvad
Ringkøbing Faster Arnborg 18 Fasterholt Hjøllur
Fjord 41 NATURRESERVAT 439 61 Ejstrupholm
Bjerregard Skjern 178 Torris Sønder 20 411 2009 29
Hemmet 423 Tarm 21 Høven Felding Blåhøj Filskov Give
Nymindegab 38 Lyne 28 Sønder
Nørre Ølgod Omme 473 30
Nebel 181

3

4

A B C

ÖSTERGÖTLAND
KALMAR
SMÅLAND
NJUDUNG
KINDA
TJUST
MÖRE
BLEKINGE
Öland
Stora Alvaret
190
234
181
D
E
F
1
2
3
4
Väderstad
Mjölby
SVANEHÖLM
Skeda udde
Nykil
Björsäter
Röster
Yxnerum
Ringarum
Gusum
S:t Anna
Tyrislöt
Rök
Rinna
Ekeby
Strålsnäs
Bestorp
Brokind
Vidaberg
Valdemarsvik
Nora
Gryt
Trehörna
Boxholm
HÅLAVEDEN
Sommen
Ulrika
Rimforsa
Kättilstad
Tryserum
FÅGELVIK
Falerum
Sten
Rosendal
Somvik
Broddebo
Skedshult
Edsbruk
Östra Ed
Tranås
BRIPENBERG
Blåvik
Malexander
Örsebo
Oppeby
Björkefors
Dalhem
SÄBY
Hestra
Gripenberg
Kisa
Åsunden
Överum
Björnsholm
Lofta
Loftahammar
Frinnaryd
Sundhultsbrunn
Tidersrum
Horn
Hycklinge
Vireda
Asby
Odensvi
Gamleby
Kälvik
Marbäck
Liden
N. Vi
Aneby
Askeryd
Österbymo
Ydrefors
Gullringen
Höghult
Blackstad
Almvik
Flisby
Rydsnäs
Västervik
Solberga
Anneberg
Svinhult
NORRA KVILL NATIONALPARK
Södra Vi
Gladhammar
Gunnebo
SKURUGATA
Frödinge
Nässjö
Eksjö
Hult
Vimmerby
Ankarsrum
Västrum
Bruzaholm
Totebo
HELGERUM
Mariannelund
Hjorted
Stensjön
Storebro
Blankaholm
Bellö
Tuna
Mellby
Karlstorp
Silverdalen
Mörtfors
Björkö
Ekenässjön
Hultsfred
Vena
Stenbo
Paulistrom
Krokstorp
N.Sandsjö
Misterhult
Vetlanda
Holsbybrunn
Kvillsfors
Järnforsen
Skirö
Målilla
Kristdala
Landsbro
Visby
Nabbelund
Ölands norra udde
Fårbo
Figeholm
Hultsjö
Nye
STENSJÖ
Byxelkrok
Grankullavik
Fröderyd
Virserum
Mörlunda
Björnhult
Saltvik
Korsberga
Bockara
Oskarshamn
Böda
Lemnhult
Döderhult
Byrum
BLÅ JUNGFRUN NATIONALPARK
Emån
Berga
Asa
Ramkvilla
Hultanäs
Fågelfors
Finsjö
Åseda
Fagerhult
Högsby
Påskallavik
Löttorp-Högby
Norrhult
Emsfors
Berg
Tolg
Böcksholm
Nottebäck
Mjösebo
Fliseryd
Källa
Braås
Ruda
Grönskåra
Allgunnen
Långemåla
Sandvik
Rottne
Dädesjö
Älghult
Mönsterås
Gårdsby
Lenhovda
Sävsjöström
Kråksmåla
Alstermo
Blomstermåla
Alböke
Föra
Växjö
Öjaby
Herråkra
Alsterbro
Fröseke
Ålem
Timmernabben
Måleras
STRÖMSRUM
Löt
Furuby
Kosta
Gullaskruv
Häggemåla
Köpingsvik
Bäckebo
Kåremo
TELEBORG
Bergdala
Hälleberga
Flerahopp
Orrefors
SOLLIDEN
Borgholm
KAPELLUDDEN
Hovmantorp
Kristvallabrunn
Rockneby
Lessebo
Eriksmåla
Boda glasbruk
Nybro
Läckeby
Rälla
Gärdslösa
Ingelstad
Linsdal
Rottnen
Nöbbele
Johansfors
Örsjö
Trekanten
Kalmar
SMANTORP
Långlöt
Glömminge
Algutsrum
GRÄBORG
Jät
Linneryd
KLÄCKEBERGA
Emmaboda
Färjestaden
Ljungbyholm
Skogsby
Åsnen
Väckelsång
Korrö
Lindås
Oskar
Vassmolösa
KARLEVISTENEN
Gårdby
Tvärskog
Hagby
Urshult
Tingsryd
Rävemåla
Vissefjärda
Påryd
Resmo
Dångebo
Mörbylånga
Konga
Halltorp
BÅRBYBORG
Alby
Djuramåla
Söderåkra
Gullabo
Mien
Holmsjö
Torsås
Kastlösa
Skärlöv
Eringsboda
Bergkvara
Hallabro
Bidalite
GETTLINGE
Segerstad
Ronnebyån
Degerhamn
Flymen
Ringamåla
Bökemåla
Tving
Brömsebro
Mellstaby
Rödeby
Kallinge
Sälleryd
Grönhögen
Bräkne-Hoby
Hjortsberga
Kristianopel
Ottenby
Näsby
Asarum
Rödeby
Lyckeby
LÅNGE JAN
Listerby
Nättraby
Jämjöslätt
Ölands södra udde
Karlshamn
Ronneby
Sonekulla
Karlskrona
Norrje
Kuggeboda
Tjurkö
Drottningskär
Torhamn
Pukaviksbukten
Liepāja
Klaipėda
Mjällby
Gdynia
E22

NASIONALPARK LÅTEFOSSEN

Rubbestadneset Jektevik Uskedal Dimmelsvik
Stord Sunda Husnes Matersdalen Fjæra Steinberg bru
Siggjarvåg Sågvåg Leirvik Valen Åkra Solfonn Seljestad SANDFLOT
Mosterhamn Sæbøvik Skånevik Kyrping 192 KYRKJENUTEN Hordalia Røldal HAUKELIFJELL
Bomlo Valevåg Mauro Kårhus E134 Etne Breioborg Lono Haukeliseter
Langevåg Utbjoa Saudasjøen Sauda Nesflaten Bleskestad Vågslid Haukeligr
Eltravåg Førde Ølen Sandeid Bjerga SKAULEN Suldalsvatn Bråtveit Bjåen
Bergen Newcastle upon Tyne Hanstholm Skjold Øvre Vats Vikedal Bopeid Vanvik Suldalsen Kvilldal Hovden
Haugesund Aksdal Skjoldastraumen Imsland Sand Suldal Suldalsosen SNONUTEN
Avaldsnes Yrkje Marvik Lovraeid Øvre Moen Hoslemo Berdale
Vedavågen Kopervik Slåttevik Hebnes Jelsa Erfjord SKARJENFOSSEN Blåsjo Bykle Bjørneva
Åkrehamn Vågå Hervik Karstø Jøsenfjorden Trydal Flatel
Karmøy Alvestad Eik Ombo Nesvik Vindsvik Tøtlandsvik URDALSNUTEN Rotemo Va
Sandve Arsvågen Eidsund Skor Hjelmeland LYSEKAMMEN HALLANDSFOSSEN
Skudeneshavn Finnøy Judaberg   Årdalsosen Roskreppfjorden Myklestøyl Hyles
Bergen Newcastle upon Tyne Hirtshals Sørbø Rennesøy Lastein Tveit Håhellarhytta Langeie
UTSTEIN Hanasand Tysdal Eide Ådneram Aust
Mosterøy Tau Lysebotn N
Randaberg **STAVANGER** Jørpeland PREKESTOL Søngesand
Tananger Hommersak Eiane Øvre Espedal Heddern
Sola Oanes Lauvvik Sinnes Ånebjør Ose
Gandal Vatne Elle Tverrå Tjørhom Espeli
Sandnes Oltedal Gilja Handeland Frøy
Orre Figgjo Ven Øvstebø Øvre Sirdal Hedderen
Bryne Kloppe Ålgård Byrkjedal VEST-AGDER Ljosland Øvre Dås
Time Oppsal Espeland Austrumdal SKORE Åseral Flystveit Senum
Søyland Nærbø Bue Bjordal Bjørnestad Knaben Bredland Bjelland
Varhaug Myrane Vikeså Vassbø Visland Haughom Risnes Eiken Stainsland Åpåsdal
Vigrestad Bjerkrein Gya Rusdal Lindefjell Kvinlog Sveindal Skeiè
Brusand Gravdal Helleland Heskestad Ramsli Kråkeland Kvinlog Kylland Snartemo Audnedal
Sirevåg Heigrestad **Egersund** Moi Helle BLÅBERGET Birkeland Bjelland Skarpengland
Ystebrød Eida Eide Sira Sandvatn Tjørnhom Råna Konsmo Laudal
Hovland Ålgård Åvedal Loga Kvinesdal Snartemo Øyslebø Nodeland
Stapnes Rekeland Hauge Åna-Sira Vigeland Mosb
Sogndalstrand Flekkefjord Feda Førland Kvås Vigmostad Elkeland Lyngdal
Hanstholm Kirkehamn Hidra Sandvikal Rørvik Lindesnes Jåsund Vigeland Krossen Høllen Sogne
Listafjorden Abelnes Heskestad Penne Herad Vanse Spind Minde Austad Spangereid Mandal Ormestad
Vestbygd Farsund Alleen Våge

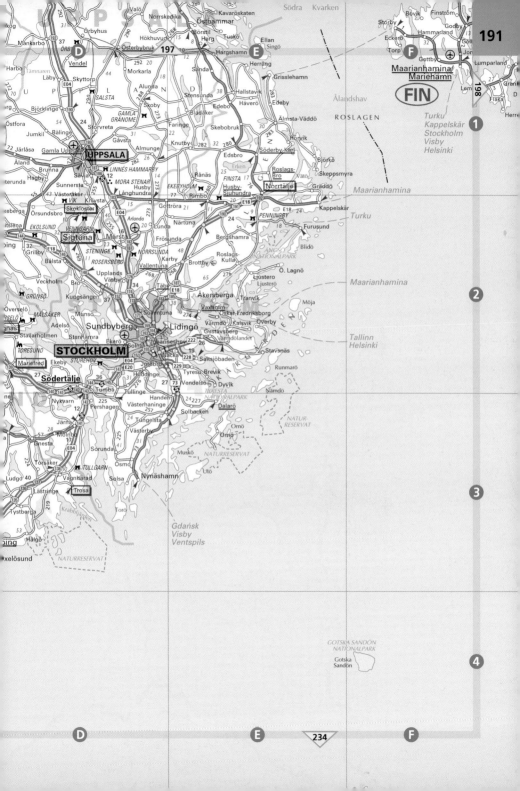

SOGN OG FJORDANE

HORDALAND

BERGEN

Voss

Newcastle upon Tyne

Haugesund
Stavanger
Hansholm
Hirtshals

Tórshavn

Florø

Førde

Sula

Stord

Odda

Leikanger

Sogndal

JOSTEDALSBR. NASJONALPA

FOLGEFONNI NASJONALPARK

HAUKELIFJELL

Fjærland

Balestrand

Gudvangen

Stalheim

Fresvik

Myrdal

Flåm

Sandane

Utvik

Skrede

Stryn

Innvik

Olden

Birksdal

Førde

Naustdal

Vevring

Stongfjorden

Askvoll

Atløya

Værlandet

Fure

Hellevik

Eide

Øn

Krakhella

Leirvik

Bø

Lavik

Torvund

Nordeide

Måren

Kongsnes

Hella

Vangsnes

Slinde

Feios

Viksøyri

Fjærestad

Arnafjord

Bjordal

Ortnevik

Soreide

Oppedal

Brekke

Rutledal

Nordgulen

Eivindvik

Hisarøy

Byrknes

Fedje

Hopplandsjøen

Rossnes

Hellesøy

Radøy

Manger

Bø

Lindås

Sæværåg

Vikanes

Mongstad

Molde

Steine

Risnes

Dueøsund

Masfjordnes

Fjon

Mo

Eksingedal

Eidslandet

Brekkhus

Evanger

Bulken

Tvinde

Mjølfjell

Uppsete

Vossestrand

Ulvik

Osa

Granvin

Kvanndal

Ålvik

Utne

Brimnes

Eidfjord

Ringøy

Sæbø

Kinsarvik

Lofthus

Aga

Nå

Hovland

Espe

Tyssedal

Odda

Hildal

Solfonn

Seljestad

Røldal

Haukeliseter

Haukeligrend

Vågslid

Nesflaten

Sauda

Saudasjøen

Etne

Ølen

Skånevik

Åkra

Utåker

Husnes

Valen

Matersdalen

Fjæra

Uskedal

Dimmelsvik

Rosendal

Løfallstrand

Sunde

Leirvik

Sagvåg

Siggjarvåg

Mosterhamn

Valevåg

Buavåg

Langevåg

Eltravåg

Stord

Fitjar

Rubbestadneset

Flatråker

Herøysund

Jektevik

Husa

Tysnesøy

Uggdal

Våge

Ingenes

Lygre

Gjermundshamn

Varaldsøy

Sunndal

Flatabø

Brattabø

Jondal

Torvikbygd

Strandebarm

Øystese

Norheimsund

Tørvikbygd

Mundheim

Sævareid

Fusa

Eikelandsosen

Hatvik

Osøyro

Halhjem

Hufthamar

Huftarøy

Gjøvåg

Reksteren

Kvalvåg

Sandvikvåg

Bjørnafjorden

Fana

Løningdalen

Nesttun

Haukeland

Espeland

Tysse

Tokagjelet

Tveita

Hagavik

Hamlagrøosen

Vaksdal

Stanghelle

Dale

Osterøy

Lonevåg

Bruvik

Steinestø

Knarvik

Salhus

Breistein

Ytre Arna

Indre Arna

Trengereid

Kleppestø

Ask

Florvåg

Solsvik

Fjell

Straume

Fieland

Flesland

Klokkarvik

Telavåg

Sotra

Hellestad

Fana

Stord

Sogndalsfjøra

Skjolden

Svedje
Brämön
Galtström
52

Gnarp
Sörfjärden
Jättendal
Harmånger
Stocka
Strömsbruk
Välsta
nna
diksvall
Arnön
NATURRESERVAT
Hornslandet
anger
Hölick
Agön

Bottniska viken /

ångvind

Pohjanlahti

lerhamn
andarne

üsne
Vallvik

xmarby

orrsundet
ångefjärden

Trödje

Hille   Utvalnäs

GÄVLE
Gävlebukten
Furuvik
76 26
Skutskär   Gårdskär
Älvkarleby
Fågelsundet
E04
35
195
Karlholmsbruk   Hällnäs
Marma
Skarplinge   Ångskär
Finnböle   195
17   Västland
13   Lövstabruk
292   Tolfta
Tierp   193

AHVENANMAA

Ahvenanmaa/Åland

FIN
ÅLAND

Geta
BOLSTAHOLM
Saltvik
Storby   Bovik   Finström   Sund
Eckerö   Godby   KASTELHOLM
Torp   Hammarland   18
Sölby   Jomala
Gottby   Lumparland

Norrboda
Söderboda
Gräsö
Forsmark
Öregrund   Gräsö
Valö   Bjurön
Norrskedika   Kavaröskaten
Östhammar
Örbyhus   Rörstil   Herg   Tuskö
292   Hökhuvud   15   Ellan
ÖRBYHUS   Österbybruk   Gimo   Singö
Vendel   292   Morkarla
191   Sunda   Herräng
Läby   Torp   Alunda   D
D   E04   SALSTA   Stensunda   Hallstavik
Björklinge   190   Skoby   Bladaker   Edebo   Häverö   Edeby   Ålmsta-Väddö
Östfora   GAMLA   Faringe   Skebobruk
GRÄNOME

Södra Kvarken

Maarianhamina/
Mariehamn
F
Lemland   Flaka

Turku
Kappelskär/
Stockholm
Visby
Helsinki

ROSLAGEN   Ålandshav

Å A   B   C

1

2

3

4

Små
Gos
Haroy
Myklebust
Nordøyane
Kjerstad   Nogva   Mids
Austnes   Hildre   Ørsnes   661
Roald   Skjelten   Brattvåg
Ålesund   Vatne   28   Ton
Søvik
Valderøy   Ålesund   Skodje
Langevåg   Spjelkavik   Digernes
Kvalsvik   Runde   Brandal   Magerholm   Ørs
Nerlandsøy   Ulsteinvik   Hareid   Sulesund   Solevåg   Aursnes
Fosnavåg   Hareidlandet   Vartdal   Sykkylven
Gurskøy   Eiksund   Årsnes   Velle   Drottninghau
Honningsvåg   Larsnes   Riånes   KOLÅSTIND   Storestandal   Stran
Ervik   Arvik   EIKSUND-   1461
Borgund   Åram   TUNNELEN   Ørsta   Furset
STADLANDET   Koparnes   Lauvstad   Sæbø   Leknes   33
Leikanger   Fiska   BÅTMUSEUM   Volda   Øye
Selje   Vik   Vatne   Bjørke
KLOSTERRUINER   Syvde   Folkestad   Viddal
Raudeberg   Aheim   SØSTRE
Vågsøy   Steinsvik   Austefjord   Hellesylt
Måløy   Bryggja   Botnen   Kalvatn   Trygge-
HELLERISTNINGER   Bjørkedal   stad
Oldeide   Maurstad   Navelsaker   Grodås   Lyngvoll
Davik   Kjølsdal   Hjelle   Hornindal   SVORMUSEET
Bremangerlandt   NORDFJORD   Stårheim   Nor   Skrede
Leirgulen   Bortnen   Isane   Nordfjordeid   Lote   Stryn   Lunde
Frøya   Ålfoten   Hestenesøyri   Anda   Innvik   Loen
Kalvåg   1670   GRAVHAUG   Utvik   Olden
Smørhamn   Svelgen   GJEGNALUNDSBREEN   Sandane   1717
Midtgulen   CECILIEKRU
Howden   Grøndal   Staume   Brein
Damba   Myklebust   Hyen   Gimmestad   Tyrkjelo
Årebrot   Haukå   Hjorteset   192
Skorpa   B   NONSFOSSEN   C   Birksdal
Reksta   Florø   Gjerde   1572   JOSTE
Eikefjord   Eidiet   Nes
Askrova   Stavanger   Storebru   SOGN OG   JOSTEDALSBREEN
Svanøy   Vevring   Hove   Aksla   NASJONALPARK
Bergen   Naustdal   Årdal   Skei   Klakegg

213

A · B · C

Hillsand · Alanäs · Flåsjön · Hoting · Östernoret
Vedjeön · Alavattnet · Havnäs · Störnaset · Svanabyn · Granåsen · V. Gafsele · Överrissjö
Öjarn · Renålandet · Lövberga · Grundsjö · Häggsjö
Strand · Hössjön · Rossön · Övra · Hälla · Holmträ
Älviken · Tuvattnet · Flykälen · Strömsund · Uriksfors · Rudsjön · Brattsele
Ålåsen · Laxviken · Näsviken · Rusksand · Gulsele
Skärvången · Ottsjön · Hallviken · Stamsele · Bäcke · Junsele · Lillsele · Degersjö
Storholmsjö · Kakuåsen · Gåxsjö · Täxan · Vängel · Sil · Ysjö · Kläppsjö · Holmsvall
Fällinge · Raftsjöhöjden · Silkås · Gisselås · Flyn · Nässjö · Eden · Håfaforsen
Lillholmsjö · Landön · Hammerdal · Ede · Görvik · Sörviken · Ramsele · Omsjö · Grundtjärn
Lundsjön · Munkflohögen · Edefors · Vallen · Ovanmo · Imfors · Nasåker · Norrtannflo · Aspeå
Norderåsen · Skyttmon · Lungsjön · Edsele · Resele · Byvatten
Böle · Häggenås · Storhögen · Borgvattnet · Björkhöjden · Nordanåker · Ås · Selsjön · Ållsjön
Aspås · Krokom · Gränningen · Mårdsjö · Boberg · Lövåsen · Årtrik · Mo · Forsmo · Ed · Sånga
Dvärsätt · Lit · Bye · Fjäl · Selsälandet · Överammer · Långsele · Multrå
Ås · Stugun · Strömsnäs · Höglunda · Krångede · Krokvåg · Österforse · Sollefteå · Helgum
Östersund · Ope · Eriksberg · Bomsund · Hammarstrand · Graninge
Marieby · Brunflo · Rissna · Valla · Ragunda · Österede · Västansjö
Orrviken · Tandsbyn · Pilgrimstad · Holmsjö · Håsjö · Bollstabruk
Hackås · Tunvågen · Revsund · Gällö · Kälarne · DÖDAFALLET · Bispgården · Östergraninge
Kövra · Bodsjö · Nor · Stavre · Nyhem · Rotsjö · Hällesjö · Boda · Laxsjön · Viksjö
Skucku · Ringsta · Hunge · Gimdalen · Sörbygden · Järkvissle · Sillre · Klärke · Nordanå · Liland
Rör · Gillhov · Ocksjön · Åsen · Gråssjön · Albacken · Liden · Backen · Bredsjö
Digerberget · Löningsberg · Bräcke · Bensjö · Sandnäset · Holm · Östlöning · Ljustorp
Åsarna · Nästeln · Handsjö · Byberget · Ovansjö · Ånge · Borgsjö · Näset · Marktjärn · Sunnansjö · Indal · Stavreviken · Äsäng
Rätan · Ytterturingen · Överturingen · Kölsillre · Alby · Erikslund · Fränsta · Hullsjön · Nyland · Gåltjärn · Bergeforsen · Söråker
Sörtjärn · Viken · Malsjöbodarna · Grundsjön · Oxsjön · Hjältanstorp · Backen · Torpshammar · Stöde · Huljen · Kovland · Timrå
Överhogdal · Torflönäs · Mellansjö · Naggen · Gässåsen · Västansjön · Fanbyn · Nedansjö · Vattjom · Sundsvall
Minne · Ramsjö · Valsjön · Kolsjön · Nyrå · Matfors · Tunbyn · Attmar · Lucksta · Alnön · Svartvik
Ytterhogdal · Flor · Sund · Skän · Västan · Malungen · Njurunda · Kvissleby · Njurundabommen · Svedje
Sänna · Andåsen · Hennan · Hassela · Grängsjö · Galtström
Alvros · Finneby · Gåda · Hen · Brändbo · Älvsund · Älgered · Gnarp · Sörfjärden
Ytterberg · Kolsätter · Vansjö · Kårböle · Letsbo · Ängebo · Strömbacka · Bergsjö · Jättendal
Ängersjö · Laforsen · Tallåsen · Friggesund · Föneby · Vattlång · Harmånger · Stocka

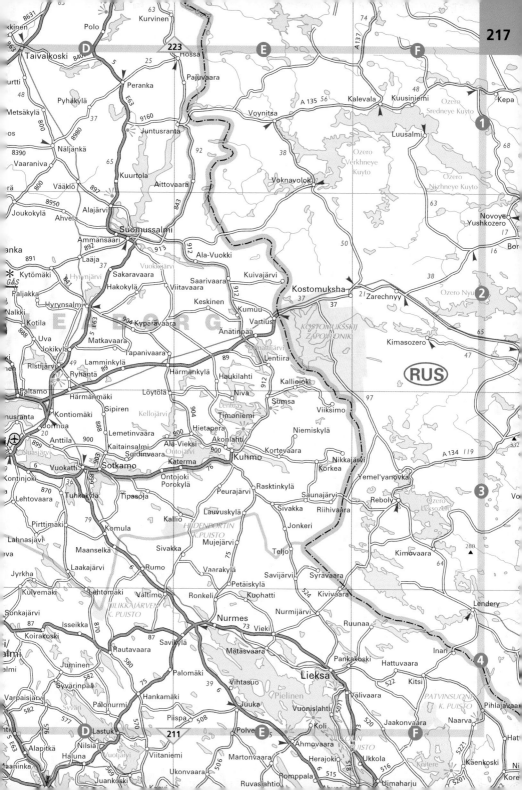

A   B   C

1

ÍSLAND

Bolungarvík
Ísafjörður
60
Bjargtangar   Patreksfjörður
63
61
Grímsey
0

Hólmavík
Flatey
Breidafjörður
Húnaflói
Siglufjörður
Skagaströnd
Ólafstjörður
Blönduós   Sauðárkrókur
Dalvík
Húsavík
Kópaske

SNÆFELLSJÖKULL
NASJONALPARK
Ólafsvík   Stykkishólmur
Hvammstangi
61
78
82
54   56
Búdardalur
57
146
Akureyri
86
JÖKULSÁRGLJÚFUR
NASJONALPARK

2

54
228
1
IS
GODAFOSS ✳
Reykjalið ✳
DET
Myvatn
271

Faxaflói

Borgárnes

Akranes
1355
1763
HERDUBREID
1510   1682
LANGJÖKULL
HOFSJÖKULL
Skjálfandafljót

REYKJAVÍK
Keflavík
Thingvellir
THINGVELLIR
NASJONALPARK
ASKJA
41
Thingvallavatn
GEYSIR
✳   ✳ GULLFOSS
42
Grindavík   Hveragerdi   51   35
Hvíta
Selfoss
Eyrarbakki
Thjórsá
Thórisvatn
1833
GRIMSFJALL   SNÆFELL
1719
Hella
VATNAJÖKULL
Hvolsvöllur

3

Heimaey
VESTMANNAEYJAR   Heimaey   MÝRDALS-   Kirkjubæjarklaustur
SKAFTAFELL
NASJONALPARK
JÖKULSARLON ✳
Surtsey   SKOGAFOSS   JÖKULL
Skogar   418   Skaftafell   Höfn
Vík   1
Fagurhólsmyri

4

A   B   C

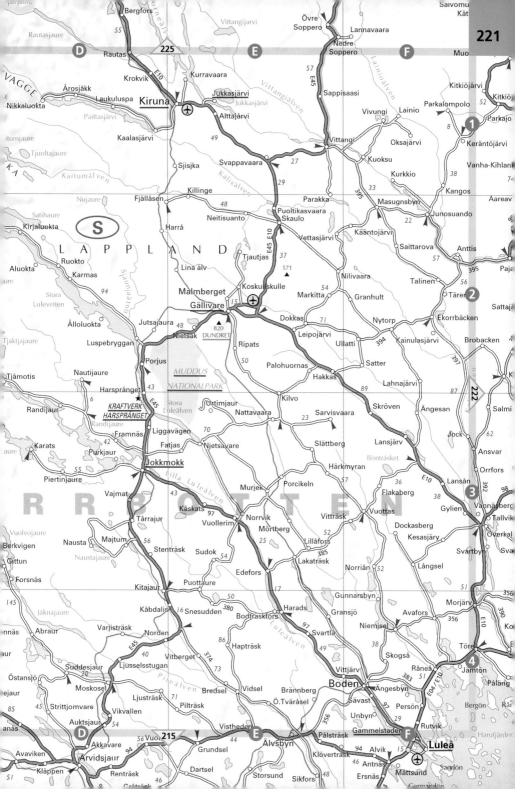

A B C

1

2

3

4

Mefjordvær
Bø
Straumsnes 862 22
28 Sætra 86
Fjor
86
La
G
Gryllefjord 40
Kaldfarnes
Senja
ANDERDALEN
N.P.
Flakkstadvågen 860
Gjøvik
69
Vaggsvik
Sjursvika 50
Stonglandseidet
Dyrøya
Bjarkøya
Mikkelbostad
Kastnesha
Grøtavær
Sandsøy
Klåpen
41 848
Grytøya
862 Andørja
25
Elgsnes
15 Sørvik
Lavangn
Harstad
Ibestad 848
Rolla 16
Mybotn 33
Børkenes 852 Grovfjord
25 Rensa Tenne
32
35 83
Refnes 852 825 53
Gausvik 39 Øse 31
SKITTENDAL 829 Gr
Hinnøya STINDEN
1306
Ulvika 50 Bøgen E10 Bjerkv
61 65 N
Kanstad E10 R
Narvik Leirvik
Heldøya HN
Tjeldnes Ankenesstrand 19
Kjeldebotn 9
43 Hakvika Grindjorda
Kjæringvika Ballangen 29
E06 Bleis
Forsa Rånvassbotn
Bognes STORS
Starberget

Andenes
Bleik
Stave Skarstein
Andøya
Nordmela
82
57 52 Myre
Bøgard Åse
Langenes Risøyhamn
Myre Alsvåg Buksnes
Skogsøya 54
81
Hovden 52
Sund Langøya 23 Bremnes
Straumsjøen 820 Sortland 82 Maurnes
73 Strand Elesnes
Straumsnes 44 Bø 36
Bitterstad Austpollen
Stokmarknes MOYSALEN
Hadseløya NAS. PARK
Melbu 34
Kaljord 1266
MØYSALEN
E10 18
Austvågøy 22
Kongselva
Piskebø 19
Øksnes 57
Eggum Vestpollen Rinøya
Gimsøya
Vestvågøy Sandsletta
70 Sundklakk 34
Borg Svolvær Store
Leknes 12 A Molla Tranøya 220
815 Henningsvær B 219 C
Stamsund
Flakstadøya Kjøpsvik
Ramberg Gravdal 21 38
Ballstad 36 Fjellbu
jorden 64 Kvalnes Skutvik 81 Presteid
Mørkveden Bodø Lundøya Ulvsvåg Drag Ájluokta

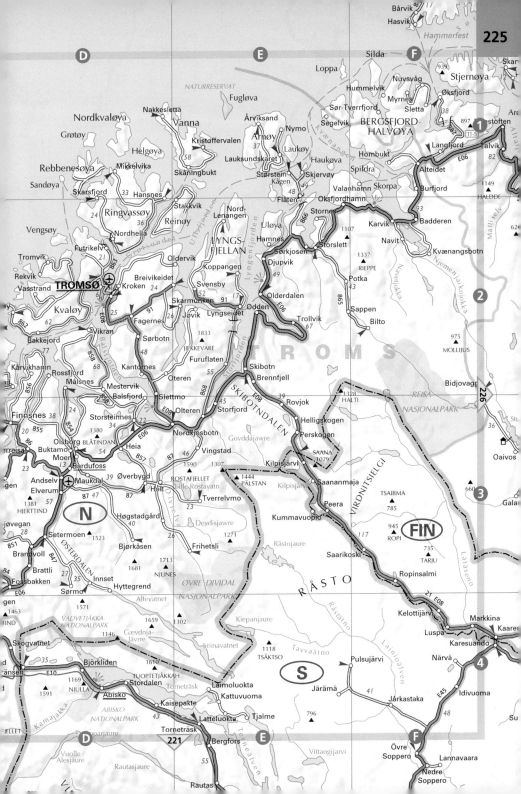

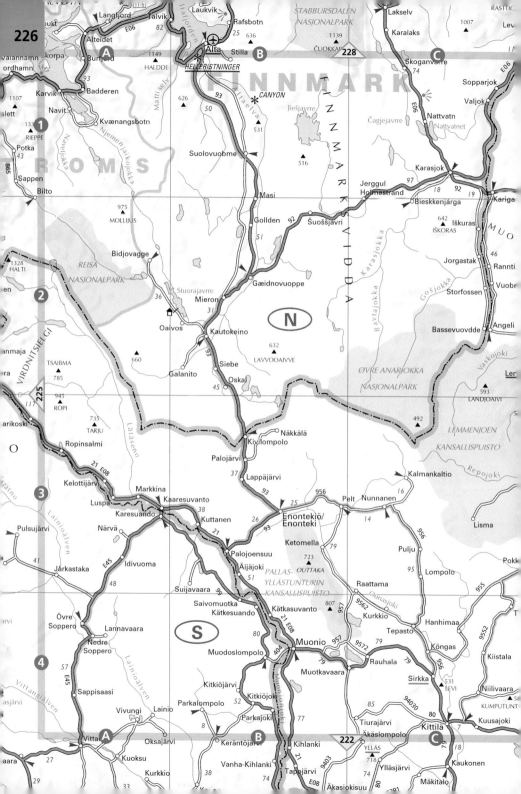

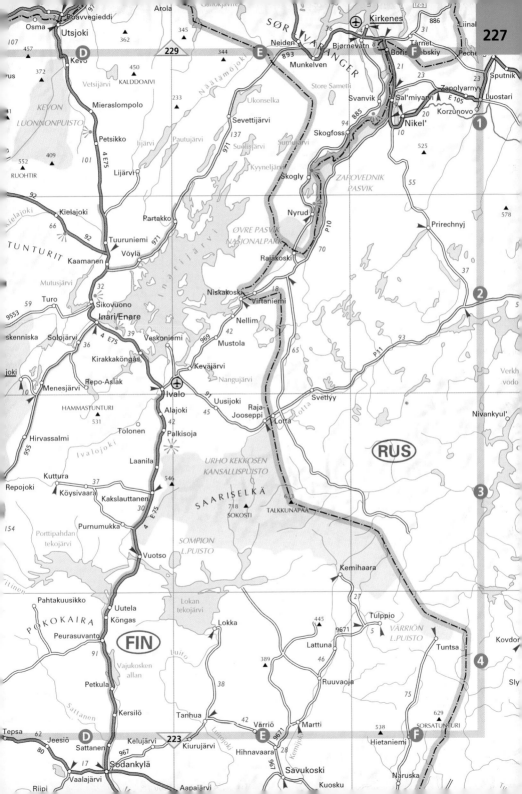

Nordkapp

A   B   C

1

Gjesvær
Skipsfjordfjell 312
Pass
Magerøya
Hjelmsøya
Ingøya
145
Havøysund
Måsøya
Honningsvåg
Tufjord
Kalven
Kåfjord
Rolvsøya
319
SVÆR
491
HALV

Tarhalsen
Reinøya
Revsbotn
315
Skavik
Snefjord
PORSANGER-
Repvåg
578
Akkarfjord
Forsøl
HALVØYA
Stranda
Veidnesklubb
Langstrand
Hammerfest
Lillefjord
89
Storelv
16
Kvaløya
Selkopp
SKARVBERG-
Kjæsvatne
Sørvær
607
Rypefjord
Masterelv
TUNNELEN
Ytre
Breivikbotn 656
Sørøya
557
Brennsvik
Kjæs
Breivik
882
Størtinden
57
Smørfjord
76
Indre Brenna
Bårvik 17
Kvalsund
94
Markop
Klokker
Hasvik
Seiland
Skaidi
Olderfjord
1079
Neverfjord
23
Silda
939
776
698
63
Indre
81
Nuvsvåg
SEILAND / SIEVJU
Saraby
Billefjord
Stjernøya
NASJONALPARK / ALBOTMEAHC
Lerresfjord
E06
Reynøya
Børselv
Hummelvik
Skarveberg
DUODDAR
Bibaktad
Sør-Tverrfjord
Hakkstabben
SION
PORSANGER
Myrnes
Øksfjord
SENNALAND
Stabbursnes
Sletta
38
Storekorsnes
E06
42
GÁISSÁT
egelvik
Arøya
60
Levdun
Hamnbukt
10
BERGSFJORD-
897
Isnestoften
62
Læktojavre
98
RÁSTT
HALVØYA
11-5
Leirbotn
Laksrelv
Spildra
Langfjord
Laukvik
STABBURSDALEN
øva
Hombukt
E06
Talvik
Rafsbotn
NASJONALPARK
1007
Le
Valan
Skorpa
82
25
636
1139
Karalaks
Sopparjok
sfjordhamn
1149
Alta
N
Čuokkarašša
Valjok
nes
HALDDE
Stilla
Skoganvarre
E06
1107
Karvik
HELLERISTNINGER
74
Nattvatn
Navit
93
Nattvatnet
1337
Badderen
626
93
CANYON
Jiešjavrre
RIEPPE
Kvænangsbotn
50
531
Čagjejavrre
Po
865
225
Sappen
Karasjok
Bilto
Suolovuobme
516
Jerggul
837
Kario
975
Holmestrand
18   92   19
MOLLIJUS
Masi
Bieskkenjárga
642
Iškuras
Bidjovagge
Gollden
92
Šuoššjávri
IŠKORAS
MU
51
46
1328
Jorgastak
Rann
HALTI
REISA
Stuorajavrre
Jorgastak
Vuo
NASJONALPARK
36
Gæidnovuoppe
Storfossen
Ange
ananmaja
Mieron
226
Bassevuovdde
31
TSIELGI
Oaivos
Kautokeino
632

A   B   C

D E F

1

Nordkinn Stettnet fyr
Skjøtningberg Mehamn Gamvik
26 31
Kjøllefjord NORDKINN- Skarveneset Berlevåg
HALVØYA Tyfjord
894 Dego 890 Nålneset Seiboneset
Kifjord 888
Màrøya Hopseldet Skjånes Store Kongsfjord Båtsfjord 402 Korsneset
Molvik Hamingberg
Langfjordnes Gulgofjorden 60 LÆSI 891 33 Nordfjord 39
888 Davggejavrre 12-5 12-5 31 Kroknes Vardø
90 Smelror
Kalak Boksjok 668 Gædnja- Svartnes
jelvik FLATTIND Tamanes 74 890 javrre Kramvik
Lebesby Leirpollskogen 633 Kiberg
Sjursjok 98 Jakobselva SKIPSKJØLEN Komagvær
370 Rustefjelbma Komageelva Skallelv
Ifjord 11-6 Sandnes 501 Skallneset
Landersfjorden Ifjordfjell 88 Maskjok Skallelv
Pass Tana E75 98
Stuora Gæssejavrre Tanabru Varangerbotn Nesseby Vestre 138 Krampenes
Søbmerjavrre Skiippagurra Jakobselv Vadsø Ekkerøy
Gæidno 25 Grasbakken Varangerfjorden Murmansk
401 E06/E75 68 895 E06 ZAPOVEDNIK
Sirma Polmak Gandvik Bugøynes
463 Nuorgam 400 Garsjøen 98 Grense-
Goržžam 910 KORGÅSEN Skoger- Jakobselv
Bøavvegieddi Arola Gallokjavrre øya 886
Osma Utsjoki 345 Bugøyfjord Kirkenes Liinahamari
107 457 362 SØR 36 Tårnet
Kevo 344 Neiden Bjørnevatn 8 Borisoglebskiy Pečenga
372 450 893 VARANGER 21 23 23 Sputni
KALDDOAIVI Munkelven Zapolyarnyy Luostari
641 Mieraslompolo 233 Store Sametti Svanvik Sal'miyarvi E 105 Korzunovo
KEVON Ukonselva 885 94 Nikel'
LUONNONPUISTO Petsikko Sevettijärvi Skogfoss 10 525
552 409 137 Suolisjärvi Skogly ZAPOVEDNIK
RUOHTIR 101 Lijärvi Kyyneljärvi PASVIK 55
FIN 92 Nyrud Prirechny
Kielajoki Partakko ØVRE PASVIK RUS 578
66 92 NASJONALPARK 70
Tuuruniemi 971 Rajäkoski 37
Kaamanen Võylä
ATUNTURIT Mutusjärvi 32
ved Turo D Sikovuono 227 Niskakoski E Rtaniemi F
9553 59 Inari/Enare Nellim
Koskenniska Solojärvi 4 E75 39 Veskoniemi Mustola
36 969 42 65 93

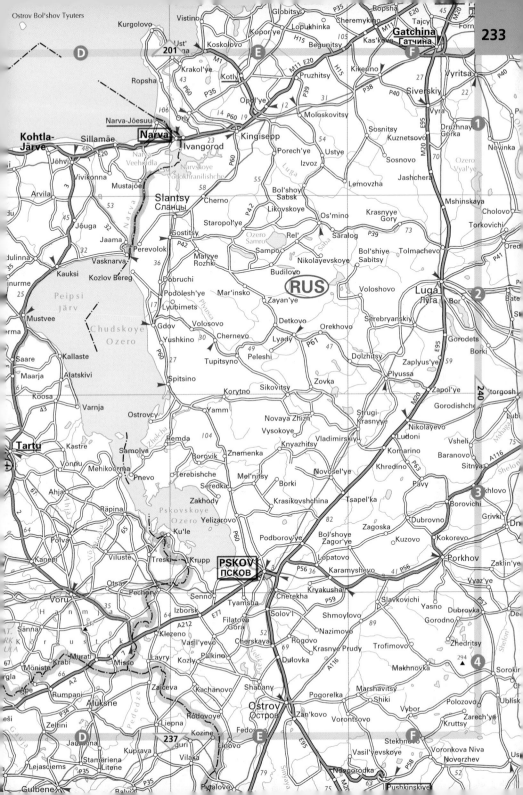

A ▲191 B C

1

185

GOTSKA SANDÖN
NATIONALPARK

Gotska
Sandön

Lauter Holmudden
Hallshuk Fårö Fårö
Kappelshamn Fårösund
Nynäshamn Lickershamn
Maarianhamina 48 Lärbro 20
35
LUMMELUNDAGROTTORNA 148 Tingstäde Kyllaj
2 Slite
Visby 147
Bro Bäl S
Högklint 45
143 Gothem
Gnisvärd 140 Barlingbo 51 G O T L A N D
Eskelhem Roma
Oskarshamn 35 48 Isums 44 Ala 146 Katthammarsvik
Hejde
Klintehamn 142 Buttle 143 TORSBURGEN
Fröjel 141 Lojsta
L. Karslö 22 Ljugarn
St. Karlsö 30 Lye
DJAUVIK Sproge Burs Gotland
140 Hemse
Hablingbo 47 Ronehamn
Havdhem

3 142 25 Burgsvik
Faludden
Sallmunds
✳ Sundre
Hoburgen

Pa

Ziemu

M

Liepāja
Rostock
Karlshamn

4

Berna

A B C Pa

Pala

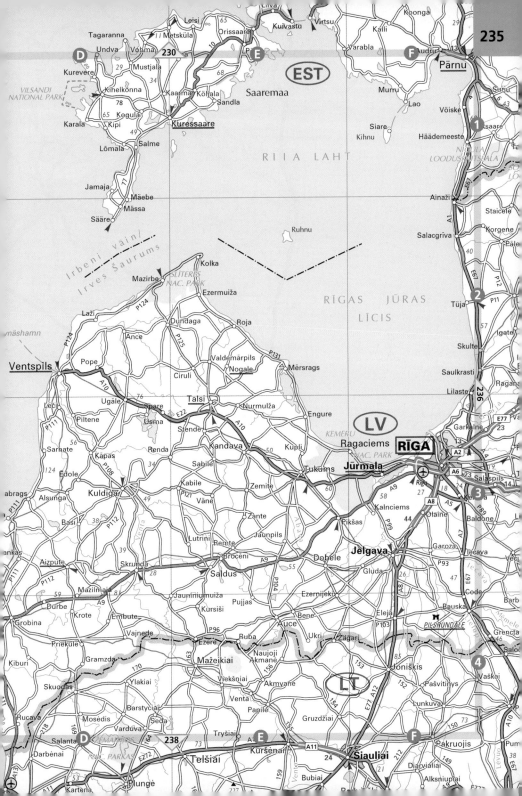

EST

Saaremaa

RIIA LAHT

RĪGAS JŪRAS LĪCIS

LV

RĪGA

Ventspils

Kuldīga

Jelgava

Jūrmala

LT

Šiauliai

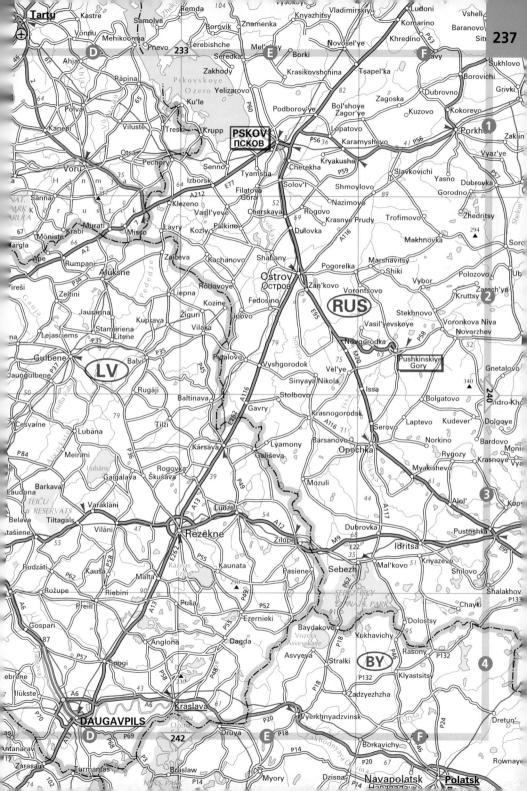

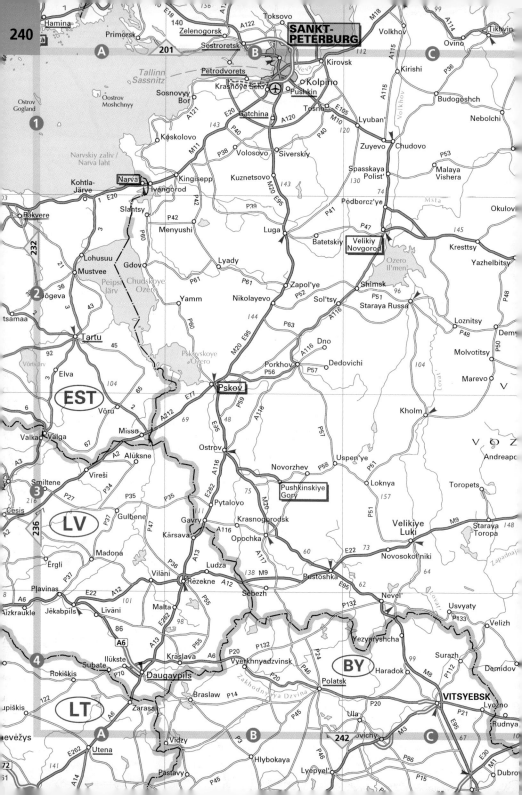

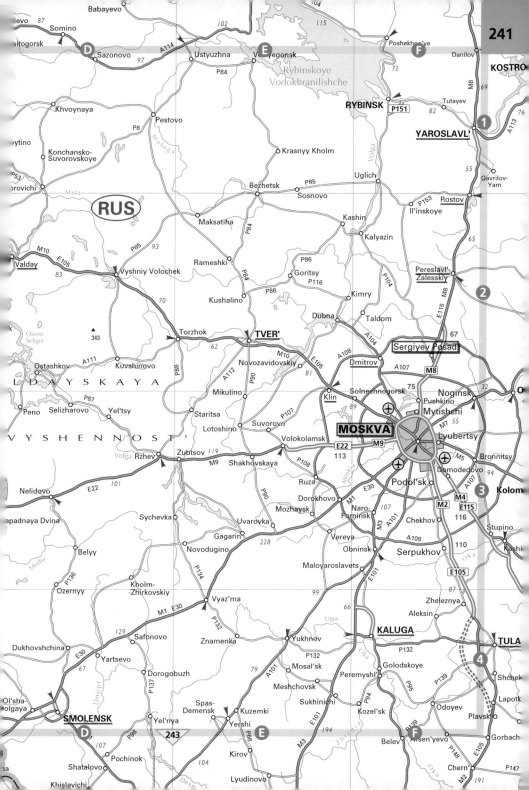

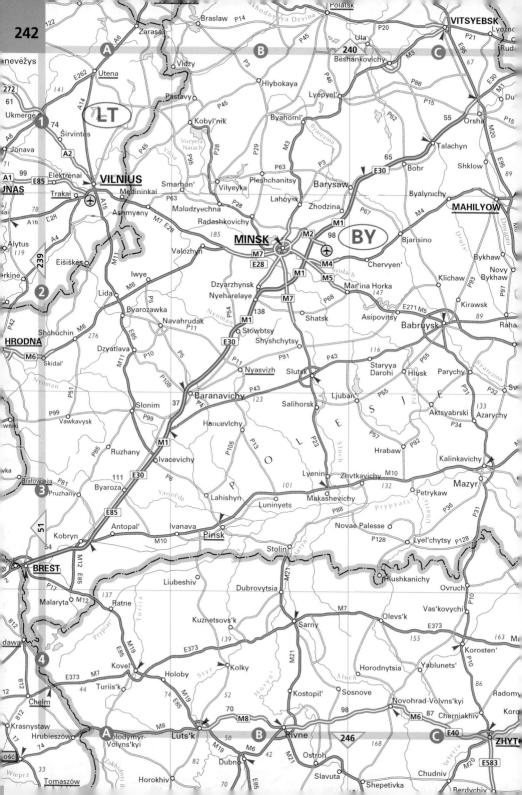

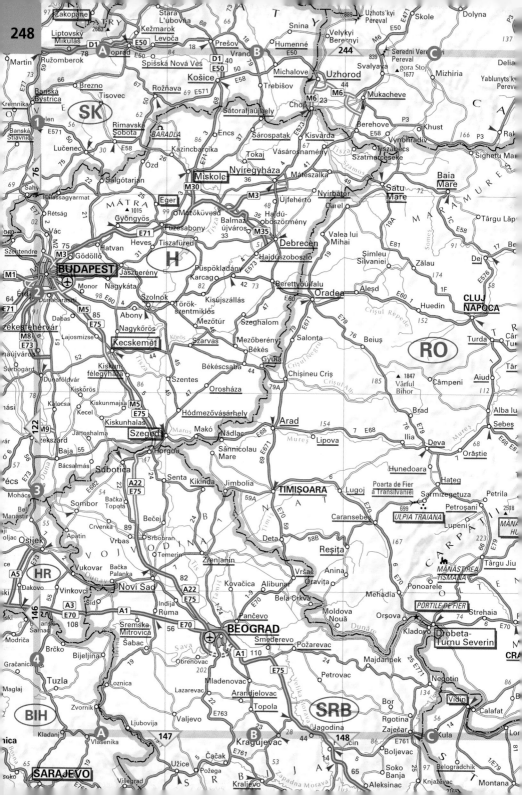

Yuzhnoukrains'k
Vossijatskoye
Rohachyk
Oleksandrivka
Domanivka
M23
Voznesens'k
Bereznehuvate
Velyka
Lepetykha
Nyzhni
Sirohozy
E58
Veselynove
P16
Bashtanka
E
F
84
M26

Nova
Odes
247
Snihurivka
Beryslav
M14
89
E105
Zhovten'
Berezivka
Voskresens'ke
Kakhovka
Chkalove
Heniches'k
1

E58
M14
MYKOLAÏV
87
Nova
Kakhovka
UA
Radisne
62
Tsiurupyns'k
Askaniia-
-Nova
M20
KHERSON
M24
63
E95
Hola
Prystan'
192
Armyansk
Ochakiv
E97
Kalanchak
Krasnoperekops'k
99
M16
Skadovs'k
E97
Dzhankoï
E87
Voinka
M26
ODESSA
Razdol'e
Pervomais'ke
KRYM S'KI
Illichivs'k
Sterehushche
Krasnohvardiis'ke
Varna
M24
E105
M26
Oktiabrs'ke
PIVOSTRIV
Bilhorod
Dnistrovs'kyi
Zatoka
Chornomors'ke
Saky
Bilohirsk
121
93
Sarata
M15
mys Tarkhankut
Myrnyi
Yevpatoria
P7
71
SIMFE POL'
2
Batumi
Mikolaivka
83
45
Alushta
Bakhchysarai
Varna
İstanbul
SEVASTOPOL'
75
Alupka
Yalta
mys khersones
41
Vylkove
mys Saryzh

Sulina
3
DELTA DUNĂRII

urighiol

TANŢA

alia
Odessa
Illichivs'k
4

Nos Kaliakra

Č E R N O
D
E
F
TR
Cide
M O R E
Kurucaşile
Azdavay

How to use the index • Avvertenze per la ricerca • Instrucciones para la consulta
Notices pour la recherche • Erläuterungen des Suchsystems

The index lists the place names, tourist sites, main tunnels and passes contained in the atlas, followed by the abbreviation of the country name to which they belong.
All names contained in two adjoining pages are referenced to the even page number.

L'indice elenca i toponimi dei centri abitati, dei siti turistici, dei principali tunnel e passi presenti nell'atlante, accompagnati dalla sigla della nazione di appartenenza.
Tutti i nomi contenuti in due pagine affiancate sono riferiti alla pagina di numero pari.

El índice presenta los topónimos de localidades, lugares turísticos, principales túneles y puertos de montaña que figuran en el atlas, seguidos de la sigla que indica el País de pertenencia. Todos los nombres contenidos en dos páginas juntas éstan referidos a la página de número par.

L'index récense les noms des localités, sites touristiques, principales tunnels et cols contenus dans l'atlas, suivis par le sigle qui indique le Pays d'appartenance.
Tous les noms contenus dans deux pages l'une à côté de l'autre sont rapportés à la page avec nombre pair.

Der Index enthält die im Atlas vorhandenen Ortsnamen, Sehenswürdigkeiten, wichtigsten Tunnels und Pässe, von dem zugehörigen Staatskennzeichen gefolgt.
Alle in zwei anliegenden Seiten enthaltenen Namen sind auf die Seite mit gerader Zahl bezogen.

A

23 August [RO] 150 F2
Å [N] 202 F2
Å [N] 218 E2
Aabenraa [DK] 178 B3
Aabybro [DK] 182 D2
Aachen [D] 42 B4
Aakirkeby [DK] 180 E3
Aalborg [DK] 182 D2
Aalburg [NL] 30 B4
Aalen [D] 72 A1
Aalestrup [DK] 182 D3
Aalsmane [LV] 236 C2
Aalsmeer [NL] 30 B3
Aalst (Alost) [B] 40 D3
Aalten [NL] 30 D4
Aalter [B] 40 C3
Äänekoski [FIN] 208 F2
Aapajärvi [FIN] 222 D2
Aarau [CH] 70 D3
Aarberg [CH] 70 C4
Aarburg [CH] 70 D3
Aareavaraa [S] 222 A2
Aareschlucht [CH] 116 D1
Aarlen (Arlon) [B] 56 D2
Aars [DK] 182 D3
Aarschot [B] 40 E3
Aarup [DK] 178 C2
Aavasaksa [FIN] 222 B3
Aba [H] 122 A1
Åbacka [S] 214 A1
Abades [E] 92 E3
Abadín [E] 82 D2
Abadíno [E] 86 E3
Abádszalók [H] 76 D4
A Baña [E] 82 B2
Abanades [E] 94 B3
Abanilla [E] 106 C2
Abano Terme [I] 118 C4
Abarán [E] 106 D2
Abárzuza [E] 86 E4
Abaújszántó [H] 76 D2
Abbadía [I] 130 E2
Abbadía San Salvatore [I]
  130 E2
Abbasanta [I] 142 B3

Abbekås [S] 180 C2
Abbeville [F] 40 A4
Abbeydorney [IRL] 10 B3
Abbeyfeale [IRL] 10 B3
Abbeyleix [IRL] 10 E2
Abbiategrasso [I] 116 D4
Abborrträsk [S] 214 C1
Abdürrahim [TR] 158 A4
Abejar [E] 94 B2
Abela [P] 98 B2
Abéliéra [F] 126 C2
Abelnes [N] 186 B3
Abelvær [N] 212 C3
Abenberg [D] 58 E4
Abengibre [E] 102 B3
Abenójar [E] 100 D3
Abensberg [D] 72 D1
Aberaeron [GB] 22 C4
Aberchirder [GB] 14 F3
Aberdare [GB] 26 D2
Aberdeen [GB] 18 F2
Aberfeldy [GB] 18 D3
Abergavenny [GB] 26 E1
Abergele [GB] 22 E2
Aberlour [GB] 14 E3
Abersee [A] 72 E3
Abersoch [GB] 22 C3
Aberspier [D] 44 D3
Aberystwyth [GB] 22 D4
Abetone [I] 128 B3
Abide [TR] 162 F2
Abide [TR] 164 F3
Abiego [E] 94 F2
Abild [DK] 178 B3
Abild [S] 184 B3
Abingdon [GB] 28 B2
Abington [GB] 20 D2
Abisko [S] 224 D4
Abiúl [P] 90 C2
Abja–Paluoja [EST] 230 D3
Abla [E] 106 B3
Ablanitsa [BG] 148 F4
Ablis [F] 54 D4
Åbo [S] 204 D1
Åbo / Turku [FIN] 198 C3
Åboland [S] 188 C3
Abondance [F] 116 B2
Abony [H] 122 C1

Åbosjö [S] 206 D1
Aboyne [GB] 14 F4
Abrantes [P] 90 C3
Abraur [S] 220 D4
Abreschviller [F] 70 D1
Abric d'Ermites [E] 96 A4
Abriès [F] 126 C1
Abrigo de la Peña del Escrito
  [E] 102 C2
Abriola [I] 134 F4
Absdorf [A] 74 C2
Abtei [A] 120 A2
Abtenau [A] 72 E4
Abtsgmünd [D] 72 A1
Abtshagen [D] 32 F2
Åby [N] 186 E3
Åby [S] 184 C3
Åby [S] 190 C3
Abyarowshchyna [BY] 38 D4
Åbyn [S] 214 D2
A Cañiza [E] 82 B3
Acate [I] 140 D3
Accadia [I] 134 E3
Acceglio [I] 126 C2
Accettura [I] 134 F4
Acciaroli [I] 136 A3
Accous [F] 88 B3
Accumoli [I] 132 D2
Acedera [E] 100 B2
Acedo [E] 86 E4
Acehuche [E] 90 F3
Acerenza [I] 134 F3
Acerno [I] 134 D4
Acerra [I] 134 C3
Aceuchal [E] 98 E2
Acey, Abbaye d'– [F] 70 B3
Acharnés [GR] 168 B2
Achenkirch [A] 72 C4
Achensee [A] 72 C4
Achenwald [A] 72 C3
Achern [D] 70 E1
Acheux–en–Amiénois [F]
  54 E1
Achilleio [GR] 160 F4
Achillium [TR] 162 F2
Achim [D] 32 B4
Achinós [GR] 156 C4
Achladóchóri [GR] 156 B3

Achladókampos [GR] 172 D2
Achleiten [A] 74 A3
Achnasheen [GB] 14 D3
Achtrup [D] 178 B3
Aci Castello [I] 140 E3
Aci Catena [I] 140 E2
Acinipo [E] 104 C3
Acıpayam [TR] 170 E3
Acireale [I] 140 E2
Aci Trezza [I] 140 E2
Acksi [S] 194 E3
A Coruña / La Coruña [E]
  82 C1
Acqua Doria [F] 130 A3
Acquafredda, Castello di– [I]
  142 B5
Acqualagna [I] 128 E4
Acquanegra sul Chiese [I]
  118 A4
Acquapendente [I] 130 F2
Acquaro [I] 138 D3
Acquasanta Terme [I] 132 E2
Acquasparta [I] 132 C2
Acquaviva delle Fonti [I]
  136 D2
Acquedolci [I] 138 B4
Acqui Terme [I] 126 E2
Acri [I] 138 E1
Acropolis Iberica [E] 94 E3
Ács [H] 74 F3
Acsa [H] 76 B3
Acsád [H] 74 D4
Ada [SRB] 122 C3
Adaköy [TR] 176 C1
Adalsbruk [N] 194 C3
Ådalsvollen [N] 204 C1
Adámas [GR] 174 C1
Adamclisi [RO] 150 E1
Adamuz [E] 100 C4
Adanero [E] 92 D3
Adare [IRL] 10 C3
Adaševci [SRB] 146 C1
Adelberg [D] 72 A1
Adelboden [CH] 116 C2
Adelebsen [D] 44 B3
Adelfia [I] 136 D2
Adelsheim [D] 58 C3
Adelsö [S] 190 D2

Adelsried [D] 72 B2
Ademuz [E] 102 C2
Adenau [D] 56 E1
Adjud [RO] 244 E4
Admont [A] 74 A4
Ådneram [N] 186 C2
Adolfsström [S] 220 B3
Adony [H] 122 B1
Adorf [D] 60 B2
Adra [E] 106 A4
Adradas [E] 94 B3
Adrall [E] 96 C1
Adramittium Thebe [TR]
  164 B3
Adrano [I] 138 B4
Adria [I] 128 D1
Adrigole [IRL] 10 A4
A. Drosini [GR] 156 E3
Adunații–Copăceni [RO]
  150 B1
Adutiškis [LT] 238 F2
Aegviidu [EST] 230 D2
Aerinó [GR] 162 A4
Ærøskøbing [DK] 178 C3
Aerzen [D] 44 B2
Aesoo [EST] 230 D3
A Estrada [E] 82 B3
Aetópetra [GR] 160 C4
Aetós [GR] 160 D2
Aetós [GR] 166 C3
Äetsä [FIN] 198 D2
Afáia [GR] 168 B3
Afántou [GR] 176 C2
Åfarnes [N] 202 D3
Afife [P] 82 B4
Afiónas [GR] 160 B4
Aflenz Kurort [A] 74 B4
A Fonsagrada [E] 82 D2
Afoss [N] 186 E2
Africo [I] 138 D4
Afritz [A] 118 F2
Afsluitdijk [NL] 30 C2
Afumați [RO] 150 C1
Áfysos [GR] 162 B4
Áfytos [GR] 162 B2
Aga [N] 192 C3
Ağaçbeyli [TR] 170 E1
Ağaçlı [TR] 158 D3

Agaete [E] 112 E3
Agalás [GR] 172 B2
Agalatovo [RUS] 200 F3
Ág. Anárgyroi [GR] 160 E4
Ág. Antónios [GR] 162 B2
Ág. Athanásios [GR] 160 F2
Agay [F] 126 B3
Agazzano [I] 126 F1
Ág. Charálampos [GR] 156 E4
Agde [F] 124 C3
Ag. Dimítrios [GR] 166 D3
Ág. Dionýsios [GR] 160 E3
Ag. Dionysíou, Moní– [GR] 162 C2
Agen [F] 88 E1
Agéranos [GR] 172 D3
Agerbæk [DK] 178 B2
Ág. Fokás [GR] 176 B1
Ag. Fotiá [GR] 174 E4
Ág. Geórgios [GR] 166 D2
Agger [DK] 182 B3
Aggersund [DK] 182 C2
Aggíus [I] 142 C2
Aggsbach–Dorf [A] 74 C2
Aggsbach–Markt [A] 74 C2
Aggstein [A] 74 C2
Aggtelek [H] 76 C2
Aghadoe [IRL] 10 B3
Aghleam / An Eachléim [IRL] 12 A2
Agiá [GR] 160 F4
Agía Ánna [GR] 166 F3
Agía Ánna [GR] 168 A1
Agía Efimía [GR] 166 B3
Agía Galíni [GR] 174 C4
Agía Marína [CY] 176 D3
Agía Marína [GR] 168 A3
Agía Marína [GR] 170 B4
Agía Nápa [CY] 176 E3
Agía Paraskeví [GR] 164 A3
Agía Pelagía [GR] 172 E4
Agiásmata [GR] 168 E1
Agiásos [GR] 164 B3
Agía Triáda [GR] 160 F2
Agía Triáda [GR] 166 C2
Agía Triáda [GR] 166 D4
Agía Varvára [GR] 174 D4
Agigea [RO] 150 F1
Ág. Ioánnis [GR] 166 F3
Ág. Ioánnis [GR] 176 A1
Agiófyllo [GR] 160 D4
Ágioi Déka [GR] 174 D4
Agiókampos [GR] 160 F4
Agiókampos [GR] 166 F2
Ágio Pnévma [GR] 156 C4
Ágios Amvrósios (Esentepe) [CY] 176 E3
Ágios Andréas [GR] 172 E2
Ágios Apóstoloi [GR] 172 E3
Agios Athanásios [GR] 160 D2
Ágios Dimítrios [GR] 160 E3
Ágios Dimítrios [GR] 172 E3
Ágios Efstrátios [GR] 162 E3
Ágios Germanos [GR] 160 D2
Ágios Górdis [GR] 166 A1
Agios Konstantínos [GR] 166 F3
Agios Konstantínos [GR] 170 A3
Ágios Kýrikos [GR] 168 F3
Ágios Léon [GR] 172 B2
Ágios Márkos [GR] 156 B4
Ágios Matthaíos [GR] 166 A1
Ágios Mýron [GR] 174 D4
Ágios Nikítas [GR] 166 B3
Ágios Nikólaos [GR] 160 B4
Ágios Nikólaos [GR] 166 C3
Ágios Nikólaos [GR] 168 A3
Ágios Nikólaos [GR] 172 D3
Ágios Nikólaos [GR] 174 E3
Ágios Pétros [GR] 166 B3
Ágios Pétros [GR] 172 D2

Ágios Theodoros (Çayırova) [CY] 176 E3
Agios Vlásios [GR] 166 D3
Agira [I] 140 D2
Ag. Kyriakí [GR] 168 F2
Ağla [TR] 170 D4
Aglasterhausen [D] 58 C3
Ag. Lávra [GR] 166 E4
Äglen [BG] 148 F3
Aglen [N] 212 C3
Agliano [I] 126 D1
Agliate [I] 116 E3
Aglona [LV] 236 D4
Ag. Loukás [GR] 168 B2
Ag. Marína [GR] 166 E2
Ag. Marína [GR] 168 B2
Ag. Marína [GR] 176 A4
Agnánta [GR] 166 C1
Agnanteró [GR] 160 E4
Agnäs [S] 206 E1
Ág. Nikólaos [GR] 162 B2
Agnita [RO] 244 D4
Agno [CH] 116 D3
Agnone [I] 132 F4
Agnone Bagni [I] 140 E3
Agnóntas [GR] 162 C4
Agoitz / Aoiz [E] 88 A3
Agolada [E] 82 C3
Agoncillo [E] 86 E4
Agon–Coutainville [F] 52 E2
Agordo [I] 118 C2
Ágosegyháza [H] 122 C2
Agost [E] 106 F2
Ag. Panteleïmonas [GR] 160 D2
Ag. Pelagía [GR] 174 D3
Ag. Pétros [GR] 160 F2
Ág. Pródromos [GR] 162 B2
Agramón [E] 106 D1
Agramunt [E] 96 C2
Ágras [GR] 160 E2
Agreda [E] 94 C2
Agreliá [GR] 160 E4
Agriá [GR] 162 B3
Agrigento [I] 140 C3
Agrilía [GR] 166 D3
Agrínio [GR] 166 D3
Agriovótano [GR] 162 B4
Agropoli [I] 134 D4
Ag. Roúmeli [GR] 174 B4
Ag. Stéfanos [GR] 168 D3
Ág. Theódoroi [GR] 162 B4
Ág. Theódoroi [GR] 166 F4
Ag. Thomás [GR] 174 D4
Ag. Triáda [GR] 168 B2
Ag. Triáda [GR] 174 C4
Agua, Cueva del– [E] 106 B2
Agua Amarga [E] 106 C4
Aguadulce [E] 106 B4
A Guarda / La Guardia [E] 82 A4
A Guarda / La Guardia [E] 100 E2
Aguasmestas [E] 82 E3
Aguas Nuevas [E] 102 B4
Aguda [P] 84 A3
A Gudiña [E] 82 C4
Agudo [E] 100 C2
Águeda [P] 84 A3
Agüero [E] 88 B4
Aguiar [P] 98 C2
Aguiar da Beira [P] 84 B3
Águila, Cuevas del– [E] 92 C4
Aguilafuente [E] 92 E2
Aguilar de Campoo [E] 86 C3
Aguilar de la Frontera [E] 104 D2
Aguilar del Alfambra [E] 102 D1
Águilas [E] 106 D3
Agüimes [E] 112 E4
Agulo [E] 112 C2

Agurain / Salvatierra [E] 86 E3
Aguzadera [E] 104 C2
Ağva / Yeşilçay [TR] 158 F3
Aha [D] 70 E3
Ahascragh [IRL] 10 D1
Ahat [TR] 170 E1
Ahaus [D] 30 D4
Åheim [N] 202 B4
Aheloy [BG] 150 E4
Ahigal [E] 92 B3
Ahıthisar [TR] 170 F1
Ahja [EST] 230 F3
Ahjärvi [FIN] 200 D1
Ahkiolahti [FIN] 210 B1
Ahlainen [FIN] 198 C1
Ahlbeck [D] 34 D3
Ahlbeck [D] 34 D2
Ahlen [D] 42 E2
Ahlerstedt [D] 32 B3
Ahlhorn [D] 30 F3
Ahlolahti [GR] 166 C3
Ahmetbey [TR] 158 C3
Ahmetbeyler [TR] 164 C3
Ahmetçe [TR] 164 B3
Ahmetler [TR] 164 F4
Ahmetli [TR] 164 D4
Ahmoo [FIN] 198 E3
Ahmovaara [FIN] 210 D1
Ahnsen [D] 44 C1
Ahokylä [FIN] 216 C3
Ahola [FIN] 208 D2
Ahola [FIN] 222 E4
Ahonkylä [FIN] 208 C2
Ahrensbök [D] 32 C2
Ahrensburg [D] 32 C2
Ahrhütte [D] 56 E1
Ähtäri / Etseri [FIN] 208 D3
Ähtärinranta [FIN] 208 D2
Ähtävä / Esse [FIN] 214 F4
Åhus [S] 180 D2
Ahvela [FIN] 216 D2
Ahveninen [FIN] 208 E4
Ahveninen [FIN] 210 B2
Ahvensalmi [FIN] 210 D3
Ahvenselkä [FIN] 222 E2
Ahverinen [FIN] 210 E2
Aianí [GR] 160 E3
Aibar [E] 88 A3
Aich [D] 72 D2
Aicha [D] 72 E2
Aichach [D] 72 C2
Aichstetten [D] 72 A3
Aidenbach [D] 72 E2
Aidone [I] 140 D3
Aigen [A] 72 F2
Aigiáli [GR] 168 E4
Aigialoúsa (Yenierenköy) [CY] 176 E2
Aígina [GR] 168 A3
Aigínio [GR] 160 F2
Aígio [GR] 166 E3
Aigle [CH] 116 B2
Aiglsbach [D] 72 C2
Aignay–le–Duc [F] 68 C2
Aigósthena [GR] 168 A2
Aigre [F] 78 D2
Aigrefeuille–d'Aunis [F] 66 C4
Aigrefeuille–sur–Maine [F] 66 C2
Aiguablava [E] 96 F2
Aiguebelle [F] 80 F3
Aiguebelle [F] 126 B4
Aigueperse [F] 80 B2
Aigues–Mortes [F] 124 D3
Aigues–Vives [F] 124 B3
Aiguevives [F] 68 A2
Aiguilles [F] 126 C1
Aiguillon [F] 88 D1
Aigurande [F] 68 A4
Äijäjoki [FIN] 226 B3
Äijälä [FIN] 208 D2
Ailefroide [F] 80 F4

Aillant–sur–Tholon [F] 68 D2
Aime [F] 116 B3
Ainaži [LV] 230 D4
Ainet [A] 118 D1
Ainhoa [F] 88 A2
Ainsa [E] 88 C4
Airaines [F] 54 E1
Airan [F] 54 B2
Airasca [I] 116 B4
Aire–sur–l'Adour [F] 88 C2
Aire–sur–la–Lys [F] 40 B3
Airolo [CH] 116 D2
Airvault [F] 66 D3
Aisey–sur–Armançon [F] 68 E2
Aisey–sur–Seine [F] 68 E2
Aïssey [F] 70 B3
Aistaig [D] 70 E2
Aisými [GR] 156 F4
Aiterhofen [D] 72 E1
Aitolikó [GR] 166 C3
Aitrach [D] 72 A3
Aitrang [D] 72 B3
Aittojärvi [FIN] 216 C4
Aittolahti [FIN] 210 E3
Aittoperä [FIN] 216 B4
Aittovaara [FIN] 216 E1
Aiud [RO] 244 C4
Åivo / Oivu [FIN] 214 F4
Aix–en–Othe [F] 68 D1
Aix–en–Provence [F] 124 E3
Aixe–sur–Vienne [F] 78 E2
Aix–les–Bains [F] 80 F3
Aizanoi [TR] 164 F3
Aizenay [F] 66 C3
Aizkraukle [LV] 236 C3
Aizpute [LV] 234 D3
Ajaccio [F] 130 A3
Ajaur [S] 214 C2
Ajaureforsen [S] 212 F2
Ajdovščina [SLO] 118 F3
Ajka [H] 120 E1
Ajnovce [KS] 154 D2
Ajo [E] 86 D2
Ajos [FIN] 216 A1
Akáki [CY] 176 D3
Akalan [TR] 158 D3
Akalan [TR] 170 D3
Akanthoú (Tatlısu) [CY] 176 E3
Akarca [TR] 170 E1
Äkasjokisuu [FIN] 222 B1
Äkäslompolo [FIN] 222 B1
Akaszto [H] 122 B2
Akbaş [TR] 164 C2
Akbaş [TR] 170 E3
Akbük [TR] 170 B4
Akçakavak [TR] 170 D4
Akçakese [TR] 158 F3
Akçaköy [TR] 170 C2
Akçaköy [TR] 170 F3
Akçaova [TR] 158 F3
Akçaova [TR] 170 C3
Akçay [TR] 164 B3
Akçay [TR] 176 E1
Akdere [TR] 170 D2
Akdoğan (Lysi) [CY] 176 E3
Aken [D] 44 E3
Åker [S] 184 C2
Åkersberga [S] 190 E2
Åkersjön [S] 204 E1
Åkers styckerbruk [S] 190 D2
Akharım [TR] 170 F1
Akhisar [TR] 164 D3
Akhtopol [BG] 158 C1
Akkarfjord [N] 228 B2
Akkavare [S] 214 C1
Akkent [TR] 170 E2
Akköy [TR] 170 B3
Akköy [TR] 170 E2
Akland [N] 186 E3
Aklı [H] 120 F1
Akmyane [LT] 234 E4

Akniste [LV] 236 C4
Akonlahti [FIN] 216 E3
Akonpohja [FIN] 210 E4
Akoúmia [GR] 174 C4
Åkra [N] 186 B1
Akrai [I] 140 E3
Akraifia [GR] 166 F3
Akraífnio [GR] 166 F3
Åkran [N] 204 C1
Akranes [IS] 218 A2
Akrapol [TR] 164 C3
Åkre [N] 194 C1
Åkrehamn [N] 186 A2
Akr. Évinos [GR] 166 D3
Akrogiáli [GR] 162 C1
Akropótamos [GR] 162 C1
Akrotíri [CY] 176 D4
Akrotíri [GR] 174 D2
Akrovoúni [GR] 156 C4
Aksakal [TR] 164 D1
Aksakovo [BG] 150 E3
Akşar [TR] 170 E3
Aksaz [TR] 164 B1
Aksaz [TR] 164 E3
Aksaz Kaplıca [TR] 170 E2
Aksdal [N] 186 A1
Aksla [N] 192 C1
Aktsyabrski [BY] 242 C3
Åkullsjön [S] 214 D3
Akureyri [IS] 218 C2
Akyazı [TR] 176 E1
Ål [N] 192 E3
Ala [I] 118 B3
Ala [S] 234 A2
Alaattin [TR] 170 E3
Alabanda [TR] 170 C3
Alabodarna [S] 178 F1
Alacadağ [TR] 176 F1
Alacant / Alicante [E] 106 F2
Alacat [TR] 164 C3
Alaçatı [TR] 168 F1
Alà dei Sardi [I] 142 C3
Ala di Stura [I] 116 B3
Aladzha Manastir [BG] 150 E3
Alaejos [E] 84 F3
Alagna–Valsésia [I] 116 C3
A Lagoa / Campo Lameiro [E] 82 B3
Alagón [E] 90 F3
Alagón [E] 94 D2
Alahärmä [FIN] 208 C1
Ala–Honkajoki [FIN] 208 C4
Alajärvi [FIN] 208 D2
Alajärvi [FIN] 216 D2
Alajoki [FIN] 216 B3
Alajoki [FIN] 226 D3
Alakurtti [RUS] 222 F2
Alakylä [FIN] 216 A4
Alakylä [FIN] 216 B2
Alakylä [FIN] 222 B2
Alalampi [RUS] 210 F3
Ala–Livo [FIN] 216 C1
Alamaa [FIN] 208 F2
Alameda [E] 104 D2
Alamedilla [E] 106 A2
Alanäs [S] 212 F4
Alancık [TR] 164 C2
Åland [N] 190 D1
Alandroal [P] 90 D4
Ålandsbro [S] 206 D3
Alange [E] 98 F2
Alaniemi [FIN] 216 B1
Alanís [E] 100 A4
Alanta [LT] 238 E2
Alap [H] 122 B2
Alapitkä [FIN] 210 C1
Alaquàs [E] 102 D3
Alaraz [E] 92 C3
Alarcón [E] 102 B2
Alaşehir [TR] 170 D2
Ålåsen [S] 204 E1
Alássio [I] 126 D3
Alastaro [FIN] 198 D2

Ala–Temmes [FIN] 216 B2
Alatoz [E] 102 C3
Alatri [I] 132 D4
Alatskivi [EST] 230 F2
Alattu [RUS] 210 F3
Ala-Valli [FIN] 208 C3
Alavattnet [S] 212 F4
Alaveteli / Nedervetil [FIN] 214 F4
Ala–Vieksi [FIN] 216 D3
Alavieska [FIN] 216 A3
Ala–Vuokki [FIN] 216 E2
Alavus [FIN] 208 D3
Alba [I] 126 D1
Alba Adriatica [I] 132 E2
Albacete [E] 102 B3
Albaching [D] 72 D3
Albacken [S] 206 B3
Alba de Tormes [E] 84 E4
Álbæk [DK] 182 E2
Alba Fucens [I] 132 E3
Albaida [E] 102 D4
Albaina [E] 86 E4
Alba Iulia [RO] 244 C4
Albaladejo [E] 100 F4
Albalate de Cinca [E] 94 F3
Albalate del Arzobispo [E] 94 E4
Albalate de las Nogueras [E] 102 B1
Albalate de Zorita [E] 102 A1
Alban [F] 124 B2
Albánchez [E] 106 C3
Albanella [I] 134 D4
Albano di Lucania [I] 134 F4
Albano Laziale [I] 132 C4
Albaredo d'Adige [I] 118 B4
Albarella [I] 128 E1
Albares [E] 92 F4
Albarracín [E] 102 C1
Albarracín, Cuevas de– [E] 102 C1
Albatana [E] 106 D1
Albena [BG] 150 E2
Albenga [I] 126 D3
Albens [F] 80 F2
Albentosa [E] 102 D2
Alberga [S] 190 C2
Albergaria-a–Velha [P] 84 A3
Alberic [E] 102 D4
Albernoa [P] 98 C3
Albero Alto [E] 94 E2
Alberobello [I] 136 D2
Alberoni [I] 118 D4
Albersdorf [D] 32 B2
Albert [F] 54 E1
Albertacce [F] 130 B2
Albertirsa [H] 76 B4
Albertville [F] 80 F3
Albeşti [RO] 150 D1
Albeşti [RO] 150 F2
Albi [F] 124 A2
Albier Montrond [F] 80 F4
Albignasego [I] 118 C4
Albinea [I] 128 B2
Albissola Marina [I] 126 E2
Albo [F] 130 B2
Albocácer / Albocàsser [E] 102 E2
Albocàsser / Albocácer [E] 102 E2
Albōke [S] 184 F3
Alboraia / Alboraya [E] 102 D3
Alboraya / Alboraia [E] 102 D3
Alborea [E] 102 C3
Albox [E] 106 C3
Albrechtice nad Vltavou [CZ] 60 D4
Albrechtsburg [A] 74 C2
Albudeite [E] 106 D2
Albufeira [P] 98 B4
Albujón [E] 106 E3

Albuñol [E] 104 F3
Albuñuelas [E] 104 F3
Alburquerque [E] 90 E3
Alby [S] 184 F4
Alby [S] 204 F3
Alcácer do Sal [P] 98 C2
Alcáçovas [P] 98 C2
Alcadozo [E] 102 B4
Alcafores [P] 90 E2
Alcaide [E] 106 C2
Alcalá de Chivert / Alcalá de Xivert [E] 102 E2
Alcalá de Guadaíra [E] 104 C2
Alcalá de Henares [E] 92 E4
Alcalá de la Selva [E] 102 D2
Alcalá del Júcar [E] 102 C3
Alcalá de los Gazules [E] 104 B3
Alcalá del Río [E] 98 I-4
Alcalá del Valle [E] 104 C2
Alcalá de Xivert / Alcalá de Chivert [E] 102 E2
Alcalá la Real [E] 104 E2
Álcamo [I] 140 B2
Alcanar [E] 96 A4
Alcanede [P] 90 B2
Alcanena [P] 90 C2
Alcañices [E] 84 E2
Alcañiz [E] 94 E4
Alcántara [E] 90 E3
Alcántara, Gole d'– [I] 138 C4
Alcantarilla [E] 106 E2
Alcantud [E] 94 B4
Alcaracejos [E] 100 B3
Alcaraz [E] 100 F4
Alcaria Ruiva [P] 98 C3
Alcarràs [E] 94 F3
Alçaşehir [TR] 164 F2
Alcaudete [E] 104 E2
Alcaudete de la Jara [E] 100 C1
Alcázar de San Juan [E] 100 E2
Alcı [TR] 170 E4
Alçitepe [TR] 162 F2
Alcobaça [P] 90 B2
Alcoba de los Montes [E] 100 D2
Alcobendas [E] 92 E4
Alcobertas [P] 90 B2
Alcocéber / Alcossebre [E] 102 E2
Alcocer [E] 94 A4
Alcochete [P] 90 B3
Alcoentre [P] 90 B3
Alcofra [P] 84 B3
Alcoi / Alcoy [E] 106 F1
Alcolea [E] 106 B3
Alcolea del Pinar [E] 94 B3
Alcolea del Río [E] 98 H4
Alconchel [E] 98 E2
Alcora / l'Alcora [E] 102 E2
Alcorcón [E] 92 E4
Alcorisa [E] 94 E4
Alcossebre / Alcocèber [E] 102 E2
Alcoutim [P] 98 C3
Alcover [E] 96 C3
Alcoy / Alcoi [E] 106 F1
Alcubierre [E] 94 D3
Alcubilla de Avellaneda [E] 94 A2
Alcubillas [E] 100 E3
Alcublas [E] 102 D2
Alcúdia [E] 108 D3
Alcúdia de Guadix [E] 106 A3
Alcuéscar [E] 90 F4
Alda [E] 86 E4
Aldeacentenera [E] 100 B1
Aldeadávila de la Ribera [E] 84 D3
Aldea del Cano [E] 90 F4
Aldea del Fresno [E] 92 D4

Aldea del Rey [E] 100 D3
Aldea de Trujillo [E] 100 B1
Aldealpozo [E] 94 C2
Aldeanueva de Ebro [E] 94 C1
Aldeaquemada [E] 100 E4
Aldeatejada [E] 84 E4
Aldeavieja [E] 92 D3
Aldeburgh [GB] 28 F2
Aldeia da Ponte [P] 90 F2
Aldeia do Bispo [P] 90 F2
Aldeias das Neves [E] 98 C3
Aldenhoven [D] 42 C4
Aldernäset [S] 212 F4
Aldershot [GB] 28 C3
Aldinci [MK] 154 D4
Aldtsier [NL] 30 C2
Åled [S] 184 B3
Aledo [E] 106 D2
Alegranza [E] 114 F2
Alekovo [BG] 150 B3
Alekovo [BG] 150 D2
Aleksandrovac [SRB] 146 F2
Aleksandrovo [SRB] 150 A3
Aleksandrów [PL] 48 E2
Aleksandrów [PL] 48 F4
Aleksandrów [PL] 64 D2
Aleksandrów Kujawski [PL] 36 D4
Aleksandrów Łódzki [PL] 48 D3
Aleksin [RUS] 240 F4
Aleksinac [SRB] 148 B3
Álem [S] 184 E3
Alemdağ [TR] 158 E3
Ålen [N] 204 C3
Alençon [F] 54 B3
Alenquer [P] 90 B3
Aléria [F] 130 B3
Aléria [F] 130 B3
Alès [F] 124 D2
Åles [I] 142 B4
Alesd [RO] 122 F1
Alessandria [I] 126 E1
Alessandria del Carretto [I] 136 C3
Alessándria della Rocca [I] 140 C2
Ålesund [N] 202 C3
Alexándreia [GR] 160 E2
Alexandria [RO] 150 B2
Alexándria Troas [TR] 162 F2
Alexandroúpoli [GR] 156 F4
Alf [D] 56 E2
Alfafar [E] 102 D3
Alfaites [P] 90 E2
Alfajarín [E] 94 E3
Alfambra [E] 102 D1
Alfambras [P] 98 A3
Alfândenga da Fé [P] 84 D3
Alfano [I] 136 B3
Alfarela de Jales [P] 84 C2
Alfaro [E] 94 C2
Alfarràs [E] 96 B2
Alfas [E] 102 D4
Alfatar [BG] 150 D2
Alfedena [I] 132 E4
Alfeizerão [P] 90 B2
Alfeld [D] 44 B2
Alfeld [D] 58 F3
Alfena [P] 84 A2
Alfés [E] 96 B2
Alfonsine [I] 128 D2
Alford [GB] 14 F4
Alforja [E] 96 B3
Ålfoten [N] 202 B4
Alfreton [GB] 24 C3
Alfstad [N] 186 E1
Alfta [S] 196 C2
Algaida [E] 108 D3
Algar [E] 104 C3

Algar [E] 108 F3
Ålgarås [S] 188 E3
Ålgård [N] 186 B2
Ålgård [N] 186 B3
Algarinejo [E] 104 E2
Algarra [E] 102 C2
Algatocín [E] 104 C3
Algeciras [E] 104 C4
Algemesí [E] 102 D4
Ålgered [S] 196 C1
Alghero [I] 142 B3
Ålghult [S] 184 E3
Alginet [E] 102 D3
Algodonales [E] 104 C2
Algodor [P] 98 C3
Algora [E] 94 B3
Algoso [P] 84 D3
Älgsjö [S] 214 B3
Alguazas [E] 106 E2
Algutsrum [S] 184 E4
Algyő [H] 122 D2
Alhama de Almería [E] 106 B3
Alhama de Aragón [E] 94 C3
Alhama de Granada [E] 104 E3
Alhama de Murcia [E] 106 D2
Alhambra [E] 100 E3
Alhamillo [E] 100 C3
Alhaurín de la Torre [E] 104 D3
Alhaurín el Grande [E] 104 D3
Alhojärvi [FIN] 208 E4
Alholm Slot [DK] 32 E1
Ålhus [N] 192 C1
Alía [E] 100 C2
Ália [I] 140 C2
Aliaga [E] 102 D1
Aliağa [TR] 164 B4
Aliartos [GR] 166 F3
Alibeyli [TR] 164 D4
Alibunar [SRB] 146 E1
Aliç [TR] 158 A3
Alicante / Alacant [E] 106 F2
Alicudi Porto [I] 138 B3
Áliden [S] 214 D2
Alife [I] 134 C2
Alija del Infantado [E] 84 F2
Alijó [P] 84 C3
Alíkampos [GR] 174 B3
Alikanás [GR] 172 B1
Alikylä [FIN] 216 A4
Alil Abasi [MK] 154 E2
Aliman [RO] 150 E1
Alimena [I] 138 A4
Alinci [MK] 160 D1
Alinda [TR] 170 C3
Alingsås [S] 184 B1
Aíno [BG] 156 B2
Alinyá [E] 96 C2
Aliseda [E] 90 E3
Alistráti [GR] 156 C4
Ali Terme [I] 138 C4
Alivéri [GR] 168 B2
Aljaraque [E] 98 D4
Aljezur [P] 98 A3
Aljinovići [SRB] 152 F1
Aljubarrota [P] 90 B2
Aljucén [E] 90 F4
Aljustrel [P] 98 C3
Alkmaar [NL] 30 B3
Alkotz [E] 86 F3
Alkoven [A] 74 A2
Alkpınar [TR] 158 C2
Aksniupiai [LT] 238 C2
Alkvettern [S] 188 E2
Állai [I] 142 B4
Allaines [F] 54 D4
Allainville [F] 54 D4
Allan [F] 124 E1
Allanche [F] 80 B3
Alland [A] 74 C3
Allariz [E] 82 C4
Allauch [F] 124 F3

Alleen [N] 186 C4
Álleghe [I] 118 C2
Allejaur [S] 214 C1
Allemont [F] 80 F4
Allenbach [D] 56 E2
Allentsteig [A] 74 B2
Allepuz [E] 102 D1
Aller–Heiligen [D] 70 E1
Allersberg [D] 58 E4
Allershausen [D] 72 C2
Allerum [S] 178 F1
Alleuze, Château d'– [F] 80 B3
Allevard [F] 80 F3
Allgunnen [S] 184 E3
Allihies [IRL] 10 A4
Allingåbro [DK] 182 D4
Allinge [DK] 180 F3
Allo [E] 86 E4
Alloa [GB] 18 D3
Álloluokta [S] 220 D2
Allonnes [F] 54 D4
Allonnes [F] 66 E2
Ållonö [S] 190 C3
Allos [F] 126 B2
Alloue [F] 78 D2
Ållsjön [S] 206 C2
Allstedt [D] 44 D3
Almacelles [E] 96 B2
Almada [P] 90 A3
Almadén [E] 100 C3
Almadén de la Plata [E] 98 F3
Almadenes, Cañón de los– [E] 106 D2
Almadenojos [E] 100 C3
Almadrones [E] 94 A3
Almagreira [P] 110 E2
Almagro [E] 100 D3
Almancil [P] 98 B4
Almandoz [E] 86 F3
Almansa [E] 102 C4
Almanza [E] 86 B3
Almaraz [E] 92 B4
Almargen [E] 104 D2
Almarza [E] 94 B2
Almås [N] 204 B2
Almásfüzitő [H] 74 F3
Almassora / Almazora [E] 102 E2
Almazán [E] 94 B2
Almazora / Almassora [E] 102 E2
Almedina [E] 100 E4
Almeida [E] 84 C4
Almeida de Sayago [E] 84 E3
Almeirim [P] 90 C3
Almelo [NL] 30 D3
Almenar [E] 96 B2
Almenara [E] 102 D3
Almenara [E] 104 D1
Almenara de Tormes [E] 84 E4
Almenar de Soria [E] 94 C2
Almendinilla [E] 104 E2
Almendra [P] 84 C3
Almendral [E] 98 E2
Almendralejo [E] 98 F2
Almenno S. Salvatore [I] 116 E3
Almere [NL] 30 B3
Almería [E] 106 B4
Almerimar [E] 106 B4
Almesåkra [S] 184 D2
Ålmestad [S] 184 B1
Älmhult [S] 184 C4
Almodôvar [P] 98 C3
Almodóvar del Campo [E] 100 D3
Almodóvar del Pinar [E] 102 B2
Almodóvar del Río [E] 104 D1
Almogía [E] 104 D3
Almograve [P] 98 B3
Almoharín [E] 90 F4

Almonaster la Real [E] 98 E3
Almonte [E] 104 B1
Almoradí [E] 106 E2
Almoraima [E] 104 C3
Almorox [E] 92 D4
Almourol [P] 90 C3
Almsee [S] 214 B3
Älmsta–Väddö [S] 190 E1
Almudévar [E] 94 E2
Almuñécar [E] 104 E3
Almunge [S] 190 D1
Almuradiel [E] 100 E4
Almwik [S] 184 E1
Almyró [GR] 172 D3
Almyropótamos [GR] 168 B2
Almyrós [GR] 162 A4
Alness [GB] 14 E3
Alnwick [GB] 20 E2
Aloja [LV] 230 D4
Alol' [RUS] 236 F3
Alónnisos [GR] 162 C4
Álora [E] 104 D3
Alosno [E] 98 D3
Alost (Aalst) [B] 40 D3
Alozaina [E] 104 D3
Alp [E] 96 D1
Alpalhão [P] 90 D3
Alpbach [A] 72 D4
Alpedrinha [P] 90 E2
Alpe du Grand Serre [F] 80 E4
Alpen [D] 42 C2
Alpengarten [D] 72 C4
Alpera [E] 102 C4
Alphen–aan den Rijn [NL]
  30 B3
Alpiarca [P] 90 C3
Alpirsbach [D] 70 E2
Alportel [P] 98 C4
Alpua [FIN] 216 B3
Alpuente [E] 102 C2
Alpullu [TR] 158 B3
Alqueva [P] 98 D2
Alquézar [E] 94 F2
Als [DK] 182 D3
Alsager [GB] 22 F3
Alsasua / Altsasu [E] 86 E3
Alsen [S] 204 E2
Alsenz [D] 56 F3
Alsfeld [D] 42 F4
Ålshult [S] 184 D4
Alsleben [D] 44 E3
Ålsø [DK] 182 E4
Alsóörs [H] 120 F1
Alsótold [H] 76 B3
Alsózsolca [H] 76 D3
Ålstad [N] 220 A1
Ålstad [S] 180 C2
Alstahaug [N] 212 D1
Alstätte [D] 30 D4
Alsterbro [S] 184 D2
Alstermo [S] 184 E3
Alston [GB] 20 D3
Alsunga [LV] 234 D3
Alsvåg [N] 224 B3
Alsvik [N] 218 F3
Alta [N] 228 B3
Altafulla [E] 96 C3
Altamira, Cuevas de– [E]
  86 C2
Altamura [I] 136 C2
Altarejos [E] 102 B2
Altaussee [A] 72 F3
Altavilla Silentina [I]
  134 E4
Altdahn [D] 56 F4
Altdorf [CH] 116 D1
Altdorf [D] 58 E4
Alt Duvenstedt [D] 32 B1
Altea [E] 108 C2
Altedo [I] 128 C2
Alteidet [N] 224 F1
Altena [D] 42 D3

Altenahr [D] 56 E1
Altenau [D] 44 C3
Altenberg [D] 60 D1
Altenberge [D] 30 E4
Altenberger Dom [D] 42 D3
Altenburg [A] 74 C2
Altenburg [D] 44 E4
Altenfelden [A] 72 F2
Altenglan [D] 56 F3
Altenhundem [D] 42 E3
Altenkirchen [D] 34 C1
Altenkirchen [D] 42 D4
Altenklingen [CH] 70 F3
Altenmarkt [A] 72 E4
Altenmarkt [A] 74 B3
Altenmarkt [D] 72 D3
Altenstadt [D] 72 A2
Altenstadt [D] 72 B3
Altensteig [D] 70 E1
Altentreptow [D] 34 C3
Altenwalde [D] 32 A2
Alter do Chão [P] 90 D3
Alteren [N] 218 F4
Althegnenberg [D] 72 C2
Altheim [A] 72 E2
Althofen [A] 120 A2
Alti [TR] 170 B4
Altimir [BG] 148 E3
Altınoluk [TR] 164 B3
Altınova [TR] 158 F4
Altınova [TR] 164 B3
Altınyaka [TR] 176 F1
Altınyayla [TR] 170 F4
Altıpiani di Arcinazzo [I]
  132 D4
Altkirch [F] 70 D3
Altlandsberg [D] 46 B1
Altmörbitz [D] 44 E4
Altmünster [A] 72 F3
Altnaharra [GB] 14 E2
Alto de los Leones de Castilla
  [E] 92 E3
Altomonte [I] 136 C4
Alton [GB] 28 B3
Altopascio [I] 128 B3
Altorricón [E] 94 F3
Altötting [D] 72 E2
Altrier [L] 56 D2
Alt Ruppin [D] 32 F4
Altsasu / Alsasua [E] 86 E3
Alt Schadow [D] 46 C2
Altstätten [CH] 70 F4
Alttajärvi [S] 220 E1
Altuna [S] 190 C1
Altura [E] 102 D2
Altwarp [D] 34 D3
Altwindeck [D] 70 C1
Alüksne [LV] 230 F4
Ålum [DK] 182 D3
Ålund [S] 214 D2
Alunda [S] 190 D1
Aluokta [S] 220 D2
Aluste [EST] 230 D3
Alvaiázere [P] 90 C2
Alvajärvi [FIN] 208 E1
Alvalade [P] 98 B2
Älvan [S] 188 D4
Alvastra [S] 188 E4
Alvdal [N] 204 B4
Älvdalen [S] 194 E2
Alvechurch [GB] 28 B1
Alverca do Ribatejo [P] 90 B3
Alversund [N] 192 B3
Alvesta [S] 184 D3
Alvestad [N] 186 A2
Älvhem [S] 184 A1
Alvignac [F] 78 E4
Ålvik [N] 192 C3
Alvik [S] 194 F3
Alvik [S] 214 E1
Älviken [S] 204 E1

Alvito [I] 132 E4
Alvito [P] 98 C2
Älvkarleby [S] 196 D3
Alvor [P] 98 B4
Älvros [S] 194 D1
Älvros [S] 194 F1
Älvsbacka [S] 188 E2
Älvsbyn [S] 214 D1
Älvsered [S] 184 B2
Älvsund [S] 196 C1
Ålvundeid [N] 202 E3
Alyekshytsy [BY] 38 D3
Alykí [GR] 162 D1
Alykí [GR] 162 D1
Alykí [GR] 168 D4
Alytus [LT] 238 D4
Alzenall [D] 58 C2
Alzey [D] 58 B3
Alzira [E] 102 D4
Alzon [F] 124 C2
Alzonne [F] 124 A3
Åmådalen [S] 194 F2
Amadora [P] 90 B3
Åmål [S] 188 D3
Amalfi [I] 134 D4
Amaliáda [GR] 172 C1
Amaliápoli [GR] 162 B4
Åmalo [GR] 168 E3
Amance [F] 70 B2
Amancey [F] 70 B4
Amandola [I] 132 E2
Amantea [I] 138 D2
Amantia [AL] 160 B3
Amarante [P] 84 B2
Amárantos [GR] 166 D2
Amǎrǎştii de Sus [RO] 148 E2
Amareleja [P] 98 D2
Amári [GR] 174 C4
Amárynthos [GR] 168 B2
Amatrice [I] 132 D3
Amay [B] 40 E4
Ambarès [F] 78 B3
Ambazac [F] 78 E2
Amberg [D] 58 F4
Ambérieu–en–Bugey [F] 80 E2
Ambert [F] 80 C2
Ambiörnarp [S] 184 B2
Ambjörby [S] 194 D3
Ambla [EST] 230 E2
Amble [GB] 20 F2
Ambleside [GB] 20 D4
Amboise [F] 66 F2
Âmbra [EST] 230 E2
Ambrières [F] 52 F4
Åmdal [N] 186 D3
Ameixial [P] 98 C3
Amel [B] 56 D1
Amélia [I] 132 C3
Amélie–les–Bains [F] 96 E1
Amelinghausen [D] 32 C3
Amendolara [I] 136 C3
Amer [E] 96 E2
A Merca [E] 82 C3
Åmilden [S] 214 C2
Åminne [S] 234 A2
Amiternum [I] 132 D3
Amlach [A] 118 D2
Åmli [N] 186 D3
Åmli [N] 186 D3
Amlwch [GB] 22 D2
Ammanford [GB] 26 D1

Ämmänsaari [FIN] 216 D2
Ammarnäs [S] 220 B4
Åmmeberg [S] 188 F3
Ammersricht [D] 58 F3
Ammóchostos (Gazimağusa)
  [CY] 176 E3
Ammótopos [GR] 166 C2
Ammoudára [GR] 174 D3
Ammoudára [GR] 174 E4
Åmnes [N] 186 E2
Amorbach [D] 58 C3
Amòreira, Acueducto de– [P]
  90 D4
Amorgós [GR] 168 E4
Amorosi [I] 134 D3
Åmot [N] 186 F1
Åmot [N] 186 F1
Åmot [N] 192 F3
Åmot [N] 192 F2
Åmot [N] 194 C2
Åmot [S] 196 C3
Åmotfors [S] 188 C1
Åmotsdal [N] 186 D1
Amou [F] 88 C2
Ampelákia [GR] 156 F3
Ampelákia [GR] 160 F4
Ampelikó [GR] 164 A4
Ampelónas [GR] 160 E4
Ampezzo [I] 118 D2
Ampfing [D] 72 D2
Amphion [F] 116 B2
Amplepuis [F] 80 D2
Amposta [E] 96 B4
Ampudia [E] 92 D1
Ampuero [E] 86 D2
Ampuis [F] 80 D3
Ampus [F] 126 B3
Amriswil [CH] 70 F3
Am See [A] 118 B1
Amsele [S] 214 C3
Amsteg [CH] 116 D1
Amsterdam [NL] 30 B3
Amstetten [A] 74 B3
Amtoft [DK] 182 C2
Amurrio [E] 86 D3
Amvrosía [GR] 156 E4
Amygdaleónas [GR] 156 C4
Amygdaliá [GR] 166 E3
Amýkles [GR] 172 D3
Amýntaio [GR] 160 D2
Amzacea [RO] 150 F2
Anadia [P] 84 A4
Anáfi [GR] 174 E2
Anafonítria [GR] 172 A1
Anagni [I] 132 D4
Anáktora Néstoros [GR]
  172 C3
Análipsi [GR] 174 E1
Anan'ïv [UA] 246 E2
Anárgyroi [GR] 160 D2
Anarráchi [GR] 160 D3
Anascaul [IRL] 10 A3
Ånåset [S] 214 D3
Åna–Sira [N] 186 B3
Anastazewo [PL] 48 B2
Änätinpää [FIN] 216 E2
Anatolí [GR] 160 F4
Anatolikó [GR] 160 D2
Anávra [GR] 162 A4
Anávra [GR] 166 D2
Anávyssos [GR] 168 B3
Anaya [E] 92 E3
An Cabhán / Cavan [IRL]
  12 D3
Anc. Batterie [F] 126 B2
Ance [LV] 234 D2
Ancenis [F] 66 C2
Ancerville [F] 56 C4
An Charraig / Carrick [IRL]
  12 C1
An Cheathrú Rua / Carraroe
  [IRL] 10 C1

An Chloich Mhór / Cloghmore
  [IRL] 12 A2
Anchuras [E] 100 C2
An Clochán Liath / Dunglow
  [IRL] 12 D1
An Coireán / Waterville [IRL]
  10 A3
Ancona [I] 128 F4
Ancy–le–Franc [F] 68 E2
Anda [N] 202 C4
An Daingean / Dingle [IRL]
  10 A3
Andalo [I] 118 B3
Åndalsnes [N] 202 D3
Andåsen [S] 204 E4
Andau [A] 74 E3
Åndebol [S] 190 C3
Andebu [N] 186 F2
Andechs [D] 72 C3
Andelot [F] 70 A2
Andenes [N] 224 B3
Andenne [B] 40 E4
Andermatt [CH] 116 D1
Andernach [D] 56 F1
Andernos–les–Bains [F] 78 B3
Andersfors [S] 214 D3
Anderslöv [S] 180 C2
Anderstorp [S] 184 C2
Andijk [NL] 30 B2
Andilla [E] 102 D2
Andocs [H] 120 F2
Andolsheim [F] 70 D2
Andornaktálya [H] 76 C3
Andorno Micca [I] 116 C3
Andorra [E] 94 E4
Andorra la Vella (AND) 96 D1
Andover [GB] 28 B3
Andrade, Castillo de– [E]
  82 C2
Andraitx [E] 108 C3
Andravída [GR] 166 C4
Andreapol' [RUS] 240 D3
Andrespol [PL] 48 D3
Andretta [I] 134 E3
Andrézieux–Bouthéon [F]
  80 C3
Ándria [I] 134 F3
Andriake [TR] 176 F2
Andritsaina [GR] 172 C2
Ándros [GR] 168 C2
Androússa [GR] 172 C3
Andrychów [PL] 62 E3
Andselv [N] 224 D3
Andújar [E] 104 F1
Anduze [F] 124 D2
An Eachléim / Aghleam [IRL]
  12 A2
Ånebjør [N] 186 C2
Åneby [N] 194 B4
Aneby [S] 184 D1
Ånes [N] 202 E2
Anet [F] 54 D3
An Fhairche / Clonbur [IRL]
  12 B3
Anfo [I] 118 A3
Anga [S] 234 A2
Ånge [S] 204 E2
Ånge [S] 206 B3
Ånge [S] 220 C4
Ångebo [S] 196 C3
Angeja [P] 84 A3
Ängelholm [S] 178 F1
Angeli [FIN] 226 C2
Angelókastro [GR] 166 C3
Angelókastro [GR] 172 E1
Angelsberg [S] 190 B3
Ängelsfors [S] 196 C3
Angelstad [S] 184 C3
Angenstein [CH] 70 D3
Anger [A] 74 C4
Angermünde [D] 34 D4

Angern [A] 74 D2
Angers [F] 66 D2
Ängersjö [S] 194 F1
Ängersjö [S] 206 E1
Angerville [F] 54 D4
Ängesan [S] 220 F3
Ängesbyn [S] 214 E1
Anghelo Ruíu, Necropoli– [I] 142 B2
Anghiari [I] 128 D4
Angiari [I] 118 B4
Anglès [E] 96 E2
Angles–sur–l'Anglin [F] 66 F4
Anglet [F] 88 A2
Anglona [LV] 236 D4
Anglure [F] 56 A4
Ango, Manoir d'– [F] 54 C1
Angoulême [F] 78 D2
Angra do Heroísmo [P] 110 C4
Ängskär [S] 196 D4
Ängsö [S] 190 C2
Angueira [P] 84 D3
Anglés [E] 94 F2
Anguiano [E] 94 B1
Anguillara Sabazia [I] 130 F3
Anguillara Veneta [I] 128 D1
Angulo [E] 86 D3
Angvika [N] 202 E2
Anholt [DK] 182 F3
Aníane [F] 124 C3
Aniche [F] 40 C4
Anina [RO] 248 C3
Anjala [FIN] 200 B3
Anjalankoski [FIN] 200 C2
Anjan [S] 204 D1
Anjos [P] 110 E2
Anjum [NL] 30 D2
Ankaran [SLO] 118 F4
Ankarede [S] 212 E3
Ankarsrum [S] 184 E2
Ankarvattnet [S] 212 E3
Ankenesstrand [N] 224 C4
Anklam [D] 34 C2
Ankum [D] 30 E3
Anlezy [F] 68 D3
Änn [S] 204 D2
Anna [EST] 230 D2
Annaberg [A] 72 E4
Annaberg [A] 74 C3
Annaberg–Buchholz [D] 60 C2
Annadalsvagen [N] 212 D2
Annalong [NIR] 12 F3
Annan [GB] 20 D3
Anna Paulowna [NL] 30 B2
An Nás / Naas [IRL] 10 F2
Anneberg [S] 184 A2
Anneberg [S] 184 D2
Annecy [F] 80 F2
Annefors [S] 196 C2
Annelund [S] 184 B1
Annemasse [F] 80 F2
Annenheim [A] 118 F2
Annerstad [S] 184 C3
Annestown [IRL] 10 D4
Annonay [F] 80 D3
Annopol [PL] 50 B4
Annot [F] 126 B2
Annoux [F] 68 E2
Annweiler [D] 58 A4
Anógeia [GR] 174 C3
Ánoixi [GR] 160 D3
Áno Kalentíni [GR] 166 C2
Áno Kastrítsi [GR] 166 D4
Áno Merá [GR] 168 D3
Anópoli [GR] 174 B4
Áno Sagkri [GR] 168 D4
Áno Sýros [GR] 168 D3
Anould [F] 70 C2
Añover de Tajo [E] 100 E1
Áno Viánnos [GR] 174 D4
Áno Vrontoú [GR] 156 C3
Anquela del Ducado [E] 94 B3

An Rinn / Ringville [IRL] 10 D4
Ans [DK] 182 D4
Ansager [DK] 178 B2
Ansarve [S] 234 A3
Ansbach [D] 58 D4
Anse [F] 80 D2
Ansedónia [I] 130 E2
Anserall [E] 96 C1
Anseremme [B] 56 C1
Ansfelden [A] 74 A3
Ansião [P] 90 C2
Ansó [E] 88 B3
An Spidéal / Spiddal [IRL] 10 C1
Anstad [N] 192 E1
Anstey [GB] 24 C4
Anstruther [GB] 18 E3
Ansvar [S] 222 A3
Antakalnis [LT] 238 D3
Antanarav [LT] 238 E1
Antandros [TR] 164 B3
Antas [P] 84 C3
Antas, Tempio di– [I] 142 B5
Antas de Ulla [E] 82 C3
Antegnate [I] 116 F4
Anten [S] 184 A1
Antequera [E] 104 D3
Anterselva / Antholz [I] 118 D1
Antey St. André [I] 116 C3
Anthéor [F] 126 B3
Anthí [GR] 156 B4
Antholz / Anterselva [I] 118 D1
Anthótopos [GR] 162 A4
Antibes [F] 126 C3
Antigonea [AL] 160 B3
Antigua [E] 118 D3
Antigua Bilbilis [E] 94 C3
Antigüedad [E] 92 E1
Antíkýra [GR] 166 E3
Antimáchia [GR] 176 A1
An Tinbhear Mór / Arklow [IRL] 10 F3
Antinchia [TR] 170 D3
Antíparos [GR] 168 D4
Antírrio [GR] 166 D3
Ántissa [GR] 162 F3
Ántissa [GR] 162 F3
Antjärn [S] 206 D3
Antnäs [S] 214 E1
Anton [BG] 156 C1
Antonin [PL] 48 B3
Antoniów [PL] 64 C1
Antonovo [BG] 150 C3
Antopal' [BY] 50 E2
Antraigues [F] 80 C4
Antrain [F] 52 E3
Antrim [NIR] 12 F2
Antrodoco [I] 132 D3
Antsla [EST] 230 E4
Anttila [FIN] 216 D3
Anttis [S] 220 F2
Anttola [FIN] 200 C1
Anttola [FIN] 210 D3
Antwerpen (Anvers) [B] 40 E3
An Uaimh / Navan [IRL] 10 F1
Anundshögen [S] 190 C2
Anvers (Antwerpen) [B] 40 E3
Anvin [F] 40 B4
Anykščiai [LT] 238 E2
Anzi [I] 134 F4
Anzio [I] 134 A2
Aoiz / Agoitz [E] 88 A3
Aosta / Aoste [I] 116 B3
Aosta / Aoste [I] 116 B3
Apaj [H] 122 D3
Apamea [TR] 158 E4
Åpåsdal [N] 186 C3
Apátfalva [H] 122 D3

Apatin [SRB] 122 B4
Apchon [F] 80 A3
Ape [LV] 230 F4
Apécchio [I] 128 D4
Apeírathos [GR] 168 E4
Apeldoorn [NL] 30 C3
Apen [D] 30 E2
Apensen [D] 32 B3
Aperlai [TR] 176 E2
Aphendrika, Panagia– [CY] 176 E2
Aphrodisias [TR] 170 D3
Apice [I] 134 D3
Apinac [F] 80 C3
Aplared [S] 184 B2
A Pobra de Brollón / Puebla del Brollón [E] 82 C3
A Pobra de Navia [E] 82 D3
A Pobra de Trives [E] 82 C4
Apoíkia [GR] 168 C2
Apolakkiá [GR] 176 B2
Apolda [D] 44 D4
Apollo Aléo, Tempio di– [I] 138 F1
Apóllon [GR] 168 E3
Apollonia [AL] 160 A2
Apollonía [GR] 162 B1
Apollonía [GR] 168 C4
Apollonía [GR] 174 C1
Apollonía [TR] 164 C3
Apollonía [TR] 164 E1
Apollonía [TR] 176 E2
A Pontenova [E] 82 D2
Apostolove [UA] 244 F2
Apothicairerie, Grotte de l'– [F] 66 A1
Äppelbo [S] 194 E4
Appelhülsen [D] 42 D2
Appenweier [D] 70 E1
Appenzell [CH] 70 F4
Appiano / Eppan [I] 118 B2
Appingedam [NL] 30 D2
Appleby–in–Westmorland [GB] 20 D3
Apremont, Gorges d'– [F] 54 E4
Aprica [I] 116 F2
Apricena [I] 134 E2
Aprigliano [I] 138 E2
Aprilia [I] 134 A2
Aprilovo [BG] 150 C3
Apróhomok [H] 76 E2
Ápsalos [GR] 160 E2
Apt [F] 124 E3
Áptera [GR] 174 B3
Áquila [CH] 116 E2
Aquileia [I] 118 E3
Aquilonia [I] 134 E3
Aquino [I] 134 C2
Ar [S] 234 B2
Arabba [I] 118 C2
Araburg [A] 74 C3
Araceli [E] 104 E2
Aracena [E] 98 E3
Aráchova [GR] 166 D3
Aráchova [GR] 166 E3
Aračinovo [MK] 154 D3
Arad [RO] 248 D2
Aradíppou [CY] 176 E3
Aragona [I] 140 C3
Aragonese, Castello– [I] 138 F1
Arahal [E] 104 C3
Arakapás [CY] 176 D4
Áraksbø [N] 186 C2
Áram [N] 202 B3
Aramits [F] 88 B3
Araña, Cueva de la– [E] 102 C4
Aranda de Duero [E] 92 F2
Arandjelovac [SRB] 146 E3

Aranjuez [E] 100 E1
Arantzazu [E] 86 E3
Aranyosapáti [H] 76 F2
Aras de Alpuente [E] 102 C2
Áratos [GR] 156 E4
Aravaca [E] 92 E4
Aravissós [GR] 160 E2
Arazede [P] 90 C1
Arbanasi [BG] 150 B3
Arbatax [I] 142 C4
Arbesbach [A] 74 B2
Arbetera [E] 94 B4
Arboga [S] 190 B2
Arbois [F] 70 B4
Arbon [CH] 70 F3
Arboréa [I] 142 B4
Arbrå [S] 196 C2
Arbroath [GB] 18 E3
Arbúcies [E] 96 E2
Árbus [I] 142 B5
Arc, Pont d'– [F] 124 D2
Arcachon [F] 78 B3
Arcas [E] 102 B2
Arc de Berà [E] 96 C3
Arce [I] 134 B2
Arcen [NL] 42 C3
Arc–en–Barrois [F] 68 F2
Arcévia [I] 128 E4
Archánes [GR] 174 D4
Archángelos [GR] 166 B2
Archángelos [GR] 176 C2
Archar [BG] 148 D3
Archena [I] 106 D2
Arches [F] 70 C2
Archiac [F] 78 C2
Archidona [E] 104 E2
Archivel [E] 106 C2
Arcidosso [I] 130 E2
Arcille [I] 130 E2
Arcinazzo Romano [I] 132 D4
Arcis–sur–Aube [F] 56 B4
Arco [I] 118 B3
Arco de Baúlhe [P] 84 B2
Arconville [F] 54 D2
Arcos de Jalón [E] 94 B3
Arcos de la Frontera [E] 104 B2
Arcos de la Sierra [E] 102 B1
Arcos de Valdevez [P] 82 B4
Årdal [N] 192 C1
Årdal [N] 186 D3
Ardala [S] 188 D4
Ardala [S] 190 C3
Ardales [E] 104 D3
Ardalsosen [N] 186 B2
Ardalstangen [N] 192 D2
Ardara [IRL] 12 C1
Ardea [I] 134 A2
Ardee [IRL] 10 F1
Arden [DK] 182 D3
Ardenciès [AL] 160 A2
Ardentes [F] 68 B3
Ardez [CH] 118 A1
Ardfert [IRL] 10 B3
Ardfinnan [IRL] 10 D3
Ardglass [NIR] 12 F3
Ardino [BG] 156 D3
Ardisa [E] 94 E2
Ardon [F] 70 B4
Ardore [I] 138 D3
Ardres [F] 40 B3
Ardrossan [GB] 18 B4
Åre [S] 204 D2
Areas [E] 82 B3
Areatza [E] 86 E3
Årebrot [N] 192 B1
Arén [E] 96 B1
Arenals del Sol / Los Arenales del Sol [E] 106 F2
Arenas [E] 86 B2

Arenas del Rey [E] 104 E3
Arenas de San Pedro [E] 92 C4
Arendal [N] 186 D3
Arendonk [B] 40 E3
Arendsee [D] 32 D4
Arene / Arrankudiaga [E] 86 D3
Arenenberg [CH] 70 F3
Areños [E] 86 B3
Arenys de Mar [E] 96 E3
Arenzano [I] 126 E2
Areópoli [GR] 172 D3
Ares [E] 82 C1
Arès [F] 78 B3
Ares del Maestrat / Ares del Maestre [E] 102 E2
Ares del Maestre / Ares del Maestrat [E] 102 E2
Aréthousa [GR] 162 B1
Areti [GR] 162 B1
Aretxabaleta [E] 86 E3
Arevalillo [E] 92 C3
Arévalo [E] 92 D2
Arezzo [I] 128 D4
Arfará [GR] 172 D2
Árfora [N] 212 C3
Argalastí [GR] 162 B4
Argállon [E] 100 B3
Argamasilla de Alba [E] 100 E4
Argamasilla de Calatrava [E] 100 D3
Argancy [F] 56 D3
Arganda del Rey [E] 92 E4
Arganil [P] 84 A4
Argási [GR] 172 B2
Argegno [I] 116 E3
Argelès–Gazost [F] 88 C3
Argelès–Plage [F] 96 F1
Argelès–sur–Mer [F] 96 F1
Argenta [I] 128 D2
Argentan [F] 54 B3
Argentat [F] 78 F3
Argentella [F] 130 A2
Argentera [I] 126 C2
Argentiera [I] 142 B2
Argentière [I] 116 B2
Argenton–Château [F] 66 D3
Argenton–sur–Creuse [F] 68 A4
Argentré [F] 52 F4
Argent–sur–Sauldre [F] 68 C2
Argés [E] 100 D1
Arginónta [GR] 176 A1
Argithéa [GR] 166 D2
Argomariz [E] 86 E3
Árgos [GR] 172 E2
Árgos Orestikó [GR] 160 D3
Argostóli [GR] 166 B4
Arguedas [E] 88 A4
Arguís [E] 88 B4
Arguisuelas [E] 102 B2
Argy [F] 68 A3
Argyrádes [GR] 166 A2
Argyroúpoli [GR] 174 C4
Arhéa Olimbía [GR] 172 C2
Århus [DK] 178 C1
Ariano Irpino [I] 134 D3
Ariano nel Polésine [I] 128 D1
Aritzo [I] 142 C4
Ariza [E] 94 C3
Årjäng [S] 188 C2
Arjeplog [S] 220 C4
Arjona [E] 104 E1
Arjonilla [E] 104 E1
Arkádi [GR] 174 C3

Arkadia [PL] 48 E2
Arkalochóri [GR] 174 D4
Arkása [GR] 176 B3
Arkesíni [GR] 168 E4
Arkítsa [GR] 166 F3
Arklow / An Tinbhear Mór
  [IRL] 10 F3
Arkösund [S] 190 C4
Arkutino [BG] 158 C1
Ärla [S] 190 C2
Arlanc [F] 80 C3
Arlberg Tunnel [A] 72 A4
Arlempdes [F] 80 C4
Arlena di Castro [I] 130 E2
Arles [F] 124 D3
Arles–sur–Tech [F] 96 E1
Arló [H] 76 C3
Arlon (Aarlen) [B] 56 D2
Arlöv [S] 180 C2
Armadale [GB] 14 C3
Armagh [NIR] 12 E3
Armarção de Pera [P] 98 B4
Arméni [GR] 160 F4
Armenioí [GR] 172 C2
Armenistís [GR] 168 E3
Arménoi [GR] 174 C4
Armentières [F] 40 C3
Armilla [E] 104 F3
Armiñon [E] 86 D4
Armólia [GR] 168 E2
Armoy [NIR] 12 F1
Armuña de Tajuña [E] 92 F4
Armutcuk [TR] 164 C2
Armutlu [TR] 158 E4
Armutlu [TR] 164 C1
Armutlu [TR] 170 B2
Armyansk [UA] 246 F3
Árna [GR] 172 D3
Arna [N] 192 B3
Arnac [F] 78 C4
Arnac–Pompadur [F] 78 E3
Arnafjord [N] 192 C2
Arnage [F] 54 B4
Arnager [DK] 180 E3
Arnaía [GR] 162 B2
Árnäs [S] 188 E3
Arnäs [S] 206 D2
Arnavutköy [TR] 158 D3
Arnavutköy [TR] 158 E4
Arnay–le–Duc [F] 68 E3
Arnborg [DK] 178 B1
Arneberg [N] 194 B3
Arneburg [D] 44 E1
Arnedillo [E] 94 C1
Arnedo [E] 94 C1
Arnes [E] 94 F4
Årnes [N] 194 C4
Årnes [N] 212 B4
Årnes [N] 212 C3
Arnhem [NL] 30 C4
Árnissa [GR] 160 E2
Arnoldstein [A] 118 F2
Arnön [S] 196 D1
Arnsberg [D] 42 E3
Arnsburg [D] 58 C1
Arnschwang [D] 60 B4
Ärnset [N] 204 A1
Arnstadt [D] 44 D4
Arnstein [D] 58 D2
Arnuera [E] 86 D2
Aroania [GR] 166 D4
Aroche [E] 98 D3
Árokt [H] 76 D3
Arola [FIN] 228 E3
Arolla [CH] 116 C2
Arolsen [D] 42 F3
Arona [I] 116 D3
Aronkylä [FIN] 208 C3
Åros [N] 188 B1
Arosa [CH] 116 F1
Årosjåkk [S] 220 D1
Årøsund [DK] 178 C2

Arouca [P] 84 B3
Arøysund [N] 186 F2
Arpacık [TR] 170 E4
Arpajon [F] 54 D4
Árpás [H] 74 E4
Arpela [FIN] 222 B4
Arquà Petrarca [I] 118 C4
Arquata del Tronto [I] 132 D2
Arquata Scrivia [I] 126 E2
Arquillinos [E] 106 A1
Arrabal / Oia [E] 82 A3
Arracourt [F] 56 D4
Arraiolos [P] 90 C4
Arrakoski [FIN] 198 F1
Arrankorpi [FIN] 198 F2
Arrankudiaga / Arene [E] 86 D3
Arrans [F] 68 E2
Arras [F] 40 B4
Arrasate o Mondragón [E]
  86 E3
Arrate [E] 86 E3
Årre [DK] 178 B2
Arreau [F] 88 D3
Arrecife [E] 114 E3
Arrens–Marsous [F] 88 C3
Arrentela [P] 90 A4
Arriate [E] 104 C3
Arríaundi [E] 86 E3
Arriba Fóssil [P] 90 A4
Arrifana [P] 98 A3
Arriondas [E] 86 B2
Arroba de los Montes [E]
  100 C2
Arromanches–les–Bains
  [F] 54 A2
Arronches [P] 90 D4
Arròs [E] 88 D4
Arròs [F] 88 D4
Arroyo de la Luz [E] 90 E3
Arroyo de la Miel–
  Benalmádena Costa [E]
  104 D3
Arroyo de San Serván [E]
  98 F2
Arruda dos Vinhos [P] 90 B3
Årsandøy [N] 212 D2
Ars–en–Ré [F] 66 C4
Arsen'yevo [RUS] 242 F1
Arsiè [I] 118 C3
Arsiero [I] 118 B3
Årslev [DK] 178 C2
Årsnes [N] 202 C3
Arsoli [I] 132 D4
Ars–sur–Moselle [F] 56 D3
Årsunda [S] 196 C4
Arsvågen [N] 186 A2
Arsy [F] 54 E2
Artà [E] 108 D3
Árta [GR] 166 C2
Artà, Coves d'– [E] 108 E3
Artajona [E] 86 F4
Artana [E] 102 D3
Ártánd [H] 122 E1
Arta Terme [I] 118 E2
Arteixo [E] 82 B2
Artemare [F] 80 E2
Artemísia [GR] 172 D3
Artemísio [GR] 162 B4
Artemónas [GR] 168 C4
Artena [I] 132 D4
Artenay [F] 68 B1
Artern [D] 44 D3
Artesa de Segre [E] 96 C2
Artesa de Segre / Montargull
  [E] 96 C2
Arth [CH] 70 E4
Arth [D] 72 D2
Arthous, Ancient Prieure d'–
  [F] 88 B2
Arthurstown [IRL] 10 E4
Arties [E] 88 D4
Artix [F] 88 C2

Artjärvi / Artsjö [FIN] 200 B3
Artotína [GR] 166 D3
Artouste–Fabrèges [F] 88 C3
Ärtrik [S] 206 C2
Artsjö / Artjärvi [FIN] 200 B3
Artsyz [UA] 246 C4
A Rúa [E] 82 D4
Arucas [E] 112 E3
Arudy [F] 88 C3
Arundel [GB] 28 C4
Arva [E] 98 F4
Årvåg [N] 202 E2
Arvagh [IRL] 12 D3
Arversund [S] 204 E2
Árvi [GR] 174 D4
Arvidsjaur [S] 214 C1
Arvieux [F] 126 B1
Árvik [N] 202 B3
Arvika [S] 188 D2
Årviksand [N] 224 E1
Arvila [EST] 230 F2
Arville [F] 54 C4
Arykanda [TR] 176 F1
Arzachena [I] 142 C2
Arzacq–Arraziguet [F] 88 C2
Aržano [HR] 144 E4
Arzberg [D] 60 B2
Arze–Arce / Uriz [E] 88 A3
Arzignano [I] 118 B4
Arzl [A] 72 B4
Arzúa [E] 82 C2
As [B] 40 F3
Aš [CZ] 60 B2
Ås [N] 188 B1
Ås [N] 204 C2
Ås [S] 204 E2
Ås [S] 206 C2
Aså [DK] 182 E2
Åsa [N] 192 F4
Åsa [S] 184 A2
Asa [S] 184 D3
Ağaçobanisa [TR] 164 C4
Ağağçgörle [TR] 170 D3
Ağağırınova [TR] 164 C2
Åsan [N] 212 D4
Åsäng [S] 206 C3
Aşanja [SRB] 146 D2
Åsarna [S] 204 E3
Asarum [S] 180 E1
Åsbro [S] 188 F3
Asby [S] 184 D1
Ascain [F] 88 A2
Ascea [I] 136 A3
Ascha [D] 72 D2
Aschach [A] 72 F2
Aschaffenburg [D] 58 C2
Aschau [A] 72 C4
Aschau [D] 72 D3
Aschbach Markt [A] 74 B3
Ascheberg [D] 32 C2
Ascheberg [D] 42 D2
Aschendorf [D] 30 E2
Aschersleben [D] 44 D3
Asciano [I] 130 E1
Ascó [E] 94 F4
Asco [F] 130 B2
Áscoli Piceno [I] 132 E2
Ascoli Satriano [I] 134 E3
Ascona [CH] 116 D2
Ascou Pailhères [F] 88 F4
Ase [N] 224 B3
Åsebyn [S] 188 C2
Åseda [S] 184 D3
Åsele [S] 214 B3
Åseli [N] 218 F3
Asemankylä [FIN] 210 C3
Asemanseutu [FIN] 208 D2
Åsen [N] 204 B1
Åsen [S] 194 E2
Åsen [S] 206 B3
Asendorf [D] 32 A4
Asenovgrad [BG] 156 D2

Asenovo [BG] 148 F3
Åsensbruk [S] 188 C3
Åseral [N] 186 C3
Åserund [N] 188 C1
Asfáka [GR] 160 C4
Asfeld [F] 56 B2
Åsgårdstrand [N] 186 F2
Asha (Pasaköy) [CY] 176 E3
Ashbourne [GB] 24 B3
Ashbourne [IRL] 10 F2
Åsheim [N] 194 C1
Ashford [GB] 28 D4
Ashington [GB] 20 E3
Ashmyany [BY] 238 F3
Ashton–under–Lyne [GB]
  24 B2
Asiago [I] 118 C3
Asikkala [FIN] 198 F2
Asila [FIN] 210 C4
Asíni [GR] 172 E2
Asipovitsy [BY] 242 C2
Ask [N] 192 A3
Ask [N] 192 F4
Ask [S] 180 C1
Aska [FIN] 222 D2
Askainen / Villnäs [FIN]
  198 C3
Askaniia–Nova [RUS] 246 F3
Askanija Nova [UA] 246 F3
Askeaton [IRL] 10 C2
Askeby [DK] 178 E3
Asker [N] 186 F1
Askersund [S] 188 F3
Askeryd [S] 184 D1
Askim [N] 188 B2
Askim [S] 182 F2
Askland [N] 186 D3
Asklepiyon [TR] 164 C3
Asklipíeio [GR] 176 A1
Askola [FIN] 200 A3
Åsköping [S] 190 C3
Askós [GR] 162 B1
Askum [S] 188 B4
Askvoll [N] 192 B1
Askýfou [GR] 174 B4
Aslestad [N] 186 D2
Åsli [N] 192 F3
Åsljunga [S] 180 C1
Åsmansbo [S] 196 B4
Asmunti [FIN] 222 D4
Asnæs [DK] 178 E2
Åsnes [N] 194 D3
As Nogais [E] 82 D3
Åsola [I] 118 A4
Asolo [I] 118 C3
Asopía [GR] 168 A2
Asopós [GR] 172 E3
Asoru, Nuraghe– [I] 142 C5
Åsons [GR] 166 B3
Åsotthalom [H] 122 C3
Aspa [S] 190 D3
Aspang Markt [A] 74 C4
Asparuhovo [BG] 150 D4
Asparukovo [BG] 150 D3
Aspås [S] 204 E2
Aspe [E] 106 E2
Åspeå [S] 206 C2
Aspet [F] 88 D3
Aspnes [N] 212 D4
Aspö [S] 190 C2
As Pontes de
  García Rodríguez / Puentes de
  García Rodríguez [E] 82 C2
Aspres–sur–Buëch [F] 124 F2
Asprópyrgos [GR] 168 A2
Aspróvalta [GR] 162 B1
Aspsele [S] 206 C1
Assamalla [EST] 230 E2
Assel [D] 32 B2
Assé–le–Boisne [F] 54 B3
Assemini [I] 142 B5
Assen [NL] 30 D2

Assens [DK] 178 C2
Assens [DK] 182 D3
Asserbo [DK] 178 E1
Assergi [I] 132 E3
Asseria [HR] 144 C3
Assessos [TR] 170 B3
Ássiros [GR] 160 F2
Assisi [I] 132 D2
Assling [D] 72 D3
Assmannshausen [D] 58 A2
Assoro [I] 140 D2
Assos [TR] 164 A3
Åsta [N] 194 C2
Astaffort [F] 88 E2
Astakós [GR] 166 C3
Åstan [N] 202 F1
Åstan [N] 204 A2
Asten [A] 74 A3
Asten [NL] 40 F3
Asti [I] 126 D1
Astira [TR] 164 B3
Astorga [E] 82 E4
Åstorp [S] 178 F1
Åstrand [S] 194 C4
Astravyets [BY] 238 F3
Ástros [GR] 172 E2
Astrup [DK] 182 D3
Astryna [BY] 38 E2
Astudillo [E] 86 B4
Astura, Torre– [I] 134 C2
Astypálaia [GR] 174 E1
Asvyeya [BY] 236 E4
Ászár [H] 74 F4
Aszód [H] 76 B3
Aszófő [H] 120 F2
Atalaia [P] 90 B4
Atalánti [GR] 166 F3
Atanneus [TR] 164 B3
Atapuerca [E] 86 C4
Atarfe [E] 104 F3
Atašiene [LV] 236 D3
Atburgazi [TR] 170 B3
Atça [TR] 170 C3
Ateca [E] 94 C3
Atella [I] 134 E3
Atessa [I] 132 F4
Ath [B] 40 D4
Athboy [IRL] 10 F1
Athea [IRL] 10 B3
Athenry [IRL] 10 C1
Athéras [GR] 166 B3
Athiénou [CY] 176 E3
Athína [GR] 168 B2
Athleague [IRL] 10 D1
Athlone / Baile Átha Luain
  [IRL] 10 D1
Athy [IRL] 10 E2
Atienza [E] 94 A3
Atina [I] 134 C2
Atkár [H] 76 C3
Åtlo [N] 204 B1
Atnbrua [N] 194 B1
Atnosen [N] 194 B1
Atouguia de Baleia [P] 90 B2
A Toxa [E] 82 B3
Åtran [S] 184 B3
Åträsk [S] 214 D3
Atri [I] 132 E3
Atripalda [I] 134 D3
Atsalarma [EST] 230 F2
Áttali [GR] 168 B1
Attel [D] 72 D3
Attendorn [D] 42 E3
Attersee [A] 72 F3
Attigny [F] 56 B3
Attleborough [GB] 28 E1
Attmar [S] 206 C4
Attnang–Puchheim [A] 72 F3
Attre [B] 40 D4
Attrup [DK] 182 D2
Åtvidaberg [S] 190 B4
Atzara [I] 142 C4

Atzendorf [D] 44 D2
Atzeneta del Maestrat [E] 102 E2
Au [A] 74 B4
Au [D] 72 C2
Aub [D] 58 D3
Aubagne [F] 124 F4
Aubange [B] 56 D3
Aubenas [F] 80 C4
Aubérive [F] 56 B3
Auberive [F] 68 F2
Aubeterre-sur-Dronne [F] 78 C3
Aubiet [F] 88 E2
Aubigny [F] 66 C3
Aubigny-les-Pothées [F] 56 B2
Aubigny-sur-Nère [F] 68 C2
Auboué [F] 56 D3
Aubrac [F] 80 B4
Aubusson [F] 80 A1
Auce [LV] 234 E4
Aucelon [F] 124 F1
Auch [F] 88 D2
Auchinleck [GB] 20 C1
Auchterarder [GB] 18 D3
Auchtermuchty [GB] 18 D3
Audelange [F] 70 A3
Audenarde (Oudenaarde) [B] 40 D3
Audenge [F] 78 B3
Auderville [F] 52 E1
Audeux [F] 70 B3
Audierne [F] 52 A3
Audincourt [F] 70 C3
Audlem [GB] 22 F3
Audnedal [N] 186 C3
Audressein [F] 88 E4
Audru [EST] 230 C3
Audruicq [F] 40 B3
Audun-le-Roman [F] 56 D3
Aue [D] 60 B2
Auen [CH] 72 C4
Auer / Ora [I] 118 C2
Auerbach [D] 58 F3
Auerbach [D] 60 B2
Auerbacher Schloss [D] 58 B3
Auffach [A] 72 D4
Augher [NIR] 12 D2
Aughnacloy [NIR] 12 E2
Aughrim [IRL] 10 F3
Augsburg [D] 72 B2
Augusta [I] 140 E3
Augustenborg [DK] 178 C3
Augustów [PL] 38 C2
Augustusburg [D] 60 C1
Aukra [N] 202 D2
Aukštadvaris [LT] 238 D3
Auktsjaur [S] 214 C1
Auletta [I] 134 E4
Aulla [I] 128 A3
Aullène [F] 130 B3
Aulnay [F] 78 C4
Aulstad [N] 192 F2
Ault [F] 40 A4
Aulus-les-Bains [F] 88 E4
Auly [RUS] 246 E1
Auma [D] 60 A1
Aumale [F] 54 D1
Aumetz [F] 56 D3
Aumont-Aubrac [F] 80 B4
Aunay-sur-Odon [F] 54 A2
Auneau [F] 54 D4
Aunet [N] 204 B1
Aunet [N] 204 C2
Aunet [N] 212 C4
Aunet [N] 212 D3
Auneuil [F] 54 D2
Aunfoss [N] 212 D4
Auning [DK] 182 D4
Aups [F] 126 A3
Aura [FIN] 198 D3

Aurach [A] 72 D4
Aurach [D] 58 D4
Auray [F] 66 A1
Aurdal [N] 192 E3
Aure [N] 202 E2
Aurejärvi [FIN] 208 D4
Aurich [D] 30 E2
Aurignac [F] 88 E3
Aurillac [F] 80 A3
Auriol [F] 124 F3
Auris-en-Oisans [F] 80 F4
Auritz / Burguete [E] 88 B3
Aurlandsvangen [N] 192 C2
Auron [F] 126 B2
Auronzo di Cadore [I] 118 D2
Aursjøhytta [N] 202 E3
Aursmoen [N] 188 C1
Aursnes [N] 202 C3
Áusa Corno [I] 118 E3
Ausejo [E] 94 C1
Ausentum [I] 136 E3
Aussernbrünst [D] 72 F2
Austad [N] 186 C2
Austad [N] 186 C4
Austanå [N] 186 D3
Austborg [N] 212 E4
Austbygda [N] 192 E4
Austefjord [N] 202 C4
Austerlitz (Slavkov u Brna) [CZ] 62 B4
Austmarka [N] 194 C4
Austnes [N] 202 C3
Austpollen [N] 224 B4
Austrått [N] 204 A1
Austrumdal [N] 186 B3
Auterive [F] 88 E3
Authon [F] 126 A2
Authon-du-Perche [F] 54 C4
Autio [S] 222 A2
Autol [E] 94 C1
Autti [FIN] 222 D3
Auttoinen [FIN] 198 F1
Autun [F] 68 E3
Auve [F] 56 B3
Auvers-s-Oise [F] 54 D3
Auvila [FIN] 200 D1
Auxerre [F] 68 D2
Auxi-le-Château [F] 40 B4
Auxonne [F] 68 F3
Auxy [F] 68 E4
Auzances [F] 80 A1
Auzon [F] 80 B3
Avå [FIN] 198 B3
Ava [S] 206 D2
Avafors [S] 220 F4
Availles-Limouzine [F] 78 D1
Aval, Falaise d' [F] 54 B1
Avala [SRB] 146 E2
Avaldsnes [N] 186 A1
Avallon [F] 68 D3
Ávas [GR] 156 F4
Avaträsk [S] 214 A3
Avaviken [S] 214 C1
Avcılar [TR] 158 D3
Avdímou [CY] 176 D4
Ávdira [GR] 156 D4
Ávdira [GR] 156 D4
Åvedal [N] 186 B3
A Veiga [E] 82 D4
Aveiras de Cima [P] 90 B3
Aveiro [P] 84 A3
Avelengo / Hafling [I] 118 B2
Avellino [I] 134 D3
Aven Armand [F] 124 C2
Avenches [CH] 70 C4
Aven de Marzal [F] 124 D2
Aven d'Orgnac [F] 124 D2
Avène [F] 124 B2
Averbode [B] 40 E3
Aversa [I] 134 C3
Avesnes-le-Comte [F] 40 B4

Avesnes-sur-Helpe [F] 56 B1
Avesta [S] 190 C1
Avetrana [I] 136 E3
Avezzano [I] 132 E4
Avgerinós [GR] 160 D3
Avía [GR] 172 D3
Aviano [I] 118 D3
Aviemore [GB] 14 E4
Avigliana [I] 116 B4
Avigliano [I] 134 E4
Avigna [I] 118 C2
Avignon [F] 124 E2
Ávila [E] 92 D3
Avilés [E] 82 F2
Avinurme [EST] 230 E2
Avinyó [E] 96 D2
Avio [I] 118 B3
Avión [E] 82 B3
Avis [P] 90 C3
Avláklá [GR] 170 A3
Avlémonas [GR] 172 E4
Avlí [GR] 156 C4
Avliótes [GR] 160 B4
Avlóna [GR] 168 B2
Avlonári [GR] 168 B1
Avlum [DK] 182 C4
Avola [I] 140 E4
Avonmouth [GB] 26 E2
Avord [F] 68 C3
Avoriaz [F] 116 B2
Avradsberg [S] 194 E4
Avramov [BG] 150 D4
Avranches [F] 52 E3
Avril [F] 56 D3
Avşar [TR] 170 B3
Avtovac [BIH] 152 E2
Axat [F] 88 F4
Axel [NL] 40 D3
Axioúpoli [GR] 156 A4
Ax-les-Thermes [F] 88 F4
Axmarby [S] 196 D3
Axminster [GB] 26 D3
Axós [GR] 174 C3
Axvall [S] 188 D4
Ay [F] 56 B3
Ayagalip [TR] 162 F2
Ayamonte [E] 98 C4
Ayas [I] 116 C3
Aydın [TR] 170 C3
Aydıncık [TR] 162 F2
Ayerbe [E] 88 B4
Aylesbury [GB] 28 C2
Ayllón [E] 92 F2
Aylsham [GB] 28 E1
Ayna [E] 102 A4
Ayoó de Vidriales [E] 84 E2
Ayora [E] 102 C4
Ayr [GB] 20 C1
Ayrancı [TR] 164 F3
Ayrancılar [TR] 170 B2
Ay. Seryios (Yenibogaziçi) [CY] 176 E3
Äyskoski [FIN] 210 B2
Äystö [FIN] 208 C3
Aytos [BG] 150 D4
Ayvacık [TR] 164 A3
Ayvalık [TR] 164 B3
Ayvatlar [TR] 164 B3
Azaila [E] 94 E3
Azambuja [P] 90 B3
Azannes-et-Soumazannes [F] 56 C3
Azanúy [E] 94 F2
Azaruja [P] 90 C4
Azath [TR] 158 A3
Azay-le-Ferron [F] 66 F3
Azay-le-Rideau [F] 66 E3
Azeitão [P] 90 B4
Azervadinha [P] 90 C3
Azinheira dos Barros [P] 98 B2
Aztepe [TR] 170 D2
Aziziye [TR] 158 B2

Aznalcóllar [E] 98 E4
Azpeitia [E] 86 E3
Azuaga [E] 100 A3
Azuara [E] 94 D3
Azuel [E] 100 C4
Azul, Cueva- [E] 108 D4
Azuqueca de Henares [E] 92 F4
Azur [F] 88 B1
Azyory [BY] 38 D2
Azzano Decimo [I] 118 D3
Azzurra, Grotta- [I] 134 C4
Azzurra, Grotta- [I] 136 A3

B

Baad [A] 72 A4
Baal [D] 42 C3
Baamonde [E] 82 C2
Baar [D] 72 C2
Baarle Nassau [NL] 40 E2
Baarn [NL] 30 B3
Babadag [RO] 248 F3
Babadağ [TR] 170 D3
Babaeski [TR] 158 B3
Babaköy [TR] 164 D3
Babek [BG] 156 D1
Babenhausen [D] 58 C2
Babenhausen [D] 72 B2
Babiak [PL] 36 E2
Babiak [PL] 48 C2
Babica [PL] 64 C3
Babice [PL] 62 A3
Băbiciu [RO] 148 F2
Babięta [PL] 38 A2
Babigoszcz [PL] 34 E3
Babimost [PL] 46 E2
Babin Potok [HR] 144 C2
Babjen [AL] 160 B2
BabnoPolje [SLO] 120 A4
Babócsa [H] 120 F3
Bábolna [H] 74 F4
Babríškes [LT] 38 D1
Babruysk [BY] 242 C2
Babta [LT] 238 D3
Babušnica [SRB] 148 C4
Babylon [CZ] 60 B4
Babylón [CZ] 74 C1
Bač [MK] 160 D2
Bač [SLO] 118 F4
Bač [SRB] 122 B4
Bača [SLO] 118 F3
Bacău [RO] 244 E4
Baccarat [F] 70 C1
Baceno [I] 116 D2
Bacharach [D] 58 A2
Bachkovo [BG] 156 D2
Bachkovski Manastir [BG] 156 D2
Bachórz [PL] 64 D3
Băcina [SRB] 146 F4
Backåkra [S] 180 D1
Bačka Palanka [SRB] 146 C1
Bäckaskog [S] 180 D1
Bačka Topola [SRB] 122 C3
Bäckby [FIN] 214 F4
Backe [S] 206 B1
Bäckebo [S] 184 E3
Bäckefors [S] 188 C3
Backen [S] 206 B3
Backen [S] 206 C2
Bäckhammar [S] 188 E2
Bački Breg [SRB] 122 B3
Bački Petrovac [SRB] 122 C4
Bački Sokolac [SRB] 122 C3
Backnang [D] 58 C4
Bačko Gradište [SRB] 122 C4
Bačko Novo Selo [SRB] 146 C1

Bačko Petrovo Selo [SRB] 122 C4
Bąćkowice [PL] 50 A4
Bacoli [I] 134 C3
Bacova mahala [BG] 150 A3
Bacqueville-en-Caux [F] 54 C1
Bácsalmás [H] 122 B3
Bácsbokod [H] 122 B3
Bácsborsód [H] 122 B3
Baczyna [PL] 46 D1
Bad Abbach [D] 72 D1
Badacsonytomaj [H] 120 E2
Bad Aibling [D] 72 D3
Badajoz [E] 90 E4
Badalona [E] 96 D3
Badalucco [I] 126 D3
Bad Aussee [A] 72 F4
Dad Dederkesa [D] 32 A2
Bad Bentheim [D] 30 D3
Bad Bergzabern [D] 58 A4
Bad Berka [D] 44 D4
Bad Berleburg [D] 42 E4
Bad Berneck [D] 58 F2
Bad Bertrich [D] 56 E2
Bad Bevensen [D] 32 C4
Bad Bibra [D] 44 D4
Bad Blankenburg [D] 58 E1
Bad Brambach [D] 60 B2
Bad Bramstedt [D] 32 C2
Bad Breisig [D] 56 F1
Bad Brückenau [D] 58 D2
Badderen [N] 224 F2
Bad Deutsch-Altenburg [A] 74 D3
Bad Doberan [D] 32 E2
Bad Driburg [D] 42 F2
Bad Düben [D] 44 F3
Bad Dürkheim [D] 58 B3
Bad Dürrenberg [D] 44 E4
Bad Dürrheim [D] 70 E2
Bad Elster [D] 60 B2
Bademli [TR] 164 A3
Bademli [TR] 164 B3
Bademli [TR] 170 C2
Bad Ems [D] 58 A2
Baden [A] 74 D3
Baden [CH] 70 E3
Baden (Rheinfelden) [D] 70 D3
Baden-Baden [D] 70 E1
Bad Endorf [D] 72 D3
Badenweiler [D] 70 D2
Baderna [HR] 144 A1
Bädeshte [BG] 156 E1
Bad Essen [D] 30 F4
Bad Frankenhausen [D] 44 D3
Bad Freienwalde [D] 46 C1
Bad Friedrichshall [D] 58 C4
Bad Gandersheim [D] 44 C2
Badgastein [A] 118 E1
Bad Gleichenberg [A] 120 C2
Bad Godesberg [D] 42 D4
Bad Goisern [A] 72 F4
Bad Gottleuba [D] 60 D1
Bad Grund [D] 44 C2
Bad Hall [A] 74 A3
Bad Harzburg [D] 44 C2
Bad Herrenalb [D] 70 E1
Bad Hersfeld [D] 44 B4
Bad Hofgastein [A] 118 E1
Bad Homburg [D] 58 B2
Bad Honnef [D] 42 D4
Bad Hönningen [D] 56 F1
Badia Gran [E] 108 D4
Badia Polésine [I] 128 C3
Badia Tedalda [I] 128 D4
Bad Iburg [D] 30 E4
Bad Ischl [A] 72 F3
Bad Karlshafen [D] 44 B3
Bad Kissingen [D] 58 D2
Bad Kleinen [D] 32 C2
Bad Kleinkirchheim [A] 118 F2

Bad König [D] 58 C3
Bad Königshofen [D] 58 D2
Bad Kösen [D] 44 E4
Bądkowo [PL] 48 C1
Bad Kreuznach [D] 58 A2
Bad Krozingen [D] 70 D2
Bad Laasphe [D] 42 E4
Bad Langensalza [D] 44 C4
Bad Lauchstädt [D] 44 E3
Bad Lausick [D] 44 F4
Bad Lauterberg [D] 44 C3
Bad Leonfelden [A] 74 A2
Bad Liebenstein [D] 44 C4
Bad Liebenwerda [D] 46 B3
Bad Liebenzell [D] 70 F1
Bad Lippspringe [D] 42 F2
Badljevina [HR] 120 E4
Bad Marienberg [D] 42 E4
Bad Meinberg [D] 42 F2
Bad Mergentheim [D] 58 D3
Bad Mitterndorf [A] 72 F4
Bad Münder [D] 44 B2
Bad Münster Ebernburg
   [D] 58 A2
Bad Münstereifel [D] 56 E1
Bad Muskau [D] 46 C3
Bad Nauheim [D] 58 C2
Bad Nenndorf [D] 44 B2
Bad Neuenahr [D] 56 F1
Bad Neustadt [D] 58 D2
Bad Oeynhausen [D] 42 F2
Badolato [I] 138 E3
Badolato Marina [I] 138 E3
Bad Oldesloe [D] 32 C2
Badonviller [F] 70 C1
Bad Orb [D] 58 C2
Badovinci [SRB] 146 C2
Badow [D] 32 D3
Bad Peterstal [D] 70 E2
Bad Pirawarth [A] 74 D2
Bad Pyrmont [D] 44 B2
Bad Radkersburg [A] 120 C2
Bad Ragaz [CH] 116 E1
Bad Reichenhall [D] 72 E3
Bad Rippoldsau [D] 70 E2
Bad Rothenfelde [D] 30 F4
Bad Saarow–Pieskow [D]
   46 C2
Bad Sachsa [D] 44 C3
Bad Säckingen [D] 70 D3
Bad Salzdetfurth [D] 44 C2
Bad Salzuflen [D] 42 F2
Bad Salzungen [D] 44 C4
Bad Schallerbach [A] 72 F2
Bad Schandau [D] 60 D1
Bad Schmiedeberg [D] 44 F3
Bad Schönau [A] 74 D3
Bad Schönborn [D] 58 B4
Bad Schussenried [D] 72 A3
Bad Schwalbach [D] 58 B2
Bad Schwartau [D] 32 D2
Bad Segeberg [D] 32 C2
Bad Sooden–Allendorf [D]
   44 B3
Bad St. Leonhard [A] 120 B1
Bad Sülze [D] 32 F2
Bad Tatzmannsdorf [A] 74 D4
Bad Tennstedt [D] 44 D4
Bad Tölz [D] 72 C3
Badu Andria [I] 142 C2
Badules [E] 94 D3
Bad Vöslau [A] 74 D3
Bad Waldsee [D] 72 A3
Bad Wiessee [D] 72 C3
Bad–Wildungen [D] 42 F4
Bad Wilsnack [D] 32 E4
Bad Wimpfen [D] 58 C4
Bad Windsheim [D] 58 D3
Bad Wörishofen [D] 72 B3
Bad Wurzach [D] 72 A3
Bad Zwischenahn [D] 30 F2
Bække [DK] 178 B2

Bækmarksbro [DK] 182 B3
Baelen [B] 42 B4
Baells [E] 96 B2
Baelo Claudia [E] 104 B4
Baena [E] 104 E2
Bæverfjord [N] 202 E2
Baeza [E] 106 A1
Bagà [E] 96 D2
Bagamér [H] 76 E4
Bağarası [TR] 170 C3
Bägarin [BG] 156 F2
Bågede [S] 212 E4
Bagenalstown / Muine Bheag
   [IRL] 10 E3
Bagenkop [DK] 178 D3
Baggård [S] 206 E1
Bagh a Chaisteil / Castlebay
   [GB] 14 A3
Bagheria [I] 140 C2
Bagn [N] 192 F3
Bagnacavallo [I] 128 D2
Bagnara Calabra [I] 138 D3
Bagnères–de–Bigorre [F]
   88 C3
Bagnères–de–Luchon [F]
   88 D4
Bagni Contursi [I] 134 E4
Bagni del Másino [I] 116 E2
Bagni di Bormio [I] 118 A2
Bagni di Craveggia [I] 116 D2
Bagni di Lucca [I] 128 B3
Bagni di Rabbi [I] 118 B2
Bagni di Salomone [I] 118 D2
Bagni di Vinadio [I] 126 C2
Bagno a Ripoli [I] 128 C3
Bagno di Romagna [I] 128 D3
Bagnoles–de–l'Orne [F] 54 A3
Bagnoli di Sopra [I] 128 D1
Bagnolo Mella [I] 116 F4
Bagnolo Piemonte [I] 126 C1
Bagnolo San Vito [I] 128 C1
Bagnols–en–Forêt [F] 126 B3
Bagnols–les–Bains [F] 80 B4
Bagnols–sur–Cèze [F] 124 E2
Bagnone [I] 128 A2
Bagnoregio [I] 130 F2
Bagno Vignoni [I] 130 E1
Bagny [PL] 38 C2
Bågø [DK] 178 C2
Bagod [H] 120 D2
Bagolino [I] 118 A3
Bagrationovsk [RUS] 36 F2
Bagsund [N] 212 C3
Báguena [E] 94 C3
Bağyaka [TR] 170 D4
Bağyurdu [TR] 170 B2
Bağyüzü [TR] 170 B3
Bahabón de Esgueva [E] 92 F1
Baharlar [TR] 164 B2
Bahçecik [TR] 158 F3
Bahçeköy [TR] 158 B4
Bahçeköy [TR] 158 C2
Bahíllo [E] 86 B3
Baia delle Zagare [I] 134 F2
Báia Domízia [I] 134 C3
Baia Mare [RO] 244 C3
Baiano [I] 134 D3
Baião [P] 84 B3
Báia Sardínia [I] 142 C2
Baiersbronn [D] 70 E2
Baigneux–les–Juifs [F] 68 E2
Baile an Sceilg / Ballinskelligs
   [IRL] 10 A3
Baile Átha Cliath / Dublin
   [IRL] 10 F2
Baile Átha Luain / Athlone
   [IRL] 10 D1
Bäile Felix [RO] 122 F1
Bäile Herculane [RO] 148 C1
Bailén [E] 104 F1
Bäilești [RO] 148 D2
Bäile Tușnad [RO] 244 E4

Bailieborough [IRL] 10 F1
Bailleul [F] 40 C3
Bailleul [F] 54 C1
Bain–de–Bretagne [F] 66 C1
Bains–les–Bains [F] 70 B2
Baio [E] 82 B2
Baiona [E] 82 A3
Bais [F] 54 A3
Baisogala [LT] 238 C2
Baix [F] 80 D4
Baixas [F] 96 E1
Baja [H] 122 B3
Bajánsenye [H] 120 D2
Bajč [SK] 74 F3
Bajina Bašta [SRB] 146 C3
Bajmok [SRB] 122 C3
Bajna [H] 76 A3
Bajram Curri [AL] 154 B3
Bajša [SRB] 122 C3
Bajzë [AL] 152 F3
Bak [H] 120 D2
Bakacak [TR] 164 B1
Bakar [HR] 144 B1
Bakewell [GB] 24 C3
Bakhchysarai [UA] 246 F4
Bakhmach [UA] 242 E3
Bakio [E] 86 E2
Bakirköy [TR] 158 E3
Bakka [N] 186 E1
Bakke [N] 186 D3
Bakke [N] 188 C3
Bakkejord [N] 224 D2
Bakken [N] 204 B2
Bakko [N] 192 E4
Baklan [TR] 170 E2
Bakonszeg [H] 76 E4
Bakonybél [H] 120 F1
Bakonycsernye [H] 74 F4
Bakonygyepes [H] 120 E1
Bakonyjákó [H] 120 E1
Bakonypeterd [H] 74 F4
Bakonysárkány [H] 74 F4
Bakonyszombatheley [H] 74 F4
Bakovac [HR] 144 C2
Baks [H] 122 C2
Baksa [H] 120 F3
Baksjöliden [S] 214 C3
Baktakékk [H] 76 D2
Baktalórántháza [H] 76 E3
Baktsjaur [S] 214 C2
Bakum [D] 30 F3
Bakvattnet [S] 204 E1
Bäl [S] 234 A2
Bala [GB] 22 D3
Balaban [TR] 158 C2
Balabancik [TR] 158 B4
Balaci [RO] 148 F1
Balaguer [E] 96 B2
Balanegra [E] 106 B4
Bälänești [RO] 148 F2
Balassagyarmat [H] 76 B3
Balástya [H] 122 C2
Balat [TR] 170 B3
Balatonakali [H] 120 F2
Balatonalmádi [H] 120 F1
Balatonbereny [H] 120 E2
Balatonboglár [H] 120 E2
Balatonederics [H] 120 E2
Balatonföldvár [H] 120 F2
Balatonfüred [H] 120 F1
Balatonfüzfö [H] 120 F1
Balatongyörök [H] 120 E2
Balatonkenese [H] 120 F1
Balatonkeresztúr [H] 120 E2
Balatonlelle [H] 120 F2
Balatonszemes [H] 120 F2
Balazote [E] 102 A4
Balbigny [F] 80 C2
Balboa [E] 82 D3
Balbriggan [IRL] 12 E4
Bälby [S] 188 F3
Bälceşti [RO] 148 E1

Balchik [BG] 150 E3
Balcılar [TR] 164 B2
Balcon de Europa [E] 104 E3
Baldenstein [CH] 116 E1
Balderschwang [D] 72 A3
Baldock [GB] 28 D2
Baldone [LV] 236 B3
Bale [HR] 144 A1
Baleines, Phare des– [F] 66 B4
Baleira [E] 82 D2
Baleizão [P] 98 C2
Balestrand [N] 192 C2
Balestrate [I] 140 B2
Balewo [PL] 36 D2
Bälgviken [S] 190 C2
Balice [PL] 62 F3
Balıkesir [TR] 164 D2
Balıklıova [TR] 168 F1
Balıköy [TR] 164 E2
Bälinge [S] 180 C1
Bälinge [S] 184 B1
Bälinge [S] 190 D1
Balingen [D] 70 F2
Balinț [RO] 122 F3
Balio Chitarra [I] 140 B2
Baljvine [BIH] 144 F2
Balkanec [BG] 148 F4
Balkanski [BG] 150 C3
Balkány [H] 76 E3
Balkıca [TR] 170 E3
Balla [IRL] 12 B3
Ballaban [AL] 160 B3
Ballachulish [GB] 18 C2
Ballaghaderreen [IRL] 12 C3
Ballangen [N] 224 C4
Ballantrae [GB] 20 B2
Ballao [I] 142 C5
Ballater [GB] 14 E4
Ballebro [DK] 178 C3
Bällefors [S] 188 E3
Ballen [DK] 178 D2
Ballenstedt [D] 44 D3
Balleroy [F] 52 F2
Ballerup [DK] 178 F2
Balli [TR] 158 B4
Ballina [IRL] 10 D2
Ballina [IRL] 12 B2
Ballinafad [IRL] 12 C3
Ballinagh [IRL] 12 D3
Ballinahinch [NIR] 12 F3
Ballinakill [IRL] 10 E3
Ballinamore [IRL] 12 D3
Ballinascarty [IRL] 10 B4
Ballinasloe [IRL] 10 D2
Ballindine [IRL] 12 B3
Ballindooly Castle [IRL] 10 C1
Ballingarry [IRL] 10 C3
Ballingarry [IRL] 10 D3
Ballinhassig [IRL] 10 C4
Ballinrobe [IRL] 12 B3
Ballinskelligs / Baile an Sceilg
   [IRL] 10 A3
Ballinspittle [IRL] 10 C4
Ballintober, Abbey– [IRL]
   12 B3
Ballintra [IRL] 12 D2
Ballio Zaffarana [I] 140 B2
Ballivor [IRL] 10 E2
Ballobar [E] 94 F3
Ballon [F] 54 B4
Ballon [IRL] 10 E3
Ballsh [AL] 160 B2
Ballshi [AL] 160 B2
Ballstad [N] 218 F1
Ballum [DK] 178 B3
Ballybay [IRL] 12 D1
Ballybofey [IRL] 12 D2
Ballybunion [IRL] 10 B2
Ballycanew [IRL] 10 F3
Ballycastle [IRL] 12 B2
Ballycastle [NIR] 12 F1
Ballyclare [NIR] 12 F2

Ballyconneely [IRL] 12 A3
Ballycotton [IRL] 10 C4
Ballycumber [IRL] 10 E2
Ballydehob [IRL] 10 B4
Ballydesmond [IRL] 10 B3
Ballyduff [IRL] 10 B2
Ballyduff [IRL] 10 D3
Ballyemund [IRL] 10 F3
Ballyfarnan [IRL] 12 C2
Ballygawley [NIR] 12 E2
Ballyglass [IRL] 12 B3
Ballygowan [NIR] 12 F3
Ballyhaunis [IRL] 12 B3
Ballyheige [IRL] 10 B2
Ballyjamesduff [IRL] 10 E1
Ballykeeran [IRL] 10 D1
Ballylanders [IRL] 10 C3
Ballylongford [IRL] 10 B2
Ballylynan [IRL] 10 E2
Ballymacoda [IRL] 10 C4
Ballymahon [IRL] 10 E1
Ballymena [NIR] 12 F2
Ballymoe [IRL] 10 D1
Ballymoney [NIR] 12 E1
Ballymore [IRL] 10 E1
Ballymore Eustace [IRL] 10 F2
Ballymote [IRL] 12 C2
Ballyragget [IRL] 10 E3
Ballyronan [IRL] 12 E2
Ballyroon [IRL] 10 A4
Ballysadare [IRL] 12 C2
Ballyshannon [IRL] 12 C2
Ballyvaughan [IRL] 10 C2
Ballywalter [NIR] 20 A3
Balmaseda [E] 86 D3
Balmazújváros [H] 76 E3
Balme [I] 116 B3
Balmúccia [I] 116 C3
Balogunyom [H] 120 D1
Balota [RO] 148 C1
Balsareny [E] 96 D2
Balsfjord [N] 224 D3
Balsicas [E] 106 E3
Balsjö [S] 206 E1
Balsorano [I] 132 E4
Bålsta [S] 190 D2
Balsthal [CH] 70 D3
Balta [RO] 148 C1
Baltaköy [TR] 170 C3
Baltanás [E] 92 E1
Baltar [E] 82 C4
Bältaţii de Sus [RO] 148 D3
Bălţi [MD] 244 E3
Baltimore [IRL] 10 B4
Baltinava [LV] 236 E3
Baltinglass [IRL] 10 E3
Baltiysk [RUS] 36 E1
Baltoji Vokė [LT] 238 E3
Balvano [I] 134 E3
Bålvatn [D] 30 E1
Balugães [P] 82 A4
Balvan [BG] 150 B4
Balvany [SK] 74 F3
Balvi [LV] 236 D2
Balya [TR] 164 C2
Balzers [FL] 70 F4
Bamberg [D] 58 E3
Bamble [N] 186 E2
Bana [H] 74 F4
Banafjäll [S] 206 E2
Banagher [IRL] 10 D2
Banarli [TR] 158 B3
Banatski Karlovac [SRB]
   146 E1
Banatsko Aranđelovo [SRB]
   122 D3
Banatsko Karadjordjevo [SRB]
   122 D4
Banatsko Novo Selo [SRB]
   146 E1
Banbridge [NIR] 12 E3
Banbury [GB] 28 B2

Banchory [GB] 18 E2
Bandaksli [N] 186 D2
Bande [E] 82 B4
Bandholm [DK] 178 D3
Bandırma [TR] 164 C1
Bandol [F] 124 F4
Bandon [IRL] 10 C4
Bāneasa [RO] 150 C2
Bāneasa [RO] 150 E2
Banff [GB] 14 F3
Bångnäs [S] 212 F3
Bangor [F] 66 A2
Bangor [GB] 22 D2
Bangor [NIR] 12 F2
Bangor Erris [IRL] 12 B2
Bangsbo [DK] 182 E2
Bánhalma [H] 76 D4
Banica [BG] 148 E3
Banie [PL] 34 D4
Banie Mazurskię [PL] 38 R1
Baniska [BG] 150 B3
Banja [SRB] 146 C4
Banja [SRB] 154 B1
Banja Koviljača [SRB] 146 C2
Banjaloka [SLO] 120 B4
Banja Luka [BIH] 144 F2
Banjani [SRB] 146 D2
Banjska [KS] 148 A4
Bánk [H] 76 E4
Banka [SK] 74 F2
Bankeryd [S] 184 C1
Bankháza [H] 122 B1
Bankya [BG] 154 F2
Bannalec [F] 52 B4
Banne [F] 124 D2
Bannesdorf [D] 32 D1
Bañolas / Banyoles [E] 96 E2
Banon [F] 124 F2
Baños de Alicún de las Torres
[E] 106 B2
Baños de Cerrato [E] 92 E1
Baños de la Encina [E] 104 F1
Baños de Montemayor [E]
92 B3
Baños de Panticosa [E] 88 C3
Baños de Rio Tobia [E] 86 D4
Bánov [CZ] 74 E1
Bánovce nad Bebravou [SK]
74 F2
Banovići [BIH] 146 B3
Bánréve [H] 76 C2
Bansin [D] 34 D2
Banská Bystrica [SK] 76 B2
Banská Štiavnica [SK] 76 A2
Banské [SK] 76 E1
Bansko [BG] 156 B3
Bansko [MK] 154 F4
Banteer [IRL] 10 C3
Bantheville [F] 56 C3
Ban. Topola [SRB] 122 D4
Bantry [IRL] 10 B4
Bantry House [IRL] 10 B4
Banya [BG] 150 E4
Banya [BG] 156 B2
Banya [BG] 156 D1
Banya [BG] 156 E1
Banyalbufar [E] 108 C3
Banyeres de Mariola [E]
106 F1
Banyoles / Bañolas [E] 96 E2
Banyuls-sur-Mer [F] 96 F2
Banz [D] 58 E2
Bapaume [F] 54 F1
Bar [MNE] 152 E4
Bara [RO] 122 F3
Baradla [H] 76 C2
Barajas [E] 92 E4
Barajas de Melo [E] 100 F1
Barakaldo [E] 86 D3
Baralla [E] 82 D3
Baranavichy [BY] 242 B3
Báránd [H] 76 D4

Baranovo [RUS] 232 F3
Baranowo [PL] 38 A3
Baranów Sandomierski [PL]
64 C2
Baraona [E] 94 B3
Baraqueville [F] 124 B1
Bårared [S] 184 B3
Barásoain [E] 86 F4
Barbadillo de Herreros [E]
94 B1
Barban [HR] 144 A1
Barbarano Vicentino [I] 118 C4
Barbaros [TR] 158 C4
Barba–Rossahöhle [D] 44 D3
Barbaste [F] 88 D1
Barbastro [E] 94 F2
Barbat [HR] 144 B2
Barbate [E] 104 B3
Bärbele [LV] 236 B4
Barberino Val d'Elsa [I] 128 C4
Barbezieux–St–Hilaire [F]
78 C2
Barbing [D] 72 D1
Barbizon [F] 54 E4
Barbotan–les–Thermes [F]
88 D2
Barby [D] 44 E2
Bårbyborg [S] 184 E4
Bârca [RO] 148 D2
Bárcabo [E] 94 F2
Barca de Alva [P] 84 C3
Barcarrota [E] 98 B2
Barcellona–Pozzo di Gotto
[I] 138 C3
Barcelona [E] 96 D3
Barcelonnette [F] 126 B2
Barcelos [P] 84 A2
Bárcena de Pie de Concha
[E] 86 C2
Barchfeld [D] 44 C4
Barchon [B] 40 F4
Barciany [PL] 38 A1
Barcin [PL] 36 C4
Barcino [PL] 36 B2
Bárcis [I] 118 D3
Barcoñes [E] 94 B3
Barcs [H] 120 E3
Barczewo [PL] 36 F2
Bardakçi [TR] 164 E3
Bardejov [SK] 64 C4
Bardejovské Kúpele [SK]
64 C4
Bardi [I] 128 A2
Bardo [PL] 62 B2
Bardolino [I] 118 B4
Bardonécchia [I] 116 A4
Bardovo [RUS] 236 F3
Bardowick [D] 32 C3
Bardufoss [N] 224 D3
Bärenalm [A] 74 A3
Barenburg [D] 32 A4
Barendrecht [NL] 30 A4
Barentin [F] 54 C2
Barenton [F] 52 F3
Bärfendal [S] 188 B3
Barfleur [F] 52 F1
Barga [I] 128 B3
Bargas [E] 100 E1
Barge [I] 126 C1
Bargteheide [D] 32 C2
Bari [I] 136 D1
Barič [SRB] 146 D2
Båring [DK] 178 C2
Bari Sardo [I] 142 C4
Barisciano [I] 132 E3
Bariyevo [BG] 150 A4
Barjac [F] 124 D2
Barjas [E] 82 D3
Barjols [F] 126 A3
Barkåker [N] 186 F2
Barkald [N] 204 B4
Barkarö [S] 190 C2

Barkava [LV] 236 D3
Barkowo [PL] 36 B3
Bârlad [RO] 244 E4
Bar–le–Duc [F] 56 C4
Barles [F] 126 B2
Barletta [I] 134 F3
Barlinek [PL] 34 E4
Barlingbo [S] 234 A2
Barmash [AL] 160 C3
Barmouth [GB] 22 D3
Barmstedt [D] 32 C2
Barnard Castle [GB] 20 E4
Bärnau [D] 60 B3
Barneberg [D] 44 D2
Barneveld [NL] 30 C4
Barneville–Carteret [F] 52 E2
Barnewitz [D] 44 F1
Barnówko [PL] 46 C1
Barnsley [GB] 24 C2
Barnstaple [GB] 26 C2
Barnstorf [D] 30 F3
Barntrup [D] 42 F2
Baroña, Castro de– [E] 82 A2
Barovo [MK] 160 E1
Barquilla de Pinares [E] 92 C4
Barr [F] 70 D2
Barracas [E] 102 D2
Barraco [E] 92 D3
Barrafranca [I] 140 D3
Barranco do Velho [P] 98 C4
Barrancos [P] 98 A3
Barrax [E] 102 A3
Barre–des–Cévennes [F]
124 C2
Barreiro [P] 90 B4
Barreiros / San Cosme [E]
82 D2
Barrême [F] 126 B2
Barrosa [E] 104 B3
Barrow–in–Furness [GB]
20 C4
Barruecopardo [E] 84 D3
Barruera [E] 88 D4
Barry [F] 124 E2
Barry [GB] 26 D2
Barryporeen [IRL] 10 D3
Barsanovo [RUS] 236 E3
Barsele [S] 214 B2
Barsinghausen [D] 44 B2
Barssel [D] 30 E2
Barstyciai [LT] 234 D4
Bar–sur–Aube [F] 68 C1
Bar–sur–Seine [F] 68 E2
Barsviken [S] 206 D3
Barth [D] 32 F2
Barton–upon–Humber [GB]
24 D2
Bartoszyce [PL] 36 F2
Barúmini [I] 142 B4
Barussa, Nuraghe– [I] 142 B6
Baruth [D] 46 B2
Barvaux–sur–Ourthe [B] 56 D1
Barver [D] 30 F3
Bårvik [N] 228 A2
Barwice [PL] 34 F3
Barysaw [BY] 242 C1
Baryshevo [RUS] 200 D2
Barza [RO] 148 F2
Bârzava [RO] 122 F3
Bârzina [BG] 148 E3
Barzio [I] 116 E3
Bas [E] 96 E2
Bås [N] 186 D3
Bašaid [SRB] 122 D4
Başalan [TR] 170 D3
Basarabi [RO] 150 F1
Basauri [E] 86 D3
Basconcillos del Tozo [E]
86 C3
Basdahl [D] 32 B3
Basel [CH] 70 D3
Baselga di Pinè [I] 118 B3

Båsheim [N] 192 E4
Bashtanka [UA] 246 E1
Basi [LV] 234 D3
Basildon [GB] 28 D3
Basilice [I] 134 D2
Bäsinge [S] 190 C1
Basingstoke [GB] 28 B3
Baška [HR] 144 B2
Baška Voda [HR] 152 B1
Baške Ostarije [HR] 144 C2
Bäsksjö [S] 214 B3
Başlamış [TR] 164 D3
Başmakçı [TR] 170 F2
Bäsna [S] 194 F4
Bassacutena [I] 142 C2
Bassano del Grappa [I] 118 C3
Bassenheim [D] 56 F2
Bassevuovdde [N] 226 C2
Bassoues [F] 88 D2
Bassum [D] 32 A4
Båstad [N] 188 B1
Båstad [S] 184 B4
Bastelica [I] 130 B3
Bastenaken (Bastogne) [B]
56 D2
Baştepe [TR] 170 F1
Bastfallet [S] 196 C4
Bastia [I] 130 B2
Bastia [I] 132 C2
Bastnäs [S] 188 D1
Bastogne (Bastenaken) [B]
56 D2
Bastuny [BY] 38 E1
Bastuträsk [S] 214 C4
Bastuträsk [S] 214 D2
Bata [RO] 122 F3
Batajnica [SRB] 146 D2
Batak [BG] 156 C2
Batakiai [LT] 238 B2
Batalha [P] 90 C2
Batanovtsi [BG] 154 F2
Batär [RO] 122 D1
Bátaszék [H] 122 B3
Baté [H] 120 F2
Batca [E] 94 F4
Batelov [CZ] 60 E4
Batetskiy [RUS] 240 B2
Bath [GB] 26 E2
Batin [BG] 150 B2
Batina [HR] 122 B3
Batlava [KS] 154 C2
Bátmonostor [H] 122 B3
Bátmuseum [N] 202 C3
Batočina [SRB] 146 E3
Bátonyterenye [H] 76 C3
Batorz [PL] 50 C4
Bátovce [SK] 76 A2
Batrina [HR] 144 F1
Båtsfjord [N] 228 E2
Båtsjaur [S] 220 C4
Bátya [H] 122 B2
Batyk [H] 120 E1
Batz–sur–Mer [F] 66 B2
Baud [F] 52 C4
Baugé [F] 66 E2
Baugy [F] 68 C3
Baume, Cirque de– [F] 70 A4
Baume, Grotte de la– [F] 70 B3
Baume–les–Dames [F] 70 B3
Baume–les Messieurs, Abbaye
de– [F] 70 A4
Baumholder [D] 56 F3

Baunei [I] 142 C4
Bauska [LV] 234 F4
Bautzen [D] 46 C4
Bavanište [SRB] 146 E2
Bavay [F] 40 D4
Baveno [I] 116 D3
Bavorov [CZ] 60 D4
Bawtry [GB] 24 C3
Bayard [F] 80 B3
Baydakovo [RUS] 236 E4
Bayerisch Eisenstein [D] 60 C4
Bayeux [F] 54 A2
Bayındır [TR] 158 F4
Bayındır [TR] 170 C2
Bayır [TR] 170 D4
Bayırköy [TR] 158 F4
Bayırköy [TR] 164 B1
Baykal [BG] 148 F3
Bayon [F] 70 C1
Bayonne [F] 88 B2
Bayrakçi Mağarasi [TR] 170 B3
Bayramdere [TR] 164 D1
Bayramiç [TR] 164 B2
Bayreuth [D] 58 F3
Bayrischzell [D] 72 D3
Baza [E] 106 B2
Bazas [F] 78 C4
Bazenheid [CH] 70 F3
Baziaş [RO] 146 F2
Bazoches–sur–Hoëne [F]
54 B3
Bazolles [F] 68 D3
Baztan / Elizondo [E] 86 E3
Bazzano [I] 128 C2
Beaconsfield [GB] 28 C2
Béal an Mhuirthead / Belmullet
[IRL] 12 A2
Beariz [E] 82 B3
Beas [E] 98 D4
Beasain [E] 86 E3
Beas de Segura [E] 106 B1
Beateberg [S] 188 E3
Beaucaire [F] 124 D3
Beaufort [IRL] 10 B3
Beaufort–en–Vallée [F] 66 E2
Beaufort–sur–Doron [F]
116 A3
Beaugency [F] 68 B2
Beaujeu [F] 80 D2
Beaulieu–sur–Dordogne
[F] 78 E4
Beaulieu–sur–Mer [F] 126 C3
Beaumaris [GB] 22 D2
Beaumes de Venise [F] 124 E2
Beaumesnil [F] 54 C2
Beaumetz [F] 40 B4
Beaumont [B] 56 B1
Beaumont [F] 52 E1
Beaumont [F] 78 D4
Beaumont–de–Lomagne
[F] 88 E2
Beaumont–le–Roger [F] 54 C2
Beaumont–sur–Sarthe [F]
54 B4
Beaune [F] 68 E3
Beaune–la–Rolande [F] 68 C1
Beaupréau [F] 66 D2
Beauraing [B] 56 C2
Beauregard, Manoir de– [F]
68 A2
Beaurepaire [F] 80 D3
Beaurepaire–en–Bresse
[F] 68 F4
Beausite [F] 56 C3
Beauvais [F] 54 D2
Beauvallon [F] 126 B4
Beauvène [F] 80 D4
Beauvezer [F] 126 B2
Beauville [F] 88 E1
Beauvoir–sur–Mer [F] 66 B3
Beauvoir–sur–Niort [F] 66 D4
Beba Veche [RO] 122 D3

Bebenhausen [D] **70** F2
Bebra [D] **44** B4
Bebrene [LV] **236** D4
Beccles [GB] **28** F2
Becedas [E] **92** C3
Bečej [SRB] **122** C4
Becerreá [E] **82** D3
Bécherel [F] **52** D3
Bechet [RO] **148** E3
Bechhofen [D] **58** D4
Bechyně [CZ] **60** D4
Becicherecu Mic [RO] **122** E3
Becilla de Valderaduey [E] **86** A4
Beçin Kalesi [TR] **170** C4
Beciu [RO] **148** F2
Beckenried [CH] **70** E4
Beckum [D] **42** E3
Beckum [D] **42** E2
Beclean [RO] **244** D3
Bécon–les–Granits [F] **66** D2
Bečov nad Teplou [CZ] **60** B2
Becsehely [H] **120** D2
Becske [H] **76** B3
Bédarieux [F] **124** B3
Bedburg [D] **42** C3
Beddingestrand [S] **180** C2
Bédée [F] **52** D4
Bedemler [TR] **168** F1
Beden [BG] **156** D3
Bedenac [F] **78** C3
Bedenica [NR] **120** D3
Bedford [GB] **28** C2
Będgoszcz [PL] **34** D4
Będków [PL] **48** D3
Bedlington [GB] **20** E3
Bednarka [PL] **64** C3
Bédole [I] **118** B2
Bedonia [I] **126** F2
Bedous [F] **88** B3
Bedsted [DK] **182** C3
Bedworth [GB] **24** B4
Będzin [PL] **62** E2
Będzino [PL] **34** F2
Beek [NL] **40** F3
Beekbergen [NL] **30** C4
Beek en Donk [NL] **40** F2
Beelitz [D] **44** F2
Beenz [D] **34** C3
Beerfelden [D] **58** C3
Beersel [B] **40** D3
Beeskow [D] **46** C2
Beesten [D] **30** E3
Befreiungshalle [D] **72** D1
Bégard [F] **52** C3
Beglezh [BG] **148** F3
Beg–Meil [F] **52** B4
Begndal [N] **192** F3
Begoncourt [F] **70** B2
Begonte [E] **82** C2
Begov Han [BIH] **146** A3
Begunitsy [RUS] **200** E4
Begur [E] **96** F2
Behramkale [TR] **164** A3
Behramlı [TR] **164** A2
Behringersmühle [D] **58** E3
Beilen [NL] **30** D2
Beilngries [D] **58** F4
Beinwil [CH] **70** D3
Beith [GB] **18** C4
Beitostølen [N] **192** E2
Beitstad [N] **212** C4
Beiuş [RO] **122** F2
Beja [P] **98** C2
Béjar [E] **92** B3
Bejís [E] **102** D2
Bekas [LV] **236** C3
Bekçiler [TR] **170** E4
Békés [H] **122** E2
Békéscsaba [H] **122** E2

Békésszentandrás [H] **122** D2
Bekilli [TR] **170** E2
Bekken [N] **194** C2
Bélâbre [F] **66** F4
Bela Crkva [SRB] **146** F2
Bel–Air [F] **52** D4
Bel–Air [F] **78** E1
Bel–Aire [F] **52** E4
Belalcázar [E] **100** B3
Bělá nad Radbuzou [CZ] **60** B3
Bela Palanka [SRB] **148** C4
Bélapátfalva [H] **76** C3
Bělá pod Bezdězem [CZ] **60** E2
Bělá pod Pradědem [CZ] **62** C3
Belava [LV] **236** D3
Belbaşı [TR] **176** F1
Belcaire [F] **88** F4
Bełchatów [PL] **48** D4
Belchin [BG] **156** B2
Belchite [E] **94** D3
Belčišta [MK] **160** C1
Belcoo [NIR] **12** D2
Beldibi [TR] **176** F1
Belecke [D] **42** E3
Beled [H] **74** E4
Belej [HR] **144** B2
Belence [TR] **170** F1
Belene [BG] **150** A3
Bélesta [F] **88** F4
Belev [RUS] **242** F1
Belevi [TR] **170** B2
Belevren [BG] **158** B2
Belfast [NIR] **12** E2
Belfir [RO] **122** F2
Belfort [F] **70** C3
Belgern [D] **44** F3
Belgirate [I] **116** D3
Belgodère [F] **130** B2
Belgooly [IRL] **10** C4
Beli [HR] **144** B1
Belianes [E] **96** C3
Belianska Jaskyňa [SK] **64** A4
Belica [BG] **150** C2
Belica [HR] **120** D2
Belica [MK] **154** C4
Belica [MK] **154** D4
Beli Iskâr [BG] **156** B2
Belikij Novgorod [RUS] **240** C2
Belımanastır [HR] **122** B3
Beli Manastir [HR] **122** B3
Belimel [BG] **148** D3
Belin–Béliet [F] **78** B4
Belinchón [E] **100** F1
Beliny [RO] **122** F3
Belišče [HR] **122** A4
Belitsa [BG] **156** B2
Beliu [RO] **122** F2
Beljakovci [MK] **154** D3
Beljina [SRB] **146** D2
Bella [I] **134** E3
Bellac [F] **78** E2
Bellaghy [NIR] **12** E2
Bellágio [I] **116** E3
Bellaguarda [E] **96** B3
Bellamont [D] **72** A3
Bellamonte [I] **118** C2
Bellano [I] **116** E3
Bellante [I] **132** E2
Bellapaïs (Beylerbeyi) [CY] **176** D3
Bellária [I] **128** E3
Bellcaire d'Urgell [E] **96** B2
Belleek [NIR] **12** D2
Bellegarde [F] **68** C1
Bellegarde [F] **124** D3
Bellegarde–en–Marche [F] **80** A1
Bellegarde–sur–Valserine [F] **80** F2
Belle–Isle–en–Terre [F] **52** C3

Bellême [F] **54** B3
Bellenaves [F] **80** B1
Bellencombre [F] **54** D1
Bellengreville [F] **54** D1
Bellevesvre [F] **68** F4
Belleville [F] **80** D2
Belleville–sur–Vie [F] **66** C3
Belley [F] **80** E2
Bellinge [DK] **178** C2
Bellínzona [CH] **116** E2
Bell–lloc d'Urgell [E] **96** B2
Bello [E] **94** C4
Bellò [S] **184** D2
Bellpuig [E] **96** C2
Belluno [I] **118** D3
Bellver, Castell de– [E] **108** C3
Bellver de Cerdanya [E] **96** D1
Bellvik [S] **214** A3
Belmez [E] **100** B4
Belmez de la Moraleda [E] **106** A2
Belmonte [E] **82** E2
Belmonte [E] **100** F2
Belmonte [P] **84** C4
Belmont–sur–Rance [F] **124** B2
Belmullet / Béal an Mhuirthead [IRL] **12** A2
Belœil [B] **40** D4
Belogradchik [BG] **148** C3
Belokamensk [UA] **246** F4
Beloljin [SRB] **148** B4
Belopolci [MK] **156** C3
Belo Pole [BG] **148** D3
Belo Polje [KS] **154** B2
Belopol'ye [UA] **242** F3
Belorado [E] **86** D4
Bělotín [CZ] **62** C3
Belovec [BG] **150** C2
Belovo [BG] **156** C2
Belozem [BG] **156** D2
Belpasso [I] **140** E2
Belsen [D] **32** B4
Belsk Duży [PL] **48** F3
Beltinci [SLO] **120** D2
Belturbet [IRL] **12** D3
Beluša [SK] **74** F1
Belušić [SRB] **146** F4
Belvedere Campomoro [F] **130** A3
Belvedere du Cirque [F] **126** C1
Belvedere Marittimo [I] **136** B4
Belvedere Ostrense [I] **128** E4
Belver [P] **90** D3
Belvès [F] **78** D4
Belvis de la Jara [E] **100** C1
Belyy [RUS] **240** D3
Belz [F] **52** C4
Belz [UA] **64** F2
Bełżec [PL] **64** C2
Belzig [D] **44** F2
Bełżyce [PL] **50** B3
Bembibre [E] **82** E3
Bembirre [E] **82** B2
Bemposta [P] **84** D3
Bemposta [P] **90** C3
Benabarre [E] **96** B1
Benalmádena [E] **104** B3
Benalup [E] **104** B3
Benamaurel [E] **106** B2
Benaojón [E] **104** C3
Benasque [E] **88** D4
Benassal [E] **102** E2
Benassay [E] **66** E4
Benátky nad Jezerou [CZ] **60** E2
Bencık [TR] **170** C4

Bene [LV] **234** E4
Benediktbeuern [D] **72** C3
Benediktiner–Abtei [D] **72** D3
Benedikt v Slovenskih goricah [SLO] **120** C2
Beneixama / Benejama [E] **106** E1
Benejama / Beneixama [E] **106** E1
Benešov [CZ] **60** E3
Benešov [CZ] **74** B2
Benešov nad Ploučnicí [CZ] **60** D1
Benestad [S] **180** D2
Benetutti [I] **142** C3
Bénévent l'Abbaye [F] **78** F2
Benevento [I] **134** D3
Benfeld [F] **70** D2
Bengtsfors [S] **188** C3
Beničanci [HR] **120** F4
Benicarló [E] **102** F2
Benicasim / Benicàssim [E] **102** E2
Benicàssim / Benicasim [E] **102** E2
Benidorm [E] **108** C2
Beniel [E] **106** E2
Benifaió [E] **102** D3
Benifallet [E] **94** F4
Benifassá, Monestir de– [E] **96** A4
Beniganím [E] **102** D4
Benilloba [E] **106** F1
Benimarfull [E] **106** F1
Benissa [E] **108** C2
Benkovac [HR] **144** C3
Benkovski [BG] **150** E2
Benneckenstein [D] **44** C3
Bennstedt [D] **44** E3
Bénodet [F] **52** B4
Benòs [E] **88** D4
Benòs [E] **88** D4
Benquerencia de la Serena [E] **100** B3
Benrath [D] **42** C3
Bensafrim [P] **98** A3
Bensberg [D] **42** D4
Bensersiel [D] **30** E1
Bensheim [D] **58** B3
Bensjö [S] **204** F3
Benzú [MA] **104** C4
Beočin [SRB] **146** D1
Beograd [SRB] **146** E2
Bera / Vera de Bidasoa [E] **86** F3
Berane [MNE] **154** B2
Beranúy [E] **96** B1
Berat [AL] **160** B2
Beratón [E] **94** C2
Berbenno di Valtellina [I] **116** F2
Berberana [E] **86** D3
Bercedo [E] **86** D3
Bercel [H] **76** B3
Berceto [I] **128** A2
Berchem [L] **56** D3
Berching [D] **58** E4
Berchtesgaden [D] **72** E3
Bercinos del Real Camino [E] **86** A3
Berck–Plage [F] **40** A3
Berdalen [N] **186** C2
Berducedo [E] **82** E2
Berducido [E] **82** B3
Berdún [E] **88** B4
Berdychiv [UA] **244** E1
Berechiu [RO] **122** F2
Beregsurány [H] **76** F2
Berehomet [UA] **244** D3
Berehove [UA] **76** F2
Berek [H] **122** D1

Berek [HR] **120** D4
Berest [PL] **64** B3
Berettyószentmárton [H] **76** E4
Berettyóújfalu [H] **76** E4
Berezan' [UA] **242** E4
Berezhany [UA] **244** D2
Berezivka [UA] **246** D3
Berezna [UA] **242** E3
Berg [CH] **70** E3
Berg [D] **58** F2
Berg [D] **72** C3
Berg [N] **188** B2
Berg [N] **192** C1
Berg [N] **194** C4
Berg [N] **212** D2
Berg [S] **184** D3
Berg [S] **188** D3
Berga [D] **44** D3
Berga [E] **96** D2
Berga [S] **184** E2
Bergama [TR] **164** C3
Bergamo [I] **116** E3
Bergara [E] **86** E3
Berg bei Neamarkt [D] **58** F4
Bergby [S] **196** C3
Bergdala [S] **184** D3
Berge [N] **186** D1
Berge [S] **204** D2
Bergedorf [D] **32** C3
Bergeforsen [S] **206** C3
Bergen [D] **32** C4
Bergen [D] **32** D4
Bergen [D] **34** C1
Bergen [D] **56** E3
Bergen [D] **60** B2
Bergen [N] **192** B3
Bergen [NL] **30** B3
Bergen (Mons) [B] **40** D4
Bergen aan Zee [NL] **30** B3
Bergen op Zoom [NL] **40** E2
Berger [N] **186** F2
Bergerac [F] **78** D4
Berget [N] **204** B1
Berget [N] **218** F4
Bergheim [D] **42** C4
Berghem [S] **184** B2
Bergisch Gladbach [D] **42** D3
Bergkvara [S] **184** E4
Bergland [S] **214** A2
Berglern [D] **72** D2
Berglia [N] **212** E4
Berglinden [S] **214** D2
Berg–Neustadt [D] **42** D4
Bergö [FIN] **208** B2
Bergö [FIN] **208** B2
Bergondo [E] **82** C2
Bergsäter [S] **214** B2
Bergshamra [S] **190** E2
Bergsjö [S] **188** E2
Bergsjö [S] **196** C1
Bergsjøstøl [N] **192** E3
Berg slussar [S] **190** B4
Bergsmoen [N] **212** D3
Bergstad [FIN] **198** E4
Bergstrøm [N] **188** C2
Bergsviken [S] **214** D2
Bergues [F] **28** F4
Bergum [NL] **30** C2
Bergün [CH] **116** F2
Bergunda [S] **184** D3
Bergundhaugen [N] **194** B2
Bergvik [S] **196** C2
Berhida [H] **120** F1
Beringel [P] **98** C2
Beringen [B] **40** E3
Berini [RO] **122** E4
Bérisal [CH] **116** C2
Berja [E] **106** B3
Berkåk [N] **204** A3
Berkenthin [D] **32** C2
Berkesz [H] **76** E3
Berkheim [D] **72** A3

Berkhof [D] 44 B1
Berkovići [BIH] 152 D2
Berkovitsa [BG] 148 D4
Berkvigen [S] 220 D3
Berlanga [E] 98 F3
Berlanga de Duero [E] 94 B2
Berlevåg [N] 228 E1
Berlin [D] 46 B2
Berlingen [CH] 70 F3
Bermeo [E] 86 E2
Bermillo de Sayago [E] 84 E3
Bern [CH] 70 D4
Bernalda [I] 136 C3
Bernartice [CZ] 60 D4
Bernati [LV] 234 C4
Bernau [D] 46 B1
Bernau [D] 72 D3
Bernaville [F] 40 B4
Bernay [F] 54 C2
Bernburg [D] 44 E3
Berndorf [A] 74 C3
Berne [D] 30 F2
Bernedo [E] 86 E4
Bernek [A] 72 B4
Bernhardsthal [A] 74 D2
Bernsdorf [D] 46 C3
Bernstein [A] 74 D4
Bernués [E] 88 B4
Beromünster [CH] 70 E4
Beronovo [BG] 150 D4
Beroun [CZ] 60 D3
Berovo [MK] 154 F4
Berre–l'Etang [F] 124 E3
Berrien [F] 52 B3
Berriozar [E] 86 F4
Berrocal [E] 98 E4
Berrocalejo [E] 92 C4
Berroquejo [E] 104 B3
Bersenbrück [D] 30 E3
Beršići [SRB] 146 D3
Bertinoro [I] 128 D3
Bertrix [B] 56 C2
Berwang [A] 72 B4
Berwick–upon–Tweed [GB]
  20 E2
Beryslav [UA] 246 E2
Berzasca [RO] 148 B1
Berzaune [LV] 236 C3
Berzeme [F] 80 D4
Berzosa [E] 94 A2
Berzovia [RO] 122 E4
Besalú [E] 96 E2
Besançon [F] 70 B3
Besande [E] 86 B3
Besenyőtelek [H] 76 C3
Besenyszög [H] 76 C4
Besigheim [D] 58 C4
Běšiny [CZ] 60 C4
Beška [SRB] 146 D1
Bessan [F] 124 C3
Bessans [F] 116 B3
Bessay–sur–Allier [F] 68 C4
Besse–en–Chandesse [F]
  80 B2
Besse–sur–Issole [F] 126 A3
Bessheim [N] 192 E1
Bessines–sur–Gartempe
  [F] 78 E2
Best [NL] 40 F2
Bestida [P] 84 A3
Bestorp [S] 190 B4
Beszowa [PL] 64 B2
Betancuria [E] 114 D3
Betanzos [E] 82 C2
Betelu [E] 86 F3
Bétera [E] 102 D3
Beteta [E] 94 B4
Bétharram, Grottes de– [F]
  88 C3
Bethausen [RO] 122 F3

Bethesda [GB] 22 D2
Béthune [F] 40 B4
Betliar [SK] 76 C2
Betna [N] 202 E2
Betna [N] 202 E2
Betsele [S] 214 C3
Bettenburg [D] 58 E2
Bettna [S] 190 C3
Bettola [I] 126 F2
Bettyhill [GB] 14 E1
Betws–y–Coed [GB] 22 D3
Betz [F] 54 E3
Betzdorf [D] 42 D4
Betzigau [D] 72 B3
Beuel [D] 42 D4
Beuil [F] 126 C2
Beulich [D] 56 F2
Beuron [D] 70 F2
Beuzeville [F] 54 B2
Bevagna [I] 132 D2
Bévercé–Malmedy [B] 56 D1
Beverley [GB] 24 D2
Beverstedt [D] 32 A3
Beverungen [D] 44 B3
Beverwijk [NL] 30 B3
Bevtoft [DK] 178 B2
Bewdley [GB] 22 F4
Bex [CH] 116 B2
Bexhill [GB] 28 D4
Beyağaç [TR] 170 E4
Beyarmudu (Pergamos) [CY]
  176 E3
Beyazköy [TR] 158 C3
Beycayırı [TR] 164 B1
Beyce Sultan [TR] 170 E2
Beydağı [TR] 170 C2
Beydilli [TR] 170 F1
Beyel [TR] 164 E2
Beyköy [TR] 170 F3
Beykoz [TR] 158 E3
Beylerbeyi (Bellapaïs) [CY]
  176 D3
Beynac–et–Cazenac [F] 78 E4
Beynat [F] 78 E3
Beyobaşı [TR] 170 E4
Bezau [A] 72 A4
Bezdan [SRB] 122 B3
Bezden [BG] 148 D4
Bezděz [CZ] 60 E2
Bezdonys [LT] 238 E3
Bezdružice [CZ] 60 C3
Bezhetë–Makaj [AL] 152 F3
Bezhetsk [RUS] 240 E2
Béziers [F] 124 B3
Béznar [E] 104 F3
Bezzecca [I] 118 B3
B. Hornberg [D] 58 C4
Biała [PL] 62 C2
Białaczów [PL] 48 E4
Biała Piska [PL] 38 B2
Biała Podlaska [PL] 50 C2
Biała Rawska [PL] 48 E3
Białawy Wielkie [PL] 46 F3
Białobrzegi [PL] 48 F3
Białogard [PL] 34 F2
Białogóra [PL] 36 C1
Białowieża [PL] 38 D4
Biały Bór [PL] 36 A2
Białystok [PL] 38 C3
Biancavilla [I] 140 E2
Bianco [I] 138 D4
Biar [E] 106 E1
Biarritz [F] 88 A2
Bias [F] 88 B1
Biasca [CH] 116 E2
Biasteri / Laguardia [E] 86 E4
Biatigala [LT] 238 C2
Biatorbágy [H] 76 A4
Bibaktad [N] 228 E2
Bibbiena [I] 128 D4
Bibbiona [I] 128 B4
Biberach [D] 70 E2

Biberach an der Riss [D] 72 A2
Biberwier [A] 72 B4
Bibione [I] 118 E4
Bibrka [UA] 64 F3
Bibury [GB] 26 F2
Bič [SLO] 120 B3
Bicaj [AL] 154 B3
Bicaz [RO] 244 D3
Bicester [GB] 28 B2
Bichl [D] 72 C3
Bicos [P] 98 B2
Bicske [H] 76 A4
Bidache [F] 88 B2
Bidalite [S] 184 E4
Bidart [F] 88 A2
Biddinghuizen [NL] 30 C3
Biddulph [GB] 22 F3
Bideford [GB] 26 C2
Bidjovagge [N] 226 A2
Bidovce [SK] 76 E2
Bidziny [PL] 50 B4
Bie [S] 190 C3
Bieber [D] 58 C2
Biebersdorf [D] 46 C2
Biecz [PL] 64 C3
Biedenkopf [D] 42 E4
Biegen [D] 46 C2
Biegen [D] 46 C2
Biejkvasslia [N] 212 E1
Biel [E] 88 B4
Biel / Bienne [CH] 70 C4
Bielany Wrocł. [PL] 46 F4
Bielawa [PL] 62 B2
Bielawy [PL] 48 D2
Bielczyny [PL] 36 C4
Bielefeld [D] 30 F4
Bielino [PL] 38 A4
Biella [I] 116 C3
Bielmonte [I] 116 C3
Bielopolje [HR] 144 D2
Bielowy [PL] 64 C3
Bielsa [E] 88 C4
Bielsa, Tunnel de– [E/F]
  88 C4
Bielsk [PL] 48 D1
Bielsko–Biała [PL] 62 E3
Bielsk Podlaski [PL] 38 C4
Biely Kameň [SK] 74 E3
Bienenbüttel [D] 32 C3
Bieniów [PL] 46 D3
Bienne / Biel [CH] 70 C4
Bienvenida [E] 98 F3
Bienvenida [E] 100 C3
Bierberchren [D] 58 D3
Bierdzany [PL] 62 D1
Biermé [F] 66 D1
Bierre–Lès–Semur [F] 68 E3
Bierutów [PL] 48 B4
Bierzwnik [PL] 34 E4
Biescas [E] 88 C4
Biesenthal [D] 46 B1
Biesiekierz [PL] 34 F2
Bieskkenjárga [N] 226 C2
Bietigheim [D] 58 C4
Bieżuń [PL] 36 E4
Biga [TR] 164 B1
Bigadiç [TR] 164 D3
Bigastro [E] 106 E2
Biggar [GB] 20 D1
Biggleswade [GB] 28 D2
Bignasco [CH] 116 D2
Bigor [MNE] 152 E3
Bihać [BIH] 144 D2
Biharia [RO] 76 E4
Biharkeresztes [H] 122 E1
Biharnagybajom [H] 76 D4
Bijambarska Pećina [BIH]
  146 B3
Bijeljani [BIH] 152 D2
Bijeljina [BIH] 146 C2
Bijelo Brdo [HR] 122 B4
Bijelo Polje [MNE] 152 F2

Bikava [LV] 236 D3
Bikovo [SRB] 122 C3
Bílá [CZ] 62 D4
Bila Tserkva [UA] 244 F1
Bilbao / Bilbo [E] 86 E3
Bilbo / Bilbao [E] 86 E3
Bileća [BIH] 152 D2
Biled [RO] 122 E3
Bílenec [CZ] 60 C2
Bitgoraj [PL] 64 D2
Bilhorod Dnistrovs'kyi [UA]
  246 D3
Bílina [CZ] 60 D2
Bilisht [AL] 160 C2
Biljanovac [SRB] 146 E4
Bilje [HR] 122 B4
Bilka [BG] 150 D3
Billdal [S] 182 F2
Billerbeck [D] 30 E4
Billericay [GB] 28 D3
Billesholm [S] 178 F1
Billingen [N] 202 D4
Billingsfors [S] 188 C3
Billom [F] 80 B2
Billsta [S] 206 D2
Billum [DK] 178 A2
Bilopillia [UA] 242 E3
Bilousivka [UA] 242 E4
Bílovec [CZ] 62 D3
Bilska [LV] 230 E4
Bilsko [PL] 64 B3
Bilto [N] 224 F2
Bíňa [SK] 76 A3
Binas [F] 68 A1
Binasco [I] 116 E4
Binche [B] 40 D4
Bindslev [DK] 182 D2
Binéfar [E] 94 F3
Bingen [D] 58 A2
Bingen [N] 186 F1
Binghöhle [D] 58 E3
Bingsjö [S] 196 B3
Bingsta [S] 204 E3
Binibeca Vell [E] 108 F3
Binic [F] 52 D3
Binkos [BG] 150 C4
Bin Tepeler [TR] 164 D4
Binz [D] 34 C2
Binzen [D] 70 D3
Bioče [MNE] 152 F3
Biograd [MNE] 152 F3
Biograd [HR] 144 C3
Bionaz [I] 116 C3
Bioska [SRB] 146 D3
Birchiş [RO] 122 F3
Bircza [PL] 64 D3
Birgi [TR] 170 C2
Birgittelyst [DK] 182 C3
Biri [N] 194 B3
Birini [EST] 230 D3
Birini [LV] 236 B2
Biristrand [N] 194 B2
Birkala / Pirkkala [FIN] 198 D1
Birkeland [N] 186 C3
Birkeland [N] 186 D4
Birkenfeld [D] 56 E3
Birkenfeld [D] 58 C3
Birkenhead [GB] 22 E2
Birkenwerder [D] 46 B1
Birkerød [DK] 178 F2
Birkfeld [A] 74 C4
Birksdal [N] 192 C1
Birmingham [GB] 22 F4
Birnau [D] 70 F3
Biron, Château de– [F] 78 D4
Birr [IRL] 10 D2
Birstein [D] 58 C2
Birštonas [LT] 238 D3
Biržai [LT] 236 A4
Birżebbuga [M] 140 C2
Birži [LV] 236 C3
Birzuli [LV] 230 E4

Bisaccia [I] 134 E3
Bisacquino [I] 140 C2
Biscarrosse [F] 78 A4
Biscarrosse–Plage [F] 78 A4
Biscéglie [I] 136 C1
Bischoffen [D] 42 E4
Bischofsgrün [D] 58 F2
Bischofsheim [D] 58 D2
Bischofshofen [A] 72 E4
Bischofswerda [D] 46 C4
Biscoitos [P] 110 C3
Biserci [BG] 150 C2
Bishop Auckland [GB] 20 E3
Bishop's Castle [GB] 22 E4
Bishop's Cleeve [GB] 26 F2
Bishop's Stortford [GB] 28 D2
Bisignano [I] 136 C4
Bisko [HR] 144 E4
Biskupice Oławskie [PL] 48 B4
Biskupice Radłowskico [PL]
  64 B2
Biskupiec [PL] 36 D3
Biskupiec [PL] 36 F2
Biskupin [PL] 48 B1
Bisław [PL] 36 C3
Bislev [DK] 182 D3
Bismark [D] 44 E1
Bismo [N] 202 E4
Bispingen [D] 32 C3
Bistrec [BG] 158 B1
Bistreţ [RO] 148 D2
Bistrica [MNE] 152 F2
Bistrica [SRB] 146 D4
Bistrica ob S. [SLO] 120 C3
Bistriţa [RO] 244 D3
Bistritsa [BG] 156 B1
Bisztynek [PL] 36 F2
Bitburg [D] 56 E2
Bitche [F] 56 F4
Bitetto [I] 136 C2
Bithia [I] 142 B6
Bitola [MK] 160 D2
Bitonto [I] 136 C1
Bitov [CZ] 74 C1
Ritterfeld [D] 44 E3
Bitterstad [N] 224 B4
Bitti [I] 142 C3
Bıvıkali [TR] 158 C3
Bivio [CH] 116 F2
Bivio Manganaro [I] 140 C2
Bivona [I] 140 C2
Bıyıklı [TR] 170 C3
Bizovac [HR] 122 A4
Bjåen [N] 186 C1
Bjala Cherkva [BG] 150 B3
Bjalizvor [BG] 156 E2
Bjär [N] 186 E1
Bjarisino [BY] 242 C2
Bjärklunda [S] 188 D4
Bjärnå / Perniö [FIN] 198 D3
Bjärnum [S] 180 D1
Bjärred [S] 180 C2
Bjärtrå [S] 206 D3
Bjästa [S] 206 D2
Bjelland [N] 186 C3
Bjelovar [HR] 120 D3
Bjerga [N] 186 B1
Bjergby [DK] 182 D2
Bjerkreim [N] 186 B3
Bjerkvik [N] 224 C4
Bjerre [DK] 178 C1
Bjerregård [DK] 178 A1
Bjerringbro [DK] 182 C3
Bjoenstrand [N] 186 B1
Bjølstad [N] 192 E1
Bjoneroa [N] 192 F3
Bjonevika [N] 192 F3
Bjørånes [N] 194 B3
Björbo [S] 194 F4
Bjordal [N] 186 B3
Bjordal [N] 192 B2
Bjørgo [N] 192 E3

Björka [S] 194 F3
Bjørkåsen [N] 224 D3
Björkberg [S] 194 F2
Björkberg [S] 214 B3
Bjørke [N] 202 C4
Bjørkedal [N] 202 C4
Björkefors [S] 184 E1
Bjørkelangen [N] 188 C1
Bjørkflåta [N] 192 E4
Björkfors [S] 212 F1
Björkhöjden [S] 206 B2
Björkliden [S] 224 D4
Björklinge [S] 190 D1
Bjørknes [N] 188 C1
Björkö [FIN] 198 B3
Björkö [S] 184 D2
Björkö [S] 190 E1
Björköby [FIN] 208 B1
Björksele [S] 214 C2
Björksjön [S] 206 C2
Björkvattnet [S] 212 E3
Björkvik [S] 190 C3
Bjørlia [N] 212 D3
Bjørn [N] 212 D1
Björna [S] 206 D2
Björneborg [S] 188 E2
Björneborg / Pori [FIN] 198 C1
Bjørnestad [N] 186 B3
Bjørnevasshytta [N] 186 C2
Bjørnevatn [N] 228 F3
Björnhult [S] 184 E2
Björnlunda [S] 190 D3
Björnrike [S] 204 E4
Björnsholm [S] 184 E1
Björnsjö [S] 206 D2
Bjørnstad [N] 212 D3
Björsäter [S] 188 E3
Björsäter [S] 190 B4
Bjørsvik [N] 192 B3
Bjuråker [S] 196 C1
Bjurberget [S] 194 D3
Bjurfors [S] 214 D3
Bjurholm [S] 178 F1
Bjurholm [S] 206 E1
Bjuröklubb [S] 214 E3
Bjurön [S] 196 E4
Bjursås [S] 196 B3
Bjursele [S] 214 C2
Bjurselet [S] 214 D2
Bjurträsk [S] 214 C2
Bjuv [S] 178 F1
Blace [SRB] 148 A4
Blachownia [PL] 62 E1
Blackburn [GB] 22 F2
Blacklion [IRL] 12 D2
Blackpool [GB] 22 E2
Blackstad [S] 184 E1
Blackwater [IRL] 10 F4
Bladåker [S] 190 E1
Blaenau Ffestiniog [GB] 22 D3
Blagaj [BIH] 152 D2
Blagaj Japra [BIH] 144 E1
Blagoevgrad [BG] 154 F3
Blagoevo [BG] 150 D3
Blagoveštenje, Manastir–
[SRB] 146 E3
Blagovica [SLO] 120 B3
Blåhøj [DK] 178 B1
Blaiken [S] 214 A4
Blaikliden [S] 212 F3
Blain [F] 66 C2
Blair Atholl [GB] 18 D2
Blairgowrie [GB] 18 D3
Blaisy–Bas [F] 68 E3
Blaj [RO] 244 D4
Blajan [F] 88 D3
Błąkały [PL] 38 B1
Blakstad [N] 186 D3
Blåmont [F] 70 C1
Blanca [E] 106 D2
Blandford Forum [GB] 26 E3
Blanes [E] 96 E3

Blangy–sur–Bresle [F] 54 D1
Blanických Rytířů, Jeskyně–
[CZ] 62 B4
Blankaholm [S] 184 E2
Blankenberge [B] 40 C2
Blankenburg [D] 44 D3
Blankenfelde [D] 46 B2
Blankenhain [D] 44 D4
Blankenheim [D] 56 E1
Blanquefort [F] 78 B3
Blansko [CZ] 62 B4
Blanzac [F] 78 C2
Blarney [IRL] 10 C4
Blarney Castle [IRL] 10 C4
Blascosancho [E] 92 D3
Blåsjön [S] 212 E3
Błaszki [PL] 48 C3
Blatná [CZ] 60 D4
Blatnica [BIH] 146 A2
Blatnica [SK] 76 B1
Blatnice pod Sv. Antonínkem
[CZ] 74 E1
Blato [HR] 144 E4
Blato [HR] 152 B2
Blattniksele [S] 214 B2
Blaubeuren [D] 72 A2
Blaufelden [D] 58 D4
Blaustein [D] 72 A2
Blåvand [DK] 178 A2
Blåvik [S] 184 D1
Blaye [F] 78 B3
Błażowa [PL] 64 D3
Blazquez [E] 100 B3
Bleckåsen [S] 204 E2
Bleckede [D] 32 C3
Blecksnäs [FIN] 208 B2
Bled [SLO] 118 F2
Bleiburg [A] 120 B2
Bleicherode [D] 44 C3
Bleik [N] 224 B3
Bleistjord [N] 224 C4
Blejeşti [RO] 150 B1
Blendija [SRB] 148 B3
Bléneau [F] 68 C2
Blentarp [S] 180 C2
Blera [I] 130 F3
Blérancourt [F] 54 F2
Bléré [F] 66 F3
Blériot–Plage [F] 28 E4
Bleskestad [N] 186 C1
Blesle [F] 80 B3
Blessington [IRL] 10 F2
Bletterans [F] 68 F4
Blévy [F] 54 C3
Blexen [D] 32 A3
Bliesbruck–Reinheim, Parc
Archéol. de– [F] 56 E4
Blieskastel [D] 56 E3
Bligny–sur–Ouche [F] 68 E3
Blikstorp [S] 188 E4
Blinisht [AL] 154 B3
Blinja [HR] 120 D4
Blintrop [D] 42 E3
Bliznaci [BG] 150 D3
Bliznak [BG] 150 E3
Bliznak [BG] 158 B1
Blizne [PL] 64 C3
Błogoszów [PL] 62 F1
Blois [F] 68 A2
Blokhus [DK] 182 D2
Blokzijl [NL] 30 C3
Blombacka [S] 188 E2
Blomberg [D] 42 F2
Blomsholms–Skeppet [S]
188 B3
Blomstermåla [S] 184 E3
Blönduós [IS] 218 B2
Błonie [PL] 46 F4
Błonie [PL] 48 E2
Błonie [PL] 50 D2
Bloška Polica [SLO] 120 A3
Blötberget [S] 188 F1

Błotnica [PL] 34 E2
Błotnica [PL] 48 E4
Błotno [PL] 34 E3
Blovice [CZ] 60 C3
Bludenz [A] 72 A4
Bludov [CZ] 62 B3
Blumberg [D] 70 E3
Blyth [GB] 20 F3
Bø [N] 186 E2
Bø [N] 186 E2
Bø [N] 192 B2
Bø [N] 192 B3
Bø [N] 224 B4
Bø [N] 224 C2
Bo [S] 190 B3
Boadilla del Monte [E] 92 E4
Boal [E] 82 E2
Boalt [S] 184 C4
Boário Terme [I] 116 F3
Bóbbio [I] 126 F1
Bobbio Pellice [I] 126 C1
Boberg [S] 206 B2
Bobice [PL] 64 D3
Bobin [PL] 64 B2
Bobingen [D] 72 B2
Bobitz [D] 32 D2
Böblingen [D] 70 F1
Bobolice [PL] 36 A2
Boboshevo [BG] 154 F3
Bobovdol [BG] 154 F2
Bobr [BY] 242 C1
Bobrová [CZ] 62 A4
Bobrovytsia [UA] 242 D4
Bobrowice [PL] 46 D3
Bobrowniki [PL] 38 D3
Bobrowniki [PL] 48 C1
Bobrynets' [UA] 246 D2
Bočac [BIH] 144 E2
Boca de Huergano [E] 86 B2
Bocairent [E] 106 F1
Boceguillas [E] 92 F2
Böçen [TR] 164 F2
Bochnia [PL] 64 B3
Bocholt [B] 40 F3
Bocholt [D] 30 D4
Bochov [CZ] 60 C2
Bochum [D] 42 D3
Bocigas [E] 92 D2
Bockara [S] 184 E2
Bockel [D] 32 B3
Bockenem [D] 44 C2
Bočki [PL] 38 C4
Böcksholm [S] 184 D3
Böckstein [A] 118 E1
Bockum Hövel [D] 42 E2
Bocognano [I] 130 B3
Boconád [H] 76 C4
Bócsa [H] 122 C2
Boçsa [RO] 122 F4
Boçsa Vasiovei [RO] 122 F4
Bocsig [RO] 122 F2
Böda [S] 184 F2
Boda [S] 188 D2
Boda [S] 194 F1
Boda [S] 206 C3
Bodaczów [PL] 50 C4
Bodafors [S] 184 D2
Boda glasbruk [S] 184 E3
Bodarsjön [S] 194 F1
Bodegraven [NL] 30 B3
Boden [S] 214 E1
Bodenmais [D] 72 E1
Bodenteich [D] 32 C4
Bodenwerder [D] 44 B2
Bodenwöhr [D] 60 B4
Bodjani [SRB] 122 B4
Bodman [D] 70 F3
Bodmin [GB] 26 B3
Bodø [N] 218 F2
Bodom [N] 212 C4
Bodrogkeresztúr [H] 76 D3
Bodrum [TR] 170 C4

Bodsjö [S] 204 F3
Bodsjöedet [S] 204 D2
Bodträskfors [S] 220 E4
Bodzanów [PL] 48 E2
Bodzanowice [PL] 62 D1
Bodzentyn [PL] 48 F4
Boëge [F] 116 A2
Boën [F] 80 C2
Bogács [H] 76 C3
Bøgard [N] 224 B3
Bogarra [E] 102 A4
Bogatić [SRB] 146 C2
Bogatovo [RUS] 36 E2
Bogatynia [PL] 60 E1
Boğaz (Bogázi) [CY] 176 E3
Boğazcık [TR] 176 E1
Bogázi (Boğaz) [CY] 176 E3
Boğaziçi [TR] 170 B2
Boğazköy [TR] 164 F1
Bogda [RO] 122 E3
Bogdana [RO] 150 A2
Bogdanci [MK] 156 A4
Bogdaniec [PL] 46 D1
Bogë [AL] 152 F3
Boge [S] 234 A2
Bogen [D] 72 E1
Bogen [N] 220 A1
Bogen [N] 224 C4
Bogen [S] 188 D1
Bogense [DK] 178 C2
Bogetići [MNE] 152 E3
Bogge [N] 202 E3
Böglosa [S] 190 D2
Bognanco [I] 116 D2
Bognes [N] 224 B4
Bognor Regis [GB] 28 C4
Bogojevo [SRB] 122 B4
Bogojevo [SRB] 148 B4
Bogoria [PL] 64 B2
Bogorodica [MK] 156 A4
Bogovina [SRB] 148 B3
Bogovina Pećina [SRB]
148 B3
Bograngen [S] 194 D3
Boguchwałów [PL] 62 D3
Bogumiłowice [PL] 48 D4
Boguszów–Gorce [PL] 62 B1
Bogutovačka Banja [SRB]
146 E4
Bogyiszló [H] 122 B2
Bohain–en–Vermandois
[F] 56 A1
Bohal [F] 52 D4
Bohdalov [CZ] 60 F4
Boheeshil [IRL] 10 A3
Bohinjska Bela [SLO] 118 F2
Bohinjska Bistrica [SLO]
118 F3
Böhmenkirch [D] 72 A1
Bohmte [D] 30 F4
Bohonal [E] 100 C2
Bohonal de Ibor [E] 92 B4
Böhönye [H] 120 E2
Bohula [MK] 160 E1
Boialvo [P] 84 A4
Boichinovtsi [BG] 148 D3
Bois–du–Four [F] 124 B1
Boitzenburg [D] 34 C3
Böixols [E] 96 C2
Boizenburg [D] 32 C3
Böja [S] 188 E4
Bojano [I] 134 D2
Bojanów [PL] 64 C2
Bojanowo [PL] 46 F3
Bøjden [DK] 178 C3
Bojkovice [CZ] 74 E1
Bojnica [BG] 148 C2
Bojnice [SK] 76 A2
Bojnik [SRB] 148 B4
Bojtiken [S] 212 F2
Bokel [D] 32 B2
Bökemåla [S] 180 E1

Bökenäs [S] 188 C4
Bokinić [HR] 144 B2
Böklund [D] 32 B1
Bokod [H] 74 F4
Bokod [H] 74 F4
Bököny [H] 76 E3
Bokros [H] 122 C2
Boksitogorsk [RUS] 240 D1
Boksjok [N] 228 D2
Bol [HR] 152 B2
Bolaños de Calatrava [E]
100 D3
Bolayır [TR] 164 B1
Bolbec [F] 54 C2
Bolca [I] 118 B3
Bölcek [TR] 164 D3
Boldekow [D] 34 C3
Boldogasszonyfa [H] 120 F3
Boldva [H] 76 D3
Bøle [N] 212 B3
Böle [S] 204 E2
Bolekhiv [UA] 64 F4
Bolemin [PL] 46 D1
Bolesławiec [PL] 46 D4
Bolesławiec [PL] 48 C4
Bolesławów [PL] 62 B2
Boleszkowice [PL] 46 C1
Bolfiar [P] 84 A3
Bolfoss [N] 188 C1
Bolgatovo [RUS] 236 F3
Bolgheri [I] 130 D1
Bolhrad [UA] 244 F4
Boliden [S] 214 D2
Bolimów [PL] 48 E2
Bolinglanna / Buaile an
Ghleanna [IRL] 12 A2
Bolintin Vale [RO] 150 B1
Boljanići [MNE] 152 E1
Boljevac [SRB] 148 B3
Boljun [HR] 118 F4
Bolkesjø [N] 186 E1
Bolkhov [RUS] 242 F1
Bolków [PL] 62 A1
Bollebygd [S] 184 B2
Bollène [F] 124 E2
Böllerkirche [D] 58 B3
Bollerup [S] 180 D2
Bollnäs [S] 196 C2
Bollstabruk [S] 206 C3
Bollullos de la Mitación [E]
104 B1
Bollullos Par del Condado
[E] 98 E4
Bologna [I] 128 C2
Bologne [F] 68 F2
Bolótana [I] 142 B3
Bolsena [I] 130 F2
Bol'shakovo [RUS] 238 B3
Bol'shaya Izhora [RUS] 200 E3
Bol'shaya Pustomerzha [RUS]
232 E1
Bol'shaya Yashchera [RUS]
232 F1
Bol'shie Sabicy [RUS] 232 F2
Bol'shiye Kolpany [RUS]
200 F4
Bol'shoye Zagor'e [RUS]
232 F3
Bol'shoy Sabsk [RUS] 232 E1
Bolstad [S] 188 C3
Bolstadøyri [N] 192 B3
Bolstaholm [FIN] 196 F4
Bolsward [NL] 30 C2
Bolszewo [PL] 36 C1
Boltaña [E] 88 C4
Boltenhagen [D] 32 D2
Boltigen [CH] 116 C1
Bolton [GB] 22 F2
Bolungarvík [IS] 218 B1
Bóly [H] 122 A3
Bolyarovo [BG] 158 A2
Bolyartsi [BG] 156 D2

Bolzano / Bozen [I] 118 C2
Bømarka [N] 212 B4
Bømarken [S] 188 C3
Bomarsund [FIN] 198 A3
Bomarzo [I] 130 F2
Bombarral [P] 90 B3
Bominago [I] 132 E3
Bom Jesus do Monte [P] 84 B2
Bomsund [S] 206 B2
Bonaduz [CH] 116 E1
Bonaguil, Château de– [F] 78 D4
Bonanza [E] 104 B2
Boñar [E] 86 A2
Bonar Bridge [GB] 14 E2
Bonares [E] 98 D4
Bonäs [S] 188 D2
Bonäs [S] 194 F3
Bonåset [S] 204 D2
Bonåsjøen [N] 220 B1
Bonassola [I] 126 F2
Bonaval [E] 92 F3
Bończa [PL] 48 F3
Bondal [N] 186 D1
Bondemon [S] 188 C3
Bondeno [I] 128 C2
Bondstorp [S] 184 C2
Bonefro [I] 134 D2
Bonete [E] 102 C4
Bonhamn [S] 206 D3
Bonhomme, Col du– [F] 70 C2
Bonifacio [F] 130 B4
Bonifati Marina [I] 136 B4
Bonilla [E] 102 A1
Bönitz [D] 46 B3
Bonlieu [F] 80 F1
Bonn [D] 42 D4
Bonnat [F] 68 A4
Bonndorf [D] 70 E3
Bønnerup Strand [DK] 182 E3
Bonnesvalyn [F] 54 F3
Bonnétable [F] 54 B4
Bonneuil–Matours [F] 66 E4
Bonneval [F] 54 C4
Bonneval–sur–Arc [F] 116 B3
Bonnéville [F] 116 A2
Bonnières [F] 54 D3
Bonnieux [F] 124 E3
Bonnigheim [D] 58 C4
Bonny–sur–Loire [F] 68 C2
Bono [I] 142 C3
Bonorva [I] 142 B3
Bonport, Abbaye de– [F] 54 C2
Bonyhád [H] 122 A3
Bonzov [CZ] 62 B3
Boom [B] 40 E3
Boos [D] 56 E2
Boos [D] 72 A2
Boos [F] 54 C2
Booth of Toft [GB] 16 E3
Bootle [GB] 22 E2
Bopfingen [D] 72 B1
Boppard [D] 56 F2
Bor [CZ] 60 B3
Bor [RUS] 232 F2
Bor [S] 184 C3
Bor [SRB] 148 B2
Borås [N] 186 E3
Borås [S] 184 B2
Borãscu [RO] 148 D1
Borba [P] 90 D4
Borbona [I] 132 D3
Borchen [D] 42 F3
Borci [BIH] 146 A4
Borculo [NL] 30 D4
Bordány [H] 122 C3
Bordeaux [F] 78 B3
Bordeira [P] 98 A3
Bordères [F] 88 D3
Bordesholm [D] 32 C2

Bordighera [I] 126 C3
Bording [DK] 178 B1
Borduşani [RO] 150 E1
Bore [I] 128 A2
Boreci [SLO] 120 D2
Borek Wielkopolski [PL] 48 A3
Borello [I] 128 D3
Borensberg [S] 188 F4
Borg [N] 218 F1
Borga [S] 212 F3
Borgå / Porvoo [FIN] 200 B3
Borgafjäll [S] 212 F3
Borgarnes [IS] 218 A2
Borgeby [S] 180 C2
Borgen [N] 186 D2
Borgentreich [D] 42 F3
Börger [D] 30 E3
Borger [NL] 30 D2
Börgermoor [D] 30 E2
Borggård [S] 190 B3
Borgharen [S] 188 F4
Borghetto di Borbera [I] 126 E2
Borgholm [S] 184 F3
Borgholzhausen [D] 30 F4
Borghorst [D] 30 E4
Børglumkloster [DK] 182 D2
Borgo Callea [I] 140 C2
Borgoforte [I] 128 B1
Borgomanero [I] 116 D3
Borgond [H] 122 A1
Borgonovo Val Tidone [I] 126 F1
Borgorose [I] 132 D3
Borgo San Dalmazzo [I] 126 C2
Borgo San Lorenzo [I] 128 C3
Borgosésia [I] 116 D3
Borgo Ticino [I] 116 D3
Borgo Tossignano [I] 128 C3
Borgo Val di Taro [I] 128 A2
Borgo Valsugana [I] 118 C3
Borgo Vercelli [I] 116 D4
Borgsjö [S] 206 B3
Borgsjö [S] 214 B3
Borgstena [S] 184 B1
Borgund [N] 192 D2
Borgund [N] 202 B3
Borgvattnet [S] 206 B2
Borgvik [S] 188 D2
Borielsbyn [S] 222 A4
Borima [BG] 148 F4
Borino [BG] 156 C3
Borislavtsi [BG] 156 E3
Borisoglebskiy [RUS] 228 F3
Borisovo [RUS] 200 F2
Borja [E] 94 D2
Borken [D] 42 D2
Borken [D] 42 F4
Borkenes [N] 224 C3
Borki [RUS] 232 E3
Børkop [DK] 178 C2
Borków [PL] 64 B1
Borkum [D] 30 D1
Borlänge [S] 196 B4
Borlaug [N] 192 D2
Børlía [N] 204 B3
Borlu [TR] 164 E4
Bormes–les–Mimosas [F] 126 A4
Bórmio [I] 118 A2
Borna [D] 44 E4
Borneiro, Castro de– [E] 82 B2
Borne Sulinowo [PL] 36 A3
Bornhöved [D] 32 C2
Börnicke [D] 44 F1
Bornlitz [D] 32 B2
Bornos [E] 104 B2
Bornova [TR] 170 B2
Borodianka [UA] 242 D4
Borodinskoye [RUS] 200 E2
Boronów [PL] 62 E2
Borová Lada [CZ] 72 F1

Borovan [BG] 148 E3
Borovany [CZ] 74 B1
Borovets [BG] 156 B2
Borovica [BG] 148 C3
Borovichi [RUS] 232 F3
Borovik [RUS] 232 E3
Borovo [BG] 150 B3
Borovo [HR] 122 B4
Borovtsi [BG] 148 D3
Borów [PL] 50 B4
Borowa [PL] 48 B4
Borrby [S] 180 D2
Borre [DK] 178 F3
Borre [N] 186 F2
Borreby [DK] 178 D3
Borredà [E] 96 D2
Borremose [DK] 182 D3
Borriana / Burriana [E] 102 E3
Börringe [S] 180 C2
Borriol [E] 102 E2
Borris [DK] 178 B1
Borris [IRL] 10 E3
Borris–in–Ossory [IRL] 10 D2
Borrisokane [IRL] 10 D2
Borrisoleigh [IRL] 10 D2
Börrum [S] 190 C4
Borş [RO] 122 E1
Børs [RO] 244 B4
Børsa [N] 204 B2
Borşa [RO] 244 D3
Børselv [N] 228 C2
Borsfa [H] 120 D2
Borsh [AL] 160 B3
Borsodiánka [H] 76 D3
Borsodnádasd [H] 76 C3
Börstil [S] 196 E4
Bortholoma [D] 72 A1
Bort–les–Orgues [F] 80 A2
Börtnan [S] 204 E3
Bortnen [N] 202 B4
Borup [DK] 178 E2
Borynia [UA] 64 E4
Boryslav [UA] 64 E4
Boryspil' [UA] 242 D4
Borzechowo [PL] 36 C2
Borzone, Abbazia di– [I] 126 F2
Borzysław [PL] 36 A2
Bosa [I] 142 B3
Bosanci [HR] 120 B4
Bosanska Bojna [BIH] 144 D1
Bosanska Dubica [BIH] 144 E1
Bosanska Gradiška [BIH] 144 F1
Bosanska Kostajnica [BIH] 144 E1
Bosanska Krupa [BIH] 144 D2
Bosanska Rača [BIH] 146 C2
Bosanski Brod [BIH] 146 A1
Bosanski Novi [HR] 144 D1
Bosanski Petrovac [BIH] 144 D2
Bosanski Šamac [BIH] 146 B1
Bosansko Grahovo [BIH] 144 D3
Bošany [SK] 74 F2
Bősárkány [H] 74 E3
Bosc–Mesnil [F] 54 D2
Bosco Chiesanuova [I] 118 B3
Bösel [D] 30 F2
Bosgouet [F] 54 C2
Bosilegrad [SRB] 154 E2
Bosiljevo [HR] 120 B4
Bosjökloster [S] 180 C2
Bosjön [S] 188 E1
Boskoop [NL] 30 B4
Boskovice [CZ] 62 B4
Bosna Klanac [BIH] 146 A3
Bošnjace [SRB] 148 B4
Bošnjaci [HR] 146 B1
Bosruck Tunnel [A] 74 A4
Bössbo [S] 194 E2

Bossbøen [N] 186 D1
Bossea [I] 126 D2
Bossòst [E] 88 D4
Bostandere [TR] 164 B2
Boštanj [SLO] 120 B3
Böste [S] 180 C2
Boston [GB] 24 D4
Bostrak [N] 186 E2
Bosut [SRB] 146 C2
Bőszénfa [H] 120 F3
Boteå [S] 206 D2
Botevgrad [BG] 148 E4
Botevo [BG] 150 E3
Boticas [P] 84 C2
Botinec [HR] 120 C3
Botnen [N] 202 C4
Botngård [N] 204 A1
Bótoa [E] 90 E4
Bötom / Karijoki [FIN] 208 B3
Botoroaga [RO] 150 B2
Botorrita [E] 94 D3
Botoşani [RO] 244 E3
Botricello [I] 138 E2
Botsmark [S] 214 D3
Böttberg [D] 72 C3
Botten [S] 188 D2
Bottheim [N] 202 E4
Bottidda [I] 142 C3
Bottnaryd [S] 184 C1
Bottrop [D] 42 D3
Botun [MK] 160 C1
Botunets [BG] 156 B1
Bouaye [F] 66 C2
Bouchair [F] 54 E2
Bouconville–sur–Madt [F] 56 D4
Boudry [CH] 70 C4
Bouesse [F] 68 A3
Bouges–le–Château [F] 68 A3
Bouguenais [F] 66 C2
Bouillon [B] 56 E1
Bouilly [F] 68 E1
Boulay–Moselle [F] 56 E3
Bouligny [F] 56 D3
Boulogne–sur–Gesse [F] 88 D3
Boulogne–sur–Mer [F] 40 A3
Bouloire [F] 54 B4
Boumois, Château de– [F] 66 E2
Bouniagues [F] 78 D4
Bourbon–Lancy [F] 68 D4
Bourbon–l'Archambault [F] 68 C4
Bourbonne–les–Bains [F] 70 B2
Bourbourg [F] 28 F4
Bourbriac [F] 52 C3
Bourdeaux [F] 124 E1
Bourdeilles [F] 78 D3
Bourg [F] 78 B3
Bourg–Achard [F] 54 C2
Bourganeuf [F] 78 F2
Bourg–Argental [F] 80 D3
Bourg–de–Péage [F] 80 D4
Bourg–en–Bresse [F] 80 E2
Bourges [F] 68 B3
Bourg–et–Comin [F] 56 A2
Bourg–Lastic [F] 80 A2
Bourg–Madame [F] 96 D1
Bourgneuf–en–Retz [F] 66 B2
Bourgogne [F] 56 B3
Bourgoin–Jallieu [F] 80 E3
Bourg–St–Andéol [F] 124 E2
Bourg–St–Maurice [F] 116 B3
Bourgtheroulde–Infreville [F] 54 C2
Bourgueil [F] 66 E2
Bourideys [F] 78 B4
Bourmont [F] 70 B2
Bourne [GB] 24 D4
Bournemouth [GB] 26 F4

Bourneville [F] 54 C2
Bournezeau [F] 66 C3
Boussac [F] 68 B4
Boussens [F] 88 E3
Bouvignes [B] 56 C1
Bouvron [F] 66 C2
Bouxwiller [F] 56 F4
Bouzonville [F] 56 E3
Bova [I] 138 D4
Bovalino [I] 138 D3
Bovallstrand [S] 188 B4
Bova Marina [I] 138 D4
Bovan [SRB] 148 B3
Bovec [SLO] 118 E2
Bóveda [E] 82 C3
Bóvegno [I] 116 F3
Bovense [DK] 178 D2
Bøverbru [N] 194 B3
Bøverdal [N] 192 E1
Boves [I] 126 C2
Bović [HR] 120 C4
Bovik [FIN] 196 F4
Bovino [I] 134 E3
Bovolenta [I] 118 C4
Bovolone [I] 118 B4
Bovrup [DK] 178 C3
Boxberg [D] 58 C3
Boxholm [S] 188 F4
Boxmeer [NL] 42 B2
Boxtel [NL] 40 F2
Boyalı [TR] 164 D4
Boyalıca [TR] 158 F4
Boyalıca [TR] 164 E2
Boyalık [TR] 158 D3
Boyle [IRL] 12 C3
Bøylefoss [N] 186 D3
Bøyum [N] 192 C1
Božaj [MNE] 152 F3
Bozalan [TR] 170 D2
Bozan [TR] 170 F2
Božava [HR] 144 C3
Bozburun [TR] 176 C1
Bozcaada [TR] 162 F2
Bozcaatlı [TR] 164 E4
Bozdağ [TR] 170 C2
Bozdoğan [TR] 170 D3
Bozel [F] 116 A3
Bozen / Bolzano [I] 118 C2
Bozhane [TR] 158 E3
Bozhenci [BG] 150 B4
Bozhurishte [BG] 154 F2
Božica [SRB] 154 E2
Boží Dar [CZ] 60 C2
Bozkurt [TR] 170 E2
Bozkuş [TR] 164 F4
Bozkuş [TR] 164 F4
Bozlar [TR] 164 C1
Bozolan [TR] 168 F1
Bozouls [F] 80 A4
Bozouls, Trou de– [F] 80 A4
Bozovici [RO] 148 B1
Bozveliisko [BG] 150 E3
Bozyaka [TR] 170 E4
Bózzolo [I] 128 B1
Bra [B] 56 D1
Bra [I] 126 D1
Brå [N] 204 B2
Braås [S] 184 D3
Brabecke [D] 42 E3
Brabova [RO] 148 D2
Bracciano [I] 130 F3
Brachlewo [PL] 36 D3
Bracieux [F] 68 A2
Bracigovo [BG] 156 C2
Bräcke [S] 204 F3
Brackenheim [D] 58 C4
Brackley [GB] 28 D2
Bracknell [GB] 28 C3
Brackwede [D] 30 F4
Brad [RO] 244 C3
Bradford [GB] 24 C2
Bradina [BIH] 146 A4

Bradvari [BG] 150 D2
Brae [GB] 16 E3
Brædstrup [DK] 178 C1
Braemar [GB] 14 E4
Braga [P] 84 B2
Bragança [P] 84 D2
Brahestad / Raahe [FIN] 216 A2
Brahetrolleborg [DK] 178 C3
Brail [CH] 116 F2
Brăila [RO] 248 F3
Braine [F] 54 F3
Braine–le–Comte [B] 40 D4
Braintree [GB] 28 D2
Brake [D] 30 F2
Brakel [B] 40 D3
Brakel [D] 42 F3
Bräkne–Hoby [S] 180 E1
Brålanda [S] 188 C3
Bram [F] 88 F3
Bramberg [A] 72 D4
Bramberg [CH] 72 D4
Brämhult [S] 184 B2
Bramming [DK] 178 B2
Brampton [GB] 20 D3
Bramsche [D] 30 E3
Branč [SK] 74 E2
Branč [SK] 74 F3
Branca [I] 132 D1
Brancaleone Marina [I] 138 D4
Brancion [F] 80 D1
Brancoli, Pieve di– [I] 128 B3
Brâncoveni [RO] 148 E2
Brand [A] 116 F1
Brandal [N] 202 C3
Brändåsen [S] 204 D4
Brändbo [S] 196 C1
Brandbu [N] 194 B3
Brande [DK] 178 B1
Bränden [S] 194 E1
Brandenberg [A] 72 D4
Brandenburg [D] 44 F2
Brand–Erbisdorf [D] 60 C1
Brandhof [A] 74 B4
Brandis [D] 46 B3
Brändö [FIN] 198 B3
Brandomil [E] 82 B2
Brandon [F] 80 D1
Brandon [GB] 20 E3
Brandstorp [S] 184 C1
Brandval [N] 194 C4
Brandvoll [N] 224 D3
Brandýsek [CZ] 60 D2
Brandýs n Labem [CZ] 60 E2
Bráneşti [RO] 150 C1
Branica [BG] 156 F2
Braničevo [SRB] 146 F2
Braniewo [PL] 36 E2
Branik [SLO] 118 F3
Branišovice [CZ] 74 D1
Branitz, Schloss– [D] 46 C3
Brankovice [CZ] 62 C4
Brännåker [S] 212 F3
Brännberg [S] 214 D1
Branne [F] 78 C3
Brannenburg [D] 72 D3
Brännland [S] 206 E1
Brännland [S] 206 E1
Brañosera [E] 86 C3
Brańsk [PL] 38 C4
Brantôme [F] 78 D3
Branzi [I] 116 F3
Bras–d'Asse [F] 126 A2
Braskereidfoss [N] 194 C3
Braslaw [BY] 240 B4
Braşov [RO] 248 D3
Brassac [F] 124 B2
Brassac–Jumeaux [F] 80 B3
Brasschaat [B] 40 E3
Bras–sur–Meuse [F] 56 C3
Brastad [S] 188 B4
Břasy [CZ] 60 C3

Brąszewice [PL] 48 C3
Brataj [AL] 160 B3
Bråte [N] 188 C1
Bratislava [SK] 74 E3
Bratków Dolny [PL] 48 C3
Bratovoeşti [RO] 148 E2
Brattabø [N] 192 C3
Brattåker [S] 214 A2
Brattbäcken [S] 212 F4
Bratten [S] 214 B3
Brattfors [S] 188 E2
Brattingsborg [DK] 178 D2
Brattjær [N] 212 B4
Brattli [N] 224 D3
Brattsele [S] 206 C1
Brattset [N] 202 E2
Brattvåg [N] 202 C3
Bratunac [BIH] 146 C3
Bråtveit [N] 186 C1
Bratya Daskolovi [BG] 156 D2
Braubach [D] 56 F2
Braunau [A] 72 E2
Braunfels [D] 58 B1
Braunlage [D] 44 C3
Braunschweig [D] 44 C2
Braus, Col de– [F] 126 C3
Bravone [F] 130 B3
Bray / Bré [IRL] 10 F2
Bray–sur–Seine [F] 54 E4
Bray–sur–Somme [F] 54 E1
Brazatortas [E] 100 C3
Brazii [RO] 122 F2
Brbinj [HR] 144 C3
Brčko [BIH] 146 B2
Brdjani [SRB] 146 E3
Bré / Bray [IRL] 10 F2
Brebeni [RO] 148 E2
Brebina [RO] 148 F2
Brebu [RO] 122 F4
Brebu Nou [RO] 122 F4
Brécey [F] 52 F3
Brechin [GB] 18 E3
Brecht [B] 40 E3
Břeclav [CZ] 74 D2
Brecon [GB] 26 E1
Brécy [F] 68 C3
Bred [S] 190 C2
Breda [NL] 40 E2
Bredaryd [S] 184 C2
Bredbyn [S] 206 D2
Breddin [D] 32 E4
Bredebro [DK] 178 B3
Bredelar [D] 42 F3
Bredevad [DK] 178 B3
Bredland [N] 186 C3
Bredsel [S] 214 D1
Bredsjö [S] 188 F1
Bredsjön [S] 206 C3
Bredstedt [D] 178 B3
Bredsten [DK] 178 B2
Bredträsk [S] 206 D1
Bree [B] 40 F3
Breg [SLO] 120 B3
Bregana [HR] 120 C3
Breganze [I] 118 C3
Bregare [BG] 148 E3
Bregenz [A] 32 A3
Bregovo [BG] 148 C2
Bréhal [F] 52 F3
Brehna [D] 44 E3
Breidablik [N] 202 D4
Breidvik [N] 220 A2
Breil–sur–Roya [F] 126 C3
Brein [N] 192 C1
Breióborg [N] 186 C1
Breisach [D] 70 D2
Breisen [D] 44 F1
Breisjøberget [N] 194 D3
Breistein [N] 192 B3
Breitachklamm [D] 72 A4
Breite [CH] 70 E3
Breitenbrunn [D] 72 B2

Breitengussbach Hallstadt [D] 58 E3
Breitenhees [D] 32 C4
Breitungen [D] 58 D1
Breivik [N] 228 A2
Breivikbotn [N] 228 A2
Breivikeidet [N] 224 E2
Brekke [N] 192 B2
Brekken [N] 204 C3
Brekkhus [N] 192 B3
Brekkvassely [N] 212 D3
Brekovica [BIH] 144 D2
Brekstad [N] 202 F1
Bremen [D] 32 A3
Bremerhaven [D] 32 A3
Bremervörde [D] 32 B3
Bremke [D] 42 E3
Bremke [D] 42 E3
Bremnes [N] 224 B3
Bremsnes [N] 202 D2
Breń [PL] 34 E4
Brenes [E] 98 F4
Brenica [BG] 148 E3
Brenna [N] 204 C4
Brenna [N] 212 D2
Brennero, Passo del– / Brenner Pass [A/I] 118 C1
Brenner Pass / Brennero, Passo del– [A/I] 118 C1
Brennfjell [N] 224 E2
Brennsvik [N] 228 B2
Breno [I] 118 A3
Brénod [F] 80 E2
Brentwood [GB] 28 D3
Brenzone [I] 118 B3
Brescello [I] 128 B1
Bréscia [I] 116 F3
Bresdon [F] 78 C2
Breskens [NL] 40 D2
Bresles [F] 54 E2
Breslovec [BG] 148 F3
Bresnica [SRB] 146 E3
Bressanone / Brixen [I] 118 C2
Bressuire [F] 66 D3
Brest [BG] 148 F3
Brest [BY] 50 D2
Brest [F] 52 B3
Brestova [HR] 144 B1
Brestovac [HR] 120 E4
Brestovac [SRB] 148 B4
Brestovac [SRB] 148 B2
Brestovačka Banja [SRB] 148 B2
Brestovăţ [RO] 122 E3
Brestovik [SRB] 146 E2
Breteau [F] 68 C2
Bretenoux [F] 78 E4
Bretesche, Château de la– [F] 66 B2
Breteuil [F] 54 C3
Breteuil [F] 54 E2
Brétignolles–sur–Mer [F] 66 B3
Bretten [D] 58 B4
Breuberg [D] 58 C3
Breuil–Cervinia [I] 116 C3
Breukelen Ut [NL] 30 B3
Breuna [D] 42 F3
Brevens Bruk [S] 190 B3
Brevik [N] 186 E2
Brevik [S] 188 E4
Brevik [S] 190 E2
Breza [BIH] 146 B3
Breza [SK] 62 E4
Brezičani [BIH] 144 E2
Brežice [SLO] 120 C3
Brežiški Grad [SLO] 120 C3
Breznica [BG] 156 B3
Breznica [HR] 120 D3
Breznica Dak. [HR] 120 F4
Březnice [CZ] 60 D3
Breznik [BG] 154 F2

Brezno [SK] 76 B2
Brézolles [F] 54 C3
Brezová [SK] 74 E2
Brezovica [KS] 154 C3
Brezovica [SK] 64 B4
Brezovica [SLO] 120 A3
Brezovo [BG] 156 D1
Brezovo Polje [BIH] 146 C2
Brezovo Polje [HR] 144 D1
Briançon [F] 116 A4
Briare [F] 68 C2
Briatico [I] 138 D2
Bribir [HR] 144 D3
Bribirske Mostine [HR] 144 D3
Briceni [MD] 244 E2
Bricquebec [F] 52 E2
Bridgend [GB] 26 D2
Bridgnorth [GB] 22 F4
Bridgwater [GB] 26 E3
Bridlington [GB] 24 D2
Bridport [GB] 26 E3
Briec [F] 52 B3
Brie–Comte–Robert [F] 54 E3
Brielle [NL] 30 A4
Brienne–le–Château [F] 68 E1
Brienz [CH] 116 D1
Brienza [I] 134 E4
Brieskow–Finkenheerd [D] 46 C2
Brieves [E] 82 E2
Briey [F] 56 D3
Brig [CH] 116 C2
Brigg [GB] 24 D3
Brighouse [GB] 24 C2
Brighton [GB] 28 C4
Brignogan–Plage [F] 52 B2
Brignoles [F] 126 A3
Brignoud [F] 80 E3
Brihuega [E] 94 A3
Brijesta [HR] 152 C2
Brilon [D] 42 E3
Brimnes [N] 192 C3
Brinay [F] 68 B3
Brinches [P] 98 D3
Bríndisi [I] 136 E2
Brinje [HR] 144 C2
Brinkum [D] 32 A3
Brinon [F] 68 D3
Brintbodarna [S] 194 E3
Briones [E] 86 D4
Brione Verzasca [CH] 116 D2
Brionne [F] 54 C2
Brioude [F] 80 B3
Brioux–sur–Boutonne [F] 78 C1
Briouze [F] 54 A3
Brisighella [I] 128 D3
Brissac–Quincé [F] 66 D2
Brissago [CH] 116 D2
Bristol [GB] 26 E2
Bristvica [HR] 144 D4
Brive–la–Gaillarde [F] 78 E3
Briviesca [E] 86 D4
Brixen / Bressanone [I] 118 C2
Brixham [GB] 26 D4
Brixlegg [A] 72 D4
Brka [BIH] 146 B2
Brnaze [HR] 144 E4
Brněnec [CZ] 62 B3
Brno [CZ] 62 B4
Bro [S] 190 D2
Bro [S] 234 A2
Broadford [IRL] 10 C2
Broadstairs [GB] 28 E3
Broager [DK] 178 C3
Brobacken [S] 222 A2
Broby [S] 180 D1
Broby [S] 190 C3
Bročanac [HR] 144 E4
Broćeni [LV] 234 B3
Brock [D] 30 E4
Bröckel [D] 44 C1

Brockenhurst [GB] 26 F4
Brockhöfe [D] 32 C4
Brod [BIH] 146 B4
Brod [KS] 154 C3
Brodarevo [SRB] 152 F2
Brodarica [HR] 144 D4
Broddbo [S] 190 C1
Broddebo [S] 184 E1
Brode [SLO] 120 A3
Brodenbach [D] 56 F2
Broderup [DK] 178 B3
Brodestorf [D] 32 E2
Brodica [SRB] 148 B2
Brodick [GB] 18 B4
Brod na Kupi [HR] 120 B4
Brodnica [PL] 36 D3
Brodowe Łąka [PL] 38 A3
Brody [PL] 46 C3
Brody [PL] 46 D2
Brody [PL] 48 F4
Broglie [F] 54 B2
Brohl [D] 56 F1
Brojce [PL] 34 E2
Brok [PL] 38 B4
Brokind [S] 190 B4
Brolo [I] 138 B3
Bromarv [FIN] 198 D4
Brome [D] 44 D1
Bromma [N] 192 E3
Brommat [F] 80 A3
Bromölla [S] 180 D1
Brömsebro [S] 180 F1
Bromsgrove [GB] 26 F1
Bron [F] 80 D2
Brønderslev [DK] 182 D2
Broni [I] 116 E4
Bronice [PL] 46 D3
Bronikowo [PL] 34 F3
Bronisławów [PL] 48 E3
Bronken [N] 194 C3
Bronkow [D] 46 B3
Bronnbach [D] 58 C3
Brønnøysund [N] 212 D2
Brøns [DK] 178 B2
Bronte [I] 138 B4
Broons [F] 52 D3
Brørup [DK] 178 B2
Brösarp [S] 180 D2
Broshniv–Osada [UA] 64 F4
Brossac [F] 78 C3
Brossasco [I] 126 C2
Broşteni [RO] 148 C1
Brøstrud [N] 192 E3
Brötjemark [S] 184 C1
Broto [E] 88 C4
Broträsk [S] 214 D3
Brottby [S] 190 E2
Brøttem [N] 204 B2
Brotterode [D] 58 E1
Brøttum [N] 194 B2
Brou [F] 54 C4
Brouage [F] 78 B1
Brough [GB] 20 D4
Broughshane [NIR] 12 F2
Broughton in Furness [GB] 20 C4
Brouis, Col de– [F] 126 C3
Broumov [CZ] 62 B2
Brouvelieures [F] 70 C2
Brouwershaven [NL] 40 D2
Brovary [UA] 242 D4
Brovst [DK] 182 D2
Brownhills [GB] 22 F4
Brozas [E] 90 E3
Brseč [HR] 144 B1
Brtnice [CZ] 60 F4
Brua [N] 204 B4
Bruchhausen–Vilsen [D] 32 A4
Bruchhauser Steine [D] 42 E3
Bruchsal [D] 58 B4
Bruck [A] 118 D2

Brück [D] 44 F2
Bruck [D] 60 B4
Bruck an der
 Grossglocknerstrasse [A]
 72 E4
Bruck an der Leitha [A] 74 D3
Bruck an der Mur [A] 74 B4
Brückl [A] 120 B2
Brudzeń Duży [PL] 48 D1
Brudzewo [PL] 46 E2
Brüel [D] 32 E3
Bruère–Allichamps [F] 68 B3
Bruff [IRL] 10 C3
Bruflat [N] 192 F3
Bruges (Brugge) [B] 40 C3
Brugg [CH] 70 E3
Brugge (Druges) [B] 40 C3
Brugnato [I] 126 F2
Bruhagen [N] 202 D2
Brühl [D] 42 C4
Brújula, Puerto de la– [E]
 86 C4
Bruksvallarna [S] 204 D3
Brûlon [F] 54 A4
Brumath [F] 70 D1
Brummen [NL] 30 C4
Brumov Bylnice [CZ] 74 F1
Brumunddal [N] 194 B3
Brunau [S] 190 D1
Bruneck / Brunico [I] 118 C2
Brunehamel [F] 56 B2
Brunete [E] 92 E4
Brunflo [S] 204 F2
Brunheda [P] 84 C3
Brunico / Bruneck [I] 118 C2
Bruniquel [F] 88 F2
Brunkeberg [N] 186 D2
Brunlund [DK] 178 B3
Brunna [S] 190 D1
Brunnby [S] 178 F1
Brunnen [CH] 70 E4
Brunnsberg [S] 194 E2
Brunsbüttel [D] 32 B2
Brunskog [S] 188 D2
Brunssum [NL] 42 B3
Bruntál [CZ] 62 C3
Bruravik [N] 192 C3
Brus [SRB] 146 E4
Brusand [N] 186 A3
Brušane [HR] 144 C2
Brusarci [BG] 148 D3
Brusasco [I] 116 C4
Brúsio [CH] 116 F2
Bruška [HR] 144 C3
Brusnichnoye [RUS] 200 D2
Brusník [SK] 76 B2
Brussel / Bruxelles [B] 40 D3
Brüssow [D] 34 D3
Brusy [PL] 36 B2
Bruvno [HR] 144 D3
Bruvoll [N] 194 C3
Bruxelles / Brussel [B] 40 D3
Bruyères [F] 70 C2
Bruzaholm [S] 184 D2
Bruzzano Zeffirio [I] 138 D4
Brvenik [SRB] 154 C1
Brwinów [PL] 48 E2
Brydal [N] 204 B4
Bryggia [N] 202 B4
Bryne [N] 186 A3
Bryrup [DK] 178 C1
Brza Palanka [SRB] 148 C2
Brzeće [SRB] 148 A4
Brzeg [PL] 62 C1
Brzeg Dolny [PL] 46 F4
Brześć Kujawski [PL] 48 C1
Brzesko [PL] 64 B3
Brzeszcze [PL] 62 E3
Brzezie [PL] 36 B3
Brzezie [PL] 48 B3
Brzeziny [PL] 48 C3

Brzeziny [PL] 48 D3
Brzeźnica [PL] 62 F3
Brzeźnica [PL] 64 C2
Brzeźno [PL] 48 B2
Brzostek [PL] 64 C3
Brzoza [PL] 36 C4
Brzóza [PL] 48 F3
Brzozie Lubawskie [PL] 36 D3
Brzozów [PL] 64 D3
Bua [S] 184 A2
Buaile an Ghleanna /
 Bolinglanna [IRL] 12 A2
Buavåg [N] 186 A1
Buberget [S] 214 D3
Bubiai [LT] 238 C2
Bubry [F] 52 C4
Buca [TR] 170 B2
Buçaco [P] 84 A4
Bučany [SK] 74 E2
Buccheri [I] 140 E3
Bucchianico [I] 132 F3
Buchach [UA] 244 D2
Bucheben [A] 118 E1
Büchen [D] 32 C3
Buchen [D] 58 C3
Buchenwald [D] 44 D4
Buchholz [D] 32 C3
Buchin [RO] 122 F4
Buchin Prohod [BG] 148 D4
Buchloe [D] 72 B3
Buchlov [CZ] 74 E1
Büchold [D] 58 D2
Buchs [CH] 70 F4
Buchy [F] 54 D2
Bučin [MK] 160 D1
Búcine [I] 128 C4
Bučiste [MK] 154 E3
Bučje [SRB] 146 C4
Bučje [SRB] 148 C3
Bückeburg [D] 42 F2
Bücken [D] 32 B4
Buckfastleigh [GB] 26 C3
Buckie [GB] 14 F3
Buckingham [GB] 28 C2
Buckow [D] 46 C1
Bückwitz [D] 32 E4
Bučovice [CZ] 62 B4
Bucquoy [F] 40 B4
Bucsa [H] 76 D4
Bucşani [RO] 150 B1
Bucureşti [RO] 150 C1
Bucureşti [RO] 248 E3
Buczek [PL] 48 D3
Buczyna [PL] 64 E3
Bud [N] 202 D2
Buda [I] 128 D2
Budakeszi [H] 76 B4
Budakovo [MK] 160 D1
Budal [N] 204 B3
Budaörs [H] 76 B4
Budapest [H] 76 B4
Búðardalur [IS] 218 B2
Buddusò [I] 142 C3
Bude [GB] 26 C3
Budeč [CZ] 74 C1
Budeşti [RO] 150 C1
Budilovo [RUS] 232 E2
Budimci [HR] 122 A4
Budimić Japra [BIH] 144 E2
Budimir [HR] 144 E4
Büdingen [D] 58 C2
Budišičina [HR] 120 D3
Budišov nad Budišovkou
 [CZ] 62 C3
Budjevo [SRB] 154 B1
Budkovce [SK] 64 F2
Budmirici [MK] 160 D2
Budogoshch [RUS] 240 C1
Budoi [RO] 76 F4
Budomierz [PL] 64 E2
Budoni [I] 142 C3
Budowo [PL] 36 B2

Budožeļja [SRB] 146 D4
Budrio [I] 128 C2
Budrovci [HR] 146 B1
Budry [PL] 38 B1
Budva [MNE] 152 E3
Budynĕ nad Ohří [CZ] 60 D2
Budziszewice [PL] 48 E3
Budzyń [PL] 36 B4
Bue [N] 186 B3
Bue Marino, Grotta del– [I]
 142 C3
Bueña [E] 94 C4
Buen Amor, Castillo– [E] 84 E4
Buenavista del Norte [E]
 112 C2
Buëndia [E] 94 A4
Bufón de Arenillas [E] 86 B2
Buftea [RO] 150 B1
Bugac [H] 122 C2
Buğdayli [TR] 164 C1
Bugeat [F] 78 F3
Buggerru [I] 142 B5
Bugojno [BIH] 144 F3
Bugøyfjord [N] 228 E3
Bugøynes [N] 228 E3
Bugyi [H] 122 B1
Bühl [D] 70 E1
Buhuşi [RO] 244 E3
Builth Wells [GB] 22 D4
Buis–les–Baronnies [F] 124 E2
Buitenpost [NL] 30 D2
Buitrago [E] 92 F3
Buj [H] 76 E3
Bujalance [E] 104 E1
Bujanovac [SRB] 154 D2
Bujaraloz [E] 94 E3
Buje [HR] 118 E4
Bujoru [RO] 150 B2
Bük [H] 74 D4
Buk [PL] 34 D3
Buk [PL] 46 E2
Bükkábrány [H] 76 D3
Bükkösd [H] 120 F3
Bukonys [LT] 238 C3
Bukovi [SRB] 146 D3
Bukovice [CZ] 62 B3
Bukovo, Manastir– [SRB]
 148 C2
Bukowiec [PL] 46 E2
Bukowina Tatrzańska [PL]
 62 F4
Bukowo Morskie [PL] 34 F2
Bukowsko [PL] 64 D3
Buksnes [N] 224 B3
Bukta [N] 204 B1
Buktamo [N] 224 D3
Bülach [CH] 70 E3
Bulat–Pestivien [F] 52 C3
Buldan [TR] 170 D2
Bülgarene [BG] 148 F4
Bülgarene [BG] 150 A3
Bülgarevo [BG] 150 F2
Bülgarovo [BG] 150 E4
Bülgarska Polyana [BG]
 156 F2
Bülgarski Izvor [BG] 148 F4
Bulgnéville [F] 70 B2
Bulinac [HR] 120 E3
Bulinovac [SRB] 148 C3
Bulken [N] 192 C3
Bulkowo [PL] 48 E1
Bullarby [S] 188 C3
Bullas [E] 106 D2
Bulle [CH] 116 B1
Bullendorf [A] 74 D2
Bullmark [S] 214 D4
Bulqizë [AL] 154 B4
Bülstringen [D] 44 D2
Bultei [I] 142 C3
Buna [BIH] 152 D2
Bunclody [IRL] 10 E3

Buncrana [IRL] 12 E1
Bunde [D] 30 E2
Bünde [D] 30 F4
Bundoran [IRL] 12 C2
Bungay [GB] 28 F2
Bunge [S] 234 B2
Bunić [HR] 144 C2
Bunkris [S] 194 E2
Bunleix [F] 78 F2
Bunmahon [IRL] 10 D4
Bun na Abhna / Bunnahowen
 [IRL] 12 B2
Bunnahowen / Bun na Abhna
 [IRL] 12 B2
Bunnyconnellan [IRL] 12 B2
Buñol [E] 102 D3
Bunratty [IRL] 10 C2
Bunratty Castle [IRL] 10 C2
Buonalbergo [I] 134 D3
Buonconvento [I] 130 E1
Buonfornello [I] 138 A4
Buonvicino [I] 136 B4
Buoux, Fort de– [F] 124 E3
Bur [DK] 182 B3
Burano [I] 118 D4
Burbach [D] 42 E4
Burcei [I] 142 C5
Bureå [S] 214 B1
Bureå [S] 214 D3
Burela [E] 82 D1
Büren [CH] 70 D4
Büren [D] 42 E3
Burfjord [N] 224 F1
Burford [GB] 28 B2
Burg [D] 32 B2
Burg [D] 32 D1
Burg [D] 44 E3
Burg [D] 46 C3
Burgas [BG] 150 E4
Burgau [A] 120 D1
Burgau [D] 72 B2
Burgau [P] 98 A4
Burgbernheim [D] 58 D3
Burgdorf [CH] 70 D4
Burgdorf [D] 44 C1
Burgebrach [D] 58 E3
Bürgel [D] 44 E4
Bürgeln [D] 70 D3
Burgelu / Elburgo [E] 104 D3
Burghaun [D] 58 D1
Burghausen [D] 72 E3
Burg Hessenstein [D] 42 F4
Burgh–Haamstede [NL] 40 D2
Búrgio [I] 140 C2
Burgistein [CH] 116 C1
Burgjoss [D] 58 C2
Burg Klam [A] 74 B3
Burgkunstadt [D] 58 E2
Burglengenfeld [D] 60 A4
Burg Metternich [D] 56 F2
Burgoberbach [D] 58 D4
Burgos [E] 86 C4
Burgsinn [D] 58 D2
Burg Stargard [D] 34 C3
Burgsvik [S] 234 A3
Burguete / Auritz [E] 88 B3
Burgui / Burgi [E] 88 B3
Burguillos [E] 98 F4
Burguillos del Cerro [E] 98 C2
Burhan [TR] 164 F2
Burhaniye [TR] 164 B3
Burharkent [TR] 170 D2
Burie [F] 78 C2
Burila Mare [RO] 148 C2
Burlada [E] 86 F4
Burladingen [D] 70 F2
Burlo [D] 30 D4
Burnham–on–Crouch [GB]
 28 E3
Burnham–on–Sea [GB] 26 E2
Burnley [GB] 24 B2
Burón [E] 86 B2

Buron, Château de– [F] 80 B2
Buronzo [I] 116 D3
Burravoe [GB] 16 F3
Burrel [AL] 154 B4
Burriana / Borriana [E] 102 E3
Burs [S] 234 A3
Burs [S] 234 A2
Bursa [TR] 164 E1
Burseryd [S] 184 B2
Bürstadt [D] 58 B3
Burtenbach [D] 72 B2
Burton upon Trent [GB] 24 B4
Burträsk [S] 214 D3
Burvik [S] 214 E3
Burwell [GB] 28 D2
Bury [GB] 22 F2
Buryn′ [UA] 242 E3
Bury St Edmunds [GB] 28 E2
Burzenin [PL] 48 C3
Burziya [BG] 148 D4
Busalla [I] 126 E2
Busana [I] 128 B2
Busca [I] 126 C2
Busdorf [D] 32 B1
Buseto Palizzolo [I] 140 B2
Buševec [HR] 120 C4
Bushat [AL] 152 F4
Bushmills [NIR] 12 F1
Bushtricë [AL] 154 B3
Bus′k [UA] 244 C1
Busko–Zdrój [PL] 64 B2
Bušno [PL] 50 D4
Busot [E] 106 F2
Busovača [BIH] 146 A3
Bussang [F] 70 C2
Bussang, Col de– [F] 70 C2
Busseto [I] 128 B1
Bussolengo [I] 118 B4
Bussoleno [I] 116 B4
Bussum [NL] 30 B3
Bustnes [N] 218 F4
Busto Arsízio [I] 116 D3
Busto Garolfo [I] 116 D3
Büsum [D] 32 B2
Butan [BG] 148 E3
Buteni [RO] 122 F2
Butenky [UA] 242 F4
Butera [I] 140 D3
Bütgenbach [B] 56 D1
Buthrotum [AL] 160 B4
Butler′s Bridge [IRL] 12 D3
Butrint [AL] 160 B4
Butryny [PL] 36 F3
Butsyn [UA] 50 E3
Buttapietra [I] 118 B4
Buttelstedt [D] 44 D4
Buttevant [IRL] 10 C3
Buttingsrud [N] 192 F3
Buttlar [D] 58 D1
Buttle [S] 234 A2
Buttstädt [D] 44 D4
Butzbach [D] 58 B2
Bützow [D] 32 E2
Buvarp [N] 212 C4
Buvika [N] 204 B2
Buvika [N] 204 C4
Buxtehude [D] 32 B3
Buxton [GB] 24 B3
Buxu, Cueva del– [E] 86 B2
Buxy [F] 68 E4
Büyükada [TR] 158 E3
Büyükbelen [TR] 164 D4
Büyükçekmece [TR] 158 D3
Büyükkaraağaç [TR] 176 C1
Büyükkarıştıran [TR] 158 C3
Büyükkonak [TR] 170 E3
Büyükkonuk (Komi Kebir)
 [CY] 176 E3
Büyükorhan [TR] 164 E2
Büyüksöğle [TR] 176 F1
Büyükyenice [TR] 164 C3
Buyükyoncalı [TR] 158 C3

Buz [AL] 160 B3
Buzançais [F] 68 A3
Buzancy [F] 56 C3
Buzău [RO] 248 E3
Buzescu [RO] 150 A2
Buzet [HR] 118 F4
Buziaş [RO] 122 E3
Buzyakovtsi [BG] 156 C1
By [S] 188 D1
By [S] 196 C4
Byahoml' [BY] 242 B1
Byala [BG] 150 B3
Byala [BG] 150 B3
Byala Slatina [BG] 148 E3
Byal Izvor [BG] 156 D3
Byaroza [BY] 38 E4
Byarozawka [BY] 38 F2
Byarum [S] 184 C2
Byberget [S] 204 F3
Bybjerg [DK] 178 E2
Bychawa [PL] 50 C4
Byczki [PL] 48 E3
Byczyna [PL] 48 C4
Bydgoszcz [PL] 36 C4
Bye [S] 204 F2
Bye [S] 206 C3
Byelaazyorsk [BY] 38 F4
Byelitsa [BY] 38 E2
Byenyakoni [BY] 38 E1
Byershty [BY] 38 D2
Bygdeå [S] 214 D4
Bygdin [N] 192 E2
Bygdsiljum [S] 214 D3
Bygland [N] 186 B3
Byglandsfjord [N] 186 D3
Bygstad [N] 192 B1
Bykle [N] 186 C2
Byllis [AL] 160 B3
Byrkjedal [N] 186 B3
Byrkjelo [N] 192 C1
Byrknes [N] 192 A2
Byrness [GB] 20 E2
Byrum [DK] 182 E2
Byrum [S] 184 F2
Byšice [CZ] 60 E2
Byske [S] 214 D2
Bystré [CZ] 62 B3
Bystřianska Jaskyňa [SK]
   76 B2
Bystřice [CZ] 60 E3
Bystřice nad Pernštejnem
   [CZ] 62 B4
Bystřice pod Hostýnem [CZ]
   62 C4
Bystřička [CZ] 62 D4
Bystrzyca Kłodzka [PL] 62 B2
Byszki [PL] 36 A3
Byszyno [PL] 34 F2
Bytča [SK] 62 D4
Bytnica [PL] 46 D2
Bytom [PL] 62 E2
Bytom Odrzański [PL] 46 E3
Bytonia [PL] 36 C2
Bytów [PL] 36 B2
Bytsyen' [BY] 38 F3
Byvattnet [S] 206 C2
Byxelkrok [S] 184 F2
Bzenec [CZ] 74 E1
Bzovík [SK] 76 B2

C

Caaveiro, Monasterio de– [E]
   82 C2
Cabação [P] 90 C3
Cabaço [E] 90 C2
Cabaj–Čápor [SK] 74 F3

Cabañaquinta [E] 82 F3
Cabañas [E] 82 C1
Cabanes [E] 102 E2
Čabar [HR] 120 R4
Cabeço de Vide [P] 90 D3
Cabertarar [TR] 170 D2
Căbeşti [RO] 122 F2
Cabeza del Buey [E] 100 B3
Cabezamesada [E] 100 F2
Cabezarados [E] 100 D3
Cabezarrubias del Puerto [E]
   100 D3
Cabezas Rubias [E] 98 D3
Cabezo de Torres [E] 106 E2
Cabezón de la Sal [E] 86 C2
Cabezuela del Valle [E] 92 B3
Cabo de Gata [E] 106 C4
Cabo de Palos [E] 106 E3
Cabourg [F] 54 B2
Cabra [E] 104 E2
Cabra del Santo Cristo [E]
   106 A2
Cabranes [E] 86 A2
Cábras [I] 142 B4
Cabreiros [E] 82 C2
Cabrela [P] 90 B4
Cabrera [E] 108 D4
Cabrerets [F] 88 F1
Cabrillas [E] 84 D4
Cacabelos [E] 82 D3
Čačak [SRB] 146 D3
Cáccamo [I] 140 C2
Cacemes [P] 90 A3
Cáceres [E] 90 F3
Čachtice [CZ] 60 E2
Cachopo [P] 98 C4
Čachtice [SK] 74 F2
Čačini [HR] 120 F4
Cadaqués [E] 96 F2
Cadaval [P] 90 B3
Cadavedo [E] 82 E2
Čaďavica [BIH] 144 E2
Čaďavica [HR] 120 F3
Čadca [SK] 62 E4
Cadelbosco di Sopra [I]
   128 B2
Cadenábbia [I] 116 E3
Cadenberge [D] 32 B2
Cadenet [F] 124 E3
Cadeuil [F] 78 B2
Cadí, Túnel de– [E] 96 D2
Cádiar [E] 106 A3
Cadillac [F] 78 C4
Cadipietra [I] 118 D1
Cádiz [E] 104 B3
Cadrete [E] 94 D3
Caen [F] 54 B2
Caernarfon [GB] 22 D2
Caerphilly [GB] 26 E2
Čafasan [MK] 160 C2
Çağış [TR] 164 D2
Cagli [I] 128 E4
Cágliari [I] 142 C5
Çağman [TR] 176 F1
Cagnano Varano [I] 134 E2
Cagnes–sur–Mer [F] 126 C3
Caherdaniel / Cathair Dónall
   [IRL] 10 A3
Cahermurphy [IRL] 10 C2
Cahersiveen [IRL] 10 A3
Cahir [IRL] 10 D3
Cahors [F] 88 F1
Cahul [MD] 244 F4
Caiazzo [I] 134 C3
Cairnryan [GB] 20 B2
Cairo Montenotte [I] 126 D2
Cais do Pico [P] 110 B3
Caister-on-Sea [GB] 28 F1
Caivano [I] 134 C3
Čajetina [SRB] 146 D4
Čajniče [BIH] 146 C4
Čakajovce [SK] 74 F2

Çakallar [TR] 164 C2
Çakılı [TR] 158 C2
Çakır [TR] 164 C2
Çakırbeyli [TR] 170 C3
Çakırlı [TR] 164 B1
Çakmak [TR] 170 D4
Čakovec [HR] 120 D2
Çal [TR] 170 E2
Cala [E] 98 E3
Cala Blanca [E] 108 E3
Cala Blava [E] 108 D3
Calabor [E] 84 D2
Calabritto [I] 134 E3
Calaceite [E] 94 F4
Calacuccia [F] 130 B2
Cala d'Oliva [I] 142 B2
Cala d'Or [E] 108 D4
Calaf [E] 96 C2
Calafat [E] 96 B4
Calafat [RO] 148 D2
Calafell [E] 96 C3
Cala Galdana [E] 108 E3
Cala Gonone [I] 142 C3
Calahonda–Chaparral [E]
   104 D3
Calahonda–Chaparral [E]
   104 F3
Calahorra [E] 94 C1
Calais [F] 28 F4
Cala Liberotto [I] 142 D3
Cala Mesquida [E] 108 E3
Cala Millor [E] 108 D3
Calamocha [E] 94 C4
Calamonte [E] 98 F2
Cala Moreia–Cala Morlanda
   [E] 108 D3
Cala Morell [E] 108 E3
Calañas [E] 98 D3
Calanda [E] 94 E4
Calangiánus [I] 142 C2
Cala'n Porter [E] 108 F3
Cala Pi [E] 108 D4
Călăraşi [RO] 150 D1
Cala Ratjada [E] 108 E3
cala Sa Calobra [E] 108 D3
Cala Santanyí [E] 108 D4
Calascibetta [I] 140 D2
Calasetta [I] 142 A5
Calasparra [E] 106 D2
Calatafimi [I] 140 B2
Calatañazor [E] 94 B2
Cala Tarida [E] 108 E2
Calatayud [E] 94 C3
Calatorao [E] 94 D3
Calatrava, Convento de– [E]
   100 D3
Calatrava la Vieja [E] 100 D3
Calau [D] 46 C3
Cala Vadella [E] 108 E2
Calbe [D] 44 E2
Çalca [TR] 170 F1
Caldarola [I] 132 D2
Caldas da Rainha [P] 90 B2
Caldas de Monchique [E]
   98 B3
Caldas de Reis [E] 82 B3
Caldas de Vizela [P] 84 B2
Caldelas [P] 82 B4
Caldes de Boi [E] 88 D4
Caldes de Malavella [E] 96 E3
Caldes de Montbui [E] 96 D3
Caldes d'Estrac [E] 96 E3
Caldirola [I] 126 F2
Calella [E] 96 E3
Calella de Palafrugell [E] 96 F3
Calenzana [F] 130 A2
Calera y Chozas [E] 100 C1
Caleruega [E] 92 F2
Cales de Mallorca [E] 108 D4
Calheta [P] 110 B3
Calheta [P] 110 D3
Çali [TR] 164 E1

Càlig [E] 96 A4
Calignac [F] 88 D1
Çalıklı [TR] 164 E4
Călimăneşti [RO] 248 D3
Calimera [I] 136 F3
Calitri [I] 134 E3
Calízzano [I] 126 D2
Callac [F] 52 C3
Callan [IRL] 10 D3
Callander [GB] 18 C3
Callington [GB] 26 C3
Callosa d'en Sarrià [E] 108 C2
Callosa de Segura [E] 106 E2
Calma [SRB] 146 C1
Călmăţuiu [RO] 148 F2
Calne [GB] 26 F2
Calolziocorte [I] 116 E3
Calonge [E] 96 E3
Calp / Calpe [E] 108 C2
Calpe / Calp [E] 108 C2
Caltabellotta [I] 140 C2
Caltagirone [I] 140 D3
Caltanissetta [I] 140 D3
Caltavuturo [I] 138 A4
Çaltepe [TR] 170 F3
Çaltılıbük [TR] 164 D2
Caltra [IRL] 10 D1
Călugăreni [RO] 150 B2
Calui [RO] 148 E1
Caluso [I] 116 C4
Calvello [I] 134 F4
Calvi [F] 130 A2
Calvià [E] 108 C3
Calvörde [D] 44 D2
Calw [D] 70 F1
Calzadilla de la Cueza [E]
   86 B4
Camacha [P] 110 F3
Camaiore [I] 128 B3
Camaldoli [I] 128 D3
Camaldoli, Eremo di– [I]
   128 D3
Çamaltı [TR] 170 A2
Camarasa [E] 96 B2
Camarena de la Sierra [E]
   102 D2
Camarès [F] 124 B2
Camaret-sur-Mer [F] 52 A3
Camarillas [E] 102 D1
Camariñas [E] 82 A2
Camarzana de Tera [E] 84 E2
Camas [E] 98 E4
Cambados [E] 82 B3
Cambeo [E] 82 C3
Camberg [D] 58 B2
Camberley [GB] 28 C3
Cambo–les–Bains [F] 88 B2
Camborne [GB] 26 B3
Cambrai [F] 54 F1
Cambre [E] 82 C2
Cambremer [F] 54 B2
Cambridge [GB] 28 D2
Cambrils [E] 96 B3
Camburg [D] 44 D4
Çamdere [TR] 164 F4
Camelford [GB] 26 B3
Çameli [TR] 170 E4
Camenca [MD] 244 F2
Camerino [I] 132 D2
Çamiçi [TR] 170 C3
Camigliatello [I] 138 E1
Camin [D] 32 D3
Caminha [P] 82 A4
Caminomorisco [E] 92 B3
Caminreal [E] 94 C4
Çamköy [TR] 170 C4
Çamlıbel (Mýrtou) [CY]
   176 D3

Campagna [I] 134 D4
Campagnático [I] 130 E2
Campan [F] 88 D3
Campana [I] 138 E1
Campanario [F] 100 B2
Campanas / Kanpaneta
   [E] 86 F4
Campanet, Coves de– [E]
   108 D3
Campaspero [E] 92 E2
Campbeltown [GB] 18 B4
Câmpeni [RO] 244 C4
Câmpia Turzii [RO] 244 C4
Campi Bisenzio [I] 128 C6
Campiglia Marittima [I] 130 D1
Campiglia Soana [I] 116 C3
Campillo de Altobuey [E]
   102 B2
Campillo de Arenas [E] 104 F2
Campillo de Llerena [E]
   100 A3
Campillos [E] 104 D2
Câmpina [RO] 248 E3
Campione d'Italia [I] 116 E3
Campisábalos [E] 94 A3
Campi Salentina [I] 136 E3
Campo [E] 96 B1
Campo [P] 98 D2
Campobasso [I] 134 D2
Campobecerros [E] 82 C4
Campobello di Licata [I]
   140 D3
Campobello di Mazara [I]
   140 B2
Campocologno [CH] 116 F2
Campo Coy [E] 106 D2
Campodarsego [I] 118 C4
Campo de Caso / Caso
   [E] 86 A2
Campo de Criptana [E] 100 F2
Campofelice di Fitalia [I]
   140 C2
Campofilone [I] 132 E2
Campofiorito [I] 140 C2
Campoformido [I] 118 E3
Campogalliano [I] 128 C2
Campohermoso [E] 106 C4
Campo Lameiro / A Lagoa
   [E] 82 B3
Campo Ligure [I] 126 C2
Campo Maior [P] 90 E4
Campomanes [E] 82 F3
Campomarino [I] 134 D1
Campomarino [I] 136 E3
Camponaraya [E] 82 D3
Campora San Giovanni [I]
   138 D2
Campo Real [E] 92 F4
Camporeale [I] 140 B2
Camporrobles [E] 102 C3
Campos [E] 108 D4
Camposampiero [I] 118 C4
Camposanto [I] 128 C2
Campotéjar [E] 104 F2
Campo Túres / Sand in Taufers
   [I] 118 C1
Camprodón [E] 96 E2
Câmpulung [RO] 248 D3
Câmpulung Moldovenesc
   [RO] 244 D3
Câmpu Mare [RO] 148 C1
Çamyayla [TR] 170 D3
Çamyuva [TR] 164 F3
Camyuva [TR] 176 F1
Çan [TR] 164 B2
Cañada de Benatanduz [E]
   102 D1
Cañadajuncosa [E] 102 B2
Cañaíca del Calar [E] 106 C2
Čanak [HR] 144 C2
Çanakçı [TR] 164 E3
Çanakkale [TR] 164 A2

Canale [I] 126 D1
Canales de Molina [E] 94 C4
Canal S. Bovo [I] 118 C3
Canaples [F] 40 B4
Canas de Senhorim [P] 84 B4
Cañaveral [E] 90 F3
Cañaveral de León [E] 98 E3
Cañaveras [E] 102 B1
Canazei [I] 118 C2
Cancale [F] 52 E3
Cancon [F] 78 D4
Candamo [E] 82 F2
Candamo, Cueva de– [E] 82 F2
Candanchú [E] 88 B3
Çandarlı [TR] 158 F4
Çandarlı [TR] 164 B4
Candás [E] 82 F2
Candasnos [E] 94 F3
Candé [F] 66 D2
Candela [I] 134 E3
Candelária [P] 110 A3
Candelario [E] 92 B3
Candeleda [E] 92 C4
Candia Lomellina [I] 116 D4
Çandır [TR] 176 C1
Canelli [I] 126 D1
Canelobre, Cueva de– [E] 106 F2
Canero [E] 82 E2
Canet [F] 124 C3
Canet de Mar [E] 96 E3
Cañete [E] 102 C2
Cañete la Real [E] 104 D2
Canet–Plage [F] 96 F1
Canfranc [E] 88 B3
Cangas [E] 82 A3
Cangas [E] 82 D1
Cangas del Narcea [E] 82 E3
Cangas de Onís [E] 86 B2
Canha [P] 90 B4
Caniçada [P] 84 B2
Canicatti [I] 140 C3
Canicattini Bagni [I] 140 E3
Caniles [E] 106 B3
Canillas del Aceituno [E] 104 E3
Canino [I] 130 E2
Cañizal [E] 84 F4
Cañizares [E] 94 B4
Canjáyar [E] 106 B3
Canlia [RO] 150 D1
Cannai [I] 142 B5
Cannara [I] 132 C2
Canne [I] 134 F3
Cánnero Riviera [I] 116 D2
Cannes [F] 126 B3
Canneto [I] 130 D1
Canneto sull'Óglio [I] 118 A4
Cannich [GB] 14 D3
Cannigione [I] 142 C2
Cannóbio [I] 116 D2
Cannock [GB] 22 F4
Canolo [I] 138 D3
Canosa di Púglia [I] 134 F3
Canossa [I] 128 B2
Canossa, Castello di– [I] 128 B2
Can Pastilla [E] 108 C3
Can Picafort [E] 108 D3
Cansano [I] 132 E4
Cantalapiedra [E] 84 F4
Cantalejo [E] 92 E2
Cantalpino [E] 84 F4
Cantanhede [P] 84 A4
Cantavieja [E] 90 E1
Çantavir [SRB] 122 C3
Canterbury [GB] 28 E3
Cantillana [E] 98 F4
Cantoral de la Peña [E] 86 B3
Cantoria [E] 106 C3
Cantù [I] 116 E3

Canvey Island [GB] 28 D3
Cany–Barville [F] 54 C1
Canyet de Mar [E] 96 E3
Canyon [N] 226 B1
Caoria [I] 118 C3
Cáorle [I] 118 D4
Caorso [I] 128 A1
Capaccio [I] 134 D4
Capaci [I] 140 C1
Capalbio [I] 130 E2
Capannoli [I] 128 B4
Caparde [BIH] 146 C3
Caparra, Ruinas de– [E] 92 B3
Caparroso [E] 94 D1
Capbreton [F] 88 B2
Cap–d'Ail [F] 126 C3
Capdella [E] 96 C1
Cap d'en Font [E] 108 F3
Capdepera [E] 108 E3
Capelas [P] 110 E1
Capellades [E] 96 C3
Capendu [F] 124 B3
Capens [F] 88 E3
Capestang [F] 124 B3
Capestrano [I] 132 E3
Cap Ferret [F] 78 A3
Capinha [P] 90 E2
Capistrello [I] 132 D4
Capizzi [I] 138 B4
Čapljina [BIH] 152 C2
Capmany [F] 96 E2
Capo Cavallo [F] 130 A2
Capodimonte [I] 130 F2
Capo di Ponte [I] 118 A3
Capodiponte [I] 128 B3
Capo d'Orlando [I] 138 B3
Capoferrato [I] 142 C5
Capolíveri [I] 130 C2
Capo Rizzuto [I] 138 F2
Caposile [I] 118 D4
Capoterra [I] 142 D5
Cappamore [IRL] 10 C3
Cappenberg [D] 42 D2
Cappoquin [IRL] 10 D4
Capracotta [I] 132 F4
Capráia [I] 130 C1
Capranica [I] 130 F3
Capri [I] 134 C4
Capriati a Volturno [I] 134 C2
Capriccioli [I] 142 C2
Căpruța [RO] 122 F3
Captieux [F] 88 C1
Capua [I] 134 C3
Capurso [I] 136 D2
Čara [HR] 152 B2
Caracal [RO] 148 E2
Caracenilla [E] 102 A1
Caracovo [BG] 156 D2
Caracuel de Calatrava [E] 100 D3
Caraglio [I] 126 C2
Čarakovo [BIH] 144 E2
Caraman [F] 88 F3
Caramulo [P] 84 B3
Cărand [RO] 122 F2
Caranga [E] 82 F3
Caransebeș [RO] 122 F4
Carantec [F] 52 B2
Car Asen [BG] 150 C3
Carassai [I] 132 E2
Caraula [RO] 148 D2
Caravaca [E] 106 D2
Caravaggio [I] 116 E4
Carbajales de Alba [E] 84 E3
Carbajo [E] 90 E3
Carballo [E] 82 B2
Carbon–Blanc [F] 78 B3
Carboneras [E] 106 C4
Carboneras de Guadazaón [E] 102 B2

Carbónia [I] 142 B5
Carbonin / Schluderbach [I] 118 D2
Carbonne [F] 88 E3
Cârbunari [RO] 146 F2
Carcaboso [E] 92 B3
Carcabuey [E] 104 E2
Carcaixent [E] 102 D4
Carcans [F] 78 B3
Carcans–Plage [F] 78 B3
Carcar [E] 94 C1
Carcare [I] 126 D2
Carcassonne [F] 124 A3
Carcastillo [E] 88 A4
Carcavelo [P] 90 A3
Carcelén [E] 102 C3
Carceri, Eremo delle– [I] 132 D2
Carcès [F] 126 A3
Carcoforo [I] 116 C3
Çardak [TR] 164 B1
Çardak [TR] 164 F4
Çardak [TR] 170 F2
Çardaklı [TR] 170 D3
Cardedeu [I] 96 D3
Cardejón [E] 94 C2
Cardelleda de Valdeorras [E] 82 D4
Cardeña [E] 100 C4
Cardenete [E] 102 B2
Cardiff [GB] 26 E2
Cardigan [GB] 22 C4
Cardito [I] 134 C2
Cardona [I] 96 D2
Carei [RO] 76 F3
Carene [TR] 164 B3
Carennac [F] 78 E4
Carentan [F] 52 F2
Carevac [BIH] 144 E3
Carev Dvor [MK] 160 C2
Carezza al Lago / Karersee [I] 118 C2
Cargèse [F] 130 A3
Carhaix–Plouguer [F] 52 C3
Caria [P] 90 E2
Cariati [I] 138 F1
Cariçin Grad [SRB] 148 B4
Cariçino [BG] 150 E2
Carignan [F] 56 C2
Carignano [I] 126 D1
Cariñena [E] 94 D3
Cariño [E] 82 C1
Carinola [I] 134 C3
Carlantino [I] 134 D2
Carlentini [I] 140 E3
Carlet [E] 102 D4
Carling [F] 56 D4
Carlingford [IRL] 12 E3
Carlisle [GB] 20 D3
Carloforte [I] 142 A5
Carlow [D] 32 D2
Carlow / Ceatharlach [IRL] 10 E3
Carlton [GB] 24 C2
Carmagnola [I] 126 D1
Carmarthen [GB] 26 C1
Carmaux [F] 124 A2
Cármenes [E] 82 F3
Carmona [E] 104 C1
Carnac [F] 66 A1
Carndonagh [IRL] 12 E1
Carnew [IRL] 10 E3
Carnia [I] 118 E2
Carnlough [NIR] 12 F2
Carnota [E] 82 A2
Carnoustie [GB] 18 E3
Caro [F] 52 D4
Carolei [I] 138 D2
Carolinensiel [D] 30 F1
Carona [I] 116 F3
Caronía [I] 138 B4
Casa Branca [P] 90 C4
Casa Branca [P] 90 C4

Carpaneto Piacentino [I] 128 A1
Carpegna [I] 128 D3
Carpenédolo [I] 118 A4
Carpentras [F] 124 E2
Carpi [I] 128 C2
Carpignano Sesia [I] 116 D3
Carpineti [I] 128 B2
Carpineto Romano [I] 134 B2
Cârpiniș [RO] 122 D3
Carpino [I] 134 F2
Carpinone [I] 134 C2
Carpio [E] 84 F4
Carquefou [F] 66 C2
Carqueiranne [F] 124 F4
Carralg Airt / Carrickart [IRL] 12 D1
Carral [E] 82 C2
Carranza / Karrantza [E] 86 D3
Carrapateira [P] 98 A3
Carrara [I] 128 A3
Carraroe / An Cheathrú Rua [IRL] 10 C1
Carrascalejo [E] 100 C1
Carrascosa del Campo [E] 102 A1
Carrazeda de Ansiães [P] 84 C3
Carrazedo [P] 84 C2
Carrbridge [GB] 14 E4
Carregado [P] 90 B3
Carregal do Sal [P] 84 B4
Carrega Ligure [I] 126 F2
Carregueiro [P] 98 C3
Carrick / An Charraig [IRL] 12 C1
Carrickart / Carraig Airt [IRL] 12 D1
Carrickfergus [NIR] 12 F2
Carrickmacross [IRL] 10 F1
Carrick–on–Shannon [IRL] 12 C3
Carrick–on–Suir [IRL] 10 D3
Carriço [P] 90 C2
Carrigaline [IRL] 10 C4
Carrigallen [IRL] 12 D3
Carriganimmy [IRL] 10 B3
Carrigans [IRL] 12 D1
Carrión de Calatrava [E] 100 D3
Carrión de los Condes [E] 86 B4
Carrizo [E] 82 E4
Carrizosas [E] 100 E3
Carro [F] 124 E3
Carros [F] 126 C3
Carrouges [F] 54 B3
Carrowkeel [IRL] 12 E1
Carrù [I] 126 D2
Carryduff [NIR] 12 F2
Carry–le–Rouet [F] 124 E3
Çarshovë [AL] 160 C3
Carsoli [I] 132 D3
Carsulae [I] 132 C3
Cartagena [E] 106 E3
Cártama [E] 104 D3
Cartaxo [P] 90 B3
Cartaya [E] 98 D4
Cartelle [E] 82 B3
Carteret [F] 52 E2
Cartoixa de Porta Coeli [E] 102 D3
Cartoixa d'Escaldei [E] 96 B3
Cartuja de Aula Dei [E] 94 E3
Carviçais [P] 84 D3
Carvin [F] 40 C4
Carvoeiro [P] 98 B4
Carwitz [D] 34 C3
Casabermeja [E] 104 D3
Casabona [I] 138 F2
Casa Branca [P] 90 C4

Casa Branca [P] 98 B2
Casacalenda [I] 134 D2
Casáccia [CH] 116 F2
Casaholc [H] 76 F3
Casalabate [I] 136 E3
Casalarreina [E] 86 D4
Casalbordino [I] 132 F3
Casal Borsetti [I] 128 D2
Casalbuono [I] 136 B3
Casalciprano [I] 134 D2
Casale [I] 140 B2
Casalecchio di Reno [I] 128 C2
Casale Monferrato [I] 116 D4
Casalmaggiore [I] 128 B1
Casalpusterlengo [I] 116 F4
Casal Velino [I] 136 A3
Casamáina [I] 132 E3
Casamari, Abbazia di– [I] 134 B2
Casamássima [I] 136 D2
Casamicciola Terme [I] 134 C3
Casamozza [F] 130 B2
Casarabonela [E] 104 D3
Casarano [I] 136 F3
Casar de Cáceres [E] 90 F3
Casar de las Hurdes [E] 92 B3
Casares [E] 104 C3
Casares, Cueva de los– [E] 94 B3
Casariche [E] 104 D2
Casarubios del Monte [E] 92 E4
Casas Cueva [E] 106 A2
Casas de Benitez [E] 102 C3
Casas de Don Pedro [E] 100 B2
Casas de Fernando Alonso [E] 102 A3
Casas de Jorós [E] 114 D3
Casas de Juan Núñez [E] 102 B3
Casas del Puerto [E] 106 E1
Casas de Reina [E] 98 F3
Casas–Ibáñez [E] 102 C3
Casatejada [E] 92 B4
Cascais [P] 90 A3
Cascante [E] 94 C2
Cascia [I] 132 D2
Casciana Terme [I] 128 B4
Cáscina [I] 128 B3
Căscioarele [RO] 150 C2
Casekow [D] 34 D4
Caselle [I] 116 C4
Caserta [I] 134 C3
Cashel [IRL] 10 D3
Cashel, Rock of– [IRL] 10 D3
Casillas del Ángel [E] 114 E3
Casina [I] 128 B2
Casinina [I] 128 E3
Casino di Terra [I] 128 B4
Casinos [E] 102 D3
Čáslav [CZ] 60 E3
Caso / Campo de Caso [E] 86 A2
Casola Valsenio [I] 128 D3
Casoli [I] 132 F4
Casoria [I] 134 C3
Caspe [E] 94 E4
Cassà de la Selva [E] 96 E2
Cassagnes–Bégonhès [F] 124 B1
Cassano allo Ionio [I] 136 C4
Cassano d'Adda [I] 116 E3
Cassano delle Murge [I] 136 C2
Cassel [F] 40 B3
Cassibile [I] 140 E3
Cassine [I] 126 E1
Cassino [I] 134 C2
Cassis [F] 124 E4
Cassuéjouls [F] 80 A4

Castagneto Carducci [I] 130 D1
Castalla [E] 106 F1
Castañar de Ibor [E] 100 B1
Castanet-Tolosan [F] 88 E3
Castanheira de Pera [P] 90 D2
Castasegna [CH] 116 E2
Casteu [B] 40 D4
Casteggio [I] 126 F1
Castejón de Monegros [E] 94 E3
Castejón de Sos [E] 88 D4
Castejón de Valdejasa [E] 94 D2
Castel Bolognese [I] 128 D3
Castelbouc [F] 124 C1
Castelbuono [I] 138 A4
Casteldelfino [I] 126 C1
Castel del Piano [I] 130 E2
Castel del Rio [I] 128 C3
Castel di Sangro [I] 132 E4
Castel di Tora [I] 132 D3
Castel Doria, Terme di– [I] 142 C2
Castelejo [P] 98 A3
Castelfidardo [I] 128 F4
Castelfiorentino [I] 128 C4
Castelflorite [E] 94 F3
Castelfranco Emilia [I] 128 C2
Castelfranco in Miscano [I] 134 D3
Castelfranco Véneto [I] 118 C3
Castel Goffredo [I] 118 A4
Casteljaloux [F] 88 D1
Castellabate [I] 136 A3
Castellammare del Golfo [I] 140 B2
Castellammare di Stábia [I] 134 D4
Castelamonte [I] 116 C3
Castellana, Grotte di– [I] 136 D2
Castellana Grotte [I] 136 D2
Castellana Sícula [I] 138 A4
Castellane [F] 126 B3
Castellaneta [I] 136 D2
Castellar [E] 106 B1
Castellar de la Frontera [E] 104 C3
Castellar de la Muela [E] 94 C4
Castellar de Santiago [E] 100 E4
Castell'Arquato [I] 128 A1
Castell'Azzara [I] 130 E2
Castellazzo Bormida [I] 126 E1
Castelldans [E] 96 B3
Castell d'aro [E] 96 E3
Castell de Cabres [E] 96 A4
Castelldefels [E] 96 D3
Castel de Ferro [E] 104 F3
Castell de Mur / Cellers [E] 96 C2
Castelleone [I] 116 E4
Castelletto d'Orba [E] 126 E2
Castellfollit de la Roca [E] 96 E2
Castellina in Chianti [I] 128 C4
Castelló de la Plana / Castellón de la Plana [E] 102 E2
Castelló de la Ribera [E] 102 E4
Castelló d'Empúries [E] 96 F2
Castellón de la Plana / Castelló de la Plana [E] 102 E2
Castellote [E] 102 E1
Castello Tesino [I] 118 C3
Castellterçol [E] 96 D3
Castellúccio dei Sáuri [I] 134 E3
Castelluccio Sup. [I] 136 B3
Castelluzzo [I] 140 B1

Castelmagno [I] 126 C2
Castelmassa [I] 128 C1
Castelmauro [I] 134 D2
Castelmoron [F] 88 D1
Castelnau [F] 78 E4
Castelnaudary [F] 88 F3
Castelnau–de–Médoc [F] 78 B3
Castelnau-de–Montmiral [F] 88 F2
Castelnau d'Estretefonds [F] 88 E2
Castelnau-Magnoac [F] 88 D3
Castelnau–Montratier [F] 88 F1
Castelnovo ne' Monti [I] 128 B2
Castelnuovo Berardenga [I] 128 C4
Castelnuovo della Dáunia [I] 134 E2
Castelnuovo di Garfagnana [I] 128 B3
Castelnuovo di Porto [I] 132 C3
Castelnuovo di Val di Cecina [I] 130 D1
Castelnuovo Don Bosco [I] 116 C4
Castelnuovo Monterotaro [I] 134 E2
Castelnuovo Scrívia [I] 126 E1
Castelo [P] 90 C2
Castelo Branco [P] 84 D3
Castelo Branco [P] 90 D2
Castelo Branco [P] 110 A3
Castelo de Paiva [P] 84 B3
Castelo de Vide [P] 90 D3
Castelo do Neiva [P] 82 A4
Castel Porziano [I] 130 F4
Castelraimondo [I] 132 D2
Castel San Giovanni [I] 126 F1
Castel San Lorenzo [I] 134 E4
Castel San Pietro Terme [I] 128 C2
Castelsaraceno [I] 136 B3
Castelsardo [I] 142 B2
Castelsarrasin [F] 88 E2
Castelseprio [I] 116 D3
Castelserás [E] 94 E4
Casteltérmini [I] 140 C2
Castelvecchio Subequo [I] 132 E3
Castelverde [I] 116 F4
Castelvetere in Val Fortore [I] 134 D2
Castelvetrano [I] 140 B2
Castel Volturno [I] 134 C3
Castenaso [I] 128 C2
Castets [F] 88 B1
Castiádas [I] 142 C5
Castigliole d'Orcia [I] 130 E1
Castiglioncello [I] 128 B4
Castiglione dei Pepoli [I] 128 C3
Castiglione del Lago [I] 130 F1
Castiglione della Pescáia [I] 130 D2
Castiglione delle Stiviere [I] 118 A4
Castiglione Messer Marino [I] 132 F4
Castiglione Olona [I] 116 D3
Castiglion Fibocchi [I] 128 D4
Castiglion Fiorentino [I] 128 D4
Castilblanco [E] 100 C2
Castilblanco de los Arroyos [E] 98 F4
Castillejo de Martín Viejo [E] 84 D4
Castilliscar [E] 88 A4

Castillo de Locubín [E] 104 E2
Castillo de Matajudíos [E] 86 B4
Castillo de Tajarja [E] 104 E3
Castillo de Villamalefa [E] 102 D2
Castillon–la–Bataille [F] 78 C3
Castillonnès [F] 78 D4
Castillo Pasiega las Chimenas, Cuevas el– [E] 86 C2
Castione della Presolana [I] 116 F3
Castlebar [IRL] 12 B2
Castlebay / Bagh a Chaisteil [GB] 14 A3
Castlebellingham [IRL] 12 E3
Castleblayney [IRL] 12 E3
Castlebridge [IRL] 10 E4
Castlecomer [IRL] 10 E3
Castledermot [IRL] 10 E3
Castle Douglas [GB] 20 C2
Castleisland [IRL] 10 B3
Castlemaine [IRL] 10 B3
Castlemartyr [IRL] 10 C4
Castleplunkett [IRL] 12 C3
Castlepollard [IRL] 10 E1
Castlerea [IRL] 12 C3
Castletown [GBM] 20 B4
Castletownbere [IRL] 10 A4
Castletown House [IRL] 10 F2
Castletownroche [IRL] 10 C3
Castletownshend [IRL] 10 B4
Castlewellan [NIR] 12 F3
Castrejón [E] 84 F4
Castres [F] 124 A2
Castricum [NL] 30 B3
Castries [F] 124 D3
Castril [E] 106 B2
Castrillo de Don Juan [E] 92 E1
Castrillo de la Reina [E] 94 A1
Castrillón [E] 82 E2
Castro [I] 130 E2
Castro / Dozón [E] 82 C3
Castrobarto [E] 86 D3
Castrocalbón [E] 84 E2
Castrocaro Terme [I] 128 D3
Castrocontrigo [E] 84 E2
Castro da Cola [P] 98 B3
Castro Daire [P] 84 B3
Castro dei Volsci [I] 134 B2
Castro de Rei [E] 82 D2
Castrojeriz [E] 86 B4
Castro Marim [P] 98 C4
Castromil [E] 84 D2
Castromonte [E] 92 D1
Castronuevo [E] 84 F3
Castronuño [E] 84 F3
Castropol [E] 82 D2
Castrop-Rauxal [D] 42 D3
Castroreale [I] 138 C4
Castrotorafe, Ruinas de– [E] 84 E3
Castro–Urdiales [E] 86 D2
Castroverde [E] 82 D2
Castro Verde [P] 98 C3
Castroverde de Cerrato [E] 92 E1
Castrovillari [I] 136 C4
Castuera [E] 100 B3
Cataéggio [I] 116 E2
Çatalca [TR] 158 D3
Çatallar [TR] 176 F1
Catane [RO] 148 D2
Catánia [I] 140 E3
Catanzaro [I] 138 E2
Catanzaro Marina [I] 138 E2
Catarroja [E] 102 D3
Catenanuova [I] 140 E2
Cateraggio [I] 130 B3

Cathair Dónall / Caherdaniel [IRL] 10 A3
Catoira [E] 82 B2
Catterick [GB] 20 E4
Cattólica [I] 128 E3
Cattólica Eraclea [I] 140 C3
Catus [F] 88 F1
Cáuaş [RO] 76 F3
Caudebec–en–Caux [F] 54 C2
Caudete [E] 106 E1
Caudeval [F] 88 F4
Caudry [F] 56 A1
Caulonia [I] 138 E3
Caulonia [I] 138 E3
Caumont [F] 52 F2
Caumont [F] 88 E3
Caunes–Minervois [F] 124 A3
Cauro [F] 130 A3
Cáuşani [MD] 244 F3
Caussade [F] 88 F2
Cauterets [F] 88 C3
Cauville [F] 54 B1
Cava [E] 96 B4
Cava de' Tirreni [I] 134 D4
Cava d'Ispica [I] 140 E4
Cavaglià [I] 116 C3
Cavaillon [F] 124 E3
Cavalaire–sur–Mer [F] 126 B4
Cavalese [I] 118 C2
Cavalière [F] 126 B4
Cavallino [I] 118 D4
Cavallino [I] 136 F3
Cavalls, Cova dels– [E] 102 E2
Cavan / An Cabhán [IRL] 12 D3
Cävärän [RO] 122 F4
Cavárzere [I] 128 D1
Çavdarhisar [TR] 164 F3
Çavdir [TR] 170 E3
Cave del Predil [I] 118 E2
Cavi [I] 126 F2
Caviaga [I] 116 E4
Cavo [I] 130 D2
Cavour [I] 126 C1
Cavriglia [I] 128 C4
Cavtat [HR] 152 D3
Çavuş [TR] 176 F1
Çayağzı [TR] 158 E3
Çaybaşı [TR] 170 B2
Çayçinge [TR] 164 F3
Çayhisar [TR] 170 E4
Çayırova (Ágios Theodoros) [CY] 176 E3
Caylus [F] 88 F2
Cayrols [F] 78 F4
Çayyaka [TR] 164 F1
Cazalegas [E] 92 D4
Cazalla de la Sierra [E] 98 F3
Cazals [F] 78 F4
Cazane Plavişeviţa [RO] 148 C1
Cazaubon [F] 88 D2
Cazeneuve, Château de– [F] 78 C4
Cazères [F] 88 E3
Cazin [BIH] 144 D2
Čazma [HR] 120 D4
Cazorla [E] 106 B2
Cea [E] 82 C3
Cea [E] 86 A3
Ceatharlach / Carlow [IRL] 10 E3
Cebolla [E] 100 D1
Čebovce [SK] 76 B3
Cebreiro [E] 82 D3
Cebreros [E] 92 D3
Cebrones del Rio [E] 84 F2
Ceccano [I] 134 B2
Cece [H] 122 B2
Čečejovce [SK] 76 D2
Čechtice [CZ] 60 E3
Čechtín [CZ] 60 F4

Cécina [I] 128 B4
Ceclavín [E] 90 E3
Cecos [E] 82 D3
Cedeira [E] 82 C1
Cedillo [E] 90 D3
Cedros [P] 110 A3
Cedynia [PL] 34 D4
Cee [E] 82 A2
Cefalù [I] 138 A4
Cegléd [H] 122 C1
Céglie Messápica [I] 136 E2
Cegrane [MK] 154 C3
Cehegín [E] 106 D2
Ceica [RO] 122 F1
Ceillac [F] 126 B1
Ceira [P] 84 A4
Čejč [CZ] 74 D1
Čekiške [LT] 238 C3
Ceków Kolonia [PL] 48 C3
Čelákovice [CZ] 60 E2
Celano [I] 132 E4
Celanova [E] 82 B4
Čelarevo [SRB] 146 C1
Celaru [RO] 148 E2
Celbowo [PL] 36 C1
Celbridge [IRL] 10 F2
Čelebić [BIH] 144 E3
Celerina [CH] 116 F2
Čelić [BIH] 146 B2
Celico [I] 138 E1
Čelinac [BIH] 144 F2
Celjahavi [BY] 242 B3
Celje [SLO] 120 B3
Cella [E] 102 C1
Celldömölk [H] 74 E4
Celle [D] 44 C1
Celle di Bulgheria [I] 136 B3
Celle Lígure [I] 126 E2
Cellers / Castell de Mur [E] 96 C2
Celles [B] 40 C3
Celles–sur–Belle [F] 66 D4
Čelopeci [MK] 154 C4
Celorico da Beira [P] 84 C4
Celorico de Basto [P] 84 B2
Celsoy [F] 70 A2
Çeltek [TR] 170 F3
Çeltikköy [TR] 158 A4
Čemerno [BIH] 152 E2
Cemke [TR] 158 E3
Cenad [RO] 122 D3
Cencenighe [I] 118 C2
Cenei [RO] 122 D3
Ceneköy [TR] 158 B3
Cenicentos [E] 92 D4
Cenicero [E] 86 E4
Cenizzate [E] 102 B3
Čenta [SRB] 146 D1
Centallo [I] 126 C2
Centelles [E] 96 D2
Cento [I] 128 C2
Centuri [F] 130 B1
Centúripe [I] 140 E2
Cepagatti [I] 132 E3
Čepan [AL] 160 B3
Čepin [HR] 122 A4
Čepovan [SLO] 118 F3
Ceprano [I] 134 B2
Cer [MK] 154 C4
Čeralije [HR] 120 F4
Cerami [I] 138 B4
Ceranów [PL] 38 B4
Ceraso [I] 136 A3
Cerbère [F] 96 F2
Cerbu [RO] 148 F1
Cerceda [E] 82 B2
Cerceda [E] 92 E3
Cercedilla [E] 92 E3

Cerchiara di Calábria [I]
136 C4
Cerda [I] 138 A4
Cerdedo [E] 82 B3
Cerdeira [P] 84 C4
Cerdon [F] 68 B2
Cerea [I] 118 B4
Cerecinos de Campos [E]
84 F2
Cered [H] 76 C3
Cereixo [E] 82 B2
Ceremosnja [SRB] 146 F2
Ceres [I] 116 B4
Ceresole Reale [I] 116 B3
Céret [F] 96 E1
Cerfontaine [B] 56 B1
Ceriale [I] 126 D2
Cerignola [I] 134 F3
Cérilly [F] 68 C4
Čerín [SK] 76 B2
Cerisiers [F] 68 D1
Cerizay [F] 66 D3
Cerkezköy [TR] 158 C3
Cerknica [SLO] 120 A3
Cerkno [SLO] 118 F3
Cerkovitsa [BG] 148 F3
Cerkvenjak [SLO] 120 C2
Cerkwica [PL] 34 E2
Çermë [AL] 160 A2
Cermei [RO] 122 F2
Cerna [HR] 146 B1
Cernache do Bom Jardim
[P] 90 C2
Černá Hora [CZ] 62 B4
Cernăteşti [RO] 148 D1
Cernavodă [RO] 150 E1
Černá v Pošumaví [CZ] 74 A2
Cernay [F] 70 C3
Cernégula [E] 86 C3
Cernica [RO] 150 C1
Černičevo [BG] 148 C3
Cerniébaud [F] 70 B4
Cernik [HR] 144 F1
Cernóbbio [I] 116 E3
Černookovo [BG] 150 E2
Černošín [CZ] 60 C3
Černovice [CZ] 60 E4
Černuc [CZ] 60 D2
Cerósimo [I] 136 C3
Cerovačke Špilje [HR] 144 D3
Cerovica [BIH] 152 C2
Çërravë [AL] 160 C2
Cerreto Laziale [I] 132 D4
Cérrik [AL] 160 B2
Cerro de los Angeles [E] 92 E4
Cerro de los Santos [E] 102 B4
Cerro Muriano [E] 100 B4
Certaldo [I] 128 C4
Cervatos [E] 86 C3
Cervatos de la Cueza [E] 86 B4
Červená [CZ] 60 D4
Červená Lhota [CZ] 60 E4
Červená–Řečice [CZ] 60 E4
Červená Skala [SK] 76 C1
Červená Voda [CZ] 62 B3
Červený Hrádek [CZ] 60 C2
Červený Hrádek [CZ] 60 D3
Červený Kameň [SK] 74 F2
Červený Kameň [SK] 74 F1
Červený Kláštor [SK] 64 B4
Červený Kostelec [CZ] 62 A2
Cervera [E] 96 C2
Cervera de la Cañada [E]
94 C3
Cervera del Llano [E] 102 A2
Cervera del Río Alhama
[E] 94 C2
Cervera de Pisuerga [E] 86 B3
Cerveteri [I] 130 F3
Cérvia [I] 128 D3
Cervignano del Friuli [I]
118 E3

Cervinara [I] 134 D3
Cervione [F] 130 B2
Cervo [E] 82 D1
Cervo [I] 126 D3
Cesana Torinese [I] 116 B4
Cesarica [HR] 144 C2
Cesarò [I] 138 B4
Cesarzowice [PL] 46 E4
Cesena [I] 128 D3
Cesenático [I] 128 E3
Ceserhát–Suráni [H] 76 B3
Cēsis [LV] 236 C2
Česká Bělá [CZ] 60 F3
Česká Kamenice [CZ] 60 D1
Česká Lípa [CZ] 60 E2
Česká Skalice [CZ] 62 A2
Česká Třebová [CZ] 62 B3
České Budějovice [CZ] 74 A1
České Libchavy [CZ] 62 B3
České Velenice [CZ] 74 B2
Český Brod [CZ] 60 E3
Český Krumlov [CZ] 74 A2
Český Šternberk [CZ] 60 E3
Český Těšín [CZ] 62 D3
Çeşme [TR] 168 E1
Çeşmealti [TR] 168 F1
Cespedosa [E] 92 C3
Cessalto [I] 118 D3
Cessenon–sur–Orb [F]
124 B3
Čestimensko [BG] 150 D2
Čestobrodica [SRB] 146 D3
Cestona / Zestoa [E] 86 E3
Cesvaine [LV] 236 D3
Cetate [RO] 148 D2
Çetibeli [TR] 170 D4
Cetinje [MNE] 152 E3
Cetóbriga [P] 90 B4
Cetona [I] 130 F2
Cetraro [I] 136 B4
Ceuta [E] 104 C4
Ceuti [E] 106 D2
Ceva [I] 126 D2
Cevico Navero [E] 92 E1
Čevo [MNE] 152 E3
Cewków [PL] 64 D2
Ceylan [TR] 170 F4
Ceyrat [F] 80 C2
Ceyzériat [F] 80 E2
Chaalis, Abbaye de– [F] 54 E3
Chabanais [F] 78 D2
Chabeuil [F] 80 D4
Chablis [F] 68 D2
Chabreloche [F] 80 C2
Chabris [F] 68 A2
Chachersk [BY] 242 D2
Chagny [F] 68 E4
Chailland [F] 66 C4
Chaillé–les–Marais [F] 66 C4
Chailley–Turny [F] 68 D1
Chailluz, Fort de– [F] 70 B3
Chairóneia [GR] 166 F3
Chajkola [RUS] 216 F1
Chalabre [F] 88 F4
Chalais [F] 78 C3
Chalamont [F] 80 E2
Chalampé [F] 70 D3
Chalandrítsa [GR] 166 D4
Chálki [GR] 160 F4
Chálki [GR] 176 B2
Chalkiádes [GR] 162 A3
Chalkída [GR] 168 A2
Chalkidóna [GR] 160 F2
Challans [F] 66 B3
Challes–les–Eaux [F] 80 F3
Chalonnes–sur–Loire [F]
66 D2
Châlons–en–Champagne
[F] 56 B3
Chalon–sur–Saône [F] 68 E4
Chalupy [PL] 48 D1
Châlus [F] 78 E2

Chalusset, Château de– [F]
78 E2
Cham [CH] 70 E4
Cham [D] 60 B4
Chamberet [F] 78 F3
Chambéry [F] 80 F3
Chambilly [F] 80 C1
Chambley–Bussières [F]
56 D3
Chambon–sur–Lac [F] 80 B2
Chambon–sur–Voueize
[F] 80 A1
Chambord [F] 68 A2
Chambord, Parc de– [F] 68 B2
Chamelet [F] 80 D2
Chameregg [D] 60 B4
Chammünster [D] 60 B4
Chamonix–Mont–Blanc [F]
116 B2
Champagnac–le–Vieux
[F] 80 B3
Champagne–Mouton [F] 78 D2
Champagnole [F] 70 B4
Champaubert [F] 56 A3
Champdeniers [F] 66 D4
Champ du Bataille, Château
du– [F] 54 C2
Champ du Feu [F] 70 D2
Champeix [F] 80 B2
Champéry [CH] 116 B2
Champex [CH] 116 B2
Champier [F] 80 E3
Champigné [F] 66 D2
Champigny–sur–Veude
[F] 66 E3
Champillon [F] 56 A3
Champlan [F] 54 D3
Champlitte [F] 70 A3
Champlon [B] 56 D2
Champoluc [I] 116 C3
Champorcher [I] 116 C3
Champrond–en–Gâtine [F]
54 C4
Champtoceaux [F] 66 C2
Champvent [CH] 70 B4
Chamrousse [F] 80 E4
Chamusca [P] 90 C3
Chanaleilles [F] 80 B4
Chanas [F] 80 D3
Chandrinós [GR] 172 C3
Chaniá [GR] 174 B3
Chaniótis [GR] 162 B2
Channel Tunnel / La Manche,
Tunnel sous– [F/GB] 28 E4
Chantada [E] 82 C3
Chantelle [F] 80 B1
Chantemerle [F] 116 A4
Chantilly [F] 54 E3
Chantonnay [F] 66 C3
Chão de Codes [P] 90 D2
Chaource [F] 68 E2
Chapelle–Royale [F] 54 C4
Chárakas [GR] 174 D4
Charavgí [GR] 160 E3
Charavines [F] 80 E3
Charbonnières–les–Bains
[F] 80 D2
Charbowo [PL] 48 B1
Chard [GB] 26 D3
Charenton–du–Cher [F] 68 B4
Charité, Abbaye de la– [F]
70 B3
Charleroi [B] 40 D4
Charlestown [IRL] 12 C2
Charleville / Rath Luirc [IRL]
10 C3
Charleville–Mézières [F] 56 C2
Charlieu [F] 80 C2
Charlottenberg [S] 188 C1
Charly [F] 54 F3
Charly [F] 68 C3
Charmes [F] 70 C1

Charnawchytsy [BY] 50 D2
Charneca [P] 90 A3
Charny [F] 68 C2
Charnyany [BY] 50 E2
Charolles [F] 80 D1
Chârost [F] 68 B3
Charpentry [F] 56 C3
Charrières [CH] 116 B1
Charron [F] 66 C4
Charroux [F] 78 D1
Chartres [F] 54 C4
Charvarica [BG] 154 F3
Charzykowy [PL] 36 B3
Chassant [F] 54 C4
Chasseneuil–s.–Bonnieure
[F] 78 D2
Chasse sur Rhone [F] 80 D3
Chassigny [F] 68 F2
Château–Arnoux [F] 126 A2
Châteaubourg [F] 52 E4
Châteaubriant [F] 66 C1
Château–Chinon [F] 68 D3
Château d'Oex [CH] 116 B2
Château–du–Loir [F] 66 E2
Châteaudun [F] 54 C4
Châteaugiron [F] 52 E4
Château–Gontier [F] 66 D1
Château–Landon [F] 68 C1
Château–la–Vallière [F]
66 E2
Château–l'Évêque [F] 78 D3
Châteaulin [F] 52 B3
Châteaumeillant [F] 68 B4
Châteauneuf [F] 78 C2
Châteauneuf–de–Randon
[F] 80 B4
Châteauneuf–du–Faou [F]
52 B3
Châteauneuf–du–Pape [F]
124 E2
Châteauneuf–en–Thymerais
[F] 54 C3
Châteauneuf–sur–Cher [F]
68 B3
Châteauneuf–sur–Loire
[F] 68 B2
Châteauneuf–sur–Sarthe
[F] 66 D2
Châteauponsac [F] 78 E2
Château–Porcien [F] 56 B2
Château–Queyras [F] 126 B1
Château–Regnault [F] 56 C2
Châteaurenard [F] 68 C2
Château–Renault [F] 66 F2
Châteauroux [F] 68 A3
Château–Salins [F] 56 D4
Château–Thierry [F] 54 F3
Châteauvillain [F] 68 F2
Châtel [F] 116 B2
Châtelaillon–Plage [F] 66 C4
Châtelet [B] 40 D4
Châtelguyon [F] 80 B2
Châtellerault [F] 66 E3
Châtel–Montagne [F] 80 C2
Châtel–St–Denis [CH] 116 B1
Châtelus–Malvaleix [F] 68 B4
Châtenois [F] 70 B2
Chatham [GB] 28 D3
Châtillon [I] 116 C3
Châtillon–Coligny [F] 68 C2
Châtillon–en–Bazois [F] 68 D3
Châtillon–en–Diois [F] 124 F1
Châtillon–sur–Chalaronne
[F] 80 D2
Châtillon–sur–Indre [F] 66 F3
Châtillon–sur–Loire [F] 68 C2
Châtillon–sur–Marne [F] 56 A3
Châtillon–sur–Seine [F] 68 E2
Châtre, Église de– [F] 78 C2
Chatteris [GB] 28 D1
Chaudes–Aigues [F] 80 B3
Chauffailles [F] 80 D2

Chaufour–lès–Bonnières
[F] 54 D3
Chaumergy [F] 68 F4
Chaumont [F] 68 F2
Chaumont–sur–Aire [F] 56 C4
Chaumont–sur–Loire [F] 68 A2
Chaunay [F] 78 D1
Chauny [F] 54 F2
Chaussin [F] 68 F4
Chauvigny [F] 66 E4
Chaux–Neuve [F] 80 F1
Chavaleč [CZ] 60 F2
Chavdar [BG] 156 C3
Chavec [P] 04 C2
Chavusy [BY] 242 D2
Chayki [RUS] 236 F4
Chazelles–sur–Lyon [F] 80 D2
Cheb [CZ] 60 B2
Chęciny [PL] 64 B1
Cheddar [GB] 26 E2
Chef–Boutonne [F] 78 D1
Cheglevici [RO] 122 D3
Cheímarros [GR] 156 B4
Chekhov [RUS] 240 F3
Chekhovo [RUS] 36 F1
Cheles [E] 98 D2
Chełm [PL] 50 D3
Chełmek [PL] 62 E3
Chełmno [PL] 36 C3
Chelmsford [GB] 28 D3
Chełmża [PL] 36 C4
Chełst [PL] 46 E1
Cheltenham [GB] 26 F2
Chelva [E] 102 C2
Chémery–sur–Bar [F] 56 C2
Chemillé [F] 66 D2
Chemin [F] 68 F4
Chemnitz [D] 60 C1
Chenaux [CH] 70 C4
Clière–Pignier [F] 78 E2
Chénérailles [F] 80 A1
Chenonceaux [F] 66 F3
Chepelare [BG] 156 D3
Chepstow [GB] 26 E2
Chera [E] 102 C3
Cherasco [I] 126 D1
Cherbourg [F] 52 E1
Cherekha [RUS] 232 E3
Cheremykino [RUS] 200 E4
Cherepovo [BG] 156 F2
Chereshovo [BG] 156 B2
Cherkasovo [RUS] 200 D2
Cherkasy [UA] 246 D1
Cherna Mesta [BG] 156 B2
Chernaya Rechka [RUS]
232 E3
Chernevo [RUS] 232 E2
Cherniakhiv [UA] 242 C4
Chernihiv [UA] 242 D3
Cherni rid [BG] 156 F3
Chernivtsi [UA] 244 D2
Cherno [RUS] 232 E1
Chernomorets [BG] 158 B1
Chernovskoye [RUS] 232 E1
Chernyakhovsk [RUS] 238 B3
Chéroy [F] 68 C1
Cherskaya [RUS] 232 E4
Chérso [GR] 156 A4
Cherveix–Cubas [F] 78 E3
Chervena Voda [BG] 150 C2
Cherven Bryag [BG] 148 E3
Cherves–Richemont [F] 78 C2
Chervonohrad [UA] 64 F2
Chervyen' [BY] 242 C2
Cherykaw [BY] 242 D2
Chester [GB] 22 E3
Chesterfield [GB] 24 C3
Chester–le–Street [GB] 20 E3
Chevagnes [F] 68 D4
Chevanceaux [F] 78 C3
Chevenez [CH] 70 C3

Chevilly, Château de- [F] 68 B1
Chevreuse [F] 54 D3
Chézal-Benoît [F] 68 B3
Chialamberto [I] 116 B3
Chiampo [I] 118 B4
Chianca, Dolmen di- [I] 136 C1
Chianciano Terme [I] 130 F1
Chiaramonti [I] 142 B2
Chiaramonti Gulfi [I] 140 E3
Chiaravalle [I] 128 E4
Chiaravalle [I] 128 F4
Chiaravalle Centrale [I] 138 E3
Chiaravalle della Colomba [I] 128 A1
Chiari [I] 116 F3
Chiaromonte [I] 136 C3
Chiasso [CH] 116 E3
Chiavari [I] 126 F2
Chiavenna [I] 116 E2
Chichester [GB] 28 B4
Chiclana de la Frontera [E] 104 B3
Chiclana de Segura [E] 106 B1
Chieming [D] 72 D3
Chieri [I] 116 C4
Chiesa [I] 128 D2
Chiesa in Valmalenco [I] 116 F2
Chiessi [I] 130 C2
Chieti [I] 132 F3
Chigny [F] 56 B2
Chiliadoú [GR] 168 B1
Chiliandaríou, Moní- [GR] 162 C2
Chiliomódi [GR] 166 F4
Chillarón de Cuenca [E] 102 B2
Chillon [CH] 116 B2
Chillón [E] 100 C3
Chimaera [TR] 176 F1
Chimay [B] 56 B2
Chinadievo [UA] 244 C3
Chinchilla de Monte-Aragón [E] 102 B4
Chinchón [E] 100 E1
Chinon [F] 66 E3
Chióggia [I] 128 D1
Chíos [GR] 168 E1
Chipiona [E] 104 A2
Chippenham [GB] 26 F2
Chipping Norton [GB] 28 B2
Chipping Sodbury [GB] 26 E2
Chiprana [E] 94 E4
Chiprovtsi [BG] 148 D3
Chiren [BG] 148 E3
Chirivel [E] 106 C2
Chirpan [BG] 156 E2
Chisa [F] 130 B3
Chiselet [RO] 150 D2
Chişinău [MD] 244 F3
Chişineu Criş [RO] 122 E2
Chiusa / Klausen [I] 118 C2
Chiusa di Pesio [I] 126 D2
Chiusaforte [I] 118 E2
Chiusa Scláfani [I] 140 C2
Chiusi [I] 130 F1
Chiva [E] 102 D3
Chivasso [I] 116 C4
Chkalove [RUS] 246 F3
Chkalovo [RUS] 238 B3
Chlebowo [PL] 46 D2
Chlemoútsi [GR] 166 C4
Chlewice [PL] 62 F2
Chlewiska [PL] 48 F4
Chlewo [PL] 48 C3
Chlmec [SK] 76 E2
Chlumec nad Cidlinou [CZ] 60 F2
Chlum u Třeboně [CZ] 74 B1
Chmielnik [PL] 64 B2

Chmielno [PL] 46 D4
Chobienia [PL] 46 E3
Chobienice [PL] 46 E2
Choceň [CZ] 62 B3
Choceń [PL] 48 C2
Chochołów [PL] 62 F4
Chocianów [PL] 46 E4
Chociwel [PL] 34 E3
Choczewo [PL] 36 C1
Chodecz [PL] 48 C2
Chodel [PL] 50 B4
Chodos / Xodos [E] 102 E2
Chodov [CZ] 60 B2
Chodová Planá [CZ] 60 B3
Chodzież [PL] 36 B4
Chojna [PL] 34 D4
Chojnice [PL] 36 B3
Chojnów [PL] 46 E4
Cholet [F] 66 D3
Chomakovtsi [BG] 148 E3
Chomęciska Małe [PL] 50 D4
Chomutov [CZ] 60 C2
Chop [UA] 76 E2
Chóra [GR] 172 C3
Chorbadzhijsko [BG] 156 E3
Choreftó [GR] 162 B3
Chorges [F] 126 B1
Chorio [I] 138 D4
Choristí [GR] 156 C4
Chorley [GB] 22 F2
Chornobyl [UA] 242 D3
Chornomors'ke [UA] 246 E3
Choroszcz [PL] 38 C3
Chorro, Garganta del- [E] 104 D3
Chorros, Cueva de los- [E] 106 C1
Chorros del Mundo [E] 100 F4
Chortkiv [UA] 244 D2
Chorzele [PL] 36 F3
Chorzów [PL] 62 E2
Chorzyna [PL] 48 C4
Choszczno [PL] 34 E4
Chotěboř [CZ] 60 F3
Chotětín [CZ] 60 D3
Choumnikó [GR] 156 B4
Chouto [P] 90 C3
Chouvigny, Gorges de- [F] 80 B1
Choye [F] 70 B3
Chozoviótissa [GR] 168 E4
Chrast [CZ] 60 F3
Chrastava [CZ] 60 E1
Chrepiski Manastir [BG] 148 E4
Christchurch [GB] 26 F4
Christianoúpoli [GR] 172 C3
Christiansfeld [DK] 178 B2
Christinehof [S] 180 D2
Christkindl [A] 74 A3
Christós [GR] 168 E3
Chrudim [CZ] 60 F3
Chrýsafa [GR] 172 D3
Chrysochóri [GR] 156 C4
Chrysorrogiatissa, Panagia- [CY] 176 C4
Chrysoskalítissa [GR] 174 A4
Chrysoúpoli [GR] 156 D4
Chrząchówek [PL] 50 B3
Chrzan [PL] 48 B2
Chrzanów [PL] 62 E2
Chudenice [CZ] 60 C4
Chudniv [UA] 244 E1
Chudoba [PL] 62 D1
Chudomir [BG] 150 C3
Chudovo [RUS] 240 C1
Chułkovo [RUS] 200 D2
Chuprene [BG] 148 C3
Chur [CH] 116 E1
Church Stretton [GB] 22 E4
Churchtown [IRL] 10 E4
Churchtown [IRL] 10 E4

Churek [BG] 156 B1
Chvagnes-en-Paillers [F] 66 C3
Chwaszczyno [PL] 36 C1
Chyhyryn [UA] 246 D1
Chyňava [CZ] 60 D3
Chýnov [CZ] 60 E4
Chýnovská Jeskyně [CZ] 60 E4
Chyże [PL] 62 F4
Chyžne [PL] 62 F4
Cianciana [I] 140 C2
Ciasna [PL] 62 D1
Ciążeń [PL] 48 B2
Cibakháza [H] 122 C1
Ciborro [P] 90 C4
Ciboure [F] 88 A2
Cicciano [I] 134 D3
Cicerone, Tomba di- [I] 134 B3
Ćićevac [SRB] 146 F4
Čičevci [BIH] 146 C3
Čičevo [BIH] 146 A4
Cichy [PL] 38 B1
Čičíl [BG] 148 C2
Ćiciuk [SRB] 146 F4
Ciclopi, Isole dei- [I] 140 E2
Čičmany [SK] 76 A1
Cidones [E] 94 B2
Ciechanów [PL] 36 F4
Ciechanowiec [PL] 38 B4
Ciechocinek [PL] 36 D4
Ciemnik [PL] 34 E3
Ciempozuelos [E] 100 E1
Ciepielów [PL] 50 B3
Cieplice Śląskie-Zdrój [PL] 60 F1
Čierny Balog [SK] 76 B2
Cierp-Gaud [F] 88 D3
Cieśle [PL] 48 E2
Cieszanów [PL] 64 E2
Cieszyn [PL] 48 B3
Cieszyn [PL] 62 D3
Cieszyno [PL] 34 F3
Cieza [E] 106 D2
Ciężkowice [PL] 64 B3
Čiftlikköy [TR] 158 E4
Cifuentes [E] 94 B3
Cifuentes [E] 94 B4
Cigales [E] 92 D1
Cigánd [H] 76 E2
Cigliano [I] 116 C4
Cilipi [HR] 152 D3
Cill Airne / Killarney [IRL] 10 B3
Cillas [E] 94 C3
Cill Chainnigh / Kilkenny [IRL] 10 E3
Cill Charthaigh / Kilcar [IRL] 12 C1
Cill Chiaráin / Kilkieran [IRL] 10 B1
Cilleros [E] 90 F2
Cimadevilla [E] 82 B2
Cimburk [CZ] 62 B3
Cimburk [CZ] 74 E1
Cimino, Monte- [I] 130 F3
Cimitero Militare Britannico [I] 134 C2
Cimochy [PL] 38 C2
Cimoláis [I] 118 D2
Cîmpeni [RO] 244 C4
Cinco Casas [E] 100 E3
Cindere [TR] 170 E2
Çine [TR] 170 C3
Činěves [CZ] 60 E2
Ciney [B] 56 C1
Cinfães [P] 84 B3
Cingoli [I] 128 E4
Cinigiano [I] 130 E2
Cínisi [I] 140 B1
Cinquefrondi [I] 138 D3

Cintegabelle [F] 88 E3
Cintei [RO] 122 E2
Cintruénigo [E] 94 C2
Ciocăneşti [RO] 150 D1
Ciocârlia [RO] 150 E1
Ciółkowo [PL] 48 D1
Ciorogârla [RO] 150 B1
Cîrali [TR] 176 F1
Circo de Barrosa [E] 88 C4
Cirella [I] 136 B4
Cirencester [GB] 26 F2
Cirey [F] 70 C1
Ciria [E] 94 C2
Ciriè [I] 116 C4
Ćirkovicy [RUS] 200 E4
Cirò [I] 138 F1
Cirò Marina [I] 138 F1
Ciron [F] 66 F4
Çırpı [TR] 170 B2
Ciruli [LV] 234 E2
Cisa, Passo della- [I] 128 A2
Cisna [PL] 64 D4
Cisnădie [RO] 248 D3
Cisneros [E] 86 B4
Cista Provo [HR] 144 E4
Cista Velika [HR] 144 E4
Cisterna di Latina [I] 134 A2
Cisternino [I] 136 D2
Cisterna [E] 86 A3
Ciszyca [PL] 48 F2
Citak [TR] 164 D3
Cîteaux, Abbaye de- [F] 68 F3
Çıtlık [TR] 170 D4
Čitluk [BIH] 152 C2
Cittadella [I] 118 C3
Città della Pieve [I] 130 F2
Città del Vaticano [V] 132 C4
Città di Castello [I] 128 D4
Cittaducale [I] 132 D3
Cittanova [I] 138 D3
Città Sant'Angelo [I] 132 E3
Ciudad Real [E] 100 D3
Ciudad Rodrigo [E] 84 D4
Ciudad Romana [E] 94 C3
Ciudad Romana [E] 98 E3
Ciulniţa [RO] 150 D1
Ciumeghiu [RO] 122 E2
Ciutadella de Menorca [E] 108 E3
Civica [E] 94 A3
Cividale del Friuli [I] 118 E3
Çivili [TR] 164 C2
Civita [I] 130 F2
Civita Castellana [I] 132 C3
Civitanova Marche [I] 132 E1
Civitavécchia [I] 130 E3
Civitella del Tronto [I] 132 E2
Civitella di Romagna [I] 128 D3
Civitella in Val di Chiana [I] 128 D4
Civitella Paganico [I] 130 E1
Civitella Roveto [I] 132 E4
Civray [F] 78 D1
Civrieux-d'Azergues [F] 80 D2
Çivril [TR] 170 F2
Clacton-on-Sea [GB] 28 E3
Clairvaux-les-Lacs [F] 80 F1
Clamecy [F] 68 D2
Clamerey [F] 68 E3
Clamouse, Grotte de- [F] 124 C2
Clane [IRL] 10 E2
Clara [IRL] 10 E2
Clarecastle [IRL] 10 C2
Claremorris [IRL] 12 B3
Clarinbridge [IRL] 10 C1
Claros [TR] 170 B3
Clashmore [IRL] 10 D4
Claudy [NIR] 12 E1

Clausholm [DK] 182 D4
Clausthal-Zellerfeld [D] 44 C3
Claviere [I] 116 A4
Cleanovu [RO] 148 D2
Clécy [F] 54 A2
Cleethorpes [GB] 24 D3
Clefmont [F] 70 B2
Clefs [F] 66 E2
Clejani [RO] 150 B1
Clelles [F] 80 E4
Clementino, Porto- [I] 130 E3
Cléon-d'Andran [F] 124 E1
Clères [F] 54 C2
Clermont [F] 54 E2
Clermont-de-Beauregarde [F] 78 D3
Clermont-en-Argonne [F] 56 C3
Clermont-Ferrand [F] 80 B2
Clermont-l'Hérault [F] 124 C3
Clerval [F] 70 C3
Clervaux [L] 56 D2
Cléry [F] 68 B2
Cles [I] 118 B2
Clevedon [GB] 26 E2
Clifden [IRL] 12 A3
Cliffoney [IRL] 12 C2
Clisson [F] 66 C2
Clitheroe [GB] 22 F2
Clitunno, Fonti del- [I] 132 D2
Clitunno, Tempio del- [I] 132 D2
Clogan [IRL] 10 D2
Clogh [IRL] 10 E3
Clogheen [IRL] 10 D3
Cloghmore / An Chloich Mhór [IRL] 12 A2
Clohars-Carnöet [F] 52 B4
Clonakilty [IRL] 10 B4
Clonalis House [IRL] 12 C3
Clonard [IRL] 10 E2
Clonaslee [IRL] 10 D2
Clonbur / An Fhairche [IRL] 12 B3
Clondalkin [IRL] 10 F2
Clones [IRL] 12 D3
Clonfert [IRL] 10 D2
Clonmacnoise [IRL] 10 D2
Clonmany [IRL] 12 E1
Clonmel / Cluain Meala [IRL] 10 D3
Clonmellon [IRL] 10 E1
Clonroche [IRL] 10 E3
Cloonbannin [IRL] 10 B3
Cloonkeen [IRL] 10 B3
Cloonlara [IRL] 10 C2
Cloppenburg [D] 30 F3
Clough [NIR] 12 F3
Cloughjordan [IRL] 10 D2
Cloyes-sur-le-Loir [F] 68 A1
Cloyne [IRL] 10 C4
Cluain Meala / Clonmel [IRL] 10 D3
Cluina [E] 94 A2
Cluj Napoca [RO] 244 C4
Clun [GB] 22 E4
Cluny [F] 80 D1
Cluses [F] 116 B2
Clusone [I] 116 E3
Ćmielów [PL] 50 B4
Cmolas [PL] 64 C2
Cnocán na Líne / Knocknalina [IRL] 12 B2
Coachford [IRL] 10 C4
Coalville [GB] 24 C4
Coaña [E] 82 E2
Cobadin [RO] 150 E1
Çobanlar [TR] 164 D3
Cobh [IRL] 10 C4
Coburg [D] 58 E2
Coca [E] 92 D2
Coceges del Monte [E] 92 E2

Cocentaina [E] 106 F1
Cochem [D] 56 F2
Cockermouth [GB] 20 C3
Code [LV] 234 F4
Codigoro [I] 128 D2
Codogno [I] 116 E4
Codos [E] 94 D3
Codróipo [I] 118 E3
Coesfeld [D] 30 D4
Coevorden [NL] 30 D3
Coflans [F] 116 A3
Cofrentes [E] 102 C3
Coghinas [I] 142 C2
Cognac [F] 78 C2
Cogne [I] 116 B3
Cogolin [F] 126 B4
Cogollos [E] 86 C4
Cogolludo [E] 94 A3
Cogul, Cova del- [E] 96 B3
Cohiniac [F] 52 C3
Coimbra [P] 84 A4
Coín [E] 104 D3
Coina [P] 90 B4
Coirós [E] 82 C2
Čoka [SRB] 122 C3
Colares [P] 90 A3
Colareţu [RO] 148 D1
Cólbe [D] 42 F4
Colbitz [D] 44 E2
Colcerasa [I] 132 D1
Colchester [GB] 28 E2
Colditz [D] 44 F4
Coldstream [GB] 20 E2
Colembert [F] 40 B3
Colera [E] 96 F2
Coleraine [NIR] 12 E1
Colfiorito [I] 132 D2
Colfosco [I] 118 C2
Colfosco [I] 118 C2
Colico [I] 116 E2
Coligny [F] 80 E1
Colindres [E] 86 D2
Colintraive [GB] 18 B3
Collado Villalba [E] 92 E3
Coll de Nargó [E] 96 C2
Collécchio [I] 128 B2
Colledimezzo [I] 132 F4
Colle di Val d'Elsa [I] 128 C4
Colleferro [I] 132 D4
Collegno [I] 116 C4
Colle Isarco / Gossensass
[I] 118 C1
Collesalvetti [I] 128 B4
Colle Sannita [I] 134 D2
Collesano [I] 138 A4
Colletorto [I] 134 D2
Colliano [I] 134 E4
Collinée [F] 52 D3
Cóllio [I] 116 F3
Collioure [F] 96 F1
Collodi [I] 128 B3
Collonges [F] 80 F2
Collonges-la-Rouge [F] 78 E3
Collooney [IRL] 12 C2
Colmar [F] 70 D2
Colmars [F] 126 B2
Colmenar [E] 104 E3
Colmenar de Oreja [E] 100 E1
Colmenar Viejo [E] 92 E3
Cologna Véneta [I] 118 B4
Cologne [F] 88 E2
Cololgno al Serio [I] 116 E3
Colombey-les-Belles [F]
70 B1
Colombey-les-Deux-Églises
[F] 68 F2
Colomiers [F] 88 E2
Coloneşti [RO] 148 F1
Colònia de Sant Jordi [E]
108 D4
Colonia Selladores [E] 100 D4
Colorno [I] 128 B1

Colosimi [I] 138 E2
Colunga [E] 86 B2
Colwyn Bay [GB] 22 E2
Comácchio [I] 128 D2
Comana [RO] 150 C2
Comana [RO] 150 F2
Comăneşti [RO] 244 E4
Comano Terme [I] 118 B3
Coma-ruga [E] 96 C3
Combarro [E] 82 B3
Combeaufontaine [F] 70 B3
Comber [NIR] 12 F2
Combourg [F] 52 E3
Combronde [F] 80 B2
Comburg [D] 58 C4
Comeglians [I] 118 E2
Comelico Superiore [I] 118 D2
Comillas [E] 86 C2
Cómiso [I] 140 E4
Comloşu Mare [RO] 122 D3
Commentry [F] 80 B1
Commequiers [F] 66 B3
Commercy [F] 56 C4
Como [I] 116 E3
Comorişte [RO] 146 F1
Cómpeta [E] 104 E3
Compiègne [F] 54 E2
Comporta [P] 90 B4
Comps-sur-Artuby [F] 126 B3
Comrat [MD] 244 F3
Comunanza [I] 132 E2
Conca [F] 130 B3
Concarneau [F] 52 B4
Concesio [I] 116 F3
Conches-en-Ouche [F] 54 C3
Concordia Sagittaria [I] 118 D3
Condat [F] 80 A3
Condé-en-Brie [F] 54 F3
Condeixa-a-Nova [P] 84 A4
Condé-sur-Noireau [F] 54 A2
Condino [I] 118 B3
Condofuri [I] 138 C4
Condofuri Marina [I] 138 D4
Condom [F] 88 D2
Condove [I] 116 B4
Condrieu [F] 80 D3
Conegliano [I] 118 D3
Conflans en Jarnisy [F] 56 D3
Conflans-sur-Lanterne
[F] 70 B2
Confolens [F] 78 D2
Cong [IRL] 10 C1
Congleton [GB] 22 F3
Congosto de Valdavia [E]
86 B3
Congresbury [GB] 26 E2
Conil de la Frontera [E] 104 B3
Conímbriga [P] 90 C1
Coningsby [GB] 24 D3
Conlie [F] 54 A4
Conna [IRL] 10 C4
Connantre [F] 56 A4
Connerré [F] 54 B4
Čonoplja [SRB] 122 B3
Conquista [E] 100 C4
Conquista de la Sierra [E]
100 B2
Conselice [I] 128 D2
Conselve [I] 118 C4
Consett [GB] 20 E3
Constanţa [RO] 150 F1
Constantí [E] 96 C3
Constantina [E] 100 A4
Constantine [F] 56 D3
Consuegra [E] 100 E2
Consuma [I] 128 C3
Contarina [I] 128 D1
Contay [F] 54 E1
Contea [I] 128 C3
Conţeşti [RO] 150 B2

Contigliano [I] 132 D3
Contis-Plage [F] 88 B1
Contres [F] 68 A2
Contrexéville [F] 70 B2
Controne [I] 134 E4
Contursi Terme [I] 134 E4
Conty [F] 54 E2
Conversano [I] 136 D2
Conwy [GB] 22 D2
Cookstown [NIR] 12 E2
Coole [IRL] 10 E1
Cooraclare [IRL] 10 B2
Cootehill [IRL] 12 D3
Cope [E] 106 D3
Copertino [I] 136 F3
Cöpköy [TR] 158 B3
Copparo [I] 128 D2
Coppenbrügge [D] 44 B2
Corabia [RO] 148 F2
Corato [I] 136 C1
Coray [F] 52 B3
Corbalán [E] 102 D1
Corbeil-Essonnes [F] 54 E4
Corbeny [F] 56 A2
Corbera d'Ebre [E] 94 F4
Corbie [F] 54 E1
Corbigny [F] 68 D3
Corbii Mari [RO] 150 B3
Corbridge [GB] 20 E3
Corby [GB] 28 C1
Corcaigh / Cork [IRL] 10 C4
Corciano [I] 132 C2
Corcieux [F] 70 C2
Corcomroe Abbey [IRL] 10 C2
Corconne [F] 124 D2
Corconte [E] 86 C3
Corcubión [E] 82 A2
Cordenons [I] 118 D3
Cordes [F] 124 A2
Córdoba [E] 104 D1
Cordobilla de Lácara [E] 90 F4
Corella [E] 94 C2
Cori [I] 134 B2
Coria [E] 90 F2
Coria del Río [E] 104 B1
Coriano [I] 128 E3
Corigliano Calabro [I] 136 C4
Corinaldo [I] 128 E4
Coripe [E] 104 C2
Cork / Corcaigh [IRL] 10 C4
Corlăţel [RO] 148 C2
Corlay [F] 52 C3
Corleone [I] 140 C2
Corleto Perticara [I] 134 F4
Çorlu [TR] 158 C3
Cormainville [F] 54 C4
Cormeilles [F] 54 B2
Cormery [F] 66 F3
Cornau [D] 30 F3
Cornellana [E] 82 E2
Córniglio [I] 128 B2
Cornimont [F] 70 C2
Cornuda la Valle [I] 118 C3
Cornudella de Montsant
[E] 96 B3
Cornus [I] 142 B3
Corofin [IRL] 10 C2
Corovodë [AL] 160 B3
Corps [F] 80 E4
Corral de Almaguer [E] 100 F2
Corralejo [E] 114 E3
Corrales [E] 84 E3
Corral Rubio [E] 102 B4
Corre [F] 70 B2
Corréggio [I] 128 B2
Corridonia [I] 132 E2
Corsano [I] 136 F4
Corseul [F] 52 D3
Corte [F] 130 B2
Corte Brugnatella [I] 126 F2
Corte Figueira [P] 98 C3
Cortegada [E] 82 B3

Cortegana [E] 98 E3
Cortemaggiore [I] 128 A1
Cortemília [I] 126 D2
Cortes [E] 94 D2
Cortes de la Frontera [E]
104 C3
Cortes de Pallás [E] 102 C3
Cortes de Peleas [E] 98 E2
Corte Zorrinha [P] 98 C3
Cortijos de Abajo [E] 100 D2
Cortina d'Ampezzo [I] 118 D2
Cortona [I] 130 F1
Coruche [P] 90 B3
Coruña del Conde [E] 94 A2
Corvara in Badia [I] 118 C2
Corvera [E] 106 E2
Corvey [D] 44 B2
Corwen [GB] 22 E3
Cosa [E] 94 D4
Cosa [I] 130 E2
Cosenza [I] 138 E1
Cosne-Cours-sur-Loire
[F] 68 C2
Cosne d'Allier [F] 68 C4
Coşoveni [RO] 148 E2
Coşoveni [RO] 148 E2
Cospeito [E] 82 D2
Cossato [I] 116 C3
Cossé-le-Vivien [F] 66 D1
Cossonay [CH] 116 B1
Costa da Caparica [P] 90 A4
Costa de los Pins [E] 108 D3
Costeşti [RO] 148 F1
Costigliole Saluzzo [I] 126 C2
Costineşti [RO] 150 F2
Coswig [D] 44 E3
Coswig [D] 46 B4
Cote [E] 104 C2
Cotignac [F] 126 A3
Cotronei [I] 138 E2
Cottbus [D] 46 C3
Couches [F] 68 E4
Couço [P] 90 C3
Coucy-le-Château-Auffrique
[F] 54 F2
Coudray-Montbault, Château
de- [F] 66 D3
Couflenz [F] 88 E4
Cougnac, Grottes de- [F]
78 E4
Couhé [F] 66 E4
Couilly [F] 54 E3
Couiza [F] 124 A3
Coulanges-la-Vineuse [F]
68 D2
Coulmier-le-Sec [F] 68 E2
Coulommiers [F] 54 E3
Coulon [F] 66 D4
Coulonges [F] 66 D4
Coupar Angus [GB] 18 D3
Couptrain [F] 54 A3
Courboyer, Manoir de- [F]
54 B3
Courceau [F] 68 E3
Courchevel [F] 116 A3
Cour-Cheverny [F] 68 A2
Courçon [F] 66 C4
Cour-et-Buis [F] 80 D3
Courgains [F] 54 B4
Courmayeur [I] 116 B3
Courpière [F] 80 C2
Courrière [B] 40 E4
Coursan [F] 124 B3
Courseulles-sur-Mer [F]
54 A2
Cours-la-Ville [F] 80 D2
Courson-les-Carrières [F]
68 D2
Courtacon [F] 54 F4
Courtanvaux, Château de-
[F] 66 F2
Courteilles [F] 54 B2

Courtelevant [F] 70 C3
Courtenay [F] 68 C1
Courtmacsherry [IRL] 10 B4
Courtomer [F] 54 B3
Courtown Harbour [IRL] 10 F3
Courtrail (Kortrijk) [B] 40 C3
Courville [F] 54 C4
Coutances [F] 52 E2
Couterne [F] 54 A3
Coutevroult [F] 54 E3
Coutras [F] 78 C3
Couvet [CH] 70 C4
Couvin [B] 56 B2
Covadonga [E] 86 B2
Covadonga [E] 86 B2
Covaleda [E] 94 B2
Covarrubias [E] 94 A1
Covarrubias [E] 94 B2
Covăsinţ [RO] 122 E3
Covci [RO] 148 D2
Coventry [GB] 28 B1
Covide [P] 82 B4
Covilhã [P] 90 E2
Cowes [GB] 28 B4
Cox [F] 88 E2
Cózar [E] 100 E4
Cozes [F] 78 B2
Cozia, Mănăstirea– [RO]
248 D3
Cozzano [F] 130 B3
Craco [I] 136 C3
Craidorolţ [RO] 76 F3
Craigavon [NIR] 12 E2
Crail [GB] 18 E3
Crailsheim [D] 58 D4
Craiova [RO] 122 F2
Craiova [RO] 148 E2
Crângeni [RO] 148 F2
Crângu [RO] 150 A2
Crans [CH] 116 C2
Craon [F] 66 D1
Craponne-sur-Arzon [F]
80 C3
Crato [P] 90 D3
Craughwell [IRL] 10 C1
Crawley [GB] 28 C3
Crea, Santuario di– [I] 116 C4
Crêches-sur-Saône [F] 80 D2
Crécy [F] 54 E3
Crécy-en-Ponthieu [F] 40 A4
Crécy-sur-Serre [F] 56 A2
Crediton [GB] 26 D3
Creevagh [IRL] 12 B2
Creglingen [D] 58 D3
Creil [F] 54 E2
Crema [I] 116 E4
Cremaste [TR] 164 B2
Crémieu [F] 80 E2
Cremona [I] 116 F4
Crenšovci [SLO] 120 D2
Créon [F] 78 C3
Crepaja [SRB] 146 E1
Crépy-en-Valois [F] 54 E2
Cres [HR] 144 B2
Crésantignes [F] 68 E1
Crescentino [I] 116 C4
Crespin [F] 40 D4
Crespino [I] 128 D1
Cressensac [F] 78 E3
Cresslough [IRL] 12 D1
Crest [F] 80 D4
Cresta [CH] 116 E2
Creussen [D] 58 F3
Creutzwald [F] 56 E3
Creuzburg [D] 44 C4
Crevalcore [I] 128 C2
Crevecoeur [F] 54 D2
Crevecœur-en-Auge [F]
54 B2
Crevedia Mare [RO] 150 B1
Crevillent / Crevillente [E]
106 E2

Crevillente / Crevillent [E] 106 E2
Crevoladossola [I] 116 D2
Crewe [GB] 22 F3
Crewkerne [GB] 26 E3
Criação Velha [P] 110 A3
Crianlarich [GB] 18 C3
Cricklade [GB] 26 F2
Crieff [GB] 18 D3
Crikvenica [HR] 144 B1
Crillon [F] 54 D2
Crišnjeva [HR] 144 B1
Crispiano [I] 136 D2
Crissolo [I] 126 C1
Cristo, Monasterio del– [E] 82 E2
Cristo del Espíritu–Santo [E] 100 D2
Crivitz [D] 32 D3
Crkvice [BIH] 146 A3
Crkvina [BIH] 146 B2
Crkvina Prolaz [MNE] 152 F2
Crmljan [KS] 154 C2
Črmošnjice [SLO] 120 B4
Črna [SLO] 120 B2
Crna Bara [SRB] 122 D3
Crna Trava [SRB] 154 E2
Crnča [SRB] 146 C3
Crni Lug [BIH] 144 E3
Crni Vrh [SLO] 118 F3
Črnkovci [HR] 122 A4
Crnoklište [SRB] 148 C4
Črnomelj [SLO] 120 B4
Crocq [F] 80 A2
Crodo [I] 116 D2
Croithlí / Crolly [IRL] 12 D1
Croix Haute, Col de la– [F] 124 F1
Crolly / Croithlí [IRL] 12 D1
Cro–Magnon [F] 78 D3
Cromarty [GB] 14 E3
Cromer [GB] 24 F4
Crook [GB] 20 E3
Crookedwood [IRL] 10 E1
Crookhaven [IRL] 10 A4
Crookstown [IRL] 10 B4
Croom [IRL] 10 C3
Cropalati [I] 136 C4
Cropani [I] 138 E2
Crosia [I] 136 D4
Crossakeel [IRL] 10 F1
Crosshaven [IRL] 10 C4
Crossmaglen [NIR] 10 F1
Crossmolina [IRL] 12 B2
Crotone [I] 138 F2
Crowborough [GB] 28 D4
Croydon [GB] 28 C3
Crozant [F] 68 A4
Crozon [F] 52 A3
Cruas [F] 80 D4
Cruceni [RO] 122 D4
Cruces [E] 82 C2
Crucoli [I] 138 F1
Crumlin [NIR] 12 F2
Cruseilles [F] 80 F2
Crusheen [IRL] 10 C2
Cruzy [F] 68 E2
Cruzy [F] 124 B3
Crvenka [SRB] 122 C4
Csabacsüd [H] 122 D2
Csákánydoroszló [H] 120 D1
Csakvár [H] 76 A4
Csanádapáca [H] 122 D2
Csanádpalota [H] 122 D3
Csanytelek [H] 122 C2
Csapod [H] 74 D4
Csárdaszállás [H] 122 D2
Csaroda [H] 76 F2
Császártöltés [H] 122 B2
Csávoly [H] 122 B3

Csenger [H] 76 F3
Csengersima [H] 76 F3
Csépa [H] 122 C2
Cserebökény [H] 122 D2
Cserkeszőlő [H] 122 C2
Csernely [H] 76 C3
Csesznek [H] 74 F4
Csobád [H] 76 D2
Csókakői Varrom [H] 74 F4
Csökmő [H] 122 E1
Csokonyavisonta [H] 120 E3
Csongrád [H] 122 C2
Csopak [H] 120 F1
Csór [H] 122 A1
Csorna [H] 74 E4
Csorvás [H] 122 D2
Csót [H] 74 E4
Csurgó [H] 120 E3
Cuadros [E] 82 F4
Cualedro [E] 82 C4
Cuba [P] 98 C2
Cubel [E] 94 C3
Cubells [E] 96 C2
Cubo de Bureba [E] 86 D4
Çubuklu [TR] 170 E4
Cucueți [RO] 148 E1
Cudillero [E] 82 F2
Cuéllar [E] 92 E2
Cuenca [E] 102 B2
Cuers [F] 124 F4
Cuerva [E] 100 D2
Cuesta Blanca de Arriba [E] 106 E3
Cuevas del Almanzora [E] 106 C3
Cuevas del Becerro [E] 104 D3
Cuevas de San Clemente [E] 92 F1
Cuevas de San Marcos [E] 104 E2
Cúglieri [I] 142 B3
Cugnon–sur–Semois [B] 56 C2
Cuhom [F] 40 B3
Cuijk [NL] 42 B2
Cuillé [F] 66 D1
Cuiseaux [F] 80 E1
Cuisery [F] 80 E1
Cujmir [RO] 148 C2
Cukurini [LV] 236 D4
Çukurköi [TR] 158 B3
Çukurköy [TR] 170 E3
Culaccio [I] 128 B3
Culan [F] 68 B4
Culdaff [IRL] 12 E1
Culemborg [NL] 30 B4
Cúllar [E] 106 B2
Cullen [GB] 14 F3
Cullera [E] 102 D4
Cullompton [GB] 26 D3
Culoz [F] 80 E2
Cuma [I] 134 C3
Cumbernauld [GB] 18 C4
Cumbres de S. Bartolomé [E] 98 E3
Cumbres Mayores [E] 98 E3
Ćumić [SRB] 146 E3
Cumnock [GB] 20 C1
Cumpăna [RO] 150 F1
Cunault [F] 66 E2
Cúneo [I] 126 C2
Čuništa [BIH] 146 B3
Ćunski [HR] 144 B2
Cuntis [E] 82 B3
Cuorgnè [I] 116 C3
Cupar [GB] 18 E3
Cupello [I] 134 D1
Cupra Marittima [I] 132 E2
Cupramontana [I] 128 E4
Čuprija [SRB] 146 F3
Cura, Santuari de– [E] 108 D3
Cura Nuova [I] 130 D1

Curcani [RO] 150 C2
Curel [F] 124 F2
Curia [P] 84 A4
Ćurlovac [HR] 120 E3
Curon Venosta / Graun im Vinschgau [I] 118 B1
Curraghmore [IRL] 10 D3
Curtatone [I] 118 B4
Curtea de Argeş [RO] 248 D3
Curtici [RO] 122 E2
Curtis [E] 82 C2
Curtişoara [RO] 148 E1
Čurug [SRB] 122 C4
Cusset [F] 80 C1
Custines [F] 56 D4
Custonaci [I] 140 B1
Cutigliano [I] 128 B3
Cutro [I] 138 F2
Cutting [F] 56 E4
Çüvenli [TR] 158 C3
Cuveşdia [RO] 122 E3
Cuvilly [F] 54 E2
Cuxhaven [D] 32 A2
Cuzzola [I] 142 C2
Cvikov [CZ] 60 E1
Cwmbran [GB] 26 E2
Cybinka [PL] 46 C2
Cyców [PL] 50 C3
Cytonium [TR] 164 C3
Czacz [PL] 46 E2
Czajków [PL] 48 C3
Czaplinek [PL] 34 F3
Czarna [PL] 50 B3
Czarnków [PL] 36 A4
Czarnożyły [PL] 48 C4
Czarny Dunajec [PL] 62 F4
Czastary [PL] 48 C4
Czchów [PL] 64 B3
Czechowice–Dziedzice [PL] 62 E3
Czeladź [PL] 62 E2
Czemierniki [PL] 50 C3
Czempiń [PL] 46 F2
Częremcha [PL] 38 C4
Czerniejewo [PL] 48 B2
Czernikowo [PL] 36 D4
Czernin [PL] 36 D2
Czersk [PL] 36 C3
Czersk [PL] 48 F2
Czerwieńsk [PL] 46 D2
Czerwionka–Leszczyny [PL] 62 D3
Czerwony–Dwór [PL] 38 B1
Częstochowa [PL] 62 E1
Człopa [PL] 34 F4
Człuchów [PL] 36 B3
Czorsztyn [PL] 64 A4
Czudec [PL] 64 C3
Czyżew–Osada [PL] 38 B4

D

Daaden [D] 42 E4
Dabarska Spilja [BIH] 144 E2
Dabas [H] 122 B1
Dabern [D] 46 B3
Dąbie [PL] 34 D3
Dąbie [PL] 48 C2
Dabilja [MK] 154 F4
Dąbki [PL] 36 A2
Dąbki [PL] 46 F3
Dabo [F] 70 D1
Dabo, Roch. de– [F] 70 D1
Dăbovan [BG] 148 F3

Dabovets [BG] 156 F2
Dăbovo [BG] 156 E1
Dąbrowa [PL] 48 B1
Dąbrowa [PL] 48 C3
Dąbrowa [PL] 50 C2
Dąbrowa [PL] 62 C2
Dąbrowa Białostocka [PL] 38 C2
Dąbrowa Górnicza [PL] 62 E2
Dąbrowa Tarnowska [PL] 64 B2
Dąbrówca Warszawska [PL] 48 F4
Dabrówka [PL] 64 D2
Dąbrówka Kościelna [PL] 38 C3
Dąbrówka Leśna [PL] 46 F1
Dąbrówka Wielkopolska [PL] 46 E2
Dąbrówno [PL] 36 E3
Dăbuleni [RO] 148 E2
Dachau [D] 72 C2
Dachnów [PL] 64 E2
Dachsteinhöhlen [A] 72 F4
Dačice [CZ] 74 C1
Dad [H] 74 F4
Dadaglı [TR] 170 D2
Dädesjö [S] 184 D3
Dáfnes [GR] 166 D4
Dáfni [GR] 162 C2
Dáfni [GR] 162 E2
Dáfni [GR] 168 B2
Dáfni [GR] 172 D1
Dafnónas [GR] 156 D3
Dafnotí [GR] 166 C2
Dağakça [TR] 164 E1
Dagali [N] 192 D3
Dağardı [TR] 164 E2
Dagda [LV] 236 E4
Dagebüll [D] 178 B3
Dağkızılca [TR] 170 B2
Dahlem [D] 56 E1
Dahlen [D] 44 F3
Dahlenburg [D] 32 C3
Dahme [D] 32 D2
Dahme [D] 46 B3
Dahmen [D] 32 F3
Dahn [D] 56 F4
Dähre [D] 32 D4
Daia [RO] 150 B2
Daikanvik [S] 214 A2
Daimiel [E] 100 E3
Daimoniá [GR] 172 E3
Daingean [IRL] 10 E2
Đakovica / Gjakove [KS] 154 B3
Đakovo [HR] 146 B1
Daksti [LV] 230 E4
Dal [N] 186 E1
Dal [N] 194 B4
Dala [S] 188 E4
Dalaas [A] 72 A4
Dala–Floda [S] 194 F4
Dala–Husby [S] 196 C4
Dala–Järna [S] 194 E3
Dalama [TR] 170 C3
Dalaman [TR] 176 D1
Dalarö [S] 190 E3
Dalbeattie [GB] 20 C2
Dalberg [D] 56 F2
Dalboşet [RO] 148 B1
Dalby [DK] 178 D2
Dalby [S] 180 C2
Dalbyn [S] 194 F2
Dale [GB] 26 B1
Dale [N] 186 D3
Dale [N] 192 B3
Dale [N] 192 B1
Dale [N] 202 C4
Dalen [N] 186 D2
Dalen [N] 202 E3
Daleszyce [PL] 50 A4

Dalfors [S] 196 B2
Dalhem [S] 184 E1
Dalhem [S] 234 A2
Dalholen [N] 202 F4
Dalías [E] 106 B4
Daliowa [PL] 64 C4
Dalj [HR] 122 B4
Daljani [BIH] 144 F4
Dalkeith [GB] 18 D4
Dalkey [IRL] 10 F2
Dalmine [I] 116 E3
Dalmose [DK] 178 D2
Daløy [N] 192 A2
Dalry [GB] 18 C4
Dalsbruk / Taalintehdas [FIN] 198 D4
Dalselv [N] 218 F4
Dalseter [N] 192 F2
Dalseter [N] 204 A4
Dalsjöfors [S] 184 B2
Dalskog [S] 188 C3
Dals Långed [S] 188 C3
Dals Rostock [S] 188 C3
Dalstein [F] 56 D3
Daluis, Gorges de– [F] 126 B2
Dalum [S] 184 B1
Dalvík [S] 218 C2
Daly [CY] 176 D3
Dalyan [TR] 162 F2
Dalyan [TR] 176 D1
Damási [GR] 160 E4
Damaskiniá [GR] 160 D3
Damasławek [PL] 48 B1
Damba [N] 202 B4
Dambaslar [TR] 158 B3
Dambeck [D] 32 E3
Dammartin–en–Goële [F] 54 E3
Damme [B] 40 C2
Damme [D] 30 F3
Dammen [N] 186 E2
Dammendorf [D] 46 C2
Damno [PL] 36 B1
Damp 2000 [D] 32 C1
Damparis [F] 68 F3
Dampierre [F] 54 D3
Dampierre [F] 70 B3
Dampierre–sur–Boutonne [F] 78 C1
Dampierre–sur–Salon [F] 70 B3
Damville [F] 54 C3
Damvillers [F] 56 C3
Dănciuleşti [RO] 148 E1
D. Andrijevci [HR] 146 B1
Dăneasa [RO] 148 F2
Daneţi [RO] 148 E2
Dångebo [S] 184 D4
Dangé–St–Romain [F] 66 F3
Danilovgrad [MNE] 152 E3
Danişment [TR] 164 C2
Daniszyn [PL] 48 B3
Danków [PL] 34 E4
Dannäs [S] 184 C3
Dannemarie [F] 70 C3
Dannenberg [D] 32 D4
Dannenwalde [D] 32 F4
Dannike [S] 184 B2
Dánszentmiklós [H] 122 C1
Daon [F] 66 D2
Daoulas [F] 52 B3
Darabani [RO] 244 C2
Darány [H] 120 E3
Darbénai [LT] 238 A1
Darbu [M] 186 F1
Darda [HR] 122 B4
Dardesheim [D] 44 D2
Dardhë [AL] 160 C3
Darfo [I] 116 F3
Dargilan, Grotte de– [F] 124 C2
Dargun [D] 32 F2

Darıca [TR] 158 E3
Darıca [TR] 164 C2
Dariveren [TR] 170 E3
Därligen [CH] 116 C1
Darlington [GB] 20 E4
Darłówko [PL] 36 A2
Darłowo [PL] 36 A2
Darmstadt [D] 58 B2
Darney [F] 70 B2
Darnius [E] 96 E2
Daroca [E] 94 C3
Darque [P] 82 A4
Darro [E] 106 A2
Dartford [GB] 28 D3
Dartmouth [GB] 26 D4
Dartsel [S] 214 D1
Daruvar [HR] 120 E4
Darvas [H] 122 E1
Darwen [GB] 22 F2
Dasburg [D] 56 D2
Dascălu [RO] 150 C1
Dashkavichy [BY] 38 E3
Dašice [CZ] 60 F3
Dasing [D] 72 C2
Daskalovo [BG] 154 F2
Dasochóri [GR] 156 D4
Dassel [D] 44 B2
Dassow [D] 32 D2
Dasswang [D] 58 F4
Daszyna [PL] 48 D2
Datça [TR] 176 B1
Datteln [D] 42 D2
Daugai [LT] 238 D4
Daugård [DK] 178 C2
Daugavgrīva [LV] 234 F3
Daugavpils [LV] 236 D4
Dauguli [LV] 230 D4
Daun [D] 56 E2
Dautphetal [D] 42 E4
Daventry [GB] 28 C1
Daviá [GR] 172 D2
Davik [N] 202 B4
Daviot [GB] 14 E3
Davle [CZ] 60 D3
Dávleia [GR] 166 E3
Davos [CH] 116 F1
Davutlar [TR] 170 B3
Dawlish [GB] 26 D3
Dax [F] 88 B2
Dazkırı [TR] 170 F2
D. Bukovića [SRB] 146 C3
Ddrinci [BG] 150 E2
Deal [GB] 28 E4
Deão [P] 82 A4
Deauville [F] 54 B2
Debar [MK] 154 C4
Debeburnu [TR] 164 D3
Debeikiai [LT] 238 E2
Debelets [BG] 150 B4
Dębe Wielkie [PL] 48 F2
Dębica [PL] 64 C3
Dębina [PL] 62 C2
Dęblin [PL] 50 B3
Dębno [PL] 150 A4
Dębnica Kaszubska [PL] 36 B2
Dębno [PL] 46 C1
Dębno [PL] 64 A4
Dębno [PL] 64 B3
Debovo [BG] 150 A3
Dębowo [PL] 38 C2
Debrc [SRB] 146 D2
Debrecen [H] 76 E4
Debrznica [PL] 46 D2
Debrzno [PL] 36 B3
Debůr [BG] 156 D2
Dęby [PL] 38 A3
Dečani [KS] 154 B2
Dechtice [SK] 74 E2
Decimomannu [I] 142 B5
Děčín [CZ] 60 D1
Decines [F] 80 D2

Decize [F] 68 D4
De Cocksdorp [NL] 30 B2
Dedaj [AL] 152 F3
Dedebaği [TR] 170 E3
Dedelow [D] 34 C3
Dedemsvaart [NL] 30 D3
Dédestapolcsány [H] 76 C3
Dedinci [BG] 150 C4
Dedino [MK] 154 E4
Dedovichi [RUS] 240 B2
Defile de L'Ecluse [F] 80 E2
Dég [H] 122 A2
Degaña [E] 82 E3
Degeberga [S] 180 D2
Degerby [FIN] 198 B4
Degerby [FIN] 198 E4
Degerfors [S] 188 C2
Degerhamn [S] 184 E4
Degerndorf [D] 72 D3
Degernes [N] 188 C2
Degersjö [S] 206 C1
Degerträsk [S] 214 D2
Deggendorf [D] 72 E1
Dego [N] 228 D1
De Haan [B] 40 C2
Dehesa de Campoamor [E] 106 E2
Deià / Deyá [E] 108 C3
Deidesheim [D] 58 B3
Deifontes [E] 104 F2
Deining [D] 58 F4
Deinze [B] 40 D3
Dej [RO] 244 C3
Deje [S] 188 D2
Dejoi [RO] 148 E1
Dekéleia [CY] 176 E3
De Koog [NL] 30 B2
De Kooy [NL] 30 B2
Dekov [BG] 150 A3
Delary [S] 184 C4
Delbrück [D] 42 E2
Delčevo [MK] 154 F3
Delden [NL] 30 D4
Delebäck [S] 188 E3
Delégyháza [H] 76 B4
Deleitosa [E] 100 B1
Đelekovec [HR] 120 D3
Delémont [CH] 70 D3
Delfoí [GR] 166 E3
Delfoí [GR] 166 E3
Delft [NL] 30 A4
Delfzijl [NL] 30 D2
Délia [I] 140 D3
Delianuova [I] 138 D3
Deliatyn [UA] 244 D2
Deliblato [SRB] 146 E2
Deliceto [I] 134 E3
Deliler [TR] 164 D3
Delitzsch [D] 44 E3
Dellach [A] 118 E2
Delle [F] 70 C3
Delme [F] 56 D2
Delmenhorst [D] 32 A3
Delnice [HR] 120 B4
Delouze–Rosières [F] 70 B1
Delsbo [S] 196 C1
Delvin [IRL] 10 E1
Delvina [AL] 160 B4
Delvináki [GR] 160 C4
Demandice [SK] 76 A3
Demánová [SK] 76 B1
Demänovská Jaskyňa Slobody [SK] 76 B1
Demecser [H] 76 E2
Demidov [RUS] 240 C4
Demigny [F] 68 E4
Demirci [TR] 164 E3

Demirci [TR] 164 E2
Demirhanlı [TR] 158 A2
Demir Kapija [MK] 154 E4
Demirköy [TR] 158 C2
Demirören [TR] 164 F4
Demirtaş [TR] 164 E1
Demjansk [RUS] 240 C2
Demmin [D] 32 F2
Demoiselles, Grotte des– [F] 124 C2
Demonte [I] 126 C2
Demre [TR] 176 F1
Demyansk [RUS] 240 C2
Denain [F] 40 C4
Don Andel [NL] 30 D2
Denbigh [GB] 22 E2
Den Burg [NL] 30 B2
Dendermonde (Termonde) [B] 40 D3
Denekamp [NL] 30 D3
Đeneral Janković [KS] 154 D3
Den Haag [NL] 30 A3
Den Helder [NL] 30 B2
Dénia [E] 108 C1
Denizgören [TR] 164 A2
Denizkent [TR] 164 C1
Denizler [TR] 170 E2
Denizli [TR] 170 E3
Denkendorf [D] 72 C1
Denkingen [D] 70 F3
Den Oever [NL] 30 B2
Denzlingen [D] 70 D2
De Panne [B] 40 B3
Derbent [TR] 170 D2
Derby [GB] 24 C3
Derebağ [TR] 170 D3
Derecske [H] 76 D4
Dereham [GB] 28 E1
Dereköy [TR] 158 B2
Dereköy [TR] 164 F3
Dereköy [TR] 170 D2
Dereköy [TR] 170 F3
Dereköy [TR] 170 F3
Dereli [TR] 164 D2
Deringaj [HR] 144 D3
Dermantsi [BG] 148 E4
Dermbach [D] 58 D1
Dermulo [I] 118 B2
Derneburg [D] 44 C2
Deronje [SRB] 122 B4
Derreada [P] 98 B2
Derry (Londonderry) [NIR] 12 E1
Deruta [I] 132 C2
Derval [F] 66 C1
Dervéni [GR] 166 E4
Derventa [BIH] 146 A2
Dervishka mogila [BG] 156 F2
Dervíziana [GR] 166 C2
Descartes [F] 66 F3
Desenzano del Garda [I] 118 A4
Deset [N] 194 C2
Desfína [GR] 166 E3
Desimirovac [SRB] 146 E3
Desio [I] 116 E3
Deskáti [GR] 160 E3
Deskle [SLO] 118 E3
Desmond's Castle [IRL] 10 C3
Desná [CZ] 60 E1
Dešov [CZ] 74 C1
Despeñaperros [E] 100 D4
Despotovac [SRB] 146 F3
Despotovo [SRB] 122 C4
Dessau [D] 44 E3
Deštné [CZ] 62 B2
Destriana [E] 82 E4
Destrnik [SLO] 120 C2
Désulo [I] 142 C4
Desvres [F] 40 B3
Deszk [H] 122 D3
Deta [RO] 122 E4

Detk [H] 76 C3
Detkovo [RUS] 232 E2
Detmold [D] 42 F2
Dětřichov nad Bystřicí [CZ] 62 C3
Dettelbach [D] 58 D3
Dettifoss [IS] 218 C2
Detva [SK] 76 B2
Deurne [NL] 42 B3
Deutschkreutz [A] 74 D4
Deutschlandsberg [A] 120 B2
Deutsch–Wagram [A] 74 D2
Deva [E] 86 E3
Deva [RO] 240 C3
Dévaványa [H] 122 D1
Devčići [HR] 144 C2
Devecikonağı [TR] 164 D2
Devecser [H] 120 E1
Devene [BG] 148 E3
Deventer [NL] 30 C3
Deveselu [RO] 148 E2
Devetaki [BG] 150 A3
Devic [MK] 154 D4
Devin [BG] 156 C3
Devizes [GB] 26 F3
Devnya [BG] 150 E3
Dewsbury [GB] 24 C2
Deyá / Deià [E] 108 C3
Deza [E] 94 C3
Dezzo [I] 116 F3
Dhërmi [AL] 160 A3
Diafáni [GR] 176 B3
Diagučiai [LT] 238 E2
Diakoftó [GR] 166 E4
Dialampí [GR] 156 E4
Diamante [I] 136 B4
Dianalund [DK] 178 E2
Diano Marina [I] 126 C3
Diarvialiai [LT] 238 C2
Diásellu [GR] 160 E4
Diatlovo [BY] 242 A2
Diavatá [GR] 160 F2
Dichiseni [RO] 150 D1
Dicomano [I] 128 C3
Didcot [GB] 28 C2
Didesti [RO] 148 F2
Dídyma [GR] 168 A3
Didyma [TR] 170 B4
Didymóteicho [GR] 158 A3
Die [F] 80 E4
Dieburg [D] 58 C2
Diedorf [D] 44 C4
Diego Alvaro [E] 92 C3
Diekirch [L] 56 D2
Diemelstadt [D] 42 F3
Dienne [F] 80 A3
Dienten [A] 72 E4
Diepholz [D] 30 F3
Dieppe [F] 54 C1
Dierdorf [D] 58 A1
Dieren [NL] 30 C4
Dierhagen [D] 32 E2
Diesdorf [D] 32 D4
Diessen [D] 72 C3
Diest [B] 40 E3
Dietenheim [D] 72 A2
Dietfurt [D] 58 F4
Dietikon [CH] 70 E3
Dietmannsdorf [A] 120 C2
Dietmannsried [D] 72 B3
Dieue–sur–Meuse [F] 56 C3
Dieulefit [F] 124 E1
Dieulouard [F] 56 D4
Dieuze [F] 56 E4
Dieveniškės [LT] 38 F1
Diez [D] 58 B2
Differdange [L] 56 D3
Digerberget [S] 204 E3
Digermulen [N] 224 B4
Digernes [N] 202 C3
Dignac [F] 78 D2

Dignano [I] 118 E3
Digne–les–Bains [F] 126 B2
Digny [F] 54 C3
Digoin [F] 80 C1
Dijon [F] 68 F3
Díkaia [GR] 156 F2
Dikanäs [S] 212 F2
Dikance [KS] 154 C3
Dikili [TR] 164 B3
Dikli [LV] 230 D4
Diksmuide [B] 40 C3
Diktalo Ántro [GR] 174 D4
Diktýnaion [GR] 174 B3
Dílesi [GR] 168 B2
Dillenberg [D] 42 E4
Dillingen [D] 56 E3
Dillingen [D] 72 B2
Dílos [GR] 168 D3
Dilwyn [GB] 26 E1
Dímaina [GR] 168 A3
Dimaro [I] 118 B2
Dímitra [GR] 160 F4
Dimitrovgrad [BG] 156 E2
Dimitrovgrad [SRB] 148 D4
Dimmelsvik [N] 192 B4
Dimovo [BG] 148 C3
Dinami [I] 138 D3
Dinan [F] 52 D3
Dinant [B] 56 C1
Dinard [F] 52 D3
Dingelstädt [D] 44 C3
Dingle [S] 188 C3
Dingle / An Daingean [IRL] 10 A3
Dingli [M] 140 C4
Dingolfing [D] 72 D2
Dingwall [GB] 14 D3
Dinkelsbühl [D] 58 D4
Dinklage [D] 30 F3
Dinozé [F] 70 C2
Dinslaken [D] 42 C2
Dio [S] 184 C3
Díon [GR] 160 E3
Diosgyör [H] 76 D3
Dipkarpaz (Rizokárpasox) [CY] 176 E2
Dipótamos [GR] 156 D3
Dippoldiswalde [D] 60 D1
Dirgenler [TR] 176 E1
Dirnaich [D] 72 D2
Diseñä [N] 194 C4
Disentis / Mustér [CH] 116 E1
Disneyland [F] 54 E3
Dispíli [GR] 160 D3
Diss [GB] 28 E2
Dístomo [GR] 166 E3
Dístrato [GR] 160 C3
Ditzingen [D] 70 F1
Diva Slatina [BG] 148 D3
Divci [SRB] 146 D3
Divčibare [SRB] 146 D3
Dívčí Hrady [CZ] 74 D1
Dives–sur–Mer [F] 54 B2
Divič [SRB] 146 C3
Divínski Hrad [SK] 76 B2
Divjakë [AL] 160 A2
Divonne–les–Bains [F] 80 F2
Divri [GR] 162 A4
Divuša [HR] 144 E1
Dixence [CH] 116 C2
Dizy–le–Gros [F] 56 B2
Djäkneböle [S] 206 E1
Djala [SRB] 122 C3
Djauvik [S] 234 A3
Djupfest [N] 202 F1
Djupfors [S] 214 A1
Djúpivogur [IS] 218 D3
Djupsjö [S] 204 D1
Djupvik [N] 224 E2
Djura [S] 194 F3
Djurakovac [KS] 154 B2
Djuramåla [DK] 184 D4

Djurås [S] 194 F3
D. Kronovo [SLO] 120 B3
Dłoń [PL] 46 F3
Dlouhá Loučka [CZ] 62 C3
Długie [PL] 34 E4
Długołęka [PL] 46 F4
Długosiodło [PL] 38 B4
Dmitriyev-L'govckiy [RUS] 242 F2
Dmitrov [RUS] 240 F2
Dmitrovsk-Orlovskiy [RUS] 242 F2
Dniprodzerzhyns'k [UA] 246 E1
Dnipropetrovs'k [UA] 246 F1
Dniproprudne [UA] 246 F2
Dno [RUS] 240 B2
Doba [RO] 76 F3
Dobanovci [SRB] 146 D2
Dobapuszta [H] 76 C4
Dobbiaco / Toblach [I] 118 D2
Dobbrikow [D] 44 F2
Dobczyce [PL] 62 F3
Dobel [D] 70 E1
Dobele [LV] 234 E3
Döbeln [D] 44 F4
Doberlug Kirchhain [D] 46 B3
Döbern [D] 46 C3
Dobersberg [A] 74 B1
Dobiegniew [PL] 34 F4
Doboj [BIH] 146 A2
Doboz [H] 122 E2
Dobra [PL] 34 E3
Dobra [PL] 48 C3
Dobra [PL] 64 A3
Dobra [RO] 148 D2
Dobra [SRB] 148 B1
Dobra Gora [MNE] 152 E3
Dobrá Niva [SK] 76 B2
Dobřany [CZ] 60 C3
Dobrčane [KS] 154 D2
Dobrcz [PL] 36 C3
Dobre [PL] 50 B2
Dobre Miasto [PL] 36 E2
Döbriach [A] 118 F2
Dobrich [BG] 150 E2
Dobřichovice [CZ] 60 D3
Dobri Do [SRB] 154 D2
Dobri dol [BG] 148 D3
Dobrin [BG] 150 E2
Dobrinishte [BG] 156 B3
Dobrinja [BIH] 144 E2
Dobriš [CZ] 60 D3
Dobrits [BG] 158 A2
Dobrna [SLO] 120 B2
Dobrodan [BG] 148 F4
Dobrodzień [PL] 62 D2
Döbrököz [H] 122 A2
Dobromani [BIH] 152 D2
Dobromierz [PL] 48 E4
Dobromierz [PL] 62 B1
Dobromirka [BG] 150 B4
Dobromirtsi [BG] 156 E3
Dobromyl' [UA] 64 D3
Dobron [UA] 76 F2
Dobro Polje [BIH] 146 B4
Dobroselica [SRB] 146 D4
Dobrošinci [MK] 154 F4
Dobrosloveni [RO] 148 E3
Dobrosołowo [PL] 48 B2
Dobrosyn [UA] 64 F2
Dobroszyce [PL] 48 B4
Dobroteasa [RO] 148 E1
Dobroteşti [RO] 148 F2
Dobrotitsa [BG] 150 D2
Dobrovelychkivka [UA] 246 D2
Dobrovnik [SLO] 120 D2
Dobrovodský Hrad [SK] 74 E2
Dobrovol'sk [RUS] 238 B3
Dobrš [CZ] 60 C4
Dobruchi [RUS] 232 D2
Dobrun [BIH] 146 C4
Dobrush [BY] 242 D2

Dobrush [UA] 242 D2
Dobruška [CZ] 62 A2
Dobrzany [PL] 34 E3
Dobrzejewice [PL] 36 D4
Dobrzeń Wielki [PL] 62 C1
Dobrzyca [PL] 48 B3
Dobrzyń nad Wisłą [PL] 48 D1
Dobšinská ľadová Jaskyňa [SK] 76 C1
Dóc [H] 122 C2
Dochamps [B] 56 D1
Dockasberg [S] 220 F3
Docksta [S] 206 D2
Doclea [MNE] 152 E3
Doclin [RO] 122 E4
Dödafallet [S] 206 C3
Döderhult [S] 184 E2
Dodóni [GR] 160 C4
Dodši [H] 144 D1
Doe Castle [IRL] 12 D1
Doesburg [NL] 30 C4
Doetinchem [NL] 30 C4
Doğanbey [TR] 170 A3
Doğanbey [TR] 170 B3
Doganović [KS] 154 C3
Döge [H] 76 E2
Dogliani [I] 126 D2
Dogueno [P] 98 C3
Dohňany [SK] 62 D4
Doiber [A] 120 D2
Dojč [SK] 74 E2
Dojeviće [SRB] 154 B1
Dojrenci [BG] 150 A3
Dokka [N] 192 F3
Dokkas [S] 220 E2
Dokkedal [DK] 182 D3
Dokkum [NL] 30 C2
Doksy [CZ] 60 E2
Doktorce [PL] 38 C3
Dolac [KS] 154 C2
Dólar [E] 106 B3
Dolceácqua [I] 126 C3
Dol-de-Bretagne [F] 52 E3
Dole [F] 68 F3
Dølemo [N] 186 D3
Dolenci [MK] 160 C1
Dolenja Vas [SLO] 120 B4
Dolga Vas [SLO] 120 D2
Dolgellau [GB] 22 D3
Dolgorukovo [RUS] 36 E1
Dolhobyczów [PL] 64 F1
Doli [HR] 152 D2
Doliná [GR] 160 C4
Dolianova [I] 142 C5
Dolice [PL] 34 E4
Dolíchi [GR] 160 E3
Doljani [HR] 144 D2
Doljani [MNE] 152 F3
Doljevac [SRB] 148 B4
Döllach [A] 118 E1
Döllbach [D] 58 D2
Dolle [D] 44 E2
Dølli [N] 202 F4
Döllstädt [D] 44 D4

Dolno Kamartsi [BG] 156 C1
Dolno Kosovrasti [MK] 154 C4
Dolno Levski [BG] 156 C2
Dolno Novkovo [BG] 150 C3
Dolno Osenovo [BG] 156 B2
Dolno Tserovene [BG] 148 D3
Dolno Ujno [BG] 154 E2
Dolný Kubín [SK] 62 E4
Dolo [I] 118 C4
Dolores [E] 106 E2
Doloscy [RUS] 236 F4
Dolovo [SRB] 146 E2
Dolsk [PL] 46 F3
Dołubowo [PL] 38 C4
Dolyna [UA] 64 F4
Dolyns'ka [UA] 246 E2
Dolzhicy [RUS] 232 F2
Dołżyca [PL] 64 D4
Dom [A] 120 A2
Domaháza [H] 76 C3
Domaj–Has [AL] 154 B3
Domanic [TR] 164 F2
Domanovići [BIH] 152 C2
Domašov [CZ] 62 C3
Domaszowice [PL] 48 B4
Domažlice [CZ] 60 C4
Dombas [N] 202 E4
Dombasle [F] 70 C1
Dombegyház [H] 122 E2
Dombóvár [H] 120 F2
Dombrád [H] 76 E2
Dombrot-le-Sec [F] 70 B2
Domburg [NL] 40 D2
Doméniko [GR] 160 E4
Domèvre-en-Haye [F] 56 D4
Domfront [F] 52 F3
Domingão [P] 90 C3
Dömitz [D] 32 D3
Domme [F] 78 E4
Dommitzsch [D] 44 F3
Domnitsa [GR] 166 D3
Domnovo [RUS] 36 F1
Domodedovo [RUS] 240 F3
Domodóssola [I] 116 D2
Domokós [GR] 166 E2
Domousnice [CZ] 60 E2
Dompaire [F] 70 B2
Dompierre [F] 68 D4
Dompierre–du–Chemin [F] 52 E4
Dompierre–sur–Besbre [F] 68 D4
Dompierre–sur–Mer [F] 66 C4
Domrémy–la–Pucelle [F] 70 B1
Dömsöd [H] 122 B1
Domurcali [TR] 158 B2
Dómus de Maria [I] 142 B6
Domusnóvas [I] 142 B5
Domžale [SLO] 120 B3
Donado [E] 84 E2
Donaghadee [NIR] 20 A2
Donaghmore [IRL] 10 D2
Doña Mencía [E] 104 E2
Donaueschingen [D] 70 E2
Donaustauf [D] 72 D1
Donauwörth [D] 72 B1
Don Benito [E] 100 A2
Doncaster [GB] 24 C3
Dondurma [TR] 164 B2
Donegal / Dún na nGall [IRL] 12 D2
Donja Brela [HR] 152 B1
Donja Brezna [MNE] 152 E2
Donja Bukovica [MNE] 152 E2
Donja Kamenica [SRB] 146 D3
Donja Kamenica [SRB] 148 C3
Donja Ljubata [SRB] 154 E2
Donja Šatornja [SRB] 146 E3
Donja Suvaja [HR] 144 D3
Donja–Vrijeska [HR] 120 E4
Donje Ljupče [KS] 154 C2

Donje Petrčane [HR] 144 C3
Donji Koričani [BIH] 144 F3
Donji Krcin [SRB] 146 F4
Donji Lapac [HR] 144 D2
Donji Lipovik [MK] 154 E4
Donji Miholjac [HR] 120 F3
Donji Milanovac [SRB] 148 B2
Donji Stajevac [SRB] 154 E2
Donji Vakuf [BIH] 144 F3
Donji Zemunik [HR] 144 C3
Don Juan, Cueva de– [E] 102 C3
Donnalucata [I] 140 E4
Donnersbach [A] 74 A4
Donnersbachwald [A] 74 A4
Donostia–San Sebastián [E] 86 F3
Donovaly [SK] 76 B1
Dontilly [F] 54 E4
Donurme [EST] 230 E2
Donzenac [F] 78 E3
Donzère [F] 124 E1
Donzy [F] 68 C3
Doohooma / Dumha Thuama [IRL] 12 A2
Doonbeg [IRL] 10 B2
Doonloughan [IRL] 12 A3
Doorn [NL] 30 B4
Doornik (Tournai) [B] 40 C4
Dörarp [S] 184 C3
Dorchester [GB] 26 E3
Dordives [F] 68 C1
Dordrecht [NL] 30 B4
Dorēž [AL] 160 B1
Dorfen [D] 72 D2
Dorfmark [D] 32 B4
Dorgali [I] 142 C3
Doria, Castello– [I] 126 E2
Dório [GR] 172 C2
Dorkáda [GR] 156 B4
Dorking [GB] 28 C3
Dorkovo [BG] 156 C2
Dormagen [D] 42 C3
Dormánd [H] 76 C3
Dormans [F] 54 F3
Dor Mărunt [RO] 150 D1
Dornas [F] 80 C4
Dornauberg [A] 118 C1
Dornava [SLO] 120 C2
Dornbirn [A] 72 A4
Dornburg [D] 44 D4
Dorndorf [D] 44 C4
Dornes [F] 68 C4
Dorno [I] 116 D4
Dornoch [GB] 14 E3
Dornstetten [D] 70 E2
Dornum [D] 30 E1
Dorobanţu [RO] 150 E1
Dorog [H] 76 A3
Dorogobuzh [RUS] 240 D4
Dorohoi [RO] 244 D3
Dorohucza [PL] 50 C3
Dorokhovo [RUS] 240 E3
Dorosyny [UA] 50 F4
Dorotea [S] 214 A3
Dörpen [D] 30 E2
Dörpstedt [D] 32 B1
Dorsten [D] 42 D2
Dortan [F] 80 E2
Dortmund [D] 42 D3
Dörtyol (Prastio) [CY] 176 E3
Dorum [D] 32 A2
Dörverden [D] 32 B4
Dörzbach [D] 58 D3
Dosbarrios [E] 100 E1
Döşeme [TR] 176 B1
Dos Hermanas [E] 104 B2
Dospat [BG] 156 C3
Dos Torres [E] 100 C3
Døstrup [DK] 178 B3
Dotnuva [LT] 238 D2
Douai [F] 40 C4

Douamont, Fort du– [F] 56 C3
Douarnenez [F] 52 B3
Douchy [F] 68 C2
Doucier [F] 80 F1
Doudeville [F] 54 C1
Doué–la–Fontaine [F] 66 D3
Douglas [GB] 20 C1
Douglas [GBM] 20 B4
Doulaincourt [F] 68 F1
Doulevant–le–Château [F] 68 F1
Doullens [F] 40 B4
Dourdan [F] 54 D4
Dourgne [F] 124 A3
Doussard [F] 80 F3
Douvaine [F] 116 A2
Douzy [F] 56 C2
Dover [GB] 28 E4
Dovre [N] 202 E4
Downham Market [GB] 28 D1
Downings [IRL] 12 D1
Downpatrick [NIR] 12 F3
Dowra [IRL] 12 C2
Dowsk [BY] 242 D2
Doxáto [GR] 156 C4
Dozón / Castro [E] 82 C3
Dozulé [F] 54 B2
Drabiv [UA] 242 E4
Drac, Coves del– [E] 108 D3
Dračevo [MK] 154 D3
Drachenfels [D] 42 D4
Drachenwand [A] 72 E3
Drachselsried [D] 60 C4
Drachten [NL] 30 D2
Drag [N] 212 C3
Dragalevtsi [BG] 156 B1
Dragalina [RO] 150 D1
Drăgăneşti de Vede [RO] 150 A2
Drăgăneşti–Olt [RO] 148 F2
Drăgăneşti–Vlaşca [RO] 150 B2
Draganici [HR] 120 C4
Dragaš [KS] 154 C3
Drăgăşani [RO] 148 E1
Dragatuš [SLO] 120 B4
Drăgeşti [RO] 122 F1
Dragichevo [BG] 154 F2
Draginje [SRB] 146 D2
Draginovo [BG] 156 C2
Dragocvet [SRB] 146 F3
Dragoevo [MK] 154 E4
Dragoman [BG] 148 D4
Dragomir [BG] 156 C2
Dragomirovo [BG] 150 B3
Dragomirovo [BG] 150 B3
Dragomirovo [BG] 154 F2
Dragon, Caverne du– [F] 56 A2
Dragør [DK] 178 F2
Dragoş Vodă [RO] 150 D1
Drăgoteşti [RO] 148 D1
Dragotina [RO] 148 D1
Dragov Doll [MK] 154 D4
Dragovishtitsa [BG] 154 E2
Dragsfjärd [FIN] 198 D3
Dragsholm Slot [DK] 178 E2
Dragușnan [Dit] [?] 76 B3
Drahanovice [CZ] 62 C3
Drahichyn [BY] 50 F2
Drahonice [CZ] 60 D4
Drahovce [SK] 74 E2
Draka [BG] 158 B1
Drakčići [SRB] 146 E4
Draksenić [BIH] 144 E1
Dráma [GR] 156 C4
Dramče [MK] 154 E3
Drammen [N] 186 F1
Drangedal [N] 186 E2
Drängsered [S] 184 B3
Drängsmark [S] 214 D2
Drănic [RO] 148 E2
Dransfeld [D] 44 B3

Dranske [D] 34 C1
Drasenhofen [A] 74 D2
Drávafok [H] 120 F3
Drávaszabolcs [H] 122 A3
Dravískos [GR] 156 C4
Dravograd [SLO] 120 B2
Drawno [PL] 34 F4
Drawsko Pomorskie [PL] 34 F3
Drążdżewo [PL] 36 F4
Draženov [CZ] 60 B4
Dražniew [PL] 50 C1
Drebkau [D] 46 C3
Drégelypalánk [H] 76 B3
Drei [D] 44 C4
Dreilingen [D] 32 C4
Dren [KS] 154 C1
Dren [MK] 160 D1
Drenchia [I] 118 E3
Drencova [RO] 148 B1
Drenovac [SRB] 154 D2
Drenovets [BG] 148 D3
Drenovci [HR] 146 B2
Drensteinfurt [D] 42 E2
Drépano [GR] 160 E3
Dresden [D] 46 B4
Dretyń [PL] 36 B2
Dreux [F] 54 C3
Drevsjø [N] 194 C1
Drewitz [D] 44 E2
Drewitz [D] 46 B2
Drezdenko [PL] 46 E1
Drežnica [HR] 144 C1
Dreznik-Grad [HR] 144 D2
Driebergen [NL] 30 B4
Drienovo [SK] 76 B3
Driffield [GB] 24 D2
Drimoleague [IRL] 10 B4
Drina Kanjon [BIH] 146 C3
Drinjača [BIH] 146 C3
Drinovci [BIH] 152 C1
Driny [SK] 74 E2
Drionville [F] 40 B3
Driva [N] 202 F3
Drivstua [N] 202 F3
Drizë [AL] 160 B2
Drlače [SRB] 146 C3
Drnholec [CZ] 74 D2
Drniš [HR] 144 D4
Drnovo [SLO] 120 C3
Drøbak [N] 188 B1
Drobeta-Turnu Severin [RO]
 148 C1
Drobin [PL] 48 E1
Drochtersen [D] 32 B2
Drogheda / Droichead Átha
 [IRL] 12 E4
Drohiczyn [PL] 50 C1
Drohobych [UA] 64 E3
Droichead Átha / Drogheda
 [IRL] 12 E4
Droichead Nua / Newbridge
 [IRL] 10 E2
Droitwich [GB] 26 F1
Droftowice [PL] 48 B4
Dromahair [IRL] 12 C2
Dromcolliher [IRL] 10 C3
Dromore [NIR] 12 D2
Dromore West [IRL] 12 C2
Dronero [I] 126 C2
Dronninglund [DK] 182 D2
Dronten [NL] 30 C3
Dropla [BG] 150 E2
Drosáto [GR] 156 A4
Drosbacken [S] 194 D1
Drosendorf Stadt [A] 74 C1
Drosiá [GR] 168 A2
Drosopigí [GR] 160 D2
Drosopigí [GR] 166 C2
Drosselbjerg [DK] 178 D2
Drottninghaug [N] 202 F2
Droúseia [CY] 176 C4
Drozdowo [PL] 36 A1

Drugan [BG] 154 F2
Drumconrath [IRL] 10 F1
Drumevo [BG] 150 D3
Drumkeeran [IRL] 12 C2
Drumlish [IRL] 10 E1
Drummore [GB] 20 B3
Drumnadrochit [GB] 14 D3
Drumshanbo [IRL] 12 C3
Drumsna [IRL] 12 C3
Drusenheim [F] 70 E1
Druskininkai [LT] 38 D1
Drusti [LV] 236 C2
Druten [NL] 30 C4
Druya [BY] 236 E4
Družetic [SRB] 146 D2
Druzhba [DG] 150 E3
Druzhba [RUS] 36 F1
Druzhnaja Gorka [RUS] 232 F1
Drvar [BIH] 144 E3
Drvenik [HR] 152 C2
Dryanovo [BG] 150 B4
Drygały [PL] 38 B2
Drymós [GR] 160 F2
Dryópi [GR] 168 A3
Dryopída [GR] 168 C3
Dryós [GR] 168 D4
Drzewce [PL] 48 C2
Drzewiany [PL] 36 A2
Drzewica [PL] 48 E3
D. Stupnica [HR] 144 D1
Duagh [IRL] 10 B3
Duas Igrejas [P] 84 D3
Dub [SRB] 146 D3
Dubá [CZ] 60 E2
Dubac [HR] 152 D3
Dubăsari [MD] 244 F3
Dubechne [UA] 50 E3
Duben [D] 46 B3
Dubí [CZ] 60 D2
Dubica [HR] 144 E1
Dubienka [PL] 50 D4
Dubin [PL] 46 F3
Dubinino [RUS] 200 E2
Dubliany [UA] 64 E3
Dublin / Baile Átha Cliath
 [IRL] 10 F2
Dubna [RUS] 240 E2
Dub nad Moravou [CZ] 62 C4
Dubňany [CZ] 74 E1
Dubnica nad Váhom [SK]
 74 F1
Dübnitsa [BG] 156 C3
Dubno [UA] 244 D1
Dubočka Pećina [SRB] 148 B1
Dubovac [SRB] 146 E2
Dubovsko [BIH] 144 D2
Dubrava [BIH] 144 F2
Dubrava [HR] 120 D3
Dubrava [HR] 120 D3
Dubrava [RUS] 238 B4
Dubrave [BIH] 146 B2
Dubravica [BIH] 146 A3
Dubravka [HR] 152 D3
Dubrovka [RUS] 236 F3
Dubrovnik [HR] 152 D3
Dubrovno [RUS] 232 F3
Dubrovytsia [UA] 242 B4
Dubrowna [BY] 242 C1
Ducey [F] 52 E3
Duchcov [CZ] 60 D2
Ducherow [D] 34 C3
Duclair [F] 54 C2
Dudar [H] 74 F4
Dudelange [L] 56 D3
Düdenköy [TR] 176 E1
Duderstadt [D] 44 C3
Dudeştii Vechi [RO] 122 D3
Dudince [SK] 76 A3
Düdingen [CH] 70 C4
Dudley [GB] 22 F4
Due Carrare [I] 118 C4
Dueñas [E] 92 E1

Duesund [N] 192 B2
Dueville [I] 118 C3
Dufftown [GB] 14 F3
Duga Poljana [SRB] 154 B1
Duga Resa [HR] 120 C4
Duge Njive [HR] 152 C2
Dugi Rat [HR] 144 E4
Dugła [TR] 164 C3
Dugopolje [HR] 144 E4
Dugo Selo [HR] 120 D3
Duhnen [D] 32 A2
Duingen [D] 44 B2
Duingt [F] 80 F2
Duino [I] 118 E3
Duisburg [D] 47 C3
Duka [H] 120 E1
Dukat [AL] 160 A3
Dukat [SRB] 154 E2
Dukhovshchina [RUS] 240 D4
Dukla [PL] 64 C3
Dukovany [CZ] 74 D1
Dükštas [LT] 238 F2
Dukštos [LT] 238 E3
Dülbok Izvor [BG] 156 D2
Duleek [IRL] 10 F2
Dülken [D] 42 C3
Dülmen [D] 42 D2
Dulnain Bridge [GB] 14 E4
Dulovka [RUS] 232 E4
Dulovo [BG] 150 D2
Dulpetorpet [N] 194 C3
Dumača [SRB] 146 D2
Dumakömlöd [H] 122 B2
Dumanlı [TR] 164 F4
Dumbarton [GB] 18 C3
Dumbrava [RO] 122 F3
Dumbrăveni [RO] 150 E2
Dumfries [GB] 20 E1
Dumha Thuama / Doohooma
 [IRL] 12 A2
Dümpelfeld [D] 56 E1
Dun [F] 56 C3
Duna [N] 212 C3
Dunaengus [IRL] 10 B1
Dunaföldvár [H] 122 B2
Dunaharaszti [H] 76 B4
Dunaivtsi [UA] 244 E2
Dunajská Streda [SK] 74 E3
Dunakeszi [H] 76 B3
Dunakiliti [H] 74 E3
Dunany [IRL] 12 E3
Dunapataj [H] 122 B2
Dunărea [RO] 150 E1
Dunas de São Jacinto [P]
 84 A3
Dunaszeg [H] 74 E3
Dunaszekcső [H] 122 B3
Dunaszentbenedek [H] 122 B2
Dunasziget [H] 74 E3
Dunatetétlen [H] 122 B2
Dunaújváros [H] 122 B1
Dunavecse [H] 122 B2
Dunavtsi [BG] 148 C2
Dunbar [GB] 18 E4
Dunbeath [GB] 14 F2
Dunblane [GB] 18 D3
Dunboy Castle [IRL] 10 A4
Dunboyne [IRL] 10 F2
Dunbrody Abbey [IRL] 10 E4
Duncormick [IRL] 10 E4
Dundaga [LV] 234 D2
Dundalk / Dún Dealgan [IRL]
 12 E3
Dún Dealgan / Dundalk [IRL]
 12 E3
Dundee [GB] 18 E3
Dunderland [N] 218 F4
Dunfanaghy [IRL] 12 D1
Dunfermline [GB] 18 D4
Dungannon [NIR] 12 E2
Dungarvan [IRL] 10 D4

Dungiven [NIR] 12 E2
Dunglow / An Clochán Liath
 [IRL] 12 D1
Dungourney [IRL] 10 C4
Dunje [MK] 160 D1
Dunjica [MK] 154 E4
Dunker [S] 190 C3
Dunkerque [F] 28 F4
Dunkerque Ouest [F] 28 F4
Dunkineely [IRL] 12 C2
Duńkowice [PL] 64 E3
Dún Laoghaire [IRL] 10 F2
Dunlavin [IRL] 10 E2
Dunleer [IRL] 12 E3
Duun-le-Palestel [F] 68 A4
Dunloe, Gap of- [IRL] 10 B3
Dunloy [NIR] 12 F2
Dunmanway [IRL] 10 B4
Dunmore [IRL] 10 D1
Dunmore Caves [IRL] 10 E3
Dunmore East [IRL] 10 E4
Dunmurry [NIR] 12 F2
Dún na nGall / Donegal [IRL]
 12 D2
Dunoon [GB] 18 B3
Duns [GB] 20 E1
Dunshaughlin [IRL] 10 F2
Dunstable [GB] 28 C2
Dun-sur-Auron [F] 68 B3
Dunure [GB] 20 B1
Dunvegan [GB] 14 B3
Duoddar Sion [N] 228 B2
Dupnitsa [BG] 154 F3
Duquesa, Castillo de la- [E]
 104 C3
Durabeyler [TR] 164 E2
Durach [BG] 150 D2
Duran [BG] 150 D3
Durance [F] 88 D1
Durango [E] 86 F3
Durankulak [BG] 150 F2
Duras [F] 78 C4
Durasıllı [TR] 164 D4
Durban-Corbières [F] 124 B3
Durbe [LV] 234 D2
Durbuy [B] 56 D1
Dúrcal [E] 104 F3
Đurđenovac [HR] 120 F4
Đurđevac [HR] 120 D3
Đurđevića Tara [MNE] 152 F2
Đurđevik [BIH] 146 B3
Durdevi Stupovi [SRB] 154 B1
Düren [D] 42 C4
Durham [GB] 20 E3
Durhasan [TR] 164 E3
Durlas / Thurles [IRL] 10 D3
Durness [GB] 14 E1
Dürnkrut [A] 74 D2
Dürnstein [A] 74 C2
Durnstein [A] 120 A1
Durón [E] 94 A4
Durrës [AL] 160 A1
Durrow [IRL] 10 E3
Durrow Abbey [IRL] 10 E2
Durrus [IRL] 10 B4
Dursunbey [TR] 164 E2
Durtal [F] 66 E2
Duruelo de la Sierra [E] 94 B2
Dusetos [LT] 238 E2
Düskotna [BG] 150 D4
Dusnok [H] 122 B2
Dusocin [PL] 36 D2
Düsseldorf [D] 42 C3
Duszniki [PL] 46 E2
Duszniki-Zdrój [PL] 62 B2
Dutluca [TR] 164 E2
Dutluca [TR] 170 D2
Dutovlje [SLO] 118 F3
Duved [S] 204 D2
Düvertepe [TR] 164 D3
Duztarla [TR] 164 C3
Dvärsätt [S] 204 E2

Dve Mogili [BG] 150 B3
Dverberg [N] 224 B3
Dvor [HR] 144 D1
Dvor [SLO] 120 B3
Dvorce [CZ] 62 C3
Dvory nad Žitavou [SK] 74 F3
Dvůr Králové nad Labem
 [CZ] 60 F2
Dwingeloo [NL] 30 D3
Dyat'kovo [RUS] 242 E1
Dyatlitsy [RUS] 200 E4
Dybäck [S] 180 C2
Dyblin [PL] 48 D1
Dyce [GB] 18 F2
Dyck [D] 42 C3
Dygowo [PL] 34 F2
Dylewo [PL] 38 A3
Dymchurch [GB] 28 E4
Dymniki [BY] 38 D4
Dynów [PL] 64 D3
Dyranut [N] 192 D3
Dyrnes [N] 202 E1
Dyrráchio [GR] 172 D2
Dysbodarna [S] 194 E2
Dýstos [GR] 168 B2
Dyulino [BG] 150 E4
Dyuni [BG] 158 C1
Dyvik [S] 190 E2
Dzelzava [LV] 236 D3
Džepišta [MK] 154 C4
Dzhankoi [UA] 246 F3
Dzhebel [BG] 156 E3
Dzhurovo [BG] 148 E4
Dzhuryn [UA] 244 E2
Dziadkowice [PL] 38 C4
Dziadowa Kłoda [PL] 48 B4
Działdowo [PL] 36 E3
Działoszyce [PL] 64 A2
Działoszyn [PL] 48 C4
Dziemiany [PL] 36 B2
Dzierzgoń [PL] 36 D2
Dzierzki [PL] 36 F3
Dzierżoniów [PL] 62 B2
Dzietrzychowo [PL] 36 F2
Dźigolj [SRB] 148 B4
Dzivin [BY] 50 E2
Dziwnów [PL] 34 D2
Dziwnówek [PL] 34 E2
Dźuľunica [BG] 150 C3
Džumajlija [MK] 154 D4
Dźwierzuty [PL] 36 F3
Dźwirzyno [PL] 34 E2
Dzyarechyn [BY] 38 E3
Dzyarzhynsk [BY] 242 B2
Dzyatlava [BY] 38 F2

E

Easingwold [GB] 24 C2
Easky [IRL] 12 C2
Eastbourne [GB] 28 D4
East Grinstead [GB] 28 C3
East Kilbride [GB] 18 C4
Eastleigh [GB] 28 B5
Eaux-Bonnes [F] 88 C3
Eaux-Chaudes [F] 88 C3
Eauze [F] 88 D2
Ebberup [DK] 178 C2
Ebbo / Epoo [FIN] 200 B3
Ebbw Vale [GB] 26 E1
Ebecik [TR] 170 E3
Ebeleben [D] 44 C3
Ebelsbach [D] 58 E2
Ebeltoft [DK] 178 D1
Ebeltoft Færge [DK] 178 D1
Eben [A] 72 C4
Ebenfurth [A] 74 D3
Eben im Pongau [A] 72 E4
Ebensee [A] 72 F3
Eberbach [D] 58 B2

Eberbach [D] 58 C3
Eberdingen [D] 58 C4
Ebergötzen [D] 44 C3
Ebermannstadt [D] 58 E3
Ebern [D] 58 E2
Eberndorf [A] 120 B2
Ebersbach [D] 46 C4
Ebersberg [D] 72 D3
Eberschwang [A] 72 F3
Ebersdorf [D] 32 B3
Ebersdorf [D] 72 E2
Eberstein [A] 120 B2
Eberstein [D] 70 E1
Eberswalde [D] 34 C4
Ebes [H] 76 E4
Ebeylı [TR] 158 F4
Ebingen [D] 70 F2
Éboli [I] 134 D4
Ebrach [D] 58 D3
Ebreïchsdorf [A] 74 D3
Ebreuil [F] 80 B1
Ebstorf [D] 32 C4
Eceabat [TR] 164 A2
Echallens [CH] 116 B1
Echallon [F] 80 E2
Echarri / Etxarri [E] 86 F4
Échevennoz [I] 116 B3
Echínos [GR] 156 D3
Échourgnac [F] 78 C3
Echternach [L] 56 E2
Écija [E] 104 D1
Eck [A] 72 F3
Ečka [SRB] 122 D4
Eckartsau [A] 74 D3
Eckartsberga [D] 44 D4
Eckernförde [D] 32 C1
Eckerö [FIN] 196 F4
Eckersholm [S] 184 C2
Eckwarden [D] 30 F2
Ecole Valentine [F] 70 B3
Ecommoy [F] 66 E2
Ecouis [F] 54 D2
Ecoust–St–Mein [F] 40 C4
Ecsegfalva [H] 122 D1
Ecthe [D] 44 C3
Ecueillé [F] 68 A3
Ecury [F] 56 B3
Ed [S] 188 C3
Ed [S] 206 C2
Eda [S] 188 C1
Eda glasbruk [S] 188 C1
Edam [NL] 30 B3
Edane [S] 188 D2
Eddelak [D] 32 B2
Ede [NL] 30 C4
Ede [S] 204 F2
Edebäck [S] 188 E1
Edebo [S] 190 E1
Edeby [S] 190 E1
Edefors [S] 204 F2
Edefors [S] 220 E3
Edelény [H] 76 D2
Eden [S] 206 C1
Edenbridge [GB] 28 D3
Edenderry [IRL] 10 E2
Edenkoben [D] 58 B3
Edersee [D] 42 F3
Édessa [GR] 160 E2
Edevik [S] 212 D4
Edewecht [D] 30 F2
Edgeworthstown [IRL] 10 E1
Edhem [S] 188 E4
Edinburgh [GB] 18 D4
Edincik [TR] 164 C1
Edineţ [MD] 244 E2
Edirne [TR] 158 A2
Edland [N] 186 D1
Ēdole [LV] 234 F4
Édolo [I] 118 A2
Édon [F] 78 D2
Edremit [TR] 164 B3
Edsbro [S] 190 E1

Edsbruk [S] 184 E1
Edsbyn [S] 196 B2
Edsele [S] 206 B2
Edsleskog [S] 188 C3
Edsta [S] 196 C1
Edsvalla [S] 188 D2
Eeklo [B] 40 D3
Eelde [NL] 30 D2
Een [NL] 30 D2
Efendiköprüsü [TR] 164 F3
Eferding [A] 72 F2
Effeløt [N] 186 F2
Effelsberg, Radioteleskop–
   [D] 56 E1
Efkarpía [GR] 156 A4
Eforie [RO] 250 C3
Eforie Nord [RO] 150 F1
Eforie Sud [RO] 150 F1
Efpálio [GR] 166 D3
Eftimie Murgu [RO] 148 B1
Efýra [GR] 172 C1
Éfyras [GR] 166 B2
Egebæk [DK] 178 B2
Egeln [D] 44 D2
Egense [DK] 182 D3
Eger [H] 76 C3
Egerlövö [H] 76 D3
Egernsund [DK] 178 C3
Egersund [N] 186 B3
Egervár [H] 120 D2
Egesheim [D] 70 F2
Egeskov [DK] 178 C3
Egestorf [D] 32 C3
Egg [A] 72 A4
Egg [A] 118 C1
Eggedal [N] 192 E4
Eggenburg [A] 74 C2
Eggenfelden [D] 72 E2
Eggesin [D] 34 D3
Eggjaseteren [N] 212 D4
Egglham [D] 72 E2
Eggum [N] 218 F1
Eghezée [B] 40 E4
Egiertowo [PL] 36 C2
Egilsstaðir [IS] 218 D3
Egletons [F] 78 F3
Eglinton [NIR] 12 E1
Egmond aan Zee [NL] 30 B3
Egna / Neumarkt [I] 118 B2
Egremont [GB] 20 C3
Ejea de los Caballeros [E]
   94 D2
Egsdorf [D] 46 B2
Egtved [DK] 178 B2
Eguzon [F] 68 A4
Egyek [H] 76 D3
Ehingen [D] 72 A2
Ehnen [L] 56 D3
Ehra–Lessien [D] 44 D1
Ehrenburg [A] 72 B4
Ehrenburg [D] 32 A2
Ehrenhausen [A] 120 C2
Ehrwald [A] 72 B4
Eiane [N] 186 B2
Eibar [E] 86 E3
Eibenstock [D] 60 B2
Eibergen [NL] 30 D4
Eibiswald [A] 120 B2
Eich [D] 58 B3
Eichendorf [D] 72 E2
Eichstätt [D] 72 C1
Eid [N] 212 B4
Eida [N] 186 B3
Eidanger [N] 186 E2
Eide [N] 186 B2
Eide [N] 186 B3
Eide [N] 192 B2
Eide [N] 202 D2
Eide [N] 212 E3
Eidem [N] 212 C2
Eidet [N] 202 F2
Eidfjord [N] 192 C3
Eiði [FR] 182 B1
Eidiet [N] 192 B1

Eidsborg [N] 186 D2
Eidsbugarden [N] 192 E2
Eidsbygda [N] 202 D3
Eidsdal [N] 202 D3
Eidsfoss [N] 186 F2
Eidskog [N] 188 C1
Eidslandet [N] 192 B2
Eidsøra [N] 202 E3
Eidstod [N] 186 D2
Eidsund [N] 186 B2
Eidsvåg [N] 202 E3
Eidsvoll [N] 194 B4
Eidsvoll verk [N] 194 B4
Eifa [D] 42 E4
Eigenrieden [D] 44 C4
Eik [N] 186 B2
Eikefjørd [N] 192 B1
Eikelandsosen [N] 192 B3
Eiken [N] 186 C3
Eikenes [N] 192 B1
Eiksund [N] 202 C3
Eilenburg [D] 44 F3
Eilsleben [D] 44 D2
Eimisjärvi [FIN] 210 F2
Eina [N] 194 B3
Einastrand [N] 194 B3
Einavoll [N] 194 B3
Einbeck [D] 44 B2
Eindhoven [NL] 40 F3
Einsiedeln [CH] 70 E4
Einzinger Boden [A] 72 D4
Eisenach [D] 44 C4
Eisenbach [D] 58 C1
Eisenbach [D] 70 E2
Eisenberg [D] 44 E4
Eisenerz [A] 74 B4
Eisenhüttenstadt [D] 46 C2
Eisenkappel [A] 120 B2
Eisenstadt [A] 74 D3
Eisensteinhöhle [A] 74 C3
Eisfeld [D] 58 E2
Eisgarn [A] 74 B1
Eišiškės [LT] 38 E1
Eislingen [D] 72 A1
Eisriesenwelt [A] 72 E4
Eitorf [D] 42 D4
Eivindvik [N] 192 B2
Eivissa / Ibiza [E] 108 E2
Ejby [DK] 178 C2
Ejheden [S] 194 F2
Ejstrupholm [DK] 178 B1
Ejulve [E] 94 D4
Ek [S] 188 E3
Ekáli [GR] 168 B2
Ekeby [S] 178 F1
Ekeby [S] 188 F4
Ekeby [S] 190 D2
Ekebyholm [S] 190 E1
Ekedal [N] 190 C1
Ekedalen [S] 188 E4
Ekenäs [S] 188 D3
Ekenäs / Tammisaari [FIN]
   198 D4
Ekenässjön [S] 184 D2
Ekerö [S] 190 D2
Ekinhisar [TR] 170 F1
Ekkerøy [N] 228 F2
Ekne [N] 204 B1
Ekolsund [S] 190 D2
Ekornavallen [S] 188 D4
Ekorrbäcken [S] 220 F2
Ekorrträsk [S] 214 C3
Ekshärad [S] 194 E4
Eksingedal [N] 192 B2
Eksjö [S] 184 D2
Ekträsk [S] 214 C3
Ekzarh Antimovo [BG] 158 B1
Elaía [GR] 172 E3
Elaiochória [GR] 162 B2
Elaiónas [GR] 166 E3

El Alamo [E] 92 E4
El Alcornocal [E] 100 B4
El Altet [E] 106 F2
Elämäjärvi [FIN] 208 F1
Elanets' [UA] 246 D2
Elantxobe [E] 86 E3
Elassóna [GR] 160 E3
El Astillero [E] 86 C2
Eláteia [GR] 166 E3
Eláti [GR] 160 D4
Eláti [GR] 160 E3
Elatoú [GR] 166 D3
El Ballestero [E] 100 F4
El Barco de Ávila [E] 92 C3
El Barraco [E] 92 D3
El Berrón [E] 82 F2
Elbeuf [F] 54 C2
Elbigenalp [A] 72 B4
Elbingerode [D] 44 D3
Elbląg [PL] 36 D2
El Bodón [E] 90 F2
El Bonillo [E] 100 F3
El Bosque [E] 104 C3
Elburg [NL] 30 C3
Elburgo / Burgelu [E] 104 D3
El Burgo de Ebro [E] 94 D3
El Burgo de Osma [E] 94 A2
El Burgo Ranero [E] 86 A3
El Cabaco [E] 92 B3
el Campello [E] 106 F2
El Canal [E] 108 E2
El Cañavate [E] 102 A2
El Carpio [E] 104 E1
El Carpio de Tajo [E] 100 D1
El Casar de Talamanca [E]
   92 F3
El Castillo de las Guardas
   [E] 98 E4
El Castor [E] 104 C2
El Centenillo [E] 100 D4
El Cerro de Andévalo [E] 98 D3
Elche / Elx [E] 106 E2
Elche de la Sierra [E] 106 D1
Elçili [TR] 158 A3
El Coronil [E] 104 C2
El Cotillo [E] 114 E3
El Cubo de Don Sancho
   [E] 84 D4
El Cubo de Tierra del Vino
   [E] 84 E3
El Cuervo [E] 104 B2
El'cy [RUS] 240 D3
Elda [E] 106 E1
Eldalsosen [N] 192 C1
Eldena [D] 32 D3
Eldforsen [S] 194 E4
Eldrehaug [N] 192 D2
Elefsína [GR] 168 A2
Eleftherés [GR] 168 A2
Elefthério [GR] 160 F4
Eleftherochóri [GR] 160 D3
Eleftheroúpoli [GR] 156 C4
Eleja [LV] 234 F4
El Ejido [E] 106 B4
Elek [H] 122 E2
Elektrenai [LT] 238 D3
Elena [BG] 150 C4
Elenite [BG] 150 E4
Eleoúsa [GR] 176 C2
Eleousas, Moni Panagias–
   [CY] 176 D2
El Escorial [E] 92 E3
Eléšnica [BG] 156 B2
El Espinar [E] 92 E3
el Fondó dels Frares [E]
   106 E2
Elgå [N] 204 C4
El Gargantón [E] 100 D3
El Garrobo [E] 98 E4
Elgg [CH] 70 F3

El Grado [E] 94 F2
El Grau [E] 102 D3
el Grau / Grao [E] 102 D4
Elgsnes [N] 224 C3
El Guijo [E] 100 C3
Eliaröd [S] 180 D2
Elimäki [FIN] 200 B3
Eling [S] 188 D4
Elín Pelin [BG] 156 B1
Eliseyna [BG] 148 D4
Elizondo [E] 88 A2
Elizondo / Baztan [E] 86 E3
Efk [PL] 38 B2
Elkeland [N] 186 C4
Elkhovo [BG] 158 A2
Ellan [S] 196 E4
Elle [N] 186 B2
Ellenberg [D] 58 D4
Ellesmere [GB] 22 E3
Elling [DK] 182 E2
Ellingen [D] 58 E4
Ellmau [A] 72 D4
Ellon [GB] 18 F2
Ellös [S] 188 B4
Ellrich [D] 44 C3
Ellwangen [D] 58 D4
Elm [CH] 116 E1
Elmacık [TR] 158 B2
El Madroño [E] 98 E4
Elmalı [TR] 176 E1
El Masnou [E] 96 D3
El Médano [E] 112 D3
Elmen [A] 72 B4
El Minguilllo [E] 100 E3
El Molar [E] 92 E3
El Molinillo [E] 100 D2
El Moral [E] 106 C2
Elmpt [D] 42 C3
Elmshorn [D] 32 B2
Elmstein [D] 58 A3
Elne [F] 96 F1
Elnesvågen [N] 202 D2
Elo / Monreal [E] 86 F4
Eloro [I] 140 E4
Elorz / Noain [E] 86 F4
Élos [GR] 174 B4
Előszállás [H] 122 B2
Elounta [GR] 174 E3
el Palmar [E] 102 D3
El Palmar de Troya [E] 104 C2
El Palmeral [E] 106 E2
El Palo [E] 104 D3
El Pardo [E] 92 E4
El Paular [E] 92 E3
El Pedernoso [E] 100 F2
El Pedroso [E] 98 F4
El Perelló [E] 96 B4
El Perelló [E] 102 D4
Elphin [IRL] 12 C3
El Pinar [E] 112 A2
El Piñero [E] 84 E3
el Pinós / Pinoso [E] 106 E1
El Pito [E] 82 F2
el Pla de Santa Maria [E]
   96 C3
El Pobo de Dueñas [E] 94 C4
El Pont de Suert [E] 96 B1
El Port / Sóller [E] 108 D3
el Port de la Selva [E] 96 F2
El Portil [E] 98 D4
el Prat de Llobregat [E] 96 D3
El Priorato [E] 104 C1
El Puente del Arzobispo [E]
   100 C1
El Puerto de Santa Maria [E]
   104 B3
El Ramonete [E] 106 D3
El Real de la Jara [E] 98 F3
El Real de San Vicente [E]
   92 D4
El Recuenco [E] 94 B4

El Retiro [E] 104 D3
El Robledo [E] 100 D2
El Rocío [E] 104 B2
El Rompido [E] 98 D4
El Ronquillo [E] 98 E4
El Royo [E] 94 B2
El Rubio [E] 104 D2
El Sabinar [E] 106 C1
El Saler [E] 102 D3
El Salobral [E] 102 B4
El Saucejo [E] 104 D2
Elsdorf [D] 42 C4
El Serrat [AND] 88 E4
Elsfleth [D] 18 E3
Elšica [BG] 156 C2
Elst [NL] 30 C4
Elsten [D] 30 F3
Elster [D] 44 F3
Elsterberg [D] 60 B2
Elsterwerda [D] 46 B3
El Tejar [E] 104 D2
Elten [D] 30 C4
El Tiemblo [E] 92 D3
Eltmann [D] 58 E3
El Toboso [E] 100 F2
El Tormillo [E] 94 F3
El Torno [E] 92 B3
El Torno [E] 104 B3
Eltravåg [N] 186 A1
El Tumbalejo [E] 98 E4
Eltville [D] 58 B2
Eltz [D] 56 F2
Elva [EST] 230 E3
Elvas [P] 90 D4
Elvbrua [N] 194 C1
Elvdal [N] 194 C1
Elven, Tour d'– [F] 66 B1
El Vendrell [E] 96 C3
Elverum [N] 194 C3
Elverum [N] 224 D3
Elvestad [N] 188 B2
El Villar de Arnedo [E] 94 C1
Elvira [E] 104 F2
Elviria [E] 104 D3
El Viso [E] 100 B3
El Viso del Alcor [E] 104 C1
Elvran [N] 204 B2
Elx / Elche [E] 106 E2
Ely [GB] 28 D1
Élyros [GR] 174 B4
Elzach [D] 70 E2
Elze [D] 44 B2
Emberménil [F] 70 C1
Embrun [F] 126 B1
Embute [LV] 234 D4
Emden [D] 30 E2
Emecik [TR] 176 B1
Emese [TR] 164 B2
Emet [TR] 164 F3
Emiralem [TR] 164 C4
Emlichheim [D] 30 D3
Emmaboda [S] 184 D3
Emmaljunga [S] 184 C4
Emmaste [EST] 230 B3
Emmeloord [NL] 30 C3
Emmen [NL] 30 D3
Emmendingen [D] 70 D2
Emmerich [D] 30 C4
Emmingen–Liptingen [D]
  70 F3
Emőd [H] 76 D3
Emona [BG] 150 E4
Émpa [CY] 176 C4
Empesós [GR] 166 C2
Empfingen [D] 70 E2
Empoli [I] 128 B3
Émponas [GR] 176 C2
Emporeiós [GR] 168 E2
Emporeiós [GR] 176 A1
Emporeiós [GR] 176 A1
Empúriabrava [E] 96 F2
Empúries [E] 96 F2

Emsdetten [D] 30 E4
Emsfors [S] 184 E3
Emskirchen [D] 58 E3
Emstek [D] 30 F3
Emtinghausen [D] 32 A4
Emyvale [IRL] 12 E2
Enafors [S] 204 D2
Enäjärvi [FIN] 200 C2
Enånger [S] 196 C2
Enare / Inari [FIN] 226 D2
Enarsvedjan [S] 204 E1
Encamp [AND] 96 D1
Encarnación, Santuario de
  la– [E] 102 B4
Encinas de Abajo [E] 84 E4
Encinasola [E] 98 E3
Encinedo [E] 82 D4
Enciso [E] 94 C1
Encs [H] 76 D2
Encsencs [H] 76 E3
Endelave By [DK] 178 C2
Enden [N] 194 B1
Endingen [D] 70 D2
Endrefalva [H] 76 B3
Endrinal [E] 92 B3
Endrőd [H] 122 D1
Enebakk [N] 188 B1
Enese [H] 74 E4
Enevo [BG] 150 D3
Enez [TR] 156 F4
Enfesta / Pontecesures [E]
  82 B2
Enfield [IRL] 10 F2
Engelberg [CH] 116 D1
Engelhartszell [A] 72 F2
Engelia [N] 192 F3
Engeln [D] 32 A4
Engelskirchen [D] 42 D4
Engelsviken [N] 188 B2
Engen [D] 70 E3
Enger [D] 30 F4
Enger [N] 194 B3
Engerdal [N] 194 C1
Engerneset [N] 194 C2
Engesland [N] 186 D3
Engesvang [DK] 178 B1
Enghien [B] 40 D4
Engi [CH] 70 F4
Engjane [N] 202 E2
England [D] 32 B1
Englefontaine [F] 56 A1
Engstingen [D] 70 F2
Énguera [E] 102 C4
Enguídanos [E] 102 B2
Engure [LV] 234 E3
Enkhuizen [NL] 30 C3
Enklinge [FIN] 198 B3
Enköping [S] 190 D2
Enmo [N] 204 B3
Enna [I] 140 D2
Ennezat [F] 80 B2
Ennis / Inis [IRL] 10 C2
Enniscorthy [IRL] 10 E3
Enniscrone [IRL] 12 C2
Enniskean [IRL] 10 B4
Enniskillen [NI] 12 D2
Ennistymon [IRL] 10 C2
Enns [A] 74 A3
Eno [FIN] 210 E2
Enokunta [FIN] 208 E4
Enonkoski [FIN] 210 D3
Enonkylä [FIN] 216 C3
Enonteki / Enontekiö [FIN]
  226 B3
Enontekiö / Enonteki [FIN]
  226 B3
Enschede [NL] 30 D4
Ensisheim [F] 70 D2
Entlebuch [CH] 70 D4
Entradas [P] 98 C3
Entraigues [F] 68 A3
Entranis–sur–Nohain [F] 68 C2

Entraygues–sur–Truyère
  [F] 80 A4
Entre Ambos–os–Rios [P]
  84 B3
Entrevaux [F] 126 B3
Entrèves [I] 116 B3
Entrimo [E] 82 B4
Entroncamento [P] 90 C3
Enviken [S] 196 B3
En Xoroi, Cova d'– [E] 108 F3
Enying [H] 122 A2
Eoux [F] 88 D3
Epannes [F] 66 D4
Epanomí [GR] 160 F3
Epe [D] 30 D4
Epe [NL] 30 C3
Épernay [F] 56 A3
Épernon [F] 54 D3
Ephesos [TR] 170 B3
Epídavros, Arhéa– [GR] 168 A3
Épila [E] 94 D3
Épinal [F] 70 C2
Epiry [F] 68 D3
Episcopía [I] 136 C3
Episkopí [CY] 176 D4
Episkopí [GR] 174 C3
Epitálio [GR] 172 C2
Eplény [H] 120 F1
Epône [F] 54 D3
Epoo / Ebbo [FIN] 200 B3
Eppan / Appiano [I] 118 B2
Eppenstein [A] 120 B1
Eppingen [D] 58 B4
Eptachóri [GR] 160 C3
Eptálofos [GR] 166 E3
Epuisay [F] 66 F2
Eraclea [I] 118 D4
Eraclea [I] 136 C3
Eraclea Mare [I] 118 D4
Eraclea Minoa [I] 140 C3
Eräjärvi [FIN] 198 E1
Eräslahti [FIN] 208 E4
Erateiní [GR] 166 E3
Erátyrá [GR] 160 D3
Erba [I] 116 E3
Erbach [D] 58 C3
Erbach [D] 72 A2
Erbalunga [F] 130 B2
Erbè [I] 118 B4
Erbendorf [D] 60 B3
Ercolano [I] 134 C3
Ercsi [H] 122 B1
Érd [H] 76 B4
Erdal [N] 192 B1
Erdek [TR] 164 C1
Erdevik [SRB] 146 C1
Erding [D] 72 D2
Erdöhorváti [H] 76 E2
Erdut [HR] 122 B4
Ergama [TR] 164 C2
Ergili [TR] 164 D1
Érgli [LV] 236 C3
Ergoldsbach [D] 72 D2
Erice [I] 140 B2
Erice [TR] 170 E1
Ericeira [P] 90 A3
Ericek [TR] 158 E4
Erikli [TR] 158 A4
Eriksberg [S] 190 C3
Eriksberg [S] 206 B2
Eriksberg [S] 212 F3
Erikslund [S] 206 B3
Eriksmåla [S] 184 D3

Erikstad [S] 188 C3
Eringsboda [S] 184 D4
Erka [N] 202 E4
Erkelenz [D] 42 C3
Erla [E] 94 D2
Erlangen [D] 58 E3
Erlenbach [D] 58 C3
Erlsbach [A] 118 D1
Ermelo [NL] 30 C3
Ermenonville [F] 54 E3
Ermesinde [P] 84 A2
Ermidas–Aldeia [P] 98 B2
Ermióni [GR] 168 A3
Ermitage, Grotte de l'– [F]
  70 A3
Ermoúpoli [GR] 168 D3
Ermsleben [D] 44 D3
Erndtebrück [D] 42 E4
Ernée [F] 52 F4
Ernerwald [CH] 116 D2
Ernestinovo [HR] 122 B4
Ernstbrunn [A] 74 D2
Erp [D] 42 C4
Erquy [F] 52 D3
Erratzu [E] 88 A2
Errenteria / Rentería [E] 86 F3
Erro [E] 88 A3
Erronkari / Roncal [E] 88 B3
Ersekë [AL] 160 C3
Ersmark [S] 206 F1
Ersnäs [S] 214 E1
Erstein [F] 70 D2
Ertuğrul [TR] 164 C2
Ervasti [FIN] 216 C1
Ervedal [E] 90 D3
Ervedosa [P] 84 C3
Ervenik [HR] 144 D3
Ervidel [P] 98 C2
Ervik [N] 202 B3
Ervy–le–Châtel [F] 68 D2
Erwitte [D] 42 E3
Erxleben [D] 44 D2
Erythrés [GR] 168 A2
Erzsébet [H] 122 A3
Eržvilkas [LT] 238 C2
Esa / Yesa [E] 88 B3
Esatçe [TR] 158 A4
Esatlar [TR] 164 F2
Esbjerg [DK] 178 A2
Esblada [E] 96 C3
Esbo / Espoo [FIN] 198 F3
Escairón [E] 82 C3
Escalada [E] 86 C3
Escalaplano [I] 142 C4
Escalona [E] 88 C4
Escalona [E] 92 D4
Escalonilla [E] 100 D1
Escandón, Puerto de– [E]
  102 D2
Escariche [E] 92 F4
Escároz / Ezkaroze [E] 88 B3
Escatrón [E] 94 E3
Eschede [D] 32 C4
Eschenbach [D] 58 F3
Eschenburg–Eibelshausen
  [D] 42 E4
Eschenlohe [D] 72 C3
Escherndorf [D] 58 D3
Eschershausen [D] 44 B2
Esch–sur–Alzette [L] 56 D3
Esch–sur–Sûre [L] 56 D2
Eschwege [D] 44 C3
Eschweiler [D] 42 C4
Escipions, Torre dels– [E]
  96 C3
Escombreras [E] 106 E3
Escornalbou [E] 96 B3
Escos [F] 88 B2
Es Cubells [E] 108 E2
Escucha [E] 94 D4
Escúllar [E] 106 B3
Eşen [TR] 176 E1

Esence [TR] 164 D1
Esens [D] 30 E1
Esentepe (Ágios Amvrósios)
  [CY] 176 E3
Esenyurt [TR] 158 D3
es Figueral [E] 108 F2
Esgos [E] 82 C3
Esguevillas de Esgueva
  [E] 92 E1
Eskelhem [S] 234 A2
Eskiçine [TR] 170 C3
Eskifjördur [IS] 218 D3
Eski Gediz [TR] 164 F3
Eskihisar [TR] 170 C4
Eskilstuna [S] 190 C2
Eskin [TR] 164 F3
Eskola [FIN] 216 A4
Eslared [S] 184 B3
Eslarn [D] 60 B3
Eslohe [D] 42 E3
Eslöv [S] 180 C2
Esmared [S] 184 B3
Eşme [TR] 164 E4
Es Mercadal [E] 108 F3
Esmoriz [P] 84 A3
Esnandes [F] 66 C4
Esnouvenaux [F] 70 A2
Espa [N] 194 B3
Espadilla [E] 102 D2
Espalion [F] 80 A4
Esparreguera [E] 96 D3
Espås [N] 204 B2
Espe [S] 192 C3
Espedal [N] 192 F2
Espejo [E] 104 E1
Espeland [N] 186 B3
Espeland [N] 192 B3
Espelandsfoss [N] 192 C4
Espelette [E] 88 B2
Espeli [N] 186 C3
Espelkamp [D] 30 F4
Espera [E] 104 B2
Esperia [I] 134 C2
Espezel [F] 88 F4
Espiel [E] 100 B4
Espinama [E] 86 B2
Espinheiro, Convento de– [P]
  90 C4
Espinho [P] 84 A3
Espinilla [E] 86 C3
Espinosa de los Monteros
  [E] 86 D3
Espírito Santo [P] 98 C3
Esplantas [E] 80 C3
Esponellà [E] 96 E2
Espoo / Esbo [FIN] 198 F3
Esporles [E] 108 C3
Es Port d'Alcúdia [E] 108 D3
es Port d'Andraitx [E] 108 C3
Esposende [P] 84 A2
Espot [E] 88 E4
Espot Esquí [E] 96 D2
Esprels [F] 70 B3
Esse / Ähtävä [FIN] 214 F4
Essen [D] 30 E3
Essen [D] 42 D3
Essenbach [D] 72 D2
Essertaux [F] 54 E2
Esslingen [D] 70 F1
Essoyes [F] 68 E2
Essuilles [F] 54 E2
Essunga [S] 188 D4
Estada [E] 94 F3
Estagel [F] 96 E1
Estaing [F] 80 A4
Estaïres [F] 40 B3
Estang [F] 88 D2
Estanyol [E] 108 D4
Estarreja [P] 84 A3
Estavayer–le–Lac [CH] 70 C4
Este [I] 118 C4
Estela [P] 84 A2

Estella / Lizarra [E] 86 E4
Estellenchs [E] 108 C3
Estepa [E] 104 D2
Estepar [E] 86 C4
Estepona [E] 104 C3
Esteras, Cuestas de– [E] 94 B3
Esternay [F] 54 F4
Esterri d'Àneu [E] 88 E4
Esterwegen [D] 30 E2
Estíbaliz, Santuario de– [E]
  86 E3
Estissac [F] 68 D1
Estói [P] 98 C4
Estoril [P] 90 A3
Estrées–St–Denis [F] 54 E2
Estremera [E] 100 F1
Estremoz [P] 90 D4
Esztergom [H] 76 A3
Etables–sur–Mer [F] 52 D3
Etagnac [F] 78 D2
Etain [F] 56 D3
Étalans [F] 70 B3
Etalle [B] 56 D2
Étampes [F] 54 D4
Étang–sur–Arroux [F] 68 D4
Etaples [F] 40 A3
Ete [H] 74 F4
Eteläinen [FIN] 198 E2
Etili [TR] 164 B2
Etne [N] 186 B1
Etoges [F] 56 A3
Éton [F] 56 C3
Etréaupont [F] 56 B2
Etrepagny [F] 54 D2
Etretat [F] 54 B1
Etropole [BG] 148 E4
Etseri / Ähtäri [FIN] 208 D3
Ettelbruck [L] 56 D2
Ettenheim [D] 70 D2
Ettlingen [D] 58 B4
Etxarri / Echarri [E] 86 F4
Eu [F] 40 A4
Eudorf [D] 42 F4
Euerhausen [D] 58 D3
Eugénie–les–Bains [F] 88 C2
Eulate [E] 86 E4
Eumeneia [TR] 170 F1
Eunate [E] 86 F4
Eupen [B] 42 B4
Eura [FIN] 198 C2
Euraåminne / Eurajoki [FIN]
  198 C2
Eurajoki / Euraåminne [FIN]
  198 C2
Euratsfeld [A] 74 B3
Eurialo, Castello– [I] 140 E3
Euromos [TR] 170 C4
Europa–Brücke [A] 72 C4
Europoort [NL] 30 A4
Euskirchen [D] 42 C4
Eussenhausen [D] 58 D2
Eutin [D] 32 C2
Eutzsch [D] 44 F3
Eväjärvi [FIN] 208 E4
Evangelísmos [GR] 160 F4
Evanger [N] 192 B3
Evaux–les–Bains [F] 80 A1
Evciler [TR] 164 B2
Evciler [TR] 170 F2
Évdilos [GR] 168 E3
Evendorf [D] 32 C3
Evenstad [N] 194 C2
Everöd [S] 180 D2
Everswinkel [D] 42 E2
Evertsberg [S] 194 E2
Evesham [GB] 26 F1
Evian [F] 116 B2
Evijärvi [FIN] 208 D1
Evinochóri [GR] 166 D3
Evisa [F] 130 A2
Evitskog [FIN] 198 E4
Evje [N] 186 C3

Evolène [CH] 116 C2
Évora [P] 90 C4
Évora Monte [P] 90 D4
Evran [F] 52 D3
Evrensekiz [TR] 158 C3
Evreux [F] 54 C3
Evron [F] 54 A4
Evry [F] 54 E3
Évzonoi [GR] 160 E2
Exaplátanos [GR] 160 E2
Éxarchos [GR] 166 F3
Excideuil [F] 78 E3
Exeter [GB] 26 D3
Exmes [F] 54 B3
Exmouth [GB] 26 D3
Exochí [GR] 156 C3
Exochí [GR] 160 E3
Exómvourgo [GR] 168 D3
Externsteine [D] 42 F2
Extertal [D] 42 F2
Extremo [P] 82 B4
Eydehavn [N] 186 E3
Eyemouth [GB] 18 E4
Eyguières [F] 124 E3
Eygurande [F] 80 A2
Eylie [F] 88 D4
Eymet [F] 78 D4
Eymoutiers [F] 78 F2
Eyrarbakki [IS] 218 A3
Ézaro [E] 82 A2
Ezcaray [E] 86 D4
Ezere [LV] 234 E4
Ezeriş [RO] 122 F4
Ezermuiža [LV] 230 B4
Ezernieki [LV] 236 E4
Ezernijeki [LV] 234 E4
Ezine [TR] 164 A2
Ezkaroze / Escároz [E] 88 B3

F

Faaborg [DK] 178 C3
Faak [A] 118 F2
Fabara, Mausoleo de– [E]
  94 F4
Fabbrico [I] 128 B1
Fåberg [N] 194 B2
Fabero [E] 82 E3
Fábiánháza [H] 76 F3
Fábiánsebestyén [H] 122 D2
Fabriano [I] 132 D1
Facheca [E] 108 C2
Fačkov [SK] 76 A1
Facture [F] 78 B3
Fadd [H] 122 B2
Faenza [I] 128 D3
Faeto [I] 134 E3
Fafe [P] 84 B2
Făgăraş [RO] 244 D4
Fågelfors [S] 184 E2
Fågelsjö [S] 194 F1
Fågelsundet [S] 196 D3
Fågelvik [S] 184 F1
Fageole, Col de la– [F] 80 B3
Fagerås [S] 188 D2
Fagerhaugen [N] 202 F3
Fagerheim Fjellstue [N]
  192 D3
Fagerhult [S] 184 C1
Fagerhult [S] 184 E3
Fagerhult [S] 188 C4
Fagernes [N] 192 E2
Fagernes [N] 224 D2
Fagersanna [S] 188 E4
Fagersta [S] 190 B1
Fagerstrand [N] 188 B1
Fagervik [N] 204 B1
Fagervika [N] 218 E3
Fåget [RO] 122 F3
Fäggeby [S] 196 B4

Fåglavik [S] 184 B1
Fagnano Castello [I] 136 B4
Fagurhólsmyri [IS] 218 C3
Faial [P] 110 E3
Fai della Paganella [I] 118 B2
Faido [CH] 116 D2
Fains le Sources [F] 56 C4
Faistós [GR] 174 C4
Fajã do Ouvidor [P] 110 B3
Fajã dos Cubres [P] 110 B3
Fajã Grande [P] 110 B2
Fakenham [GB] 24 E4
Fåker [S] 204 E3
Fakija [BG] 158 B1
Fakse [DK] 178 E3
Fakse Ladeplads [DK] 178 E3
Falaise [F] 54 B2
Falásarna [GR] 174 A3
Falatádos [GR] 168 D3
Falcade [I] 118 C2
Falconara, Castello di– [I]
  140 D3
Falconara Marittima [I] 128 F4
Falcone [I] 138 C3
Falcsut [H] 76 A4
Faldsled [DK] 178 C3
Falerii Novi [I] 130 F3
Falerna [I] 138 D2
Falerna Marina [I] 138 D2
Falerum [S] 184 E1
Falileevo [RUS] 200 E4
Faliráki [GR] 176 C2
Falkenberg [D] 46 B3
Falkenberg [D] 72 E2
Falkenberg [S] 184 A3
Falkenstein [A] 74 D2
Falkenstein [A] 74 D2
Falkenstein [D] 44 D3
Falkenstein [D] 56 D2
Falkenstein [D] 60 B4
Falkenstein [D] 60 B2
Falkenstein, Château de– [F]
  56 F4
Falkirk [GB] 18 D4
Falköping [S] 188 D4
Fałków [PL] 48 E4
Falla [S] 190 B3
Fällen [S] 184 C3
Fallersleben [D] 44 D2
Fallet [N] 194 C4
Fallet [N] 202 F4
Fällfors [S] 214 D2
Fallingbostel [D] 32 B4
Falmouth [GB] 26 B4
Falset [E] 96 B3
Falsterbo [S] 178 F2
Fălticeni [RO] 244 E3
Falträsk [S] 214 C2
Faludden [S] 234 A3
Falun [S] 196 B3
Falusziget [H] 122 E1
Fámjin [FR] 182 A2
Fana [N] 192 B3
Fanano [I] 128 B3
Fanári [GR] 156 E4
Fanári [GR] 166 D2
Fanbyn [S] 206 B4
Fáncs [H] 122 A2
Fanefjord [DK] 178 E3
Fångåmon [S] 204 D2
Fanjeaux [F] 88 F3
Fannrem [N] 202 F2
Fano [I] 128 E3
Fanós [GR] 156 A4
Fântânele [RO] 150 B2
Fanthyttan [S] 188 F2
Farad [H] 74 E4
Fara Novarese [I] 116 D3
Fårbo [S] 184 E2
Farcheville, Château de– [F]
  54 D4
Farébersviller [F] 56 E4

Fareham [GB] 28 B4
Fårevejle [DK] 178 E2
Farfa, Abbazia di– [I] 132 D3
Färgaryd [S] 184 B3
Färgelanda [S] 188 C3
Fargerdal [N] 212 B4
Färila [S] 196 B1
Faringdon [GB] 28 B2
Faringe [S] 190 E1
Färingtofta [S] 180 C1
Farini [I] 126 F2
Färjestaden [S] 184 E3
Farkadóna [GR] 160 E4
Farkasgyepü [H] 120 E1
Farkaždin [SRB] 146 D1
Farlete [E] 94 E3
Färliug [RO] 122 F4
Färlöv [S] 180 D1
Fårna [S] 190 B1
Färnäs [S] 194 F3
Farnese [I] 130 E2
Farnham [GB] 28 C3
Faro [P] 98 C4
Fårö [S] 234 B2
Fårösund [S] 234 B2
Farranfore [IRL] 10 B3
Farre [DK] 178 C1
Fársala [GR] 162 A4
Farsø [DK] 182 C3
Farstad [N] 202 D2
Farstorp [S] 180 D1
Farsund [N] 186 B4
Farum [DK] 178 F2
Fårvang [DK] 182 D4
Fasanerie, Schloss– [D] 58 D2
Fasano [I] 136 D2
Fåset [N] 204 B4
Fasgar [E] 82 E3
Fasovka [UA] 242 D4
Faster [DK] 178 B1
Fasterholt [DK] 178 B1
Fastov [UA] 242 D4
Fatezh [RUS] 242 F2
Fátima [E] 104 C3
Fátima [P] 90 C2
Fatjas [S] 220 E3
Fatnica [BIH] 152 D2
Fättjaur [S] 212 F2
Faucille, Col de la– [F] 80 F2
Faucogney–et–la–Mer [F]
  70 C2
Faulbach [D] 58 C3
Faulensee [CH] 116 C1
Faulquemont [F] 56 E4
Fauske [N] 220 B2
Fauville [F] 54 C1
Fåvang [N] 194 B2
Favara [E] 102 D4
Favara [I] 140 C3
Faverges [F] 80 F3
Faverney [F] 70 B2
Favignana [I] 140 A2
Favone [F] 130 B3
Favorite [D] 58 B4
Favrholt [DK] 182 C4
Fawley [GB] 28 B4
Fayence [F] 126 B3
Fayet [F] 124 B2
Fayl–Billot [F] 70 B2
Fayón [E] 94 F4
Fay–sur–Lignon [F] 80 C4
Fazendas de Almeirim [P]
  90 C3
Feakle [IRL] 10 C2
Fécamp [F] 54 C1
Feda [N] 186 B3
Fedje [N] 192 A2
Fedosino [RUS] 236 E2
Fefor [N] 192 F1

Fegen [S] 184 B3
Feggeklit [DK] 182 C3
Fegyvernek [H] 76 D4
Fehérgyarmat [H] 76 F3
Fehrbellin [D] 32 F4
Fehring [A] 120 C2
Feigumfoss [N] 192 D2
Feios [N] 192 C2
Feiring [N] 194 B3
Feistritz [A] 120 C1
Feitos [P] 84 A2
Feketić [SRB] 122 C4
Felanitx [E] 108 D4
Felben [A] 72 D4
Felber–tauern Tunnel [A]
  118 D1
Feld [A] 118 F2
Feldafing [D] 72 C3
Feldbach [A] 120 C1
Feldballe [DK] 182 E4
Feldberg [D] 34 C3
Feldberg [D] 70 E3
Feldkirch [A] 118 F2
Feldkirchen [D] 72 D3
Feldsted [DK] 178 B3
Felechosa [E] 82 F3
Feletto [I] 116 C4
Felgueiras [P] 84 B2
Felgyö [H] 122 C2
Félix [E] 106 D3
Felixstowe [GB] 28 E2
Felizzano [I] 126 E1
Fellbach [D] 70 F1
Fellern [A] 72 D4
Felletin [F] 80 A2
Fellingsbro [S] 190 B2
Felnac [RO] 122 E3
Felonica [I] 128 C1
Felsengarten [D] 58 E3
Felsöleperd [H] 120 F2
Felsönyárád [H] 76 D2
Felsőszentiván [H] 122 B3
Felsőtárkány [H] 76 C3
Felsőzsolca [H] 76 D3
Feltre [I] 118 C3
Femsjö [S] 184 B3
Femundsenden [N] 194 C1
Fenagh [IRL] 12 D3
Fenais da Ajuda [P] 110 E1
Fene [E] 82 C1
Fenékpuszta [H] 120 E2
Fener [I] 118 C3
Fenestrelle [I] 116 B4
Fénétrange [F] 56 E4
Feneu [F] 66 D2
Fénis [I] 116 C3
Fenit [IRL] 10 B3
Fenstad [N] 194 C4
Fer a Cheval, Cirque du– [F]
  70 B4
Feragen [N] 204 C3
Féraklos [GR] 176 C2
Ferbane [IRL] 10 D2
Ferdinandshof [D] 34 D3
Fére [GR] 162 A3
Fère, Château de– [F] 54 F3
Fère–Champenoise [F] 56 A4
Fère–en–Tardenois [F] 54 F3
Ferendia [RO] 122 E4
Ferentino [I] 132 D4
Ferento [I] 130 F2
Féres [GR] 156 F4
Ferez [E] 106 C3
Feria [E] 98 E2
Feričanci [HR] 120 F4
Ferla [I] 140 E3
Ferlach [A] 120 A2
Ferleiten [A] 118 E1
Fermignano [I] 128 E4
Fermo [I] 132 E2
Fermoselle [E] 84 D3
Fermoy [IRL] 10 C3

Fernancaballero [E] 100 D3
Fernán Núñez [E] 104 D1
Ferns [IRL] 10 E3
Fernstein [A] 72 B4
Ferovac [HR] 120 F4
Ferrandina [I] 136 C3
Ferrara [I] 128 D2
Ferreira [E] 82 D2
Ferreira do Alentejo [P] 98 C2
Ferreira do Zêzere [P] 90 C2
Ferreries [E] 108 E3
Ferreruela de Huerva [E] 94 D4
Ferrette [F] 70 D3
Ferriere [I] 126 F2
Ferrières [F] 68 C1
Ferrières–sur–Sichon [F] 80 C2
Ferring [DK] 182 B3
Ferrol [E] 82 C1
Fertőd [H] 74 D4
Fertőrákos [H] 74 D3
Fertőszentmiklós [H] 74 D4
Festenburg [A] 74 C4
Festøy [N] 202 C3
Festung Königstein [D] 60 D1
Festvåg [N] 218 F2
Feteşti [RO] 150 E1
Fethard [IRL] 10 D3
Fethard [IRL] 10 E4
Fethiye [TR] 176 D1
Fetsund [N] 188 B1
Feu, Roche du– [F] 52 B3
Feucht [D] 58 E4
Feuchtwangen [D] 58 D4
Feurs [F] 80 C2
Fevåg [N] 204 A1
Fevik [N] 186 D3
Fiamignano [I] 132 D3
Fiastra, Abbadia di– [I] 132 E2
Fibiş [RO] 122 E3
Fíchti [GR] 172 E1
Ficulle [I] 130 F2
Fidenza [I] 128 B1
Fidje [N] 186 D3
Fieberbrunn [A] 72 D4
Fiegler [A] 118 F4
Fier [AL] 160 A2
Fier, Gorges du– [F] 80 F2
Fiera di Primiero [I] 118 C3
Fierbinţi [RO] 150 A1
Fierzë [AL] 154 B3
Fiesch [CH] 116 D2
Fieschi, Basilica dei– [I] 126 F2
Fiésole [I] 128 C3
Fiesso Umbertiano [I] 128 D1
Figáleia [GR] 172 C2
Figari [F] 130 B4
Figeholm [S] 184 E2
Figgjo [N] 186 B2
Figline Valdarno [I] 128 C4
Figueira da Foz [P] 90 C1
Figueira de Castelo Rodrigo [P] 84 C3
Figueiró dos Vinhos [P] 90 C2
Figueras / Figueres [E] 96 E2
Figueres / Figueras [E] 96 E2
Fiholm [S] 190 C2
Fiksdal [N] 202 D3
Filadélfi [GR] 162 B1
Filadélfia [I] 138 E2
Filaga [I] 140 C2
Fil'akovo [SK] 76 C2
Filatova Gora [RUS] 232 E4
Filevo [BG] 156 E2
Filey [GB] 24 D2
Filia [GR] 164 A3
Filiaşi [RO] 148 D1
Filiátes [GR] 160 B4
Filiatrá [GR] 172 C3
Filipovci [BG] 154 E2
Filipów [PL] 38 B1

Filippiáda [GR] 166 C2
Filippoi [GR] 156 C4
Filipstad [S] 188 E2
Filisur [CH] 116 F2
Filitosa [F] 130 A3
Fillan [N] 202 E1
Fillefjell Pass [N] 192 D2
Fillýra [GR] 156 E3
Filótas [GR] 160 D2
Filóti [GR] 168 E4
Filottrano [I] 128 F4
Filskov [DK] 178 B1
Filyriá [GR] 160 E2
Filzmoos [A] 72 E4
Finale Emília [I] 128 C2
Finale Lígure [I] 126 D2
Fiñana [E] 106 B3
Finby / Särkisalo [FIN] 198 D4
Finderup [DK] 178 B1
Finestrat [E] 106 F1
Fingerboda [S] 188 F2
Finike [TR] 176 F1
Finiq [AL] 160 B4
Finisterre / Fisterra [E] 82 A2
Finja [S] 180 C1
Finnäs [S] 214 C2
Finnbo [S] 196 B3
Finnböle [S] 196 D4
Finnea [IRL] 10 E1
Finneby [S] 196 B1
Finneid [N] 220 B2
Finneidfjord [N] 212 E1
Finnentrop [D] 42 E3
Finnerödja [S] 188 E3
Finnlia [N] 186 E1
Finnøy [N] 220 B1
Finnsäter [S] 204 E1
Finnsnes [N] 224 D3
Finnstad [N] 204 B4
Finntorp [S] 188 D2
Finnvelta [N] 194 C4
Finow [D] 34 C4
Finsand [N] 192 F4
Finsjö [S] 184 E3
Finspång [S] 190 B3
Finsta [S] 190 E2
Finsterwalde [D] 46 B3
Finström [FIN] 196 F4
Fionnay [CH] 116 B2
Fionnphort [GB] 18 A2
Fiorenzuola d'Arda [I] 128 A1
Firá / Thíra [GR] 174 D1
Firbis Castle [IRL] 12 B2
Firenze [I] 128 C3
Firenzuola [I] 128 C3
Firkeel [IRL] 10 A4
Firlej [PL] 50 C3
Firminy [F] 80 C3
Fiscal [E] 88 C4
Fischamend [A] 74 D3
Fischbach [D] 56 F4
Fischbach [D] 56 F3
Fischbeck [D] 44 B2
Fischbeck [D] 44 E1
Fischen [D] 72 A4
Fischerbócsa [H] 122 C2
Fishguard [GB] 22 B4
Fisíni [GR] 162 E2
Fiska [N] 202 B3
Fiskárdo [GR] 166 B3
Fiskebäckskil [S] 188 B4
Fiskebøl [N] 224 B4
Fiskevollen [N] 194 C1
Fiskö [FIN] 198 B3
Fiskøl [N] 186 E2
Fismes [F] 56 A3
Fiss [A] 118 B1
Fisterra / Finisterre [E] 82 A2
Fıstıklı [TR] 158 E4
Fitero [E] 94 C2
Fitjar [N] 192 A4
Fiuggi [I] 132 D4

Fiumefreddo Bruzio [I] 138 D2
Fiumefreddo di Sicilia [I] 138 C4
Fiumicíno [I] 130 F4
Fivemiletown [NIR] 12 D2
Fivizzano [I] 128 B2
Fjæra [N] 192 B4
Fjærland [N] 192 C1
Fjäl [S] 204 F2
Fjälkinge [S] 180 D1
Fjällåsen [S] 220 D2
Fjällbacka [S] 188 B3
Fjällgården [S] 204 E3
Fjällnäs [S] 204 C3
Fjällnäs [S] 214 B1
Fjaltring [DK] 182 B3
Fjand Gårde [DK] 182 B4
Fjärås [S] 184 A2
Fjärdhundra [S] 190 C1
Fjeli [S] 212 C3
Fjell [N] 192 A3
Fjellerup [DK] 182 E3
Fjellheim [N] 192 E3
Fjellsrud [N] 188 B1
Fjelstrup [DK] 178 C2
Fjenneslev [DK] 178 E2
Fjerestad [N] 192 C2
Fjerritslev [DK] 182 C2
Fjon [N] 192 B2
Fjone [N] 186 D2
Fjordgård [N] 224 C2
Fjugesta [S] 188 F2
Flå [N] 192 E3
Flaçà [E] 96 E2
Fladdabister [GB] 16 E4
Fladungen [D] 58 D2
Flagy [F] 70 B3
Flaine [F] 116 B2
Flaka [FIN] 198 A4
Flakaberg [S] 220 F3
Flakaträsk [S] 214 A1
Flakk [N] 204 B2
Flakkstadvågen [N] 224 C3
Flåm [N] 192 C2
Flampourári [GR] 160 C4
Flaran [F] 88 D2
Flärke [S] 206 E2
Flatabø [N] 192 B4
Flateby [N] 188 C2
Flateland [N] 186 D3
Flåten [N] 224 E1
Flåtestøa [N] 194 C2
Flatmark [N] 202 D3
Flatøydegard [N] 192 F2
Flatråker [N] 192 B4
Flätsbo [S] 196 B2
Flått [N] 212 D3
Flattnitz [A] 118 F1
Flauenskjold [DK] 182 D2
Flaugeac [F] 78 D4
Flavigny–sur–Moselle [F] 70 B1
Fléchin [F] 40 B3
Fleckenberg [D] 42 E3
Fleckenstein, Château de– [F] 56 F4
Fleetwood [GB] 22 F1
Flehingen [D] 58 B4
Flekke [N] 192 B1
Flekkefjord [N] 186 B3
Flemma [N] 202 E2
Flen [S] 190 C3
Flensburg [D] 178 B3
Flerahopp [S] 184 E3
Flers [F] 54 A3
Flesberg [N] 186 E1
Flesje [N] 192 C2
Flesland [N] 192 A3
Flesnes [N] 224 B3
Fleurance [F] 88 D2
Fleuré [F] 66 E4
Fleurier [CH] 70 C4

Fleurus [B] 40 E4
Fleury [F] 54 D2
Flims [CH] 116 E1
Flims Waldhaus [CH] 116 E1
Flins [F] 54 D3
Flirsch [A] 72 B4
Flisa [N] 194 C3
Flisbrua [N] 194 C3
Flisby [S] 184 D1
Fliseryd [S] 184 E3
Flix [E] 94 F4
Flize [F] 56 C2
Floby [S] 184 B1
Floda [S] 184 A1
Floda [C] 190 B4
Floda [S] 214 D3
Flögåsen [S] 194 E2
Flogned [S] 188 C1
Flogny–la–Chapelle [F] 68 D2
Flöha [D] 60 C1
Flon [S] 204 D3
Flor [S] 204 F4
Florac [F] 124 C1
Florange [F] 56 D3
Florennes [B] 56 C1
Florenville [B] 56 C2
Floresti [RO] 148 C1
Florídia [I] 140 E3
Floriile [RO] 150 E1
Flórina [GR] 160 D2
Flornes [N] 204 C2
Florø [N] 192 B1
Florstadt [D] 58 C2
Florvåg [N] 192 A3
Flostrand [N] 218 E4
Flötningen [S] 194 D1
Fluberg [N] 192 F3
Flüelen [CH] 116 D1
Fluglafjørður [FR] 182 B1
Flühli [CH] 116 D1
Flumeri [I] 134 E3
Flumet [F] 116 A3
Fluminimaggiore [I] 142 B5
Flums [CH] 70 F4
Fluren [S] 196 C2
Flykälen [S] 204 F1
Flymen [S] 180 F1
Flyn [S] 206 B2
Flystveit [N] 186 C3
Flytåsen [S] 196 B2
Fnideq [MA] 104 C4
Foça [TR] 164 B4
Foča–Srbinje [BIH] 146 B4
Fockbek [D] 32 B1
Focşani [RO] 244 E4
Fódele [GR] 174 D3
Foeni [RO] 122 D4
Fogdö [S] 190 C2
Foggia [I] 134 E2
Föglö [FIN] 198 B4
Fohnsdorf [A] 120 B1
Foiano di Chiana [I] 130 F1
Foinikoúntas [GR] 172 C3
Foix [F] 88 E4
Fojnica [BIH] 146 A3
Fojnica [BIH] 152 D2
Fokstugu [N] 202 F4
Földeák [H] 122 D2
Foldereid [N] 212 D3
Földes [H] 76 E4
Foldingbro [DK] 178 B2
Folégandros [GR] 174 C1
Folelli [F] 130 B2
Folgaria [I] 118 B3
Folgarida [I] 118 B2
Folgoso [E] 82 D3
Foliá [GR] 156 C4
Foligno [I] 132 D2
Folkárna [S] 190 C1
Folkestad [N] 202 C3
Folkestone [GB] 28 F4
Folladal [N] 212 C4

Follafoss [N] 212 C4
Folldal [N] 202 F4
Follina [I] 118 D3
Föllinge [S] 204 E1
Follónica [I] 130 D2
Folmava [CZ] 60 B4
Fölsbyn [S] 188 C2
Folwarki [PL] 48 D4
Folyás [H] 76 D3
Fompedraza [E] 92 E2
Fondamente [F] 124 C2
Fondi [I] 134 B2
Fondo [I] 118 B2
Fönebo [S] 196 C1
Fonfría [E] 84 E3
Fonfría [E] 94 D4
Fonni [I] 142 C4
Fonseca, Castillo de– [E] 92 D2
Fontainebleau [F] 54 E4
Fontaine–de–Vaucluse [F] 124 E2
Fontaine–Française [F] 68 F3
Fontaine Guérard, Abbaye de– [F] 54 D2
Fontaine Henry, Château de– [F] 54 A2
Fontaine–le–Dun [F] 54 C1
Fontaine–sur–Coole [F] 56 B4
Fontanars dels Alforins [E] 102 C4
Fontanella [A] 72 A4
Fontanellato [I] 128 B1
Fontanelle [I] 118 D3
Fontanosas [E] 100 C3
Fonte Avellana, Monastero di– [I] 128 E4
Fontecha [E] 86 D3
Fonte Colombo, Convento di– [I] 132 D3
Fontedias [E] 82 B2
Fontenay, Abbaye de– [F] 68 E2
Fontenay–le–Comte [F] 66 D4
Fontenay–Trésigny [F] 54 E3
Fontevraud–l'Abbaye [F] 66 E3
Fontfroide, Abbaye de– [F] 124 B3
Fontgombault [F] 66 F4
Fontinha [P] 90 C1
Fontioso [E] 92 F1
Fontiveros [E] 84 F4
Font–Romeu [F] 96 D1
Fontstown [IRL] 10 E2
Fontvieille [F] 124 E3
Fonyód [H] 120 E2
Fonzaso [I] 118 C3
Fóppolo [I] 116 F3
Föra [S] 184 F3
Forbach [D] 70 E1
Forbach [F] 56 E3
Forbes, Castle– [IRL] 10 E1
Forcall [E] 102 E1
Forcalquier [F] 124 F2
Forcarei [E] 82 B3
Forchach [A] 72 B4
Forchheim [D] 58 E3
Forchtenstein [A] 74 D3
Ford [GB] 18 B3
Førde [N] 186 B1
Førde [N] 192 B1
Fordingbridge [GB] 26 F3
Fordongianus [I] 142 B4
Forenza [I] 134 F3
Forfar [GB] 18 E3
Forges–les–Eaux [F] 54 D2
Forino [I] 134 D3
Forio [I] 134 C3
Førland [N] 186 C3
Forlì [I] 128 D3
Forlì del Sánnio [I] 132 F4
Forlimpopoli [I] 128 D3

Formazza [I] 116 D2
Formby [GB] 22 E2
Formerie [F] 54 D2
Formia [I] 134 B3
Formigine [I] 128 C2
Formiguères [F] 96 D1
Formofoss [N] 212 D3
Fornace [I] 130 E2
Fornaci di Barga [I] 128 B3
Fornalutx [E] 108 D3
Fornelli [I] 142 B2
Fornells [E] 108 F3
Forni Avoltri [I] 118 D2
Forni di Sopra [I] 118 D2
Forni di Sotto [I] 118 D2
Forno Alpi Graie [I] 116 B3
Forno di Zoldo [I] 118 D2
Fornos de Algodres [P] 84 B4
Fornovo di Taro [I] 128 B2
Foros do Arrão [P] 90 C3
Forotic [RO] 122 E4
Forøy [N] 218 E3
Forráskút [H] 122 C2
Forres [GB] 14 E3
Fors [S] 188 C4
Fors [S] 196 C4
Fors [S] 206 D2
Forsa [N] 224 C4
Forsbacka [S] 196 C3
Forsby / Koskenkylä [FIN]
  200 B3
Forserum [S] 184 C2
Forset [N] 192 F2
Forshaga [S] 188 D2
Forsheda [S] 184 C3
Forsheden [S] 214 B2
Forshem [S] 188 D3
Förslöv [S] 184 B4
Forsmark [S] 196 D4
Forsmo [S] 206 C2
Forsnacken [S] 214 A1
Forsnäs [S] 214 B1
Forsnäs [S] 220 D3
Forsnes [N] 202 E1
Forsøl [N] 228 B2
Forssa [FIN] 198 D2
Forst [D] 46 C3
Forstinning [D] 72 D2
Forsvik [S] 188 E3
Fort Augustus [GB] 14 D4
Forte dei Marmi [I] 128 B3
Forte di Bibbiona [I] 130 D1
Forth [D] 58 E3
Fort–Mahon–Plage [F] 40 A4
Fortrose [GB] 14 E3
Fortun [N] 192 D1
Fortuna [E] 106 E2
Fortuneswell [GB] 26 E4
Fort William [GB] 14 C4
Forvik [N] 212 D1
Fos [F] 88 D4
Fösked [S] 188 E2
Foskros [N] 194 D1
Foskvallen [S] 194 D1
Fosnavåg [N] 202 B3
Fosnes [N] 212 C3
Fossano [I] 126 D2
Fossanova, Abbazia di– [I]
  134 B2
Fossbakken [N] 224 D3
Fossby [N] 188 C2
Fossen [N] 192 D1
Fosser [N] 188 C1
Fosses [B] 40 E4
Fossland [N] 212 C3
Fossombrone [I] 128 E4
Fos–sur–Mer [F] 124 E3
Foteiná [GR] 160 E3
Foucarmont [F] 54 D1
Fouesnant [F] 52 B4
Fougères [F] 52 E4
Fougerolles [F] 70 C2

Foulain [F] 68 F2
Foulum [DK] 182 D3
Fouras [F] 78 B1
Fourcès [F] 88 D2
Fourfourás [GR] 174 C4
Foúrka [GR] 160 C3
Fourmies [F] 56 B2
Fourná [GR] 166 D2
Fourneaux [F] 80 A1
Fournels [F] 80 B4
Fournés [GR] 174 B3
Foúrnoi [GR] 168 F3
Fourquet [F] 88 E1
Fours [F] 68 D4
Foústani [GR] 160 E2
Fowey [GB] 26 B3
Foxford [IRL] 12 B2
Foynes [IRL] 10 C2
Foz [E] 82 D2
Foz do Arelho [P] 90 B2
Foz Giraldo [P] 90 D2
Frabosa Soprana [I] 126 D2
Frącki [PL] 38 C2
Fraga [E] 94 F3
Fragkísta [GR] 166 D2
Fragkokástello [GR] 174 B4
Fraize [F] 70 C2
Framley [DK] 178 C1
Framlingham [GB] 28 E2
Frammersbach [D] 58 C2
Främmestad [S] 188 D4
Framnäs [S] 220 D3
Frampol [PL] 64 D1
Framzelle [F] 28 E4
Francardo [F] 130 B2
Francavilla al Mare [I] 132 F3
Francavilla di Sicilia [I] 138 C4
Francavilla Fontana [I] 136 E2
Francelos [P] 84 A3
Francofonte [I] 140 E3
Frändefors [S] 188 C4
Franeker [NL] 30 C2
Frangy [F] 80 F2
Frankenberg [D] 42 F4
Frankenberg [D] 60 C1
Frankenburg [A] 72 F3
Frankenmarkt [A] 72 E3
Frankenthal [D] 58 B3
Frankfurt (Oder) [D] 46 C2
Frankfurt am Main [D] 58 B2
Frankrike [S] 204 E1
Fränsta [S] 206 B3
Františkovy Lázně [CZ] 60 B2
Franzburg [D] 32 F2
Frasassi, Grotte di– [I] 128 E4
Frascati [I] 132 C4
Frasdorf [D] 72 D3
Fraserburgh [GB] 16 D4
Frashër [AL] 160 B3
Frăsinet [RO] 150 C1
Frasne [F] 70 B4
Frasno, Puerto de– [E] 94 D3
Frassino [I] 126 C2
Frassinoro [I] 128 B2
Frasso [I] 134 D3
Fratel [P] 90 D3
Fratte Polesine [I] 128 D1
Frauenau [D] 72 E1
Frauenberg [D] 42 E4
Frauenburg [A] 120 A1
Frauenfeld [CH] 70 F3
Frauenkirch [CH] 116 F1
Frauenkirchen [A] 74 D3
Frauenstein [A] 74 A3
Frauenstein [D] 60 C1
Frauschereck [A] 72 E3
Frayssinet [F] 78 E1
Frechen [D] 42 C4
Frechilla [E] 86 B4
Freckenhorst [D] 42 E2
Fredensborg [DK] 178 F1
Fredericia [DK] 178 C2

Frederiks [DK] 182 C4
Frederiksberg [DK] 178 E2
Frederikshavn [DK] 182 E2
Frederikssund [DK] 178 E2
Frederiksværk [DK] 178 E1
Frednowy [PL] 36 E3
Fredrika [S] 214 B3
Fredriksberg [S] 188 E1
Fredrikshamn / Hamina [FIN]
  200 C3
Fredrikstad [N] 188 B2
Fredriksten [N] 188 C2
Freest [D] 34 C2
Fregenal de la Sierra [E] 98 E3
Fregene [I] 130 F3
Frei [N] 202 D2
Freiberg [D] 60 C1
Freiburg [D] 32 B2
Freiburg im Breisgau [D]
  70 D2
Freiensteinau [D] 58 C2
Freihung [D] 58 F3
Freila [E] 106 B2
Freilassing [D] 72 E3
Freising [D] 72 C2
Freistadt [A] 74 A2
Freital [D] 46 B4
Freixedas [P] 84 C4
Freixianda [P] 90 C2
Freixo de Espada à Cinta
  [P] 84 D3
Frejev [DK] 182 D3
Frejlev [DK] 32 E1
Fréjus [F] 126 B3
Fréjus, Tunnel de– [F/I] 116 A4
Frenchpark [IRL] 12 C3
Frenštát pod Radhoštěm
  [CZ] 62 D4
Freren [D] 30 E3
Freshford [IRL] 10 E3
Fresnay–sur–Sarthe [F] 54 B4
Fresnes [F] 40 C4
Fresnes [F] 70 B2
Fresnes–en–Woëvre [F] 56 C3
Fresno Alhándiga [E] 92 C3
Fresno de la Ribera [E] 84 F3
Fresno de Sayago [E] 84 E3
Fresno de Sayago [E] 84 E3
Fresvik [N] 192 C2
Fréteval [F] 68 A1
Fretigney–et–Velloreille
  [F] 70 B3
Fretzdorf [D] 32 E4
Freudenberg [D] 42 D4
Freudenberg [D] 58 C3
Freudenstadt [D] 70 E2
Freundsberg [A] 72 C4
Frévent [F] 40 B4
Freyburg [D] 44 E4
Freyenstein [D] 32 E3
Freyming Merlebach [F] 56 E3
Freystadt [D] 58 E4
Freyung [D] 72 F2
Frías [E] 86 D3
Fribourg [CH] 116 B1
Frick [CH] 70 D3
Fridafors [S] 184 D4
Fridingen [D] 70 F2
Friedberg [A] 74 C4
Friedberg [D] 58 C2
Friedberg [D] 72 B2
Friedburg [A] 72 E3
Friedeburg [D] 30 F2
Friedersdorf [D] 46 B2
Friedewald [D] 44 B4
Friedland [D] 34 C3
Friedland [D] 44 B3
Friedland [D] 46 C2
Friedrichroda [D] 44 C4
Friedrichshafen [D] 70 F3
Friedrichskoog [D] 32 B2
Friedrichsort [D] 32 C1

Friedrichstadt [D] 32 B1
Friedrichswalde [D] 34 C4
Friedstein [A] 74 A4
Friesach [A] 120 A1
Friesack [D] 44 F1
Friesenheim [D] 70 D2
Friesoythe [D] 30 E2
Frifelt [DK] 178 B2
Friggesund [S] 196 C1
Frihetsli [N] 224 E3
Frillesås [S] 184 A2
Frinkenberg [A] 72 C4
Frinnaryd [S] 184 D1
Friol [E] 82 C2
Fristad [S] 184 B1
Fritsla [S] 184 B2
Fritzlar [D] 42 F4
Fröderyd [S] 184 D2
Frödinge [S] 184 E2
Frohburg [D] 44 E4
Frohnleiten [A] 74 B4
Froissy [F] 54 E2
Fröjel [S] 234 A3
Frombork [PL] 36 E2
Frome [GB] 26 E3
Fromental [F] 54 A3
Fromentine [F] 66 B3
Frómista [E] 86 B4
Fromy [F] 56 C2
Fronsac [F] 88 D3
Fronteira [P] 90 D4
Frontenhausen [D] 72 D2
Frontera [E] 112 A2
Frontignan [F] 124 C3
Fronton [F] 88 E2
Fröseke [S] 184 E3
Frosinone [I] 134 B2
Fröskog [S] 188 C3
Frösö [S] 204 E2
Frosolone [I] 134 D2
Frossay [F] 66 B2
Frosta [N] 204 B1
Frostavallen [S] 180 C1
Frösthult [S] 190 C2
Frøstrup [DK] 182 C2
Frösunda [S] 190 D2
Frøvi [S] 190 B2
Frøyrak [N] 186 D3
Fruges [F] 40 B4
Frutigen [CH] 116 C1
Fry [GR] 176 A3
Frýdek–Místek [CZ] 62 D3
Frýdlant [CZ] 60 E1
Frýdlant nad Ostravicí [CZ]
  62 D3
Frýdštejn [CZ] 60 E2
Frygnowo [PL] 36 E3
Frymburk [CZ] 74 A2
Fryšták [CZ] 62 D3
Frysztak [PL] 64 C3
Ftéri [GR] 166 E4
Ftterë [AL] 160 B3
Fuans [F] 70 C4
Fubine [I] 126 E1
Fucécchio [I] 128 B3
Fuencaldenas [E] 88 B4
Fuencaliente [E] 100 C4
Fuencaliente de la Palma [E]
  112 B2
Fuencaliente de Lucio [E]
  86 C3
Fuencarral [E] 92 E4
Fuendejalón [E] 94 D2
Fuendetodos [E] 94 D3
Fuengirola [E] 104 C3
Fuenlabrada [E] 92 E4
Fuenlabrada de los Montes
  [E] 100 C2
Fuenmayor [E] 86 E4
Fuensalida [E] 100 D1
Fuensanta [E] 106 E2
Fuente Álamo [E] 102 B4

Fuente Álamo de Murcia [E]
  106 D3
Fuentealbilla [E] 102 B3
Fuentecén [E] 92 F2
Fuente Dé [E] 86 B2
Fuente de Cantos [E] 98 E3
Fuente del Arco [E] 98 F3
Fuente del Maestre [E] 98 E2
Fuente del Obispo [E] 106 A1
Fuente de Pedro Naharro
  [E] 100 F2
Fuente de Santa Cruz [E]
  92 D2
Fuente el Fresno [E] 100 D2
Fuente el Sauz [E] 92 F4
Fuente el Sol [E] 84 F4
Fuenteguinaldo [E] 90 F2
Fuentelapeña [E] 84 F4
Fuentelcésped [E] 92 F2
Fuentelespino de Haro [E]
  102 A2
Fuentelespino de Moya [E]
  102 C2
Fuentemilanos [E] 92 E3
Fuente Obejuna [E] 100 B3
Fuente Palmera [E] 104 D1
Fuentepinilla [E] 94 B2
Fuenterrabía / Hondarribia
  [E] 86 F3
Fuentes [E] 102 B2
Fuentesaúco [E] 84 E4
Fuentes de Andalucía [E]
  104 C1
Fuentes de Ayódar [E] 102 D2
Fuentes de Ebro [E] 94 E3
Fuentes de Jiloca [E] 94 C3
Fuentes de León [E] 98 E3
Fuentes de Nava [E] 86 B4
Fuentes de Oñoro [E] 84 C4
Fuentes de Ropel [E] 84 F2
Fuentidueña de Tajo [E] 100 F1
Fuerte del Rey [E] 104 F1
Fügen [A] 72 C4
Fuglebjerg [DK] 178 E2
Fuglem [N] 204 B2
Fuhrberg [D] 44 C1
Fulda [D] 58 D1
Fülesd [H] 76 F3
Fulnek [CZ] 62 D3
Fülöpszállás [H] 122 B2
Fulpmes [A] 72 C4
Fulunäs [S] 194 D2
Fumay [F] 56 C2
Fumel [F] 88 E1
Funäsdalen [S] 204 D3
Funchal [P] 110 E4
Fundão [P] 90 E2
Fundres / Pfundres [I] 118 C1
Fundulea [RO] 150 C1
Furadouro [P] 84 A3
Furculeşti [RO] 150 A2
Fure [N] 192 B1
Furnes (Veurne) [B] 40 C3
Fürnitz [A] 118 F2
Fursett [N] 202 C3
Furset [N] 202 D2
Fürstenau [D] 30 E3
Fürstenfeld [A] 120 C1
Fürstenfeldbruck [D] 72 C2
Fürstenwalde [D] 46 C2
Fürstenwerder [D] 34 C3
Fürstenzell [D] 72 E2
Furta [H] 122 E1
Furtan [S] 188 D2
Fürth [D] 58 E3
Furth im Wald [D] 60 B4
Furtwangen [D] 70 E2
Furuby [S] 184 D3
Furudal [S] 194 F2
Furuflaten [N] 224 E2
Furusjö [S] 184 C1

Furusund [S] 190 E2
Furutangvik [N] 212 D3
Furuvik [S] 196 D3
Fusa [N] 192 B3
Fuscaldo [I] 138 D1
Fusch [A] 72 E4
Fushë Arrëz [AL] 154 B3
Fushë–Krujë [AL] 154 A4
Fushë–Kuqe [AL] 154 A4
Fushë Muhurr [AL] 154 B4
Fusio [CH] 116 D2
Füssen [D] 72 B3
Futog [SRB] 146 D1
Futrikelv [N] 224 D2
Füzesabony [H] 76 C3
Füzesgyarmat [H] 122 E1
Fužeta [P] 98 C4
Fylakí [GR] 162 A4
Fylákio [GR] 156 F3
Fylakopi [GR] 174 C1
Fylí [GR] 168 B2
Fylí [GR] 168 B2
Fyllinge [S] 184 B3
Fynshav [DK] 178 C3
Fyresdal [N] 186 D2
Fyrkat [DK] 182 D3
Fyteíes [GR] 166 C3

G

Gaas [A] 120 D1
Gaasbeek [B] 40 D3
Gabarc [BG] 148 E3
Gabarret [F] 88 D2
Gabčíkovo [SK] 74 E3
Gabela [BIH] 152 C2
Gaber [BG] 148 D4
Gabicce Mare [I] 128 E3
Gąbin [PL] 48 D2
Gąbino [PL] 36 B1
Gaboš [HR] 122 B4
Gabrovica [BG] 156 C2
Gabrovka [SLO] 120 B3
Gabrovo [BG] 150 B4
Gać [PL] 38 B3
Gacé [F] 54 B3
Gacko [BIH] 152 D2
Gåda [S] 196 B1
Gäddede [S] 212 E3
Gäddeholm [S] 190 C2
Gadebusch [D] 32 D3
Gadna [H] 76 D2
Gádor [E] 106 B3
Gádoros [H] 122 D2
Gadžin Han [SRB] 148 B4
Gæidno [N] 228 D2
Gæidnovuoppe [N] 226 B2
Gaël [F] 52 D4
Găeşti [RO] 248 D3
Gaeta [I] 134 B3
Gaflenz [A] 74 B3
Gagarin [RUS] 240 E3
Gaggenau [D] 70 E1
Gagliano Castelferrato [I]
138 B4
Gagliano del Capo [I] 136 F4
Gagnef [S] 194 F3
Gahro [D] 46 B3
Gaildorf [D] 58 C4
Gaillac [F] 88 F2
Gaillimh / Galway [IRL] 10 C1
Gaillon [F] 54 D2
Gainsborough [GB] 24 D3
Gaios [GR] 166 B2
Gairloch [GB] 14 C2
Gairo [I] 142 C4
Gaj [HR] 120 E4
Gaj [SRB] 146 E2
Gajary [SK] 74 D2
Gajdobra [SRB] 122 C4

Gajeva [LV] 236 E3
Gakovo [SRB] 122 B3
Gålå [N] 192 F2
Galåbodarna [S] 204 E3
Galan [F] 88 D3
Galanádo [GR] 168 D4
Galanito [N] 226 B2
Galanta [SK] 74 E3
Galapagar [E] 92 E3
Galashiels [GB] 20 D2
Galata [BG] 150 E3
Galatáki, Moní– [GR] 168 A1
Galatás [GR] 168 A3
Galaţi [RO] 244 F4
Galatia (Mehmetcik) [CY]
176 E3
Galati Marina [I] 138 C4
Galatina [I] 136 F3
Galátista [GR] 162 B2
Galatone [I] 136 E3
Galaxídi [GR] 166 E3
Galbally [IRL] 10 C3
Gålborget [S] 206 D1
Galdakao [E] 86 E3
Gáldar [E] 112 E3
Galeata [I] 128 D3
Galera [E] 106 B2
Galéria [F] 130 A2
Galgaguta [H] 76 B3
Galgagyörk [H] 76 B3
Galgamácsa [H] 76 B3
Galicea Mare [RO] 148 D2
Galinóporni (Kaleburnu) [CY]
176 E2
Galiny [PL] 36 F2
Galipsós [GR] 162 C1
Galissás [GR] 168 D3
Galisteo [E] 90 F3
Galižana [HR] 144 A2
Galizano [E] 86 D2
Gallarate [I] 116 D3
Gällared [S] 184 B3
Gallargues [F] 124 D3
Gallarus Oratory [IRL] 10 A3
Gallegos del Río [E] 84 E2
Gallegos de Solmirón [E]
92 C3
Gallenstein [A] 74 B3
Galliate [I] 116 D3
Gallípoli [I] 136 E3
Gällivare [S] 220 E2
Gallneukirchen [A] 74 A2
Gällö [S] 204 E2
Gällstad [S] 184 B2
Gallur [E] 94 D2
Galovo [BG] 148 E3
Gålsjö bruk [S] 206 D2
Galston [GB] 18 C4
Galtelli [I] 142 C3
Galten [DK] 178 C1
Galten [N] 194 C1
Gåltjärn [S] 206 C3
Galtström [S] 206 C4
Galtür [A] 118 A1
Galveias [P] 90 C3
Gálvez [E] 100 C3
Gałwawy [PL] 38 A1
Galway / Gaillimh [IRL] 10 C1
Galyatetö [H] 76 C3
Gamaches [F] 40 A4
Gambara [I] 116 F4
Gambárie [I] 138 D3
Gambatesa [I] 134 D2
Gambolò [I] 116 D4
Gaming [A] 74 B3
Gamla Gränome [S] 190 D1
Gamla Uppsala [S] 190 D1
Gamleby [S] 184 E1
Gammalsälen [S] 194 D3
Gammel Estrup [DK] 182 D4
Gammel Skagen [DK] 182 E1
Gammelskolla [N] 194 B2

Gammelstaden [S] 214 E1
Gammertingen [D] 70 F2
Gams [CH] 70 F4
Gamvik [N] 228 D1
Gamzigrad [SRB] 148 C3
Gan [F] 88 C3
Ganacker [D] 72 E2
Ganagobie, Prieuré– [F]
124 F2
Gand (Gent) [B] 40 D3
Gandal [N] 186 B2
Gåndara [P] 84 B4
Ganderkesee [D] 30 F2
Gandesa [E] 94 F4
Gandia [E] 102 D4
Gandino [I] 116 F3
Gandrup [DK] 182 D3
Gandvik [N] 228 E2
Gåneasa [RO] 148 E1
Ganges [F] 124 C2
Gangi [I] 138 B4
Gångiova [RO] 148 E2
Gangkofen [D] 72 D2
Gannat [F] 80 B1
Gänserndorf [A] 74 D2
Gap [F] 126 A1
Gaperhult [S] 188 D3
Gara [H] 122 B3
Garaballa [E] 102 C2
Garabonc [H] 120 E2
Garafía [E] 112 B1
Garaguso [I] 134 F4
Gara Khitrino [BG] 150 D3
Garani [BY] 242 B2
Garavac [BIH] 146 B2
Garbagna [I] 126 E1
Garbno [PL] 38 A1
Gârbovu [RO] 148 D1
Garbów [PL] 50 B3
Garbsen [D] 44 B1
Garching [D] 72 D3
Garcia [E] 96 B3
Garciaz [E] 100 B1
Garčin [HR] 146 B1
Gârcov [RO] 148 F2
Gard, Pont du– [F] 124 D2
Garda [I] 118 B3
Gardanne [F] 124 E3
Gårdby [S] 184 F4
Gardeja [PL] 36 D3
Gardelegen [D] 44 D1
Gardíki [GR] 166 D3
Garding [D] 32 B1
Gârdnäs [S] 212 F4
Gardone Riviera [I] 118 A3
Gardone Val Trómpia [I]
116 F3
Gárdony [H] 122 A1
Gårdsby [S] 184 D3
Gardsjöbäcken [S] 214 A2
Gårdskär [S] 196 D3
Gärdslösa [S] 184 F3
Gardstad [N] 212 C3
Gårdstånga [S] 178 C2
Garein [F] 88 C1
Gårelehöjden [S] 206 C1
Garen [N] 192 C3
Gares / Puente la Reina
[E] 86 F4
Gareŝnica [HR] 120 E4
Garéssio [I] 126 D2
Gargaliánoi [GR] 172 C3
Gargas, Grotte de– [F] 88 D3
Gargaur [S] 214 B1
Gargellen [A] 116 F1
Gargilesse–Dampierre [F]
68 A4
Gargnano [I] 118 B3
Gargnäs [S] 214 B2
Gargoles de Abajo [E] 94 B4
Gârgyán [H] 122 C2
Gargždai [LT] 238 A2

Gari [MK] 154 C4
Garibaldi, Tomba di– [I]
142 C2
Garípa [GR] 174 D4
Garkalne [LV] 236 B3
Garlasco [I] 116 D4
Garliava [LT] 238 D3
Garlin [F] 88 C2
Garlstorf [D] 32 C3
Garmisch Partenkirchen
[D] 72 C4
Garmo [N] 192 E1
Garnisch Gardens [IRL] 10 B4
Garoza [LV] 234 F3
Garpenberg [S] 196 C4
Gárrat [E] 96 D3
Garrafe de Torío [E] 82 F4
Garray [E] 94 B2
Garrel [D] 30 F3
Garristown [IRL] 10 F2
Garrotxa, Zona Volcànica de
la– [E] 96 E2
Garrovillas [E] 90 F3
Garrucha [E] 106 C3
Gars am Kamp [A] 74 C2
Garsås [S] 194 F3
Garsnas [S] 180 D2
Garten [N] 202 F1
Gartland [N] 212 D3
Gartow [D] 32 D4
Gartringen [D] 70 F1
Gartz [D] 34 D4
Garvão [P] 98 B3
Garwolin [PL] 50 B2
Garz [D] 34 C2
Gåsborn [S] 188 E1
Gåsbue [N] 202 E3
Gaschurn [A] 116 F1
Gascueña [E] 102 B1
Gasen [A] 74 C4
Gaskeluokta [S] 214 A2
Gąski [PL] 38 B2
Gąsocin [PL] 48 E1
Gaspoltshofen [A] 72 F3
Gässäsen [S] 206 B4
Gasteiner Klamm [A] 72 E4
Gastellovo [RUS] 238 B3
Gastes [F] 78 A4
Gastoúni [GR] 172 B1
Gasztony [H] 120 D1
Gata [N] 194 C3
Gata de Gorgos [E] 108 C2
Gătaia [RO] 122 E4
Gatchina [RUS] 200 F4
Gatehouse of Fleet [GB] 20 C2
Gåtér [H] 122 C2
Gateshead [GB] 20 E3
Gátova [E] 102 D3
Gatta [I] 128 B2
Gattendorf [A] 74 D3
Gattinara [I] 116 D3
Gaubert [F] 54 C4
Gaucín [E] 104 C3
Gaukås [N] 186 D3
Gaulstad [N] 212 C4
Gaupne [N] 192 D2
Gaushach [D] 58 D2
Gausvik [N] 224 C4
Gautefall [N] 186 D2
Gautestad [N] 186 D3
Gauville [F] 54 B3
Gavaloú [GR] 166 D3
Gavardo [I] 118 A3
Gavarnie [F] 88 D4
Gavarnie, Cirque de– [F] 88 C4
Gávavencselló [H] 76 E3
Gaverina Terme [I] 116 F3
Gavi [I] 126 E2
Gaviāo [P] 90 D3
Gavirate [I] 116 D3
Gävle [S] 196 D3

Gavoi [I] 142 C3
Gavorrano [I] 130 D2
Gavray [F] 52 E3
Gávrio [GR] 168 C2
Gávros [GR] 160 D2
Gavry [RUS] 236 E3
Gåvsta [S] 190 D1
Gåxsjö [S] 204 F1
Gaziköy [TR] 158 B4
Gazimağusa (Ammóchostos)
[CY] 176 E3
Gazoldo degli Ippoliti [I]
118 A4
Gázoros [GR] 156 C4
Gbelce [SK] 76 A3
Gdańsk [PL] 36 C2
Gdov [RUS] 230 F2
Gdów [PL] 64 A3
Gdynia [PL] 36 C1
Gea de Albarracín [E] 102 C1
Geashill [IRL] 10 E2
Geaune [F] 88 C2
Gebesee [D] 44 D4
Geblar [D] 58 D1
Gebze [TR] 158 E3
Geçitkale (Lefkónikon) [CY]
176 E3
Geçkınli [TR] 158 B2
Gedem [D] 58 C2
Gedesby [DK] 32 E1
Gedinne [B] 56 C2
Gediz [TR] 164 F3
Gedser [DK] 32 E1
Gedsted [DK] 182 C3
Gedved [DK] 178 C1
Geel [B] 40 E3
Geertruidenberg [NL] 30 A4
Geeste [D] 30 E3
Geesthacht [D] 32 C3
Gefell [D] 58 F2
Gefrees [D] 58 F2
Gefýra [GR] 160 F2
Gefýria [GR] 166 E2
Gehren [D] 58 E1
Geijersholm [S] 188 E1
Geilenkirchen [D] 42 B3
Geilo [N] 192 D3
Geiranger [N] 202 D4
Geisa [D] 58 D1
Geiselhöring [D] 72 D1
Geiselwind [D] 58 E3
Geisenfeld [D] 72 C2
Geisenhausen [D] 72 D2
Geisingen [D] 70 E3
Geislingen [D] 72 A2
Geisnes [N] 212 C3
Geithain [D] 44 F4
Geithus [N] 186 F1
Gela [I] 140 D3
Geldern [D] 42 C3
Geldrop [NL] 40 F3
Geleen [NL] 40 F3
Gelej [H] 76 D3
Gelembe [TR] 164 C3
Gelgaudiškis [LT] 238 C3
Gelibolu [TR] 164 B1
Gelibolu [TR] 170 D4
Gelida [E] 96 D3
Gelnhausen [D] 58 C2
Gelnica [SK] 76 D1
Gelsa [E] 94 E3
Gelsenkirchen [D] 42 D3
Gelting [D] 178 C3
Gelu [RO] 122 E3
Gembloux [B] 40 E4
Gémenos [F] 124 F4
Gemerská Poloma [SK] 76 C2
Gemerská Ves [SK] 76 C2
Gemert [NL] 40 F2
Gemikonağı (Karavostasi)
[CY] 176 D3

Gemiş [TR] 170 F2
Gemlik [TR] 158 E4
Gemmenich [B] 42 B4
Gemona del Friuli [I] 118 E3
Gémozac [F] 78 C2
Gemünd [D] 42 C4
Gemünden [D] 42 F4
Gemünden [D] 56 F2
Gemunden [D] 58 D2
Genappe [B] 40 D4
Génave [E] 100 F4
Genazzano [I] 132 D4
Gençay [F] 66 E4
Gencsapáti [H] 74 D4
Génelard [F] 68 D4
General Inzovo [BG] 156 F1
Generalski Stol [HR] 120 C4
General Toshevo [BG] 150 E2
Generli [TR] 158 B3
Genevad [S] 184 B3
Genève [CH] 80 F2
Gengenbach [D] 70 E2
Genillé [F] 66 F3
Genk [B] 40 F3
Genlis [F] 68 F3
Gennádio [GR] 176 C2
Genna Maria, Nuraghe– [I] 142 B4
Gennep [NL] 42 C2
Gennes [F] 66 E2
Génolhac [F] 124 D1
Génova [I] 126 E2
Genshagen [D] 46 B2
Gent (Gand) [B] 40 D3
Genthin [D] 44 E2
Gentioux [F] 78 F2
Genzano di Lucánia [I] 134 F3
Genzano di Roma [I] 132 C4
Georgianoí [GR] 160 E3
Georgioúpoli [CY] 176 D4
Georgi Traykov [BG] 150 E3
Georgsheil [D] 30 E2
Geotermia, Museo della– [I] 130 D1
Gera [D] 60 B1
Geraardsbergen [B] 40 D3
Gerabronn [D] 58 D4
Gerace [I] 138 D3
Gerakarou [GR] 162 B1
Gérakas [GR] 172 E3
Geráki [GR] 172 E3
Gerakiní [GR] 162 B2
Gérardmer [F] 70 C2
Geras [A] 74 C2
Gerasdorf bei Wien [A] 74 D2
Gerbéviller [F] 70 C1
Gerbstedt [D] 44 D3
Gérce [H] 120 E1
Gerchsheim [D] 58 D3
Geremeas [I] 142 C5
Gerena [E] 98 E4
Gerês [P] 82 B4
Geretsried [D] 72 C3
Gérgal [E] 106 B3
Gergelyiugornya [H] 76 F3
Gerince [TR] 176 B1
Gërkëni [LV] 236 C3
Gerlos [A] 72 D4
Germaringen [D] 72 B3
Germasogela [CY] 176 D4
Germay [F] 70 A1
Germencik [TR] 170 C3
Germering [D] 72 B2
Germering [D] 72 C2
Germersheim [D] 58 B4
Germigny-des-Pres [F] 68 B2
Gernika–Lumo [E] 86 E3
Gernrode [D] 44 D3
Gernsbach [D] 70 E1
Gernsheim [D] 58 B3
Gerola Alta [I] 116 E3
Geroliménas [GR] 172 D4

Gerolstein [D] 56 E2
Gerolzhofen [D] 58 D3
Gerona / Girona [E] 96 E2
Geroskípou [CY] 176 C4
Gerovo [HR] 120 B4
Gerri de la Sal [E] 96 C1
Gersfeld [D] 58 D2
Gersthofen [D] 72 B2
Gerswalde [D] 34 C4
Gesäter [S] 188 C3
Gesäuse [A] 74 B4
Gescher [D] 30 D4
Geseke [D] 42 E3
Gespunsart [F] 56 C2
Gestelnburg [CH] 116 C2
Gesualdo [I] 134 D3
Gesunda [S] 194 F3
Geta [FIN] 196 F4
Getafe [E] 92 E4
Getaria [E] 86 F3
Gettlinge [S] 184 E4
Gettorf [D] 32 C1
Getxo [E] 86 E3
Gévezé [F] 52 E4
Gevgelija [MK] 156 A4
Gevigney–et–Mercey [F] 70 B2
Gevrey–Chambertin [F] 68 F3
Gevsjön [S] 204 D2
Gex [F] 80 F2
Gey [D] 42 C4
Geyikli [TR] 162 F2
Geyre [TR] 170 D3
Geysir [IS] 218 B3
Gföhl [A] 74 C2
Ghedi [I] 116 F4
Gheorghieni [RO] 244 D4
Ghilarza [I] 142 B3
Ghimpați [RO] 150 B2
Ghisonaccia [F] 130 B3
Ghisoni [F] 130 B3
Giáltra [GR] 166 F2
Giannitsá [GR] 160 E2
Giannoúli [GR] 156 F3
Giardinetto [I] 134 E3
Giardini–Naxos [I] 138 C4
Giarmata [RO] 122 E3
Giarratana [I] 140 E3
Giarre [I] 138 C4
Giat [F] 80 A2
Giba [I] 142 B5
Gibellina [I] 140 B2
Gibellina, Ruderi di– [I] 140 B2
Gibilmanna, Santuario di– [I] 138 A4
Gibostad [N] 224 D2
Gibraleón [E] 98 D4
Gibraltar [GBZ] 104 C4
Gic [H] 74 E4
Gidböle [S] 206 E2
Gideå [S] 206 E2
Gideåkroken [S] 214 B3
Gidle [PL] 48 D4
Gieboldehausen [D] 44 C3
Giedraičiai [LT] 238 E3
Gielas [S] 212 F2
Gielniów [PL] 48 E3
Gien [F] 68 C2
Giengedal [N] 192 C1
Giengen [D] 72 B2
Giens [F] 126 A4
Giera [RO] 122 E4
Gierałtowice [PL] 62 E3
Gieselwerder [D] 44 B3
Giessen [D] 58 B1
Gieten [NL] 30 D2
Giethoorn [NL] 30 C3
Gietrzwałd [PL] 36 E3
Giffoni [I] 134 D4
Gifhorn [D] 44 C1
Gigen [BG] 148 F3
Giglio Porto [I] 130 D2

Gignac [F] 124 C3
Gijón / Xixón [E] 82 F2
Giksi [LV] 236 C2
Gilford [NIR] 12 E3
Gilja [N] 186 B2
Gilleleje [DK] 178 E1
Gillhov [S] 204 F3
Gills [GB] 14 F1
Gillstad [S] 188 D4
Gilserberg [D] 42 F4
Gilze [NL] 40 E2
Gimat [F] 88 E2
Gimdalen [S] 206 B3
Gimel–les–Cascades [F] 78 F3
Gimenells, Castell de– [E] 94 F3
Gimmestad [N] 202 C4
Gimo [S] 196 E4
Gimont [F] 88 E2
Ginci [BG] 148 D4
Gingst [D] 34 C1
Ginosa [I] 136 C2
Ginzling [A] 118 C1
Ginzo de Limia / Xinzo de Limia [E] 82 C4
Giões [P] 98 C3
Gióia del Colle [I] 136 D2
Gióia Táuro [I] 138 D3
Gioiosa Marea [I] 138 C3
Giornico [CH] 116 E2
Giove Anxur, Tempio di– [I] 134 B2
Giovinazzo [I] 136 C1
Giraltovce [SK] 64 C4
Girgantai [LT] 238 C4
Girifalco [I] 138 E2
Girne (Keryneia) [CY] 176 D3
Girolata [F] 130 A2
Giromagny [F] 70 C3
Girona / Gerona [E] 96 E2
Gironella [E] 96 D2
Girvan [GB] 20 B2
Gisholt [N] 186 E2
Gislaved [S] 184 B2
Gislev [DK] 178 D3
Gisors [F] 54 D2
Gisselås [S] 204 F1
Gisselfeld [DK] 178 E3
Gissi [I] 132 F4
Gisslarbo [S] 190 B2
Gistaín [E] 88 D4
Gistel [B] 40 C3
Gistrup [DK] 182 D3
Gittun [S] 220 D3
Giugliano in Campania [I] 134 C3
Giuliano di Roma [I] 134 B2
Giulianova [I] 132 E2
Giulväz [RO] 122 E4
Giurgița [RO] 148 D2
Giurgiu [RO] 150 B2
Give [DK] 178 B1
Givet [F] 56 C1
Givors [F] 80 D3
Givry [B] 40 D4
Givry [F] 68 D2
Givry [F] 68 E4
Givry–en–Argonne [F] 56 C3
Giżałki [PL] 48 B2
Gizdavac [HR] 144 E4
Gizeux [F] 66 E2
Giżycko [PL] 38 B2
Gizzeria [I] 138 E2
Gjakove / Ðakovica [KS] 154 B3
Gjelten [N] 204 B4
Gjemnes [N] 202 D2
Gjerbës [AL] 160 B2
Gjerde [N] 192 D1
Gjermundshamn [N] 192 B4
Gjern [DK] 182 D4
Gjerrild [DK] 182 E3

Gjerstad [N] 186 E3
Gjersvik [N] 212 D3
Gjesvær [N] 228 C1
Gjeving [N] 186 E3
Gjinar [AL] 160 B2
Gjirokastër [AL] 160 B3
Gjølga [N] 204 B1
Gjølme [N] 202 F2
Gjøra [N] 202 E3
Gjóv [FR] 182 B1
Gjøvag [N] 192 B4
Gjøvik [N] 194 B3
Gjøvik [N] 224 C3
G. Konjare [MK] 154 D3
Gkoritsá [GR] 172 D3
Gkoúra [GR] 166 E4
Gla [GR] 166 F3
Gladbeck [D] 42 D3
Gladenbach [D] 42 E4
Gladhammar [S] 184 E2
Gladstad [N] 212 D1
Glamoč [BIH] 144 E3
Glåmos [N] 204 C3
Glamsbjerg [DK] 178 C2
Glandorf [D] 30 E4
Glanmire [IRL] 10 C4
Glanworth [IRL] 10 C3
Glarus [CH] 70 F4
Glasgow [GB] 18 C4
Glashütte [D] 60 D1
Glashütten [A] 120 B2
Glastonbury [GB] 26 E3
Glauchau [D] 60 B1
Glava [BG] 148 E3
Glava [S] 188 D2
Glavan [BG] 156 F2
Glavanovtsi [BG] 154 E3
Glavičice [BIH] 146 C2
Glavinitsa [BG] 150 D2
Glavnik [KS] 154 C2
Gleann Cholm Cille / Glencolumbkille [IRL] 12 C1
Gleann na Muaidhe / Glenamoy [IRL] 12 B2
Głębock [PL] 36 E2
Glebychevo [RUS] 200 D3
Gleichen [D] 44 D4
Gleina [D] 44 E4
Gleinalm Tunnel [A] 74 B4
Gleisdorf [A] 120 C1
Glenamaddy [IRL] 10 D1
Glenamoy / Gleann na Muaidhe [IRL] 12 B2
Glencoe [GB] 18 C2
Glencolumbkille / Gleann Cholm Cille [IRL] 12 C1
Glendalough [IRL] 10 F3
Glenealy [IRL] 10 F3
Glengarriff [IRL] 10 B4
Glénic [F] 78 F2
Glenmore [IRL] 10 E3
Glenrothes [GB] 18 D3
Glenties [IRL] 12 C2
Glenville [IRL] 10 C3
Glesne [N] 192 F4
Gletsch [CH] 116 D2
Gletscher Garten [D] 72 E3
Glewitz [D] 32 F2
Glimåkra [S] 180 D1
Glimmingehus [S] 180 D2
Glin [IRL] 10 B2
Glina [HR] 120 C4
Glinka [PL] 62 E4
Glinojeck [PL] 36 E4
Glinsce / Glínsk [IRL] 10 B1
Glinsk / Glinsce [IRL] 10 B1
G. Lisina [SRB] 154 C2
Glissjöberg [S] 204 E4
Glitterheim [N] 192 E1
Gliwice [PL] 62 D2
Glłavë [AL] 160 B3
Globitsy [RUS] 200 E4

Globočica [KS] 154 C3
Głodowa [PL] 36 A2
Gloggnitz [A] 74 C3
Głogoczów [PL] 62 F3
Glogovac [HR] 120 D3
Głogów [PL] 46 E3
Głogówek [PL] 62 D2
Głogów Małopolski [PL] 64 C2
Glomfjord [N] 218 F3
Glommen [S] 184 A3
Glommersträsk [S] 214 C2
Glömminge [S] 184 E3
Glorup [DK] 178 D3
Glóssa [GR] 162 C4
Glössbo [S] 196 C2
Glossop [GB] 24 B2
Glostrup [DK] 178 F2
Glöte [S] 204 D4
Gloucester [GB] 26 F2
Głowaczów [PL] 48 F3
Główczyce [PL] 36 B1
Glowe [D] 34 C1
Glöwen [D] 32 E4
Głowno [PL] 48 D2
Głożan [SRB] 146 C1
Glozhene [BG] 148 E4
Glozhene [BG] 148 E3
Glozhenski Manastir [BG] 148 E4
Głubczyce [PL] 62 C2
Głuchołazy [PL] 62 C2
Głuchów [PL] 48 C3
Głuchów [PL] 48 E3
Głuchowo [PL] 46 F2
Glücksburg [D] 178 B3
Glückstadt [D] 32 B2
Gluda [LV] 234 F3
Glumsø [DK] 178 E2
Głuszyca [PL] 46 E2
Głuszyca [PL] 62 B2
Glyfá [GR] 162 B4
Glyfáda [GR] 166 E3
Glyfáda [GR] 168 B3
Glykí [GR] 166 B2
Glyngøre [DK] 182 C3
Gmünd [A] 74 B2
Gmünd [A] 118 E1
Gmund [D] 72 C2
Gmunden [A] 72 F3
Gnarp [S] 196 D1
Gnarrenburg [D] 32 B3
Gnas [A] 120 C2
Gnesau [A] 118 F2
Gnesta [S] 190 D3
Gneux [F] 56 A3
Gniechowice [PL] 46 F4
Gniew [PL] 36 D3
Gniewkowo [PL] 36 C4
Gniezno [PL] 48 B2
Gnisvärd [S] 234 A2
Gnjilane [KS] 154 D2
Gnocchetta [I] 128 E2
Gnoien [D] 32 F2
Gnojnice [BIH] 152 D2
Gnosjö [S] 184 C2
Göbel [TR] 164 D2
Göçbeyli [TR] 164 C3
Göçek [TR] 176 D1
Goch [D] 42 C2
Göd [H] 76 B3
Godafoss [IS] 218 C2
Godalming [GB] 28 C3
Godby [FIN] 196 F4
Godech [BG] 148 D4
Godegard [S] 188 F3
Godelheim [D] 44 B3
Gödenroth [D] 56 F2
Goderville [F] 54 C1
Godętowo [PL] 36 C1
Godkowo [PL] 36 E2
Gödöllő [H] 76 B4
Godovič [SLO] 118 F3

Godowa [PL] 64 C3
Godøynes [N] 218 F3
Gödre [H] 120 F3
Godziesze Wielkie [PL] 48 C3
Godziszewo [PL] 36 C2
Goes [NL] 40 D2
Góglio [I] 116 D2
Gogolin [PL] 62 D2
Gógolo [I] 118 B2
Göhren [D] 34 C2
Goieşti [RO] 148 E1
Goirle [NL] 40 E2
Góis [P] 90 D2
Góito [I] 118 B4
Goizueta [E] 86 F3
Gojani i Madh [AL] 154 R3
Gojsalići [BIH] 146 B3
Gökçedağ [TR] 164 E2
Gökçek [TR] 170 F2
Gökçen [TR] 170 C2
Gökçeören [TR] 164 E4
Gokels [D] 32 B2
Gökova [TR] 170 D4
Gökpınar [TR] 176 F1
Göksholm [S] 190 B2
Göktepe [TR] 170 D3
Gol [N] 192 E3
Gola [HR] 120 E3
Gołąb [PL] 50 B3
Gołańcz [PL] 36 B4
Gölbent [TR] 176 E1
Gölby [FIN] 196 F4
Golchen [D] 34 C3
Gölcük [TR] 158 B4
Gölcük [TR] 158 F3
Gölcük [TR] 164 D3
Gölcük [TR] 170 C2
Golçük [TR] 170 D4
Golčův Jeníkov [CZ] 60 F3
Golczewo [PL] 34 E3
Gołdap [PL] 38 B1
Goldbach [D] 50 C2
Goldberg [D] 32 E3
Goldelund [D] 178 B3
Golden [IRL] 10 D3
Goldenstedt [D] 30 F3
Gölecik [TR] 164 D1
Goleen [IRL] 10 A4
Golegã [P] 90 C3
Goleim [AL] 160 B3
Golema Crcorija [MK] 154 E3
Golemo Selo [SRB] 154 D2
Goleniów [PL] 34 E3
Goleniowy [PL] 62 F2
Golfe-Juan [F] 126 C3
Golfo Aranci [I] 142 C2
Golfo di Sogno [F] 130 B4
Gölhisar [TR] 170 F4
Golina [PL] 48 B2
Goliševa [LV] 236 E3
Golizyno [RUS] 240 F3
Goljam Dervent [BG] 158 A2
Goljam Izvor [BG] 156 E2
Goljamo Belovo [BG] 156 C2
Goljamo Kamenjane [BG]
    156 E3
Goljan Man. [BG] 156 F2
Gollden [N] 226 B2
Göllersdörf [A] 74 C2
Gollhofen [D] 58 D3
Golling [A] 72 E4
Gölmarmara [TR] 164 D4
Golmayo [E] 94 B2
Golnice [PL] 46 D4
Golnik [SLO] 120 A2
Golodskoye [RUS] 240 F4
Golpejas [E] 84 E4
Golspie [GB] 14 E2
Golssen [D] 46 B2
Göltarla [TR] 176 F1
Golubac [SRB] 146 F2
Golub Dobrzyń [PL] 36 D4

Golubinje [SRB] 148 C1
Golubovci [MNE] 152 E3
Gołuchów [PL] 48 B3
Golvesh [BG] 150 E2
Gölyaka [TR] 164 C1
Golyalo Krushevo [BG]
    158 B1
Golyam porovec [BG] 150 D2
Gölyazı [TR] 164 E1
Gołymin-Ośrodek [PL] 36 F4
Golzow [D] 44 F2
Gómara [E] 94 C2
Gombasecká Jaskyňa [SK]
    76 C2
Gombe [TR] 176 E1
Gombo [I] 128 B3
Gömeç [TR] 164 B3
Gomes Aires [P] 98 B3
Gommern [D] 44 E2
Gomunice [PL] 48 D4
Gönc [H] 76 D2
Goncelin [F] 80 F3
Gondomar [P] 84 A2
Gondrecourt [F] 70 B1
Gondrin [F] 88 D2
Gönen [TR] 164 C2
Goni, Nuraghe- [I] 142 C5
Goniá [GR] 174 B3
Goniądz [PL] 38 C2
Gónnoi [GR] 160 F3
Gonnosfanádiga [I] 142 B5
Gönyü [H] 74 F3
Gonzaga [I] 128 C1
Gooik [B] 40 D3
Goole [GB] 24 D2
Goor [NL] 30 D4
Göpfritz [A] 74 C2
Goppenstein [CH] 116 C2
Göppingen [D] 72 A1
Góra [PL] 46 E3
Góra [PL] 48 E1
Góra Kalwaria [PL] 48 F2
Goransko [MNE] 152 E2
Góra Puławska [PL] 48 E4
Góra Świętej Anny [PL] 62 D2
Goražde [BIH] 146 C4
Gördalen [S] 194 D2
Gordaliza del Pino [E] 86 A3
Gordes [F] 124 E2
Gördes [TR] 164 D3
Goren Chiflik [BG] 150 E3
Gorenja Vas [SLO] 118 F3
Goresbridge [IRL] 10 E3
Gorey [IRL] 10 F3
Görgeteg [H] 120 E3
Gorgier [CH] 70 C4
Gorgonzola [I] 116 E3
Gorica [BG] 150 E4
Gorica [BIH] 152 C1
Gorica [HR] 144 C3
Gorica [SLO] 120 D2
Gorica Jamnička [HR] 120 C4
Goričan [HR] 120 D2
Goricë [AL] 160 C2
Gorinchem [NL] 30 B4
Gorino Veneto [I] 128 C2
Goritsy [RUS] 240 E2
Göritz [D] 34 D3
Gorízia [I] 118 E3
Gorjão [P] 90 C3
Gørlev [DK] 178 D2
Gorlice [PL] 64 B3
Görlitz [D] 46 D4
Gormanston Castle [IRL] 12 E4
Gormund [CH] 70 E4
Gorna Beshovica [BG] 148 E4
Gorna Cerovene [BG] 148 D3
Gorna Dikanja [BG] 154 F2
Gorna Kremena [BG] 148 E4
Gorna Mitropoliya [BG] 148 F3
Gorna Oryakhovitsa [BG]
    150 B3

Gorna Studena [BG] 150 B3
Gornij [HR] 144 D3
Gorni Tsibur [BG] 148 D3
Gornja Grabovica [BIH] 146 A4
Gornjak, Manastir- [SRB]
    146 F3
Gornja Klina [KS] 154 C2
Gornja Ploča [HR] 144 D2
Gornja Radgona [SLO] 120 D2
Gornja Sabanta [SRB] 146 E3
Gornja Toponica [SRB] 148 B3
Gornja Tuzla [BIH] 146 B2
Gornja-Vrijeska [HR] 120 E4
Gornji Lapac [HR] 144 D2
Gornji Milanovac [SRB]
    146 E3
Gornji Podgradci [BIH] 144 E1
Gornji Ravno [BIH] 144 F4
Górno [PL] 50 A4
Gorno Alexandrovo [BG]
    150 D4
Gorno Novo Selo [BG] 156 D1
Gorno Yabălkovo [BG] 158 B2
Gorobinci [MK] 154 D3
Gorodets [RUS] 232 F2
Gorodno [RUS] 232 F4
Górowo Iławeckie [PL] 36 E2
Gorredijk [NL] 30 C2
Gorron [F] 52 F4
Gørslev [DK] 178 E2
Gort [IRL] 10 C2
Górtys [GR] 172 D2
Górtys [GR] 174 D4
Görükle [TR] 164 E1
Gorv [N] 192 B1
Görvik [S] 206 B2
Gorzanów [PL] 62 B2
Görzke [D] 44 E2
Gorzkowice [PL] 48 D4
Gorzków-Osada [PL] 50 C4
Gorzów Śląski [PL] 48 C4
Gorzów Wielkopolski [PL]
    46 D1
Gorzyca [PL] 46 C2
Gorzyce [PL] 64 C1
Gorzyń [PL] 46 E2
Goržžam [N] 228 D3
Gosaldo [I] 118 C3
Gosau [A] 72 F4
Göschenen [CH] 116 D1
Góscino [PL] 34 E2
Gosdorf [A] 120 C2
Goslar [D] 44 C2
Goślice [PL] 48 D1
Gósol [E] 96 D2
Gospari [LV] 236 D4
Gospić [HR] 144 C2
Gosport [GB] 28 B4
Gossau [CH] 70 F3
Gosselies [B] 40 D4
Gossensass / Colle Isarco
    [I] 118 C1
Gössl [A] 72 F3
Gössweinstein [D] 58 E3
Gostiliciv [RUS] 200 E4
Gostitsy [RUS] 232 E2
Gostivar [MK] 154 C4
Gostków [PL] 48 C2
Göstling [A] 74 B3
Gostomia [PL] 36 A4
Gostun [SRB] 152 F2
Gostycyn [PL] 36 C3
Gostyń [PL] 46 F3
Gostynin [PL] 48 D2
Goszcz [PL] 48 B3
Goszczanowo [PL] 46 D1
Göteborg [S] 184 A2
Götene [S] 188 D4
Gotenica [SLO] 120 B4

Gotha [D] 44 C4
Gothem [S] 234 A2
Götlunda [S] 190 B2
Gotse Delchev [BG] 156 C3
Gottböle [FIN] 208 B3
Gottby [FIN] 190 F1
Gotthard Tunnel [CH] 116 D2
Göttingen [D] 44 B3
Gottne [S] 206 D2
Gottolengo [I] 116 F4
Gottröra [S] 190 D2
Göttweig [A] 74 C2
Gouarec [F] 52 C3
Gouda [NL] 30 B4
Goulou, Col des- [F] 80 B2
Goulven [F] 52 B2
Gouménissa [GR] 156 A4
Goumois [CH] 70 C3
Gourdon [F] 78 E4
Gourin [F] 52 B3
Gournay-en-Bray [F] 54 D2
Goûrnes [GR] 174 D3
Gourniá [GR] 174 E4
Gourville [F] 78 C2
Gout-Rossignol [F] 78 D3
Gouveia [P] 84 B4
Goûves [GR] 174 D3
Gouvets [F] 52 F3
Gouviá [GR] 160 B4
Gouzon [F] 80 A1
Govedartsi [BG] 156 B2
Govedjari [HR] 152 C2
Gøvstdal [N] 192 E4
Goworowo [PL] 38 A3
Gowran [IRL] 10 E3
Göynuk [TR] 176 F1
Göynükbelen [TR] 164 E2
Gózd [PL] 48 F3
Gozdnica [PL] 46 D3
Gózd-Zaszosie [PL] 48 E4
Gözler [I H] 170 E2
Graal-Müritz [D] 32 E2
Grab [BIH] 152 D3
Grab [PL] 48 B2
Grabarka [PL] 38 C4
Grabaţ [RO] 122 D3
Graberje [HR] 120 D4
Gråbo [S] 184 A1
Gråborg [S] 184 F3
Grabovac [SRB] 146 F3
Grabow [D] 32 D3
Grabów [PL] 48 C2
Grabowiec [PL] 50 D4
Grabówka [PL] 38 C3
Grabów nad Prosną [PL] 48 B3
Grabownica Starzeńska [PL]
    64 D3
Grabowskie [PL] 38 B2
Grabrovica [SRB] 148 C1
Gračac [HR] 144 D3
Gračanica [BIH] 146 B2
Gračanica [KS] 154 C2
Gračanica [SRB] 146 C3
Graçay [F] 68 B3
Grächen [CH] 116 C2
Gračišće [HR] 144 A1
Gradac [HR] 152 C2
Gradac [MNE] 152 E1
Gradac, Manastir- [SRB]
    154 B1
Gradačac [BIH] 146 B2
Graddis [N] 220 B3
Gräddö [S] 190 E1
Gradec [BG] 148 C2
Gradec Prokupski [HR] 120 C4
Gradefes [E] 86 A3
Graderas, Cueva de las- [E]
    94 E4
Gradešnica [MK] 160 D2
Gradets [BG] 150 C4

Gradevo [BG] 156 B2
Gradignan [F] 78 B3
Gradin [SLO] 118 F4
Gradina [HR] 144 C2
Gradina [SRB] 148 D4
Grădinari [RO] 146 F1
Grădinari [RO] 148 E1
Gradinarovo [BG] 150 D3
Gradisca d'Isonzo [I] 118 E3
Gradishte [BG] 150 B3
Gradište [HR] 146 B1
Gradište [SRB] 148 C4
Grădiştea [RO] 150 D1
Gradki [PL] 36 F2
Grado [E] 82 F2
Grado [I] 118 E4
Gradówek [PL] 46 D4
Gradsko [MK] 154 E4
Græsted [DK] 178 E1
Grafenau [D] 72 E1
Gräfenberg [D] 58 E3
Grafenegg [A] 74 C2
Gräfenhainichen [D] 44 E3
Grafenwöhr [D] 58 F3
Grafenwörth [A] 74 C2
Grafing [D] 72 D3
Grafrath [D] 72 C2
Gräfsnäs [S] 184 B1
Graglia, Santuário di- [I]
    116 C3
Gragnano [I] 134 D4
Gråhaugen [N] 202 F2
Grahovo [MNE] 152 E3
Grahovo [SLO] 120 A3
Graiguenamanagh [IRL] 10 E3
Grainetière, Abbaye de la- [F]
    66 C3
Graja, Cueva de la- [E] 104 F2
Grajewo [PL] 38 C2
Gralhos [P] 84 C2
Gralla [A] 120 C2
Grallagh [IRL] 12 C3
Gram [DK] 178 B2
Gramada [BG] 148 C3
Gramat [F] 78 E4
Gramatikovo [BG] 158 C2
Grambow [D] 34 D3
Gramenos [AT] 166 E2
Grammenos [AT] 166 D3
Grammeno [GR] 160 C4
Grammichele [I] 140 E3
Gramsh [AL] 160 B2
Gram Slot [DK] 178 B2
Gramzda [LV] 234 D4
Gramzow [D] 32 F4
Gramzow [D] 34 D4
Gran [N] 194 B4
Granåbron [S] 194 E4
Granada [E] 104 F3
Granadilla de Abona [E]
    112 C3
Granard [IRL] 10 E1
Granarolo dell'Emília [I]
    128 C2
Granåsen [S] 214 A4
Granátula de Calatrava [E]
    100 D3
Granberget [S] 214 A3
Granboda [FIN] 198 A4
Grancey-le-Château [F]
    68 F2
Grandas de Salime [E] 82 D2
Grandcamp-Maisy [F] 52 F2
Grand-Champ [F] 52 C4
Grand Chartreuse, Couvent de
    la- [F] 80 E3
Grande-Fougeray [F] 66 C1
Grandjouan [F] 66 C2
Grândola [P] 98 B2
Grandpré [F] 56 C3

Grandrieu [F] 80 B4
Grand Roc [F] 78 D3
Grand-Rozoy [F] 54 F3
Grandson [CH] 70 C4
Grand-St-Bernard, Col du- [CH/I] 116 B3
Grand-St-Bernard, Tunnel du- [CH/I] 116 B3
Grandvilliers [F] 54 D2
Grañén [E] 94 E2
Grangärde [S] 194 F4
Grange [IRL] 12 C2
Grange-Bleneau, Château de la- [F] 54 E4
Grange-le-Bocage [F] 54 F4
Grängesberg [S] 188 F1
Granges-sur-Vologne [F] 70 C2
Grängsjö [S] 196 D1
Granhult [S] 220 F2
Graninge [S] 206 C2
Granitola Torretta [I] 140 B2
Granitz, Jagdschloss- [D] 34 C2
Granja [P] 84 A3
Granja [P] 98 D2
Granja de Moreruela [E] 84 E2
Granja de Torrehermosa [E] 100 A3
Grankulla / Kauniainen [FIN] 198 F3
Grankullavik [S] 184 F2
Granlunda [S] 190 D1
Gränna [S] 184 C1
Grannäs [S] 214 B1
Granne [F] 38 C4
Grannes [N] 212 E2
Gränningen [S] 204 F2
Granö [S] 214 C3
Granollers [E] 96 D3
Granowo [PL] 46 E2
Gransee [D] 32 F4
Gränsgård [S] 214 B1
Gransherad [N] 186 E1
Gransjö [S] 220 E4
Gränsjön [S] 188 C2
Gran Tarajal [E] 114 D3
Grantham [GB] 24 C4
Grantown-on-Spey [GB] 14 E4
Granträsk [S] 214 B3
Granvik [S] 188 E3
Granvika [N] 194 B1
Granville [F] 52 E3
Granvin [N] 192 C3
Granvollen [N] 194 B4
Grao / el Grau [E] 102 D4
Grasbakken [N] 228 E2
Gräsberg [S] 194 F4
Graševo [BG] 156 C2
Grašišče [SLO] 118 F4
Gräsmark [S] 188 D1
Gräsmyr [S] 206 E1
Gräsö [S] 196 E4
Gräso [S] 196 E4
Grassac [F] 78 D2
Grassano [I] 134 F4
Grassau [D] 72 D3
Grasse [F] 126 B3
Gråssjön [S] 206 B3
Gråsten [DK] 178 B3
Grästorp [S] 188 D4
Gratangen [N] 224 C4
Gråtanliden [S] 214 A2
Gratkorn [A] 120 C1
Gråträsk [S] 214 C1
Graulhet [F] 88 F2
Graun im Vinschgau / Curon Venosta [I] 118 B1
Graus [E] 94 F2
Grava [S] 188 D2
Grávalos [E] 94 C2
Gravberget [N] 194 C3

Gravdal [N] 186 B3
Gravdal [N] 218 F1
Grave [NL] 42 B2
Gravedona [I] 116 E2
Gravelines [F] 28 F4
Gravellona Toce [I] 116 D3
Gravens [DK] 178 B2
Gravesend [GB] 28 D3
Gravhaug [N] 202 C4
Graviá [GR] 166 E3
Gravina in Púglia [I] 136 C2
Gravítsa [GR] 166 D2
Gravmark [S] 214 D3
Gravoúna [GR] 156 D4
Gray [F] 70 A3
Grayan-et-Hôpital [F] 78 B2
Graz [A] 120 C1
Grazalema [E] 104 C3
Gražiškiai [LT] 238 C4
Grazzanise [I] 134 C3
Grazzano Visconti [I] 128 A1
Grčak [SRB] 146 E4
Grčarice [SLO] 120 B4
Grdelica [SRB] 148 C4
Greaca [RO] 150 C2
Greaker [N] 186 F2
Great Dunmow [GB] 28 D2
Great Malvern [GB] 26 F1
Great Torrington [GB] 26 C3
Great Yarmouth [GB] 28 F1
Grebbestad [S] 188 B3
Grebenhain [D] 58 C1
Grebenstein [D] 44 B3
Grębkowo [PL] 50 B2
Grębocin [PL] 36 D4
Greding [D] 58 E4
Greencastle [NIR] 12 E3
Greenock [GB] 18 C3
Greetsiel [D] 30 E1
Gregolímano [GR] 166 F2
Greifenburg [A] 118 E2
Greiffenberg [D] 34 D4
Greifswald [D] 34 C2
Greillenstein [A] 74 C2
Grein [A] 74 B3
Greiz [D] 60 B1
Grenaa [DK] 182 E4
Grenade [F] 88 C2
Grenade [F] 88 E2
Grenchen [CH] 70 D4
Grenctale [LV] 236 B4
Grenoble [F] 80 E3
Grense-Jakobselv [N] 228 F3
Grenzland-Turm [CZ] 60 B3
Gréolierès [F] 126 B3
Greoni [RO] 146 F1
Gréoux-les-Bains [F] 124 F3
Gressoney-la-Trinité [I] 116 C3
Gressoney-St-Jean [I] 116 C3
Gresten [A] 74 B3
Gretna Green [GB] 20 D3
Grettstadt [D] 58 D2
Greussen [D] 44 D4
Greux [F] 70 B1
Grevbäck [S] 188 E4
Greve in Chianti [I] 128 C4
Greven [D] 30 E4
Grevená [GR] 160 D3
Grevenbroich [D] 42 C3
Grevenbrück [D] 42 E3
Grevenmacher [L] 56 E3
Grevesmühlen [D] 32 D2
Greve Strand [DK] 178 E2
Greyabbey [NIR] 12 F3
Greystones [IRL] 10 F2
Grez-en-Bouère [F] 54 A4
Grezzana [I] 118 B4
Grianan of Aileach [IRL] 12 E1
Gries-am-Brenner [A] 118 C1
Griesbach [D] 72 E2
Gries in Sellrain [A] 72 C4

Grieskirchen [A] 72 F2
Griffen [A] 120 B2
Grignan [F] 124 E2
Grignols [F] 78 C4
Grigoriopol [UA] 244 F3
Grillby [S] 190 D2
Grimaldi [I] 138 D2
Grimaud [F] 126 B4
Grimdalen [N] 186 D2
Grimma [D] 44 F4
Grimmen [D] 32 F2
Grimo [N] 192 C3
Grimsås [S] 184 C2
Grimsbu [N] 204 A4
Grimsby [GB] 24 D3
Grimsdalshytta [N] 202 F4
Grimslöv [S] 184 C3
Grímsstaðir [IS] 218 C2
Grimstad [N] 186 D4
Grindaheim [N] 192 E2
Grindal [N] 202 F2
Grindavík [IS] 218 A3
Grindjorda [N] 224 C4
Grindsted [DK] 178 B1
Grinkiškis [LT] 238 C2
Griñón [E] 92 E4
Grinzane Cavour [I] 126 D2
Gripenberg [S] 184 D1
Gripenberg [S] 184 D1
Grisignano di Zocco [I] 118 C4
Grisolles [F] 88 E2
Grisslehamn [S] 190 E1
Grisvåg [N] 202 D2
Grivitsa [BG] 148 F3
Grivy [RUS] 236 E2
Grizáno [GR] 160 E4
Grižkabūdis [LT] 238 C3
Grøa [N] 202 E3
Gröbers [D] 44 E3
Grobina [LV] 234 D4
Gröbming [A] 72 F4
Grocka [SRB] 146 E2
Gródek [PL] 38 D4
Gródek [PL] 38 D3
Gródek nad Dunajcem [PL] 64 B3
Gröditz [D] 46 B3
Gródki [PL] 50 C4
Grodków [PL] 62 C2
Grodno [PL] 62 B1
Grodzeń [PL] 36 D4
Grodziec [PL] 46 D4
Grodziec [PL] 62 B3
Grodzisk Mazowieki [PL] 48 E2
Grodzisk Wielkoposki [PL] 46 E2
Groenlo [NL] 30 D4
Groix [F] 52 B4
Grojdibodu [RO] 148 E3
Grójec [PL] 48 B2
Grójec [PL] 48 F3
Grömitz [D] 32 D2
Gromnik [PL] 64 B3
Gromo [I] 116 F3
Gromovo [RUS] 200 E2
Gromovo [RUS] 238 A3
Grøna [N] 192 E1
Gronau [D] 30 D4
Gronau [D] 44 B2
Grönbo [S] 214 D2
Grønbua [N] 192 E1
Grøndal [N] 202 B4
Grong [N] 212 D3
Grönhögen [S] 184 E4
Grønhøj [DK] 182 C4
Gröningen [D] 44 D2
Groningen [NL] 30 D2
Granlja [N] 204 B1
Grønnes [N] 202 D3
Grönskåra [S] 184 E3
Grönsö [S] 190 D2

Gropen [S] 188 F3
Grósio [I] 118 A2
Grossarl [A] 72 E4
Grossbeeren [D] 46 B2
Grossbreitenbach [D] 58 E2
Grossburgwedel [D] 44 C1
Grossenbrode [D] 32 D1
Grossenhain [D] 46 B4
Grossenkneten [D] 30 F3
Grossenzersdorf [A] 74 D3
Grosseto [I] 130 E2
Gross-Gerau [D] 58 B2
Gross-Gerungs [A] 74 B2
Grossglobniz [A] 74 B2
Grosshabersdorf [D] 58 E3
Grossharras [A] 74 D2
Grosshöchstetten [CH] 70 D4
Gross Mohrdorf [D] 32 F2
Gross Oesingen [D] 44 C1
Gross-Pertenschlag [A] 74 B2
Gross-Pertholz [A] 74 B2
Grosspetersdorf [A] 120 D1
Grossraming [A] 74 B3
Gross Räschen [D] 46 C3
Gross Schönebeck [D] 34 C4
Gross-Siegharts [A] 74 C2
Gross-Umstadt [D] 58 C3
Grosswoltersdorf [D] 32 F4
Grostenquin [F] 56 E4
Grosuplje [SLO] 120 B3
Grøtavær [N] 224 C3
Grötholen [S] 194 D1
Grotli [N] 202 D4
Grotnes [S] 192 B3
Grottaglie [I] 136 D2
Grottaminarda [I] 134 D3
Grottammare [I] 132 E2
Grotteria [I] 138 E3
Grouw [NL] 30 C2
Grova [N] 186 E2
Grövelsjön [S] 204 C4
Grovfjord [N] 224 C3
Grozd'ovo [BG] 150 E3
Grožnjan [HR] 118 F4
Gr. Strömkendorf [D] 32 D2
Grua [N] 194 B4
Grubben [N] 212 E2
Grube [D] 32 D2
Grubišno Polje [HR] 120 E4
Gruda [HR] 152 D3
Grude [BIH] 152 C1
Grude [S] 184 B1
Grudusk [PL] 36 F4
Grudziądz [PL] 36 D3
Gruemirë [AL] 152 F3
Gruia [RO] 148 C2
Gruibingen [D] 72 A2
Gruissan [F] 124 B3
Grumentum [I] 136 B3
Grums [S] 188 D2
Grünau [A] 72 F3
Grünberg [D] 58 C1
Grünburg [A] 74 A3
Grundfors [S] 212 F2
Grundfors [S] 214 B2
Grundforsen [S] 194 D2
Grundlsee [A] 72 F3
Grundsel [S] 214 D1
Grundsjö [S] 214 A4
Grundsjö [S] 214 B2
Grundsjön [S] 206 B4
Grundsund [S] 188 B4
Grundsunda [S] 206 E2
Grundtjärn [S] 206 C2
Grünenplan [D] 44 B2
Grungedal [N] 186 D1
Grünheide [D] 46 B2
Grünhof [D] 34 D3
Grünstadt [D] 58 B3
Grunwald [PL] 36 E3
Grupčin [MK] 154 C3

Gruškovje [SLO] 120 C3
Gruvberget [S] 196 C3
Gruyères [CH] 116 B1
Gruža [SRB] 146 E3
Gruzdžiai [LT] 234 E4
Grybów [PL] 64 B3
Grycksbo [S] 196 B3
Gryfice [PL] 34 E2
Gryfino [PL] 34 D3
Gryfów Śląski [PL] 46 D4
Grykë [AL] 160 A2
Gryllefjord [N] 224 C2
Grymyr [N] 194 B4
Gryneion [TR] 164 C4
Gryt [S] 190 C3
Gryt [S] 190 C4
Gryta [N] 202 E1
Grytgöl [S] 190 B3
Grythyttan [S] 188 E2
Grytsjö [S] 212 F3
Grytstorp [S] 190 B3
Gryzy [PL] 38 B1
Grzmiąca [PL] 36 A3
Grzybno [PL] 36 D3
Gschnitz [A] 118 C1
Gschöder [A] 74 B4
Gschwend [D] 58 C4
Gstaad [CH] 116 C2
Gstadt [D] 72 D3
Gsteig [CH] 116 B2
Guadahortuna [E] 106 A2
Guadajoz [E] 98 F4
Guadalajara [E] 92 F4
Guadalcanal [E] 98 F3
Guadalcázar [E] 104 D1
Guadalerzas [E] 100 E2
Guadalest [E] 106 F1
Guadalmez [E] 100 C3
Guadalmina [E] 104 C3
Guadalupe [E] 100 B2
Guadalupe, Monasterio de- [E] 100 B2
Guadalupe, Santuario de- [E] 106 A1
Guadamur [E] 100 D1
Guadarrama [E] 92 E3
Guadix [E] 106 A3
Guagno [F] 130 B3
Gualdo Cattáneo [I] 132 C2
Gualdo Tadino [I] 132 D2
Guarcino [I] 132 D4
Guarda [CH] 116 F1
Guarda [P] 84 C4
Guardamar del Segura [E] 106 F2
Guardavalle [I] 138 E3
Guardiagrele [I] 132 F3
Guardialfiera [I] 134 D2
Guardia Lombardi [I] 134 E3
Guardia Piemontese [I] 138 D1
Guardia Sanframondi [I] 134 D3
Guardias Viejas [E] 106 B4
Guardo [E] 86 B3
Guareña [E] 98 F2
Guarromán [E] 104 F1
Guasila [I] 142 B5
Guastalla [I] 128 B1
Guazzora [I] 126 C1
Gubanitsy [RUS] 200 E4
Gubbhägen [S] 212 F4
Gúbbio [I] 128 E4
Gubbmyran [S] 194 D2
Gubbträsk [S] 214 B2
Guben [D] 46 C3
Guber [BIH] 144 E4
Guberevac [SRB] 146 E3
Gubin [PL] 46 C3
Guča [SRB] 146 D4
Gudavac [BIH] 144 D2
Guddal [N] 192 B2
Guderup [DK] 178 C3

Gudhjem [DK] 180 E3
Gudow [D] 32 D3
Gudvangen [N] 192 C2
Guebwiller [F] 70 D2
Güéjar Sierra [E] 104 F3
Guémené–Penfao [F] 66 C1
Guémené–sur–Scorff [F] 52 C3
Guenange [F] 56 D3
Guer [F] 52 D4
Guérande [F] 66 B2
Guéret [F] 78 F2
Guérigny [F] 68 C3
Guethary [F] 88 A2
Gueugnon [F] 68 D4
Güglingen [D] 58 C4
Guglíonesi [I] 134 D2
Gugny [PL] 38 C3
Guía de Isora [E] 112 C3
Guichen [F] 52 E4
Guidonia [I] 132 D4
Guíglía [I] 128 C2
Guignes [F] 54 E4
Guijuelo [E] 92 C3
Guildford [GB] 28 C3
Guillaumes [F] 126 B2
Guillena [E] 98 E4
Guillestre [F] 126 B1
Guils [E] 96 C1
Guilvinec [F] 52 A4
Güímar [E] 112 D3
Guimarães [P] 84 B2
Guimerà [E] 96 C3
Guimiliau [F] 52 B3
Guincho [P] 90 A3
Guînes [F] 40 B3
Guingamp [F] 52 C3
Guipry [F] 66 C1
Guísamo [E] 82 C2
Guisborough [GB] 20 F4
Guise [F] 56 A2
Guissény [F] 52 B2
Gulssona [E] 96 C2
Guitalens [F] 88 F3
Guitíriz [E] 82 C2
Guîtres [F] 78 C3
Gujan–Mestras [F] 78 B3
Gükçeyazi [TR] 164 C2
Gulbene [LV] 236 D2
Guldborg [DK] 178 E3
Gülec [TR] 164 B1
Gulgofjorden [N] 228 E2
Gulla [N] 202 E2
Gullabo [S] 184 E4
Gullaskruv [S] 184 E3
Gullbrå [N] 192 C2
Gulleråsen [S] 194 F3
Gullfoss [IS] 218 B3
Gullhaug [N] 186 F2
Gullríngen [S] 184 E1
Gullsby [S] 188 D1
Gullspång [S] 188 E3
Gullstein [N] 202 E2
Güllü [TR] 170 E2
Güllüce [TR] 164 D2
Güllük [TR] 170 C4
Gülpınar [TR] 162 F3
Gulsele [S] 206 C1
Gulsrud [N] 186 F1
Gulsvik [N] 192 F3
Gülübíntsi [BG] 156 F1
Gülúbovo [BG] 156 E2
Gulyantsi [BG] 148 F3
Gumboda [S] 214 D3
Gumhöjden [S] 188 E1
Gumiel de Hizán [E] 92 F2
Gumlösa [S] 180 D3
Gummersbach [D] 42 D4
Gumpoldskirchen [A] 74 D3
Gumtow [D] 32 E4
Gümüldür [TR] 170 B2
Gümüşpınar [TR] 158 D3
Gümüşsu [TR] 170 F2

Gümüşsuyu [TR] 158 C3
Gümüşyeni [TR] 164 F2
Gümzovo [BG] 148 C2
Gundelfingen [D] 72 B2
Gundelsheim [D] 58 C4
Güneşli [TR] 164 E3
Güney [TR] 170 E2
Güney [TR] 170 F3
Güneyköy [TR] 164 E3
Güngör (Koutsovéntis) [CY]
  176 D3
Gunja [HR] 146 B2
Günlüce [TR] 164 F2
Gunnarn [S] 214 B2
Gunnarp [S] 184 B2
Gunnarsbyn [S] 220 F4
Gunnarskog [S] 188 D1
Gunnarskulla [FIN] 198 E3
Gunnarvattnet [S] 212 E4
Gunnebo [S] 184 E2
Gunnilbo [S] 190 B1
Gunten [CH] 116 C1
Güntersberge [D] 44 D3
Guntersblum [D] 58 B3
Guntersdorf [A] 74 C2
Guntertshausen [A] 72 E3
Guntín [E] 82 C3
Günzburg [D] 72 B2
Gunzenhausen [D] 58 E4
Gurahonţ [RO] 122 F2
Gura Motrului [RO] 148 D1
Gura Motrului, Mănăstirea–
  [RO] 148 D1
Gura Väii [RO] 148 C1
Gurçeşme [TR] 164 B1
Gurcz [PL] 36 D3
Güre [TR] 164 F4
Güre [TR] 170 F1
Güreci [TR] 164 B1
Gurgazu [F] 130 B4
Gurk [A] 120 A2
Gurkovo [BG] 150 B4
Gurlevo [RUS] 232 E1
Gürpinar [TR] 158 B3
Gurrea de Gállego [E] 94 E2
Gürsu [TR] 164 E1
Gurtnellen [CH] 116 D1
Gušče [HR] 120 D4
Gusev [RUS] 238 B3
Gusinje [MNE] 154 B2
Gusmar [AL] 160 B3
Güspini [I] 142 B4
Gusselby [S] 188 F2
Güssing [A] 120 C1
Gusswerk [A] 74 B3
Gustavfors [S] 194 E4
Gustavs / Kustavi [FIN] 198 B3
Gustavsberg [S] 190 E2
Gustavsberg [S] 214 C3
Gustavsfors [S] 188 C2
Güstrow [D] 32 E2
Gusum [S] 190 C4
Gusvattnet [S] 212 E3
Guta [BY] 242 D3
Gutcher [GB] 16 F3
Gutenstein [A] 74 C3
Gütersloh [D] 42 E2
Gutštejn [CZ] 60 C3
Guttannen [CH] 116 D1
Guttormsgard [S] 192 E3
Gützkow [D] 34 C2
Güvercinlik [TR] 170 C4
Güzelbahçe [TR] 170 A2
Güzelpinar [TR] 170 F2
Güzelyalı (Vavylás) [CY]
  176 D3
Güzelyurt (Mórfou) [CY]
  176 D3
Guzet–Neige [F] 88 E4
Gvardeiskoye [RUS] 36 F1
Gvardeysk [RUS] 36 F1
Gvarv [N] 186 E2

Gvozd [HR] 120 C4
Gvozd [MNE] 152 E2
Gwatt [CH] 116 C1
Gwda Wielka [PL] 36 A3
Gy [F] 70 B3
Gya [N] 186 B3
Gyarmat [H] 74 E4
Gyermely [H] 76 A4
Gyl [N] 202 E2
Gylien [S] 220 F3
Gylling [DK] 178 C1
Gýmeš [SK] 74 F2
Gymnó [GR] 168 B2
Gyomaendrőd [H] 122 D1
Gyömrő [H] 76 B4
Gyón [H] 74 E3
Gyöngyös [I I] 76 C1
Gyöngyöspata [H] 76 C3
Gyönk [H] 122 A2
Győr [H] 74 E4
Győrtelek [H] 76 F3
Gysinge [S] 196 C4
Gýtheio [GR] 172 D3
Gyttorp [S] 188 F2
Gyueshevo [BG] 154 E3
Gyula [H] 122 E2
Gyulaj [H] 122 A2
Gzy [PL] 38 A4

H

Häädemeeste [EST] 230 D3
Haag [A] 74 B3
Haag [D] 72 D2
Haag am Hausruck [A] 72 F3
Haaksbergen [NL] 30 D4
Haapajärvi [FIN] 216 B4
Haapajoki [FIN] 216 A3
Haapa–Kimola [FIN] 200 B2
Haapakylä [FIN] 208 F2
Haapala [FIN] 216 B1
Haapamäki [FIN] 208 E3
Haapamäki [FIN] 210 A1
Haapamäki [FIN] 210 C2
Haapamäki [FIN] 210 C1
Haapasalmi [FIN] 210 E3
Haapavesi [FIN] 216 B3
Haapsalu [EST] 230 C2
Haar [D] 72 C3
Haarajoki [FIN] 198 F3
Haarajoki [FIN] 210 B3
Haarala [FIN] 208 F2
Haaraoja [FIN] 216 B3
Haarby [DK] 178 C2
Haaren [D] 42 F3
Haarlem [NL] 30 B3
Haavisto [FIN] 208 E3
Habartice [CZ] 46 D4
Habas [F] 88 B2
Habay [B] 56 D2
Habernau [A] 72 F3
Hablingbo [S] 234 A3
Habo [S] 184 C1
Håbol [S] 188 C3
Habry [CZ] 60 F3
Håby [S] 188 C3
Hachdorf [D] 70 F2
Hachenburg [D] 42 D4
Hachmühlen [D] 44 B2
Hacıdanişment [TR] 158 A2
Hacısungur [TR] 158 B3
Hacıveliler [TR] 176 F1
Hackås [S] 204 E3
Häckeberga [S] 180 C2
Hacketstown [IRL] 10 F3
Hacksjö [S] 214 B3
Håcksvik [S] 184 B2
Hadamar [D] 58 B1
Hädanberg [S] 206 D2
Haddington [GB] 18 E4
Haderslev [DK] 178 B2

Haderup [DK] 182 C4
Hadiach [UA] 242 F3
Hadım [TR] 170 E2
Hadleigh [GB] 28 E2
Hadmersleben [D] 44 D2
Hadrian's Wall [GB] 20 D3
Hadsten [DK] 182 D4
Hadsund [DK] 182 D3
Hadzhidimitrovo [BG] 150 B3
Hadzhidimovo [BG] 156 C3
Hadžići [BIH] 146 B4
Hægeland [N] 186 C3
Hærland [N] 188 C2
Hafling / Avelengo [I] 118 B2
Hafsmo [N] 202 F2
Hałorsbyggel [S] 194 E1
Haga [N] 188 C1
Hagafoss [N] 192 D3
Hagby [S] 184 E4
Hagby [S] 190 D1
Hagebro [DK] 182 C3
Hagen [D] 32 A3
Hagen [D] 42 D3
Hagenberg [A] 74 B2
Hagenburg [D] 44 B1
Hagenow [D] 32 D3
Hageri [EST] 230 D2
Hagetmau [F] 88 C2
Hagfors [S] 188 E1
Häggås [S] 214 A3
Häggemåla [S] 184 E3
Häggenås [S] 204 F2
Häggsåsen [S] 204 E2
Häggsjöbränna [S] 204 D2
Häggsjömon [S] 214 B4
Häggsjövik [S] 204 E1
Haglebu [N] 192 E3
Hagondange [F] 56 D3
Hagudi [EST] 230 D2
Haguenau [F] 56 F4
Håhellarhytta [N] 186 C2
Hahn [D] 30 F2
Hahnbach [D] 58 F3
Hahöt [H] 120 C2
Haibach ob der Donau [A]
  72 F2
Haid [A] 74 A3
Haidmuhle [D] 72 F2
Haiger [D] 42 E4
Haigerloch [D] 70 F2
Häijää [FIN] 198 D1
Hailsham [GB] 28 D4
Hailuoto / Karlö [FIN] 216 A2
Haina [D] 42 F4
Hainburg [A] 74 D3
Hainfeld [A] 74 C3
Hainichen [D] 44 F4
Hainsbach [D] 72 D1
Haithabu [D] 32 B1
Hajdúböszörmény [H] 76 E3
Hajdúdorog [H] 76 E3
Hajdúhadház [H] 76 E3
Hajdúnánás [H] 76 E3
Hajdúsámson [H] 76 E3
Hajdúszoboszló [H] 76 E4
Hajdúszovát [H] 76 E4
Hajdúvíd [H] 76 E3
Hajerdin [BG] 148 E3
Hajnówka [PL] 38 D4
Hajós [H] 122 B2
Håkafot [S] 212 E3
Håkenby [N] 188 C2
Hakkas [S] 220 E2
Hakkenpää [FIN] 198 C3
Häkkilä [FIN] 208 F2
Hakkstabben [N] 228 B2
Hakokylä [FIN] 216 D2
Håksberg [S] 194 F4
Hakuni [FIN] 208 C3
Håkvika [N] 224 C4
Halaç [TR] 176 F1

Hålaforsen [S] 206 C2
Halámky [CZ] 74 B1
Hala Sultan Tekkesi [CY]
  176 E3
Halásztelek [H] 76 B4
Halberstadt [D] 44 D2
Hald [DK] 182 D3
Halden [N] 188 B2
Haldensee [A] 72 B3
Haldensleben [D] 44 D2
Halenkov [CZ] 62 D4
Halesworth [GB] 28 F2
Håle–Täng [S] 188 D4
Hälgö [S] 190 D3
Halhjem [N] 192 B3
Halíč [SK] 76 B2
Halich [UA] 244 D2
Halifax [GB] 24 C2
Halikarnassos [TR] 170 C4
Halikko [FIN] 198 D3
Halitpaşa [TR] 164 C4
Haljala [EST] 230 E1
Halk [DK] 178 C2
Halkivaha [FIN] 198 D2
Halkosaari [FIN] 208 C2
Hälla [S] 206 C1
Hallabro [S] 184 D4
Hallaçli [TR] 158 C3
Hallandsfossen [N] 186 C2
Hallapuro [FIN] 208 D1
Hallaryd [S] 184 C4
Hällbacken [S] 220 C3
Hällbo [S] 196 C2
Halle [B] 40 D3
Halle [D] 30 F4
Halle [D] 44 E3
Hälleberga [S] 184 E3
Hällefors [S] 188 E1
Hälleforsnäs [S] 190 C3
Hallein [A] 72 E3
Hallen [S] 204 E3
Hallenberg [D] 42 E3
Hallerud [S] 188 E3
Hälljsjö [S] 206 B3
Hällestad [S] 190 B3
Hällevadsholm [S] 188 C3
Hałtevik [N] 202 E1
Hälleviksstrand [S] 188 B4
Halli [FIN] 208 E4
Hallignicourt [F] 56 B4
Hallila [FIN] 200 B3
Hallingby [N] 192 F4
Hällingsåfallet [S] 212 E3
Hall in Tirol [A] 72 C4
Hålnäs [S] 196 D3
Hällnäs [S] 214 C3
Hällnäs [S] 220 C3
Hällristningar [S] 188 B3
Hallsberg [S] 188 F3
Hallshuk [S] 234 A2
Hällsjö [S] 206 C2
Hällsta [S] 190 C2
Hallstahammar [S] 190 C2
Hallstatt [A] 72 F4
Hallstavik [S] 190 E1
Halltorp [S] 184 E4
Halluin [F] 40 C3
Hälivik [S] 220 C4
Hallviken [S] 204 F1
Halmstad [S] 184 B3
Halna [S] 188 E3
Halne [N] 192 D3
Halne Fjellstue [N] 192 D3
Hals [DK] 182 D3
Hals [N] 202 E2
Halsa [N] 202 E2
Hal'shany [BY] 238 F4
Hålsjö [S] 196 C1
Halsskov [DK] 178 D2
Halstead [GB] 28 D2
Halsteren [NL] 40 E2
Halsua [FIN] 208 D1

Haltdalen [N] 204 B2
Haltern [D] 42 D2
Haltwhistle [GB] 20 E3
Haluna [FIN] 210 C1
Halvarsgårdarna [S] 196 B4
Halver [D] 42 D3
Ham [F] 54 F2
Hamallaj [AL] 154 A4
Hamamdere [TR] 164 E4
Hamamköy [TR] 170 C2
Hamar [N] 194 B3
Hambergen [D] 32 A3
Hamburg [D] 32 C3
Hamburgsund [S] 188 B3
Hambye, Abbaye de– [F] 52 F3
Hamdibey [TR] 164 C2
Hamdorf [D] 32 B1
Hämeenkyrö / Tavastkyro [FIN] 198 D1
Hämeenlinna / Tavastehus [FIN] 198 E2
Hämeler Wald [D] 44 C2
Hameln [D] 44 B2
Hämelschenburg [D] 44 B2
Hamersleben [D] 44 D2
Hamidiye [TR] 158 A3
Hamidiye [TR] 158 C2
Hamilton [GB] 18 C4
Hamina / Fredrikshamn [FIN] 200 C3
Hamingberg [N] 228 F2
Hamitli [TR] 158 A3
Hamlagrøosen [N] 192 B3
Hamm [D] 42 E2
Hammar [S] 188 F3
Hammarland [FIN] 196 F4
Hammarn [S] 188 E1
Hammarnäs [S] 204 E2
Hammarstrand [S] 206 B2
Hammarvika [N] 202 E1
Hammaslahti [FIN] 210 E2
Hammel [DK] 182 D4
Hammelburg [D] 58 D2
Hammer [N] 204 B1
Hammer [N] 212 C4
Hammer [N] 212 C4
Hammerbach [D] 58 C2
Hammerdal [S] 204 F2
Hammerfest [N] 228 B2
Hammerhøj [DK] 182 D3
Hammershus [DK] 180 E3
Hamminkeln [D] 42 C2
Hamna [N] 202 F1
Hamnbukt [N] 228 C3
Hamnes [N] 224 E2
Hamoir [B] 56 D1
Hampetorp [S] 190 B3
Hampovica [HR] 120 E3
Hamra [S] 194 F2
Hamrångefjärden [S] 196 C3
Hamre [N] 186 D4
Hamre [S] 196 C2
Hamremoen [N] 192 F4
Hams, Coves des– [E] 108 D3
Hamula [FIN] 210 B2
Hamula [FIN] 210 C2
Hamzabey [TR] 158 B2
Hamzali [MK] 154 F4
Hamzići [BIH] 152 C2
Han [MNE] 152 E3
Hän [S] 188 C2
Hän [S] 194 E4
Hanasand [N] 186 B2
Hanaskog [S] 180 D1
Hanau [D] 58 C2
Hançalar [TR] 170 E2
Hânceşti [MD] 244 F1
Hancevichy [BY] 242 B3
Handegg [CH] 116 D1
Handeland [N] 186 C2
Handen [S] 190 E3
Handlová [SK] 76 A2

Handöl [S] 204 D2
Handsjö [S] 204 F3
Hanerau–Hademarschen [D] 32 B2
Hanestad [N] 194 B1
Hanftal [A] 74 D2
Hangaskylä [FIN] 208 C3
Hangö / Hanko [FIN] 198 D4
Hangvar [S] 234 A2
Hanhimaa [FIN] 226 C4
Hanhisalo [FIN] 216 A4
Han i Hotit [AL] 152 F3
Hank [NL] 30 B4
Hankamäki [FIN] 210 C1
Hankasalmi [FIN] 210 B3
Hanken [S] 188 E4
Hankensbüttel [D] 32 C4
Hanko / Hangö [FIN] 198 D4
Hanna [PL] 50 D3
Hannivirta [FIN] 210 D3
Hann–Münden [D] 44 B3
Hannover [D] 44 B1
Hannuit (Hannut) [B] 40 E4
Hannusranta [FIN] 216 D3
Hannut (Hannuit) [B] 40 E4
Hanoğlu [TR] 170 E1
Hânova [RO] 148 C1
Han Pijesak [BIH] 146 C3
Hanskühnenburg [D] 44 C3
Hansnes [N] 224 D1
Hanstedt [D] 32 C3
Hanstholm [DK] 182 C2
Han-sur-Lesse [B] 56 C2
Han-sur-Nied [F] 56 D4
Hantháza [H] 122 C1
Hanušovce [SK] 76 E1
Hanušovice [CZ] 62 B3
Haparanda [S] 222 B4
Häppälä [FIN] 210 B3
Hapträsk [S] 220 E4
Hara [EST] 230 C2
Härad [S] 190 C2
Haradok [BY] 240 C4
Harads [S] 220 E4
Häradsbäck [S] 184 C4
Haraneset [N] 212 C3
Haras du Pin [F] 54 B3
Hårberg [N] 204 A1
Harbergsdalen [S] 212 E3
Harbo [S] 190 D1
Harboøre [DK] 182 B3
Harburg [D] 32 C3
Harburg [D] 72 B1
Hardbakke [N] 192 A2
Hardegg [A] 74 C2
Hardegsen [D] 44 B3
Hardelot–Plage [F] 40 A3
Hardemo [S] 188 F3
Hardenberg [NL] 30 D3
Harderwijk [NL] 30 C3
Hardeshøj [DK] 178 C3
Hardheim [D] 58 C3
Hardom [FIN] 200 B3
Hareid [N] 202 C3
Haren [D] 30 E3
Haren [NL] 30 D2
Harestua [N] 194 B4
Harfleur [F] 54 B2
Harg [S] 196 E4
Hargla [EST] 230 C4
Hargnies [F] 56 C2
Hargshamn [S] 196 E4
Harhala [FIN] 198 E1
Haría [E] 114 F2
Harivaara [FIN] 210 E1
Härjänvatsa [FIN] 198 E3
Härjåsjön [S] 194 F1
Harjavalta [FIN] 198 C1
Harju [S] 220 D3
Harjula [FIN] 216 B1
Harjunmaa [FIN] 210 C4
Harjunsalmi [FIN] 200 A1

Harkány [H] 122 A3
Härkeberga [S] 190 D2
Härkmeri [FIN] 208 B3
Härkmyran [S] 220 E3
Härlec [BG] 148 E3
Harlech [GB] 22 D3
Härlev [DK] 178 E2
Harlingen [NL] 30 C2
Harlösa [S] 180 C2
Harlow [GB] 28 D2
Harmancık [TR] 164 E2
Harmandallar [TR] 164 E4
Harmanec [SK] 76 B2
Harmanecká Jaskyňa [SK] 76 B2
Harmånger [S] 196 D1
Härmänkylä [FIN] 216 D2
Härmänmäki [FIN] 216 D2
Harmelen [NL] 30 B3
Harndrup [DK] 178 C2
Härnösand [S] 206 D3
Haro [E] 86 D4
Harodz'ki [BY] 238 F4
Haroldswick [GB] 16 F3
Háromfa [H] 120 E3
Haroué [F] 70 B1
Harpefoss [N] 192 F1
Harpenden [GB] 28 C2
Harplinge [S] 184 B3
Harpstedt [D] 30 F3
Harrå [S] 220 D2
Harrachov [CZ] 60 F1
Harran [N] 212 D3
Harre [DK] 182 C3
Harrogate [GB] 24 C2
Harrsjöhöiden [S] 212 F3
Harrsjön [S] 212 F3
Harrström [FIN] 208 B2
Harsa [S] 196 B2
Härsängen [S] 188 C3
Harsefeld [D] 32 B3
Harsewinkel [D] 30 F4
Hârşova [RO] 248 F3
Harsprånget [S] 220 D3
Harstad [N] 224 C3
Harste [D] 44 B3
Harsum [D] 44 C2
Harsvik [N] 212 B4
Harta [H] 122 B2
Hartberg [A] 74 C4
Hartha [D] 44 F4
Hartland [GB] 26 C2
Hartlepool [GB] 20 F4
Hartmannshain [D] 58 C2
Hartola [FIN] 200 B3
Hârve [S] 196 B1
Harwich [GB] 28 E2
Harzgerode [D] 44 D3
Hasanağa [TR] 164 E1
Hasanbey [TR] 164 C1
Hasanpaşa [TR] 164 F1
Haselund [D] 32 B1
Haselünne [D] 30 E3
Håsjö [S] 206 B3
Hasköy [TR] 158 A4
Hasköy [TR] 158 B2
Hasköy [TR] 164 F4
Haslach [A] 74 A2
Haslach [D] 70 E2
Hasle [DK] 180 D3
Haslemden [N] 194 C3
Haslemere [GB] 28 C3
Haslev [DK] 178 E2
Hasparren [F] 88 B2
Haspe [D] 42 D3
Hasseki [TR] 164 B4
Hassel [D] 32 B4
Hassela [S] 206 C4
Hasselfelde [D] 44 D3
Hasselfors [S] 188 F3
Hasselt [B] 40 F3
Hasselt [NL] 30 C3

Hassfurt [D] 58 E2
Hassi [FIN] 200 A1
Hasslach [D] 58 E2
Hassle [S] 188 E3
Hassleben [D] 34 C3
Hässleholm [S] 180 D1
Hästbo [S] 196 C4
Hästbo [S] 196 D3
Hastersboda [FIN] 198 B4
Hästholmen [S] 188 E4
Hastiere–Lavaux [B] 56 C1
Hastings [GB] 28 D4
Hästveda [S] 180 D1
Hasvik [N] 228 A2
Hat' [UA] 76 F2
Hatě [CZ] 74 C2
Hațeg [RO] 150 E1
Hatfield [GB] 28 C2
Hatfjelldal [N] 212 E2
Hatıplar [TR] 164 C4
Hatsola [FIN] 210 C4
Hattem [NL] 30 C3
Hattingen [D] 42 D3
Hattonchâtel [F] 56 D4
Hättorp [S] 188 E3
Hattstedt [D] 32 B1
Hattula [FIN] 198 E2
Hattuselkonen [FIN] 216 E4
Hattuvaara [FIN] 210 F1
Hattuvaara [FIN] 210 F1
Hatulanmäki [FIN] 216 C3
Hatvan [H] 76 B3
Hatvik [N] 192 B3
Haug [N] 192 D2
Haugan [N] 204 B1
Haugastøl [N] 192 D3
Haugbøen [N] 202 E3
Hauge [N] 186 B3
Hau'gesund [N] 186 A1
Hauggrend [N] 186 D2
Haughom [N] 186 B3
Haugsdorf [A] 74 C2
Haugsten [N] 192 E2
Hauho [FIN] 198 E2
Haukå [N] 192 B1
Haukedal [N] 192 C1
Haukeland [N] 192 B3
Haukeligrend [N] 186 D1
Haukeliseter [N] 186 D1
Haukilahti [FIN] 216 E2
Haukipudas [FIN] 216 B2
Haukivuori [FIN] 210 C3
Hauklappi [FIN] 200 D1
Haule [NL] 30 D2
Haunersdorf [D] 72 E2
Haunia [FIN] 198 C1
Haurida [S] 184 D1
Hausach [D] 70 E2
Hausen [D] 42 D4
Hausen [D] 58 D3
Hausen [D] 72 B3
Häusern [D] 70 E3
Husham [D] 72 C3
Hausjärvi [FIN] 198 F2
Häusling [A] 74 C2
Hausmannstatten [A] 120 C1
Hautajärvi [FIN] 222 E2
Haut-Asco [F] 130 B2
Haut-Barr, Château du– [F] 70 D1
Hautecombe, Abbaye de– [F] 80 E3
Hautefort, Château de– [F] 78 E3
Haute-Nendaz [CH] 116 B2
Hauterive, Abbaye de– [CH] 116 B1
Hauteville-Lompnes [F] 80 E2
Hauteville Plage [F] 52 E2
Haut Kœnigsbourg [F] 70 D2
Hautmont [F] 56 B1
Hauzenberg [D] 72 F2

Havaj [SK] 64 C4
Havant [GB] 28 B4
Håvberget [S] 194 F4
Havdhem [S] 234 A3
Håvedalen [S] 188 B3
Havelange [B] 56 C1
Havelberg [D] 32 E4
Haverdal [S] 184 B3
Haverfordwest [GB] 26 C1
Haverhill [GB] 28 D2
Häverö [S] 190 E1
Häverud [S] 188 C3
Havířov [CZ] 62 D3
Hävla [S] 190 B3
Havlíčkův Brod [CZ] 60 F3
Havnäs [S] 212 F4
Havnbjerg [DK] 178 C3
Havneby [DK] 178 A3
Havnebyen [DK] 178 E1
Havnsø [DK] 178 D2
Havøysund [N] 228 B1
Havran [CZ] 60 C2
Havran [TR] 164 B3
Havsa [TR] 158 B3
Havstensund [S] 188 B3
Hawick [GB] 20 D2
Hayange [F] 56 D3
Hayle [GB] 26 A3
Hay-on-Wye [GB] 26 E1
Hayrabolu [TR] 158 B3
Hayriye [TR] 158 E4
Hayriye [TR] 170 F3
Haywards Heath [GB] 28 C4
Hazebrouck [F] 40 B3
Hazlov [CZ] 60 B2
Hazmburk [CZ] 60 D2
Hcıkasım [TR] 164 B2
Headford [IRL] 10 C1
Heathfield [GB] 28 D4
Hebnes [N] 186 B3
Heby [S] 190 C2
Hechingen [D] 70 F2
Hecho [E] 88 B3
Hechtel [B] 40 F3
Hechthausen [D] 32 B2
Hed [S] 190 B2
Hedal [N] 192 F3
Hedared [S] 184 B1
Hedås [S] 188 E2
Hédauville [F] 54 E1
Hedburg [D] 58 E2
Hedby [S] 194 F3
Hedbyn [S] 188 E1
Heddal [N] 186 E1
Hedderen [N] 186 C3
Hédé [F] 52 E4
Hede [S] 190 C1
Hedehusene [DK] 178 E2
Hedekas [S] 188 C3
Hedemora [S] 196 B4
Heden [S] 194 D1
Heden [S] 194 E2
Hedenäset [S] 222 B3
Hedensted [DK] 178 C2
Hedesunda [S] 196 C4
Hedeviken [S] 204 E4
Hee [DK] 182 B4
Heek [D] 30 D4
Heemstede [NL] 30 B3
Heerde [NL] 30 C3
Heerenveen [NL] 30 C2
Heerlen [NL] 42 B4
Heeze [NL] 40 F3
Hegerum [S] 184 F2
Heggenes [N] 192 E2
Heglibister [GB] 16 E3
Hegra [N] 204 B2
Hegyeshalom [H] 74 E3
Hegyhátsál [H] 120 D1
Hegykő [H] 74 D4
Heia [N] 212 D3

Heia [N] 224 D3
Heidal [N] 192 F1
Heide [D] 32 B2
Heideck [D] 58 E4
Heidelberg [D] 58 B3
Heiden [D] 42 D2
Heidenau [D] 46 B4
Heidenheim [D] 72 B1
Heidenreichstein [A] 74 B1
Heigrestad [N] 186 B3
Heikendorf [D] 32 C1
Heikkurila [FIN] 210 D4
Heiland [N] 186 E3
Heilbad Heiligenstadt [D] 44 C3
Heilbronn [D] 58 C4
Heilevong [N] 192 B1
Heiligenberg [D] 70 F3
Heiligenblut [A] 118 E1
Heiligenbösch-Kirche [D] 56 E3
Heiligenhafen [D] 32 D1
Heiligenkreuz [A] 74 C3
Heiligenkreuz [A] 74 C2
Heiligenkreuz [A] 120 D1
Heiligenroth [D] 58 B1
Heiligkreuztal [D] 70 F2
Heilsbronn [D] 58 E4
Heimaey [IS] 218 B3
Heimdal [N] 204 B2
Heimertingen [D] 72 A3
Heinääho [FIN] 210 C1
Heinämaa [FIN] 200 B3
Heinämäki [FIN] 210 B1
Heinävaara [FIN] 210 E2
Heinävesi [FIN] 210 D3
Heinersdorf [D] 46 C2
Heino [NL] 30 C3
Heinola [FIN] 200 B2
Heinoniemi [FIN] 210 E3
Heinrichsruh [D] 34 D3
Hoinsberg [D] 42 D3
Heippes [F] 56 C3
Heiterwang [A] 72 B2
Heituinlahti [FIN] 200 C2
Hejde [S] 234 A2
Hejlsminde [DK] 178 C2
Hejnice [CZ] 60 E1
Hejnsvig [DK] 178 B2
Hekal [AL] 160 B2
Hel [PL] 36 D1
Heldenberg [A] 74 C2
Heldrungen [D] 44 D3
Helechal [E] 100 B3
Helensburgh [GB] 18 C3
Helfenburk [CZ] 60 D4
Helfštýn [CZ] 62 C4
Helgen [N] 186 E2
Helgum [S] 206 C2
Hell [N] 204 B2
Hella [N] 192 C2
Helland [N] 202 F2
Helle [N] 186 C3
Helle [N] 186 E3
Helleland [N] 186 B3
Hellendoorn [NL] 30 D3
Helleristninger [N] 202 B4
Helleristninger [N] 228 B3
Hellesøy [N] 192 A2
Hellesylt [N] 202 C4
Hellevad [DK] 178 B3
Hellevik [N] 192 B1
Hellevoetsluis [NL] 30 A4
Helligskogen [N] 224 E3
Hellín [E] 106 D1
Hellinge [DK] 178 D3
Hellsö [FIN] 198 B4
Helmond [NL] 40 F2
Helmsdale [GB] 14 E2
Helmsley [GB] 24 D1
Helmstedt [D] 44 D2
Helnessund [N] 220 A1

Helsa [D] 44 B3
Helsingborg [S] 178 F1
Helsinge [DK] 178 E1
Helsingfors / Helsinki [FIN] 198 F3
Helsingør [DK] 178 F1
Helsinki / Helsingfors [FIN] 198 F3
Helstad [N] 212 D2
Helston [GB] 26 A4
Heltermaa [EST] 230 B2
Helvia Recina [I] 132 E1
Hemau [D] 58 F4
Hemel Hempstead [GB] 28 C2
Hemer [D] 42 D3
Hëming [F] 70 C1
Hemling [S] 206 D1
Hemmet [DK] 178 A1
Hemmingen [S] 214 C2
Hemmingsmark [S] 214 D2
Hemmoor [D] 32 B2
Hemnes [N] 188 C1
Hemnesberget [N] 218 E4
Hemse [S] 234 A3
Hemsedal [N] 192 E3
Hemslingen [D] 32 B3
Hen [N] 192 F4
Henån [S] 188 C4
Hencida [H] 76 E4
Hendaye [F] 86 F3
Hendrik Ido Ambacht [NL] 30 B4
Hengelo [NL] 30 D3
Hengersberg [D] 72 E2
Heniches'k [UA] 246 F3
Hénin Beaumont [F] 40 C4
Henley-on-Thames [GB] 28 C3
Hennan [S] 196 B1
Hennebjerg [D] 58 D2
Hennebont [F] 52 C4
Hennef [D] 42 D4
Hennerhöle [A] 72 E3
Henne Strand [DK] 178 A1
Hennezel [F] 70 B2
Henningsvær [N] 218 F1
Hénoville [F] 40 B3
Henrichemont [F] 68 C2
Henriksfjäll [S] 212 F2
Henryków [PL] 62 B2
Henstedt-Ulzburg [D] 32 C2
Hepoköngäs [FIN] 216 D2
Hepola [FIN] 216 A1
Heppenheim [D] 58 B3
Heraclea [MK] 160 D2
Herad [N] 186 B4
Herad [N] 192 E3
Heradsbygd [N] 194 C3
Herajoki [FIN] 210 E1
Herakleia [TR] 170 C3
Hera Lacinia, Tempio di- [I] 138 F2
Herăşti [RO] 150 C1
Hérault, Gorges de l'- [F] 124 C2
Herbault [F] 68 A2
Herberstein [A] 120 C1
Herbertingen [D] 70 F2
Herbertstown [IRL] 10 C3
Herbesthal [B] 42 B4
Herbeumont [B] 56 C2
Herbignac [F] 66 B2
Herbolzheim [D] 70 D2
Herborn [D] 42 E4
Herbrechtingen [D] 72 B2
Herby [PL] 62 E1
Herceg Novi [MNE] 152 E3
Hercegovac [HR] 120 E4
Hercegovska Goleša [SRB] 146 C4
Hercegszántó [H] 122 B3
Herdal [N] 202 C3

Herdberg [D] 42 E3
Herdla [N] 192 A3
Herdoniae [I] 134 E3
Hereford [GB] 26 E1
Herefoss [N] 186 D3
Héreg [H] 76 A4
Hereke [TR] 158 F3
Herencia [E] 100 E2
Herend [H] 120 F1
Herentals [B] 40 E3
Herfølge [DK] 178 E2
Herford [D] 30 F4
Hergiswil [CH] 70 E4
Héricourt [F] 70 C3
Heringsdorf [D] 34 D2
Ilerisau [CH] 70 F4
Hérisson [F] 68 C4
Herl'any [SK] 76 E1
Herleshausen [D] 44 C4
Herlufsholm [DK] 178 E3
Hermagor [A] 118 E2
Hermannsburg [D] 32 C4
Hermanns-Denkmal [D] 42 F2
Heřmanovice [CZ] 62 C2
Hermansverk [N] 192 C2
Herment [F] 80 A2
Hermeskeil [D] 56 E3
Hermo [E] 82 E3
Hermsdorf [D] 44 E4
Hernani [E] 86 F3
Herne [D] 42 D3
Herne Bay [GB] 28 E3
Herning [DK] 178 B1
Hernstein [A] 74 C3
Heroldsberg [D] 58 E3
Herøya [N] 186 E2
Herøysund [N] 192 B4
Herråkra [S] 184 D3
Herräng [S] 190 E1
Herraskylä [FIN] 208 D3
Herre [N] 186 E2
Herrenberg [D] 70 F1
Herrenchiemsee [D] 72 D3
Herrera [E] 100 D3
Herrera [E] 104 D2
Herrera del Duque [E] 100 C2
Herrera de los Navarros [E] 94 D3
Herrera de Pisuerga [E] 86 B3
Herrería [E] 94 C4
Herreruela [E] 90 E3
Herrestad [S] 188 C4
Herrgotts Kirche [D] 58 D3
Herrljunga [S] 184 B1
Herrnburg [D] 32 D2
Herrnhut [D] 46 C4
Herröskkatan [FIN] 198 A4
Herrsching [D] 72 C3
Herrskog [S] 206 D3
Herrvik [S] 234 B2
Hersbruck [D] 58 F3
Herselt [B] 40 E3
Hertford [GB] 28 D2
Hertnik [SK] 64 C4
Hervás [E] 92 B3
Hervik [N] 186 B2
Herzberg [D] 32 E3
Herzberg [D] 32 F4
Herzberg [D] 44 B4
Herzberg [D] 44 C3
Herzberg [D] 46 B3
Herzfeld [D] 42 E3
Herzfelde [D] 46 B2
Herzlake [D] 30 E3
Herzogenaurach [D] 58 E3
Herzogenburg [A] 74 C2
Herzsprung [D] 32 E4
Hesdin [F] 40 B4
Hesel [D] 30 E2
Heskestad [N] 186 B3
Heskestad [N] 186 B4

Hesnæs [DK] 178 E3
Hessel [DK] 182 C3
Hesselagergård [DK] 178 D3
Hessich-Lichtenau [D] 44 B3
Hess Oldendorf [D] 44 B2
Hessvik [N] 192 B4
Hestad [N] 192 B3
Hestenesøyri [N] 202 C4
Hestra [S] 184 C2
Hestra [S] 184 D1
Hetin [SRB] 122 D4
Het Loo [NL] 30 C3
Hettange-Grande [F] 56 D3
Hettstedt [D] 44 D3
Hetvehely [H] 120 F3
Heustreu [D] 58 D2
Heverlee [B] 40 E3
Heves [H] 76 E3
Hévíz [H] 120 E2
Hevlin [CZ] 74 D2
Hexentanzplatz [D] 44 D3
Hexham [GB] 20 E3
Heyrieux [F] 80 D3
Heysham [GB] 20 D4
Hidas [H] 122 A3
Hidasnémeti [H] 76 D2
Hieflau [A] 74 B4
Hiendelaencina [E] 94 A3
Hierapolis [TR] 170 C2
Hiersac [F] 78 C2
Hietakylä [FIN] 210 C3
Hietanen [FIN] 200 C1
Hietaniemi [FIN] 222 E1
Hietaperä [FIN] 216 E3
High Cross [IRL] 10 E2
High Wycombe [GB] 28 C2
Higuera, Torre de la- [E] 104 A2
Higuera de la Serena [E] 100 A3
Higuera de Vargas [E] 98 E2
Higuera la Real [E] 98 E3
Higueruela [E] 102 B4
Hihnavaara [FIN] 222 D1
Hiirola [FIN] 210 C4
Hiitinen / Hitis [FIN] 198 D4
Hijar [E] 94 E4
Hilchenbach [D] 42 E4
Hildal [N] 192 C4
Hildburghausen [D] 58 E2
Hilden [D] 42 C3
Hilders [D] 58 D1
Hildesheim [D] 44 C2
Hildre [N] 202 C3
Hilertshausen [D] 72 C2
Hilkerode [D] 44 C3
Hilla [FIN] 198 E4
Hille [S] 196 D3
Hillegom [NL] 30 B3
Hillerød [DK] 178 E1
Hillerstorp [S] 184 C2
Hillesøy [N] 224 D2
Hililä [FIN] 216 A3
Hillion [F] 52 D3
Hillsand [S] 212 F4
Hillsborough [NIR] 12 F3
Hillswick [GB] 16 E3
Hilltown [NIR] 12 E3
Hilmo [N] 204 C2
Hilpoltstein [D] 58 E4
Hilterfingen [CH] 116 C1
Hiltulanlahti [FIN] 210 C2
Hilvarenbeek [NL] 40 E2
Hilversum [NL] 30 B3
Himanka [FIN] 216 A3
Himankakylä [FIN] 216 A3
Himarë [AL] 160 B3
Himlštejn [CZ] 60 C2
Himmelkoron [D] 58 F2
Himmelpforten [D] 32 B3
Hinckley [GB] 24 C4
Hindås [S] 184 A2

Hindelang [D] 72 B3
Hinderburg [D] 32 E4
Hindsig [DK] 178 A1
Hinnerjoki [FIN] 198 C2
Hinnerup [DK] 182 D4
Hinneryd [S] 184 B3
Hinojal [E] 90 F3
Hinojos [E] 104 B1
Hinojosa del Duque [E] 100 B3
Hinojosa del Valle [E] 98 F2
Hinterbichl [A] 118 D1
Hinterrhein [CH] 116 E2
Hintersee [D] 34 D3
Hinterstoder [A] 74 A3
Hinterthal [A] 72 E4
Hintertux [A] 118 C1
Hinterweidenthal [D] 56 F3
Hinterzarten [D] 70 E3
Hío [E] 82 A3
Hırkalı [TR] 164 E3
Hirnsdorf [A] 120 C1
Hirnyk [UA] 64 F2
Hirrlingen [D] 70 F2
Hirschaid [D] 58 E3
Hirschau [D] 58 F3
Hirschberg [D] 58 F2
Hirschegg [A] 72 A4
Hirschhorn [D] 58 C3
Hirsch-Stein [D] 60 B2
Hîrseşti [RO] 148 F1
Hirsilä [FIN] 208 E4
Hirsingue [F] 70 D3
Hirson [F] 56 B2
Hîrşova [RO] 248 F3
Hirtshals [DK] 182 D2
Hirvassalmi [FIN] 226 D3
Hirvasvaara [FIN] 222 D2
Hirvensalmi [FIN] 200 B1
Hirvihaara [FIN] 198 F3
Hirvijärvi [S] 222 A3
Hirvijoki [FIN] 208 D2
Hirvisalo [FIN] 200 B2
Hisarcık [TR] 164 F3
Hisardžik [SRB] 152 F1
Hisartepe Dascylium [TR] 164 D1
Hissjön [S] 206 E1
Histria [RO] 250 C3
Hita [E] 94 A3
Hitchin [GB] 28 C2
Hitiaş [RO] 122 E3
Hitis / Hiitinen [FIN] 198 D4
Hitovo [BG] 150 E2
Hitra [N] 202 E2
Hittarp [S] 178 F1
Hitterdal [N] 204 C3
Hitzacker [D] 32 D3
Hiukkajoki [FIN] 210 E4
Hjallerup [DK] 182 D2
Hjällstad [S] 194 D3
Hjälmseryd [S] 184 C2
Hjältanstorp [S] 206 B4
Hjärnarp [DK] 178 F1
Hjartåsen [N] 220 A3
Hjärtum [S] 188 C4
Hjelle [N] 202 C4
Hjelle [N] 202 D4
Hjellestad [N] 192 A3
Hjelmeland [N] 186 B2
Hjelset [N] 202 D2
Hjerkinn [N] 202 F4
Hjerpsted [DK] 178 B3
Hjerting [DK] 178 A2
Hjo [S] 188 E4
Hjøllund [DK] 178 B1
Hjørring [DK] 182 D2
Hjorte [DK] 178 C2
Hjorted [S] 184 E2
Hjorteset [N] 192 B1
Hjortkvarn [S] 190 B3
Hjortsberga [S] 180 E1
Hjortsberga [S] 184 C3

Hjulsbro [S] 190 B4
Hjulsjø [S] 188 F1
Hlinsko [CZ] 60 F3
Hlobyne [UA] 246 E1
Hlohovec [SK] 74 E2
Hluboká nad Vltavou [CZ] 74 A1
Hlučín [CZ] 62 D3
Hluk [CZ] 74 E1
Hlukhiv [UA] 242 E3
Hlusk [BY] 242 C2
Hlybokaya [BY] 242 B1
Hlyniany [UA] 64 E3
Hniezdne [SK] 64 B4
Hnilec [SK] 76 C1
Hnúšťa [SK] 76 C2
Hobermayer–Hofen [A] 120 C1
Hobol [H] 120 F3
Hobro [DK] 182 D3
Hocalar [TR] 170 F1
Hoče [SLO] 120 C2
Hoces del Cabriel [E] 102 C3
Hoces del Duratón [E] 92 E2
Hoces del Riaza [E] 92 F2
Höchberg [D] 58 D3
Hochburg [A] 72 E3
Hochburg [D] 70 D2
Hochdonn [D] 32 B2
Hochdorf [CH] 70 E4
Höchenschwand [D] 70 E3
Hochfelden [F] 70 D1
Hochosterwitz [A] 120 A2
Hochspeyer [D] 58 A3
Höchst [D] 58 C3
Höchstadt [D] 58 E3
Höchstädt [D] 72 B2
Hochstatten [D] 58 A3
Höckendorf [D] 46 B4
Hockenheim [D] 58 B3
Hoczew [PL] 64 D4
Hodal [N] 204 B4
Hodalen [N] 204 B3
Hodejov [SK] 76 C2
Hodenhagen [D] 32 B4
Hodkovice nad Mohelkou [CZ] 60 E2
Hódmezővásárhely [H] 122 D2
Hodal [N] 204 C4
Hodonín [CZ] 74 E2
Hodoš [SLO] 120 D2
Hodošan [HR] 120 D2
Hoedekenskerke [NL] 40 D2
Hoei (Huy) [B] 40 E4
Hoek van Holland [NL] 30 A4
Hoenzethen [D] 32 D4
Hof [D] 60 A2
Hof [D] 70 F1
Hofgeismar [D] 44 B3
Hofheim [D] 58 E2
Hofles [N] 212 C3
Höfn [IS] 218 C3
Hofors [S] 194 D3
Hofstad [N] 212 B4
Höganäs [S] 178 F1
Hogdal [S] 188 B3
Höge [S] 204 E2
Högerud [S] 188 D2
Högfors [S] 188 F1
Högfors / Karkkila [FIN] 198 F3
Höghult [S] 184 E1
Högklint [S] 234 A2
Höglunda [S] 206 B2
Högnabba [FIN] 208 D1
Högsäter [S] 188 C3
Högsby [S] 184 E3
Høgset [N] 202 D2
Högsjö [S] 206 D3
Høgstadgård [N] 224 D3
Hogstorp [S] 188 C4
Høgvålen [S] 204 D4
Hőgyész [H] 122 A2

Hohenau [A] 74 D2
Hohenbachschlucht [A] 72 B4
Hohenberg [A] 74 C3
Hohenbrunn [D] 72 C3
Hohenburg [D] 58 F4
Hoheneck [D] 58 D3
Hohenfels [D] 58 A3
Hohenhewen [D] 70 E3
Höhenkirchen [D] 72 C3
Hohenlimburg [D] 42 D3
Hohenlinden [D] 72 D2
Hohenlockstedt [D] 32 B2
Hohenpeissenberg [D] 72 B3
Hohenschwangau [D] 72 B3
Hohenstein [D] 58 B2
Hohensyburg [D] 42 D3
Hohentauern [A] 74 A4
Hohentwiel [D] 70 E3
Hohen Wehrda [D] 44 B4
Hohenwerfen [A] 72 E4
Hohenwestedt [D] 32 B2
Hohenzollern [D] 70 F2
Hohne [D] 44 C1
Hohneck [F] 70 C2
Hohrodberg [F] 70 D2
Hohwacht [D] 32 D1
Hoikhankylä [FIN] 210 B3
Hoilola [FIN] 210 F2
Hoisko [FIN] 208 D2
Højby [DK] 178 E1
Højer [DK] 178 B3
Højerup [DK] 178 F3
Højslev Stby [DK] 182 C3
Hojsova Straž [CZ] 60 C4
Hok [S] 184 C2
Hökåsen [S] 190 C2
Hökhuvud [S] 196 E4
Hokka [FIN] 210 B4
Hokksund [N] 186 F1
Hökön [S] 184 C4
Hoks Herrgård [S] 184 C2
Hokusukoski [FIN] 208 E3
Hol [N] 192 D3
Hol [S] 184 B1
Holand [N] 212 E3
Hola Prystan' [UA] 246 E3
Holašovice [CZ] 74 A1
Holbæk [DK] 178 E2
Holbeach [GB] 24 D4
Holbøl [DK] 178 B3
Holckenhavn [DK] 178 D2
Holdorf [D] 30 F3
Hole [S] 188 D1
Holeby [DK] 32 D1
Holedeč [CZ] 60 C2
Holešov [CZ] 62 C4
Holíč [SK] 74 E2
Holice [CZ] 60 F3
Hölick [S] 196 D1
Holiseva [FIN] 208 E3
Holja [FIN] 198 E1
Höljes [S] 194 D3
Hollabrunn [A] 74 C2
Hollád [H] 120 C2
Høllen [N] 186 C4
Hollenbach [D] 72 C2
Hollenegg [A] 120 B2
Hollenstedt [D] 32 B3
Hollerath [D] 56 E1
Hollestein [A] 74 B3
Hollfeld [D] 58 E3
Hollingsholm [N] 202 D2
Hollola [FIN] 198 F2
Hollolan [FIN] 198 F2
Hollum [NL] 30 C1
Höllviken [S] 178 F2
Holm [DK] 178 C3
Holm [FIN] 214 F4
Holm [N] 188 B2
Holm [N] 212 D2
Holm [S] 206 C3
Hólmavík [IS] 218 B2

Holmec [SLO] 120 B2
Holmedal [S] 188 C2
Holmegil [N] 188 C2
Holmestrand [N] 186 F2
Holmfirth [GB] 24 C2
Holmfors [S] 214 B2
Holmfors [S] 214 D2
Holmön [S] 206 F1
Holmsjö [S] 184 D4
Holmsjö [S] 204 F3
Holmsjö [S] 206 C1
Holmsund [S] 206 F1
Holmsveden [S] 196 C2
Holmträsk [S] 206 C1
Holmudden [S] 234 B2
Holm–Zhirkovskij [RUS] 240 D3
Holoby [UA] 50 F3
Holod [RO] 122 F2
Holovanivs'k [UA] 246 C2
Holovne [UA] 50 D3
Holøydal [N] 204 C4
Holsætra [N] 192 F2
Holsbybrunn [S] 184 D2
Holsen [N] 192 C1
Holsljunge [S] 184 B2
Holstebro [DK] 182 C4
Holsted [DK] 178 B2
Holsworthy [GB] 26 C3
Holt [GB] 24 E4
Holt [N] 186 D3
Holt [N] 224 D3
Holten [NL] 30 D3
Holtet [N] 188 C3
Holtet [N] 194 C3
Holtsås [N] 186 E2
Holtsee [D] 32 C1
Holtslåtten [N] 194 C3
Holwerd [NL] 30 C2
Holycross [IRL] 10 D3
Holyhead [GB] 22 D2
Holywell [GB] 22 E2
Holywood [NIR] 12 F2
Holzdorf [D] 44 F3
Holzgau [A] 72 B4
Holzkirchen [D] 72 C3
Holzleitensattel [A] 72 B4
Holzminden [D] 44 B2
Holzschlag [D] 70 E3
Homberg [D] 42 F4
Homberg [D] 44 B4
Homborsund [N] 186 D4
Hombukt [N] 224 F1
Homburg [D] 56 F3
Hommelstø [N] 212 D2
Hommelvik [N] 204 B2
Hommersåk [N] 186 B2
Homokszentgyörgy [H] 120 E3
Homps [F] 124 B3
Homyel' [BY] 242 D2
Honaz [TR] 170 E3
Hondarribia / Fuenterrabía [E] 86 F3
Hönebach [D] 44 B4
Hønefoss [N] 192 F4
Honfleur [F] 54 B2
Høng [DK] 178 D2
Honiton [GB] 26 D3
Honkajoki [FIN] 208 C4
Honkakoski [FIN] 208 C4
Honkola [FIN] 208 F2
Hønning [DK] 178 B2
Honningsvåg [N] 202 B3
Honningsvåg [N] 228 C1
Honrubia [E] 102 B2
Honrubia de la Cuesta [E] 92 F2
Hontalbilla [E] 92 E2
Hontoria de la Cantera [E] 86 C4
Hontoria del Pinar [E] 94 A2
Hoofddorp [NL] 30 B3

Hoogerheide [NL] 40 E2
Hoogeveen [NL] 30 D3
Hoogezand [NL] 30 D2
Hoogkarspel [NL] 30 B3
Hoogstraten [B] 40 E2
Hooksiel [D] 30 F1
Höör [S] 180 C1
Hoorn [NL] 30 B3
Hopen [N] 202 E1
Hopfgarten [A] 72 D4
Hoplandsjøen [N] 192 A2
Hopovo, Manastir– [SRB] 146 D1
Hopperstad Stavkirke [N] 192 C2
Hopseidet [N] 228 D1
Hopsten [D] 30 E3
Hoptrup [DK] 178 B2
Hora–Sv–Šebestiána [CZ] 60 C2
Horažďovice [CZ] 60 C4
Horb [D] 70 E2
Horbelev [DK] 178 E3
Hörby [S] 180 C2
Horcajo de los Montes [E] 100 C2
Horcajo de Santiago [E] 100 F2
Horche [E] 92 F4
Horda [S] 184 C3
Hörda [S] 184 C3
Hordain [F] 40 C4
Hordalia [N] 186 C1
Horgen [CH] 70 E4
Horgevik [N] 186 D2
Horgoš [SRB] 122 C3
Horia [RO] 122 E3
Horia [RO] 150 C1
Hořice [CZ] 60 F2
Horitschon [A] 74 D4
Hörja [S] 180 C1
Horjul [SLO] 120 A3
Hörken [S] 188 F1
Horki [BY] 242 D1
Hormogos [E] 92 D4
Horn [A] 74 C2
Horn [D] 42 E3
Horn [D] 70 F3
Horn [N] 194 B3
Horn [N] 212 D2
Horn [S] 184 E1
Hornachos [E] 98 F2
Hornachuelos [E] 100 B4
Horna Štubňa [SK] 76 A2
Hornbæk [DK] 178 F1
Hornberg [D] 58 C3
Hornberg [D] 70 E2
Hornburg [D] 44 C2
Horncastle [GB] 24 D3
Horndal [S] 196 C4
Hörne [D] 32 B2
Horne [DK] 178 C3
Horneburg [D] 32 B3
Hörnefors [S] 206 E1
Hornesund [N] 186 C3
Horní Benešov [CZ] 62 C3
Horní Cerekev [CZ] 60 E4
Horní Lideč [CZ] 62 D3
Horní Loděnice [CZ] 62 C3
Hornindal [N] 202 C4
Hørning [DK] 178 C1
Horní Planá [CZ] 74 A2
Horní Vltavice [CZ] 72 F1
Hornnes [N] 186 C3
Hornos [E] 106 B1
Hornos de Peal [E] 106 B2
Hornoy [F] 54 D1
Hornsea [GB] 24 D2
Hörnsjö [S] 206 E1
Hornslet [DK] 182 D4
Hörnum [D] 178 A3

Hornum [DK] 182 D3
Horný Tisovník [SK] 76 B2
Horodenka [UA] 244 D2
Horodło [PL] 50 E4
Horodnytsia [UA] 242 C4
Horodok [UA] 64 E3
Horodyshche [UA] 246 D1
Horokhiv [UA] 244 C1
Horonkylä [FIN] 208 B3
Hořovice [CZ] 60 D3
Horred [S] 184 A2
Hörröd [S] 180 D2
Horrskog [S] 196 C4
Horsens [DK] 178 C1
Horsham [GB] 28 C3
Hørsholm [DK] 178 F2
Horslunde [DK] 178 D3
Horsmanaho [FIN] 210 D2
Horšovský Týn [CZ] 60 C3
Horst [B] 40 E3
Horst [D] 32 C3
Horst [NL] 42 C3
Hörstel [D] 30 E4
Horstmar [D] 30 E4
Horsunlu [TR] 170 D2
Hort [H] 76 C3
Horta [P] 110 A3
Horten [N] 186 F2
Hortezuela [E] 94 B3
Hortigüela [E] 94 A1
Hortobágy [H] 76 D4
Hőrup [D] 178 B3
Hørve [DK] 178 E2
Horven [N] 212 C3
Horw [CH] 70 E4
Hosby [DK] 178 C2
Hoscheid [L] 56 D2
Hosenfeld [D] 58 C1
Hoset [N] 220 A2
Hoshtevë Vithkuq [AL] 160 B3
Hosjö [S] 196 B3
Hoslemo [N] 186 C2
Hospental [CH] 116 D1
Hospice de France [F] 88 D4
Hospital [IRL] 10 C3
Hospital de Órbigo [E] 82 E4
Hossa [FIN] 216 E1
Hossegor [F] 88 B2
Hössjö [S] 206 E1
Hössjön [S] 206 B1
Hosszúpályi [H] 76 E4
Hosszú–Pereszteg [H] 120 E1
Hostalric [E] 96 E3
Hoštejn [CZ] 62 B3
Hostens [F] 78 B4
Hostěřadice [CZ] 74 D1
Hostianské Nemce [SK] 76 B2
Hostinné [CZ] 60 F2
Hostomice [CZ] 60 D3
Hoston [N] 202 F2
Hostouň [CZ] 60 B3
Hostovice [SK] 64 D4
Hostýn [CZ] 62 C4
Hotagen [S] 204 F1
Hotarele [RO] 150 C2
Hoting [S] 214 A3
Hotton [B] 56 D1
Hötzelsdorf [A] 74 C2
Hou [DK] 182 E3
Houdain [F] 40 B4
Houdan [F] 54 D3
Houdelaincourt [F] 70 B1
Houeillès [F] 88 D1
Houffalize [B] 56 D2
Houlbjerg [DK] 182 D4
Houlgate [F] 54 B2
Hourtin [F] 78 B3
Hourtin–Plage [F] 78 B2
Houthalen [B] 40 F3
Houtsala [FIN] 198 C3
Houtskär / Houtskari [FIN] 198 C3

Houtskari / Houtskär [FIN] 198 C3
Hov [DK] 178 C1
Hov [N] 194 B3
Hov [S] 188 F4
Hova [S] 188 E3
Hovborg [DK] 178 B2
Hovda [N] 192 E3
Hovdala [S] 180 D1
Hovden [N] 186 C1
Hovden [N] 224 B3
Høve [DK] 178 E2
Hove [DK] 182 B3
Hove [N] 192 B1
Hövelhof [D] 42 F2
Hoven [DK] 178 B1
Hoverberg [S] 204 E3
Hovet [N] 192 D3
Hovi [FIN] 210 C2
Hovin [N] 186 E1
Hovin [N] 204 B2
Hovinsholm [N] 194 B3
Hovland [N] 186 B3
Hovland [N] 192 C3
Hovmantorp [S] 184 D3
Hovsta [S] 188 F2
Howard, Castle– [IRL] 10 F3
Howth [IRL] 22 B1
Höxter [D] 44 B2
Hoya [D] 32 B4
Hoya–Gonzalo [E] 102 B4
Høyanger [N] 192 B3
Høydalen [N] 186 E2
Høydalsmo [N] 186 D2
Høydalsseter [N] 192 D1
Hoyerswerda [D] 46 C3
Høyjord [N] 186 F2
Høylandet [N] 212 D3
Hoym [D] 44 D3
Hoyos [E] 90 F2
Hoyos del Espino [E] 92 C3
Höytiä [FIN] 208 F3
Hozha [BY] 38 D2
Hrabaw [RUS] 242 C3
Hrachovo [SK] 76 C2
Hrad Beckov [SK] 74 F2
Hradec Králové [CZ] 50 A4
Hradec nad Moravicí [CZ] 62 D3
Hradec nad Svitavou [CZ] 62 B3
Hrádek [CZ] 60 D2
Hrádek [CZ] 60 F2
Hrádek [CZ] 74 D2
Hrádek nad Nisou [CZ] 60 E1
Hradhoviště [CZ] 74 B1
Hradvz'k [UA] 246 E1
Hranice [CZ] 62 C4
Hranovnica [SK] 76 C1
Hrastik [SLO] 120 B3
Hrastovlje [SLO] 118 F4
Hrebenne [PL] 64 C3
Hřensko [CZ] 60 D1
Hríňová [SK] 76 B2
Hrob [CZ] 60 D2
Hrochův Týnec [CZ] 60 F3
Hrodna [BY] 38 D2
Hronov [CZ] 62 B2
Hrotovice [CZ] 74 C1
Hrtkovci [SRB] 146 D2
Hrubieszów [PL] 50 D4
Hrubov [SK] 64 C4
Hrubý Rohozec [CZ] 60 E2
Hrud [PL] 50 C2
Hrušov [SK] 76 A2
Hrušovany [CZ] 74 D2
Hrvace [HR] 144 E4
Hrvatska Kostajnica [HR] 144 E1
Huaröd [S] 180 D2
Huarte [E] 86 F4
Huben [A] 118 B1

Huben [A] 118 D1
Hubenov [CZ] 60 C3
Hubertusburg [D] 44 F4
Hubertusstock, Jagdschloss– [D] 34 C4
Hucqueliers [F] 40 B3
Huda Luknja [SLO] 120 B2
Huddersfield [GB] 24 C2
Huddinge [S] 190 D2
Huddunge [S] 190 C1
Hudiksvall [S] 196 C1
Huedin [RO] 244 C4
Huélago [E] 106 A2
Huélamo [E] 102 B1
Huelgoat [F] 52 B3
Huelma [F] 106 A2
Huelva [E] 98 D4
Huércal de Almería [E] 106 B4
Huércal–Overa [E] 106 C3
Huerta del Rey [E] 94 A2
Huerta de Valdecarábanos [E] 100 E1
Huérteles [E] 94 C2
Huerto [E] 94 E2
Huesa [E] 106 B2
Huesca [E] 94 E2
Huéscar [E] 106 C2
Hueselgau [D] 44 C4
Huete [E] 102 A1
Huétor Tájar [E] 104 E2
Hüfingen [D] 70 E3
Hufthamar [N] 192 A3
Huhdasjärvi [FIN] 200 B2
Huhla [BG] 156 F3
Huhtala [FIN] 222 C4
Huhtapuhto [FIN] 216 B3
Huhti [FIN] 198 D2
Huhtilampi [FIN] 210 E2
Huhus [FIN] 210 E2
Huissinkylä [FIN] 208 C2
Huittinen [FIN] 198 D2
Huizen [NL] 30 B3
Huizen [NL] 30 B3
Huizingen [B] 40 D3
Hujakkala [FIN] 200 D2
Hukkala [FIN] 210 D2
Hukvaldy [CZ] 62 D3
Hulderbo [N] 202 E4
Hulín [CZ] 60 C4
Huljen [S] 206 C4
Hulle [N] 202 F2
Hullsjön [S] 206 C3
Hulsing [DK] 182 E1
Hulst [NL] 40 D3
Hult [S] 184 D2
Hult [S] 188 E2
Hultanäs [S] 184 D2
Hultsfred [S] 184 E2
Hultsjö [S] 184 D2
Hum [BIH] 152 E1
Hum [HR] 118 F4
Humada [E] 86 C2
Humanes [E] 92 F3
Humble [DK] 178 D3
Humenné [SK] 76 E1
Humla [S] 184 C1
Humlebæk [DK] 178 F1
Humlum [DK] 182 C3
Hümme [D] 44 B3
Hummelsta [S] 190 C2
Humpolec [CZ] 60 E2
Humppi [FIN] 208 E2
Humppila [FIN] 198 D2
Humprecht [CZ] 60 E2
Hunaudaye, Château de– [F] 52 D3
Hundåla [N] 212 D1
Hunderdorf [D] 72 E1
Hundested [DK] 178 E1
Hundorp [N] 192 F1
Hunedoara [RO] 248 C3

Hünfeld [D] 58 D1
Hunge [S] 204 F3
Hungen [D] 58 C2
Hungerford [GB] 28 B3
Hunnebostrand [S] 188 B4
Hunspach [F] 56 F4
Hunstanton [GB] 24 E4
Huntingdon [GB] 28 D1
Huntly [GB] 14 F4
Huopanankoski [FIN] 208 F2
Hurbanovo [SK] 74 F3
Hurdal [N] 194 B3
Hurdal Verk [N] 194 B3
Hurez, Mănăstirea– [RO] 248 D3
Hurczani [RO] 148 D1
Huriel [F] 68 B4
Hurissalo [FIN] 200 C1
Hurskaala [FIN] 210 C3
Hürsovo [BG] 150 D3
Hurtanmaa [FIN] 200 C2
Hurup [DK] 182 C3
Hurva [S] 180 C2
Hus [CZ] 72 F1
Husa [N] 192 B4
Huså [S] 204 D2
Husaby [S] 188 D4
Húsavík [IS] 218 C2
Husbondliden [S] 214 C2
Husby [DK] 182 B4
Husbygård [S] 190 C3
Husby Långhundra [S] 190 D2
Husby–Sjuhundra [S] 190 E2
Huşi [RO] 244 F3
Husinec [CZ] 72 F1
Huskvarna [S] 184 C1
Husnes [N] 192 B4
Husö [FIN] 198 B4
Hustopeče [CZ] 74 D1
Husum [D] 32 B1
Husum [S] 206 E2
Husvika [N] 212 D1
Huta [PL] 64 B4
Huta Zawadzka [PL] 48 E3
Hutovo [BIH] 152 D2
Hüttenberg [A] 120 B1
Hüttschlag [A] 72 E4
Huttwil [CH] 70 D4
Huutijärvi [FIN] 198 E1
Huwniki [PL] 64 D3
Huy (Hoei) [B] 40 E4
Hvalba [FR] 182 A2
Hvalpsund [DK] 182 C3
Hvalvík [FR] 182 B1
Hvam [N] 188 B1
Hvammstangi [IS] 218 B2
Hvar [HR] 152 B2
Hveragerði [IS] 218 A3
Hvidbjerg [DK] 182 C3
Hvide Sande [DK] 178 A1
Hvittingfoss [N] 186 F2
Hvolsvöllur [IS] 218 B3
Hvoznitsa [BY] 50 D2
Hybo [S] 196 C1
Hycklinge [S] 184 E1
Hyde [GB] 24 B2
Hyen [N] 202 C4
Hyères [F] 126 A4
Hyervyaty [BY] 238 F3
Hyggen [N] 186 F1
Hyhälänmäki [FIN] 216 C4
Hylestad [N] 186 C2
Hylla [N] 204 C1
Hyllested Skovgårde [DK] 178 D1
Hyltebruk [S] 184 B3
Hynnekleiv [N] 186 D3
Hyry [FIN] 216 B1
Hyrynsalmi [FIN] 216 D2
Hyssna [S] 184 A2
Hythe [GB] 28 E4
Hyttegrend [N] 224 D3

Hytti [FIN] 200 D2
Hyvinge / Hyvinkää [FIN] 198 F3
Hyvinkää / Hyvinge [FIN] 198 F3
Hyypiö [FIN] 222 D2
Hyžne [PL] 64 D3

I

Ialissós [GR] 176 C2
Iam [RO] 146 F1
Ianca [RO] 148 C3
Iaşl [RO] 244 E3
Iasmos [GR] 156 C3
Iasos [TR] 170 C4
Iátova [E] 102 C3
Ibakibka [UA] 76 F2
Ibañeta, Puerto de– [E/F] 88 B3
Ibarska Klisura [SRB] 146 E4
Ibbenbüren [D] 30 E4
Ibeas de Juarros [E] 86 C4
Ibestad [N] 224 C3
Ibi [E] 106 F1
Ibieca [E] 94 E2
Ibiza / Eivissa [E] 108 E2
Ibrány [H] 76 E3
Ibrice [TR] 158 B4
Ibrikbaba [TR] 158 A4
Ibriktepe [TR] 158 A3
Ichenhausen [D] 72 B2
Ichtratzheim [F] 70 D2
İçikler [TR] 164 E4
Icoana [RO] 148 F1
Idaío Ántro [GR] 174 C4
Idala [S] 184 A2
Idanha-a-Nova [P] 90 E2
Idar–Oberstein [D] 56 F3
Idbacka [S] 214 B3
Idensalmi / Iisalmi [FIN] 216 C4
Idivuoma [S] 224 F4
Idjoš [SRB] 122 D3
Idom [DK] 182 C4
Idre [S] 194 D1
Idrija [SLO] 118 F3
Idritsa [RUS] 236 F3
Idro [I] 118 A3
Idstein [D] 58 B2
Idyma [TR] 170 D4
Iecava [LV] 234 F3
Ieper (Ypres) [B] 40 C3
Ierápetra [GR] 174 E4
Ieropigí [GR] 160 C2
If, Château d'– [F] 124 E4
Ifaístia [GR] 162 E2
Ifjord [N] 228 D2
Igal [H] 120 F2
Igalo [MNE] 152 D3
Igate [LV] 236 B2
Igea Marina [I] 128 E3
Igelbäcken [S] 188 F3
Igelfors [S] 190 B3
Igerøy [N] 212 D2
Iggesund [S] 196 C1
Iglesias [I] 142 B5
Igliauka [LT] 238 D3
Igliczna [PL] 62 B2
Igls [A] 72 C4
Ignaberga [S] 180 D1
Ignalina [LT] 238 F2
Ignatpol [UA] 242 C4
Igneada [TR] 158 C2
Igołomia [PL] 64 A3
Igoumenítsa [GR] 166 B1
Igralište [BG] 154 F4
Igrane [HR] 152 C2
Igrejinha [P] 90 C4

Igriés [E] 94 E2
Igualada [E] 96 C3
Igualeja [E] 104 C3
Igüeña [E] 82 E3
Iharosberény [H] 120 E2
Ihlienworth [D] 32 B2
Ii [FIN] 216 B1
Iisalmi / Idensalmi [FIN] 216 C4
Iisvesi [FIN] 210 B2
Iittala [FIN] 198 E2
Iitti [FIN] 200 B2
IJmuiden [NL] 30 B3
Ikalis / Kaalinen [FIN] 208 D4
Ikast [DK] 178 B1
Ikhala [RUS] 210 E4
Ikhtiman [BG] 156 B1
Ikizköy [TR] 170 C4
Ikkala [FIN] 198 E3
Ikkeläjärvi [FIN] 208 C3
Ikornnes [N] 202 C3
Ilanz [CH] 116 E1
Iława [PL] 36 D3
Il Casalone [I] 130 F3
il Castagno [I] 128 B4
Ilchester [GB] 26 E3
Ildır [TR] 168 F1
Ileana [RO] 150 C1
Ileía [GR] 166 F2
Ilfracombe [GB] 26 C2
Ilgižiai [LT] 238 C2
Ilhan [TR] 158 C4
Ilhavo [P] 84 A3
Ilia [RO] 248 C3
Ilica [TR] 164 C2
Ilıcalı [TR] 164 D3
Ilidža [BIH] 146 B4
Ilijaš [BIH] 146 B3
Il'inskoye [RUS] 240 F2
Ilirska Bistrica [SLO] 118 F4
Ilk [H] 76 F3
Ilkley [GB] 24 C2
Illano [E] 82 E2
Illar [E] 106 B3
Illa Ravena [E] 108 D3
Illby / Ilola [FIN] 200 B3
Illertissen [D] 72 A2
Illescas [E] 92 E4
Illichivs'k [UA] 246 D3
Illiers–Combray [F] 54 C4
Illingen [D] 58 B4
Illmitz [A] 74 D3
Illo [FIN] 198 D2
Íllora [E] 104 E2
Illschwang [D] 58 F3
Illueca [E] 94 C3
Ilmajoki [FIN] 208 C2
Il'me [RUS] 200 E1
Ilmenau [D] 58 E1
Ilminster [GB] 26 E3
Ilmoila [FIN] 198 E2
Ilok [HR] 146 C1
Ilola / Illby [FIN] 200 B3
Ilomants / Ilomantsi [FIN] 210 F2
Ilomantsi / Ilomants [FIN] 210 F2
Iłowa [PL] 46 D3
Iłowiec [PL] 36 A3
Il Pulo [I] 136 C2
Il Pulo [I] 136 C1
Ilsbo [S] 196 C1
Ilsenburg [D] 44 C2
Ilseng [N] 194 B3
Ilshofen [D] 58 D4
Ilskov [DK] 182 C4
Ilükste [LV] 234 F4
Ilvesjoki [FIN] 208 C3
Ilyaslar [TR] 164 D3
Ilyaslı [TR] 164 F4
Ilz [A] 120 C1
Iłża [PL] 48 F4

Imatra [FIN] 200 D1
Ímeros [GR] 156 E4
Imfors [S] 206 C2
Immenhausen [D] 44 B3
Immenstaad [D] 70 F3
Immenstadt [D] 72 A3
Immingham [GB] 24 D3
Imola [I] 128 D2
Imotski [HR] 152 C1
Imperia [I] 126 D3
Imphy [F] 68 C3
Impilakhti [RUS] 210 F4
Imrehegy [H] 122 B2
Ímroz [TR] 162 F2
Imsenden [N] 194 B2
Imsland [N] 186 B1
Imst [A] 72 B4
Inari [FIN] 216 F4
Inari / Enare [FIN] 226 D2
Inay [TR] 164 F4
Inca [E] 108 D3
Inch [IRL] 10 B3
Inch [IRL] 10 C4
Inchigeelagh [IRL] 10 B4
Inciems [LV] 236 B2
İnciraltı [TR] 170 B2
İncirköy [TR] 170 E4
İncirliova [TR] 170 C3
Incisa in Val d'Arno [I] 128 C4
Incisioni Rupestri, Parco Nazionale delle– [I] 118 A3
Indal [S] 206 C3
Independenta [RO] 150 E2
Inđija [SRB] 146 D1
Indre Billefjord [N] 228 C2
Indre Brenna [N] 228 C2
Indura [BY] 38 D2
İnece [TR] 158 B2
İnecik [TR] 158 B3
İnegöl [TR] 164 F1
Ineu [RO] 122 F2
Infantado [P] 90 B3
Infiesto [E] 86 A2
Ingå / Inkoo [FIN] 198 E4
Ingdalen [N] 204 A2
Ingelheim [D] 58 B2
Ingelstad [S] 184 D3
Ingenes [S] 192 B4
Ingenio [E] 112 E4
Ingevallsbo [S] 196 B4
Ingolsbenning [S] 190 B1
Ingolsheim [F] 56 F4
Ingolstadt [D] 72 C1
Ingwiller [F] 56 F4
Iniesta [E] 102 B3
Iniö [FIN] 198 D3
Inis / Ennis [IRL] 10 C2
Inishannon [IRL] 10 C4
Inke [H] 120 E2
Inkerilä [FIN] 200 C2
Inkoo / Ingå [FIN] 198 E4
Innala [FIN] 208 E3
Inndyr [N] 218 F3
Innerkrems [A] 118 F1
Innerleithen [GB] 20 D2
Innertavle [S] 206 F1
Innertkirchen [CH] 116 D1
Innervik [S] 220 C4
Innfjorden [N] 202 D3
Innhavet [N] 220 B1
Innichen / San Cándido [I] 118 D2
Inning [D] 72 C3
Innsbruck [A] 72 C4
Innset [N] 204 A3
Innset [N] 224 D3
Innvik [N] 202 C4
Inowłódz [PL] 48 E3
Inowrocław [PL] 48 C1

Ins [CH] 70 C4
Insch [GB] 14 F4
Insjön [S] 194 F3
Irísko [PL] 34 E3
Însurăței [RO] 248 F3
Intepe [TR] 164 A2
Interlaken [CH] 116 C1
Intra [I] 116 D3
Inturkė [LT] 238 E2
Inveraray [GB] 18 B3
Inverbervie [GB] 18 F3
Invergarry [GB] 14 D4
Invergordon [GB] 14 E3
Invermoriston [GB] 14 D3
Inverness [GB] 14 D3
Inverurie [GB] 14 F4
Inviken [S] 212 F3
Inzell [D] 72 E3
Ioánnina [GR] 160 C4
Ion Corvin [RO] 150 E1
Ioneşti [RO] 148 D1
Ioneşti [RO] 148 F1
Ionia [GR] 160 F2
Íos [GR] 174 D1
Iphofen [D] 58 D3
Ípsala [TR] 158 A4
Ipswich [GB] 28 E2
Iraío [GR] 166 F4
Iraío [GR] 170 B3
Iraío [GR] 172 E2
Irákleia [GR] 156 B4
Irákleia [GR] 166 E2
Irákleia [GR] 168 D4
Irákleio [GR] 174 D3
Iranzu [E] 86 E4
Irdning [A] 74 A4
Iregszemcse [H] 120 F2
Ireo [GR] 170 B3
Irgıllı [TR] 170 F2
Irig [SRB] 146 D1
Irixoa [E] 82 C2
Irnfritz [A] 74 C2
Irsina [I] 134 F4
Irun [E] 86 F3
Iruña / Pamplona [E] 86 F4
Irunberri / Lumbier [E] 88 A3
Irurita [E] 88 A2
Irurtzun [E] 86 F4
Irvine [GB] 18 C4
Irvinestown [NIR] 12 D2
Isaba / Izaba [E] 88 B3
İsabey [TR] 170 E2
Isaccea [RO] 248 F3
Ísafjörður [IS] 218 B1
İşalniţa [RO] 148 E2
Isane [N] 202 B4
Isaszeg [H] 76 B4
Isbister [GB] 16 E3
Íscar [E] 92 E2
Ischgl [A] 118 A1
Ischia [I] 134 C3
Isdes [F] 68 B2
Ise [N] 188 B2
Iselle [I] 116 D2
Iselsberg [A] 118 E2
Iseltwald [CH] 116 C1
Isenvad [DK] 178 B1
Iseo [I] 116 F3
Iserlohn [D] 42 D3
Isernia [I] 134 C2
Isfjorden [N] 202 D3
İshaklı [TR] 158 B4
Isigni–sur–Mer [F] 52 F2
Işıklar [TR] 170 D2
Işıklı [TR] 170 F1
İsili [I] 142 C4
İsinda [TR] 176 E2
İskele [TR] 164 D2
Iskele (Trikomon) [CY] 176 E3
Iskra [RUS] 200 E2
İşkuras [N] 226 C2
Isla [E] 86 D2

Isla Cristina [E] 98 C4
Isla Mayor [E] 104 B2
Islares [E] 86 D2
Ismaning [D] 72 C2
Ismantorp [S] 184 F3
Isnäs [FIN] 200 B3
Isnestoften [N] 228 B3
Isny [D] 72 A3
Iso–Äiniö [FIN] 198 F1
Iso–Evo [FIN] 198 F2
Isojoki / Storå [FIN] 208 C3
Isokyla [FIN] 208 C2
Isokyla [FIN] 210 B3
Isokylä [FIN] 216 B3
Isokylä [FIN] 222 D2
Isokyrö / Storkyro [FIN] 208 C2
Isola [F] 126 C2
Isola 2000 [F] 126 C2
Isola del Gran Sasso d'Italia [I] 132 E3
Isola della Scala [I] 118 B4
Isola delle Femmine [I] 140 C1
Isola dei Liri [I] 132 E4
Isola di Capo Rizzuto [I] 138 F2
Isolahti [FIN] 208 F3
Isona [E] 96 C2
Isoperä [FIN] 198 D2
Isorella [I] 116 F4
Isosuo [FIN] 200 B1
Isperikh [BG] 150 D2
İspica [I] 140 E4
Issa [RUS] 236 F2
Isseikka [FIN] 216 D4
Isselburg [D] 30 D4
Issigeac [F] 78 D4
Isso [E] 106 D1
Issogne [I] 116 C3
Issoire [F] 80 B2
Issoudun [F] 68 B3
Is–sur–Tille [F] 68 F3
İstanbul [TR] 158 E3
Istarske Toplice [HR] 118 F4
Istebna [PL] 62 E3
Istha [D] 42 F3
Isthmía [GR] 166 F4
Istiaía [GR] 162 B4
Istibanja [MK] 154 E3
Istomino [RUS] 240 D4
Istranca [TR] 158 D3
Istres [F] 124 E3
Istria [RO] 250 C3
Istunmäki [FIN] 210 B2
Isturits et d'Oxocelhaya, Grottes d'– [F] 88 B2
Istuzu [TR] 176 C1
Isums [S] 234 A2
Itä–Aure [FIN] 208 D3
Itä–Karttula [FIN] 210 B2
Itäkylä [FIN] 208 D1
Italica [E] 98 E4
Itämen [FIN] 208 D3
Itanós [GR] 174 F3
Itéa [GR] 160 D3
Itéa [GR] 166 E1
Itéa [GR] 166 E3
Itháki [GR] 166 C3
Itieli [I] 132 C3
Itri [I] 134 B2
İttiri [I] 142 B3
Itxassou [F] 88 B2
Itzehoe [D] 32 B2
Ivacevičy [BY] 242 B3
Ivåd [H] 76 C3
Ivalo [FIN] 226 D2
Ivanava [BY] 50 F2
Ivančice [CZ] 74 D1
Ivančiský Viadukt [CZ] 74 D1
Ivančna Gorica [SLO] 120 B3
Ivanec [HR] 120 D3

Ivangorod [RUS] 232 E1
Ivanić Grad [HR] 120 D4
Ivanjica [SRB] 146 D4
Ivanjska [BIH] 144 E2
Ivankiv [UA] 242 D4
Ivankovo [HR] 146 B1
Ivano–Frankivs'k [UA] 244 D2
Ivano–Frankove [UA] 64 E3
Ivanovice na Hané [CZ] 62 C4
Ivanovo [BG] 150 D3
Ivanovo [BG] 156 E2
Ivanovo Manastir [BG] 150 B2
Ivanska [HR] 120 D3
Ivanski [BG] 150 D3
Ivanychí [UA] 50 E4
Ivarrud [N] 212 E2
Ivatsevichy [BY] 38 F3
Ivaylovgrad [BG] 156 F3
Iveland [N] 186 D3
Ivetofta [S] 180 D1
Ívira [GR] 156 C4
Ivíron, Moní– [GR] 162 C2
Ivréa [I] 116 C3
Ívrindi [TR] 164 C2
Ivry–la–Bataille [F] 54 D3
Ivybridge [GB] 26 C4
Iwaniska [PL] 64 B1
Iwla [PL] 64 C3
Iwonicz–Zdrój [PL] 64 C3
Iwye [BY] 38 F1
Ixiá [GR] 176 C2
Izaba / Isaba [E] 88 B3
Izačić [BIH] 144 D2
Izarra [E] 86 D3
Izbica Kujawska [PL] 48 C2
Izbiceni [RO] 148 F2
Izbicko [PL] 62 D2
Izbište [SRB] 146 E1
Izborsk [RUS] 232 E4
Izcar [E] 104 E2
Izeda [P] 84 D3
Izegem [B] 40 C3
Izernore [F] 80 E2
Izgrev [BG] 158 C1
Izmaïl [UA] 244 F4
İzmir [TR] 170 B2
İzmit [TR] 158 F3
İzmit (Kocaeli) [TR] 158 F3
Iznájar [E] 104 E2
İznalloz [E] 104 F2
İznik [TR] 158 F4
Izola [SLO] 118 E4
Izsák [H] 122 B2
Izvara [RUS] 232 F1
Izvoarele [RO] 150 B2
Izvor [BG] 148 C3
Izvor [BG] 154 F2
Izvor [MK] 154 C4
Izvor [MK] 154 C4
Izvor [SRB] 146 F3
Izvoz [RUS] 232 E1

J

Jaakonvaara [FIN] 210 E1
Jaala [FIN] 200 B2
Jaalanka [FIN] 216 C2
Jääli [FIN] 216 B2
Jaama [EST] 230 F2
Jääskä [FIN] 216 A4
Jääskö [FIN] 222 C2
Jabkenice [CZ] 60 E2
Jablanac [HR] 144 C2
Jablanica [BIH] 146 A4
Jablonec nad Jizerou [CZ] 60 F1
Jablonec nad Nisou [CZ] 60 E2
Jablonica [SK] 74 E2
Jabłonka [PL] 62 F4
Jabłonna [PL] 46 E2

Jablonné nad Orlicí [CZ] 62 B3
Jablonné v Podještědi [CZ] 60 E1
Jabłonowo Pomorskie [PL] 36 D3
Jablunkov [CZ] 62 E3
Jabugo [E] 98 E3
Jabukovac [BIH] 146 C4
Jabuka [MNE] 152 F2
Jabuka [SRB] 146 E2
Jabuka [SRB] 152 F1
Jabukovik [SRB] 148 C4
Jaca [E] 88 B4
Jáchymov [CZ] 60 C2
Jacinki [PL] 36 A2
Jacobsdorf [D] 46 C2
Jaczowice [PL] 62 C2
Jade [D] 30 F2
Jädraås [S] 196 C3
Jadranska Lešnica [SRB] 146 C2
Jadraque [E] 94 A3
Jægerspris [DK] 178 E2
Jaén [E] 104 F2
Jagare [BIH] 144 F2
Jagel [D] 32 B1
Jagenbach [A] 74 B2
Jagodina [SRB] 146 F3
Jagodje [SLO] 118 E4
Jagodnjak [HR] 122 A4
Jagodzin [PL] 46 D4
Jagsthausen [D] 58 C3
Jahnsfelde [D] 46 C2
Jajce [BIH] 144 F3
Ják [H] 120 D1
Jakabszállás [H] 122 C2
Jakalj [SRB] 146 D3
Jakkukylä [FIN] 216 B1
Jakkula [FIN] 208 C2
Jäkkvik [S] 220 B3
Jakobsbakken [N] 220 B2
Jakobstad / Pietarsaari [FIN] 214 F4
Jakokoski [FIN] 210 E2
Jakšić [HR] 120 F4
Jakub [CZ] 60 E3
Jakubany [SK] 64 B4
Jakubčovice nad Odrou [CZ] 62 C3
Jakuszyce [PL] 60 F1
Jalasjärvi [FIN] 208 C3
Jaligny–sur–Besbre [F] 80 C1
Jałówka [PL] 38 D3
Jamaja [EST] 230 B4
Jamena [SRB] 146 C2
Jämijärvi [FIN] 208 D4
Jäminkipohja [FIN] 208 E4
Jämjöslätt [S] 180 F1
Jammerdal [N] 194 C4
Jämsä [FIN] 208 F4
Jämsänkoski [FIN] 208 E4
Jämshög [S] 180 D1
Jämtön [S] 220 F4
Jamu Mare [RO] 122 E4
Jamurda [LV] 236 C3
Janakkala [FIN] 198 E2
Janče [MK] 154 C4
Jandía Playa [E] 114 D4
Jänese [EST] 230 E1
Janja [BIH] 146 C2
Janjina [HR] 152 C2
Jankov [CZ] 60 E3
Janków [PL] 48 B3
Jännevirta [FIN] 210 C2
Jánoshalma [H] 122 B3
Jánosháza [H] 120 E1
Jánossomorja [H] 74 E3
Janovice nad Úhlavou [CZ] 60 C4
Janów [PL] 38 C2
Janów [PL] 48 E2
Janów [PL] 62 E2

Janowiec [PL] 50 B3
Janowiec Wielkopolski [PL] 48 B1
Janów Lubelski [PL] 64 D1
Janowo [PL] 36 F3
Janów Podlaski [PL] 50 C2
Janské Lazně [CZ] 60 F2
Jämsmässholmen [S] 204 E1
Januszewice [PL] 48 E3
Janville [F] 54 D4
Janvry [F] 54 D3
Janzé [F] 52 E4
Jäppilä [FIN] 210 C3
Jarafuel [E] 102 C3
Jaraicejo [E] 100 B1
Jaraíz de la Vera [E] 92 B4
Jarak [SRB] 146 D2
Jārāma [S] 224 E4
Jarama, Circuito de– [E] 92 E3
Jarandilla de la Vera [E] 92 B4
Järbo [S] 196 C3
Jarcevo [RUS] 240 D4
Jarczew [PL] 50 B2
Jardin [F] 66 F2
Jard–sur–Mer [F] 66 C3
Jaren [N] 194 B3
Jaren [S] 188 C2
Jargeau [F] 68 B2
Järkastaka [S] 224 F4
Jarkovac [SRB] 146 E1
Järkvissle [S] 206 C3
Järlåsa [S] 190 D1
Jarmen [D] 34 C2
Jarmenil [F] 70 C2
Jarmina [HR] 122 B4
Järn [S] 188 C3
Järna [S] 190 D3
Jarnac [F] 78 C2
Jarnages [F] 80 A1
Järnäsklubb [S] 206 E2
Järnforsen [S] 184 E2
Jarny [F] 56 D3
Jarocin [PL] 48 B3
Jaroměř [CZ] 60 F2
Jaroměřice nad Rokytnou [CZ] 74 C1
Jaroslavl [RUS] 240 F1
Jarosław [PL] 64 D3
Jarosławiec [PL] 36 A1
Järpås [S] 188 D4
Järpen [S] 204 D2
Järrestad [S] 180 D2
Jarrio [E] 82 E2
Järsnäs [S] 184 E2
Jarszewko [PL] 34 D3
Järva–Jaani [EST] 230 E2
Järvakandi [EST] 230 D2
Järvelä [FIN] 198 F2
Järvenpää [FIN] 200 C1
Järvenpää [FIN] 210 C4
Järvenpää / Träskända [FIN] 198 F3
Järventausta [FIN] 216 B4
Järvikylä [FIN] 216 C3
Järvsjö [S] 214 B3
Järvsö [S] 196 C1
Järvtjärn [S] 214 D3
Jaša Tomić [SRB] 122 D4
Jasenak [HR] 144 C1
Jasenjani [BIH] 146 A4
Jasenkovo [BG] 150 D2
Jasenná [CZ] 62 D4
Jasenovac [HR] 144 E1
Jasenovets [BG] 150 C3
Jasenovo [MNE] 152 F2
Jasenovo [SRB] 146 D4
Jasenovo [SRB] 146 F2
Jasień [PL] 36 B2
Jasień [PL] 46 D3
Jasienica [PL] 62 E3
Jasienica Rosielna [PL] 64 C3
Jasienie [PL] 62 D1
Jasika [SRB] 146 F4

Jasikovo [SRB] 148 B2
Jasionówka [PL] 38 C3
Jašiūnai [LT] 238 E3
Jaskínia Raj [PL] 64 A1
Jaskyňa Domica [SK] 76 C2
Jasło [PL] 64 C3
Jasná [SK] 76 B1
Jasna Góra [PL] 62 E1
Jasno [RUS] 232 F4
Jasov [SK] 76 D2
Jasovská Jaskyňa [SK] 76 D2
Jastarnia [PL] 36 C1
Jastrebarsko [HR] 120 C4
Jastrowie [PL] 36 A3
Jastrzębia [PL] 36 C1
Jastrzębia [PL] 48 F3
Jastrzębie–Zdrói [PL] 62 D3
Jåsund [N] 186 C4
Jászágó [H] 76 C4
Jászalsószentgyörgy [H] 76 C4
Jászapáti [H] 76 C4
Jászárokszállás [H] 76 C3
Jászberény [H] 76 C4
Jászfényszaru [H] 76 C4
Jászkarajenő [H] 122 C1
Jászkisér [H] 76 C4
Jászkóhalma [H] 76 C4
Jászladány [H] 76 C4
Jászów [PL] 62 C2
Jászszentandrás [H] 76 C4
Jászszentlászló [H] 122 C2
Jásztelek [H] 76 C4
Jät [S] 184 D3
Játar [E] 106 C2
Jatko [FIN] 216 C1
Jatov [SK] 74 F3
Jättendal [S] 196 D1
Jaubrun [F] 80 B4
Jauge [F] 78 B3
Jaun [CH] 116 C1
Jaungulbene [LV] 236 D2
Jauniniumuiža [LV] 234 E4
Jaunjelgava [LV] 236 C3
Jaunpils [LV] 234 D3
Jauntsaras [E] 86 F3
Jaurakkajärvi [FIN] 216 C1
Jauranna [LV] 236 D2
Jaurplebalga [LV] 236 C2
Jausiers [F] 126 B2
Jåvall [N] 188 C2
Javarus [FIN] 222 D2
Jävenitz [D] 44 D1
Javerdat [F] 78 E2
Javier / Xabier [E] 88 B3
Javierre [E] 88 C4
Javoříčko [CZ] 62 B3
Javorník [CZ] 62 C2
Jävre [S] 214 E2
Javron [F] 54 A3
Jawor [PL] 46 F4
Jawor Solecki [PL] 50 B4
Jaworzno [PL] 62 E2
Jayena [E] 104 E3
Jażići [BIH] 146 B4
Jazvina–Puszta [H] 120 F2
Jeanménil [F] 70 C2
Jebel [RO] 122 E4
Jedburgh [GB] 20 E2
Jedeszki [PL] 38 C2
Jedlina–Zdrój [PL] 62 B2
Jedlińsk [PL] 48 F3
Jednorożec [PL] 36 F4
Jędrzejów [PL] 64 A2
Jédula [E] 104 B2
Jedwabne [PL] 38 B3
Jedwabno [PL] 36 F3
Jeesiö [FIN] 222 C1
Jegălia [RO] 150 E1
Jegłownik [PL] 36 D2
Jēkabpils [LV] 236 C3
Jektevik [N] 192 B4

Jektvik [N] 218 E3
Jelah [BIH] 146 A2
Jelcz–Laskowice [PL] 48 B4
Jelenia Góra [PL] 60 F1
Jeleniewo [PL] 38 C1
Jelenino [PL] 36 A3
Jeleśnia [PL] 62 E3
Jelgava [LV] 234 F3
Jelizarovo [RUS] 232 E3
Jelling [DK] 178 B2
Jełowa [PL] 62 D1
Jels [DK] 178 B2
Jelsa [HR] 152 B2
Jelsa [N] 186 B2
Jelšane [SLO] 118 F4
Jelšava [SK] 76 C2
Jelsi [I] 134 D2
Jemieliste [PL] 38 C1
Jemnice [CZ] 74 C1
Jena [D] 44 D4
Jenbach [A] 72 C4
Jeneč [CZ] 60 D3
Jenikowo [PL] 34 E3
Jennersdorf [A] 120 D1
Jensåsvoll [N] 204 C3
Jeppo / Jepua [FIN] 208 C1
Jepua / Jeppo [FIN] 208 C1
Jeraika [LV] 236 D4
Jerez de la Frontera [E] 104 B2
Jerez del Marquesado [E] 106 A3
Jerez de los Caballeros [E] 98 E2
Jerggul Holmestrand [N] 226 C2
Jergucati [AL] 160 B4
Jérica [E] 102 D2
Jerichow [D] 44 E1
Jerka [PL] 46 F3
Jerónimos, Monasterio de los– [E] 106 E2
Jerpoint Abbey [IRL] 10 E3
Jerslev [DK] 182 D2
Jerup [DK] 182 E2
Jerxheim [D] 44 D2
Jerzens [A] 72 B4
Jerzu [I] 142 C4
Jerzwałd [PL] 36 D3
Jesberg [D] 42 F4
Jesenice [CZ] 60 C2
Jesenice [HR] 144 E4
Jesenice [SLO] 118 F2
Jesenice [SLO] 120 C3
Jeseník [CZ] 62 C2
Jesenovac [BIH] 144 E2
Jesenské [SK] 76 C2
Jesi [I] 128 F4
Jesionowo [PL] 34 E4
Jésolo [I] 118 D4
Jessen [D] 44 F3
Jessheim [N] 194 B4
Jestřebí [CZ] 60 E2
Jettenh. [D] 44 C3
Jettingen–Scheppach [D] 72 B2
Jeumont [F] 40 D4
Jevenstedt [D] 32 B1
Jever [D] 30 F1
Jevíčko [CZ] 62 B3
Jevišovice [CZ] 74 C1
Jevnaker [N] 194 B4
Jezerane [HR] 144 C1
Jezero [BIH] 144 F3
Jezero [HR] 144 C1
Jezerski [BIH] 144 D2
Jezersko [SLO] 120 A2
Jezevo [HR] 120 D4
Jeżewo [PL] 48 D1
Jeziorany [PL] 36 F2
Jeżów [PL] 48 E3
Jeżowe [PL] 64 D2

J. F. Kennedy Memorial Forest Park [IRL] 10 E4
Jičín [CZ] 60 E2
Jieznas [LT] 238 D3
Jihlava [CZ] 60 F4
Jijona / Xixona [E] 106 F1
Jilava [RO] 150 B1
Jilemnice [CZ] 60 F2
Jílové u Prahy [CZ] 60 D3
Jiltjer [S] 214 B1
Jimbolia [RO] 122 D3
Jimena [E] 106 A2
Jimena de la Frontera [E] 104 C3
Jimramov [CZ] 62 B3
Jindřichov [CZ] 62 C2
Jindřichovice [CZ] 60 B2
Jindřichův Hradec [CZ] 60 E4
Jirkov [CZ] 60 C2
Jistebnice [CZ] 60 D4
Jitaru [RO] 148 F1
Joachimsthal [D] 34 C4
Jobbágyi [H] 76 B3
Jochberg [A] 72 D4
Jock [S] 220 F3
Jódar [E] 106 A2
Jodoigne [B] 40 E4
Joensuu [FIN] 210 E2
Joesjö [S] 212 E1
Jõgeva [EST] 230 E2
Johanheshov [S] 190 D2
Johannelund [S] 214 C3
Johanngeorgenstadt [D] 60 B2
Johannisholm [S] 194 E3
Johansfors [S] 184 D3
John o'Groats [GB] 14 F2
Johnstone [GB] 18 C4
Johnstown [IRL] 10 D3
Jõhvi [EST] 230 F1
Joigny [F] 68 D2
Joinville [F] 68 F1
Jokela [FIN] 198 F3
Jokijärvi [FIN] 210 B2
Jokikylä [FIN] 208 D3
Jokikylä [FIN] 216 B2
Jokikylä [FIN] 216 B4
Jokikylä [FIN] 216 B4
Jokikylä [FIN] 216 B4
Jokikylä [FIN] 216 D2
Jokimaa [FIN] 198 F2
Jokioinen / Jookis [FIN] 198 D2
Jokiperä [FIN] 208 C2
Jokipii [FIN] 208 C3
Jokivarsi [FIN] 208 D3
Jokkmokk [S] 220 D3
Jökulsarlon [IS] 218 C3
Jolanda di Savóia [I] 128 D2
Jomala [FIN] 196 F4
Jönåker [S] 190 C3
Jonas, Grottes de– [F] 80 B2
Jonasvollen [N] 204 C4
Jonava [LT] 238 D3
Joncy [F] 68 E4
Jondal [N] 192 B3
Joniny [PL] 64 B3
Joniškis [LT] 234 F4
Jonkeri [FIN] 216 E3
Jönköping [S] 184 C1
Jönköping [S] 184 C1
Jonsberg [S] 190 C4
Jonsrud [N] 194 B3
Jonzac [F] 78 C2
Jookis / Jokioinen [FIN] 198 D2
Jordanów [PL] 62 F3
Jordanów Śląski [PL] 62 B1
Jordbro [S] 190 D2
Jördenstorf [D] 32 F2
Jordet [N] 194 C2
Jorgastak [N] 226 C2
Jörgen–Berg [CH] 116 E1

Jörlanda [S] 182 F1
Jormua [FIN] 216 D3
Jormvattnet [S] 212 E3
Jörn [S] 214 D2
Joroinen / Jorois [FIN] 210 C3
Jorois / Joroinen [FIN] 210 C3
Jørpeland [N] 186 B2
Jorquera [E] 102 B3
Jørstad [N] 212 D4
Jošan [HR] 144 D2
Jošanica [BIH] 146 B3
Jošanica, Manastir– [SRB] 146 E3
Jošanička Banja [SRB] 154 C1
Jošavka [BIH] 144 F2
Josefov [CZ] 60 F2
Jøsenfjorden [N] 186 B2
Joševa [SRB] 146 C2
Josipdol [HR] 144 C1
Josipovac [HR] 122 A4
Jössefors [S] 188 D2
Josselin [F] 52 D4
Jøssund [N] 212 C3
Jostedal [N] 192 D1
Jósvafő [H] 76 C2
Jouarre [F] 54 F3
Jõuga [EST] 230 F2
Jougne [F] 70 B4
Joukio [FIN] 200 E1
Joukokylä [FIN] 216 D2
Joure [NL] 30 C2
Journaankylä [FIN] 200 B3
Joutsa [FIN] 210 B4
Joutseno [FIN] 200 D2
Joutsijärvi [FIN] 222 D2
Jovan [S] 214 B2
Joviac [F] 124 E1
Jøvik [N] 224 E2
Jovsa [SK] 76 E1
Joyeuse [F] 124 D1
Józefów [PL] 48 F2
Józefów [PL] 50 B4
Józefów [PL] 64 E2
Józsa [H] 76 E3
Juankoski [FIN] 210 C1
Juan–les–Pins [F] 126 C3
Judaberg [N] 186 B2
Judenburg [A] 120 B1
Judinsalo [FIN] 200 A1
Juelsminde [DK] 178 C2
Jugenbdburg [D] 58 B1
Jugon–les–Lacs [F] 52 D3
Jugorje [SLO] 120 B4
Juhtimäki [FIN] 208 D4
Juillac [F] 78 E3
Juist [D] 30 E1
Jukkasjärvi [S] 220 E1
Juknaičiai [LT] 238 B2
Juktån [S] 214 B2
Jule [N] 212 E4
Jülich [D] 42 C4
Julierpass [CH] 116 F2
Julita [S] 190 B3
Jullouville [F] 52 E3
Jumièges [F] 54 C2
Jumilla [E] 106 E1
Juminen [FIN] 210 C1
Jumisko [FIN] 222 E3
Jumkersrott [D] 30 E1
Jumkil [S] 190 D1
Jung [S] 188 D4
Jungsund [FIN] 208 B2
Junibodsand [S] 206 C4
Juniville [F] 56 B3
Junnikkala [FIN] 200 D1
Junosuando [S] 220 F2
Junqueira [PT] 84 C3
Junsele [S] 206 C1
Juntusranta [FIN] 216 E1
Juodupė [LT] 236 C4
Juojärvi [FIN] 210 D2
Juoksengi [S] 222 B3

Juoksenki [FIN] 222 B3
Juokslahti [FIN] 208 F4
Juorkuna [FIN] 216 C2
Jupiter [RO] 150 F2
Jurbarkas [LT] 238 C3
Jurignac [F] 78 C2
Jürkalne [LV] 234 D3
Jurklošter [SLO] 120 C3
Jurków [PL] 64 B3
Jürmala [LV] 234 F3
Jurmo [FIN] 198 B3
Jurmo [FIN] 198 C4
Jurovski Brod [HR] 120 B4
Jurowce [PL] 38 C3
Jurva [FIN] 208 C2
Jurvala [FIN] 200 C2
Jurvansalo [FIN] 208 F2
Jushkino [RUS] 232 D2
Jussey [F] 70 B2
Juszkowy Grád [PL] 38 D3
Juta [H] 120 F2
Jüterbog [D] 44 F2
Jutis [S] 220 C3
Jutrosin [PL] 46 F3
Jutsajaura [S] 220 D2
Juujärvi [FIN] 222 D3
Juuka [FIN] 210 D1
Juupajoki [FIN] 208 E4
Juurikka [FIN] 210 E3
Juva [FIN] 198 C2
Juva [FIN] 210 C4
Juvanum [I] 132 F4
Juvigny–le–Tertre [F] 52 F3
Juvola [FIN] 210 D3
Juvre [DK] 178 A2
Juzennecourt [F] 68 F2
Južnyj [RUS] 36 E1
Jyderup [DK] 178 E2
Jylhä [FIN] 210 B1
Jyllinge [DK] 178 E2
Jyrkäntoski [FIN] 222 F3
Jyrkha [FIN] 216 D3
Jyväskylä [FIN] 208 F3

K

Kaalamo [RUS] 210 F3
Kaalasjärvi [S] 220 D1
Kaalinen / Ikalis [FIN] 208 D4
Kaamanen [FIN] 226 D2
Kaanaa [FIN] 208 D4
Käännänmäki [FIN] 216 B4
Kääntojärvi [S] 220 F2
Kaarela [FIN] 216 B2
Kaaresuvanto [FIN] 226 A3
Kaarina [FIN] 198 C3
Kaarma [EST] 230 B3
Käärmelahti [FIN] 210 D4
Kaarssen [D] 32 D3
Kaartilankoski [FIN] 210 D4
Kaatsheuvel [NL] 40 E2
Kaavi [FIN] 210 C2
Kaba [H] 76 D4
Kabakca [TR] 158 D3
Kabalar [TR] 170 E2
Kabaltepe [TR] 162 F2
Kabböle [FIN] 200 B3
Kåbdalis [S] 220 E4
Kabelvåg [N] 218 F1
Kabile [LV] 234 E3
Kableshkovo [BG] 150 E4
Kač [SRB] 146 D1
Kačanik [KS] 154 D3
Kacelovo [BG] 150 C3
Kačeřov [CZ] 60 G3
Kachanovo [RUS] 232 E4
Kačikol [KS] 154 D2
Kačina [CZ] 60 E3
Kácov [CZ] 60 E3
Kaczorów [PL] 60 F1

Kadaň [CZ] 60 C2
Kadarkút [H] 120 E3
Kadikalesi [TR] 170 B3
Kadıköy [TR] 158 B4
Kadıköy [TR] 170 D2
Kadıköy [TR] 176 E1
Kadłubówka [PL] 38 C4
Kadłub Turawski [PL] 62 D1
Kadrifakovo [MK] 154 E3
Kadyanda [TR] 176 D1
Kadzidło [PL] 38 A3
Käenkoski [FIN] 210 F1
Kåfjord [N] 228 C1
Kaga [S] 190 B4
Kåge [S] 214 D2
Kågeröd [S] 180 C1
Kagkádi [GR] 166 D4
Kaharlyk [UA] 242 D4
Kahla [D] 58 F1
Kaïáfas [GR] 172 C2
Kaïméni Chóra [GR] 168 A3
Käina [EST] 230 B2
Kainach bei Voitsberg [A] 120 B1
Kainasto [FIN] 208 C3
Kaindorf [A] 120 C1
Kainu [FIN] 208 D1
Kainulasjärvi [S] 220 F2
Kaipiainen [FIN] 200 C2
Kairahta [FIN] 208 F3
Kairala [FIN] 222 D2
Kairila [FIN] 198 C1
Kairiškiai [LT] 234 E4
Kaisepakte [S] 224 D4
Kaiserbach [D] 58 C4
Kaisersesch [D] 56 F2
Kaiserslautern [D] 56 F3
Kaiser–Wilhelm–Koog [D] 32 B2
Kaisheim [D] 72 B1
Kaišiadoris [LT] 238 D3
Kaitainsalmi [FIN] 216 D3
Kaitsor [FIN] 208 C1
Kaiu [EST] 230 D2
Kaivanto [FIN] 216 C3
Kaivomäki [FIN] 210 C4
Kajaani / Kajana [FIN] 216 D3
Kajana / Kajaani [FIN] 216 D3
Kajánújfalu [H] 122 D2
Kajetans–Brücke [A] 118 B1
Kajoo [FIN] 210 D1
Kájov [CZ] 74 A2
Kajraly [RUS] 222 E2
Kakanj [BIH] 146 A3
Kakarríq [AL] 152 F4
Kakavi [AL] 160 B4
Kakerbeck [D] 44 D1
Kakhovka [UA] 246 E2
Käkilahti [FIN] 216 C3
Kaklıc [TR] 170 A2
Kaklik [TR] 170 E2
Kakmă [HR] 144 C3
Kąkolewnica Wschodnia [PL] 50 C2
Kakopetriá [CY] 176 D3
Kakóvatos [GR] 172 C2
Kákrina [BG] 150 A4
Kakslauttanen [FIN] 226 D3
Kaktyni [LV] 236 C3
Kakušen [S] 204 F1
Kakushöhle [D] 42 C4
Kál [H] 76 C3
Kälä [FIN] 210 B4
Kalaja [FIN] 216 B4
Kalajoki [FIN] 216 A3
Kalak [N] 228 D2
Kalakoski [FIN] 208 D3
Kalamáki [GR] 160 F4
Kalamáki [GR] 162 B3
Kalamariá [GR] 160 F2
Kalamáta [GR] 172 D3

Kalámi [GR] 174 B3
Kalamítsi [GR] 162 C2
Kálamos [GR] 168 B2
Kalamotí [GR] 168 E2
Kalampáki [GR] 156 C4
Kalampáki [GR] 160 D4
Kalanchak [RUS] 246 E3
Kalándra [GR] 162 B2
Kalá Nerá [GR] 162 B4
Kalanti [FIN] 198 C2
Kálarne [S] 206 B3
Kálathos [GR] 176 C2
Kalavárda [GR] 176 C2
Kalávryta [GR] 166 E4
Kalax [FIN] 208 B3
Kalbe [D] 44 D1
Kalce [SLO] 118 F3
Kalčevo [BG] 158 A1
Káld [H] 120 E1
Kaldfarnes [N] 224 C3
Kaldhusseter [N] 202 D4
Kale [TR] 164 D2
Kale [TR] 170 E3
Kale [TR] 176 F1
Kaleburnu (Galinóporni) [CY] 176 E2
Kalekovets [BG] 156 D2
Kaleköy [TR] 162 F2
Kalela [FIN] 198 C2
Kalenić, Manastir– [SRB] 146 E4
Kálergo [GR] 168 C2
Kalesija [BIH] 146 B2
Kalety [PL] 62 E2
Kalétzi [GR] 160 C4
Kalétzi [GR] 166 D4
Kaleva [FIN] 198 D3
Kalevala [RUS] 216 F1
Kalí [GR] 160 E2
Kaliánoi [GR] 166 E4
Kalidón [GR] 166 D3
Kaliningrad [RUS] 36 E1
Kalinkavichy [BY] 242 C3
Kalinovik [BIH] 146 B4
Kalinovka [RUS] 238 B3
Kalinovo [PL] 38 B2
Kalinovo [SK] 76 B2
Kaliráchi [GR] 160 D3
Kálisty [PL] 36 E2
Kalisz [PL] 48 B3
Kalisz Pomorski [PL] 34 F3
Kaliváni [GR] 168 C2
Kalix [S] 222 B4
Kaljord [N] 224 B4
Kalkan [TR] 176 E2
Kalkar [D] 42 C2
Kalkgruber [DK] 182 C3
Kalkım [TR] 164 C2
Kalkkinen [FIN] 200 A2
Kall [D] 42 C4
Kall [S] 204 D2
Källa [S] 184 F3
Källarbo [S] 196 B4
Kallaste [EST] 230 F2
Kallbäck [FIN] 198 F3
Källberget [S] 204 E3
Kalli [EST] 230 C3
Kallimasiá [GR] 168 E2
Kallinge [S] 180 E1
Kallio [FIN] 208 D4
Kallio [FIN] 216 E3
Kalliojoki [FIN] 216 E2
Kalliokylä [FIN] 210 B1
Kalliokylä [FIN] 216 C4
Kallíslahti [FIN] 210 D3
Kallithéa [GR] 156 C4
Kallithéa [GR] 160 F3
Kallithéa [GR] 162 B2
Kallithéa [GR] 172 C2
Kallithéa [GR] 176 C2

Kalliuskoski [FIN] 216 C2
Kallmünz [D] 58 F4
Kálló [H] 76 B3
Kallön [S] 214 B1
Kalloní [GR] 164 A3
Kalloní [GR] 168 A3
Kállósemjén [H] 76 E3
Kallsedet [S] 204 D1
Kallträsk [FIN] 208 B4
Källunga [S] 184 B1
Kallunki [FIN] 222 E2
Kalmakattio [FIN] 226 C3
Kálmánháza [H] 76 E3
Kalmar [S] 184 E3
Kalmari [FIN] 208 E2
Kalná [CZ] 60 E3
Kalna [SRB] 148 C3
Kalná nad Hronom [SK] 76 A3
Kalnciems [LV] 234 F3
Kalnik [PL] 36 E2
Kalochóri [GR] 160 D3
Kaló Chorió [GR] 174 E4
Kalocsa [H] 122 B2
Kalofer [BG] 156 D1
Kalogriá [GR] 166 C4
Kaloi Liménes [GR] 174 C4
Kalókastro [GR] 156 B4
Kalonéri [GR] 160 D3
Kaló Nero [GR] 172 C2
Kalopanagiótis [CY] 176 D3
Kaloskopí [GR] 166 E3
Kalotina [BG] 148 D4
Kaloyan [BG] 150 D3
Kaloyanovo [BG] 156 D2
Káloz [H] 122 A1
Kalpaki [GR] 160 C4
Kalpio [FIN] 216 C2
Kals [A] 118 D1
Kalsdorf [A] 120 C1
Kalsdorf [A] 120 C1
Kalsvik [S] 190 E2
Kaltanenai [LT] 238 E2
Kaltenkirchen [D] 32 C2
Kaltennordheim [D] 58 D1
Kaltinėnai [LT] 238 B2
Kaluga [RUS] 240 F4
Kalugerovo [BG] 156 C2
Kaluńerovo [SRB] 146 F2
Kalush [UA] 244 C2
Kałuszyn [PL] 50 B2
Kalv [S] 184 B2
Kalvåg [N] 202 B4
Kalvarija [LT] 38 C1
Kalvatn [N] 202 C4
Kalvehave [DK] 178 E3
Kalven [N] 228 B1
Kälvia / Kelviå [FIN] 214 F4
Kälvik [S] 184 F1
Kalvitsa [FIN] 210 C4
Kalvola [FIN] 198 E2
Kalwang [A] 74 B4
Kalwaria Zebrzydowska [PL] 62 F3
Kalyazin [RUS] 240 F2
Kalyena [UA] 50 F2
Kálymnos [GR] 176 A1
Kalynivka [UA] 244 E1
Kalývia [GR] 166 C2
Kám [H] 120 D1
Kamanski Vučiak [HR] 120 E4
Kamáres [GR] 168 C4
Kamáres [GR] 168 D4
Kamáres [GR] 174 C4
Kamariótissa [GR] 162 E1
Kamburovo [BG] 150 C3
Kámeiros [GR] 176 C2
Kamen [BG] 150 D3
Kámen [CZ] 60 E4
Kamen [D] 42 D3
Kamenari [MNE] 152 E3

Kaména Voúrla [GR] 166 E3
Kamen Bryag [BG] 150 F2
Kamengrad [BIH] 144 E2
Kamenica [MK] 154 E3
Kamenice nad Lipou [CZ] 60 E4
Kamenichý Hrad [SK] 64 B4
Kameničná [SK] 74 F3
Kamenka [RUS] 200 E3
Kamennogorsk [RUS] 200 E2
Kamenný Újezd [CZ] 74 A1
Kameno [BG] 150 E4
Kamenovo [BG] 150 C2
Kamensko [HR] 120 E4
Kamensko [HR] 144 E4
Kamenz [D] 46 C4
Kamëz [AL] 160 B1
Kamianets'–Podil's'kyi [UA] 244 D2
Kamianka [UA] 246 D1
Kamianka–Buz'ka [UA] 64 F2
Kamianka–Dniprovs'ka [UA] 246 F2
Kamičak [BIH] 144 E2
Kamień [PL] 64 D2
Kamienica [PL] 64 A3
Kamieniec Ząbkowicki [PL] 62 B2
Kamienna [SK] 64 B4
Kamień Krajeński [PL] 36 B3
Kamienna Góra [PL] 62 A1
Kamień Pomorski [PL] 34 E2
Kamieńsk [PL] 48 D4
Kamínia [GR] 160 C4
Kamínia [GR] 162 E2
Kamin'–Kashyrs'kyi [UA] 50 E2
Kamion [PL] 48 E2
Kammerstein [A] 74 B4
Kamnica [SLO] 120 B3
Kamnik [SLO] 120 B3
Kampánis [GR] 156 A4
Kampen [D] 178 A3
Kampen [NL] 30 C3
Kamperland [NL] 40 D2
Kampiá [GR] 168 E1
Kampinos [PL] 48 E2
Kamp Lintfort [D] 42 C3
Kámpos [GR] 166 D3
Kámpos [GR] 168 F3
Kámpos [GR] 172 D3
Kámpos [GR] 174 A3
Kamula [FIN] 216 C3
Kamyanyets [BY] 38 D4
Kamyanyuki [BY] 38 D4
Kamýk nad Vltavou [CZ] 60 D3
Kanal [SLO] 118 F3
Kanala [FIN] 208 E1
Kanála [GR] 168 C3
Kanália [GR] 160 F4
Kanalláki [GR] 166 B2
Kanatlarci [MK] 160 D1
Kańczuga [PL] 64 D3
Kandava [LV] 234 E3
Kandel [D] 58 B4
Kandern [D] 70 D3
Kandersteg [CH] 116 C2
Kandestederne [DK] 182 E1
Kandīla [GR] 172 D1
Kanepi [EST] 230 F3
Kanestraum [N] 202 E2
Kanfanar [HR] 144 A1
Kangas [FIN] 216 A3
Kangasaho [FIN] 208 E2
Kangasala [FIN] 198 E1
Kangashäkki [FIN] 208 F2
Kangaskylä [FIN] 208 E1
Kangaslampi [FIN] 210 D3
Kangaskylä [FIN] 216 B4
Kangasniemi [FIN] 210 B4
Kangasoja [FIN] 216 B4
Kangasvieri [FIN] 208 E1

Kangos [S] 220 F1
Kanin [PL] 36 A1
Kaninkola [FIN] 198 D3
Kaniv [UA] 242 E4
Kanižarica [SLO] 120 B4
Kanjiža [SRB] 122 C3
Kanjon Cetine [HR] 144 E4
Kanjon Ugar [BIH] 144 F2
Kankaanpää [FIN] 208 C4
Kankainen [FIN] 210 B3
Kankova [SLO] 120 C2
Kånna [S] 184 C3
Kannonkoski [FIN] 208 E2
Kannus [FIN] 216 A4
Kannuskoski [FIN] 200 C2
Kanpaneta / Campanas
  [C] 06 F4
Kansız [TR] 164 D2
Kanstad [N] 224 B4
Kantala [FIN] 210 C3
Kántanos [GR] 174 B4
Kanteemaa [FIN] 198 D2
Kántia [GR] 172 E2
Kantojoki [FIN] 222 E3
Kantokylä [FIN] 216 B3
Kantomaanpää [FIN] 222 B3
Kantornes [N] 224 D2
Kantorp [S] 190 C3
Kantti [FIN] 208 C3
Kanturk [IRL] 10 C3
Kányavár [H] 120 D2
Kaolinovo [BG] 150 D2
Kaona [SRB] 146 E4
Kaonik [BIH] 146 A3
Kaonik [SRB] 146 F4
Kąp [PL] 38 B2
Kapaklı [TR] 158 E4
Kapaklı [TR] 164 D4
Kapandriti [GR] 168 B2
Käpas [LV] 234 D3
Kapčiamiestis [LT] 38 D1
Kapelludden [S] 184 F3
Kapfenberg [A] 74 B4
Kapıkaya [TR] 164 E3
Kapıkırı [TR] 170 C3
Kapinci [HR] 120 F3
Kapini [LV] 236 D3
Kapitan Andreevo [BG] 156 F2
Kaplica (Davlós) [CY] 176 E3
Kaplice [CZ] 74 B2
Kapolcs [H] 120 E1
Kápolna [H] 76 C3
Kaposfüred [H] 120 F2
Kaposvár [H] 120 F2
Kapp [N] 194 B3
Kappel [D] 56 F2
Kappel [D] 70 D2
Kappeln [D] 32 C1
Kappelshamn [S] 234 A2
Kappelskär [S] 190 E2
Kappl [A] 72 E4
Kaprun [A] 72 E4
Kapsáli [GR] 172 E4
Kápsas [GR] 172 D2
Kapune [LV] 236 D3
Kapušany [SK] 76 D1
Kapuvár [H] 74 E4
Karaağaç [TR] 176 F1
Karabayır [TR] 170 E4
Karabeylı [TR] 164 F3
Karabiga [TR] 164 C1
Karabörtlen [TR] 170 D4
Karaburun [TR] 158 D3
Karaburun [TR] 168 F1
Karacaali [TR] 158 E4
Karacabey [TR] 164 D1
Karacaköy [TR] 158 D3
Karacalar [TR] 164 C3
Karacalar [TR] 164 C3
Karaçam [TR] 164 C3
Karacaoğlan [TR] 158 B3
Karacasu [TR] 170 D3

Karaçulha [TR] 176 D1
Karâd [H] 120 F2
Karahallı [TR] 170 E2
Karahisar [TR] 170 E3
Karainebeyli [TR] 164 A1
Karaisen [BG] 150 B3
Karakadağ [TR] 158 C2
Karakagür [TR] 158 B3
Karakamza [TR] 158 B2
Karakaya [TR] 170 C3
Karakiani [GR] 168 A3
Karakoumi (Karakum) [CY]
  176 D3
Karaköy [TR] 164 B2
Karaköy [TR] 170 C2
Karaköy [TR] 170 D2
Karakum (Karakoumi) [CY]
  176 D3
Karakür [TR] 164 E3
Karakurt [TR] 164 D3
Karakuzu [TR] 164 C4
Karala [EST] 230 A3
Karalaks [N] 228 C3
Karali [RUS] 210 F2
Karalin [BY] 38 E3
Karamanci [BG] 156 E2
Karamandere [TR] 158 D3
Karamanlı [TR] 170 F3
Karamürsel [TR] 158 F3
Karamyshevo [RUS] 232 E3
Karancslapujtő [H] 76 C3
Karaova [TR] 170 C4
Karaöz [TR] 176 F1
Karapelit [BG] 150 E2
Karasjok [N] 226 C1
Karasyn [UA] 50 F3
Kárász [H] 122 A3
Karataş [TR] 164 D4
Karats [S] 220 D3
Karavanški Predor [A/SLO]
  118 F2
Karavás [GR] 172 E4
Karaveliler [TR] 164 C3
Karavelovo [BG] 158 A1
Káravos [GR] 168 B2
Karavostasi (Gemikonağı)
  [CY] 176 D3
Karavostásis [GR] 174 C1
Karavukovo [SRB] 122 B4
Karayakuplu [TR] 158 F3
Karbasan [TR] 170 E2
Karbenning [S] 190 C1
Kårböle [S] 196 B1
Karby [DK] 182 C3
Karby [S] 190 E2
Karcag [H] 76 D4
Karczowiska [PL] 46 E4
Kardakáta [GR] 166 B4
Kardam [BG] 150 E2
Kardámaina [GR] 176 A1
Kardámyla [GR] 168 E1
Kardamýli [GR] 172 D3
Kardašova–Řečice [CZ] 60 E4
Karditsa [GR] 166 D2
Kärdla [EST] 230 B2
Kardos [H] 122 D2
Kardosküt [H] 122 D2
Kåremo [S] 184 E3
Karersee / Carezza al Lago
  [I] 118 C2
Karesuando [S] 226 A3
Kärevere [EST] 230 E3
Kargalı [TR] 158 F3
Kargı [TR] 176 D1
Kargów [PL] 64 B2
Kargowa [PL] 46 E2
Karhujärvi [FIN] 222 E3
Karhukangas [FIN] 216 B3
Karhula [FIN] 200 C3
Kárhus [N] 186 B1
Karhusjärvi [FIN] 200 D2
Kari [FIN] 210 C1

Karianí [GR] 162 C1
Karigasniemi [FIN] 226 C1
Karijoki / Bötom [FIN] 208 B3
Karilats [EST] 230 F3
Karine [TR] 170 B3
Karinkanta [FIN] 216 B2
Karis / Karjaa [FIN] 198 E4
Karise [DK] 178 E2
Karitaina [GR] 172 D2
Karjaa / Karis [FIN] 198 E4
Karjala [FIN] 198 C2
Karjalohia [FIN] 198 E3
Kärjenkoski [FIN] 208 B3
Kärkäälä [FIN] 210 B3
Karkaloú [GR] 172 D2
Kârki [LV] 230 E4
Karkkila / Högfors [FIN]
  198 E3
Karkku [FIN] 198 D1
Karklampi [FIN] 198 F1
Kärköla [FIN] 198 E3
Kärkölä [FIN] 198 F2
Karksi–Nuia [EST] 230 D3
Kärla [EST] 230 B3
Karlby [FIN] 198 B4
Karleby / Kokkola [FIN] 214 F4
Karlevistenen [S] 184 E4
Karlewo [PL] 36 E4
Karl Gustav [S] 184 B2
Karlholmsbruk [S] 196 D4
Karlino [PL] 34 F2
Karló / Hailuoto [FIN] 216 A2
Karlobag [HR] 144 C2
Karlovac [HR] 120 C4
Karlóvasi [GR] 168 F2
Karlova Studánka [CZ] 62 C3
Karlovo [BG] 156 D1
Karlovy Vary [CZ] 60 C2
Karłowice [PL] 62 C1
Karlsberg [S] 56 F2
Karlsberg [S] 184 C1
Karlsberg [S] 196 B1
Karlsborg [S] 188 E4
Karlsborg [S] 222 B4
Karlshamn [S] 180 E1
Karlshöfen [D] 32 B3
Karlskoga [S] 188 E2
Karlskrona [S] 180 E1
Karlslunde Strand [DK] 178 E2
Karlsrud [N] 192 E4
Karlsruhe [D] 58 B4
Karlstad [S] 188 D2
Karlstadt [D] 58 D2
Karlštejn [CZ] 60 D3
Karlštejn [CZ] 62 A3
Karlstift [A] 74 B2
Karlstorp [S] 184 D2
Karmas [S] 220 D2
Karmelava [LT] 238 D3
Kärnä [FIN] 208 D1
Kärnä [FIN] 208 F1
Kärnåsens Hembygdsgård
  [S] 188 E1
Karniszyn [PL] 36 E4
Karnobat [BG] 150 D4
Karojba [HR] 118 F4
Karousádes [GR] 160 B4
Karow [D] 32 E3
Karpacz [PL] 60 F1
Karpasolo [FIN] 210 D3
Kárpathos [GR] 176 B3
Karpenísi [GR] 166 D2
Karperó [GR] 160 D3
Karpuzlu [TR] 170 C3
Karrantza / Carranza [E] 86 D3
Kärrbackstrand [S] 194 D3
Kärrbö [S] 190 B1
Karrebæksminde [DK] 178 E3
Kärsämä [FIN] 216 B3
Kärsämäki [FIN] 216 B3
Karsanlahti [FIN] 210 C1
Kärsava [LV] 236 E3

Karsibór [PL] 34 D2
Karsikas [FIN] 216 B3
Karşıyaka [TR] 164 C1
Karsjö [S] 196 C2
Karstädt [D] 32 E3
Karst en Yesos [E] 106 C3
Kärstna [EST] 230 E3
Karstø [N] 186 A2
Karstula [FIN] 208 E2
Kartal [TR] 158 E3
Kartala [BG] 156 B2
Kartena [LT] 238 A2
Kartéri [GR] 166 B2
Karteros [GR] 174 D3
Karthaía [GR] 168 C3
Karttula [FIN] 210 B2
Kartuzy [PL] 36 C2
Karungi [S] 222 B4
Karunki [FIN] 222 B4
Karup [DK] 182 C4
Karuse [EST] 230 C3
Karvala [FIN] 208 D2
Kärväskylä [FIN] 208 F1
Kärvatn [N] 202 E3
Karvia [FIN] 208 C3
Karvik [N] 224 E2
Kärvikhamn [N] 224 D2
Karviná [CZ] 62 D3
Karvio [FIN] 210 D2
Karvounári [GR] 166 B2
Karwia [PL] 36 C1
Karwica [PL] 38 A2
Karyá [GR] 160 E3
Karyá [GR] 166 B3
Karyá [GR] 172 D2
Karyés [GR] 162 A4
Karyés [GR] 162 C2
Karyés [GR] 172 D2
Karyótissa [GR] 160 E2
Karyoúpoli [GR] 172 D3
Kárystos [GR] 160 C2
Kås [DK] 182 D2
Kaş [TR] 176 E2
Kasaba [TR] 176 E1
Kašalj [SRB] 154 C1
Kascyukovichy [BY] 242 D2
Kåseberga [S] 180 D2
Kasejovice [CZ] 60 C4
Kashin [RUS] 240 E2
Kashirskoye [RUS] 238 A3
Kašina [FIN] 120 D3
Kasinka Wielka [PL] 62 F3
Käsmu [EST] 230 D1
Kasnäs [FIN] 198 D4
Käspakas [GR] 162 E2
Kašperk [CZ] 60 C4
Kašperské Hory [CZ] 60 C4
Kaspichan [BG] 150 D3
Kassa [FIN] 222 B2
Kassándreia [GR] 162 B2
Kassari [EST] 230 B2
Kassel [D] 44 B3
Kassiópi [GR] 160 B4
Kassópi [GR] 166 B2
Kastabos [TR] 176 C1
Kastaniá [GR] 160 D4
Kastaniá [GR] 160 D3
Kastaniá [GR] 166 D2
Kastaniá [GR] 166 E4
Kastaniá [GR] 172 D3
Kastaniá [GR] 172 E3
Kastaniés [GR] 158 A2
Kastelholms [FIN] 198 A3
Kastellaun [D] 56 F2
Kastélli [GR] 174 B3

Kastélli [GR] 174 D4
Kaštel Stari [HR] 144 D4
Kaštel Žegarski [HR] 144 D3
Kasterlee [B] 40 E3
Kastl [D] 58 F4
Kastllösa [S] 184 E4
Kastneshamn [N] 224 C3
Kastorf [D] 32 C2
Kastoria [GR] 160 D3
Kastráki [GR] 166 C3
Kastre [EST] 230 F3
Kástro [GR] 162 B4
Kástro [GR] 166 C4
Kástro [GR] 166 F3
Kactrosykiá [GR] 166 B2
Kastrup [DK] 178 F2
Kasvandu [EST] 230 D2
Kaszaper [H] 122 D2
Katáfyto [GR] 156 B3
Katákolo [GR] 172 B2
Kataloinen [FIN] 198 F2
Kätänjoki [FIN] 208 D2
Katápola [GR] 168 E4
Katará Pass [GR] 160 D4
Katastári [GR] 172 B1
Kåtaviken [S] 212 E1
Katerbow [D] 32 F4
Kateríni [GR] 160 F3
Katerʹinska [CZ] 62 B4
Katerloch [A] 74 C4
Katerma [FIN] 216 E3
Kätkasuvanto [FIN] 226 B4
Kätkesuando [S] 226 B4
Katlanovo [MK] 154 D3
Katlanovska Banja [MK]
  154 D3
Katlenburg–Duhm [D] 44 C3
Káto Achaïa [GR] 166 D4
Káto Alepochóri [GR] 168 A2
Káto Aséa [GR] 172 D2
Katochi [GR] 166 C3
Káto Dolianá [GR] 172 E2
Káto Kleitoría [GR] 166 E4
Káto Makrinoú [GR] 166 D3
Káto Nevrokópi [GR] 156 C3
Káto Pýrgos [CY] 176 C3
Káto Samikó [GR] 172 C2
Káto Tithoréa [GR] 166 E3
Katoúna [GR] 166 C3
Káto Velitsés [GR] 166 D4
Káto Vérmio [GR] 160 E2
Katovice [CZ] 60 D4
Káto Vlasía [GR] 166 D4
Káto Vrontoú [GR] 156 C3
Katowice [PL] 62 E2
Káto Zákros [GR] 174 F4
Katrineberg [S] 196 C3
Katrineholm [S] 190 C3
Katschberg Tunnel [A] 118 E1
Kattavía [GR] 176 B2
Katthammarsvik [S] 234 B2
Kattilakoski [FIN] 208 D1
Kättilstad [S] 184 E1
Kattisavan [S] 214 B2
Kattlunds [S] 234 A3
Kattuvuoma [S] 224 E4
Katumäki [FIN] 210 B3
Katundi i Ri [AL] 160 A1
Katuntsi [BG] 156 B3
Katwijk aan Zee [NL] 30 A3
Katy [PL] 34 D3
Kąty [PL] 64 D2
Katyčiai [LT] 238 B2
Katymár [H] 122 B3
Kąty Wrocławskie [PL] 46 F4
Kaub [D] 58 A2
Kaufbeuren [D] 72 B3
Kaufering [D] 72 B2
Kaufungen [D] 44 B3
Kauhajärvi [FIN] 208 C3
Kauhajärvi [FIN] 208 D2
Kauhajoki [FIN] 208 C3

Kauhava [FIN] 208 C2
Kaukalampi [FIN] 198 F2
Kaukela [FIN] 198 F1
Kaukonen [FIN] 222 B1
Kauksi [EST] 230 F2
Kaukuri [FIN] 198 D3
Kaulbach [D] 56 F3
Kaunas [LT] 238 D3
Kaunata [LV] 236 E3
Kauniainen / Grankulla [FIN] 198 F3
Kaunos [FIN] 176 C1
Kauns [A] 72 B4
Kaupanger [N] 192 D2
Kaurajärvi [FIN] 208 C2
Kauria [FIN] 200 C1
Kauša [LV] 236 D3
Kausala [FIN] 200 B2
Kaustby / Kaustinen [FIN] 208 D1
Kaustinen / Kaustby [FIN] 208 D1
Kautokeino [N] 226 B2
Kauttio [RUS] 222 F3
Kauttua [FIN] 198 C2
Káva [H] 76 B4
Kavacık [TR] 158 A3
Kavacık [TR] 164 D2
Kavacık [TR] 170 F2
Kavadarci [MK] 154 E4
Kavajë [AL] 160 A1
Kavak [TR] 158 B4
Kavakdere [TR] 158 B2
Kavaklı [TR] 158 A3
Kavaklı [TR] 158 A3
Kavaklı [TR] 158 B2
Kavaklı [TR] 158 D3
Kavaklıdere [TR] 170 D3
Kavála [GR] 156 D4
Kavarna [BG] 150 F2
Kavaröskaten [S] 196 E4
Kåvenvallen [S] 204 D3
Kävlinge [S] 180 C2
Kávos [GR] 166 B2
Kavoúsi [GR] 174 E4
Kavşıt [TR] 170 C3
Kavýli [GR] 158 A3
Kaxholmen [S] 184 C1
Kayabaşı [TR] 170 F4
Kayaköy [TR] 170 C2
Kayaköy [TR] 176 D1
Kayalar [TR] 164 C2
Kayapa [TR] 158 A2
Kayapa [TR] 164 C3
Käyhäjoki [FIN] 216 A4
Käyhtiönmaa [FIN] 198 C1
Kayı [TR] 158 C3
Käylä [FIN] 222 E3
Kaymakçi [TR] 170 C2
Käyrämö [FIN] 222 C2
Kayran [TR] 170 D2
Kaysersberg [F] 70 D2
Kazaklar [TR] 170 E2
Kazanci [BIH] 144 E3
Kažani [MK] 160 D2
Kazanka [UA] 246 D2
Kazanlük [BG] 156 E1
Kazárma [GR] 172 C3
Kazichene [BG] 156 B1
Kazıklı [TR] 170 C4
Kazimierza Wielka [PL] 64 B2
Kazimierz Biskupi [PL] 48 C2
Kazimierz Dolny [PL] 50 B3
Kazincbarcika [H] 76 D2
Kazlowshchyna [BY] 38 E2
Kazlu–Rūda [LT] 238 C3
Kaznějov [CZ] 60 C3
Kaz'yany [BY] 238 F2
Kcynia [PL] 36 B4
Kdyně [CZ] 60 C4
Kéa [GR] 168 C3
Keadue [IRL] 12 C3

Keady [NIR] 12 E3
Kebrene [TR] 164 B2
Kecel [H] 122 B2
Kecskemét [H] 122 C2
Kėdainiai [LT] 238 D2
Kédros [GR] 166 D2
Kędzierzyn–Koźle [PL] 62 D2
Keel [IRL] 12 A2
Keenagh [IRL] 10 E1
Keenová [CZ] 60 C4
Kefalári [GR] 166 E4
Kéfalos [GR] 176 A1
Kefalóvryso [GR] 160 C3
Kefalóvryso [GR] 160 E3
Kefermarkt [A] 74 B2
Keflavík [IS] 218 A3
Kehidakustány [H] 120 E2
Kehl [D] 70 D1
Kehra [EST] 230 D2
Kehra [EST] 230 D1
Kehrig [D] 56 F2
Kehtna [EST] 230 D2
Keighley [GB] 24 C2
Keihärinkoski [FIN] 208 F1
Keihäskoski [FIN] 198 D2
Keikyä [FIN] 198 D2
Keila–Joa [EST] 230 C2
Keipene [LV] 236 C3
Keisala [FIN] 208 D2
Keitele [FIN] 210 B2
Keith [GB] 14 F3
Kekava [LV] 234 F3
Kékestető [H] 76 C3
Kelankyla [FIN] 222 D4
Kelberg [D] 56 E2
Kelbra [D] 44 D3
Këlcyrë [AL] 160 B3
Kelebia [H] 122 C3
Kelebija [SRB] 122 C3
Kelefá [GR] 172 D3
Kelekçi [TR] 170 E3
Kelemér [H] 76 C2
Keler [TR] 170 B2
Keles [TR] 164 E2
Kelheim [D] 72 D1
Kell [D] 56 E3
Kélla [GR] 160 D2
Kellemberg [D] 42 C3
Kellenhusen [D] 32 D2
Kellerberg [D] 42 E4
Kellinghusen [D] 32 B2
Kelloselkä [FIN] 222 E2
Kells [IRL] 10 A3
Kells [IRL] 10 F1
Kelmė [LT] 238 C2
Kelottijärvi [FIN] 224 F4
Kelso [GB] 20 E2
Keltaniemi [FIN] 200 A2
Kelujärvi [FIN] 222 D1
Kelvä [FIN] 210 E1
Kelviä / Kälviä [FIN] 214 F4
Kemaliye [TR] 164 E4
Kemalpaşa [TR] 170 B2
Kemberg [D] 44 F3
Kemecse [H] 76 E3
Kemence [H] 76 A3
Kemenesmagasi [H] 74 E4
Kemer [TR] 164 B1
Kemer [TR] 170 D3
Kemer [TR] 176 E1
Kemer [TR] 176 F1
Kemerburgaz [TR] 158 E3
Kemerköy [TR] 176 E1
Kémes [H] 120 F3
Kemi [FIN] 216 A1
Kemihaara [FIN] 226 E3
Kemijärvi [FIN] 222 D2
Keminmaa [FIN] 222 B4
Kemiö / Kimito [FIN] 198 D3
Kemnath [D] 58 F3
Kemnitz [D] 34 C2
Kemnitz [D] 44 F2

Kempele [FIN] 216 B2
Kempen [D] 42 C3
Kempolovo [RUS] 200 E4
Kempten [D] 72 B3
Kendal [GB] 20 D4
Kenderes [H] 76 D4
Kendice [SK] 76 D1
Kengis [S] 222 B2
Kengyel [H] 122 D1
Kenmare [IRL] 10 B3
Kento [RUS] 216 F1
Kentrikó [GR] 156 A4
Kéntro [GR] 166 D4
Kenyeri [H] 74 E4
Kenzingen [D] 70 D2
Kepez [TR] 164 A2
Kepice [PL] 36 B2
Kepno [PL] 48 B4
Kepsut [TR] 164 D2
Kerameía [GR] 164 B3
Keramídi [GR] 160 F4
Keramítsa [GR] 160 C4
Keramos [TR] 170 C4
Keramotí [GR] 156 D4
Keräntöjärvi [S] 220 F1
Kerasiá [GR] 168 A1
Kerasochóri [GR] 166 D2
Kerasóna [GR] 166 C2
Keratéa [GR] 168 B3
Keratókampos [GR] 174 D4
Kerava / Kervo [FIN] 198 F3
Kerecsend [H] 76 C3
Kerekegyháza [H] 122 C1
Kerí [GR] 172 B2
Kerien [F] 52 C3
Kerimäki [FIN] 210 D3
Kerisalo [FIN] 210 C3
Kerjean, Château de– [F] 52 B2
Kerken [D] 42 C3
Kerkíni [GR] 156 B4
Kerkonkoski [FIN] 210 B2
Kerkrade [NL] 42 B4
Kérkyra [GR] 160 B4
Kerma [FIN] 210 D3
Kermen [BG] 156 F1
Kernascléden [F] 52 C4
Kerpen [D] 42 C4
Kerpiçlik [TR] 164 E3
Kërrabë [AL] 160 B1
Kersilö [FIN] 222 C1
Kerstimbo [S] 196 C4
Kertemine [DK] 178 D2
Kertészsziget [H] 122 E1
Kertil [TR] 164 D3
Kervo / Kerava [FIN] 198 F3
Kerýneia (Girne) [CY] 176 D3
Kerzers [CH] 70 C4
Kesälahti [FIN] 210 E3
Keşan [TR] 158 B4
Kesarevo [BG] 150 C3
Kesasjäry [S] 220 F3
Kesh [NIR] 12 D2
Keskastel [F] 56 E4
Keskikylä [FIN] 216 A2
Keskinen [FIN] 216 E2
Kesselfall [A] 72 D4
Kesselsdorf [D] 46 B4
Kesteren [NL] 30 C4
Kesti [FIN] 208 D3
Kestilä [FIN] 216 C3
Keswick [GB] 20 D3
Keszthely [H] 120 E2
Kétegyháza [H] 122 E2
Ketenovo [MK] 154 E3
Ketomella [FIN] 226 B3
Kętrzyn [PL] 38 A1
Kétsoproni [H] 122 D2
Kettering [GB] 28 C1
Kettilsby [S] 188 D2
Kettwig [D] 42 D3
Kęty [PL] 62 D3
Ketzin [D] 44 F2

Keula [D] 44 C3
Keuruu [FIN] 208 E3
Keväjärvi [FIN] 226 E2
Kevelaer [D] 42 C2
Kevo [FIN] 226 D1
Kežmarok [SK] 64 B4
Khaapalampi [RUS] 210 F4
Khadziloni [BY] 38 E2
Kharava [BY] 38 E4
Kharmanli [BG] 156 E2
Khaskovo [BG] 156 E2
Khelyulya [RUS] 210 F3
Kherson [UA] 246 E3
Khisariya [BG] 156 D1
Khiytola [RUS] 200 E1
Khlebarovo [BG] 150 C3
Khmel'nyts'kyi [UA] 244 E2
Khmil'nyk [UA] 244 E1
Khodoriv [UA] 244 C2
Kholm [RUS] 240 C3
Kholm–Zhirkovsky [RUS] 240 D3
Khomsk [BY] 38 F4
Khorol [UA] 242 F4
Khotyn [UA] 244 D2
Khoyniki [BY] 242 D3
Khredino [RUS] 232 F3
Khrojna [BG] 156 D2
Khust [UA] 244 C3
Khvoynaya [RUS] 240 D1
Khyriv [UA] 64 D3
Kiáto [GR] 166 E4
Kiaunoriai [LT] 238 C2
Kibæk [DK] 178 B1
Kiberg [N] 228 F2
Kiburi [LV] 234 D4
Kibyra [TR] 170 F3
Kičevo [MK] 154 C4
Kichenitsa [BG] 150 C2
Kichevo [BG] 150 D3
Kidafovice [PL] 64 D3
Kidderminster [GB] 22 F4
Kidlington [GB] 28 B2
Kidričevo [SLO] 120 C2
Kidsgrove [GB] 22 F3
Kidwelly [GB] 26 C1
Kiefersfelden [D] 72 D3
Kiel [D] 32 C1
Kielajoki [FIN] 226 D2
Kielce [PL] 64 B1
Kienberg [A] 118 D1
Kienberg [CH] 70 D3
Kiental [CH] 116 C1
Kierinki [FIN] 222 C2
Kiernozia [PL] 48 D2
Kiesilä [FIN] 200 C1
Kietävälä [FIN] 210 D4
Kietrz [PL] 62 D3
Kiezmark [PL] 36 D2
Kifisiá [GR] 168 B2
Kifjord [N] 228 D1
Kihelkonna [EST] 230 B3
Kihlanki [FIN] 222 B1
Kihniö [FIN] 208 D3
Kiihtelysvaara [FIN] 210 E2
Kiikala [FIN] 198 E3
Kiikka [FIN] 198 D1
Kiikoinen [FIN] 198 C1
Kiiminki [FIN] 216 B2
Kiiskilä [FIN] 216 B4
Kiistala [FIN] 226 C4
Kije [PL] 64 B2
Kijevo [BIH] 146 B4
Kijevo [HR] 144 D3
Kijevo [KS] 154 C2
Kijmajärvi [FIN] 198 D1
Kikerino [RUS] 200 F4
Kikinda [SRB] 122 D3
Kikół [PL] 36 D4
Kikut [N] 192 D3
Kil [N] 186 E3

Kil [S] 188 D2
Kil [S] 188 F2
Kila [GR] 160 D3
Kila [S] 188 D2
Kila [S] 190 C1
Kilafors [S] 196 C2
Kılavuzlar [TR] 170 F3
Kilbaha [IRL] 10 B2
Kilbeggan [IRL] 10 E2
Kilberry [IRL] 10 F1
Kilboghamm [N] 218 E4
Kilcar / Cill Charthaigh [IRL] 12 C1
Kilcock [IRL] 10 F2
Kilcolman Castle [IRL] 10 C3
Kilconnell [IRL] 10 D1
Kilcoole [IRL] 10 F3
Kilcooley Abbey [IRL] 10 D3
Kilcormac [IRL] 10 D2
Kilcullen [IRL] 10 E2
Kilcurry [IRL] 12 E3
Kildare [IRL] 10 E2
Kilderss [NIR] 12 E2
Kildorrery [IRL] 10 C3
Kilebygd [N] 186 E2
Kilen [N] 186 E2
Kilfenora [IRL] 10 C2
Kilfinnane [IRL] 10 C3
Kilgarvan [IRL] 10 B3
Kilifarevo [BG] 150 B4
Kilingi–Nõmme [EST] 230 D3
Kilitbahir [TR] 164 A2
Kilkee [IRL] 10 B2
Kilkeel [NIR] 12 E3
Kilkenny / Cill Chainnigh [IRL] 10 E3
Kilkieran / Cill Chiaráin [IRL] 10 B1
Kilkinkylä [FIN] 200 B1
Kilkinlea [IRL] 10 B3
Kilkís [GR] 156 A4
Kill [IRL] 10 D4
Killadysert [IRL] 10 C2
Killala [IRL] 12 B2
Killaloe [IRL] 10 C2
Killarney / Cill Airne [IRL] 10 B3
Killashandra [IRL] 12 D3
Killashee [IRL] 10 E1
Killeberg [S] 184 C4
Killeigh [IRL] 10 E2
Killenaule [IRL] 10 D3
Killimer [IRL] 10 B2
Killimor [IRL] 10 D2
Killin [GB] 18 C3
Killinge [S] 220 E2
Killinkoski [FIN] 208 D3
Killorglin [IRL] 10 B3
Killybegs [IRL] 12 C2
Killyleagh [NIR] 12 F3
Kilmacduagh Cathedral [IRL] 10 C2
Kilmacrenan [IRL] 12 D1
Kilmacthomas [IRL] 10 D4
Kilmaganny [IRL] 10 D3
Kilmaine [IRL] 12 B3
Kilmallock [IRL] 10 C3
Kilmanahan [IRL] 10 D3
Kilmarnock [GB] 18 C4
Kilmartin [GB] 18 B3
Kilmeaden [IRL] 10 D4
Kilmeage [IRL] 10 E2
Kilmeedy [IRL] 10 C3
Kilmelford [GB] 18 B3
Kilmichael [IRL] 10 B4
Kilmore Quay [IRL] 10 E4
Kilnaleck [IRL] 10 E1
Kilpisjärvi [FIN] 224 E3
Kilpola [FIN] 210 C4
Kilpua [FIN] 216 B3
Kilrush [IRL] 10 B2
Kilshannig [IRL] 10 B3

Kilsmo [S] 190 B3
Kilsyth [GB] 18 C4
Kiltealy [IRL] 10 E3
Kilternan [IRL] 10 F2
Kiltimagh [IRL] 12 B3
Kilvakkala [FIN] 208 D4
Kilvo [S] 220 E2
Kilwinning [GB] 18 C4
Kilyos [TR] 158 E3
Kimási [GR] 168 A1
Kimasozero [RUS] 216 F2
Kiminki [FIN] 208 E2
Kimito / Kemiö [FIN] 198 D3
Kimle [H] 74 E3
Kimméria [GR] 156 D4
Kímola [FIN] 200 B2
Kímolos [GR] 174 C1
Kimonkylä [FIN] 200 B3
Kimovaara [RUS] 216 F3
Kimry [RUS] 240 F2
Kincardine [GB] 18 D3
Kindberg [A] 74 C4
Kindelbrück [D] 44 F2
Kinderdijk, Molens van– [NL] 30 B4
Kinding [D] 58 E4
Kindsjön [S] 194 D3
Kinéta [GR] 168 A2
Kingisepp [RUS] 232 E1
Kingsbridge [GB] 26 C4
Kingscourt [IRL] 10 F1
King's Lynn [GB] 24 E4
Kingston upon Hull [GB] 24 D2
Kington [GB] 22 E4
Kınık [TR] 164 C3
Kınık [TR] 164 E2
Kınık [TR] 170 F4
Kınık [TR] 176 E1
Kınıkyeri [TR] 170 E3
Kinlochborvic [GD] 14 D1
Kinlochewe [GB] 14 D3
Kinlochleven [GB] 14 C4
Kinlough [IRL] 12 C2
Kinna [S] 184 B2
Kinnadoohy [IRL] 12 A3
Kinnarp [S] 184 C1
Kinnbäck [S] 214 E2
Kinnegad [IRL] 10 E2
Kinni [FIN] 200 B1
Kinnitty [IRL] 10 D2
Kinnula [FIN] 208 E1
Kinnuranlahti [FIN] 210 C2
Kinrooi [B] 40 F3
Kinross [GB] 18 D3
Kinsale [IRL] 10 C4
Kinsarvik [N] 192 C3
Kintai [LT] 238 A2
Kintaus [FIN] 208 F3
Kinvarra [IRL] 10 C2
Kióni [GR] 166 B3
Kiónia [GR] 168 D3
Kipen' [RUS] 200 F4
Kipi [EST] 230 B3
Kipilahti [FIN] 200 A3
Kipina [FIN] 216 C1
Kipoureío [GR] 160 D3
Kirakaköngås [FIN] 226 D2
Kiralan [TR] 170 E2
Királyegyháza [H] 120 F3
Kıranköy [TR] 164 E4
Kirawsk [BY] 242 C2
Kiraz [TR] 170 C2
Kirazlı [TR] 164 B2
Kirbla [EST] 230 C3
Kircasalih [TR] 158 B3
Kirchbach [A] 118 E2
Kirchbach [A] 120 C2
Kirchberg [A] 72 D4
Kirchberg [D] 56 F2
Kirchberg [D] 58 D4

Kirchberg an der Pielach [A] 74 C3
Kirchbichl [A] 72 D4
Kirchdorf [D] 32 A4
Kirchdorf [D] 32 D2
Kirchdorf an der Krems [A] 74 A3
Kirchen [D] 30 F1
Kirchenlamitz [D] 60 A2
Kirchentellinsfurt [D] 70 F2
Kirchenthumbach [D] 58 F3
Kirchhain [D] 42 F4
Kirchheim [D] 44 B4
Kirchheimbolanden [D] 58 B3
Kirchhm i.l. [A] 72 E2
Kirchlautor [D] 50 E2
Kirchlinteln [D] 32 B4
Kirchschlag [A] 74 D4
Kirchseeon [D] 72 D3
Kirchundem [D] 42 E3
Kirchzell [D] 58 C3
Kircubbin [NIR] 12 F3
Kireç [TR] 164 D2
Kirikküla [EST] 230 C2
Kırıklar [TR] 164 C2
Kiriou, Roche de– [F] 52 C3
Kiriši [RUS] 240 C1
Kirjaluokta [S] 220 D2
Kir'jamo [RUS] 200 D4
Kırkağaç [TR] 164 C3
Kirkby Lonsdale [GB] 20 D4
Kirkcaldy [GB] 18 D4
Kirkcudbright [GB] 20 C3
Kirkeby [N] 204 C2
Kirkehamn [N] 186 B3
Kirke Hvalsø [DK] 178 E2
Kirkenær [N] 194 C3
Kirkenes [N] 228 F3
Kirkholt [DK] 182 D2
Kírki [GR] 156 E4
Kirkjubæjarklaustur [IS] 218 B3
Kirkjubøur [FR] 182 B2
Kirkkolati [RUS] 210 F3
Kirkkonummi / Kyrkslätt [FIN] 198 D3
Kırklareli [TR] 158 B2
Kirkonkylä [FIN] 198 D3
Kırkpınar [TR] 170 F3
Kirkvollen [N] 204 C2
Kirkwall [GB] 16 C2
Kirn [D] 56 F2
Kirov [RUS] 242 E1
Kirovohrad [UA] 246 D2
Kirovsk [RUS] 240 B1
Kirovskoye [RUS] 200 E3
Kirriemuir [GB] 18 E3
Kirtorf [D] 42 F4
Kiruna [S] 220 E1
Kisa [S] 184 E1
Kisar [H] 76 F3
Kisbér [H] 74 F4
Kisdobsza [H] 120 E3
Kiseljak [BIH] 146 A3
Kishartyán [H] 76 B3
Kisielice [PL] 36 D3
Kisielnica [PL] 38 B3
Kisko [FIN] 198 D3
Kisköre [H] 76 C4
Kiskőrös [H] 122 B2
Kiskundorozsma [H] 122 C3
Kiskunfélegyháza [H] 122 C2
Kiskunhalas [H] 122 C2
Kiskunlacháza [H] 122 B1
Kiskunmajsa [H] 122 C2
Kişla [TR] 164 F5
Kislang [H] 122 A1
Kisslegg [D] 72 A3
Kiszállás [H] 122 C3
Kist [D] 58 D3
Kistanje [HR] 144 D3
Kistelek [H] 122 C2

Kisújszállás [H] 76 D4
Kisvárda [H] 76 E2
Kiszkowo [PL] 48 B1
Kiszombor [H] 122 D3
Kitajaur [S] 220 D4
Kitee [FIN] 210 E3
Kiten [BG] 158 C1
Kition [CY] 176 E3
Kitkiöjärvi [S] 222 A1
Kitkiöjoki [S] 222 A1
Kítros [GR] 160 F3
Kitsi [FIN] 210 E1
Kittelfjäll [S] 212 F2
Kittendorf [D] 32 F3
Kittilä [FIN] 222 B1
Kittsee [A] 74 E3
Kitula [FIN] 198 E3
Kitula [FIN] 208 F4
Kitzbühel [A] 72 D2
Kitzingen [D] 58 D3
Kitzloch–Klamm [A] 72 E4
Kiukainen [FIN] 198 C2
Kiurujärvi [FIN] 222 D1
Kiuruvesi [FIN] 216 C4
Kiutaköngäs [FIN] 222 E3
Kivadár [H] 120 E3
Kivéri [GR] 172 E2
Kivertsi [UA] 50 F4
Kivesjärvi [FIN] 216 C2
Kiviapaja [FIN] 210 D4
Kivijärvi [FIN] 208 E1
Kivik [S] 180 D2
Kivikangas [FIN] 208 D1
Kivilahti [FIN] 210 E1
Kivilompolo [FIN] 222 B3
Kivilompolo [FIN] 226 B3
Kivioja [FIN] 222 C3
Kiviöli [EST] 230 E1
Kivisalmi [FIN] 210 B2
Kivisuo [FIN] 208 F4
Kivivaara [FIN] 216 E3
Kivi–Vigala [EST] 230 C2
Kivotós [GR] 160 D3
Kıyıkışlacık [TR] 170 C4
Kıyıköy [TR] 158 C2
Kızılca [TR] 170 E3
Kızılcabölük [TR] 170 E3
Kızılcasöğüt [TR] 170 E1
Kızılören [TR] 170 F1
Kızılyaka [TR] 170 D4
Kjeeringvika [N] 224 C4
Kjelda [N] 212 D2
Kjeldebotn [N] 224 C4
Kjelfossen [N] 192 C2
Kjellerup [DK] 182 C4
Kjellmyra [N] 194 C3
Kjernmoen [N] 194 C2
Kjerrengvoll [N] 204 B3
Kjerret [N] 188 C1
Kjerringvåg [N] 202 E1
Kjerringvik [N] 204 B1
Kjerstad [N] 202 C3
Kjøllefjord [N] 228 D1
Kjølsdal [N] 202 B4
Kjøra [N] 204 A2
Kjulo / Köyliö [FIN] 198 C2
K. Kamila [GR] 156 B4
Klacka–Lerberg [S] 188 F2
Kläckeberga [S] 184 E3
Kladanj [BIH] 146 B3
Kladnica [SRB] 146 D4
Kladnice [HR] 144 D4
Kladno [CZ] 60 D2
Kladovo [SRB] 148 C1
Kladruby [CZ] 60 C3
Klæbu [N] 204 B2
Klaffer [A] 72 F2
Klagenfurt [A] 120 A2
Klaipéda [LT] 238 A2
Klakegg [N] 192 C1
Klaksvík [FR] 182 B1

Klamila [FIN] 200 C3
Klana [HR] 120 A4
Klanac [HR] 144 C2
Klanjec [HR] 120 C3
Klanxbüll [D] 178 B3
Klåpen [N] 224 C3
Kläppen [S] 214 C1
Kläppsjö [S] 206 C1
Klarabro [S] 194 D3
Klärke [S] 206 C3
Klarup [DK] 182 D3
Klašnice [BIH] 144 F2
Klässbol [S] 188 D2
Klášterec nad Ohří [CZ] 60 C2
Klášter Teplá [CZ] 60 C3
Kláštor pod Znievom [SK] 76 A1
Klatovy [CZ] 60 C4
Klaukkala [FIN] 198 F3
Klaus an der Pyhrnbahn [A] 74 A3
Klausdorf [D] 32 F1
Klausdorf [D] 46 B2
Klausen / Chiusa [I] 118 C2
Klazienaveen [NL] 30 D3
Klazomenai [TR] 168 F1
Klębowiec [PL] 36 A3
Kłecko [PL] 48 B1
Kleczew [PL] 48 C2
Klein Glödnitz [A] 118 F2
Kleinhau [D] 42 C4
Kleinhaugsdorf [A] 74 C2
Klein Vielen [D] 32 F3
Kleinzell [A] 74 C3
Kleisoúra [GR] 166 C2
Kleive [N] 202 D2
Kleivegrend [N] 186 D2
Kleivstua [N] 188 B1
Klejniki [PL] 38 C3
Klemensker [DK] 180 E3
Klement [A] 74 D2
Klempenow [D] 34 C3
Klempicz [PL] 46 E1
Klenčí pod čerchovem [CZ] 60 B4
Klenike [SRB] 154 D2
Klenjé [AL] 160 C1
Klenovica [HR] 144 C1
Kleppe [N] 186 A2
Kleppestø [N] 192 A3
Klerken [B] 40 C3
Klešno [PL] 34 F4
Kleszczele [PL] 38 C4
Kletnya [RUS] 242 E2
Kleve [D] 42 C2
Klevshult [S] 184 C2
Klezeno [RUS] 230 F4
Klichaw [RUS] 242 C2
Kliczków [PL] 46 D4
Klietz [D] 44 E1
Klimátia [GR] 160 C4
Kliment [BG] 150 D2
Klimontów [PL] 64 A2
Klimontów [PL] 64 C1
Klimovo [RUS] 200 E2
Klimpfjäll [S] 212 E2
Klin [RUS] 240 E3
Klina [KS] 154 C2
Klinča Sela [HR] 120 C4
Klingenbach [A] 74 D3
Klingenmünster [D] 58 A4
Klingenthal [D] 60 B2
Klink [D] 32 F3
Klintehamn [S] 234 A2
Klintfors [S] 214 D2
Klintholm [DK] 178 E3
Klintsy [RUS] 242 D2
Klippan [S] 180 C1
Klippen [S] 212 F1
Klippen [S] 214 B3
Klippinge [DK] 178 E2

Klírou [CY] 176 D3
Klis [HR] 144 E4
Klisino [PL] 62 C2
Klisura [BG] 156 C1
Klisura [SRB] 154 E2
Klisura Sutjeske [BIH] 152 E2
Klitmøller [DK] 182 C2
Klixbüll [D] 178 B3
Kljajićevo [SRB] 122 B3
Ključ [BIH] 144 E2
Klobouky u Brna [CZ] 74 D1
Kłobuck [PL] 62 E1
Kłobuczyn [PL] 46 E3
Kłobuk [BIH] 152 C2
Klockestrand [S] 206 D3
Kłoczew [PL] 50 B3
Kłodawa [PL] 46 D1
Kłodawa [PL] 48 C2
Kłodzko [PL] 62 B2
Kløfta [N] 194 B4
Klokkarvik [N] 192 A3
Klokkervik [N] 228 D2
Klokočevac [SRB] 148 C2
Klokočevci [HR] 120 F4
Klokotnica [BIH] 146 B2
Kloogaranna [EST] 230 C2
Klooster [NL] 30 D3
Klos [AL] 154 B3
Klos [AL] 154 B4
Kloštar Ivanić [HR] 120 D4
Kloštar Podravski [HR] 120 E3
Kloster [S] 196 C4
Kloster Arnstein [D] 58 B2
Kloster Chorin [D] 34 C4
Klosterkirche in Altenmarkt [D] 72 E2
Klösterle [A] 72 A4
Klosterneuburg [A] 74 D2
Klosterruiner [N] 202 B4
Klosters [CH] 116 F1
Kloster Schäftlarn [D] 72 C3
Kloster Zella [D] 44 F2
Kloster Zinna [D] 44 F2
Kloten [S] 188 F1
Klötze [D] 44 D1
Klövsträsk [S] 214 D1
Kløvimoen [N] 212 E2
Klövsjö [S] 204 E3
Kl. Plasten [D] 32 F3
Kluczbork [PL] 48 C4
Klucze [PL] 62 E2
Kluczewsko [PL] 62 F1
Kluis [D] 34 C1
Kluki [PL] 36 B1
Kluki [PL] 48 D4
Klukowa Huta [PL] 36 C2
Klupe [BIH] 144 F2
Klusy [PL] 38 B2
Klutsiön [S] 204 D4
Klütz [D] 32 D2
Klyastsitsy [BY] 236 F4
Knaben [N] 186 C3
Knäm [S] 188 B3
Knapphus [N] 186 B1
Knäred [S] 184 B4
Knaresborough [GB] 24 C2
Knarvik [N] 192 B3
Knäsjö [S] 206 D1
Knätten [S] 204 E4
Knebel [DK] 178 D1
Knetzgau [D] 58 E2
Kneža [SLO] 118 F3
Knežak [SLO] 118 F4
Kneževi Vinogradi [HR] 122 B3
Kneževo [HR] 122 B3
Knezha [BG] 148 E3
Knežica [BIH] 144 F1
Knić [SRB] 146 E3
Knídi [GR] 160 D3
Knidos [TR] 176 B1
Kniebis [D] 70 E2
Knighton [GB] 22 E4

Knights Town [IRL] 10 A3
Knin [HR] 144 D3
Knislinge [S] 180 D1
Knittelfeld [A] 120 B1
Knivsta [S] 190 D2
Knjaževac [SRB] 148 C3
Knock [IRL] 12 B3
Knockcroghery [IRL] 10 D1
Knocknalina / Cnocán na Líne [IRL] 12 A2
Knocktopher [IRL] 10 E3
Knokke–Heist [B] 40 C2
Knosós [GR] 174 D3
Knottingley [GB] 24 C2
Knudshoved [DK] 178 D2
Knurów [PL] 62 D2
Knurowiec [PL] 38 B4
Knutby [S] 190 E1
Knutsford [GB] 22 F3
Knyazevo [RUS] 236 F3
Knyazhevo [BG] 156 F2
Knyazhicy [RUS] 232 E3
Knyszyn [PL] 38 C3
Kobarid [SLO] 118 E3
Kobbelveid [N] 220 B1
Kobeliaky [UA] 242 F4
København [DK] 178 F2
Koberg [S] 188 C4
Kobeřice [CZ] 62 D3
Kobiele Wielkie [PL] 48 D4
Kobilyane [BG] 156 E3
Kobišnica [SRB] 148 C2
Koblenz [D] 56 F2
Kobryn [BY] 50 E2
Kobułty [PL] 36 F2
Kobylany [PL] 50 D2
Kobylin [PL] 46 F3
Kobyłka [PL] 48 F2
Kobyl'nik [BY] 238 F3
Kocaali [TR] 158 B4
Kocabaş [TR] 170 E2
Kocaburgaz [TR] 158 C4
Kocaçeşme [TR] 158 B4
Kocaeli (İzmit) [TR] 158 F3
Kočani [MK] 154 E3
Kocapınar [TR] 164 C2
Koçarlı [TR] 170 C3
Kocbeře [CZ] 60 F2
Koceljevo [SRB] 146 D2
Kočerín [BIH] 152 C1
Kočevje [SLO] 120 B4
Kočevska Reka [SLO] 120 B4
Kochel [D] 72 C3
Kocherinovo [BG] 154 F3
Kocherov [UA] 242 D4
Kochmar [BG] 150 D2
Kock [PL] 50 C3
Kocs [H] 74 F4
Kocsér [H] 122 C1
Kocsola [H] 120 F2
Kócsújfalu [H] 76 D4
Koczała [PL] 36 B2
Kodal [N] 186 F2
Koderi [PL] 50 D2
Kodersdorf [D] 46 D4
Kodesjärvi [FIN] 208 C4
Kodrąb [PL] 48 D4
Koetschette [L] 56 D2
Kofçaz [TR] 158 B2
Köflach [A] 120 B1
Kögbo [S] 196 C3
Køge [DK] 178 E2
Kogila [MK] 160 D1
Kogula [EST] 230 B3
Kohfidisch [A] 120 D1
Kohila [EST] 230 D2
Kohtla–Järve [EST] 230 F1
Koigi [EST] 230 E2
Koijärvi [FIN] 198 E2
Koikkala [FIN] 210 C4
Koiláda [GR] 168 A3
Koilovtsi [BG] 148 F3

Kõima [EST] 230 C3
Köinge [S] 184 B3
Koirakoski [FIN] 216 D4
Köisi [EST] 230 E2
Koisjärvi [FIN] 198 E3
Koíta [GR] 172 D4
Koivu [FIN] 222 C3
Koivulahti / Kvevlax [FIN] 208 B2
Koivumäki [FIN] 210 D3
Kojetín [CZ] 62 C4
Kojola [FIN] 216 B4
Kökar [FIN] 198 B4
Kokava nad Rimavicou [SK] 76 C2
Kokemäki / Kumo [FIN] 198 C2
Kokin Brod [SRB] 146 D4
Kokkála [GR] 172 D4
Kokkário [GR] 170 B3
Kokkila [FIN] 198 D3
Kókkina (Erenköy) [CY] 176 C3
Kókkino Neró [GR] 160 F4
Kokkola / Karleby [FIN] 214 F4
Kokkolahti [FIN] 210 D3
Koklë [AL] 160 B2
Koklíoí [GR] 160 C4
Koknese [LV] 236 C3
Kokonvaara [FIN] 210 D2
Kokorevo [RUS] 232 F3
Kokořín [CZ] 60 E2
Koksijde–Bad [B] 40 C3
Kola [BIH] 144 E2
Köla [S] 188 C1
Kołacz [PL] 34 F3
Kołacze [PL] 50 D3
Koláka [GR] 166 F3
Koláre [SK] 76 B3
Kolari [FIN] 222 B2
Kolari [SRB] 146 E2
Kolárovo [SK] 74 F3
Kolåsen [S] 204 D1
Kolašin [MNE] 152 F2
Kolbäck [S] 190 C2
Kołbacz [PL] 34 E3
Kołbaskowo [PL] 34 D3
Kolbenshån [S] 204 D4
Kolbermoor [D] 72 D3
Kołbiel [PL] 50 A2
Kolbotn [N] 188 B1
Kolbudy Górne [PL] 36 C2
Kolbuszowa [PL] 64 C2
Kolby [DK] 178 D2
Kolby Kås [DK] 178 D2
Kołczewo [PL] 34 D2
Kołczygłowy [PL] 36 B2
Koldby [DK] 182 C3
Kolding [DK] 178 B2
Koleczkowo [PL] 36 C1
Koler [S] 214 D1
Kölesd [H] 122 A2
Kolešino [MK] 154 F4
Kolga–Jaani [EST] 230 E3
Kolho [FIN] 208 E3
Koli [FIN] 210 E1
Kolín [CZ] 60 E3
Kolin [PL] 34 E4
Kolind [DK] 182 D3
Kolindrós [GR] 160 E2
Kolinec [CZ] 60 C4
Kölingared [S] 184 C1
Kõljala [EST] 230 B3
Kolka [LV] 230 B4
Kolkonpää [FIN] 210 D3
Kolkontaipale [FIN] 210 C3
Kolky [UA] 242 B4
Kölleda [D] 44 D4
Kollerud [S] 194 D4
Kollínes [GR] 172 D2
Kollund [DK] 178 B3
Kolmården [S] 190 C3

Kolm–Saigurn [A] 118 E1
Köln [D] 42 C4
Kolnica [PL] 62 C1
Kolno [PL] 38 B3
Kolo [BIH] 144 F4
Koło [PL] 48 C2
Kołobrzeg [PL] 34 E2
Kolodruby [UA] 64 F3
Kolokolovo [RUS] 230 F2
Kolokot [KS] 154 D3
Kolomyia [UA] 244 D2
Kolonia Korytnica [PL] 50 B3
Kolonjë [AL] 160 A2
Kolonowskie [PL] 62 D2
Kolophon [TR] 170 B2
Kolossai [TR] 170 E2
Kolossi [CY] 176 D4
Koloveč [CZ] 60 C4
Kolpino [RUS] 240 B1
Kolsätter [S] 194 F1
Kölsillre [S] 204 F4
Kolsjön [S] 206 B4
Kolsva [S] 190 B2
Kolta [SK] 76 A3
Kolu [FIN] 208 E2
Kolunič [BIH] 144 D2
Koluszki [PL] 48 D3
Kolut [SRB] 122 B3
Koluvere [EST] 230 C2
Kolvasozero [RUS] 216 F3
Kolvereid [N] 212 C3
Kolymvári [GR] 174 B3
Komádi [H] 122 E1
Komagvær [N] 228 F2
Koman [AL] 154 B3
Komańcza [PL] 64 D4
Kómara [GR] 156 F3
Komarevo [BG] 148 F3
Komarino [RUS] 232 F3
Komárno [SK] 74 F3
Komarno [UA] 64 F3
Komárom [H] 74 F3
Komar Prolaz [BIH] 144 F3
Koma tou Yialou (Kumyalı) [CY] 176 E3
Komenda [SLO] 120 B3
Kómi [GR] 168 D3
Kómi [GR] 168 E2
Komi Kebir (Büyükkonuk) [CY] 176 E3
Komin [HR] 120 D3
Komirić [SRB] 146 C2
Kómito [GR] 168 C2
Komiža [HR] 152 A2
Komjáti [H] 76 D2
Kömlő [H] 76 C4
Komló [H] 122 A3
Komméno [GR] 166 C2
Kommerniemi [FIN] 210 D4
Kommunary [RUS] 200 E2
Komnes [N] 186 F2
Komniná [GR] 156 D4
Komniná [GR] 160 D2
Komninádes [GR] 160 C3
Komorane [KS] 154 C2
Komorowo [PL] 46 F4
Komorzno [PL] 48 B4
Komossa [FIN] 208 C1
Komotiní [GR] 156 E4
Kömpöc [H] 122 C2
Kompolje [HR] 144 C2
Kömpöti [GR] 166 C2
Komsomol'sk [RUS] 36 F1
Komsomol'skoye [RUS] 200 D2
Komula [FIN] 216 D3
Komunari [BG] 150 D3
Komuniga [BG] 156 E2
Kömürköy [TR] 158 C2
Konak [SRB] 122 D4
Konakpınar [TR] 164 D2
Konarevo [SRB] 146 E4

Konarzyny [PL] 36 B3
Končanica [HR] 120 E4
Konče [MK] 154 E4
Konchansko–Suvorovskoye [RUS] 240 D1
Kondolovo [BG] 158 C1
Kondorfa [H] 120 D2
Kondoros [H] 122 D2
Kondrić [HR] 146 B1
Koněpruské Jeskyně [CZ] 60 D3
Køng [DK] 178 E3
Konga [S] 184 D4
Köngäs [FIN] 226 C4
Köngäs [FIN] 226 D4
Kongasmäki [FIN] 216 C2
Kongensgruve [N] 186 E1
Kongensvollen [N] 202 F1
Kongerslev [DK] 182 D3
Kong Humbles Grav [DK] 178 D3
Konginkangas [FIN] 208 F2
Kongsberg [N] 186 E1
Kongselva [N] 224 B4
Kongsfjord [N] 228 E1
Kongshavn [N] 186 D3
Kongsmoen [N] 212 D3
Kongsnes [N] 192 C2
Kongsvinger [N] 194 C4
Konice [CZ] 62 B3
Koniecpol [PL] 62 F1
Konieczna [PL] 64 C4
König–Otto–Höhle [D] 58 F4
Königsbrück [D] 46 B4
Königsbrunn [D] 72 B2
Königsee [D] 58 E1
Königsfeld [D] 70 E2
Königshofen [D] 58 D3
Königslutter [D] 44 D2
Königssee [D] 72 E4
Königsstuhl [D] 34 C1
Königstein [D] 58 B2
Königstein [D] 60 D1
Königswartha [D] 46 C4
Königswiesen [A] 74 B2
Königswinter [D] 42 D4
Königs–Wusterhausen [D] 46 B2
Konin [PL] 48 C2
Koniščina [HR] 120 D3
Koniskós [GR] 160 E4
Konispol [AL] 160 B4
Kónitsa [GR] 160 C3
Köniz [CH] 70 D4
Konjevići [BIH] 146 C3
Konjic [BIH] 146 A4
Konjsko [BIH] 152 D3
Könnern [D] 44 E3
Konnerud [N] 186 F1
Konnevesi [FIN] 210 B2
Könni [FIN] 208 C2
Könnu [EST] 230 D1
Konopiště [CZ] 60 E3
Konopiste [MK] 160 E1
Konotop [PL] 34 F3
Konotop [PL] 46 E3
Końskie [PL] 48 E4
Konsko [MK] 160 E1
Konsmo [N] 186 B3
Konstancin–Jeziorna [PL] 48 F2
Konstantynów [PL] 50 C2
Konstantynów Łodzki [PL] 48 D3
Konstanz [D] 70 F3
Konteenperä [FIN] 222 D3
Kontiainen [FIN] 208 D1
Kontiäs [GR] 162 E2
Kontinjoki [FIN] 216 D3
Kontiolahti [FIN] 210 E2
Kontiomäki [FIN] 216 D3
Kontiovaara [FIN] 210 E1

Kontiovaara [FIN] 210 E1
Kontkala [FIN] 210 D2
Kontokáli [GR] 160 B4
Kontopoúli [GR] 162 E2
Konttajärvi [FIN] 222 B2
Konush [BG] 156 E2
Konyavo [BG] 154 F3
Konyshevka [RUS] 242 F2
Konz [D] 56 E3
Koonga [EST] 230 C3
Köörtilä [FIN] 208 B4
Koosa [EST] 230 F3
Kopachivka [UA] 50 F4
Koparnes [N] 202 B3
Kópasker [IS] 218 C2
Köpenick [D] 46 B2
Koper [SLO] 118 F4
Köpernitz [D] 32 F4
Kopervik [N] 186 A2
Kóphága [H] 74 D4
Kopidlno [CZ] 60 E2
Köping [S] 190 B2
Köpingsvik [S] 184 F3
Kopisto [FIN] 216 A3
Koplik [AL] 152 F3
Köpmanholmen [S] 206 D2
Köpmannebro [S] 188 C3
Koporin, Manastir– [SRB] 146 E3
Kopor'ye [RUS] 200 E4
Koppang [N] 194 B2
Koppangen [N] 224 E2
Kopparberg [S] 188 F1
Kopperå [N] 204 C2
Kopperby [D] 32 C1
Koppom [S] 188 C1
Koprivets [BG] 150 C3
Koprivlen [PL] 156 C3
Koprivnica [HR] 120 D3
Koprivnica [SRB] 148 C2
Kopřivnice [CZ] 62 D3
Koprivshtitsa [BG] 156 C1
Köprübaşı [TR] 164 E4
Köprübaşı [TR] 170 D2
Köprühisar [TR] 158 F4
Köprüören [TR] 164 F2
Koprzywnica [PL] 64 C2
Kopsa [FIN] 216 A3
Köpu [EST] 230 D3
Korbach [D] 42 F3
Korbevac [SRB] 154 E2
Korbielów [PL] 62 E3
Korbovo [SRB] 148 C1
Korbu [MD] 244 E2
Korcë [AL] 160 C2
Korčula [HR] 152 C2
Korczew [PL] 50 C1
Korczycõw [PL] 46 D2
Korczyna [PL] 64 C3
Korenica [HR] 144 D2
Korentovaara [FIN] 210 F1
Korespohja [FIN] 208 F4
Körez [TR] 164 F4
Korfantów [PL] 62 C2
Körfez [TR] 158 F3
Kórfos [GR] 168 A3
Korgen [N] 212 E1
Korgene [LV] 230 D4
Koria [FIN] 200 B2
Korinós [GR] 160 F3
Korinth [DK] 178 C3
Kórinthos [GR] 166 F4
Kórinthos, Arhéa– [GR] 166 F4
Korisós [GR] 160 D2
Korissía [GR] 168 C3
Korita [BIH] 152 D2
Korita [HR] 152 C3
Koritata [BG] 156 D2
Koritë [AL] 160 B2
Koriten [BG] 150 E2
Kórithi [GR] 166 C4

Korkea [FIN] 216 E3
Korkeakangas [FIN] 210 E3
Korlátka [SK] 74 E2
Körmend [H] 120 D1
Kormu [FIN] 198 E2
Korne [PL] 36 C2
Korneuburg [A] 74 D2
Kornevo [RUS] 36 E1
Kórnik [PL] 46 F2
Kornsjø [N] 188 C3
Kornwestheim [D] 70 F1
Kőrnye [H] 74 F4
Koromačno [HR] 144 B2
Koróni [GR] 172 D3
Kóronos [GR] 168 E4
Koronoúda [GR] 156 B4
Koronowo [PL] 36 C3
Korop [UA] 242 E3
Koropí [GR] 168 B3
Körösladány [H] 122 E1
Köröstarcsa [H] 122 D2
Korosten' [UA] 242 C4
Korostyshiv [UA] 242 D4
Korpavár [H] 120 E2
Korpi [FIN] 216 A4
Korpijärvi [FIN] 210 B4
Korpikå [S] 222 A4
Korpilahti [FIN] 208 F3
Korpilombolo [S] 222 A2
Korpo / Korppoo [FIN] 198 C4
Korpoström [FIN] 198 C4
Korppinen [FIN] 208 F1
Korppoo / Korpo [FIN] 198 C4
Korrigans [F] 66 B2
Korrö [S] 184 D3
Korsåsen [S] 196 B2
Korsberga [S] 184 D2
Korsberga [S] 188 E4
Korsen [N] 212 C4
Korsholm [S] 180 C2
Korsholm / Mustasaari [FIN]
  208 B2
Korskrogen [S] 196 B1
Korsmo [N] 194 C4
Korsnäs [FIN] 208 B2
Korsør [DK] 182 C2
Korsør [DK] 178 D2
Korsun'–Shevchenkivs'kyi
  [UA] 246 D1
Korsveien [N] 204 B2
Korsvoll [N] 202 E2
Korsze [PL] 36 F2
Körteke [TR] 170 D3
Kortekylä [FIN] 208 D2
Korten [BG] 156 E1
Kortenberg [B] 40 E3
Kortesjärvi [FIN] 208 C1
Kortevaara [FIN] 216 E3
Kórthi [GR] 168 D3
Kortrijk (Courtrai) [B] 40 C3
Korucu [TR] 164 C3
Koruköv [TR] 158 B2
Koruköy [TR] 164 B1
Korup [DK] 178 C2
Korušce [HR] 144 E4
Korva [S] 222 B3
Korvala [FIN] 222 C2
Korvaluoma [FIN] 208 C4
Korvenkylä [FIN] 216 B3
Korvensuu [FIN] 198 C3
Koryčany [CZ] 74 E1
Korycin [PL] 38 C2
Korydallós [GR] 160 D4
Koryfási [GR] 172 C3
Korytnica–Kúpele [SK] 76 B1
Korytno [RUS] 232 E3
Korzeniste [PL] 38 B3
Korzenna [PL] 64 B3
Korzybie [PL] 36 B2
Kos [GR] 176 A1
Kosanica [MNE] 152 F2
Košarovce [SK] 64 C4

Kosava [BY] 38 E3
Kościan [PL] 46 F2
Kościelec [PL] 48 C2
Kościerzyna [PL] 36 C2
Kose [EST] 230 D2
Kösedere [TR] 162 F3
Kosel [MK] 160 C1
Koserow [D] 34 D2
Košetice [CZ] 60 E3
Košice [SK] 76 D2
Kosik [RUS] 242 E1
Kosinë [AL] 160 B3
Kosjerić [SRB] 146 D3
Kösk [TR] 170 C3
Koška [HR] 122 A4
Kookeby [FIN] 208 C2
Koskela [FIN] 208 D2
Koskenkorva [FIN] 208 C2
Koskenkylä [FIN] 210 B2
Koskenkylä / Forsby [FIN]
  200 B3
Koskenniska [FIN] 226 D2
Koskenpää [FIN] 208 E3
Koski [FIN] 198 D3
Koski [FIN] 198 F2
Koski [FIN] 216 C4
Koskimäki [FIN] 208 C2
Kóskina [GR] 168 B2
Koskolovo [RUS] 200 D4
Koškovce [SK] 64 C4
Koskue [FIN] 208 C3
Koskullskulle [S] 220 E2
Kosmás [GR] 172 E3
Kósmio [GR] 156 E4
Kosmo [N] 220 A2
Kosmonosy [CZ] 60 E2
Kosola [FIN] 208 C2
Kosovo Polje [KS] 154 C2
Kosovska Mitrovica [KS]
  154 C2
Kosów Lacki [PL] 38 B4
Kössen [A] 72 B3
Kost [CZ] 60 E2
Kósta [GR] 168 A4
Kosta [S] 184 D3
Kostanjevac [HR] 120 C4
Kostanjevica [SLO] 120 C3
Kosta Perchevo [BG] 148 C3
Kostelec [CZ] 60 F4
Kostelec nad Černými [CZ]
  60 E3
Kostelec nad Labem [CZ]
  60 E2
Kostelec nad Orlicí [CZ] 62 B3
Kostelec na Hané [CZ] 62 C4
Kostenets [BG] 156 C2
Kosti [BG] 158 C2
Kostinbrod [BG] 154 F2
Kostojeviči [SRB] 146 D3
Kostolac [SRB] 146 E2
Kostomłoty [PL] 46 F4
Kostomuksha [RUS] 216 E2
Kostopil' [UA] 242 B4
Kóstos [GR] 168 D4
Kostów [PL] 48 C4
Kostrzyń [PL] 46 C1
Kostrzyn [PL] 48 A2
Kosturino [MK] 154 F4
Košumberk [CZ] 62 A3
Košutovo [KS] 154 C2
Koszalin [PL] 34 F2
Koszęcin [PL] 62 E2
Kőszeg [H] 74 D4
Kosztowo [PL] 36 B4
Koszuty [PL] 46 F2
Koszyce [PL] 64 B2
Kótaj [H] 76 E3
Kotala [FIN] 208 D3
Kótas [GR] 160 D2
Kotë [AL] 160 A3
Kotel [BG] 150 C4
Kötelec [H] 76 C4

Köthen [D] 44 E3
Kotila [FIN] 216 D2
Kotka [FIN] 200 C3
Kotlarnia [PL] 62 D2
Kotlice [PL] 50 D4
Kotlin [PL] 48 B3
Kotly [RUS] 200 E4
Kotola [FIN] 222 E2
Kotor [MNE] 152 E3
Kotorsko [BIH] 146 A2
Kotor Varoš [BIH] 144 F2
Kotovs'k [UA] 244 F2
Kotowice [PL] 62 E2
Kótronas [GR] 172 D3
Kötschach–Mauthen [A]
  118 E2
Kotten [NL] 30 D4
Köttkulla [S] 184 C2
Kotvala [FIN] 208 E1
Kötzting [D] 60 B4
Koufália [GR] 160 F2
Koufós [GR] 162 C2
Kouhi [FIN] 210 B3
Koúklia [CY] 176 C4
Koukounariés [GR] 162 B4
Koúmanis [GR] 172 C1
Koúndouros [GR] 168 C3
Koúrenta [GR] 160 C4
Kourion [CY] 176 D4
Kournás [GR] 174 C3
Kouroúta [GR] 172 B2
Koutsó [GR] 156 D4
Koutsóchero [GR] 160 E4
Koutsourás [GR] 174 E4
Koutsovéntis (Güngör) [CY]
  176 D3
Kouvola [FIN] 200 B2
Kovačevac [SRB] 146 E2
Kovachevica [BG] 156 C3
Kovachevtsi [BG] 156 B2
Kovachica [BG] 148 D3
Kovačica [SRB] 146 E1
Kovarce [SK] 74 F2
Kovarskas [LT] 238 D2
Kovel' [UA] 50 E3
Kovero [FIN] 210 E2
Kovin [SRB] 146 E2
Kovland [S] 206 C3
Kövra [S] 204 E3
Kowal [PL] 48 D2
Kowale Oleckie [PL] 38 B1
Kowalewo Pomorskie [PL]
  36 D4
Kowary [PL] 60 F1
Köyceğiz [TR] 170 D4
Köyhänperä [FIN] 216 B4
Köyliö / Kjulo [FIN] 198 C2
Köysivaara [FIN] 226 D3
Koyunhis [TR] 158 F4
Koyunköy [TR] 164 F1
Koyunoba [TR] 164 E3
Kozak [TR] 164 C3
Kozáni [GR] 160 D3
Kozarac [BIH] 144 E2
Kozarac [HR] 122 B3
Kozar Belene [BG]
  150 A3
Kozel [CZ] 60 C3
Kozel'sk [RUS] 240 F4
Koziatyn [UA] 244 E1
Kozica [HR] 152 C2
Koziebrody [PL] 36 E4
Koziegłowy [PL] 62 E2
Kozienice [PL] 50 B3
Kozí Hrádek [CZ] 60 E4
Kozina [SLO] 118 F4
Kozine [LLV] 236 E2
Kozjak [MK] 160 C2
Kozlar [TR] 170 E3
Kozlodui [BG] 148 E3
Kozlov Bereg [RUS] 230 F2
Kozłowo [PL] 36 E3

Kozluk [BIH] 146 C2
Kozly [CZ] 60 D2
Kozly [RUS] 232 E4
Kožmin [PL] 48 B3
Kozojedy [CZ] 60 C3
Kozolupy [CZ] 60 C3
Kozpınar [TR] 164 F1
Kożuchów [PL] 46 D3
Kozy [PL] 62 E3
Kozyürük [TR] 158 B3
Krääkkiö [FIN] 198 D2
Krabbesholm [DK]
  182 C3
Krabi [EST] 230 F4
Kräckelbäcken [S] 194 E2
Kraddsele [S] 214 A1
Kraftverk Harsprånget [S]
  220 D3
Krąg [PL] 36 A2
Kragelund [DK] 182 E2
Kragenæs [DK] 178 D3
Kragerø [N] 186 E3
Kragujevac [SRB] 146 E3
Krahës [AL] 160 B3
Kraište [BG] 156 B2
Krajenka [PL] 36 B3
Krajišnik [SRB] 122 D4
Krajn [AL] 152 F4
Krajna [SLO] 120 C2
Krajná Poľana [SK] 64 C4
Krajnik Gorny [PL] 34 D4
Krakača [BIH] 144 D1
Kråkan [S] 206 E2
Kråkeland [N] 186 C3
Krakés [LT] 238 C2
Krakhella [N] 192 B2
Kräklingbo [S] 234 A2
Kråklivollen [N] 204 B2
Kråkmo [N] 220 B1
Krakol'ye [RUS] 200 D4
Krakovec [UA] 244 C1
Krakovets' [UA] 64 E3
Kraków [PL] 62 F3
Krakow am See [D] 32 E3
Kråksmåla [S] 184 E3
Králíky [CZ] 62 B3
Kraljeva Sutjeska [BIH] 146 B3
Kraljevica [HR] 144 B1
Kraljevo [SRB] 146 E4
Kraľovany [SK] 62 E4
Král'ov Brod [SK] 74 F3
Královec [CZ] 60 F2
Kralovice [CZ] 60 C3
Kráľovský Chlmec [SK] 76 E2
Kralupy nad Vltavou [CZ]
  60 D2
Kramfors [S] 206 D3
Kramolin [BG] 150 A3
Krampenes [N] 228 F2
Kramsach [A] 72 C4
Kråmvik [N] 186 D1
Kramvik [N] 228 F2
Kraneá [GR] 160 E3
Kranenburg [D] 30 C4
Kranevo [BG] 150 E4
Krångede [S] 206 B2
Krani [MK] 160 C2
Kraniá [GR] 160 D4
Kraniá Elassónas [GR] 160 E3
Kranichfeld [D] 44 D4
Kranídi [GR] 168 A3
Kranj [SLO] 120 B3
Kranjska Gora [SLO] 118 F2
Krapina [HR] 120 C3
Krapinske Toplice [HR] 120 C3
Krapkowice [PL] 62 D2
Krapperup [S] 178 F1
Krasen [BG] 150 E2
Krasiczyn [PL] 64 D3
Krasikovshchina [RUS] 232 E3
Kräslava [LV] 236 D4

Krásná Hora nad Vltavou
  [CZ] 60 D3
Krásna Hôrka [SK] 76 D2
Krásná Lípa [CZ] 60 E1
Krasnasyel'ski [BY] 38 E3
Krasnaya Hora [RUS] 242 D2
Krasne Folwarczne [PL] 38 C3
Kraśniczyn [PL] 50 D4
Krašnik [PL] 50 B4
Krasnogorodsk [RUS] 236 E3
Krasnogorodskoye [RUS]
  240 B3
Krasnogorsk [RUS] 240 F3
Krasnohryvka [UA] 246 C1
Krásno nad Kysucou [SK]
  62 E4
Krasnoperekops'k [UA] 246 F3
Krasnopol [PL] 38 C1
Krasnopol'e [BY] 242 D2
Krasnosel'e [RUS] 38 B1
Krasnosielc [PL] 38 A3
Krasnovo [BG] 156 C1
Krasnoye [RUS] 236 F3
Krasnoye [RUS] 238 A3
Krasnoye Selo [RUS] 200 F4
Krasnoznamensk [RUS]
  238 B3
Krasnye Prudy [RUS] 232 E4
Krasnyje Gory [RUS] 232 F2
Krasnystaw [PL] 50 C4
Krasnyy Bor [RUS] 36 F1
Krasnyy Kholm [RUS] 240 E1
Krasnyy Luch [RUS] 232 E1
Krasocin [PL] 62 F1
Krašov [CZ] 60 C3
Krastë [AL] 160 B1
Krasulje [BIH] 144 E2
Krasznokvajda [H] 76 D2
Krátigos [GR] 164 B4
Kratovo [MK] 154 E3
Kratovska Stena [SRB] 146 D3
Krauchenwies [D] 70 F2
Kraushöhle [A] 74 B4
Krautheim [D] 58 C3
Kravaře [CZ] 60 D2
Kravaře [CZ] 62 D3
Kravarsko [HR] 120 C4
Kravik [N] 192 E4
Kravnsø [DK] 178 A2
Kraymorie [BG] 158 B1
Kražiaai [LT] 238 C2
Kreba–Neudorf [D] 46 C4
Krefeld [D] 42 C3
Kregme [DK] 178 E1
Kreje Lurës [AL] 154 B4
Krekila [FIN] 216 A4
Kremastí [GR] 172 E3
Kremastí [GR] 176 C2
Kremenchuk [UA] 246 E1
Kremenets' [UA] 244 D1
Kremmen [D] 44 F1
Kremna [SRB] 146 C3
Kremnica [SK] 76 A2
Krems [A] 74 C2
Kremsmünster [A] 74 A3
Křemže [CZ] 74 A1
Krenkerup [DK] 178 E3
Křenov [CZ] 62 B3
Krepa [PL] 48 C3
Krepcha [BG] 150 C3
Krepoljin [SRB] 146 F3
Kresna [BG] 156 B3
Kréstena [GR] 172 C2
Kresttsy [RUS] 240 C2
Kretinga [LT] 238 A2
Kreuth [D] 72 C3
Kreuzenstein [A] 74 D2
Kreuzlingen [CH] 70 F3
Kreuztal [D] 42 E4
Kreva [BY] 238 F4
Kriakénava [LT] 238 D2
Krichim [BG] 156 C2

Kričov [BY] 242 D2
Kriebstein [D] 44 F4
Krieglach [A] 74 C4
Kriezā [GR] 168 B2
Kríkello [GR] 166 D3
Krimml [A] 72 D4
Krimmler Wasserfälle [A]
72 D4
Křinec [CZ] 60 E2
Kringla [N] 192 B2
Krinídes [GR] 156 C4
Kristall–Höhle [D] 58 B1
Kristalopig [GR] 160 D2
Kristberg [S] 188 F3
Kristdala [S] 184 E2
Kristianopel [S] 180 F1
Kristiansand [N] 186 D4
Kristianstad [S] 180 D1
Kristiansund [N] 202 D2
Kristiinankaupunki /
Kristinestad [FIN] 208 B3
Kristineberg [S] 194 D2
Kristineberg [S] 214 C2
Kristinefors [S] 194 D4
Kristinehamn [S] 188 E2
Kristinehov [S] 180 D2
Kristinestad /
Kristiinankaupunki [FIN]
208 B3
Kristoffervalen [N] 224 E1
Kristóni [GR] 156 A4
Kristvallabrunn [S] 184 E3
Kritiniá [GR] 176 B2
Kritsá [GR] 174 E4
Kriva Feja [SRB] 154 E2
Kriváň [SK] 76 B2
Krivanda [LV] 236 E3
Kriva Palanka [MK] 154 E3
Kriva reka [BG] 150 F3
Krivčevo [SLO] 120 B3
Krivelj [SRB] 148 B2
Krivi Dol [MK] 154 E3
Krivodol [BG] 148 D3
Krivogaštani [MK] 160 D1
Křivoklát [CZ] 60 D3
Krivolak [MK] 154 E4
Križ [HR] 120 D4
Križanov [CZ] 62 A4
Križevci [HR] 120 D3
Krk [HR] 144 B1
Krka [SLO] 120 B3
Krklja [MK] 154 E3
Krnjača [SRB] 146 E2
Krnjak [HR] 120 C4
Krnjeuša [BIH] 144 D2
Krnov [CZ] 62 C3
Krobia [PL] 46 F3
Kroczyce [PL] 62 E2
Krøderen [N] 192 B4
Krogsbølle [DK] 178 C2
Krogsered [S] 184 B3
Krokan [N] 186 D1
Krokebol [N] 188 B1
Krokeés [GR] 172 D3
Krokek [S] 190 C3
Kroken [N] 212 E2
Kroken [N] 224 D2
Kroknes [N] 228 F2
Krokom [S] 204 E2
Krokowa [PL] 36 C1
Kroksjö [S] 214 B3
Kroksjö [S] 214 D3
Krokstad [S] 188 C3
Krokstadelva [N] 186 F1
Krokstadøra [N] 202 F2
Krokstorp [S] 184 E2
Krokstrand [N] 220 A3
Kroksund [N] 188 C2
Kroktorp [S] 194 E4
Krokvåg [S] 206 B2
Krokvik [S] 220 D1
Krolevets' [UA] 242 E3

Królewiec [PL] 48 E4
Królowy Most [PL] 38 D3
Kroměříž [CZ] 62 C4
Kromerowo [PL] 36 F2
Krompachy [SK] 76 D1
Kromy [RUS] 242 F2
Kronach [D] 58 F2
Kronegg [A] 74 B2
Kronoby / Kruunupyy [FIN]
214 F4
Kronsgaard [D] 178 C3
Kronshtadt [RUS] 200 E3
Kropa [SLO] 118 F3
Kröpelin [D] 32 E2
Kropp [D] 32 B1
Kroppenstedt [D] 44 D2
Kropstädt [D] 44 F2
Krościenko [PL] 64 D3
Krościenko nad Dunajcem
[PL] 64 B4
Krosna [LT] 38 C1
Krośniewice [PL] 48 D2
Krosno [PL] 36 D2
Krosno [PL] 64 C3
Krosno Odrzańskie [PL] 46 D2
Krossbu [N] 192 D1
Krossen [N] 186 C4
Krostitz [D] 44 E3
Krote [LV] 234 D4
Krotoszyn [PL] 48 B3
Krouna [CZ] 62 A3
Kršan [HR] 144 B1
Kršete [HR] 118 E4
Krško [SLO] 120 C3
Krstac [MNE] 152 E3
Krstac [MNE] 152 E2
Kručov [SK] 64 C4
Krucz [PL] 36 A4
Kruge [HR] 144 D2
Kruglovo [RUS] 36 E1
Kruiningen [NL] 40 D2
Kruisland [NL] 40 D2
Krujë [AL] 154 B4
Kruk [N] 192 E2
Krukowo [PL] 36 F3
Krumbach [A] 74 D4
Krumbach [D] 72 B2
Krumë [AL] 154 B3
Krummendorf [D] 32 E2
Krumovgrad [BG] 156 E3
Krumpendorf [A] 120 A2
Krün [D] 72 C4
Krupá [CZ] 60 D2
Krupac [BIH] 146 A4
Krupac [BIH] 146 B4
Krupaja [SRB] 146 F3
Krupa na Vrbasu [BIH] 144 E2
Krupanj [SRB] 146 C3
Krupe [PL] 50 D4
Krupina [SK] 76 B2
Krupište [MK] 154 E3
Krupnik [BG] 154 F3
Krupp [RUS] 232 E3
Krusá [DK] 178 B3
Kruščić [SRB] 122 B4
Kruševac [SRB] 146 F4
Kruševo [MK] 160 D1
Krusha [BG] 148 D4
Krushari [BG] 150 E2
Krushevets [BG] 158 B1
Krushovene [BG] 148 F3
Krushovica [BG] 148 E2
Kruszwica [PL] 48 C1
Kruszyna [PL] 48 D4
Krutcy [RUS] 232 F4
Krute [MNE] 152 E4
Krutneset [N] 212 E1
Kruunupyy / Kronoby [FIN]
214 F4
Kruusila [FIN] 198 D3

Krya [TR] 176 D1
Kryakusa [RUS] 232 E3
Krýa Vrýsi [GR] 160 E2
Kryekuq [AL] 160 A2
Krylbo [S] 190 C1
Kryle [DK] 182 B4
Krylovo [RUS] 38 A1
Krymne [UA] 50 E3
Krynica [PL] 64 B4
Krynica Morska [PL] 36 D2
Krynki [PL] 38 D3
Kryopigí [GR] 162 B2
Kryspinów [PL] 62 F3
Kryve Ozero [UA] 246 D2
Kryvyi Rih [UA] 246 E2
Krzęcin [PL] 34 E4
Krzeczów [PL] 48 C4
Krzelów [PL] 46 E3
Krzepice [PL] 48 C4
Krzeszów [PL] 62 A1
Krzeszów [PL] 64 D2
Krzeszowice [PL] 62 F2
Krzeszyce [PL] 46 D1
Krzynowłoga Mała [PL] 36 F4
Krzystkowice [PL] 46 D3
Krzywiń [PL] 46 F3
Krzyzewo [PL] 38 A3
Krzyż Wlkp. [PL] 34 F4
Ksar–es–Seghir [MA] 104 B4
Książ [PL] 62 B1
Książ Wielki [PL] 62 F2
Ktísmata [GR] 160 C4
Kubbe [S] 206 D2
Küblis [CH] 116 F1
Kubrat [BG] 150 C2
Kuç [AL] 160 B3
Kučevo [SRB] 146 F2
Kuchl [A] 72 E3
Kučište [KS] 154 B2
Kucovë [AL] 160 B2
Küçükbahçe [TR] 168 E1
Küçükçekmece [TR] 158 D3
Küçükkuyu [TR] 164 B3
Kuddby [S] 190 C4
Kudever' [RUS] 236 F3
Kudirkos Naumiestis [LT]
238 C3
Kudowa–Zdrój [PL] 62 B2
Kufstein [A] 72 D3
Kuggeboda [S] 180 E1
Kuggerud [N] 194 C4
Kuha [FIN] 222 D4
Kuhanen [FIN] 210 C2
Kühlungsborn [D] 32 E2
Kuhmalahti [FIN] 198 E1
Kuhmo [FIN] 216 E3
Kuhmoinen [FIN] 198 F1
Kühsen [D] 32 C3
Kuhstedt [D] 32 B3
Kühtai [A] 72 B4
Kuimetsa [EST] 230 D2
Kuivajärvi [FIN] 216 E2
Kuivaniemi [FIN] 216 B1
Kuivanto [FIN] 200 B2
Kuivasjärvi [FIN] 208 C3
Kuivasmäki [FIN] 208 E3
Kuivastu [EST] 230 C3
Kukës [AL] 154 B3
Kukinia [PL] 34 F2
Kukko [FIN] 208 D2
Kukko [FIN] 208 E2
Kukkola [FIN] 198 E1
Kukkulankoski [FIN] 222 B4
Kuklin [PL] 36 E4
Kuks [CZ] 60 F2
Kukujevci [SRB] 146 C1
Kukurečani [MK] 160 D2
Kula [BG] 148 C2
Kula [BIH] 146 B3
Kula [SRB] 122 C4
Kula [TR] 164 E4
Kula Novinska [HR] 152 C2

Kulaši [BIH] 146 A2
Kulata [BG] 156 B3
Kuldīga [LV] 234 D3
Ku'le [RUS] 232 D3
Kulefall [S] 190 C4
Kuleli [TR] 158 B3
Kulennoinen [FIN] 210 D4
Kulen Vakuf [BIH] 144 D2
Kulhuse [DK] 178 E1
Kuliai [LT] 238 B2
Kullaa [FIN] 198 C1
Kulla Gunnarstorp [S] 178 F1
Kullo / Kulloo [FIN] 200 A3
Kulloo / Kullo [FIN] 200 A3
Küllsted [D] 44 C3
Kulmain [D] 60 A3
Kulmbach [D] 58 F2
Kuloharju [FIN] 222 E3
Kultaranta [FIN] 198 C3
Kulvemäki [FIN] 216 D3
Kulykiv [UA] 64 F2
Kumanê [SRB] 122 D4
Kumanica [SRB] 146 D4
Kumanovo [MK] 154 D3
Kumarlar [TR] 164 B2
Kumbağ [TR] 158 C4
Kumburk [CZ] 60 F2
Kumburun [TR] 162 F2
Kumkale [TR] 162 F2
Kumköy [TR] 158 E3
Kumla [S] 188 F3
Kumlinge [FIN] 198 B3
Kumluca [TR] 176 F1
Kummavuopio [S] 224 E3
Kummeren [N] 218 F3
Kumo / Kokemäki [FIN]
198 C2
Kumpuvaara [FIN] 222 D4
Kumreut [D] 72 F2
Kumrovec [HR] 120 C3
Kumu [FIN] 216 E2
Kumyalı (Koma tou Yialou)
[CY] 176 E3
Kunadacs [H] 122 B1
Kunágota [H] 122 E2
Kuncsorba [H] 122 D1
Kunda [EST] 230 E1
Kunes [N] 228 D2
Kunfehértó [H] 122 C2
Kungälv [S] 184 A1
Kungsängen [S] 190 D2
Kungsäter [S] 184 B2
Kungsbacka [S] 184 A2
Kungsberg [S] 196 C3
Kungsfors [S] 196 C3
Kungshållet [S] 190 C2
Kungshamn [S] 188 B4
Kungsör [S] 190 C2
Kunhegyes [H] 76 D4
Kunín [CZ] 62 D3
Kunmadaras [H] 76 D4
Kunovice [CZ] 74 E1
Kunow [D] 34 D4
Kunów [PL] 48 F4
Kunowo [PL] 46 F3
Kunpeszér [H] 122 B1
Kunrau [D] 44 D1
Kunštát [CZ] 62 B4
Kunszentmárton [H] 122 D2
Kunszentmiklós [H] 122 B1
Kunžak [CZ] 74 B1
Künzelsau [D] 58 C4
Kuohatti [FIN] 216 E4
Kuohenmaa [FIN] 198 E1
Kuohijoki [FIN] 198 F1
Kuoksu [S] 220 F1
Kuolayarvi [RUS] 222 E2
Kuolio [FIN] 222 E3
Kuona [FIN] 216 B4
Kuopio [FIN] 210 C2

Kuora [FIN] 210 E1
Kuortane [FIN] 208 D2
Kuosku [FIN] 222 E1
Kup [H] 120 E1
Kup [PL] 62 D1
Kupferberg [D] 58 F2
Kupferzell [D] 58 C4
Kupinovo [SRB] 146 D2
Kupirovo [HR] 144 D3
Kupiškis [LT] 238 D2
Kupjak [HR] 120 B4
Kupkovo [RUS] 232 D2
Kupli [LV] 234 E3
Küplü [TR] 158 A3
Kuprava [LV] 236 D2
Kupres [BIH] 144 F3
Kupychiv [UA] 50 E4
Kurbinovo [MK] 160 C2
Kurbnesh [AL] 154 B4
Kurchatov [RUS] 242 F2
Kurd [H] 122 A2
Kürdzhali [BG] 156 E3
Kurejoki [FIN] 208 D2
Kuremäe [EST] 230 F2
Kuressaare [EST] 230 B3
Kurevere [EST] 230 B3
Kurgolovo [RUS] 200 D4
Kurianka [PL] 38 C2
Kurikka [FIN] 208 C3
Kurilo [BG] 148 D4
Kuřim [CZ] 62 B4
Kurjala [FIN] 210 C2
Kurjenkylä [FIN] 208 D3
Kurkela [FIN] 198 D3
Kurkiyeki [RUS] 200 E1
Kurkkio [FIN] 226 C4
Kurkkio [S] 220 F1
Kürnare [BG] 156 D1
Kurobasi [TR] 164 A3
Kurola [FIN] 210 C3
Kurolanahti [FIN] 210 B2
Kuropta [RUS] 222 F1
Kurovitsy [RUS] 232 E1
Kurów [PL] 50 B3
Kurowice [PL] 48 D3
Kurozwęki [PL] 64 B2
Kurravaara [S] 220 E1
Kuršėnai [LT] 238 C1
Kursiši [LV] 234 E4
Kursu [FIN] 222 E2
Kuršumlija [SRB] 148 A4
Kuršumlijska Banja [SRB]
148 A4
Kurşunlu [TR] 158 E4
Kurşunlu [TR] 164 D1
Kurtakko [FIN] 222 B2
Kurtbey [TR] 158 A3
Kurtti [FIN] 216 D1
Kuru [FIN] 198 E1
Kuru [FIN] 208 D4
Kurudere [TR] 170 B2
Kurvinen [FIN] 222 F4
Kurzelów [PL] 62 F1
Kurzeszyn [PL] 48 E3
Kurzętnik [PL] 36 D3
Kuşadası [TR] 170 B3
Kuşçayır [TR] 164 B2
Kuşcenneti [TR] 164 D1
Kusel [D] 56 F3
Kushalino [RUS] 240 E2
Kuside [MNE] 152 E2
Kusmark [S] 214 D2
Küssnacht [CH] 70 E4
Kustavi / Gustavs [FIN] 198 B3
Küstrin–Kietz [D] 46 C1
Kuşu [TR] 164 E3
Kut [HR] 120 D4
Kuta [MNE] 152 E2
Kutemajärvi [FIN] 210 B3
Kutina [FIN] 120 D4
Kutjevo [HR] 120 F4
Kutná Hora [CZ] 60 E3

Kutno [PL] 48 D2
Kuttanen [FIN] 226 B3
Kultura [FIN] 226 D3
Kúty [SK] 74 E2
Kuuksenvaara [FIN] 210 F2
Kuuminainen [FIN] 198 C1
Kuurtola [FIN] 210 E1
Kuusaa [FIN] 208 F3
Kuusaa [FIN] 216 B3
Kuusajoki [FIN] 222 C1
Kuusalu [EST] 230 D1
Kuusamo [FIN] 222 E3
Kuusankoski [FIN] 200 B2
Kuusiniemi [RUS] 216 F1
Kuusjärvi [FIN] 210 D2
Kuusjoki [FIN] 198 D3
Kuuttila [FIN] 208 C2
Kuvaskangas [FIN] 208 B4
Kuvshinovo [RUS] 240 D2
Kuyucak [TR] 170 D2
Kuyvozi [RUS] 200 F3
Kuzemki [RUS] 240 E4
Kuzma [SLO] 120 C2
Kuzmin [SRB] 146 C2
Kuźmina [PL] 64 D3
Kuznechnoye [RUS] 200 E1
Kuznetsovo [RUS] 232 F1
Kuznetsovs'k [UA] 242 B4
Kuźnia Raciborska [PL] 62 D2
Kuźnica [PL] 38 D2
Kuzovo [RUS] 232 F3
Kvačany [SK] 62 F4
Kvænangsbotn [N] 224 F2
Kværndrup [DK] 178 D3
Kvål [N] 204 B2
Kvalsund [N] 228 B2
Kvalsvik [N] 202 B3
Kvalvåg [N] 192 A4
Kvalvåg [N] 202 D2
Kvam [N] 192 F1
Kvam [N] 212 C4
Kvammen [N] 202 F2
Kvamsøy gamle Kirke [N]
192 C2
Kvanndal [N] 192 C3
Kvanne [N] 202 E2
Kvantenburg [S] 188 D3
Kvarnåsen [S] 214 C2
Kvarnberg [S] 194 F2
Kvarnberget [S] 194 E4
Kvarnbranet [S] 214 C3
Kvarsebo [S] 190 C3
Kvarstadseter [N] 194 B2
Kvås [N] 186 C4
Kvasilov [UA] 244 D1
Kvasowka [BY] 38 D2
Kveaunet [N] 212 A4
Kvèdarna [LT] 238 B2
Kveejdet [N] 212 E3
Kveina [N] 212 D2
Kvelde [N] 186 F2
Kvelia [N] 212 E3
Kvenvær [N] 202 E1
Kvernessetra [N] 194 C1
Kvetkai [LT] 236 C4
Kvevlax / Koivulahti [FIN]
208 B2
Kvicksund [S] 190 C2
Kvigno [N] 192 D2
Kvikkjokk [S] 220 C2
Kvikne [N] 204 B3
Kvilda [CZ] 60 C4
Kvilldal [N] 186 C1
Kville [S] 188 B3
Kvillsfors [S] 184 D2
Kvinesdal [N] 186 C3
Kvinlog [N] 186 C4
Kvisler [N] 194 C3
Kvissleby [S] 206 D1
Kvistgård [DK] 178 F1
Kvisvik [N] 202 E2
Kviteseid [N] 186 D2

Kvitnes [N] 202 D2
Kvitten [N] 204 C4
Kwiatkowice [PL] 48 D3
Kwidzyn [PL] 36 D3
Kwilcz [PL] 46 E2
Kybartai [LT] 238 C3
Kyburg [CH] 70 E3
Kycklingvattnet [S] 212 E3
Kyffhäuser–Denkmal [D] 44 D3
Kyїv [UA] 242 D4
Kyjov [CZ] 74 E1
Kykkou, Panagia tou– [CY]
176 D4
Kyläinpää [FIN] 208 C2
Kylämä [FIN] 208 E4
Kylänlahti [FIN] 210 D1
Kylemore Abbey [IRL] 12 A3
Kyle of Lochalsh [GB] 14 C3
Kyliia [UA] 246 C4
Kyllaj [S] 234 B2
Kylland [N] 186 C3
Kyllburg [D] 56 E2
Kyllíni [GR] 166 C4
Kylmäkoski [FIN] 198 E2
Kylmälä [FIN] 216 B2
Kylmämäki [FIN] 210 B3
Kymbo [S] 184 C1
Kyme [TR] 164 B4
Kými [GR] 168 B1
Kýmina [GR] 160 F2
Kymönkoski [FIN] 208 F1
Kynšperk nad Ohří [CZ] 60 B2
Kypäräjärvi [FIN] 210 D2
Kypärävaara [FIN] 210 D2
Kyparissía [GR] 172 C2
Kyriáki [GR] 166 F3
Kyritz [D] 32 E4
Kyrkhult [S] 180 D1
Kyrkjebygdi [N] 186 D2
Kyrksæterøra [N] 202 F2
Kyrkslätt / Kirkkonummi [FIN]
198 E3
Kyrkstad [S] 214 E3
Kyrksten [S] 188 E2
Kyrö [FIN] 198 D3
Kyrönlahti [FIN] 208 D4
Kyröskoski [FIN] 198 D1
Kyrping [N] 186 B1
Kyšice [CZ] 60 D3
Kysucké Nové Mesto [SK]
62 E4
Kytäjä [FIN] 198 F3
Kýthira [GR] 172 E4
Kýthnos [GR] 168 C3
Kytömäki [FIN] 216 D2
Kyustendil [BG] 154 E3
Kyyjärvi [FIN] 208 E2
Kyynämöinen [FIN] 208 E3
Kyzikos [TR] 164 C1
Kyznecovo [RUS] 240 B1

L

Laa an der Thaya [A] 74 D2
Laage [D] 32 E2
Laage Weitendorf [D] 32 E2
Lääja [FIN] 216 D2
Laajoki [FIN] 198 C2
Laakajärvi [FIN] 216 D3
Laakirchen [A] 72 F3
La Alameda [E] 100 D3
La Alamedilla [E] 92 D3
La Alberca [E] 92 B3
La Alberca de Záncara [E]
102 A2
La Albuera [E] 98 E2
La Aldea del Obispo [E]
100 B1
La Algaba [E] 98 E4
La Almarcha [E] 102 A2

La Almolda [E] 94 E3
La Almudena [E] 106 D2
La Almunia de Doña Godina
[E] 94 D3
Laamala [FIN] 200 D1
Laanila [FIN] 226 D3
La Antigua [E] 84 F2
La Antilla [E] 98 D4
La Azohía [E] 106 D3
Labacolla [E] 82 B2
Labajos [E] 92 D3
la Balme [F] 80 E4
La Baña [E] 82 D4
La Bañeza [E] 82 E4
La Barca de la Florida [E]
104 B3
La Barrela [E] 82 C3
La Bassée [F] 40 C4
la Bastide [F] 126 B3
Labastide–d'Armagnac [F]
88 C1
La Bastide de–Sérou [F] 88 E4
Labastide–Murat [F] 78 E4
La Bastide–Puylaurent [F]
80 C4
Labastide–Rouairoux [F]
124 B3
La Bastie d'Urfé [F] 80 C2
La Bâtiaz [CH] 116 B2
La Bâtie–Neuve [F] 126 B1
La Baule [F] 66 B2
La Bazoche–Gouet [F] 54 C4
Låbbyn [S] 188 C2
Łabędzie [PL] 34 F3
la Bégude–de–Mazenc [F]
124 E1
La Belle Etoile [F] 56 A4
Labenne [F] 88 B2
La Bérarde [F] 80 F4
L'Aber–Wrac'h [F] 52 B2
La Bien Aparecida [E] 86 D2
Labin [HR] 144 B1
Labinot Fushë [AL] 160 B1
La Bisbal de Falset [E] 96 B3
la Bisbal d'Empordà [E] 96 E2
Łabiszyn [PL] 36 C4
Labjana [KS] 154 D2
Lábod [H] 120 E3
Laboe [D] 32 C1
Laborel [F] 124 F2
Labouheyre [F] 78 B4
La Bourboule [F] 80 A2
La Bóveda de Toro [E] 84 F3
Łabowa [PL] 64 B3
Labrags [LV] 234 D3
Labrède [F] 78 B4
La Bresse [F] 70 C2
La Brillanne [F] 124 F3
Labrit [F] 88 C1
Łabunie [PL] 64 E1
Läby [S] 190 D1
Laç [AL] 154 A4
Laç [AL] 154 B4
La Cabrera [E] 92 E3
La Caillere–St–Hilaire [F]
66 C3
La Cala del Moral [E] 104 D3
La Calahorra [E] 106 B3
La Calera [E] 112 B2
La Caleta [E] 114 E2
La Caletta [I] 142 D3
Lacalm [F] 80 A4
La Calzada de Calatrava [E]
100 D3
La Calzada de Oropesa [E]
92 C4

La Campana [E] 104 C1
La Campana [E] 106 D3
La Cañada de Cañepla [E]
106 C2
La Cañada de Verich [E] 94 E4
Lacanau [F] 78 B3
Lacanau–Océan [F] 78 B3
La Canonica [F] 130 B2
La Canonja [E] 96 C3
La Canourgue [F] 80 B4
La Capelle [F] 56 B2
Lacapelle–Marival [F] 78 E4
La Capte [F] 126 A4
Lácarak [SRB] 146 C2
La Caridad [F] 82 E2
La Carlota [E] 104 D1
La Carolina [E] 100 D4
La Cartuja [E] 104 B2
Lacaune [F] 124 B2
La Cavalerie [F] 124 C2
Lacave [F] 78 E4
Lacco Ameno [I] 134 C3
Lacedonia [I] 134 E3
La Celle–Dunoise [F] 68 A4
Lăceni [RO] 150 B2
La Cerca [E] 86 D3
Láces [I] 118 B2
La Chaise–Dieu [F] 80 C3
La Chambre [F] 80 F3
Lachamp [F] 80 B4
Lachanás [GR] 156 B4
Lachaniá [GR] 176 C2
La Chapelle [F] 80 D2
La Chapelle d'Angillon
[F] 68 B2
La Chapelle–en–Valgaudemar
[F] 80 F4
La Chapelle–en–Vercors
[F] 80 E4
La Chapelle–Glain [F] 66 D2
la–Chapelle–Laurent [F] 80 B3
La Charité–sur–Loire [F] 68 C3
La Chartre–sur–le–Loir
[F] 66 F2
La Châtaigneraie [F] 66 D3
La Châtre [F] 68 B4
La Chaux–de–Fonds [CH]
70 C4
Lachendorf [D] 44 C1
La–Chevignerie [F] 66 C2
la Chèze [F] 52 D4
Lachowo [PL] 38 B2
La Ciotat [F] 124 F4
La Ciudad Encantada [E]
102 B1
Łąck [PL] 48 D2
Läckeby [S] 184 E3
Läckö [S] 188 D3
La Clayette [F] 80 D1
la Clisse [F] 78 C2
La Cluse [F] 80 E2
La Cluse–et–Mijoux [F] 70 B4
La Codosera [E] 90 E3
La Colle Noire [F] 126 B3
La Colle St. Michel [F] 126 B2
Lacona [I] 130 C2
La Concepción [E] 104 D3
Láconi [I] 142 C4
La Coquille [F] 78 E3
La Coronada [E] 100 B2
La Corrèze [F] 78 F3
La Corte [I] 142 B2
La Coruña / A Coruña [E]
82 C1
La Côte–St–André [F] 80 E3
Lacourt [F] 88 E4
La Courtine [F] 80 A2
La Couvertoirade [F] 124 C2
Lacq [F] 88 C2
La Croisière [F] 78 E2
La Croix Ferrée [F] 78 E2

La Croixille [F] 52 E4
La Croix–Valmer [F] 126 B4
La Cueva Santa [E] 102 D2
La Cumbre [E] 100 B1
La Cure [F] 80 F1
Lăcusteni de Sus [RO] 148 E1
Lad [H] 120 E3
Ląd [PL] 48 B2
Ladapeyre [F] 68 B4
Ladbergen [D] 30 E4
Ladby [DK] 178 D2
Lądek–Zdrój [PL] 62 B2
Ládi [GR] 156 F3
Ladíspoli [I] 130 F3
Ladoeiro [P] 90 E2
Ladon [F] 68 C1
Ladoye, Cirque de– [F] 70 A4
Ladushkin [RUS] 36 E1
Ladyzhyn [UA] 244 F2
La Encinilla y El Rubio [E]
104 C2
Lærdalsøyri [N] 192 D2
Laerma [GR] 176 C2
La Espina [E] 82 E2
La Estrella [E] 100 C1
Laeva [EST] 230 E3
La Felipa [E] 102 B3
La Fère [F] 54 F2
la Ferrière [F] 66 F2
la Ferrière [F] 80 F3
La Ferrière–en–Parthenay
[F] 66 D3
Laferté [F] 70 B2
La Ferté–Bernard [F] 54 B4
La–Ferté–Chevresis [F] 56 A2
La Ferté–Gaucher [F] 54 F3
la–Ferté–Loupière [F] 68 D2
La Ferté–Macé [F] 54 A3
La Ferté–Milon [F] 54 F3
La Ferté–sous–Jouarre
[F] 54 F3
La Ferté–St–Aubin [F] 68 B2
La Ferté–Vidame [F] 54 C3
La–Feuille [F] 54 D2
Laffrey [F] 80 E4
Láfka [GR] 166 E4
La Flèche [F] 66 E2
La Florida [E] 82 E2
La Flotte [F] 66 C4
La Font de la Figuera [E]
102 C4
la Foresta, Convento– [I]
132 D3
Laforsen [S] 196 B1
Lafortunada [E] 88 C4
La Franca [E] 86 C2
Lafrançaise [F] 88 E2
La Fregeneda [E] 84 C3
La Fresneda [E] 94 E4
La Frua [I] 116 D2
La Fuente de San Esteban
[E] 84 D4
Läga [BG] 148 E4
La Gacilly [F] 66 B1
La Gallega [E] 94 A2
Lagan [S] 184 C3
Laganás [GR] 172 B2
Lagarde [F] 56 E4
La Garde–Freinet [F] 126 B4
La Garriga [E] 96 D3
La Garrovilla [E] 90 E4
Lage [D] 42 F2
Łagiewniki [PL] 62 B1
Laginá [GR] 162 B1
La Gineta [E] 102 B3
L'Agiot Élancourt [F] 54 D3
Lagkáda [GR] 168 E1
Lagkáda [GR] 172 D3
Lagkádas [GR] 162 B1
Lagkádia [GR] 172 D2
Lagkadíkia [GR] 162 B1
Lagnieu [F] 80 E2

Lagnö [S] 190 C4
Lagny [F] 54 E3
Lagoa [P] 98 B4
Lagodaž [BG] 154 F3
Lagonegro [I] 136 B3
Lagonísi [GR] 168 B3
Lágos [GR] 156 E4
Lagos [P] 98 B4
Lagosanto [I] 128 D2
Łagów [PL] 46 D2
Łagów [PL] 64 B1
Łagówek [PL] 46 D2
La Granada de Rio Tinto
  [E] 98 E3
la Granadella [E] 96 B3
La Grand-Combe [F] 124 D2
La Grande-Motte [F] 124 D3
La Granja [E] 92 E3
La Granjuela [E] 100 B3
Lagrasse [F] 124 B3
La Grave [F] 80 F4
Lägsta [S] 206 D1
La Guardia / A Guarda [E]
  82 A4
La Guardia / A Guarda [E]
  100 E2
Laguardia / Biasteri [E] 86 E4
La Guardia de Jaén [E] 104 F2
Laguarres [E] 96 B1
Laguarta [E] 88 C4
Laguépie [F] 124 A1
La Guerche-de-Bretagne
  [F] 66 D1
La Guerche-sur-l'Aubois
  [F] 68 C3
Laguiole [F] 80 A4
Laguna de Duero [E] 92 D2
Laguna del Marquesado [E]
  102 C2
Laguna de Negrillos [E] 84 F2
Laguna de Santiago [E] 112 C3
Laguna Negra [E] 94 B1
Lagunas de Villafáfila [E] 84 F3
Lagýna [GR] 160 F2
La Haba [E] 100 B2
Lahane [F] 88 B1
la Haye [F] 54 D2
La Haye-du-Puits [F] 52 E2
Lahdenperä [FIN] 208 E1
Lahemmaa [EST] 230 D1
La Hermida [E] 86 B2
Laheycourt [F] 56 C4
La Higuera [E] 102 B4
Lahinch [IRL] 10 C2
La Hinojosa [E] 102 A2
Lahishyn [UA] 242 B3
Lahnajärvi [S] 220 F2
Lahnalahti [FIN] 210 C3
Lahnasjävi [FIN] 216 D3
Lahnberg [A] 118 D2
Lahnsattel [A] 74 C3
Lahnstein [D] 56 F2
Laholm [S] 184 B4
Laholuoma [FIN] 208 C4
La Horra [E] 92 F2
Lahoysk [BY] 242 B2
La Hoz de la Vieja [E] 94 D4
Lahr [D] 70 D2
Lätteenkylä [FIN] 198 C2
Lahti [FIN] 198 C2
Lahti / Lahtis [FIN] 200 A2
Lahtis / Lahti [FIN] 200 A2
La Hutte [F] 54 B4
Laibgaliai [LT] 238 C1
Laichingen [D] 72 A2
Laifour, Roches de- [F] 56 C2
L'Aigle [F] 54 C3
La Iglesuela del Cid [E] 102 E2
Laignes [F] 68 C2
Laiguéglia [I] 126 D3
L'Aiguillon [F] 66 C4
Laihela / Laihia [FIN] 208 C2

Laihia / Laihela [FIN] 208 C2
Laikko [FIN] 200 E1
Laïliás [GR] 156 B3
Laimbach [A] 74 B2
Laimoluokta [S] 224 E4
Lainate [I] 116 E3
Lainbach [A] 74 B4
Lainijaur [S] 214 C2
Lainio [S] 220 F1
Lairg [GB] 14 E2
Laisbäck [S] 214 B2
La Isla [E] 86 B2
Laissac [F] 80 A4
Laïsta [GR] 160 C3
Laisvall [S] 220 C4
Laitikkala [FIN] 198 E1
Laitila [FIN] 198 D2
Laitineva [FIN] 216 B2
Laize-la-Ville [F] 54 A2
la-Jaille-Yvon [F] 66 D2
La Jana [E] 96 A4
Lajares [E] 114 E3
La Javie [F] 126 B2
Lajes [P] 110 C3
Lajes das Flores [P] 110 B2
Lajes do Pico [P] 110 A3
Lajkovac [SRB] 146 D3
La Jonchère-St-Maurice
  [F] 78 E2
la Jonquera [E] 96 E2
Lajoskomárom [H] 122 A2
Lajosmizse [H] 122 C1
Lak [H] 76 D2
Łąka [PL] 62 E3
Lakaluoma [FIN] 208 D2
Lakaniemi [FIN] 208 D2
Łąka Prudnicka [PL] 62 C2
Lakatnik [BG] 148 D4
Lakaträsk [S] 220 E3
Lakavica [MK] 154 E4
Lakfors [N] 212 D2
Lakhdenpokh'ya [RUS] 210 E4
Laki [MK] 154 E3
Lakitelek [H] 122 C2
Lákka [GR] 166 B2
Lakkí [GR] 170 B4
Lákkoi [GR] 174 B3
Lákkoma [GR] 162 E1
Lakkópetra [GR] 166 D4
Lakócsa [H] 120 F3
Lakolk [DK] 178 A2
Laksåvik [N] 202 E1
Lakselv [N] 228 C3
Laktaši [BIH] 144 F2
La Lantejuela [E] 104 D2
Lalapaşa [TR] 158 A2
Lálas [GR] 172 C2
l'Albagés [E] 96 B3
L'Albi [E] 96 B3
l'Alcora / Alcora [E] 102 E2
L'Ampolla [E] 96 B4
l'Alguenya [E] 106 C2
La Lima [I] 128 B3
Lalín [E] 82 C3
Lalinde [F] 78 D4
La Línea de la Concepción
  [E] 104 C4
Lalkovo [BG] 158 A2
Lalm [AL] 160 B1
Lalm [N] 192 F1
Laloşu [RO] 148 E1
La Loupe [F] 54 C3
Lalouvesc [F] 80 D3
La Louvière [B] 40 D4
L'Alpe-d'Huez [F] 80 F4
Lalueza [E] 94 E2
La Luisiana [E] 104 D1
Lam [D] 60 C4

La Machine [F] 68 D3
La Maddalena [I] 142 C2
Lama dei Peligni [I] 132 F4
La Magdalena [E] 82 F3
La Malène [F] 124 C1
Lamalou-les-Bains [F] 124 B3
La Manche, Tunnel sous- /
  Channel Tunnel [F/GB] 28 E4
La Manga del Mar Menor
  [E] 106 E3
Lamarche [F] 70 B2
Lamargelle [F] 68 E3
La Marina [E] 106 E2
Lamarosa [P] 90 C3
Lamarque [F] 78 B3
Lamas do Vouga [P] 84 A3
Lamastre [F] 80 D4
La Mata [E] 106 E2
La Matanza [E] 84 F2
La Maucarrière [F] 66 D3
Lambach [A] 72 F3
Lamballe [F] 52 D3
Lambesc [F] 124 E3
Lamborn [S] 196 B3
Lambrecht [D] 58 B3
Lamego [P] 84 B3
la-Melleraye-de-Bretagne
  [F] 66 C2
L'Ametlla de Mar [E] 96 B4
Lamezia Terme [I] 138 C2
Lamía [GR] 166 E2
Lammhult [S] 184 D3
Lammi [FIN] 198 F2
Lammi [FIN] 208 D2
Lamminaho [FIN] 216 B4
Lamminkylä [FIN] 210 E2
Lamminkylä [FIN] 216 D2
Lamminkyulya [RUS] 200 E1
Lamminmaa [FIN] 208 C3
La Molina [E] 96 D2
La Mongie [F] 88 C3
La Mota [E] 104 E2
La Mothe-Achard [F] 66 B3
La-Mothe-St-Héray [F] 66 E3
Lamotte-Beuvron [F] 68 B2
La Motte-Chalancon [F]
  124 F2
la Motte-du-Caire [F] 126 A2
Lamouroux, Grottes de- [F]
  78 E3
Lampaanjärvi [FIN] 210 B1
Lampaul [F] 52 A2
Lampaul-Plouarzel [F] 52 A2
Lampedusa [I] 140 A4
Lámpeia [GR] 166 C3
Lampeter [GB] 22 D4
Lampínsaari [FIN] 216 B3
Lampíri [GR] 166 D3
La Mudarra [E] 92 D1
La Muela [E] 94 D3
La Mure [F] 80 E4
La Murta [E] 102 D4
Lana [I] 118 B2
Lanaja [E] 94 E3
La Napoule-Plage [F] 126 B3
Lanark [GB] 18 C4
La Nava [E] 98 E3
La Nava de Ricomalillo [E]
  100 C1

Lanciano [I] 132 F3
Lanciunava [LT] 238 D2
Łańcut [PL] 64 D2
Landau [D] 58 B4
Landau [D] 72 E2
Landeck [A] 72 B4
Landedo [P] 84 D2
Landendorf [A] 74 D2
Landepéreuse [F] 54 C3
Landerneau [F] 52 B3
Landersfjorden [N] 228 D2
Landeryd [S] 184 B3
Landesbergen [D] 44 B1
Landete [E] 102 C2
Landévennec [F] 52 B3
Landivisiau [F] 52 B3
Landivy [F] 52 F3
Landkirchen [D] 32 D1
Landön [S] 204 E2
Landquart [CH] 116 F1
Landrecies [F] 56 A1
Landsberg [D] 44 E3
Landsberg [D] 72 B3
Landsbro [S] 184 D2
Landshut [D] 72 D2
Landshut, Ruine– [D] 56 E2
Landskrona [S] 178 F2
Landštejn [CZ] 74 B1
Landštejn [CZ] 74 B1
Landstuhl [D] 56 F3
Landudec [F] 52 B3
Landvetter [S] 184 A2
Lane [N] 192 C2
Lanersbach [A] 72 C4
Lanesborough [IRL] 10 E1
La Neuve-Lyre [F] 54 C3
La Neuveville [CH] 70 C4
Langa [DK] 182 D4
Långå [S] 204 D3
Langa de Duero [E] 92 F2
Långáminne [FIN] 208 B2
Langangen [N] 186 E2
Langballig [D] 178 C3
Langban [S] 188 E1
Långbo [S] 196 B2
Langdal [N] 202 D3
Langeac [F] 80 B3
Langeais [F] 66 E2
Langehauk [N] 192 E3
Langeid [N] 186 C2
Länge Jan [S] 184 E4
Längelmäki [FIN] 208 E4
Langelsheim [D] 44 C2
Långemåla [S] 184 E3
Langen [A] 72 A4
Langen [D] 32 A2
Langen [D] 58 B2
Längenäs [S] 188 D1
Langenau [D] 72 A2
Langenburg [D] 58 D4
Langenes [N] 224 B3
Längenfeld [A] 118 B1
Langenfeld [D] 42 C3
Langenhahn [D] 58 B1
Langenhorn [D] 178 B3
Langenisarhofen [D] 72 E2
Langenlois [A] 74 C2
Langennaundorf [D] 46 B3
Langenorla [D] 58 F1
Langenselbold [D] 58 C2
Langenthal [CH] 70 D4
Langenwang [A] 74 C4
Langenzenn [D] 58 E3
Langeoog [D] 30 E1
Langeskov [DK] 178 D2
Langesø [DK] 178 C2
Langesund [N] 186 E2
Langevåg [N] 186 A1
Langevåg [N] 202 C3
Langewiese [D] 42 E3
Langfjord [N] 224 F1
Langfjordnes [N] 228 D2

Långflon [S] 194 D3
Langhammars [S] 234 B2
Langhirano [I] 128 B2
Langholm [GB] 20 D2
Långijöby [S] 214 A2
Långlöt [S] 184 F3
Långnäs [FIN] 198 B4
Langnau im Emmental [CH]
  70 D4
Langø [DK] 178 D3
Langogne [F] 80 C4
Langoiran [F] 78 C4
Langon [F] 78 C4
Langquaid [D] 72 D1
Langraiz Oka / Nanclares de la
  Oca [E] 86 D3
Langreo / Langréu [E] 82 F3
Langres [F] 68 F2
Langréu / Langreo [E] 82 F3
Långron [S] 206 E2
Långsel [S] 220 F3
Långsele [S] 206 C2
Långsele [S] 212 F3
Långserud [S] 188 D2
Långshyttan [S] 196 C4
Langstrand [N] 228 B2
Langstrand [S] 214 A2
Långträsk [S] 214 C2
Långträsk [S] 214 D2
Languïdou, Chapelle de- [F]
  52 A3
Langula [D] 44 C4
Långvattnet [S] 214 C3
Langviken [S] 214 D3
Långviksmon [S] 206 D1
Långvind [S] 196 D2
Langwarden [D] 30 F1
Langwedel [D] 32 B4
Langweid [D] 72 B2
Langweiler [D] 56 F3
Langwies [CH] 116 F1
Lanhelas [P] 82 A4
Lanjarón [E] 104 F3
Lankas [LV] 234 D3
Lankila [FIN] 200 C2
Länkipohja [FIN] 208 E4
Lankojärvi [FIN] 222 B2
Lankoori [FIN] 198 C1
Lankosi [FIN] 208 B4
Lanleff, Temple de– [F] 52 C3
Lanmeur [F] 52 C2
Lanna [S] 184 C2
Länna [S] 190 C2
Lannabruk [S] 188 F2
Lannavaara [S] 226 A4
Lannemezan [F] 88 D3
Lannevesi [FIN] 208 F2
Lannilis [F] 52 B2
Lannion [F] 52 C2
Lanobre [F] 80 A2
La Noguera [E] 102 C1
Lanouaille [F] 78 E3
Lansån [S] 220 F3
Lansikylä [FIN] 208 D3
Länsi–Vuokka [FIN] 210 C3
Lansjärv [S] 220 F3
Lanškroun [CZ] 62 B3
Lanslebourg-Mont-Cenis
  [F] 116 B3
Lanšperk [CZ] 62 B3
Lantosque [F] 126 C3
Lanusei [I] 142 C4
Lanvollon [F] 52 C3
Lánycsók [H] 122 B3
Lanzá [E] 82 C2
Lanzendorf [A] 74 D3
Lanžhot [CZ] 74 D2
Lanzo d'Intelvi [I] 116 E3
Lanzo Torinese [I] 116 C4
Lao [EST] 230 C3
Laodikeia [TR] 170 E2
La Oliva [E] 88 A4

La Oliva [E] 114 E3
Laon [F] 56 A2
La Orotava [E] 112 D2
La Paca [E] 106 D2
La Pacaudière [F] 80 C1
Lápafő [H] 120 F2
Lapalisse [F] 80 C1
La Pallice [F] 66 C4
La Palma [E] 106 E3
La Palma del Condado [E] 98 E4
Lapalme [F] 124 B4
La Palud-sur-Verdon [F] 126 B3
la Panouse [F] 80 B4
Łapanów [PL] 64 A3
Lápas [GR] 166 D4
La Pelechaneta / Pelejaneta [E] 102 E2
La Peraleja [E] 102 A1
la Péruse [F] 78 D2
La Petite-Pierre [F] 56 E4
Lapeyrade [F] 88 D1
Lapinjärvi / Lappträsk [FIN] 200 B3
Lapinlahti [FIN] 210 B1
Lapinsaari [FIN] 208 C2
Lapistó [H] 122 D2
Lápithos (Lápta) [CY] 176 D3
La Plagne [F] 116 B3
la Plaine-Sur-Mer [F] 66 B2
La Plaza / Teverga [E] 82 E3
Laplume [F] 88 D1
la Pobla de Lillet [E] 96 D2
La Pobla de Massaluca [E] 94 F4
la Pobla de Segur [E] 96 C1
la Pobla de Vallbona [E] 102 D3
La Pobla Llarga [E] 102 D4
la Pobla Tornesa [E] 102 E2
La Pola de Gordón [E] 82 F3
La Portera [E] 102 C3
Lapoutroie [F] 70 D2
Lapovo [SRB] 146 E3
Lappach / Lappago [I] 118 C1
Lappago / Lappach [I] 118 C1
Lappajärvi [FIN] 208 D1
Lappijärvi [FIN] 226 B3
Läppe [S] 190 B3
Lappeenranta / Villmanstrand [FIN] 200 D2
Lappfjärd / Lapväärtti [FIN] 208 B3
Lappfors [FIN] 208 C1
Lappi [FIN] 198 C2
Lappo [FIN] 198 B3
Lappo / Lapua [FIN] 208 C2
Lappohja / Lappvik [FIN] 198 D4
Lappträsk [S] 222 B4
Lappträsk / Lapinjärvi [FIN] 200 B3
Lappvattnet [S] 214 D3
Lappvik / Lappohja [FIN] 198 D4
la Primaude [F] 124 B1
Lapseki [TR] 164 B1
Lápta (Lápithos) [CY] 176 D3
Laptevo [RUS] 236 F3
Lapua / Lappo [FIN] 208 C2
La Puebla de Almoradiel [E] 100 F2
La Puebla de Castro [E] 94 F2
La Puebla de Cazalla [E] 104 C2
La Puebla de Híjar [E] 94 E3
La Puebla de los Infantes [E] 104 D1
La Puebla del Río [E] 104 B2
La Puebla de Montalbán [E] 100 D1

La Puebla de Valdavia [E] 86 B3
La Puebla de Valverde [E] 102 D2
La Pueblanueva [E] 100 D1
La Puerta del Segura [E] 106 C1
La Punt [CH] 116 F2
Lapušnik [KS] 154 C2
Lapväärtti / Lappfjärd [FIN] 208 B3
Łapy [PL] 38 C3
Laqueuille [F] 80 B2
L'Aquila [I] 132 E3
La Rábita [E] 104 F3
Laracha [C] 82 B2
Laragh [IRL] 10 F3
Laragne-Montéglin [F] 124 F2
La Rambla [E] 104 D1
l'Arbre [F] 78 D2
L'Arbresle [F] 80 D2
Lärbro [S] 234 B2
Larceveau-Arros-Cibits [F] 88 B2
Larche [F] 78 E3
Larche [F] 126 B2
Lårdal [N] 186 D2
Lardaro [I] 118 B3
Larderello [I] 130 D1
Lardero [E] 86 E4
Lárdos [GR] 176 C2
Lardosa [P] 90 E2
Laredo [E] 86 D2
La Réole [F] 78 C4
La Restinga [E] 112 A3
Largentière [F] 124 D1
L'Argentière-la-Bessée [F] 126 B1
Largs [GB] 18 B4
La Rhune [F] 88 A2
Lariano [I] 132 D4
La Rinconada [E] 98 F4
Larino [I] 134 D2
Larionovo [RUS] 200 F2
Lárisa [GR] 160 E4
Larissa [TR] 164 C4
Larkollen [N] 188 B2
L'Armellière [F] 124 D3
Larmor [F] 52 B4
Lárnaka [CY] 176 E3
Larne [NIR] 12 F2
La Robla [E] 82 F3
La Roca de la Sierra [E] 90 E4
la Roca del Vallès [E] 96 D3
La Roche [CH] 116 B1
La Roche-Bernard [F] 66 B1
La Roche-Chalais [F] 78 C3
la Roche-de-Rame [F] 126 B1
La Roche-Derrien [F] 52 C2
La Roche-en-Ardenne [B] 56 D2
La Rochefoucauld [F] 78 D2
La Rochelle [F] 66 C4
La Roche-Posay [F] 66 F3
La Roche-sur-Foron [F] 80 F2
La Roche-sur-Yon [F] 66 C3
La Rochette [F] 80 F3
Larochette [L] 56 D2
La Roda [E] 102 B3
La Roda de Andalucía [E] 104 D2
Laroquebrou [F] 78 F4
La Roquebrussanne [F] 124 F4
Laroque-des-Arcs [F] 88 F1
Laroque-d'Olmes [F] 88 F4
La Roque-Gageac [F] 78 E4
La Rösa [CH] 116 F2
La Rouche-Courbon [F] 78 C2
Larraga [E] 86 F4
Larrau [F] 88 B3
Larret [F] 70 B3
Larroque [F] 88 F2

Larsmo / Luoto [FIN] 214 F4
Larsnes [N] 202 B3
l'Artigue [F] 88 E4
La Rubia [E] 94 B2
Laruns [F] 88 C3
Lárymna [GR] 168 A1
La Salceda [E] 92 E3
la Salles-les Alpes [F] 80 F4
La Salvetat [F] 124 A1
La Salvetat-sur-Agout [F] 124 B2
la Salzadella [E] 102 E2
Läsänkoski [FIN] 210 B4
Las Anorias [E] 102 B4
Lasarte-Oria [E] 86 F3
La Sauceda [E] 104 C3
Las Bárdenas Reales [E] 88 A4
Las Batuecas [E] 92 B3
Låsby [DK] 178 C1
Las Cabezas de San Juan [E] 104 B2
Las Caldas de Besaya [E] 86 C2
Lascaux, Grotte de- [F] 78 E3
la Selve [F] 124 B2
la Sénia [E] 96 A4
Lasenice [CZ] 74 B1
La Señuela [E] 104 B2
La Serna Del Monte [E] 92 F3
La Seu d'Urgell [E] 96 C1
La Seyne [F] 124 F4
Las Fuentes [E] 102 C4
Las Huelgas [E] 86 C4
Łasin [PL] 36 D3
Łask [PL] 48 D3
Łaskarzew [PL] 50 B2
Laski [PL] 36 A2
Laski [PL] 48 B4
Łasko [SLO] 120 B3
Laskowa [PL] 64 B3
Laskowice [PL] 36 C3
Laskowice [PL] 62 C2
Laslovo [HR] 122 B4
Las Marías [E] 106 B4
Las Médulas [E] 82 D4
Las Mesas [E] 100 F3
Las Navas de la Concepción [E] 100 A4
Las Navas del Marqués [E] 92 D3
Las Negras [E] 106 C4
La Solana [E] 100 E3
La Souche [F] 80 C4
La Souterraine [F] 68 A4
Lasovo [SRB] 148 C3
Las Palas [E] 106 D3
Las Palmas de Gran Canaria [E] 112 E3
Las Pedroñeras [E] 100 F2
La Spézia [I] 128 A3
Las Rozas [E] 92 E4
Lassan [D] 34 C2
Lassay [F] 54 A3
Lassemoen [N] 212 D3
Lassigny [F] 54 E2
Lastein [N] 186 B2
La Sterza [I] 128 B4
Las Torcas [E] 102 B2
Las Torres de Cotillas [E] 106 E2
Lastovo [HR] 152 B2
Lastras de Cuéllar [E] 92 E2
Lastres [E] 86 B1
Lästringe [S] 190 D3
Lastruk [FIN] 210 C1
Lastulahti [FIN] 210 C1
Lastva [BIH] 152 D3
La Suze-sur-Sarthe [F] 54 A4

Lašva [BIH] 146 A3
Las Veguillas [E] 92 B2
Las Ventas con Peña Aguilera [E] 100 D2
Las Ventas de S. Julián [E] 92 C4
Łaszczów [PL] 64 E2
Laszki [PL] 64 E2
Laszóvar [RO] 146 F2
la Tannière [F] 52 F4
Låtefossen [N] 192 C4
Latera [I] 130 F2
Laterza [I] 136 D2
Lathen [D] 30 E3
La Thuile [I] 110 B3
Latiano [I] 136 E2
Latikberg [S] 214 B3
Latina [I] 134 B2
Latinac [SRB] 148 B3
Latisana [I] 118 E3
Látky [SK] 76 B2
Lató [GR] 174 E4
Latorpsbruk [S] 188 F2
La Torre [E] 102 C3
la Torre Baixa [E] 102 C2
La Torre de Esteban Hambrán [E] 92 D4
La Torresaviñán [E] 94 B3
La Tour-du-Pin [F] 80 E3
La Tranche-sur-Mer [F] 66 C4
Latresne [F] 78 B3
La Trimouille [F] 66 F4
La Trinité [F] 66 A1
La Trinité-Porhoët [F] 52 D4
Latronico [I] 136 B3
Latronquière [F] 78 F4
Latte, Fort la- [F] 52 D3
Latteluokta [S] 224 E4
Lattuna [FIN] 226 E4
La Turbie [F] 126 C3
Latva [FIN] 216 B3
Latvalampi [FIN] 210 D3
Latvaset [FIN] 216 B4
Laubrières [F] 66 D1
Laucha [D] 44 D4
Lauchdorf [D] 72 B3
Lauchhammer [D] 46 B3
Laudal [N] 186 C4
Lauder [GB] 20 E1
Laudio / Llodio [E] 86 D3
Laudona [LV] 236 D3
Lauenau [D] 44 B2
Lauenbrück [D] 32 B3
Lauenburg [D] 32 C3
Lauenstein [D] 60 D1
Lauf [D] 58 E3
Laufen [CH] 70 D3
Laufen [D] 72 E3
Laufenburg [CH] 70 E3
Laufenburg (Baden) [D] 70 E3
Lauffen [D] 58 B4
Laugnac [F] 88 E1
Laugarbakki [IS] 216 B2
Lauingen [D] 72 B2
Laujar de Andarax [E] 106 B3
Laukaa [FIN] 208 F3
Laukeland [N] 192 B1
Laukka [FIN] 216 B2
Laukkala [FIN] 210 B1
Lauksundskaret [N] 224 E1
Laukuluspa [S] 220 D1
Laukuva [LT] 238 B2
Laukvik [N] 224 C2
Laukvik [N] 228 D3
Laukvika [N] 220 A1
Launceston [GB] 26 C3
La Unión [E] 106 E3
Laupen [CH] 70 C4
Laupheim [D] 72 A2
Lauragh [IRL] 10 A3
Laureana di Borrello [I] 138 D3
Laurencetown [IRL] 10 D2

Laurenzana [I] 134 F4
Lauria [I] 136 B3
Laurière [F] 78 E2
Laurino [I] 134 E4
Lausanne [CH] 116 B1
Laussig [D] 44 F3
Lautaporras [FIN] 198 E2
Lautemburg [D] 42 C4
Lauter [S] 234 B2
Lauterbach [D] 58 C1
Lauterbourg [F] 58 B4
Lauterbrunnen [CH] 116 C2
Lautere [LV] 236 C3
Lauterecken [D] 56 F3
Lauterhofen [D] 58 F4
Lautrec [F] 124 A2
Lauvåsen [N] 204 B2
Lauvsjølia [N] 212 E3
Lauvsnes [N] 212 C3
Lauvstad [N] 202 C3
Lauvuskylä [FIN] 216 E3
Lauvvik [N] 186 B2
Lauwersoog [NL] 30 D2
Lauzerte [F] 88 E1
Lauzun [F] 78 D4
La Vacherie [F] 80 D4
Lavagna [I] 126 F2
Laval [F] 52 F4
la Vall d'Uixó [E] 102 D3
La Vallivana [E] 96 A4
Lavamünd [A] 120 B2
Lavangnes [N] 224 C3
Lávara [GR] 158 A3
Lavardac [F] 88 D1
Lavardin [F] 66 F2
Lavarone [I] 118 B3
Lavaur [F] 88 F2
La Vecilla [E] 82 F3
I avelanet [F] 88 F4
Lavello [I] 134 E3
Lavelsloh [D] 42 F1
La Venta [E] 106 B3
La Verna [I] 128 D4
la Veurdre [F] 68 C4
Lavia [FIN] 198 C1
Laviano [I] 134 E3
Lavik [N] 192 B2
la Vila Joiosa / Villajoyosa [E] 106 F2
la Villa / Stern [I] 118 C2
Lavinio-Lido di Enea [I] 134 A2
La Virgen del Camino [E] 82 F4
Lavis [I] 118 B3
Lavit [F] 88 E2
Lavong [N] 212 D1
Lavos [P] 90 C1
La Voulte-sur-Rhône [F] 80 D4
Lavoûte-Chilhac [F] 80 B3
Lavoûte-Polignac, Château de- [F] 80 C3
Lavoûte-sur-Loire [F] 80 C3
Lavoye [F] 56 B3
Lavra [E] 84 A2
Lávrio [GR] 168 B3
Lavry [RUS] 230 F4
Lavsjö [S] 214 A3
La Wantzenau [F] 70 D1
Ławszowa [PL] 46 D3
Laxå [S] 188 F3
Laxe [E] 82 B1
Laxne [S] 190 B2
Laxsjö [S] 204 F1
Laxsjön [S] 206 C3
Laxtjärn [S] 194 E4
Laxviken [S] 204 F1
La Yedra [E] 106 B2
La Yesa [E] 102 D2

Läyliäinen [FIN] 198 E3
La Yunta [E] 94 C4
Laza [E] 82 C4
Lazarevac [SRB] 146 D3
Lazarevo [SRB] 122 D4
Lazdijai [LT] 38 C1
Laze [SLO] 120 B3
Lázi [H] 74 F4
Laži [LV] 234 D2
Lazise [I] 118 B4
Łaziska Górne [PL] 62 E3
Lazisko [SK] 76 B1
Lazkao [E] 86 E3
Lázné Bělohrad [CZ] 60 F2
Lázné Kynžvart [CZ] 60 B3
Laz Stubički [HR] 120 D3
La Zubia [E] 104 F3
Łazy [PL] 34 F2
Leacanabuaile Stone Fort
  [IRL] 10 A3
Leamington Spa [GB] 28 B1
Leap [IRL] 10 B4
Leatherhead [GB] 28 C3
Łeba [PL] 36 B1
Lebach [D] 56 E3
Le Ballon [F] 52 E4
Lebane [SRB] 148 B4
Lebanza [E] 86 B3
Le Bar [F] 126 B3
Le Barp [F] 78 B4
Le Beausset [F] 124 F4
Lebedin [UA] 242 F3
Lěbénymiklós [H] 74 E3
Lebesby [N] 228 D2
Le Biot [F] 116 B2
Le Blanc [F] 66 F4
Łebno [PL] 36 C1
Le Boréon [F] 126 C2
Łebork [PL] 36 B1
Le Boulou [F] 96 E1
Le Bourg d'Oisans [F] 80 F4
Le Bourget [F] 80 E3
le Bousquet–d'Orb [F] 124 C2
Le Bouveret [CH] 116 B2
Lebrija [E] 104 B2
Lebring [A] 120 C2
Le Bugue [F] 78 D4
Lebus [D] 46 C2
Lebyazh'e [RUS] 200 E3
Le Calanche [F] 130 A2
le Caloy [F] 88 C1
Le Cap–d'Agde [F] 124 C3
Le Cateau–Cambrésis [F]
  56 A1
Le Catelet [F] 54 F1
Le Caylar [F] 124 C2
Lecce [I] 136 E3
Lecco [I] 116 E3
Lécera [E] 92 E4
Lech [A] 72 A4
Lechainá [GR] 166 C4
L'Echalp [F] 126 C1
le Chambon–sur–Lignon
  [F] 80 C2
Le Chateau–d'Oléron [F] 78 B1
Le Châtelard [F] 80 F3
Le Châtelet [F] 68 B4
Le Chesne [F] 56 C3
Le Cheylard [F] 80 C4
Lechlade on Thames [GB]
  28 B2
Lechmühlen [D] 72 B3
Lechovice [CZ] 74 D2
Léchovo [GR] 160 D2
Lěči [LV] 234 D3
Leciñena [E] 94 E2
Leck [D] 178 B3
Le Conquet [F] 52 A3
Le Coteau [F] 80 C2
Le Creusot [F] 68 E4
Le Croisic [F] 66 B2
Le Crotoy [F] 40 A4

Lectoure [F] 88 D2
Łęczna [PL] 50 C3
Łęczyca [PL] 34 E3
Łęczyca [PL] 48 D2
Ledal [N] 202 E2
Ledaña [E] 102 B3
Ledbury [GB] 26 F1
Ledeč nad Sázavou [CZ]
  60 E3
Ledena Pečina [MNE] 152 E2
Ledenice [CZ] 74 B1
Ledenika Peštera [BG]
  148 D4
Ledesma [E] 84 E4
Ledge [D] 32 E4
Lédignan [F] 124 D2
Ledigos [E] 86 B3
Leding [S] 206 D2
Lednica [SK] 62 D4
Lednice [CZ] 74 D2
Le Donjon [F] 80 C1
Le Dorat [F] 78 E1
Ledreborg [DK] 178 E2
Lędyczek [PL] 36 B3
Leeds [GB] 24 C2
Leek [GB] 24 B3
Leek [NL] 30 D2
Leenane [IRL] 12 A3
Leens [NL] 30 D2
Leer [D] 30 E2
Leerdam [NL] 30 B4
Leese [D] 44 B1
Leesi [EST] 230 D1
Leeuwarden [NL] 30 C2
Le Faou [F] 52 B3
Le Faouët [F] 52 B3
le Fayet [F] 116 B2
Lefka [BG] 156 F2
Léfka (Lefke) [CY] 176 D3
Lefkáda [GR] 166 B3
Lefkádia [GR] 160 E2
Lefkaditi [GR] 166 E3
Lefke (Léfka) [CY] 176 D3
Léfkes [GR] 168 D4
Lefkími [GR] 166 A2
Lefkógeia [GR] 156 C3
Lefkónikon (Geçitkale) [CY]
  176 E3
Lefkoşa (Lefkosía) [CY]
  176 D3
Lefkosía (Lefkoşa) [CY]
  176 D3
Léfktra [GR] 166 F3
le Folgoet [F] 52 B2
Le Folgoët [F] 52 B2
Le Fossat [F] 88 E3
Le Freney [F] 116 A4
le Fuilet [F] 66 C2
Leganés [E] 92 E4
Le–Gault–St–Denis [F] 54 C4
Legbąd [PL] 36 C3
Legden [D] 30 D4
Legé [F] 66 C3
Legionowo [PL] 48 F2
Léglise [B] 56 D2
Legnago [I] 118 B4
Legnano [I] 116 D3
Legnica [PL] 46 E4
Legnickie Pole [PL] 46 E4
Legoland [DK] 178 B1
le Gouray [F] 52 D3
Łęgowo [PL] 36 C2
Legrad [HR] 120 D3
Le Grand–Bourg [F] 78 F2
Le Grand–Lucé [F] 66 F2
Le Grand–Pressigny [F] 66 F3
Le Grau–du–Roi [F] 124 D3
Legrená [GR] 168 B3
le Gressier [F] 78 B3
Leguatiano [E] 86 D3
Léguevin [F] 88 E2
Łęg Wygoda [PL] 64 B2

Le Havre [F] 54 B2
Lehelitz [D] 44 E3
le–Hérie–la Vieville [F] 56 A2
Lehliu [RO] 150 C1
Lehliu Gare [RO] 150 C1
Lehmäjoki [FIN] 208 C2
Lehmen [D] 56 F2
Lehmo [FIN] 210 E2
Lehnice [SK] 74 E3
Lehnin [D] 44 F2
Le Hohwald [F] 70 D2
Le Houga [F] 88 C2
Lehrberg [D] 58 D4
Lehre [D] 44 C2
Lehrte [D] 44 C2
Lehtimäki [FIN] 208 D2
Lehtmetsa [EST] 230 D2
Lehtola [FIN] 222 D3
Lehtomäki [FIN] 216 D4
Lehtovaara [FIN] 210 F2
Lehtovaara [FIN] 216 D3
Leianokládi [GR] 166 E2
Leibnitz [A] 120 C2
Leicester [GB] 24 C4
Leiden [NL] 30 A3
Leie [EST] 230 E3
Leiferde [D] 44 C1
Leighlinbridge [IRL] 10 E3
Leighton Buzzard [GB] 28 C2
Leikanger [N] 192 C2
Leikanger [N] 202 B3
Leinefelde [D] 44 C3
Leinelä [FIN] 198 F2
Leinesodden [N] 212 D1
Leini [I] 116 C4
Leipalingis [LT] 38 D1
Leipämäki [FIN] 210 D3
Leipheim [D] 72 B2
Leipojärvi [S] 220 E2
Leipsoí [GR] 170 A4
Leipzig [D] 44 E3
Leira [N] 192 E2
Leira [N] 202 E2
Leira [N] 212 D1
Leirbotn [N] 228 B3
Leirfall [N] 204 C2
Leirgulen [N] 202 B4
Leiria [P] 90 C2
Leiro [E] 82 B3
Leirosa [P] 90 C1
Leirpollskogen [N] 228 E2
Leirvik [FR] 182 B1
Leirvik [N] 192 B4
Leirvik [N] 192 B2
Leirvik [N] 224 C4
Leirvika [N] 218 E4
Leisi [EST] 230 B3
Leisnig [D] 44 F4
Leissigen [CH] 116 C1
Leitir Meallain / Lettermullan
  [IRL] 10 B1
Leitzkau [D] 44 E2
Leivadia [CY] 176 E3
Leivadítis [GR] 156 D3
Leivonmäki [FIN] 210 B4
Lejasciems [LV] 236 D2
Lekáni [GR] 156 C2
Łękawa [PL] 48 D4
Lekeitio / Lequeitio [E] 86 E3
Lekenik [HR] 120 D4
Lekeryd [S] 184 C1
Lekhchevo [BG] 148 D3
Łęki Górne [PL] 64 B3
Leknes [N] 202 C3
Leknes [N] 218 F1
Łeknica [PL] 46 C3
Leksand [S] 194 F3
Leksberg [S] 188 E3
Leksdalen [N] 204 C2
Leksvik [N] 204 B1
Lekunberri [E] 86 F3
Lekvattnet [S] 194 D4

Leland [N] 212 D1
Le Lauzet–Ubaye [F] 126 B2
Le Lavandou [F] 126 A4
L'Elefante [I] 142 B2
Lelice [PL] 48 D1
Le Liège [F] 66 F3
Le Lion–D'Angers [F] 66 D2
Lelkowo [PL] 36 E2
Lelle [EST] 230 D2
Le Locle [CH] 70 C4
Le Logis–du–Pin [F] 126 B3
Le Loroux–Bottereau [F] 66 C2
Le Louroux [F] 66 D2
Lelów [PL] 62 F2
Le Luc [F] 126 A3
Le Ludd [F] 66 E2
Lelystad [NL] 30 C3
Lem [DK] 178 A1
Le Mans [F] 54 B4
Le Markstein [F] 70 C2
Le Mas–d'Azil [F] 88 E3
Le Mayet [F] 80 C1
Lembach [F] 56 F4
Lembeck [D] 42 D2
Lembeye [F] 88 C2
Lemele [NL] 30 D3
Le Merlerault [F] 54 B3
Le–Mesnil–Vigot [F] 52 F2
Lemesos (Limassol) [CY]
  176 D4
Lemetinvaara [FIN] 216 D3
Lemförde [D] 30 F3
Lemgo [D] 42 F2
Lemi [FIN] 200 C2
Lemke [D] 32 B4
Lemland [FIN] 198 A4
Lemmenjoki [FIN] 226 D2
Lemmer [NL] 30 C2
Lemnhult [S] 184 D2
Le Monastier [F] 80 C4
Le Monêtier–les–Bains
  [F] 80 F4
Le Monteix [F] 80 B1
Le Montet [F] 68 C4
Le Mont–St–Michel [F]
  52 E3
le Mouret [CH] 116 B1
Lemovzha [RUS] 232 E1
Lempäälä [FIN] 198 E1
Lempdes [F] 80 B3
Lempdes [F] 80 B2
Lempyy [FIN] 210 C2
le Mulins [F] 80 C2
Le Muret [F] 78 B4
Le Muy [F] 126 B3
Lemvig [DK] 182 B3
Lena [N] 194 B3
Lenart v Slovenskih goricah
  [SLO] 120 C2
Lencloître [F] 66 E3
Lencouacq [F] 88 C1
Lend [A] 72 E4
Lendava [SLO] 120 D2
Lendery [RUS] 216 F4
Lendinara [I] 128 D1
Lendum [DK] 182 E2
Lenes [N] 202 E2
Le Neubourg [F] 54 C2
Lengefeld [D] 58 F1
Lengerich [D] 30 E3
Lengerich [D] 30 E4
Lenggries [D] 72 C3
Lengnau [CH] 70 E3
Lengyeltóti [H] 120 B2
Lenhovda [S] 184 D3
Leni [I] 138 B3
Lenina [BY] 242 D3
Léning [F] 56 E4
Lenk [CH] 116 C2
Lenna [I] 116 F3

Lennartsfors [S] 188 C2
Lenningen [N] 192 F2
Lenno [I] 116 E3
Leno [I] 116 F4
Lenola [I] 134 B2
Lenora [CZ] 72 F1
Le Nouvion–en–Thiérache
  [F] 56 B2
Lenovo [BG] 156 D2
Lens [F] 40 C4
Lensahn [D] 32 D2
Lensvik [N] 204 A1
Léntas [GR] 174 D4
Lentföhrden [D] 32 C2
Lenti [H] 120 D2
Lentiira [FIN] 216 E2
Lenting [D] 72 C1
Lentini [I] 140 E3
Lentvaris [LT] 238 E3
Lenungen [S] 188 C2
Lenzburg [CH] 70 E3
Lenzen [D] 32 D4
Lenzerheide [CH] 116 E1
Lenzkirch [D] 70 E3
Leoben [A] 74 B4
Leoben [A] 118 E1
Leogang [A] 72 E4
Leominster [GB] 26 E1
León [E] 82 F4
Léon [F] 88 B1
Leonarisso (Ziyamet) [CY]
  176 F2
Leonberg [D] 70 F1
Leonessa [I] 132 D3
Leonessa [I] 134 E3
Leonforte [I] 140 D2
Leonídio [GR] 172 E2
Leontári [GR] 172 D2
Leóntio [GR] 172 D1
Leontýnský Zámek [CZ] 60 D3
Leopoldsburg [B] 40 F3
Leopoldsdorf [A] 74 D3
Leopovina [HR] 120 D3
Le Palais [F] 66 A1
Le Palmyre [F] 78 B2
L'Epau, Abbaye de– [F] 54 B4
Lepe [E] 98 D4
Le–Péage–de–Roussillon
  [F] 80 D3
Lepenica [SRB] 154 E2
Lepenicë [AL] 160 A3
Lepenoú [GR] 166 C3
Le Perthus [F] 96 E1
Lepetane [MNE] 152 E3
Le Pin–au–Haras [F] 54 B3
L'Epine [F] 56 B3
Lepistönmäki [FIN] 208 D1
le Pleynet [F] 80 F3
Lepoglava [HR] 120 C3
Le Poiré–sur–Vie [F] 66 C3
Le Pont [F] 80 F3
Le Pont–de–Beauvoisin
  [F] 80 E3
Le Pont–de–Claix [F] 80 E4
le Pont–de–Montvert [F]
  124 C1
Le Pontet [F] 78 B3
Leporano [I] 136 D3
Le Porge [F] 78 B3
Le Portel [F] 40 A3
Leposavić [KS] 148 A4
Le Pouldu [F] 52 B4
Lépoura [GR] 168 B2
Le Pouzin [F] 80 D4
Leppäkoski [FIN] 200 A1
Leppälä [FIN] 200 D2
Leppälahti [FIN] 210 B1
Leppälahti [FIN] 210 D2
Leppämäki [FIN] 210 C2
Leppäselkä [FIN] 210 B2
Leppävesi [FIN] 208 F3
Leppävirta [FIN] 210 C3

Leppiniemi [FIN] 216 B2
Lépreo [GR] 172 C2
Lepsény [H] 120 F1
Leptokaryá [GR] 160 F3
Lëpushë [AL] 152 F3
Le Puy–en–Velay [F] 80 C3
Lequeitio / Lekeitio [E] 86 E3
Leques, Col des– [F] 126 B3
Le Quesnoy [F] 40 C4
Ler [N] 204 B2
Le Rabot [F] 68 B2
Lerbäck [S] 188 F3
Lercara Friddi [I] 140 C2
Lerchenborg [DK] 178 D2
Lerdala [S] 188 E4
Lerga [E] 88 A3
Lcrici [I] 128 A3
Lérida / Lleida [E] 96 B2
Lerín [E] 94 C1
Lerma [E] 92 F1
Lerm–et–Musset [F] 88 D1
Lermoos [A] 72 B4
Lérni [GR] 172 E2
Le Rozier [F] 124 C2
Lerresfjord [N] 228 B2
Lerum [S] 184 A1
Le Russey [F] 70 C4
Lerwick [GB] 16 E4
Lés [E] 88 D4
Leş [RO] 122 F1
Lesa [I] 116 D3
Les Abrets [F] 80 E3
Les Adrets [F] 126 B3
Les Aix–d'Angillon [F] 68 C3
Lešak [KS] 154 C1
Lesaka [E] 86 F3
les Aldudes [F] 88 A3
Les Andelys [F] 54 D2
Les Antiques [F] 124 E3
Les Arcs [F] 116 B3
Les Arcs [F] 126 B3
les Avants [CH] 116 B2
les Avellanes [E] 96 B2
Les Baux–de–Provence [F] 124 E3
les Borges Blanques [E] 96 B3
Les Bouchoux [F] 80 F2
Le Boulay Lue [F] 56 D3
Les Cabannes [F] 88 E4
L'Escala [E] 96 F2
Les Calanques [F] 124 E4
Lescar [F] 88 C2
L'Escarène [F] 126 C3
Les Cases d'Alcanar [E] 96 A4
Lesce [SLO] 118 F2
Les Contamines–Montjoie [F] 116 B3
les Coves de Vinromà [E] 102 E2
Les Deux–Alpes [F] 80 F4
Les Diablerets [CH] 116 B2
Lesdins [F] 54 F2
Les Echarmeaux [F] 80 D2
Les Echelles [F] 80 E3
Le Sentier [CH] 80 F1
Les Epesses [F] 66 D2
Les Escaldes [AND] 96 D1
Les Essarts [F] 66 C3
Les Eyzies–de–Tayac [F] 78 D4
Les–Fins [F] 70 C4
Les Forges [F] 52 C4
Les Gets [F] 116 B2
Les Halles [F] 80 D2
Les Haudères [CH] 116 C2
Les Hayons [F] 54 D2
Les Herbiers [F] 66 C3
Les Houches [F] 116 B2
Lesichovo [BG] 156 C2
Lésina [I] 134 E2
Les Issambres [F] 126 B3
Lesja [N] 202 E4
Lesjärvi [FIN] 198 E2

Lesjaskog [N] 202 E3
Lesjaverk [N] 202 E4
Lesjöfors [S] 188 E1
Leskelä [FIN] 216 B3
Lesko [PL] 64 D3
Leskovac [SRB] 148 B4
Leskova Dolina [SLO] 120 A4
Leskovik [AL] 160 C3
Leskovo [BG] 150 E2
Les Laumes [F] 68 E3
Les Lecques [F] 124 F4
Les Menuires [F] 116 A3
Lesmont [F] 68 E1
Lósna [PL] 46 D4
Lesneven [F] 52 B2
Lešnica [PL] 62 D2
Lešnica [ŠRB] 146 C2
Leśniów Wielki [PL] 46 D3
Lesnovo [MK] 154 E3
Lesogorskiy [RUS] 200 D2
Lesparre–Médoc [F] 78 B2
Lesperon [F] 88 B1
Les Pieux [F] 52 E2
Les Planches–en–Montagne [F] 80 F1
les Planes d'Hostoles [E] 96 E2
l'Espluga de Francolí [E] 96 C3
Les Ponts–de–Cé [F] 66 D2
Lesquin [F] 40 C4
Les Riceys [F] 68 E2
Les Rosiers [F] 66 E2
les Rotes [E] 108 C2
Les Rousses [F] 80 F1
Les Sables–d'Olonne [F] 66 B3
Les Saisies [F] 116 A3
Les Salles [F] 80 C2
Lessay [F] 52 E2
Lessebo [S] 184 D3
Lessila [FIN] 198 C1
Lessines [B] 40 D3
l estards [F] 78 F3
l'Estartit [E] 96 F2
Lestelle Bétharram [F] 88 C3
Les–Thilliers–en–Vexin [F] 54 D2
Lestijärvi [FIN] 208 E1
Les Trois–Epis [F] 70 D2
Les Trois–Moutiers [F] 66 E3
Lesum [D] 32 A3
Lesura [BG] 148 D3
les Useres / Useras [E] 102 E2
Les Vans [F] 124 D1
Leszno [PL] 46 E3
Leszno [PL] 48 E2
Leszno Górne [PL] 46 D3
Létavértes [H] 76 E4
Letchworth [GB] 28 D2
Le Teil [F] 124 E1
Le Teilleul [F] 52 F3
le Temple [F] 78 B3
Letenye [H] 120 D2
Le Thillot [F] 70 C2
Letkés [H] 76 A3
Letku [FIN] 198 E2
Letmathe [D] 42 D3
Letnitsa [BG] 150 A3
Letohrad [CZ] 62 B3
Letoon [TR] 176 E1
Le Touquet–Paris–Plage [F] 40 A3
Le Touvet [F] 80 E3
Letovice [CZ] 62 B3
Le Trayas [F] 126 B3
Le Tremblade [F] 78 B2
Le Tréport [F] 54 D1
Letreros, Cueva de los– [E] 106 C2
Letsbo [S] 196 B1
Letschin [D] 46 C1
Letterfrack [IRL] 12 A3
Letterkenny [IRL] 12 D1

Lettermullan / Leitir Mealláin [IRL] 10 B1
Letur [E] 106 C1
Letychiv [UA] 244 E2
Letzlingen [D] 44 D2
Leu [RO] 148 E2
Leucate [F] 96 F1
Leuchtenburg [D] 58 F1
Leuglay [F] 68 E2
Leuk [CH] 116 C2
Leukerbad [CH] 116 C2
Leun [D] 58 B1
Leuna [D] 44 E3
Leussow [D] 32 D3
Leutasch [A] 72 C4
Leutenberg [D] 50 T2
Leutkirch [D] 72 A3
Leutschach [A] 120 C2
Leuven (Louvain) [B] 40 E3
Leuze [B] 40 D4
Levajok [N] 228 D3
Le Val–André [F] 52 D3
Levan [AL] 160 A2
Levänen [FIN] 200 C2
Levanger [N] 204 C1
Levanto [FIN] 198 F2
Lévanto [I] 126 F3
Levanzo [I] 140 A2
Leväranta [FIN] 222 D2
Levashovo [RUS] 200 F3
Leväsjoki [FIN] 208 C4
Le Vast [F] 52 F1
Le Vaudreuil [F] 54 C2
Levdun [N] 228 B3
Leven [GB] 18 E3
Levens [F] 126 C3
Le Verdon [F] 78 B2
Leverkusen [D] 42 C3
Levern [D] 30 F4
Le Vernet [F] 126 B2
Levet [F] 68 B3
Levice [SK] 76 A3
Levico Terme [I] 118 B3
Levídi [GR] 172 D2
Levie [F] 130 B3
Levier [F] 70 B4
Le Vigan [F] 124 C2
Levoča [SK] 76 C1
Levroux [F] 68 A3
Levski [BG] 150 A3
Levunovo [BG] 156 B3
Lewes [GB] 28 C4
Lewin Brzeski [PL] 62 C2
Leyburn [GB] 20 E4
Leypi [RUS] 222 F1
Leysin [CH] 116 B2
Leżajsk [PL] 64 D2
Ležáky [CZ] 60 F3
LežE [AL] 152 F4
Lézignan–Corbières [F] 124 B3
Lezoux [F] 80 B2
Lezuza [E] 102 A3
Lgota [PL] 62 A2
L'gov [RUS] 242 F2
Libčeves [CZ] 60 E2
Liberec [CZ] 60 E1
Libiąż [PL] 62 E3
Libochovice [CZ] 60 D2
Libohovë [AL] 160 B3

Libourne [F] 78 C3
Libramont [B] 56 C2
Librazhd [AL] 160 B1
Librilla [E] 106 D2
Libusza [PL] 64 C3
Licata [I] 140 D3
Licciana Nardi [I] 128 A2
Lich [D] 58 C1
Licháda [GR] 166 F2
Lichfield [GB] 24 B4
Lichnice [CZ] 60 F3
Lichtenau [A] 74 C2
Lichtenau [D] 42 F3
Lichtenberg [D] 58 F2
Lichtenberg [F] 56 F4
Lichtenfels [D] 42 F3
Lichtenfels [D] 58 E2
Lichtensteig [CH] 70 F4
Lichtenstein [CH] 116 E1
Lichtenstein [D] 60 B1
Lichtenstein [D] 70 F2
Lichtenvoorde [NL] 30 D4
Lickershamn [S] 234 A2
Lički Osik [HR] 144 C2
Ličko Lešče [HR] 144 C2
Licodia Eubea [I] 140 E3
Licques [F] 40 B3
Lid [S] 188 E1
Lida [BY] 38 E2
Liden [S] 184 D1
Liden [S] 206 C3
Liden [S] 214 A2
Liden [S] 214 D3
Lidhult [S] 184 B3
Lidice [CZ] 60 D2
Lidingö [S] 190 D2
Lidköping [S] 188 D4
Lido degli Estensi [I] 128 D2
Lido delle Nazioni [I] 128 D2
Lido di Camaiore [I] 128 B3
Lido di Castel Fusano [I] 130 F4
Lido di Fermo [I] 132 E2
Lido di Jésolo [I] 118 D4
Lido di Latina [I] 134 A2
Lido di Metaponto [I] 136 D3
Lido di Ostia [I] 130 F4
Lido di Pomposa [I] 128 D2
Lido di Scanzano [I] 136 C3
Lido di Spina [I] 128 D2
Lido di Torre Mileto [I] 134 E2
Lido di Venézia [I] 118 D4
Lidoríki [GR] 166 E3
Lido Silvana [I] 136 D3
Lidsjöberg [S] 212 F4
Lidzbark [PL] 36 E3
Lidzbark Warmiński [PL] 36 F2
Liebegg [CH] 70 E3
Liebenau [A] 74 B2
Liebenau [D] 32 B4
Liebenwalde [D] 34 C4
Lieberose [D] 46 C2
Liebling [RO] 122 E4
Liechtenstein Klamm [A] 72 E4
Liedakkala [FIN] 222 B4
Liedenpohja [FIN] 208 D3
Lieg [D] 56 F2
Liège (Luik) [B] 40 F4
Lieksa [FIN] 210 E1
Lielvärde [LV] 236 B3
Lienz [A] 118 D2
Liepāja [LV] 234 C4
Liepna [LV] 230 F4
Lier [B] 40 E3
Lier [N] 186 F1
Lierbyen [N] 186 F1
Liérganes [E] 86 D2
Liernais [F] 68 E3
Lierville [F] 54 D2
Liesa [E] 94 E2
Liesjärvi [FIN] 208 E3
Lieskau [D] 46 B3

Lieske [D] 46 C4
Liesniemi [FIN] 198 D3
Liesse [F] 56 A2
Liestal [CH] 70 D3
Lieto / Lundo [FIN] 198 D3
Liétor [E] 102 B4
Lieu–Restauré, Abbaye de– [F] 54 E3
Lieurey [F] 54 C2
Lievestuore [FIN] 210 B3
Lievikoski [FIN] 198 C1
Liezen [A] 74 A4
Liezere [LV] 236 C3
Lifford [IRL] 12 D1
Liffré [F] 52 E4
Liggavägen [S] 220 D3
Ligieri [LV] 236 B3
Lignano Pineta [I] 118 E4
Lignano Sabbiadoro [I] 118 E3
Ligneuville [B] 56 D1
Lignières [F] 68 B3
Ligny–en–Barrois [F] 56 C4
Ligourió [GR] 172 E2
Ligueil [F] 66 F3
Ligugé, Abbaye de– [F] 66 E4
Lihjamo [FIN] 208 E3
Lihme [DK] 182 C3
Lihula [EST] 230 C3
Liiansaari [FIN] 200 C1
Liitsola [FIN] 198 D2
Liiva [EST] 230 C3
Lijärvi [FIN] 226 D1
Lijeva Rijeka [MNE] 152 F3
Likavský Hrad [SK] 76 B1
Likenäs [S] 194 D3
Likosoúra [GR] 172 D2
Likovskoye [RUS] 232 E2
Liland [S] 206 C3
Lilaste [LV] 234 F2
Lild Strand [DK] 182 C2
L'Ile–Bouchard [F] 66 E3
L'Ile–Rousse [F] 130 B2
Lilienfeld [A] 74 C3
Liljendal [FIN] 200 B3
Lilla Edet [S] 184 A1
Lilláfors [S] 220 E3
Lillafüred [H] 76 D3
Lillaz [I] 116 B3
Lillbo [S] 196 C1
Lillby [FIN] 208 C1
Lille [DK] 178 E2
Lille [F] 40 C3
Lillebo [N] 194 C1
Lillebonne [F] 54 C2
Lillefjord [N] 228 B2
Lillehammer [N] 194 B2
Lillerød [DK] 178 F2
Lillers [F] 40 B3
Lillesand [N] 186 D4
Lillestrøm [N] 188 B1
Lille Værløse [DK] 178 F2
Lillhaga [S] 194 F1
Lillhärad [S] 190 C2
Lillhärdal [S] 194 E1
Lillholmsjö [S] 204 E1
Lillholmträsk [S] 214 C2
Lillkågesträsk [S] 214 D2
Lillkyro / Vähäkyro [FIN] 208 C2
Lillo [E] 100 E2
Lillögda [S] 214 B1
Lillpite [S] 214 D1
Lillsele [S] 206 C1
Lillsele [S] 214 C3
Lillviken [S] 220 B3
Limáni Chersonísou [GR] 174 D3
Limanköy [TR] 158 C2
Limanowa [PL] 64 B3
Limassol (Lemesos) [CY] 176 D4
Limatola [I] 134 D3

Limavady [NIR] 12 E1
Limbaži [LV] 230 D4
Limbourg [B] 40 F4
Limburg [D] 58 B2
Limedsforsen [S] 194 E3
Limenária [GR] 162 D1
Liménas [GR] 168 B1
Liméni [GR] 172 D3
Limerick / Luimneach [IRL] 10 C2
Limhamn [S] 178 F2
Limingo / Liminka [FIN] 216 B2
Liminka / Limingo [FIN] 216 B2
Liminkakylä [FIN] 216 A3
Limín Litochórou [GR] 160 F3
Limínpuro [FIN] 216 C2
Limmared [S] 184 B2
Limna [UA] 64 D4
Limnae [TR] 164 A2
Límnes [GR] 172 E1
Límni [GR] 168 A1
Limniá [GR] 156 D4
Limnítsa [GR] 166 D3
Limoges [F] 78 E2
Limogne-en-Quercy [F] 88 F1
Limone Piemonte [I] 126 C2
Limonest [F] 80 D2
Limone sul Garda [I] 118 B3
Limosano [I] 134 D2
Limours [F] 54 D3
Limoux [F] 88 F4
Lin [AL] 160 C2
Lina älv [S] 220 E2
Linares [E] 104 F1
Linares de Mora [E] 102 D2
Linares de Riofrío [E] 92 B3
Linariá [GR] 162 D4
Linate [I] 116 E4
Lincoln [GB] 24 D3
Lind [DK] 178 B1
Lindärva [S] 188 D4
Lindås [N] 192 B2
Lindås [S] 184 E3
Lindau [D] 44 E2
Lindau [D] 72 A3
Lindaunis [D] 32 C1
Linddalen [S] 188 F3
Linde [DK] 182 C2
Lindefallet [S] 196 C2
Lindefjell [N] 186 C3
Lindelbrunn [D] 56 F4
Lindelse [DK] 178 D3
Linden [BG] 156 C3
Linden [D] 56 F3
Lindenberg [D] 46 B1
Lindenberg [D] 72 A3
Lindenfels [D] 58 B3
Lindenholz [CH] 70 D4
Linderbach [D] 44 D4
Linderhof [D] 72 B3
Lindern [D] 30 E3
Linderöd [S] 180 D2
Lindesberg [S] 188 F2
Lindesnäs [S] 194 F4
Lindkoski [FIN] 200 B3
Lindlia [N] 192 F3
Lindome [S] 184 A2
Líndos [GR] 176 C2
Lindoso [P] 82 B4
Lindow [D] 32 F4
Lindsås [N] 186 D3
Lindum [DK] 182 D3
Lindved [DK] 178 C1
Líné [CZ] 60 C3
Lingbo [S] 196 C3
Linge [N] 202 D3
Lingen [D] 30 E3
Linghed [S] 196 B3
Linghem [S] 190 B4
Linguaglossa [I] 138 C4

Linken [D] 34 D3
Linköping [S] 190 B4
Linkvarnen [S] 204 E4
Linna [FIN] 208 F2
Linnankylä [FIN] 208 D3
Linnanperä [FIN] 208 F1
Linnerud [N] 194 C2
Linneryd [S] 184 D3
Linnes [N] 194 D2
Linnés Hammarby [S] 190 D1
Linova [BY] 38 E4
Linovo [RUS] 236 E2
Linsdal [S] 184 E3
Linsell [S] 204 E4
Linthal [CH] 116 E1
Lintzel [D] 32 C4
Linum [D] 44 F1
Linz [A] 74 A2
Linz [D] 56 F1
Liomseter [N] 192 F2
Lioni [I] 134 E3
Liópraso [GR] 160 E4
Lipa [BIH] 144 F4
Lípa [CZ] 62 C4
Lipa [PL] 64 C1
Lipany [SK] 64 B4
Lipar [SRB] 122 C4
Lípari [I] 138 C3
Lipcani [MD] 244 E2
Liperi [FIN] 210 D2
Liperonmäki [FIN] 210 B3
Lipiany [PL] 34 E4
Lipica [SLO] 118 F4
Lipik [HR] 120 E4
Lipinki Łużyckie [PL] 46 D3
Lipka [PL] 36 B3
Lipljan [KS] 154 C2
Lipnica [BG] 148 E3
Lipnica [PL] 36 B2
Lipnica [PL] 36 D4
Lipnice nad Sázavou [CZ] 60 E3
Lipník [PL] 64 C1
Lipník nad Bečvou [CZ] 62 C4
Lipnishki [BY] 38 F1
Lipnița [RO] 150 F2
Lipno [PL] 36 D4
Lipno nad Vltavou [CZ] 74 A2
Lipova [CZ] 62 D4
Lipova [RO] 122 E3
Lipovac [HR] 146 C1
Lipová-Lázně [CZ] 62 C2
Lipovci [SLO] 120 D2
Lipovica [SRB] 148 B4
Lipovka [RUS] 238 B3
Lipovljani [HR] 120 E4
Lipovo Polje [HR] 144 C2
Lipowina [PL] 36 E2
Lipowo [PL] 36 E3
Lippborg [D] 42 E2
Lippstadt [D] 42 E3
Lipsheim [F] 70 D1
Lipsk [PL] 38 C2
Lipsko [PL] 50 B4
Lipsko [PL] 64 E1
Liptovská Osada [SK] 76 B1
Liptovská Teplička [SK] 76 C1
Liptovské Matiašovce [SK] 62 F4
Liptovský-Mikuláš [SK] 76 B1
Lipusz [PL] 36 C2
Lis [AL] 154 B4
Lisaku [EST] 230 F2
Lisboa [P] 90 B3
Lisburn [NIR] 12 F2
Liscarroll [IRL] 10 C3
Lisdoonvarna [IRL] 10 C2
Lisec [MK] 154 C3
Liseleje [DK] 178 E1
Liselund [DK] 178 F3
Liselund [DK] 178 F3
Lisia Góra [PL] 64 B3

Lisieux [F] 54 B2
Lisinki [FIN] 222 C2
Liskeard [GB] 26 C3
Lisland [N] 186 D2
L'Isle [CH] 116 B1
Lisle [F] 78 D3
L'Isle-Adam [F] 54 E3
L'Isle-de-Noé [F] 88 D2
L'Isle-en-Dodon [F] 88 E3
l'Isle-Jourdain [F] 78 E1
L'Isle-Jourdain [F] 88 E2
Lisleset [N] 192 E3
L'Isle-sur-la-Sorgue [F] 124 E2
L'Isle-sur-le-Doubs [F] 70 C3
Lisle-sur-Tarn [F] 88 F2
Lisma [FIN] 226 C3
Lismore [IRL] 10 D3
Lišnja [BIH] 144 F2
Lison, Source du– [F] 70 B4
Lišov [CZ] 74 B1
Lisów [PL] 46 C2
Lisse [NL] 30 B3
Lissewege [B] 40 C2
Lisskogsbränden [S] 194 E3
Líst [D] 178 A3
Lista [S] 190 C2
Lişteava [RO] 148 E2
Listeid [N] 186 B4
Listerby [S] 180 E1
Liština [BIH] 152 C1
Listowel [IRL] 10 B2
Lit [S] 204 F2
Litene [LV] 236 D2
Litér [H] 120 F1
Liternum [I] 134 C3
Lit-et-Mixe [F] 88 B1
Lithakiá [GR] 172 B2
Lithínes [GR] 174 E4
Litl [GR] 160 F2
Litice [CZ] 62 B3
Litija [SLO] 120 B3
Litke [H] 76 B3
Litmalahti [FIN] 210 C2
Litmaniemi [FIN] 210 C2
Litóchoro [GR] 160 F3
Litoměřice [CZ] 60 D2
Litomyšl [CZ] 62 B3
Litovel [CZ] 62 C3
Litslena [S] 190 D2
Littlehampton [GB] 28 C4
Littleport [GB] 28 D1
Littoperä [FIN] 216 C4
Litultovice [CZ] 62 C3
Litvínov [CZ] 60 C2
Liubar [UA] 244 E1
Liubech [UA] 242 D3
Liubeshiv [UA] 50 F2
Liuboml' [UA] 50 D3
Liukoniai [LT] 238 D3
Liusselsstugan [S] 220 D4
Liuta [UA] 76 F1
Livada de Bihor [RO] 122 F1
Livade [HR] 118 F4
Livadeiá [GR] 166 F3
Livaderó [GR] 156 C3
Livadhja [AL] 160 B4
Livádi [GR] 160 E3
Livádi [GR] 162 B1
Livádi [GR] 168 C4
Livádi [GR] 172 E4
Livádia [GR] 176 B2
Livadochóri [GR] 162 E2
Līvāni [LV] 236 D3
Livari [MNE] 152 E3
Livarot [F] 54 B2
Liverá [GR] 160 D3
Livera (Sadrazamköy) [CY] 176 D3
Livernon [F] 78 E4
Liverpool [GB] 22 E2
Livigno [I] 116 F2

Livingston [GB] 18 D4
Livno [BIH] 144 E4
Livo [FIN] 216 C1
Livold [SLO] 120 B4
Livorno [I] 128 B4
Livorno Ferraris [I] 116 C4
Livov [SK] 64 B4
Livron–sur–Drôme [F] 80 D4
Liw [PL] 50 B1
Lixa [P] 84 B2
Lixoúri [GR] 166 B4
Lizard [GB] 26 A4
Lizarra / Estella [E] 86 E4
Lizartza [E] 86 F3
Lizy [F] 54 E3
Lizzano [I] 136 D3
Ljasnaja [BY] 38 F3
Lješane [KS] 154 B2
Ljig [SRB] 146 D3
Ljørdalen [N] 194 D2
Ljosland [N] 186 C3
Ljuba [SRB] 146 C1
Ljuban' [BY] 242 C3
Ljuban' [RUS] 240 C1
Ljubaništa [MK] 160 C2
Ljubenovo [BG] 156 E2
Ljubinje [BIH] 152 D2
Ljubljana [SLO] 120 A3
Ljubno [SLO] 120 A2
Ljubno [SLO] 120 B2
Ljubogošta [BIH] 146 B3
Ljubostinja, Manastir– [SRB] 146 E4
Ljubovija [SRB] 146 C3
Ljubovo [BIH] 152 D3
Ljubuški [BIH] 152 C2
Ljubytino [RUS] 240 C1
Ljudinovo [RUS] 242 E1
Ljugarn [S] 234 A3
Ljungby [S] 184 C3
Ljungbyhed [S] 180 C1
Ljungbyholm [S] 184 E3
Ljungdalen [S] 204 D3
Ljunghusen [S] 178 F2
Ljungsarp [S] 184 C2
Ljungsbro [S] 190 B4
Ljungskile [S] 188 C4
Ljusdal [S] 196 C1
Ljusfallshammar [S] 190 B3
Ljusne [S] 196 D2
Ljustero [S] 190 E2
Ljustorp [S] 206 C3
Ljusträsk [S] 214 C1
Ljutići [MNE] 152 F2
Ljuti Dol [BG] 148 E4
Ljutomer [SLO] 120 D2
Llafranc [E] 96 F3
Llagostera [E] 96 E3
Llanberis [GB] 22 D2
Llançà [E] 96 F2
Llandeilo [GB] 26 D1
Llandovery [GB] 26 D1
Llandudno [GB] 22 D2
Llanelli [GB] 26 D1
Llanes [E] 86 B2
Llangefni [GB] 22 D2
Llangollen [GB] 22 E3
Llangurig [GB] 22 D4
Llanidloes [GB] 22 D4
Llantwit Major [GB] 26 D2
Llanuwchllyn [GB] 22 D3
Llavorsí [E] 96 C1
Lleida / Lérida [E] 96 B2
Llera [E] 98 F2
Llerena [E] 98 F3
Lles de Cerdanya [E] 96 D1
Llíria [E] 102 D3
Llívia [F] 96 D1
Llodio / Laudio [E] 86 D3
Lloret de Mar [E] 96 E3

Lluc, Monestir de– [E] 108 D3
Llucena / Lucena del Cid [E] 102 E2
Llucmajor [E] 108 D3
Lnáře [CZ] 60 D4
Lniano [PL] 36 C3
Loano [I] 126 D2
Loarre, Cast. de– [E] 88 B4
Löbau [D] 46 C4
Lobenstein [D] 58 F2
Łobez [PL] 34 E3
Lobios [E] 82 B4
Löbnitz [D] 32 F2
Łobodno [PL] 62 E1
Lobón [E] 98 E2
Lobonäs [S] 196 B2
Loborika [HR] 144 A2
Lobosh [BG] 154 F2
Loburg [D] 44 E2
Łobżenica [PL] 36 B4
Locana [I] 116 C3
Locarno [CH] 116 D2
Loccum [D] 44 B1
Lochaline [GB] 18 B2
Loch Baghasdail /
Lochboisdale [GB] 14 A3
Lochboisdale / Loch
Baghasdail [GB] 14 A3
Lochearnhead [GB] 18 C3
Lochem [NL] 30 D4
Loches [F] 66 F3
Loch Garman / Wexford [IRL] 10 E4
Lochgilphead [GB] 18 B3
Lochinver [GB] 14 D2
Lochmaddy / Loch nam
Madadh [GB] 14 B2
Loch nam Madadh /
Lochmaddy [GB] 14 B2
Łochocin [PL] 48 D1
Łochów [PL] 38 B4
Lochranza [GB] 18 B4
Lochteå / Lohtaja [FIN] 214 F3
Lockenhaus [A] 74 D4
Lockerbie [GB] 20 D1
Löcknitz [D] 34 D3
Locmaria [F] 66 A2
Locmariaquer [F] 66 A1
Locminé [F] 52 C4
Locorotondo [I] 136 D2
Locquirec [F] 52 C2
Locri [I] 138 E3
Locri Epizefiri [I] 138 D3
Locronan [F] 52 B3
Loctudy [F] 52 B4
Löddeköpinge [S] 178 F2
Lode [I] 142 C3
Lode [LV] 236 C2
Löderup [S] 180 D2
Lodève [F] 124 C2
Lodi [I] 116 E4
Løding [N] 218 F2
Lødingen [N] 224 B4
Lodonero [I] 132 D3
Lodosa [E] 94 C1
Lödöse [S] 184 A1
Łódź [PL] 48 D3
Loeches [E] 92 F4
Loen [N] 202 C4
Loev [BY] 242 D3
Løfallstrand [N] 192 B4
Lofer [A] 72 D3
Lofsdal [FIN] 198 C3
Lofsdalen [S] 204 D4
Lofta [S] 184 E1
Loftahammar [S] 184 F1
Lofthus [N] 192 C3
Log [SLO] 118 E2
Loga [D] 30 E2
Loga [N] 186 B3
Logarska Dolina [SLO] 120 B2
Logatec [SLO] 118 F3

Lögda [S] 214 B3
Lögdeå [S] 206 E2
Logkaníkos [GR] 172 D2
Lognvik [N] 186 D1
Logroño [E] 86 E4
Logrosán [E] 100 B2
Løgstør [DK] 182 C3
Løgumkloster [DK] 178 B3
Lohals [DK] 178 D3
Lohberg [D] 60 C4
Lohéac [F] 52 D4
Lohikoski [FIN] 210 D4
Lohiniva [FIN] 222 B2
Lohiranta [FIN] 222 E3
Lohja [FIN] 198 E3
Lohmen [D] 32 E3
Löhne [D] 30 F4
Lohne [D] 30 F3
Lohnsfeld [D] 56 F3
Lohr [D] 58 C2
Lohtaja / Lochteå [FIN] 214 F3
Loiano [I] 128 C3
Loimaa [FIN] 198 D2
Loimaankunta [FIN] 198 D2
Loire, Gorges de la– [F] 80 C4
Lóiri [I] 142 C2
Loisirs, Parc de– [F] 78 B3
Loitz [D] 32 F2
Loja [E] 104 E2
Lojanice [SRB] 146 D2
Lojsta [S] 234 A3
Lojt Kirkeby [DK] 178 B3
Loka Brunn [S] 188 E2
Lokachi [UA] 50 E4
Lokakylä [FIN] 208 E2
Lokalahti [FIN] 198 C3
Lokca [SK] 62 E4
Loke [SLO] 120 B3
Løken [N] 188 C1
Lokeren [B] 40 D3
Loket [CZ] 60 B2
Lokhvytsia [UA] 242 E4
Lokka [FIN] 226 E4
Løkken Verk [N] 202 F2
Løkken [DK] 182 D2
Loknya [RUS] 240 C3
Løkośháza [H] 122 E2
Lokot' [RUS] 242 E2
Loksa [EST] 230 D1
Lokuta [EST] 230 D2
Lokve [HR] 120 B4
Lokve [SLO] 118 F3
Lokve [SRB] 146 E1
l'Olleria [E] 102 D4
Lölling [A] 120 B1
Lom [BG] 148 D3
Lom [CZ] 60 C2
Lom [N] 192 E1
Lõmala [EST] 230 B3
Łomazy [PL] 50 C2
Lombez [F] 88 E3
Lombrives, Grotte de– [F] 88 E4
Lom Cherkovna [BG] 150 C3
Lomello [I] 116 D4
Lomen [N] 192 E2
Lomma [S] 180 C2
Lomme [F] 40 C3
Lommel [B] 40 F3
Lom nad Rimavicou [SK] 76 B2
Lomnice nad Lužnicí [CZ] 74 B1
Lomonosov [RUS] 200 E3
Lompolo [FIN] 226 C3
Lomsjö [S] 214 B3
Łomża [PL] 38 B3
Lonato [I] 118 A4
Lončari [BIH] 146 B2
Lončarica [HR] 120 E3
Londinières [F] 54 D1
London [GB] 28 C3

Londonderry (Derry) [NIR] 12 E1
Lonevåg [N] 192 B3
Longá [GR] 160 E4
Longarone [I] 118 D2
Longeau [F] 68 F2
Longeville les St. Avold [F] 56 E3
Longford [IRL] 10 E1
Longny-au-Perche [F] 54 C3
Longobucco [I] 138 E1
Longo Mel [P] 90 C3
Longpont [F] 54 F3
Longré [F] 78 D1
Longroiva [P] 84 C3
Longsel [N] 218 E4
Longtown [GB] 20 D3
Longué [F] 66 E2
Longueau [F] 54 E1
Longuyon [F] 56 D3
Longwy [F] 56 D3
Lonigo [I] 118 C4
Lonin [N] 212 B4
Løningdalen [N] 192 B3
Löningen [D] 30 E3
Löningsberg [S] 204 F3
Łoniów [PL] 64 C2
Lono [N] 186 C1
Lönsboda [S] 184 C4
Lønsdal [N] 220 B3
Lønset [N] 202 D3
Lønset [N] 202 D3
Lons-le-Saunier [F] 68 F4
Lønstrup [DK] 182 D2
Lónya [H] 76 F2
Looberghe [F] 40 B3
Looe [GB] 26 C3
Loon Plage [F] 28 F4
Loosdorf [A] 74 C3
Lopar [HR] 144 B2
Lopare [BIH] 146 B2
Lopatica [MK] 160 D1
Lopatovo [RUS] 232 E3
Lope [LV] 236 C4
Lopera [E] 104 E1
Łopiennik [PL] 50 C4
Loppi [FIN] 198 E2
Lopud [HR] 152 D3
Lopukhinka [RUS] 200 E4
Łopuszna [PL] 62 F4
Łopuszno [PL] 48 E4
Loqueffret [F] 52 B3
Lora del Río [E] 104 C1
Lorca [E] 106 D2
Lorcé [B] 56 D1
Lorch [D] 58 A2
Lorch [D] 72 A1
Lordosa [P] 84 B3
Loredo [E] 86 D2
Loreley [D] 58 A2
Lørenskog [N] 188 B1
Lorentzen [F] 56 E4
Loreo [I] 128 D1
Loreto [I] 128 F4
Loreto Aprutino [I] 132 E3
Lórév [H] 122 B1
Lorgues [F] 126 B3
Lorica [I] 138 E2
Lorient [F] 52 B4
Lórinci [H] 76 B3
Loriol-sur-Drôme [F] 80 D4
Lorlanges [F] 80 B3
Lormes [F] 68 D3
Lormont [F] 78 B3
Loro Ciuffenna [I] 128 C4
Lorqui [E] 106 E2
Lörrach [D] 70 D3
Lorris [F] 68 C2
Lörsfeld [D] 42 C4
L'Orso [I] 142 C2
Lorup [D] 30 E3
Loryma [TR] 176 C1

Los [S] 194 F1
Losa, Nuraghe– [I] 142 B3
Los Abrigos [E] 112 C3
Los Alares [E] 100 C2
Los Alcázares [E] 106 E3
Los Arcos [E] 86 E4
Los Arcos [E] 98 E2
Losar de la Vera [E] 92 B4
Los Arenales del Sol / Arenals del Sol [E] 106 F2
Losau [D] 58 F2
Los Barrios [E] 104 B4
Los Caños de Meca [E] 104 B3
Los Corrales de Buelna [E] 86 C2
Loscos [E] 94 D4
Los Cristianos [E] 112 C3
Losenstein [A] 74 A3
Los Escullos [E] 106 C4
Losevo [RUS] 200 E1
Los Galachos [E] 94 E3
Los Gigantes [E] 112 C3
Losheim [D] 56 E1
Losheim [D] 56 E3
Los Hinojonos [E] 100 F2
Łosice [PL] 50 C2
Los Isidros [E] 102 C3
Loški Potok [SLO] 120 B4
Los Llanos de Aridane [E] 112 B1
Los Mallos [E] 88 B4
Los Millares [E] 106 B3
Los Molares [E] 104 C2
Los Navalmorales [E] 100 D1
Los Navalucillos [E] 100 D1
Los Ojuelos [E] 104 C2
Los Olmos [E] 94 E4
Losomäki [FIN] 210 D1
Łososina Dolna [PL] 64 B3
Los Palacios y Villafranca [E] 104 D2
l'Ospedale [F] 130 B3
Lossa [D] 44 D4
Los Santos de Maimona [E] 98 E2
Los Sauces [E] 112 B1
Lossburg [D] 70 D2
Losse [F] 88 D1
Lossiemouth [GB] 14 E3
Lostwithiel [GB] 26 B3
Los Urrutias [E] 106 E3
Los Villares [E] 104 F2
Los Yébenes [E] 100 E2
Löt [S] 184 F3
Lote [N] 202 C4
Løten [N] 194 C3
Lotorp [S] 190 B3
Lotoshino [RUS] 240 E3
Lotta [RUS] 226 E3
Lotte [D] 30 E4
Lottefors [S] 196 C2
Löttorp-Högby [S] 184 F3
Lotyn [PL] 36 A3
Lotzorai [I] 142 C4
Loubens-Lauragais [F] 88 F3
Loučná nad Desnou [CZ] 62 C2
Loudéac [F] 52 C3
Loudes [F] 80 C3
Loudun [F] 66 E3
Loué [F] 54 A4
Loue, Source de la– [F] 70 B4
Louejärvi [FIN] 222 C3
Loughborough [GB] 24 C4
Loughbrickland [NIR] 12 E3
Loughglinn [IRL] 12 C3
Loughmoe Castle [IRL] 10 D3
Loughrea [IRL] 10 D2
Louhans [F] 68 F4
Louhivaara [FIN] 210 E1

Louisburgh [IRL] 12 A2
Loukás [GR] 172 D2
Loukísia [GR] 168 A2
Loukusa [FIN] 222 E4
Loulay [F] 78 C1
Loulé [P] 98 B4
Louny [CZ] 60 D2
Louppy-sur-Loison [F] 56 C3
Lourdes [E] 82 C2
Lourdes [F] 88 C3
Louredo [P] 84 B2
Lourenzá [E] 82 D2
Loures [P] 90 B3
Lourical [P] 90 C2
Lourinhã [P] 90 B3
Loúros [GR] 166 C2
Lourosa [P] 84 A3
Loury [F] 68 B1
Lousa [P] 90 B3
Lousã [P] 90 D2
Lousada [P] 84 B2
Louth [GB] 24 D3
Loutrá [GR] 164 B4
Loutrá [GR] 166 D2
Loutrá [GR] 168 C3
Loutrá [GR] 172 C2
Loutrá Aidipsoú [GR] 166 F2
Loutrá Aridaías [GR] 160 E2
Loutrá Elefthéron [GR] 162 C1
Loutrá Kaïtsas [GR] 166 E2
Loutráki [GR] 166 C3
Loutráki [GR] 166 F4
Loutrá Kounoupélli (Yrmínis) [GR] 166 C4
Loutrá Kyllínis [GR] 172 B1
Loutrá Lagkadá [GR] 162 B1
Loutrá Smokóvou [GR] 166 D2
Loutrá Vólvis [GR] 162 B1
Loutrá Ypátis [GR] 166 E2
Loutró Elénis [GR] 166 F4
Loutrós [GR] 156 F4
Loútsa [GR] 168 B2
Louvain (Leuven) [B] 40 E3
Louviers [F] 54 C2
Louvigné-du-Desert [F] 52 E3
Lövånger [S] 214 E3
Lovasberény [H] 76 A4
Lövåsen [S] 196 B4
Lövåsen [S] 206 B2
Lovászi [H] 120 D2
Lövberg [S] 212 E2
Lövberga [S] 206 B1
Lovech [BG] 148 F4
Lovére [I] 116 F3
Lovestad [S] 180 D2
Loviisa / Lovisa [FIN] 200 B3
Løvik [N] 202 D2
Lovisa / Loviisa [FIN] 200 B3
Loviště [HR] 152 B2
Lövnäs [S] 194 E2
Lövnäs [S] 212 F3
Lövnäs [S] 214 B3
Lövnäs [S] 220 C3
Lövnäsvallen [S] 194 E1
Lövö [FIN] 198 B3
Lövö [H] 74 D4
Lovosice [CZ] 60 D2
Lovraeid [N] 186 B1
Lovran [HR] 120 A4
Lovrenc na Pohorju [SLO] 120 C2
Lovrin [RO] 122 D3
Lövsjö [S] 212 F3
Lövsjön [S] 194 F4
Lövstabruk [S] 196 D4
Lövstad [S] 190 B4
Lövstrand [S] 212 F4
Lövvik [S] 212 F4
Łowcza [PL] 50 C4
Löwenberg [D] 32 F4
Löwenfreigehege [D] 42 B3

Lowenstein [D] 42 F4
Lowestoft [GB] 28 F2
Łowicz [PL] 48 E2
Łowinek [PL] 36 C3
Łowyń [PL] 46 E2
Löytänä [FIN] 208 F1
Löytölä [FIN] 216 D3
Loż [SLO] 120 A4
Lozarevo [BG] 150 D4
Lozari [F] 130 B2
Lozen [BG] 156 C2
Lozen [BG] 156 F2
Lozenets [BG] 158 C1
Loznica [BG] 150 C3
Loznica [SRB] 146 C2
Loznica [SRB] 146 D3
Lozovac [HR] 144 D4
Lozovik [SRB] 146 E2
Lozoya [E] 92 E3
Lozoyuela [E] 92 F3
Lozzo di Cadore [I] 118 D2
Luanco [E] 82 F2
Luarca [E] 82 E2
Lubaczów [PL] 64 E2
Lubań [PL] 46 D4
Lubāna [LV] 236 D3
Lubartów [PL] 50 C3
Lubasz [PL] 36 A4
Lubawa [PL] 36 E3
Lubawka [PL] 62 A2
Lübbecke [D] 30 F4
Lübben [D] 46 B3
Lübbenau [D] 46 C3
Lübbow [D] 32 D4
Lübeck [D] 32 C2
Lubenec [CZ] 60 C2
Lubenice [HR] 144 B2
Lubersac [F] 78 E3
Lubia [E] 94 B2
Łubianka [PL] 34 E4
Łubianka [PL] 36 C4
Lubiatowo [PL] 34 E4
Lubiąż [PL] 46 E4
Lubichowo [PL] 36 C3
Lubień [PL] 62 F3
Lubień Kujawski [PL] 48 D2
Lubieszyn [PL] 34 D3
Lubin [PL] 46 E3
Lubiń [PL] 46 F3
Lublin [PL] 50 C3
Lubliniec [PL] 62 D2
Lubmin [D] 34 C2
Łubnice [PL] 48 C4
Lubniewice [PL] 46 D2
Łubno [PL] 36 B2
Lubny [UA] 242 E4
Lubomino [PL] 36 E2
Luboń [PL] 46 F2
Luboniek [PL] 48 C2
Luboradz [PL] 46 E4
Luboszów [PL] 46 D3
Luboszyce [PL] 46 E3
Ľubotín [SK] 64 B4
Lubowidz [PL] 36 E4
Lubowitz [PL] 62 D3
Łubowo [PL] 36 A3
Łubowo [PL] 48 B2
Lubraniec [PL] 48 C2
Lubrín [E] 106 C3
Lubsko [PL] 46 D3
Lubsza [PL] 62 C3
Lübtheen [D] 32 D3
Lubuczewo [PL] 36 B1
Luby [PL] 36 E4
Lübz [D] 32 E3
Lucainena de las Torres [E] 106 C3
Lucan [IRL] 10 F2
Lucaret [RO] 122 E3
Lucca [I] 128 B3
Luče [SLO] 120 B2

Lucena [E] 104 E2
Lucena del Cid / Llucena
[E] 102 E2
Lucenay [F] 68 E3
Luc–en–Diois [F] 124 F1
Lučenec [SK] 76 B2
Lucera [I] 134 E2
Luciana [E] 100 D3
Lucianca [RO] 150 B1
Lucignano [I] 130 E1
Lucija [SLO] 118 E4
Lucito [I] 134 D2
Luckau [D] 46 B3
Luckenwalde [D] 46 B2
Lucksta [S] 206 C4
Lückstedt [D] 32 D4
Luco dei Marsi [I] 132 E4
Luçon [F] 66 C3
Luc–sur–Mer [F] 54 B2
Lucus Feroniae [I] 132 C3
Ludanice [SK] 74 F2
Ludbreg [HR] 120 D3
Lüdenscheid [D] 42 D3
Lüderitz [D] 44 E1
Ludgo [S] 190 D3
Lüdinghausen [D] 42 D2
Ludlow [GB] 22 E4
Ludomy [PL] 46 F1
Ludoni [RUS] 232 F3
Ludów Polski [PL] 62 C1
Ludvika [S] 188 F1
Ludwigsburg [D] 58 C4
Ludwigshafen [D] 58 B3
Ludwigshafen [D] 70 F3
Ludwigslust [D] 32 D3
Ludwigsstadt [D] 58 F2
Ludwin [PL] 50 C3
Ludza [LV] 236 E3
Luesia [E] 88 B4
Lug [BIH] 152 D2
Lug [HR] 122 B4
Luga [RUS] 232 F2
Lugagnano Val d'Arda [I]
128 A1
Lugano [CH] 116 E3
Lügde [D] 44 B2
Luggau [A] 72 E4
Lugnås [S] 188 E3
Lugo [E] 82 C2
Lugo [I] 128 D2
Lugoj [RO] 122 F3
Lugones [E] 82 F2
Luhačovice [CZ] 74 E1
Luhalahti [FIN] 208 D4
Luhanka [FIN] 208 F4
Luhtanen [FIN] 200 B1
Luhtapohja [FIN] 210 E2
Luhtikylä [FIN] 198 F2
Luica [RO] 150 C1
Luidja [EST] 230 B2
Luigny [F] 54 C4
Luik (Liège) [B] 40 F4
Luikonlahti [FIN] 210 D2
Luimneach / Limerick [IRL]
10 C2
Luino [I] 116 D3
Luisenburg [D] 60 B3
Luka [SRB] 148 C2
Lukač [HR] 120 E3
Lukanja [SLO] 120 C2
Lukare [KS] 154 C2
Lukavac [BIH] 146 B2
Lüki [BG] 156 D2
Lukiv [UA] 50 E3
Łukom [PL] 48 B2
Lukov [CZ] 62 C4
Lukovë [AL] 160 B3
Lukovica [SLO] 120 B3
Lukovit [BG] 148 E3
Lukovo [HR] 144 C2
Lukovo [MK] 160 C1

Lukovo [SRB] 148 A4
Lukovo [SRB] 148 B3
Lukovo Šugarje [HR] 144 C2
Łuków [PL] 50 B2
Lukšić [HR] 144 D4
Lukta [PL] 36 E3
Luktvatnet [N] 212 E1
Luleå [S] 214 E1
Lüleburgaz [TR] 158 B3
Lumbarda [HR] 152 C2
Lumbier / Irunberri [E] 88 A3
Lumbrales [E] 84 D4
Lumbrein [CH] 116 E1
Lumbres [F] 40 B3
Lumby [DK] 178 C2
Lumezzane [I] 116 F3
Lumijoki [FIN] 216 B2
Lumivaara [RUS] 200 E1
Lumivaara [RUS] 210 E4
Lummelundagrottorna [S]
234 A2
Lummen [B] 40 E3
Lummenlunda [S] 234 A2
Lumparland [FIN] 198 A4
Lumsås [DK] 178 E1
Lumsheden [S] 196 C3
Lun [HR] 144 B2
Luna [E] 94 E2
Lunas [F] 124 C2
Lunca Corbului [RO] 148 F1
Lund [DK] 178 C1
Lund [S] 180 C2
Lunda [S] 190 D2
Lundamo [N] 204 B2
Lunde [N] 186 E2
Lunde [N] 192 C1
Lunde [N] 202 C4
Lunde [S] 206 D3
Lundeborg [DK] 178 D3
Lunden [D] 32 B1
Lunden [N] 186 E3
Lunderseter [N] 194 C4
Lunderskov [DK] 178 B2
Lundo / Lieto [FIN] 198 D3
Lundsjön [S] 204 E2
Lüneburg [D] 32 C3
Lunel [F] 124 D3
Lünen [D] 42 D3
Lunéville [F] 70 C1
Lungern [CH] 116 D1
Lungro [I] 136 C4
Lungsjön [S] 206 B2
Lungsund [S] 188 E2
Lungvik [S] 206 D3
Lunino [RUS] 238 B3
Luninyets [BY] 242 B3
Lunkkaus [FIN] 222 D2
Lunkuva [LT] 234 F4
Lunna [BY] 38 D2
Lünne [D] 30 E3
Lunteren [NL] 30 C4
Lunz [A] 74 B3
Luode [FIN] 208 D4
Luogosanto [I] 142 C2
Luopa [FIN] 208 C3
Luopioinen [FIN] 198 E1
Luosto [FIN] 222 D2
Luoto / Larsmo [FIN] 214 F4
Luotola [FIN] 200 C2
Luotolahti [FIN] 200 C1
Lupac [RO] 122 F4
Lupara [I] 134 F2
Lupawa [PL] 36 B2
Lupeni [RO] 248 C3
Lupiac [F] 88 D2
Lupiana [E] 92 F4
Lupoglav [HR] 120 D3
Lupperode [I] 104 E2
Lura e Vjetër [AL] 154 B4
Lurcy–Lévis [F] 68 C4
Lure [F] 70 C3
Lureuil [F] 66 F4

Lurgan [NIR] 12 E2
Lurgrotte [A] 120 C1
Luri [F] 130 B1
Lušci Palanka [BIH] 144 E2
Lüsens [A] 72 C4
Lushnjë [AL] 160 B2
Lusi [FIN] 200 B2
Lusignan [F] 66 E4
Lusigny [F] 68 E1
Lusina [PL] 46 E4
Lusk [IRL] 12 E4
Lus–la–Croix–Haute [F]
124 F1
Luso [P] 84 A4
Luspa [FIN] 224 F4
Luspebryggan [S] 220 D2
Lussac–les–Châteaux [F]
66 E4
Lussac–les–Églises [F] 78 E1
Lussan [F] 124 D2
Luster [N] 192 D1
Łuszczów [PL] 50 C3
Lutago / Luttach [I] 118 C1
Lutcza [PL] 64 C3
Lutherstadt Eisleben [D] 44 D3
Lutherstadt Wittenberg [D]
44 F3
Lütjenburg [D] 32 C1
Lutnes [N] 194 D2
Lutojärvi [FIN] 210 D3
Lutol Suchy [PL] 46 E2
Lutomek [PL] 46 E1
Lutomiersk [PL] 48 D3
Luton [GB] 28 C2
Lutowo [PL] 36 B3
Lutrini [LV] 234 E3
Lutry [PL] 36 F2
Luts'k [UA] 50 F4
Lutta [FIN] 198 C2
Luttach / Lutago [I] 118 C1
Lutterworth [GB] 28 C1
Lututów [PL] 48 C4
Lützen [D] 44 E4
Lutzmannsburg [A] 74 D4
Lützow [D] 32 D3
Luukkola [FIN] 200 D1
Luukkonen [FIN] 200 D1
Luumäki [FIN] 200 C2
Luupuvesi [FIN] 216 C4
Luusalmi [RUS] 216 F1
Luusniemi [FIN] 210 B4
Luusua [FIN] 222 D3
Luvia [FIN] 198 C1
Luvozero [RUS] 216 F2
Lux [F] 68 E4
Luxembourg [L] 56 D3
Luxeuil–les–Bains [F] 70 C2
Luxey [F] 88 C1
Luz [P] 110 B3
Luzaide / Valcarlos [E] 88 B3
Lužani [HR] 146 A1
Luzarches [F] 54 E3
Luže [CZ] 62 A3
Luzeret [F] 68 A4
Luzern [CH] 70 E4
Luzhayka [RUS] 200 D2
Luzhki [RUS] 38 A1
Luzi Madhi [AL] 160 A2
Łużki [PL] 50 C2
Luz–St–Sauveur [F] 88 D4
Luzy [F] 68 D4
Luzzara [I] 128 B1
Luzzi [I] 138 E1
L'viv [UA] 64 F3
Lvubertsy [RUS] 240 F3
Lwówek [PL] 46 E2
Lwówek Śląski [PL] 46 D4
Lyady [RUS] 232 E2
Lyamony [RUS] 236 E3
Lyaskelya [RUS] 210 F3
Lyaskovets [BG] 150 B3
Lyatno [BG] 150 D2

Lychen [D] 34 C3
Lyckeby [S] 180 F1
Lycksaberg [S] 214 B2
Lycksele [S] 214 C3
Lydd [GB] 28 D4
Lye [S] 234 A3
Lyel'chytsy [BY] 242 C3
Lyenin [BY] 242 B3
Lyepyel' [BY] 242 B1
Lygna [N] 194 B3
Lygre [N] 192 B4
Lykófos [GR] 156 F3
Lykorráchi [GR] 160 C3
Lyme Regis [GB] 26 D3
Lymington [GB] 26 F4
Lynderupgård [DK] 182 C3
Lyne [DK] 178 B1
Lyngby [DK] 178 F2
Lyngby [DK] 182 B3
Lyngdal [N] 186 C4
Lyngør [N] 186 E3
Lyngså [DK] 182 E2
Lyngseidet [N] 224 E2
Lyngvoll [N] 202 C4
Lynton [GB] 26 D2
Lyntupy [BY] 238 F2
Lyon [F] 80 D2
Lyons–la–Forêt [F] 54 D2
Lyozno [BY] 240 C4
Lypova Dolyna [UA] 242 F3
Lysá nad Labem [CZ] 60 E2
Łysa Polana [PL] 64 A4
Łyse [PL] 38 A3
Lysebotn [N] 186 B2
Lysekil [S] 188 B4
Lysi (Akdoğan) [CY] 176 E3
Łysianka [UA] 242 F4
Łysomice [PL] 36 C4
Lysøysund [N] 212 B4
Lyss [CH] 70 C4
Lysvik [S] 188 D1
Lytham St Anne's [GB] 22 E2
Lyuban' [RUS] 240 C1
Lyubcha [BY] 38 F2
Lyuben [BG] 156 D2
Lyubertsy [RUS] 240 F3
Lyubimets [BG] 156 F2
Lyubimets [RUS] 232 E2
Lyubytino [RUS] 240 C1
Lyudinovo [RUS] 242 E1
Lyulyakovo [BG] 150 D4

M

Maalahti / Malax [FIN] 208 B2
Maaninka [FIN] 210 B1
Maaninkavaara [FIN] 222 E3
Maanselkä [FIN] 216 D3
Maardu [EST] 230 D1
Maarianhamina / Mariehamn
[FIN] 190 F1
Maarianvaara [FIN] 210 D2
Maarja [EST] 230 E2
Maasbree [NL] 42 B3
Maaseik [B] 40 F3
Maasland [N] 30 A4
Maasmechelen [B] 40 F3
Maassluis [NL] 30 A4
Maastricht [NL] 40 F4
Maavesi [FIN] 210 C3
Mablethorpe [GB] 24 E3
Macael [E] 106 C3
Maçanet de Cabrenys [E]
96 E2
Maçanet de la Selva [E]
96 E3
Mação [P] 90 D3
Maccagno [I] 116 D2
Macclesfield [GB] 22 F3
Maceda [E] 82 C4

Macedo de Cavaleiros [P]
84 D2
Macelj [HR] 120 C3
Macerata [I] 132 E1
Macerata Féltria [I] 128 E3
Mãceşu de Jos [RO] 148 E2
Machair Loistche / Rosepenna
[IRL] 12 D1
Machault [F] 56 B3
Mâchecourt [F] 66 B2
Macherádo [GR] 172 B2
Machico [P] 110 E3
Machliny [PL] 34 F3
Machynlleth [GB] 22 D3
Maciejowice [PL] 50 B3
Macinaggio [F] 130 B1
Mackenrode [D] 44 C3
Mačkovci [SLO] 120 D2
Macocha [CZ] 62 B4
Macomer [I] 142 B3
Mâcon [F] 80 D1
Macotera [E] 92 C3
Macoviște [RO] 146 F2
Macroom [IRL] 10 B4
Macugnaga [I] 116 C3
Mád [H] 76 D3
Madalena [P] 110 A3
Madan [BG] 156 D3
Mädängsholm [S] 184 C1
Madara [BG] 150 D3
Maddaloni [I] 134 D3
Made [NL] 30 B4
Madekoski [FIN]
216 B2
Maderuelo [E] 92 F2
Madésimo [I] 116 E2
Madieres [F] 124 C2
Madliena [LV] 236 C3
Madona [LV] 236 C3
Madonna dell'Acero [I] 128 B3
Madonna della Civita [I]
134 B2
Madonna della Neve [I] 132 D2
Madonna del Ponte [I] 128 C3
Madonna del Rosario [I]
140 C2
Madonna del Sasso [I] 116 D3
Madonna di Bracciano [I]
130 F3
Madonna di Campíglio [I]
118 B2
Madonna di Canneto [I]
132 F4
Madonna di Senales /
Unserfrau [I] 118 B2
Madonna di Tirano [I] 116 F2
Madrid [E] 92 F4
Madridejos [E] 100 E2
Madrigal de las Altas Torres
[E] 84 F4
Madrigalejo [I] 100 B3
Madrigalejo del Monte [E]
92 F1
Mãdrigeşti [RO] 122 F3
Mãdrino [BG] 150 D4
Madrono [E] 100 B1
Mäebe [EST] 230 B4
Mælen [N] 204 B1
Maella [E] 94 F4
Mære [N] 212 C4
Maetzu [E] 86 E4
Mafra [P] 90 A3
Maga Circe, Grotta della– [I]
134 B3
Magallón [E] 94 D2
Magalluf [E] 108 C3
Magaña [E] 94 C2
Magasa [I] 118 B3
Magaz de Pisuerga [E] 92 E1
Magdalensberg [A] 120 A2
Magdbäcken [S] 206 D2

Magdeburg [D] 44 E2
Magellarë [AL] 154 C4
Magenta [I] 116 D3
Magerholm [N] 202 C3
Magescq [F] 88 B2
Maggia [CH] 116 D2
Maghera [NIR] 12 E2
Magherafelt [NIR] 12 E2
Magierowa Wola [PL] 48 F3
Magione [I] 130 F1
Magkanári [GR] 174 D1
Maglaj [BIH] 146 A2
Maglavit [RO] 148 D2
Maglehem [S] 180 D2
Maglehøj Strand [DK] 178 D3
Magliano dei Marsi [I] 132 D3
Magliano in Toscana [I] 130 E2
Magliano Sabina [I] 132 C3
Maglić [SRB] 146 E4
Máglie [I] 136 F3
Magnac-Laval [F] 78 E1
Magnesia [TR] 170 B3
Magneux Haute Rive [F] 80 C2
Magnières [F] 70 C1
Magnor [N] 188 C1
Magny-Cours [F] 68 C3
Magny-en-Vexin [F] 54 D2
Magny-Jobert [F] 70 C3
Maguelone [F] 124 C3
Maguiresbridge [NIR] 12 D2
Magura [BG] 148 C3
Magyarbánhegyes [H] 122 D2
Magyarboly [H] 122 A3
Magyarkeszi [H] 120 F2
Magyarmecske [H] 120 F3
Magyarszombatfa [H] 120 D2
Maheriv [UA] 64 E2
Mahide [E] 84 E2
Mahilyow [BY] 242 C2
Mahlow [D] 46 B2
Mahlsdorf [D] 32 D4
Mahlu [FIN] 208 C2
Mahmutlar [TR] 170 C2
Mahmutsevketpaşa [TR] 158 E3
Mahnala [FIN] 198 D1
Mahón / Maó [E] 108 F3
Mahora [E] 102 B3
Mahovo [H] 120 D4
Maia [P] 84 A2
Maia [P] 110 E1
Maia [P] 110 E2
Maiaky [UA] 50 F4
Maials [E] 94 F4
Maïche [F] 70 C3
Máida [I] 138 E2
Maidenhead [GB] 28 C3
Maidstone [GB] 28 D3
Maienfeld [CH] 70 F4
Maierato [I] 138 D2
Maijanen [FIN] 222 C2
Maillezais [F] 66 D4
Mailly-le-Camp [F] 56 B4
Mailly-le-Château [F] 68 D2
Mainburg [D] 72 C2
Mainhardt [D] 58 C4
Maintenon [F] 54 D3
Mainua [FIN] 216 C3
Mainz [D] 58 B2
Maiori [I] 134 D4
Maiori, Nuraghe- [I] 142 C2
Mair de Diu de Montgarri [E] 88 D4
Mairena del Alcor [E] 104 C1
Mairena del Aljarafe [E] 104 B1
Maisach [D] 72 C2
Maishofen [A] 72 E4
Maišiogala [LT] 238 E3
Maison-Neuve [F] 68 E1
Maissau [A] 74 C2
Máistir Gaoithe / Mastergeeby [IRL] 10 A3

Maja [HR] 144 D1
Majadahonda [E] 92 E4
Majadas [E] 90 F4
Majadas [E] 92 B4
Majaelrayo [E] 92 F3
Majavatn [N] 212 D2
Majdan [MK] 160 E1
Majdanek [PL] 50 C3
Majdan Królewski [PL] 64 C2
Majdanpek [SRB] 148 B2
Majtum [S] 220 D3
Majur [SRB] 146 C2
Makarska [HR] 152 B2
Makaševičy [BY] 242 B3
Makce [SRB] 146 F2
Makedonski Brod [MK] 154 D4
Mäkela [FIN] 222 E3
Makhnovka [RUS] 232 F4
Mäkikylä [FIN] 208 F3
Mäkitalo [FIN] 222 B1
Mäkkiikylä [FIN] 208 E3
Makkola [FIN] 210 D3
Makljenovac [BIH] 146 A2
Makó [H] 122 D3
Makó-Rákos [H] 122 D2
Makov [SK] 62 D4
Maková Hora [CZ] 60 D3
Makoviš [SRB] 146 D3
Makovo [MK] 160 D1
Maków [PL] 62 F2
Mąkowarsko [PL] 36 C3
Maków Mazowiecki [PL] 36 F4
Maków Podhalański [PL] 62 F3
Makrakómi [GR] 166 E2
Makreš [MK] 154 D3
Mákri [GR] 156 E4
Mákri [GR] 172 D2
Makrochóri [GR] 160 E2
Makryámmos [GR] 162 D1
Makrygialós [GR] 174 E4
Makrynítsa [GR] 162 B3
Makryplágio [GR] 156 C3
Maksatiha [RUS] 240 C2
Malå [S] 214 C2
Mala Bosna [SRB] 122 C3
Malacky [SK] 74 E2
Mala Domaša [SK] 76 E1
Maladzyechna [BY] 242 B2
Málaga [E] 104 D3
Malagón [E] 100 D3
Malahide [IRL] 12 E4
Málainn Mhóir / Malin More [IRL] 12 C1
Mała Karczma [PL] 36 D3
Mala Kladuša [BIH] 144 D1
Maläk Porovec [BG] 150 D2
Mala Krsna [SRB] 146 E2
Malalbergo [I] 128 C2
Malá Lehota [SK] 76 A2
Malamoneda [E] 100 D2
Malandríno [GR] 166 E3
Mälarhusen [S] 180 D2
Malaryta [BY] 50 D2
Mala Subotica [HR] 120 D2
Malaucène [F] 124 E2
Malax / Maalahti [FIN] 208 B2
Malaya Vishera [RUS] 240 C1
Malbork [PL] 36 D2
Malbouzon [F] 80 B4
Malbuisson [F] 70 B4
Malcésine [I] 118 B3
Malchin [D] 32 F3
Malchow [D] 32 E3
Malcocinado [E] 100 A4
Malcontenta [I] 118 D4
Malcov [SK] 64 B4
Maldegem [B] 40 D3
Maldon [GB] 28 D3
Małdyty [PL] 36 E2
Malé [I] 118 B2

Malechowo [PL] 36 A2
Máleme [GR] 174 B3
Malenovice [CZ] 62 C4
Malente-Gremsmühlen [D] 32 C2
Målerås [S] 184 D3
Máles [GR] 174 E4
Malesco [I] 116 D2
Malesherbes [F] 54 D4
Malesína [GR] 166 F3
Malestroit [F] 52 D4
Maletto [I] 138 B4
Malexander [S] 184 D1
Malfourat, Mine de- [F] 78 D4
Malgovik [S] 214 A3
Malhadas [P] 84 D3
Malhao [P] 84 B4
Mália [GR] 174 D3
Malicorne [F] 66 E2
Mali Idjos [SRB] 122 C4
Malíkovo [HR] 144 E4
Mälilla [S] 184 E2
Mali Lošinj [HR] 144 B2
Malin [IRL] 12 E1
Malin [UA] 242 D4
Málinec [SK] 76 B2
Malines (Mechelen) [B] 40 E3
Malingsbo [S] 190 B1
Maliniec [PL] 48 C2
Malin More / Málainn Mhóir [IRL] 12 C1
Malinska [HR] 144 B1
Mali Prolog [HR] 152 C2
Maliq [AL] 160 C2
Mal'kovo [RUS] 236 F3
Mališevo / Malisheve [KS] 154 C2
Malisheve / Mališevo [KS] 154 C2
Mališkylä [FIN] 216 B3
Mali Štupelj [KS] 154 B2
Malix [CH] 116 E1
Mali Zvornik [SRB] 146 C3
Maljevac [HR] 144 D1
Maljovica [BG] 156 B2
Malkara [TR] 158 B4
Małkinia Górna [PL] 38 B4
Malkkila [FIN] 210 D3
Malko Gradishte [BG] 156 F2
Malko Tŭrnovo [BG] 158 B2
Mal'kovo [RUS] 236 F3
Malla [E] 96 D2
Mallaig [GB] 14 C4
Mallersdorf [D] 72 D1
Málles Venosta / Mals im Vinschgau [I] 118 B2
Malling [DK] 178 C1
Mallnitz [A] 118 E1
Mallow [IRL] 10 C3
Malm [N] 212 C4
Malmbäck [S] 184 C2
Malmberget [S] 220 E2
Malmédy [B] 56 D1
Malmesbury [GB] 26 F2
Malmköping [S] 190 C3
Malmö [S] 178 F2
Malmslätt [S] 188 F4
Malo [I] 118 C3
Małogoszcz [PL] 64 A1
Maloja [CH] 116 F2
Malo-les-Bains [F] 28 F4
Malomirovo [BG] 158 A2
Malónas [GR] 176 C2
Malonno [I] 118 A3
Małopolski [PL] 62 F2
Malorad [BG] 148 E3
Małowidz [PL] 36 F4
Måløy [N] 202 B4
Maloyaroslavets [RUS] 240 F3
Malpartida de Cáceres [E] 90 F3
Malpartida de Plasencia [E] 92 B4

Malpica de Bergantiños [E] 82 B1
Malpica de Tajo [E] 100 D1
Mälpils [LV] 236 B3
Mälsåker [S] 190 D2
Malšice [CZ] 60 E4
Mals im Vinschgau / Málles Venosta [I] 118 B2
Malsjö [S] 188 D2
Malsjöbodarna [S] 204 F4
Målsnes [N] 224 D2
Malta [A] 118 E1
Malta [LV] 236 D3
Maltat [F] 68 D4
Maltepe [TR] 158 E3
Maltepe [TR] 164 B2
Maltesholm [S] 180 D2
Malton [GB] 24 D2
Malu [RO] 148 E2
Malung [S] 194 E3
Malungen [N] 194 C3
Malungen [S] 206 C4
Malungsfors [S] 194 E3
Maluszyn [PL] 62 F1
Malva [E] 84 F3
Malveira [P] 90 A3
Malvik [N] 204 B2
Mályi [H] 76 D3
Mały Płock [PL] 38 B3
Malyye Rozhki [RUS] 232 E2
Mamaia [RO] 150 F1
Mamarrosa [P] 84 A3
Mamers [F] 54 B3
Mammola [I] 138 E3
Mamone [I] 142 C3
Mamonovo [RUS] 36 E1
Mám Trasna / Maumtrasna [IRL] 12 B3
Mamyra [N] 212 B4
Mána [GR] 166 E4
Maňa [SK] 74 F3
Manacor [E] 108 D3
Manadas [P] 110 B3
Manamansalo [FIN] 216 C3
Manasija, Manastir- [SRB] 146 F3
Mănăstirea [RO] 150 D1
Mancha Real [E] 104 F2
Manchester [GB] 22 F2
Manching [D] 72 C2
Manciano [I] 130 E2
Mancier [F] 88 D2
Mandal [N] 186 C4
Måndalen [N] 202 D3
Mándas [I] 142 C4
Mandelieu [F] 126 B3
Mandello del Lario [I] 116 E3
Mandelsloh [D] 44 B1
Manderscheid [D] 56 E2
Mandira [TR] 158 B3
Mándok [H] 76 E2
Mándra [GR] 156 F3
Mándra [GR] 168 A2
Mandráki [GR] 176 A1
Mandrikó [GR] 176 B2
Manduria [I] 136 E3
Manerba del Garda [I] 118 A4
Manérbio [I] 116 F4
Manětín [CZ] 60 C3
Manevychi [UA] 50 F3
Mánfa [H] 122 A3
Manfredónia [I] 134 F2
Mangalia [RO] 150 F2
Mångbyn [S] 214 E3
Mangen [N] 192 A3
Manger [N] 192 A3
Mangfall Brücke [D] 72 C3
Mångsbodarna [S] 194 E2
Mangskog [S] 188 D1
Mangualde [P] 84 B4
Manguilla [E] 100 A3
Máni [GR] 158 A3

Maniago [I] 118 D3
Manilva [E] 104 C3
Manisa [TR] 164 C4
Manita Peć [HR] 144 C3
Mank [A] 74 B3
Månkarbo [S] 196 D4
Mańki [PL] 36 E3
Manlleu [E] 96 D2
Mannheim [D] 58 B3
Mano [F] 78 B4
Manoláda [GR] 166 C4
Mañón [E] 82 D1
Manorhamilton [IRL] 12 C2
Manosque [F] 124 F3
Manrèsa [Ł] 96 D2
Månsåsen [S] 204 E2
Manschnow [D] 46 C2
Mansfeld [D] 44 D3
Mansfield [GB] 24 C3
Mansilla de las Mulas [E] 82 F4
Mansle [F] 78 D2
Manso [F] 130 A2
Mansoniemi [FIN] 208 C4
Mantamádos [GR] 164 A3
Manteigas [P] 84 B4
Mantes-la-Jolie [F] 54 D3
Mantila [FIN] 208 C3
Mantíneia [GR] 172 D2
Mäntlahti [FIN] 200 C3
Mantorp [S] 188 F4
Mantoúdi [GR] 168 A1
Mantova [I] 118 B4
Mäntsälä [FIN] 198 F2
Mänttä [FIN] 208 E3
Mäntyharju [FIN] 200 B1
Mäntyjärvi [FIN] 222 D3
Mäntylahti [FIN] 210 C1
Mäntyluoto [FIN] 198 B1
Manyas [TR] 164 D2
Manzanares [E] 100 E3
Manzanares el Real [E] 92 E3
Manzaneda [E] 82 C4
Manzanera [E] 102 D2
Manzanilla [E] 98 E4
Manzat [F] 80 B2
Maó / Mahón [E] 108 F3
Maqueda [E] 92 D4
Maranchón [E] 94 B3
Maranello [I] 128 C2
Marano di Napoli [I] 134 C3
Marano Lagunare [I] 118 E3
Marans [F] 66 C4
Maratea [I] 136 B3
Marateca [P] 90 B4
Marathiás [GR] 166 D3
Marathókampos [GR] 168 F2
Marathónas [GR] 168 B2
Marathópoli [GR] 172 C3
Márathos [GR] 174 D3
Marathóvounos (Ulukışla) [CY] 176 E3
Maravillas, Cueva de las- [E] 98 E3
Marbach [D] 58 C4
Marbäck [S] 184 B1
Marbäck [S] 184 C1
Marbacka [S] 188 D1
Mårbacken [S] 194 D4
Marbella [E] 104 C3
Marboz [F] 80 E1
Marburg [D] 42 E4
Marcali [H] 120 F2
Marčana [HR] 144 A2
Marceddì [I] 142 B4
Marcenais [F] 78 C3
March [GB] 28 D1
Marchaux [F] 70 B3
Marche-en-Famenne [B] 56 C1
Marchegg [A] 74 D2
Marchena [E] 104 C2

Marchenilla [E] 104 C2
Marcheprime [F] 78 B3
Marciac [F] 88 D2
Marciana Marina [I] 130 C2
Marcianise [I] 134 C3
Marcigny [F] 80 C1
Marcilla [E] 94 D1
Marcillac–Vallon [F] 124 B1
Marcillat–en–Combraille
  [F] 80 B1
Marcilly–le–Hayer [F] 68 D1
Marcinowice [PL] 62 B1
Marciszów [PL] 62 A1
Marckolsheim [F] 70 D2
Mardalsfoss [N] 202 E3
Mardie [F] 68 B1
Mårdsele [S] 214 C3
Mårdsjö [S] 206 B2
Mårdsund [S] 204 E2
Marebbe / St Vigil [I] 118 C2
Máre de Déu de la Balma
  [E] 102 E1
Mare de Déu del Toro [E]
  108 F3
Mårem [N] 192 E4
Måren [N] 192 B2
Marennes [F] 78 B2
Maréttimo [I] 140 A2
Mareuil [F] 66 C3
Mareuil [F] 78 D3
Marevo [RUS] 240 C2
Margarítes [GR] 174 C3
Margaríti [GR] 166 B2
Margate [GB] 28 E3
Margecany [SK] 76 D1
Margherita di Savoia [I] 134 F2
Marghita [RO] 76 F4
Margina [RO] 122 F3
Margonin [PL] 36 B4
Marhaň [SK] 64 C4
Marhanets' [UA] 246 F2
Marhet [B] 56 D2
María [E] 106 C2
Maria Birnbaum [D] 72 C2
Maria de la Salut [E] 108 D3
María Dreierchen [A] 74 C2
Mariager [DK] 182 D3
Maria Laach [D] 56 F1
Maria Laach [D] 56 F1
Marialva [P] 84 C3
Maria Martenthal [D] 56 E2
Mariannelund [S] 184 E2
Marianopoli [I] 138 A4
Mariànos [P] 90 D2
Mariánské Lázně [CZ] 60 B3
Máriapócs [H] 76 E3
Maria Saal [A] 120 A2
Mariastein [A] 72 D4
Maria Taferl [A] 74 B3
Maria Trost [A] 120 C1
Maria Wörth [A] 118 F2
Mariazell [A] 74 B3
Maribo [DK] 178 D3
Maribor [SLO] 120 C2
Marieby [S] 204 E2
Mariedal [S] 188 D4
Mariedamm [S] 188 F3
Mariefred [S] 190 D2
Mariehamn / Maarianhamina
  [FIN] 190 F1
Marieholm [S] 180 C2
Marieholm [S] 184 C2
Marielyst [DK] 32 E1
Mariëmont [B] 40 D4
Marienberg [D] 60 C2
Marienberg, Kloster– / Monte
  Maria, Abbazia di– [I] 118 B2
Marienborn [D] 44 D2
Marienburg [D] 56 E2
Marienheide [D] 42 D3
Marienstatt [D] 42 D4
Marienthal [D] 42 D4

Mariestad [S] 188 E3
Marieux [F] 40 B4
Marifjøra [N] 192 D2
Marignane [F] 124 E3
Marigny–le–Châtel [F] 54 F4
Marihn [D] 32 F3
Marija Bistrica [HR] 120 D3
Marijampolé [LT] 238 C3
Marikostinovo [BG] 156 B3
Marilles [B] 40 E4
Marín [E] 82 B3
Marina [EST] 230 D3
Marina [HR] 144 D4
Marina di Alberese [I] 130 D2
Marina di Amendolara [I]
  136 C3
Marina di Árbus [I] 142 B4
Marina di Ardea [I] 134 A2
Marina di Camerota [I] 136 B3
Marina di Campo [I] 130 C2
Marina di Caronía [I] 138 B4
Marina di Carrara [I] 128 A3
Marina di Castagneto–
  Donorático [I] 130 D1
Marina di Chiéuti [I] 134 E2
Marina di Gáiro [I] 142 C4
Marina di Ginosa [I] 136 D3
Marina di Gioiosa Iónica [I]
  138 E3
Marina di Grosseto [I] 130 D2
Marina di Léuca [I] 136 F4
Marina di Massa [I] 128 A3
Marina di Pietrasanta [I]
  128 B3
Marina di Pisa [I] 128 B3
Marina di Ragusa [I] 140 D4
Marina di Ravenna [I] 128 D2
Marina di Schiavonea [I]
  136 C4
Marina di Vasto [I] 134 D1
Mar'ina Horka [BY] 242 C2
Marinaleda [E] 104 D2
Marina Palmense [I] 132 E2
Marina Romea [I] 128 D2
Marine de Sisco [F] 130 B2
Marinella [I] 140 B2
Marineo [I] 140 C2
Marines [F] 54 D3
Maringues [F] 80 B2
Marinha Grande [P] 90 B2
Marinhais [P] 90 B3
Marinkainen [FIN] 214 F4
Mar'insko [RUS] 232 E2
Mariotto [I] 136 C2
Maristella [I] 142 B2
Maristova [N] 192 D2
Máriuţa [RO] 150 C1
Marjalija [E] 100 D2
Märjamaa [EST] 230 C2
Marjaniemi [FIN] 216 A2
Marjovaara [FIN] 210 E2
Markabygd [N] 204 C1
Markaryd [S] 184 B4
Markdorf [D] 70 F3
Marke [B] 40 C3
Market Deeping [GB] 24 D4
Market Drayton [GB] 22 F3
Market Harborough [GB]
  28 C1
Markethill [NIR] 12 E3
Market Rasen [GB] 24 D3
Market Weighton [GB] 24 D2
Marki [PL] 48 F2
Markina–Xemein [E] 86 E3
Märkisch Buchholz [D] 46 B2
Markitta [S] 220 C2
Markkina [FIN] 224 F4
Markleugast [D] 58 F2
Markneukirchen [D] 60 B2
Markop [N] 228 B2
Markópoulo [GR] 166 C4
Markópoulo [GR] 168 B3

Markovac [SRB] 146 E3
Markova Sušica [MK] 154 D3
Markovci pri Ptuju [SLO]
  120 C2
Markov Manastir [MK] 154 D3
Markovo [BG] 150 D3
Markovo Kale [SRB] 154 D2
Markranstädt [D] 44 E4
Marksburg [D] 56 F2
Markt Bibart [D] 58 D3
Marktbreit [D] 58 D3
Markt Erlbach [D] 58 E3
Marktheidenfeld [D] 58 C3
Markt–Indersdorf [D] 72 C2
Marktjärn [S] 206 B3
Marktl [D] 72 E2
Marktoberdorf [D] 72 B3
Marktredwitz [D] 60 B3
Markt St Florian [A] 74 A3
Markt St Martin [A] 74 D4
Marktzeuln [D] 58 E2
Markušica [HR] 122 B4
Markušovce [SK] 76 D1
Markvarerc [CZ] 74 C1
Marl [D] 42 D2
Marlborough [GB] 26 F2
Marle [F] 56 A2
Marlenheim [F] 70 D1
Marlens [F] 80 F3
Marlow [D] 32 F2
Marma [S] 196 D4
Marmande [F] 78 C4
Marmara [TR] 158 C4
Marmaraereğlisi [TR] 158 C3
Marmári [GR] 168 C2
Marmaris [TR] 176 C1
Mármaro [GR] 168 E1
Marmelete [P] 98 B3
Marmolejo [E] 104 E1
Marmore, Cascata delle– [I]
  132 D3
Marmoutier [F] 70 D1
Marmuri, Grotta su– [I] 142 C4
Marnay [F] 70 B3
Marne [D] 32 B2
Marnitz [D] 32 E3
Maróneia [GR] 156 E4
Maroslele [H] 122 D3
Maróstica [I] 118 C3
Marotta [I] 128 E4
Marpíssa [GR] 168 D4
Marquartstein [D] 72 D3
Marquion [F] 40 C4
Marquise [F] 40 A3
Marradi [I] 128 C3
Marrebæk [DK] 32 E1
Marrúbiu [I] 142 B4
Marsala [I] 140 A2
Mârşani [RO] 148 E2
Marsberg [D] 42 F3
Marschlins [CH] 116 F1
Marsciano [I] 132 C2
Marseillan [F] 124 C3
Marseillan–Plage [F] 124 C3
Marseille [F] 124 E4
Marseille–en–Beauvaisis
  [F] 54 D2
Marshavitsy [RUS] 232 F4
Marsico Nuovo [I] 134 E4
Marsico Vetere [I] 134 F4
Marsiliana [I] 130 E2
Marsjö [S] 190 B3
Marsliden [S] 212 F3
Märsta [S] 190 D2
Marstal [DK] 178 C3
Marstrand [S] 182 F1
Mårsylä [FIN] 216 A3
Marta [I] 130 F2
Martano [I] 136 F3
Martel [F] 78 E4
Martelange [B] 56 D2
Mártely [H] 122 D2

Marten [BG] 150 C2
Martfü [H] 122 D1
Marthille [F] 56 D4
Marthon [F] 78 D2
Martigné–Ferchuad [F] 66 C1
Martigny [CH] 116 B2
Martigues [F] 124 E3
Martim Longo [P] 98 C3
Martin [SK] 76 A1
Martina / Martinsbruck [CH]
  118 B1
Martina Franca [I] 136 D2
Martinci Čepinski [HR] 122 A4
Martín de la Jara [E] 104 D2
Martín de Yeltes [E] 84 D4
Martinet [E] 96 D1
Martinje [SLO] 120 D2
Martíno [GR] 166 F3
Martinsbruck / Martina [CH]
  118 B1
Martinsicuro [I] 132 E2
Martinszell [D] 72 D2
Martinvast [F] 52 E1
Mártis [I] 142 B2
Martjanci [SLO] 120 D2
Martna [EST] 230 C2
Martofte [DK] 178 D2
Martonvaara [FIN] 210 D1
Martonvásár [H] 76 A4
Martorell [E] 96 D3
Martos [E] 104 F2
Mårtsviken [S] 194 D3
Martti [FIN] 222 E1
Marttila [FIN] 198 D3
Maruflar [TR] 164 C3
Maruševec [HR] 120 D3
Marvão [P] 90 E3
Marvejols [F] 80 B4
Marvik [S] 186 B1
Marwałd [PL] 36 E3
Marxwalde [D] 46 C1
Marxzell [D] 58 B4
Marynin [PL] 50 D3
Maryport [GB] 20 C3
Marzabotto [I] 128 C2
Marzahna [D] 44 F2
Marzahne [D] 44 F1
Marzamemi [I] 140 E4
Marzocca [I] 128 E4
Mâsca [RO] 122 E2
Maschen [D] 32 C3
Mas d'Azil, Grotte du– [F]
  88 E3
Mas de Barberans [E] 96 A4
Mas de las Matas [E] 94 E4
Masegoso de Tajuña [E] 94 B3
Maser [I] 118 C3
Masevaux [F] 70 C3
Masfjordnes [N] 192 B2
Mashan [AL] 160 B2
Masi [N] 226 B2
Maside [E] 82 C3
Masi Torello [I] 128 D2
Maskjok [N] 228 D2
Masku [FIN] 198 C3
Maslarevo [BG] 150 B3
Maslenica [HR] 144 C3
Maslinica [HR] 152 A1
Maslovare [BIH] 144 F2
Maso [FIN] 208 F2
Maspalomas [E] 112 D4
Massa [I] 128 B3
Massa Fiscaglia [I] 128 D2
Massafra [I] 136 D2
Massa Lubrense [I] 134 C4
Massamagrell [E] 102 D3
Massa Marittima [I] 130 D1
Massat [F] 88 E4
Massay [F] 68 B3
Masseret [F] 78 E3
Masseube [F] 88 D3
Massiac [F] 80 B3

Mastaura [TR] 170 D2
Masterelv [N] 228 B2
Mastergeeby / Máistir Gaoithe
  [IRL] 10 A3
Masterud [N] 194 C4
Mas Thibert [F] 124 E3
Mastichári [GR] 176 A1
Mästocka [S] 184 B3
Masty [BY] 38 C2
Masugnsbyn [S] 220 F2
Maszewo [PL] 34 E3
Maszewo [PL] 46 D2
Matabuena [E] 92 E3
Mata de Alcántara [E] 90 E3
Mátala [GR] 174 C4
Matalascañas [E] 104 A2
Matalebreras [E] 94 C2
Matallana de Torío [E] 86 A3
Matallana de Toríos [E] 82 F3
Mataporquera [E] 86 C3
Matara [FIN] 210 D1
Matarágka [GR] 166 D2
Mataró [E] 96 D3
Mataruška Banja [SRB] 146 E4
Mätäsvaara [FIN] 216 E4
Matejče, Manastir– [MK]
  154 D3
Matelica [I] 132 D1
Matera [I] 136 C2
Matersdalen [N] 192 B4
Mateševo [MNE] 152 F2
Matészalka [H] 76 F3
Matfors [S] 206 C4
Matha [F] 78 C2
Mathay [F] 70 C3
Mathildedal [FIN] 198 D3
Matignon [F] 52 D3
Matîši [LV] 230 D4
Matka, Manastir– [MK] 154 D3
Matkavaara [FIN] 216 D2
Matlock [GB] 24 C3
Matochina [BG] 158 A2
Matos [P] 98 C2
Matour [F] 80 D1
Mátrafüred [H] 76 C3
Mátraháza [H] 76 C3
Mátraszentimre [H] 76 C3
Mátraterenye [H] 76 C3
Mátraverebély [H] 76 C3
Matre [N] 186 B1
Matre [N] 192 B2
Matrei am Brenner [A] 72 C4
Matrei in Osttirol [A] 118 D1
Matrosovo [RUS] 238 A3
Mattaur [S] 220 C3
Matteröd [S] 180 C1
Mattersburg [A] 74 D3
Mattighofen [A] 72 E3
Mattila [FIN] 200 D1
Mattilanmäki [FIN] 222 E2
Mattinata [I] 134 F2
Mattinen [FIN] 198 C3
Mattmar [S] 204 E2
Mattsee [A] 72 F3
Måttsund [S] 214 E1
Matulji [HR] 120 A4
Matyli [BY] 38 E2
Matzen [A] 72 C4
Matzen [A] 74 D2
Maubeuge [F] 40 D4
Maubourguet [F] 88 C2
Mauchline [GB] 18 C4
Mauerkirchen [A] 72 E2
Maukdal [N] 224 D3
Maula [FIN] 222 C4
Maulbronn [D] 58 B4
Mauléon [F] 66 D3
Mauléon–Licharre [F] 88 B3
Maulévrier [F] 66 D3
Maumtrasna / Mám Trasna
  [IRL] 12 A3

Maunujärvi [FIN] 222 C2
Maupas, Château de- [F]
68 C3
Maupertus-sur-Mer [F] 52 F1
Maura [N] 194 B4
Maurach [A] 72 C4
Maure [F] 52 D4
Mäureni [RO] 122 E4
Mauriac [F] 78 F3
Maurnes [N] 224 B3
Mauron [F] 52 D4
Maurs [F] 78 F4
Maurstad [N] 202 B4
Maurvangen [N] 192 E2
Maury [F] 96 E1
Mautern [A] 74 B4
Mauterndorf [A] 118 F1
Mauth [D] 72 F1
Mauthausen [A] 74 B2
Mauvezin [F] 88 E2
Mauvoisin [CH] 116 B2
Mauzé-sur-le-Mignon [F]
66 D4
Mavikent [TR] 176 F1
Mavréli [GR] 160 E4
Mavrochóri [GR] 160 D3
Mavrokklísi [GR] 156 F3
Mavroléfki [GR] 156 C4
Mavromáta [GR] 166 D2
Mavromáti [GR] 172 C3
Mavrothálassa [GR] 156 C4
Mavrovi Hanovi [MK] 154 C4
Mavrovo [MK] 154 C4
Mavrovoúni [GR] 160 E4
Mavrovoúni [GR] 172 D3
Maximiliana [E] 104 E3
Maximilians–Grotte [D] 58 F3
Maxmo [FIN] 208 C1
Maybole [GB] 20 B2
Mayen [D] 56 F2
Mayenne [F] 52 F4
Mayet [F] 66 E2
Maynooth [IRL] 10 F2
Mayoralgo [E] 90 F4
Mayorga [E] 86 A4
Mayrhofen [A] 72 C4
Mäyry [FIN] 208 D2
Mazagón [E] 104 A1
Mazagran [F] 56 B3
Mazamet [F] 124 A3
Mazara del Vallo [I] 140 B2
Mazarrón [E] 106 D3
Mažeikiai [LT] 234 E4
Mazères [F] 88 F3
Mazerulles [F] 56 D4
Mázia [GR] 160 C4
Mazières–en–Gâtine [F] 66 D4
Maziha [RUS] 232 E2
Mazıköy [TR] 170 C4
Mazilmaja [LV] 234 D4
Mazirbe [LV] 230 B4
Mazotos [CY] 176 E4
Mazsalaca [LV] 230 D4
Mazurki [PL] 50 B2
Mazyr [BY] 242 C3
Mazzalve [LV] 236 C4
Mazzarino [I] 140 D3
Mazzaró [I] 138 C4
Mazzarrone [I] 140 D3
M. Bondone [I] 118 B3
Mchowo [PL] 36 F4
M. D. de la Salut [E] 96 E2
M. D. de Pinós [E] 96 C2
M. D. de Queralt [E] 96 D2
Mdzewo [PL] 36 E4
Mealhada [P] 84 A4
Méandre de Queuille [F] 80 B2
Meaux [F] 54 E3
Mechelen (Malines) [B] 40 E3
Mechernich [D] 42 C4
Mechka [BG] 150 B2
Mechowo [PL] 34 E2

Mecidiye [TR] 164 C4
Mecikal [PL] 36 B3
Mecsér [H] 74 E3
Meda [P] 84 C3
Medak [HR] 144 C2
Mede [I] 116 D4
Medebach [D] 42 E3
Medelim [P] 90 E2
Medellín [E] 100 A2
Medelser Schlucht [CH]
116 E1
Medemblik [NL] 30 B2
Medena Selišta [BIH] 144 E3
Medeni Poljani [BG] 156 C2
Meden Rudnik [BG] 158 B1
Medenychi [UA] 64 Г3
Medet [TR] 170 E3
Medevi [S] 188 F3
Medgidia [RO] 150 E1
Medgyesegyháza [H] 122 E2
Medhamn [S] 188 E3
Mediaş [RO] 244 D4
Medicina [I] 128 D2
Medina [H] 122 B2
Medina Azahara [E] 104 D1
Medinaceli [E] 94 B3
Medina del Campo [E] 92 D2
Medina de Pomar [E] 86 D3
Medina de Rioseco [E] 86 A4
Medina–Sidonia [E] 104 B3
Medininkai [LT] 238 E3
Medle [S] 214 D2
Médole [I] 118 A4
Médous, Grotte de– [F] 88 C3
Médousa [GR] 156 D3
Medovina [BG] 148 C3
Medskogen [S] 194 D3
Medstugan [S] 204 D2
Medugorje [BIH] 152 C2
Medulin [HR] 144 A2
Medvedja [SRB] 154 D2
Medveď'ov [SK] 74 E3
Medvida [HR] 144 D3
Medvode [SLO] 120 A3
Medyka [PL] 64 E3
Medze [LV] 234 D3
Medzev [SK] 76 D2
Medzilaborce [SK] 64 C4
Medžitlija [MK] 160 D2
Meerane [D] 60 B1
Meerkerk [NL] 30 B4
Meersburg [D] 70 F3
Meeuwen [B] 40 F3
Mefjordvær [N] 224 C2
Méga Chorió [GR] 166 D3
Méga Déreio [GR] 156 F3
Megáli Vólvi [GR] 162 B1
Megalochóri [GR] 160 E4
Megálo Chorió [GR] 176 B3
Megálo Livádi [GR] 168 C4
Megalópoli [GR] 172 D2
Mégara [GR] 168 A2
Megara Hyblaea [I] 140 E3
Méga Spílaio [GR] 166 E4
Megève [F] 116 B2
Megísti [GR] 176 E2
Megístis Lávras, Moní– [GR]
162 D2
Megorjelo [BIH] 152 C2
Meg. Panagía [GR] 162 C2
Megyaszó [H] 76 D3
Mehadia [RO] 148 C1
Mehamn [N] 228 D1
Mehikoorma [EST] 230 F3
Mehmetcik (Galatia) [CY]
176 E3
Mehov Krš [SRB] 154 B2
Mehring [D] 56 B3
Mehtäkylä [FIN] 216 A3
Mehun–sur–Yèvre [F] 68 B3
Meiåvollen [N] 204 B3

Meijel [NL] 42 B3
Meilen [CH] 70 E4
Meillant, Château de– [F]
68 B3
Meilleraye, Abbaye de– [F]
66 C2
Meina [I] 116 D3
Meine [D] 44 C2
Meinerzhagen [D] 42 D3
Meiningen [D] 58 E1
Meira [E] 82 D2
Meiräni [LV] 236 D3
Meiringen [CH] 116 D1
Meisenheim [D] 56 F3
Meisingset [N] 202 E2
Melssen [D] 46 B4
Meitingen [D] 72 B2
Męka [PL] 48 C3
Mekinje [SLO] 120 B3
Mekrijärvi [FIN] 210 F2
Meksa Šantić [SRB] 122 B3
Mel [I] 118 C3
Mélampes [GR] 174 C4
Melaniós [GR] 168 E1
Melátes [GR] 166 C2
Melbeck [D] 32 C3
Melbu [N] 224 B4
Meldal [N] 202 F2
Meldola [I] 128 D3
Meldorf [D] 32 B2
Melegnano [I] 116 E4
Melenci [SRB] 122 D4
Melene [TR] 164 B3
Melfi [I] 134 E3
Melgaço [P] 82 B4
Melgar de Arriba [E] 86 A4
Melgar de Fernamental [E]
86 B4
Melgarejo [E] 104 B2
Melholt [DK] 182 E2
Melhus [N] 202 E2
Melhus [N] 204 B2
Melide [E] 82 C2
Melides [P] 98 B2
Meligalás [GR] 172 D2
Melíki [GR] 160 E2
Melilli [I] 140 E3
Melineşti [RO] 148 D1
Melisenda [I] 142 C4
Mélisey [F] 70 C3
Mélissa [GR] 156 D4
Melissáni [GR] 166 B4
Melíssi [GR] 160 D3
Melissópetra [GR] 160 C3
Melissourgós [GR] 162 B1
Melito di Porto Salvo [I]
138 D4
Melívoia [GR] 156 D3
Melk [A] 74 C3
Melksham [GB] 26 F2
Mellakoski [FIN] 222 B3
Mellanel [S] 206 D2
Mellansjö [S] 206 B4
Mellanström [S] 214 B1
Mellau [A] 72 A4
Mellby [S] 184 B4
Mellbystrand [S] 184 B4
Melle [D] 30 F4
Melle [F] 66 D4
Mellendorf [D] 44 B1
Mellerud [S] 188 C3
Mellieha [M] 140 C4
Mellilä [FIN] 198 D2
Mellin [D] 44 D1
Melloussa [MA] 104 B4
Mellrichstadt [D] 58 D2
Mellstaby [S] 184 E4
Melnica [SRB] 146 F2
Melnik [BG] 156 B3
Mělník [CZ] 60 D2
Mel'nikovo [RUS] 200 E2
Mel'nitsy [RUS] 232 E3

Melrand [F] 52 C4
Melrose [GB] 20 E2
Melsomvik [N] 186 F2
Melsungen [D] 44 B4
Meltaus [FIN] 222 C2
Melton Mowbray [GB] 24 C4
Meltosjärvi [FIN] 222 B3
Melun [F] 54 E4
Melvich [GB] 14 E1
Mélykút [H] 122 B3
Melzo [I] 116 E3
Membrilla [E] 100 E3
Membrío [E] 90 E3
Memer [F] 124 A1
Mem Martins [P] 90 A3
Memmingen [D] 72 A3
Mémorial du Omaha Beach
[F] 54 A2
Mena [UA] 242 E3
Menággio [I] 116 E3
Menai Bridge [GB] 22 D2
Ménaičiai [LT] 238 C2
Menasalbas [E] 100 D2
Menat [F] 80 B1
Mencshely [H] 120 F1
Mendavia [E] 86 E4
Mende [F] 80 B4
Menden [D] 42 E3
Menderes [TR] 170 B2
Mendig [D] 56 F1
Mending [A] 74 B3
Mendrisio [CH] 116 E3
Ménéac [F] 52 D4
Menec [F] 66 A1
Menemen [TR] 164 C4
Menen [B] 40 C3
Menesjärvi [FIN] 226 D2
Menetés [GR] 176 B3
Ménez Hom [F] 52 B3
Menfi [I] 140 B2
Ménfőcsanak [H] 74 E4
Menga, Cueva de– [E] 104 D3
Mengamuñoz [E] 92 C3
Mengen [D] 70 F2
Mengeš [SLO] 120 B3
Mengíbar [E] 104 F1
Mengishevo [BG] 150 D3
Menídi [GR] 166 C2
Ménigoute [F] 66 D4
Ménina [GR] 166 B1
Menonen [FIN] 198 D2
Mens [F] 80 A4
Menstrup [DK] 178 E3
Menthon [F] 80 F2
Menton [F] 126 C3
Méntrida [E] 92 D4
Menyushi [RUS] 232 E2
Menz [D] 32 F4
Meppel [NL] 30 C3
Meppen [D] 30 E3
Mequinenza [E] 94 F3
Mequinenza, Castillo de– [E]
94 F3
Mer [F] 68 A2
Mera de Boixo [E] 82 C1
Meräker [N] 204 C2
Meran / Merano [I] 118 B2
Merano / Meran [I] 118 B2
Merate [I] 116 E3
Mercatale [I] 130 F1
Mercatino Conca [I] 128 E3
Mercato San Severino [I]
134 D3
Mercato Saraceno [I] 128 D3
Merčéz [SRB] 148 A4
Merdrignac [F] 52 D4
Méréville [F] 54 D4
Merges [H] 74 E4
Mergozzo [I] 116 D3
Méribel-les-Allues [F] 116 A3
Meriç [TR] 158 A3
Mérichas [GR] 168 C3

Merichleri [BG] 156 E2
Mericler [TR] 170 C3
Mérida [E] 98 F2
Merijärvi [FIN] 216 A3
Merikarvia / Sastmola [FIN]
208 B4
Merimasku [FIN] 198 C3
Měřín [CZ] 60 F4
Mering [D] 72 B2
Mérk [H] 76 F3
Merkendorf [D] 58 E4
Merkine [LT] 38 D1
Merklingen [D] 72 A2
Merlara [I] 128 C1
Merlo, Tours de– [F] 78 F4
Merlevenez [F] 52 C4
Merligen [CH] 116 C1
Mern [DK] 178 E3
Mernye [H] 120 F2
Merošina [SRB] 148 B4
Merrahalsen [N] 192 C2
Mersch [D] 42 C3
Mersch [L] 56 D2
Merseburg [D] 44 E3
Mersinbeleni [TR] 170 C3
Mērsrags [LV] 234 E2
Merthyr Tydfil [GB] 26 D2
Mértola [P] 98 C3
Méru [F] 54 D2
Mervans [F] 68 F4
Merville [F] 40 B3
Méry [F] 56 A4
Meryemana [TR] 170 B3
Merzig [D] 56 E3
Mesagne [I] 136 E2
Mesão Frio [P] 84 B3
Mesariá [GR] 168 C2
Meschede [D] 42 E3
Meschers–sur–Gironde
[F] 78 B2
Mešeišta [MK] 160 C1
Mesenikólas [GR] 166 D2
Meshchovsk [RUS] 240 E4
Mési [GR] 156 E4
Mesić [SRB] 146 F1
Mesillas [E] 92 B4
Mesimvría [GR] 156 E4
Mesinge [DK] 178 D2
Meškasalis [LT] 38 D1
Mesklá [GR] 174 B3
Meškuičiazi [LT] 234 F4
Meslay [F] 66 D1
Mesnalien [N] 194 B2
Mesnil–Val [F] 54 D1
Mesocco [CH] 116 E2
Mesochóra [GR] 166 C1
Mesochóri [GR] 160 E4
Mesochóri [GR] 176 B3
Mésola [I] 128 D2
Mesolóngi [GR] 166 D3
Mesón do Vento [E] 82 B2
Mesopótamo [GR] 166 B2
Mespelbrunn [D] 58 C2
Messancy [B] 56 D3
Messas [F] 68 B1
Messdorf [D] 44 E1
Messelt [N] 194 B2
Messina [I] 138 C3
Messines de Baixo [P] 98 B4
Messíni [GR] 172 D3
Messkirch [D] 70 F2
Messlingen [S] 204 D3
Messtetten [D] 70 F2
Mesta [BG] 156 B3
Mestá [GR] 168 E2
Mestanza [E] 100 D3
Městec Králové [CZ] 60 E2
Mestervik [N] 224 D2
Mésti [GR] 156 E4
Mestilä [FIN] 198 C3
Mestlin [D] 32 E3
Město Albrechtice [CZ] 62 C3

Město Libavá [CZ] 62 C3
Mestre [I] 118 D4
Mesvres [F] 68 E4
Mesztegnyő [H] 120 E2
Metabief [F] 70 B4
Metagkitsi [GR] 162 B2
Metaljka [BIH] 146 C4
Metamórfosi [GR] 162 B2
Metanjac [MNE] 152 F2
Metapontium [I] 136 D3
Metaxádes [GR] 156 F3
Metaxás [GR] 160 E3
Metéora [GR] 160 D4
Méteren [F] 40 B3
Méthana [GR] 168 A3
Methóni [GR] 160 F3
Methóni [GR] 172 C3
Metković [HR] 152 C2
Metličina [BG] 150 E3
Metlika [SLO] 120 B4
Metnitz [A] 120 A1
Metóchi [GR] 162 B4
Metóchi [GR] 166 D4
Metsäkylä [FIN] 200 C3
Metsäkylä [FIN] 216 D1
Metsälä / Ömossa [FIN]
  208 B3
Metsküla [EST] 230 B3
Métsovo [GR] 160 D4
Metten [D] 72 E1
Mettet [B] 56 C1
Mettingen [D] 30 E4
Mettlach [D] 56 E3
Mettmann [D] 42 D3
Metz [F] 56 D3
Metzervisse [F] 56 D3
Metzingen [D] 70 F2
Meulan [F] 54 D3
Meung-sur-Loire [F] 68 B1
Meuselwitz [D] 44 E4
Meux [B] 40 E4
Mexilhoeira Grande [P] 98 B3
Meximieux [F] 80 E2
Meyenburg [D] 32 E3
Meylan [F] 80 E3
Meymac [F] 78 F3
Meyrargues [F] 124 F3
Meyrueis [F] 124 C2
Meyzieu [F] 80 D2
Mézapos [GR] 172 D4
Mezdra [BG] 148 E4
Mèze [F] 124 C3
Mézel [F] 126 A2
Mężenin [PL] 38 B3
Mežica [SLO] 120 B2
Mézières [F] 78 E2
Mézières-en-Brenne [F] 66 F4
Mézilhac [F] 80 C4
Mézin [F] 88 D1
Mezőberény [H] 122 E2
Mezőcsát [H] 76 D3
Mezőfalva [H] 122 B2
Mezőhegyes [H] 122 D2
Mezőhék [H] 122 D1
Mezőkeresztes [H] 76 D3
Mezőkovácsháza [H] 122 D2
Mezőkövesd [H] 76 D3
Mezőlak [H] 74 E4
Mezőnyárád [H] 76 D3
Mezőőrs [H] 74 F4
Mèzos [F] 88 B1
Mezősas [H] 122 E1
Mezőszilas [H] 122 A2
Mezőtúr [H] 122 D1
Mezquita de Jarque [E] 94 D4
Mezzojuso [I] 140 C2
Mezzolombardo [I] 118 B2
Mgarr [M] 140 B4
Mięczyn [PL] 50 D4
Miami Platja [E] 96 B3
Mianowice [PL] 36 B1
Miasteczko Śląskie [PL] 62 E2

Miastko [PL] 36 B2
Miastkowo [PL] 38 B3
Michałkowo [PL] 38 A1
Michalovce [SK] 76 E1
Michałów [PL] 48 F4
Michałów [PL] 64 B2
Michałowo [PL] 38 D3
Micheldorf [A] 74 A3
Michelstadt [D] 58 C3
Michendorf [D] 44 F2
Michów [PL] 50 B3
Michurinskoye [RUS] 200 E2
Middelburg [NL] 40 D2
Middelfart [DK] 178 C2
Middelharnis [NL] 30 A4
Middelkerke-Bad [B] 40 C2
Middlesbrough [GB] 20 F4
Middlewich [GB] 22 F3
Midéa [GR] 172 E2
Midhurst [GB] 28 C3
Midleton [IRL] 10 C4
Midlum [D] 32 A2
Midsland [NL] 30 C1
Midsund [N] 202 C3
Midtgulen [N] 202 B4
Midtskogberget [N] 194 C2
Miechów [PL] 62 F2
Mieders [A] 72 C4
Miedes [E] 94 C3
Międzdroje [PL] 34 D2
Miedzno [PL] 48 C4
Międzybórz [PL] 48 B3
Międzybrodzie Bialskie [PL]
  62 E3
Międzychód [PL] 46 E1
Międzygórze [PL] 62 B2
Międzylesie [PL] 62 B3
Międzyrzec Podlaski [PL]
  50 C2
Międzyrzecz [PL] 46 D2
Miehikkälä [FIN] 200 C2
Miejsce Piastowe [PL] 64 C3
Miejska Górka [PL] 46 F3
Miélan [F] 88 D3
Mielec [PL] 64 C2
Mielno [PL] 34 F2
Mielno [PL] 46 D3
Mieluskylä [FIN] 216 B3
Mieraslompolo [FIN] 226 D1
Miercurea Ciuc [RO] 244 D4
Mieres [E] 82 F3
Mierkenis [S] 220 B3
Mieron [N] 226 B2
Mieroszów [PL] 62 B2
Miersig [RO] 122 F1
Mierzyno [PL] 36 C1
Miesbach [D] 72 C3
Mieścisko [PL] 48 B1
Mieste [D] 44 D1
Miesterhorst [D] 44 D1
Mieszkowice [PL] 46 C1
Mietoinen [FIN] 198 C3
Mieussy [F] 116 B2
Mifol [AL] 160 A2
Migennes [F] 68 D2
Migliacciaro [F] 130 B3
Migliarino [I] 128 B3
Migliarino [I] 128 D2
Migliónico [I] 136 C2
Mignano Monte Lungo [I]
  134 C2
Migne [F] 66 F4
Miguel Esteban [E] 100 F2
Miguelturra [E] 100 D3
Mihăeşti [RO] 148 F2
Mihai Bravu [RO] 150 C2
Mihăileşti [RO] 150 C1
Mihail Kogălniceanu [RO]
  150 F1
Mihajlovac [SRB] 148 C2
Mihályi [H] 74 E4
Mihla [D] 44 C4

Miiluranta [FIN] 216 B3
Mijares [E] 92 D4
Mijares [E] 102 C3
Mijas [E] 104 D3
Mijoux [F] 80 F2
Mikaelshulen [N] 186 E2
Mikalavas [LT] 238 D4
Mikalavas [LT] 238 F2
Mike [H] 120 E3
Mikhalkovo [BG] 156 C2
Mikhaylovo [BG] 148 E3
Mikkelbostad [N] 224 C3
Mikkeli / St Michel [FIN]
  210 C4
Mikkelvika [N] 224 D1
Mikleuš [HR] 120 F4
Mikóháza [H] 76 E2
Mikolaivka [UA] 246 F4
Mikołajki [PL] 38 A2
Mikołajki Pomorskie [PL]
  36 D2
Mikolin [PL] 62 C1
Mikołów [PL] 62 E2
Mikoszewo [PL] 36 D2
Mikre [BG] 148 F4
Mikrevo [BG] 156 B3
Mikró Chorió [GR] 166 D2
Mikró Déreio [GR] 156 F3
Mikrókampos [GR] 160 F2
Mikrópoli [GR] 156 C4
Mikrothíves [GR] 162 A4
Mikstat [PL] 48 B3
Mikulčice [CZ] 74 E2
Mikulov [CZ] 74 D2
Mikulovice [CZ] 62 C2
Mikulovice [CZ] 74 C1
Miłakowo [PL] 36 E2
Miland [N] 186 E1
Milano [I] 116 E4
Milano Marittima [I] 128 D3
Milanovac [HR] 120 F4
Milanówek [PL] 48 E2
Milâs [TR] 170 C4
Milatos [GR] 174 D3
Milavidy [BY] 38 F3
Milazzo [I] 138 C3
Mildenhall [GB] 28 C2
Milejczyce [PL] 38 C4
Milejewo [PL] 36 D2
Milena [I] 140 C3
Mileševa, Manastir– [SRB]
  152 F1
Mileševo [SRB] 122 C3
Milet [TR] 170 B3
Miletići [HR] 144 C3
Mileto [I] 138 D3
Miletopolis [TR] 164 D1
Milevsko [CZ] 60 D4
Milford [IRL] 12 D1
Milford Haven [GB] 26 C1
Milharadas [P] 98 B3
Milići [BIH] 146 C3
Milicz [PL] 48 B3
Miliés [GR] 162 B4
Milín [CZ] 60 D3
Milina [GR] 162 B4
Milino [MK] 154 D3
Militello in Val di Catania
  [I] 140 E3
Miljevina [BIH] 146 B4
Millares [E] 102 C3
Millas [F] 96 E1
Millau [F] 124 C2
Millesimo [I] 126 D2
Millesvik [S] 188 D3
Millevaches [F] 78 F3
Millinge [DK] 178 C3
Millom [GB] 20 C4
Millstatt [A] 118 E2
Millstreet [IRL] 10 B3
Milltown [IRL] 10 B3
Milltown Malbay [IRL] 10 C2

Milmarcos [E] 94 C3
Milmersdorf [D] 34 C4
Milna [HR] 152 B1
Miločer [MNE] 152 E3
Miłocin [PL] 50 B3
Miłomłyn [PL] 36 E3
Milos [GR] 174 B1
Milosavci [BIH] 144 F2
Miloševa Kula [SRB] 148 C2
Miłosław [PL] 48 B2
Milovice u Hořic [CZ] 60 F2
Milow [D] 32 D3
Milówka [PL] 62 E3
Milreu [P] 98 C4
Milseburg [D] 58 D1
Milštejn [CZ] 60 E1
Miltach [D] 60 B4
Miltenberg [D] 58 C3
Milton Keynes [GB] 28 C2
Milutinovac [SRB] 148 C1
Mimizan [F] 78 A4
Mimizan–Plage [F] 78 A4
Mimoň [CZ] 60 E2
Mina de São Domingos
  [P] 98 C3
Minas de Oro (Romanas)
  [E] 82 E2
Minas de Riotinto [E] 98 E3
Minateda, Cuevas de– [E]
  106 D1
Minateda–Horca [E] 106 D1
Minaya [E] 102 A3
Minde [N] 186 B4
Mindelheim [D] 72 B3
Minden [D] 42 F2
Mindin [F] 66 B2
Mindszent [H] 122 C2
Minehead [GB] 26 D2
Mineo [I] 140 E3
Mineralni Bani [BG] 156 E2
Minerbio [I] 128 C2
Minervino di Lecce [I] 136 F3
Minervino Murge [I] 134 F3
Minervio [F] 130 B1
Minglanilla [E] 102 B3
Mingorria [E] 92 D3
Minićevo [SRB] 148 C3
Minne [S] 204 F4
Minnesund [N] 194 B4
Minnetler [TR] 164 C3
Miño [E] 82 C2
Mínoa [GR] 168 E4
Minot [F] 68 F2
Minsen [D] 30 F1
Minsk [BY] 242 B2
Mińsk Mazowiecki [PL] 50 B2
Minturnae [I] 134 C3
Minturno [I] 134 C3
Miočić [HR] 144 D3
Miočinovići [HR] 144 D1
Miokovićevo [HR] 120 E4
Mionica [SRB] 146 D3
Mira [E] 102 C2
Mira [I] 118 C4
Mira [P] 90 C1
Mirabel [E] 90 F3
Mirabella Imbàccari [I] 140 D3
Mirabello [I] 128 C2
Miradolo Terme [I] 116 E4
Mirador del Fito [E] 82 F2
Miraflores [E] 86 C4
Miraflores [E] 100 D3
Miraflores de la Sierra [E]
  92 E3
Miramar [F] 126 B3
Miramare [I] 128 E3
Miramare, Castello di– [I]
  118 E3
Miramas [F] 124 E3
Mirambeau [F] 78 C2
Miramont–de–Guyenne
  [F] 78 C4

Miranda [E] 94 C1
Miranda de Ebro [E] 86 D4
Miranda do Corvo [P] 90 C2
Miranda do Douro [P] 84 E3
Mirande [F] 88 D2
Mirandela [P] 84 C2
Mirándola [I] 128 C1
Mirano [I] 118 C4
Mirantes [E] 82 F3
Miravci [MK] 160 E1
Miravet [E] 94 F4
Mirebeau [F] 66 E3
Mirebeau [F] 68 F3
Mirecourt [F] 70 B2
Mirepoix [F] 88 F3
Mิřkov [CZ] 60 B3
Mirna [SLO] 120 B3
Mirna Peč [SLO] 120 B3
Mirnice [HR] 152 B1
Miróbriga [P] 98 B2
Miroč [SRB] 148 C2
Mirocin Šrední [PL] 46 D3
Miroslav [CZ] 74 D1
Mirosławiec [PL] 34 F3
Mirošov [CZ] 60 C3
Mirovice [CZ] 60 D4
Mirovo [BG] 156 C2
Mirow [D] 32 F3
Mirów [PL] 62 E2
Mirsk [PL] 60 E1
Mirto [I] 136 D4
Mirueña [E] 92 C3
Mişca [RO] 122 E2
Misi [FIN] 222 D3
Mišićevo [SRB] 122 C3
Misilmeri [I] 140 C2
Miskolc [H] 76 D3
Miskolctapolca [H] 76 D3
Mislata [E] 102 C3
Mislinja [SLO] 120 B2
Missanello [I] 136 C3
Misso [EST] 230 F4
Mistelbach [A] 74 D2
Misten [N] 220 A2
Misterbianco [I] 140 E3
Misterhult [S] 184 F2
Mistretta [I] 138 B4
Misurina [I] 118 D2
Misvær [N] 220 A2
Miszewo [PL] 36 C2
Mitchelstown [IRL] 10 C4
Mitchelstown Caves [IRL]
  10 D3
Míthymna [GR] 164 A3
Mitrašinci [MK] 154 F3
Mitrópoli [GR] 166 D2
Mitrova Reka [SRB] 154 B1
Mitrovo [SRB] 146 E4
Mitseh [A] 120 B1
Mittåádalen [S] 204 D3
Mittelberg [A] 72 A4
Mittelberg [A] 118 B1
Mittelberg [D] 72 B3
Mittelsaida [D] 60 C1
Mittelstenahe [D] 32 B2
Mittelwald [D] 72 C4
Mittenwalde [D] 34 C4
Mittenwalde [D] 46 B2
Mittersill [A] 72 D4
Mitterteich [D] 60 B3
Mittet [N] 202 D3
Mittewald [A] 118 D2
Mittweida [D] 44 F4
Mitwitz [D] 58 E2
Mizhiria [UA] 244 C2
Mizil [RO] 248 E3
Miziya [BG] 148 E3
Mjåland [N] 186 D4
Mjällby [S] 180 D1
Mjällom [S] 206 D3
Mjåvatn [N] 186 D3
Mjell [N] 192 C2

Mjöbäck [S] 184 B2
Mjölby [S] 188 F4
Mjølfjell [N] 192 C3
Mjölkbäcken [S] 212 E1
Mjölkvattnet [S] 204 D1
Mjönäs [S] 188 E1
Mjøndalen [N] 186 F1
Mjønes [N] 202 F1
Mjørlund [N] 194 B3
Mjøsebo [S] 184 E3
Mjösjöby [S] 206 D1
M. Kalývia [GR] 160 E4
Mladá Boleslav [CZ] 60 E2
Mladá Vožice [CZ] 60 E4
Mladé Buky [CZ] 60 F2
Mladečská Jeskyně [CZ] 62 B3
Mladenovac [SRB] 146 E2
Mlado Nagoričane [MK] 154 D3
Mlamolovo [BG] 154 F2
Mława [N] 36 E4
Mleczno [PL] 46 E3
Mlekarevo [BG] 156 F1
Mlini [HR] 152 D3
Mliniště [BIH] 144 E3
Młodasko [PL] 46 E2
Młogoszyn [PL] 48 D2
Młynary [PL] 36 E2
Młynarze [PL] 38 A3
Mnich [CZ] 60 E4
Mnichovice [CZ] 60 E3
Mnichovo Hradiště [CZ] 60 E2
Mnichów [PL] 64 A2
Mniów [PL] 48 E4
Mníšek nad Hnilcom [SK] 76 D2
Mníšek pod Brdy [CZ] 60 D3
Mniszek [PL] 48 F3
Mo [N] 186 D2
Mo [N] 192 B2
Mo [N] 194 C4
Mo [N] 202 D3
Mo [S] 188 C3
Mo [S] 188 D3
Mo [S] 188 E3
Mo [S] 196 C2
Mo [S] 206 C2
Moan [N] 204 B4
Moaña [E] 82 B3
Moate [IRL] 10 E2
Moča [SK] 76 A3
Mocejón [E] 100 E1
Móchlos [GR] 174 E3
Mochós [GR] 174 D3
Mochowo [PL] 48 D1
Mochy [PL] 46 E2
Möckern [D] 44 E2
Mockfjärd [S] 194 F4
Möckmühl [D] 58 C3
Möckow [D] 34 C2
Moclín [E] 104 F2
Modane [F] 116 A4
Modave [B] 40 E4
Módena [I] 128 C2
Módi [GR] 166 E3
Módica [I] 140 E4
Modigliana [I] 128 D3
Modlęcin [PL] 46 D2
Modliborzyce [PL] 50 C4
Mödling [A] 74 D3
Modliszewko [PL] 48 B1
Modra [SK] 74 E2
Modra Špilja [HR] 152 A2
Modrava [CZ] 72 F1
Modrča [BIH] 146 B2
Modrište [MK] 154 D4
Modron [BIH] 146 A2
Modruš [HR] 144 C1
Modrý Kameň [SK] 76 B2
Modugno [I] 136 C2

Moeche, Castillo de– [E] 82 C1
Moelv [N] 194 B3
Moen [N] 224 D3
Moena [I] 118 C2
Moesgård [DK] 178 C1
Mofalla [S] 188 E4
Moffat [GB] 20 D2
Mofjell [N] 186 D3
Moftinu Mic [RO] 76 F3
Mogadouro [P] 84 D3
Mogán [E] 112 D4
Mogielnica [PL] 48 E3
Mogilica [BG] 156 D3
Mogilište [BG] 150 F2
Mogilno [PL] 48 B1
Móglia [I] 128 C1
Mogliano Veneto [I] 118 D4
Moglicë [AL] 160 C2
Mogno [CH] 116 D2
Mogno [CH] 116 D2
Mogón [E] 106 B1
Mogorella [I] 142 B4
Mogorić [HR] 144 C2
Mogoro [I] 142 B4
Mogoşoaia [RO] 150 B1
Moguer [E] 98 D4
Moha [H] 74 F4
Mohács [H] 122 B3
Mohärad [S] 184 C2
Moharras [E] 102 A3
Moheda [S] 184 D3
Mohelnice [CZ] 62 B3
Moher, Cliffs of– [IRL] 10 C2
Mohill [IRL] 12 C3
Möhkö [FIN] 210 F2
Moholm [S] 188 E3
Mohora [H] 76 B3
Mohyliv-Podilis'kyi [UA] 244 E2
Mui [N] 186 B3
Moià [E] 96 D2
Moikipää / Molpe [FIN] 208 B2
Moimenta da Beira [P] 84 B3
Mo-i-Rana [N] 218 F4
Moirans [F] 80 E3
Moirans–en–Montagne [F] 80 F1
Moíres [GR] 174 C4
Mõisaküla [EST] 230 D3
Moissac [F] 88 E2
Moita [P] 90 B4
Moitas [P] 90 D2
Moixent [E] 102 C4
Mojácar [E] 106 C3
Mojados [E] 92 D2
Mojęcice [PL] 46 E4
Mojkovac [MNE] 152 F2
Mojonera [E] 106 B4
Mojstrana [SLO] 118 F2
Moklište [MK] 154 E4
Mokobody [PL] 50 B2
Mokra Gora [SRB] 146 C4
Mokren [BG] 150 D4
Mokresh [BG] 148 D3
Mokrin [SRB] 122 D3
Mokronog [SLO] 120 B3
Mokrzyska [PL] 64 B3
Möksy [FIN] 208 E2
Mol [B] 40 E3
Mol [SRB] 122 C3
Mola [I] 116 F3
Mola di Bari [I] 136 D2
Moland [N] 186 D1
Moláoi [GR] 172 E3
Molare [I] 126 E2
Mold [GB] 22 E3
Moldava n. Bodvou [SK] 76 D2
Molde [N] 192 B2
Molde [N] 202 D3
Moldova Nouă [RO] 146 F2

Moldova Veche [RO] 146 F2
Moldovița [RO] 146 F2
Moldovița, Mănăstirea– [RO] 244 D3
Møldrup [DK] 182 D3
Moldusen [N] 194 D4
Moledo [P] 82 A4
Molenheide [B] 40 F3
Molétai [LT] 238 E2
Molfetta [I] 136 C1
Moliden [S] 206 D2
Molières [F] 88 F2
Moliets–et–Maa [F] 88 B1
Molina de Aragón [E] 94 C4
Molina de Segura [E] 106 E2
Mulinella [I] 128 D2
Molinicos [E] 106 C1
Molino de Villobas [E] 88 C4
Molinos [E] 94 E4
Molinos [E] 100 E2
Molinos de Duero [E] 94 B2
Molíns de Reí [E] 96 D3
Moliterno [I] 136 B3
Molkom [S] 188 E2
Mollafeneri [TR] 158 E3
Mollas [AL] 160 B2
Mollas [AL] 160 C3
Möllbrücke [A] 118 E2
Mölle [S] 178 F1
Molledo [E] 86 C2
Möllenbeck [D] 34 C3
Mollerussa [E] 96 B2
Mollet del Vallès [E] 96 D3
Molliens [F] 54 E1
Mollina [E] 104 D2
Mölln [D] 32 C3
Mollósund [S] 182 F1
Mölltorp [S] 188 E4
Mölnbo [S] 190 D3
Mölndal [S] 184 A2
Mölnlycke [S] 184 A2
Mołodycz [PL] 64 D2
Mólos [GR] 166 E2
Moloskovitsy [RUS] 232 E1
Moloy [F] 68 F3
Molpe / Moikipää [FIN] 208 B2
Molsheim [F] 70 D1
Moltifao [F] 130 B2
Moltolieu [F] 124 A3
Molveno [I] 118 B3
Molvotitsy [RUS] 240 C2
Mombaroccio [I] 128 E3
Mombeltrán [E] 92 C4
Mombuey [E] 84 E2
Momchilgrad [BG] 156 E3
Momín Prohod [BG] 156 C2
Mommark [DK] 178 C3
Momo [I] 116 D3
Momrak [N] 186 D2
Monachil [E] 104 F3
Monaco [MC] 126 C3
Monaghan [IRL] 12 E3
Monäs [FIN] 208 C1
Monasterace Marina [I] 138 E3
Monasterboice [IRL] 10 F1
Monasterevin [IRL] 10 E2
Monasterio de Leyre [E] 88 B3
Monastir [BG] 156 D3
Monastir [I] 142 B5
Monastiráki [GR] 156 F4
Monastiráki [GR] 166 C3
Monbiel [CH] 116 F1
Moncada [E] 102 D3
Moncalieri [I] 116 C4
Moncalvo [I] 116 C4
Monção [P] 82 B4
Moncarapacho [P] 98 C4
Moncayo [E] 94 C2
Mönchdorf [A] 74 B2
Mönchengladbach [D] 42 C3
Mönchhof [A] 74 D3
Mónchio d. Cortio [I] 128 B2

Monchique [P] 98 B3
Monclova [E] 104 C1
Moncofa [E] 102 E3
Moncontour [F] 52 D3
Moncoutant [F] 66 D3
Mondariz [E] 82 B3
Mondariz–Balneario [E] 82 B3
Mondatoríccio [I] 138 E1
Mondaye, Abbaye de– [F] 54 A2
Mondéjar [E] 92 F4
Mondello [I] 140 C1
Mondeŀlos [SRB] 146 C1
Mondim de Basto [P] 84 B2
Mondolfo [I] 128 E4
Mondoñedo [E] 82 D2
Mondorf–les–Bains [L] 56 D3
Mondoubleau [F] 66 F2
Mondoví [I] 126 D2
Mondragone [I] 134 C3
Mondsee [A] 72 E3
Moneasa [RO] 122 F2
Monéglia [I] 126 F2
Monegrillo [E] 94 E3
Monemvasía [GR] 172 E3
Monesi [I] 126 D2
Monesterio [I] 98 E3
Monestier–de–Clermont [F] 80 E4
Monêtier–Allemont [F] 126 A2
Moneygall [IRL] 10 D2
Moneymore [NIR] 12 E2
Monfalcone [I] 118 E3
Monfarracinos [E] 84 E3
Monfero [E] 82 C2
Monflanquin [F] 78 D4
Monforte [P] 90 D4
Monforte da Beira [P] 90 E3
Monforte de Lemos [E] 82 C3
Monghidoro [I] 128 C3
Mönichkirchen [A] 74 C4
Moní Élonís [GR] 172 E3
Móniste [EST] 230 E4
Monistrol–d'Allier [F] 80 B3
Monistrol de Montserrat [E] 96 D3
Monistrol–sur–Loire [F] 80 C3
Monívea [IRL] 10 D1
Moŋki [PL] 38 C3
Mönlas [D] 58 F3
Monmouth [GB] 26 E2
Monnai [F] 54 B3
Mönni [FIN] 210 E2
Monnickendam [NL] 30 B3
Monninkylä [FIN] 200 A3
Monodéndri [GR] 160 C4
Monódryo [GR] 168 B1
Monólithos [GR] 176 B2
Monopoli [I] 136 D2
Monor [H] 76 B4
Monóvar / Monòver [E] 106 E1
Monòver / Monóvar [E] 106 E1
Monpazier [F] 78 D4
Monplaisir [F] 66 F2
Monreal [E] 100 E2
Monreal / Elo [E] 86 F4
Monreal del Campo [E] 94 C4
Monreale [I] 140 C1
Monroy [E] 90 F3
Monroyo [E] 102 E1
Monrupino [I] 118 F3
Mons (Bergen) [B] 40 D4
Monsanto [P] 90 E2
Monsaraz [P] 98 D2
Monschau [D] 42 C4
Monségur [F] 78 C4

Monsélice [I] 118 C4
Mons En Baroeul [F] 40 C3
Monsheim [D] 58 B3
Mønsted [DK] 182 C3
Mönsterås [S] 184 E3
Monsummano Terme [I] 128 B3
Montabaur [D] 58 A1
Montagnac [F] 124 C3
Montagnana [I] 118 C4
Montagny [F] 80 D2
Montagut [E] 96 E2
Montaigu [F] 66 C3
Montaigu–de–Quercy [F] 88 E1
Montaigut [F] 80 B1
Montaigut–sur–Save [F] 88 E2
Montaione [I] 128 B4
Montalbán [E] 94 D4
Montalbán [E] 100 D1
Montalbano Elicona [I] 138 C4
Montalbano Jonico [I] 136 C3
Montalbo [E] 102 A2
Montalcino [I] 130 E1
Montalto di Cosola [I] 126 F2
Montalegre [P] 82 B4
Montalieu [F] 80 E2
Montalivet–les–Bains [F] 78 B2
Montallegro [I] 140 C3
Montalto delle Marche [I] 132 E2
Montalto di Castro [I] 130 E3
Montalto Ligure [I] 126 D3
Montalto Uffugo [I] 138 D1
Montalvão [P] 90 D3
Montamarta [E] 84 E3
Montana [BG] 148 D3
Montana [CH] 116 C2
Montaña [E] 94 D3
Montánchez [t] 90 f4
Montanejos [E] 102 D2
Montaren [F] 124 D2
Montargil [P] 90 C3
Montargis [F] 68 C1
Montargull / Artesa de Segre [E] 96 C2
Montastruc la–Conseillère [F] 88 F2
Montauban [F] 52 D4
Montauban [F] 88 E2
Montauriol [F] 88 E2
Montbard [F] 68 E2
Montbazens [F] 124 B1
Montbazon [F] 66 F3
Montbéliard [F] 70 C3
Montbenoît [F] 70 B4
Montblanc [E] 96 C3
Mont-Blanc, Tunnel du– [F/I] 116 B3
Montbonnot [F] 80 E3
Montbrison [F] 80 C2
Montbron [F] 78 D2
Montbrun–les–Bains [F] 124 F2
Montceau–les–Mines [F] 68 E4
Montchanin [F] 68 E4
Montcornet [F] 56 B2
Montcuq [F] 88 E1
Mont-de-Marsan [F] 88 C2
Montdidier [F] 54 E2
Mont–Dol [F] 52 E3
Monte, Castel de– [I] 134 F3
Montealegre [E] 92 D1
Montealegre del Castillo [E] 102 B4
Monte Arabí, Cueva de– [E] 102 C4
Montebelluna [I] 118 C3
Montebourg [F] 52 F2
Montebruno [I] 126 F2

Monte–Carlo [MC] 126 C3
Montecassino, Abbazia di– [I] 134 C2
Montecatini–Terme [I] 128 B3
Montécchio [I] 128 E3
Montecchio Emilia [I] 128 B2
Montécchio Maggiore [I] 118 C4
Montechiaro, Castello di– [I] 140 C3
Monte Codi, Cant.– [I] 142 C4
Montecorice [I] 136 A3
Montecorvino Rovella [I] 134 D4
Monte da Pedra [P] 90 D3
Monte do Trigo [P] 98 D2
Montefalco [I] 132 D2
Montefalcone nel Sannio [I] 132 F4
Montefiascone [I] 130 F2
Montefiorentino, Convento di– [I] 128 D3
Montefiorino [I] 128 B2
Monteforte Irpino [I] 134 D3
Montefrío [E] 104 E2
Montegabbione [I] 130 F2
Montegiordano Marina [I] 136 C3
Montegiorgio [I] 132 E2
Monte Gordo [P] 98 C4
Montegrotto Terme [I] 118 C4
Montehermoso [E] 90 F2
Monteil [F] 80 D4
Monte Isola [I] 116 F3
Montejícar [E] 104 F2
Montelabbate [I] 130 F2
Montelaver [P] 90 A3
Montel–de–Gelat [F] 80 A2
Montélimar [F] 124 E1
Montella [I] 134 D3
Montellano [E] 104 C2
Montemaggiore Belsito [I] 138 A4
Monte Maria, Abbazia di– / Marienberg, Kloster– [I] 118 B2
Montemassi [I] 130 E1
Montemíccioli, Torre di– [I] 128 C4
Montemolín [E] 98 F3
Montemor–o–Novo [P] 90 C4
Montemor–o–Velho [P] 90 C1
Montemurlo [I] 128 C3
Montendre [F] 78 C3
Montenegro de Cameros [E] 94 B1
Montenero di Bisáccia [I] 134 D1
Monte Oliveto Maggiore, Abbazia di– [I] 130 E1
Montepulciano [I] 130 F1
Monterde [E] 94 C3
Montereale [I] 132 D3
Montereale Valcellina [I] 118 D3
Montereau [F] 68 C2
Montereau–Faut–Yonne [F] 54 E4
Monte Redondo [P] 90 C2
Monterenzio [I] 128 C2
Monteriggioni [I] 128 C4
Monteroda [D] 44 C3
Monteroni d'Arbia [I] 130 E1
Monteroni di Lecce [I] 136 E3
Monterosso al Mare [I] 126 F3
Monterosso Almo [I] 140 E3
Monterosso Grana [I] 126 C2
Monterotondo [I] 132 C4
Monterotondo Marittimo [I] 130 D1
Monterroso [E] 82 C3

Monterrubio de la Serena [E] 100 B3
Monterubbiano [I] 132 E2
Monte San Biagio [I] 134 B2
Montesano sulla Marcellana [I] 136 B3
Monte San Savino [I] 128 D4
Monte Sant'Angelo [I] 134 F2
Monte Santiago [E] 86 D3
Montesarchio [I] 134 D3
Montescaglioso [I] 136 C2
Montesclaros [E] 92 C4
Montese [I] 128 C3
Monte Senario, Convento– [I] 128 C3
Montesilvano Marina [I] 132 F3
Montesinos, Cueva de– [E] 100 F3
Montesquieu–Volvestre [F] 88 E3
Montesquiou [F] 88 D2
Montevarchi [I] 128 C4
Montevecchio Marina [I] 142 B4
Monteverde [I] 134 E3
Monte Vergine, Santuario di– [I] 134 D3
Montevil [P] 90 B4
Montfaucon–en–Velay [F] 80 C3
Montferrat [F] 126 B3
Montfort [F] 52 D4
Montfort [F] 88 E2
Montfort–en–Chalosse [F] 88 B2
Montfort l'Amaury [F] 54 D3
Mont Gargan [F] 78 F3
Montgat [E] 96 D3
Montgenèvre [F] 116 A4
Montgenèvre, Col de– [F/I] 116 A4
Montgeoffroy, Château de– [F] 66 E2
Montgesoye [F] 70 B4
Montgiscard [F] 88 F3
Montgrí, Castell de– [E] 96 F2
Montguyon [F] 78 C3
Monthermé [F] 56 C2
Monthey [CH] 116 B2
Monthois [F] 56 B3
Monthureux–sur–Saône [F] 70 B2
Monti [I] 142 C2
Monticelli Terme [I] 128 B2
Montichiari [I] 118 A4
Monticiano [I] 130 E1
Montiel [E] 100 F4
Montier–en–Der [F] 68 F1
Montignac [F] 78 E3
Montigny–le–Roi [F] 70 A2
Montigny–sur–Aube [F] 68 E2
Montijo [E] 90 E4
Montijo [P] 90 B4
Montilla [E] 104 D2
Montilleja [E] 102 B3
Monti–Sion, Santuari de– [E] 108 D3
Montivilliers [F] 54 B1
Montizón [E] 100 E4
Montlieu–la–Garde [F] 78 C3
Mont–Louis [F] 96 D1
Montluçon [F] 68 B4
Montluel [F] 80 E2
Montmajour, Abbaye de– [F] 124 D3
Montmarault [F] 80 B1
Montmédy [F] 56 C3
Montmélian [F] 80 F3
Montmeyan [F] 126 A3
Montmirail [F] 54 B4
Montmirail [F] 54 F3

Montmirey [F] 70 A3
Montmoreau–St–Cybard [F] 78 C3
Montmorillon [F] 66 F4
Montmort [F] 56 A3
Montoire–sur–le–Loir [F] 66 F2
Montoito [P] 98 D2
Montorio [E] 86 C3
Montorio al Vomano [I] 132 E3
Montoro [E] 104 E1
Montoy–Flanville [F] 56 D3
Montpellier [F] 124 C3
Montpellier–le–Vieux [F] 124 C2
Montpezat–de–Quercy [F] 88 F1
Montpon–Ménestérol [F] 78 C3
Montpont–en–Bresse [F] 80 E1
Mont–Ras [I] 96 F2
Montréal [F] 68 D2
Montréal [F] 88 D2
Montréal [F] 88 F3
Montredon–Labessonnie [F] 124 A2
Montréjeau [F] 88 D3
Montrésor [F] 68 A3
Montresta [I] 142 B3
Montret [F] 68 F4
Montreuil [F] 40 A3
Montreuil–aux–Lions [F] 54 F3
Montreuil–Bellay [F] 66 E3
Montreux [CH] 116 B2
Montrevault [F] 66 D2
Montrevel–en–Bresse [F] 80 E1
Montrichard [F] 68 A2
Montrøen [N] 204 B4
Montroi / Montroy [E] 102 D3
Mont–roig del Camp [E] 96 B3
Montrond–les–Bains [F] 80 C2
Montrose [GB] 18 E3
Montroy / Montroi [E] 102 D3
Montsalvy [F] 80 A4
Montsauche–les–Settons [F] 68 D3
Montségur [F] 88 F4
Montseny [E] 96 D3
Montserrat [E] 96 D3
Montsoreau [F] 66 E3
Mont–sous–Vaudrey [F] 70 A4
Monts–s–Guesnes [F] 66 E3
Mont–Ste–Odile [F] 70 D2
Montsûrs [F] 52 F4
Montuenga [E] 92 D2
Montuïri [E] 108 D3
Monturque [E] 104 E2
Monza [I] 116 E3
Monze [F] 124 A3
Monzón [E] 94 F3
Monzón de Campos [E] 86 B4
Monzuno [I] 128 C2
Moon–sur–Elle [F] 52 F2
Moordorf [D] 30 E2
Moosburg [D] 72 D2
Moosham [A] 118 F1
Moosinning [D] 72 D2
Moos in Passeier / Moso in Passiria [I] 118 B1
Mór [H] 74 F4
Mora [E] 100 E2
Mora [E] 100 E2
Mora [P] 90 C3
Mora [S] 194 F3
Mora [S] 196 B4
Mora, Puerto de la– [E] 104 F3
Morača, Manastir– [MNE] 152 F2
Móra d'Ebre [E] 94 F4

Mora de Rubielos [E] 102 D2
Moradillo de Roa [E] 92 F2
Morąg [PL] 36 E2
Mórahalom [H] 122 C3
Moraïtika [GR] 166 A1
Morakovo [MNE] 152 E2
Morakowo [PL] 36 B4
Móra la Nova [E] 94 F4
Moral de Calatrava [E] 100 E3
Moraleda de Zafayona [E] 104 E3
Moraleja [E] 90 F2
Morales del Vino [E] 84 E3
Morano Cálabro [I] 136 C4
Mora Stenar [S] 190 D1
Morasverdes [E] 92 B3
Moratalla [E] 106 D2
Morava [SLO] 120 B4
Moravče pri Gabrovki [SLO] 120 B3
Moravice [HR] 120 B4
Moraviţa [RO] 122 E4
Morávka [CZ] 62 D3
Moravská Třebová [CZ] 62 B3
Moravské Budějovice [CZ] 74 C1
Moravské Lieskové [SK] 74 E2
Moravský Beroun [CZ] 62 C3
Moravský Krumlov [CZ] 74 D1
Morawica [PL] 64 B1
Morbach [D] 56 E2
Mörbacka [S] 194 D3
Morbegno [I] 116 E2
Mörbisch [A] 74 D3
Mörbylånga [S] 184 E4
Morcenx [F] 88 C1
Morciano di Romagna [I] 128 C3
Morcone [I] 134 D2
Morcote [CH] 116 D3
Mordelles [F] 52 D4
Mordoğan [TR] 168 F1
Mordy [PL] 50 C2
Morecambe [GB] 20 D4
Moreda [E] 106 A2
Moreira [P] 84 A2
Morella [E] 102 E1
Morella la Vella [E] 102 E1
Moreno, Col de la– [F] 80 B2
Moreruela, Monasterio de– [E] 84 E2
Móres [I] 142 B3
Morestel [F] 80 E3
Moret–sur–Loing [F] 54 E4
Moretta [I] 126 C1
Moreuil [F] 54 E2
Morez [F] 80 F1
Mörfelden [D] 58 B2
Mórfi [GR] 166 B2
Mórfou (Güzelyurt) [CY] 176 D3
Morgantina [I] 140 D3
Morgat [F] 52 A3
Morgedal [N] 186 D2
Morges [CH] 116 B1
Morgex [I] 116 B3
Morgins [CH] 116 B2
Morgny [F] 54 D2
Morgongåva [S] 190 C1
Morhange [F] 56 E4
Mori [I] 118 B3
Moriani–Plage [F] 130 B2
Mórichida [H] 74 E4
Morigny Champigny [F] 54 D4
Morimondo, Abbazia di– [I] 116 D4
Moritzburg [D] 44 E4
Moritzburg [D] 46 B4
Moritzburg, Schloss– [D] 46 B4
Moriville [F] 70 C2
Morjärv [S] 222 A4

Mørk [N] 188 B2
Morkarla [S] 190 D1
Mørke [DK] 182 D4
Mørkøv [DK] 178 E2
Morkovice Slížany [CZ] 62 C4
Mörkret [S] 194 D1
Mørkveden [N] 218 E1
Morla [E] 82 E4
Morlaàs [F] 88 C2
Morlaix [F] 52 B2
Mörlunda [S] 184 E2
Mormanno [I] 136 B4
Mormant [F] 54 E4
Mornay–Berry [F] 68 C3
Mornese [I] 126 E2
Morón de Almazán [E] 94 B3
Morón de la Frontera [E] 104 C2
Morosaglia [P] 130 B2
Morovič [SRB] 146 C2
Morøya [N] 220 A1
Morozzo [I] 126 D2
Morpeth [GB] 20 E3
Morra [I] 128 D4
Morral de Cabrafeixet [E] 96 B4
Marriaunet [N] 212 B4
Morro del Jable [E] 114 D4
Mörrum [S] 180 C1
Mörsburg [CH] 70 E3
Morshyn [UA] 64 F4
Mörsil [S] 204 E2
Morskoga krog [S] 190 B2
Mörskom / Myrskylä [FIN] 200 B3
Morskoye [RUS] 238 A3
Morsum [D] 178 A3
Mørsvikbotn [N] 220 B1
Mortagne–au–Perche [F] 54 B3
Mortagne–sur–Sèvre [F] 66 D3
Mortágua [P] 84 A4
Mortain [F] 52 F3
Mortara [I] 116 D4
Mörtberg [S] 220 E3
Morteau [F] 70 C4
Mortegliano [I] 118 E3
Mörtfors [S] 184 E2
Mortier–Crolle, Château de– [F] 66 D1
Mortrée [F] 54 B3
Mörtschach [A] 118 E1
Morud [DK] 178 C2
Morup [S] 184 A3
Moryń [PL] 34 D4
Morzine [F] 116 B2
Morzyczyn [PL] 34 E3
Mosal'sk [RUS] 240 F1
Mosås [S] 188 F2
Mosätt [S] 204 E4
Mosbach [D] 58 C3
Mosbekk [N] 188 C1
Mosby [N] 186 C4
Moščanci [SLO] 120 D2
Moscavide [P] 90 B3
Moščenica [HR] 120 D4
Moščenice [HR] 144 B1
Moščenička Draga [HR] 144 B1
Moschendorf [A] 120 D1
Moschopótamos [GR] 160 E3
Moscufo [I] 132 E3
Mosédis [LT] 234 D4
Mosel [D] 60 B1
Moshult [S] 184 B3
Mosina [PL] 46 F2
Mosjø [S] 206 D2
Mosjøen [N] 212 D1
Moškanjci [SLO] 120 C2
Mosko [BIH] 152 D2
Moskog [N] 192 B1
Moskosel [S] 214 C1

Moskva [RUS] 240 F3
Moslavina [HR] 120 F3
Mosna [SRB] 148 C2
Moso in Passiria / Moos in
  Passeier [I] 118 B1
Mosonmagyaróvár [H] 74 E3
Mosqueruela [E] 102 D2
Moss [D] 70 F3
Moss [N] 188 B2
Mossiberg [S] 194 E2
Mössingen [D] 70 F2
Most [PL] 156 E2
Most [CZ] 60 C2
Mosta [M] 140 C4
Mostar [BIH] 152 C1
Mosteiros [P] 110 E1
Mosterhamn [N] 186 A1
Mostesquiu [E] 96 D2
Mostki [PL] 64 B2
Most na Soči [SLO] 118 F3
Móstoles [E] 92 E4
Mostowo [PL] 36 A2
Mosty [PL] 50 D3
Mostys'ka [UA] 64 E3
Mosune [HR] 144 C1
Moszczanka [PL] 50 B3
Mota, Cast. de la– [E] 92 D2
Mota del Cuervo [E] 100 F2
Mota del Marqués [E] 84 F3
Motal' [BY] 38 F4
Motala [S] 188 F4
Motherwell [GB] 18 C4
Motilla del Palancar [E] 102 B3
Motjärnshyttan [S] 188 E1
Motovun [HR] 118 F4
Motricoux [F] 88 F2
Motril [E] 104 F3
Motru [RO] 148 C1
Motta di Livenza [I] 118 D3
Motta Montecorvino [I] 134 E2
Motta Visconti [I] 116 D4
Motte–Glain, Château de la–
  [F] 66 D2
Móttola [I] 136 D2
Möttönen [FIN] 208 E1
Mou [DK] 182 D3
Mouchard [F] 70 B4
Moudon [CH] 116 B1
Moúdros [GR] 162 E2
Mougins [F] 126 B3
Mouhijärvi [FIN] 198 D1
Mouliherne [F] 66 E2
Moulins [F] 68 C4
Moulins–Engilbert [F] 68 D3
Moulins–la–Marche [F] 54 B3
Moulismes [F] 78 E1
Moult [F] 54 B2
Mountallen [IRL] 12 C3
Mount Bellew [IRL] 10 D1
Mount Charles [IRL] 12 D2
Mountmellick [IRL] 10 E2
Mountrath [IRL] 10 E2
Mountshannon [IRL] 10 D2
Moura [P] 98 D2
Mourão [P] 98 D2
Mouriés [GR] 156 A4
Mouros, Cast. dos– [P] 90 A3
Mourujärvi [FIN] 222 E3
Moustey [F] 78 B4
Moustiers–Ste–Marie [F]
  126 B3
Mouthe [F] 80 F1
Mouthier [F] 70 B4
Mouthoumet [F] 124 A3
Moutier [CH] 70 D3
Moutier–d'Ahun [F] 78 F2
Moutiers [F] 66 C3
Moûtiers [F] 116 A3
Mouton–Rothschild [F] 78 B3
Moutoullás [CY] 176 D3
Moutsoúna [GR] 168 E4
Mouy [F] 54 E2

Mouzakaíoi [GR] 160 C4
Mouzáki [GR] 166 D2
Mouzáki [GR] 172 C1
Mouzon [F] 56 C2
Moville [IRL] 12 E1
Mowchadz' [BY] 38 F2
Moy [NIR] 12 E2
Moyenvic [F] 56 D4
Moynalty [IRL] 10 F1
Moyne Abbey [IRL] 12 B2
Moyuela [E] 94 D3
Moyvore [IRL] 10 E1
Mozáceni [RO] 150 A1
Mozhaysk [RUS] 240 E3
Mozia [I] 140 A2
Mozirje [SLO] 120 B2
Mozuli [RUS] 236 E3
Mozyr' [RUS] 38 A1
Mpalí [GR] 174 C3
Mpampalió [GR] 166 C3
Mpampíni [GR] 166 C3
Mpatsí [GR] 168 C2
Mpenítses [GR] 166 A1
Mpórsio [GR] 166 D4
Mpoúkka [GR] 166 C2
Mprálos [GR] 166 E3
Mragowo [PL] 38 A2
Mrakovica [BIH] 144 E2
Mramor [BIH] 152 D2
Mrazovac [BIH] 144 D2
Mrčajevci [SRB] 146 E3
Mrežičko [MK] 160 E1
Mrkonjić–Grad [BIH] 144 E3
Mrkopalj [HR] 120 B4
Mrocza [PL] 36 B4
Mroczeń [PL] 48 B4
Mrzeżyno [PL] 34 E2
Mrzygłód [PL] 64 D3
Mšeno [CZ] 60 E2
Mshinskaya [RUS] 232 F2
Mstislavl' [BY] 242 D1
Mstów [PL] 62 E1
Mszana Dolna [PL] 62 F3
Mszczonów [PL] 48 E2
Mt–Dauphin [F] 126 B1
Mt. Melleray Monastery
  [IRL] 10 D3
Mtsensk [RUS] 242 F1
Mt. St. Joseph Abbey [IRL]
  10 D2
Muć [HR] 144 E4
Muccia [I] 132 D2
Much [D] 42 D4
Mücheln [D] 44 E3
Muchówka [PL] 64 B3
Muciélagos, Cava de los– [E]
  106 C3
Mücka Mikow [D] 46 C4
Muckross [IRL] 10 B3
Muckross House [IRL] 10 B3
Mudanya [TR] 158 E4
Mudau [D] 58 C3
Mudela, Castillo de– [E]
  100 E4
Müden [D] 32 C4
Müdrets [BG] 156 F2
Muel [E] 94 D3
Muela de Cortes [E] 102 C4
Muelas del Pan [E] 84 E3
Muff [IRL] 12 E1
Muge [P] 90 B3
Mügeln [D] 44 F4
Muggendorf [D] 58 E3
Múggia [I] 118 F4
Mugiro [E] 86 F3
Muğla [TR] 170 D4
Müglizh [BG] 156 E1
Mugnano [I] 130 F1
Mugron [F] 88 C2
Mühlacker [D] 58 B4
Mühlbach [A] 72 E4

Mühlberg [D] 46 B3
Mühldorf [D] 72 D2
Mühlen [A] 120 B1
Mühlhausen [D] 44 C4
Mühlhausen [D] 58 F4
Mühlhausen [D] 72 A2
Muhola [FIN] 208 E1
Muhos [FIN] 216 B2
Muhovo [BG] 156 C1
Muine Bheag / Bagenalstown
  [IRL] 10 E3
Muiños [E] 82 B4
Muir of Ord [GB] 14 D3
Mujdžić [BIH] 144 E3
Mujejärvi [FIN] 216 E3
Mukachove [UA] 76 F2
Mula [E] 106 D2
Mulazzo [I] 128 A2
Mulba [E] 98 F4
Mulegns [CH] 116 E2
Mülheim [D] 42 C3
Mülheim [D] 56 E2
Mulhouse [F] 70 D3
Muljava [SLO] 120 B3
Muljula [FIN] 210 E3
Möllheim [D] 70 D3
Mullinavat [IRL] 10 E3
Mullingar [IRL] 10 E1
Müllrose [D] 46 C2
Mullsjö [S] 184 C1
Mullyttan [S] 188 F3
Mulseryd [S] 184 C2
Multia [FIN] 208 E3
Multrå [S] 206 C2
Mumor [H] 120 D2
Muñana [E] 92 C3
Münchberg [D] 58 F2
Müncheberg [D] 46 C2
München [D] 72 C2
Münchhausen [D] 42 E4
Münchhausen [D] 46 B3
Mundaka [EST] 86 E3
Munderkingen [D] 72 A2
Mundheim [N] 192 B3
Munera [E] 102 A3
Mungia [E] 86 E3
Muniaczkowice [PL] 64 A2
Muñico [E] 92 D3
Muniellos, Bosque de– [E]
  82 E3
Muniesa [E] 94 D4
Munka–Ljungby [S] 178 F1
Munkebo [DK] 178 D2
Munkedal [S] 188 C4
Munkelven [N] 226 E1
Munkflohögen [S] 204 F2
Munkfors [S] 188 E1
Münnerstadt [D] 58 D2
Munsala [FIN] 208 C1
Münsingen [CH] 70 D4
Munsö [S] 190 D2
Münster [CH] 116 D2
Münster [D] 30 E4
Munster [D] 32 C4
Munster [F] 70 C2
Münstertal [D] 70 D3
Münzenberg [D] 58 C2
Münzkirchen [A] 72 F2
Muodoslompolo [S] 222 A1
Muonio [FIN] 226 B4
Muotkalahti [RUS] 222 E1
Muotkavaara [FIN] 222 B1
Muradiye [TR] 164 C4
Murakeresztúr [H] 120 E2
Muráň [SK] 76 C2
Murano [I] 118 D4
Muras [E] 82 D2
Murat [F] 80 A3
Murati [EST] 230 F4
Muratlar [TR] 164 B2
Muratlar [TR] 170 D3
Muratlı [TR] 158 C3

Murato [F] 130 B2
Murat–sur–Vèbre [F] 124 B2
Murau [A] 118 F1
Muravera [I] 142 C5
Murazzano [I] 126 D2
Mürchevo [BG] 148 D3
Murchin [D] 34 C2
Murcia [E] 106 E2
Murciélagos, Cueva de los–
  [E] 104 E2
Murciélagos, Cueva de los–
  [E] 104 F3
Murczyn [PL] 36 C4
Mur–de–Barrez [F] 80 A3
Mur–de–Bretagne [F] 52 C3
Mureck [A] 120 C2
Mürefte [TR] 158 B4
Muret [F] 88 E3
Murga [H] 122 A2
Murgados [E] 82 C1
Murgaševo [MK] 160 D1
Murgia / Murguía [E] 86 E3
Murg–Kraftwerk [D] 70 E1
Murguía / Murgia [E] 86 E3
Muri [CH] 70 E4
Murias de Paredes [E] 82 E3
Murieta [E] 86 E4
Murighiol [RO] 250 D3
Murino [MNE] 154 B2
Muriquan [AL] 152 F4
Murjek [S] 220 E3
Murlo [I] 130 E1
Murnau [D] 72 C3
Muro [E] 108 D3
Muro [F] 130 B2
Muro de Alcoy / Muro del
  Comtat [E] 106 F1
Muro del Comtat / Muro de
  Alcoy [E] 106 F1
Murole [FIN] 208 D4
Muro Lucano [I] 134 E3
Murony [H] 122 E2
Muros [E] 82 A2
Murowana Goślina [PL] 46 F2
Mürren [CH] 116 C2
Murrhardt [D] 58 C4
Murrisk Abbey [IRL] 12 B2
Murru [EST] 230 C3
Murska Sobota [SLO] 120 D2
Mursko Središće [HR] 120 D2
Murta [RO] 148 E2
Murtas [E] 106 A3
Murten [CH] 70 C4
Murter [HR] 144 C4
Murtinheira [P] 90 C1
Murtolahti [FIN] 210 C2
Murtosa [P] 84 A3
Murtovaara [FIN] 216 F3
Murvica [HR] 144 C3
Mürzzuschlag [A] 74 C4
Musamaa [FIN] 208 D2
Musasău de Tinca [RO] 122 F2
Musetrene [N] 192 E1
Mussalo [FIN] 200 C3
Musselkanaal [NL] 30 E2
Mussidan [F] 78 D3
Mussomeli [I] 140 C2
Mussy [F] 68 E2
Mustafa Kemal Paşa [TR]
  164 D2
Müstair [CH] 118 A2
Mustajärvi [FIN] 208 D4
Mustajõe [EST] 230 F1
Mustalahti [FIN] 208 E3
Mustasaari / Korsholm [FIN]
  208 B2
Mustér / Disentis [CH] 116 E1
Mustikkaperä [FIN] 208 E2
Mustinmäki [FIN] 210 C3
Mustinsalo [FIN] 210 C3

Mustjala [EST] 230 B3
Mustla [EST] 230 E3
Mustola [FIN] 226 E2
Mustvee [EST] 230 E2
Muszaki [PL] 36 F3
Muszyna [PL] 64 B4
Muszynka [PL] 64 B4
Muta [SLO] 120 B2
Mutalahti [FIN] 210 F2
Mutanj [SRB] 146 E3
Mutilva [E] 86 F4
Mutlangen [D] 72 A1
Mutriku [E] 86 E3
Mutterstadt [D] 58 B3
Muurame [FIN] 208 F3
Muurasjärvi [FIN] 216 B4
Muurikkala [FIN] 200 D2
Muurla [FIN] 198 D3
Muurola [FIN] 200 C2
Muurola [FIN] 222 C3
Muuruvesi [FIN] 210 C2
Muxía [E] 82 A2
Múzeum Oravskej Dediny
  [SK] 62 F4
Muzillac [F] 66 B1
Mužla [SK] 76 A3
Mužlja [SRB] 122 D4
Myakishevo [RUS] 236 F3
Mybotn [N] 224 C3
Myckelgensjö [S] 206 C2
Myczków [PL] 64 D4
Myggenäs [S] 182 F1
Myhinpää [FIN] 210 B3
Myjava [SK] 74 E2
Mýkines [GR] 172 E1
Myking [N] 192 E3
Myklebust [N] 202 B4
Myklebust [N] 202 C2
Myklestøyl [N] 186 C2
Mykolaïv [UA] 64 F3
Mykolaïv [UA] 246 E3
Mýkonos [GR] 168 D3
Myllyaho [FIN] 208 E1
Myllykoski [FIN] 200 B2
Myllykselä [FIN] 198 F1
Myllymaa [FIN] 198 D1
Myllymäki [FIN] 208 E3
Mýloi [GR] 172 E2
Mylopótamos [GR] 172 E4
Mylund [DK] 182 D2
Mynämäki [FIN] 198 C3
Myndos [TR] 170 B4
Myonnesos [TR] 170 A3
Myos [TR] 170 B3
Myra [TR] 176 F1
Myrane [N] 186 B3
Myrås [S] 220 C4
Myrdal [N] 192 C3
Myre [N] 224 B3
Myre [N] 224 B3
Myren [S] 194 D4
Myrhorod [UA] 242 F4
Mýrina [GR] 162 E2
Myrina [TR] 164 B4
Myrkky [FIN] 208 B3
Myrmoen [N] 204 C3
Myrnes [N] 224 F1
Myrnyi [UA] 246 E4
Myronivka [UA] 246 C1
Myrskylä / Mörskom [FIN]
  200 B3
Myrtiés [GR] 176 A1
Mýrtos [GR] 174 E4
Mýrtou (Çamlıbel) [CY]
  176 D3
Myrvika [N] 212 C3
Myrviken [S] 204 E3
Mysen [N] 188 B2
Mysenec [CZ] 60 D4
Myshall [IRL] 10 E3
Myshuryn Rih [UA] 246 E1
Myślenice [PL] 62 F3

Myślibórz [PL] 34 E4
Myślice [PL] 36 D2
Mysłowice [PL] 62 E2
Mysovka [RUS] 238 A3
Mystegná [GR] 164 B3
Mystrás [GR] 172 D3
Mysubyttseter [N] 192 D1
Myszków [PL] 62 E2
Myszyniec [PL] 38 A3
Mýtikas [GR] 166 C3
Mytilíni [GR] 164 B3
Mytishchi [RUS] 240 F3
Mýtna [SK] 76 B2
Mýto [BY] 38 E2
Mýto [CZ] 60 D3
Mzdowo [PL] 36 A2
Mzurki [PL] 48 D3

Nå [N] 192 C3
Naamijoki [FIN] 222 B2
Naantali / Nådend [FIN]
198 C3
Naarajärvi [FIN] 210 B3
Naarajärvi [FIN] 216 F4
Naarden [NL] 30 B3
Naarva [FIN] 210 F1
Nääs [S] 184 A1
Naas / An Nás [IRL] 10 F2
Nabaskoze / Navascués
[E] 88 B3
Nabbelund [S] 184 F2
Nabburg [D] 60 B4
Nábrád [H] 76 F3
Náchod [CZ] 62 B2
Nacivelioba [TR] 164 C2
Nacka [S] 190 E2
Nadarzyn [PL] 48 E2
Nadąş [RO] 122 F3
Naddvik [N] 192 D2
Nadela [E] 82 D2
Nådend / Naantali [FIN]
198 C3
Nădlac [RO] 122 D3
Nădlac [RO] 248 B3
Nadrin [B] 56 D2
Nádudvar [H] 76 D4
Nærbø [N] 186 A3
Næstved [DK] 178 E3
Náfels [CH] 70 F4
Náfpaktos [GR] 166 D3
Náfplio [GR] 172 E2
Naggen [S] 206 B4
Naglarby [S] 196 B4
Nagłowice [PL] 62 F2
Nagold [D] 70 F2
Nagu / Nauvo [FIN] 198 C3
Nagyatád [H] 120 E3
Nagybajom [H] 120 E2
Nagybaracska [H] 122 B3
Nagycenk [H] 74 D4
Nagycserkesz [H] 76 E3
Nagydorog [H] 122 B2
Nagyecsed [H] 76 F3
Nagyér [H] 122 D2
Nagyfüged [H] 76 C3
Nagygyanté [H] 122 E1
Nagygyimót [H] 74 E4
Nagyhalász [H] 76 E3
Nagyhegyes [H] 76 E4
Nagyhomok [H] 76 E2
Nagyigmánd [H] 74 F4
Nagyiván [H] 76 D4
Nagykálló [H] 76 E3
Nagykanizsa [H] 120 E2
Nagykáta [H] 76 C4
Nagykereki [H] 76 E4
Nagyköllked [H] 120 D1

Nagykónyi [H] 120 F2
Nagykőrös [H] 122 C1
Nagylak [H] 122 D3
Nagylóc [H] 76 B3
Nagymágocs [H] 122 D2
Nagymaros [H] 76 B3
Nagyoroszi [H] 76 B3
Nagypuszta [H] 120 E3
Nagyrábé [H] 76 E4
Nagyszénás [H] 122 D2
Nagyvázsony [H] 120 E1
Naharros [E] 94 A3
Naharros [E] 102 A2
Nahe [D] 32 C2
Nahkiaisoja [FIN] 222 B3
Naidăş [RO] 146 F2
Naila [D] 58 F2
Nailloux [F] 88 F3
Nailsworth [GB] 26 F2
Naipu [RO] 150 B2
Nairn [GB] 14 E3
Najac [F] 124 A1
Nájera [E] 86 D4
Näkkälä [FIN] 226 B3
Nakkesletta [N] 224 D1
Nakkila [FIN] 198 C1
Naklik [PL] 64 D2
Naklo [SLO] 120 A3
Nakło nad Notecią [PL] 36 B4
Nakovo [SRB] 122 D3
Nakskov [DK] 178 D3
Nålden [S] 204 E2
Nałęczów [PL] 50 B3
Nálepkovo [SK] 76 D1
Näljänkä [FIN] 216 D1
Nalkki [FIN] 216 D2
Nalzen [F] 88 F4
Nalžovké Hory [CZ] 60 C4
Nalžovské Hory [CZ] 60 C4
Nambroca [E] 100 E1
Namdalseid [N] 212 C4
Namen (Namur) [B] 40 E4
Náměšť nad Oslavou [CZ]
62 A4
Námestovo [SK] 62 E4
Namlos [A] 72 B4
Namma [N] 194 C3
Nämpnäs [FIN] 208 B3
Namsos [N] 212 C3
Namsskogan [N] 212 D3
Namsvassgardån [N] 212 E3
Namur (Namen) [B] 40 E4
Namysłów [PL] 48 B4
Nanclares de la Oca / Langraiz
Oka [E] 86 D3
Nancy [F] 56 D4
Nangis [F] 54 E4
Nannestad [N] 194 B4
Nans–les–Pins [F] 124 F3
Nant [F] 124 C2
Nantes [F] 66 C2
Nanteuil–le–Haudouin [F]
54 E3
Nantiat [F] 78 E2
Nantua [F] 80 E2
Nantwich [GB] 22 F3
Naours, Grottes de– [F] 54 E1
Náousa [GR] 160 E2
Náousa [GR] 168 D4
Nåpagård [N] 186 E1
Napi [EST] 230 B2
Naples [F] 158 B3
Nápoli [I] 134 C3
Na Pomezí [CZ] 62 C2
Naposenaho [FIN] 208 E2
När [S] 234 A3
Nåra [N] 192 A2
Naraio, Castelo de– [E] 82 C1
Narberth [GB] 26 C1
Narbolía [I] 142 B4
Narbonne [F] 124 B3
Narbonne–Plage [F] 124 B3

Narbuvollen [N] 204 C4
Narcao [I] 142 B5
Nardis, Cascata di– [I] 118 B2
Nardò [I] 136 E3
Narechenski Bani [BG] 156 D2
Narew [PL] 38 D3
Narewka [PL] 38 D3
Närhilä [FIN] 210 B2
Narila [FIN] 210 C3
Narjordet [N] 204 C3
Narkaus [FIN] 222 C3
Narlica [TR] 158 F4
Narni [I] 132 C3
Naro [I] 140 C3
Naro–Fominsk [RUS] 240 F3
Narol [PL] 64 E2
Narón [E] 82 C3
Närpes / Närpiö [FIN] 208 B3
Närpiö / Närpes [FIN] 208 B3
Narta [HR] 120 D3
Nartháki [GR] 162 A4
Nartkowo [PL] 34 E2
Närtuna [S] 190 E2
Naruska [FIN] 222 E1
Narva [EST] 232 E1
Narva [FIN] 198 D1
Närva [FIN] 200 A1
Närvä [S] 224 F4
Narva–Jõesuu [EST] 230 F1
Närvijoki [FIN] 208 B2
Narvik [N] 224 C4
Näs [S] 184 C1
Näs [S] 188 E2
Näs [S] 194 E4
Näs [S] 214 D3
Näs [S] 234 A3
Naşa [TR] 164 E3
Näsåker [S] 206 C2
N. Åsarp [S] 184 C1
Näsåud [RO] 244 D3
Nasbinals [F] 80 B4
Näsby [S] 184 E4
Näsbyholm [S] 184 C2
Nascimiento del Río Cuervo
[E] 102 B1
Näset [S] 206 B3
Nashulta [S] 190 C2
Našice [HR] 120 F4
Nasielsk [PL] 48 E1
Näsinge [S] 188 B3
Näsland [S] 214 C4
Näsledovice [CZ] 74 D1
Naso [I] 138 B3
Na Špičáku [CZ] 62 C2
Nassau [D] 58 A2
Nassereith [A] 72 B4
Nässja [S] 188 F4
Nässjö [S] 184 D2
Nässjö [S] 206 D2
Nässvallen [S] 204 E3
Nasswald [A] 74 C3
Nastan [BG] 156 C3
Nästansjö [S] 214 A2
Nastazin [PL] 34 E3
Nästeln [S] 204 E3
Nästi [FIN] 198 C2
Nastola [FIN] 200 B2
Nasūm [S] 180 D1
Näsviken [S] 196 C1
Näsviken [S] 204 F1
Nata [CY] 176 C4
Natalinci [SRB] 146 E3
Nätra Fjällskog [S] 206 D2
Nattavaara [S] 220 D3
Nättraby [S] 180 E1
Nattvatn [N] 226 C1
Naturno / Naturns [I] 118 B2
Naturns / Naturno [I] 118 B2
Naucelle [F] 124 B1
Nauders [A] 118 B1
Nauen [D] 44 F1
Naujoji Akmanė [LT] 234 E4

Naul [IRL] 10 F2
Naumburg [D] 44 E4
Naumestis [LT] 238 D2
Naunhof [D] 44 F4
Nausta [S] 220 D3
Naustbukta [N] 212 C3
Naustdal [N] 192 B1
Nauste [N] 202 E3
Naustvika [N] 202 E3
Nautijaure [S] 220 D2
Nautsi [RUS] 226 E2
Nautsung [N] 192 B2
Nauvo / Nagu [FIN] 198 C3
Nava [E] 86 A2
Navacelles, Cirque de– [F]
124 C2
Navacerrada [E] 92 E3
Nava de la Asunción [E] 92 D2
Nava del Rey [E] 84 F4
Navahermosa [E] 100 D2
Navahrudak [BY] 38 F2
Naval [E] 94 F2
Navalagamella [E] 92 E4
Navalcán [E] 92 C4
Navalcarnero [E] 92 E4
Navaleno [E] 94 B2
Navalguijo [E] 92 C3
Navalmanzano [E] 92 E2
Navalmoral [E] 92 D3
Navalmoral de la Mata [E]
92 B4
Navalón [E] 102 C4
Navalperal de Pinares [E]
92 D3
Navalpino [E] 100 C2
Navalvillar de Ibor [E] 100 B1
Navalvillar de Pela [E] 100 B2
Navan / An Uaimh [IRL] 10 F1
Nåvårdalen [N] 204 B3
Navarredonda de Gredos
[E] 92 C3
Navarrenx [F] 88 B2
Navarrés [E] 102 D4
Navarrete [E] 86 E4
Navàs [S] 96 D2
Navascués / Nabaskoze
[E] 88 B3
Navas de Estena [E] 100 D2
Navas del Madroño [E] 90 E3
Navas del Rey [E] 92 D4
Navas de Oro [E] 92 E2
Navas de San Juan [E] 106 B1
Navata [E] 96 E2
Navatalgordo [E] 92 D3
Navayel'nya [BY] 38 F2
Nävekvarn [S] 190 C3
Navelli [I] 132 E3
Navelsaker [N] 202 C4
Nave Redonda [P] 98 B3
Näverkärret [S] 190 B2
Naverstad [S] 188 C2
Naveta des Tudons [E] 108 E3
Navia [E] 82 E2
Navilly [F] 68 F4
Navit [N] 224 F2
Navlya [RUS] 242 E2
Năvodari [RO] 150 F1
Navruz [TR] 164 C2
Naxås [S] 204 E2
Náxos [GR] 168 D4
Naxos [I] 138 C4
Nazaré [P] 90 B2
Nazıfoaşa [TR] 164 F1
Nazıllı [TR] 170 D3
Nazimovo [RUS] 232 E4
N. Bukovica [HR] 120 F4
N.–D. de Clausis [F] 126 C1
N.–D. de Kerdevot [F] 52 B3
N.D. de la Salette [F] 80 E4
N.–D. de Lure [F] 124 F2
N.–D. de Miracles [F] 126 C3
N.–D.–du–Haut [F] 70 C3

N.–D. du Mai [F] 124 F4
Ndroq [AL] 160 A1
Néa Anchiálos [GR] 162 A4
Néa Artáki [GR] 168 B1
Néa Epídavros [GR] 168 A3
Néa Fókaia [GR] 162 B2
Néa Kallikráteia [GR] 162 B2
Néa Karváli [GR] 156 D4
Néa Kerdýllia [GR] 162 C1
Néa Koróni [GR] 172 C3
Neale [IRL] 12 B3
Néa Liosia [GR] 168 B2
Néa Mádytos [GR] 162 B1
Néa Mákri [GR] 168 B2
Néa Michanióna [GR] 160 F2
Néa Moní [GR] 168 E1
Néa Moudaniá [GR] 162 B2
Neamţ, Mănăstirea– [RO]
244 E3
Neandria [TR] 164 A2
Néa Péramos [GR] 156 C4
Néa Péramos [GR] 168 A2
Néa Plágia [GR] 162 B2
Neápoli [GR] 160 D3
Neápoli [GR] 172 C3
Neápoli [GR] 174 B3
Neapolis [TR] 170 D3
Néa Poteídaia [GR] 162 B2
Néa Róda [GR] 162 C2
Néa Roúmata [GR] 174 B3
Néa Sánta [GR] 156 E3
Néa Stýra [GR] 168 B2
Neath [GB] 26 D2
Néa Tríglia [GR] 162 B2
Néa Výssa [GR] 158 A3
Néa Zíchni [GR] 156 C4
Nebiler [TR] 164 B3
Nebolchi [RUS] 240 C1
Nebra [D] 44 D4
Nechanice [CZ] 60 F2
Neckarelz [D] 58 C3
Neckargemünd [D] 58 B3
Neckargerach [D] 58 C3
Neckarsteinach [D] 58 B3
Neckarsulm [D] 58 C4
Neckenmarkt [A] 74 D4
Necşeşti [RO] 150 A2
Nečtiny [CZ] 60 C3
Neda [E] 82 C1
Nedansjö [S] 206 C4
Nedde [F] 78 F2
Neddemin [D] 34 C3
Nedebø [SK] 74 F3
Nedelišce [HR] 120 D2
Nederhögen [S] 204 E4
Nedervetil / Alaveteli [FIN]
214 F4
Neder Vindinge [DK]
178 E3
Nedre Eggedal [N] 192 E4
Nedre Gårdsjö [S] 194 F3
Nedre Soppero [S] 226 A4
Nedstrand [N] 186 B2
Nedvědíce [CZ] 62 B4
Nędza [PL] 62 D2
Neede [NL] 30 D4
Neermoor [D] 30 E2
Neeroeteren [B] 40 F3
Nefyn [GB] 22 C3
Negoiești [RO] 148 E1
Negorci [MK] 156 A4
Negoslavci [HR] 146 C1
Negotin [SRB] 148 C2
Negotino [MK] 154 F4
Negovanovci [BG] 148 C2
Negrar [I] 118 B4
Negraşi [RO] 150 A1
Negreira [E] 82 B2
Negren–Tino [CH] 116 E2
Négrondes [F] 78 D3
Negru Vodă [RO] 150 E2
Neheim–Hüsten [D] 42 E3

Nehoiu [RO] 248 E3
Neiden [N] 228 E3
Neitisuanto [S] 220 E2
Neittävä [FIN] 216 C2
Nejdek [CZ] 60 B2
Nekromanteío [GR] 166 B2
Neksø [DK] 180 E3
Nelas [P] 84 B4
Nelidovo [RUS] 240 D3
Nellim [FIN] 226 E2
Nellingen [D] 72 A2
Neltaa [FIN] 198 E3
Neman [RUS] 238 B3
Nembro [I] 116 F3
Neméa [GR] 166 E4
Neméa [GR] 166 E4
Nemenčinė [LT] 238 E3
Nemesnádudvar [H] 122 B3
Nemesszalók [H] 74 E4
Németkér [H] 122 B2
Nemila [BIH] 146 A3
Nemours [F] 54 E4
Nemrutkale [TR] 164 C4
Nemška Loka [SLO] 120 B4
Nemšová [SK] 74 F1
Nemti [H] 76 C3
Nemyriv [UA] 64 E2
Nenagh [IRL] 10 D2
Nendeln [FL] 70 F4
Neochóri [GR] 160 E4
Neochóri [GR] 162 B4
Neochóri [GR] 166 C4
Neochóri [GR] 166 C3
Neochóri [GR] 166 D2
Neochóri [GR] 168 B2
Néo Monastíri [GR] 166 E2
Néos Marmarás [GR] 162 C2
Nepi [I] 130 F3
Nepomuk [CZ] 60 C4
Neptun [RO] 150 F2
Nérac [F] 88 D1
Neratovice [CZ] 60 D2
Néré [F] 78 C1
Neresheim [D] 72 B1
Nereta [LV] 236 C4
Nereto [I] 132 E2
Neretva Kanjon [BIH] 146 A4
Nerezine [HR] 144 B2
Nerežišča [HR] 152 B1
Neringa [LT] 238 A2
Neringa–Nida [LT] 238 A2
Néris–les–Bains [F] 80 B1
Nerja [E] 104 E3
Nerja, Cueva de– [E] 104 E3
Nérondes [F] 68 C3
Nerpio [E] 106 C1
Nerpio, Cuevas de– [E] 106 C2
Nersingen [D] 72 A2
Nerskogen [N] 202 F3
Nerva [E] 98 E4
Nervesa della Battaglia [I] 118 D3
Nervi [I] 126 E2
Nerviano [I] 116 D3
Nes [N] 186 E2
Nes [N] 192 C1
Nes [N] 192 C1
Nes [N] 192 C1
Nes [N] 192 F3
Nes [NL] 30 C1
Nesactium [HR] 144 A2
Nesaseter [N] 212 D3
Nesbyen [N] 192 E3
Nesebür [BG] 150 E4
Neset [N] 220 A3
Nesflaten [N] 186 C1
Nesheim [N] 192 B2
Neskaupstaður [IS] 218 D3
Neslandsvatn [N] 186 E2
Nesle [F] 54 F2
Nesna [N] 218 E4
Nesoddtangen [N] 188 B1
Nespereira [P] 84 B2

Nesseby [N] 228 E2
Nesselwang [D] 72 B3
Nestáni [GR] 172 D2
Nestavoll [N] 202 F3
Nesterov [RUS] 238 C3
Nestório [GR] 160 C3
Nesttun [N] 192 B3
Nesvik [N] 186 B2
Neszmély [H] 74 F3
Netolice [CZ] 74 A1
Netretić [HR] 120 C4
Nettancourt [F] 56 C4
Netta Pierwsza [PL] 38 C2
Nettetal [D] 42 C3
Nettuno [I] 134 A2
Nettuno, Grotta di– [I] 142 A2
Neubeckum [D] 42 E2
Neuberg [A] 74 C4
Neuberg an der Mürz [A] 74 C3
Neubrandenburg [D] 34 C3
Neubukow [D] 32 E2
Neubulach [D] 70 F1
Neuburg [D] 72 C1
Neuburg [D] 72 E2
Neuchâtel [CH] 70 C4
Neu Darchau [D] 32 D3
Neudorf [D] 44 D3
Neudorf [D] 58 B4
Neudorf–Platendorf [D] 44 C1
Neuenburg [D] 30 F2
Neuenbürg [D] 58 B4
Neuenburg [D] 70 D3
Neuenhaus [D] 30 D3
Neuenkirchen [D] 32 B4
Neuenstein [D] 44 B4
Neuenstein [D] 58 C4
Neuenstein [D] 58 C4
Neuenwalde [D] 32 A2
Neuer Weg [D] 30 E2
Neufahrn [D] 72 D2
Neuf–Brisach [F] 70 D2
Neufchâteau [B] 56 C2
Neufchâteau [F] 70 B1
Neufchâtel–en–Bray [F] 54 D1
Neufchâtel–sur–Aisne [F] 56 B2
Neufeld [D] 32 B2
Neufelden [A] 72 F2
Neuffen [D] 70 F2
Neugersdorf [D] 46 C4
Neuhaus [D] 32 B2
Neuhaus [D] 32 D3
Neuhaus [D] 44 B3
Neuhaus [D] 58 E2
Neuhaus [D] 58 F3
Neuhaus [D] 72 E2
Neuhausen am Rheinfall [CH] 70 E3
Neuhof [D] 46 B2
Neuhofen an der Krems [A] 74 A3
Neuillé Port–Pierre [F] 66 F2
Neuilly–l'Évêque [F] 70 A2
Neuilly–St–Front [F] 54 F3
Neu–Isenburg [D] 58 B2
Neukalen [D] 32 F2
Neukirch [D] 46 C4
Neukirchen [A] 72 D4
Neukirchen [A] 72 E3
Neukirchen [D] 42 F4
Neukirchen [D] 178 B3
Neukloster [D] 32 E2
Neuland [D] 32 B2
Neulengbach [A] 74 C3
Neulingen [D] 58 B4
Neu Lübbenau [D] 46 B2
Neum [BIH] 152 C2
Neumarkt [A] 72 E3
Neumarkt [A] 120 A1
Neumarkt [D] 58 F4
Neumarkt / Egna [I] 118 B2

Neumarkt–St Veit [D] 72 D2
Neu–Moresnet [B] 42 B4
Neumorschen [D] 44 B4
Neu Mukran [D] 34 C1
Neumünster [D] 32 C2
Neunagelberg [A] 74 B2
Neunburg [D] 60 B4
Neung–sur–Beuvron [F] 68 B2
Neunkirchen [A] 74 C3
Neunkirchen [D] 56 E3
Neunkirchen–Seelscheid [D] 42 D4
Neuötting [D] 72 E2
Neupölla [A] 74 C2
Neuruppin [D] 32 F4
Neu Schrepkow [D] 32 E4
Neuschwanstein [D] 72 B3
Neusiedl am See [A] 74 D3
Neuss [D] 42 C3
Neustadt [D] 32 D2
Neustadt [D] 32 E4
Neustadt [D] 42 F4
Neustadt [D] 46 C4
Neustadt [D] 58 C2
Neustadt [D] 58 E2
Neustadt [D] 58 F1
Neustadt [D] 70 E3
Neustadt [D] 72 C1
Neustadt am Rübenberge [D] 44 B1
Neustadt an der Aisch [D] 58 E3
Neustadt an der Waldnaab [D] 60 B3
Neustadt an der Weinstrasse [D] 58 B3
Neustadt–Glewe [D] 32 D3
Neustift [A] 118 C1
Neustift / Novacella [I] 118 C2
Neustrelitz [D] 32 F3
Neu–Ulm [D] 72 A2
Neuvéglise [F] 80 B3
Neuves–Maisons [F] 70 B1
Neuvic [F] 78 D3
Neuvic [F] 78 F3
Neuville [F] 66 E3
Neuville [F] 80 D2
Neuville–aux–Bois [F] 68 B1
Neuvilly–en–Argonne [F] 56 C3
Neuvola [FIN] 210 B3
Neuvy [F] 68 A4
Neuvy–Bouin [F] 66 D3
Neuvy–sur–Barangeon [F] 68 B2
Neuwied [D] 56 F1
Neuzelle [D] 46 C2
Neveklov [CZ] 60 D3
Nevel' [RUS] 240 C4
Neverfjord [N] 228 B2
Nevers [F] 68 C3
Nevès [E] 96 D2
Nevesinje [BIH] 152 D2
Nevlunghavn [N] 186 E3
Nevossuo [FIN] 200 B3
New Alresford [GB] 28 B3
Newark–on–Trent [GB] 24 C3
Newbiggin–by–the–Sea [GB] 20 F3
Newbliss [IRL] 12 D3
Newbridge / Droichead Nua [IRL] 10 E2
Newburgh [GB] 18 D3
Newbury [GB] 28 B3
Newcastle [NIR] 12 F3
Newcastle Emlyn [GB] 22 C4
Newcastle–under–Lyme [GB] 22 F3
Newcastle upon Tyne [GB] 20 E3
Newcastle West [IRL] 10 C3
New Galloway [GB] 20 C2

Newgrange [IRL] 10 F1
Newhaven [GB] 28 C4
Newinn [IRL] 10 D3
Newmarket [GB] 28 D2
Newmarket [IRL] 10 C3
Newmarket [IRL] 10 C3
Newmarket–on–Fergus [IRL] 10 C2
Newport [GB] 22 F3
Newport [GB] 26 B4
Newport [GB] 28 B4
Newport [IRL] 10 C2
Newport [IRL] 12 B2
Newport–on–Tay [GB] 18 E3
Newport Pagnell [GB] 28 C2
New Quay [GB] 22 C4
Newquay [GB] 26 B3
New Romney [GB] 28 D4
New Ross / Ros Mhic Thriúin [IRL] 10 E3
Newry [NIR] 12 E3
Newton Abbot [GB] 26 D3
Newton Le Willows [GB] 22 F2
Newtonmore [GB] 14 D4
Newton Stewart [GB] 20 B2
Newtown [GB] 22 E4
Newtownabbey [NIR] 12 F2
Newtownards [NIR] 12 F2
Newtown Butler [NIR] 12 D3
Newtownhamilton [NIR] 12 E3
Newtown Mount Kennedy [IRL] 10 F3
Newtownstewart [NIR] 12 D2
Nexon [F] 78 E2
Nežilovo [MK] 154 D4
Niadinge [LT] 38 D1
Niana [I] 116 C3
Nianfors [S] 196 C2
Niaux, Grotte de– [F] 88 E4
Nibe [DK] 182 D3
Nicaj–Shalë [AL] 154 B3
Nicaj Shoshë [AL] 152 F3
Nicastro [I] 138 E2
Nice [F] 126 C3
Nickelsdorf [A] 74 E3
Nicknoret [S] 214 C2
Nicolosi [I] 140 C2
Nicopolis ad Istrum [BG] 150 B3
Nicosia [I] 138 B4
Nicotera [I] 138 D3
Nidda [D] 58 C2
Nidderau [D] 58 C2
Nideck, Château du– [F] 70 D1
Nideggen [D] 42 C4
Nidzica [PL] 36 E3
Niebla [E] 98 D4
Nieborow [PL] 48 E2
Niebüll [D] 178 B3
Nieby [D] 178 C3
Niechanowo [PL] 48 B2
Niechorze [PL] 34 E2
Niedalino [PL] 34 F2
Niederalben [D] 56 F3
Niederalteich [D] 72 E1
Niederau [A] 72 D4
Niederaula [D] 44 B4
Niederbronn–les–Bains [F] 56 F4
Niederelsungen [D] 42 F3
Niederkleen [D] 58 B1
Niederkrüchten [D] 42 C3
Niederndorf [A] 72 D3
Niederoderwitz [D] 46 C4
Nieder Stotzingen [D] 72 A1
Nieder–Wöllstadt [D] 58 C2
Niederwinkling [D] 72 E1
Nieder–Wöllstadt [D] 58 C2
Niederwölz [A] 120 A1
Niedrzwica Duża [PL] 50 C4
Niedźwiedź [PL] 36 D3
Niemce [PL] 50 C3
Niemcza [PL] 62 B2
Niemegk [D] 44 F2

Niemica [PL] 36 A2
Niemijärvi [FIN] 210 F1
Niemis [S] 222 B3
Niemisel [S] 220 F4
Niemisjärvi [FIN] 210 B3
Niemiskylä [FIN] 216 E3
Niemodlin [PL] 62 C2
Nienburg [D] 32 B4
Nienhagen [D] 32 E2
Niepołomice [PL] 64 A3
Nieppe [F] 40 C3
Niepruszewo [PL] 46 F2
Nierstein [D] 58 B2
Niesky [D] 46 C4
Nieszawa [PL] 48 C1
Nietsak [S] 220 E2
Nieuil [F] 78 D2
Nieuweschans [NL] 30 E2
Nieuwpoort [B] 40 C3
Nigrán [E] 82 A3
Nigríta [GR] 156 B4
Nihattula [FIN] 198 E2
Niilivaara [FIN] 222 C1
Niinilahti [FIN] 208 F2
Niinimäki [FIN] 210 C3
Niinisalo [FIN] 208 C4
Niinivesi [FIN] 210 B2
Niirala [FIN] 210 F3
Niittumaa [FIN] 198 C1
Níjar [E] 106 C3
Nijemci [HR] 146 C1
Nijkerk [NL] 30 C3
Nijmegen [NL] 30 C4
Nijverdal [NL] 30 D3
Nikaia [GR] 160 F4
Nikaia [TR] 158 F4
Nikaranperä [FIN] 208 E2
Nikel' [RUS] 226 F1
Niki [GR] 160 D2
Nikiá [GR] 176 A1
Nikifóros [GR] 156 C4
Nikil [S] 190 B4
Nikísiani [GR] 156 C4
Nikitári [CY] 176 D3
Nikítas [GR] 162 C2
Nikkajärvi [FIN] 216 E3
Nikkala [S] 222 B4
Nikkaluokta [S] 220 D1
Nikkaroinen [FIN] 200 A1
Nikla [H] 120 E2
Nikolaevo [BG] 156 F1
Nikolaevskoye [RUS] 232 C2
Nikola Kozlevo [BG] 150 D2
Nikolayevo [RUS] 232 F3
Nikopol [BG] 150 A3
Nikopol' [UA] 246 F2
Nikópoli [GR] 166 B2
Nikšić [MNE] 152 E2
Nilivaara [S] 220 E2
Nilsiä [FIN] 210 C2
Nim [DK] 178 C1
Nîmes [F] 124 D2
Nin [HR] 144 C3
Ninfa [I] 134 B2
Ninove [B] 40 D3
Niort [F] 66 D4
Niquidetto [I] 116 B4
Niroú Kháni [GR] 174 D3
Niš [SRB] 148 B4
Nisa [P] 90 D3
Nisáki [GR] 160 B4
Niscemi [I] 140 C2
Niška Banja [SRB] 148 B4
Niskakoski [RUS] 226 E2
Niska–Pietilä [FIN] 200 D1
Nisko [PL] 64 C2
Nissafors [S] 184 C2
Nissi [EST] 230 C2
Nissilä [FIN] 216 C1
Nissoria [I] 138 B4
Nitaure [LV] 236 C3
Nitlax [FIN] 198 D4

Nitra [SK] **74** F2
Nitrianske Pravno [SK] **76** A1
Nitrianske Rudno [SK] **76** A2
Nitry [F] **68** D2
Nittedal [N] **194** B4
Nittenau [D] **60** B4
Nittendorf [D] **58** F4
Nittkvarn [S] **188** F1
Nivå [DK] **178** F1
Niva [FIN] **216** E3
Nivala [FIN] **216** B3
Nivelles [B] **40** D4
Niversac [F] **78** D3
Nixhöhle [A] **74** B3
Nizhyn [UA] **242** E3
Nižná [SK] **62** F4
Nižná Boca [SK] **76** B1
Nižná Polianka [SK] **64** C4
Nižná Slaná [SK] **76** C2
Nizy-le-Comte [F] **56** B2
Nizza Monferrato [I] **126** D1
Njavve [S] **220** C2
Njegoševo [SRB] **122** C3
Njetsavare [S] **220** E3
Njivice [HR] **144** B1
Njupeskärs Vattenfall [S] **194** D1
Njurandabommen [S] **206** C4
Njurunda [S] **206** C4
Njutånger [S] **196** C2
Noailles [F] **54** E2
Noain / Elorz [E] **86** F4
Noale [I] **118** C4
Noasca [I] **116** B3
Nöbbele [S] **184** D3
Nöbbelöv [S] **180** D1
Noceda [E] **82** E3
Nocera [I] **134** D3
Nocera Umbra [I] **132** D2
Noceto [I] **128** B2
Noci [I] **136** D2
Nocito [E] **88** C4
Nodeland [N] **186** C4
Nods [F] **70** B4
Noé [F] **88** E3
Noépoli [I] **136** C3
Noeux [F] **40** B4
Nofuentes [E] **86** D3
Nogale [LV] **234** E2
Nogales [E] **98** E2
Nogara [I] **118** B4
Nogaro [F] **88** D2
Nogarole Rocca [I] **118** B4
Nogent [F] **68** F2
Nogent-le-Roi [F] **54** D3
Nogent-le-Rotrou [F] **54** C4
Nogent-sur-Seine [F] **54** F4
Nogersund [S] **180** E1
Noginsk [RUS] **240** F3
Nogva [N] **202** C3
Noharre [E] **92** D2
Nohfelden [D] **56** E3
Noia Noya [E] **82** B2
Noidans-le-Ferroux [F] **70** B3
Noirétable [F] **80** C2
Noirmoutier-en-l'Ile [F] **66** B2
Noja [E] **86** D2
Nokia [FIN] **198** D1
Nokka [FIN] **200** B1
Nokkamäli [FIN] **216** D4
Nokkosmäenkulma [FIN] **208** C4
Nola [I] **134** D3
Nol Alafors [S] **184** A1
Nolay [F] **68** E4
Noli [I] **126** D2
Nomeny [F] **56** D4
Nomexy [F] **70** C2
Nômme [EST] **230** D2
Nonancourt [F] **54** C3
Nonant-le-Pin [F] **54** B3
Nonantola [I] **128** C2

Nonaspe [E] **94** F4
Nonsfossen [N] **192** C1
Nontron [F] **78** D2
Nonza [F] **130** B2
Noordwijk aan Zee [NL] **30** A3
Noormarkku / Norrmark [FIN] **198** C1
Nopankylä [FIN] **208** C2
Noppikoski [S] **194** F2
Nor [N] **194** C4
Nor [N] **202** C4
Nor [S] **204** F3
Nora [I] **142** B6
Nora [S] **184** E1
Nora [S] **188** F2
Nørager [DK] **182** D3
Norberg [S] **190** B1
Norbi [EST] **230** C2
Norcia [I] **130** F3
Norcia [I] **132** D2
Nordagutu [N] **186** E2
Nordanå [S] **184** B4
Nordanå [S] **206** C3
Nordanåker [S] **206** B2
Nordanås [S] **214** A1
Nordanås [S] **214** B3
Nordanås [S] **214** C1
Nordanholen [S] **194** F4
Nordankäl [S] **206** B1
Nordanrå [S] **214** A3
Nordansjö [S] **214** A3
Nordausques [F] **40** B3
Nordberg [N] **202** D4
Nordborg [DK] **178** C3
Nordbotn [N] **202** F1
Nordbottnen [S] **204** D2
Nordby [DK] **178** A2
Nordby [DK] **178** D1
Nordby [N] **188** B1
Nordby [N] **188** B2
Nordby [N] **194** C2
Norddeich [D] **30** E1
Nordeide [N] **192** B2
Norden [D] **30** E1
Norden [S] **220** D4
Nordenham [D] **30** F2
Norderåsen [S] **204** F2
Norderney [D] **30** E1
Norderö [S] **204** E2
Norderstedt [D] **32** C2
Nordeste [P] **110** E1
Nord Etnedal [N] **192** F2
Nordfjord [N] **228** E2
Nordfjordeid [N] **202** C4
Nordfold [N] **220** A1
Nordgulen [N] **192** B2
Nordhalben [D] **58** F2
Nordhallen [S] **204** D2
Nordhausen [D] **44** C3
Nordhella [N] **224** D2
Nordhorn [D] **30** D3
Nordingrå [S] **206** D3
Nordkapp [N] **228** C1
Nordkirchen [D] **42** D2
Nordkisa [N] **194** B4
Nordkjosbotn [N] **224** D3
Nord-Lenangen [N] **224** C2
Nordli [N] **212** E3
Nördlingen [D] **72** B1
Nordmaling [S] **206** C2
Nordmark [S] **188** E1
Nordmela [N] **224** B3
Nordøyvågen [N] **218** E4
Nordre Osen [N] **194** C2
Nordseter [N] **194** B2
Nordsinni [N] **192** F3
Nordsjö [S] **196** C2
Nordskjørin [N] **212** B4
Nordskov [DK] **178** D2
Nordvik [N] **202** C2
Nordvika [N] **202** E1

Nore [S] **196** C1
Noresund [N] **192** F4
Norg [NL] **30** D2
Norheimsund [N] **192** B3
Nørholm [N] **186** D4
Norhyttan [S] **194** F4
Norinkylä [FIN] **208** C3
Norje [S] **180** D1
Norkino [RUS] **236** F3
Norma [I] **134** B2
Normjöle [S] **206** E1
Norn [S] **196** B4
Norra Bergnäs [S] **220** C3
Norra Finnskoga [S] **194** D3
Norrahammar [S] **184** C2
Norraker [S] **212** F3
Norrala [S] **196** C2
Norra Löten [S] **194** D3
Norra Mellby [S] **180** D1
Norra Råda [S] **188** E1
Norra Tresund [S] **214** A2
Norrback [FIN] **208** B2
Norrbäck [S] **214** B3
Norrberg [S] **214** B2
Norrboda [S] **194** F2
Norrboda [S] **196** E4
Norrby [FIN] **214** F4
Norrby [S] **214** B2
Nørre Aaby [DK] **178** C2
Nørre Alslev [DK] **178** E3
Nørre Broby [DK] **178** C2
Nørre Lyndelse [DK] **178** C2
Nørre Nebel [DK] **178** A1
Nørre Snede [DK] **178** B1
Nørresundby [DK] **182** D2
Nørre Vejrup [DK] **178** B2
Nørre Vorupør [DK] **182** C3
Norrfjärden [S] **214** E1
Norrfors [S] **206** E1
Norrgravsjö [S] **214** B3
Norr Hede [S] **204** D3
Norrhult [S] **184** D3
Norriån [S] **220** F3
Norrköping [S] **190** C3
Norrmark / Noormarkku [FIN] **198** C1
Norrnäs [FIN] **208** B3
Norrskedika [S] **196** E4
Norrsunda [S] **190** D2
Norrsundet [S] **196** D3
Norrtälje [S] **190** E1
Norrtannflo [S] **206** C2
Norrvik [S] **220** E3
Nors [DK] **182** C2
Norsholm [S] **190** B4
Norsjö [S] **214** C2
Norsjövallen [S] **214** C2
Nörten–Hardenberg [D] **44** C3
Northallerton [GB] **20** E4
Northam [GB] **26** C2
Northampton [GB] **28** C1
North Berwick [GB] **18** E4
Northeim [D] **44** C3
North Ferriby [GB] **24** D2
Northleach [GB] **26** F2
North Walsham [GB] **28** F1
Northwich [GB] **22** F3
Nortorf [D] **32** C2
Nort-sur-Erdre [F] **66** C2
Norvik [S] **204** E1
Norwich [GB] **28** E1
Nos [N] **186** E2
Nøsen [N] **192** E2
Nosivka [UA] **242** E3
Nossa Senhora da Conceição [P] **98** C2
Nossa Senhora da Serra [P] **84** D2
Nossa Senhora De Taúde [P] **84** A3
Nossa Senhora do Cabo [P] **90** A4

Nossebro [S] **188** D4
Nössemark [S] **188** C2
Nossen [D] **46** B4
Nótia [GR] **160** E1
Nötö [FIN] **198** C4
Noto [I] **140** E4
Noto Antica [I] **140** E4
Notodden [N] **186** E2
Notre–Dame de Consolation [F] **70** C4
Notre–Dame de-la-Roquette [F] **126** B3
Notre–Dame des Fontaines [F] **126** C2
Nottebäck [S] **184** D3
Nøtterøy [N] **186** F2
Nottingham [GB] **24** C3
Nottuln [D] **30** E4
Nouan–le–Fuzelier [F] **68** B2
Nouans-les-Fontaines [F] **68** A3
Nousu [FIN] **222** E2
Nouvaillé–Maupertuis [F] **66** E4
Nouvion [F] **40** A4
Nova [EST] **230** C2
Nova [H] **120** D2
Nová Baňa [SK] **76** A2
Nova Breznica [MK] **154** D3
Nová Bystrica [CZ] **74** B1
Nová Bystrica [SK] **62** E4
Novacella / Neustift [I] **118** C2
Novacene [BG] **148** E4
Novaci [MK] **160** D2
Nova Crnja [SRB] **122** D4
Novae Palesse [BY] **242** C3
Novaféltria [I] **128** D3
Nova Gorica [SLO] **118** E3
Nova Gradiška [HR] **144** F1
Novaja Kakhovka [UA] **246** E3
Novajidrány [H] **76** D2
Nova Kakhovka [RUS] **246** E3
Nova Kapela [HR] **144** F1
Nova Kasaba [BIH] **146** C3
Novakovo [BG] **156** D2
Nováky [SK] **76** A2
Novales [E] **94** E2
Novalesa, Abbazia di– [I] **116** B4
Nova Levante / Welschnofen [I] **118** C2
Novalja [HR] **144** C2
Nova Odesa [UA] **246** D2
Nová Paka [CZ] **60** F2
Nova Pazova [SRB] **146** D2
Nova Peć [CZ] **72** F2
Nova Praha [UA] **246** E1
Nova Varoš [SRB] **146** D4
Nova Zagora [BG] **156** E1
Nové Hrady [CZ] **74** B2
Novelda [E] **106** C2
Novellara [I] **128** B2
Nové Město nad Metují [CZ] **62** A2
Nové Mesto nad Váhom [SK] **74** F2
Nové Město na Moravě [CZ] **62** A3
Nové Město pod Smrkem [CZ] **60** E1
Nové Mitrovice [CZ] **60** C3
Noventa Vicentina [I] **118** C4
Novés [E] **92** D4
Noves [F] **124** E2
Nové Sady [SK] **74** F2

Nové Strašecí [CZ] **60** D2
Nové Zámky [SK] **74** F3
Novgorodka [RUS] **236** E2
Novgrad [BG] **150** B3
Novhorodka [UA] **246** E2
Novhorod–Siverskyi [UA] **242** E2
Novi Bečej [SRB] **122** C4
Novi di Módena [I] **128** C1
Novi Dojran [MK] **156** A4
Noviergas [E] **94** C2
Novi Grad [BIH] **146** B1
Novigrad [HR] **118** E4
Novigrad [HR] **144** C3
Novigrad Podravski [HR] **120** E3
Novi Han [BG] **156** B1
Novi Iskăr [BG] **156** B1
Novi Kazarci [SRB] **122** D3
Novi Kneževac [SRB] **122** C3
Novi Krichim [BG] **156** D2
Novi Ligure [I] **126** E1
Novi Marof [HR] **120** D3
Novion–Porcien [F] **56** B2
Novi Pazar [BG] **150** D3
Novi Pazar [SRB] **154** B1
Novi Sad [SRB] **146** D1
Novi Senkovac [HR] **120** F4
Novi Travnik [BIH] **144** B1
Novi Vinodolski [HR] **144** B1
Novoarkhanhel's'k [UA] **246** D2
Novobobruysk [RUS] **238** A4
Novo Brdo [KS] **154** D2
Novodugino [RUS] **240** E3
Novohrad–Volvns'kyi [UA] **242** C4
Novoiavorivs'ke [UA] **64** E3
Novo mesto [SLO] **120** B3
Novo Miloševo [SRB] **122** D3
Novomoskovs'k [UA] **246** F1
Novomyrhorod [UA] **246** D1
Novo Panicharovo [BG] **158** B1
Novorzhev [RUS] **236** F2
Novoselë [AL] **160** A2
Novoselets [BG] **156** F1
Novo Selo [BG] **148** C2
Novo Selo [BG] **150** A4
Novo Selo [BG] **150** C2
Novo Selo [BG] **156** B2
Novo Selo [MK] **154** F4
Novoseltsi [BG] **158** B1
Novosel'ye [RUS] **232** E3
Novosokol'niki [RUS] **240** C3
Novoukraïnka [UA] **64** F2
Novovolyns'k [UA] **50** E4
Novovorontsovka [UA] **246** E2
Novozavidovskiy [RUS] **240** E2
Novo Zvečevo [HR] **120** E4
Novozybkov [RUS] **242** D2
Novska [HR] **120** E4
Nový Bohumín [CZ] **62** D3
Nový Bor [CZ] **60** E1
Nový Bydžov [CZ] **60** F2
Nový Bykhaw [BY] **242** C2
Nový Hrad [CZ] **62** B4
Novyi Buh [UA] **246** E2
Novyi Bykiv [UA] **242** E4
Novyi Rozdil [UA] **64** F3
Nový Jičín [CZ] **62** D3
Nový Knín [CZ] **60** D3
Novyy Dvor [BY] **38** E2
Nowa Brzeźnica [PL] **48** D4
Nowa Cerekwia [PL] **62** D3
Nowa Dęba [PL] **64** C2
Nowa Karczma [PL] **36** C2
Nowa Karczma [PL] **36** D1
Nowa Ruda [PL] **62** B2
Nowa Sarzyna [PL] **64** D2
Nowa Słupia [PL] **50** A4

Nowa Sól [PL] 46 D3
Nowa Wieś [PL] 38 A3
Nowa Wieś Ełcka [PL] 38 B2
Nowa Wieś Lęborska [PL]
  36 B1
Nowe [PL] 36 D3
Nowe Brzesko [PL] 64 A2
Nowe Czarnowo [PL] 34 D4
Nowe Miasteczko [PL] 46 D3
Nowe Miasto [PL] 48 E1
Nowe Miasto Lubawskie
  [PL] 36 E3
Nowe Miasto nad Pilicą
  [PL] 48 E3
Nowe Miasto nad Wartą
  [PL] 48 B2
Nowe Piekuty [PL] 38 C4
Nowe Polichno [PL] 46 D1
Nowe Skalmierzyce [PL]
  48 B3
Nowe Warpno [PL] 34 D3
Nowica [PL] 36 E2
Nowogard [PL] 34 E3
Nowogród [PL] 38 B3
Nowogród Bobrzański [PL]
  46 D3
Nowogród Bobrzański [PL]
  46 D3
Nowogrodziec [PL] 46 D4
Nowosady [PL] 38 D3
Nowosielec [PL] 64 D2
Nowosiółki [PL] 64 F2
Nowowola [PL] 38 C2
Nowy Duninów [PL] 48 D1
Nowy Dwór [PL] 38 D2
Nowy Dwór Gdański [PL]
  36 D2
Nowy Dwór Mazowiecki
  [PL] 48 E2
Nowy Korczyn [PL] 64 B2
Nowy Majdan [PL] 64 D2
Nowy Orzechów [PL] 50 C3
Nowy Sącz [PL] 64 B3
Nowy Staw [PL] 36 D2
Nowy Targ [PL] 62 F4
Nowy Tomyśl [PL] 46 E2
Nowy Wiśnicz [PL] 64 B3
Nowy Żmigród [PL] 64 C3
Noyant [F] 66 E2
Noyers [F] 68 D2
Noyers–sur–Jabron [F] 124 F2
Noyon [F] 54 F2
Nozay [F] 66 C2
Nozdrzec [PL] 64 D3
Nozeroy [F] 70 B4
Nožičko [BIH] 144 F2
N. Petrítsi [GR] 156 B3
N. Rubeža [MNE] 152 E2
N. Sandsjö [S] 184 D2
N. S. de Angosto [E] 86 D3
N. S. de Chilla [E] 92 C4
N. S. de Cortés [E] 100 F4
N. S. de Hontanares [E] 92 F2
N. S. de la Bienvenida [E]
  94 B4
N. S. de la Cabeza [E] 106 B2
N. S. de la Estrella [E] 106 B1
N. S. del Remedio [E] 102 C3
N. S. del Valle [E] 86 B3
N. Selo [BIH] 146 A1
N. Senhora da Azinheira
  [P] 84 C2
N. Senhora d'Abadia [P] 84 B2
N. Senhora da Graça [P] 84 B2
N. Senhora dos Remédios
  [P] 84 B3
N. Señora de Irache [E] 86 E4
N. Skärvången [S] 204 E1
N. Skióni [GR] 162 B2
Nubledo [E] 82 F2
Nueil–les–Aubiers [F] 66 D3
Nueno [E] 94 E2

Nuestra Señora de Arcos [E]
  100 D3
Nuestra Señora de la Antigua
  [E] 100 E4
Nuestra Señora de la
  Anunciada [E] 84 F3
Nuestra Señora de la
  Misericordia [E] 94 C2
Nuestra Señora de la Vega
  [E] 102 D2
Nuestra Señora del Rocío
  [E] 104 B1
Nuestra Señora del Yugo
  [E] 88 A4
Nuestra Señora de Monlora
  [E] 94 E2
Nuestra Señora de Piedra
  Albas [E] 98 D3
Nueva–Carteya [E] 104 E2
Nuévalos [E] 94 C3
Nuevo Baztán [E] 92 F4
Nufringen [D] 70 F1
Nuijamaa [FIN] 200 D2
Nuino [UA] 50 E3
Nuits–St–Georges [F] 68 E3
Nules [E] 96 C3
Nules [E] 102 E3
Nulvi [I] 142 B2
Numana [I] 128 F4
Numancia [E] 94 B2
Nummela [FIN] 198 E3
Nummenkylä [FIN] 198 E2
Nummi [FIN] 198 E3
Nummijärvi [FIN] 208 C3
Nummikoski [FIN] 208 C3
Nuneaton [GB] 24 B4
Nunkirchen [D] 56 E3
Nunnanen [FIN] 226 C3
Nunnanlahti [FIN] 210 D1
Nuño Gómez [E] 92 D4
Nunsdorf [D] 46 B2
Nunspeet [NL] 30 C3
Nuojua [FIN] 216 C2
Nuoramoinen [FIN] 200 B1
Nuorgam [FIN] 228 D3
Nuoritta [FIN] 216 C2
Nuoro [I] 142 C3
Nupaky [CZ] 60 E3
Nur [PL] 38 B4
Nuragus [I] 142 B4
Nurallao [I] 142 C4
Nuraminis [I] 142 B5
Nuraxi, Nuraghe su– [I] 142 B4
Nürburg [D] 56 E1
Nürburgring [D] 56 E1
Núria, Santuari de– [E] 96 D1
Nurmaa [FIN] 200 B1
Nurmes [FIN] 216 E4
Nurmi [FIN] 198 D1
Nurmijärvi [FIN] 198 F3
Nurmijärvi [FIN] 216 E4
Nurmo [FIN] 208 C2
Nurmuža [LV] 234 E3
Nürnberg [D] 58 E3
Nurri [I] 142 C4
Nürtingen [D] 70 F1
Nus [I] 116 C3
Nusnäs [S] 194 F3
Nusret [TR] 164 D2
Nuštar [HR] 122 B4
Nutheim [N] 186 D1
Nuttlar [D] 42 E3
Nuupas [FIN] 222 D3
Nuvsvåg [N] 224 F1
Nuvvus [FIN] 226 C1
N. Vånga [S] 188 D4
N. Vi [S] 184 D1
Nw. Ludzicko [PL] 34 F3
Nyåker [S] 206 E1
Nyakhachava [BY] 38 F4
Nyárád [H] 74 E4
Nyárlőrinc [H] 122 C2

Nyasvizh [BY] 242 B2
Nybergsund [N] 194 D2
Nyborg [DK] 178 D2
Nyborg [N] 212 E4
Nyborg [S] 214 F1
Nybro [S] 184 E3
Nyby [DK] 178 E3
Nyby [FIN] 208 B2
Nyby [S] 214 C3
Nybyn [S] 204 E2
Nydala [S] 184 C2
Nydrí [GR] 166 B3
Nye [S] 184 D2
Nyeharelaye [BY] 242 B2
Nyékládháza [H] 76 D3
Nyergesujfalu [H] 76 A3
Nygård [N] 192 B2
Nygård [N] 224 C4
Nygarden [N] 194 B1
Nyhammar [S] 194 F4
Nyhem [S] 206 B3
Nyhyttan [S] 188 F2
Nyírábrány [H] 76 E4
Nyíracsád [H] 76 E3
Nyíradony [H] 76 E3
Nyírbátor [H] 76 E3
Nyírbéltek [H] 76 E3
Nyírbogát [H] 76 E3
Nyíregyháza [H] 76 E3
Nyírkáta [H] 76 F3
Nyírlugos [H] 76 E3
Nyírmada [H] 76 F3
Nyírtelek [H] 76 E3
Nyírtura [H] 76 E3
Nykälä [H] 210 B3
Nykarleby / Uusikaarlepyy
  [FIN] 208 C1
Nyker [DK] 180 E3
Nykirke [N] 194 B3
Nykøbing [DK] 178 B3
Nykøbing [DK] 178 E1
Nykøbing [DK] 182 C3
Nyköping [S] 190 C3
Nykrogen [S] 190 C1
Nykroppa [S] 188 E2
Nykvarn [S] 190 D3
Nyland [S] 206 C3
Nyland [S] 206 D3
Nyland [S] 206 D2
Nylars [DK] 180 E3
Nyluspen [S] 214 A2
Nymburk [CZ] 60 E2
Nymfaía [GR] 156 E3
Nymindegab [DK] 178 A1
Nymo [N] 224 E1
Nynäshamn [S] 190 D3
Nyneset [N] 212 D3
Nyon [CH] 80 F2
Nyons [F] 124 E2
Nyrå [S] 206 C4
Nýrsko [CZ] 60 C4
Nyrud [N] 226 E2
Nysa [PL] 62 C2
Nysa [TR] 170 C3
Nysäter [S] 188 D2
Nyseter [N] 202 D3
Nyskoga [S] 194 D4
Nyskolla [N] 194 B2
Nyslott / Savonlinna [FIN]
  210 D3
Nystad / Uusikaupunki [FIN]
  198 C2
Nysted [DK] 32 E1
Nystova [N] 192 D2
Nytorp [S] 220 F2
Nytrøa [N] 204 B3
Nyúl [H] 74 E4
Nyvollen [N] 204 C2
Nyzhankovychi [UA]
  64 D3
Nyzhni Sirohozy [UA]
  246 F2

O

O, Château d'– [F] 54 B3
Oafae e Stillës [AL] 160 B1
Oafae Kemzës [AL] 154 B4
Oaivos [N] 226 B2
Oakham [GB] 24 C4
Oandu [EST] 230 E2
Oanes [N] 186 B2
Oban [GB] 18 B2
O Barco de Valdeorras [E]
  82 D4
Óbarok [H] 76 A4
Obbekær [DK] 178 B2
Obbola [S] 206 F1
Obdach [A] 120 B1
Obedinenie [BG] 150 B3
Obejo [E] 100 C4
Obel [MK] 154 F3
Obeliai [LT] 236 C4
Oberammergau [D] 72 B3
Oberau [D] 72 C3
Oberaudorf [D] 72 D3
Oberdrauburg [A] 118 E2
Oberei [CH] 116 C1
Obergrafendorf [A] 74 C3
Obergünzburg [D] 72 B3
Obergurgl [A] 118 B1
Oberhaslach [F] 70 D1
Oberhausen [D] 42 C3
Oberhof [A] 118 F1
Oberhof [D] 58 E1
Oberhofen [CH] 116 C1
Oberjoch [D] 72 B3
Oberkirch [D] 70 E1
Oberkochen [D] 72 A1
Obermünchen [D] 72 D2
Obernai [F] 70 D2
Obernberg [A] 72 E2
Obernberg am Brenner [A]
  118 C1
Obernburg [D] 58 C3
Oberndorf [A] 72 E3
Oberndorf [D] 70 E2
Obernholz [D] 32 C4
Obernzell [D] 72 F2
Oberpullendorf [A] 74 D4
Oberried [CH] 116 C1
Oberriet [CH] 70 F4
Ober–Roden [D] 58 C2
Obersickte [D] 44 C2
Obersinn [D] 58 D2
Obersontheim [D] 58 D4
Oberstaufen [D] 72 A3
Oberstdorf [D] 72 A4
Oberstenfeld [D] 58 C4
Obersuhl [D] 44 B4
Obertauern [A] 72 F4
Obertraubling [D] 72 D1
Obertraun [A] 72 F4
Obervellach [A] 118 E1
Oberviechtach [D] 60 B4
Oberwald [CH] 116 D2
Oberwart [A] 74 D4
Oberwasser [D] 70 E2
Oberwesel [D] 56 F2
Oberwiesenthal [D] 60 C2
Oberwölzstadt [A] 120 A1
Oberzeiring [A] 74 A4
Óbidos [P] 90 B2
Obing [D] 72 D3
Objat [F] 78 E3
Objazda [PL] 36 B1
Ob. Kindberg [A] 74 C4
Öblarn [A] 72 F4
Obleševo [MK] 154 E3
Obljaj [HR] 144 D1
Obninsk [RUS] 240 F3
Obnova [BG] 150 A3
Ö. Bodane [S] 188 D3
Obodowo [PL] 36 B3

O Bolo [E] 82 D4
Oborishte [BG] 156 C1
Oborniki [PL] 46 F1
Oborniki Śląska [PL] 46 F4
Oborovo [HR] 120 D4
Obory [CZ] 60 D3
Obreja [RO] 122 F4
Obrenovac [SRB] 146 D2
Obretenik [BG] 150 B3
Obrochishte [BG] 150 E3
Obrov [SLO] 118 F4
Obrovac [HR] 144 D3
Obrovac [HR] 144 E4
Obrovac [SRB] 122 C4
Obruchishte [BG] 156 C2
Obsteig [A] 72 B4
Obukhiv [UA] 242 D4
Obzor [BG] 150 E4
Ocaklar [TR] 164 C1
Ocaklı [TR] 164 B1
Ocaña [E] 100 E1
O Carballiño [E] 82 B3
Occhiobello [I] 128 D1
Ochagavía / Otsagi [E]
  88 B3
Ochakiv [UA] 246 D3
Ochojec [PL] 62 D2
Ochozská Jesk. [CZ] 62 B4
Ochoz u Brna [CZ] 62 B4
Ochsattel [A] 74 C3
Ochsenburg [A] 74 C3
Ochsenfurt [D] 58 D3
Ochsenhausen [D] 72 A2
Ochtrup [D] 30 D4
Ocieski [PL] 64 B1
Ockelbo [S] 196 C3
Ocksjön [S] 204 F3
Ocolna [RO] 148 E2
O Convento / Poio [E] 82 B3
O Corgo [E] 82 D3
Ócsa [H] 76 B4
Öcsöd [H] 122 D1
Ocypel [PL] 36 C3
Od [S] 184 B1
Odda [N] 192 C4
Odden [N] 194 C1
Odden [N] 224 E2
Odder [DK] 178 C1
Oddesund [DK] 182 C3
Ödeby [S] 190 B2
Odeceixe [P] 98 B3
Odeleite [P] 98 C4
Odelzhausen [D] 72 C2
Odemira [P] 98 B3
Ödemiş [TR] 170 C2
Öden [E] 96 C2
Ödenäs [S] 184 B1
Odenbach [D] 56 F3
Odensbacken [S] 190 B3
Odense [DK] 178 C2
Odensjö [S] 184 C3
Odensvi [S] 184 E1
Odensvi [S] 190 B2
Oderberg [D] 34 D4
Oderljunga [S] 180 C1
Oderzo [I] 118 E3
Ödeshög [S] 188 E4
Odessa [UA] 246 D3
Ödestugu [S] 184 C2
Odivelas [P] 90 A3
Odivelas [P] 98 C2
Odnes [N] 192 F3
Odolanów [PL] 48 B3
Odoorn [NL] 30 D3
Odorheiu Secuiesc [RO]
  244 D4
Odoyev [RUS] 240 F4
Odranci [SLO] 120 D2
Ödrn [CZ] 62 C3
Odrzywół [PL] 48 E3
Ødsted [DK] 178 B2
Odum [DK] 182 D4

Odžaci [SRB] 122 B4
Odžak [BIH] 146 B2
Odžak [MNE] 152 F2
Ödzemirci [TR] 170 F2
Odziena [LV] 236 C3
Oebisfelde [D] 44 D2
Oederan [D] 60 C1
Oeding [D] 30 D4
Oeijenbraak [B] 40 E3
Oelde [D] 42 E2
Oelsnitz [D] 60 B2
Oensinger Klus [CH] 70 D3
Oersberg [D] 178 D4
Oetmannshausen [D] 44 B4
Oëtre, Roche d'– [F] 54 A2
Oettingen [D] 72 B1
Oetz [A] 72 B4
Öfehértó [H] 76 E3
Offenbach [D] 58 B2
Offenburg [D] 70 E2
Offenheim [D] 58 B3
Offida [I] 132 E2
Ofir [P] 84 A2
Oforsen [S] 188 E1
Ofte [N] 186 D2
Ogenbargen [D] 30 E1
Oğlansini [TR] 170 E4
Ogliastro Cilento [I] 134 D4
Ognica [PL] 34 D4
Ognjanovo [BG] 156 C3
Ogradena [RO] 148 C1
Ogre [LV] 236 B3
Ogrodzieniec [PL] 62 E2
Ogrosen [D] 46 C3
O Grove [E] 82 A3
Ogulin [HR] 144 C1
Ohat [H] 76 D3
Oheb [CZ] 60 F3
Ohlava [FIN] 216 B1
Ohordorf [D] 44 D1
Ohrdruf [D] 58 E1
Ohrid [MK] 160 C2
Öhringen [D] 58 C4
Ohtanajärvi [S] 222 A2
Ohtola [FIN] 208 D3
Óhuta [H] 76 E2
Oía [GR] 174 D1
Oiä [P] 84 A3
Oia / Arrabal [E] 82 A3
Oijärvi [FIN] 216 B1
Oikarainen [FIN] 222 C3
Oímbra [E] 84 C2
Oinasjärvi [FIN] 198 E3
O Incio [E] 82 D3
Oinoanda [TR] 170 F4
Oinói [GR] 168 A2
Oinoskylä [FIN] 208 E2
Oiron [F] 66 E3
Oirschot [NL] 40 F2
Oisemont [F] 54 D1
Oissel [F] 54 C2
Oisterwijk [NL] 40 F2
Oitti [FIN] 198 F2
Öitylo [GR] 172 D3
Oivu / Åivo [FIN] 214 F4
Öja [FIN] 214 F4
Öjaby [S] 184 C4
Ojakylä [FIN] 216 B4
Ojakylä [FIN] 216 C2
Ojala [FIN] 208 D2
Öjarn [S] 204 F1
Ojców [PL] 62 F2
Öje [S] 194 E3
Öjebyn [S] 214 D2
Ojén [E] 104 D3
Ojo Guareña [E] 86 C3
Ojós [E] 106 D2
Ojos Negros [E] 94 C4
Ojrzeń [PL] 48 E1
Öjung [S] 196 B2
Öjvasslan [S] 194 D1
Okalewo [PL] 36 E4

Okalewo [PL] 36 E4
Okány [H] 122 E1
Økdal [N] 204 B2
Okehampton [GB] 26 C3
Oker [D] 44 C2
Okhtyrka [UA] 242 F3
Okkelberg [N] 204 B1
Oklaj [HR] 144 D3
Okol [AL] 152 F3
Okonek [PL] 36 A3
Okonin [PL] 36 D3
Okons'k [UA] 50 F3
Okopy [PL] 50 D3
Okoř [CZ] 60 D2
Okors [BG] 150 D2
Okrug [HR] 144 D4
Oksajärvi [S] 220 F1
Oksakoski [FIN] 208 E1
Oksava [FIN] 216 B4
Oksböl [DK] 178 A2
Oksdøl [N] 212 C3
Øksendalen [N] 194 B1
Øksendrup [DK] 178 D3
Øksfjord [N] 224 F1
Øksfjordhamn [N] 224 E2
Øksna [N] 194 C3
Øksnes [N] 224 B4
Økstad [N] 204 B2
Oksvoll [N] 202 F1
Oktiabrs'ke [UA] 246 F3
Oktoniá [GR] 168 B1
Okučani [HR] 144 F1
Okulovka [RUS] 240 D2
Okuninka [PL] 50 D3
Ólafsfjörður [IS] 218 C2
Ólafsvík [IS] 218 A2
Ö. Lagnö [S] 190 E2
Olaine [LV] 234 F3
Olargues [F] 124 B3
Olaszfalu [H] 120 F1
Oława [PL] 62 C1
Olazagutia / Olazti [E] 86 E4
Olazti / Olazagutia [E] 86 E4
Olba [E] 102 D2
Olbasa [TR] 170 F3
Olbernhau [D] 60 C2
Ólbia [I] 142 C2
Olbięcin [PL] 50 B4
Oldcastle [IRL] 10 E1
Oldeberkoop [NL] 30 C2
Oldeide [N] 202 B4
Olden [N] 202 C4
Olden [S] 204 E1
Oldenburg [D] 30 F2
Oldenburg [D] 32 D2
Oldenzaal [N] 30 D3
Olderdalen [N] 224 E2
Olderfjord [N] 228 C2
Oldervik [N] 224 E2
Oldham [GB] 24 B2
Oldmeldrum [GB] 18 F2
Old Mellifont Abbey [IRL] 10 F1
Oldřichovice [CZ] 62 E3
Oleby [S] 194 D4
Olecko [PL] 38 B2
Oléggio [I] 116 D3
Oleiros [E] 82 A2
Oleiros [E] 82 C2
Oleiros [P] 90 D2
Oleksandriia [UA] 246 E1
Oleksandrivka [UA] 246 D1
Oleksandrivka [UA] 246 E2
Olen [B] 40 E3
Ølen [N] 186 B1
Olèrdola [E] 96 C3
Olesa de Montserrat [E] 96 D3
Olešnica [PL] 48 B4
Olešnice [CZ] 62 B3
Olesno [PL] 62 D1
Oleszno [PL] 48 E4
Oleszyce [PL] 64 E2

Oletta [F] 130 B2
Olette [F] 96 E1
Olevs'k [UA] 242 C4
Ølgod [DK] 178 B1
Olhain, Château Féodal d'–
   [F] 40 B4
Olhão [P] 98 C4
Ol'hopil' [UA] 244 F2
Oliana [E] 96 C2
Olía Speciosa [I] 142 C5
Oliena [I] 142 C3
Olingdal [S] 194 E1
Olingsjövallen [S] 194 E1
Olite [E] 88 A4
Oliva [E] 102 D4
Oliva de la Frontera [E] 98 E2
Oliva de Mérida [E] 98 F2
Olivadi [I] 138 E2
Olivares [E] 98 E4
Olivares de Júcar [E] 102 A2
Oliveira de Azeméis [P] 84 A3
Oliveira de Frades [P] 84 B3
Oliveira do Bairro [P] 84 A3
Oliveira do Hospital [P] 84 B4
Olivenza [E] 98 E2
Olivet [F] 68 B1
Olivone [CH] 116 E2
Ol'ka [SK] 64 C4
Olkkala [FIN] 198 E3
Olkusz [PL] 62 F2
Ollerup [DK] 178 C3
Olliergues [F] 80 C2
Ollikkala [FIN] 200 C3
Ollila [FIN] 198 D3
Ölölä [FIN] 210 F2
Ölmbrotorp [S] 188 F2
Ölme [S] 188 E2
Olmedilla de Alarcón [E]
   102 B2
Olmedillo de Roa [E] 92 F1
Olmedo [E] 92 D2
Olmedo [I] 142 B2
Olmeto [F] 130 A3
Ölmhult [S] 188 D2
Olmillos de Sasamón [E]
   86 C4
Olocau del Rey [E] 102 E1
Olofsbäck [S] 214 A3
Olofsfors [S] 206 E2
Olofström [S] 180 D1
Olombrada [E] 92 E2
Olomouc [CZ] 62 C3
Olon / Oyon [E] 86 E4
Olonzac [F] 124 B3
Oloron–Ste-Marie [F] 88 C3
Olos Fthiotidos [GR] 166 E2
Olost [E] 96 D2
Olot [E] 96 E2
Olovo [BIH] 146 B3
Olownik [PL] 38 B1
Olpe [D] 42 D4
Øls [DK] 182 D3
Olsätter [S] 188 D2
Olsberg [D] 42 E3
Olsborg [N] 224 D3
Olseröd [S] 180 D2
Ölserud [S] 188 D3
Olší [CZ] 62 B4
Olsøy [N] 204 B1
Ölsremma [S] 184 C2
Olst [NL] 30 C3
Østykke [DK] 178 E2
Olszowa Wola [PL] 48 E3
Olsztyn [PL] 36 E3
Olsztyn [PL] 62 E1
Olsztynek [PL] 36 E3
Olszyna [PL] 46 C3
Olszyna [PL] 46 D4
Oltedal [N] 186 B2
Olten [CH] 70 D3

Olteni [RO] 150 A2
Olteniţa [RO] 150 C2
Olteren [N] 224 E3
Oltina [RO] 150 E1
Oltre il Colle [I] 116 F3
Ölüdeniz [TR] 176 D1
Olula del Río [E] 106 C3
Olvega [E] 94 C2
Olvera [E] 104 C3
Olympía [GR] 172 C2
Olympiáda [GR] 162 C1
Ólympos [GR] 176 B3
Ólympos [TR] 176 F1
Ólynthos [GR] 162 B2
Olza [PL] 62 D3
Oma, Bosque de– [E] 86 E3
Omagh [NIR] 12 D2
Omalí [GR] 160 D3
Omalós [GR] 174 B4
Oman [BG] 158 B1
Omarska [BIH] 144 E2
Ömböly [H] 76 F3
Ombygget Stavkirke [N]
   192 C2
Omegna [I] 116 D3
Ömerköy [TR] 164 D2
Ömerli [TR] 158 E3
Omiš [HR] 144 E4
Omišalj [HR] 144 B1
Ommen [NL] 30 D3
Ommunddalen [N] 212 B4
Omodos [CY] 176 D4
Omoljica [SRB] 146 C2
Ómossa / Metsälä [FIN]
   208 B3
Omsjö [S] 206 C2
Omurtag [BG] 150 C3
Øn [N] 192 B2
Oña [E] 86 D3
Oñati [E] 86 E3
Onda [E] 102 D2
Ondara [E] 108 C1
Ondarroa [E] 86 E3
Ondić [HR] 144 D2
Ö Nësberg [S] 194 E4
Oneşti [RO] 244 E4
Onguera [E] 86 C2
Onil [E] 106 F1
Onkamo [FIN] 210 E3
Onkamo [FIN] 222 E2
Onkiniemi [FIN] 200 B1
Onnaing [F] 40 C4
Önneköp [S] 180 D2
Onoranza [I] 134 E2
Onsaker [N] 192 F4
Onsevig [DK] 178 D3
Ontiñena [E] 94 F3
Ontinyent [E] 102 D4
Ontojoki Porokylä [FIN]
   216 D3
Ontur [E] 106 D1
Önusberg [S] 214 C2
Onuškis [LT] 238 D3
Onzonilla [E] 82 F4
Ooidonk [B] 40 D3
Oola [IRL] 10 D3
Oostburg [NL] 40 D2
Oostduinkerke [B] 40 C3
Oostende (Ostende) [B] 40 C2
Oosterbeek [NL] 30 C4
Oosterend [NL] 30 C1
Oosterhout [NL] 40 E2
Oosterwolde [NL] 30 D2
Oostmalle [B] 40 E2
Ootmarsum [NL] 30 D3
Opaka [BG] 150 C3
Opalenica [PL] 46 E2
Opařany [CZ] 60 D4
Oparić [SRB] 146 F4
Opatija [HR] 120 A4
Opatów [PL] 48 B4
Opatów [PL] 50 B4

Opatówek [PL] 48 C3
Opatowiec [PL] 64 B2
Opava [CZ] 62 D3
Ope [S] 204 F2
Opglabbek [B] 40 F3
Opi [I] 132 E4
O Pino [E] 82 B2
Opinogóra Górna [PL] 36 F4
Opishnia [UA] 242 F4
Opladen [D] 42 D3
Oplenac, Manastir– [SRB]
   146 E3
Opletnya [BG] 148 D4
Oploo [NL] 42 B2
Oplotnica [SLO] 120 C2
Opochka [RUS] 236 F3
Opočno [CZ] 62 A2
Opoczno [PL] 48 E3
Opole [PL] 62 D2
Opole Lubelskie [PL] 50 B4
Opol'ye [RUS] 232 E1
Oporów [PL] 48 D2
Opovo [SRB] 146 D1
Oppach [D] 46 C4
Oppaker [N] 194 C4
Oppdal [N] 202 F3
Oppdøl [N] 202 E3
Oppeby [S] 184 E1
Oppedal [N] 192 B2
Oppegård [N] 188 B1
Oppenau [D] 70 E2
Oppenheim [D] 58 B3
Opphaug [N] 202 F1
Opphiem [N] 192 C2
Opphus [N] 194 C2
Oppido Lucano [I] 134 F3
Oppido Mamertina [I] 138 D3
Oppidum d'Ensérune [F]
   124 B3
Oppola [RUS] 210 E4
Opponitz [A] 74 B3
Oppsal [N] 186 B3
Opsa [BY] 238 F2
Opusztazser [H] 122 C2
Opuzen [HR] 152 C2
Ör [H] 76 F3
Ora [CY] 176 D4
Öra [S] 184 B1
Ora / Auer [I] 118 C2
Oradea [RO] 122 F1
Orahovac [KS] 154 C3
Orahov Do [BIH] 152 D2
Orahovica [HR] 120 F4
Orahovlje [BIH] 152 C2
Oraison [F] 124 F3
Orajärvi [FIN] 222 B2
Orange [F] 124 E2
Orani [I] 142 C3
Oranienbaum [D] 44 E3
Oranienburg [D] 46 B1
Oranmore [IRL] 10 C1
Oraovica [SRB] 154 E3
Öras [N] 204 C2
Orašac [BIH] 144 D2
Orašac [MK] 154 D3
Orašac [SRB] 148 C4
Orasi [F] 130 A4
Orašje [BIH] 146 B2
Orăşti [RO] 150 C1
Orăştie [RO] 248 C3
Oravainen / Oravais [FIN]
   208 C1
Oravais / Oravainen [FIN]
   208 C1
Öravan [S] 214 B3
Oravasaari [FIN] 208 F3
Oravi [FIN] 210 D3
Oravijoki [FIN] 216 D2
Oravikoski [FIN] 210 C2
Oravisalo [FIN] 210 E3
Oraviţa [RO] 146 F1

Oravská Lesná [SK] 62 E4
Oravská Polhora [SK] 62 E4
Oravský Podzámok [SK] 62 E4
Orba [E] 108 C2
Ørbæk [DK] 178 D2
Orbassano [I] 116 B4
Orbe [CH] 116 B1
Orbeasca [RO] 150 B2
Orbec [F] 54 B2
Orbetello [I] 130 E2
Orbey [F] 70 D2
Ørby [DK] 178 D1
Örbyhus [S] 196 D4
Örbyhus [S] 196 D4
Orca [P] 90 E2
Orcera [E] 106 C1
Orches [F] 66 E3
Orchies [F] 40 C4
Orchomenós [GR] 166 F3
Orchomenós [GR] 166 F3
Orchomenós [GR] 172 D2
Orcières [F] 126 B1
Orderud [N] 188 C2
Ordes [E] 82 B2
Ordino [AND] 96 D1
Orduña [E] 86 D3
Ore [S] 206 E2
Orebić [HR] 152 C2
Örebro [S] 188 F2
Öregrund [S] 196 E4
Orehova vas Rače [SLO] 120 C2
Orehoved [DK] 178 E3
Orehovica [SG] 148 D3
Orehovno [RUS] 232 E2
Oreiní [GR] 156 B4
Orel [RUS] 242 F1
Ören [TR] 164 B3
Ören [TR] 170 C4
Ören [TR] 170 F4
Örencik [TR] 164 B2
Örencik [TR] 164 F3
Örenkaya [TR] 170 F1
Orense / Ourense [E] 82 C3
Oreoi [GR] 162 B4
Oresak [BG] 148 F4
Oreshari [BG] 156 E3
Orestiáda [GR] 158 A3
Öreström [S] 214 C3
Oresvika [N] 218 E4
Öreyd [S] 184 C2
Orgáni [GR] 156 E3
Organyà [E] 96 C2
Orgaz [E] 100 E2
Orgelet [F] 80 E1
Orgenvika [N] 192 F4
Orgeval [F] 54 D3
Orgjost [AL] 154 C3
Orgnac–l'Aven [F] 124 D2
Orgon [F] 124 E3
Orgosolo [I] 142 C3
Orgovány [H] 122 C2
Orhaneli [TR] 164 C2
Orhangazi [TR] 158 E4
Orhaniye [TR] 158 A4
Orhanlar [TR] 164 C2
Orhanlı [TR] 170 B2
Orhei [MD] 244 F3
Ør. Hvidbjerg [DK] 182 C3
Oria [E] 106 C3
Oria [I] 136 E3
Orihuela [E] 106 E2
Orihuela del Tremedal [E] 102 C1
Orikhiv [UA] 246 F2
Orikum [AL] 160 A3
Orimattila [FIN] 200 B2
Orio [E] 86 F3
Oriolo [I] 136 C3
Oripää [FIN] 198 D2
Orismala [FIN] 208 C2
Orissaare [EST] 230 B3

Oristano [I] 142 B4
Öriszentpéter [H] 120 D2
Orivesi [FIN] 208 E4
Orizare [BG] 150 E4
Ørjarvik [N] 202 D2
Ørje [N] 188 C2
Örjiva [E] 104 F3
Orkanger [N] 204 A2
Örkelljunga [S] 180 C1
Örkény [H] 122 B1
Orléans [F] 68 B1
Orlík nad Vltavou [CZ] 60 D4
Orlovat [SRB] 146 E1
Orly [F] 54 E3
Orly [RUS] 232 E1
Örlya [BY] 38 E2
Orlyak [BG] 150 D2
Orlyane [BG] 148 F4
Ormanlı [TR] 158 D3
Ormea [I] 126 D2
Ormemyr [N] 186 E1
Örménykút [H] 122 D2
Ormestad [N] 186 C4
Órmos [GR] 160 F3
Órmos [GR] 168 D3
Órmos Panagías [GR] 162 C2
Órmos Prínou [GR] 162 D1
Ormož [SLO] 120 D2
Ormsjö [S] 212 F3
Ormskirk [GB] 22 F2
Ornans [F] 70 B4
Örnäs [S] 196 B4
Ornavasso [I] 116 D3
Örnberg [FIN] 208 C2
Ornes [N] 212 E3
Ørnes [N] 218 F3
Orneta [PL] 36 E2
Ørnhøj [DK] 182 C4
Ornö [S] 190 E3
Örnsköldsvik [S] 206 D2
Orolik [HR] 146 C1
Oron–la–Ville [CH] 116 B1
Oropa, Santuário d'– [I] 116 C3
Oropesa [E] 92 C4
Oropesa del Mar / Orpesa [E] 102 E2
Orošac [HR] 152 D3
Orosei [I] 142 C3
Orosháza [H] 122 D2
Oroso [E] 82 B2
Oroszlány [H] 74 F4
Oroszló [H] 120 F3
Ørpen [N] 192 F4
Orpesa / Oropesa del Mar [E] 102 E2
Orpington [GB] 28 D3
Orre [N] 186 A3
Orrefors [S] 184 E3
Orrfors [S] 222 A1
Orrliden [S] 194 D2
Orroli [I] 142 C4
Orrviken [S] 204 E2
Orsa [S] 194 F2
Orsala [S] 194 E4
Orsara di Púglia [I] 134 E3
Örsås [S] 184 B2
Örsbäck [S] 206 E1
Orscholz [D] 56 E3
Örsebo [S] 184 D1
Örserum [S] 184 D1
Orsha [BY] 242 C1
Orsières [CH] 116 B2
Örsjö [S] 184 E3
Ørskog [N] 202 D3
Ørslev [DK] 178 E3
Örslösa [S] 188 D4
Ørsnes [N] 202 C3
Orsogna [I] 132 F3
Orsomarso [I] 136 B4
Orşova [RO] 148 C1

Orsoya [BG] 148 D3
Ørsta [N] 202 C3
Orsta [S] 190 B2
Ørsted [DK] 182 D3
Örsundsbro [S] 190 C2
Ort [A] 72 E2
Ortaca [TR] 164 B2
Ortaca [TR] 176 D1
Ortakent [TR] 170 B4
Ortaklar [TR] 170 B3
Ortaköy [TR] 170 C3
Orta Nova [I] 134 E3
Ortaoba [TR] 164 C2
Orta San Giúlio [I] 116 D3
Orte [I] 132 C3
Ortenberg [D] 58 C2
Ortenburg [D] 72 E2
Orth [A] 74 D3
Orthez [F] 88 B2
Orthovoúni [GR] 160 D4
Ortigueira [E] 82 D1
Ørting [DK] 178 C1
Ortisei / St Ulrich [I] 118 C2
Ortişoara [RO] 122 E3
Ortnevik [N] 192 C2
Orto [F] 130 A2
Örtomta [S] 190 B4
Ortona [I] 132 F3
Ortona dei Marsi [I] 132 E4
Ortrand [D] 46 B3
Örträsk [S] 214 C3
Ortu [I] 142 B4
Ortueri [I] 142 B4
Öru [EST] 230 E3
Oruçoğlu [TR] 158 E3
Ørum [DK] 182 D3
Ørum [DK] 182 E4
Orume [I] 142 C3
Örup [S] 180 D2
Orval, Abbaye d'– [B] 56 C2
Orvalho [P] 90 D2
Ørvella [N] 186 E1
Orvieto [I] 130 F2
Örviken [S] 214 D3
Orvinio [I] 132 D3
Oryahovec [BG] 156 D3
Oryakhovo [BG] 148 E3
Ö. Ryd [S] 190 C4
Orzechowo [PL] 36 D4
Orzesze [PL] 62 E2
Orzhytsia [UA] 242 E4
Orzinuovi [I] 116 F4
Orzola [E] 114 F2
Orzysz [PL] 38 B2
Os [N] 204 B3
Os [S] 184 C2
Osa [N] 192 C3
Osby [S] 184 C4
Oschatz [D] 44 F4
Oschersleben [D] 44 D2
Öschiri [I] 142 C2
Ošćiłowo [PL] 36 E4
Ose [N] 186 C2
Øse [N] 224 C4
Osečina [SRB] 146 C3
Oseja de Sajambre [E] 86 B2
Osen [N] 212 B3
Osenets [BG] 150 C3
Osera de Ebro [E] 94 E3
Osidda [I] 142 C3
Osie [PL] 36 C3
Osieczna [PL] 36 C3
Osieczna [PL] 46 F3
Osiecznica [PL] 46 D2
Osiek [PL] 36 C3
Osiek [PL] 64 C2
Osijek [HR] 122 B4
Osikovitsa [BG] 148 E4
Ósilo [I] 142 B2
Ósimo [I] 128 F4
Osinja [BIH] 146 A2
Osinów [PL] 34 D4

Osíou Louká, Moní– [GR] 166 E3
Osipaonica [SRB] 146 E2
Osjaków [PL] 48 C4
Osječenica [MNE] 152 E3
Oskal [N] 226 B2
Oskar [S] 184 E3
Oskar–Fredriksborg [S] 190 E2
Oskarshamn [S] 184 E2
Oskarström [S] 184 B3
Øskendalsøra [N] 202 E3
Oskowo [PL] 36 B2
Osl'any [SK] 76 A2
Osli [H] 74 E4
Oslo [N] 188 B1
Osløs [DK] 182 C2
Osma [FIN] 228 D3
Osmancalı [TR] 164 C4
Osmankalfalar [TR] 170 F3
Osmanki [FIN] 216 C4
Osmanlar [TR] 164 C2
Osmanli [TR] 158 B3
Os'mino [RUS] 232 E2
Osmjany [BY] 242 A2
Ösmo [S] 190 D3
Osmoy–St–Valery [F] 54 D1
Osnabrück [D] 30 E4
Osnäs [FIN] 198 B3
Ošno Lubuskie [PL] 46 D2
Osoblaha [CZ] 62 C2
Osor [E] 96 E2
Osor [HR] 144 B2
Osorhei [RO] 122 F1
Osorno la Mayor [E] 86 B4
Osowiec [PL] 38 C2
Osowo Lęborskie [PL] 36 B1
Osowo Leśne [PL] 36 C2
Osøyro [N] 192 B3
Os Peares [E] 82 C3
Ospedaletti [I] 126 C3
Ospitaletto [I] 118 F3
Oss [NL] 30 C4
Óssa [AP] 162 B1
Ossa de Montiel [E] 100 F3
Ossiach [A] 118 F2
Ossjøen [N] 192 D3
Östanjö [S] 188 F3
Östansjö [S] 194 E1
Östansjö [S] 214 C1
Östanvik [S] 194 F2
Oštarije [HR] 144 C1
Ostashkov [RUS] 240 D2
Ostaszewo [PL] 36 D2
Östavall [S] 204 F4
Ostbevern [D] 30 E4
Østbirk [DK] 178 C1
Østby [N] 194 D2
Osted [DK] 178 E2
Ostellato [I] 128 D2
Østenå [N] 186 D2
Ostende (Oostende) [B] 40 C2
Österbo [N] 188 C2
Österbø [N] 192 D2
Osterburg [D] 32 E4
Osterburken [D] 58 C3
Østerbybruk [S] 196 D4
Østerby Havn [DK] 182 E2
Österbymo [S] 184 D1
Österede [S] 206 C2
Österfärnebo [S] 196 C4
Österforse [S] 206 C2
Östergraninge [S] 206 C3
Osterhever [D] 32 B1
Osterhofen [D] 72 E2
Osterholz–Scharmbeck [D] 32 A3

Östermark / Teuva [FIN] 208 B3
Ostermiething [A] 72 E3
Osterncappeln [D] 30 F4
Östernoret [S] 214 B3
Österö [FIN] 208 C1
Osterode [D] 44 C3
Österreichisches Freilichtmuseum [A] 120 C1
Östersund [S] 204 E2
Östersundom [FIN] 198 F3
Østerud [N] 186 F1
Øster Ulslev [DK] 32 E1
Österunda [S] 190 D1
Österväla [S] 196 D4
Östervallskog [S] 188 C2
Øster Vrå [DK] 182 D2
Ostfildern [D] 70 F1
Östfora [S] 190 D1
Osthammar [S] 196 E4
Ostheim [D] 58 D2
Osthofen [D] 58 B3
Ostia [I] 130 F4
Ostíglia [I] 128 C1
Ostiz [E] 86 F4
Ostland [D] 30 D1
Östloning [S] 206 C3
Östmark [S] 194 D4
Ostnäs [S] 206 F1
Östomsjön [S] 194 D1
Ostra [I] 128 E4
Östraby [S] 180 C2
Ostrach [D] 70 F3
Östra Ed [S] 184 F1
Östra Frölunda [S] 184 B2
Östra Husby [S] 190 C4
Östra Kärne [S] 188 E2
Östra Luka [BIH] 144 E2
Ostrava [CZ] 62 D3
Östra Yttermark [FIN] 208 B3
Østre Kile [N] 186 D2
Oštrelj [BIH] 144 E2
Ostritz [D] 46 D4
Ostróda [PL] 36 E4
Ostrog, Manastir– [MNE] 152 E3
Ostroh [UA] 244 D1
Ostrołęka [PL] 38 A3
Ostromecko [PL] 36 C4
Ostroróg [PL] 46 E1
Ostros [MNE] 152 F4
Ostrov [CZ] 60 C2
Ostrov [RO] 150 D2
Ostrov [RUS] 200 E2
Ostrov [RUS] 232 E3
Ostrovcy [RUS] 230 F3
Ostrov nad Oslavou [CZ] 60 F4
Ostrovo [BG] 150 C2
Ostrowice [PL] 34 F3
Ostrowiec [PL] 36 A2
Ostrowiec Świętokrzyski [PL] 50 A4
Ostrowite [PL] 36 C3
Ostrowite [PL] 48 B2
Ostrów Lubelski [PL] 50 C3
Ostrów Mazowiecka [PL] 38 B4
Ostrów Wielkopolski [PL] 48 B3
Ostrožac [BIH] 144 D2
Ostrožac [BIH] 146 A4
Ostrożany [PL] 38 C4
Ostrzeszów [PL] 48 B3
Ostuni [I] 136 E2
Ostvik [S] 214 D2
Østvika [N] 212 E3
Ostwald [F] 70 D1
Osuna [E] 104 E2
Oswestry [GB] 22 E3
Oświęcim [PL] 62 F3
Osztopán [H] 120 E2
Otalampi [FIN] 198 E3
Otanki [FIN] 216 C3

Otanów [PL] 34 E4
Otava [FIN] 200 C1
Otelec [RO] 122 D4
Otepää [EST] 230 E3
Oteren [N] 224 D2
Oterma [FIN] 216 C2
Otero de Bodas [E] 84 E2
Oteševo [MK] 160 C2
Otetelişu [RO] 148 E1
Otivar [E] 104 E3
Otley [GB] 24 C2
Otmuchów [PL] 62 C2
Otnes [N] 194 C1
Otočac [HR] 144 C2
Otočec [SLO] 120 B3
Otok [HR] 146 B1
Otok [SLO] 120 A3
Otoka [BIH] 144 D2
Otopeni [RO] 150 B1
Otorowo [PL] 46 E2
Otradnoye [RUS] 200 F2
Otranto [I] 136 F3
Otrić [HR] 144 D3
Otrokovice [CZ] 62 C4
Otsa [EST] 230 F3
Otsagi / Ochagavía [E] 88 B3
Otta [N] 192 F1
Ottana [I] 142 C3
Ottaviano [I] 134 D3
Ottenby [S] 184 E4
Ottenschlag [A] 74 B2
Ottensheim [A] 74 A2
Ottenstein [A] 74 B2
Otterbach [D] 56 F3
Otterbäcken [S] 188 E3
Otterlo [NL] 30 C4
Otterndorf [D] 32 B2
Ottersberg [D] 32 B3
Ottersøy [N] 212 C3
Otterup [DK] 178 C2
Öttevény [H] 74 E3
Ottnang [A] 72 F3
Ottobeuren [D] 72 B3
Ottobiano [I] 116 D4
Ottone [I] 126 F2
Ottsjö [S] 204 D2
Ottsjön [S] 204 F1
Ottweiler [D] 56 E3
Ö. Tväråsel [S] 214 D1
Otwock [PL] 48 F2
Ouanne [F] 68 D2
Oucques [F] 68 A1
Oud Beijerland [NL] 30 A4
Ouddorp [NL] 40 D2
Oudenaarde (Audenarde)
   [B] 40 D3
Oude-Pekela [NL] 30 E2
Oudewater [NL] 30 B4
Oughterard [IRL] 10 C1
Ouistreham [F] 54 B2
Oulainen [FIN] 216 B3
Oullins [F] 80 D2
Oulu / Uleåborg [FIN] 216 B2
Oulujoki [FIN] 216 B2
Oulunsalo [FIN] 216 B2
Oulx [I] 116 B4
Ounas [FIN] 216 C3
Oundle [GB] 28 D1
Oura [P] 84 C2
Ouranóupoli [GR] 162 C2
Ourense / Orense [E] 82 C3
Ourique [P] 98 B3
Ouroi [E] 82 D1
Ourscamps, Abbaye d'– [F]
   54 F2
Oust [F] 88 E4
Outes [E] 82 B2
Outokumpu [FIN] 210 D2
Ouzouer–le–Marché [F] 68 B1
Ovacik [TR] 170 C2
Ovacik [TR] 170 D2
Ovada [I] 126 E2

Ovakent [TR] 170 C2
Ovakışlacik [TR] 170 C4
Ovanåker [S] 196 B2
Ovanmo [S] 206 B2
Ovansjö [S] 206 B3
Ovar [P] 84 A3
Ovčar Banja [SRB] 146 D3
Övedskloster [S] 180 C2
Ovelgönne [D] 32 B3
Ovenstädt [D] 42 F1
Överammer [S] 206 B2
Overåneset [N] 202 D3
Överäng [S] 204 D1
Overath [D] 42 D4
Överberg [S] 204 E4
Överbo [S] 196 B2
Overby [DK] 178 C2
Överby [S] 190 E2
Øverbygd [N] 224 D3
Överbyn [S] 194 D4
Overgård [DK] 182 D3
Överhogdal [S] 204 F4
Överhörnäs [S] 206 D2
Overijse [B] 40 E3
Överjeppo [FIN] 208 C1
Over Jerstal [DK] 178 B2
Överkalix [S] 222 A3
Överlännäs [S] 206 C2
Överlida [S] 184 B2
Övermark / Ylimarkku [FIN]
   208 B3
Överö [FIN] 198 B4
Øverøye [N] 202 D3
Överrissjö [S] 214 B4
Överröda [S] 214 D3
Överselö [S] 190 D2
Övertänger [S] 196 B3
Overton [GB] 28 B3
Övertorneå [S] 222 B3
Övertorneå / Ylitornio [FIN]
   222 B3
Överturingen [S] 204 F3
Överum [S] 184 E1
Oveselu [RO] 148 E1
Ovidiu [RO] 150 F1
Oviedo [E] 82 F2
Ovindoli [I] 132 E3
Övra [S] 206 C1
Övralid [S] 188 E2
Øvre Årdal [N] 192 D2
Övre Bäck [S] 214 D3
Øvre Dåsvatn [N] 186 C3
Øvre Espedal [N] 186 B2
Øvre Jervan [N] 204 B2
Øvre Moen [N] 186 C2
Øvre Rendal [N] 194 B1
Øvre Sirdal [N] 186 C3
Övre Soppero [S] 226 A4
Øvrestøl [N] 202 D2
Øvre Vats [N] 186 B1
Ovruch [UA] 242 C3
Ovsishche [RUS] 232 E2
Øvstebø [N] 186 B2
Øvstedal [N] 202 D3
Ovtrup [DK] 178 A1
Owschlag [D] 32 B1
Öxabäck [S] 184 B2
Oxbakken [S] 190 C3
Oxberg [S] 194 D2
Oxelösund [S] 190 D3
Oxford [GB] 28 B2
Oxie [S] 180 C2
Oxsjön [S] 206 B4
Oxyá [GR] 166 D2
Oxýneia [GR] 160 D4
Øy [N] 186 D3
Oyace [I] 116 C3
Øyan [N] 204 C2
Øyangen [N] 202 F1
Øye [N] 192 E2
Øye [N] 202 C3
Øyenkilen [N] 188 B2

Øyer [N] 194 B2
Øyermoen [N] 194 D4
Øyestad [N] 186 D3
Øyfjell [N] 186 D1
Øylo [N] 192 E2
Øymark [N] 188 C2
Oyntdartfjørður [FR] 182 B1
Oyon / Olon [E] 86 E4
Oyonnax [F] 80 E2
Oyonnax [F] 80 E2
Oyrières [F] 70 A3
Øyslebø [N] 186 C4
Øystese [N] 192 B3
Oyten [D] 32 B3
Ozalj [HR] 120 C4
Ożarów [S] 50 B4
Ozarów [PL] 50 B4
Ożarów Mazowieki [PL] 48 F2
Ožbalt [SLO] 120 C2
Ózd [H] 76 C3
Ożd'any [SK] 76 C2
Özdere [TR] 170 B3
Ozegna [I] 116 C3
Ozerki [RUS] 200 E3
Ozernyy [RUS] 240 D3
Ozersk [RUS] 38 B1
Ozerskoye [RUS] 200 E2
Ozieri [I] 142 C3
Ozimek [PL] 62 D2
Ozora [H] 122 A2
Ozorków [PL] 48 D3
Ozren, Manastir– [BIH] 146 B2

P

Pääjärvi [FIN] 208 E2
Paakkila [FIN] 210 D2
Paakkola [FIN] 222 C4
Paanala [FIN] 210 B3
Paaso [FIN] 200 B1
Paatela [FIN] 210 C4
Paatinen [FIN] 198 C3
Paavola [FIN] 216 B2
Pabianice [PL] 48 D3
Pabiarže [LT] 238 E3
Pabradė [LT] 238 E3
Pabuçlu [TR] 164 E4
Paceco [I] 140 B2
Pacentro [I] 132 E4
Pachiá Ámmos [GR] 174 E4
Pachino [I] 140 E4
Páchna [CY] 176 D4
Pachyammos [CY] 176 C3
Pácin [H] 76 E2
Paços de Ferreira [P] 84 B2
Pacov [CZ] 60 E4
Pacsa [H] 120 E2
Pacyna [PL] 48 D2
Pacy–sur–Eure [F] 54 D3
Paczków [PL] 62 C2
Pădarevo [BG] 150 D4
Padarosk [BY] 38 E3
Padasjoki [FIN] 198 F1
Padborg [DK] 178 B3
Padej [SRB] 122 D3
Paderborn [D] 42 F2
Paderne [P] 98 B4
Paderno Dugnano [I] 116 E3
Padiham [GB] 24 B2
Padina [SRB] 146 E1
Padinska Skela [SRB] 146 D2
Padirac, Gouffre de– [F] 78 E4
Padjenne [N] 144 D3
Padova [I] 118 C4
Padrenda [E] 82 B4
Padrógão Grande [P] 90 D2
Padrón [E] 82 B2
Padru [I] 142 C2
Padru Mannu [I] 142 B3
Padstow [GB] 26 B3

Padul [E] 104 F3
Padula [I] 134 E4
Padules [E] 106 B3
Paesana [I] 126 C1
Paestum [I] 134 D4
Paestum [I] 134 D4
Páfos [CY] 176 C4
Pag [HR] 144 C2
Pägaia [RO] 76 F4
Pagani [I] 134 D3
Pagánico [I] 130 E2
Pagasaí [GR] 162 B4
Pagėgiai [LT] 238 B3
Pagnoz [F] 70 B4
Pagny–sur–Moselle [F] 56 D4
Páhi [H] 122 B2
Pahkakumpu [FIN] 222 D2
Pahkamäki [FIN] 208 F1
Pahtakuusikko [FIN] 226 D4
Paianía [GR] 168 B2
Paide [EST] 230 D2
Paignton [GB] 26 D4
Paijärvi [FIN] 200 C3
Pailhès [F] 88 E3
Paimbœuf [F] 66 B2
Paimio / Pemar [FIN] 198 D3
Paimpol [F] 52 C2
Paisievo [BG] 150 D2
Paisley [GB] 18 C4
Paisua [FIN] 216 D4
Pajala [S] 222 A2
Pájara [E] 114 D3
Pajares, Puerto de– [E] 82 F3
Pajęczno [PL] 48 C4
Pajukoski [FIN] 216 D4
Pajulahti [FIN] 210 C1
Pajulankylä [FIN] 210 C4
Pajuskylä [FIN] 210 B1
Pajuvaara [FIN] 216 E1
Pakość [PL] 48 B1
Pakosławice [PL] 62 C2
Pakoštane [HR] 144 C3
Pakosze [PL] 36 E2
Pakrac [HR] 120 E4
Pakruojis [LT] 238 D1
Paks [H] 122 B2
Palacios del Sil [E] 82 E3
Palacios de Sanabria [E] 84 E2
Paladru [F] 80 E3
Pala e Rughes, Nuraghe– [I]
   142 C3
Palafrugell [E] 96 F2
Palagianello [I] 136 D2
Palagiano [I] 136 D2
Palagonia [I] 140 E3
Palaiá Epídavros [GR] 168 A3
Palaiá Messíni [GR] 172 C2
Palaíkastro [GR] 174 F3
Palaiochóra [GR] 174 B4
Palaiochóri [GR] 162 B2
Palaiochóri [GR] 166 B2
Palaiochóri [GR] 166 C2
Palaiochóri [GR] 172 C2
Palaiokastrítsa [GR] 160 B4
Palaiomonastíri [GR] 166 D1
Palaiópoli [GR] 162 C1
Palaiópoli [GR] 168 C3
Palaiópyrgos [GR] 160 E4
Palaiópyrgos [GR] 166 D3
Palairos [GR] 166 C3
Palaiseau [F] 54 D3
Palamás [GR] 166 D1
Palamós [E] 96 F3
Palamut [TR] 164 C3
Palancar, Monasterio del– [E]
   90 F3
Pålänge [S] 222 A4
Palanga [LT] 238 A2
Palas de Rei [E] 82 C2
Palasi [EST] 230 E2
Palatitsa [GR] 160 E2

Palatna [KS] 148 A4
Palau [I] 142 C2
Palavas–les–Flots [F] 124 C3
Palazzo Adriano [I] 140 C2
Palazzolo Acréide [I] 140 E3
Palazzolo sull'Oglio [I] 116 F3
Palazzo San Gervasio [I]
   134 F3
Paldiski [EST] 230 C2
Pale [BIH] 146 B4
Pâle [LV] 230 D4
Palena [I] 132 F4
Palencia [E] 86 B4
Paleócastro [GR] 156 B4
Palermo [AL] 160 B3
Palermo [I] 140 C1
Palestrina [I] 132 C4
Palfau [A] 74 B3
Pálháza [H] 76 E2
Páli [H] 74 E4
Palić [SRB] 122 C3
Palikkala [FIN] 198 D2
Palín [SK] 76 E2
Palinuro [I] 136 A3
Paliouriá [GR] 160 D3
Palioúrion [GR] 162 C2
Paliseul [B] 56 C2
Paljakka [FIN] 200 B2
Paljakka [FIN] 216 D2
Paljakka [FIN] 222 F3
Pälkäne [FIN] 198 E1
Palkino [RUS] 232 E4
Palkisoja [FIN] 226 D3
Pallagório [I] 138 E1
Pallanza [I] 116 D3
Pallarés [E] 98 F3
Palларuelo de Monegros
   [E] 94 E3
Pallas Grean [IRL] 10 C3
Pallestrina [I] 118 D4
Pallíni [GR] 168 B2
Pallosenvaara [FIN] 210 F1
Palluau [F] 66 C3
Palma del Río [E] 104 D1
Palma de Mallorca [E] 108 C3
Palma di Montechiaro [I]
   140 C3
Palmadula [I] 142 B2
Palma Nova [E] 108 C3
Palmanova [I] 118 E3
Pálmas Arboreá [I] 142 B4
Palmela [P] 90 B4
Palmi [I] 138 D3
Palo del Colle [I] 136 C2
Palohuornas [S] 220 E2
Páloi [GR] 176 A1
Palojärvi [FIN] 226 B3
Palojoensuu [FIN] 226 B3
Palokangas [FIN] 210 C2
Palokastër [AL] 160 B3
Palokka [FIN] 208 F3
Palokki [FIN] 210 D2
Palomäki [FIN] 210 D1
Palomares [I] 106 C3
Palomares del Campo [E]
   102 A2
Palomas [E] 98 F2
Palombara Sabina [I] 132 D4
Palonurmi [FIN] 210 C1
Palos de la Frontera [E] 98 D4
Palota [SK] 64 D4
Pals [E] 96 F2
Pålsboda [S] 190 B3
Pålstrandudden [S] 214 D2
Pålsträsk [S] 214 D1
Paltamo [FIN] 216 D3
Paltanen [FIN] 210 B3
Paltaniemi [FIN] 216 D3
Pältiniş [RO] 122 F4
Pal'tsevo [RUS] 200 D2
Palumir [SRB] 146 E4
Palus [FIN] 198 C1

Paluzza [I] 118 E2
Palviainen [FIN] 210 C3
Påmark / Pomarkku [FIN] 198 C1
Pamhagen [A] 74 D3
Pamiątkowo [PL] 46 F2
Pamiers [F] 88 E3
Pamiętowo [PL] 36 B3
Pamma [EST] 230 B3
Pampaneira [E] 104 F3
Pamparato [I] 126 D2
Pampílhosa da Serra [P] 90 D2
Pamplona / Iruña [E] 86 F4
Pamporovo [BG] 156 D3
Pampow [D] 32 D3
Pamucak [TR] 170 B3
Pamukça [TR] 164 D2
Pamukkale [TR] 170 E2
Pamukyazı [TR] 170 B2
Panagía [GR] 156 D4
Panagía [GR] 160 D3
Panagía [GR] 168 B2
Panagía [GR] 174 D4
Panagyurishte [BG] 156 C1
Panaitólio [GR] 166 D3
Panajë [AL] 160 A3
Panasówka [PL] 64 D2
Panassac [F] 88 D3
Panayır [TR] 164 D3
Pancallo [I] 138 B4
Pancar [TR] 170 B2
Pančevo [SRB] 146 E2
Pancharevo [BG] 156 B1
Pancorbo, Garganta de– [E] 86 D4
Pancorvo [E] 86 D4
Pandélys [LT] 236 C4
Pandino [I] 116 E4
Pandrup [DK] 182 D2
Panemunis [LT] 236 C4
Panenský Týnec [CZ] 60 D2
Panes [E] 86 B2
Panevėžys [LT] 238 D2
Panga [EST] 230 B3
Panicale [I] 130 F1
Paničkovo [BG] 156 D2
Paniza [E] 94 D3
Paniza, Puerto de– [E] 94 D3
Pankajärvi [FIN] 216 E4
Pankakoski [FIN] 210 E1
Pankala [FIN] 216 A3
Panker [D] 32 C1
Panki [PL] 62 E1
Pannonhalma [H] 74 E4
Pannonhalma [H] 74 E4
Panoias [P] 84 C3
Páno Léfkara [CY] 176 D4
Páno Panagiá [CY] 176 C4
Páno Plátres [CY] 176 D4
Panormítis [GR] 176 B1
Pánormos [GR] 168 D3
Pánormos [GR] 174 C3
Pantaleo [I] 142 B5
Pantalica, Necropoli di– [I] 140 E3
Pantánassa [GR] 172 E3
Päntäne [FIN] 208 C3
Pantelej, Manastir– [MK] 154 E3
Pantelleria [I] 140 A3
Panticosa [E] 88 C3
Pantón [E] 82 C3
Pantów [PL] 48 F4
Panxón [E] 82 A3
Panyola [H] 76 F3
Páola [I] 138 D1
Pápa [H] 74 E4
Papadiánika [GR] 172 E3
Paparzyn [PL] 36 C3
Papasídero [I] 136 B4

Pápateszeir [H] 74 E4
Pape [LV] 234 D4
Papenburg [D] 30 E2
Papile [LT] 234 E4
Papiliai [LT] 238 E2
Papilys [LT] 236 C4
Paplin [PL] 38 B4
Papowo Biskupie [PL] 36 C3
Papozze [I] 128 D1
Pappenheim [D] 72 C1
Páprád [H] 120 F3
Paprotnia [PL] 50 C2
Papvesiai [LT] 236 B4
Parábita [I] 136 E3
Paraćin [SRB] 146 F3
Parád [H] 76 C3
Parada del Sil [E] 82 C3
Paradas [E] 104 C2
Paradeísi [GR] 176 C2
Paradeísia [GR] 172 D2
Parádeisos [GR] 156 D4
Paradela [E] 82 C3
Paradela [P] 84 C2
Paradies [D] 72 A3
Paradisgård [S] 188 E1
Paradyż [PL] 48 E4
Parainen / Pargas [FIN] 198 C3
Parakka [S] 220 E1
Parákoila [GR] 164 A3
Paralía [GR] 160 F3
Paralía [GR] 166 D4
Paralía [GR] 166 F3
Paralía [GR] 172 E3
Paralía Akrátas [GR] 166 E4
Paralía Iríon [GR] 172 E2
Paralía Kýmis [GR] 168 B1
Paralía Platánou [GR] 166 E4
Paralía Skotínas [GR] 160 F3
Paralímni [CY] 176 E3
Paralío Ástros [GR] 172 E2
Páramo del Sil [E] 82 F3
Paramythiá [GR] 166 B2
Paranésti [GR] 156 D3
Parantala [FIN] 208 F2
Parapótamos [GR] 160 B4
Parassapuszta [H] 76 B3
Parata, Tour de la– [F] 130 A3
Paravóla [GR] 166 D3
Paray–le–Monial [F] 80 C1
Parc de Chambord [F] 68 A2
Parcent [E] 108 C2
Parcé sur Sarthe [F] 54 A4
Parchim [D] 32 E3
Parc Ornithologique [F] 80 E2
Parczew [PL] 50 C3
Pardubice [CZ] 60 F3
Parechcha [BY] 38 D2
Paredes [E] 82 D2
Paredes [P] 84 B2
Paredes de Coura [P] 82 B4
Paredes de Nava [E] 86 B4
Paredes de Sigüenza [E] 94 B3
Parentis–en–Born [F] 78 B4
Paretón [E] 106 D3
Parey [D] 44 E2
Párga [GR] 166 B2
Pargas / Parainen [FIN] 198 C3
Pargny–sur–Saulx [F] 56 B4
Pargolovo [RUS] 200 F3
Parikkala [FIN] 210 E4
Paris [F] 54 E3
Parisot [F] 88 F2
Parje [SLO] 118 F4
Parkajoki [S] 222 A1
Parkalompolo [S] 220 F1
Parkano [FIN] 208 D4
Parkkila [FIN] 216 B4
Parkkima [FIN] 216 B4
Parknasilla [IRL] 10 A3
Parkumäki [FIN] 210 D3

Parla [E] 92 E4
Parlak [TR] 168 E1
Parlówko [PL] 34 D2
Parma [I] 128 B2
Parndorf [A] 74 D3
Pärnu [EST] 230 D3
Pärnu–Jaagupi [EST] 230 D3
Parola [FIN] 200 C2
Páros [GR] 168 D4
Paroveia [LT] 236 B4
Parpan [CH] 116 E1
Parsberg [D] 58 F4
Partakko [FIN] 226 E2
Partakoski [FIN] 200 C1
Partanna [I] 140 B2
Partenen [A] 116 F1
Parthenay [F] 66 D3
Parthéni [GR] 170 B4
Parthéni [GR] 172 D2
Partille [S] 184 A1
Partinello [F] 130 A2
Partinico [I] 140 B2
Partizani [SRB] 146 E3
Partizánske [SK] 74 F2
Partizanske Vode [SRB] 146 D4
Partry [IRL] 12 B3
Pårup [DK] 178 B1
Parychy [BY] 242 C2
Påryd [S] 184 E4
Pasaia [E] 86 F3
Pasaköy (Asha) [CY] 176 E3
Pas Limáni [GR] 168 E2
Paşayiğit [TR] 158 A4
Paşcani [RO] 244 E3
Pas de la Casa [AND] 96 D1
Paseęk [PL] 36 E2
Pas–en–Artois [F] 40 B4
Pasewalk [D] 34 D3
Pasha Liman [AL] 160 A3
Pasi [FIN] 200 C2
Pasiecznik [PL] 60 F1
Pasiene [LV] 236 E3
Pasjak [HR] 118 F4
Pasjane [KS] 154 D2
Påskallavik [S] 184 E3
Pasmajärvi [FIN] 222 B2
Pašman [HR] 144 C3
Paspolo [TR] 158 C2
Passage East [IRL] 10 E4
Passage West [IRL] 10 C4
Passandra [TR] 164 B3
Passau [D] 72 F2
Passignano sul Trasimeno [I] 130 F1
Passow [D] 34 D4
Pasta Monte Granata [I] 134 E2
Pastavy [BY] 238 F2
Pastena, Grotte di– [I] 134 B2
Pastor [E] 82 C2
Pastoriza [E] 82 D2
Pastrana [E] 94 A4
Păstrovo [BG] 156 E1
Pasvalys [LT] 236 B4
Pašvitinys [LT] 234 F4
Pasym [PL] 36 F3
Pásztó [H] 76 B3
Pasztowa Wola [PL] 50 A4
Patana [FIN] 208 D1
Patara [TR] 176 E2
Patavesi [FIN] 198 F1
Patay [F] 68 B1
Paterek [PL] 36 B4
Patergassen [A] 118 F2
Paterna [E] 102 D3
Paterna del Madera [E] 100 F4
Paterna de Rivera [E] 104 B3
Paternion [A] 118 E2
Paternò [I] 140 E2
Paternopoli [I] 134 D3

Patersdorf [D] 72 E1
Patio [RUS] 200 C3
Patiópoulo [GR] 166 C2
Patitiri [GR] 162 C4
Pátka [H] 76 A4
Patlangıç [TR] 170 F4
Pátmos [GR] 168 F3
Pątnów [PL] 48 C4
Pato [FIN] 198 C2
Patog [AL] 154 A4
Patosi [AL] 160 A2
Pátra [GR] 166 D4
Patreksfjörður [IS] 218 A1
Patrickswell [IRL] 10 C2
Patrikka [FIN] 210 F2
Patsch [A] 72 C4
Pattada [I] 142 C3
Pattensen [D] 44 B2
Patterdale [GB] 20 D3
Patti [I] 138 C3
Pattijoki [FIN] 216 A2
Pătulele [RO] 148 C2
Páty [H] 76 A4
Pau [F] 88 C3
Pauillac [F] 78 B3
Paukarlahti [FIN] 210 C2
Paularo [I] 118 E2
Paulhaguet [F] 80 B3
Paulilatino [I] 142 B4
Paulinzella [D] 58 E1
Pāuliş [RO] 122 E3
Pauliström [S] 184 D2
Pauls–Kirche [D] 56 E2
Paulstown [IRL] 10 E3
Paulx [F] 66 C3
Paupys [LT] 238 C2
Pausa [D] 60 B2
Pausin [D] 44 F1
Pauträsk [S] 214 B2
Påvalsby [FIN] 198 D4
Pavel [BG] 150 B3
Pavel Banya [BG] 156 D1
Pavia [I] 116 E4
Pavia [P] 90 C4
Pavia, Certosa di– [I] 116 E4
Pavilly [F] 54 D2
Pavilosta [LV] 234 D3
Pávliani [GR] 166 E3
Pavlice [CZ] 74 C1
Pavlikeni [BG] 150 B3
Pavlivka [UA] 64 F1
Pávlos [GR] 166 F3
Pavlovsk [RUS] 200 F4
Pavullo nel Frignano [I] 128 B2
Pavy [RUS] 232 F3
Pawłowiczki [PL] 62 D2
Pawłowo [PL] 36 B4
Pawłowo [PL] 36 B3
Pawonków [PL] 62 D2
Payerne [CH] 70 C4
Paymogo [E] 98 D3
Payrac [F] 78 E4
Pazardzhik [BG] 156 C2
Pazarić [BIH] 146 B4
Pazarköy [TR] 164 A2
Pazarköy [TR] 164 C2
Pazin [HR] 144 A1
Pazo de Oca [E] 82 B2
P. Cachorro [P] 110 A3
Pchelarovo [BG] 156 D2
Pchelino [RUS] 200 E2
Pchelnik [BG] 150 E3
Pcim [PL] 62 A3
Pčinja [MK] 154 D3
Peal de Becerro [E] 106 B2
Peáule [F] 66 B1
Péc / Peje [KS] 154 B2
Pećane [HR] 144 D2
Peccioli [I] 128 B4
Pečenjevce [SRB] 148 B4
Pechina [E] 106 B3

Pech–Merle, Grotte du– [F] 88 F1
Pecica [RO] 122 E3
Pecineaga [RO] 150 F2
Peciu Nou [RO] 122 E4
Pecka [SRB] 146 C3
Peckelsheim [D] 42 F3
Pecorini a Mare [I] 138 B3
Pečŏry [RUS] 232 D3
Pec pod Sněžkou [CZ] 60 F2
Pécs [H] 122 A3
Pécsvárad [H] 122 A3
Pedagaggi [I] 140 E3
Pedaso [I] 132 E2
Pederobba [I] 118 C3
Pedersker [DK] 180 E3
Pedersöre / Pedersören k [FIN] 208 C1
Pedersören k / Pedersöre [FIN] 208 C1
Pédi [GR] 176 B1
Pedoulás [CY] 176 D3
Pedrafita do Cebreiro, Puerto– [E] 82 D3
Pedralba [E] 102 D3
Pedraza [E] 92 E3
Pedreguer [E] 108 C2
Pedreira [E] 82 C2
Pedrera [E] 100 C2
Pedrera [E] 104 D2
Pedrizas, Puerto de las– [E] 104 D3
Pedro Abad [E] 104 E1
Pedro Andrés [E] 106 C1
Pedro Bernardo [E] 92 C4
Pedroche [E] 100 C3
Pedrógão [P] 90 C2
Pedrógão [P] 98 D2
Pedro Martínez [E] 106 A2
Pedro Muñoz [E] 100 F2
Pedrosillo el Ralo [E] 84 E4
Pocblcs [GB] 20 D1
Peel [GBM] 20 B3
Peenemünde [D] 34 C2
Peera [FIN] 224 E3
Péfkos [GR] 160 C3
Péfkos [GR] 174 D4
Pega [P] 90 E2
Pegau [D] 44 E4
Pégeia [CY] 176 C4
Peggau [A] 120 C1
Pegli [I] 126 E2
Pegnitz [D] 58 F3
Pego [E] 108 C1
Pegões [P] 90 B4
Peguera [E] 108 C3
Peguerinos [E] 92 E3
Pehčevo [MK] 154 F3
Peheim [D] 30 E3
Pehlivanköy [TR] 158 B3
Peine [D] 44 C2
Peipohja [FIN] 198 C2
Peippu [FIN] 208 B4
Peira–Cava [F] 126 C3
Peiraiás [GR] 168 B2
Peiss [D] 72 C2
Peissenberg [D] 72 C3
Peiting [D] 72 B3
Peitz [D] 46 C3
Peje / Péc [KS] 154 B2
Pejo [I] 118 B2
Pekkala [FIN] 222 D3
Pelagićevo [BIH] 146 B2
Pelasgía [GR] 162 B4
Pelatíkovo [BG] 154 F3
Pełczyce [PL] 34 E4
Pełczyn [PL] 46 F3
Pelejaneta / La Pelechaneta [E] 102 E2
Pélekas [GR] 160 B4
Peleshi [RUS] 232 E2
Peletá [GR] 172 E3

Pelhřimov [CZ] 60 E4
Peliciego, Cueva de– [E]
  106 E1
Peligros [E] 104 F3
Pelince [MK] 154 D3
Pelkosenniemi [FIN] 222 D2
Pélla [GR] 160 E2
Péllaro [I] 138 D4
Pellegrino Parmense [I]
  128 A2
Pellegrue [F] 78 C4
Pellérd [H] 120 F3
Pellesmäki [FIN] 210 C2
Pellevoisin [F] 68 A3
Pellinge / Pellinki [FIN] 200 B3
Pellinki / Pellinge [FIN] 200 B3
Pello [FIN] 222 B2
Pello [S] 222 B2
Pellosniemi [FIN] 200 C1
Polovo [BG] 148 E3
Pelplin [PL] 36 C2
Pelt [FIN] 226 B3
Peltosalmi [FIN] 210 B1
Pélussin [F] 80 D3
Pély [H] 76 C4
Pemaninos [TR] 164 D2
Pemar / Paimio [FIN] 198 D3
Pembroke [GB] 26 C1
Pembroke Dock [GB] 26 C1
Peñacerrada [E] 86 E4
Penacova [P] 84 A4
Peña Escrita, Cuevas de– [E]
  100 C4
Peñafiel [E] 92 E2
Peñafiel [P] 84 B2
Peñaflor [E] 104 D1
Penaguião [P] 84 B3
Peñalén [E] 94 B4
Peñalsordo [E] 100 B3
Penalva do Castelo [P] 84 B4
Penamacor [P] 90 C2
Peñaranda de Bracamonte
  [E] 84 F4
Peñaranda de Duero [E] 92 F2
Peñarroya, Castillo de– [E]
  100 E3
Peñarroya de Tastavins [E]
  96 A4
Peñarroya–Pueblonuevo [E]
  100 B3
Penarth [GB] 26 E2
Peñascosa [E] 100 F4
Peñas de San Pedro [E]
  102 A4
Peñausende [E] 84 E3
Penc [H] 76 B3
Pendik [TR] 158 E3
Pendine [GB] 26 C1
Pendus, Rocher des– [F] 80 A3
Penedono [P] 84 C3
Penela [P] 90 C2
Penestin [F] 66 B1
Penészlek [H] 76 F3
Peniche [P] 90 B2
Penicuik [GB] 18 D4
Penig [D] 44 F4
Peníscola / Peñíscola [E]
  102 F2
Peñíscola / Peníscola [E]
  102 F2
Penkum [D] 34 D3
Penmarch, Pointe de– [F]
  52 A4
Pennabilli [I] 128 D3
Pennala [FIN] 200 A2
Penne [I] 132 E3
Penne [N] 186 B4
Penningby [S] 190 E2
Peno [RUS] 240 D3
Penrith [GB] 20 D3
Penryn [GB] 26 B4
Pensala [FIN] 208 C1

Pentagioí [GR] 166 D3
Pentálofo [GR] 160 D3
Pentálofo [GR] 166 C3
Pénte Vrýses [GR] 162 B1
Pentrez–Plage [F] 52 B3
Penyige [H] 76 F3
Penzance [GB] 26 A3
Penzberg [D] 72 C3
Penzlin [D] 32 F3
Pepelow [D] 32 E2
Pępowo [PL] 46 F3
Peqin [AL] 160 B2
Pér [H] 74 F4
Perachóra [GR] 166 F4
Péra Choríon [CY] 176 D3
Perafita [P] 84 A2
Perä–Hyyppä [FIN] 208 C3
Peraía [GR] 160 F2
Perälä [FIN] 208 B3
Peraleda del Zaucejo [E]
  100 B3
Peralejos [E] 102 D1
Peralejos de las Truchas
  [E] 94 B4
Perales del Alfambra [E]
  102 D1
Perales de Tajuña [E] 100 F1
Peralta [E] 94 C1
Peralva [P] 98 C4
Pérama [GR] 160 C4
Pérama [GR] 174 C3
Peranka [FIN] 216 D1
Peränkylä [FIN] 198 C1
Peränne [FIN] 208 D3
Perä–Posio [FIN] 222 E3
Peräseinäjoki [FIN] 208 D3
Perast [MNE] 152 E3
Perchauer Sattel [A] 120 A1
Perchtoldsdorf [A] 74 D3
Percy [F] 52 F3
Perdasdefogu [I] 142 C4
Perdifumo [I] 136 A3
Perdigão [P] 90 D2
Perdíguera [E] 94 E3
Pérdika [GR] 166 B2
Pérdika [GR] 166 C1
Pérdika [GR] 168 A3
Perechyn [UA] 76 F1
Pereda de Ancares [E] 82 D3
Père de Montfort, Grotte du–
  [F] 66 D3
Peredo [P] 84 D3
Pereiaslav–Khmel'nyts'kyi
  [UA] 242 E4
Pereiro [P] 98 C3
Peremozhne [UA] 64 F3
Peremyshl' [RUS] 240 F4
Pereruela [E] 84 E3
Pereslavl'–Zalesskiy [RUS]
  240 F2
Pereta [I] 130 E2
Peretu [RO] 150 A2
Perevolok [RUS] 230 F2
Perfugas [I] 142 B2
Perg [A] 74 B2
Pergamos (Beyarmudu) [CY]
  176 E3
Pérgine Valsugana [I] 118 B3
Pergola [I] 128 C2
Perho [FIN] 208 E1
Periam [RO] 122 D3
Periana [E] 104 E3
Périers [F] 52 E2
Pérignác [F] 78 E3
Périgueux [F] 78 D3
Perii Broşteni [RO] 150 A2
Periš [SRB] 148 C3
Perisgrund [FIN] 208 B2
Perişoru [RO] 148 D2
Perişoru [RO] 150 D1
Períssa [GR] 174 D2
Peristerá [GR] 162 B1

Peristeróna [CY] 176 D3
Perivóli [GR] 160 D3
Perjasica [HR] 144 C1
Perjen Tunnel [A] 72 B4
Perkáta [H] 122 B1
Perkpolder [NL] 40 D2
Perle [LV] 236 C2
Perleberg [D] 32 E4
Perles'e [RUS] 200 E4
Perlez [SRB] 146 D1
Perly [PL] 38 A1
Përmet [AL] 160 C3
Pernå / Pernaja [FIN] 200 B3
Pernaa [FIN] 208 C2
Pernacha de Cima [P] 90 C3
Pernaja / Pernå [FIN] 200 B3
Pernat [HR] 144 B2
Pernek [SK] 74 E2
Pernes [P] 90 C3
Pernes–les–Fontaines [F]
  124 E2
Pernik [BG] 154 F2
Pernink [CZ] 60 B2
Perniö / Bjärnå [FIN] 198 D3
Pernitz [A] 74 C3
Pernštejn [CZ] 62 B4
Pernu [FIN] 222 D3
Pérolles, Pont de– [CH]
  116 B1
Peron [F] 80 F2
Péronne [F] 54 F1
Perosa Argentina [I] 116 B4
Pérouges [F] 80 E2
Perpignan [F] 96 E1
Perrero [I] 116 B4
Perros–Guirec [F] 52 C2
Persberg [S] 188 E1
Persenbeug [A] 74 B3
Pershagen [S] 190 D3
Perskogen [N] 224 E3
Persön [S] 214 E1
Perstorp [S] 180 C1
Perstorp [S] 206 E2
Perth [GB] 18 D3
Pertisau [A] 72 C4
Pertočа [SLO] 120 C2
Pertosa, Grotta di– [I] 134 E4
Pertoúli [GR] 160 D4
Perttaus [FIN] 222 C2
Pertteli [FIN] 198 D3
Pertuis [F] 124 F3
Pertunmaa [FIN] 200 B1
Pertusa [E] 94 F2
Peruc [CZ] 60 D2
Perúgia [I] 132 C2
Perunika [BG] 156 E3
Perushtica [BG] 156 D2
Peršić [HR] 144 C2
Péruwelz [B] 40 C4
Pervomais'k [UA] 246 D2
Pervomais'ke [UA] 246 F3
Pervomayskoye [RUS] 200 E3
Perwez [B] 40 E4
Pesac [RO] 122 D3
Pesadas de Burgos [E] 86 C3
Pesados [TR] 170 C4
Pesaguero [E] 86 B2
Pésaro [I] 128 E3
Pescaglia [I] 128 B3
Pescara [I] 132 F3
Pescasseroli [I] 132 E4
Péschici [I] 134 F1
Peschiera [I] 136 C3
Peschiera del Garda [I] 118 B4
Péscia [I] 128 B3
Pescina [I] 132 E4
Pescocostanzo [I] 132 E4
Pescolanciano [I] 134 C2
Pescopagano [I] 134 E3
Pescorocchiano [I] 132 D3
Peshkëpija [AL] 160 A3
Peshkopi [AL] 154 B4

Peshtera [BG] 156 C2
Pesio, Certosa di– [I] 126 C2
Peski [RUS] 200 E3
Pesmes [F] 70 A3
Pesnica pri Mariboru [SLO]
  120 C2
Pesočani [MK] 160 C1
Pesochnyy [RUS] 200 F3
Peso da Régua [P] 84 B3
Pesoz [E] 82 D2
Pesquera del Duero [E] 92 E2
Pesqueza [E] 90 F3
Pessáni [GR] 156 F3
Pessin [D] 44 F1
Peštani [MK] 160 C2
Peşteana Jiu [RO] 148 D1
Peştera [RO] 150 E1
Pestovo [RUS] 240 D1
Pešurići [BIH] 146 C4
Petäiskylä [FIN] 216 E3
Petäjämäki [FIN] 210 C2
Petäjävesi [FIN] 208 E3
Petalídi [GR] 172 C3
Petaloúdes [GR] 176 C2
Pétange [L] 56 D3
Petehi [RH] 144 A1
Peteranec [HR] 120 E3
Peterborough [GB] 28 D1
Peterlee [GB] 20 F3
Petersburg [A] 72 B4
Petersdorf [D] 32 D1
Petersfield [GB] 28 B3
Petershagen [D] 42 F1
Petershagen [D] 46 C2
Petershausen [D] 72 C2
Pétervására [H] 76 C3
Pethelinós [GR] 156 C4
Pétifürdő [H] 120 F1
Petikträsk [S] 214 C2
Petilia Policastro [I] 138 E2
Petino [RUS] 238 A3
Petko Karavelov [BG] 150 B3
Petko Slaveykov [BG] 150 A4
Petkula [FIN] 222 C1
Petkus [D] 46 B2
Petlovac [RH] 122 A3
Petlovača [SRB] 146 C2
Petőháza [H] 74 D4
Petoúsi [GR] 166 B1
Petra [E] 108 D3
Pétra [GR] 160 E3
Pétra [GR] 164 A3
Petra [RO] 148 D2
Petralia Soprana [I] 138 A4
Petrálona [GR] 162 B2
Petraná [GR] 160 E3
Petrelë [AL] 160 B1
Petrella Tifernina [I] 134 D2
Petrelle [I] 130 F1
Petrer [E] 106 E1
Petreşti [RO] 76 F3
Petreşti [RO] 150 A1
Petreto–Bicchisano [F] 130 A3
Petrich [BG] 156 B3
Petrich [BG] 156 C1
Petrikov [BY] 242 C3
Petrila [RO] 248 C3
Petrina [SLO] 120 B4
Petrinja [HR] 120 D4
Petrodvorets [RUS] 200 F3
Petrohan [BG] 148 D4
Pétrola [E] 102 B4
Petromäki [FIN] 210 C2
Petronell–Carnuntum [A]
  74 D3
Petroşani [RO] 248 C3
Petrosino [I] 140 A2
Petrotá [GR] 156 F2
Petroússa [GR] 156 C4
Petrovac [MNE] 152 E3
Petrovac [SRB] 146 F2

Petrovaradin [SRB]
  146 D1
Petrove [UA] 246 E2
Petrovice [CZ] 60 C4
Petrovice [CZ] 60 D3
Petrovići [BIH] 144 F4
Petrovo [BG] 156 B3
Petřvald [CZ] 62 D3
Petrykaw [RUS] 242 C3
Petrykivka [RUS] 246 E1
Petsákoi [GR] 166 E4
Petsikko [FIN] 226 D1
Pettenbach [A] 72 F3
Pettigo [NIR] 12 D2
Pettneu am A. [A] 72 B4
Peuerbach [A] 72 F2
Peura [FIN] 222 C3
Peurajärvi [FIN] 216 E3
Peurasuvanto [FIN] 226 D4
Pevensey [GB] 28 D4
Peveragno [I] 126 C2
Peypin [F] 124 F3
Peyragudes [F] 88 D4
Peyrat–le–Chateaux [F] 78 F2
Peyrehorade [F] 88 B2
Peyriac–Minervois [F] 124 B3
Peyrolles [F] 124 F3
Peyruis [F] 126 A2
Peyrusse–le–Roc [F] 124 A1
Pézenas [F] 124 C3
Pezinok [SK] 74 E2
Pezoúla [GR] 156 D4
Pezovo [MK] 154 D3
Pezuela de las Torres [E] 92 F4
Pfaffendorf [D] 58 E2
Pfaffenhofen [D] 72 C2
Pfaffen–hoffen [F] 56 F4
Pfäffikon [CH] 70 E4
Pfäffikon [CH] 70 E4
Pfafflar [A] 72 B4
Pfalzfeld [D] 56 F2
Pfalzgrafen Weiler [D] 70 E2
Pfänder Tunnel [A] 72 A3
Pfarrkirchen [D] 72 E2
Pfatter [D] 72 D1
Pfeffenhausen [D] 72 D2
Pforzheim [D] 58 B4
Pfreimd [D] 60 B3
Pfronten [D] 72 B2
Pfullendorf [D] 70 F3
Pfullingen [D] 70 F2
Pfundres / Fundres [I] 118 C1
Pfunds [A] 118 B1
Pfungstadt [D] 58 B3
P. Gynaikókastro [GR] 156 A4
Phalsbourg [F] 56 E4
Phaselis [TR] 176 F1
Phellos [TR] 176 E1
Philippeville [B] 56 C1
Philippsreut [D] 72 F1
Philippsthal [D] 44 B4
Phokaia [TR] 164 B4
Phönike [AL] 160 B4
Piacenza [I] 128 A1
Piádena [I] 118 A4
Piaggine [I] 134 E4
Piana [F] 130 A2
Piana Crixia [I] 126 D2
Piana degli Albanesi [I] 140 C2
Pian Castagna [I] 126 E2
Piancavallo [I] 118 D3
Pian d'Alma [I] 130 D2
Piàn di Scò [I] 128 C4
Pianella [I] 128 C4
Pianello Val Tidone [I] 126 F1
Pianiccia [I] 130 B3
Piani Resinelli [I] 116 E3
Pianoro [I] 128 C2
Pianotolli–Caldarello [F]
  130 B4
Pias [P] 98 D2
Pias [P] 98 D3

Piasecznik [PL] 34 E4
Piaseczno [PL] 34 D4
Piaseczno [PL] 48 F2
Piaski [PL] 46 F3
Piaski [PL] 50 C3
Piastów [PL] 48 F2
Piaszczyna [PL] 36 B2
Piątek [PL] 48 D2
Piatra [RO] 150 A2
Piatra Neamţ [RO] 244 E3
Piatra Olt [RO] 148 E2
Piazza al Serchio [I] 128 B3
Piazza Armerina [I] 140 D3
Piazza Brembana [I] 116 E3
Piazzatorre [I] 116 E3
Piazzola sul Brenta [I] 118 C4
Pićan [HR] 144 A1
Picassent [E] 102 D3
Picerno [I] 134 E4
Pichoux, Gorges de– [CH] 70 D4
Pickering [GB] 24 D1
Pico [I] 134 B2
Picquigny [F] 54 E1
Pidna [GR] 160 F3
Piechowice [PL] 60 F1
Piecki [PL] 38 A2
Piedade, Ponta da– [P] 98 B4
Piedicavallo [I] 116 C3
Piedicroce [F] 130 B2
Piediluco [I] 132 D3
Piedimonte Etneo [I] 138 C4
Piedimonte Matese [I] 134 C2
Piedimulera [I] 116 D2
Piedra, Monasteiro de– [E] 94 C3
Piedrabuena [E] 90 E3
Piedrabuena [E] 100 D3
Piedrafita de Babia [E] 82 E3
Piedrahita [E] 92 C3
Piedralaves [E] 92 D4
Piedras Albas [E] 90 E3
Piekary Śląskie [PL] 62 E2
Piekło [PL] 36 D2
Pieksämäki [FIN] 210 C3
Pielavesi [FIN] 210 B1
Pieniężno [PL] 36 E2
Piennes [F] 56 D3
Pieńsk [PL] 46 D4
Pienza [I] 130 E1
Pierre–Buffière [F] 78 E2
Pierre–de–Bresse [F] 68 F4
Pierrefitte–Nestalas [F] 88 C3
Pierrefitte–sur–Aire [F] 56 C4
Pierrefonds [F] 54 E2
Pierrefort [F] 80 A3
Pierrefort, Château de– [F] 56 D4
Pierrelatte [F] 124 E2
Pierroton [F] 78 B3
Piertinjaure [S] 220 D3
Piesalankylä [FIN] 208 E3
Pieski [PL] 46 D2
Pieskowa Skala [PL] 62 F2
Piessling Urspr. [A] 74 A3
Piešťany [SK] 74 F2
Pieszyce [PL] 62 B2
Pietarsaari / Jakobstad [FIN] 214 F4
Pietra Bismantova [I] 128 B2
Pietragalla [I] 134 F4
Pietralba [F] 130 B2
Pietra Ligure [I] 126 D2
Pietralunga [I] 128 D4
Pietramelara [I] 134 C3
Pietraperzia [I] 140 D3
Pietrasanta [I] 128 B3
Pietravairano [I] 134 C2
Pietreni [RO] 150 E1
Pietroşani [RO] 150 B2
Pietrowice [PL] 62 C3
Pietrzwałd [PL] 36 E3

Pieve di Bono [I] 118 B3
Pieve di Cadore [I] 118 D2
Pieve di Teco [I] 126 D3
Pievepelago [I] 128 B3
Pieve Santo Stéfano [I] 128 D4
Pievescola [I] 128 C4
Pieve S. Giacomo [I] 116 F4
Pigádi [GR] 162 B4
Pigés [GR] 166 C2
Pigí [GR] 166 D3
Píglio [I] 132 D4
Pigna [I] 126 C3
Pignola [I] 134 E4
Pihkainmäki [FIN] 210 C2
Pihkala [FIN] 216 B3
Pihlajalahti [FIN] 208 D4
Pihlajalahti [FIN] 210 D4
Pihlajavaara [FIN] 210 F1
Pihlajaveden as. [FIN] 208 E3
Pihlava [FIN] 198 C1
Pihtipudas [FIN] 208 F1
Piikkiö / Pikis [FIN] 198 D3
Piipola [FIN] 216 B3
Piippaharju [FIN] 210 B3
Piispa [FIN] 210 D1
Piispala [FIN] 208 E2
Pikasilla [EST] 230 E3
Pikis / Piikkiö [FIN] 198 D3
Pikšas [LV] 234 E3
Piła [I] 116 B3
Piła [I] 128 E1
Piła [PL] 36 A4
Pilar de la Horadada [E] 106 E2
Pilar de la Mola [E] 108 E2
Pilas [E] 104 B1
Pilastri [I] 128 C1
Pilastro [I] 128 B2
Pilat, Dune de– [F] 78 A3
Pilat–Plage [F] 78 A3
Pileta, Cueva de la– [E] 104 C3
Pilgrimstad [S] 204 F3
Pilica [PL] 62 F2
Pílio [GR] 168 A1
Pilis [H] 76 B4
Piliscsaba [H] 76 A4
Pilisvörösvár [H] 76 B4
Piliuona [LT] 238 D3
Pilpala [FIN] 198 E3
Pilsrundāle [LV] 234 F4
Pilštanj [SLO] 120 C3
Piltene [LV] 234 D3
Pilträsk [S] 214 D1
Pilu [RO] 122 E2
Pilviškiai [LT] 238 C3
Pilzno [PL] 64 C3
Pina de Ebro [E] 94 E3
Piñar [E] 104 F2
Pınara [TR] 176 E1
Pinarejos [E] 92 E2
Pinarello [F] 130 B3
Pınarhisar [TR] 158 C2
Pınarköy [TR] 170 C4
Pince [SLO] 120 D2
Pincehely [H] 122 A2
Pińczów [PL] 64 B2
Pindal, Cueva del– [E] 86 C2
Pineda de la Sierta [E] 94 A1
Pineda de Mar [E] 96 E3
Pinerolo [I] 126 C1
Pineto [I] 132 E3
Piney [F] 68 E1
Pinhal Novo [P] 90 B4
Pinhão [E] 84 C3
Pinhel [P] 84 C4
Pinkafeld [A] 74 C4
Pinneberg [D] 32 B2
Pino [E] 82 F3
Pino [F] 130 B1
Pino do Val [E] 82 B2
Pinofranqueado [E] 90 F2
Pinols [F] 80 B3

Piñor [E] 82 C3
Pinoso / el Pinós [E] 106 E1
Pinos Puente [E] 104 F2
Pinsk [BY] 242 B3
Pinsoro [E] 88 A4
Pinto [E] 92 E4
Pinzio [P] 84 C4
Pinzolo [I] 118 B3
Pióbbico [I] 128 E4
Piombino [I] 130 D1
Piona, Abbazia di– [I] 116 E2
Pionki [PL] 50 A3
Pionsat [F] 80 B1
Pióraco [I] 132 D2
Piorunkowice [PL] 62 C2
Piossasco [I] 116 B4
Piotrków [PL] 50 C4
Piotrkowice [PL] 46 F3
Piotrkowice [PL] 64 B2
Piotrków Kujawski [PL] 48 C2
Piotrków Trybunalski [PL] 48 D3
Piotrowice [PL] 48 F2
Piotrowo [PL] 46 E1
Piotta [CH] 116 D2
Piove di Sacco [I] 118 C4
Piovene–Rocchette [I] 118 C3
Pipriac [F] 66 C1
Piqeras [AL] 160 B3
Piqueras, Puerto de– [E] 94 B1
Piran [SLO] 118 E4
Piras [I] 142 C3
Pirčiupiai [LT] 238 E4
Pirdop [BG] 156 C1
Pirgovo [BG] 150 B2
Piriac–sur–Mer [F] 66 B2
Piriatin [UA] 242 E4
Pirin [BG] 156 B3
Pirkkala / Birkala [FIN] 198 D1
Pirlibey [TR] 170 D3
Pirîtijärvi [FIN] 208 B4
Pirmasens [D] 56 F3
Pirna [D] 46 B4
Pirnesperä [FIN] 216 B3
Pirok [MK] 154 C3
Pirot [SRB] 148 C4
Pirou–Plage [F] 52 E2
Pirovac [HR] 144 C1
Pirtó [H] 122 C2
Piteşti [RO] 248 D3
Pithiviers [F] 68 C1
Pitigliano [I] 130 E2
Pitkäjärvi [FIN] 198 D3

Pitkälahti [FIN] 210 C2
Pitlochry [GB] 18 D2
Pitomača [HR] 120 E3
Pitsiäna [GR] 166 C2
Pitvaros [H] 122 D2
Pivka [SLO] 118 F4
Pivnica [HR] 120 E4
Pivski Manastir [MNE] 152 E2
Piwniczna [PL] 64 B4
Pizarra [E] 104 D3
Pizhma [RUS] 200 F4
Pizzighettone [I] 116 E4
Pizzo [I] 138 D2
Pizzoli [I] 132 D3
Pjatihatki [UA] 246 E1
Pjätteryd [S] 184 C3
Plabennec [F] 52 B2
Placis [LV] 236 B2
Plage de Pineto [F] 130 B2
Plagiá [GR] 156 A4
Plagiá [GR] 156 E3
Plaigne [F] 88 F3
Plaisance [F] 78 D4
Plaisance [F] 88 D2
Pláka [GR] 162 E2
Plakia [GR] 164 D1
Plakiás [GR] 174 C4
Plana [BIH] 152 D2
Planá [CZ] 60 B3
Planá nad Lužnicí [CZ] 60 E4
Plancios [I] 118 C2
Plancoët [F] 52 D3
Plandište [SRB] 146 E1
Plan d'Orgon [F] 124 E3
Plan–du–Lac [F] 116 B2
Plánice [CZ] 60 C4
Planina [SLO] 120 A3
Planina pri Sevnici [SLO] 120 C3
Planinica [SRB] 148 C3
Planjane [HR] 144 D4
Plankenburk [CZ] 62 B3
Plankenstein [A] 74 B3
Planoles [E] 96 D2
Plansee [A] 72 B4
Plasencia [E] 92 B4
Plasencia de Jalón [E] 94 D2
Plasencia del Monte [E] 94 E2
Plaški [HR] 144 C1
Plassen [N] 194 D2
Plassenburg [D] 58 F2
Plášťovce [SK] 76 B3
Plasy [CZ] 60 C3
Plataiés [GR] 168 A2
Platamona Lido [I] 142 B2
Platamónas [GR] 156 D4
Platamónas [GR] 160 F3
Platanákia [GR] 156 A4
Platanés [GR] 174 C3
Plataniá [GR] 162 B4
Platánia [GR] 172 C2
Plataniás [GR] 174 B3
Platanistós [GR] 168 C2
Plátanos [GR] 172 C2
Plátanos [GR] 172 E2
Plátanos [GR] 174 A3
Platariá [GR] 166 B2
Platerów [PL] 50 C2
Pláti [GR] 156 F3
Plati [I] 138 D3
Platiána [GR] 172 C2
Platíčevo [SRB] 146 D2
Platja d'Aro [E] 96 E3
Platja des Canar [E] 108 F2
Plátsa [GR] 172 D3
Platta [CH] 116 E1
Plattling [D] 72 E2
Platygyáli [GR] 166 C3
Platýkampos [GR] 160 F4
Platýs Gialós [GR] 168 C4
Platys Gialós [GR] 168 D3
Platýstomo [GR] 166 E2

Plau [D] 32 E3
Plaue [D] 44 E2
Plauen [D] 60 B2
Plav [MNE] 154 B2
Plava [KS] 154 C3
Plavas [LV] 234 E3
Plave [SLO] 118 E3
Plavecký Hrad [SK] 74 E2
Plavecký Mikuláš [SK] 74 E2
Plavinas [LV] 236 C3
Plavna [SRB] 148 C2
Pławna [PL] 46 D4
Playa Blanca [E] 114 E3
Playa de Las Américas [E] 112 C3
Playa del Inglés [C] 112 C4
Playa de San Juán [E] 106 F2
Płazów [PL] 64 E2
Pleaux [F] 78 F3
Plech [D] 58 F3
Plecka Dąbrowa [PL] 48 D2
Pleinfeld [D] 58 E4
Plélan–le–Grand [F] 52 D4
Plémet [F] 52 D3
Pleniţa [RO] 148 D2
Plentzia [E] 86 E2
Plépi [GR] 168 A3
Pleshchanitsy [RUS] 242 B1
Plešivec [SK] 76 C2
Pleşoiu [RO] 148 E1
Plesse [F] 66 C2
Plessenburg [D] 44 C3
Plessis–Bourré, Château du– [F] 66 D2
Plestin–les–Grèves [F] 52 C2
Pleszew [PL] 48 B3
Pleternica [HR] 146 A1
Plettenberg [D] 42 E3
Pleumartin [F] 66 F4
Pleven [BG] 148 F3
Plevna [RO] 150 D1
Pleyben [F] 52 B3
Pliego [E] 106 D2
Pliešovce [SK] 76 B2
Plikáti [GR] 160 C3
Plina Jezero [HR] 152 C2
Pliska [BG] 150 D2
Plitvice [HR] 144 D2
Plitvički Ljeskovac [HR] 144 C2
Pljevlja [MNE] 152 F1
Pllake [AL] 160 B4
Ploaghe [I] 142 B2
Ploča [SRB] 146 E4
Ploče [HR] 152 C2
Płochocin [PL] 48 E2
Płock [PL] 48 E2
Ploërmel [F] 52 D4
Ploieşti [RO] 248 E3
Plomári [GR] 164 B4
Plombières–les–Bains [F] 70 C2
Plomin [HR] 144 B1
Plön [D] 32 C2
Plonéour Lanvern [F] 52 B3
Płońsk [PL] 48 E1
Plopii Slăviteşti [RO] 148 F2
Plopşoru [RO] 148 D1
Płoskinia [PL] 36 E2
Plosky [BG] 156 B3
Ploştina [RO] 148 C1
Płotno [PL] 34 E4
Płoty [PL] 34 E3
Plouaret [F] 52 C2
Plouay [F] 52 C4
Ploubalay [F] 52 D3
Ploudalmézeau [F] 52 A2
Plouescat [F] 52 B2
Plougasnou [F] 52 C2
Plougastel–Daoulas [F] 52 B3
Plougonven [F] 52 B3
Plouguenast [F] 52 D3

Plouguerneau [F] 52 B2
Plouha [F] 52 C3
Plouigneau [F] 52 B3
Ploumanac'h [F] 52 C2
Plounévez–Quintin [F] 52 C3
Plouray [F] 52 C3
Plovdiv [BG] 156 D2
Plozévet [F] 52 A3
Plungė [LT] 238 B2
Pluty [PL] 36 E2
Pluviers [F] 78 D2
Pluvigner [F] 52 C4
Plužine [BIH] 152 D2
Plužine [MNE] 152 E2
Płużnica [PL] 36 D3
Plymouth [GB] 26 C4
Płytnica [PL] 36 A3
Plýtra [GR] 172 E3
Plyussa [RUS] 232 F2
Plzeň [CZ] 60 C3
Pnevo [RUS] 230 F3
Pniewo [PL] 38 A4
Pniewy [PL] 46 E2
Pobedino [RUS] 238 C3
Pobes [E] 86 D3
Pobiedziska [PL] 48 B2
Pobierowo [PL] 34 E2
Pobikry [PL] 38 C4
Pobiti Kamŭni [BG] 150 E3
Pobit Kamŭk [BG] 156 C2
Poblado Celtico [E] 82 E2
Poblado Iberico [E] 96 B3
Poblado Iberico [E] 96 E2
Pobladura de la Sierra [E] 82 E4
Pobladura del Valle [E] 84 F2
Poblet [E] 96 C3
Pobra do Caramiñal / Puebla del Caramiñal [E] 82 A2
Počátky [CZ] 60 E4
Poceirão [P] 90 B4
Pochep [RUS] 242 E2
Pochinok [RUS] 242 D1
Pöchlarn [A] 74 B3
Pocinho [P] 84 C3
Počitelj [BIH] 152 C2
Pocking [D] 72 E2
Pocklington [GB] 24 D2
Počkuny [PL] 38 C1
Poço do Inferno [P] 84 B4
Pocrnje [BIH] 152 D2
Pocsaj [H] 76 E4
Počuta [SRB] 146 D3
Poczesna [PL] 62 E2
Podari [RO] 148 E2
Podbanské [SK] 62 F4
Podberez'ye [RUS] 240 C2
Podbořany [CZ] 60 C2
Podborje [BIH] 144 F4
Podborov'ye [RUS] 232 E3
Podbožur [MNE] 152 E2
Podbrdo [SLO] 118 F3
Podbrezová [SK] 76 B2
Poddębice [PL] 48 C3
Poděbrady [CZ] 60 E3
Podelzig [D] 46 C2
Podem [BG] 148 F3
Podence [P] 84 D2
Podensac [F] 78 C4
Podersdorf am See [A] 74 D3
Podgaje [PL] 36 B3
Podgarić [HR] 120 D4
Podgora [HR] 152 C2
Podgorač [HR] 122 A4
Podgorac [SRB] 148 B2
Podgorica [MNE] 152 E3
Podgorie [AL] 160 C2
Podgornoye [RUS] 238 B3
Podgor'ye [RUS] 230 F3
Podgrad [SLO] 118 F4
Podgradec [AL] 160 C2
Podhorod' [SK] 76 F1

Podivín [CZ] 74 D2
Podklasztorze [PL] 48 E3
Podkoren [SLO] 118 F2
Podkova [BG] 156 E3
Podkrepa [BG] 156 E2
Podkriváň [SK] 76 B2
Podlehnik [SLO] 120 C3
Podljubelj [SLO] 120 A2
Podlugovi [BIH] 146 B3
Podnovlje [BIH] 146 A2
Podochóri [GR] 156 C4
Podogorá [GR] 166 C2
Podolesh'e [RUS] 232 D2
Podolínec [SK] 64 B4
Podol'sk [RUS] 240 F3
Podosoje [HR] 144 E3
Podrašnica [BIH] 144 E3
Podromanija [BIH] 146 B3
Podslon [BG] 156 E1
Podsreda [SLO] 120 C3
Podujevo [KS] 154 C2
Podunavci [SRB] 146 E4
Podvinje [HR] 146 A1
Podvolovljek [SLO] 120 B2
Podwilcze [PL] 34 F2
Podwilk [PL] 62 F3
Poeldijk [NL] 30 A4
Poetto [I] 142 C5
Poggendorf [D] 32 F2
Poggibonsi [I] 128 C4
Póggio Renatico [I] 128 C2
Póggio Rusco [I] 128 C1
Pöggstall [A] 74 B2
Pogonianí [GR] 160 C3
Pogorelka [RUS] 232 E4
Pogoritsa [BG] 150 C3
Pogórska Wola [PL] 64 B3
Pogórze [PL] 62 C2
Pogorzela [PL] 48 A3
Pogrodzie [PL] 36 D2
Pohja [FIN] 198 E1
Pohja / Pojo [FIN] 198 E4
Pohja–Lankila [FIN] 200 D1
Pohjankylä [FIN] 198 D3
Pohjansaha [FIN] 208 B4
Pohjaslahti [FIN] 208 E3
Pohjaslahti [FIN] 222 D3
Pohjoinen [FIN] 198 F2
Pohjoislahti [FIN] 208 E3
Pohjola [FIN] 200 B1
Pohorelá [SK] 76 C1
Pohořelice [CZ] 74 D1
Pohoří [A] 74 B2
Pohoskylä [FIN] 210 B3
Pohrebyshche [UA] 244 F1
Pohtola [FIN] 208 D4
Poiana Brașov [RO] 248 D3
Poiana Mare [RO] 148 D2
Poibrene [BG] 156 C1
Poijula [FIN] 216 C1
Poikelus [FIN] 208 D4
Poikko [FIN] 198 D4
Point [A] 74 B3
Pointe des Poulains [F] 66 A1
Point Sublime [F] 124 C1
Poirino [I] 126 D1
Poissons [F] 68 F1
Poitiers [F] 66 E4
Poix [F] 54 D2
Poix–Terron [F] 56 B2
Pojate [SRB] 146 F4
Pojejena [RO] 146 F2
Pojo / Pohja [FIN] 198 E4
Pókaszepetk [H] 120 E2
Pokka [FIN] 226 D3
Pokój [PL] 62 C1
Pokorská Ves [A] 74 B2
Pokupsko [HR] 120 C4
Pol [E] 82 D2
Polača [HR] 144 D3
Polače [HR] 152 C2

Pola de Allande [E] 82 E2
Pola de Laviana [E] 82 F3
Pola de Lena [E] 82 F3
Pola de Siero [E] 82 F2
Pola de Somiedo [E] 82 E3
Połajewo [PL] 46 F1
Polán [E] 100 D1
Polanica–Zdrój [PL] 62 B2
Połaniec [PL] 64 C2
Polanów [PL] 36 A2
Polatsk [BY] 240 B4
Polcenigo [I] 118 D3
Połczno [PL] 36 B2
Połczyn–Zdrój [PL] 34 F3
Pölde [EST] 230 B3
Polémi [CY] 176 C4
Polena [BG] 154 F3
Polepy [CZ] 60 D2
Polesella [I] 128 D1
Polessk [RUS] 238 A3
Polgár [H] 76 D3
Polgárdi [H] 122 A1
Poli [GR] 166 B3
Polianí [GR] 172 D3
Poliçan [AL] 160 B2
Poliçan [AL] 160 B3
Policastro Bussentino [I] 136 B3
Police [PL] 34 D3
Police nad Metují [CZ] 62 B2
Polička [CZ] 62 B3
Poličnik [HR] 144 C3
Policoro [I] 136 C3
Polida, Cova de na– [E] 108 F3
Polientes [E] 86 C3
Polignano [I] 128 B2
Polignano a Mare [I] 136 D2
Poligny [F] 70 A4
Polikrayshte [BG] 150 B3
Pólis [CY] 176 C3
Polistena [I] 138 D3
Polistílo [GR] 156 C4
Politiká [GR] 168 A1
Politikón [CY] 176 D3
Poljana [BG] 158 A1
Poljana [HR] 120 E4
Poljana [SRB] 146 F2
Poljanak [HR] 144 C2
Poljčane [SLO] 120 C3
Polje [BIH] 146 A2
Poljica [HR] 152 B2
Poljice [BIH] 144 E3
Polkowice [PL] 46 E3
Pölläkkä [FIN] 210 B3
Pölläkkä [FIN] 210 D3
Pöllau [A] 74 C4
Polle [D] 44 B2
Pollença [E] 108 D3
Pollentia [E] 108 D3
Pollfoss [N] 202 D4
Polmak [N] 228 D3
Polná [CZ] 60 F4
Polomka [SK] 76 C1
Polop [E] 108 C2
Pološko [MK] 160 E1
Polska Cerekiew [PL] 62 D2
Polski Gradets [BG] 156 F2
Polski Trŭmbesh [BG] 150 B3
Polsko Kosovo [BG] 150 B3
Polso [FIN] 208 E1
Poltár [SK] 76 C2
Poltava [UA] 242 F4
Põltsamaa [EST] 230 D2
Polusperä [FIN] 216 A3
Põlva [EST] 230 F3
Polvela [FIN] 210 D1
Polvijärvi [FIN] 210 D2
Polyany [RUS] 200 E3
Polýchnitos [GR] 164 A4
Polýgyros [GR] 162 B2
Polykárpi [GR] 160 E2

Polykástano [GR] 160 D3
Polýkastro [GR] 156 A4
Polymedium [TR] 164 A3
Polypótamo [GR] 160 D2
Polýrracho [GR] 160 E3
Polyrrinía [GR] 174 B3
Polzela [SLO] 120 B3
Pomar [E] 94 F3
Pomarance [I] 128 B4
Pomarico [I] 136 C2
Pomarkku / Påmark [FIN] 198 C1
Pomáz [H] 76 B4
Pombal [P] 90 C2
Pomellen [D] 34 D3
Pomézia [I] 132 C4
Pomigliano d'Arco [I] 134 D3
Pommersfelden [D] 58 E3
Pomorie [BG] 150 E4
Pomoy [F] 70 B3
Pompaples [CH] 116 B1
Pompei [I] 134 D3
Pompey [F] 56 D4
Pómpia [GR] 174 C4
Pompiano [I] 116 F4
Pomposa, Abbazia di– [I] 128 D2
Pomysk Wielki [PL] 36 B2
Poncin [F] 80 E2
Ponferrada [E] 82 D3
Pon'goguba [RUS] 216 E1
Poniatowa [PL] 50 B3
Ponicova, Peşteră– [RO] 148 C1
Poniec [PL] 46 F3
Ponikve [MK] 154 E3
Ponikve [SLO] 120 B3
Poniky [SK] 76 B2
Ponoarele [RO] 248 C3
Pons [F] 78 C2
Ponsa [FIN] 198 E1
Ponsacco [I] 128 B4
Pont [F] 68 F3
Pont [I] 116 B3
Ponta [P] 110 E3
Pontacq [F] 88 C3
Ponta Delgada [P] 110 E1
Pontailler–sur–Saône [F] 68 F3
Pontal [P] 98 B4
Pont–à–Mousson [F] 56 D4
Pontão [P] 90 C2
Pontarion [F] 78 F2
Pontarlier [F] 70 B3
Pontarso [I] 118 C3
Pontassieve [I] 128 C3
Pontaubault [F] 52 E3
Pont–Audemer [F] 54 C2
Pontaumur [F] 80 B2
Pont–Aven [F] 52 B4
Pont Canavese [I] 116 C3
Pont Cellier [F] 68 C4
Pontcharra [F] 80 E3
Pontchartrain [F] 54 D3
Pontchâteau [F] 66 B2
Pont–Croix [F] 52 A3
Pont–d'Ain [F] 80 E2
Pont–de–Briques [F] 40 A3
Pont–de–Dore [F] 80 C2
Pont–de–l'Arche [F] 54 C2
Pont del Diable [E] 96 C3
Pont–de–Roide [F] 70 C3
Pont–de–Salars [F] 124 B1
Pont–d'Espagne [F] 88 C3
Pont–de–Vaux [F] 80 E1
Ponte Arche [I] 118 B3
Ponteareas [E] 82 B3
Pontebba [I] 118 E2
Ponte–Caldelas [E] 82 B3
Ponteceno di Sopra [I] 126 F2
Ponteceso [E] 82 B1

Pontecesures / Enfesta [E] 82 B2
Pontechianale [I] 126 C1
Pontecorvo [I] 134 C2
Ponte da Barca [P] 82 B4
Pontedecimo [I] 126 E2
Ponte de Lima [P] 82 B4
Ponte della Venturina [I] 128 C3
Ponte dell'Ólio [I] 126 F1
Pontedera [I] 128 B4
Ponte de Sôr [P] 90 C3
Pontedeume [E] 82 C2
Ponte di Legno [I] 118 A2
Ponte di Piave [I] 118 D3
Ponteland [GB] 20 E3
Pontelandolfo [I] 134 D3
Ponte–Leccia [F] 130 B2
Pontelongo [I] 118 C4
Ponte nelle Alpi [I] 118 D3
Pont–en–Royans [F] 80 E4
Ponte Nuovo [F] 130 B2
Pontenx–les–Forges [F] 78 A4
Ponte Oliveras [E] 82 B2
Ponte S. Pietro [I] 116 E3
Ponte Tresa [CH] 116 D3
Ponte Ulla [E] 82 B2
Pontevedra [E] 82 B3
Pontevico [I] 116 F4
Pontgibaud [F] 80 B2
Pontigny [F] 68 D2
Pontinia [I] 134 B2
Pontinvrea [I] 126 E2
Pontisméno [GR] 156 B4
Pontivy [F] 52 C4
Pont–l'Abbé [F] 52 B4
Pont–l'Evêque [F] 54 B2
Pontlevoy [F] 68 A2
Pontoise [F] 54 D3
Pontokómi [GR] 160 D3
Pontones [GB] 106 C1
Pontoon [IRL] 12 B2
Pontorson [F] 52 E3
Pontpierre [L] 56 D3
Pont–Réan [F] 52 E4
Pontremoli [I] 128 A2
Pontresina [CH] 116 F2
Pontrieux [F] 52 C2
Ponts [E] 96 C2
Pont–Scorff [F] 52 C4
Pont–St–Esprit [F] 124 E2
Pont–St–Martin [I] 116 C3
Pont–St–Vincent [F] 70 B1
Pont–sur–Yonne [F] 68 D1
Pontvallain [F] 66 E2
Pontypool [GB] 26 E2
Pontypridd [GB] 26 C2
Ponza [I] 134 A3
Poole [GB] 26 F4
Pope [LV] 234 D2
Poperinge [B] 40 C3
Popesti [RO] 76 F4
Popeşti Leordeni [RO] 150 C1
Popilnya [UA] 244 F1
Popina [BG] 150 D2
Popintsi [BG] 156 C1
Popiołówka [PL] 38 C3
Popoli [I] 132 E3
Popovac [HR] 120 D4
Popovača [HR] 120 D4
Popovitsa [BG] 156 D2
Popovo [BG] 150 C3
Popovo [BG] 158 A1
Popovo [RUS] 200 D3
Popów [PL] 48 C4
Poppenhausen [D] 58 D2
Poppi [I] 128 C3
Poprad [SK] 76 C1
Popsko [BG] 156 E3
Populónia [I] 130 D1
Poraj [PL] 62 E2
Poranem [FIN] 208 D2

Porasa [FIN] 198 F1
Porazava [BY] 38 E3
Porcikeln [S] 220 E3
Porcsalma [H] 76 F3
Porcuna [E] 104 E1
Porczyny [PL] 48 C3
Pordenone [I] 118 D3
Pordim [BG] 148 F3
Pordoi, Passo– [I] 118 C2
Poręba [PL] 62 E2
Poreč [HR] 128 F1
Porech'ye [RUS] 232 E1
Pori / Björneborg [FIN] 198 C1
Porjus [S] 220 D2
Porkala / Porkkala [FIN] 198 E4
Porkhov [RUS] 232 F3
Porkkala [FIN] 216 B3
Porkkala / Porkala [FIN] 198 E4
Poroszló [H] 76 D3
Porozina [HR] 144 B1
Pórpi [GR] 156 E4
Porquerolles [F] 126 A4
Porraskoski [FIN] 198 F1
Porrentruy [CH] 70 C3
Porretta Terme [I] 128 C3
Porsgrunn [N] 186 E2
Pörszombat [H] 120 D2
Port a' Chlóidh / Portacloy [IRL] 12 B2
Portacloy / Port a' Chlóidh [IRL] 12 B2
Portadown [NIR] 12 E2
Portaferry [NIR] 12 F3
Portalegre [P] 90 D3
Portalrubio [E] 94 D4
Portariá [GR] 162 B3
Portarlington [IRL] 10 E2
Port Askaig [GB] 18 A3
Port Aventura [E] 96 C3
Portbail [F] 52 E2
Port-Barcarès [F] 96 F1
Portbou [E] 96 F2
Port-Camargue [F] 124 D3
Port–Cros [F] 126 A4
Port d'Adaia [E] 108 F3
Port-de-Bouc [F] 124 E3
Port de Pollença [E] 108 D3
Portel [P] 98 D2
Portela [P] 82 B4
Portela do Home [E] 82 B4
Port Ellen [GB] 18 A3
Portelo [P] 84 D2
Port–en–Bessin [F] 54 A2
Port Erin [GBM] 20 B4
Pórtes [GR] 168 A3
Portes les Valence [F] 80 D4
Pörtet [S] 188 D1
Port Eynon [GB] 26 C2
Portezuelo [E] 90 F3
Portglenone [NIR] 12 E2
Port-Grimaud [F] 126 B4
Porthcawl [GB] 26 D2
Porthmadog [GB] 22 D3
Portíccio [F] 130 A3
Portile de Fier [RO] 148 C1
Portilla de la Reina [E] 86 B2
Portillo [E] 92 D2
Portimão [P] 98 B4
Portimo [FIN] 222 D3
Portinatx [E] 108 F1

Portinho da Arrábida [P] 90 B4
Port-Joinville [F] 66 B3
Port Lairge / Waterford [IRL] 10 E4
Port–la–Nouvelle [F] 124 B4
Portlaoise [IRL] 10 E2
Port–Leucate [F] 96 F1
Port–Louis [F] 52 C4
Portman [E] 106 E3
Port–Manech [F] 52 B4
Portmarnock [IRL] 12 E4
Pörtmossen [FIN] 208 B2
Portnahaven [GB] 18 A3
Port–Navalo [F] 66 A1
Port Nis / Port of Ness [GB] 14 C1
Porto [E] 82 D4
Porto [F] 130 A2
Porto [I] 142 C2
Porto [P] 84 A2
Porto Alto [P] 90 B3
Porto Azzurro [I] 130 D2
Portobello [I] 142 C2
Portocelo [E] 82 D1
Porto Ceresio [I] 116 D3
Porto Cervo [I] 142 C2
Porto Cesareo [I] 136 E3
Pórto Chéli [GR] 168 A4
Porto Colom [E] 108 D4
Porto Corallo [I] 142 C5
Porto Corsini [I] 128 D2
Porto Covo [P] 98 B2
Porto Cristo [E] 108 D3
Porto d'Áscoli [I] 132 E2
Porto de Mós [P] 90 B2
Porto di Levante [I] 138 C3
Porto do Son [E] 82 A2
Porto Empedocle [I] 140 C3
Pórto Ércole [I] 130 D2
Portoferráio [I] 130 C2
Portofino [I] 126 E2
Port of Ness / Port Nis [GB] 14 C1
Porto Garibaldi [I] 128 D2
Pórto Germenó [GR] 168 A2
Portogruaro [I] 118 D3
Porto Judeu [P] 110 C4
Pórto Kágio [GR] 172 D4
Pórto Karrás [GR] 162 C2
Porto Levante [I] 128 E1
Pörtom / Pirttikylä [FIN] 208 B2
Portomaggiore [I] 128 D2
Portomarín [E] 82 C3
Porto Moniz [P] 110 D3
Portomouro [E] 82 B2
Porto Novo [P] 90 B3
Portopalo di Capo Pássero [I] 140 E4
Porto-Pollo [F] 130 A3
Porto Potenza Picena [I] 132 E1
Portør [N] 186 E3
Pórto Ráfti [GR] 168 B3
Porto Recanati [I] 128 F4
Porto Rotondo [I] 142 C2
Portorož [SLO] 118 E4
Porto San Giorgio [I] 132 E2
Porto Sant'Elpídio [I] 132 E2
Porto Santuru [I] 142 C5
Porto Santo Stéfano [I] 130 E2
Portoscuso [I] 142 B5
Portos dos Fusos [P] 98 C4
Porto Tolle [I] 128 E1
Porto Tórres [I] 142 B2
Porto–Vecchio [F] 130 B4
Portovenere [I] 128 A3
Porto Viro [I] 128 D1
Portpatrick [GB] 20 B2
Portree [GB] 14 C3
Portroe [IRL] 10 D2
Portrush [NIR] 12 E1

Portsalon [IRL] 12 D1
Pörtschach [A] 118 F2
Portsmouth [GB] 28 B4
Port–Ste–Marie [F] 88 D1
Portstewart [NIR] 12 E1
Port–St–Louis–du–Rhône [F] 124 E3
Port–St–Marie, la Chartreuse de– [F] 80 B2
Port–sur–Saône [F] 70 B3
Port Talbot [GB] 26 D2
Portumna [IRL] 10 D2
Port–Vendres [F] 96 F1
Port William [GB] 20 B3
Porvola [FIN] 208 E4
Porvoo / Borgå [FIN] 200 B3
Porządzie [PL] 38 A4
Porzuna [E] 100 D2
Posada [E] 82 F2
Posada [I] 86 B2
Posada [I] 142 D3
Posada de Valdeón [E] 86 B2
Posadas [E] 104 D1
Posavski Podgajci [HR] 146 B2
Poschiavo [CH] 116 F2
Posedarje [HR] 144 C3
Poseídio [GR] 162 B2
Poseidonía [GR] 168 D3
Pósfa [H] 74 D4
Poshnjë [AL] 160 B2
Posio [FIN] 222 E3
Positano [I] 134 D4
Possagno [I] 118 C3
Pössneck [D] 58 F1
Posta [I] 132 D3
Postojna [SLO] 118 F3
Postojnska Jama [SLO] 118 F3
Postoloprty [CZ] 60 C2
Postomino [PL] 36 A1
Postuša [MK] 154 C4
Posušje [BIH] 144 F4
Poświętne [PL] 38 C3
Potamiá [GR] 162 D1
Potamiés [GR] 174 D3
Potamoí [GR] 156 C3
Potamós [GR] 172 E4
Potamós [GR] 174 A3
Potamoúla [GR] 166 D3
Potcoava [RO] 148 F1
Potenstejn [CZ] 60 C4
Potenza [I] 134 E4
Potenza Picena [I] 132 E1
Potes [E] 86 B2
Potġčiky [CZ] 60 B2
Potka [N] 224 E2
Potlogi [RO] 150 B1
Potnjani [HR] 122 A4
Potoci [BIH] 152 D1
Potok [PL] 64 C3
Potok [SK] 76 B3
Potsdam [D] 44 F2
Potštát [CZ] 62 B3
Pottenbrunn [A] 74 C3
Pottenstein [A] 74 C3
Pottenstein [D] 58 F3
Pöttmes [D] 72 C2
Potula [FIN] 198 F2
Potworów [PL] 48 E3
Pouancé [F] 66 D1
Pougues–les–Eaux [F] 68 C3
Pouilly [F] 68 C3
Pouilly–en–Auxois [F] 68 B2
Pouilly–sous–Charlieu [F] 80 C2
Poúnta [GR] 168 D4
Pourtalet, Col du– [E/F] 88 C3
Poussay [F] 70 B2
Pouyastruc [F] 88 D3
Pouy–de–Touges [F] 88 E3

Pouzauges [F] 66 D3
Pouzihac [F] 124 D2
Považská Bystrica [SK] 76 A1
Považský Hrad [SK] 62 D4
Poviglio [I] 128 B1
Povlja [HR] 152 B1
Póvoa [P] 98 D2
Povoação [P] 110 E1
Póvoa de Lanhoso [P] 84 B2
Póvoa de Varzim [P] 84 A2
Povors'k [UA] 50 F3
Powburn [GB] 20 E2
Powerscourt House [IRL] 10 F2
Powidz [PL] 48 B2
Powlalice [PL] 34 E2
Powodow [PL] 48 D2
Poyatos [E] 102 B1
Poynton [GB] 22 E2
Poyntzpass [NIR] 12 E3
Poyracık [TR] 164 C3
Poyrali [TR] 158 C2
Poyraz [TR] 164 D4
Poyrazdamları [TR] 164 D4
Poysdorf [A] 74 D2
Pöytyä [FIN] 198 D2
Poza de la Sal [E] 86 D3
Požane [HR] 118 F4
Požarevac [SRB] 146 E2
Pozazal, Puerto– [E] 86 C3
Pozdrezde [PL] 38 B1
Požega [HR] 120 F4
Požega [SRB] 146 D3
Pożerunje [KS] 154 D3
Poznań [PL] 46 F2
Pozo Alcón [E] 106 B2
Pozoblanco [E] 100 C3
Pozo–Cañada [E] 102 B4
Pozohondo [E] 102 B4
Pózondon [E] 94 C4
Pozondón [E] 102 C1
Pozo Negro [E] 114 D3
Poźrzadło [PL] 46 D2
Pozuel de Ariza [E] 94 C3
Pozuelo [E] 102 A4
Pozuelo de Zarzón [E] 90 F2
Pozzallo [I] 140 E4
Pózzis [I] 118 E2
Pozzomaggiore [I] 142 B3
Pozzo S. Nicola [I] 142 B2
Pozzuoli [I] 134 C3
Prabuty [PL] 36 D3
Prača [BIH] 146 B4
Prachatice [CZ] 72 F1
Prácheň [CZ] 60 C4
Pracký Kopec [CZ] 74 D1
Pradell [E] 96 B3
Pradelle [F] 124 F1
Pradelles [F] 80 C4
Prádena [E] 92 F3
Prades [E] 96 E1
Pradillo [E] 94 B1
Pradła [PL] 62 F2
Prado del Rey [E] 104 C3
Pradoluengo [E] 86 D4
Præstø [DK] 178 D3
Pragersko [SLO] 120 C2
Prägraten [A] 118 D1
Praha [CZ] 60 D3
Prahecq [F] 66 D4
Prahovo [SRB] 148 C2
Praia a Mare [I] 136 B4
Praia da Tocha [P] 90 C1
Praia da Vieira [P] 90 B2
Praia da Vitória [P] 110 C3
Praia de Monte Clérigo [P] 98 A3
Praia de Santa Cruz [P] 90 A3
Praia do Norte [P] 110 A3
Praia Grande [P] 90 A3
Praiano [I] 134 D4
Praias–Sado [P] 90 B4

Prainha [P] 110 B3
Praisós [GR] 174 E4
Prakovce [SK] 76 D1
Prali [I] 116 B4
Pralognan–la–Vanoise [F] 116 B3
Prámanta [GR] 160 D4
Pranjani [SRB] 146 D3
Prapatnica [HR] 144 D4
Prasiá [GR] 166 D2
Prašice [SK] 74 F2
Prasiés [GR] 174 C3
Prastio (Dörtyol) [CY] 176 E3
Praszka [PL] 48 C4
Prat de Compte [E] 94 F4
Pıatlella [I] 134 C2
Prati di Tivo [I] 132 E3
Prato [I] 128 C3
Prats de Lluçanès [E] 96 D2
Prats–de–Mollo–la–Preste [F] 96 E2
Prauthoy [F] 68 F2
Pravdinsk [RUS] 36 F1
Pravets [BG] 148 E4
Pravia [E] 82 F2
Pravlov [CZ] 74 D1
Preajba [RO] 150 A1
Prebold [SLO] 120 B3
Préchac [F] 78 B4
Précy–sous–Thil [F] 68 E3
Precy sur Vrin [F] 68 D2
Predappio [I] 128 D3
Predazzo [I] 118 C2
Preddvor [SLO] 120 A3
Predeal [RO] 248 D3
Predejane [SRB] 154 E2
Predel [SLO] 118 E2
Predeşti [RO] 148 D2
Preding [A] 120 C2
Predlitz [A] 118 F1
Predoi / Prettau [I] 118 D1
Pré–en–Pail [F] 54 A3
Preetz [D] 32 C2
Pregarten [A] 74 B2
Preili [LV] 236 C3
Preitenštejn [CZ] 60 C3
Prekal [AL] 152 F3
Prekestol [N] 186 B2
Preko [HR] 144 C3
Prekonoška Pećina [SRB] 148 C3
Prelau [A] 72 E4
Prelog [HR] 120 D3
Prelon [BG] 150 A4
Přelouč [CZ] 60 D3
Prem [SLO] 118 F4
Premantura [HR] 144 A2
Prémery [F] 68 C3
Premià de Mar [E] 96 D3
Premnitz [D] 44 E1
Prenjas [AL] 160 C2
Prénouvellon [F] 68 B1
Prenzlau [D] 34 C3
Preobrazhenski Manastir [BG] 150 B3
Přerov [CZ] 62 C4
Prerow [D] 32 F1
Preselentsi [BG] 150 E2
Preševo [SRB] 154 D3
Presicce [I] 136 F4
Prešov [SK] 76 D1
Pressac [F] 78 B1
Pressath [D] 58 F3
Pressbaum [A] 74 C3
Pré St–Didier [I] 116 B3
Prestfoss [N] 192 F4
Prestice [I] 128 A3
Preston [GB] 22 F2
Prestwick [GB] 18 C4
Prettau / Predoi [I] 118 D1
Prettin [D] 44 F3
Pretul [A] 74 C4

Pretzsch [D] 44 F3
Preuilly–sur–Claise [F] 66 F3
Prevalje [SLO] 120 B2
Préveli, Moní– [GR] 174 C4
Préveranges [F] 68 B4
Préveza [GR] 166 C2
Prevršac [HR] 144 E1
Prezid [HR] 120 B4
Priaranza del Bierzo [E] 82 D4
Přibĕnice [CZ] 60 E4
Pribeta [SK] 74 F3
Priboj [BIH] 146 B2
Priboj [SRB] 146 C4
Priboj [SRB] 154 D2
Příbor [CZ] 62 D3
Prichaly [RUS] 238 B3
Prichsenstadt [D] 58 D3
Pridvorci [BIH] 152 D1
Pridvorica [SRB] 146 E4
Priego [E] 94 B4
Priego de Córdoba [E] 104 E2
Priekulė [LT] 238 A2
Priekule [LV] 234 D4
Priekuli [LV] 236 C2
Prien [D] 72 D3
Prienai [LT] 238 D3
Priene [TR] 170 B3
Priero [I] 126 D2
Prievidza [SK] 76 A2
Prignano Cilento [I] 136 A3
Prigrevica [SRB] 122 B4
Prijeboj [HR] 144 D2
Prijedor [BIH] 144 E2
Prijepolje [SRB] 152 F1
Prikraj [HR] 120 D3
Prilep [MK] 160 D1
Prilike [SRB] 146 D4
Priluka [BIH] 144 E3
Přimda [CZ] 60 B3
Primel–Trégastel [F] 52 B2
Primišlje [HR] 144 C1
Primolano [I] 118 C3
Primorsk [RUS] 36 E1
Primorsk [RUS] 200 D3
Primošten [HR] 144 D4
Primstal [D] 56 E3
Prínos [GR] 162 D1
Priolo Gargallo [I] 140 E3
Prioro [E] 86 B3
Priozersk [RUS] 200 E2
Pripek [BG] 156 E3
Prirechnyj [RUS] 226 F2
Prisad [MK] 154 D4
Prisadets [BG] 158 A2
Priseltsi [BG] 158 D3
Prisoja [MNE] 154 A2
Prisoje [BIH] 144 E4
Prisovice [CZ] 60 E2
Prissac [F] 66 F4
Priština [KS] 154 C2
Pritzerbe [D] 44 E2
Pritzier [D] 32 D3
Pritzwalk [D] 32 E4
Privas [F] 80 D4
Priverno [I] 134 B2
Privlaka [HR] 144 C3
Privlaka [HR] 146 B1
Prizren [KS] 154 C3
Prizzi [I] 140 C2
Prnjavor [BIH] 144 F2
Prnjavor [SRB] 146 C2
Probištip [MK] 154 E3
Probstzella [D] 58 F2
Próchoma [GR] 160 F2
Prochowice [PL] 46 E4
Pródromos [CY] 176 D3
Pródromos [GR] 166 F3
Proença–a–Nova [P] 90 D2

Profilia [GR] 176 C2
Profitis [GR] 162 B1
Profondeville [B] 40 E4
Progled [BG] 156 D3
Prohor Pčinjski [SRB] 154 D3
Prokópi [GR] 168 A1
Prokuplje [SRB] 148 B4
Prolaz [BG] 150 C2
Prómachoi [GR] 160 E2
Promachónas [GR] 156 B3
Promna [PL] 48 F3
Promnik [PL] 64 B1
Pronsfeld [D] 56 E2
Propriano [F] 130 A3
Proseč [CZ] 62 A3
Prosenik [BG] 150 E4
Prosotsáni [GR] 156 C4
Prostĕjov [CZ] 62 C4
Prostki [PL] 38 B2
Prószków [PL] 62 C2
Proszowice [PL] 64 A2
Protarás [CY] 176 E3
Próti [GR] 156 C4
Protići [BIH] 144 E3
Protivanov [CZ] 62 B4
Protivín [CZ] 60 D4
Protokklísi [GR] 156 F3
Prötzel [D] 46 C1
Prouille [F] 88 F3
Prousós [GR] 166 D3
Provins [F] 54 F4
Prozor–Rama [BIH] 144 F4
Pruchnik [PL] 64 D3
Prudhoe [GB] 20 E3
Prudnik [PL] 62 C2
Prügy [H] 76 D3
Průhonice [CZ] 60 D3
Prüm [D] 56 E2
Pruna [E] 104 C2
Prundu [RO] 150 C2
Prunet [F] 80 A3
Prunete [F] 130 B2
Prunet–et–Belpuig [F] 96 E1
Prunetta [I] 128 B3
Prunn [D] 72 D1
Prunn, Schloß– [D] 72 C1
Prusice [PL] 46 F4
Pruské [SK] 74 F1
Pruszcz [PL] 36 C3
Pruszcz Gdański [PL] 36 C2
Pruszków [PL] 48 F2
Prutting [D] 72 D3
Prüzen [D] 32 E2
Pruzhany [BY] 38 E4
Pruzhitsy [RUS] 200 E4
Pryluky [UA] 242 E4
Prypiat' [UA] 242 D3
Pryvitne [UA] 50 E4
Przasnysz [PL] 36 F4
Przechlewo [PL] 36 B3
Przedbórz [PL] 48 E4
Przedecz [PL] 48 C2
Przełęk [PL] 62 C2
Przemków [PL] 46 E3
Przemocze [PL] 34 E3
Przemyśl [PL] 64 D3
Przemyśl [PL] 64 D3
Przesmyki [PL] 50 C2
Przewale [PL] 64 E1
Przewłoka [PL] 50 B3
Przeworsk [PL] 64 D2
Przewóz [PL] 46 D3
Przezmark [PL] 36 D2
Prześmierowo [PL] 46 F2
Przodkowo [PL] 36 C2
Przybiernów [PL] 34 D3
Przybychowo [PL] 46 F1
Przygodzice [PL] 48 B3
Przyłęk [PL] 64 C2
Przylesie [PL] 62 C1
Przystajń [PL] 62 D1

Przysucha [PL] 48 E3
Przyszów [PL] 64 C2
Przyszowa [PL] 64 B3
Przytoczna [PL] 46 D2
Przytoczno [PL] 50 B3
Przytuły [PL] 38 B3
Przytyk [PL] 48 F3
Przywory [PL] 62 D2
Pšaca [MK] 154 E3
Psachná [GR] 168 B1
Psará [GR] 168 D1
Psarádes [GR] 160 C2
Psáthi [GR] 174 C1
Psathópyrgos [GR] 166 D3
Psathotópi [GR] 166 C2
Pskov [RUS] 232 E3
Psychikó [GR] 166 E1
Psychró [GR] 174 D4
Pszczew [PL] 46 E2
Pszczyna [PL] 62 E3
Pszów [A] 72 E4
Pszów [PL] 62 D3
Ptéleá [GR] 156 D3
Ptolemáïda [GR] 160 D2
Ptóo [GR] 168 A2
Ptuj [SLO] 120 C2
Ptujska Gora [SLO] 120 C2
Puchberg [A] 74 C3
Púchov [SK] 74 F1
Pučišća [HR] 152 B1
Puck [PL] 36 C1
Puçol [E] 102 D3
Pudasjärvi [FIN] 216 C1
Puebla de Alcocer [E] 100 B2
Puebla de Don Fadrique [E]
   106 C2
Puebla de Don Rodrigo [E]
   100 C2
Puebla de Guzmán [E] 98 D3
Puebla de la Calzada [E] 90 E4
Puebla de la Reina [E] 98 F2
Puebla del Brollón / A Pobra
   de Brollón [E] 82 C3
Puebla del Caramiñal / Pobra
   do Caramiñal [E] 82 A2
Puebla de Lillo [E] 86 A2
Puebla del Maestre [E] 98 F3
Puebla del Príncipe [E] 100 E4
Puebla de Obando [E] 90 E4
Puebla de Sanabria [E] 84 D2
Puebla de Vallés [E] 92 F3
Pueblica de Valverde [E] 84 E2
Pueblonuevo del Guadiana
   [E] 90 E4
Pueblonuevo del Guadiana
   [E] 90 E4
Puente Almuhey [E] 86 B3
Puente de Domingo Flórez
   [E] 82 D4
Puente de Génave [E] 106 B1
Puente de Montañana [E]
   96 B1
Puente Genil [E] 104 D2
Puente la Reina / Gares
   [E] 86 F4
Puente la Reina de Jaca
   [E] 88 B4
Puentelarra [E] 86 D3
Puentenansa [E] 86 D2
Puente Romano [E] 90 E3
Puentes de García
   Rodríguez / As Pontes de
   García Rodríguez [E] 82 C2
Puente Viesgo [E] 86 C2
Puerta de Levante [E] 102 D4
Puerto Banús [E] 104 C3
Puerto Castilla [E] 92 B3
Puerto de Béjar [E] 92 B3
Puerto de la Cruz [E] 112 D2
Puerto del Carmen [E] 114 E3
Puerto del Rosario [E] 114 E3
Puerto de Mazarrón [E] 106 D3

Puerto de Santa Cruz [E]
   100 B2
Puerto de San Vicente [E]
   100 C1
Puerto Lajas [E] 114 E3
Puerto Lápice [E] 100 E2
Puertollano [E] 100 D3
Puerto Lumbreras [E] 106 C3
Puertomingalvo [E] 102 D2
Puerto Real [E] 104 B3
Puerto Rey [E] 106 C3
Puerto Rico [E] 112 D4
Puertoserrano [E] 104 C2
Pueyo, Monasterio de– [E]
   94 F2
Puffendorf [D] 42 C3
Puget–sur–Argens [F] 126 B3
Puget–Théniers [F] 126 B3
Puget–Ville [F] 126 A4
Pugnochiuso [I] 134 F2
Puhja [EST] 230 E3
Puhos [FIN] 210 E3
Puhos [FIN] 216 C1
Puig [E] 102 D3
Puigcerdà [E] 96 D1
Puig–reig [E] 96 D2
Puise [EST] 230 C2
Puiseaux [F] 54 E4
Puivert [F] 88 F4
Pujjas [LV] 234 E4
Pukavik [S] 180 D1
Pukë [AL] 154 B3
Pukiš [BIH] 146 B2
Pukkila [FIN] 200 A3
Pula [HR] 144 A2
Pula [I] 142 B6
Puławy [PL] 50 B3
Pulborough [GB] 28 C4
Pulgar [E] 100 D2
Pulju [FIN] 226 C3
Pulkau [A] 74 C2
Pulkkila [FIN] 198 F1
Pulkkila [FIN] 216 B3
Pulkovo [RUS] 200 F4
Pulpí [E] 106 D3
Pulsa [FIN] 200 D2
Pulsnitz [D] 46 C4
Pulsujärvi [S] 224 E4
Puttusk [PL] 38 A4
Pumpėnai [LT] 238 D1
Pumpula [FIN] 200 C2
Punat [HR] 144 B1
Punkaharju [FIN] 210 E4
Punkalaidun [FIN] 198 D2
Punta, Château de la– [F]
   130 A3
Punta Ala [I] 130 D2
Punta de Moraira [E] 108 C2
Puntagorda [E] 112 B1
Punta Križa [HR] 144 B2
Punta Marina [I] 128 D2
Punta Prima [E] 108 F3
Puntas de Calnegre [E] 106 D3
Punta Umbría [E] 98 D4
Punxin [E] 82 C3
Puokio [FIN] 216 C2
Puolanka [FIN] 216 C2
Puoltikasvaara [S] 220 E2
Puottaure [S] 220 E3
Puralankylä [FIN] 208 E1
Purbach [A] 74 D3
Purchena [E] 106 C3
Pürg [A] 72 F4
Purgstall [A] 74 B3
Purkersdorf [A] 74 C3
Purkjaur [S] 220 D3
Purmerend [NL] 30 B3
Purmojärvi [FIN] 208 D1
Pürnstein [A] 72 F2
Purnumukka [FIN] 226 D3
Purnuvaara [FIN] 222 E3
Purontaka [FIN] 216 A4

Purroy [E] 94 C3
Purroy de Solana [E] 96 B2
Purujärvi [FIN] 210 E3
Purullena [E] 106 A3
Pürvomay [BG] 156 D2
Puša [LV] 236 D4
Puščava [SLO] 120 C2
Pushkin [RUS] 200 F4
Pushkinskiye Gory [RUS]
   236 F2
Püski [H] 74 E3
Puškino [RUS] 240 F3
Püspökládány [H] 76 D4
Pustevny [CZ] 62 D4
Pustków [PL] 64 C2
Pustoshka [RUS] 240 B3
Pusula [FIN] 198 E3
Puszcza [PL] 38 B1
Puszczykowo [PL] 46 F2
Pusztamérges [H] 122 C3
Pusztamiske [H] 120 E1
Pusztamonostor [H] 76 C4
Puszta–Szabolcs [H] 122 B1
Pusztaszemes [H] 120 F2
Putaja [FIN] 198 D1
Putanges–Pont–Ecrepin
   [F] 54 A3
Putbus [D] 34 C2
Putgarten [D] 34 C1
Putignano [I] 136 D2
Putignano, Grotta di– [I]
   136 D2
Putikko [FIN] 210 E4
Putim [CZ] 60 D4
Putim [CZ] 60 D4
Putinci [SRB] 146 D2
Putineiu [RO] 150 A2
Putineiu [RO] 150 B2
Putkela [FIN] 210 F2
Putlitz [D] 32 E3
Putnok [H] 76 C2
Puttelange [F] 56 E4
Putten [NL] 30 C3
Puttgarden [D] 32 D1
Putyvl' [UA] 242 E3
Putzu Idu [I] 142 B4
Puumala [FIN] 200 D1
Puurmani [EST] 230 E3
Puvyalador [F] 96 D1
Puyguilhem [F] 78 D3
Puy–Guillaume [F] 80 C2
Puykkola [RUS] 210 F3
Puylaurens [F] 88 F3
Puy–l'Evêque [F] 88 E1
Puymorens, Col de– [F] 96 D1
Puze [LV] 234 D2
Puzzittu, Nuraghe– [I] 142 C4
Pwllheli [GB] 22 D3
Pyaski [BY] 38 D3
Pyatchino [RUS] 200 D4
Pyatidorozhnoye [RUS] 36 E1
Pydhaitsi [UA] 244 D2
Pydnay [TR] 176 D1
Pyelishcha [BY] 50 D1
Pyhäjärvi [FIN] 216 B4
Pyhäjoki [FIN] 198 C2
Pyhäjoki [FIN] 216 A3
Pyhäkylä [FIN] 216 D1
Pyhältö [FIN] 200 C2
Pyhämaa [FIN] 198 B2
Pyhänsivu [FIN] 216 B2
Pyhäntä [FIN] 216 C3
Pyhäntaka [FIN] 200 B2
Pyhäranta [FIN] 198 C2
Pyhäsalmi [FIN] 216 B3
Pyhäselkä [FIN] 210 E2
Pyhtää / Pyttis [FIN] 200 B3
Pyla [CY] 176 E3
Pyla–sur–Mer [F] 78 A3
Pylés [GR] 176 B3
Pýli [GR] 160 C2
Pýli [GR] 166 D1

Pýli [GR] 168 A2
Pylí [GR] 176 A1
Pylkönmäki [FIN] 208 E2
Pýlos [GR] 172 C3
Pyntäinen [FIN] 208 C4
Pyöreinen [FIN] 210 C1
Pyörny [FIN] 208 C2
Pyramides [CH] 116 C2
Pyrgá [CY] 198 D7
Pyrgadíkia [GR] 162 C2
Pyrgáki [GR] 168 D4
Pyrgío [GR] 168 E2
Pýrgoi [GR] 160 E2
Pýrgos [GR] 160 F2
Pýrgos [GR] 170 A3
Pýrgos [GR] 172 C2
Pýrgos [GR] 174 D4
Pýrgos Gerakioú [GR] 172 E3
Pyrsógianni [GR] 160 C3
Pyrzyce [PL] 34 E4
Pyšely [CZ] 60 E3
Pyskowice [PL] 62 D2
Pytalovo [RUS] 236 E2
Pythagóreio [GR] 170 B3
Pyttis / Pyhtää [FIN] 200 B3
Pyyrinlahti [FIN] 208 F2
Pyzdry [PL] 48 B2

Q

Qiselay-et-Graciaux [F] 70 B3
Quadri [I] 132 F4
Quakenbrück [D] 30 E3
Qualitz [D] 32 E2
Quarona [I] 116 D3
Quarrata [I] 128 C3
Quarré-les-Tombes [F] 68 D3
Quarteira [P] 98 B4
Quartu Sant'Elena [I] 142 C5
Qudeschild [NL] 30 B2
Quebradas [P] 90 B3
Quedlinburg [D] 44 D3
Quelaines-St. Gault [F] 66 D1
Queluz [P] 90 A3
Quercamps [F] 40 B3
Quercianella [I] 128 B4
Querenca [P] 98 C4
Querfurt [D] 44 D3
Quéribus, Château de- [F] 124 B4
Quermanço [E] 96 F2
Quéroy, Grottes du- [F] 78 D2
Quesada [E] 106 B2
Questembert [F] 66 B1
Quettehou [F] 52 F2
Quiberon [F] 66 A1
Quickborn [D] 32 C2
Quillan [F] 88 F4
Quimper [F] 52 B3
Quimperlé [F] 52 B4
Quin Abbey [IRL] 10 C2
Quinéville [F] 52 F2
Quingey [F] 70 B4
Quinta da Bacalhôa [P] 90 B4
Quintana de la Serena [E] 100 B3
Quintana del Castillo [E] 82 E4
Quintana del Puente [E] 86 B4
Quintanar de la Orden [E] 100 F2
Quintanar de la Sierra [E] 94 B1
Quintanar del Rey [E] 102 B3
Quintana Redonda [E] 94 B2
Quintanilha [P] 84 D2
Quintanilla de las Viñas [E] 94 A1

Quintanilla de Onésimo [E] 92 E2
Quintanilla-Sobresierra [E] 86 C4
Quintin [F] 52 C3
Quinto [E] 94 E3
Quiroga [E] 82 D3
Quirra, Castello di- [I] 142 C5
Quissac [F] 124 D2

R

Råå [S] 178 F1
Raab [A] 72 F2
Raabs an der Thaya [A] 74 C2
Raahe / Brahestad [FIN] 216 A2
Rääkkylä [FIN] 210 E3
Raalte [NL] 30 D3
Raanujärvi [FIN] 222 B3
Raattama [FIN] 226 C3
Rab [HR] 144 B2
Rabac [HR] 144 B1
Råbäck [S] 188 D3
Rabade [E] 82 C2
Rábade [E] 82 C2
Rábafüzes [H] 120 D1
Rábagani [RO] 122 F2
Rábahidvég [H] 120 D1
Rabastens [F] 88 F2
Rabastens-de-Bigorre [F] 88 D3
Rabat [M] 140 C4
Rábatamasi [H] 74 E4
Rabbalshede [S] 188 B3
Rabča [SK] 62 E4
Rabí [CZ] 60 C4
Rábida, Monasterio de la- [E] 98 D4
Rabisha [BG] 148 C3
Rabka [PL] 62 F3
Rabrovo [BG] 148 C2
Rabrovo [SRB] 146 F2
Rabštejn [CZ] 60 F3
Rabsztyn [PL] 62 F2
Råby-Rönö [S] 190 C3
Rača [SK] 74 E3
Rača [SRB] 146 E3
Rača [SRB] 148 B4
Rácalmás [H] 122 B1
Racalmuto [I] 140 C3
Rácari [RO] 150 B1
Răcarii de Sus [RO] 148 D1
Răcășdia [RO] 122 F1
Racconigi [I] 126 D1
Rače [SLO] 120 C2
Ráches [GR] 166 E2
Raciąż [PL] 48 E1
Raciążek [PL] 48 C1
Racibórz [PL] 62 D3
Ráckeve [H] 122 B1
Racławice [PL] 64 A2
Rączki [PL] 36 E3
Raczki [PL] 38 C2
Råda [S] 194 D4
Radalj [SRB] 146 C3
Radanje [MK] 154 E3
Radanovići [MNE] 152 E3
Radashkovichy [BY] 242 B2
Rădăuți [RO] 244 D3
Radawnica [PL] 36 B3
Radcliffe-on-Trent [GB] 24 C3
Raddusa [I] 140 D3
Rade [D] 32 B3
Råde [N] 188 B2
Radeberg [D] 46 B4
Radebeul [D] 46 B4
Radeburg [D] 46 B4
Radeče [SLO] 120 B3
Radęcin [PL] 34 F4

Radegast [D] 44 E3
Radehiv [UA] 244 C1
Radenci [SLO] 120 C2
Radenthein [A] 118 F2
Radevormwald [D] 42 D3
Radimlja [BIH] 152 D2
Rădineşti [RO] 148 D1
Radisne [UA] 246 F1
Radiviliv [UA] 244 D1
Radko Dimitrievo [BG] 150 D3
Radkow [PL] 62 B2
Radlje ob Dràvi [SLO] 120 B2
Radłów [PL] 62 D1
Radmirje [SLO] 120 B2
Radna [RO] 122 E3
Radnejaur [S] 220 C4
Radnevo [BG] 156 E1
Radnica [PL] 46 D2
Radnice [CZ] 60 C3
Radolfzell [D] 70 F3
Radom [PL] 48 F3
Rådom [S] 194 D4
Radomin [PL] 36 D4
Radomir [AL] 154 B4
Radomir [BG] 154 E2
Radomiru [RO] 148 E2
Radomsko [PL] 48 D4
Radomyshl' [UA] 242 D4
Radomyśl Wielki [PL] 64 C2
Radošina [SK] 74 F2
Radošovce [SK] 74 E2
Radostowo [PL] 36 F2
Radoszewice [PL] 48 C4
Radoszyce [PL] 48 E4
Radotín [CZ] 60 D3
Radovanu [RO] 148 D2
Radovašnica [SRB] 146 C2
Radovets [BG] 158 A2
Radovići [MNE] 152 E3
Radoviš [MK] 154 E4
Radovljica [SLO] 118 F2
Radowo Wielkie [PL] 34 E3
Radruz [PL] 64 E2
Radstadt [A] 72 E4
Radstock [GB] 26 E5
Radučić [HR] 144 D3
Raduczyce [BG] 48 C4
Radujevac [SRB] 148 C2
Radun' [BY] 38 E1
Radunci [BG] 150 B4
Raduša [MK] 154 C3
Radviliškis [LT] 238 C2
Radwanca [PL] 48 E3
Radymno [PL] 64 D3
Radzanów [PL] 36 E4
Radziądz [PL] 46 F3
Radziejów [PL] 48 C1
Radziłów [PL] 38 B3
Radziwie [PL] 48 D2
Radzovce [SK] 76 C3
Radzymin [PL] 48 F2
Radzyń Chełmiński [PL] 36 D3
Radzyń Podlaski [PL] 50 C2
Raec [MK] 154 D4
Rærh [DK] 182 C2
Raesfeld [D] 42 C2
Raffadali [I] 140 C3
Rafina [GR] 168 B2
Rafsbotn [N] 228 B3
Raftsjöhöjden [S] 204 F1
Ragaciems [LV] 234 F3
Ragály [H] 76 C2
Ragama [E] 84 F4
Ragana [LV] 236 B2
Rågeleje [DK] 178 E1
Råglanda [S] 188 D3
Ragunda [S] 206 B2
Ragusa [I] 140 E4
Raguva [LT] 238 D2
Rahachow [BY] 242 C2
Raharney [IRL] 10 E2
Rahaugen [N] 188 B2

Rahden [D] 30 F3
Rahikka [FIN] 208 C3
Råholt [N] 194 B4
Raijala [FIN] 198 C2
Raikküla [EST] 230 D2
Raimat [E] 96 B2
Rain [D] 72 B2
Raippaluoto / Replot [FIN] 208 B1
Raippo [FIN] 200 D2
Räisälä [FIN] 222 D3
Raisio / Reso [FIN] 198 C3
Raistakka [FIN] 222 E3
Raitaperä [FIN] 208 E2
Raival [F] 56 C4
Raivala [FIN] 200 C4
Raivala [FIN] 208 C4
Raja-Jooseppi [FIN] 226 E3
Rajákoski [RUS] 226 E2
Rajamäki [FIN] 198 F3
Rajanovci [BG] 148 C3
Rajastrand [S] 212 F3
Rajë [AL] 154 B3
Rajec [SK] 76 A1
Rajecké Teplice [SK] 76 A1
Rajgród [PL] 38 C2
Rajić [HR] 144 E1
Rajka [H] 74 E3
Rajkova Pećina [SRB] 148 B2
Raka [SLO] 120 C3
Rakaka [H] 76 D2
Rakamaz [H] 76 E3
Rakek [SLO] 120 A3
Rakhiv [UA] 244 C3
Rakitna [SLO] 120 A3
Rakitnica [BG] 156 E1
Rakitovec [SLO] 118 F4
Rakitovo [BG] 156 C2
Rakke [EST] 230 E2
Rakkestad [N] 188 B2
Rákóczifalva [H] 122 D1
Rakoniewice [PL] 46 E2
Rakoš [KS] 154 C2
Rakoszyce [PL] 46 F4
Rakova [SK] 62 E4
Rakovica [HR] 144 D2
Rakovitsa [BG] 148 C3
Rakovník [CZ] 60 D3
Rakovo [BG] 150 C4
Rakovski [BG] 156 D2
Rakovskovo [BG] 150 E4
Raków [PL] 64 B2
Raksi [H] 120 F2
Rakvere [EST] 230 E1
Ralja [SRB] 146 E2
Rälla [S] 184 F3
Ram [SRB] 146 F2
Ramacastañas [E] 92 C4
Ramacca [I] 140 E3
Rämälä [FIN] 210 C4
Ramales de la Victoria [E] 86 D2
Ramallosa [E] 82 A3
Ramallosa / Teo [E] 82 B2
Ramberg [N] 218 E1
Rambervillers [F] 70 C2
Rambin [D] 34 C2
Rambouillet [F] 54 D3
Rameshki [RUS] 240 E2
Ramfo [N] 202 E3
Ramirás [E] 82 B4
Ramkvilla [S] 184 D2
Ramljane [HR] 144 D4
Rämmen [S] 188 E1
Rammerskirchen [D] 42 C3
Ramnäs [S] 190 C1
Râmne [S] 188 B2
Râmnicu Sărat [RO] 248 E3
Râmnicu Vâlcea [RO] 248 D3
Ramnous [GR] 168 B2
Ramosch [CH] 118 A1
Ramsau [A] 72 F4

Ramsberg [S] 188 F1
Ramsele [S] 206 B2
Ramsey [GBM] 20 B3
Ramsgate [GB] 28 E3
Rämshyttan [S] 194 F4
Ramsjö [S] 206 B4
Ramsli [N] 186 B3
Ramstein [D] 56 F3
Ramučiai [LT] 238 C2
Ramundberget [S] 204 C3
Ramvik [S] 206 D3
Ramygala [LT] 238 D2
Ramzova-Petrikov [CZ] 62 C2
Råna [N] 186 B3
Ranalt [A] 118 B1
Rånäs [S] 190 E1
Rancǐrov [CZ] 74 C1
Randaberg [N] 186 A2
Randalstown [NIR] 12 E2
Randamonys [LT] 38 D1
Randan [F] 80 B2
Randazzo [I] 138 C4
Rånddalen [S] 204 D4
Randegg [A] 74 B3
Randen [N] 192 E1
Randers [DK] 182 D3
Randijaur [S] 220 D3
Randín [E] 82 B4
Randos [GR] 160 C2
Randsfjorden [N] 194 B3
Randsjö [S] 204 E4
Randsverk [N] 192 E1
Råneå [S] 220 F4
Ranemsletta [N] 212 C3
Rânes [F] 54 A3
Ranft [CH] 116 D1
Rångedala [S] 184 B1
Rangendingen [D] 70 F2
Rangstrup [DK] 178 B3
Rani List [BG] 156 E3
Raniżów [PL] 64 C2
Rankinen [FIN] 216 B3
Rannankyla [FIN] 208 D3
Rannannmäki [FIN] 198 C2
Rannsundet [S] 204 D4
Ranntila [FIN] 226 C2
Ransäter [S] 188 D1
Ransby [S] 194 D3
Ranshofen [A] 72 E2
Ransta [S] 190 C1
Rantajärvi [S] 222 B3
Rantasalmi [FIN] 210 D3
Rantsila [FIN] 216 B3
Rantun [D] 178 A3
Ranua [FIN] 222 D4
Ranum [DK] 182 C3
Rånvassbotn [N] 224 C4
Ranzo [I] 126 D2
Raon-l'Étape [F] 70 C2
Råossi [I] 118 B3
Rapallo [I] 126 F2
Rápina [EST] 230 F3
Rapla [EST] 230 D2
Rapolla [I] 134 E3
Raposa [P] 90 C3
Rapotice [CZ] 62 B4
Rappenloch-Schlucht [A] 72 A4
Rapperswil [CH] 70 E4
Rappottenstein [A] 74 B2
Rapsáni [GR] 160 F3
Raron [CH] 116 D2
Raša [HR] 144 B1
Räsälä [FIN] 210 C2
Rascafría [E] 92 E3
Raseiniai [LT] 238 C2
Räsele [S] 214 A3
Rašica [SLO] 120 B3
Rasimbegov [MK] 160 D1
Rasines [E] 86 D2
Rasivaara [FIN] 210 E3
Raška [SRB] 154 C1

Rasktinkylä [FIN] 216 E3
Raslavice [SK] 64 C4
Rásná [CZ] 60 E4
Rasony [BY] 236 F4
Rasova [RO] 150 E1
Raspay [E] 106 E1
Rasquera [E] 94 F4
Rast [RO] 148 D2
Rästa [S] 190 B2
Rastatt [D] 58 B4
Råsted [DK] 182 D3
Rastede [D] 30 F2
Rastenfeld [A] 74 B2
Rasteš [MK] 154 C4
Rasti [FIN] 210 E3
Rastošnica [BIH] 146 C2
Rastovac [MNE] 152 E2
Rasueros [E] 84 F4
Räsvani [RO] 150 D1
Rasy [PL] 48 D3
Raszków [PL] 48 B3
Rätan [S] 204 E3
Ratan [S] 214 D4
Ratau [S] 206 F1
Rateče [SLO] 118 F2
Ratekau [D] 32 D2
Rathangen [IRL] 10 E2
Rathcoole [IRL] 10 F2
Rathcormack [IRL] 10 C3
Rathcroghan [IRL] 12 C3
Rathdrum [IRL] 10 F3
Rathenow [D] 44 E1
Rathfran Abbey [IRL] 12 B2
Rathfriland [NIR] 12 E3
Rathkeale [IRL] 10 C3
Rath Luirc / Charleville [IRL] 10 C3
Rathmelton [IRL] 12 D1
Rathmolyon [IRL] 10 F2
Rathmullan / Rathmullen [IRL] 12 D1
Rathmullen / Rathmullan [IRL] 12 D1
Rathnew [IRL] 10 F3
Rath of Mullamast [IRL] 10 E2
Rathvilty [IRL] 10 E3
Ratibor [CZ] 62 D4
Ratingen [D] 42 C3
Ratipera [FIN] 208 E2
Ratková [SK] 76 C2
Ratkovo [SRB] 122 C4
Ratne [UA] 50 E2
Ratsichy [BY] 38 D2
Rattenberg [A] 72 D4
Ratten–Unterdorf [A] 74 C4
Rattersdorf [A] 74 D4
Rattosjärvi [FIN] 222 C2
Rättvik [S] 194 F3
Ratzeburg [D] 32 D3
Raubling [D] 72 D3
Raudaskylä [FIN] 216 B3
Raudeberg [N] 202 B4
Raudlia [N] 212 E1
Raufarösn [IS] 218 D2
Raufoss [N] 194 B3
Rauha [FIN] 200 D1
Rauhala [FIN] 210 E1
Rauhala [FIN] 222 B1
Rauhaniemi [FIN] 210 D4
Raulach [E] 80 A3
Rauland Høyfjellshotell [N] 186 D1
Rauma / Raumo [FIN] 198 C2
Raumala [FIN] 198 D3
Raumo / Rauma [FIN] 198 C2
Raumünzach [D] 70 E1
Rauna [LV] 236 C2
Rauris [A] 72 E4
Raustå [N] 192 E4
Rautajärvi [FIN] 198 E1
Rautalampi [FIN] 210 B2

Rautaniemi [FIN] 198 D2
Rautavaara [FIN] 216 D4
Rautila [FIN] 198 C3
Rautio [FIN] 216 A3
Rautjärvi [FIN] 200 D1
Rauvatn [N] 218 F4
Ravanica, Manastir– [SRB] 146 F3
Ravanička Pećina [SRB] 146 F3
Ravanusa [I] 140 D3
Rava–Rus'ka [UA] 64 E2
Ravatn [N] 212 D1
Ravattila [FIN] 200 D2
Ravazd [H] 74 E4
Ravča [HR] 152 C2
Ravda [BG] 150 E4
Ravel [F] 80 B2
Ravello [I] 134 D4
Rävemåla [S] 184 D4
Ravenglass [GB] 20 C4
Ravenna [I] 128 D2
Ravensbrück [D] 32 F4
Ravensburg [D] 58 B4
Ravioskorpi [FIN] 200 B1
Rävmarken [S] 188 C3
Ravna Dubrava [SRB] 148 C4
Ravna Reka [SRB] 146 F3
Ravne [SLO] 120 B2
Ravnholt [DK] 178 D2
Ravno [BIH] 152 D2
Ravno Rašće [HR] 144 D1
Ravno Selo [SRB] 122 C4
Rawa Mazowiecka [PL] 48 E3
Rawicz [PL] 46 F3
Rayleigh [GB] 28 D3
Rayol [F] 126 B4
Räyrinki [FIN] 208 D1
Räyskälä [FIN] 198 E2
Rayvio [RUS] 210 E4
Razboj [BIH] 144 F1
Razbojna [SRB] 148 A4
Razbojna Dupka [MK] 160 D1
Razdol'e [UA] 246 F3
Razdol'ye [RUS] 200 F2
Razdrto [SLO] 118 F3
Razgrad [BG] 150 C3
Razhanka [BY] 38 E2
Rãžica [BG] 150 C4
Razkriže [SLO] 120 D2
Razlog [BG] 156 B2
Razlovci [MK] 154 F3
Ráztočno [SK] 76 A2
Reading [GB] 28 C3
Réalmont [F] 124 A2
Realp [CH] 116 D2
Reanaclogheen / Ré na gCloichín [IRL] 10 D4
Réau, Ancient Abbaye de la– [F] 78 D1
Réaup–Lisse [F] 88 D1
Reay [GB] 14 E1
Rebais [F] 54 F3
Rebolledo de la Torre [E] 86 C3
Reboly [RUS] 216 F3
Rebordelo [P] 84 D2
Rebrovo [BG] 148 D4
Rebürkovo [BG] 148 E4
Reç [AL] 154 B4
Recanati [I] 128 F4
Rečane [KS] 154 C3
Recas [E] 100 E1
Recaş [RO] 122 E3
Recea [RO] 148 C2
Recea [RO] 150 A1
Recey–sur–Ource [F] 68 F2
Rechnitz [A] 74 D4
Rechytsa [BY] 242 D3
Recke [D] 30 E3

Recklinghausen [D] 42 D2
Recoaro Terme [I] 118 B3
Recologne [F] 70 B3
Recópolis [E] 94 A4
Recsk [H] 76 C3
Recueda [E] 94 A2
Recz [PL] 34 E3
Ręczno [PL] 48 D4
Reda [PL] 36 C1
Redalen [N] 194 B3
Redcar [GB] 20 F4
Redditch [GB] 28 B1
Redea [RO] 148 E2
Redefin [D] 32 D3
Rédics [H] 120 D2
Redipuglia [I] 118 E3
Redon [F] 66 B1
Redondela [E] 82 B3
Redondo [P] 98 D2
Redruth [GB] 26 B3
Rędzikowo [PL] 36 B1
Rees [D] 42 C2
Reetz [D] 32 E3
Refnes [N] 224 B3
Reftele [S] 184 C2
Regalbuto [I] 140 E2
Regéc [H] 76 D2
Regen [D] 72 E1
Regensburg [D] 72 D1
Regenstauf [D] 60 B4
Reggello [I] 128 B1
Règgio di Calábria [I] 138 D3
Reggiolo [I] 128 B1
Règgio nell'Emilia [I] 128 B2
Reghin [RO] 244 D4
Regis–Breitingen [D] 44 E4
Regkínio [GR] 166 F3
Regna [S] 190 B3
Regonkylä [FIN] 208 C2
Reguengos de Monsaraz [P] 98 D2
Rehau [D] 60 B2
Rehborn [D] 56 F3
Rehden [D] 30 F3
Rehna [D] 32 D2
Reichéa [GR] 172 E3
Reichenau [D] 70 F3
Reichenau an der Rax [A] 74 C3
Reichenbach [D] 44 B4
Reichenbach [D] 46 C4
Reichenbach [D] 60 B2
Reichenberg [D] 46 C1
Reichertshausen [D] 72 C2
Reichertshofen [D] 72 C2
Reichstett [F] 70 D1
Reigate [GB] 28 C3
Reigersburg [A] 74 C2
Reignier [F] 80 F2
Reijola [FIN] 210 E2
Reila [FIN] 198 B2
Reillanne [F] 124 F3
Reims [F] 56 B3
Rein [A] 120 C1
Reinach [CH] 70 D3
Reinach [CH] 70 E4
Reinberg [D] 34 C2
Reine [N] 218 E1
Reinfeld [D] 32 C2
Reinhardshagen [D] 44 B3
Reinheim [D] 58 C3
Reinosa [E] 86 C3
Reinsfeld [D] 56 E3
Reinslisætra [N] 204 B4
Reinsvik [N] 202 D2
Reinsvoll [N] 194 B3
Reirat [N] 212 E3
Reisach [A] 118 E2
Reisbach [D] 72 E2
Reischach [D] 72 E2
Reischenhart [D] 72 D3
Reisjärvi [FIN] 216 B4

Reitan [N] 204 C3
Reit im Winkl [D] 72 D3
Reittiö [FIN] 210 C1
Reitzehain [D] 60 C2
Rejmyre [S] 190 B3
Rejowiec [PL] 50 D4
Rejowiec Fabryczny [PL] 50 D4
Rejštejn [CZ] 60 C4
Reka [HR] 120 D3
Reka [SLO] 118 F3
Rekeland [N] 186 B3
Reken [D] 42 D2
Rekijoki [FIN] 198 D3
Rekovac [SRB] 146 F3
Rekvik [N] 224 D2
Rel' [RUS] 232 E2
Rely [F] 40 B3
Remagen [D] 56 C1
Rémalard [F] 54 C3
Remda [RUS] 232 D3
Remels [D] 30 E2
Remeskylä [FIN] 216 C4
Remetea Mare [RO] 122 E3
Remich [L] 56 D3
Remígia, Cova– [E] 102 E2
Remiremont [F] 70 C2
Remmarn [S] 206 D1
Remmet [S] 204 E4
Remnes [N] 212 D1
Remolinos [E] 94 D2
Remouchamps [B] 40 F4
Remoulins [F] 124 D2
Remscheid [D] 42 D3
Remte [LV] 234 E3
Rémuzat [F] 124 F2
Rena [N] 194 C2
Ré na gCloichín / Reanacloqheen [IRL] 10 D4
Renaison [F] 80 C2
Renaix (Ronse) [B] 40 D3
Renålandet [S] 204 F1
Renbygda [N] 204 C3
Rencēni [LV] 230 D4
Renchen [D] 70 E1
Renda [LV] 234 D3
Rendal [N] 202 E2
Rende [I] 138 D1
Rendsburg [D] 32 B1
Renfors [S] 214 D2
Rengsjö [S] 196 C2
Reni [UA] 244 F4
Renko [FIN] 198 E2
Renkum [NL] 30 C4
Rennebu [N] 202 F3
Rennerod [D] 58 B1
Rennertshofen [D] 72 C1
Rennes [F] 52 E4
Rennweg [A] 118 E1
Renon / Ritten [I] 118 C2
Rens [DK] 178 B3
Rensä [N] 224 C3
Rentería / Errenteria [E] 86 F3
Rentína [GR] 162 B1
Rentína [GR] 166 D2
Rentjärn [S] 214 C2
Renträsk [S] 214 C1
Renvyle [IRL] 12 A3
Reolid [E] 100 F4
Répáshuta [H] 76 D3
Répcelak [H] 74 E4
Repino [RUS] 200 E3
Replot / Raippaluoto [FIN] 208 B1
Repo–Aslak [FIN] 226 D2
Repojoki [FIN] 226 D3
Reposaari [FIN] 198 B1
Reppen [N] 192 C2
République, Col de la– [F] 80 D3
Repvåg [N] 228 C2

Requena [E] 102 C3
Réquista [F] 124 B2
Rerik [D] 32 E2
Reşadiye [TR] 176 B1
Resana [I] 118 C3
Resanovci [BIH] 144 D3
Resavska Pećina [SRB] 146 F3
Resele [S] 206 C2
Resen [MK] 160 C2
Resende [E] 84 B3
Reshetylivka [UA] 242 F4
Reşiţa [RO] 122 F4
Reskjem [N] 186 C2
Resko [PL] 34 E3
Resmo [S] 184 E4
Resna [MNE] 152 E3
Reso / Raisio [FIN] 198 C3
Ressons [F] 54 E2
Reszel [PL] 36 F2
Retama [E] 100 C3
Retama, Garganta de– [E] 100 C2
Retamal de Llerena [E] 100 A3
Retamar [E] 106 B4
Retamosa [E] 100 B1
Retford [GB] 24 C3
Rethel [F] 56 B2
Rethem [D] 32 B4
Réthymno [GR] 174 C3
Retie [B] 40 E3
Retiers [F] 66 C1
Retortillo de Soria [E] 94 A3
Retournac [F] 80 C3
Rétság [H] 76 B3
Retuerta [E] 92 F1
Retuerta del Bullaque [E] 100 D2
Retuneri [FIN] 210 D2
Retz [A] 74 C2
Reuilly [F] 68 B3
Reus [E] 96 B3
Reusel [NL] 40 E3
Reuterstadt Stavenhagen [D] 32 F3
Reutlingen [D] 70 F2
Reutte [A] 72 B4
Revel [F] 88 F3
Révfülöp [H] 120 E2
Révigny–sur–Ornain [F] 56 C4
Revin [F] 56 C2
Revište [SK] 76 A2
Řevničov [CZ] 60 D2
Revò [I] 118 B2
Revonkylä [FIN] 210 E2
Revonlahti [FIN] 216 B2
Revsnes [N] 192 D2
Revsnes [N] 212 B4
Revsund [S] 204 F3
Revúca [SK] 76 C2
Rewal [PL] 34 E2
Rexbo [S] 196 B3
Rexnin [AL] 160 B3
Reykjahlíd [IS] 218 C2
Reykjavík [IS] 218 A3
Rey Moro, Cueva del– [E] 102 C4
Rēzekne [LV] 236 E3
Rezovo [BG] 158 C2
Rgotina [SRB] 148 C2
Rhade [D] 32 B3
Rhayader [GB] 22 D4
Rheda [D] 42 E2
Rhede [D] 42 C2
Rheinau [D] 70 E1
Rheinbach [D] 42 C4
Rheinberg [D] 42 C3
Rheinböllen [D] 56 F2
Rheindahlen [D] 42 C3
Rheine [D] 30 E2
Rheinfall [D] 70 E3
Rheinfelden [CH] 70 D3

Rheinfelden (Baden) [D] **70** D3
Rheinsberg [D] **32** F4
Rhein-Weser-Turm [D] **42** E3
Rheinzabern [D] **58** B4
Rhêmes-Notre-Dame [I] **116** B3
Rhenen [NL] **30** C4
Rhens [D] **56** F2
Rheydt [D] **42** C3
Rhinau [F] **70** D2
Rhinow [D] **44** E1
Rho [I] **116** E3
Rhoon [NL] **30** A4
Rhosneigr [GB] **22** D2
Rhyl [GB] **22** E2
Rhynern [D] **42** E3
Ria Formosa [P] **98** C4
Riaillé [F] **66** C2
Rialp [E] **96** C1
Riaño [E] **86** B2
Rians [F] **124** F3
Rianxo [E] **82** B2
Riaza [E] **92** F2
Ribabellosa [E] **86** D4
Ribadavia [E] **82** B3
Ribadelago [E] **82** D4
Ribadeo [E] **82** D2
Ribadesella [E] **86** B2
Ribaflecha [E] **94** C1
Ribaforada [E] **94** D2
Ribarci [SRB] **154** E2
Ribariče [SRB] **154** B2
Ribaritsa [BG] **148** F4
Riba-roja de Túria [E] **102** D3
Ribarska Banja [SRB] **146** F4
Ribas de Sil [E] **82** C3
Ribas do Miño, Monasterio
  de- [E] **82** C3
Ribčev Laz [SLO] **118** F3
Ribe [DK] **178** B2
Ribeauvillé [F] **70** D2
Ribécourt [F] **54** F2
Ribeira Brava [P] **110** D3
Ribeira de Pena [P] **84** C2
Ribeira Grande [P] **110** E1
Ribeiras [P] **110** B3
Ribeirinha [P] **110** A3
Ribemont [F] **56** A2
Ribera [I] **140** C2
Ribérac [F] **78** D3
Ribera de Cardós [E] **88** E4
Ribera del Fresno [E] **98** F2
Ribes de Freser [E] **96** D2
Ribnica [BIH] **146** B3
Ribnica [SLO] **118** F4
Ribnica [SLO] **120** B3
Ribniţa [MD] **244** F2
Ribolla [I] **130** D1
Ricadi [I] **138** D3
Říčany [CZ] **60** E3
Riccia [I] **134** D2
Riccione [I] **128** E3
Richelieu [F] **66** E3
Richky [UA] **64** E2
Richmond [GB] **20** E4
Richtenberg [D] **32** F2
Rickarum [S] **180** D1
Rickling [D] **32** C2
Ricla [E] **94** D3
Ricse [H] **76** E2
Riddarhyttan [S] **190** B1
Ridderkerk [NL] **30** B4
Ridjica [SRB] **122** B3
Ridzewo [PL] **38** B2
Riebini [LV] **236** D3
Ried [A] **118** B1
Ried [CH] **72** B4
Riedbach [D] **58** D3
Riedenburg [D] **72** C1
Rieder [D] **72** B3
Riedern [D] **70** E3

Ried im Innkreis [A] **72** F2
Riegel [D] **46** C3
Riegel [D] **70** D2
Riegersburg [A] **120** C1
Riego de Ambrós [E] **82** E4
Riekki [FIN] **222** F3
Riello [E] **82** E3
Rieneck [D] **58** D2
Riesa [D] **46** B4
Riesi [I] **140** D3
Riestedt [D] **44** D3
Rietavas [LT] **238** B2
Rietberg [D] **42** E2
Rieth [D] **34** D3
Rieti [I] **132** D3
Rietschen [D] **46** C3
Rieumes [F] **88** E3
Rieupeyroux [F] **124** A1
Rieussec [F] **124** B3
Rieux [F] **88** E3
Riez [F] **126** A3
Riezlern [A] **72** A4
Riffian [MA] **104** B4
Rīga [LV] **234** F3
Rīgaio [GR] **162** A4
Rigáni [GR] **166** D3
Riglos [E] **88** B4
Rignac [F] **124** B1
Rignano Flaminio [I] **132** C3
Riihimäki [FIN] **198** F2
Riihivaara [FIN] **216** C3
Riihivalkama [FIN] **198** E2
Riiho [FIN] **208** E3
Riipi [FIN] **222** C1
Riispyy [FIN] **208** B4
Riistavesi [FIN] **210** C2
Rijeka [BIH] **146** B3
Rijeka [HR] **120** A4
Rijeka Crnojevića [MNE]
  152 E3
Rijssen [NL] **30** D3
Rikava [LV] **236** D3
Řikonín [CZ] **62** B4
Riksgränsen [S] **224** D4
Rila [BG] **154** F3
Rilci [BG] **150** E2
Rillé [F] **66** E2
Rillo [E] **94** D4
Rilski Man. [BG] **156** B2
Rima [I] **116** C3
Rimaucourt [F] **70** A2
Rimavská Baňa [SK] **76** C2
Rimavská Sobota [SK] **76** C2
Rimbach [D] **72** E2
Rimbo [S] **190** E2
Rimella [I] **116** D3
Rimforsa [S] **184** E1
Rímini [I] **128** E3
Rimito / Rymättylä [FIN]
  198 C3
Rimske Toplice [SLO] **120** B3
Rincón de la Victoria [E]
  104 E3
Rincón de Soto [E] **94** C1
Rindal [N] **202** F2
Rindown Castle [IRL] **10** D1
Ringamåla [S] **180** E1
Ringarum [S] **190** C4
Ringaskiddy [IRL] **10** C4
Ringe [DK] **178** C2
Ringebu [N] **192** F1
Ringkøbing [DK] **178** A1
Ringnäs [S] **194** E2
Ringnes [N] **192** F4
Ringøy [N] **192** C3
Ringsheim [D] **70** D2
Ringstad [S] **190** B3
Ringsted [DK] **178** E2
Ringville / An Rinn [IRL] **10** D4
Ringwood [GB] **26** F3
Rinkilä [FIN] **210** D3
Rinna [S] **188** F4

Rinøya [N] **224** B4
Rinteln [D] **42** F2
Río [GR] **166** D3
Riobianco / Weissenbach
  [I] **118** C2
Río de Losa [E] **86** D3
Riofrío [E] **82** E4
Riofrío de Llano [E] **94** B3
Riola Sardo [I] **142** B4
Riolobos [E] **90** F3
Río Lobos, Cañón del- [E]
  94 A2
Riolo Terme [I] **128** D3
Riom [F] **80** B2
Riomaggiore [I] **126** F3
Rio Maior [P] **90** B3
Riomar [I] **96** B4
Rio Marina [I] **130** D2
Rio Mau [P] **84** A2
Riom-ès-Montagnes [F]
  80 A3
Rion-des-Landes [F] **88** B1
Rionegro del Puente [E] **84** E2
Rionero in Vúlture [I] **134** E3
Riópar [E] **100** F4
Riós [E] **82** C4
Riosa [E] **82** F3
Rio Saliceto [I] **128** B2
Rioseco de Tapia [E] **82** F4
Rio Torto [P] **84** B4
Rioz [F] **70** B3
Ripač [BIH] **144** D2
Ripacandida [I] **134** E3
Ripanj [SRB] **146** E2
Riparbella [I] **128** B4
Ripatransone [I] **132** E2
Ripats [S] **220** E2
Ripky [UA] **242** E1
Ripley [GB] **24** C3
Ripoll [E] **96** D2
Ripon [GB] **24** C1
Riposto [I] **138** C4
Ripsa [S] **190** C3
Riquewihr [F] **70** D2
Risan [MNE] **152** E3
Risasvallen [S] **204** D4
Risbäck [S] **212** F3
Risberg [S] **194** E2
Riscle [F] **88** C2
Riseberga [S] **180** C1
Riseberga Kloster [S] **188** F2
Risede [S] **212** F3
Rish [BG] **150** D3
Risinge [S] **190** B3
Risliden [S] **214** C2
Risnes [N] **186** C3
Risnes [N] **192** B2
Rišňovce [SK] **74** F2
Risør [N] **186** E3
Risøyhamn [N] **224** B3
Rissa [N] **204** A1
Rissna [S] **204** F2
Risti [EST] **230** C2
Ristiina [FIN] **200** C1
Ristijärvi [FIN] **216** D2
Ristilä [FIN] **210** B3
Ristinge [DK] **178** D3
Ristinkylä [FIN] **210** D2
Ristna [EST] **230** B2
Ristovac [SRB] **154** D2
Risträsk [S] **214** B3
Risulahti [FIN] **210** C4
Risum-Lindholm [D] **178** B3
Risuperä [FIN] **208** E1
Rítíni [GR] **160** E3
Ritola [FIN] **208** D2
Ritsem [S] **220** C1
Ritten / Renon [I] **118** C2
Rittmanshausen [D] **44** C4
Riuttala [FIN] **198** C1
Riva-Bella [F] **54** B2
Riva dei Tarquini [I] **130** E3

Riva del Garda [I] **118** B3
Riva di Solto [I] **116** F3
Rivanazzano [I] **126** E1
Rivarolo Canavese [I] **116** C4
Rivarolo Mantovano [I] **128** B1
Riva Valdobbia [I] **116** C3
Rive-de-Gier [F] **80** D3
Rivello [I] **136** B3
Rivergaro [I] **126** F1
Rivesaltes [F] **96** E1
Rivinperä [FIN] **216** C3
Rivne [UA] **242** B4
Rívoli [I] **116** B4
Rizári [GR] **160** E2
Rízia [GR] **156** F2
Riznkárpasox (Dipkarpaz)
  [CY] **176** E2
Rízoma [GR] **160** D4
Rizómata [GR] **160** E3
Rizómylos [GR] **160** F4
Rizómylos [GR] **172** C3
Rjånes [N] **202** C3
Rjukan [N] **186** D1
Ro [I] **128** D1
Roa [E] **92** F2
Roa [N] **194** B4
Roald [N] **202** C3
Røan [N] **202** F2
Roana [I] **118** C3
Roanne [F] **80** C2
Roasjö [S] **184** B2
Roavvegieddi [N] **228** D3
Robănești de Jos [RO] **148** E2
Robbio [I] **116** D4
Röbel [D] **32** F3
Robella [I] **116** C4
Røberg [N] **204** B1
Robertingue [F] **40** A3
Robertsfors [S] **214** D3
Robleda [E] **90** F2
Robledillo de Gata [E] **90** F2
Robledo [E] **100** F4
Robledo de Chavela [E] **92** D3
Robledo del Buey [E] **100** C2
Robles de la Valcueva [E]
  82 F3
Robliza de Cojos [E] **84** E4
Robres [E] **94** E2
Robres del Castillo [E] **94** C1
Robru [N] **192** E3
Rocamadour [F] **78** E4
Roccabianca [I] **128** B1
Roccadáspide [I] **134** E4
Rocca di Cambio [I] **132** E3
Rocca di Mezzo [I] **132** E3
Rocca di Neto [I] **138** F2
Rocca Imperiale [I] **136** C3
Roccalbegna [I] **130** E2
Roccalumera [I] **138** C4
Rocca Malatina, Sassi di- [I]
  128 C2
Roccamonfina [I] **134** C3
Roccanova [I] **136** C3
Roccapalumba [I] **140** C2
Rocca Pia [I] **132** E4
Roccaraso [I] **132** E4
Rocca San Casciano [I] **128** D3
Roccastrada [I] **130** E1
Rocca Vecchia [I] **136** F3
Roccella Iónica [I] **138** E3
Roccelletta del Vescovo di
  Squillace [I] **138** E2
Rocche di Cusa [I] **140** B2
Rocchetta Belbo [I] **126** D2
Rocella Valdemonte [I] **138** C4
Roche [E] **104** B3
Rochebloine, Château de- [F]
  80 D3
Rochechouart [F] **78** E2

Rochecourbière, Grotte de- [F]
  124 E2
Rochefort [B] **56** C2
Rochefort [F] **78** B1
Rochefort, Grotte de- [F] **54** A4
Rochefort-en-Terre [F] **66** B1
Rochefort-s-Nenon [F] **70** A3
Rochehaut [B] **56** C2
Rochemaure [F] **124** E1
Rocher, Château du- [F] **52** F4
Rocherolle, Château de la-
  [F] **68** A3
Rochers, Château des- [F]
  52 E4
Rocheservière [F] **66** C3
Rochester [GB] **28** D3
Rochlitz [D] **44** F4
Rochsburg [D] **44** F4
Rociana del Condado [E] **98** E4
Rociu [RO] **150** A1
Rockcorry [IRL] **12** D3
Rockenhausen [D] **56** F3
Rockhammar [S] **190** B2
Rockneby [S] **184** E3
Rocroi [F] **56** B2
Rød [N] **188** B3
Róda [GR] **160** B4
Rodach [D] **58** E2
Roda de Eresma [E] **92** E3
Roda de Isábena [E] **96** B1
Rødal [N] **202** D4
Rodalice [HR] **144** D3
Ródanas, Sant. de- [E] **94** D3
Rodange [L] **56** D3
Ródão, Portas de- [P] **90** D3
Rødberg [N] **192** E4
Rødby [DK] **32** D1
Rødby [S] **180** E1
Rødbyhavn [DK] **32** D1
Rødding [DK] **178** B2
Rødding [DK] **182** C3
Rødeby [S] **180** E1
Rodeiro [E] **82** C3
Rødekro [DK] **178** B3
Rodellar [E] **94** F2
Roden [NL] **30** D2
Rodenkirchen [D] **30** F2
Rodewald [D] **32** B4
Rodewisch [D] **60** B2
Rodez [F] **80** A4
Rodgau [D] **58** C2
Rødhus Klit [DK] **182** D2
Rodiá [GR] **160** E4
Rodi Gargánico [I] **134** F2
Roding [D] **60** B4
Rødkærsbro [DK] **182** D4
Rodolívos [GR] **156** B2
Rodópoli [GR] **156** B4
Ródos [GR] **176** C2
Rodovoye [RUS] **232** E4
Rodrigatos de la Obispalía
  [E] **82** E4
Rodrigo, Castelo- [P] **84** C4
Rødsjøen [N] **204** B1
Rødven [N] **202** D3
Rødvig [DK] **178** E3
Roela [EST] **230** E2
Roermond [NL] **42** B3
Roeselare (Roulers) [B] **40** C3
Roeulx [D] **40** D4
Roffiac [F] **80** B3
Roflaschlucht [CH] **116** E2
Röfors [S] **188** F3
Rofrano [I] **136** B3
Rogač [HR] **152** A1
Rogačica [SRB] **146** C3
Rogalice [PL] **62** C4
Rogalin [PL] **46** F2
Rogaška Slatina [SLO] **120** C3
Rogatec [SLO] **120** C3
Rogatica [BIH] **146** C4
Rogätz [D] **44** E2

Roggenburg [D] 72 B2
Rogil [P] 98 B3
Røgind [DK] 178 A1
Rögla [S] 180 C2
Rogliano [F] 130 B1
Rogliano [I] 138 E2
Rognac [F] 124 E3
Rognan [N] 220 B2
Rogne [N] 192 E2
Rognes [N] 204 B2
Rogova [RO] 148 C2
Rogovka [LV] 236 E3
Rogovo [RUS] 232 E4
Rogowo [PL] 48 B1
Rogozhinë [AL] 160 A2
Rogoznica [HR] 144 D4
Rogoźno [PL] 46 F1
Rogoźno [PL] 48 C3
Roguszyn [PL] 50 B1
Rohan [F] 52 C4
Rohatec [CZ] 74 E1
Rohatyn [UA] 244 C2
Rohožník [SK] 74 E2
Rohr [A] 72 C4
Rohrbach [A] 72 F2
Rohrbach-lès-Bitche [F] 56 E4
Rohrberg [D] 32 D4
Rohrenfels [D] 72 C2
Rohr in Niederbayern [D]
   72 D1
Rohuküla [EST] 230 C2
Rohuneeme [EST] 230 D1
Roisel [F] 54 F2
Roja [LV] 234 E2
Rojales [E] 106 E2
Röjan [S] 204 E3
Rojão Grande [P] 84 A4
Röjdåfors [S] 194 D4
Rojiştea [RO] 148 E2
Rök [S] 188 F4
Röka [S] 214 C2
Röke [S] 180 C1
Rokiciny [PL] 48 D3
Rokietnica [PL] 64 D3
Rokiškis [LT] 236 C4
Rokity [PL] 36 B2
Rökkum [N] 202 E2
Røkland [N] 220 A2
Roknäs [S] 214 D2
Rokua [FIN] 216 C2
Rokytnice [CZ] 62 B3
Rolandstorp [S] 212 E3
Rold [DK] 182 D3
Røldal [N] 186 C1
Rolfstorp [S] 184 A2
Rolle [CH] 116 A1
Rølvåg [N] 218 E4
Rolvsøy [N] 188 B2
Roma [I] 132 C4
Romagnano Sésia [I] 116 D3
Romakkajärvi [FIN] 222 B3
Romakloster [S] 234 A2
Roman [BG] 148 E4
Roman [RO] 244 E3
Romangordo [E] 92 B4
Romanija [BIH] 146 B3
Romanshorn [CH] 70 F3
Romans-sur-Isère [F] 80 D4
Romashki [RUS] 200 E2
Rombas [F] 56 D3
Rom By [DK] 182 B3
Romena, Castello di- [I]
   128 C3
Romena, Pieve di- [I] 128 D3
Romeral [E] 100 E2
Romfartuna [S] 190 C1
Romilly-sur-Seine [F] 54 F4
Romiou, Petra tou- [CY]
   176 C4
Romny [UA] 242 E3
Romont [CH] 116 B1

Romorantin-Lanthenay
   [F] 68 B2
Romppala [FIN] 210 E2
Romsey [GB] 26 F3
Romtemplom [H] 76 A4
Røn [N] 192 E2
Roncade [I] 118 D4
Roncadelle [I] 116 F4
Roncal / Erronkari [E] 88 B3
Roncegno [I] 118 C3
Roncesvalles [E] 88 B3
Ronchamp [F] 70 C3
Ronchi dei Legionari [I] 118 E3
Ronciglione [I] 130 F3
Ronco Canavese [I] 116 C3
Roncofreddo [I] 128 D3
Ronco Scrivia [I] 126 E2
Ronda [E] 104 C3
Rønde [DK] 182 E4
Ronehamn [S] 234 A3
Rong [N] 192 C3
Röngu [EST] 230 E3
Ronkeli [FIN] 216 E4
Rönnäng [S] 182 F1
Rönnäs [FIN] 200 B3
Rønne [DK] 180 D3
Ronneburg [D] 60 B1
Ronneby [S] 180 E1
Rønnede [DK] 178 E3
Rönnigsåsen [S] 204 D3
Rönnliden [S] 214 C2
Rönnöfors [S] 204 E1
Rönnskär [S] 214 D3
Rönnynkylä [FIN] 208 F1
Rönö [S] 190 C4
Ronsberg [D] 72 B3
Ronse (Renaix) [B] 40 D3
Roodeschool [NL] 30 D2
Roonah Quay [IRL] 12 A2
Roosendaal [NL] 40 E2
Roosky [IRL] 12 C3
Ropa [PL] 64 B3
Ropaži [LV] 236 B3
Ropczyce [PL] 64 C3
Ropeid [N] 186 B1
Ropinsalmi [FIN] 224 F3
Ropotovo [MK] 154 D4
Ropsha [RUS] 200 D4
Ropsha [RUS] 200 F4
Roque, Pointe de la- [F] 54 C2
Roquebillière [F] 126 C2
Roquebrune-Cap-Martin
   [F] 126 C3
Roquefort [F] 88 C1
Roquefort-sur-Soulzon [F]
   124 B2
Roquemaure [F] 124 E2
Roquesteron [F] 126 C3
Roquetaillade, Château-de-
   [F] 78 C4
Roquetas de Mar [E] 106 B4
Roquetes [E] 96 B4
Røra [N] 204 C1
Rörbäcksnäs [S] 194 D2
Rore [BIH] 144 E3
Rörön [S] 204 E3
Røros [N] 204 B1
Rorschach [CH] 70 F3
Rörum [S] 180 D2
Rørvig [DK] 178 E1
Rørvik [N] 186 B4
Rørvik [N] 204 B1
Rørvik [N] 212 C3
Rörvik [S] 190 E1
Ros' [BY] 38 E3
Rosais [P] 110 B3
Rosala [FIN] 198 D4
Rosal de la Frontera [E] 98 D3
Rosa Marina [I] 136 E2
Rosans [F] 124 F2
Rosarno [I] 138 D3
Rosas / Roses [E] 96 F2

Rosbach [D] 58 B2
Rosche [D] 32 C4
Rościszewo [PL] 36 E4
Roscoff [F] 52 B2
Roscommon [IRL] 10 D1
Roscrea [IRL] 10 D2
Rosdorf [D] 44 B3
Rosegg [A] 118 F2
Roselle [I] 130 E2
Roselle Módica [I] 140 E4
Rosen [BG] 158 B1
Rosenberg [D] 58 D4
Rosenburg [A] 74 C2
Rosendal [N] 192 B4
Rosendal [S] 178 F1
Rosendal [S] 184 D1
Rosenheim [D] 72 D3
Rosenhof [A] 74 B2
Rosenholm [DK] 182 D4
Rosentorp [S] 194 F2
Rosepenna / Machair Loiscthe
   [IRL] 12 D1
Rosersberg [S] 190 D2
Roses / Rosas [E] 96 F2
Roseţi [RO] 150 D1
Roseto Capo Spúlico [I] 136 C3
Roseto degli Abruzzi [I] 132 E3
Roseto Valfortore [I] 134 D2
Roshchino [RUS] 200 E3
Rosica [BG] 150 E2
Rosice [CZ] 62 B4
Rosignano-Maríttimo [I] 128 B4
Rosignano Solvay [I] 128 B4
Rosino [BG] 156 C1
Roşiori [RO] 76 E4
Roşiori de Vede [RO] 150 A2
Roskilde [DK] 178 E2
Rosko [PL] 36 A4
Roslags-Bro [S] 190 E1
Roslags-kulla [S] 190 E2
Roslavl' [RUS] 242 D1
Roslev [DK] 182 C3
Rosli [N] 192 F1
Rosmaninhal [P] 90 E3
Ros Mhic Thriúin / New Ross
   [IRL] 10 E3
Rosnowo [PL] 34 F2
Rosny sur Seine [F] 54 D3
Rosolina Mare [I] 128 E1
Rosolini [I] 140 E4
Rosoman [MK] 154 E4
Rosporden [F] 52 B3
Rossano [I] 136 C4
Rossas [P] 84 B3
Ross Carbery [IRL] 10 B4
Rosscor [NIR] 12 D1
Rosserk Abbey [IRL] 12 B2
Rosses Point [IRL] 12 C2
Rossfjord [N] 224 D2
Rosshaupten [D] 72 B3
Rossiglione [I] 126 E2
Rossio [P] 90 C3
Rossla [D] 44 D1
Rossland [N] 192 A3
Rosslare Harbour [IRL] 10 E4
Rosslau [D] 44 E3
Rosslea [NIR] 12 D3
Rossnes [N] 192 A2
Rossön [S] 206 B1
Ross-on-Wye [GB] 26 E1
Rossosz [PL] 50 C2
Rossoszyca [PL] 48 C3
Rəssvassbukt [N] 212 E1
Röstånga [S] 180 C1
Rostassac [F] 88 F1
Roštejn [CZ] 60 F4
Roštejn [CZ] 60 F4
Röster [S] 190 B4
Rostock [D] 32 E2
Rostov [RUS] 240 F2

Rostrenen [F] 52 C3
Rostrevor [NIR] 12 E3
Röström [S] 214 A3
Rastvollen [N] 204 C4
Rosvik [N] 220 B2
Rosvik [S] 214 E1
Rosyth [GB] 18 D4
Röszke [H] 122 C3
Roszki-Wodźki [PL] 38 C3
Rot [S] 194 E2
Rota [E] 104 B2
Rotberget [N] 194 D3
Roteberg [S] 190 D1
Rotemo [N] 186 C2
Rotenburg [D] 32 B3
Rotenburg [D] 44 B4
Rotenfels [D] 58 A2
Rotgülden [A] 118 E1
Roth [D] 58 E4
Rötha [D] 44 E4
Rothaus [D] 70 E3
Rothemühl [D] 34 C3
Rothenburg [D] 46 D4
Rothenburg, Ruine- [D] 58 E3
Rothenburg ob der Tauber
   [D] 58 D3
Rothéneuf [F] 52 E3
Rothenstein [D] 72 C1
Rotherham [GB] 24 C3
Rothes [GB] 14 E3
Rothesay [GB] 18 B3
Rotondella [I] 136 C3
Rótova [E] 102 D4
Rotsjö [S] 206 B3
Rott [D] 72 B3
Rott [D] 72 D3
Rottach [D] 72 C3
Rötteln [D] 70 D3
Rottenbach [D] 58 E2
Rottenbuch [D] 72 B3
Rottenburg [D] 70 F2
Rottenburg [D] 72 D2
Rottenmann [A] 74 A4
Rotterdam [NL] 30 A4
Rotthalmünster [D] 72 E2
Röttingen [D] 58 D3
Rottne [S] 184 D3
Rottneros [S] 188 D1
Rottweil [D] 70 E2
Rotvoll [N] 204 C2
Rötz [D] 60 B4
Roubaix [F] 40 C3
Rouchovany [CZ] 74 C1
Roudnice nad Labem [CZ]
   60 D2
Rouen [F] 54 C2
Rouffach [F] 70 D2
Rouffignac, Grotte de- [F]
   78 D3
Rougé [F] 66 C1
Rougemont [F] 70 B3
Rougemont [F] 70 C3
Rouillac [F] 78 C2
Roujan [F] 124 C3
Roukavichy [BY] 242 D2
Roulers (Roeselare) [B] 40 C3
Roundstone [IRL] 10 B1
Roundwood [IRL] 10 F3
Roússa [GR] 156 F3
Roussillon [F] 80 F3
Roussillon [F] 124 E3
Rouvres-en-Xaintois [F]
   70 B2
Rovakka [S] 222 B2
Rovaniemi [FIN] 222 C3
Rovanjska [HR] 144 C3
Rovastinaho [FIN] 222 C4
Rovato [I] 116 F3
Roverbella [I] 118 B4
Rovereto [I] 118 B3
Rövershagen [D] 32 E2
Roverud [N] 194 C4

Roviés [GR] 166 F2
Rovigo [I] 128 D1
Rovinj [HR] 128 F1
Rovišće [HR] 120 D3
Rovjok [N] 224 E3
Rovte [SLO] 118 F3
Rów [PL] 34 D4
Rowy [PL] 36 B1
Rowy [PL] 48 C3
Royan [F] 78 B2
Royat [F] 80 B2
Royaumont, Abbaye de- [F]
   54 E3
Roybon [F] 80 E3
Roye [F] 54 E2
Royère-de-Vassivière [F]
   78 F2
Røyken [N] 188 B1
Röykkä [FIN] 198 E3
Røyrvik [N] 212 E3
Røyse [N] 192 F4
Røysheim [N] 192 E1
Royston [GB] 28 D2
Roza [BG] 156 F1
Rožaj [MNE] 154 B2
Różan [PL] 38 A3
Różanki [PL] 46 D1
Rožanstvo [SRB] 146 D4
Rozay-en-Brie [F] 54 E4
Rozdil [UA] 64 F3
Rozdory [RUS] 246 F1
Roženski Manastir [BG]
   156 B3
Rozhniativ [UA] 64 F4
Rozhyshche [UA] 50 F4
Rožmberk nad Vltavou [CZ]
   74 A2
Rožmitál pod Třemšínen
   [CZ] 60 D3
Rožňava [SK] 76 C2
Rožnov pod Radhoštěm [CZ]
   62 D4
Rożnów [PL] 64 B3
Rozogi [PL] 38 A3
Rozoy [F] 56 B2
Rozprza [PL] 48 D4
Roztoky [CZ] 60 D2
Rožupe [LV] 236 D3
Rozvadov [CZ] 60 B3
Rozzano [I] 116 E4
Rrëshen [AL] 154 B4
Rtanj [SRB] 148 B3
Ru [E] 82 C2
Ruba [LV] 234 E4
Rubbestadneset [N] 192 A4
Rubena [E] 86 C4
Rubielos de Mora [E] 102 D2
Rubiera [I] 128 B2
Rucava [LV] 234 D4
Ruciane-Nida [PL] 38 A2
Rud [N] 188 B1
Rud [N] 192 E3
Rud [N] 192 F4
Rud [S] 188 E2
Ruda [PL] 38 B2
Ruda [S] 184 E3
Ruda Maleniecka [PL] 48 E4
Rudare [SRB] 148 B4
Rudawica [PL] 46 D3
Rudawka [PL] 38 C2
Ruda Wolińska [PL] 50 B2
Ruda Yavarskaya [BY] 38 E2
Rudelsburg [D] 44 E4
Rudenica [SRB] 146 E4
Rüdersdorf [D] 46 B2
Rudesheim [D] 58 A2
Rüdiškės [LT] 238 E3
Rudka [PL] 38 C4
Rudka [PL] 50 D3
Rudkøbing [DK] 178 D3
Rudky [UA] 64 E3
Rudna [PL] 36 B3

Rudna [PL] 46 E3
Rudna Glava [SRB] 148 B2
Rudnica [MNE] 152 F1
Rudnica [SRB] 154 C1
Rudnik [BG] 158 E3
Rudnik [KS] 154 C2
Rudnik [PL] 62 D3
Rudnik [PL] 64 D2
Rudnik [SRB] 146 E3
Rudniki [PL] 48 C4
Rudnik Szlachecki–Kol.
 [PL] 50 B4
Rudno [PL] 36 D2
Rudno [PL] 50 C2
Rudno [SLO] 118 F3
Rudnya [RUS] 240 C4
Rudo [BIH] 146 C4
Rudolphstein [D] 58 F2
Rudolstadt [D] 58 F1
Rudozem [BG] 156 D3
Rudsgrendi [N] 186 E1
Rudsjön [S] 206 B1
Rudskoga [S] 188 E3
Ruds–Vedby [DK] 178 D2
Rudy [PL] 62 D2
Rudy–Rysie [PL] 64 B3
Rudzāti [LV] 236 D3
Rue [F] 40 A4
Rueda [E] 92 D2
Rueda, Monasterio de– [E] 94 E3
Rueda de Jalón [E] 94 D3
Ruelle–sur–Touvre [F] 78 D2
Ruen [BG] 150 D4
Ruffano [I] 136 F3
Ruffec [F] 78 D2
Ruffieux [F] 80 F2
Rugāji [LV] 236 D2
Rugby [GB] 28 C1
Rugldalen [N] 204 C3
Rugles [F] 54 C3
Rugvica [HR] 120 D4
Ruha [FIN] 208 C2
Ruhala [FIN] 208 E4
Ruhällen [S] 190 C1
Rühen [D] 44 D1
Ruhland [D] 46 B3
Ruhmannsfelden [D] 72 E1
Ruhpolding [D] 72 D3
Ruidera [E] 100 F3
Ruínas [I] 142 B4
Ruinas Romanas [E] 94 A2
Ruinas Romanas [E] 100 C1
Ruinas Romanas [E] 102 B2
Ruínas Romanas [P] 98 C2
Rüjiena [LV] 230 D4
Rujište [SRB] 148 B3
Rujište [SRB] 148 B3
Ruju, Nuraghe– [I] 142 C3
Ruka [FIN] 222 E3
Rukke [S] 192 E3
Rullbo [S] 194 F1
Rülzheim [D] 58 B4
Rum [H] 120 D1
Ruma [SRB] 146 D2
Rumboci [BIH] 144 F4
Rumburk [CZ] 60 E2
Rumelifeneri [TR] 158 E3
Rumia [PL] 36 C1
Rumigny [F] 56 B2
Rumilly [F] 80 F2
Rummen [B] 40 E3
Rummukkala [FIN]
 210 D3
Rumo [FIN] 216 D3
Rumont [F] 56 C4
Rumpani [CZ] 230 F4
Runcorn [GB] 22 F2
Runde [N] 202 B3
Rundfloen [N] 194 D2
Rundvik [S] 206 E2
Runni [FIN] 216 C4

Runović [HR] 152 C1
Ruokojärvi [FIN] 222 B2
Ruokojärvi [S] 222 A3
Ruokolahti [FIN] 200 D1
Ruokto [S] 220 D2
Ruona [FIN] 208 D2
Ruopsa [FIN] 222 D2
Ruorasmäki [FIN] 200 B1
Ruotaanmäki [FIN] 210 B1
Ruoti [I] 134 E4
Ruøtsinkylä Svenskby [FIN]
 200 B3
Ruotsinpyhää Strömfors [FIN]
 200 B3
Ruovesi [FIN] 208 D4
Rupa [HR] 120 A4
Rupea [RO] 244 D4
Rupt [F] 70 C2
Rus [E] 106 A1
Rusalka [BG] 150 F2
Rusanivka [UA] 242 F3
Rúscio [I] 132 D3
Rusdal [N] 186 B3
Ruse [BG] 150 B2
Ruše [SLO] 120 C2
Rusele [S] 214 B2
Ruševo [HR] 146 A1
Rusfors [S] 214 B3
Rush [IRL] 12 E4
Rushden [GB] 28 C1
Rusiec [PL] 48 C4
Rusinowo [PL] 34 E3
Rusinowo [PL] 34 F4
Rusjasi [MK] 154 C4
Ruská Volová [SK] 76 F1
Ruskeala [RUS] 210 F3
Ruski Krstur [SRB] 122 C4
Ruskila [FIN] 210 C2
Rusksand [S] 206 C1
Rusksele [S] 214 C2
Ruskträsk [S] 214 C2
Rusné [LT] 238 A2
Rusokastro [BG] 158 B1
Rüsselsheim [D] 58 B2
Russi [I] 128 D2
Russliseter [N] 192 E1
Rust [A] 74 D3
Rust [D] 70 D2
Rustad [N] 194 B4
Rustefjelbma [N] 228 D2
Rusvekk [N] 194 C3
Ruswil [CH] 70 E4
Ruszów [PL] 46 D3
Rutalahti [FIN] 208 F3
Rute [E] 104 E2
Rutenbrock [D] 30 E3
Rüthen [D] 42 E3
Ruthin [GB] 22 E3
Rüthnick [D] 32 F4
Rüti [CH] 70 E4
Rüti [CH] 116 E1
Rutigliano [I] 136 D2
Rutka–Tartak [PL] 38 C1
Rutki–Kossaki [PL] 38 B3
Rutledal [N] 192 B2
Rutvik [S] 214 E1
Ruukki [FIN] 216 B2
Ruunaa [FIN] 216 F4
Ruurlo [NL] 30 D4
Ruutana [FIN] 198 E1
Ruutana [FIN] 210 B1
Ruuvaoja [FIN] 222 E1
Ruvallen [S] 204 D3
Ruvanaho [FIN] 222 E3
Ruvasiahtio [FIN] 210 D2
Ruvo di Púglia [I] 136 C1
Ruwer [D] 56 E2
Ruza [RUS] 240 E3
Ruzhany [BY] 38 E3
Ruzhintsi [BG] 148 D3
Ruzhyn [UA] 244 E1
Růžkovy Lhotice [CZ] 60 E3

Ružomberok [SK] 76 B1
Ry [DK] 178 C1
Ryå [DK] 182 D2
Ryabovo [RUS] 200 E3
Ryakhovo [BG] 150 C2
Ryákia [GR] 160 E3
Rybachiy [RUS] 238 A3
Rybarzowice [PL] 62 E3
Rybinsk [RUS] 240 F1
Rybnica [PL] 60 F1
Rybnik [PL] 62 D3
Rybnik [SK] 76 C2
Rybno [PL] 36 E3
Ryboły [PL] 38 C3
Rychliki [PL] 36 D2
Лychmburk [CZ] 62 A3
Rychnov nad Kněžnou [CZ]
 62 B2
Rychnowo [PL] 36 E3
Rychtal [PL] 48 B4
Rychwał [PL] 48 C2
Ryczywół [PL] 50 A3
Ryd [S] 184 D4
Rydaholm [S] 184 C3
Ryde [GB] 28 B4
Rydet [S] 184 A2
Rydland [N] 194 B1
Rydsnäs [S] 184 D1
Rydułtowy [PL] 62 D3
Rydzyna [PL] 46 F3
Rye [GB] 28 D4
Ryen [N] 186 D4
Ryfoss [N] 192 E2
Rygge [N] 188 B2
Rygozy [RUS] 236 F3
Ryhälä [FIN] 210 D4
Ryhäntä [FIN] 216 D2
Rykene [N] 186 D3
Ryki [PL] 50 B3
Ryl'sk [RUS] 242 F3
Rymań [PL] 34 E2
Rymanów [PL] 64 C3
Rýmařov [CZ] 62 C3
Rymättylä / Rimito [FIN]
 198 C3
Rýmnio [GR] 160 E3
Ryn [PL] 38 A2
Rynarzewo [PL] 36 C4
Ryomgård [DK] 182 E4
Rypefjord [N] 228 B2
Rypin [PL] 36 D4
Ryslinge [DK] 178 D2
Ryssby [S] 184 C3
Rysum [D] 30 E2
Rytel [PL] 36 C3
Rytinki [FIN] 222 D4
Rytkynkylä [FIN] 216 B3
Rytro [PL] 64 B4
Ryzmberk [CZ] 60 C4
Rząśnik [PL] 38 A4
Rzecin [PL] 46 E1
Rzeczenica [PL] 36 B3
Rzeczyca [PL] 48 E3
Rzegnowo [PL] 36 F4
Rzemień [PL] 64 C2
Rzepin [PL] 46 D2
Rzesznikowo [PL] 34 E2
Rzeszów [PL] 64 C3
Rzewnowo [PL] 34 E2
Rzgów [PL] 48 D3
Rzhev [RUS] 240 D3
Rzhishchiv [UA] 242 E4

S

Sääksjärvi [FIN] 208 D1
Sääksmäki [FIN] 198 E2
Saal [D] 72 D1
Saalbach [A] 72 D4

Saalburg [D] 58 B2
Saales [F] 70 D2
Saalfeld [D] 58 F1
Saalfelden [A] 72 E4
Saamatti [FIN] 198 E3
Saananmaja [FIN] 224 E3
Saanen [CH] 116 B2
Saaramaa [FIN] 200 C2
Saarbrücken [D] 56 E3
Saarburg [D] 56 E3
Sääre [EST] 230 B4
Saare [EST] 230 E2
Saarela [FIN] 210 B1
Saarela [FIN] 216 E3
Saarenkylä [FIN] 222 C3
Saarenmaa [FIN] 198 C2
Saaresmäki [FIN] 216 C3
Saari [FIN] 210 E4
Saarijärvi [FIN] 208 E2
Saarikko [FIN] 198 D2
Saarikoski [FIN] 224 F3
Saarinen [FIN] 216 D2
Saario [FIN] 210 E3
Saarivaara [FIN] 210 F3
Saarivaara [FIN] 216 E2
Saarlouis [D] 56 E3
Saas Almagell [CH] 116 C2
Saas–Fee [CH] 116 C2
Saas Grund [CH] 116 C2
Sääskjärvi [FIN] 222 D3
Sääskjärvi [FIN] 200 B2
Sababurg [D] 44 B3
Šabac [SRB] 146 C2
Sabadell [E] 96 D3
Sabaro [E] 86 A3
Sabáudia [I] 134 B2
Sabbioneta [I] 128 B1
Sabbucina [I] 140 D3
Sabile [LV] 234 E3
Sabiñánigo [E] 88 C4
Sabinarde Calatañazor [E]
 94 B2
Sabinosa [E] 112 A2
Sabinov [SK] 64 B4
Sabiote [E] 106 B1
Sables–d'Or–les–Pins [F]
 52 D3
Sablé–sur–Sarthe [F]
 54 A4
Sábole [S] 204 D2
Saborsko [HR] 144 C2
Sabres [F] 88 C1
Sabrosa [P] 84 C3
Sabugal [P] 90 E2
Saby [S] 184 D1
Šaca [SK] 76 D2
Săcălaz [RO] 122 E3
Sacavém [P] 90 B3
Sacecorbo [E] 94 B4
Sacedón [E] 94 A4
Sacerueía [E] 100 C3
Sacile [I] 118 E3
Sacra di San Michele [I]
 116 B4
Săcueni [RO] 76 F4
Sada [E] 82 C2
Sádaba [E] 88 A4
Sadala [EST] 230 E2
Sadikov Bunar [SRB] 148 C4
Sadina [BG] 150 C3
Sadki [PL] 36 B4
Sadova [RO] 148 E2
Sadovets [BG] 148 F3
Sadovo [BG] 150 E3
Sadovo [BG] 156 D2
Sądów [PL] 46 D2
Sadrazamköy (Livera) [CY]
 176 D3
S. Adriano [I] 128 D3
Sadská [CZ] 60 E3
Sädvaluspen [S] 220 B3

Sæbø [N] 192 C3
Sæbø [N] 202 C3
Sæbøvik [N] 192 B4
Sæby [DK] 182 E2
Sæd [DK] 178 B3
Sædinenie [BG] 156 D2
Sædinenie [BG] 156 E1
Saelices [E] 100 F2
Sælvig [DK] 178 D1
Saepinum [I] 134 D2
Saerbeck [D] 30 E4
Sætra [N] 224 C2
Sætre [N] 188 B1
Sætre [N] 194 C2
Sætteråsen [N] 204 B1
Saeul [L] 56 U2
Sævareid [N] 192 B3
Sævråsvåg [N] 192 B2
Safa [TR] 164 F2
Safara [P] 98 D3
Safary–Park [A] 74 D2
Säffle [S] 188 D2
Saffron Walden [GB] 28 D2
Safonovo [RUS] 240 D4
Şag [RO] 122 E4
Sagard [D] 34 C1
S'Agaró [E] 96 E3
S. Agata di Esaro [I] 136 B4
Saggrenda [N] 186 E1
Sagiáda [GR] 160 B4
Sågmyra [S] 196 B3
Sagone [F] 130 A3
Sagres [P] 98 A4
Sagu / Sauvo [FIN] 198 D3
Sagunt / Sagunto [E] 102 D3
Sagunto / Sagunt [E] 102 D3
Sagvåg [N] 192 A4
Ságvár [H] 120 F2
Sahagún [E] 86 A3
Sahalahti [FIN] 198 E1
Sahankylä [FIN] 208 C3
Sahavaara [S] 222 A2
Sahilköy [TR] 158 E3
Şahin [TR] 158 B3
Sahinburgaz [TR] 158 C4
Sahrajärvi [FIN] 208 E3
Šahy [SK] 76 B3
Saignelégier [CH] 70 C3
Saija [FIN] 222 E2
Saikari [FIN] 210 B2
Saillagouse [F] 96 D1
Saillans [F] 80 D4
Sailly Flibeaucourt [F] 40 A4
Säimen [FIN] 210 D3
Sains [F] 56 A2
Saint Abbain [B] 80 D1
Sainte–Lucie–de–Tallano
 [F] 130 B3
Sainte–Marie–Siché [F]
 130 B3
Saintes [F] 78 C2
Saintfield [NIR] 12 F3
Saint–Ghislain [B] 40 D4
Saint Hilaire de la Côte
 [F] 80 E3
Saint–Jacques [I] 116 C3
Sairinen [FIN] 198 C2
Saissac [F] 124 A3
Saittarova [S] 222 A1
Saivomuotka [S] 226 B4
Sajaniemi [FIN] 198 E2
Sajenek [PL] 38 C2
Šajkaš [SRB] 146 D1
Sajószentpéter [H] 76 D2
Sakaravaara [FIN] 216 D2
Šakiai [LT] 238 C1
Säkinmäki [FIN] 210 B3
Sakıremer [TR] 170 B3
Sakızlık [TR] 164 F2
Sakowczyk [PL] 64 C4
Sakskøbing [DK] 178 E3

Saky [UA] 246 F4
Säkylä [FIN] 198 C2
Sala [S] 190 C1
Šal'a [SK] 74 F3
Salaberg [A] 74 B3
Salacgrīva [LV] 230 D4
Sala Consilina [I] 134 E4
Salahmi [FIN] 216 C3
Salakas [LT] 238 F2
Salakovac [SRB] 146 F2
Salamajärvi [FIN] 208 E1
Salamanca [E] 84 E4
Salamína [GR] 168 A2
Salamis [CY] 176 E3
Salantai [LT] 238 B1
Salaóra [GR] 166 C2
Salar [E] 104 E3
Sälärd [RO] 76 E4
Salardú [E] 88 D4
Salas [E] 82 E2
Salaš [SRB] 148 C2
Salas de los Infantes [E] 94 A1
Salaspils [LV] 236 B3
Salau [F] 88 E4
Salbohed [S] 190 C1
Salbris [F] 68 B2
Salcia [RO] 148 D2
Šalčininkai [LT] 238 E4
Salcombe [GB] 26 C4
Sălcuţa [RO] 148 D2
Sălcuţa [RO] 150 B1
Saldaña [E] 86 B3
Salduba [E] 94 D3
Saldus [LV] 234 F3
Sale [I] 126 E1
Saleby [S] 188 D4
Salem [D] 70 F3
Salema [P] 98 A4
Salemi [I] 140 B2
Sälen [S] 194 D2
Salernes [F] 126 A3
Salerno [I] 134 D4
Salers [F] 80 A3
S. Alessio Sículo [I] 138 C4
Saletta [I] 116 B4
Salgótarján [H] 76 C3
Šalgovík [SK] 76 D1
Salhus [N] 192 B3
Sali [HR] 144 C3
Salice [F] 130 A3
Salice Terme [I] 126 E1
Salies-de-Béarn [F] 88 B2
Salies-du-Salat [F] 88 E3
Salignac-Eyvigues [F] 78 E4
Salihli [TR] 164 D4
Salihorsk [BY] 242 B3
Salinas [E] 82 F2
Salinas [E] 106 E1
Salinas de Pinilla [E] 100 F3
Salinas de Pisuerga [E] 86 B3
Salin-de-Giraud [F] 124 D3
Saline di Volterra [I] 128 B4
Sälinkää [FIN] 198 F2
Salins-les-Bains [F] 70 B4
Salir [P] 98 C4
Salisbury [GB] 26 F3
Salka [SK] 76 A3
Salla [FIN] 222 E2
Sallanches [F] 116 B2
Sallent de Gállego [E] 88 C3
Sälleryd [S] 180 F1
Salles [F] 78 B4
Salles-Curan [F] 124 B2
Salles-s.-l'Hers [F] 88 F3
Sällinge [S] 190 B2
Sallmunds [S] 234 A3
Salme [EST] 230 B3
Salmenkylä [FIN] 208 E3
Salmenniemi [FIN] 208 E2
Salmerón [E] 94 B4
Salmi [FIN] 208 D2

Salmi [S] 222 A3
Salmivaara [FIN] 222 E2
Sal'miyarvi [RUS] 226 F1
Salmoral [E] 92 C3
Salo [FIN] 198 D3
Salò [I] 118 A3
Salobreña [E] 104 F3
Saločiai [LT] 236 B4
Saloínen [FIN] 216 A2
Salon [F] 56 A4
Salona [HR] 144 E4
Salon-de-Provence [F] 124 E3
Salonta [RO] 122 E2
Salorino [E] 90 E3
Salou [E] 96 B3
Salovci [SLO] 120 D2
Salsåker [S] 206 D3
Salse di Nirano [I] 128 B2
Salses-le-Château [F] 96 F1
Salsnes [N] 212 C3
Salsomaggiore Terme [I] 128 A1
Salsta [S] 190 D1
Salt [E] 96 E2
Saltash [GB] 26 C3
Saltbæk [DK] 178 D2
Saltoluokta [S] 220 C2
Saltrød [N] 186 D3
Saltsjöbaden [S] 190 E2
Saltum [DK] 182 D2
Saltvik [FIN] 198 A3
Saltvik [S] 184 E2
Salubőle [S] 206 E2
Saluzzo [I] 126 C1
Salvacañete [E] 102 C2
Salvada [P] 98 C3
Salvagnac [F] 88 F2
Salvarola, Terme di– [I] 128 B2
Salvaterra de Magos [P] 90 B3
Salvaterra de Miño [E] 82 B3
Salvatierra [E] 100 D3
Salvatierra / Agurain [E] 86 E3
Salvatierra de los Barros [E] 98 E2
Salviac [F] 78 E4
Salzburg [A] 72 E3
Salzburg [D] 58 D2
Salzgitter-Bad [D] 44 C2
Salzgitter-Lebenstedt [D] 44 C2
Salzhausen [D] 32 C3
Salzkotten [D] 42 E3
Salzwedel [D] 32 D4
Salzweg [D] 72 F2
Sama de Langreo [E] 82 F3
Samadet [F] 88 C2
Samadet [F] 88 C2
Samailli [TR] 170 D2
Samandıra [TR] 158 F3
Samarína [GR] 160 C3
Samassi [I] 142 B5
Samatan [F] 88 E3
Sambiase [I] 138 E2
Sambir [UA] 64 E3
Sambuca di Sicília [I] 140 B2
Sambucheto [I] 132 D3
Sambuci [I] 132 D4
Sambucina, Abbazia della– [I] 138 E1
Samedan [CH] 116 F2
Samer [F] 40 A3
Sámi [GR] 166 B4
Samitier [E] 94 F2
Şamlı [TR] 164 C2

Samoëns [F] 116 B2
Samokłęski [PL] 50 C3
Samokov [BG] 156 B2
Samokov [MK] 154 C4
Samolva [RUS] 230 F3
Samoranovo [BG] 154 F3
Šamorín [SK] 74 E3
Samos [E] 82 D3
Sámos [GR] 170 B3
Samoš [SRB] 146 E1
Samos, Monasterio de– [E] 82 D3
Samostan Pleterje [SLO] 120 C3
Samothráki [GR] 162 E1
Samovodene [BG] 150 B3
Sampatiki [GR] 172 C2
Samper [E] 88 C4
Samper de Calanda [E] 94 E4
Sampéyre [I] 126 C2
Sampo [RUS] 232 E2
Samtens [D] 34 C2
Samugheo [I] 142 B4
Saná [GR] 162 B1
Sanad [SRB] 122 C3
San Adrián [E] 94 C1
San Agustín [E] 102 B3
San Agustín [E] 112 E4
San Andrés [E] 82 C1
San Anton Leitza [E] 86 F3
Sanary-sur-Mer [F] 124 F4
San Asensio [E] 86 D4
Sanat Eufemia [E] 86 B3
Sanaüja [E] 96 C2
San Bartolomé de las Abiertas [E] 100 D1
San Bartolomé de la Torre [E] 98 D4
San Bartolomeo in Galdo [I] 134 D2
San Benedetto dei Marsi [I] 132 E4
San Benedetto del Tronto [I] 132 E2
San Benedetto in Alpe [I] 128 D3
San Benedetto Po [I] 128 C1
San Benito [E] 100 C3
San Bernardino [CH] 116 E2
San Bernardino, Tunnel del– [CH] 116 E2
San Biagio di Callalta [I] 118 D3
San Biágio Plátani [I] 140 C2
San Bonifácio [I] 118 B4
San Bruzio [I] 130 E2
San Calogero [I] 140 B2
San Cándido / Innichen [I] 118 D2
San Carlos del Valle [E] 100 E3
San Casciano dei Bagni [I] 130 F2
San Casciano in Val di Pesa [I] 128 C4
San Cataldo [I] 136 F3
San Cataldo [I] 140 D3
Sancergues [F] 68 C3
Sancerre [F] 68 C3
Sancey-le-Grand [F] 70 C3
Sanchidrián [E] 92 D3
San Chírico Raparo [I] 136 C3
San Cipirello [I] 140 C2
San Claudio al Chienti [I] 132 E1
San Clemente [E] 102 A3
San Clemente a Casuria [I] 132 E3
San Clemente al Vomano [I] 132 E3
San Clodio, Monasterio de– [E] 82 B3

Sancoins [F] 68 C3
San Cosme / Barreiros [E] 82 D2
San Cristóbal de la Laguna [E] 112 D2
San Cristóbal de la Vega [E] 92 D2
Sancti Petri [E] 104 B3
Sancti–Spíritus [E] 84 D4
Sancti–Spíritus [E] 100 B2
Sancti Spíritus, Convent del– [E] 102 D3
Sancy–sur–Nied [F] 56 D4
Sand [N] 186 B1
Sand [N] 194 C4
Sånda [N] 186 D3
Sanda [N] 186 E2
Sanda [S] 190 E1
San Damiano d'Asti [I] 126 D1
Sandane [N] 202 C4
San Daniele del Friuli [I] 118 E3
San Daniele Po [I] 128 B1
Sandanski [BG] 156 B3
Sandared [S] 184 B2
Sandarne [S] 196 D2
Sandau [D] 32 E4
Sandaucourt [F] 70 B2
Sandbach [GB] 22 F3
Sande [D] 30 F2
Sande [N] 186 F2
Sande [N] 192 B1
Sandefjord [N] 186 F2
Sandeid [N] 186 B1
Sandem [N] 188 C1
San Demetrio Corone [I] 136 C4
Sanden [N] 186 E2
Sander [N] 194 C4
Sandhem [S] 184 C1
Sandías [E] 82 C4
Sand in Taufers / Campo Túres [I] 118 C1
Sandizell [D] 72 C2
Sandl [A] 74 B2
Sandla [EST] 230 B3
Sandmoen [N] 212 C3
Sandnäset [S] 206 B3
Sandnes [N] 186 B2
Sandnes [N] 186 E2
Sandnes [N] 228 D2
Sandness [GB] 16 E3
Sandnessjøen [N] 212 D1
Sando [E] 84 D4
Sandö Bro [S] 206 D3
Sandomierz [PL] 64 C1
San Dónaci [I] 136 E3
San Donà di Piave [I] 118 D4
San Donato Milanese [I] 116 F4
Sandøreng [N] 212 E2
Sándorfalva [H] 122 C2
Sandown [GB] 28 B4
S. Andrea [I] 118 B3
S. Andrea [I] 134 C3
S. Andrea Apostolo dello Iónio [I] 138 E3
S. Andrés del Rabanedo [E] 82 F4
Sandrigo [I] 118 C3
Šandrovac [HR] 120 E3
Sandsbraten [N] 192 E4
Sandsjö [S] 194 F2
Sandsjö [S] 214 B3
Sandsjön [S] 188 E1
Sandsjönas [S] 214 B2
Sandslån [S] 206 D3
Sandsletta [N] 218 F1
Sandsøy [N] 224 C3
Sandstad [N] 194 C3
Sandstad [N] 202 F1
Sandstedt [D] 32 A3

Sandur [FR] 182 A2
Sandvatn [N] 186 B3
Sandve [N] 186 A2
Sandvig [DK] 180 E3
Sandvik [N] 194 C2
Sandvik [S] 184 F3
Sandvika [N] 188 B1
Sandvika [N] 204 C1
Sandvika [N] 212 D1
Sandvikal [N] 186 B4
Sandviken [S] 196 C3
Sandviken [S] 204 D1
Sandvikvåg [N] 192 A4
Sandwich [GB] 28 E3
San Emiliano [E] 82 E3
San Esteban [E] 86 F3
San Esteban de Gormaz [E] 94 A2
San Fele [I] 134 E3
San Felice Circeo [I] 134 B3
San Felice in Balsignano [I] 136 D2
San Felice sul Panaro [I] 128 C2
San Ferdinando di Púglia [I] 134 F3
San Fernando [E] 104 B3
San Francisco [E] 86 A4
San Fratello [I] 138 B4
San Fruttuoso [I] 126 E2
Sånga [S] 206 C2
San Galgano, Abbazia di– [I] 130 E1
Sangarcía [E] 92 D3
San Gavino Monreale [I] 142 B5
Sangazi [TR] 158 E3
San Gemini [I] 132 C3
San Gemini Fonte [I] 132 C3
Sangerhausen [D] 44 D3
San Germano [I] 116 D4
San Gimignano [I] 128 C4
San Ginesio [I] 132 D2
Sanginkylä [FIN] 216 C2
San Giorgio [I] 142 C5
San Giorgio di Livenza [I] 118 D4
San Giórgio di Nogaro [I] 118 E3
San Giorgio Iónico [I] 136 D3
San Giovanni, Grotta– [I] 136 E2
San Giovanni, Grotta di– [I] 142 B5
San Giovanni al Mavone [I] 132 E3
San Giovanni a Piro [I] 136 B3
San Giovanni di Sínis [I] 142 B4
San Giovanni in Croce [I] 128 B1
San Giovanni in Fiore [I] 138 E2
San Giovanni in Persiceto [I] 128 C2
San Giovanni in Venere [I] 132 F3
San Giovanni Lupatoto [I] 118 B4
San Giovanni Rotondo [I] 134 E2
San Giovanni Suergiu [I] 142 B5
San Giovanni Valdarno [I] 128 C4
San Giovenale [I] 130 F3
Sangis [S] 222 B4
San Giuliano Terme [I] 128 B3
San Giuseppe Jato [I] 140 C2
San Giustino [I] 128 D4
San Giusto [I] 132 D2
Sangla [EST] 230 E3

San Godenzo [I] **128** C3
Sangonera la Verde [E]
106 D2
Sangüesa / Zangoza [E] **88** A3
Sanguinet [F] **78** B4
Sáni [GR] **162** B2
San Ignacio de Loiola [E]
86 E3
Sanitz [D] **32** E2
San Javier [E] **106** E3
San José [E] **106** C4
San José / Sant Josep [E]
108 E2
San José del Valle [E] **104** B3
San Juan de Alicante /
Sant Joan d'Alacant [E] **106** F2
San Juan del Olmo [E] **92** C3
San Juan de los Terreros [E]
106 D3
San Juan del Puerto [E] **98** D4
San Juan de Muskiz [E] **86** D2
San Juan de Ortega [E] **86** D4
Sankovo [RUS] **240** E1
Sankt Andrä [A] **74** D3
Sankt Gertraud /
Santa Gertrude [I] **118** B2
Sankt Kathrein am Hauenstein
[A] **74** C4
Sankt Leonhard [A] **118** B1
Sankt Leonhard in Passeier /
San Leonardo in Passiria
[I] **118** B1
Sankt Magdalena / Santa
Maddalena Vallalta [I] **118** D2
Sankt Margareten [A] **120** A2
Sankt Martin [A] **72** E4
Sankt–Michaelisdonn [D]
32 B2
Sankt–Peterburg [RUS] **200** F3
Sankt Valentin auf der Haide /
San Valentino alla Muta [I]
118 B1
San Lazzaro di Savena [I]
128 C2
San Leo [I] **128** D3
San Leonardo [I] **134** E2
San Leonardo, Monasterio
de– [E] **92** C2
San Leonardo de Yagüe
[E] **94** A2
San Leonardo in Passiria /
Sankt Leonhard in Passeier
[I] **118** B1
San Lorenzo [I] **138** D4
San Lorenzo de Calatrava
[E] **100** D4
San Lorenzo de El Escorial
[E] **92** E3
San Lorenzo de la Parrilla
[E] **102** B2
San Lorenzo in Campo [I]
128 E2
San Lorenzo Nuovo [I] **130** F2
San Luca [I] **138** D3
Sanlúcar de Barrameda [E]
104 B2
Sanlúcar la Mayor [E] **98** E4
San Lúcido [I] **138** D1
Sanluri [I] **142** B4
San Marcello Pistoiese [I]
128 B3
San Marco Argentano [I]
136 C4
San Marco dei Cavoti [I]
134 D3
San Marco in Lamis [I] **134** E2
San Marino [RSM] **128** E3
Sànmartin [RO] **122** F1
San Martín de la Vega [I]
92 E4
San Martín del Pedroso
[E] **84** D2

San Martín del Rey Aurelio /
Sotrondio [E] **82** F3
San Martín de Pusa [E]
100 D1
San Martín de Unx [E] **88** A3
San Martín de Valdeiglesias
[E] **92** D4
San Martino Buon Albergo
[I] **118** B4
San Martino dei Colli [I]
130 F1
San Martino della Battaglia
[I] **118** B4
San Martino delle Scale [I]
140 C1
San Martino di Castrozza [I]
118 C2
San Martino di Lupari [I]
118 C3
San Mateo de Gállego [E]
94 E2
San Mauro Castelverde [I]
138 A4
San Michele all'Ádige [I]
118 B2
San Michele di Plaianu [I]
142 B2
San Michele Salentino [I]
136 E2
San Miguel de Bernúy [E]
92 E2
San Miguel de las Dueñas
[E] **82** E3
San Miguel de Salinas [E]
106 E2
San Millan [E] **86** D3
San Millán de la Cogolla
[E] **86** D4
San Miniato [I] **128** B4
Sänna [EST] **230** F4
Sänna [S] **188** F3
Sänna [S] **196** D1
Sänna [S] **204** F4
S. Anna di Alfaedo [I] **118** B3
Sannazzaro de' Burgondi [I]
116 D4
Sannenmöser [CH] **116** C1
Sannicandro di Bari [I] **136** D2
Sannicandro Gargánico [I]
134 E2
San Nicolás de Tolentino [E]
112 D3
Sànnicolau Mare [RO] **122** D3
Nicolò [I] **128** D2
San Nicolò di Trullas [I]
142 B3
San Nicolò Gerrei [I] **142** C5
Sannidal [N] **186** E3
Sanniki [PL] **48** D2
Sanok [PL] **64** D3
San Pancrazio Salentino [I]
136 E2
San Paolo [I] **142** C2
San Paolo di Civitate [I]
134 E2
San Paolo di Peltuino [I]
132 E2
San Pedro [E] **86** B2
San Pedro [I] **102** A4
San Pedro de Alcántara [E]
104 C3
San Pedro de Arlanza [E]
94 A1
San Pedro de la Nave [E] **84** E3
San Pedro del Arroyo [E]
92 D3
San Pedro del Pinatar [E]
106 E3
San Pedro de Mérida [E] **98** F2
San Pelayo [E] **92** E1
San Pellegrino in Alpe [I]
128 B3

San Pellegrino Terme [I]
116 E3
San Piero a Sieve [I] **128** C3
San Pietro, Badia di– [I]
128 F4
San Pietro di Simbranos [I]
142 B2
San Pietro di Sorres [I] **142** B3
San Pietro in Casale [I] **128** C2
San Pietro in Valle [I] **132** D2
San Pietro Vernotico [I] **136** E3
San Polo d'Enza [I] **128** B2
San Priamo [I] **142** C5
San Prospero [I] **128** C2
Sanquhar [GB] **20** C2
San Quírico d'Orcia [I] **130** E1
San Rafael [E] **92** E3
San Rafael del Río [E] **96** A4
Sanremo [I] **126** D3
San Roman de Cameros
[E] **94** B1
San Roque [E] **82** B2
San Roque [E] **104** C4
San Roque de Riomera [E]
86 D2
San Rufo [I] **134** E4
San Sadurniño [E] **82** C1
San Salvatore Monferrato
[I] **116** D4
San Salvo [I] **134** D1
San Sebastián de la Gomera
[E] **112** C2
San Sebastiano Curone [I]
126 E1
Sansepolcro [I] **128** D4
San Servando, Castillo de– [E]
100 E1
San Severino Marche [I]
132 D2
San Severo [I] **134** E2
San Sicario [I] **116** B4
Sanski Most [BIH] **144** E2
San Sosti [I] **136** B4
Santa, Cova– [E] **108** E2
Santa Amalia [E] **100** A2
Santa Ana de Cambas [P]
98 C3
Santa Bàrbara [I] **96** B4
Santa Bárbara [E] **98** D3
Santa Bárbara [P] **110** C3
Santacara [E] **88** A4
Santa Caterina di Pittinuri
[I] **142** B3
Santa Caterina Valfurva [I]
118 A2
Santa Caterina Villarmosa
[I] **140** D2
Santa Cesarea Terme [I]
136 F3
Santa Clara–a–Velha [P] **98** B3
Santa Coloma [AND] **96** C1
Santa Coloma de Farners
[E] **96** E2
Santa Coloma de Queralt
[E] **96** C3
Santa Colomba de Somoza
[E] **82** E4
Santa Comba [E] **82** B2
Santa Comba Dão [P] **84** A4
Santa Comba de Rossas
[P] **84** D2
Santa Cristina / St Christina
[I] **118** C2
Santa Cristina d'Aro [E] **96** E3
Santa Croce Camerina [I]
140 D4
Santa Croce di Magliano [I]
134 D2
Santa Croce d. Sannio [I]
134 D2
Santa Croce sull'Arno [I]
128 B3

Santa Cruz [P] **110** E4
Santa Cruz da Graciosa [P]
110 B3
Santa Cruz das Flores [P]
110 B2
Santa Cruz de Campezo /
Santi Kurutze Kanpezu
[E] **86** E4
Santa Cruz de la Palma [E]
112 B1
Santa Cruz de la Serós [E]
88 B4
Santa Cruz de la Sierra [E]
100 B2
Santa Cruz de la Zarza [E]
100 F1
Santa Cruz del Retamar [E]
92 D4
Santa Cruz de Moya [E]
102 C2
Santa Cruz de Mudela [E]
100 E4
Santa Cruz de Tenerife [E]
112 D2
Santadi [I] **142** B5
Santa Domenica Vittoria [I]
138 C4
Santa Elena [E] **100** D4
Santaella [E] **104** D2
Santa Eufemia [E] **100** C3
Santa Eulalia [E] **82** F3
Santa Eulália [P] **90** D4
Santa Eulalia del Río /
Santa Eulària des Riu [E]
108 E2
Santa Eulalia de Oscos [E]
82 D2
Santa Eulària des Riu / Santa
Eulalia del Río [E] **108** E2
Santa Fé [E] **104** F3
Santafiora [I] **130** F2
Sant'Agata dè Goti [I] **134** D3
Sant'Ágata di Militello [I]
138 B4
Sant'Agata di Púglia [I] **134** E3
Santa Gertrude /
Sankt Gertraud [I] **118** B2
Sant'Agostino [I] **128** C2
Sant Agusti de Lluçanes
[E] **96** D2
Santa Iría [P] **98** D3
Santa Justa [P] **90** C4
Sant'Alberto di Butrio [I]
126 F1
Santa Luce [I] **128** B4
Santa Lucía [E] **112** E4
Santa Lucía del Mela [I]
138 C3
Santa Luzia [P] **82** A4
Santa Luzia [P] **98** B3
Santa Maddalena Vallalta /
Sankt Magdalena [I] **118** D2
Santa Magdalena de Polpis
[E] **102** E2
Santa Margalida [E] **108** D3
Santa Margarida de Montbui
[E] **96** C3
Santa Margarida do Sado
[P] **98** C2
Santa Margherita [I] **142** B6
Santa Margherita di Bélice
[I] **140** B2
Santa Margherita Lígure [I]
126 F2
Santa María [E] **108** D3
Santa María a Piè di Chienti
[I] **132** E1
Santa María Arabona [I]
132 E3
Santa María Cápua Vetere
[I] **134** C3

Santa Maria da Feira [P] **84** A3
Santa Maria d'Anglona [I]
136 C3
Santa María de Cayón [E]
86 C2
Santa María de Huerta [E]
94 B3
Santa Maria dei Lattani [I]
134 C2
Santa María de las Hoyas
[E] **94** A2
Santa María del Campo
[E] **86** C4
Santa María del Páramo
[E] **82** E4
Santa María de Nieva [E]
106 C3
Santa María di Bressanoro
[I] **116** E4
Santa María di Corte, Abbazia
di– [I] **142** B3
Santa María di Portonovo
[I] **128** F4
Santa María di Propezzano
[I] **132** E3
Santa María di Rambona [I]
132 E1
Santa María di Ronzano [I]
132 E3
Santa María di Siponto [I]
134 F2
Santa María in Valle Porclaneta
[I] **132** D3
Santa María la Real de Nieva
[E] **92** D2
Santa María Maggiore [I]
116 D2
Santa Maria Mayor [P] **84** B3
Santa Maria Navarrese [I]
142 C4
Santa Maria Nuova [I] **128** F4
Santa Marinella [I] **130** F3
Santa Marta [E] **98** E2
Santa Marta [E] **102** A3
Santa Marta [P] **98** C3
Santa Marta de Tormes
[E] **84** E4
Santana [P] **110** E3
Sântana [RO] **122** E2
Santana da Serra [P] **98** B3
Santana do Mato [P] **90** C3
Santander [E] **86** D2
Sant'Andrea [I] **136** F3
Sant'Andrea Bagni [I] **128** B2
Sant'Andrea di Conza [I]
134 E3
Sant'Andrea Fríus [I] **142** C5
Sant'Ángelo in Vado [I] **128** D4
Sant'Angelo Lodigiano [I]
116 E4
Santa Ninfa [I] **140** B2
Sant'Anna, Santuario di– [I]
126 C2
Sant'Anna Arresi [I] **142** B5
Sant'Antimo, Abbazia di– [I]
130 E1
Sant'Antine, Nuraghe– [I]
142 B3
Sant'Antíoco [I] **142** B5
Sant Antoni de Portmany
[E] **108** E2
Sant'António di Gallura [I]
142 C2
Santanyí [E] **108** D4
Santa Olalla [E] **92** D4
Santa Olalla del Cala [E] **98** E3
Santa Pau [E] **96** E2
Santa Pola [E] **106** F2
Sant'Apollinare in Classe [I]
128 D2
Santa Ponça [E] **108** C3
Sant'Arcangelo [I] **136** C3

Santarcángelo di Romagna [I] 128 E3
Santarém [P] 90 B3
Santa Restituta [I] 130 F2
Santa Sabina, Nuraghe~ [I] 142 B3
Santa Severa [F] 130 B1
Santa Severa [I] 130 F3
Santas Martas [E] 82 F4
Santa Sofia [I] 128 D3
Santa Susanna [E] 96 E3
Santa Tegra, Monte de~ [E] 82 A4
Santa Teresa di Riva [I] 138 C4
Santa Teresa Gallura [I] 130 B4
Santa Uxía de Ribeira [E] 82 A3
Santa Vitória [P] 98 C2
Sant Boi de Llobregat [E] 96 D3
Sant Carles de la Ràpita [E] 96 B4
Sant Celoni [E] 96 E3
Sant Cugat Sesgarrigues [E] 96 D3
Santed [E] 94 C3
Sant'Elia a Pianisti [I] 134 D2
Sant'Elia Fiumerapido [I] 134 C2
San Telmo [E] 98 D3
Santena [I] 116 C4
San Teodoro [I] 142 C2
Santéramo in Colle [I] 136 C2
Santervás de Campos [E] 86 A4
Santes Creus [E] 96 C3
Sant'Eufémia Lamézia [I] 138 E2
Sant'Eutizio, Abbazia di~ [I] 132 D2
Sant Feliu de Codines [E] 96 D3
Sant Feliu de Guíxols [E] 96 E3
Sant Feliu de Llobregat [E] 96 D3
Sant Ferran de Ses Roquetes [E] 108 E2
Sant Francesc de Formentera [E] 108 E2
Sant Grau [E] 96 E3
Santhià [I] 116 C4
Sant Hilari Sacalm [E] 96 E2
Sant Hipòlit de Voltregà [E] 96 D2
Santiago [P] 84 D3
Santiago, Cuevas de~ [E] 98 F3
Santiago de Alcántara [E] 90 E3
Santiago de Calatrava [E] 104 E1
Santiago de Compostela [E] 82 B2
Santiago de la Espada [E] 106 C1
Santiago de la Ribera [E] 106 E3
Santiago del Campo [E] 90 F3
Santiago do Cacém [P] 98 B2
Santiago do Escoural [P] 90 C4
Santibáñez [E] 86 B3
Santibáñez de Ayllón [E] 92 F2
Santibáñez de la Sierra [E] 92 B3
Santibáñez de Vidriales [E] 84 E2
Santibáñez Zarzaguda [E] 86 C4
Santi Kurutze Kanpezu / Santa Cruz de Campezo [E] 86 E4

Santillana del Mar [E] 86 C2
Santimamiñe [E] 86 E3
Santiponce [E] 98 E4
Santissima Trinitá di Saccargia [I] 142 B2
Santisteban del Puerto [E] 106 B1
Sant Joan d'Alacant / San Juan de Alicante [E] 106 F2
Sant Joan de les Abadesses [E] 96 E2
Sant Joan de Llabritja [E] 108 F2
Sant Joan de Vilatorrada [E] 96 D2
Sant Josep, Gruta de~ [E] 102 D3
Sant Josep / San José [E] 108 E2
Sant Juliá de Lória [AND] 96 D1
Sant Llorenç de Morunys [E] 96 D2
Sant Lluís [E] 108 F3
Sant Martí Sarroca [E] 96 C3
Sant Mateu [E] 96 A4
Sant Miquel de Balansat [E] 108 E2
Santo Aleixo [P] 90 D4
Santo Aleixo da Restauração [P] 98 D3
Santo Amador [P] 98 D2
Santo André [P] 98 B2
Santo Domingo [E] 100 B4
Santo Domingo de la Calzada [E] 86 D4
Santo Domingo de Silos [E] 94 A1
Santo Estevão [P] 90 E2
Santo Estevo [E] 82 C3
Santo Estevo, Monasterio de~ [E] 82 C3
Santok [PL] 46 D1
S. Antolín [E] 86 B2
Santomera [E] 106 E2
Santoméri [GR] 166 D4
Santoña [E] 86 D2
S. Antoni de Calonge [E] 96 E3
S. Antonio di Santadí [I] 142 B4
Santo Stefano [I] 142 C5
Santo Stefano Belbo [I] 126 D1
Santo Stéfano di Cadore [I] 118 D2
Santo Stefano di Camastra [I] 138 B4
Santo Stéfano Quisquina [I] 140 C2
Santo Stino di Livenza [I] 118 D3
Santo Tirso [P] 84 B2
Santo Tomé [E] 106 B1
Santo Tomé del Puerto [E] 92 F3
Santovenia [E] 84 F2
Santovenia de Pisuerga [E] 92 D1
Sant Pau de Seguries [E] 96 E2
Sant Pere de Rodes [E] 96 F2
Sant Pere Pescador [E] 96 F2
Sant Pol de Mar [E] 96 E3
Sant Quirze de Besora [E] 96 D2
Sant Quirze de Colera [E] 96 F2
Sant Rafel [E] 108 E2
Sant Sadurní d'Anoia [E] 96 D3
Sant Salvador [E] 108 D4
Sant Tomàs [E] 108 E4
Santu Lussúrgiu [I] 142 B3
Santurce / Santurtzi [E] 86 D3
Santurtzi / Santurce [E] 86 D3

Sant Vicenç de Castellet [E] 96 D3
Sant Vicent del Raspeig / San Vicente del Raspeig [E] 106 F2
Sant Vicent de sa Cala [E] 108 F2
San Urbez, Santuario de~ [E] 88 C4
San Valentino alla Muta / Sankt Valentin auf der Haide [I] 118 B1
San Venanzo [I] 130 F2
San Vicente de Alcántara [E] 90 E3
San Vicente de la Barquera [E] 86 C2
San Vicente del Raspeig / Sant Vicent del Raspeig [E] 106 F2
San Vincenzo [I] 130 D1
San Vincenzo, Abbazia di~ [I] 134 C2
San Vito [I] 142 C5
San Vito al Tagliamento [I] 118 D3
San Vito Chietino [I] 132 F3
San Vito dei Normanni [I] 136 E2
San Vito di Cadore [I] 118 D2
San Vito lo Capo [I] 140 B1
San Vito Romano [I] 132 D4
San Vittore delle Chiuse [I] 128 E4
Sanxay [F] 66 D4
Sanxenxo [E] 82 A3
Sanza [I] 136 B3
Sanzay [F] 66 D3
São Barnabé [P] 98 B3
São Bartolomeu [P] 98 C3
São Bartolomeu da Serra [E] 98 B2
São Bartolomeu de Messines [P] 98 B3
São Brás de Alportel [P] 98 C4
São Cristóvão [P] 90 B4
São Domingos [P] 98 B2
São Francisco da Serra [P] 98 B2
São Gregório [P] 82 B4
São Jacinto [P] 84 A3
São João [P] 110 A3
São João da Madeira [P] 84 A3
São João da Pesqueira [P] 84 C3
São João da Serra [P] 84 B3
São João dos Caldeireiros [P] 98 C3
São Luís [P] 98 B3
São Manços [P] 98 C2
São Marcos [P] 84 A4
São Marcos da Ataboeira [P] 98 C3
São Marcos da Serra [P] 98 B3
São Martinho [P] 84 A4
São Martinho das Amoreiras [P] 98 B3
São Martinho do Porto [P] 90 B2
São Mateus [P] 110 A3
São Mateus da Calheta [P] 110 C3
São Matias [P] 98 C2
São Miguel de Acha [P] 90 E2
São Miguel de Machede [P] 90 C4
São Miguel do Pinheiro [P] 98 C3
São Pedro [P] 84 A4
São Pedro da Cadeira [P] 90 A3
São Pedro de Balsemão [P] 84 B3

São Pedro de Muel [P] 90 B2
São Pedro de Solis [P] 98 C3
São Pedro do Sul [P] 84 B3
Saorge [F] 126 C3
São Romão [P] 90 C4
São Romão [P] 98 C2
São Sebastião [P] 110 C4
São Teotónio [P] 98 B3
Saou [F] 124 E1
São Vicente [P] 110 D3
São Vicente da Beira [P] 90 D2
Sapareva Banya [BG] 156 B2
Sapernoye [RUS] 200 E2
Sápes [GR] 156 E4
Saphane [TR] 164 F3
Sápjane [HR] 120 A4
sa Pobla [E] 108 D3
Sapotskin [BY] 38 D2
Sappada [I] 118 D2
Sappee [FIN] 198 E1
Sappee [FIN] 198 F1
Sappemeer [NL] 30 D2
Sappen [N] 224 E2
Sappisaasi [S] 220 E1
Sappu [FIN] 210 D3
Sapri [I] 136 B3
Saqués [E] 88 C4
Saraby [N] 228 B2
Sarafovo [BG] 150 E4
Säräisniemi [FIN] 216 C3
Sarajevo [BIH] 146 B3
Saráikino [GR] 168 B1
Saráikinoí [GR] 160 E2
Saralog [RUS] 232 E2
Saramon [F] 88 E2
Sáránd [H] 76 E4
Saranda [AL] 160 B4
Saransko [BG] 158 A1
Sarantsi [BG] 156 B1
Sarata [UA] 246 D4
Saray [TR] 158 C3
Saraycık [TR] 164 E4
Sarayçık [TR] 176 F1
Sarayköy [TR] 170 D2
Šarbanovac [SRB] 148 B2
Sarbia [PL] 36 A4
Sarbinowo [PL] 34 F2
Sarbinowo [PL] 46 C1
Sárbogárd [H] 122 A2
Sarby [PL] 62 C2
Sarceda [E] 86 C2
Sárdara [I] 142 B4
Sardara, Terme di~ [I] 142 B4
Sardes [TR] 164 D4
Sardínia [GR] 166 C2
Sardoal [P] 90 C3
S'Arenal [E] 108 D3
S'Arenal d'en Castell [E] 108 F3
Sárengrad [HR] 146 C1
Sarentino / Sarnthein [I] 118 C2
Sárenz [BG] 150 E2
Sarga, Cova de la~ [E] 106 F1
Sargans [CH] 70 F4
Sári [H] 76 B4
Sari d'Orcino [F] 130 A3
Sarıgöl [TR] 170 D2
Sarıkaya [TR] 170 D2
Sarıköy [TR] 164 C1
Sariñena [E] 94 E3
Šarišský Hrad [SK] 76 D1
Sarısu [TR] 158 F4
Sarıyer [TR] 158 E3
Sarkad [H] 122 E2
Sarkadkeresztúr [H] 122 E2
Särkijärvi [FIN] 216 C2
Särkilahti [FIN] 198 F1

Särkilahti [FIN] 210 D4
Särkimo [FIN] 208 C1
Särkisalmi [FIN] 210 E4
Särkisalo [FIN] 208 F2
Särkisalo / Finby [FIN] 198 D4
Särkkä [FIN] 210 C1
Šarkovo [BG] 158 A2
Şarköy [TR] 158 B4
Sarlat–la–Canéda [F] 78 E4
Sarmizegetuza [RO] 248 C3
Särna [S] 194 D1
Sarnaki [PL] 50 C1
Sarnano [I] 132 D2
Sarnate [LV] 234 D3
Sarnen [CH] 116 D1
Sarnes [E] 86 B2
Sárnico [I] 116 F3
Särnino [BG] 150 F2
Sarno [I] 134 D3
Sarnow [D] 34 C3
Sarnow [PL] 46 F3
Sarnówek [PL] 50 A4
Sarnthein / Sarentino [I] 118 C2
Sarny [UA] 242 B4
Särö [S] 182 F2
Saronída [GR] 168 B3
Saronno [I] 116 E3
Sárospatak [H] 76 E2
Šarovce [SK] 76 A3
Sarpsborg [N] 188 B2
Sarracín [E] 86 C4
Sarral [E] 96 C3
Sarralbe [F] 56 E4
Sarrebourg [F] 56 E4
Sarreguemines [F] 56 E4
Sárrétudvari [H] 76 D4
Sarre–Union [F] 56 E4
Sarria [E] 82 D3
Sarrión [E] 102 D2
Sarroch [I] 142 B5
Sarron [F] 88 C2
Sarsila İskele [TR] 176 D1
Sársina [I] 128 D3
Sarstedt [D] 44 C2
Sárszentlőrinc [H] 122 A2
Sarteano [I] 130 F1
Sartène [I] 130 A3
Sárti [GR] 162 C2
Sartilly [F] 52 E3
Sartmustafa [TR] 164 D4
Saruhanli [TR] 164 C4
Sárvár [H] 74 D4
Sarvela [FIN] 208 C3
Sarvijoki [FIN] 208 B2
Sarvikumpu [FIN] 210 D2
Sarvinki [FIN] 210 E2
Sarvisvaara [S] 220 E3
Sárvsjön [S] 204 D3
Sarzana [I] 128 A3
Sarzeau [F] 66 B1
Sarzedas [P] 90 D2
Sasa [MK] 154 E3
Sa Savina [E] 108 E2
Sasca Montană [RO] 146 F2
Sásd [H] 120 F3
Šášov [SK] 76 A2
Sassari [I] 142 B2
Sassello [I] 126 E2
Sassenage [F] 80 E3
Sassenberg [D] 30 B4
Sassenheim [NL] 30 B3
Sassnitz [D] 34 C1
Sassocorvaro [I] 128 E3
Sassoferrato [I] 128 E4
Sassofortino [I] 130 E1
Sasso Marconi [I] 128 C2
Sassonero [I] 128 C3
Sassuolo [I] 128 B2
Šaštín–Stráže [SK] 74 E2
Sastmola / Merikarvia [FIN] 208 B4

Såtåhaugvoll [N] 204 B3
Sataniv [UA] 244 D2
Sátão [P] 84 B3
Satchinez [RO] 122 E3
Såtenäs [S] 188 D4
Säter [S] 188 E4
Säter [S] 196 B4
Sätila [S] 184 A2
Satırlar [TR] 164 C4
Sätofta [S] 180 C2
Sátoraljaújhely [H] 76 E2
Satovcha [BG] 156 C3
Satow [D] 32 E2
Sätra brunn [S] 190 C1
Sátres [GR] 156 D3
Satrup [D] 178 B3
Sattajärvi [S] 222 A2
Sattanen [FIN] 222 C1
Sattendorf [A] 118 F2
Satter [S] 220 F2
Satu Mare [RO] 244 C3
Saturn [RO] 150 F2
Saturnia [I] 130 E2
Saturnia, Terme di– [I] 130 E2
Saucats [F] 78 B4
Sauclières [F] 124 C2
Sauda [N] 186 B1
Sauðárkrókur [IS] 218 B2
Saudasjøen [N] 186 B1
Saudron [F] 70 A1
Saue [EST] 230 C2
Saue [EST] 230 C2
Sauerbrunn [A] 120 B1
Sauerlach [D] 72 C3
Saugos [LT] 238 A2
Saugues [F] 80 B3
Saujon [F] 78 B2
Saukkola [FIN] 198 E3
Saukonkyla [FIN] 208 D2
Sauland [N] 186 E1
Saulieu [F] 68 E3
Saulkrasti [LV] 236 B2
Sault [F] 124 F2
Sault–de–Navailles [F] 88 C2
Saulvaux [F] 56 C4
Saulx [F] 70 B3
Saulxures [F] 70 C2
Saumur [F] 66 E2
Saunajärvi [FIN] 216 E3
Saunakylä [FIN] 208 C4
Saunalahti [FIN] 210 C3
Saunavaara [FIN] 222 D2
Saus [N] 212 D2
Sausheim [F] 70 D3
Sauvagnat [F] 80 A2
Sauve [F] 124 D2
Sauveterre–de–Béarn [F] 88 B2
Sauveterre–de–Guyenne [F] 78 C4
Sauviat–sur–Vige [F] 78 F2
Sauvo / Sagu [FIN] 198 D3
Sauxillanges [F] 80 B2
Sauze d'Oulx [I] 116 B4
Sauzet [F] 88 E1
Sauzé–Vaussais [F] 78 D1
Sauzon [F] 66 A1
Sava [BG] 150 E3
Sava [I] 136 E3
Sävar [S] 206 F1
Sävärşin [RO] 122 F3
Sävast [S] 214 E1
Savaştepe [TR] 164 C3
Savci [SLO] 120 C2
Säve [S] 182 F1
Savelletri [I] 136 D2
Savelli [I] 138 E1
Savenaho [FIN] 210 B4
Savenay [F] 66 C2
Saverdun [F] 88 E3
Saverne [F] 70 D1
Savero [FIN] 200 C2

Savi [FIN] 198 D1
Sävia [FIN] 210 B1
Savigliano [I] 126 D1
Savignac–les–Eglises [F] 78 D3
Savignano Irpino [I] 134 E3
Savignano sul Rubicone [I] 128 D3
Savigny–sur–Braye [F] 66 F2
Savijärvi [FIN] 216 E3
Savikoski [FIN] 198 D2
Savikylä [FIN] 216 E4
Savines–le–Lac [F] 126 B1
Savine Vode [KS] 154 B2
Savinlemi [FIN] 198 E2
Savino Selo [SRB] 122 C4
Saviore dell'Adamello [I] 118 A3
Savitaipale [FIN] 200 C2
Sävja [S] 190 D1
Šavnik [MNE] 152 E2
Savognin [CH] 116 E2
Sávoly [H] 120 E2
Savona [I] 126 E2
Savonlinna / Nyslott [FIN] 210 D3
Savonranta [FIN] 210 D3
Sävsjö [S] 184 D2
Sävsjön [S] 188 F1
Sävsjöström [S] 184 D3
Savudrija [HR] 118 E4
Savukoski [FIN] 222 D1
Sax [E] 106 E1
Saxdalen [S] 188 F1
Saxnäs [S] 212 F3
Saxtorpsskogen [S] 178 F2
Saxvallen [S] 204 D1
Säynätsalo [FIN] 208 F3
Säyneinen [FIN] 210 C1
Sázava [CZ] 60 E3
Sazonovo [RUS] 240 D1
S. Baudelio, Ermita de– [E] 94 B2
S. Benito de la Contienda [E] 98 E2
S. Biágio [I] 128 D2
Scaër [F] 52 B3
Scafa [I] 132 E3
Scalasaig [GB] 18 A3
Scalea [I] 136 B4
Scaletta Zanclea [I] 138 C4
Scålevik [N] 186 D4
Scalloway [GB] 16 E4
Scandiano [I] 128 B2
Scanno [I] 132 E4
Scansano [I] 130 E2
Scanzano Jónico [I] 136 C3
Scarborough [GB] 24 D1
Scardovari [I] 128 D2
Scarinish [GB] 14 A4
S. Carlo [I] 140 C2
Scarperia [I] 128 C3
Scarriff [IRL] 10 C2
Šćepan Polje [MNE] 152 E1
Scepsis [TR] 164 B2
Schaan [FL] 70 F4
Schachendorf [A] 74 D4
Schackenborg [DK] 178 B3
Schackendorf [D] 32 C2
Schaffhausen [CH] 70 E3
Schafstädt [D] 44 E3
Schäftlarn [D] 72 C3
Schagen [NL] 30 B2
Schalkholz [D] 32 B1
Schalkau [A] 74 C3
Schallstadt [D] 70 D2
Schangnau [CH] 116 C1
Schaprode [D] 34 C1
Scharbeutz [D] 32 E2
Schärding [A] 72 F2
Scharfeneck [A] 74 D3
Scharnitz [A] 72 C4

Scharnstein [A] 72 F3
Schaumberg [A] 72 F2
Scheer [D] 70 F2
Scheessel [D] 32 B3
Schéggia [I] 128 E4
Scheibbs [A] 74 B3
Scheifling [A] 120 A1
Scheinfeld [D] 58 D3
Schellenberger Eishöhle [D] 72 E3
Schemmerhofen [D] 72 A2
Schenefeld [D] 32 B2
Scherfede [D] 42 F3
Schermbeck [D] 42 D2
Scherneck [D] 72 B2
Schesslitz [D] 58 E3
Scheveningen [NL] 30 A3
Scheyern [D] 72 C2
Schieder [D] 42 F2
Schierling [D] 72 D1
Schiermonnikoog [NL] 30 D1
Schiers [CH] 116 F1
Schifferstadt [D] 58 B3
Schilde [B] 40 E3
Schilpário [I] 116 F3
Schiltach [D] 70 E2
Schio [I] 118 C3
Schirets' [UA] 64 F3
Schirmeck [F] 70 D1
Schirnding [D] 60 B2
Schitu [RO] 150 B2
Schkeuditz [D] 44 E3
Schladen [D] 44 C2
Schladming [A] 72 F4
Schläg [A] 72 F2
Schlaining [A] 74 D4
Schlaiten [A] 118 D1
Schlaitz [D] 44 E3
Schlanders / Silandro [I] 118 B2
Schlangenbad [D] 58 B2
Schleching [D] 72 D3
Schleiden [D] 42 C4
Schleiz [D] 58 F2
Schleswig [D] 32 B1
Schleusingen [D] 58 E2
Schlieben [D] 46 B3
Schlierbach [A] 74 A3
Schliersee [D] 72 C3
Schlitz [D] 32 E3
Schlitz [D] 58 D1
Schlierten [D] 44 C2
Schloss [D] 58 B3
Schlosshof [A] 74 D3
Schlosspark [F] 56 F4
Schlotheim [D] 44 C3
Schluchsee [D] 70 E3
Schlüchtern [D] 58 C2
Schluderbach / Carbonin [I] 118 D2
Schluderns / Sluderno [I] 118 B2
Schlüssberg [A] 72 F3
Schlüsselfeld [D] 58 E3
Schlutup [D] 32 D2
Schmalkalden [D] 58 E1
Schmallenberg [D] 42 E3
Schmidmühlen [D] 58 F4
Schmilka [D] 60 D1
Schmölln [D] 34 D3
Schmölln [D] 44 E4
Schnackenburg [D] 32 D4
Schnaittenbach [D] 60 A3
Schneeberg [D] 60 B2
Schneverdingen [D] 32 B3
Schober Pass [A] 74 B4
Schöder [A] 118 F1
Schöllkrippen [D] 58 C2
Schönau [D] 70 D3
Schönbach [A] 74 B2
Schönbeck [D] 34 C3
Schönberg [A] 72 C4

Schönberg [D] 32 C1
Schönberg [D] 32 D2
Schönberg [D] 60 B2
Schönberg [D] 72 E1
Schönbergerstrand [D] 32 C1
Schönborn [A] 74 D2
Schönebeck [D] 32 E4
Schönebeck [D] 44 E2
Schönecken [D] 56 E2
Schongau [D] 72 B3
Schönhagen [D] 32 C2
Schöningen [D] 44 D2
Schönleiten [D] 72 C2
Schönmünzach [D] 70 E1
Schöntal [D] 58 C3
Schönthal [D] 60 B4
Schönwald [D] 70 E2
Schönwalde [D] 32 D2
Schönwalde [D] 46 B1
Schoondijke [NL] 40 D2
Schoonebeek [NL] 30 D2
Schoonhoven [NL] 30 B4
Schoonoord [NL] 30 D3
Schopfheim [D] 70 D3
Schopfloch [D] 58 D4
Schöppenstedt [D] 44 D2
Schoppernau [A] 72 A4
Schöppingen [D] 30 E4
Schorndorf [D] 72 A1
Schotten [D] 58 C1
Schramberg [D] 70 E2
Schrems [A] 74 B2
Schriesheim [D] 58 B3
Schrobenhausen [D] 72 C2
Schröcken [A] 72 A4
Schruns [A] 72 A4
Schull [IRL] 10 B4
Schüpfheim [CH] 70 D4
Schuttertal [D] 70 E2
Schüttorf [D] 30 E3
Schwaan [D] 32 E2
Schwabach [D] 58 E4
Schwabhausen [D] 44 C4
Schwabhausen [D] 72 C2
Schwäbisch Gmünd [D] 72 A1
Schwäbisch Hall [D] 58 C4
Schwabmünchen [D] 72 B2
Schwaförden [D] 32 A4
Schwaigern [D] 58 C4
Schwalenberg [D] 42 F2
Schwalmstadt–Treysa [D] 42 F4
Schwalmstadt–Ziegenhain [D] 42 F4
Schwanbeck [D] 34 C3
Schwanden [CH] 70 F4
Schwandorf [D] 60 B4
Schwanebeck [D] 44 D2
Schwanenstadt [A] 72 F3
Schwanewede [D] 32 A3
Schwaney [D] 42 F3
Schwarmstedt [D] 32 B4
Schwarzach [A] 72 E4
Schwarzburg [D] 58 E1
Schwarzenau [A] 74 B2
Schwarzenbach [D] 60 A2
Schwarzenbek [D] 32 C3
Schwarzenfeld [D] 60 B4
Schwarzenfels [D] 58 D2
Schwarze Pumpe [D] 46 C3
Schwarzsee [CH] 116 C1
Schwaz [A] 72 C4
Schwechat [A] 74 D3
Schweden–Stein [D] 44 E4
Schwedt [D] 34 D4
Schwegenheim [D] 58 B3
Schweich [D] 56 E2
Schweinfurt [D] 58 D2
Schweitenkirchen [D] 72 C2
Schwelm [D] 42 D3
Schwenningen [D] 70 E2

Schwerin [D] 32 D3
Schwerte [D] 42 D3
Schwetzingen [D] 58 B3
Schwittersdorf [D] 44 E3
Schwuelper [D] 44 C2
Schwyz [CH] 70 E4
Sciacca [I] 140 B2
Sciara del Fuoco [I] 138 C2
Scicli [I] 140 E4
Scilla [I] 138 D3
Ścinawa [PL] 46 E3
Scoglitti [I] 140 D4
S. Colombano al Lambro [I] 116 E4
Scopello [I] 116 C3
Scopello [I] 140 B1
Scurdia [I] 140 E3
Scornicești [RO] 148 F1
Scorzè [I] 118 C4
Scotch Corner [GB] 20 E4
Scourie [GB] 14 D1
Scrabster [GB] 14 F1
Scrignac [F] 52 B3
Scritto [I] 132 C1
Scunthorpe [GB] 24 D3
Scuol [CH] 118 A1
Scupi [MK] 154 D4
S. Damiano Macra [I] 126 C2
S. Doménico [I] 116 D2
Seaford [GB] 28 C4
Seaham [GB] 20 F3
Seara [E] 82 D3
Seatoller [GB] 20 D3
Seaton [GB] 26 D3
Sebbersund [DK] 182 D3
Sebečevo [SRB] 154 B1
Sebeş [RO] 248 C3
Sebezh [RUS] 236 F3
Sebiş [RO] 122 F2
Sebnitz [D] 46 C4
Seč [CZ] 60 C3
Seč [CZ] 60 F3
Sečanj [SRB] 122 D4
Secășeni [RO] 146 F1
Secemin [PL] 62 F1
Séchault [F] 56 B3
Seckau [A] 74 B4
Seclin [F] 40 C4
Secondigny [F] 66 D3
Sečovce [SK] 76 E2
Sečovlje [SLO] 118 E4
Seda [LT] 234 D4
Sedan [F] 56 C2
Sedbergh [GB] 20 D4
Sedelsberg [D] 30 E2
Sedemte Prestola, Manastir– [BG] 148 D3
Séderon [F] 124 F2
Sédico [I] 118 C3
Sédilo [I] 142 B3
Sédini [I] 142 B2
Sedlčany [CZ] 60 D3
Sedlec [CZ] 60 E3
Sedlec–Prčice [CZ] 60 D3
Sedlice [CZ] 60 D4
Sedrun [CH] 116 D1
Šeduva [LT] 238 C2
Sędziszów [PL] 64 C2
See [A] 72 B4
Seebach [A] 118 F1
Seeboden [A] 118 E2
Seebruck [D] 72 D3
Seefeld in Tyrol [A] 72 C4
Seehausen [D] 32 E4
Seehausen [D] 44 D2
Seehausen [D] 44 F2
Seehof [A] 74 B3
Seekirchen [A] 72 E3
Seelbach [D] 70 E2
Seelingstadt [D] 60 B1
Seelisberg Tunnel [CH] 116 D1
Seelow [D] 46 C2

Seem [DK] 178 B2
Seeon [D] 72 D3
Seeon [D] 72 D3
Seerhausen [D] 46 B4
Sées [F] 54 B3
Seesen [D] 44 C2
Seeshaupt [D] 72 C3
Seethal [A] 118 F1
Seewalchen [A] 72 F3
Seewiesen [A] 74 B4
Seferihisar [TR] 170 A2
Sefrivatnet [N] 212 D2
Segalstad [N] 194 B2
Segarcea [RO] 148 E2
Segård [N] 194 B3
Segelvik [N] 224 E1
Segerstad [S] 184 E4
Segesd [H] 120 E3
Segesta [I] 140 B2
Seget [HR] 144 D4
Seggau [A] 120 C2
Seglinge [FIN] 198 B3
Segmon [S] 188 D2
Segni [I] 132 D4
Segóbriga [E] 100 F2
Segonzac [F] 78 C2
Segorbe [E] 102 D2
Segovia [E] 92 E3
Segré [F] 66 D2
Seğucak [TR] 164 D2
Ségur [F] 124 B1
Segura [E] 106 C1
Segura [P] 90 E3
Segura de León [E] 98 E3
Segura de los Baños [E] 94 D4
Segurilla [E] 92 C4
Şehirlioğlu [TR] 164 E4
Sehnde [D] 44 C2
Seia [P] 84 B4
Seiches-sur-le-Loir [F] 66 E2
Seifhennersdorf [D] 60 E1
Seilhac [F] 78 E3
Seilleraye, Château de la– [F] 66 C2
Seim [N] 192 B3
Seinäjoki [FIN] 208 C2
Seira [E] 88 D4
Seis / Siusi [I] 118 C2
Seissan [F] 88 D2
Seitenstetten Markt [A] 74 B3
Seixal [P] 90 B4
Seixo [P] 84 B4
Sejerby [DK] 178 D1
Sejny [PL] 38 C1
Sejs [DK] 178 C1
Seki [TR] 170 F4
Sel [N] 192 F1
Sela [N] 212 C4
Seland [N] 186 D3
Selanovtsi [BG] 148 E3
Selänpää [FIN] 200 B2
Selargius [I] 142 C5
Selaste [EST] 230 E1
Selb [D] 60 B2
Selbitz [D] 58 F2
Selbu [N] 204 B2
Selby [GB] 24 C2
Selca [SLO] 118 F3
Selce [HR] 144 B1
Selchow [D] 46 B2
Selçuk [TR] 170 B3
Selde [DK] 182 C3
Selendi [TR] 164 D4
Selendi [TR] 164 E4
Selenicë [AL] 160 A3
Selent [D] 32 C1
Sélestat [F] 70 D2
Selet [S] 214 D2
Seleuş [RO] 122 E2
Seleuš [SRB] 146 E1
Selevac [SRB] 146 E2

Selfjorden [N] 218 E1
Selfoss [IS] 218 B3
Selgua [E] 94 F2
Séli [GR] 160 E2
Selianítika [GR] 166 D3
Seligenstadt [D] 58 C2
Selimağa [TR] 164 E2
Selimiye [TR] 170 C3
Selínia [GR] 168 A2
Selinunte [I] 140 B2
Selishtë [AL] 154 B4
Selishte [BG] 154 F3
Selište [SRB] 148 B3
Selitë [AL] 160 B2
Selizharovo [RUS] 240 D3
Selje [N] 202 B4
Seljestad [N] 192 C4
Seljord [N] 186 D2
Selkie [FIN] 210 E2
Selkirk [GB] 20 D2
Selkopp [N] 228 B2
Sella [E] 106 F1
Sella di Corno [I] 132 D3
Sellasía [GR] 172 D2
Selles [F] 68 A2
Sellía [GR] 174 C4
Sellières [F] 68 F4
Sellin [D] 34 C2
Sellye [H] 120 F5
Selm [D] 42 D2
Šelmberk [CZ] 60 E3
Selmsdorf [D] 32 D2
Selnes [N] 212 B4
Selneset [N] 204 B1
Selnica [SLO] 120 C2
Selongey [F] 68 F3
Selonnet [F] 126 B2
S. Elpidio a Mare [I] 132 E2
Selsälandet [S] 206 B2
Selseng [N] 192 C2
Selsingen [D] 32 B3
Selsjön [S] 206 C2
Selsø Slot [DK] 178 E2
Selsverket [N] 192 F1
Seltjärn [S] 206 D2
Seltz [F] 58 A4
Selva [N] 202 F1
Selva di Cadore [I] 118 C2
Selva di Val Gardena / Wolkenstein in Gröden [I] 118 C2
Selvik [N] 192 B1
Selvino [I] 116 F3
Sem [N] 186 F2
Šember [CZ] 60 E3
Semblana [P] 98 C3
Semeljci [HR] 122 A4
Semeyskoye [RUS] 200 E4
Semily [CZ] 60 E2
Semizovac [BIH] 146 B3
Semmering [A] 74 C4
Semmering Pass [A] 74 C4
Sempas [SLO] 118 F3
Sempeter [SLO] 118 E3
Šempeter v Savinjski dolini [SLO] 120 B3
Semur-en-Auxois [F] 68 E3
Seña [SK] 76 D2
Sena de Luna [E] 82 F3
Sénas [F] 124 E3
Şencöy [TR] 158 E4
Sencur [SLO] 120 A3
Senden [D] 42 D2
Sendenhorst [D] 42 E2
Sendim [P] 84 D3
Senec [SK] 74 E3
Seneffe [B] 40 D4
Senez [F] 126 B2
Senftenberg [D] 46 C3
Senica [SK] 74 E2
Senigállia [I] 128 F4
Senise [I] 136 C3

Senj [HR] 144 C2
Senlis [F] 54 E3
Sennecey–le–Grand [F] 68 E4
Sennelager [D] 42 F2
Sennestadt [D] 42 F2
Sennewitz [D] 44 E3
Sennik [BG] 150 A4
Senno [RUS] 232 E4
Sénnori [I] 142 B2
Senohrad [SK] 76 B2
Senokos [BG] 150 E2
Senonches [F] 54 C3
Senoncourt [F] 70 B2
Senones [F] 70 C2
Senorbì [I] 142 C5
Señorío de Bértiz [E] 88 A2
Senovo [BG] 150 C2
Senovo [SLO] 120 C3
Senožaty [CZ] 60 E3
Senožeče [SLO] 118 F3
Sens [F] 68 D1
Sens-de-Bretagne [F] 52 E4
Senseruth [B] 56 C2
Senta [SRB] 122 C3
Senterada [E] 96 C1
Šentilj [SLO] 120 C2
Šentjur [SLO] 120 C3
Senum [N] 186 C3
Sepekov [CZ] 60 D4
Sepino [I] 134 D2
Sępopol [PL] 36 F2
Sępreuş [RO] 122 E2
Septemvri [BG] 156 C2
Septemvriyci [BG] 148 D3
Sept–Saulx [F] 56 B3
Sepúlveda [E] 92 F2
Sequeros [E] 92 B3
Serain [F] 54 F1
Seraincourt [F] 56 B2
Seraing [B] 40 F4
Seraserli [TR] 170 F2
Seravezza [I] 128 B3
Şerbăneşti [RO] 148 F2
Sercééren [TR] 164 D2
Serebryanskiy [RUS] 232 F2
Sered' [SK] 74 E2
Seredka [RUS] 232 E3
Seredžius [LT] 238 C3
Seregélyes [H] 122 A1
Seregno [I] 116 E3
Sérent [F] 52 D4
Serfaus [A] 118 B1
Sergen [TR] 158 C2
Sergiyev Posad [RUS] 240 F2
Serhat [TR] 164 B2
Seriaji [LT] 38 D1
Seriate [I] 116 E3
Sérifos [GR] 168 C4
Serinhisar [TR] 170 E3
Serino [I] 134 D3
Sermaize–les–Bains [F] 56 C4
Sermenin [MK] 160 E1
Sérmide [I] 128 C1
Sermoneta [I] 134 B2
Serock [PL] 38 A4
Seroczyn [PL] 50 B2
Seroick Jezioro Zegrzyńskie [PL] 38 A4
Serón [E] 106 B3
Serón de Nágima [E] 94 C2
Seròs [E] 94 A3
Serovo [RUS] 236 F3
Serpa [P] 98 D3
Serpins [P] 84 A4
Serpukhov [RUS] 240 F3
Serra [E] 102 D3
Serracapriola [I] 134 E2
Serrada [E] 92 D2
Serra de Água [P] 110 D3

Serra dè Conti [I] 128 E4
Serradifalco [I] 140 C3
Serradilla [E] 92 B4
Serramazzoni [I] 128 B2
Serra Nova [E] 108 D3
Serrant, Château de– [F] 66 D2
Serra Orrios [I] 142 C3
Serra San Bruno [I] 138 E3
Serra San Quirico [I] 128 E4
Serrastretta [I] 138 E2
Serravalle [CH] 116 E2
Serravalle Pistoiese [I] 128 B3
Serrenti [I] 142 B5
Serres [F] 124 F2
Sérres [GR] 156 B4
Serreta [P] 110 C3
Serri [I] 142 C4
Serrières [F] 80 D3
Sersale [I] 138 E2
Sertã [P] 90 D2
Sertolovo [RUS] 200 F3
Seruci, Nuraghe– [I] 142 B5
Sérvia [GR] 160 E3
Servian [F] 124 C3
Serviana [I] 160 C4
Servigliano [I] 132 E2
Serwy [PL] 38 C2
Sesa [E] 94 E2
Seseña Nuevo [E] 100 E1
Sesimbra [P] 90 A4
Seskinore [NIR] 12 D2
Sésklo [GR] 162 B4
Sesma [E] 86 E4
Sessa Aurunca [I] 134 C3
Sessvatn [N] 186 C1
Šestani [MNE] 152 E3
Šestanovac [HR] 144 E4
Sestao [E] 86 D3
Sesto / Sexten [I] 118 D2
Sesto al Reghena [I] 118 D3
Sesto Calende [I] 116 D3
Sesto Fiorentino [I] 128 C3
Sestola [I] 128 B3
Sesto S. Giovanni [I] 116 E3
Sestriere [I] 116 B4
Sestri Levante [I] 126 F2
Sestroretsk [RUS] 200 F3
Sestu [I] 142 B5
Sesué [E] 88 D4
Sesvete [HR] 120 D3
Séta [GR] 168 B1
Šéta [LT] 238 D2
Setcases [E] 96 E2
Sète [F] 124 D3
Seter [N] 204 B1
Seter [N] 204 C4
Setermoen [N] 224 D3
Setihovo [BIH] 146 C4
Setpsindiği [TR] 158 A2
Setså [N] 220 B2
Settebagni [I] 132 C4
Settimo Torinese [I] 116 C4
Settle [GB] 24 C1
Setúbal [P] 90 B4
Seui [I] 142 C4
Seulo [I] 142 C4
Seurre [F] 68 F4
Sevar [BG] 150 C2
Sevaster [AL] 160 B3
Sevastopol' [UA] 246 F4
Sevast'yanovo [RUS] 200 E2
Sevel [DK] 182 C3
Sevenoaks [GB] 28 D3
Sever [P] 84 A3
Sévérac–le–Château [F] 124 C1
Severin [F] 32 E3
Severin [HR] 120 E3
Ševětín [CZ] 74 B1
Sevettijärvi [FIN] 226 E1
Sevilla [E] 104 B1
Sevilleja de la Jara [E] 100 C1

Şevketiye [TR] 164 B1
Şevketiye [TR] 164 C2
Sevlievo [BG] 150 A4
Sevnica [SLO] 120 C3
Sevojno [SRB] 146 D3
Sevrier [F] 80 F2
Sevsk [RUS] 242 F2
Sexdrega [S] 184 B2
Sexten / Sesto [I] 118 D2
Seyches [F] 78 C4
Seyda [D] 44 F3
Seydiköy [TR] 170 B2
Seyðisfjörður [IS] 218 D3
Seymen [TR] 158 C3
Seyne [F] 126 B2
Seynod [F] 80 F2
Seyssel [F] 80 F2
Seysses [F] 88 E3
Şeytan Sofrasi [TR] 164 B3
Sežana [SLO] 118 F3
Sézanne [F] 54 F4
Sezimovo Ústí [CZ] 60 E4
Sezze [I] 134 B2
S. Fãgelås [S] 188 E4
Stáka [GR] 174 B4
Sfakiá [GR] 174 B4
Sfântu Gheorghe [RO] 244 E4
S. Felices de los Gallegos [E] 84 D4
Sforzacosta [I] 132 E2
S. Geraldo [P] 90 C4
S. Ginés de la Jara, Monasterio de– [E] 106 E3
S. Giorgio della Richinvelda [I] 118 D3
S. Giorgio d. Sannio [I] 134 D3
S. Giovanni Bianco [I] 116 E3
S. Giusta [I] 142 B4
S. Gregòrio [I] 142 C5
S. Gregorio Magno [I] 134 E4
S. Gusmé [I] 128 C4
Shabany [RUS] 232 E4
Šhabla [BG] 150 F2
Shaftesbury [GB] 26 F3
Shahovskaja [RUS] 240 E3
Shakhovskaya [RUS] 240 E3
Shanagolden [IRL] 10 C2
Shanklin [GB] 28 B4
Shannon [IRL] 10 C2
Shannonbridge [IRL] 10 C2
Sharashova [BY] 38 D4
Sharnevo [BG] 156 E1
Shatalovo [RUS] 242 F3
Shatsk [BY] 242 B2
Shats'k [UA] 50 D3
Shchors [UA] 242 E3
Shchors'k [UA] 246 D2
Shchuchin [BY] 38 E2
Shchuchyn [BY] 242 A2
's Heerenberg [NL] 30 C4
Sheerness [GB] 28 D3
Sheffield [GB] 24 C3
Shefford [GB] 28 C2
Shëmhill [AL] 160 B2
Shëngjergj [AL] 154 B3
Shëngjergj [AL] 160 B1
Shëngjin [AL] 152 F4
Shënmëri [AL] 154 B3
Shepetivka [UA] 244 D1
Shepton Mallet [GB] 26 E3
Sherborne [GB] 26 E3
Shercock [IRL] 10 F1
Sheringham [GB] 24 F4
's–Hertogenbosch [NL] 40 F2
Shetaj [AL] 154 A4
Shijak [AL] 160 A1
Shiki [RUS] 232 F4
Shilkovci [BG] 150 B4
Shillelagh [IRL] 10 E3
Shilovo [RUS] 236 F3
Shimsk [RUS] 240 C2
Shinrone [IRL] 10 D2

Shipchenski Manastir [BG] 150 B4
Shipchenski Prokhad [BG] 150 B4
Shipka [BG] 150 B4
Shipkovo [BG] 148 F4
Shiroka Lŭka [BG] 156 D3
Shirokë [AL] 152 F4
Shirokoye [RUS] 36 F2
Shivatsevo [BG] 150 C4
Shkalle [AL] 160 B4
Shklow [BY] 242 C1
Shkodër [AL] 152 F4
Shkorpilovtsi [BG] 150 E3
Shmoylovo [RUS] 232 F4
Shøde [DK] 178 D3
Shoshan [AL] 154 B3
Shostka [UA] 242 E3
Shpola [UA] 246 D1
Shranamanragh Bridge [IRL] 12 B2
Shrewsbury [GB] 22 E3
Shrule [IRL] 10 C1
Shtëpëz [AL] 160 B3
Shtërmen [AL] 160 B2
Shumen [BG] 150 D3
Shumsk [UA] 244 D1
Shyroke [UA] 246 E2
Shyshchytsy [BY] 242 B2
Siána [GR] 176 B2
Sianów [PL] 34 F2
Siare [EST] 230 C3
Siátista [GR] 160 D3
Siaulenai [LT] 238 C2
Siauliai [LT] 238 C1
Sibabravas [LT] 238 D2
Sibari [I] 136 C4
Sibbhult [S] 180 D1
Sibbo / Sipoo [FIN] 198 F3
Šibenik [HR] 144 D4
Sibilla, Ruderi di– [I] 134 B2
Sibinj [HR] 146 A1
Sibiu [RO] 248 D3
Sibo [S] 196 C2
Sićevo [SRB] 148 C3
Sicignano degli Alburni [I] 134 E4
Siculiana [I] 140 C3
Šid [SRB] 146 C1
Sidári [GR] 160 B4
Siddeburen [NL] 30 D2
Sideby / Siipyy [FIN] 208 B4
Sidensjö [S] 206 D2
Siderno [I] 138 E3
Sidertjärn [S] 194 F1
Sidiró [GR] 156 F3
Sidirókastro [GR] 156 B4
Sidirónero [GR] 156 C3
Sidlyšče [UA] 50 F2
Sidmouth [GB] 26 D3
Sidra [PL] 38 C2
Sidra [PL] 38 D2
Sidyma [TR] 176 D1
Sidzina [PL] 62 C2
Siebe [N] 226 B2
Siebenberg [D] 56 E1
Siecq [F] 78 C2
Siedlce [PL] 50 B2
Siedlinghausen [D] 42 E3
Siedliska [PL] 36 A4
Siedlisko [PL] 46 E3
Siegburg [D] 42 D4
Siegen [D] 42 E4
Siegenburg [D] 72 D1
Sieggraben [A] 74 D4
Siegsdorf [D] 72 D3
Siekierki [PL] 46 C1
Siekkinen [FIN] 222 E4
Sielec [PL] 50 D4
Sielpia Wlk [PL] 48 E4
Siemiany [PL] 36 D3

Siemiatycze [PL] 38 C4
Siena [I] 128 C4
Sieniawa [PL] 64 D2
Sieniawka [PL] 60 E1
Sieniec [PL] 48 C4
Siennica [PL] 50 B2
Siennica Różana [PL] 50 D4
Sienno [PL] 50 B4
Sieppijärvi [FIN] 222 B2
Sieradz [PL] 48 C3
Sieraków [PL] 46 E1
Sieraków [PL] 62 D1
Sierakowice [PL] 36 C2
Sierck–les–Bains [F] 56 D3
Sierentz [F] 70 D3
Sierning [A] 74 A3
Sierpc [PL] 36 E4
Sierra Bermeja [E] 104 C3
Sierra de Fuentes [E] 90 F3
Sierra de Luna [E] 94 D2
Sierra de Yeguas [E] 104 D2
Sierra Nevada [E] 104 F3
Sierre [CH] 116 C2
Siete Aguas [E] 102 C3
Sievi [FIN] 216 A4
Siewierz [PL] 62 E2
Sifferbo [S] 196 B3
Siğacik [TR] 168 F2
Sigean [F] 124 B3
Sigena, Monasterio de– [E] 94 F3
Siggjarvåg [N] 192 A4
Sighetu Marmaţiei [RO] 244 C3
Sighişoara [RO] 244 D4
Siglufjörður [IS] 218 B2
Sigmaringen [D] 70 F2
Signes [F] 124 F4
Signy–l'Abbaye [F] 56 B2
Sígri [GR] 162 F3
Sigtuna [S] 190 D2
Sigüeiro [E] 82 B2
Sigüenza [E] 94 B3
Sigües [E] 88 B3
Sigulda [LV] 236 B2
Sihtuuna [FIN] 222 B3
Siikainen [FIN] 208 C4
Siikajoki [FIN] 216 A2
Siilakoski [FIN] 210 D4
Siikala [FIN] 198 E3
Siilinjärvi [FIN] 210 C2
Siipyy / Sideby [FIN] 208 B4
Siivikko [FIN] 216 C1
Sijarinska Banja [SRB] 154 D2
Sikeå [S] 214 D3
Sikfors [S] 214 D1
Síkinos [GR] 174 D1
Siklós [H] 122 A3
Sikórz [PL] 48 D1
Sikovitsy [RUS] 232 E3
Sikovuono [FIN] 226 D2
Siksjö [S] 214 B3
Siksjön [S] 214 C1
Sil [S] 206 B1
Šilale [LT] 238 B2
Silandro / Schlanders [I] 118 B2
Silánus [I] 142 B3
Silbaš [SRB] 122 C4
Silberstedt [D] 32 B1
Şile [TR] 158 F3
Siles [E] 106 C1
Şilindia [RO] 122 F2
Silíqua [I] 142 B5
Silişţea [RO] 150 E1
Silişţea–Gumeşti [RO] 150 A1
Silistra [BG] 150 D2
Silivri [TR] 158 D3
Siljan [N] 186 E2
Siljansnäs [S] 194 F3
Silkås [S] 204 F1
Silkeborg [DK] 178 C1

Silla [E] 102 D3
Silla de Felipe II [E] 92 E3
Sillamäe [EST] 230 F1
Sillans–la–Cascade [F] 126 A3
Silleda [E] 82 B3
Sillé–le–Guillaume [F] 54 A4
Sillerud [S] 188 C2
Sillian [A] 118 D2
Sillre [S] 206 C3
Silnica [PL] 62 F1
Silno [PL] 36 B3
Šilo [HR] 144 B1
Sils [E] 96 E3
Silsand [N] 224 D3
Sils–Maria [CH] 116 F2
Siltala [FIN] 216 C3
Šilutė [LT] 238 A2
Šiluva [LT] 238 C2
Silva [E] 82 B2
Silvacane [F] 124 E3
Silvaplana [CH] 116 F2
Silvares [P] 90 D2
Silvenski Bani [BG] 150 C4
Silverdalen [S] 184 E2
Silvermines [IRL] 10 D2
Silves [P] 98 B4
Silvi Marina [I] 132 E3
Silz [A] 72 B4
Simagino [RUS] 200 E3
Simanala [FIN] 210 D3
Simancas [E] 92 D1
Şimand [RO] 122 E2
Simasåg [N] 74 D4
Simav [TR] 164 E3
Simaxis [I] 142 B4
Simbach [D] 72 E2
Simbach [D] 72 E2
Simena [TR] 176 F2
Simeonovgrad [BG] 156 E2
Simferopol' [UA] 246 F4
Simići [BIH] 146 C3
Simitli [BG] 154 F3
Šimkaičiai [LT] 238 C3
Simlångsdalen [S] 184 B3
Şimleu Silvaniei [RO] 244 C3
Simmelkaer [DK] 182 C4
Simmerath [D] 42 C4
Simmerberg [D] 72 A3
Simmern [D] 56 F2
Simnas [LT] 38 D1
Simo [FIN] 216 A1
Símonos Pétras, Moní– [GR] 162 C2
Simonstorp [S] 190 C3
Simontornya [H] 122 A2
Simorre [F] 88 D3
Simpele [FIN] 200 E1
Simplon Dorf [CH] 116 C2
Simplonpass [CH] 116 C2
Simrishamn [S] 180 D2
Simuna [EST] 230 E2
Šimuni [HR] 144 C2
Sinaia [RO] 248 D1
Sinalunga [I] 130 E1
Sinanaj [AL] 160 B3
Sinarcas [E] 102 C2
Sıncansarnıç [TR] 164 E1
Sindal [DK] 182 D2
Sindelfingen [D] 70 F1
Sindi [EST] 230 D3
Sındırgı [TR] 164 D3
Sinekçi [TR] 164 C1
Sinekli [TR] 158 D3
Sinemorets [BG] 158 C2
Sines [P] 98 B2
Sineşti [RO] 150 C1
Sinetta [FIN] 222 C3
Sineu [E] 108 D3
Sinevo [RUS] 200 E2
Singen [D] 70 F3
Singerin [A] 74 C3

Singsås [N] 204 B2
Singusdal [N] 186 E2
Sinilähde [FIN] 200 B2
Siniscola [I] 142 C3
Sinj [HR] 144 E4
Sinnai [I] 142 C5
Sinnes [N] 186 C2
Sinópoli [I] 138 D3
Sinsen [A] 72 B4
Sinsheim [D] 58 B4
Sintea Mare [RO] 122 E2
Sintra [P] 90 A3
Sintsi [FIN] 210 E3
Sinuessa [I] 134 C2
Sinyaya Nikola [RUS] 236 E2
Sinziq [D] 56 F1
Siófok [H] 120 F2
Sion [CH] 116 C2
Sion [CZ] 60 H3
Sion [F] 70 B1
Siorac–en–Périgord [F] 78 D4
Sip [SRB] 148 C1
Sipahi [TR] 158 B3
Šipči [SRB] 154 B2
Sipiren [FIN] 216 D3
Sipoo / Sibbo [FIN] 198 F3
Šipovo [BIH] 144 E3
Sippola [FIN] 200 C2
Sira [N] 186 B3
Sirač [HR] 120 E4
Siracusa [I] 140 F3
Siret [RO] 244 D3
Sirevåg [N] 186 B3
Sirgala [EST] 230 F1
Şiria [RO] 122 E2
Sirig [SRB] 122 C4
Sirishtnik [BG] 154 F2
Širitovci [HR] 144 D3
Sirkka [FIN] 222 B1
Sirkön [S] 184 D3
Sırma [N] 228 D3
Sirmione [I] 118 B4
Sirnach [CH] 70 F3
Sirok [N] 76 C3
Široké [SK] 76 D1
Široki Brijeg [BIH] 152 C1
Sirolo [I] 128 F4
Siruela [E] 100 C2
Širvintos [LT] 238 E3
Sisak [HR] 120 D4
Sisamón [E] 94 B4
Sisante [E] 102 B3
Sisättö [FIN] 208 D4
Sisbacka [FIN] 208 C1
S. Isidoro del Campo [E] 98 E4
Šišljavič [H] 120 C4
Sissa [I] 128 B1
Sissach [CH] 70 D3
Sissonne [F] 56 B2
Sisteron [F] 126 A2
Sistiana [I] 118 E3
Sistranda [N] 202 E1
Sit. Anna [S] 190 C4
Sitasjaurestugorna [S] 220 C1
Sitelä [GR] 174 E3
Sitges [E] 96 C3
Sitno [HR] 144 D4
Sitovo [BG] 150 D2
Sitrama de Tera [E] 84 E2
Sittard [NL] 40 F3
Sitten [D] 44 F4
Sittensen [D] 32 B3
Sittersdorf [A] 120 B2
Sittingbourne [GB] 28 D2
Sitzendorf [A] 74 D2
Siuntio / Sjundea [FIN] 198 E3
Siurua [FIN] 216 B1
Siusi / Seis [I] 118 C2
Sivac [SRB] 122 C4

Sivakka [FIN] 216 E3
Sivakka [FIN] 216 E3
Sivakkavaara [FIN] 210 D2
Sivaslı [TR] 170 E1
Siverskiy [RUS] 232 F1
Síviri [GR] 162 B2
Sivriler [TR] 158 C2
Sivry–sur–Meuse [F] 56 C3
Six–Fours–les–Plages [F] 124 F4
Sixmilebridge [IRL] 10 C2
Sizun [F] 52 B3
Sjenica [SRB] 154 B1
S. Jeroni, Monestir de– [E] 102 D4
Siisika [S] 220 E1
Sjoa [N] 192 F1
Sjøåsen [N] 212 C3
Sjöberg [S] 214 A2
Sjöbo [S] 180 C2
Sjøholt [N] 202 C3
Sjøli [N] 194 C2
Sjölunda [S] 214 B2
Sjørring [DK] 182 C3
Sjørup [DK] 182 C3
Sjötofta [S] 184 B2
Sjötorp [S] 188 E3
Sjoutnäset [S] 212 E3
Sjøvegan [N] 224 C3
Sjøvik [S] 184 A1
S. Juan, Castillo de– [E] 106 D3
S. Juan de la Peña [E] 88 B4
Sjundea / Siuntiol [FIN] 198 E3
Sjursjok [N] 228 D2
Sjursvika [N] 224 C3
Sjusjøen [N] 194 B2
Skabland [N] 194 B3
Skåbu [N] 192 F1
Skadovs'k [UA] 246 E3
Skælskør [DK] 178 D3
Skærbæk [DK] 178 B2
Skafídia [GR] 172 B2
Skaftafell [IS] 218 C3
Skaftung [FIN] 208 B3
Skagaströnd [IS] 218 B2
Skage [N] 212 C3
Skagen [DK] 182 E1
Skaidi [N] 228 B2
Skaista [LV] 236 E4
Skaistkalne [LT] 236 B4
Skakavac [HR] 120 C4
Skála [GR] 164 A3
Skála [GR] 166 C4
Skála [GR] 166 F3
Skála [GR] 168 F3
Skála [GR] 172 E3
Skala [PL] 62 F2
Skalabiňa [SK] 76 B1
Skála Eresoú [GR] 162 F3
Skála Kalliráchis [GR] 162 D1
Skålan [S] 204 E3
Skála Oropoú [GR] 168 B2
Skala–Podil'ska [UA] 244 D2
Skálavík [FR] 182 B2
Skalbmierz [PL] 64 B2
Skaldö [FIN] 198 E4
Skalica [SK] 74 E2
Skalité [SK] 62 E4
Skalitsa [BG] 156 F1
Skallelv [N] 228 F2
Skälleröd [S] 188 B3
Skållerud [S] 188 C3
Skallerup Kit [DK] 182 D2
Skallskog [S] 194 F3
Skalmodal [S] 212 E2
Skalmsjö [S] 206 D2
Skalochóri [GR] 160 D3
Skalotí [GR] 156 C3
Skalotí [GR] 174 C4
Skals [DK] 182 D3

Skålsjön [S] 196 B2
Skalstugan [S] 204 C1
Skammestein [N] 192 E2
Skän [S] 206 B4
Skandáli [GR] 162 E2
Skanderborg [DK] 178 C1
Skånes Fagerhult [S] 184 B4
Skåne–Tranås [S] 180 D2
Skånevik [N] 186 B1
Skåningbukt [N] 224 E1
Skånninge [S] 188 F4
Skanör [S] 178 F2
Skansbachen [S] 194 E4
Skansen [N] 204 C1
Skansholm [S] 214 A3
Skansnäs [S] 214 B1
Skåpafors [S] 188 C3
Skåpe [PL] 46 D2
Skar [N] 192 C2
Skara [S] 188 D4
Skäran [S] 214 D3
Skarberget [N] 224 C4
Skärblacka [S] 190 B4
Skard [N] 202 E2
Skarda [S] 214 C3
Skåre [S] 188 D2
Skåret [N] 194 D2
Skärhamn [S] 182 F1
Skarhult [S] 180 C2
Skarínou [CY] 176 D4
Skarjenfossen [N] 186 C2
Skårlöv [S] 184 E4
Skarmunken [N] 224 E2
Skarnes [N] 194 C4
Skarpengland [N] 186 C4
Skärplinge [S] 196 D4
Skarsfjord [N] 224 D1
Skarstein [N] 224 B3
Skarszewy [PL] 36 C2
Skårup [DK] 178 D3
Skärvången [S] 204 E1
Skarvberg–Tunnelen [N]
    228 C2
Skarveberg [N] 228 B2
Skarvsjö [S] 214 B2
Skaryszew [PL] 48 F3
Skarżynek [PL] 36 F4
Skarżysko-Kamienna [PL]
    48 F4
Skasberget [N] 194 C4
Skata [FIN] 198 D4
Skattungbyn [S] 194 F2
Skatval [N] 204 B1
Skaudvilė [LT] 238 B2
Skaulo [S] 220 E2
Skave [DK] 182 C3
Skavik [N] 228 B2
Skawina [PL] 62 F3
Skeda udde [S] 190 B4
Skedevi [S] 190 B3
Skedshult [S] 184 E1
Skedsmokorset [N] 188 B1
Skee [S] 188 B3
Skegness [GB] 24 E3
Skehobruk [S] 190 E1
Skei [N] 192 C1
Skei [N] 202 E2
Skei [N] 212 C2
Skeie [N] 186 C3
Skela [SRB] 146 D2
Skelani [BIH] 146 C3
Skelde [DK] 178 C3
Skellefteå [S] 214 D2
Skelleftehamn [S] 214 D2
Skelleftestrand [S] 214 D2
Skelmersdale [GB] 22 F2
Skender Vakuf [BIH] 144 F2
Skene [S] 184 B2
Skenshyttan [S] 196 B4
Skepastó [GR] 162 B1
Skepe [PL] 36 D4
Skeppshult [S] 184 B3

Skeppsmyra [S] 190 E1
Skeppsvik [S] 206 F1
Skerping [DK] 182 C2
Skerries [IRL] 12 E4
Ski [N] 188 B1
Skiáthos [GR] 162 B4
Skibbereen [IRL] 10 B4
Skibbild [DK] 182 C4
Skibby [DK] 178 E2
Skibniew–Podawce [PL] 38 B4
Skibotn [N] 224 E2
Skidal' [BY] 38 D2
Skien [N] 186 E2
Skierbieszów [PL] 50 D4
Skierniewice [PL] 48 C2
Skiippagurra [N] 228 E2
Skille [N] 212 D2
Skillingaryd [S] 184 C2
Skillinge [S] 180 D2
Skillingmark [S] 188 C1
Skiniás [GR] 174 D4
Skinnarbu [N] 186 D1
Skinnerup [DK] 182 C2
Skinnskatteberg [S] 190 B1
Skiønne [N] 192 E4
Skipnes [N] 202 E2
Skipton [GB] 24 C2
Skiptvet [N] 188 B2
Skirö [S] 184 D2
Skivarp [S] 180 C2
Skive [DK] 182 C3
Skiveren [DK] 182 E2
Skivjane [KS] 154 B3
Skjærhalden [N] 188 B3
Skjånes [N] 228 D1
Skjåvika [N] 212 E2
Skjeberg [N] 188 B2
Skjeggedal [N] 186 D3
Skjelbreid [N] 212 D3
Skjelstad [N] 212 C4
Skjelten [N] 202 C3
Skjelvik [N] 228 D2
Skjern [DK] 178 B1
Skjervefossen [N] 192 C3
Skjervøy [N] 224 E1
Skjold [N] 186 B1
Skjoldastraumen [N] 186 B1
Skjolden [N] 192 D1
Skjønhaug [N] 188 B2
Skjøtningberg [N] 228 D1
Sklithro [GR] 160 F4
Skoby [S] 190 D1
Skočivir [MK] 160 D2
Škocjanske Jame [SLO]
    118 F4
Skoczów [PL] 62 E3
Skodje [N] 202 C3
Skødstrup [DK] 182 D4
Škofije [SLO] 118 F4
Škofja Loka [SLO] 120 A3
Škofljica [SLO] 120 B3
Skog [S] 196 C2
Skógafoss [IS] 218 B3
Skoganvarre [N] 226 C1
Skogar [S] 218 B3
Skogen [S] 188 C2
Skoger [N] 188 F1
Skogfoss [N] 226 E1
Skoghall [S] 188 D2
Skogli [N] 192 D3
Skogly [N] 226 E1
Skogn [N] 204 C1
Skogså [S] 220 F4
Skogsby [S] 184 E3
Skogstad [N] 192 E2
Skogstorp [S] 184 A3
Skogstorp [S] 190 C2
Skogvatnet [N] 224 D4
Skoki [PL] 46 F1
Skokloster [S] 190 D2
Skole [UA] 64 E4
Skollenborg [N] 186 E1

Sköllersta [S] 188 F3
Skomdal [N] 186 D2
Skomielna Biała [PL] 62 F3
Skomlin [PL] 48 C4
Skönberga [S] 190 C4
Skópelos [GR] 162 C4
Skópelos [GR] 164 B4
Skopí [GR] 174 E3
Skopiá [GR] 162 A4
Skopje [MK] 154 D3
Skopós [GR] 160 D2
Skopun [FR] 182 A2
Skor [N] 186 B2
Skórcz [PL] 36 C3
Skórka [PL] 36 A4
Skoroszów [PL] 46 F3
Skorovatn [N] 212 D3
Skorped [S] 206 D2
Skørping [DK] 182 D3
Skörstorp [S] 184 C1
Skórzec [PL] 50 B2
Skotnes [N] 212 C2
Skotnoye [RUS] 200 F3
Skotoússa [GR] 156 B4
Skoträsk [S] 214 B2
Skotselv [N] 186 F1
Skotterud [N] 188 C1
Skoulikariá [GR] 166 C2
Skoúra [GR] 172 D3
Skoútari [GR] 156 B4
Skovballe [DK] 178 D3
Skovby [DK] 178 C3
Skövde [S] 188 E4
Skra [GR] 160 E1
Skrad [HR] 120 B4
Skradin [HR] 144 D4
Skradinski Buk [HR] 144 D4
Skråmestø [N] 192 A3
Skravena [BG] 148 E4
Skrea [S] 184 B3
Skrede [N] 202 C4
Skreia [N] 194 B3
Skríveri [LV] 236 C3
Skröven [S] 220 F3
Skrunda [LV] 234 D3
Skucku [S] 204 E3
Skudeneshavn [N] 186 A2
Skulsk [PL] 48 C2
Skulte [LV] 236 B2
Skultorp [S] 188 E4
Skultuna [S] 190 C2
Skuodas [LT] 234 D4
Skurugata [S] 184 D2
Skurup [S] 180 C2
Škušava [LV] 236 D3
Skute [N] 192 F3
Skuteč [CZ] 60 F3
Skutskär [S] 196 D3
Skutvik [N] 220 B1
Skvyra [UA] 244 F1
Skwierzyna [PL] 46 D1
Skýcov [SK] 76 A2
Skýdra [GR] 160 E2
Skylloura (Yılmazköy) [CY]
    176 D3
Skýros [GR] 162 D4
Skyttmon [S] 206 B2
Skyttorp [S] 190 D1
Sládkovičovo [SK] 74 E3
Śladów [PL] 48 E2
Slagavallen [S] 204 D4
Slagelse [DK] 178 D2
Slagnäs [S] 214 B1
Slane [IRL] 10 F1
Slangerup [DK] 178 E2
Slănic Moldova [RO] 244 E4
Slano [HR] 152 D2
Slantsy [RUS] 232 E2
Slaný [CZ] 60 D2
Ślapanice [CZ] 60 D2
Slåstad [N] 194 C4
Slatina [HR] 120 F4

Slatina [MNE] 152 E2
Slatina [RO] 148 E1
Slatina [SRB] 146 C2
Slatina [SRB] 146 E3
Slatina [SRB] 148 C2
Slatina de Mureş [RO] 122 F3
Slatiňany [CZ] 60 F3
Slatino [MK] 154 C3
Slatinski Drenovac [HR]
    120 F4
Slättåkra [S] 184 B3
Slättberg [S] 194 F2
Slättberg [S] 220 E3
Slåttevik [N] 186 A2
Slätthog [S] 184 C3
Slattum [N] 188 B1
Slåttvik [N] 212 E3
Släveşti [RO] 150 A1
Slavětín [CZ] 62 B3
Slavhostice [CZ] 60 E2
Slavičín [CZ] 74 F1
Slavín [CZ] 60 D2
Slavkovichi [RUS] 232 F4
Slavkov u Brna (Austerlitz)
    [CZ] 62 B4
Slavonice [CZ] 74 C1
Slavonski Brod [HR] 146 A1
Slavotin [BG] 148 D3
Slavsk [RUS] 238 B3
Slavuta [UA] 244 D1
Slavutych [UA] 242 D3
Slavyanovo [BG] 150 A3
Sława [PL] 46 E3
Sławatycze [PL] 50 D2
Slawharad [BY] 242 D2
Sławków [PL] 62 E2
Sławno [PL] 36 A2
Sławoborze [PL] 34 F2
Sleaford [GB] 24 D4
Sleme [SLO] 120 B2
Slemmestad [N] 188 B1
Ślepać most [MNE] 152 F2
Slepčević [SRB] 146 C2
Ślesin [PL] 36 C4
Ślesin [PL] 48 C2
Sleszów [PL] 62 C1
Sletta [N] 224 F1
Slettafoss [N] 202 E3
Slette [N] 202 D4
Slettestrand [DK] 182 D2
Slettmo [N] 224 D2
Slettvik [N] 204 D1
Sliedrecht [NL] 30 B4
Sliema [M] 140 C4
Sligeach / Sligo [IRL] 12 C2
Sligo / Sligeach [IRL] 12 C2
Slinde [N] 192 C2
Slipra [N] 204 B1
Slite [S] 234 B2
Sliven [BG] 150 C4
Slivnica [SLO] 120 C2
Slivnitsa [BG] 148 D4
Slivno [HR] 152 C1
Slivo Pole [BG] 150 C2
Slivovo [KS] 154 C2
Śliwa [PL] 36 E3
Śliwice [PL] 36 C3
Slobozia [RO] 150 B2
Slobozia Mândra [RO] 148 F2
Slobozia Moara [RO] 150 B1
Słomniki [PL] 62 F2
Slonim [BY] 38 F3
Słonowice [PL] 34 E3
Słońsk [PL] 46 C2
Sloten [NL] 30 C2
Slottsbron [S] 188 D2
Slough [GB] 28 C3
Sloup [CZ] 62 B4
Sloupsko–Šošuvské Jeskyně
    [CZ] 62 B4
Slovac [SRB] 146 D3
Slovenj Gradec [SLO] 120 B2

Slovenska Bistrica [SLO]
    120 C2
Slovenská Ľupča [SK] 76 B2
Slovenske Konjice [SLO]
    120 C2
Slovenské Nové Mesto [SK]
    76 E2
Slovinci [HR] 144 E1
Słubice [PL] 46 C2
Słubice [PL] 48 E2
Sluderno / Schluderns [I]
    118 B2
Sluis [NL] 30 A4
Sluis [NL] 40 C2
Šluknov [CZ] 46 C4
Slůnchev Bryag [BG] 150 E4
Slunj [HR] 144 C1
Słupca [PL] 48 B2
Słupia [PL] 64 B2
Słupiec [PL] 62 B2
Słupno [PL] 48 D2
Słupsk [PL] 36 B1
Slušovice [CZ] 62 C4
Slutsk [BY] 242 B2
Stuzewo [PL] 36 C4
Slyuda [RUS] 222 F1
Småge [N] 202 D2
Smålandsstenar [S] 184 B2
Smålåsen [N] 212 D2
Smalininkai [LT] 238 B3
Smârdioasa [RO] 150 B2
Smarhon' [BY] 238 F3
S. Maria della Versa [I]
    126 F1
S. Maria in Calanca [CH]
    116 E2
S. Marina Salina [I] 138 C3
Šmarje [SLO] 118 E4
Šmarje [SLO] 120 C3
S. Martino in Pensilis [I]
    134 D2
Šmartno [SLO] 120 B2
Šmartno [SLO] 120 B3
S. Mauro Forte [I] 134 F4
S. M. de Naranco [E] 82 F2
Smedås [N] 204 B3
Smedbyn [S] 188 D2
Smederevo [SRB] 146 E2
Smederevska–Palanka [SRB]
    146 E3
Smedjebacken [S] 190 B1
Smedjeviken [S] 204 D1
Smedstorp [S] 180 D2
Smęgorzów [PL] 64 B2
Smeland [N] 186 D2
Smelror [N] 228 F2
S. Michele di Ganzaria [I]
    140 D3
Smídary [CZ] 60 F2
Šmígiel [PL] 46 E2
S. Miguel [E] 86 F3
S. Miguel de Escalada [E]
    82 F4
S. Miguel del Arroyo [E] 92 E2
S. Miguel de las Victorias
    [E] 94 B4
Smila [UA] 246 D1
Smilde [N] 30 D2
Smiljan [BG] 156 D3
Šmilovo [PL] 36 B4
Smiltene [LV] 232 C4
Smínthi [GR] 156 D2
Smirnenski [BG] 148 D3
Smögen [S] 188 B4
Smogulec [PL] 36 B4
Smokvica [MK] 156 A4
Smołdzino [PL] 36 B1
Smoleń [PL] 62 F2
Smolensk [RUS] 240 D3
Smolevitschi [BY] 242 B2
Smolnica [PL] 46 C1
Smolník [SK] 76 D2

Smolyan [BG] 156 D3
Smolyanovtsi [BG] 148 D3
Smørfjord [N] 228 C2
Smørhamn [N] 202 B4
Smuka [SLO] 120 B3
Smyadovo [BG] 150 D3
Smygehamn [S] 180 C2
Snappertuna [FIN] 198 E4
Snaptun [DK] 178 C1
Snåre [FIN] 214 F4
Snartemo [N] 186 C3
Snarup [DK] 178 C3
Snåsa [N] 212 D4
Snausen [N] 202 F2
Snavlunda [S] 188 F3
Snedsted [DK] 182 C3
Sneek [NL] 30 C2
Sneem [IRL] 10 A3
Snefjord [N] 228 B2
Snerta [N] 194 C1
Snesudden [S] 220 E4
Sněžné [CZ] 62 A3
S. Nicola da Crissa [I] 138 E3
S. Nicolás del Puerto [E] 100 A4
Snihurivka [UA] 246 E2
Snilldal [N] 202 F2
Snina [SK] 76 E1
Snjatyn [UA] 244 D2
Šnjegotina Gornja [BIH] 144 F2
Snogebæk [DK] 180 E3
Snössvallen [S] 194 E1
Snöstorp [S] 184 B3
S. Ny [S] 188 D2
Soajo [P] 82 B4
Soanlakhti [RUS] 210 F3
Soave [I] 118 B4
Söbbön [S] 188 C3
Sober [E] 82 C3
Soběslav [CZ] 60 E4
Sobibór [PL] 50 D3
Sobieszewo [PL] 36 D2
Sobieszów [PL] 60 F1
Sobki [PL] 48 D3
Sobków [PL] 64 B2
Sobotín [CZ] 62 C3
Sobotište [SK] 74 E2
Sobotka [CZ] 60 E2
Sobótka [PL] 62 B1
Sobowidz [PL] 36 C2
Sobra [HR] 152 C3
Sobrado [E] 82 C2
Sobrado dos Monxes [E] 82 C2
Sobrance [SK] 76 E1
Sobreira Formosa [P] 90 D2
Søby [DK] 178 C3
Soča [SLO] 118 E2
Sočanica [KS] 148 A4
Sočerga [SLO] 118 F4
Sochaczew [PL] 48 E2
Sochaux [F] 70 C3
Sochocin [PL] 48 E1
Sochós [GR] 162 B1
Socodor [RO] 122 E2
Socol [RO] 146 F2
Socovos [E] 106 D1
Socuéllamos [E] 100 F3
Sodankylä [FIN] 222 C1
Söderåkra [S] 184 E4
Söderala [S] 196 C2
Söderås [S] 194 F3
Söderbärke [S] 190 B1
Söderboda [S] 196 E4
Söderby [FIN] 200 B3
Söderby-Karl [S] 190 E1
Söderfors [S] 196 D4
Söderhamn [S] 196 C2

Söderköping [S] 190 C4
Södertälje [S] 190 D2
Söderudden [FIN] 208 B1
Södra Vallgrund [FIN] 208 B2
Södra Vi [S] 184 E2
Sodražica [SLO] 120 B3
Sødring [DK] 182 D3
Soest [D] 42 E3
Soest [NL] 30 B3
Soestdijk [NL] 30 B3
Sofádes [GR] 166 D2
Sofiero [S] 178 F1
Sofíivka [UA] 246 E2
Sofikó [GR] 166 F4
Sofiya-Grad [BG] 156 B1
Sofó [GR] 160 F4
Sögel [D] 30 E3
Sogge bru [N] 202 D3
Sogliano al Rubicone [I] 128 D3
Sogndal [N] 192 C2
Sogndalstrand [N] 186 B3
Søgne [N] 186 C4
Sogn Folkemuseum [N] 192 D2
Sogn Gions [CH] 116 E2
Sögüdlüdere [TR] 170 E4
Soğukpınar [TR] 164 E1
Söğüt [TR] 170 F4
Söğüt [TR] 176 C1
Söğütalan [TR] 164 D1
Sohren [D] 56 F2
Soidinkumpu [FIN] 222 E3
Soidinvaara [FIN] 216 D3
Soignies [B] 40 D4
Soini [FIN] 208 D2
Soinlahti [FIN] 216 C4
Soissons [F] 54 F2
Sokal' [UA] 64 F2
Söke [TR] 170 B3
Suklul [FIN] 208 C1
Sokna [N] 192 F4
Soknedal [N] 204 B2
Soko Banja [SRB] 148 B3
Sokolac [BIH] 144 D2
Sokolac [BIH] 146 B3
Sokolany [PL] 38 C2
Sokółka [PL] 38 C2
Sokolniki [PL] 48 C4
Sokolov [CZ] 60 B2
Sokolovo [BG] 148 F4
Sokolovo [BG] 150 E2
Sokołów Małopolski [PL] 64 D2
Sokołów Podlaski [PL] 50 B1
Sokoły [PL] 38 C3
Sokovaara [FIN] 210 E1
Sol [SK] 76 E1
Sola [N] 186 A2
Solacolu [RO] 150 C1
Solana de los Barros [E] 98 E2
Solana del Pino [E] 100 D4
Solánas [I] 142 C5
Solares [E] 86 D2
Solarolo [I] 128 D2
Solbacken [S] 190 E3
Solberg [N] 186 E2
Solberg [S] 206 C1
Solberga [S] 184 D2
Solbjerg [DK] 182 C3
Solbjerg [DK] 182 D3
Solčava [SLO] 120 B2
Solda / Sulden [I] 118 B2
Şoldanu [RO] 150 C1
Sölden [A] 118 B1
Soldeu [AND] 96 D1
Solec Kujawski [PL] 36 C4
Solec nad Wisłą [PL] 50 B4
Solec-Zdrój [PL] 64 B2
Solem [N] 212 C4
Solenzara [F] 130 B3

Solera del Gabaldón [E] 102 B2
Solesmes [F] 56 A1
Solesmes, Abbaye de- [F] 54 A4
Solevåg [N] 202 C3
Solf / Sulva [FIN] 208 B2
Solfonn [N] 192 C4
Solheim [N] 192 B2
Solignac [F] 78 E2
Solihull [GB] 22 F4
Solijani [HR] 146 C2
Solin [HR] 144 E4
Solingen [D] 42 D3
Solivella [E] 96 C3
Söll [A] 72 D4
Sollana [E] 102 D3
Sollebrunn [S] 184 B1
Sollefteå [S] 206 C2
Sollenau [A] 74 D3
Sollentuna [S] 190 D2
Soller [D] 42 C4
Sóller [E] 108 D3
Sóller / el Port [E] 108 D3
Søllerød [DK] 178 F2
Sollerön [S] 194 F3
Søllested [DK] 178 D3
Sollia [N] 194 B1
Solliden [S] 184 F3
Solliès-Pont [F] 124 F4
Sollihøgda [N] 186 F1
Solmaz [TR] 170 E3
Solmyra [S] 190 B2
Solna [S] 190 D2
Solnechnogorsk [RUS] 240 F3
Solnhofen [D] 72 C1
Solnice [CZ] 62 B2
Solojärvi [FIN] 226 D2
Solonka [UA] 244 C2
Solosancho [E] 92 D3
Sološnica [SK] 74 E2
Solothurn [CH] 70 D4
Solovi [RUS] 232 E4
Solovychi [UA] 50 E3
Solöz [TR] 158 F4
Solrød Strand [DK] 178 E2
Solsa [S] 190 D3
Sølsnes [N] 202 D3
Solsona [E] 96 C2
Solsvik [N] 192 A3
Solt [H] 122 B2
Soltau [D] 32 B4
Sol'tsy [RUS] 240 C2
Soltvadkert [H] 122 B2
Solum [N] 186 F1
Solunto [I] 140 C1
Solutré, Roche de- [F] 80 D1
Solvang [N] 202 F4
Sölvesborg [S] 180 D1
Solvik [S] 188 C3
Solvorn [N] 192 D2
Soma [TR] 164 C3
Sømådal [N] 204 C4
Somaglia [I] 116 E4
Sømåseter [N] 194 C1
Sombernon [F] 68 E3
Sombor [SRB] 122 B3
Someren [NL] 40 F3
Somerniemi [FIN] 198 E3
Somero [FIN] 198 D3
Sommariva del Bosco [I] 126 D1
Sommarset [N] 220 B2
Sommatino [I] 140 D3
Sommen [S] 184 D1
Sommepy-Tahure [F] 56 B3
Sömmerda [D] 44 D4
Sommerfeld [D] 32 F4
Sommersted [DK] 178 B2
Sommery [F] 54 D2
Sommesous [F] 56 B4

Sommières [F] 124 D2
Somo [E] 86 D2
Somogyacsa [H] 120 F2
Somogyapáti [H] 120 F3
Somogyjád [H] 120 F2
Somogyszob [H] 120 E3
Somogytarnóca [H] 120 E3
Somogyvár [H] 120 E2
Somosierra [E] 92 F3
Somosierra, Puerto de- [E] 92 F3
Somovit [BG] 148 F3
Sompolno [PL] 48 C2
Sompuis [F] 56 B4
Sompujärvi [FIN] 222 C4
Somvik [S] 184 D1
Son [N] 188 B2
Son Bou [E] 108 F3
Sonceboz [CH] 70 C4
Soncillo [E] 86 C3
Soncino [I] 116 F4
Sóndalo [I] 118 A2
Sondby [FIN] 200 B3
Søndeled [N] 186 E3
Sønder Balling [DK] 182 C3
Sønderborg [DK] 178 C3
Sønderby [DK] 178 C3
Sønderby [DK] 178 E3
Sønderby [DK] 182 B4
Sønder Dråby [DK] 182 C3
Sønder Felding [DK] 178 B1
Sønderho [DK] 178 A2
Sønder Omme [DK] 178 B1
Sondershausen [D] 44 D3
Søndersø [DK] 178 C2
Søndervig [DK] 182 B4
Søndervika [N] 204 C3
Sondrio [I] 116 F2
Søndrum [S] 184 B3
Sonekulla [S] 180 E1
Songe [N] 186 E3
Songesand [N] 186 B2
Sonkaja [FIN] 210 E2
Sonkajärvi [FIN] 216 D4
Sonneberg [D] 58 E2
Sonntagberg [A] 74 B3
Sonogno [CH] 116 D2
Sonsbeck [D] 42 C2
Sonseca [E] 100 E2
Sonta [SRB] 122 B4
Sonthofen [D] 72 A3
Sontra [D] 44 B4
Son Xoriguer [E] 108 E3
Sopeira [E] 96 B1
Sopela [E] 86 E2
Sophienhöhle [D] 58 F3
Sople [PL] 64 E2
Sopoćani [SRB] 154 B1
Sopoćani, Manastir- [SRB] 154 B1
Soponya [H] 122 A1
Šoporňa [SK] 74 F2
Sopot [BG] 156 D1
Sopot [MK] 154 D3
Sopot [PL] 36 C2
Sopot [SRB] 146 E2
Sopotnica [MK] 160 C1
Şopotu Nou [RO] 148 B1
Sopparjok [N] 226 C1
Sopron [H] 74 D3
Sora [I] 132 E4
Soragna [I] 128 B1
Söräker [S] 206 C3
Sorano [I] 130 E2
Sorbas [E] 106 C3
Sorbie [GB] 20 B3
Sørbø [N] 186 B2
Sörbo [S] 188 C3
Sørbotn [N] 224 D2
Sörbygden [S] 206 B3
Sørbymagle [DK] 178 E2

Sørdal [N] 220 B2
Sore [F] 78 B4
Söréd [H] 74 F4
Søre Herefoss [N] 186 D3
Soreide [N] 192 B2
Søre Moen [N] 204 D1
Sørenget [N] 212 C3
Soresina [I] 116 F4
Sörfjärden [S] 196 D1
Sør-Flatanger [N] 212 C3
Sörfors [S] 206 E1
Sörforsa [S] 196 C1
Sórgono [I] 142 C4
Sorgues [F] 124 E2
Sörgutvik [N] 212 C2
Sørhella [N] 202 E4
Soria [I] 94 B2
Soriano Calabro [I] 138 E3
Soriano nel Cimino [I] 130 F3
Sorica [SLO] 118 F3
Sorihuela del Guadalimar [E] 106 B1
Sorita [E] 102 E1
Sørkjosen [N] 224 E2
Sorkun [TR] 170 F1
Sorkwity [PL] 36 F2
Sørli [N] 212 E4
Sörmjöle [S] 206 E1
Sørmo [N] 224 D3
Sorø [DK] 178 E2
Soroca [MD] 244 E2
Soroní [GR] 176 C2
Sorpe [E] 88 E4
Sørreisa [N] 224 D3
Sorrento [I] 134 C4
Sorsakoski [FIN] 210 C3
Sorsele [S] 214 B1
Sörsjön [S] 194 D2
Sorso [I] 142 B2
Sort [E] 96 C1
Sortavala [RUS] 210 F4
Sortino [I] 140 E3
Sörtjärn [S] 204 E4
Sortland [N] 224 B3
Sør-Tverrfjord [N] 224 F1
Sørumsand [N] 188 B1
Sorunda [S] 190 D3
Sörup [DK] 178 C3
Sørup [DK] 182 D3
Sørvær [N] 228 A2
Sørværøy [N] 218 E2
Sørvågen [N] 218 E2
Sørvágur [FR] 182 A1
Sörvattnet [S] 204 D4
Sørvik [N] 202 F1
Sørvik [N] 224 C3
Sörviken [S] 206 B2
Sørvollen [N] 204 B4
Sösdala [S] 180 C1
Sos del Rey Católico [E] 88 A4
Soses [E] 94 F3
Sošice [HR] 120 C3
Sošnica [SK] 34 F3
Sošnica [PL] 62 D2
Sośnicowice [PL] 62 D2
Sosnicy [RUS] 232 F1
Sosnivka [UA] 64 F2
Sosnove [UA] 242 B4
Sosnovo [RUS] 200 F2
Sosnovo [RUS] 232 F1
Sosnovy Bor [RUS] 200 E4
Sosnowica [PL] 50 C3
Sosnowiec [PL] 62 E2
Sospel [F] 126 C3
Sossano [I] 118 C4
Šoštanj [SLO] 120 B2
Sóstis [GR] 156 E3
Søstrefoss [N] 202 D4
Sostrup [DK] 182 E3
Sot [SRB] 146 C1
Sotaseter [N] 192 D1
Soteska [SLO] 120 B3

Søtholmen [N] 188 C3
Sotilla de la Adrada [E] 92 D4
Sotillo de las Palomas [E] 92 C4
Sotin [HR] 146 C1
Sotkamo [FIN] 216 D3
Sotkuma [FIN] 210 D2
Sotobañado y Priorato [E] 86 B3
Soto del Barco [E] 82 F2
Soto de los Infantes [E] 82 E2
Soto del Real [E] 92 E3
Sotos [E] 102 B1
Sotresgudo [E] 86 C3
Sotrondio / San Martín del Rey Aurelio [E] 82 F3
Sotta [F] 130 B4
Sotteville les Rouen [F] 54 C2
Sottomarina [I] 128 D1
Sottrum [D] 32 B3
Sottunga [FIN] 198 B4
Sotuélamos [E] 100 F3
Soual [F] 124 A2
Soúda [GR] 174 B3
Souesmes [F] 68 B2
Soufflenheim [F] 56 F4
Soufli [GR] 156 F3
Soúgia [GR] 174 B4
Souillac [F] 78 E4
Souilly [F] 56 C3
Soulac–sur–Mere [F] 78 B2
Soulaines–Dhuys [F] 68 F1
Soulópoulo [GR] 160 C4
Soultz [F] 56 F4
Soultz [F] 70 D2
Soumoulou [F] 88 C3
Soúnio [GR] 156 D4
Soúnio [GR] 168 B3
Souppes–sur–Loing [F] 68 C1
Sourdeval [F] 52 F3
Sourdon [F] 54 E2
Soure [P] 90 C1
Sournia [F] 96 E1
Sourotí [GR] 162 B2
Soúrpi [GR] 162 B4
Sousceyrac [F] 78 F4
Sousel [P] 90 D4
Soustons [F] 88 B2
Soutelo [E] 82 B3
Southampton [GB] 28 B3
Southend–on–Sea [GB] 28 D3
South Molton [GB] 26 D3
Southport [GB] 22 E2
South Shields [GB] 20 F3
Southwold [GB] 28 F2
Soutomaior, Castillo de– [E] 82 B3
Souvála [GR] 168 A3
Souvigny [F] 68 C4
Søvang [DK] 178 B3
Søvassli [N] 202 F2
Sovata [RO] 244 D4
Sövdeborg [S] 180 C2
Söve [TR] 164 D2
Sover [I] 118 C2
Soverato [I] 138 E3
Soveria Mannelli [I] 138 E2
Sövestad [S] 180 D2
Sovetsk [RUS] 238 B3
Sovetskiy [RUS] 200 D3
Søvik [N] 202 C2
Sovinec [CZ] 62 C3
Sovjan [AL] 160 C2
Sowia Góra [PL] 46 E1
Sowiniec [PL] 34 E4
Soyen [D] 72 D3
Søyland [N] 186 A3
Sozoro [TR] 158 B2
Sozopol [BG] 158 C1
Spa [B] 40 F4
Spacco della Regina [I] 130 C2
Spaichingen [D] 70 E2

Spakenburg [NL] 30 B3
Spalding [GB] 24 D4
Spálené Poříčí [CZ] 60 C3
Spalt [D] 58 E4
Spanchevci [BG] 148 D4
S. Pancrázio [I] 118 B2
Spandau [D] 46 B1
Spånga [S] 190 C2
Spangenberg [D] 44 B4
Spangereid [N] 186 C4
Spannberg [A] 74 D2
Španovica [HR] 120 E4
S. Pantaleón de Losa [E] 86 D3
Sparanise [I] 134 C3
Spare [LV] 234 D3
Sparreholm [S] 190 C3
Sparresholm [DK] 178 E3
Spárta [GR] 168 A2
Spartà [I] 138 C3
Spárti [GR] 172 D3
Spárto [GR] 166 C2
Spas [AL] 154 B3
Spasovo [BG] 150 F2
Spasskaya Polist' [RUS] 240 C1
Spáta [GR] 168 B2
Spätaru [RO] 148 E1
Spatharaíoi [GR] 170 A3
Spean Bridge [GB] 14 D4
Specke [S] 188 D1
S. Pedro [P] 98 D2
S. Pedro de Cardeña [E] 86 C4
S. Pedro de Teverga [E] 82 E3
Speinshart [D] 58 F3
Spekedalssetra [N] 204 B4
Spello [I] 132 D2
Spenge [D] 30 F4
Spennymoor [GB] 20 E3
Spenshult [S] 184 B3
Spentrup [DK] 182 D3
Spercheiáda [GR] 166 E2
S. Pere de Ribes [E] 96 C3
Sperlonga [I] 134 B3
Spétses [GR] 168 A4
Speyer [D] 58 B3
Spezzano Albanese [I] 136 C4
Spícino [RUS] 232 D2
Spickendorf [D] 44 E3
Spiddal / An Spidéal [IRL] 10 C1
Spiegelau [D] 72 E1
Spiekeroog [D] 30 E1
Spielbg [D] 58 D3
Spielfeld [A] 120 C2
S. Pietro al Natisone [I] 118 E3
Spiez [CH] 116 C1
Spijkenisse [NL] 30 A4
Spílaia Diroú [GR] 172 D3
Spíli [GR] 174 C4
Spilimbergo [I] 118 E3
Spilja Hrustovača [BIH] 144 E2
Spillum [N] 212 C3
Spina, Necropoli di– [I] 128 D2
Spinalógka [GR] 174 E3
Spinazzola [I] 134 F3
Spincourt [F] 56 D3
Spind [N] 186 B4
Špindlerův–Mlýn [CZ] 60 F2
Spineta Nuova [I] 134 D4
Špionica Donja [BIH] 146 B2
Špišić Bukovica [HR] 120 E3
Spiss [A] 118 B1
Spišská Belá [SK] 64 B4
Spišská Nová Ves [SK] 76 B1
Spišské Podhradie [SK] 76 D1
Spišský Hrad [SK] 76 D1
Spišský Štvrtok [SK] 76 C1
Spital am Pyhrn [A] 74 A3
Spittal an der Drau [A] 118 E2
Spitz [A] 74 C2
Spjærøy [N] 188 B2

Spjald [DK] 178 B1
Stade [D] 32 B3
Spjelkavik [N] 202 C3
Spjutsund [FIN] 200 A3
Split [HR] 144 E4
Splügen [CH] 116 E2
Spodnja Idrija [SLO] 118 F3
Spodsbjerg [DK] 178 D3
Špogi [LV] 236 D4
Spohle [D] 30 F2
Spoleto [I] 132 D2
Spoltore [I] 132 F3
Spotorno [I] 126 D2
Spøttrup [DK] 182 C3
Sprakensehl [D] 32 C4
Sprecowo [PL] 36 E2
Spreenhagen [D] 46 B2
Spremberg [D] 46 C3
Spresiano [I] 118 D3
Springe [D] 44 B2
Sproge [S] 234 A3
Spy [B] 40 E4
Spychowo [PL] 38 A2
Spydeberg [N] 188 B2
Spytkowice [PL] 62 F3
Squillace [I] 138 E2
Squinzano [I] 136 E3
Srahmore [IRL] 12 B2
Srbac [BIH] 144 F1
Srbica [KS] 154 C2
Srbobran [SRB] 122 C4
Srđevići [BIH] 144 E4
Srdiečko [SK] 76 B1
Srebărna [BG] 150 D2
Srebrenica [BIH] 146 C3
Srebrenik [BIH] 146 B2
Sredets [BG] 156 E2
Sredets [BG] 158 B1
Središče ob Dravi [SLO] 120 D2
Sredishte [BG] 150 D2
Srednje [BIH] 146 B3
Srednogortsi [BG] 156 D3
Sredno Gradishte [BG] 156 E2
Sredogriv [BG] 148 C3
Šrem [PL] 46 F2
Sremska Kamenica [SRB] 146 D1
Sremska Mitrovica [SRB] 146 C2
Sremska Rača [SRB] 146 C2
Sremski Karlovci [SRB] 146 D1
Sribne [UA] 242 E3
Srni [CZ] 72 F1
Środa Śląska [PL] 46 E4
Środa Wielkopolska [PL] 48 B2
Srokowo [PL] 38 A1
S. Roque do Pico [P] 110 B3
Srpci [MK] 160 D1
Srp. Itebej [SRB] 122 D4
Srpska Crnja [SRB] 122 C3
Srpski Miletić [SRB] 122 B4
S. Salvador de Leyre [E] 88 B3
S. Silvestre de Guzmán [E] 98 D4
S. Stefano d'Aveto [I] 126 F2
Sta [S] 204 D2
Staaken [D] 46 B2
Sta. Ana, Monasterio de– [E] 106 E1
Staatz [A] 74 D2
Stabbestad [N] 186 E3
Stabbursnes [N] 228 C3
Stabekk [N] 188 B1
Sta. Casilda [E] 86 D4
Stachy [CZ] 60 C4
Sta. Coloma [AND] 96 D1
Sta. Coloma de G. [E] 96 D3

Sta. Cristina de Lena [E] 82 F3
Stade [D] 32 B3
Stadl a. d. Mur [A] 118 F1
Stadra [S] 188 F2
Stadskanaal [NL] 30 D2
Stadt Allendorf [D] 42 F4
Stadthagen [D] 44 B2
Stadtilm [D] 58 E1
Stadtkyll [D] 56 E1
Stadtlauringen [D] 58 D2
Stadtlohn [D] 30 D4
Stadtoldendorf [D] 44 B2
Stadtroda [D] 58 F1
Stadtsteinach [D] 58 F2
St Aegyd [A] 74 C3
Sta. Elena [E] 88 C4
Sta. Espina, Monasterio de– [E] 92 D1
Stäfa [CH] 70 E4
Staffanstorp [DK] 180 C2
Staffarda, Abbazia di– [I] 126 C1
Staffelstein [D] 58 E2
Stafford [GB] 22 F3
St–Affrique [F] 124 B2
Stágeira [GR] 162 C1
St–Agnant [F] 78 B1
St–Agrève [F] 80 C3
Stahle [D] 44 B2
Stai [N] 194 B2
Staicele [LV] 230 D4
St–Aignan [F] 66 D1
St–Aignan [F] 68 A2
Staigue Fort [IRL] 10 A3
Stainach [A] 74 A4
Staines [GB] 28 C3
Stainsland [N] 186 C3
Stainville [F] 56 C4
Stainz [A] 120 B2
Stakčín [SK] 76 E1
Stakenjokk [S] 212 E2
Stakkvik [N] 224 E2
Stalać [SRB] 146 F4
St–Alban [F] 80 B4
St Albans [GB] 28 C2
Stalden [CH] 116 C2
Stalheim [N] 192 C2
Stalheims–Klievene Museum [N] 192 C2
Stalida [GR] 174 D3
Stall [A] 118 E1
Stallarholmen [S] 190 D2
Stallberg [D] 34 D3
Stållberg [S] 188 F1
Ställdalen [S] 188 F1
Stalon [S] 212 F3
Stalowa Wola [PL] 64 C2
St–Amand–en–Puisaye [F] 68 C2
St–Amand–les–Eaux [F] 40 C4
St–Amand–Longpré [F] 68 A2
St–Amand–Montrond [F] 68 B4
St–Amans [P] 80 B4
St–Amant–Roche–Savine [F] 80 C2
S. Silvestre de Guzmán [E]
Sta. María a Real [E] 82 C3
Sta. María de Bellpuig de les Avellanes [E] 96 B2
Sta. María de Conxo [E] 82 B2
Sta. María de la Vega [E] 84 F3
Sta. María de Lebeña [E] 86 B2
Sta. María de Melque [E] 100 D1
Sta. María de Mezonzo [E] 82 C2
Sta. María la Real [E] 86 C3
Sta. María la Real [E] 94 C2
Stambolovo [BG] 150 D3
St–Ambroix [F] 124 D2
St–Amé [F] 70 C2
Stameriena [LV] 236 D2

Stamford [GB] 24 D4
Stamná [GR] 166 C3
St–Amour [F] 80 E1
Stampfen [A] 118 E1
Stams [A] 72 B4
St Andrä [A] 120 B2
St–André [F] 54 C3
St Andreasberg [D] 44 C3
St–André–de–Cubzac [F] 78 C3
St–André–les–Alpes [F] 126 B2
St Andrews [GB] 18 E3
Stänga [S] 234 A3
Stange [N] 194 B3
Stangerum [DK] 182 D3
Stanghelle [N] 192 B3
Staniewice [PL] 36 A2
Stanisławów [PL] 50 A2
Stanišić [SRB] 122 B3
Stanjel [SLO] 118 F3
Stanjevci [MK] 154 E3
Staňkov [CZ] 60 C3
St Annaparochie [NL] 30 C2
Stanós [GR] 162 B1
Stans [CH] 70 E4
Stansstad [CH] 70 E4
St–Anthème [F] 80 C3
St–Antoine [F] 80 D3
St.–Antoine, Chapelle– [F] 88 B3
St Anton [A] 72 A4
St–Antonin–Noble–Val [F] 88 F2
St. Antonino [F] 130 B2
Stany [PL] 64 C2
Stanzach [A] 72 B4
St–Août [F] 68 B3
Stapar [SRB] 122 B4
Staphorst [NL] 30 D3
Stapnes [N] 186 B3
Stąporków [PL] 48 E4
Stara [PL] 48 E4
Stará Bystrica [SK] 62 E4
Stara Cerlev [SLO] 120 B4
Starachowice [PL] 48 F4
Stara Gradiška [HR] 144 F1
Stara Krašnica [PL] 46 E4
Stará L'ubovňa [SK] 64 B4
Stara Moravica [SRB] 122 C3
Stara Novalja [HR] 144 C2
Stara Pazova [SRB] 146 D1
Stara Reka [BG] 150 C4
Stará Turá [SK] 74 E2
Stará Voda [CZ] 60 B3
Staravolya [BY] 38 E4
Stara Wrona [PL] 48 E1
Staraya Russa [RUS] 240 C2
Staraya Toropa [RUS] 240 C3
Stara Zagora [BG] 156 E1
Starcevo [BG] 156 D3
Stare Czarnowo [PL] 34 D3
Stare Dębno [PL] 34 F2
Stare Hory [SK] 76 B1
Stare Jeżewo [PL] 38 C3
Staré Město [CZ] 62 B3
Staré Město [CZ] 62 B3
Staré Město [CZ] 74 E1
Stare Osiecno [PL] 34 F4
Stargard–Szczeciński [PL] 34 E3
Stårheim [N] 202 B4
Stari Bar [MNE] 152 E4
Stari Dojran [MK] 156 A4
Starigrad [HR] 144 C2
Stari Grad [HR] 152 B2
Stari Gradac [HR] 120 E3
Starigrad Paklenica [HR] 144 C3
Stari Mikanovci [HR] 146 B1

Stari Slankamen [SRB] **146** D1
Staritsa [RUS] **240** E3
Starjak [HR] **120** C4
Starkov [CZ] **62** B3
Starnberg [D] **72** C3
Starod [SLO] **118** F4
Starodub [RUS] **242** E2
Starogard [PL] **34** E3
Starogard Gdański [PL] **36** C2
Starokostiantyniv [UA] **244** E1
Staromieśtcie [PL] **62** F2
Staro Nagoričane, Manastir–
   [MK] **154** D3
Staro Oryakhovo [BG] **150** E3
Staropol'ye [RUS] **232** E2
Starosel [BG] **156** C1
Staroselci [BG] **148** E3
Staro selo [BG] **148** F4
Staro Selo [BG] **150** C2
Starożreby [PL] **48** E1
Starup [DK] **178** B2
Starup [DK] **178** C2
Starý Bernštejn [CZ] **60** E2
Stary Borek [PL] **64** D3
Starychi [UA] **64** E3
Stary Dzierzgoń [PL] **36** D2
Stary Gózd [PL] **48** F3
Starý Hrozenkov [CZ] **74** F1
Staryi Sambir [UA] **64** E3
Stary Plzenec [CZ] **60** C3
Stary Sącz [PL] **64** B3
Starý Smokovec [SK] **64** A4
Stary Szelków [PL] **38** A4
Starý Vestec [CZ] **60** E2
Stary Wieś [PL] **50** C4
Staryya Darohi [BY] **242** C2
Starzyny [PL] **62** F2
St-Astier [F] **78** D3
Staszów [PL] **64** B2
Stat. Angístis [GR] **156** C4
Stathelle [N] **186** E2
Statland [N] **212** C3
Statte [I] **136** D2
St-Aubane [F] **126** B3
St-Auban-sur-l'Ouvèze [F]
   124 F2
St-Aubin-d'Aubigné [F] **52** E4
St-Aubin-du-Cormier [F]
   52 E4
St-Aubin-sur-Mer [F] **54** B2
St.-Augustin, Château de– [F]
   68 C4
St-Aulaye [F] **78** C3
Staume [N] **202** B4
Staupitz [D] **46** B3
St Austell [GB] **26** B3
Stava [S] **184** D1
Stavang [N] **192** B1
Stavanger [N] **186** B2
Stavaträsk [S] **214** D2
Stave [N] **224** B3
Staveley [GB] **24** C3
Stavelot [B] **56** D1
Stavenisse [NL] **40** D2
Staveren [NL] **30** C2
Stavern [D] **30** E3
Stavern [N] **186** F3
Stavertsi [BG] **148** E3
Stavkirke [N] **186** E1
Stavkirke [N] **192** D2
St-Avold [F] **56** E4
Stavre [N] **204** F3
Staveviken [S] **206** C3
Stavrochóri [GR] **174** E4
Stavrodrómi [GR] **172** C2
Stavrós [GR] **160** E2
Stavrós [GR] **162** B1
Stavrós [GR] **166** B3
Stavrós [GR] **166** D3
Stavrós [GR] **168** A1
Stavrós [GR] **168** B2
Stavrós [GR] **174** B3

Stavrós tis Psókas [CY]
   176 C3
Stavroúpoli [GR] **156** D3
Stavsjø [N] **194** B3
Stavsnäs [S] **190** E2
Stawiguda [PL] **36** E3
Stawiski [PL] **38** B3
Stawiszyn [PL] **48** B3
St–Aygulf [F] **126** B3
St–Bard [F] **80** A2
St. Barthèlemy [CH] **116** B1
St.–Barthélemy [F] **52** F3
St. Bartholomá [D] **72** E4
St–Béat [F] **88** D3
St–Beauzély [F] **124** B2
St–Benin [F] **68** D3
St–Benoît–du–Sault [F] **66** F4
St–Benoît–sur–Loire [F] **68** B2
St–Bertrand–de–Comminges
   [F] **88** D3
St.–Blaise [F] **124** E3
St Blasien [D] **70** E3
St–Blin [F] **70** A1
St–Bonnet–de–Joux [F] **80** D1
St–Bonnet–en–Champsaur
   [F] **126** B1
St–Bonnet–le–Château [F]
   80 C3
St–Brevin–les–Pins [F] **66** B2
St–Brice–en–Coglès [F] **52** E3
St–Brieuc [F] **52** D3
St–Calais [F] **66** F2
St–Cast–le–Guildo [F] **52** D3
St–Céré [F] **78** E4
St–Cergue [CH] **80** F1
St–Cernin [F] **80** A3
St–Chamas [F] **124** E3
St–Chamond [F] **80** D3
St–Chély–d'Apcher [F] **80** B4
St–Chély–d'Aubrac [F] **80** A4
St–Chinian [F] **124** B3
St Christina / Santa Cristina
   [I] **118** C2
St Christoph [A] **72** A4
St. Christophe–en–Oisans
   [F] **80** F4
St–Ciers–sur–Gironde [F]
   78 C3
St–Cirq–Lapopie [F] **88** F1
St.–Clair [F] **54** A2
St–Clar [F] **88** E2
St–Claud [F] **78** D2
St–Claude [F] **80** F1
St Clears [GB] **26** C1
St–Clément [F] **70** C1
St–Clément–sur–Durance
   [F] **126** B1
St–Côme–d'Olt [F] **80** A4
St.–Cosme–en–Vairais [F]
   54 B4
St–Cyprien [F] **78** D4
St–Cyprien–Plage [F] **96** F1
St. David's [GB] **22** B4
St–Denis [F] **54** E3
St–Denis–d'Oléron [F] **66** C4
St–Denis–d'Orques [F] **54** A4
St–Didier–en–Velay [F] **80** C3
St–Dié [F] **70** C2
St–Dizier [F] **54** F4
St–Donat–sur–l'Herbasse
   [F] **80** D3
St. Doulagh's Church [IRL]
   12 E4
Steane [N] **186** D2
Ste–Anne–d'Auray [F] **52** C4
Ste–Anne–la–Palud [F] **52** B3
Ste.–Barbe [F] **52** B3
Stechelberg [CH] **116** C2
Štěchovice [CZ] **60** D3
Steckborn [CH] **70** F3
Ste–Croix [CH] **70** B4
Ste–Croix–Volvestre [F] **88** E3

Steeg [A] **72** A4
Steenbergen [NL] **40** E2
Ste.–Engrâce [F] **88** B3
Ste–Enimie [F] **124** C1
Steenvoorde [F] **40** B3
Steenwijk [NL] **30** C3
Stefáni [GR] **166** C2
Štefaníkova Mohyla [SK] **74** E2
Stefaniná [GR] **162** B1
Stefanovo [BG] **150** E2
Ste–Foy–la–Grande [F] **78** C3
Stegaros [N] **192** D4
Ste–Gauburge–Ste–Colombe
   [F] **54** B3
Stege [DK] **178** E3
Stegeborg [S] **190** C4
Stegersbach [A] **120** D1
Stegna [PL] **36** D2
St–Egrève [F] **80** E3
Ste–Hélène [F] **78** B3
Ste–Hermine [F] **66** C3
Stehnovo [RUS] **236** F2
Steigen [N] **220** A1
Steilwände [D] **72** A3
Stein [A] **74** C2
Stein [D] **58** E3
Stein [N] **192** F4
Stein [N] **212** B4
Steinaberg bru [N] **192** C4
Steinach [A] **118** C1
Stein am Rhein [CH] **70** F3
Steinau [D] **58** C2
Steinbach [D] **58** F2
Stëinberg [A] **74** D4
Steinberg [D] **178** C3
Steinberg am Rofan [A] **72** C4
Steine [N] **192** B2
Steinestø [N] **192** B3
Steinfeld [A] **118** E2
Steinfeld [D] **30** F3
Steinfeld [D] **56** E1
Steinfurt [D] **30** E4
Steingaden [D] **72** B3
Steinhagen [D] **32** F2
Steinhausen [D] **72** A3
Steinheim [D] **42** F2
Steinhorst [D] **32** C4
Steinibach [CH] **116** E1
Steinkjer [N] **212** C4
Steinløysa [N] **202** D2
Steinsåsen [N] **204** C3
Steinsberg [D] **58** B4
Steinsburg [D] **58** E2
Steinsdal [N] **202** F1
Steinshøle [S] **192** E4
Steinsholt [N] **186** F2
Steinsøynes [N] **202** E1
Steinsvik [N] **202** B4
Ste.– Jalle [F] **124** E2
Steknica [PL] **36** B1
Ste–Livrade–sur–Lot [F] **88** E1
Stellendam [NL] **30** A4
St–Eloy–les–Mines [F] **80** B1
Ste–Marie–aux–Mines [F]
   70 D2
Ste–Marie–de–Campan
   [F] **88** D3
Ste–Marie–du–Mont [F] **52** F2
Ste–Maure–de–Touraine
   [F] **66** F3
Ste–Maxime [F] **126** B4
Ste–Menehould [F] **56** C3
Ste–Mère–Eglise [F] **52** F2
St–Emilion [F] **78** C3
Sten [S] **184** D1
Stenay [F] **56** C3
Stenbjerg [DK] **182** B3
Stenbo [S] **184** E2
Stendal [D] **44** E1
Stende [LV] **234** E3
Steneby [S] **188** C3

Stengelsrud [N] **186** E1
St Englmar [D] **72** E1
Stenhammar [S] **190** C3
Stenhamra [S] **190** D2
Stení [GR] **168** B1
Steninge [S] **184** B3
Steninge [S] **190** D2
Stenlille [DK] **178** E2
Stenløse [DK] **178** E2
Stennäs [S] **206** D1
Stenó [GR] **172** D2
Stènoma [GR] **166** D2
Stensele [S] **214** B2
Stensjö [S] **184** E2
Stensjön [S] **184** D2
St–Georges [F] **66** D2
Stenstorp [S] **188** E4
Stenträsk [S] **214** C2
Stenstrup [DK] **178** C3
Stensund [S] **214** B1
Stensund [S] **220** C4
Stensunda [S] **190** E1
Stenträsk [S] **220** D3
Stenudden [S] **220** C3
Stenungsund [S] **182** F1
Steornabhagh / Stornoway
   [GB] **14** C1
Stepanci [MK] **154** D4
Stepnica [PL] **34** D3
Stepojevac [SRB] **146** D2
Sterdyń–Osada [PL] **38** B4
Sterehushche [UA] **246** E3
Sterławki Wielkie [PL] **38** A2
Stern, Manastir– [BIH] **144** F2
Stern / la Villa [I] **118** C2
Stérna [GR] **156** D3
Sternberg [D] **32** E3
Šternberk [CZ] **60** E4
Šternberk [CZ] **62** C3
Stérnes [GR] **174** B3
Stérnia [GR] **168** D3
Sterringi [N] **202** E4
Sterzing / Vipiteno [I] **118** C1
Ste–Sévère [F] **68** B4
Stes–Maries–de–la–Mer [F]
   124 D3
St. Estèphe [F] **78** B2
Ste–Suzanne [F] **54** A4
Stęszew [PL] **46** F2
Štětí [CZ] **60** D2
St–Étienne [F] **80** D3
St–Étienne–de–Baïgorry
   [F] **88** B2
St–Etienne–de–St–Geoirs
   [F] **80** E3
St–Etienne–de–Tinée [F]
   126 B2
St–Étienne–les–Orgues [F]
   124 F2
Ste–Tulle [F] **124** F3
Stevenage [GB] **28** D2
Stevrek [BG] **150** C4
Stewarton [GB] **18** C4
Steyerberg [D] **42** F1
Steyersberg [A] **74** C4
Steyr [A] **74** A3
Steyr–Durchbruch [A] **74** A3
Stezherovo [BG] **150** A3
St–Fargeau [F] **68** C2
St.–Fiacre [F] **52** B4
St–Firmin [F] **80** E4
St–Florent [F] **66** D2
St–Florent [F] **68** B3
St–Florent [F] **130** B2
St.–Florent–des–Bois [F]
   66 C3
St–Florentin [F] **68** D2
St. Florian [A] **72** F2
St–Flour [F] **80** B3
St–Fort–sur–Gironde [F] **78** B2
St.–Fort–sur–le–Né [F] **78** C2
St–Fulgent [F] **66** C3
St Gallen [A] **74** B3

St Gallen [CH] **70** F4
St Gallenkirch [A] **116** F1
St–Galmier [F] **80** C3
St. Gangolf [D] **56** E3
St–Gaudens [F] **88** D3
St–Gaultier [F] **68** A3
St–Geniez–d'Olt [F] **80** A4
St–Genis–de–Saintonge
   [F] **78** C2
St–Genix–sur–Guiers [F]
   80 E3
St. George [CH] **116** A1
St Georgen [A] **72** F3
St Georgen [A] **120** B1
St Georgen [D] **70** E2
St–Georges [F] **66** D2
St–Georges–de–Didonne
   [F] **78** B2
St. Georges–on–Couzan
   [F] **80** C2
St–Geours–de–Maremne
   [F] **88** B2
St–Germain [F] **54** D3
St–Germain [F] **78** E3
St–Germain–de–Calberte
   [F] **124** D2
St–Germain–de–Joux [F]
   80 E2
St–Germain–des–Fossés
   [F] **80** C1
St–Germain–des–Vaux
   [F] **52** E1
St–Germain–du–Bois [F]
   68 F4
St–Germain–du–Plain [F]
   68 E4
St–Germain–Laval [F] **80** C2
St–Germain–Lembron [F]
   80 B3
St–Germain–l'Herm [F] **80** B3
St–Germain–Plage [F] **52** E2
St–Germer–de–Fly [F] **54** D2
St–Gervais [F] **124** B2
St–Gervais–d'Auvergne
   [F] **80** B1
St–Gervais–les–Bains [F]
   116 B2
St–Géry [F] **88** F1
St–Gildas–des–Bois [F] **66** B2
St Gilgen [A] **72** E3
St–Gilles [F] **124** D3
St–Gilles–Croix–de–Vie
   [F] **66** B3
St–Gilles–Pligeaux [F] **52** C3
St–Gingolph [CH] **116** B2
St–Girons [F] **88** E3
St–Girons–en–Marensin
   [F] **88** B1
St–Girons–Plage [F] **88** B1
St Goar [D] **56** F2
St Goarshausen [D] **56** F2
St–Gobain [F] **54** F2
St–Gorgon–Main [F] **70** B4
St–Guénolé [F] **52** A4
St–Guilhem–le–Desert [F]
   124 C2
St Helens [GB] **22** F2
St Helier [GBJ] **52** E2
St. Hilaire Cottes [F] **40** B3
St–Hilaire–de–Villefranche
   [F] **78** C2
St–Hilaire–du–Harcouët
   [F] **52** F3
St–Hippolyte [F] **70** C3
St–Hippolyte–du–Fort [F]
   124 C2
St. Höga [S] **182** F1
St–Honoré les–Bains [F]
   68 D4
St–Hubert [B] **56** C2
Stia [I] **128** D3
Sticciano Scalo [I] **130** E2

Stiefern [A] 74 C2
Stiens [NL] 30 C2
Stift Zwettl [A] 74 B2
Stigen [N] 194 D2
Stigen [S] 188 C3
Stigfoss [N] 202 D3
Stigliano [I] 134 F4
Stigliano, Bagni di- [I] 130 F3
Stignano [I] 138 E3
Stigsjö [S] 206 C3
Stigtomta [S] 190 C3
Stiklestad [N] 204 C1
Stilla [N] 226 B1
Stilo [I] 138 E3
St-Imier [CH] 70 C4
Stimlje [KS] 154 C2
St Ingbert [D] 56 E3
Stintino [I] 142 B2
Štip [MK] 154 E4
Stirling [GB] 18 D3
Štirovača [HR] 144 C2
Štitary [CZ] 74 C1
Štitnik [SK] 76 C2
Štíty [CZ] 62 B3
Ştiuca [RO] 122 F4
St Ives [GB] 26 A3
St Ives [GB] 28 D1
Stixenstein [A] 74 C3
St-Jacut [F] 52 D3
St. Jakob [A] 118 D1
St Jakob im Rosental [A]
118 F2
St-James [F] 52 E3
Stjärnsund [S] 188 F3
Stjärnsund [S] 196 C4
St. Jaume d'Enveja [E] 96 B4
St-Jean-Brévelay [F] 52 C4
St-Jean-Cap-Ferrat [F]
126 C3
St-Jean-d'Angély [F] 78 C1
St-Jean-de-Bournay [F]
80 E3
St-Jean-de-Losne [F] 68 F3
St-Jean-de-Luz [F] 88 A2
St-Jean-de-Maurienne
[F] 80 F3
St-Jean-de-Monts [F] 66 B3
St-Jean-du-Bruel [F] 124 C2
St-Jean-du-Gard [F] 124 D2
St-Jean-du-Liget, Chapelle-
[F] 66 F3
St-Jean-en-Royans [F] 80 E4
St-Jean-le-Thomas [F] 52 E3
St-Jean-Pied-de-Port
[F] 88 B3
St. Jeans-d'Arves [F] 80 F3
St-Jeoire [F] 116 A2
St. Joan de Penyagolosa [E]
102 D2
St Johann am Tauern [A] 74 A4
St Johann im Pongau [A] 72 E4
St Johann in Tirol [A] 72 D4
St Johnstown [IRL] 12 D1
Stjørdal [N] 204 B2
St-Jores [F] 52 E2
St-Jorioz [F] 80 F2
St-Jory [F] 88 E2
St-Jouan-de-l'Isle [F] 52 D3
St-Jouin-de-Marnes [F]
66 E3
St-Juéry [F] 124 A2
St-Julien [F] 80 E1
St-Julien [F] 88 E3
St-Julien-Chapteuil [F] 80 C3
St-Julien-de-Vouvantes
[F] 66 C2
St. Julien-du-Verdon [F] 126 B3
St-Julien-en-Beauchêne
[F] 124 F1
St.-Julien-en-Born [F] 88 B1
St-Julien-en-Genevois
[F] 80 F2

St-Julien-l'Ars [F] 66 E4
St-Junien [F] 78 E2
St Just [GB] 26 A3
St-Just-en-Chaussée [F]
54 E2
St-Just-en-Chevalet [F]
80 C2
St-Justin [F] 88 C1
St. Kanzian [A] 120 B2
St Lambrecht [A] 120 A1
St-Lary-Soulan [F] 88 D4
St-Laurent [F] 52 F2
St-Laurent [F] 78 E2
St.-Laurent-de-la-Cabrerisse
[F] 124 B3
St.-Laurent-de-la-Salanque
[F] 96 F1
St-Laurent-des-Autels
[F] 66 C2
St.-Laurent-en-Gâtines
[F] 66 F2
St-Laurent-en-Grandvaux
[F] 80 F1
St-Laurent-les-Bains [F]
80 C4
St-Laurent-Médoc [F] 78 B3
St-Léger [F] 68 D3
St.-Léon, Chapelle- [F] 70 D1
St-Léonard-de-Noblat
[F] 78 E2
St Leonhard [A] 74 B3
St-Leu-d'Esserent [F] 54 E3
St-Lizier [F] 88 E3
St-Lô [F] 52 F2
St Lorenzen [A] 118 D2
St-Louis [F] 70 D3
St-Loup-sur-Semouse
[F] 70 B2
St-Luc [CH] 116 C2
St-Lunaire [F] 52 D3
St-Lys [F] 88 E3
St-Macaire [F] 78 C4
St-Maclou [F] 54 C2
St-Maixent-l'Ecole [F] 66 D4
St. Malm [S] 190 C3
St-Malo [F] 52 E3
St-Mamest [F] 78 D3
St. Marcel [F] 116 A3
St-Marcellin [F] 80 E3
St. Marcellin-en-Forez [F] 80 C3
St. Marein [A] 120 C1
St Margaret's Hope [GB] 16 C2
St Märgen [D] 70 E2
St. Maria [D] 58 D4
St. Maria zu den Engeln
[CH] 70 D4
St-Mars-la-Jaille [F] 66 C2
St. Martin [A] 74 B2
St. Martin [F] 66 B1
St-Martin-d'Auxigny [F] 68 B3
St-Martín-de-Crau [F] 124 E3
St-Martin-de-Londres [F]
124 C2
St. Martin-d'Entraunes [F]
126 B2
St-Martin-de-Ré [F] 66 C4
St.-Martin-du-Canigou
[F] 96 E1
St-Martin-Lestra [F] 80 D2
St-Martin-l'Heureux [F] 56 B3
St. Martin Tennengebirge
[A] 72 E4
St-Martin-Vésubie [F] 126 C2
St-Martory [F] 88 E3
St. Mathieu [F] 78 D2
St-Mathieu, Pointe de- [F]
52 A3
St-Mathieu-de-Tréviers [F]
124 C2
St-Maurice [CH] 116 B2
St-Maurice-la-Clouère
[F] 66 E4

St. Maurice la Sotterraine
[F] 68 A4
St-Maurice-Navacelles [F]
124 C2
St Maurice-sur-Moselle
[F] 70 C2
St Mawes [GB] 26 B4
St-Maximin-la-Ste-Baume
[F] 124 F3
St-Méen [F] 52 D4
St. Meinrad [CH] 70 E4
St. Mellösa [S] 190 B2
St Michael [A] 74 B4
St Michael [A] 120 D1
St Michael i. Lungau [A]
118 F1
St Michel / Mikkeli [FIN]
210 C4
St.-Michel-de Cuxa [F] 96 E1
St-Michel-de-Maurienne
[F] 80 F4
St. Michel de Rieufret [F]
78 B4
St-Michel-en-Grève [F]
52 C2
St-Michel-en-l'Herm [F]
66 C4
St-Michel-Mont-Mercure
[F] 66 D3
St-Mihiel [F] 56 C4
St. Miquel del Fai [E] 96 D3
St-Morand [F] 70 D3
St Moritz [CH] 116 F2
St-Nazaire [F] 66 B2
St. Nazaire les Eymes [F] 80 E3
St-Nectaire [F] 80 B2
St Neots [GB] 28 D2
St.-Nicodème [F] 52 C4
St-Nicolas [F] 66 B1
St.-Nicolas (St-Niklaas)
[B] 40 D3
St Nicolas-de-Port [F] 70 C1
St-Nicolas-de-Redon [F]
66 B1
St-Nicolas-du-Pélem [F]
52 C3
St-Niklaas (St.-Nicolas)
[B] 40 D3
St Niklaus [CH] 116 C2
St Nikolai [A] 72 F4
Støa [N] 194 D2
Stobeč [HR] 144 E4
Stobi [MK] 154 E4
Stoby [S] 180 D1
Stocka [S] 196 D1
Stockaryd [S] 184 D2
Stockbridge [GB] 28 B3
Stöcke [S] 206 F1
Stockelsdorf [D] 32 C2
Stockenboy [A] 118 E2
Stockerau [A] 74 D2
Stockheim [D] 58 E2
Stockholm [S] 190 D2
Stockport [GB] 24 B2
Stocksbo [S] 196 B1
Stocksbo [S] 196 C3
Stockton on Tees [GB] 20 E4
Stoczek Klasztorny [PL] 36 F2
Stoczek Łukowski [PL] 50 B2
Stod [CZ] 60 C3
Stod [N] 212 C4
Stöde [S] 206 C4
Stødi [N] 220 A3
St Oedenrode [NL] 40 F2
Stoina [RO] 148 D1
Stojan Mikhaylovski [BG]
150 D3
Stojmirovo [MK] 154 F3
Stoke-on-Trent [GB] 22 F3
Stokite [BG] 150 A4
Stokkasjøen [N] 212 D1

Stokke [N] 186 F2
Stokkemarke [DK] 178 D3
Stokkland [N] 186 E2
Stokkvågen [N] 218 E4
Stokmarknes [N] 224 B4
Štoky [CZ] 60 F4
Stola [S] 188 D3
Stolac [BIH] 152 D2
Stolberg [D] 42 C4
Stolbovo [RUS] 236 E3
Stolbzy [BY] 242 B2
Stolin [BY] 242 B3
Stollberg [D] 60 B2
Stollberg [D] 60 B1
Stöllet [S] 194 D4
Stolno [PL] 36 C3
St Olof [S] 180 D2
Stolpe [D] 34 D4
Stolpe [D] 46 B1
Stolpen [D] 46 C4
Stołpie [PL] 50 D3
Stolzenau [D] 42 F1
St-Omer [F] 40 B3
Stómio [GR] 160 F3
Stömne [S] 188 D2
Stomorska [HR] 152 B1
Ston [HR] 152 C2
Stonařov [CZ] 60 F4
Stone [GB] 22 F3
Stonehaven [GB] 18 F2
Stongfjorden [N] 192 B1
Stonglandseidet [N] 224 C3
Stønjumfoss [N] 192 D2
Stopanja [SRB] 146 F4
Stopnica [PL] 64 B2
Storå [S] 188 F2
Storå / Isojoki [FIN] 208 C3
Stora Blåsjön [S] 212 E3
Storås [N] 202 F2
Stora Sjöfallet [S] 220 C2
Storbäck [S] 212 F3
Storborgaren [S] 206 D1
Storby [FIN] 196 F4
Stord [N] 192 B4
Stordal [N] 202 D3
Stordalen [S] 224 D4
Storebro [S] 184 E2
Storebru [N] 192 B1
Store Darum [DK] 178 B2
Storehaug [N] 192 B1
Store Heddinge [DK] 178 F2
Storekorsnes [N] 228 B3
Storelv [N] 228 A2
Storelvavoll [N] 204 C3
Store Merløse [DK] 178 E2
Store Molvik [N] 228 E1
Støren [N] 204 B2
Storestandal [N] 202 C3
Storestølen [N] 192 D3
Stor-Evdal [N] 194 B2
Storfall [S] 206 E1
Storfjellseter [N] 194 B1
Storfjord [N] 224 E3
Storfors [S] 188 E2
Storforshei [N] 218 F4
Storfosna [N] 202 F1
Storfossen [N] 226 C2
Storhallaren [N] 202 E1
Storhögen [S] 204 F2
Storholmsjö [S] 204 E1
Storjola [S] 212 E3
Storjord [N] 220 A2
Storjord [N] 220 B3
Storjorda [N] 218 F3
Storkow [D] 46 B2
Storkyro / Isokyrö [FIN]
208 C2
Storlægda [N] 204 C4
Storli [N] 202 E3
Storlien [S] 204 D2
Stormi [FIN] 198 D1
Stornara [I] 134 E3

Störnaset [S] 214 A3
Stornes [N] 224 E2
Stornorrfors [S] 206 E1
Stornoway / Steornabhagh
[GB] 14 C1
Storo [I] 118 B3
Storoddan [N] 202 F2
Storsätern [S] 204 E4
Storsävdträsk [S] 214 D3
Storseterfossen [N] 202 D4
Storsjö [S] 204 D3
Storslett [N] 224 E2
Størstein [N] 224 E1
Storsteinnes [N] 224 D3
Storsund [S] 214 D1
Stortinden [N] 228 D2
Storuman [S] 214 B2
Storvallen [S] 204 C2
Storvik [S] 196 C3
Storvika [N] 212 B4
Storvollen [N] 202 F3
Storvorde [DK] 182 D3
Storvreta [S] 190 D1
Stössen [D] 44 E4
St Oswald [A] 74 B2
St.-Oswald [A] 120 B2
St.-Oswald [F] 56 E3
Stotel [D] 32 A3
Sto. Toribio de Liébana [E]
86 B2
Stotternheim [D] 44 D4
St. Ottilien [D] 72 C2
Stouby [DK] 178 C2
St-Ouen [F] 40 B4
Stourbridge [GB] 22 F4
Stournaraíika [GR] 166 D1
Støvring [DK] 182 D3
Støvringgård [DK] 182 D3
Stowbtsy [BY] 242 B2
Stowmarket [GB] 28 E2
Stow-on-the-Wold [GB]
28 B2
Stožec [CZ] 72 F1
Stozher [BG] 150 E3
St-Palais [F] 88 B2
St-Palais-sur-Mer [F]
78 B2
St. Pankraz [A] 74 A3
St-Pardoux-la-Rivière [F]
78 D3
St Paul [A] 120 B2
St-Paul [F] 126 B2
St-Paul [F] 126 C3
St-Paul-Cap-de-Joux
[F] 88 F3
St-Paul-de-Fenouillet
[F] 96 E1
St-Paulien [F] 80 C3
St-Paul-lès-Dax [F] 88 B2
St-Pé [F] 88 C3
St-Péray [F] 80 D4
St-Père [F] 68 D3
St-Père-en-Retz [F] 66 B2
St. Peter [A] 118 F2
St. Peter [CH] 116 F1
St Peter-Ording [D] 32 A1
St Peter Port [GBG] 52 D1
St-Péver [F] 52 C3
St-Philbert [F] 66 C2
St-Pierre-d'Albigny [F] 80 F3
St-Pierre-de-Chartreuse
[F] 80 E3
St-Pierre-de-Chignac [F]
78 D3
St. Pierre d'Extravache [F]
116 B4
St-Pierre-d'Oléron [F] 78 B1
St-Pierre-Église [F] 52 F1
St-Pierre-en-Port [F] 54 C1
St-Pierre-le-Moûtier [F]
68 C4
St-Pierre-Quiberon [F] 66 A1

St-Pierre–sur-Dives [F] 54 B2
St-Pois [F] 52 F3
St-Pol–de-Léon [F] 52 B2
St-Pol-sur-Ternoise [F] 40 B4
St Pölten [A] 74 C3
St-Pons–de-Thomieres [F] 124 B3
St-Porchaire [F] 78 C2
St-Pourçain sur-Sioule [F] 80 B1
St. Priest [F] 80 D2
St-Privat [F] 78 F3
St-Quay–Portrieux [F] 52 D3
St.-Quen–en-Belin [F] 66 E2
St-Quentin [F] 54 F2
St. Quirin [D] 60 B3
Strà [I] 118 C4
Straach [D] 44 F2
Strabane [NIR] 12 D2
Strachówka [PL] 50 B1
Stracia [I] 138 D4
Stracin [MK] 154 E3
Strådalen [S] 204 D4
Stradalovo [BG] 154 F3
Stradbally [IRL] 10 A3
Stradbally [IRL] 10 E2
Stradella [I] 116 E4
Stradinš [LV] 236 D2
Stradone [IRL] 12 D3
Strádov [CZ] 60 F3
Straduny [PL] 38 B2
Straelen [D] 42 C3
Strakonice [CZ] 60 D4
Straldzha [BG] 150 D4
Stralki [BY] 236 E4
Strålsnäs [S] 188 F4
Stralsund [D] 20 D2
St-Rambert [F] 80 C3
St-Rambert–d'Albon [F] 80 D3
St-Rambert–en-Bugey [F] 80 E2
Stramnes [N] 192 B3
Strand [N] 194 C2
Strand [N] 224 B3
Strand [S] 206 B1
Stranda [N] 202 D3
Stranda [N] 228 C2
Strandby [DK] 182 C3
Strandby [DK] 182 E2
Strandcally Castle [IRL] 10 D4
Strande [D] 32 C1
Strandebarm [N] 192 B3
Strandhill [IRL] 12 C2
Strandlykkja [N] 194 C3
Strangford [NIR] 12 F3
Strängnäs [S] 190 C2
Strängsered [S] 184 C1
Strångsjö [S] 190 C3
Stráni [CZ] 74 E1
Stranice [SLO] 120 C2
Stranorlar [IRL] 12 D1
Stránov [CZ] 60 E2
Stranraer [GB] 20 B2
St-Raphaël [F] 126 B3
Strasbourg [F] 70 D1
Strasburg [D] 34 C3
Straševina [MNE] 152 E2
Stråsjö [S] 196 B1
Strassburg [A] 120 A1
Strassengel [A] 120 C1
Strassfurt [D] 44 D3
Strasswalchen [A] 72 E3
Stratford-upon-Avon [GB] 28 B1
Strathaven [GB] 18 C4
Stratinska [BIH] 144 E2
Stratóni [GR] 162 C1
Stratoníki [GR] 162 C1
Strátos [GR] 166 C3
Straubenhardt [D] 58 B4
Straubing [D] 72 D1
Straum [N] 212 D1

Straume [N] 186 D1
Straume [N] 186 E2
Straume [N] 192 A3
Straumen [N] 202 E2
Straumen [N] 204 C1
Straumen [N] 212 C3
Straumen [N] 218 E4
Straumen [N] 220 B2
Straumfjorden [N] 220 B1
Straumsjøen [N] 224 B3
Straumsnes [N] 224 B4
Straumsnes [N] 224 C2
Straupitz [D] 46 C3
Strausberg [D] 46 B1
Straussfurt [D] 44 D4
Stravaj [AL] 160 B2
Straža [SRB] 146 F1
Straža [SRB] 148 B3
Strazh [RUS] 242 D2
Stražica [BG] 150 C3
Strážky [SK] 64 B4
Strážnice [CZ] 74 E1
Strážný [CZ] 72 F1
Strážske [SK] 76 E1
Štrba [SK] 76 C1
Štrbské Pleso [SK] 62 F4
Street [GB] 26 E3
Strehaia [RO] 148 D1
Strehla [D] 46 B3
Streitberg [D] 58 E3
Strękowa Góra [PL] 38 C3
Strelcha [BG] 156 C1
Strelci [BG] 156 D1
Střelište [CZ] 60 F4
Strel'na [RUS] 200 F3
Strem [A] 120 D1
St-Rémy-de-Provence [F] 124 E3
St-Renan [F] 52 A2
Strenči [LV] 230 E4
Strendene [N] 212 D2
Strengberg [A] 74 B3
Stresa [I] 116 D3
S. Tresund [S] 214 A2
Streufdorf [D] 58 E2
St.-Révérien [F] 68 D3
Strezimirovci [SRB] 154 E2
Strezovce [SRB] 154 D3
Strib [DK] 178 C2
Stříbro [CZ] 60 C3
Štrigova [HR] 120 D2
Strilky [UA] 64 E4
Strimasund [S] 212 E1
St-Riquier [F] 40 A4
Strittjomvare [S] 214 C1
Strittmat [D] 70 D2
Striževac [SRB] 148 C4
Strmica [HR] 144 D3
Strmilov [CZ] 60 E4
Strobl [A] 72 E3
Strøby Egede [DK] 178 E2
Stroevo [BG] 156 D2
Strofyliá [GR] 168 A1
Ströhem [D] 42 F1
Strokestown [IRL] 10 D1
Strøm [N] 202 E1
Ström [S] 188 C2
Strömåker [S] 214 A3
St.-Roman, Abbaye de– [F] 124 D2
Strömbacka [S] 196 C1
Stromberg [D] 56 F2
Strómboli [I] 138 C2
St-Rome-de-Tarn [F] 124 B2
Strömfors [S] 214 D2
Strömholm [S] 214 B1
Strømmen [N] 188 B1
Strömmen [S] 194 D1
Strömnäs [S] 214 A2
Stromness [GB] 14 F1
Strompdalen [N] 212 D3

Strömsbruk [S] 196 D1
Stromsfors [S] 190 C3
Strömsholm [S] 190 C2
Strömsillret [S] 194 D1
Strömsnäs [S] 206 B2
Strömsnäsbruk [S] 184 C4
Strømsood [N] 192 F4
Strömsrum [S] 184 E3
Strömstad [S] 188 B3
Strömsund [S] 206 B1
Strömsund [S] 214 A2
Strond [N] 186 D2
Strongoli [I] 138 F2
Stronie Śląskie [PL] 62 B2
Stroove [IRL] 12 E1
Stropkov [SK] 64 C4
Stroppo [I] 126 C2
Stroud [GB] 26 F2
Strόvles [GR] 174 B4
Stróża [PL] 62 F3
Str. Pole [PL] 36 D2
Strub Pass [A] 72 D3
Strücklingen [D] 30 E2
Struer [DK] 182 C3
Struga [MK] 160 C1
Strugi–Krasnyye [RUS] 232 F3
Strugovo [MK] 160 D1
Struha [BY] 38 D2
Struhařov [CZ] 60 E3
Struino [BG] 150 D3
Strumica [MK] 154 F4
Strumień [PL] 62 E3
Strupina [PL] 46 F4
Stružec [HR] 120 D4
Stryama [BG] 156 D2
Stryckséle [S] 214 C3
Stryi [UA] 244 C2
Stryj [UA] 64 F4
Stryjów [PL] 50 D4
Stryków [PL] 48 D3
Strymonikó [GR] 156 B4
Stryn [N] 202 C4
Strzałkowo [PL] 48 B2
Strzegocin [PL] 48 E1
Strzegom [PL] 62 B1
Strzegowo [PL] 36 E4
Strzelce [PL] 34 F4
Strzelce [PL] 48 D2
Strzelce Krajeńskie [PL] 34 E4
Strzelce Małe [PL] 48 D4
Strzelce Opolskie [PL] 62 D2
Strzelin [PL] 62 C1
Strzelno [PL] 48 C1
Strzyżów [PL] 50 D4
Strzyżów [PL] 64 C3
St.-Sabin, Chapelle– [F] 88 D1
St-Saëns [F] 54 D2
St. Salvator [A] 120 A1
St.-Samson–la-Poterie [F] 54 D2
St-Satur [F] 68 C3
St-Saturnin–lès-Apt [F] 124 E2
St-Saulge [F] 68 D3
St-Sauvant [F] 66 E4
St-Sauveur-en-Puisaye [F] 68 C2
St-Sauveur-le-Vicomte [F] 52 E2
St-Sauveur-sur-Tinée [F] 126 C2
St-Savin [F] 78 C3
St-Savin-sur-Gartempe [F] 66 F4
St-Seine-l'Abbaye [F] 68 E3
St-Sernin–sur-Rance [F] 124 B2
St-Sever [F] 52 F3
St-Sever [F] 88 C2
St. Slatnik [HR] 146 A1
St-Sulpice [F] 88 F2

St. Sulpice–les-Feuilles [F] 78 E1
St. Sundby [S] 190 C2
St. Susanna [E] 96 C2
St-Symphorien [F] 78 B4
St-Symphorien-de-Lay [F] 80 C2
St-Symphorien–d'Ozon [F] 80 D3
St-Symphorien–sur-Coise [F] 80 D2
St-Thégonnec [F] 52 B3
St-Thiébault [F] 70 B2
St-Trivier-de-Courtes [F] 80 E1
St.-Trond (St.–Truiden) [B] 40 E4
St-Tropez [F] 126 B4
St.–Truiden (St.–Trond) [B] 40 E4
Stubalj [HR] 144 E1
Stubbekøbing [DK] 178 E3
Stubbergård [DK] 182 C3
Stuben [A] 72 A4
Štubik [SRB] 148 C2
Stubline [SRB] 146 D2
Studánky [CZ] 74 A2
Studena [BG] 154 F2
Studená [CZ] 60 E4
Studenec [CZ] 60 F2
Studenica [SRB] 146 E4
Studénka [CZ] 62 D3
Studenzen [A] 120 C1
Studina [RO] 148 F2
Studsviken [S] 206 D1
Studzienice [PL] 36 B2
Studzienki [PL] 36 B4
Stugudal [N] 204 C3
Stuguflåten [N] 202 E3
Stugun [S] 206 B2
Stuguvollmoen [N] 204 C3
Stühlingen [D] 70 E3
Stuibenfall [A] 72 B4
Stukenbrock [D] 42 F2
Stülpe [D] 46 B2
St.–Ulrich, Château– [F] 70 D2
St Ulrich / Ortisei [I] 118 C2
Stupari [BIH] 146 B3
Stupinigi [I] 116 C4
Stupnik [HR] 120 C3
Stuposiany [PL] 64 D4
Sturehov [S] 190 D2
Ŝturovo [SK] 76 A3
St-Ursanne [CH] 70 C3
Stuttgart [D] 70 F1
St-Vaast–la-Hougue [F] 52 F2
St Valentin [A] 74 A3
St-Valery-en-Caux [F] 54 C1
St-Valery-sur-Somme [F] 40 A4
St-Vallier-de-Thiey [F] 126 B3
St-Vallier-sur-Rhône [F] 80 D3
St-Vaury [F] 68 A4
St. Veit [A] 118 D1
St Veit [A] 120 A2
St-Véran [F] 126 C1
St Vigil / Marebbe [I] 118 C2
St-Vincent [I] 116 C3
St-Vincent, Grotte de– [F] 126 A2
St-Vincent-de-Tyrosse [F] 88 C3
St. Vincent-du-Lorouër [F] 66 F2
St-Vincent-les-Forts [F] 126 B2
St Vith [B] 56 D1
St-Vivien-de-Médoc [F] 78 B2

St-Wandrille [F] 54 C2
St Wendel [D] 56 E3
St Wolfgang [A] 72 E3
St–Yan [F] 80 C1
Stykkishólmur [IS] 218 A2
Stylída [GR] 166 E2
Stymfalía [GR] 166 E4
St-Yorre [F] 80 C2
Stýpsi [GR] 164 A3
Stýra [GR] 168 B2
Styri [N] 194 B4
St–Yrieix-la-Perche [F] 78 E3
Styrnäs [S] 206 D2
Styrsö [S] 182 F2
Suances [E] 86 C2
Suaredda [I] 142 C2
Subačius [LT] 238 D2
Subaşı [TR] 158 D3
Subaşı [TR] 170 B2
Subate [LV] 236 C4
Subbiano [I] 128 D4
Suben [A] 72 E2
Subiaco [I] 132 D4
Subkowy [PL] 36 D2
Subotica [SRB] 122 C3
Subotište [SRB] 146 D2
Sučany [SK] 76 B1
Suceava [RO] 244 D3
Suceviţa, Mănăstirea– [RO] 244 D3
Sucha [PL] 46 D4
Sucha Beskidzka [PL] 62 F3
Suchá Hora [SK] 62 F4
Suchań [PL] 34 E3
Suchdol nad Lužnicí [CZ] 74 B1
Suchedniów [PL] 48 F4
Suchorze [PL] 36 B2
Suchowola [PL] 38 C2
Suchożebry [PL] 50 B2
Süchteln [D] 42 C3
Sucina [E] 106 E2
Sućuraj [HR] 152 C2
Sudbø [N] 186 D1
Sudbury [GB] 28 E2
Suddesjaur [S] 220 D4
Süden [D] 32 B1
Süderbrarup [D] 32 C1
Süderende [D] 178 A3
Süderlügum [D] 178 B3
Sudok [S] 220 E2
Sudova Vyshnia [UA] 64 E3
Sueca [E] 102 D4
Suelli [I] 142 C5
Sugères [F] 80 B2
Suhindol [BG] 150 B3
Suhinichi [RUS] 240 E4
Suhl [D] 58 E1
Suho Polje [BIH] 146 C2
Suhopolje [HR] 120 E3
Šuica [BIH] 144 F4
Suijavaara [S] 226 B3
Suikka [FIN] 200 D1
Suinula [FIN] 198 E1
Suinula [FIN] 208 E4
Suio, Terme di– [I] 134 C3
Suippes [F] 56 B3
Sukeva [FIN] 216 C3
Sukhinichi [RUS] 240 E4
Sukhlovo [RUS] 232 F3
Sukobin [MNE] 152 F4
Sukošan [HR] 144 C3
Sükösd [H] 122 B3
Sukovo [SRB] 148 C4
Sul [N] 204 C1
Šula [MNE] 152 E1
Sulâmo [N] 204 C1
Suldal [N] 186 B1
Suldalseid [N] 186 B1
Suldalsosen [N] 186 B1

Sulden / Solda [I] 118 B2
Suldrup [DK] 182 D3
Sulechów [PL] 46 D2
Sulęcin [PL] 46 D2
Sulęczyno [PL] 36 B2
Sulejów [PL] 48 E4
Sulejówek [PL] 48 F2
Sulesund [N] 202 C3
Süleymaniye [TR] 158 B3
Süleymanlı [TR] 164 D3
Sulina [RO] 246 D4
Sulingen [D] 32 A4
Suliszewo [PL] 34 E4
Sulitjelma [N] 220 B2
Sulkava [FIN] 210 B1
Sulkava [FIN] 210 D4
Sulkavanjärvi [FIN] 208 F1
Sulkavankylä [FIN] 208 D3
Sulkavanpera [FIN] 216 B4
Sułkowice [PL] 62 F3
Süller [TR] 164 D3
Süller [TR] 170 E2
Sully [F] 68 E3
Sully–sur–Loire [F] 68 C2
Sulmierzyce [PL] 48 B3
Sulmierzyce [PL] 48 D4
Sulmona [I] 132 E4
Süloğlu [TR] 158 B2
Sul'Ovské Skaly [SK] 62 D4
Sułów [PL] 46 F3
Sultançayırı [TR] 164 D2
Sultanhisar [TR] 170 C3
Sultanıca [TR] 162 F1
Sultanköy [TR] 158 A3
Sultanköy [TR] 158 C3
Sülümenli [TR] 164 F4
Sulva / Solf [FIN] 208 B2
Sulviken [S] 204 D1
Sülysáp [H] 76 B4
Sulz [D] 70 E2
Sulzbach [A] 120 C2
Sulzbach [D] 58 C4
Sulzbach [D] 58 D4
Sulzbach–Rosenberg [D] 58 F3
Sumacarcer [E] 102 D4
Sumartin [HR] 152 B2
Sümeg [H] 120 E1
Sumer [BG] 148 D3
Sumiainen [FIN] 208 F2
Sumiswald [CH] 70 D4
Summa [FIN] 200 C3
Šumperk [CZ] 62 B3
Sumsa [FIN] 216 E3
Šumvald [CZ] 62 C3
Sumy [UA] 242 F3
Sund [FIN] 198 A3
Sund [N] 224 B3
Sund [S] 188 C2
Sund [S] 206 B4
Sundborn [S] 196 B3
Sundby [FIN] 208 C1
Sundbyberg [S] 190 D2
Sundbyholm [S] 190 C2
Sunde [N] 192 B4
Sunde [N] 192 C1
Sunde [N] 202 F1
Sundebru [N] 186 E3
Sunderland [GB] 20 F3
Sundern [D] 42 E3
Sundet [S] 204 D1
Sundhultsbrunn [S] 184 D1
Sundklakk [N] 218 F1
Sundnäs [S] 220 C3
Sundö [S] 214 C3
Sundre [S] 234 A3
Sunds [DK] 182 C4
Sundsbø [N] 202 D2
Sundsli [N] 186 D2
Sundsøre [DK] 182 C3
Sundsvall [S] 206 C4
Sundsvoll [N] 212 C1
Sundvollen [N] 192 F4

Sungurlare [BG] 150 D4
Suni [I] 142 B3
Sunja [HR] 120 D4
Sunnanå [S] 194 E1
Sunnansjö [S] 194 F4
Sunnansjö [S] 206 B3
Sunnaryd [S] 184 C3
Sunndal [N] 192 B4
Sunndalsøra [N] 202 E3
Sunne [S] 188 D1
Sunnemo [S] 188 E1
Sunnersta [S] 190 D1
Suntaži [LV] 236 B3
Suodenniemi [FIN] 198 D1
Suojoki [FIN] 208 B4
Suokonmäki [FIN] 208 D2
Suolahti [FIN] 208 F2
Suolovuobme [N] 226 B1
Suomenlinna / Sveaborg [FIN] 198 F3
Suomenniemi [FIN] 200 C1
Suomijärvi [FIN] 208 C3
Suomusjärvi [FIN] 198 E3
Suomussalmi [FIN] 216 D2
Suonenjoki [FIN] 208 F2
Suontaka [FIN] 198 C2
Suontee [FIN] 210 B3
Suopelto [FIN] 198 F1
Suoperya [RUS] 222 F3
Suorva [S] 220 C2
Šuoššjávri [N] 226 B2
Suotuperä [FIN] 216 B3
Suovanlahti [FIN] 208 F2
Superga [I] 116 C4
Supetar [HR] 152 B1
Supino [I] 134 B2
Suplacu de Barcău [RO] 76 F4
Suprašl [PL] 38 C3
Surahammar [S] 190 C2
Šurany [SK] 74 F3
Suraż [PL] 38 C3
Surazh [BY] 240 C4
Surazh [RUS] 242 D2
Surbo [I] 136 E3
Surčin [SRB] 146 D2
Surduk [SRB] 146 D1
Surdulica [SRB] 154 E2
Surgères [F] 66 C4
Súria [E] 96 D2
Šurice [SK] 76 C2
Surju [EST] 230 D3
Šurlane [KS] 154 D3
Surnadalsøra [N] 202 E2
Sürnitsa [BG] 156 C3
Sursee [CH] 70 E4
Surtainville [F] 52 E2
Surte [S] 184 A1
Survilliers [F] 54 E3
Susa [I] 116 B4
Šušara [SRB] 146 E2
Susch [CH] 116 F1
Suscínio, Château de– [F] 66 B1
Susek [SRB] 146 C1
Suševo [MK] 154 F3
Sushitsa [BG] 150 B3
Sušice [CZ] 60 C4
Suso y Yuso, Monasterios de– [E] 86 D4
Süssen [D] 72 A1
Susurluk [TR] 164 D2
Susz [PL] 36 D3
Sutivan [HR] 152 B1
Sutjeska [SRB] 122 D4
Sütlaç [TR] 170 F2
Sutomore [MNE] 152 E3
Sutri [I] 130 F3
Sutrieu [F] 80 E2
Sutton Coldfield [GB] 22 F4
Süttorf [D] 32 C4
Suure–Jaani [EST] 230 D3
Suurejõe [EST] 230 D3

Suuremõisa [EST] 230 B2
Suurlahti [FIN] 200 C1
Suurmäki [FIN] 210 D2
Suva Reka [KS] 154 C3
Suvekas [LT] 238 E1
Suvereto [I] 130 D1
Suvorove [UA] 244 F4
Suvorovo [BG] 150 E3
Suvorovo [RUS] 240 E3
Suwałki [PL] 38 C1
Suystamo [RUS] 210 F3
Suzzara [I] 128 B1
Svabensverk [S] 196 B3
Svalöv [S] 180 C2
Svalyava [UA] 244 C2
Svanabyn [S] 214 A3
Svaneholm [S] 180 C2
Svanehölm [S] 188 F4
Svaneke [DK] 180 E3
Svanesund [S] 188 C4
Svängsta [S] 180 E1
Svaningen [S] 212 E4
Sv. Anna [CZ] 60 F3
Svannäs [S] 220 C4
Svanskog [S] 188 D2
Svanstein [S] 222 B3
Svanvik [N] 226 F1
Svappavaara [S] 220 E1
Svarar [FIN] 208 B2
Svärdsjö [S] 196 B3
Svarstad [N] 186 F2
Svartå [S] 188 E3
Svärta [S] 190 D3
Svartå Mustio [FIN] 198 E3
Svartberget [S] 222 A3
Svartbyn [S] 222 A3
Svärte [S] 180 C2
Svärtinge [S] 190 B3
Svartisdalen [N] 218 F4
Svartlå [S] 220 E4
Svartnäs [S] 196 C3
Svartnäs [S] 214 C2
Svartnes [N] 218 F3
Svartnes [N] 228 F2
Svarttjärn [S] 214 B1
Svartvik [S] 206 C4
Svatá Hora [CZ] 60 D3
Svatá Kateřina [CZ] 60 B3
Svategjel [N] 192 D2
Svätý Anton [SK] 76 B2
Svätý Jur [SK] 74 E2
Svatý Mikuláš [CZ] 62 A3
Svätý Peteř [SK] 74 F3
Sv. Barbora [CZ] 60 E4
Sveaborg / Suomenlinna [FIN] 198 F3
Svedala [S] 180 C2
Svedasai [LT] 238 E2
Svedje [S] 206 C4
Svedje [S] 206 D2
Svedje [S] 212 F4
Sveg [S] 194 E1
Sveindal [N] 186 C3
Sveio [N] 186 A1
Švékšna [LT] 238 B2
Svelgen [N] 202 B4
Svellingen [N] 202 E1
Svelvik [N] 186 F2
Svenarum [S] 184 C2
Švenčionėliaj [LT] 238 E2
Švenčionys [LT] 238 F2
Svendborg [DK] 178 D3
Svenes [N] 186 D3
Svenkerud [N] 192 E3
Svenljunga [S] 184 B2
Svennevad [S] 190 B3
Svensby [N] 224 E2
Svensbyn [FIN] 198 D4
Svensköp [S] 180 D2
Svenstavik [S] 204 E3
Svenstorp [S] 180 C2
Svenstrup [DK] 182 D3

Sveom [N] 192 E1
Švermov [CZ] 60 D2
S. Vero Milis [I] 142 B4
Sveta Petka [SRB] 146 F3
Svëtciems [LV] 230 D4
Sveti Andrejaš [MK] 154 D3
Sveti Ivan Žabno [HR] 120 D3
Sveti Jovan Bigorski [MK] 154 C4
Sveti Konstantin [BG] 156 C2
Sveti Naum [AL] 160 C2
Sveti Nikita [MK] 154 D3
Sveti Nikole [MK] 154 E3
Sveti Pantelejmon [MK] 154 D3
Sveti Rok [HR] 144 D3
Sveti Stefan [MNE] 152 E3
Světlá nad Sázavou [CZ] 60 E3
Svetlen [BG] 150 C3
Svetlice [SK] 64 D4
Svetlina [BG] 156 F2
Svetlina [BG] 158 B1
Svetlyy [RUS] 36 E1
Svetlyy [RUS] 226 E2
Svetogorsk [RUS] 200 D2
Svetozar Miletic [SRB] 122 B3
Svetvinčenat [HR] 144 A1
Svežen [BG] 156 D1
Svib [HR] 144 E4
S. Vicente de la Cabeza [E] 84 E2
Svidnik [SK] 64 C4
Švihov [CZ] 60 C4
Svilajnac [SRB] 146 F3
Svilengrad [BG] 156 F2
Svilojevo [SRB] 122 B4
Svinesund [S] 188 B2
Svingstad [N] 192 F3
Svingvoll [N] 192 F2
Svinhult [S] 184 D2
Sviniţa [RO] 148 D2
Svinná [SK] 74 F2
Svinndal [N] 188 B2
Svinninge [DK] 178 E2
Svir [BY] 238 F3
Svishtov [BG] 150 B3
Svislach [BY] 38 D3
Svitavy [CZ] 62 B3
Svitlovods'k [UA] 246 E1
Sv. Juraj [HR] 144 C2
Sv. Jurij [SLO] 120 C2
Sv. Martin [HR] 120 D2
Sv. Nikola [MNE] 152 E4
Svoboda [BG] 150 E2
Svoboda [RUS] 238 B4
Svobodnoye [RUS] 200 E2
Svode [BG] 148 E4
Svodín [SK] 76 A3
Svodje [SRB] 148 C4
Svoge [BG] 148 D4
Svolvær [N] 218 F1
Svorkmo [N] 202 F2
Svormuseet [N] 202 C4
Svratka [CZ] 62 A3
Svrčinovec [SK] 62 E4
Svrljig [SRB] 148 C3
Svullrya [N] 194 C3
Sv. Vid [HR] 144 B1
Svyataya Volya [BY] 38 F4
Svyetlahorsk [BY] 242 C2
Swaffham [GB] 28 E1
Swalmen [NL] 42 B3
Swanage [GB] 26 E4
Swanlinbar [IRL] 12 D2
Swansea [GB] 26 C2
Swarożyn [PL] 36 C2
Swarzędz [PL] 46 F2
Swarzewo [PL] 36 C1
Świdnica [PL] 46 D3
Świdnica [PL] 62 B1
Świdnik [PL] 50 C3
Świdwin [PL] 34 F3

Świebodzice [PL] 62 B1
Świebodzin [PL] 46 D2
Świecie [PL] 36 C3
Świecko [PL] 46 C2
Świeradów–Zdrój [PL] 60 E1
Świerczów [PL] 62 C1
Świerki [PL] 62 B2
Świerzawa [PL] 46 E4
Świerzno [PL] 34 E2
Święta [PL] 34 D4
Święta Anna [PL] 62 E1
Święta Lipka [PL] 36 F2
Święte [PL] 48 C2
Świętno [PL] 46 E2
Swindon [GB] 26 F2
Swinford [IRL] 12 B2
Świnoujście [PL] 34 D2
Swords [IRL] 10 F2
Swornegacie [PL] 36 B3
Swory [PL] 50 C2
Syalyets [BY] 38 E4
Sybaris–Copia [I] 136 C4
Sychevka [RUS] 240 E3
Syców [PL] 48 B4
Sydanmää [FIN] 198 C2
Sykaminéa [GR] 164 A3
Sykäräinen [FIN] 216 A4
Syke [D] 32 A4
Sykéa [GR] 172 E3
Sykéa [GR] 174 E4
Sykiá [GR] 160 E4
Sykiá [GR] 162 C2
Sykióna [GR] 166 E4
Sykkylven [N] 202 C3
Sykoúri [GR] 160 F4
Sylling [N] 186 F1
Sylte [N] 202 D2
Symbister [GB] 16 F3
Sými [GR] 176 B1
Synsiö [FIN] 210 B3
Syötekylä [FIN] 222 E4
Sypnievo [PL] 36 B3
Sypniewo [PL] 38 A3
Syrau [D] 60 B2
Syrävaara [FIN] 216 E3
Sysmä [FIN] 200 A1
Sysslebäck [S] 194 D3
Syston [GB] 24 C4
Syväjärvi [FIN] 222 C2
Syvänniemi [FIN] 210 B2
Syvärinpää [FIN] 210 C1
Syvde [N] 202 B4
Sývota [GR] 166 B2
Sysvsten [DK] 182 E2
Syyspohja [FIN] 200 D1
Szabadegyháza [H] 122 B1
Szabadszállás [H] 122 B2
Szabolcsbáka [H] 76 E2
Szada [H] 76 B4
Szadek [PL] 48 C3
Szakály [H] 122 A2
Szakcs [H] 120 F2
Szakmár [H] 122 B2
Szalánta [H] 122 A3
Szalkszentmárton [H] 122 B1
Szalonna [H] 76 D2
Szamocin [PL] 36 B4
Szamotuły [PL] 46 E1
Szandaszőlős [H] 122 C1
Szank [H] 122 C2
Szany [H] 74 E4
Szápár [H] 74 F4
Szarvas [H] 122 D2
Szarvasi Arboretum [H] 122 D2
Szarvaskő [H] 76 C3
Szászvár [H] 122 A3
Szatmárceseke [H] 76 F3
Százhalombatta [H] 76 B4
Szczaniec [H] 122 C1
Szczawne [PL] 64 D4
Szczawnica [PL] 64 B4
Szczebrzeszyn [PL] 64 D1

Szczecin [PL] 34 D3
Szczecinek [PL] 36 A3
Szczekociny [PL] 62 F2
Szczerców [PL] 48 D4
Szczucin [PL] 64 B2
Szczuczyn [PL] 38 B2
Szczurowa [PL] 64 B2
Szczyrk [PL] 62 E3
Szczytna [PL] 62 B2
Szczytno [PL] 36 F3
Szécsény [H] 76 B3
Szederkény [H] 122 A3
Szedres [H] 122 B2
Szeged [H] 122 C3
Szeghalom [H] 122 E1
Szegvár [H] 122 D2
Székely [H] 76 E3
Székesfehérvár [H] 122 A1
Székkutas [H] 122 D2
Szekszárd [H] 122 B2
Szemere [H] 76 D2
Szendehely [H] 76 B3
Szendrő [H] 76 D2
Szendrőlád [H] 76 D2
Szentendre [H] 76 B3
Szentes [H] 122 D2
Szentliszló [H] 120 D2
Szentliszló [H] 120 F3
Szentlőrinc [H] 120 F3
Szenyér [H] 120 E2
Szephalom [H] 76 E2
Szerencs [H] 76 D3
Szestno [PL] 38 A2
Szetlew [PL] 48 B2
Szigetszentmiklós [H] 76 B4
Szigetvár [H] 120 F3
Szigliget [H] 120 E2
Szikszó [H] 76 D2
Szil [H] 74 E4
Szilvágy [H] 120 D2
Szilvásvárad [H] 76 C3
Szirák [H] 76 B3
Szittyóúrbő [H] 122 B1
Szklarska Poręba [PL] 60 F1
Szklary [PL] 64 D3
Szklary Górne [PL] 46 E3
Szlichtyngowa [PL] 46 E3
Szob [H] 76 A3
Szolnok [H] 122 C1
Szombathely [H] 120 D1
Szonowice [PL] 62 D2
Szőny [H] 74 F3
Szpetal Górny [PL] 48 D1
Szprotawa [PL] 46 D3
Szreńsk [PL] 36 E4
Szropy [PL] 36 D2
Sztabin [PL] 38 C2
Sztum [PL] 36 D2
Sztutowo [PL] 36 D2
Sztynort [PL] 38 A1
Szubin [PL] 36 B4
Szúcs [H] 76 C3
Szulmierz [PL] 36 F4
Szumirad [PL] 62 D1
Szumowo [PL] 38 B3
Szurdokpüspöki [H] 76 C3
Szwecja [PL] 36 A3
Szydłów [PL] 48 D3
Szydłów [PL] 64 B2
Szydłowiec [PL] 48 F4
Szydłowo [PL] 36 A4
Szymbark [PL] 36 D3
Szypliszki [PL] 38 C1

T

Taalintehdas / Dalsbruk [FIN] 198 D4
Taastrup [DK] 178 E2
Taavetti [FIN] 200 C2

Tab [H] 120 F2
Tabaja [BIH] 152 D2
Tabanovce [MK] 154 D3
Tábara [E] 84 E2
Taberg [S] 184 C2
Tabernas [E] 106 B3
Tabiano Bagni [I] 128 A2
Taboada [E] 82 C3
Tábor [CZ] 60 E4
Tábua [P] 84 B4
Tabuaço [P] 84 C3
Tabuenca [E] 94 C2
Tabula Traiana [SRB] 148 C1
Täby [S] 190 D2
Tachov [CZ] 60 B3
Täckåsen [S] 194 F2
Tadcaster [GB] 24 C2
Tådene [S] 188 D4
Tafalla [E] 88 A3
Tafira [E] 112 E3
Tafjord [N] 202 D3
Täftëå [S] 206 D2
Täftëå [S] 206 F1
Tagaranna [EST] 230 B3
Tagenac [F] 80 B3
Taggia [I] 126 D3
Taghmon [IRL] 10 E4
Tagliacozzo [I] 132 D4
Táglio di Po [I] 128 D1
Tahal [E] 106 C3
Tahitótfalu [H] 76 B3
Tahivilla [E] 104 B3
Tahtacı [TR] 164 B3
Tahtaköprü [TR] 164 F1
Tai di Cadore [I] 118 D2
Tailfingen [D] 70 F2
Taillebois [F] 54 A3
Taimoniemi [FIN] 208 F1
Tain [GB] 14 E3
Taininiemi [FIN] 222 C4
Tain–l'Hermitage [F] 80 D3
Taipadas [P] 90 B4
Taipale [FIN] 198 D1
Taipale [FIN] 208 E2
Taipale [FIN] 210 B2
Taipale [FIN] 210 B1
Taipaleenharju [FIN] 216 C1
Taipaleenkyla [FIN] 208 D3
Taipalsaari [FIN] 200 D2
Taírbeart / Tarbert [GB] 14 B2
Taivalkoski [FIN] 222 E4
Taivalmaa [FIN] 208 C3
Taivassalo / Tövsala [FIN] 198 C3
Taizé [F] 80 D1
Tajada, Cuevas de la– [E] 102 C2
Tajcy [RUS] 200 F4
Tajo de las Figuras, Cueva del– [E] 104 B3
Takácsi [H] 74 E4
Takamaa [FIN] 198 D1
Takene [S] 188 D2
Takmak [TR] 164 E4
Talachyn [BY] 242 C1
Talalaïvka [UA] 242 F3
Talamone [I] 130 E2
Tál ar Groaz [F] 52 B3
Talarrubias [E] 100 B2
Talaván [E] 90 F3
Talavera de la Reina [E] 92 C4
Talavera la Real [E] 90 E4
Talaveruela [E] 92 C4
Talayuela [E] 92 B4
Talayuelas [E] 102 C2
Talcy [F] 68 A2
Tali [EST] 230 D3
Táliga [E] 98 E2
Talinen [S] 220 F2
Talla [I] 128 D4
Tallaght [IRL] 10 F2
Tallard [F] 126 A2

Tållas [S] 214 B1
Tallåsen [S] 194 D3
Tallåsen [S] 196 C1
Tällberg [S] 194 F3
Tallberg [S] 206 E1
Tallhed [S] 194 F2
Tallinn [EST] 230 D1
Talloires [F] 80 F2
Tallow [IRL] 10 D4
Tallsjö [S] 214 B3
Tallträsk [S] 214 B3
Talluskylä [FIN] 210 B2
Tallvik [S] 222 A3
Tállya [H] 76 D2
Talmont [F] 78 B2
Talmont–St–Hilaire [F] 66 D3
Talpaki [RUS] 238 A3
Talsi [LV] 234 E3
Talty [PL] 38 A2
Talvik [N] 228 B3
Tamajón [E] 92 F3
Tamames [E] 84 D4
Tamanes [N] 228 D2
Tamarë [AL] 152 F3
Tamarino [BG] 158 A1
Tamarit [E] 96 C3
Tamarite de Litera [E] 94 F3
Tamási [H] 122 A2
Tambohuse [DK] 182 C3
Taminaschlucht [CH] 116 E1
Tamis [TR] 164 A3
Tammela [FIN] 198 E2
Tammensiel [D] 32 A1
Tammerfors / Tampere [FIN] 198 E1
Tammijärvi [FIN] 208 F4
Tammilahti [FIN] 210 B4
Tammisaari / Ekenäs [FIN] 198 D4
Tamna [RO] 148 D1
Tamnič [SRB] 148 C2
Tampere / Tammerfors [FIN] 198 E1
Tamsalu [EST] 230 E2
Tamsweg [A] 118 F1
Tämta [S] 184 B1
Tamworth [GB] 24 B4
Tanabru [N] 228 D2
Tanágra [GR] 168 A2
Tananger [N] 186 A2
Tancarville [F] 54 C2
Tãncovo [BG] 156 E2
Tanda [SRB] 148 C2
Tandö [S] 194 E3
Tandragee [NIR] 12 E3
Tandsbyn [S] 204 F3
Tandsjöborg [S] 194 F1
Tånga [S] 178 F1
Tångaberg [S] 184 A2
Tangen [N] 188 B2
Tangen [N] 188 C1
Tangen [N] 194 C3
Tangen [N] 224 D3
Tanger [MA] 104 B4
Tangerhütte [D] 44 E2
Tangermünde [D] 44 E1
Tanhua [FIN] 222 D1
Taninges [F] 116 B2
Tankolampi [FIN] 208 F2
Tanlay [F] 68 E2
Tann [D] 58 D1
Tannåker [S] 184 C3
Tännäs [S] 204 D3
Tänndalen [S] 204 C3
Tanne [D] 44 C3
Tannenhof [D] 32 F3
Tännforsen [S] 204 D2
Tannheim [A] 72 B3
Tannila [FIN] 216 B1
Tänno [S] 184 C3
Tanowo [PL] 34 D3
Tanttila [FIN] 198 F2

Tanum [N] 186 F2
Tanum [S] 188 B3
Tanumshede [S] 188 B3
Tanus [F] 124 B2
Tanvald [CZ] 60 E2
Taormina [I] 138 C4
Tapa [EST] 230 E2
Tapanivaara [FIN] 216 D2
Taptheim [D] 72 B2
Tapia de Casariego [E] 82 E2
Tapionkylä [FIN] 222 C2
Tápiószecső [H] 76 B4
Tápiószele [H] 76 C4
Tápiószentmárton [H] 76 B4
Tápiószőlős [H] 76 C4
Tapojärvi [FIN] 222 B1
Tapolca [H] 120 E2
Tapolcafő [H] 74 E4
Taponas [F] 80 D2
Tapperøje [H] 178 E3
Taps [DK] 178 B2
Tapsony [H] 76 B4
Tapsony [H] 120 E2
Tara [IRL] 10 F2
Taraguilla [E] 104 C3
Tarajalejo [E] 114 D3
Tara Kanjon [MNE] 152 E2
Tara Kanjon [MNE] 152 F2
Taramundi [E] 82 D2
Tarancón [E] 100 F1
Táranto [I] 136 D3
Tarare [F] 80 D2
Tarascon [F] 124 D3
Tarascon–sur–Ariège [F] 88 E4
Tarasp [CH] 118 A1
Tarazona [E] 94 C2
Tarazona de la Mancha [E] 102 B3
Tårbæk [DK] 178 F2
Tarbert [GB] 18 B3
Tarbert [IRL] 10 B2
Tarbert / Taírbeart [GB] 14 B2
Tarbes [F] 88 C3
Tarcea [RO] 76 F4
Tarcento [I] 118 E3
Tarčin [BIH] 146 A4
Tarczyn [PL] 48 F2
Tardets–Sorholus [F] 88 B3
Tardienta [E] 94 E2
Tårendö [S] 220 F2
Târgoviște [RO] 248 D3
Târgu Frumos [RO] 244 E3
Târgu Jiu [RO] 248 C3
Târgu Lăpuș [RO] 244 C3
Târgu Mureș [RO] 244 D3
Târgu Neamț [RO] 244 E3
Târgu Secuiesc [RO] 244 E4
Tarhos [H] 122 E2
Tarhos [H] 122 E2
Tarifa [E] 104 B4
Tarján [H] 76 A4
Tarlo [PL] 50 C3
Tarm [DK] 178 B1
Tarmstedt [D] 32 B3
Tärna [S] 190 C1
Tärnaby [S] 212 F2
Tarnala [FIN] 200 E2
Tarnalelesz [H] 76 C3
Tarnaméra [H] 76 C3
Tárnamo [S] 212 F2
Tarnaörs [H] 76 C4
Tarnaszentmiklós [H] 76 C4
Tărnăveni [RO] 244 D4
Tarnawa Duża [PL] 50 C4
Tarnawatka [PL] 50 C4
Tarnawka [PL] 50 C4
Tårnet [N] 228 F3
Tarnobrzeg [PL] 64 C2
Tarnogród [PL] 64 D2
Tárnok [H] 76 A4
Tarnos [F] 88 B2
Târnova [RO] 122 F2

Tărnovci [BG] 150 C2
Tarnów [PL] 46 D1
Tarnów [PL] 50 A2
Tarnów [PL] 64 B3
Tarnów Jez. [PL] 46 E3
Tarnowo Podgórne [PL] 46 F2
Tarnowskie Góry [PL] 62 E2
Tärnsjö [S] 190 C1
Tärnvik [N] 220 A1
Tarouca [P] 84 B3
Tarp [D] 178 B3
Tarpa [H] 76 F3
Tarquínia [I] 130 E3
Tarquinia [I] 130 E3
Tarquinia Lido [I] 130 E3
Tàrrega [E] 96 C3
Tärrajur [S] 220 D3
Tarrasa / Terrassa [E] 96 D3
Tàrrega [E] 96 C2
Tårs [DK] 178 D3
Tårs [DK] 182 D2
Tarsia [I] 136 C4
Tartas [F] 88 C2
Tărtăşeşti [RO] 150 B1
Tartu [EST] 230 E3
Tårup [DK] 178 D3
Tarutino [UA] 244 F3
Tarvainen [FIN] 198 C3
Tarvasjoki [FIN] 198 D3
Tarvisio [I] 118 E2
Tarvola [FIN] 208 D1
Tasapää [FIN] 210 E3
Tǎsbŭku [TR] 170 D4
Täsch [CH] 116 C2
Tåsjö [S] 212 F4
Taşköy [TR] 164 E4
Taşkule [TR] 164 B4
Taşlıca [TR] 176 C1
Tåşnad [RO] 76 F4
Tasovice [CZ] 74 D2
Tassjö [S] 180 C1
Tata [H] 74 F4
Tatabánya [H] 76 A4
Tataháza [H] 122 B3
Tătărăştii de Sus [RO] 150 A1
Tatlısu (Akanthoú) [CY] 176 E3
Tatranská Kotlina [SK] 64 A4
Tatranská Lomnica [SK] 64 A4
Tau [N] 186 B2
Taubenlochschlucht [CH] 70 C4
Tauberbischofsheim [D] 58 C3
Taubes [LV] 230 D4
Taucha [D] 44 E3
Tauern Tunnel [A] 72 E4
Tauerntunnel [A] 118 E1
Taufers / Tubre [I] 118 A2
Taufkirchen [A] 72 F2
Taufkirchen [D] 72 D2
Taujénai [LT] 238 D2
Taüll [E] 88 D4
Taunton [GB] 26 D3
Taunusstein [D] 58 B2
Tauplitz [A] 72 F4
Taurage [LT] 238 B3
Taurasi [I] 134 D3
Taurianova [I] 138 D3
Taurine, Terme– [I] 130 E3
Taurisano [I] 136 F3
Taurkalns [LV] 236 B3
Tauros [GR] 168 B2
Tauste [E] 94 D2
Tautušiai [LT] 238 C2
Tauves [F] 80 A2
Tavaklı [TR] 162 F3
Tavannes [CH] 70 C4
Tavarnelle Val di Pesa [I] 128 C4
Tavas [TR] 170 E3
Tavascan [E] 88 E4

Tavastehus / Hämeenlinna [FIN] 198 E2
Tavastila [FIN] 200 C3
Tavastkenka [FIN] 216 C3
Tavastkyro / Hämeenkyrö [FIN] 198 D1
Tavaux [F] 68 F4
Tavelsjö [S] 214 D4
Taverna [I] 138 E2
Tavernelle [I] 130 F1
Tavernes [F] 126 A3
Tavernes de la Valldigna [E] 102 D4
Taviano [I] 136 E3
Tavira [P] 98 C4
Tavistock [GB] 26 C3
Tavna, Manastir– [BIH] 146 C2
Tavole Palatine [I] 136 D3
Tavşancil [TR] 158 F3
Tavşanli [TR] 164 F2
Täxan [S] 206 B1
Taxenbach [A] 72 E4
Taxiarchón, Moní– [GR] 168 C4
Tayfur [TR] 164 A1
Taytan [TR] 164 D4
Täzha [BG] 156 D1
Tázlár [H] 122 C2
Tazones [E] 86 B1
Tczew [PL] 36 D2
Tczów [PL] 50 A3
Teano [I] 134 C3
Tearce [MK] 154 C3
Teascu [RO] 148 E2
Techendorf [A] 118 E2
Techirghiol [RO] 150 F1
Tecklenburg [D] 30 E4
Tecuci [RO] 244 E4
Teerijärvi / Terjärv [FIN] 208 D1
Teféli [GR] 174 D4
Tefenni [TR] 170 F3
Tegéa [GR] 172 D2
Tegelen [NL] 42 C3
Tegelträsk [S] 206 D1
Tegernsee [D] 72 C3
Teggiano [I] 134 E4
Téglás [H] 76 E3
Teglaszin [H] 120 D2
Teglio [I] 116 F2
Teguise [E] 114 E3
Tehi [FIN] 198 F1
Teichel [D] 58 F1
Teichiussa [TR] 170 B3
Teignmouth [GB] 26 D3
Teillay [F] 66 C1
Teillet [F] 124 A2
Teisendorf [D] 72 E3
Teisko [FIN] 208 D4
Teixeiro [E] 82 C2
Tejeda [E] 112 E3
Tejn [DK] 180 E3
Teke [TR] 158 F3
Tekeriš [SRB] 146 C2
Tekija [SRB] 148 C1
Tekin [TR] 170 F2
Tekirdağ [TR] 158 C3
Tekovské Lužany [SK] 76 A3
Telana [I] 142 C4
Telavåg [N] 192 A3
Telč [CZ] 60 F4
Teldau [D] 32 D3
Telde [E] 112 E4
Teleborg [S] 184 D3
Telekháza [H] 76 D3
Telese Terme [I] 134 D3
Telford [GB] 22 F4
Telfs [A] 72 B4
Telgte [D] 30 E4
Telheiro [P] 98 B3
Telish [BG] 148 E3
Teljo [FIN] 216 E3

Tellingstedt [D] 32 B1
Tellskap [CH] 116 D1
Telmessos [TR] 176 D1
Telšiai [LT] 238 B1
Telti [I] 142 C2
Tembleque [E] 100 E2
Temelín [CZ] 60 D4
Temerin [SRB] 122 C4
Temmes [FIN] 216 B2
Temnata Dupka [BG] 148 D4
Témpi [GR] 160 F3
Témpio Pausánia [I] 142 C2
Templemore [IRL] 10 D2
Templetouhy [IRL] 10 D3
Templin [D] 34 C4
Templom [H] 76 A3
Temse [B] 40 D3
Temska [SRB] 148 C4
Tenala / Tenhola [FIN] 198 D4
Tenby [GB] 26 C1
Tence [F] 80 C3
Tenda, Colle di– / Tende, Col de– [F/I] 126 C2
Tende [F] 126 C2
Tende, Col de– / Tenda, Colle di– [F/I] 126 C2
Tendilla [E] 94 A4
Tenebrón [E] 84 D4
Tenero [CH] 116 D2
Tenevo [BG] 156 F1
Tenhola / Tenala [FIN] 198 D4
Tenhult [S] 184 C2
Tenja [HR] 122 B4
Tenk [H] 76 C3
Tennänget [S] 194 E3
Tennevol [N] 224 C3
Tenterden [GB] 28 D4
Tentudia, Monasterio de– [E] 98 E3
Teo / Ramallosa [E] 82 B2
Teofipol' [UA] 244 D1
Teolo [I] 118 C4
Teos [TR] 168 F2
Teovo [MK] 154 D4
Tepasto [FIN] 226 C4
Tepecik [TR] 158 F3
Tepecik [TR] 164 D1
Tepecik [TR] 164 E2
Tepecik [TR] 164 F2
Tepeköy [TR] 170 D2
Tepelenë [AL] 160 B3
Tepeören [TR] 158 E3
Teplá [CZ] 60 C3
Teplice [CZ] 60 D2
Teplice nad Metují [CZ] 62 A2
Tepsa [FIN] 222 C1
Téramo [I] 132 E3
Ter Apel [NL] 30 E3
Teratyn [PL] 50 D4
Terchová [SK] 62 E4
Terebiń [PL] 50 D4
Terebišče [RUS] 232 E3
Terebovlia [UA] 244 D2
Terem [H] 76 F3
Teremia Mare [RO] 122 D3
Terena [P] 98 D2
Teresa de Confrentes [E] 102 C4
Teresin [PL] 48 E2
Teresin [PL] 50 D4
Terespol [PL] 50 D2
Terezín [CZ] 60 D2
Terezino Polje [HR] 120 E3
Tergnier [F] 54 F2
Terebiń [PL] 50 D4
Terkoz [TR] 158 D3
Terland [N] 186 B3
Terlizzi [I] 136 C1
Termal [TR] 158 E4
Termas de Monfortinho [P] 90 E2

Terme di Lurisia [I] 126 D2
Terme di Valdieri [I] 126 C2
Terme Luigiane [I] 138 D1
Termes–d'Armagnac [F] 88 D2
Terme S. Lucia [I] 132 D2
Terme Vigliatore [I] 138 C3
Términi Imerese [I] 140 C2
Terminillo [I] 132 D3
Terminón [E] 86 C4
Térmoli [I] 134 D1
Termolovo [RUS] 200 F3
Termonde (Dendermonde) [B] 40 D3
Termonfeckin [IRL] 12 E4
Ternberg [A] 74 A3
Terndrup [DK] 182 D3
Terneuzen [NL] 40 D2
Terni [I] 132 D3
Ternitz [A] 74 C3
Ternopil' [UA] 244 D2
Térovo [GR] 166 C2
Terpan [AL] 160 B3
Terpezita [RO] 148 D2
Terpilitsy [RUS] 200 E4
Terpní [GR] 156 B4
Terracina [I] 134 B2
Terradillos de los Templarios [E] 86 B3
Terråk [N] 212 D2
Terralba [I] 142 B4
Terra Mala [I] 142 C5
Terra Mitica [E] 108 D2
Terranova di Pollino [I] 136 C3
Terrassa / Tarrasa [E] 96 D3
Terrasson–la–Villedieu [F] 78 E3
Terrateig [E] 102 D4
Terrazos [E] 86 D4
Terriente [E] 102 C1
Terskanperä [FIN] 216 B3
Tersløse [DK] 178 E2
Tertenía [I] 142 C4
Teruel [E] 102 C2
Tervahauta [FIN] 198 C1
Tervakoski [FIN] 198 E2
Tervel [BG] 150 D2
Tervo [FIN] 210 B2
Tervola [FIN] 222 C3
Terwuren [B] 40 E3
Terz [A] 74 C3
Terzaga [E] 94 C4
Tesárske Mlyňany [SK] 74 F2
Tesejerague [E] 114 D3
Těškovice [CZ] 62 D3
Teslić [BIH] 146 A2
Teslui [RO] 148 E2
Tessenberg [A] 118 D2
Tesseosen [N] 192 E1
Tessin [D] 32 E2
Tessy–sur–Vire [F] 52 F3
Tét [H] 74 E2
Tetbury [GB] 26 F2
Teterow [D] 32 F3
Teteven [BG] 148 F4
Tetovo [BG] 150 C2
Tetovo [MK] 154 C3
Tetrálofo [GR] 160 C2
Teuchrania [TR] 164 C3
Teufelshöhle [D] 58 F3
Teufen [CH] 70 F4
Teulada [E] 108 C2
Teulada [I] 142 B6
Teupitz [D] 46 B2
Teurnia [A] 118 E2
Teuro [FIN] 198 E2
Teuva / Östermark [FIN] 208 B3
Tevaniemi [FIN] 208 D4
Tevel [H] 122 A2
Teverga / La Plaza [E] 82 E3
Tevfikiye [TR] 164 A2
Tewkesbury [GB] 26 F1

Tewli [BY] 50 E1
Texeiro [E] 82 D2
Texing [A] 74 B3
Teysset [F] 78 D4
Thal [A] 118 D2
Thale [D] 44 D3
Thalfang [D] 56 E2
Thalheim [D] 60 C1
Thalmässing [D] 58 E4
Thalwil [CH] 70 E4
Thame [GB] 28 C2
Thann [F] 70 C3
Thannhausen [D] 72 B2
Tharandt [D] 46 B4
Tharigné–sur–Dué [F] 54 B4
Thárros [I] 142 B4
Tharsis [E] 98 D3
Thásos [GR] 156 D4
Thatcham [GB] 28 B3
Thaumiers [F] 68 C3
Theessen [D] 44 E2
Them [DK] 178 C1
Themar [D] 58 E2
Thénezay [F] 66 E3
Thenon [F] 78 E3
Theológos [GR] 162 D1
Theológos [GR] 166 F3
Théoule [F] 126 B3
Thera [TR] 170 D4
Thermá [GR] 162 E1
Thérma [GR] 168 F3
Thérmi [GR] 160 F2
Thermí [GR] 164 B3
Thermisía [GR] 168 A3
Thérmo [GR] 166 D3
Thermopýles [GR] 166 E3
Thermopýles [GR] 166 E2
Thernberg [A] 74 D4
Thérouanne [F] 40 B3
Thespiés [GR] 166 F3
Thesprotia [GR] 166 B1
Thessaloníki [GR] 160 F2
Thetford [GB] 28 E1
The Turoe Stone [IRL] 10 D2
Theuley [F] 70 B3
Theux [B] 40 F4
Thevet–St–Julien [F] 68 B4
Theze [F] 88 C2
Thiaucourt–Regniéville [F] 56 D4
Thiberville [F] 54 B2
Thiélbemont–Farémont [F] 56 B4
Thiendorf [D] 46 B4
Thiene [I] 118 C3
Thiers [F] 80 C2
Thiersee [A] 72 D3
Thiersheim [D] 60 B2
Thiesi [I] 142 B3
Thiessow [D] 34 C2
Thingvellir [IS] 218 B3
Thionville [F] 56 D3
Thíra [GR] 174 D2
Thíra / Firá [GR] 174 D1
Thirette [F] 80 E2
Thirsk [GB] 24 C1
Thisted [DK] 182 C3
Thísvi [GR] 166 F3
Thíva [GR] 168 A2
Thivars [F] 54 C4
Thiviers [F] 78 D3
Thizy [F] 80 D2
Tho, Pieve del– [I] 128 D3
Thoard [F] 126 A2
Thoissey [F] 80 D2
Tholey [D] 56 E3
Tholó [GR] 172 C2
Thomasberg [A] 74 D4
Thomas Street [IRL] 10 D1
Thomastown [IRL] 10 E3
Thônes [F] 80 F2
Thonon–les–Bains [F] 116 B2

Thorens–Glières, Château de– [F] 80 F2
Thorigné–en–Charnie [F] 54 A4
Thorikó [GR] 168 B3
Thörl [A] 74 B4
Thornbury [GB] 26 E2
Thorney [GB] 28 D1
Thornhill [GB] 20 C2
Thoronet, Abbaye du– [F] 126 A3
Thors [F] 68 F1
Thórshöfn [IS] 218 D2
Thouarcé [F] 66 D2
Thouars [F] 66 D3
Thouría [GR] 172 D3
Thoúrio [GR] 158 A3
Thueyts [F] 80 C4
Thuín [B] 40 D4
Thuir [F] 96 E1
Thum [D] 60 C2
Thun [CH] 116 C1
Thuret [F] 80 B2
Thürkow [D] 32 F2
Thurles / Durlas [IRL] 10 D3
Thurnau [D] 58 F2
Thurn Pass [A] 72 D4
Thurso [GB] 14 F1
Thury–Harcourt [F] 54 A2
Thusis [CH] 116 E2
Thyborøn [DK] 182 B3
Thymariá [GR] 156 F4
Thymianá [GR] 168 E1
Thyregod [DK] 178 B1
Tiana [I] 142 C4
Tibaes [P] 84 B2
Tibarrié [F] 124 B2
Tibava [SK] 76 E1
Tiberio, Grotta di– [I] 134 B3
Tibro [S] 188 E4
Ticha [BG] 150 C4
Tidaholm [S] 188 E4
Tidan [S] 188 E3
Tidersrum [S] 184 D1
Tidö [S] 190 C2
Tiefenbronn [D] 70 F1
Tiefencastel [CH] 116 E2
Tiefensee [D] 46 B1
Tiel [NL] 30 B4
Tielt [B] 40 C3
Tiemassaari [FIN] 210 C3
Tienen (Tirlemont) [B] 40 E3
Tiengen [D] 70 E3
Tiercé [F] 66 D2
Tierga [E] 94 C3
Tiermas [E] 94 A2
Tierp [S] 196 D4
Tieva [FIN] 226 C4
Tigănaşi [RO] 148 C2
Tighina [MD] 244 F3
Tigkáki [GR] 176 A1
Tignes [F] 116 B3
Tihany [H] 120 F2
Tihilă [FIN] 216 C3
Thusniemi [FIN] 210 C3
Tiironkyla [FIN] 208 E2
Tiistenjoki [FIN] 208 D2
Tijarafe [E] 112 B1
Tíjola [E] 106 B3
Tikkakoski [FIN] 208 F3
Tikkala [FIN] 208 F3
Tikkala [FIN] 210 E3
Tilberga [S] 190 C2
Tilburg [NL] 40 E2
Tilbury [GB] 28 D3
Til–Châtel [F] 68 F3
Tileagd [RO] 122 F1
Tilloy Lès Mofflaines [F] 40 B4
Tiltagals [LV] 236 D3
Tiltrem [N] 212 B4
Tilži [LV] 236 D3
Timahoe [IRL] 10 E2

Time [N] 186 A3
Tími [CY] 176 C4
Timiryazevo [RUS] 238 B3
Timişoara [RO] 122 E3
Timişoara [RO] 248 B3
Timmel [D] 30 E2
Timmele [S] 184 B1
Timmendorfer Strand [D] 32 D2
Timmernabben [S] 184 E3
Timmersdala [S] 188 E4
Timmervik [S] 188 C4
Timoleague [IRL] 10 B4
Timoniemi [FIN] 216 E3
Timovaara [FIN] 210 D1
Timrå [S] 206 C3
Timsfors [S] 184 B4
Tinahely [IRL] 10 F3
Tinajo [E] 114 E2
Tinca [RO] 122 F2
Tinchebray [F] 52 F3
Tindaya [E] 114 E3
Tineo [E] 82 E2
Tingelstad [N] 194 B3
Tinglev [DK] 178 B3
Tingnes [N] 194 B3
Tingsryd [S] 184 D4
Tingstad [S] 190 C4
Tingstäde [S] 234 A2
Tingvoll [N] 202 E2
Tinnoset [N] 186 E1
Tínos [GR] 168 D3
Tiñosillos [E] 92 D3
Tinţăreni [RO] 148 D1
Tintern Abbey [IRL] 10 E4
Tintigni [B] 56 D2
Tinuži [LV] 236 B3
Tiobraid Arann / Tipperary [IRL] 10 D3
Tione di Trento [I] 118 B3
Tipasjoki [FIN] 216 D3
Tipasoja [FIN] 216 D3
Tipperary / Tiobraid Arann [IRL] 10 D3
Tiranë [AL] 160 B1
Tirano [I] 116 F2
Tiraspol [MD] 246 C3
Tire [TR] 170 C2
Tirgo [E] 86 D4
Tiriolo [I] 138 E2
Tirlemont (Tienen) [B] 40 E3
Tirmo [FIN] 200 B3
Tirol [RO] 122 E4
Tirol / Tirolo [I] 118 B2
Tirolo / Tirol [I] 118 B2
Tirrénia [I] 128 B4
Tirschenreuth [D] 60 B3
Tirstrup [DK] 182 E4
Tiryntha [GR] 172 E2
Tišča [BIH] 146 B3
Tiscar–Don Pedro [E] 106 B2
Tishevica [BG] 148 E3
Tishino [RUS] 36 F1
Tismana, Mănăstirea– [RO] 248 C3
Tisno [HR] 144 D4
Tišnov [CZ] 62 B4
Tisovec [SVK] 76 C2
Tistrup [DK] 178 B1
Tisvilde [DK] 178 E1
Tiszaalpár [H] 122 C2
Tiszabábolna [H] 76 D3
Tiszabüra [H] 76 C4
Tiszacsege [H] 76 D3
Tiszacsermely [H] 76 E2
Tiszadob [H] 76 D3
Tiszaföldvár [H] 122 D1
Tiszafüred [H] 76 D3
Tiszajenő [H] 122 C1
Tiszakécske [H] 122 C1
Tiszalök [H] 76 E3
Tiszalúc [H] 76 D3

Tiszanána [H] 76 D4
Tiszaörs [H] 76 D4
Tiszaroff [H] 76 C4
Tiszasüly [H] 76 C4
Tiszaszőlős [H] 76 D4
Tiszatelek [H] 76 E2
Tiszaújváros [H] 76 D3
Tiszavasvári [H] 76 E3
Titaguas [E] 102 C2
Titel [SRB] 146 D1
Titisee [D] 70 E3
Tito [I] 134 E4
Tito Bustillo, Cueva de– [E] 86 B2
Titova Spilja [BIH] 144 E3
Titov Veles [MK] 154 D4
Titran [N] 202 E1
Tittling [D] 72 E2
Tittmoning [D] 72 E3
Titu [RO] 150 B1
Titz [D] 42 C3
Tiuccia [F] 130 A3
Tiukka / Tjöck [FIN] 208 B3
Tiurajärvi [FIN] 222 B1
Tivadar [H] 76 F3
Tivat [MNE] 152 E3
Tived [S] 188 E3
Tiverton [GB] 26 D3
Tivoli [I] 132 D4
Tizzano [F] 130 A4
Tjæreborg [DK] 178 B2
Tjällmo [S] 188 F3
Tjalme [S] 224 E4
Tjåmotis [S] 220 D2
Tjautjas [S] 220 E2
Tjeldnes [N] 224 C4
Tjele [DK] 182 D3
Tjelle [N] 202 D3
Tjentište [BIH] 152 E1
Tjöck / Tiukka [FIN] 208 B3
Tjolöholm [S] 184 A2
Tjøme [N] 186 F2
Tjong [N] 218 E3
Tjønnefoss [N] 186 D2
Tjørhom [N] 186 C2
Tjørnhom [N] 186 C3
Tjørnuvik [FR] 182 A1
Tjøtta [N] 212 D1
Tjugum [N] 192 C2
Tjultrask [S] 220 B4
Tjuvkil [S] 182 F1
Tkon [HR] 144 C3
Tlachene [BG] 148 E3
Tleń [PL] 36 C3
Tlmače [SK] 76 A2
Tlos [TR] 176 E1
Tłuchowo [PL] 48 D1
Tlumačov [CZ] 62 C4
Tłuszcz [PL] 48 F2
Tobarra [E] 102 B4
Tobercurry [IRL] 12 C2
Tobermory [GB] 14 B4
Tobias [A] 74 C3
Toblach / Dobbiaco [I] 118 D2
Tocha [P] 90 C1
Tocina [E] 98 F4
Töcksfors [S] 188 C2
Todal [N] 202 E2
Todalen [N] 202 E2
Todi [I] 132 C2
Todorići [BIH] 144 F3
Tødsø [DK] 182 C3
Todtmoos [D] 70 E3
Todtnau [D] 70 E3
Tõdva [EST] 230 D2
Toftbyn [S] 196 B3
Tofte [N] 188 B2
Tofterup [DK] 178 B2
Tofteryd [S] 184 C2
Tofteseter [N] 192 F2
Toftesetra [N] 202 F4
Toftir [FR] 182 B2

Toftlund [DK] 178 B2
Togher [IRL] 10 D2
Tóház [H] 122 A2
Tōhela [EST] 230 C3
Tohmajärvi [FIN] 210 E3
Toholampi [FIN] 216 A4
Tohvri [EST] 230 D3
Toichío [GR] 160 D2
Toijala [FIN] 198 E2
Toijola [FIN] 200 C1
Toikkala [FIN] 200 C2
Toikkala [FIN] 200 C2
Toirano, Grotte di– [I] 126 D2
Toitz [D] 32 F2
Toivakka [FIN] 210 B3
Toivola [FIN] 200 B1
Töjby [FIN] 208 B3
Tojšići [BIH] 146 B2
Tokačka [BG] 156 E3
Tokagjelet [N] 192 B3
Tokaj [H] 76 E3
Tokarnia [PL] 62 F3
Tokarnia [PL] 64 B1
Tokary [PL] 48 C3
Tokary [PL] 50 C1
Tokod [H] 76 A3
Toksovo [RUS] 200 F3
Tolcsva [H] 76 E2
Toledo [E] 100 D1
Tolentino [I] 132 D2
Tolfa [I] 130 F3
Tolfta [S] 196 D4
Tolg [S] 184 D3
Tolga [N] 204 B3
Tolkis / Tolkkinen [FIN] 200 A3
Tolkkinen / Tolkis [FIN] 200 A3
Tolkmicko [PL] 36 D2
Tollarp [S] 180 C2
Tølløse [DK] 178 E2
Tolmachevo [RUS] 232 F2
Tolmezzo [I] 118 E2
Tolmin [SLO] 118 F3
Tolna [H] 122 B2
Tolne [DK] 182 E2
Toló [GR] 172 E2
Tolob [GB] 16 E4
Tolonen [FIN] 226 D3
Tolosa [E] 86 F3
Tolosa [P] 90 D3
Tolosenmäki [FIN] 210 E3
Tolox [E] 104 D3
Tolve [I] 134 F4
Tomar [P] 90 C2
Tomaševac [SRB] 122 D4
Tomaševo [MNE] 152 F2
Tomášikovo [SK] 74 E3
Tomaszów Lubelski [PL] 64 E2
Tomaszów Mazowiecki [PL] 48 E3
Tomatin [GB] 14 E3
Tombebœuf [F] 78 D4
Tomelilla [S] 180 D2
Tomelloso [E] 100 F3
Tomerdingen [D] 72 A2
Tomintoul [GB] 14 E4
Tomislavgrad [BIH] 144 F4
Tømmernes [N] 220 B1
Tommerup [DK] 178 C2
Tømmervåg [N] 202 E2
Tommola [FIN] 200 C1
Tompa [H] 122 C3
Tømra [N] 204 B2
Tomter [N] 188 B2
Tona [E] 96 D2
Tonara [I] 142 C4
Tonbridge [GB] 28 D3
Tønder [DK] 178 B3
Tongeren (Tongres) [B] 40 F4
Tongres (Tongeren) [B] 40 F4
Tongue [GB] 14 E1

Tonnay–Boutonne [F] 78 C1
Tonnay–Charente [F] 78 B1
Tonneins [F] 88 D1
Tonnerre [F] 68 D2
Tonnes [N] 218 E4
Tönning [D] 32 B1
Tonquédec, Château de– [F] 52 C2
Tønsberg [N] 186 F2
Tonstad [N] 186 B3
Toomyvara [IRL] 10 D2
Toourmakeady / Tuar Mhic Éadaigh [IRL] 12 B3
Topares [E] 106 C2
Topchii [BG] 150 C2
Töpchin [D] 46 B2
Topczewo [PL] 38 C3
Toplet [RO] 148 C1
Topli Dol [SRB] 148 C3
Topliţa [RO] 244 D3
Toplou [GR] 174 E3
Topo [P] 110 B3
Topoľ [SRB] 146 C3
Topolčani [MK] 160 D1
Topolʹčany [SK] 74 F2
Topolčiansky Hrad [SK] 74 F2
Topólia [GR] 174 B3
Topolnica [SRB] 148 C2
Topolniţa [RO] 148 C1
Topolovăţu Mare [RO] 122 E3
Topolovec [BG] 148 D3
Topolovgrad [BG] 156 F2
Topolovica [HR] 120 E3
Topolovnik [SRB] 146 F2
Topolovo [BG] 156 D2
Toporu [RO] 150 B2
Topraisar [RO] 150 F1
Topusko [HR] 144 D1
Toques [E] 82 C2
Torà [E] 96 C2
Toral de los Vados [E] 82 D3
Torbalı [TR] 170 B2
Tørberget [N] 194 C2
Torbole [I] 118 B3
Torcello [I] 118 D4
Torchyn [UA] 50 F4
Tordera [E] 96 E3
Tordesillas [E] 92 D2
Tordesilos [E] 94 C4
Töre [S] 222 A4
Töreboda [S] 188 E3
Toreby [DK] 178 D3
Torekov [S] 184 A4
Torelló [E] 96 D2
Toreno [E] 82 E3
Toresund [S] 190 D2
Torf [A] 118 F1
Torfyanovka [RUS] 200 D3
Torgåsmon [S] 194 D3
Torgau [D] 44 F3
Torgelow [D] 34 D3
Torgiano [I] 132 C2
Torhamn [S] 180 F1
Torhout [B] 40 C3
Tori [EST] 230 D3
Torigni–sur–Vire [F] 52 F3
Torija [E] 94 A3
Toril [E] 102 C2
Torino [I] 116 C4
Torino di Sangro [I] 132 F3
Torino di Sangro Marina [I] 132 F3
Torís / Turís [E] 102 D3
Torla [E] 88 C4
Torma [EST] 230 E2
Tormac [RO] 122 E4
Törmäkylä [FIN] 216 C2
Törmänki [FIN] 222 C2
Tormánmäki [FIN] 216 D2
Tormos [E] 94 E2
Tornaľa [SK] 76 C2

Tornavacas [E] 92 B3
Tornby [DK] 182 D2
Torneå / Tornio [FIN] 222 B4
Tørnes [N] 186 F2
Tørnes [N] 202 D2
Torneträsk [S] 224 E4
Tornio / Torneå [FIN] 222 B4
Tornioniemi [FIN] 210 D3
Tornjoš [SRB] 122 C3
Toro [E] 84 F3
Törökszentmiklós [H] 122 D1
Toróni [GR] 162 C2
Torony [H] 120 D1
Toropec [RUS] 240 C3
Toropets [RUS] 240 C3
Toros [BG] 148 E4
Toros de Guisando [E] 92 D4
Torp [FIN] 196 F4
Torp [S] 188 C3
Torpa [S] 184 B3
Torpa Stenhus [S] 184 B2
Torpo [N] 192 E3
Torpoint [GB] 26 C3
Torpsbruk [S] 184 D3
Torpshammar [S] 206 B3
Torquay [GB] 26 D4
Torquemada [E] 86 B4
Torralba [E] 94 B3
Torralba [E] 100 D3
Torralba de el Burgo [E] 94 B2
Torralba de Oropesa [E] 92 C4
Torrão [P] 98 C2
Torre [E] 104 E3
Torre Annunziata [I] 134 D3
Torre Beretti [I] 116 D4
Torre Beretti [I] 116 D4
Torreblanca [E] 102 E2
Torrecaballeros [E] 92 E3
Torrecampo [E] 100 C3
Torre Canne [I] 136 D2
Torrechiara, Castello di– [I] 128 B2
Torrecilla [E] 102 B1
Torrecilla de la Orden [E] 84 F4
Torrecilla del Pinar [E] 94 B4
Torrecillas de la Tiesa [E] 100 B1
Torreciudad, Santuario de– [E] 94 F2
Torre de Dona Chama [P] 84 D2
Torre de Juan Abad [E] 100 E4
Torre del Bierzo [E] 82 E4
Torre del Compte [E] 104 F2
Torre del Greco [I] 134 C3
Torre del Lago Puccini [I] 128 B3
Torre dell'Impiso [I] 140 B1
Torre del Mar [E] 104 E3
Torredembarra [E] 96 C3
Torre de Moncorvo [P] 84 C3
Torre de' Pásseri [I] 132 E3
Torre de Sta. María [E] 90 F4
Torredonjimeno [E] 104 F2
Torre Faro [I] 138 D3
Torrefarrera [E] 96 B2
Torregamones [E] 84 E3
Torre Grande [I] 142 B4
Torreguadiaro [E] 104 C3
Torreiglesias [E] 92 E3
Torreira [P] 84 A3
Torrejoncillo [E] 90 F3
Torrejón de Ardoz [E] 92 E4
Torrejón de la Calzada [E] 92 E4
Torrejón del Rey [E] 92 F4
Torrejón el Rubio [E] 92 B4
Torrelaguna [E] 92 F4
Torrelapaja [E] 94 C2
Torrelavega [E] 86 C2
Torrelobatón [E] 92 D1
Torrelodones [E] 92 E3
Torremaggiore [I] 134 E2

Torremejia [E] 98 F2
Torre Melissa [I] 138 F1
Torremocha [E] 90 F4
Torremocha de Jiloca [E] 102 C1
Torremocha del Pinar [E] 94 B4
Torremolinos [E] 104 D3
Torremormojón [E] 86 A4
Torrenostra [E] 102 E2
Torrent [E] 102 D3
Torrente de Cinca [E] 94 F3
Torrenueva [E] 100 E4
Torrenueva [E] 104 F3
Torre Orsaia [I] 136 B3
Torre-Pacheco [E] 106 E3
Torre Pellice [I] 126 C1
Torreperogil [E] 106 B1
Torrequemada [E] 90 F4
Torre Santa Susanna [I] 136 E3
Torres Cabrera [E] 104 E1
Torre S. Gennaro [I] 136 E2
Torres Novas [P] 90 C2
Torre S. Sabina [I] 136 E2
Torres Vedras [P] 90 B3
Torretta [I] 138 F1
Torrette di Fano [I] 128 E3
Torre Vã [P] 98 B3
Torrevieja [E] 106 E2
Torrflonås [S] 204 F4
Torricella [I] 136 E3
Torri del Benaco [I] 118 B3
Torríglia [I] 126 E2
Torrijas [E] 102 D2
Torrijos [E] 100 D1
Tørring [DK] 178 C1
Tørring [N] 212 C4
Torrita di Siena [I] 130 F1
Torröedet [S] 204 D1
Torroella de Montgrí [E] 96 F2
Torrox [E] 104 E3
Torrubia [E] 100 C4
Torsåker [S] 190 D3
Torsåker [S] 196 C4
Torsängen [S] 188 D3
Torsås [S] 184 E4
Torsborg [S] 204 D3
Torsburgen [S] 234 A2
Torsby [S] 188 D1
Torsby [S] 194 D4
Torsfjärden [S] 212 E4
Torshälla [S] 190 C2
Tórshavn [FR] 182 B2
Torslanda [S] 182 F1
Torsminde [DK] 182 B3
Törtel [H] 122 C1
Tortinmäki [FIN] 198 C3
Tórtola de Henares [E] 92 F4
Tórtoles de Esgueva [E] 92 E1
Tortolì [I] 142 C4
Tortona [I] 126 E1
Tortora [I] 136 B3
Tortoreto [I] 132 E2
Tortoreto Lido [I] 132 E2
Tortorici [I] 138 B4
Tortosa [E] 96 B4
Tortosendo [P] 90 E2
Toruń [PL] 36 C4
Torup [S] 180 C2
Torup [S] 184 B3
Torup Strand [DK] 182 C2
Tõrva [EST] 230 E3
Tor Vaiánica [I] 134 A2
Torvikbukt [N] 202 D2
Tørvikbygd [N] 192 B3
Torvinen [FIN] 222 D2
Torvsjö [S] 214 B3
Torvund [N] 192 B2
Torzhok [RUS] 240 E2
Torzym [PL] 46 D2
Tosbotn [N] 212 D2
Toscolano Maderno [I] 118 B3

Tösens [A] 118 B1
Toses, Collado de- [E] 96 D2
Tosno [RUS] 240 B1
Toso [N] 192 F4
Tossa de Mar [E] 96 E3
Tossåsen [S] 204 E3
Tossavanlahti [FIN] 208 F1
Tösse [S] 188 D3
Tostedt [D] 32 B3
Tosterup [S] 180 D2
Tószeg [H] 122 C1
Toszek [PL] 62 D2
Totana [E] 106 D2
Totebo [S] 184 E2
Tôtes [F] 54 C1
Tótkomlós [H] 122 D2
Tøtlandsvik [N] 186 B2
Totleben [BG] 150 A3
Totnes [GB] 26 C4
Tøttdal [N] 212 C3
Tottijärvi [FIN] 198 D1
Totvázsony [H] 120 F1
Toucy [F] 68 D2
Touffou [F] 66 E4
Toul [F] 56 D4
Toulon [F] 124 F4
Toulon sur Allier [F] 68 C4
Toulon-sur-Arroux [F] 68 D4
Toulouse [F] 88 E3
Tourcoing [F] 40 C3
Tourmalet, Col du- [F] 88 C3
Tournai (Doornik) [B] 40 C4
Tournan [F] 54 E3
Tournay [F] 88 D3
Tournon [F] 80 D3
Tournon-d'Agenais [F] 88 E1
Tournon-St-Martin [F] 66 F4
Tournus [F] 80 E1
Tourny [F] 54 D2
Tours [F] 66 F2
Tourves [F] 124 F3
Toury [F] 54 D3
Toutes Aures, Col de- [F] 126 B3
Touvois [F] 66 C3
Toužim [CZ] 60 C3
Tovačov [CZ] 62 C4
Tovarnik [HR] 146 C1
Tøvik [N] 202 D2
Tövsala / Taivassalo [FIN] 198 C3
Tovste [UA] 244 D2
Towcester [GB] 28 C2
Töysä [FIN] 208 D2
Trabada [E] 82 D2
Trabadelo [E] 82 D3
Trabanca [E] 84 D3
Trabazos [E] 84 D2
Traben-Trarbach [D] 56 E2
Trabía [I] 140 C2
Trabotivište [MK] 154 F3
Trabuc, Grottes de- [F] 124 D2
Tracheiá [GR] 168 A3
Trachíli [GR] 168 B1
Tracino [I] 140 A3
Trädet [S] 184 C1
Trælleborg [DK] 178 D2
Trættlia [N] 204 C1
Trafaria [P] 90 A3
Trafoi [I] 118 B2
Tragacete [E] 102 B1
Traian [RO] 150 A2
Traian Vuia [RO] 122 F3
Traiguera [E] 96 A4
Traisen [A] 74 C3
Traiskirchen [A] 74 D3
Traismauer [A] 74 C2
Trajano [E] 104 B2
Trakai [LT] 238 E3
Trakošćan [HR] 120 C3
Trakyeli [BY] 38 E1
Tralee / Trá Lí [IRL] 10 B3

Trá Lí / Tralee [IRL] 10 B3
Tralleis [TR] 170 C3
Tramariglio [I] 142 B2
Tramelan [CH] 70 C4
Tramonti di Sopra [I] 118 D2
Tramore [IRL] 10 D4
Tranås [S] 184 D1
Tranby [N] 186 F1
Tranco [E] 106 B1
Trancoso [P] 84 C4
Tranderup [DK] 178 C3
Tranekær [DK] 178 D3
Tranekær Slot [DK] 178 D3
Tranemo [S] 184 B2
Trångmon [S] 212 E3
Trångslet [S] 194 E2
Trångsviken [S] 204 E2
Tranhult [S] 184 C2
Trani [I] 136 C1
Trankil [S] 188 C2
Tranóvalto [GR] 160 E3
Transtrand [S] 194 D2
Tranum Strand [DK] 182 D2
Tranvik [S] 190 F2
Trápani [I] 140 B2
Trapishte [BG] 150 C3
Trappe d'Aiguebelle, Monastère de la- [F] 124 E1
Trappes [F] 54 D3
Taryd [S] 184 C4
Träskända / Järvenpää [FIN] 198 F3
Träskvik [FIN] 208 B3
Träslövsläge [S] 184 A3
Trasmiras [E] 82 C4
Trassem [D] 56 E3
Tråstenik [BG] 148 F3
Trate [SLO] 120 C2
Tratzberg [A] 72 C4
Traun [A] 74 A3
Traunkirchen [A] 72 F3
Traunreut [D] 72 D3
Traunstein [D] 72 D3
Trautenfels [A] 72 F4
Trautmannsdorf [A] 74 D3
Travemünde [D] 32 D2
Travers [CH] 70 C4
Travnik [BIH] 144 F3
Travo [F] 130 B3
Travo [I] 126 F1
Trazo [E] 82 B2
Trbovlje [SLO] 120 B3
Trbušani [E] 68 C4
Trebatsch [D] 46 C2
Trebbin [D] 46 B2
Třebechovice pod Orebem [CZ] 60 F2
Trebenice [CZ] 60 D2
Trébeurden [F] 52 C2
Třebíč [CZ] 60 F4
Trebija [SLO] 118 F3
Trebinje [BIH] 152 D3
Trebisacce [I] 136 C4
Trebišov [SK] 76 E2
Trebnje [SLO] 120 B3
Třeboň [CZ] 74 B1
Tréboul [F] 52 B3
Třebovice [CZ] 62 B3
Trebujena [E] 104 B2
Trecastagni [I] 140 E2
Trecate [I] 116 D3
Trecenta [I] 128 C1
Trecesson, Château de- [F] 52 D4
Treffurt [D] 44 C4
Tregaron [GB] 22 D4
Trégastel [F] 52 C2
Tregnago [I] 118 B4
Tréguier [F] 52 C2
Trehörna [S] 184 D1
Trehörningsjö [S] 206 D1
Treia [D] 32 B1

Treibach [A] 120 A2
Treignac [F] 78 F3
Treillieres [F] 66 C2
Treis [D] 56 F2
Trekanten [S] 184 E3
Trelde [DK] 178 C2
Trelleborg [S] 180 C2
Tremês [P] 90 B3
Tremestieri [I] 138 C3
Tremezzo [I] 116 E3
Tremisht [AL] 160 C3
Třemošná [CZ] 60 C3
Tremp [E] 96 C2
Trenčianska Turná [SK] 74 F2
Trenčianske Bohuslavice [SK] 74 F2
Trenčianske Teplice [SK] 74 F1
Trenčín [SK] 74 F1
Trend [DK] 182 C3
Trendelburg [D] 44 B3
Trengereid [N] 192 B3
Trent [CH] 116 B2
Trenta [SLO] 118 F2
Trento [I] 118 B3
Treppeln [D] 46 C2
Trept [F] 80 E3
Tres Cantos [E] 92 E3
Trescore Balneario [I] 116 F3
Tresenda [I] 116 F2
Tresfjord [N] 202 D3
Tresigallo [I] 128 D2
Treski [EST] 230 F3
Treskog [S] 188 D1
Treskovec, Manastir- [MK] 154 D4
Tresnurághes [I] 142 B3
Trespaderne [E] 86 D3
Třešť [CZ] 60 F4
Tresta [GB] 16 F3
Tresta Rzadowa [PL] 48 E3
Trets [F] 124 F3
Tretten [N] 194 B2
Treuchtlingen [D] 72 B1
Treuenbrietzen [D] 44 F2
Treungen [N] 186 D2
Trevélez [E] 104 F3
Tréveray [F] 56 C4
Trevi [I] 132 D2
Treviglio [I] 116 E3
Trevignano Romano [I] 130 F3
Treviño [E] 86 E4
Treviso [I] 118 D3
Trévoux [F] 80 D2
Trezelles [F] 80 C1
Trezzano sul Naviglio [I] 116 E4
Trezzo sull'Adda [I] 116 E3
Trgovište [SRB] 154 E2
Trhová Kamenice [CZ] 60 F3
Trhové Sviny [CZ] 74 B1
Trhovište [SK] 76 E2
Triacastela [E] 82 D3
Triaíze [F] 66 C4
Triánta [GR] 176 C2
Triaucourt-en-Argonne [F] 56 C3
Tribanj Krušćica [HR] 144 C3
Triberg [D] 70 E2
Tribsees [D] 32 F2
Tricárico [I] 134 F4
Tricase [I] 136 F3
Tricesimo [I] 118 E3
Trichiana [I] 118 D3
Trie [F] 88 D3
Trieben [A] 74 A4
Trier [D] 56 E2
Trieste [I] 118 F4
Trifels [D] 58 A4
Trignac [F] 66 B2
Trígono [GR] 160 D2
Trigueros [E] 98 D4
Tríkala [GR] 160 E4

Tríkala [GR] 160 F2
Tríkala [GR] 166 E4
Trikéri [GR] 162 B4
Trikomon (Iskele) [CY] 176 E3
Trilj [HR] 144 E4
Trillevallen [S] 204 D2
Trillo [E] 94 B4
Trillofo [GR] 166 E2
Trim [IRL] 10 F2
Trimburg [D] 58 D2
Trindade [P] 84 C3
Trindade [P] 98 C3
Třinec [CZ] 62 D3
Trinidad [E] 86 F4
Trinità d'Agultu e Vignola [I] 142 C2
Trinitápoli [I] 134 F2
Trinité, Ermitage de la- [F] 130 B4
Trino [I] 116 D4
Triollo [E] 86 B3
Triora [I] 126 D3
Trípoli [GR] 172 D2
Triponzo [I] 132 D2
Tripótama [GR] 166 D4
Triptis [D] 60 A1
Trisanna-Brücke [A] 72 B4
Trisulti, Abbazia di- [I] 132 D4
Trittau [D] 32 C3
Trittenheim [D] 56 E2
Trivatea-Moşteni [RO] 150 A2
Trivento [I] 132 F4
Trnava [CZ] 60 F4
Trnava [SK] 74 E2
Trnovec nad Váhom [SK] 74 F3
Trnovo [BIH] 146 B4
Trnovo ob Soci [SLO] 118 E3
Troarn [F] 54 B2
Trödje [S] 196 D3
Troense [DK] 178 D3
Trofa [P] 84 A3
Trofaiach [A] 74 B4
Trofimovo [RUS] 232 F4
Trofors [N] 212 D2
Trogir [HR] 144 E4
Troia [I] 134 E2
Tróia [P] 90 B4
Troina [I] 138 B4
Troisdorf [D] 42 D4
Trois Fontaines, Abbaye des- [F] 56 C4
Trois-Ponts [B] 56 D1
Troits'ke [UA] 246 D2
Troizína [GR] 168 A3
Trojane [SLO] 120 B3
Trøjborg [DK] 178 B3
Trolla [N] 204 B2
Trollböle [FIN] 198 D4
Trolleholm [S] 180 C2
Trolle Ljungby [S] 180 D1
Trollenäs [S] 180 C2
Trollhättan [S] 188 C4
Trollkyrkja [N] 202 D2
Trollvik [N] 224 E2
Tromello [I] 116 D4
Tromøy [N] 186 D3
Tromsø [N] 224 D2
Tromvik [N] 224 D2
Tronco [P] 84 C2
Trondheim [N] 204 B2
Trones [N] 218 F3
Trönninge [S] 184 A2
Trönninge [S] 184 B3
Tronvik [N] 204 B1
Trôo [F] 66 F2
Troódos [CY] 176 D4
Troon [GB] 18 C4
Tropæum Traiani [RO] 150 E1
Tropea [I] 138 D3
Tropfstein-Höhle [A] 120 B2
Tropojë [AL] 154 B3
Trosa [S] 190 D3

Troškūnai [LT] 238 D2
Trosky [CZ] 60 E2
Trössing [A] 120 C2
Trossingen [D] 70 E2
Tröstau [D] 60 A3
Trostberg [D] 72 D3
Trosterud [N] 188 C2
Trostianets' [UA] 242 F3
Trostianets' [UA] 244 F2
Trouville [F] 54 B2
Trowbridge [GB] 26 F3
Troyan [BG] 148 F4
Troyanovo [BG] 150 D4
Troyanski Manastir [BG]
  148 F4
Troyanski Pateka [BG] 148 F4
Trøyen [N] 204 B2
Troyes [F] 68 E1
Troyon [F] 56 C3
Trpanj [HR] 152 C2
Trpinja [HR] 122 B4
Tršić [SRB] 146 C2
Trstená [SK] 62 F4
Trstena [SRB] 154 D2
Trstenik [SRB] 146 E4
Trsteno [HR] 152 D3
Trstín [SK] 74 E2
Trubchevsk [RUS] 242 E2
Trubia [E] 82 F2
Truchas [E] 82 D4
Truchtersheim [F] 70 D1
Trud [BG] 156 D2
Trujillo [E] 100 B1
Trulben [D] 56 F4
Trün [BG] 154 E2
Trun [CH] 116 E1
Trun [F] 54 B3
Truro [GB] 26 B3
Truskavets' [UA] 64 E4
Trustrup [DK] 182 E4
Trutnov [CZ] 60 F2
Trutnowy [PL] 36 D2
Truva [TR] 164 A2
Tryavna [BG] 150 B4
Trydal [N] 186 C2
Tryde [S] 180 D2
Tryggelev [DK] 178 D3
Tryggestad [N] 202 C4
Tryńcza [PL] 64 D2
Trýpi [GR] 172 D3
Trypití [GR] 162 C2
Trysa [TR] 176 F1
Tryserum [S] 184 F1
Tryšiai [LT] 238 B1
Trysil Innbygda [N] 194 D2
Tryszczyn [PL] 36 C4
Trzcianka [PL] 36 A4
Trzciel [PL] 46 E2
Trzcinna [PL] 34 E2
Trzcińsko Zdrój [PL] 34 D4
Trzebiatów [PL] 34 E2
Trzebiel [PL] 46 C3
Trzebież [PL] 34 D3
Trzebina [PL] 62 C2
Trzebinia [PL] 62 E2
Trzebnica [PL] 46 F4
Trzebów [PL] 46 D2
Trzemeszno [PL] 48 B2
Trzepnica [PL] 48 D4
Trzepowo [PL] 36 C2
Trześcianka [PL] 38 D3
Tržič [SLO] 120 A2
Trzin [SLO] 120 B3
Tržišče [SLO] 120 B3
Tsagkaráda [GR] 162 B3
Tsamandás [GR] 160 C4
Tsampíka, Moní– [GR] 176 C2
Tsangário [GR] 166 B2
Tsapel'ka [RUS] 232 E3
Tsarevets [BG] 150 B3
Tsarevo [BG] 158 C1
Tsaríthani [GR] 160 E4

Tschernitz [D] 46 C3
Tschierv [CH] 118 A2
Tsenovo [BG] 150 B3
Tsiurupyns'k [UA] 246 E3
Tsotíli [GR] 160 D3
Tsoútsouros [GR] 174 D4
Tsvelodubovo [RUS] 200 E3
Tua [N] 212 C4
Tua [P] 84 C3
Tuaim / Tuam [IRL] 10 D1
Tuam / Tuaim [IRL] 10 D1
Tuar Mhic Éadaigh /
  Toourmakeady [IRL] 12 B3
Tubilla del Agua [E] 86 C3
Tübingen [D] 70 F2
Tubre / Taufers [I] 118 A2
Tučepi [HR] 152 C2
Tuchan [F] 124 B4
Tüchen [D] 32 E4
Tuchola [PL] 36 C3
Tuchomie [PL] 36 B2
Tuchów [PL] 64 B3
Tuckur [FIN] 208 C1
Tuczno [PL] 34 F4
Tuddal [N] 186 E1
Tudela [E] 94 D2
Tudela de Duero [E] 92 E2
Tudu [EST] 230 E2
Tudulinna [EST] 230 F2
Tuffé [F] 54 B4
Tufjord [N] 228 B1
Tuhkakylä [FIN] 216 D3
Tui [E] 82 B3
Tuin [MK] 154 C4
Tuineje [E] 114 D3
Tuiskula [FIN] 208 C2
Tuixén [E] 96 D2
Tūja [LV] 232 B4
Tukums [LV] 234 E3
Tulare [SRB] 154 D2
Tuławki [PL] 36 F2
Tulca [RO] 122 E2
Tulcea [RO] 248 F3
Tul'chyn [UA] 244 F2
Tulešice [CZ] 74 D1
Tuliszków [PL] 48 C2
Tulla [IRL] 10 C2
Tullamore [IRL] 10 E2
Tulle [F] 78 E3
Tullebolle [DK] 178 D3
Tulleråsen [S] 204 E2
Tullgarn [S] 190 D3
Tullinge [S] 190 D2
Tullins [F] 80 E3
Tulln [A] 74 C2
Tullow [IRL] 10 E3
Tułowice [PL] 62 C2
Tulppio [FIN] 226 F4
Tulsk [IRL] 12 C3
Tum [PL] 48 D2
Tumba [S] 190 D2
Tummsjøen [N] 212 E3
Tumulus de Gavrinis [F] 66 A1
Tun [S] 188 D4
Tuna [S] 184 E2
Tunaberg [S] 190 C3
Tuna Hästberg [S] 194 F4
Tunbridge Wells [GB] 28 D3
Tunbyn [S] 206 C4
Tunçbilek [TR] 164 F2
Tune [DK] 178 E2
Tunge [S] 184 A1
Tungelsta [S] 190 D3
Tunhovd [N] 192 E3
Tunnerstad [S] 184 C1
Tunnsjørørvika [N] 212 D3
Tung By [DK] 178 D1
Tuntsa [FIN] 226 F4
Tunvågen [S] 204 E3
Tuohikotti [FIN] 200 C2
Tuohittu [FIN] 198 D3
Tuomioja [FIN] 216 B2

Tuonj [HR] 144 C1
Tuorila [FIN] 208 B4
Tuornoel, Château de– [F]
  80 B2
Tupadły [PL] 48 C1
Tupitsyno [RUS] 232 E2
Tuplice [PL] 46 C3
Tuppurinmäki [FIN] 210 C2
Tura [H] 76 B4
Turaj [AL] 154 C3
Turalići [BIH] 146 B3
Turan [TR] 164 E1
Turanlı [TR] 164 C3
Turany [SK] 76 B1
Türas [TR] 158 F3
Turawa [PL] 62 D2
Turba [EST] 230 C2
Turbe [BIH] 144 F3
Turčianske Teplice [SK] 76 A1
Turckheim [F] 70 D2
Turda [RO] 244 C4
Turégano [E] 92 E2
Turek [PL] 48 C2
Turenki [FIN] 198 E2
Turenne [F] 78 E3
Turgeliai [LT] 238 E3
Türgovishte [BG] 150 C3
Turgut [TR] 170 C3
Turgutbey [TR] 158 B3
Turgutlu [TR] 170 C2
Turgutreis [TR] 176 A1
Turhala [FIN] 216 C4
Türi [EST] 230 D2
Turi [I] 136 D2
Turiis'k [UA] 50 E3
Turija [SRB] 146 F2
Turís / Toris [E] 102 D3
Turjaci [HR] 144 E4
Turjak [SLO] 120 B3
Turka [PL] 50 D3
Turka [UA] 64 E4
Türkeli [TR] 158 C4
Túrkeve [H] 122 D1
Türkheim [D] 72 B3
Türkmen [TR] 164 C4
Turkovići [BIH] 146 B4
Turku / Åbo [FIN] 198 C3
Turleque [E] 100 E2
Turlough [IRL] 12 B2
Turmantas [LT] 238 F2
Turňa nad Bodvou [SK] 76 D2
Turnberry [GB] 20 B2
Turnhout [B] 40 E3
Türnitz [A] 74 C3
Turnov [CZ] 60 E2
Turnu Măgurele [RO] 148 F2
Turo [FIN] 226 D2
Turobin [PL] 50 C4
Túrony [H] 122 A3
Turośl [PL] 38 A2
Turów [PL] 50 C2
Turrach [A] 118 F1
Turre [E] 106 C3
Turriff [GB] 14 F3
Turtagrø [N] 192 D1
Turtel [MK] 154 E3
Turtola [FIN] 222 B3
Turunç [TR] 176 C1
Turunçova [TR] 176 F1
Turzovka [SK] 62 D4
Tusa [I] 138 B4
Tusby / Tuusula [FIN] 198 F3
Tuscánia [I] 130 F2
Tušilovic [HR] 120 C4
Tuskö [S] 196 E4
Tustervatnet [N] 212 E1
Tuszów Narodowy [PL] 64 C2
Tuszyn [PL] 48 D3
Tuszyny [PL] 36 C3
Tutajev [RUS] 240 F1
Tutayev [RUS] 240 F1
Tutin [SRB] 154 B2

Tutjunniemi [FIN] 210 E2
Tutrakan [BG] 150 C2
Tutting [D] 72 E2
Tuttlingen [D] 70 F2
Tútugi [E] 106 B2
Tutzing [D] 72 C3
Tützpatz [D] 32 F3
Tuukkala [FIN] 200 C1
Tuukkala [FIN] 210 B4
Tuulos [FIN] 198 E2
Tuupovaara [FIN] 210 E2
Tuuruniemi [FIN] 226 D2
Tuusjärvi [FIN] 210 C2
Tuuski [FIN] 200 B3
Tuusniemi [FIN] 210 D2
Tuusula / Tusby [FIN] 198 F3
Tuv [N] 192 E3
Tuvaltnet [S] 204 F1
Tuvas [FIN] 208 B3
Tuvnes [N] 202 E1
Tuzi [MNE] 152 F3
Tuzla [BIH] 146 B2
Tuzla [TR] 158 E3
Tuzla [TR] 162 B2
Tuzlata [BG] 150 F3
Tuzsér [H] 76 E2
Tvååker [S] 184 A3
Tväråbäck [S] 214 C4
Tvärålund [S] 214 C3
Tvärträsk [S] 214 B2
Tvärminne [FIN] 198 D4
Tvärskog [S] 184 E3
Tvärud [S] 188 D1
Tvede [DK] 182 D3
Tvedestrand [N] 186 E3
Tveit [N] 186 B2
Tveita [N] 192 B3
Tveitsund [N] 186 D2
Tver' [RUS] 240 E2
Tverai [LT] 238 B2
Tverrå [N] 186 B2
Tverrå [N] 212 E1
Tverrelvmo [N] 224 E3
Tversted [DK] 182 D2
Tvinde [N] 192 C3
Tvindehaugen [N] 192 E2
Tving [S] 180 E1
Tvis [DK] 182 C4
Tvøroyri [FR] 182 A2
Tvrdošovce [SK] 74 F3
Tv–Torony [H] 120 D2
Tvürditsa [BG] 150 C4
Twann–Schlucht [CH] 70 C4
Twardogóra [PL] 48 B4
Tweng [A] 118 F1
Twimberg [A] 120 B1
Twist [D] 30 D3
Twistringen [D] 32 A4
Tworków [PL] 62 D3
Tworóg [PL] 62 D2
Tyamsha [RUS] 232 E4
Tychowo [PL] 34 F2
Tychy [PL] 62 E3
Tyczyn [PL] 64 C3
Tyfjord [N] 228 D1
Tyfors [S] 194 E4
Tyholland [NIR] 12 E3
Tyin [N] 192 D2
Tyinosen [N] 192 D2
Tykocin [PL] 38 C3
Tykocin [PL] 38 C3
Tylawa [PL] 64 C4
Týlisos [GR] 174 D3
Tylldal [N] 204 B4
Tylösand [S] 184 B3
Tylstrup [DK] 182 D2
Tymbark [PL] 64 A3
Tymfristós [GR] 166 D2
Tympáki [GR] 174 D4
Tyndaris [I] 138 C3
Tynderö [S] 206 C4
Tyndrum [GB] 18 C3

Týnec nad Labem [CZ] 60 E3
Tynemouth [GB] 20 F3
Tyngsjö [S] 194 E4
Tyniec [PL] 62 F3
Týniště nad Orlicí [CZ] 62 A2
Tynkä [FIN] 216 A3
Týn nad Vltavou [CZ] 60 D4
Tynnelsö [S] 190 D2
Tynset [N] 204 B4
Typpö [FIN] 216 A3
Tyresö [S] 190 E2
Tyringe [S] 180 C1
Tyrislöt [S] 190 C4
Tyristrand [N] 192 F4
Tyrjänsaari [FIN] 210 E2
Tyrnävä [FIN] 216 B2
Týrnavos [GR] 160 E4
Tyrós [GR] 172 E2
Týřov [CZ] 60 D3
Tyrrellspass [IRL] 10 E2
Tyry [FIN] 208 F4
Tysdal [N] 186 B2
Tysken [N] 194 D3
Tysse [N] 192 B1
Tysse [N] 192 B3
Tyssebotn [N] 192 B3
Tyssedal [N] 192 C4
Tystberga [S] 190 D3
Tyszki–Nadbory [PL] 38 B3
Tytuvėnai [LT] 238 C2
Tyulenovo [BG] 150 F2
Tyvsen [DK] 178 B3
Tywyn [GB] 22 D3
Tzermiádo [GR] 174 D4
Tzummarum [NL] 30 C2

Ub [SRB] 146 D2
Úbeda [E] 106 A1
Ubergsmoen [N] 186 D3
Überhamn [D] 32 A3
Überlingen [D] 70 F3
Ubľa [SK] 76 F1
Ubli [HR] 152 B2
Ubrique [E] 104 C3
Uccellina, Torre dell–' [I]
  130 E2
Ucero [E] 94 B2
Uchanie [PL] 50 D4
Uchorowo [PL] 46 F1
Uchte [D] 42 F1
Uckange [F] 56 D3
Uckfield [GB] 28 D4
Uclés [E] 100 F2
Uçmakdere [TR] 158 C4
Üçpınar [TR] 164 C4
Ucria [I] 138 B4
Udavské [SK] 76 E1
Udbina [HR] 144 D2
Udbyhøj [DK] 182 D3
Udbyhøj Vasehuse [DK]
  182 D3
Uddeholm [S] 188 E1
Uddel [NL] 30 C3
Udden [S] 188 D3
Uddevalla [S] 188 C4
Uddheden [S] 188 D1
Uden [NL] 40 F2
Udine [I] 118 E3
Údlice [CZ] 60 C2
Udorpie [PL] 36 B2
Udovo [MK] 154 E4
Údrupij [LV] 236 C2
Udvar [H] 122 B3
Ueckermünde [D] 34 D3
Ueffeln [D] 30 E3
Uelsen [D] 30 D3
Uelzen [D] 32 C4
Uetersen [D] 32 B2

Uetze [D] 44 C1
Uffenheim [D] 58 D3
Uga [E] 114 E3
Ugåle [LV] 234 D3
Ugao-Miraballes [E] 86 E3
Ugento [I] 136 E3
Ugerløse [DK] 178 E2
Uggdal [N] 192 B4
Uggerby [DK] 182 D2
Uggersjev [DK] 178 C2
Ugglarpshavsbad [S] 184 B3
Ugíjar [E] 106 A3
Ugine [F] 116 A3
Uglich [RUS] 240 F1
Ugljan [HR] 144 C3
Ugljane [HR] 144 E4
Ugny-sur-Meuse [F] 56 C4
Ugrinovci [SRB] 162 E2
Uğürchin [BG] 148 F4
Uğurluca [TR] 164 F3
Uğurlutepe [TR] 162 E2
Uherčice [CZ] 74 C1
Uherse Mineralne [PL] 64 D3
Uherské Hradiště [CZ] 74 E1
Uherský Brod [CZ] 74 E1
Uherský Ostroh [CZ] 74 E1
Uhlířské Janovice [CZ]
    60 E3
Uhniv [UA] 64 E2
Uhřínéves [CZ] 60 E3
Uhrovec [SK] 74 F2
Uhrovský Hrad [SK] 74 F2
Uhrsleben [D] 44 D2
Uhyst [D] 46 C3
Uig [GB] 14 C2
Úihartyán [H] 76 B4
Uimaharju [FIN] 210 E2
Uimila [FIN] 200 B2
Úitelep [H] 122 A2
Uithoorn [NL] 30 B3
Uithuizen [NL] 30 D2
Ujazd [PL] 48 E3
Ujazd [PL] 62 D2
Ujazd [PL] 64 C1
Újfehértó [H] 76 E3
Újiráz [H] 122 E1
Újkígyós [H] 122 E2
Újléta [H] 76 E3
Ujma Duża [PL] 48 C1
Újmajor [H] 74 E4
Újpetre [H] 122 A3
Ujście [PL] 36 A4
Újszász [H] 76 C4
Újué [E] 88 A4
Ukhovets'k [UA] 50 E3
Ukk [H] 120 E1
Ukkola [FIN] 210 E1
Ukmerge [LT] 238 D2
Ükmez [TR] 170 B2
Ukonvaara [FIN] 210 D1
Ukri [LV] 234 E4
Ukta [PL] 38 A2
Ula [BY] 240 C4
Ula [TR] 170 D4
Ul'anka [SK] 76 B2
Ulan Majorat [PL] 50 C2
Ulanów [PL] 64 D2
Ulaş [TR] 158 C3
Ulbjerg [DK] 182 C3
Ulcinj [MNE] 152 E4
Uldum [DK] 178 C1
Uleåborg / Oulu [FIN] 216 B2
Ulefoss [N] 186 E2
Uleila del Campo [E] 106 C3
Ulëzë [AL] 154 B4
Ulfborg [DK] 182 B4
Ulgardereköyü [TR] 164 A1
Ulhówek [PL] 64 E2
Úlibice [CZ] 60 F2
Ulič [SK] 76 F1
Ulinia [PL] 36 B1

Ulivar [RO] 122 D4
Uljanik [HR] 120 E4
Ul'janovo [RUS] 238 B3
Uljma [SRB] 146 E1
Ullånger [S] 206 D3
Ullapool [GB] 14 D2
Ullared [S] 184 B3
Ullatti [S] 220 F2
Ullava [FIN] 216 A4
Ulldecona [E] 96 A4
Ulldemolins [E] 96 B3
Ullene [S] 188 D4
Ullerslev [DK] 178 D2
Ullervad [S] 188 E3
Üllés [H] 122 C2
Üllő [H] 76 B4
Ulm [D] 72 A2
Ulme [P] 90 C3
Ulmen [D] 56 E2
Ulmeni [RO] 150 C2
Ulnes [N] 192 E2
Ulog [BIH] 152 D1
Ulpiana [KS] 154 C2
Ulpia Traiana [RO] 248 C3
Ulricehamn [S] 184 B1
Ulrika [S] 184 D1
Ulriksfors [S] 206 B1
Ulsberg [N] 204 A3
Ulsrud [N] 188 B1
Ulsted [DK] 182 D2
Ulsteinvik [N] 202 C3
Ulstrup [DK] 178 D2
Ulstrup [DK] 182 D4
Uluabat [TR] 164 D1
Ulubey [TR] 164 F4
Uludağ [TR] 164 E1
Ulukışla (Marathóvounos)
    [CY] 176 E3
Ulvålia [N] 194 C2
Ulvåsa [S] 188 F4
Ulverston [GB] 20 C4
Ülvesbüll [D] 32 B1
Ulvestad [N] 192 C2
Ulvik [N] 192 C3
Ulvika [N] 224 C4
Ulvila / Ulvsby [FIN] 198 C1
Ulvsby / Ulvila [FIN] 198 C1
Ulvsjön [S] 194 E2
Umag [HR] 118 E4
Uman' [UA] 244 F2
Umasjö [S] 212 F1
Umbertide [I] 132 C1
Umbukta [N] 212 E1
Umčari [SRB] 146 E2
Umeå [S] 206 F1
Umfors [S] 212 F1
Umgransele [S] 214 C3
Umhausen [A] 72 B4
Umka [SRB] 146 D2
Umkirck [D] 70 D2
Umurbey [TR] 158 E4
Umurbey [TR] 164 B2
Umurlu [TR] 170 C3
Uña [E] 102 B1
Unaja [FIN] 198 C2
Unari [FIN] 222 C2
Unbyn [S] 214 E1
Uncastillo [E] 88 B4
Undenäs [S] 188 E3
Undersåker [S] 204 D2
Undva [EST] 230 B3
Úněšov [CZ] 60 C3
Ungheni [RO] 148 F1
Unhošt' [CZ] 60 D3
Unichowo [PL] 36 B2
Uničov [CZ] 62 C3
Uniejów [PL] 48 C3
Unirea [RO] 148 D2
Unisław [PL] 36 C4
Unna [D] 42 D3
Unnaryd [S] 184 B3

Unserfrau / Madonna di
    Senales [I] 118 B2
Unset [N] 194 C1
Unsholtet [N] 204 C3
Untamala [FIN] 208 C2
Unterach [A] 72 E3
Unterbergen [A] 74 C4
Unterlüss [D] 32 C4
Unterradlberg [A] 74 C2
Unterschächen [CH] 116 D1
Unter-Schleissheim [D] 72 C2
Unteruhldingen [D] 70 F3
Unterwasser [CH] 70 F4
Unterweissenbach [A] 74 B2
Unterwössen [D] 72 D3
Untorp [S] 194 E2
Uors [CH] 116 E1
Úpice [CZ] 62 A2
Upiłka [PL] 36 B2
Upper Largo [GB] 18 E3
Upphärad [S] 188 C4
Upplands Väsby [S] 190 D2
Uppsala [S] 190 D1
Uppsete [N] 192 C3
Upyna [LT] 238 B2
Urachi, Nuraghe s'– [I] 142 B4
Uraiújfalu [H] 74 D4
Úras [I] 142 B4
Ura Vajgurore [AL] 160 B2
Urbánia [I] 128 E4
Urbeis [F] 70 D2
Úrbel del Castillo [E] 86 C3
Urbino [I] 128 E4
Urbise [F] 80 C1
Urbø [S] 186 D1
Urçay [F] 68 B4
Urda [E] 100 E2
Urdaibai [E] 86 E3
Urdari [RO] 148 D1
Urdos [F] 88 B3
Urechești [RO] 148 E1
Uriage–les–Bains [F] 80 E4
Uriz / Arze–Arce [E] 88 A3
Urjala [FIN] 198 D2
Urjalankylä [FIN] 198 D2
Urk [NL] 30 C3
Úrkút [H] 120 F1
Urla [TR] 168 F1
Urlingford [IRL] 10 D3
Urnäsch [CH] 70 F4
Urnes [N] 192 D2
Uroševac [KS] 154 C3
Urpila [FIN] 208 E1
Urroz [E] 88 A3
Urshult [S] 184 D4
Ursus [PL] 48 F2
Urtimjaur [S] 220 E3
Ürünlü [TR] 158 B2
Ururi [I] 134 D2
Ury [F] 54 E4
Urzędów [PL] 50 B4
Urzelina [P] 110 B3
Urziceni [RO] 76 F3
Urzicuța [RO] 148 D2
Urzulei [I] 142 C4
Usagre [E] 98 F3
Uşak [TR] 164 F4
Uŝče [SRB] 146 E4
Uŝcie Gorlickie [PL] 64 B3
Usedom [D] 34 D2
Uséllus [I] 142 B4
Useras / les Useres [E] 102 E2
Ushakovo [RUS] 36 E1
Uŝi [MK] 154 D4
Uŝinci [BG] 150 C3
Usingen [D] 58 B2
Uskali [TR] 162 C4
Uskedal [N] 192 B4
Uski [FIN] 200 C3
Uskopolie [BIH] 144 F3
Üsküdar [TR] 158 E3
Üsküp [TR] 158 B2

Usküpdere [TR] 158 B2
Uslar [D] 44 B3
Usma [LV] 234 D3
Usmate Velate [I] 116 E3
Úsov [CZ] 62 B3
Uspen'ye [RUS] 240 B3
Ussé [F] 66 E3
Usseglio [I] 116 B4
Ussel [F] 80 A2
Ussel [I] 116 C3
Usseln [D] 42 E3
Usson–du–Poitou [F] 78 D1
Usson–en–Forez [F] 80 C3
Usson–les–Bains [F] 88 F4
Ustaoset [N] 192 D3
Ustaritz [F] 88 B2
Uŝtĕk [CZ] 60 D2
Uster [CH] 70 E4
Ústí [CZ] 62 B4
Ustibar [BIH] 146 C4
Ústí nad Labem [CZ] 60 D2
Ústí nad Orlicí [CZ] 62 B3
Ustipraĉa [BIH] 146 C4
Ustje [RUS] 232 E1
Ustjuzha [RUS] 240 E1
Utĺáker [N] 192 B4
Utansjö [S] 206 D3
Utbjoa [N] 186 B1
Utebo [E] 94 D3
Utena [LT] 238 E2
Utersum [D] 178 A3
Úterý [CZ] 60 C3
Uthlede [D] 32 A3
Utiel [E] 102 C3
Utne [N] 192 C3
Utrecht [NL] 30 B4
Utrera [E] 104 C2
Utrillas [E] 94 D4
Utrine [SRB] 122 C3
Utsjö [S] 194 E3
Utsjoki [FIN] 228 D3
Utstein [N] 186 A2
Uttendorf [A] 72 D4
Uttendorf [A] 72 E3
Uttermossa [FIN] 208 B3
Uttersberg [S] 190 B2
Utti [FIN] 200 C2
Utting [D] 72 C3
Uttoxeter [GB] 24 B3
Utula [FIN] 200 D1
Utvalnäs [S] 196 D3
Utvängstorp [S] 184 C1
Utvik [N] 202 C4
Utvorda [N] 212 C3
Uukuniemen Kk. [FIN] 210 E3
Uukuniemi [FIN] 210 E4
Uulu [EST] 230 D3
Uurainen [FIN] 208 F1
Uuro [FIN] 208 C3
Uuro [FIN] 210 E2
Uuro [FIN] 216 E4
Uusijoki [FIN] 226 C2
Uusikaarlepyy / Nykarleby
    [FIN] 208 C1
Uusikartano [FIN] 198 C2
Uusikaupunki / Nystad [FIN]
    198 C2
Uusikylä [FIN] 200 B2

Uusi–Värtsilä [FIN] 210 E3
Uutela [FIN] 226 D4
Uva [FIN] 216 D2
Uvac [BIH] 146 C4
Úvaly [CZ] 60 E3
Uvanå [S] 194 E4
Uvarovka [RUS] 240 E3
Uvdal [N] 192 E4
Uvernet–Fours [F] 126 B2
Uyeasound [GB] 16 F3
Uzdowo [PL] 36 E3
Uzel [F] 52 C3
Uzerche [F] 78 E3
Uzès [F] 124 D2
Uzeste [F] 78 C4
Uzhhorod [UA] 76 F2
Uzhots'kyi, Pereval– [UA]
    64 F4
Užice [SRB] 146 D3
Uzlovoye [RUS] 238 B3
Uŝpaliai [LT] 238 E2
Üzümlü [TR] 176 D1
Uzunköprü [TR] 158 A3
Uzunkuyu [TR] 168 F1
Uzunpınar [TR] 170 E2
Uŝventis [LT] 238 B2

Vå [N] 186 D1
Vå [S] 180 D1
Vaajakoski [FIN] 208 F3
Vaajasalmi [FIN] 210 B2
Vääkiö [FIN] 216 D1
Vääksy [FIN] 198 F2
Vaala [FIN] 216 C2
Vaalajärvi [FIN] 222 C1
Vaalimaa [FIN] 200 C3
Vaaljoki [FIN] 198 C2
Vaarakylä [FIN] 216 E3
Vaaraniva [FIN] 216 D1
Väärinmaja [FIN] 208 E4
Vaas [F] 66 E2
Vaasa / Vasa [FIN] 208 B2
Vaassen [NL] 30 C3
Väättäiskylä [FIN] 208 E2
Vabalninkas [LT] 236 B4
Vabres–l'Abbaye [F] 124 B2
Vác [H] 76 B3
Vacha [D] 44 C4
Váchartyán [H] 76 B3
Väckelsäng [S] 184 D3
Vad [S] 190 B1
Vadaktai [LT] 238 D2
Vădastra [RO] 148 E2
Vadépuszta [H] 120 F2
Väderstad [S] 188 F4
Vadheim [N] 192 B2
Vadili (Vatili) [CY] 176 E3
Vadna [H] 76 C2
Vadokliai [LT] 238 D2
Vado Ligure [I] 126 D2
Vadsø [N] 228 E2
Vadstena [S] 188 F4
Vaduz [FL] 70 F4
Væggerløse [DK] 32 E1
Vafaïika [GR] 156 D4
Vafiochóri [GR] 156 A4
Våg [H] 74 E4
Våga [N] 186 A2
Vågåmo [N] 192 E1
Vagan [BIH] 144 E3
Våge [N] 186 A1
Våge [N] 186 C4
Våge [N] 192 B4
Våge [N] 202 D3
Vågen [N] 202 E1
Vägeva [EST] 230 D2
Vaggeryd [S] 184 C2

Vaggsvik [N] 224 C3
Vágia [GR] 166 F3
Vagiónia [GR] 174 D4
Vaglio Basilicata [I] 134 F4
Vagnhärad [S] 190 D3
Vagos [P] 84 A3
Vågsbygd [N] 186 D4
Vägsele [S] 214 B3
Vägsjöfors [S] 194 D4
Vågslid [N] 186 C1
Vähäkyrö / Lillkyro [FIN]
   208 C2
Vahanka [FIN] 208 E2
Vahastu [EST] 230 D2
Vaheri [FIN] 208 F4
Väi [GR] 174 F3
Vaiano [I] 128 C3
Vaiges [F] 54 A4
Vaiguva [LT] 238 C2
Vaihingen [D] 58 B4
Väike-Maarja [EST] 230 E2
Väike Rakke [EST] 230 E3
Vaikko [FIN] 210 D1
Vailly [F] 54 F2
Vailly [F] 68 C2
Vainikkala [FIN] 200 D2
Vainupea [EST] 230 E1
Vainutas [LT] 238 B2
Vaison-la-Romaine [F] 124 E2
Vaite [F] 70 B3
Vaja [H] 76 E3
Vajmat [S] 220 D3
Vajnede [LV] 234 D4
Vajont [I] 118 D3
Vajszló [H] 120 F3
Vajtešin [BY] 38 E4
Vajzë [AL] 160 B3
Vakarel [BG] 156 B1
Vakern [S] 194 E4
Vakiflar [TR] 158 C3
Vaksdal [N] 192 B3
Vaksevo [BG] 154 F3
Vakumonë [AL] 160 B1
Vålådalen [S] 204 D2
Valajanaapa [FIN] 222 C4
Valajaskoski [FIN] 222 C3
Valandovo [MK] 156 A4
Valanhamn [N] 224 F1
Valareña [E] 88 A4
Valaská Belá [SK] 74 F1
Valašská Polanka [CZ] 62 D4
Valašské Klobouky [CZ] 74 F1
Valašské Meziříčí [CZ] 62 D4
Valbella [CH] 116 E1
Valberg [F] 126 B2
Vålberg [S] 188 D2
Valbiska [HR] 144 B1
Valbo [S] 196 C3
Valbondione [I] 116 F3
Valbonë [AL] 154 B2
Valbonnais [F] 80 E4
Vâlcani [RO] 122 D3
Valcarlos / Luzaide [E] 88 B3
Val-Claret [F] 116 B3
Valcum [H] 120 E2
Valdagno [I] 118 B3
Valdahon [F] 70 B4
Valdaj [RUS] 240 D2
Valdalen [N] 204 C4
Valday [RUS] 240 D2
Valdeazores [E] 100 C2
Valdecaballeros [E] 100 C2
Valdecabras [E] 102 B2
Valdecarros [E] 92 C3
Valdedios [E] 86 A1
Valdeganga [E] 102 B3
Valdeinfierno [E] 100 B4
Valdelacas de Tajo [E] 100 C1
Val del Charco del Agua
   Amarga, Cueva de la- [E]
   94 E4
Valdeltormo [E] 94 E4

Valdemadera [E] 94 C2
Valdemärpils [LV] 234 E2
Valdemarsvik [S] 190 C4
Valdemorillo [E] 92 E3
Valdemoro [E] 92 E4
Valdemoro Sierra [E] 102 B2
Valdenoceda [E] 86 D2
Valdepeñas [E] 100 E3
Valdepeñas de Jaén [E] 104 F2
Valdepolo [E] 86 A3
Valderas [E] 84 F2
Valderice [I] 140 B2
Valderoure [F] 126 B3
Valderöy [N] 202 C3
Valderrobres [E] 96 A3
Valdesalor [E] 90 F3
Val d'Esquières [F] 126 B4
Valdeverdeja [E] 100 C1
Valdgale [LV] 234 E2
Valdieri [I] 126 C2
Val d'Isère [F] 116 B3
Val-d'Izé [F] 52 E4
Valdobbiádene [I] 118 C3
Valdoviño [E] 82 C1
Valdštejn [CZ] 60 E2
Valdunquillo [E] 84 F2
Valea Argovei [RO] 150 C1
Valea lui Mihai [RO] 150 C1
Valea lui Mihai [RO] 76 F4
Valea Rea [RO] 150 E2
Valebø [N] 186 E2
Valečov [CZ] 60 E2
Vale da Rosa [P] 98 C4
Vale de Açor [P] 98 C3
Vale de Cambra [P] 84 A3
Vale de Lobos [P] 98 B4
Vale de Santarém [P] 90 B3
Vale do Arco [P] 90 D3
Vale do Côa, Parque
   Arqueológico do- [P] 84 C3
Vale do Poço [P] 98 D3
Vålega [P] 84 A3
Valéggio sul Míncio [I] 118 B4
Valen [N] 192 B4
Valença do Minho [P] 82 A4
Valençay [F] 68 A3
Valence [F] 80 D4
Valence [F] 88 E2
Valence d'Albigeois [F] 124 B2
Valence-sur-Baïse [F] 88 D2
València [E] 102 D3
Valencia de Alcántara [E] 90 E3
Valencia de Don Juan [E]
   84 F2
Valencia de las Torres [E]
   98 F3
Valencia del Ventoso [E] 98 E3
Valencia de Mombuey [E]
   98 D2
Valenciennes [F] 40 C4
Văleni [RO] 148 F2
Vălenii de Munte [RO] 248 E3
Valensole [F] 126 A3
Valentano [I] 130 E2
Valentigney [F] 70 C3
Valenza [I] 116 D4
Våler [N] 188 B2
Våler [N] 194 C3
Valeria [I] 102 B2
Vales Mortos [P] 98 D3
Valevåg [N] 186 B1
Valfábbrica [I] 132 D2
Valga [EST] 230 E4
Valgeristi [EST] 230 C2
Valgrisenche [I] 116 B3
Välijoki [FIN] 200 C2
Välijoki [FIN] 212 C3
Välikyla [FIN] 216 A4
Valimítika [GR] 166 E4
Väliug [RO] 122 F4

Välivaara [FIN] 210 E1
Valjevo [SRB] 146 D3
Valjimena [E] 92 C3
Valjok [N] 226 C1
Valka [LV] 230 E4
Valkeajärvi [FIN] 208 E3
Valkeakoski [FIN] 198 E1
Valkeala [FIN] 200 B2
Valkeavaara [FIN] 210 E3
Valkenburg [NL] 40 F4
Valkenswaard [NL] 40 F3
Valkiamäki [FIN] 200 D1
Valkininkai [LT] 238 E4
Valko / Valkom [FIN]
   200 B3
Valkom / Valko [FIN] 200 B3
Valla [S] 204 E2
Valla [S] 206 B2
Vallada [E] 82 E3
Valladolid [E] 92 D1
Vállaj [H] 76 F3
Vallåkra [S] 178 F1
Vallargärdet [S] 188 E2
Vallata [I] 134 E3
Vallbona de les Monges
   [E] 96 C3
Valldal [N] 202 D3
Valldemossa [E] 108 C3
Valle [LV] 236 B3
Valle [N] 186 C2
Valle de Abdalajís [E] 104 D3
Valle de Cabuérniga [E] 86 C2
Valle dei Templi [I] 140 C3
Valle de la Serena [E] 100 A3
Valle de los Caídos [E] 92 E3
Valle de Matamoros [E] 98 E2
Valledoria [I] 142 B2
Vallehermoso [E] 112 C2
Vallelunga Pratameno [I]
   138 A4
Vallen [S] 206 B2
Vallentuna [S] 190 D2
Valleraugue [F] 124 C2
Vallet [F] 66 C2
Valletta [M] 140 C4
Vallfogona de Ripollès [E]
   96 E2
Vallheim [N] 212 E3
Vallivana [E] 96 A4
Vallo di Lucania [I] 136 A3
Valloire [F] 80 F4
Valloires, Abbaye de- [F]
   40 A4
Vallombrosa [I] 128 C3
Vallon-en-Sully [F] 68 B4
Vallon-Pont-d'Arc [F] 124 D1
Vallorbe [CH] 116 A1
Vallorcine [F] 116 B2
Valla Slot [DK] 178 E2
Vallouise [F] 80 F4
Vallrun [S] 204 E1
Valls [E] 96 C3
Vallsbo [S] 196 C3
Vallset [N] 194 C3
Vallsta [S] 196 C2
Vallter 2000 [E] 96 E1
Vallvik [S] 196 D2
Valmadrid [E] 94 D3
Valmiera [LV] 230 D4
Valmigère [F] 124 A3
Valmojado [E] 92 D4
Valmontone [I] 132 D4
Valmorel [F] 80 F3
Val Moutier [CH] 70 D3
Valö [S] 196 D4
Valognes [F] 52 F2
Valongo [P] 84 A2
Valoria la Buena [E] 92 E1
Valøy [N] 212 C3
Valøya [N] 212 C4
Valozhyn [BY] 238 F4
Valpaços [P] 84 C2

Valpelline [I] 116 B3
Valporquero de Torío [E] 82 F3
Valpovo [HR] 122 A4
Valras-Plage [F] 124 C3
Valréas [F] 124 E2
Vals [CH] 116 E2
Valsamónero [GR] 174 C4
Valsavaranche [I] 116 B3
Valsebo [S] 188 C3
Valset [N] 202 F1
Valsinni [I] 136 C3
Valsjöbyn [S] 212 E4
Valsjön [S] 206 B4
Valskog [S] 190 B2
Vals-les-Bains [F] 80 C4
Valsøybotn [N] 202 F2
Vålsta [S] 196 D1
Val-Suzon [F] 68 E3
Valtesíniko [GR] 172 D2
Val Thorens [F] 116 A3
Valtiendas [E] 92 E2
Valtierra [E] 88 A4
Valtimo [FIN] 216 D4
Valtola [FIN] 200 C2
Váltos [GR] 156 F3
Valtournenche [I] 116 C3
Valvanera, Monasterio de-
   [E] 94 B1
Valverde [E] 112 A2
Valverde, Santuario di- [I]
   142 B3
Valverde de Cervera [E] 94 C2
Valverde de Júcar [E] 102 B2
Valverde del Camino [E] 98 D4
Valverde de Leganés [E] 98 E2
Valverde del Fresno [E] 90 E2
Valywewka [BY] 38 F2
Valzul [A] 118 A1
Vama Veche [RO] 150 F2
Vamberk [CZ] 62 B3
Vamdrup [DK] 178 B2
Våmhus [S] 194 E2
Vamlingbo [S] 234 A3
Vammala [FIN] 198 D1
Vámos [GR] 174 B3
Vámosmikola [H] 76 A3
Vámospércs [H] 76 E4
Vámosszabadi [H] 74 E3
Vampula [FIN] 198 D2
Vandoies / Vintl [I] 118 C2
Vändra [EST] 230 D3
Vandžegala [LT] 238 D3
Väne [LV] 234 E3
Vanebu [N] 186 E2
Vänersborg [S] 188 C4
Väne-Ryr [S] 188 C4
Vaneskoski [FIN] 208 C4
Vånga [S] 180 D1
Vangaži [LV] 236 B3
Vängel [S] 206 B1
Vangså [DK] 182 C2
Vänjaurbäck [S] 214 C3
Vänju Mare [RO] 148 C2
Vankiva [S] 180 D1
Vännacka [S] 188 C2
Vännäs [S] 206 E1

Vännäsberget [S] 222 A3
Vännäsby [S] 206 E1
Vannes [F] 66 B1
Vansbro [S] 194 E3
Vanse [N] 186 B4
Vansjö [S] 190 C1
Vänsjö [S] 194 F1
Vanstad [S] 180 D2
Vantaa / Vanda [FIN] 198 F3
Vanttauskoski [FIN] 222 D3
Vanvik [N] 186 B1
Vanvikan [N] 204 B1
Vanyarc [H] 76 B3
Vaplan [S] 204 E2
Vara [EST] 230 E3
Vara [S] 188 D4
Varabla [EST] 230 C3
Varades [F] 66 C2
Varages [F] 124 F3
Varakläni [LV] 236 D3
Varaldsøy [S] 192 B4
Varallo [I] 116 D3
Varanava [BY] 38 E1
Varangerbotn [N] 228 E2
Varano de' Melegari [I] 128 A2
Väräşti [RO] 150 C1
Varaždin [HR] 120 D3
Varaždinske Toplice [HR]
   120 D3
Varazze [I] 126 E2
Varberg [S] 184 A3
Várbola [EST] 230 C3
Vărbovo [BG] 156 E2
Varbyane [BG] 150 D3
Varces [F] 80 E4
Várda [GR] 166 D4
Varde [DK] 178 A2
Vardim [BG] 150 B3
Vardište [BIH] 146 C4
Vårdö [FIN] 198 B3
Vardø [N] 228 F2
Vårdomb [II] 122 B3
Värdsberg [S] 190 B4
Varduva [LT] 234 D4
Varekil [S] 188 C4
Varel [D] 30 F2
Varellaíoi [GR] 168 C2
Varena [LT] 38 E1
Varengeville-sur-Mer [F]
   54 C1
Varenna [I] 116 E3
Varennes-en-Argonne [F]
   56 C3
Varennes-sur-Allier [F] 80 C1
Vareš [BIH] 146 B3
Varese [I] 116 D3
Varese Ligure [I] 126 F2
Vårgårda [S] 184 B1
Vargön [S] 188 C4
Vargträsk [S] 214 C3
Varhaug [N] 186 A3
Várhus [N] 204 B3
Vári [GR] 168 D3
Varias [RO] 122 D3
Varilhes [F] 88 E3
Varín [SK] 62 E4
Väring [S] 188 F4
Váris [GR] 160 D3
Varjakka [FIN] 216 B2
Varjisträsk [S] 220 D4
Varkaus [FIN] 210 C3
Várkiza [GR] 168 B3
Varland [N] 186 D1
Värmdö [S] 190 E2
Värmlandsbro [S] 188 D2
Varmo [I] 118 E3
Värmskog [S] 188 D2
Varna [BG] 150 F3
Varna [SRB] 146 C2
Varna (Vahrn) [I] 118 C2
Varnamo [S] 184 C2
Varnany [BY] 238 F3

Varnhem [S] 188 E4
Varniai [LT] 238 B2
Varnja [EST] 230 F3
Varnsdorf [CZ] 60 E1
Varntresk [N] 212 E1
Väröbacka [S] 184 A2
Väroserdö [H] 122 E2
Városföld [H] 122 C2
Varoška Rijeka [BIH] 144 D1
Városlőd [H] 120 E1
Varovnik [BG] 158 B1
Varp [S] 188 B3
Varpaisjärvi [FIN] 210 C1
Várpalota [H] 120 F1
Varpanen [FIN] 200 B1
Varparanta [FIN] 210 D3
Varparanta [FIN] 210 E2
Varpsjö [S] 214 A3
Värriö [FIN] 222 D1
Vars [F] 126 B1
Vårşand [RO] 122 E2
Värsås [S] 188 E4
Varshko [RUS] 200 E2
Varsi [I] 128 A2
Värska [EST] 230 F3
Varsseveld [NL] 30 D4
Vartdal [N] 202 C3
Vartemyagi [RUS] 200 F3
Vartius [FIN] 216 E2
Vårtopu [RO] 148 D2
Värtsilä [FIN] 210 F3
Varv [S] 188 F4
Varvara [BG] 156 C2
Varvara [BG] 158 C1
Varvára [GR] 162 B1
Varzi [I] 126 F1
Varzy [F] 68 D3
Vasa / Vaasa [FIN] 208 B2
Vasalemma [EST] 230 C2
Vasankari [FIN] 216 A3
Vasarapera [FIN] 222 E3
Vasarás [GR] 172 D2
Vásárosnamény [H] 76 F3
Vasbotna [N] 212 D3
Väse [S] 188 E2
Vasiláki [GR] 172 C2
Vasilevo [BG] 150 E2
Vasil'evskoye [RUS] 236 F2
Vasiliká [GR] 162 B2
Vasiliká [GR] 162 B4
Vasiliká [GR] 164 A3
Vasilikí [GR] 166 B3
Vasilikó [GR] 168 B2
Vasilikós [GR] 172 B2
Vasilíshki [BY] 38 E2
Vasilítsi [GR] 172 C3
Vasil Levski [BG] 156 E2
Vasil'yevo [RUS] 232 E4
Vaškai [LT] 236 B4
Vaskelovo [RUS] 200 F3
Vaskio [FIN] 198 D3
Vaskivesi [FIN] 208 D3
Vasknarva [EST] 230 F2
Vaskút [H] 122 B3
Vasles [F] 66 E4
Vaslui [RO] 244 E3
Vassbø [N] 186 B3
Vassbotten [S] 188 C3
Vassenden [N] 192 C1
Vassenden [N] 192 C2
Vásses [GR] 172 C2
Vassli [N] 202 F2
Vassmolösa [S] 184 E4
Vassnäs [S] 204 D1
Vasstrand [N] 224 D2
Vassurány [H] 74 D4
Vassy [F] 52 F3
Västan [S] 206 C4
Västansfors [S] 190 B1
Västansjö [S] 206 C3
Västansjö [S] 212 F1

Västansjö [S] 212 F2
Västansjö [S] 214 B3
Västansjön [S] 206 C4
Västbacka [S] 194 F2
Västbacken [S] 204 E2
Västeräker [S] 190 D2
Väster–Arådalen [S] 204 E3
Västerås [S] 190 C2
Västerby [S] 190 D3
Västerfärnebo [S] 190 C1
Västergärn [S] 234 A2
Västerhaninge [S] 190 D3
Västerhus [S] 206 D2
Västermyckeläng [S] 194 E2
Västermyrriset [S] 214 B3
Västerrottna [S] 188 D1
Västersel [S] 206 D2
Västervik [S] 184 F2
Vastila [FIN] 200 B3
Västillä [FIN] 208 E4
Västland [S] 196 D4
Vasto [I] 134 D1
Västra Yttermark [FIN] 208 B3
Västrum [S] 184 E2
Vasvár [H] 120 D1
Vasylivka [UA] 246 F2
Vasyl'kiv [UA] 242 D4
Vasyl'kivka [UA] 246 D3
Vát [H] 74 D4
Vatan [F] 68 B3
Vaterá [GR] 164 A4
Váthi [GR] 156 B4
Vathiý [GR] 168 A2
Vathý [GR] 170 B3
Vathý [GR] 174 E1
Vathýlakkos [GR] 156 C3
Vathýlakkos [GR] 160 E3
Vathýpetro [GR] 174 D4
Vatili (Vadili) [CY] 176 E3
Vatin [SRB] 146 E1
Vatne [N] 186 B2
Vatne [N] 186 D3
Vatne [N] 202 C3
Vatnstraum [N] 186 D3
Vatólakkos [GR] 160 D3
Vatopedíou, Moní– [GR] 162 C2
Vatoúsa [GR] 162 F3
Vatra Dornei [RO] 244 D3
Vatta [H] 76 D3
Vättershus [S] 184 C1
Vattjom [S] 206 C4
Vattlång [S] 196 C1
Vattnäs [S] 194 F3
Vatvet [N] 188 C2
Vau [P] 98 B4
Vaucelles, Abbaye de– [F] 54 F1
Vauclaix [F] 68 D3
Vaucluse [F] 70 C3
Vaucouleurs [F] 56 C4
Vaudoy en Brie [F] 54 E4
Vau i Dejës [AL] 152 F4
Vauldalen [N] 204 C3
Vauvenargues [F] 124 F3
Vauvert [F] 124 D3
Vauville [F] 52 E1
Vauvillers [F] 70 B2
Vaux–Le Vicomte [F] 54 E4
Vavylás (Güzelyalı) [CY] 176 D3
Vawkavysk [BY] 38 E3
Vaxholm [S] 190 E2
Växjö [S] 184 D3
Växtorp [S] 184 B4
Vayrac [F] 78 E4
Vaysal [TR] 158 B2
Važecká Jaskyňa [SK] 76 C1
V. Bodarna [S] 184 B1
Vean [N] 202 E2
Vebbestrup [DK] 182 D3

Veberöd [S] 180 C2
Veblungsnes [N] 202 D3
Vebomark [S] 214 D3
Vecbebri [LV] 236 C3
Večelkov [SK] 76 C3
Vechta [D] 30 F3
Vecilla de Valderaduey [E] 86 B3
Vecinos [E] 84 E4
Veckholm [S] 190 D2
Vecpiebalga [LV] 236 C3
Vecsés [H] 76 B4
Vecumnieki [LV] 236 B3
Veda [S] 206 D3
Vedavågen [N] 186 A2
Vedbæk [DK] 178 F2
Veddelev [DK] 178 E2
Veddige [S] 184 A2
Věde [LV] 234 D2
Vedea [RO] 150 B2
Vedelago [I] 118 C3
Vedersø Klit [DK] 182 B4
Vedevåg [S] 188 F2
Vedjeön [S] 212 F4
Vedum [S] 188 D4
Veendam [NL] 30 D2
Veenendaal [NL] 30 C4
Veere [NL] 40 D2
Vegacervera [E] 82 F3
Vega de Espinareda [E] 82 D3
Vega de los Árboles [E] 100 F3
Vegadeo [E] 82 D2
Vega de Pas [E] 86 C3
Vega de Valcarce [E] 82 D3
Vegårshei [N] 186 E3
Vegas de Coria [E] 92 B3
Vegas del Condado [E] 82 F4
Vegger [DK] 182 D3
Veggli [N] 192 E4
Veghel [NL] 40 F2
Veglie [I] 136 E3
Vegset [N] 212 D4
Vegusdal [N] 186 D3
Vehkajärvi [FIN] 198 E1
Vehkalah [FIN] 200 B1
Vehkaperä [FIN] 208 E2
Vehmaa [FIN] 198 C3
Vehmaa [FIN] 210 C4
Vehmasjärvi [FIN] 216 D4
Vehmasmäki [FIN] 210 C2
Vehmersalmi [FIN] 210 C2
Vehniä [FIN] 208 F3
Vehu [FIN] 208 E2
Vehuvarpee [FIN] 208 C4
Veidholmen [N] 202 E1
Veidnesklubben [N] 228 C2
Veikkola [FIN] 198 E3
Veinge [S] 184 B4
Veio [I] 130 F3
Veiros [P] 90 D4
Veisiejai [LT] 38 D1
Veitshöchheim [D] 58 D3
Vejano [I] 130 F3
Vejby [S] 178 E1
Vejbystrand [S] 178 F1
Vejen [DK] 178 B2
Vejer de la Frontera [E] 104 B3
Vejers Strand [DK] 178 A2
Vejinac [BIH] 144 D1
Vejle [DK] 178 C2
Vejprty [CZ] 60 C2
Vekilski [BG] 150 D2
Velada [E] 92 C4
Velagići [BIH] 144 E2
Vela Luka [HR] 152 C3
Velanídia [GR] 172 E4
Velas [P] 110 B3
Velbert [D] 42 D3
Velburg [D] 58 F4
Velbuzhdki Pateka (Velbuzhdki Prolaz) [BG/MK] 154 E3

Velbuzhdki Prolaz (Velbuzhdki Pateka) [BG/MK] 154 E3
Velchevo [BG] 150 A4
Velden [A] 118 F2
Velden [D] 58 F3
Velden [D] 72 D2
Veldhoven [NL] 40 F3
Velebit [SRB] 122 C3
Velefigue [E] 106 B3
Velehrad [CZ] 74 E1
Velēna [LV] 236 D2
Velence [H] 76 A4
Velenje [SLO] 120 B2
Velešín [CZ] 74 A2
Velešta [MK] 160 C1
Velestíno [GR] 162 A3
Vélez–Blanco [E] 106 C2
Vélez–Málaga [E] 104 E3
Vélez–Rubio [E] 106 C2
Velgošti [MK] 160 C1
Vel. Grđevac [HR] 120 E3
Velhartice [CZ] 60 C4
Vel. Horozhanka [UA] 64 F3
Veličani [BIH] 152 D2
Velika [HR] 120 E4
Velika Brusnica [BIH] 146 A1
Velika Dapčevica [HR] 120 E4
Velika Drenova [SRB] 146 F4
Velika Gorica [HR] 120 D3
Velika Kladuša [HR] 144 D1
Velika Kopanica [HR] 146 B1
Velika Kruša [KS] 154 C3
Velika Plana [SRB] 146 E3
Velika Remeta, Manastir– [SRB] 146 D1
Velika Slatina [KS] 154 C2
Velike Lašče [SLO] 120 B3
Veliki Gradište [SRB] 146 F2
Veliki Preslav [BG] 150 D3
Veliki Šiljegovac [SRB] 146 F4
Veliki Tabor [HR] 120 C3
Velikiye Luki [RUS] 240 C3
Veliki Zdenci [HR] 120 E4
Veliko Orašje [SRB] 146 E2
Veliko Tŭrnovo [BG] 150 B3
Velí Lošinj [HR] 144 B2
Velimlje [MNE] 152 E2
Velingrad [BG] 156 C2
Velipojë [AL] 152 F4
Veliternë [AL] 160 C2
Velizh [RUS] 240 C3
Veljun [HR] 144 C1
Velka Biteš [CZ] 62 B4
Velká Hleď'sebe [CZ] 60 B3
Velká nad Veličkou [CZ] 74 E1
Velké Bílovice [CZ] 74 D2
Velké Brezno [CZ] 60 D2
Velké Heraltice [CZ] 62 C3
Velké Kapušany [SK] 76 E2
Velké Karlovice [CZ] 62 D4
Vel'ké Levére [SK] 74 D2
Velké Losiny [CZ] 62 C3
Velké Meziříčí [CZ] 60 F4
Velké Němčice [CZ] 74 D1
Velké Opatovice [CZ] 62 B3
Vel'ké Raškovce [SK] 76 E2
Vel'ké Ripňany [SK] 74 F2
Velké Uherce [SK] 76 A2
Velkua [FIN] 198 C3
Velký Beranov [CZ] 60 F4
Velký Bor [CZ] 60 C4
Velký Folkmar [SK] 76 D1
Vel'ký Krtíš [SK] 76 B3
Vel'ký Meder [SK] 74 E3
Vel'ký Šariš [SK] 76 D1
Velký Újezd [CZ] 62 C3
Velle [N] 202 C3
Velleclaire [F] 70 B3
Velleia [I] 128 A1
Velles [F] 68 A3
Velletri [I] 132 D4

Vellinge [S] 178 F2
Vel. Ljubin [UA] 64 E3
Velp [NL] 30 C4
Velpke [D] 44 D2
Velta [N] 194 C3
Vel. Trnovac [SRB] 154 D2
Veltrusy [CZ] 60 D2
Veluće [SRB] 146 F4
Velušina [MK] 160 D2
Velvary [CZ] 60 D2
Velventós [GR] 160 E3
Vel'ye [RUS] 236 E2
Velyka Hlusha [UA] 50 E2
Velyka Lepetykha [UA] 246 E2
Velyki Mosty [UA] 64 F2
Velykyi Bereznyi [UA] 76 F1
Vemb [DK] 182 B3
Vemdalen [S] 204 E3
Vemhán [S] 204 E4
Vemmelev [DK] 178 D2
Vemmenæs [DK] 178 D3
Ven [N] 186 B3
Vena [S] 184 E2
Venabu [N] 192 F1
Venaco [F] 130 B2
Venafro [I] 134 C2
Venäjä [FIN] 198 D2
Venaria Reale [I] 116 C4
Venåsen [N] 192 F1
Včančane [SRB] 146 E2
Vence [F] 126 C3
Venda Nova [P] 84 B2
Vendargues [F] 124 D3
Vendas de Galizes [P] 84 B4
Vendas Novas [P] 90 B4
Vendays–Montalivet [F] 78 B2
Vendel [S] 190 D1
Vendelsö [S] 190 E2
Vendeuvre [F] 68 E1
Vendinha [E] 98 D2
Vendôme [F] 68 A1
Vendranges [F] 80 C2
Veneheitto [FIN] 216 C3
Veneskoski [FIN] 208 D2
Venetpalo [FIN] 216 B3
Venets [BG] 150 D4
Venets [BG] 150 D2
Venets [BG] 156 E2
Venevere [EST] 230 E2
Venézia [I] 118 D4
Venialbo [E] 84 E3
Venjan [S] 194 E3
Venlo [NL] 42 C3
Venn [N] 204 B2
Vénna [GR] 156 E4
Vennesla [N] 186 D4
Vennesund [N] 212 D2
Venngarn [S] 190 D2
Venosa [I] 134 E3
Venoy [N] 168 D2
Venray [NL] 42 B2
Vent [A] 118 B1
Venta de Arraco [E] 88 B3
Venta de Baños [E] 92 E1
Venta del Moro [E] 102 C3
Venta de los Santos [E] 100 E4
Venta del Pobre [E] 106 C3
Ventadour, Château de– [F] 78 F3
Venta el Alto [E] 98 E4
Venta Nueva [E] 82 D3
Ventas de Huelma [E] 104 E3
Ventas de Zefarraya [E] 104 E3
Venté [I] 132 B2
Ventimíglia [I] 126 C3
Ventiseri [F] 130 B3
Ventnor [GB] 28 B4
Vento, Grotta del– [I] 128 B3
Ventosa de Pisuerga [E] 86 B3
Ventspils [LV] 234 D2
Venus [RO] 150 F2
Venzone [I] 118 E2

Vepsä [FIN] 216 B2
Vera [E] 106 C3
Vera [N] 204 D1
Vera de Bidasoa / Bera [E] 86 F3
Vera de Moncayo [E] 94 C2
Verba [UA] 50 E4
Verbania [I] 116 D3
Verberie [F] 54 E2
Verbicaro [I] 136 B4
Verbier [CH] 116 B2
Vercelli [I] 116 D4
Verch. Syn'ovydne [UA] 64 E4
Verdalsøra [N] 204 C1
Verdelles, Château de– [F] 54 A4
Verden [D] 32 B4
Verdenberg [CH] 70 F4
Verdens Ende [N] 186 F2
Verdikoússa [GR] 160 E4
Verdun [F] 56 C3
Verea [E] 82 B4
Vereja [RUS] 240 E3
Veresegyház [H] 76 B3
Vereya [RUS] 240 E3
Verfeil [F] 88 F3
Vergato [I] 128 C3
Vergeletto [CH] 116 D2
Verghia [F] 130 A3
Vergi [EST] 230 E1
Vérgi [GR] 156 B4
Vergiate [I] 116 D3
Vergína [GR] 160 E2
Vergt [F] 78 D3
Verguleasa [RO] 148 E1
Verh. Osel'ki [RUS] 200 F3
Verín [E] 82 C4
Verinsko [BG] 156 B1
Verket [N] 186 F2
Verkhn'odniprovs'k [UA] 246 E1
Verl [D] 42 E2
Verma [N] 202 D3
Vermafoss [N] 202 D3
Vermenton [F] 68 D2
Vermeş [RO] 122 E4
Vermiglio [I] 118 B2
Vermosh [AL] 152 F3
Vermuntila [FIN] 198 C2
Vernazza [I] 126 F3
Vern–d'Anjou [F] 66 D2
Vernes [N] 202 F1
Vernet [F] 88 E3
Vernet–les–Bains [F] 96 E1
Verneuil–sur–Avre [F] 54 C3
Verningen [N] 186 F2
Vernio [I] 128 C3
Vernon [F] 54 D3
Vernoux–en–Gâtine [F] 66 D3
Verny [F] 56 D4
Veróce [H] 76 B3
Véroia [GR] 160 E2
Verolanuova [I] 116 F4
Veroli [I] 132 D4
Verona [I] 118 B4
Verpelét [H] 76 C3
Verrabotn [N] 204 B1
Verran [N] 204 B1
Verrès [I] 116 C3
Verrières–de–Joux [F] 70 B4
Versailles [F] 54 D3
Verseg [H] 76 B3
Versmold [D] 30 F4
Versoix [CH] 80 F2
Versols–et–Lapeyre [F] 124 B2
Vertaala [FIN] 208 F3
Verteillac [F] 78 D3
Vertop [AL] 160 B2
Vertou [F] 66 C2
Vertus [F] 56 A3
Verucchio [I] 128 E3
Veruela, Monasterio de– [E] 94 C2
Verum [S] 180 D1
Verviers [B] 40 F4
Vervins [F] 56 B2
Vervnäs [S] 194 D2
Verwood [GB] 26 F3
Verzej [SLO] 120 D2
Verzuolo [I] 126 C2
Verzy [F] 56 B3
Vesala [FIN] 222 E3
Vesamäki [FIN] 210 B2
Vesanka [FIN] 208 F3
Vesanto [FIN] 210 B2
Vescovato [F] 130 B2
Vescovato [I] 116 F4
Vése [H] 120 E2
Veselec [BG] 150 C2
Veselie [BG] 158 B1
Veselí nad Lužnicí [CZ] 60 E4
Veselí nad Moravou [CZ] 74 E1
Veselinovo [BG] 150 D3
Veselynove [UA] 246 D2
Veshchevo [RUS] 200 E2
Veshtica [BG] 148 C3
Vesivehmaa [FIN] 200 A2
Veskoniemi [FIN] 226 D2
Vesnovo [RUS] 238 B3
Vesoul [F] 70 B3
Véssa [GR] 168 E2
Vessingebro [S] 184 B3
Vestbjerg [DK] 182 D2
Vestby [N] 188 B2
Vestbygd [N] 186 B4
Vester Åby [DK] 178 C3
Vesterby [DK] 178 C2
Vesterby [DK] 178 D3
Vester Egense [DK] 178 C2
Vester Egesborg [DK] 178 E3
Vesterli [N] 220 A2
Vesterø Havn [DK] 182 E2
Veste Rosenberg [D] 58 F2
Vestervig [DK] 182 B3
Vestfossen [N] 186 F1
Vestmanna [FR] 182 A1
Vestmarka [N] 188 C1
Vestnes [N] 202 D3
Vestone [I] 118 A3
Vestpollen [N] 224 B4
Vestre Jakobselv [N] 228 E2
Ves'yegonsk [RUS] 240 E1
Veszprém [H] 120 F1
Veszprémvársány [H] 74 F4
Vésztő [H] 122 E1
Veteli / Vetil [FIN] 208 D1
Vetil / Veteli [FIN] 208 D1
Vetlanda [S] 184 D2
Vetlefjorden [N] 192 C2
Vetovo [BG] 150 C2
Vetovo [HR] 120 F4
Vetralla [I] 130 E4
Vetren [BG] 150 E4
Vetren [BG] 156 E1
Vetrino [BG] 150 D3
Vetriolo Terme [I] 118 B3
Větrný Jeníkov [CZ] 60 F4
Vetschau [D] 46 C3
Vettasjärvi [S] 220 E2
Vetti [N] 192 D2
Vettisfossen [N] 192 D2
Vetulónia [I] 130 D2
Vetunica [MK] 154 E3
Veules–les–Roses [F] 54 C1
Veulettes–sur–Mer [F] 54 C1
Veurne (Furnes) [B] 40 C3
Vevang [N] 202 D2
Vevey [CH] 116 B2
Vévi [GR] 160 D2
Vevring [N] 192 B1
Veynes [F] 124 F2
Veyrier [F] 80 F2
Vezdemarbán [E] 84 F3
Vézelay [F] 68 D3
Vézelise [F] 70 B1
Vézénobres [F] 124 D2
Vezin le Coquet [F] 52 E4
Vezzano [I] 118 B3
Vezzolano, Abbazia di– [I] 116 C4
V. Gafsele [S] 214 B4
V. Husby [S] 190 C4
Viadana [I] 128 B1
Viaduc du Millau [F] 124 B2
Viais [F] 66 C2
Vial. Berestavica [BY] 38 D3
Via Mala [CH] 116 E2
Viana [E] 86 E4
Viana de Duero [E] 94 B2
Viana do Alentejo [P] 98 C2
Viana do Castelo [P] 82 A4
Viana do Bolo [E] 82 D4
Vianden [L] 56 D2
Viane [F] 124 B2
Vianen [NL] 30 B4
Vianne [F] 88 D1
Vianos [E] 100 F4
Viaréggio [I] 128 B3
Vias [F] 124 C3
Viator [E] 106 B4
Viborg [DK] 182 C3
Vibo Valentia [I] 138 D3
Vibraye [F] 54 B4
Viby [DK] 178 D2
Viby [S] 188 F3
Vic [E] 96 D2
Vič [SLO] 120 B2
Viča [SRB] 146 D4
Vicarello [I] 130 F3
Vicchio [I] 128 C3
Vicdessos [F] 88 E4
Vicedo [E] 82 D1
Vic–en–Bigorre [F] 88 D3
Vicenza [I] 118 C4
Vic–Fezensac [F] 88 D2
Vichtis / Vihti [FIN] 198 E3
Vichy [F] 80 C1
Vickan [S] 184 A2
Vic–le–Comte [F] 80 B2
Vico [E] 94 C1
Vico [F] 130 A3
Vico del Gargano [I] 134 F2
Vico Equense [I] 134 D4
Vicoforte, Santuario di– [I] 126 D2
Vicovaro [I] 132 D4
Vic–sur–Aisne [F] 54 F2
Vic–sur–Cère [F] 80 A3
Victoire, Abbaye de la– [F] 54 E3
Victoria [M] 140 B4
Vidaga [LV] 230 E4
Vidago [P] 84 C2
Vidale [LV] 234 E2
Vidamlya [BY] 50 D1
Viđareiđi [FR] 182 B1
Vidauban [F] 126 B3
Viddal [N] 202 C4
Viddalba [I] 142 C2
Vide [P] 84 B4
Videbæk [DK] 178 B1
Videle [RO] 150 B2
Videseter [N] 202 D4
Vidhas [AL] 160 B2
Vidigueira [P] 98 C2
Vidin [BG] 148 C2
Vidlin [GB] 16 E3
Vidnava [CZ] 62 C2
Vidra [RO] 150 C1
Vidsel [S] 214 D1
Vidzy [BY] 238 F2
Viechtach [D] 60 B4
Vieira [P] 90 C2
Vieja, Cueva de la– [E] 102 C4
Vieki [FIN] 216 E4
Viekšniai [LT] 234 E4
Vielīkie Lazy [UA] 244 B3
Viella [E] 88 D4
Viella, Túnel de– [E] 88 D4
Vielsalm [B] 56 D1
Vienenburg [D] 44 C2
Vienne [F] 80 D3
Vieremä [FIN] 216 C4
Viernheim [D] 58 B3
Viersen [D] 42 C3
Vieru [RO] 150 B2
Vierumäki [FIN] 200 B2
Vierville [F] 52 F2
Vierzehnheiligen [D] 58 E2
Vierzon [F] 68 B3
Viesimo [FIN] 210 E2
Viešintos [LT] 238 E2
Viešīte [LV] 236 C4
Viesites [LV] 236 C3
Vieste [I] 134 F2
Vietas [S] 220 C2
Vietri di Potenza [I] 134 E4
Vietri sul Mare [I] 134 D4
Vieux–Boucau–les–Bains [F] 88 B1
Vif [F] 80 E4
Vig [DK] 178 E2
Vigeland [N] 186 C4
Vigévano [I] 116 D4
Vigge [S] 204 E3
Viggianello [I] 136 C3
Viggiano [I] 134 F4
Vigla [GR] 166 C2
Vigl'aš [SK] 76 B2
Vigmostad [N] 186 C4
Vignale Monferrato [I] 116 D4
Vignanello [I] 130 F3
Vigneulles [F] 56 D4
Vignola [I] 128 C2
Vignola Mare [I] 142 C2
Vignory [F] 68 F1
Vigo [E] 82 B3
Vigo di Fassa [I] 118 C2
Vigrestad [N] 186 A3
Viguera [E] 94 B1
Vihantasalmi [FIN] 200 B1
Vihanti [FIN] 216 B3
Vihasjärvi [FIN] 198 E1
Vihiers [F] 66 D3
Vihren [BG] 156 B3
Vihtari [FIN] 210 D3
Vihtasuo [FIN] 210 D1
Vihti / Vichtis [FIN] 198 E3
Vihtijärvi [FIN] 198 E3
Vihtiäjärvi [FIN] 208 C4
Viiala [FIN] 198 E2
Viiksimo [FIN] 216 E3
Viinijärvi [FIN] 210 D2
Viinikoski [FIN] 216 C2
Viinistu [EST] 230 D1
Viisarimäki [FIN] 210 B3
Viitaila [FIN] 198 F2
Viitajärvi [FIN] 208 F1
Viitaniemi [FIN] 210 C1
Viitasaari [FIN] 208 F1
Viitavaara [FIN] 216 D2
Viitna [EST] 230 E1
Vijciems [LV] 230 E4
Vijenac [MNE] 152 F1
Vík [IS] 218 B3
Vik [N] 186 D4
Vik [N] 192 C2
Vik [N] 202 B3
Vik [N] 202 E2
Vik [N] 212 D2
Vik [S] 180 D2
Vik [S] 190 D2
Vika [N] 186 C2
Vika [S] 194 E3
Vika [S] 196 B4
Vikajärvi [FIN] 222 C3
Vikan [N] 202 E2
Vikane [N] 188 B2
Vikanes [N] 192 B2
Vikarbyn [S] 194 F3
Vikby [FIN] 208 B2
Vike [N] 202 E3
Vikebukt [N] 202 D3
Vikedal [N] 186 B1
Viken [S] 178 F1
Viken [S] 204 F4
Viken [S] 212 E3
Viker [N] 192 F3
Viker [S] 188 F2
Vikersund [N] 186 F1
Vikeså [N] 186 B3
Vikmanshyttan [S] 196 B4
Vikoč [BIH] 152 E1
Vikran [N] 224 D2
Viksjö [S] 206 C3
Viksøyri [N] 192 C2
Vikštejn [CZ] 62 C3
Viksvatn [N] 212 B4
Viktring [A] 120 A2
Vikvallen [S] 214 C1
Vikvarvet [N] 204 B2
Vila Baleira [P] 110 F3
Viladamat [E] 96 F2
Viladecans [E] 96 D3
Vila de Rei [P] 90 C2
Vila do Bispo [P] 98 A3
Vila do Conde [P] 84 A2
Vila do Porto [P] 110 E2
Vilafamés [E] 102 E2
Vila Fernando [P] 84 C4
Vila Flor [P] 84 C3
Vilafranca de Bonany [E] 108 D3
Vilafranca del Maestrat / Villafranca del Cid [E] 102 E2
Vilafranca del Penedès [E] 96 C3
Vila Franca de Xira [P] 90 B3
Vila Franca do Campo [P] 110 E1
Vila Fresca de Azeitão [P] 90 B4
Vilagarcía de Arousa [E] 82 B3
Vilaka [LV] 236 E2
Vilaller [E] 88 D4
Vila Meã [P] 84 C2
Vilameán [E] 82 A3
Vilamor [E] 96 C1
Vilamoura [P] 98 B4
Vilāni [LV] 236 D3
Vilanova d'Alcolea [E] 102 E2
Vilanova de Arousa [E] 82 B3
Vila Nova de Cerveira [P] 82 A4
Vila Nova de Famalicão [P] 84 B2
Vila Nova de Foz Côa [P] 84 C3
Vila Nova de Gaia [P] 84 A2
Vilanova de la Barca [E] 96 B2
Vila Nova de Milfontes [P] 98 B3
Vila Nova de Ourém [P] 90 C2
Vila Nova de Paiva [P] 84 B3
Vila Nova de S. André [P] 98 B2
Vila Nova de São Bento [P] 98 D3
Vila Nova do Corvo [P] 110 B1
Vilanova i la Geltrú [E] 96 C3
Vila Pouca de Aguiar [P] 84 C2
Vila Praia de Âncora [P] 82 A4
Vilarandelo [P] 84 C2
Vilar de Barrio [E] 82 C4
Vilardevós [E] 84 C2
Vila Real [P] 84 C3
Vila Real de Santo António [P] 98 C4
Vilar Formoso [P] 84 C4
Vila–rodona [E] 96 C3
Vilarouco [P] 84 C3

Vilars, Cova dels– [E] 96 B2
Vila–seca [E] 96 C3
Vilassar de Mar [E] 96 D3
Vila Velha de Ródão [P] 90 D3
Vila Verde [P] 84 B2
Vila Verde [P] 84 D2
Vila Verde da Raia [P] 84 C2
Vila Verde de Ficalho [P] 98 D3
Vila Viçosa [P] 90 D4
Vilches [E] 106 A1
Vildbjerg [DK] 182 C4
Vilémov [CZ] 60 F3
Vilhelmina [S] 214 A3
Vilia [GR] 168 A2
Vilinska Jama [HR] 120 C3
Viljakkala [FIN] 208 D4
Viljandi [EST] 230 D3
Viljolahti [FIN] 210 D3
Vilkaviškis [LT] 238 C3
Vilkija [LT] 238 C3
Villa Adriana [I] 132 D4
Villaba del Rey [E] 102 A1
Villa Bartolomea [I] 128 C1
Villablanca [E] 98 D4
Villablino [E] 82 E3
Villabona [E] 86 F3
Villacañas [E] 100 E2
Villa Cancellieri [I] 140 D3
Villacarrillo [E] 106 B1
Villa Castelli [I] 136 D2
Villacastín [E] 92 D3
Villach [A] 118 F2
Villacidro [I] 142 B5
Villada [E] 86 A4
Villadangos del Páramo
  [E] 82 F4
Villa del Prado [E] 92 D4
Villa del Río [E] 104 E1
Villa de Ves [E] 102 C3
Villadiego [E] 86 C4
Villadoro [I] 138 B4
Villadossola [I] 116 D2
Villaeles de Valdavia [E] 86 B3
Villaescusa de Haro [E] 102 A2
Villa Estense [I] 128 D1
Villa Formosa [E] 90 D3
Villafranca del Bierzo [E] 82 D3
Villafranca del Cid / Vilafranca
  del Maestrat [E] 102 E2
Villafranca de los Barros
  [E] 98 F2
Villafranca de los Caballeros
  [E] 100 E2
Villafranca di Verona [I]
  118 B4
Villafranca Montes de Oca
  [E] 86 D4
Villafranca Piemonte [I]
  126 C1
Villafranca Tirrena [I] 138 C3
Villafrati [I] 140 C2
Villafrechós [E] 84 F3
Villafruela [E] 92 F1
Villafuerte [E] 92 E1
Villagarcía de la Torre [E]
  98 F3
Village, Roche aux– [F] 56 C2
Villaggio Apulo [I] 136 D2
Villaggio Mancuso [I] 138 E2
Villagonzalo Pedernales
  [E] 86 C4
Villagordo [E] 104 F1
Villagrains [F] 78 B4
Villagrande Strisaili [I] 142 C4
Villaharta [E] 100 B4
Villahermosa [E] 100 F4
Villahoz [E] 92 F1
Villaines la Gonais [F] 54 B4
Villaines–la–Juhel [F] 54 A3
Villajos, Ermita de– [E] 100 F2
Villajoyosa / la Vila Joiosa
  [E] 106 F2

Villala [FIN] 210 E3
Villalba Alta [E] 82 C2
Villalba de Duero [E] 92 F2
Villalba de Guardo [E] 86 B3
Villalba del Alcor [E] 98 E4
Villalba de la Sierra [E] 102 B1
Villalba de los Alcores [E] 92 D1
Villalba de los Barros [E] 98 E2
Villalcázar de Sirga [E] 86 B4
Villalgordo del Marquesado
  [E] 102 A2
Villa Literno [I] 134 C3
Villalón de Campos [E] 86 A4
Villalpando [E] 84 F3
Villalpardo [E] 102 B3
Villaluenga [E] 100 E1
Villamalea [E] 102 B3
Villamañán [E] 84 F2
Villamanín de la Tercia [E]
  82 F3
Villamanrique [E] 100 E4
Villamanrique de la Condesa
  [E] 104 B1
Villamar [I] 142 B4
Villamartín [E] 104 C2
Villamartín de Campos [E]
  86 B4
Villamartín de Don Sancho
  [E] 86 A3
Villamassargia [I] 142 B5
Villamayor [E] 84 E4
Villamayor de Santiago [E]
  100 F2
Villamediana de Iregua [E]
  86 E4
Villamesías [E] 100 B2
Villa Minozzo [I] 128 B2
Villamuelas [E] 100 E1
Villandraut [F] 78 B4
Villandry [F] 66 F2
Villanova [I] 136 E2
Villanova d'Asti [I] 126 D1
Villanova Monteleone [I]
  142 B3
Villanova Tulo [I] 142 C4
Villanúa [E] 88 B3
Villanubla [E] 92 D1
Villanueva de Alcardete [E]
  100 F2
Villanueva de Algaidas [E]
  104 E2
Villanueva de Argaño [E]
  86 C4
Villanueva de Cameros [E]
  94 B1
Villanueva de Cañedo [E]
  84 E4
Villanueva de Córdoba [E]
  100 C4
Villanueva de Gállego [E]
  94 D2
Villanueva de Huerva [E] 94 D3
Villanueva del Aceral [E] 84 F4
Villanueva de la Fuente [E]
  100 F4
Villanueva de la Jara [E]
  102 B3
Villanueva de la Reina [E]
  104 F1
Villanueva del Arzobispo [E]
  106 B1
Villanueva de las Cruces
  [E] 98 D3
Villanueva de la Serena [E]
  100 B2
Villanueva de la Sierra [E]
  90 F2
Villanueva de las Torres [E]
  106 B2
Villanueva de la Vera [E] 92 C4
Villanueva del Campo [E]
  84 F2

Villanueva del Duque [E] 100 B3
Villanueva del Fresno [E] 98 D2
Villanueva de los Castillejos
  [E] 98 D4
Villanueva de los Infantes
  [E] 100 E4
Villanueva del Rey [E] 100 B4
Villanueva del Río Segura
  [E] 106 D2
Villanueva del Río y Minas
  [E] 98 F4
Villanueva del Trabuco [E]
  104 E3
Villanueva de San Carlos
  [E] 108 F3
Villanueva de Sigena [E] 94 F3
Villanueva de Tapia [E] 104 E2
Villanuño de Valdavia [E]
  86 B3
Villány [H] 122 A3
Villa Opicina [I] 118 F3
Villapalacios [E] 100 F4
Villapiana Scalo [I] 136 C4
Villaplana [I] 136 C4
Villa Potenza [I] 132 E1
Villapriolo [I] 140 D2
Villaputzu [I] 142 C5
Villaquejida [E] 84 F2
Villaquilambre [E] 82 F4
Villarcayo [E] 86 D3
Villard–de–Lans [F] 80 E4
Villardebelle [F] 124 A3
Villar de Cantos [E] 102 A3
Villar de Ciervo [E] 84 D4
Villardeciervos [E] 84 E2
Villar de Domingo García
  [E] 102 B1
Villardefrades [E] 84 F3
Villar del Arzobispo [E] 102 D3
Villar del Pedroso [E] 100 C1
Villar del Pozo [E] 102 B3
Villar del Rey [E] 90 E4
Villar de Olalla [E] 102 B2
Villar de Peralonso [E] 84 D4
Villar de Rena [E] 100 B2
Villar de Río [E] 94 C2
Villarejo de Fuentes [E] 102 A2
Villarejo de Salvanés [E]
  100 F1
Villares de la Reina [E] 84 E4
Villares del Saz [E] 102 A2
Villargordo del Cabriel [E]
  102 C3
Villaricos [E] 106 C3
Villarino [E] 84 D3
Villariño de Conso [E] 82 C4
Villarluengo [E] 102 D1
Villarmayor [E] 84 E4
Villa Romana del Casale [I]
  140 D3
Villarosa [I] 140 D2
Villar Perosa [I] 116 B4
Villarquemado [E] 102 C1
Villarramiel [E] 86 A4
Villarreal de San Carlos
  [E] 92 B4
Villarreal– la Vila Reial [E]
  102 E2
Villarrobledo [E] 100 F3
Villarroga de los Pinares [E]
  102 D1
Villarroja [E] 94 C2
Villarroya de la Sierra [E]
  94 C3
Villarrubia de los Ojos [E]
  100 E3
Villars [CH] 116 B2
Villars–les–Dombes [F] 80 E2
Villars–sur–Var [F] 126 C3
Villarta [E] 102 B3
Villarta de los Montes [E]
  100 C2

Villarta de San Juan [E] 100 E3
Villarubia de Santiago [E]
  100 E1
Villasadino [E] 86 C4
Villasalto [I] 142 C5
Villasana de Mena [E] 86 D3
Villa San Giovanni [I] 138 D3
Villa Santa Maria [I] 132 F4
Villasante [E] 86 D3
Villa Santina [I] 118 E2
Villaseco de los Gamitos
  [E] 84 E4
Villaseco de los Reyes [E]
  84 D3
Villasequilla [E] 100 E1
Villasimíus [I] 142 C5
Villa S. Lucia degli Abruzzi
  [I] 132 E3
Villasor [I] 142 B5
Villasrubias [E] 90 F2
Villastar [E] 102 C2
Villatobas [E] 100 E2
Villatoro [E] 86 C4
Villatoya [E] 102 C3
Villava [E] 86 F4
Villavelayo [E] 94 B1
Villaverde del Río [E] 98 F4
Villaverde de Trucios [E] 86 D3
Villaviciosa [E] 86 A1
Villaviciosa [E] 100 B4
Villavieja [E] 84 D4
Villa Vomano [I] 132 E3
Villé [F] 70 D2
Villebois–Lavalette [F] 78 D2
Ville–Devant–Chaumont
  [F] 56 C3
Villedieu–les–Poëles [F] 52 F3
Villédomain [F] 68 A3
Ville–en–Tardenois [F] 56 A3
Villefagnan [F] 78 D2
Villefontaine [F] 80 E3
Villefort [F] 124 D1
Villefranche [F] 126 C3
Villefranche–d'Albigeois [F]
  124 A2
Villefranche–de–Conflent
  [F] 96 E1
Villefranche–de–Lauragais
  [F] 88 F3
Villefranche–de–Lonchat
  [F] 78 C3
Villefranche–de–Panat [F]
  124 B2
Villefranche–de–Rouergue
  [F] 124 A1
Villefranche–du–Périgord
  [F] 78 D4
Villefranche–sur–Cher [F]
  68 B2
Villefranche–sur–Saône
  [F] 80 D2
Villegats [F] 78 D2
Villel [E] 102 C2
Villemur [F] 88 E2
Villena [E] 106 E1
Villenauxe–la–Grande [F]
  54 F4
Villeneuve [F] 124 A1
Villeneuve [F] 124 B2
Villeneuve d'Ascq [F] 40 C3
Villeneuve–de–Berg [F] 124 E1
Villeneuve–de–Marsan [F]
  88 C2
Villeneuve–l'Archevêque
  [F] 68 D1
Villeneuve–Loubet [F] 126 C3
Villeneuve–sur–Allier [F]
  68 C4
Villeneuve–sur–Lot [F] 88 E1
Villeneuve–sur–Yonne [F]
  68 D1
Villerbon [F] 68 A2

Villeréal [F] 78 D4
Villeromaine [F] 68 A2
Villers [B] 40 E4
Villers [F] 54 B2
Villers–Bocage [F] 54 A2
Villers–Bretonneux [F] 54 E1
Villers–Cotterêts [F] 54 F3
Villersexel [F] 70 C3
Villers–le–Lac [F] 70 C4
Villerville [F] 54 B2
Villeseque [F] 88 F1
Ville–sur–Illon [F] 70 B2
Villetta Barrea [I] 132 E4
Villiers–St–Georges [F] 54 F4
Villingen [D] 70 E2
Villingsberg [S] 188 F2
Villmanstrand / Lappeenranta
  [FIN] 200 D2
Villnäs / Askainen [FIN]
  198 C3
Villoldo [E] 86 B4
Villon [F] 68 E2
Villorba [I] 118 D3
Villoria [E] 84 F4
Villoslada de Cameros [E]
  94 B1
Villstad [S] 184 B2
Villvattnet [S] 214 D3
Vilmajor [H] 122 D2
Vilmány [H] 76 D2
Vilnius [LT] 238 C3
Vilobacka [FIN] 208 C1
Volovo [SRB] 146 D1
Vilppula [FIN] 208 E3
Vils [DK] 182 C3
Vilsbiburg [D] 72 D2
Vilseck [D] 58 F3
Vilshofen [D] 72 E2
Vilshult [S] 180 D1
Vilsund [DK] 182 C3
Vilunai [LT] 238 D3
Vilusi [MNE] 152 E2
Viluste [EST] 230 F3
Vilyeyka [BY] 242 B1
Vimianzo [E] 82 B1
Vimieiro [P] 90 C4
Vimioso [P] 84 D3
Vimmerby [S] 184 E2
Vimoutiers [F] 54 B2
Vimpeli [FIN] 208 D2
Vimperk [CZ] 72 F1
Vina [SRB] 154 D2
Vinac [BIH] 144 F3
Vinádio [I] 126 C2
Vinaixa [E] 96 B3
Vinaròs [E] 96 A4
Vinarsko [BG] 150 D4
Vinay [F] 80 E3
Vinça [F] 96 E1
Vinchiaturo [I] 134 D2
Vinci [I] 128 B3
Vindbyholt [DK] 178 E3
Vindelgransele [S] 214 B2
Vindeln [S] 214 C3
Vinderslev [DK] 182 C4
Vinderup [DK] 182 C3
Vindsvik [N] 186 B2
Vinebre [E] 94 F4
Vinga [RO] 122 E3
Vinga [RO] 122 F3
Vingåker [S] 190 B3
Vingelen [N] 204 B3
Vingnes [N] 194 B2
Vingrau [F] 96 E1
Vingrom [N] 194 B2
Vingstad [N] 224 E3
Vinhais [P] 84 D2
Vinica [BG] 150 D3
Vinica [MK] 154 D1
Vinica [SK] 76 B3
Vinica [SLO] 120 B4
Viničani [MK] 154 D4

Viniegra de Abajo [E] 94 B1
Vinishte [BG] 148 D3
Vinjani [HR] 152 C1
Vinje [N] 186 D1
Vinje [N] 192 C2
Vinjeøra [N] 202 E2
Vinkovci [HR] 146 B1
Vinliden [S] 214 B3
Vinnytsia [UA] 244 E2
Vinon–sur–Verdon [F] 124 F3
Vinslöv [S] 180 D1
Vinsnes [N] 186 D2
Vinsternes [N] 202 E2
Vinstra [N] 192 F1
Vintgar [SLO] 118 F2
Vintjärn [S] 196 C3
Vintl / Vandoies [I] 118 C2
Vintrosa [S] 188 F2
Viñuela de Sayago [E] 84 E3
Viñuelas [E] 92 F3
Vinuesa [E] 94 B2
Vinzelberg [D] 44 E1
Violès [F] 124 E2
Viozene [I] 126 D2
Vipava [SLO] 118 F3
Vipiteno / Sterzing [I] 118 C1
Vira [HR] 152 B2
Virdois / Virrat [FIN] 208 D3
Vire [F] 52 F3
Viré [F] 80 D1
Vire Court [F] 52 B3
Vireda [S] 184 D1
Vireši [LV] 230 E4
Virestad [S] 184 C3
Virgen [A] 118 D1
Virgen de Criptana [E] 100 F2
Virgen de la Cabeza [E] 100 D4
Virgen de la Cabeza [E] 102 A3
Virgen de la Cabeza [E] 106 B2
Virgen de la Montaña [E] 90 F3
Virgen de la Muela [E] 100 F2
Virgen de la Peña [E] 94 F2
Virgen de la Peña [E] 98 D3
Virgen del Castillo [E] 92 E2
Virginia [IRL] 10 F1
Viriat [F] 80 E2
Virieu [F] 80 E3
Virieu–le–Grand [F] 80 E2
Virje [HR] 120 E3
Virkby / Virkkala [FIN] 198 E3
Virkëni [LV] 230 D4
Virkkala / Virkby [FIN] 198 E3
Virkkula [FIN] 222 E3
Virklund [DK] 178 C1
Virmaanpää [FIN] 210 B2
Virmaila [FIN] 198 F1
Virmutjoki [FIN] 200 D1
Virojoki [FIN] 200 C3
Virolahti [FIN] 200 C3
Vironvay [F] 54 C2
Virpazar [MNE] 152 E3
Virrat / Virdois [FIN] 208 D3
Virsbo [S] 190 C1
Virsbo bruk [S] 190 B1
Virserum [S] 184 E2
VirŠuliškiai [LT] 238 E3
Virtaniemi [RUS] 226 E2
Virtasalmi [FIN] 210 C3
Virton [B] 56 C3
Virtsu [EST] 230 C3
Virttaa [FIN] 198 D2
Viru–Jaagupi [EST] 230 E2
Virvoru [RO] 148 D2
Vis [HR] 152 A2
Visaginas [LT] 238 F2
Višakio Rūda [LT] 238 C3
Visbek [D] 30 F3
Visby [DK] 178 B3
Visby [S] 234 A2
Visé [B] 40 F4
Višegrad [BIH] 146 C4

Visegrád [H] 76 B3
Viseu [P] 84 B3
Vishaj [AL] 160 B1
Vishnyeva [BY] 238 F4
Vishovgrad [BG] 150 B3
Vishtytis [LT] 238 C4
Visiedo [E] 94 D4
Vişina Veche [RO] 148 F2
Visingsborg [S] 184 C1
Viskafors [S] 184 B2
Viskinge [DK] 178 D2
Viškovci [HR] 122 A4
Viškovo [HR] 120 A4
Visland [N] 186 B3
Vislanda [S] 184 C3
Višnja Gora [SLO] 120 B3
Visočka Ržana [SRB] 148 C4
Viso del Marqués [E] 100 D4
Visoka [SRB] 146 D4
Visoki Dečani, Manastir– [KS]
154 B2
Visoko [BIH] 146 B3
Visoko [SLO] 120 A3
Visp [CH] 116 C2
Vissefjärda [S] 184 D4
Visselhövede [D] 32 B4
Visseltofta [S] 184 C4
Vissenbjerg [DK] 178 C2
Visso [I] 132 D2
Vistdal [N] 202 D3
Vistheden [S] 214 D1
Vistino [RUS] 200 D4
Visuvesi [FIN] 208 D3
Visz [H] 120 F2
Vitalahti [FIN] 208 F3
Vitănești [RO] 150 B2
Vitanovac [SRB] 146 E4
Vitberget [S] 220 E4
Vitemölla [S] 180 D2
Viterbo [I] 130 F2
Viterbo, Bagni di– [I]
130 F2
Vithkuq [AL] 160 C3
Vitigudino [E] 84 D4
Vitina [BIH] 152 C2
Vitina [KS] 154 D3
Vitis [A] 74 B2
Vitkov [CZ] 62 C3
Vitkovo [SRB] 146 E4
Vitolište [MK] 160 D1
Vitomirica [KS] 154 B2
Vitoria–Gasteiz [E] 86 E3
Vitré [F] 52 E4
Vitrupe [LV] 230 D4
Vitry–le–François [F] 56 B4
Vitsand [S] 194 D4
Vitskøl Kloster [DK] 182 C3
Vitsyebsk [BY] 240 C4
Vittangi [S] 220 E4
Vittarp [DK] 178 A1
Vittaryd [S] 184 C3
Vitteaux [F] 68 E3
Vittel [F] 70 B2
Vittinge [S] 190 C1
Vittjärn [S] 194 D4
Vittjärv [S] 220 E4
Vittória [I] 140 D4
Vittoriosa [M] 140 C4
Vittório Véneto [I] 118 D3
Vitträsk [S] 220 F3
Vittsjö [S] 180 C1
Vittskövle [S] 180 D2
Vitvattnet [S] 206 E1
Vitvattnet [S] 222 B4
Vitzenburg [D] 44 D3
Vitznau [CH] 70 E4
Viù [I] 116 B4
Viuhkola [FIN] 200 C2
Vivario [F] 134 B2
Viveiro [E] 82 D1
Vivel del Río Martín [E] 94 D4
Viver [E] 102 D2

Víverols [F] 80 C3
Viverone [I] 116 C3
Viveros [E] 100 F4
Vivier, Château du– [F] 54 E3
Viviers [F] 124 E1
Vivikonna [EST] 230 F1
Vivonne [F] 66 E4
Vivungi [S] 220 F1
Vixía Herbeira [E] 82 C1
Vize [TR] 158 C2
Vizica [BG] 158 C1
Vizille [F] 80 E4
Vižinada [HR] 118 F4
Vizovice [CZ] 62 D4
Vizsoly [H] 76 D2
Vizzavona [F] 130 B3
Vizzini [I] 140 E3
Vjetrenica [BIH] 152 D2
Vlaardingen [NL] 30 A4
Vlacháva [GR] 160 D4
Vlacherná [GR] 166 C2
Vlachiótis [GR] 172 E3
Vlachokerasiá [GR] 172 D2
Vlachovo Březí [CZ] 60 D4
Vladičin Han [SRB] 154 E2
Vlădila [RO] 148 F2
Vladimir [MNE] 152 F4
Vladimirescu [RO] 122 E3
Vladimirovac [SRB] 146 E2
Vladimirovka [RUS] 200 F2
Vladimirovo [BG] 148 D3
Vladimirovo [BG] 150 E2
Vladimirskiy [RUS] 232 F3
Vladinos [MNE] 152 E4
Vlad Țepeș [RO] 150 D1
Vlagtweed [NL] 30 E2
Vlahovo [BG] 156 D3
Vlakovič [HR] 144 D1
V. Laole [SRB] 146 F3
Vlas [BG] 150 E4
Vlasenica [BIH] 146 C3
Vlašim [CZ] 60 E3
Vlașin [RO] 150 B2
Vlasina Okruglica [SRB]
154 E2
Vlasotince [SRB] 148 C4
Vlieland [NL] 30 B2
Vlissingen [NL] 40 D2
Vlkava [CZ] 60 E2
Vlkolinec [SK] 76 B1
Vllahinë [AL] 160 A3
Vlochós [GR] 160 E4
Vlorë [AL] 160 A3
Vlotho [D] 42 F2
Vlychó [GR] 166 B3
V. Nedelja [SLO] 120 D2
Vočin [HR] 120 E4
Vöcklabruck [A] 72 F3
Voden [BG] 158 B2
Vodice [HR] 144 D4
Vodice [SLO] 120 A3
Vodňanci [HR] 146 B3
Vodița, Mănăstirea– [RO]
148 C1
Voditsa [BG] 150 C3
Vodňany [CZ] 60 D4
Vodnjan [HR] 144 A2
Vodskov [DK] 182 D2
Voergård [DK] 182 E2
Voerså [DK] 182 E2
Vogatsikó [GR] 160 D3
Vogelsdorf [D] 46 B2
Voghera [I] 126 E1
Vognillan [N] 202 F3
Vogogna [I] 116 D2
Vogorno [CH] 116 D2
Vogošća [BIH] 146 B3
Vohburg [D] 72 C1
Vohenstrauss [D] 60 B3
Võhma [EST] 230 B3
Võhma [EST] 230 D3

Void [F] 56 C4
Voikoski [FIN] 200 B2
Voiluoto [FIN] 198 C2
Voïnka [UA] 246 F3
Voiron [F] 80 E3
Voise [F] 54 D4
Vöiske [EST] 230 D3
Voiteg [RO] 122 E4
Voitsberg [A] 120 B1
Voix [F] 124 F3
Vojakkala [FIN] 198 E2
Vojany [SK] 76 E2
Vojčice [SK] 76 E2
Vojens [DK] 178 B2
Vojenské Prírodne Múzeum
[SK] 64 C4
Vojlovica [SRB] 146 E2
Vojmån [S] 214 A2
Vojnić [HR] 120 C4
Vojnik [SLO] 120 B3
Vojtanov [CZ] 60 B2
Vojtjajaure [S] 212 F2
Voknavolok [RUS] 216 E1
Voláda [GR] 176 B3
Vólakas [GR] 156 C3
Volary [CZ] 72 F1
Volda [N] 202 C3
Voldby [DK] 182 E4
Volders [A] 72 C4
Volendam [NL] 30 B3
Volfštejn [CZ] 60 B3
Volgosovo [RUS] 232 E2
Volimes [GR] 172 B1
Volissós [GR] 168 E1
Volkach [D] 58 D3
Völkermarkt [A] 120 B2
Völklingen [D] 56 E3
Volkmarsen [D] 42 F3
Volkovija [MK] 154 C4
Vollenhove [NL] 30 C3
Volmsjö [S] 214 B3
Volochys'k [UA] 244 D2
Volodarka [UA] 244 F1
Volodymyr-Volyns'kyi [UA]
50 E4
Volokolamsk [RUS] 240 E3
Vólos [GR] 162 B3
Voloshovo [RUS] 232 F2
Volosovo [RUS] 232 F1
Volovo [BG] 150 B3
Volpiano [I] 116 C4
Volterra [I] 128 B4
Volterraio [I] 130 D2
Voltri [I] 126 E2
Voltti [FIN] 208 C1
Volturara Appula [I] 134 D2
Volvic [F] 80 B2
Volyně [CZ] 60 D4
Voněche [B] 56 D2
Voneshta voda [BG] 150 B4
Vónitsa [GR] 166 C2
Vönnu [EST] 230 F3
Vönöck [H] 74 E4
Voorschoten [NL] 30 A3
Voorst [NL] 30 C4
Vopnafjördur [IS] 218 D2
Vorau [A] 74 C4
Vorbasse [DK] 178 B2
Vorbourg [CH] 70 D3
Vorchdorf [A] 72 F3
Vörden [D] 30 F3
Vordernberg [A] 74 B4
Vorderriss [D] 72 C3
Vordingborg [DK] 178 E3
Vorë [AL] 160 A1
Voreinó [GR] 160 E4
Voreppe [F] 80 E3
Vorey [F] 80 C3
Vöringsfossen [N] 192 D3
Vormsele [S] 214 C2
Vormstad [N] 202 F2

Vormsund [N] 194 C4
Voroneț, Mănăstirea– [RO]
244 D3
Voronkova Niva [RUS] 236 F2
Vorontsovo [RUS] 232 E4
Vorsfelde [D] 44 D1
Võru [EST] 230 F4
Voruča [BIH] 146 B3
Vosawtsy [BY] 50 F2
Voskopojë [AL] 160 C2
Voss [N] 192 C3
Vossijatskoje [UA] 246 D2
Votice [CZ] 60 E3
Votonósi [GR] 160 D4
Vouillé [F] 66 E4
Voukoliés [GR] 174 B3
Voúla [GR] 168 B3
Vouliagméni [GR] 168 B3
Voulpaix [F] 56 B2
Voúlpi [GR] 166 D2
Voulx [F] 54 E4
Vourkári [GR] 168 C3
Vourvouroú [GR] 162 C2
Voutás [GR] 166 F2
Vouvant [F] 66 D3
Vouvray [F] 66 F2
Vouzela [P] 84 B3
Vouziers [F] 56 B3
Voves [F] 54 C4
Vovoúsa [GR] 160 C3
Vowpa [BY] 38 D2
Voxna [S] 196 B2
Voxtorp [S] 184 C3
Vöylä [FIN] 226 D2
Voynica [BG] 148 C2
Voynitsa [RUS] 216 E1
Voynovo [BG] 150 D2
Võyri / Vörå [FIN] 208 C2
Voz [HR] 144 B1
Vozarci [MK] 154 E4
Voznesens'k [UA] 246 D2
Vozrozhdenie [RUS] 200 D2
Vrå [DK] 182 D2
Vrå [S] 184 B3
Vrabinec [CZ] 60 D1
Vráble [SK] 74 F3
Vračev Gaj [SRB] 146 F2
Vračevšnica [SRB] 146 E3
Vrachnaíika [GR] 166 D4
Vrådal [N] 186 D2
Vråliosen [N] 186 D2
Vrams Gunnarstorp [S] 178 F1
Vrana [N] 144 B2
Vrana [HR] 144 C3
Vranduk [BIH] 146 A3
Vranilovci [BG] 150 B4
Vranino [BG] 150 F2
Vranisht [AL] 154 B3
Vranja [HR] 118 F4
Vranjak [HR] 144 C2
Vranje [SRB] 154 D2
Vranjina [MNE] 152 E3
Vranjska Banja [SRB] 154 E2
Vranov nad Dyjí [CZ] 74 C1
Vranov nad Topľou [SK] 76 1
Vransko [SLO] 120 B3
Vrapčíci [BIH] 152 D1
Vrapčíšte [MK] 154 C4
Vrástama [GR] 162 B2
Vratarnica [SRB] 148 C3
Vratkovići [BIH] 152 E2
Vratna [SK] 62 E4
Vratna, Manastir– [SRB]
148 C2
Vratnica [MK] 154 C3
Vratno [HR] 120 D2
Vratsa [BG] 148 E4
Vravróna [GR] 168 B2
Vražogrnac [SRB] 148 C2
Vrba [SLO] 118 F2
Vrbanja [BIH] 144 F2
Vrbanja [HR] 146 B2

Vrbanje [MNE] 152 D3
Vrbas [SRB] 122 C4
Vrbaška [BIH] 144 F1
Vrbnica [KS] 154 C3
Vrbnik [HR] 144 B1
Vrbno pod Pradědem [CZ]
62 C3
Vrboska [HR] 152 B2
Vrbovce [SK] 74 E2
Vrbové [SK] 74 E2
Vrbovec [HR] 120 D3
Vrbovsko [HR] 120 B4
Vrchlabí [CZ] 60 F2
Vrčice [SLO] 120 B4
Vrčin [SRB] 146 E2
Vrdnik [SRB] 146 D1
Vreden [D] 30 D4
Vrees [D] 30 E3
Vrelo [HR] 144 D2
Vrelo Bune [BIH]
152 D2
Vrena [S] 190 C3
Vreoci [SRB] 146 D2
Vresovo [BG] 150 D4
Vresse [B] 56 C2
Vreta Kloster [S] 190 B4
Vretstorp [S] 188 F3
Vrgorac [HR] 152 C2
Vrhnika [SLO] 120 A3
Vrhpolje [BIH] 144 E2
Vriezenveen [NL] 30 D3
Vrigny [F] 56 A3
Vrigstad [S] 184 C2
Vrilisia [GR] 168 B2
Vrilissia [GR] 166 E2
Vrin [CH] 116 E2
Vrlika [HR] 144 E3
Vrnjačka Banja [SRB]
146 E4
Vron [F] 40 A4
Vrontádos [GR] 168 E1
Vrontoú [GR] 160 E3
Vroomshoop [NL] 30 D3
Vrosína [GR] 160 C4
Vrouchás [GR] 174 E3
Vroutek [CZ] 60 C2
Vroville [F] 70 B2
Vrpolje [HR] 144 D4
Vrpolje [HR] 146 B1
Vršac [SRB] 146 F1
Vršani [BIH] 146 C2
Vrsar [HR] 128 F1
Vrtoče [BIH] 144 D2
Vrtojba [SLO] 118 E3
Vrútky [SK] 76 A1
Vrův [BG] 148 C2
Vry [F] 56 D3
Vrýses [GR] 174 B3
Vrysoúla [GR] 166 B2
Vrýtaina [GR] 162 B4
Vsetín [CZ] 62 D4
Vsheli [RUS] 232 F3
V. Sjulsmark [S] 214 D3
V.središte [RO] 146 F1
V. Torsås [S] 184 C3
V. Trebeljevo [SLO] 120 B3
V. Trgovišce [HR] 120 C3
Vučitrn [KS] 154 C2
Vučjavas [SLO] 120 C2
Vučkovci [BIH] 146 B2
Vuckovica [SRB] 146 E3
Vue [F] 66 B2
Vufflens, Château de– [CH]
116 B1
Vught [NL] 40 F2
Vüglevtsi [BG] 150 B4
Vujanovo [SRB] 148 B4
Vuka [HR] 122 A4
Vukojevica [HR] 120 F4
Vukovar [HR] 122 B4
Vukovec [HR] 120 D3
Vuku [N] 204 C1

Vulcăneşti [MD] 244 F4
Vülchedrüm [BG] 148 D3
Vülchidol [BG] 150 E3
Vulci [I] 130 E2
Vultureşti [RO] 148 E1
Vuobmaved [FIN] 226 C2
Vuohtomäki [FIN] 210 A1
Vuojalahti [FIN] 210 B4
Vuojärvi [FIN] 222 D2
Vuokatti [FIN] 216 D3
Vuolenkoski [FIN] 200 B2
Vuolijoki [FIN] 216 C3
Vuolle [FIN] 214 F4
Vuollerim [S] 220 E3
Vuonislahti [FIN] 210 E1
Vuorenkylä [FIN] 200 A1
Vuorenmaa [FIN] 198 C2
Vuorenmaa [FIN] 210 C3
Vuorijärvi [FIN] 208 D3
Vuorilahti [FIN] 208 F2
Vuoriniemi [FIN] 210 E4
Vuostimojärvi [FIN] 222 D2
Vuotner [S] 214 C1
Vuotsino [FIN] 222 D2
Vuotso [FIN] 226 D3
Vuottas [S] 220 F3
Vuottolahti [FIN] 216 C3
Vürbitsa [BG] 150 D4
Vürshets [BG] 148 D4
Vyalikaryta [BY] 50 D2
Vyanta [LT] 234 E4
Vyartsilya [RUS] 210 F3
Vyaz'ma [RUS] 240 E4
Vyazy [RUS] 200 D3
Vybor [RUS] 232 F4
Vyborg [RUS] 200 D2
Vybranivka [UA] 64 F3
Vyerkhnyadzvinsk [BY] 236 E4
Vyhonochy [RUS] 242 E2
Vynnyky [UA] 64 F3
Vynohradiv [UA] 244 C3
Vyra [RUS] 232 F1
Vyritsa [RUS] 200 F4
Vyróneia [GR] 156 B4
Vyshgorodok [RUS] 236 E2
Vyshhorod [UA] 242 D4
Vyshniy Volochek [RUS]
240 D2
Vyskatka [RUS] 232 E2
Vyškov [CZ] 62 B4
Vyskytná [CZ] 60 E4
Vyšná Revúca [SK] 76 B1
Vyšné Nemecké [SK] 76 F2
Vysock [RUS] 200 D2
Vysoká [CZ] 60 E3
Vysoká u Příbr. [CZ] 60 D3
Vysokaye [BY] 50 C1
Vysoké Mýto [CZ] 62 A3
Vysokoe [RUS] 238 B3
Vysokoye [RUS] 232 E3
Vysoký Chlumec [CZ] 60 D3
Vysoký Hrádek [CZ] 74 A1
Vyšší Brod [CZ] 74 A2
Vyssinéá [GR] 160 D2
Vytína [GR] 172 D2

W

Waabs [D] 32 C1
Waalwijk [NL] 40 E2
Wabern [D] 44 B4
Wąbrzeźno [PL] 36 D3
Wachenroth [D] 58 E3
Wąchock [PL] 48 F4
Wachow [D] 44 F1
Wächtersbach [D] 58 C2
Wachtum [D] 30 E3
Wackersdorf [D] 60 B4
Wadebridge [GB] 26 B3
Wädenswil [CH] 70 E4

Wadlew [PL] 48 D3
Wadowice [PL] 62 E3
Wagenfeld [D] 30 F3
Wageningen [NL] 30 C4
Waging [D] 72 E3
Wagrain [A] 72 E4
Wągrowiec [PL] 46 F1
Wahlwies [D] 70 F3
Wahrenholz [D] 44 C1
Waiblingen [D] 70 F1
Waidhaus [D] 60 B3
Waidhofen an der Thaya
[A] 74 B2
Waidhofen an der Ybbs
[A] 74 B3
Waldring [A] 72 D3
Waischenfeld [D] 58 E3
Wakefield [GB] 24 C2
Walbeck [D] 44 D2
Wałbrzych [PL] 62 B1
Walchensee [D] 72 C3
Walchsee [A] 72 D3
Walcourt [B] 56 B1
Wałcz [PL] 36 A3
Wald [A] 72 D4
Wald [CH] 70 F4
Waldangelloch [D] 58 B4
Waldbröl [D] 42 D4
Waldburg [D] 72 A3
Waldeck [D] 42 F3
Waldenbuch [D] 70 F1
Waldenburg [D] 58 C4
Waldenburg [D] 60 B1
Waldfischbach [D] 56 F3
Waldhausen [D] 58 C3
Waldheim [D] 44 F4
Waldkirch [D] 70 E2
Waldkirchen [D] 72 F2
Waldkraiburg [D] 72 D2
Waldmünchen [D] 60 B4
Waldowice [PL] 46 D1
Waldsassen [D] 60 B3
Waldshut [D] 70 E3
Waldweiler [D] 56 E3
Walenstadt [CH] 70 F4
Walhalla [D] 60 B4
Wallasey [GB] 22 E2
Walldorf [D] 58 B3
Walldürn [D] 58 C3
Wallenfels [D] 58 F2
Wallern [A] 74 D3
Wallersdorf [D] 72 E2
Wallerstein [D] 72 B1
Wallfahrtskirche [D] 72 B1
Wallingford [GB] 28 B2
Wallsbüll [D] 178 B3
Wals [A] 72 E3
Walsall [GB] 22 F4
Walsrode [D] 32 B4
Waltrop [D] 42 D2
Waltsberg [A] 120 C2
Wambach [D] 42 F4
Wambierzyce [PL] 62 B2
Wanderup [D] 178 B3
Wandlitz [D] 46 B1
Wanfried [D] 44 C4
Wangen [D] 72 A3
Wangenbourg [F] 70 D1
Wangerooge [D] 30 F1
Wangersen [D] 32 B3
Wängi [CH] 70 F3
Wankendorf [D] 32 C2
Wantage [GB] 28 B2
Wanzleben [D] 44 D2
Warburg [D] 42 F3
Wardenburg [D] 30 F2
Ware [GB] 28 D2
Waregem [B] 40 C3
Wareham [GB] 26 E4
Waremme [B] 40 E4
Waren [D] 32 F3
Warendorf [D] 30 E4

Warin [D] 32 E2
Warka [PL] 48 F3
Warlubie [PL] 36 C3
Warmbad Villach [A] 118 F2
Warmensteinach [D] 58 F3
Warminster [GB] 26 F3
Warmsen [D] 42 F1
Warnemünde [D] 32 E2
Warner Bros Park [E] 92 E4
Warnice [PL] 34 D4
Warnice [PL] 34 E3
Warnsveld [NL] 30 C4
Warrenpoint [NIR] 12 E3
Warrington [GB] 22 F2
Warstein [D] 42 E3
Warszawa [PL] 48 F2
Warszkowo [PL] 36 A2
Warta [PL] 48 C3
Warta Bolesławiecka [PL]
46 D4
Wartburg [D] 44 C4
Wartensee [CH] 70 E4
Wartenstein [A] 74 C4
Warth [A] 72 A4
Wartha [D] 44 C4
Warwick [GB] 28 B1
Washington [GB] 20 E3
Wasigenstein, Château de–
[F] 56 F4
Wasilków [PL] 38 C3
Wąsosz [PL] 38 B2
Wąsosz [PL] 46 F3
Wasselonne [F] 70 D1
Wassen [CH] 116 D1
Wassenaar [NL] 30 A3
Wassenberg [D] 42 C3
Wasseralfingen [D] 72 B1
Wasserbillig [L] 56 E2
Wasserburg [D] 72 D3
Wasserfall Groppenstn. [A]
118 E1
Wasserkuppe [D] 58 D2
Wasserleonberg [A] 118 E2
Wasserschloss [D] 42 D2
Wasserschloss [D] 44 F3
Wassertrüdingen [D] 58 D4
Wassy [F] 68 F1
Wastl am Wald [A] 74 B3
Wasungen [D] 58 D1
Waterford / Port Lairge [IRL]
10 E4
Watergrasshill [IRL] 10 C4
Waterloo [B] 40 D4
Waterlooville [GB] 28 B4
Waterville / An Coireán [IRL]
10 A3
Watford [GB] 28 C2
Watten [F] 40 B3
Wattens [A] 72 C4
Watton [GB] 28 E1
Wattwil [CH] 70 F4
Watzelsdorf [A] 74 C2
Waulsort [B] 56 C1
Waver (Waver) [B] 40 E4
Wavre (Waver) [B] 40 E4
Waxenberg [A] 74 A2
Waxweiler [D] 56 E2
Ważne Młyny [PL] 48 D4
Wda [PL] 36 C3
Wdzydze Kiszewskie [PL]
36 C2
Węchadłów [PL] 64 A2
Wechselburg [D] 44 F4
Weddelsborg [DK] 178 C2
Wedel [D] 32 B3
Wedemark [D] 44 B1
Weener [D] 30 E2
Weert [NL] 40 F3
Weesen [CH] 70 F4
Weeze [D] 42 C2
Wegberg [D] 42 C3
Wegeleben [D] 44 D2

Wegenstedt [D] 44 D2
Weggis [CH] 70 E4
Węgliniec [PL] 46 D4
Węgorzewo [PL] 38 A1
Węgorzyno [PL] 34 E3
Węgrów [PL] 50 B1
Węgrzynice [PL] 46 D2
Wegscheid [D] 72 F2
Wehr [D] 56 F1
Wehr [D] 70 D3
Weichselboden [A] 74 B3
Weichshofen [D] 72 D2
Weida [D] 60 B1
Weiden [D] 60 B3
Weidenberg [D] 58 F3
Weidensees [D] 58 F3
Weidenstetten [D] 72 A2
Weigetschlag [A] 74 A2
Weikersheim [D] 58 D3
Weil [D] 70 F1
Weilar [D] 58 D1
Weilburg [D] 58 B1
Weilheim [D] 72 C3
Weilmünster [D] 58 B1
Weimar [D] 42 E4
Weimar [D] 44 D4
Weinfelden [CH] 70 F3
Weingarten [D] 72 A3
Weinheim [D] 58 B3
Weinsberg [D] 58 C4
Weintor [D] 58 A4
Weirenstein [A] 118 D1
Weismain [D] 58 E2
Weissbriach [A] 118 E2
Weissenbach [A] 72 B4
Weissenbach [A] 118 E2
Weissenbach / Riobianco
[I] 118 C2
Weissenberg [D] 46 C4
Weissenburg [D] 58 E4
Weissenegg [A] 120 C2
Weissenfels [D] 44 E4
Weissenhorn [D] 72 A2
Weissenkirchen [A] 74 C2
Weissensee [D] 44 D4
Weissenstadt [D] 58 F2
Weissenstein [D] 58 E3
Weisskirchen [A] 120 B1
Weisstannen [CH] 70 F4
Weisswasser [D] 46 C3
Weitensfeld [A] 118 F2
Weitersfelden [A] 74 B2
Weitra [A] 74 B2
Weiz [A] 120 C1
Wejherowo [PL] 36 C1
Welden [D] 72 B2
Wełdkowo [PL] 36 A2
Well [NL] 42 C2
Wellaune [D] 44 E3
Welle [D] 32 B3
Wellin [B] 56 C2
Wellingborough [GB] 28 C1
Wellington [GB] 26 D3
Wells [GB] 26 E3
Wells-next-the-Sea [GB]
24 E4
Wels [A] 72 F3
Welsberg / Monguelfo [I]
118 D2
Welschnofen / Nova Levante
[I] 118 C2
Welshpool [GB] 22 E3
Weltenburg [D] 72 D1
Welwyn Garden City [GB]
28 C2
Welzheim [D] 72 A1
Wemding [D] 72 B2
Wemperhaardt [L] 56 D2
Wenddorf [D] 44 E2
Wenecja [PL] 48 B1
Wengen [CH] 116 C2
Wennigsen [D] 44 B2

Wenns [A] 72 B4
Wépion [B] 40 E4
Weppersdorf [A] 74 D4
Werben [D] 32 E4
Werbomont [B] 56 D1
Werdau [D] 60 B1
Werder [D] 44 F2
Werdohl [D] 42 D3
Werfen [A] 72 E4
Werl [D] 42 E3
Werlte [D] 30 E3
Wermelskirchen [D] 42 D3
Wernberg [D] 60 B3
Werne [D] 42 D2
Werneck [D] 58 D2
Werneuchen [D] 46 B1
Wernigerode [D] 44 D3
Wertach [D] 72 B3
Wertheim [D] 58 C3
Werther [D] 30 F4
Wertingen [D] 72 B2
Wesel [D] 42 C2
Wesenberg [D] 32 F3
Wesendorf [D] 44 C1
Wesoła [PL] 64 B2
Wesselburen [D] 32 B1
Wesseling [D] 42 C4
Wessobrunn [D] 72 C3
West Bridgford [GB] 24 C3
West Bromwich [GB] 22 F4
Westbury [GB] 26 F3
Westende–Bad [B] 40 C3
Westendorf [A] 72 D4
Westenholz [D] 32 B4
Westensee [D] 32 C1
Westerhever [D] 32 A1
Westerholt [D] 30 E1
Westerland [D] 178 A3
Westerlo [B] 40 E3
Westerstede [D] 30 F2
Westkapelle [NL] 40 D2
Weston–super–Mare [GB] 26 E2
Westport [IRL] 12 B2
West Sandwick [GB] 16 F3
West–Terschelling [NL] 30 C1
Wetherby [GB] 24 C2
Wetlina [PL] 64 D4
Wetter [D] 42 D3
Wetter [D] 42 E4
Wetteren [B] 40 D3
Wettringen [D] 30 E4
Wetzikon [CH] 70 E4
Wetzlar [D] 58 B1
Wexford / Loch Garman
   [IRL] 10 E4
Weyer [A] 74 B4
Weyerburg [A] 72 D4
Weyer–Markt [A] 74 B3
Weyhausen [D] 32 C4
Weymouth [GB] 26 E4
Weyregg [A] 72 F3
Whitby [GB] 24 D4
Whitchurch [GB] 22 E3
Whitegate [IRL] 10 C4
Whitehead [NIR] 12 F2
Whithorn [GB] 20 B3
Whiting Bay [GB] 18 B4
Whitley Bay [GB] 20 F3
Whitstable [GB] 28 E3
Wiartel [PL] 38 A2
Wiązownica [PL] 64 D2
Wiblingen [D] 72 A2
Wicie [PL] 36 A1
Wicimice [PL] 34 E2
Wick [GB] 14 F2
Wickham Market [GB] 28 E2
Wicklow [IRL] 10 F3
Wicko [PL] 36 B3
Widawa [PL] 46 F4
Widawa [PL] 48 C3
Widdern [D] 58 C3
Widnes [GB] 22 F2

Widoma [PL] 62 F2
Widuchowa [PL] 34 D4
Więcbork [PL] 36 B3
Wiechowice [PL] 62 C3
Wiedenbrück [D] 42 E2
Wiefelstede [D] 30 F2
Wiehe [D] 44 D4
Wiehler Tropfsteinhöle [D] 42 D4
Wiek [D] 34 C1
Większyce [PL] 62 D2
Wielbark [PL] 36 F3
Wiele [PL] 36 C2
Wieleń [PL] 34 F4
Wielgie [PL] 48 C4
Wielgie [PL] 50 B3
Wielichowo [PL] 46 E2
Wieliczka [PL] 62 F3
Wieliczki [PL] 38 B2
Wielka Piaśnica [PL] 36 C1
Wielogłowy [PL] 64 B3
Wielogóra [PL] 48 F3
Wielowieś [PL] 62 D2
Wieluń [PL] 48 C4
Wien [A] 74 D3
Wiener Neustadt [A] 74 D3
Wienhausen [D] 44 C1
Wieniawa [PL] 48 F3
Wiepke [D] 44 D1
Wierden [NL] 30 D3
Wieruszów [PL] 48 C4
Wierzbica [PL] 48 F4
Wierzbice [PL] 62 B1
Wierzbowo [PL] 36 E3
Wierzchowo [PL] 36 A3
Wierzchucin Krolewski [PL]
   36 C3
Wierzchucino [PL] 36 C1
Wies [D] 72 B3
Wiesau [D] 60 B3
Wiesbaden [D] 58 B2
Wiesberg [A] 72 B4
Wieselburg [A] 74 B3
Wiesen [CH] 116 F1
Wiesenburg [D] 44 E2
Wiesentheid [D] 58 D3
Wieskirche [D] 72 B3
Wiesloch [D] 58 B3
Wiesmath [A] 74 D4
Wiesmoor [D] 30 E2
Wietze [D] 32 B4
Wietzendorf [D] 32 C4
Wigan [GB] 22 F2
Wigston [GB] 24 C4
Wigton [GB] 20 D3
Wigtown [GB] 20 B2
Wijhe [NL] 30 C3
Wikingerburg [D] 56 E2
Wil [CH] 70 F3
Wilanów [PL] 48 F2
Wilczków [PL] 46 E4
Wilczkowo [PL] 36 E2
Wilczyska [PL] 64 B3
Wildalpen [A] 74 B3
Wildbad [D] 70 E1
Wildberg [D] 70 F1
Wildeck [D] 58 C4
Wildenburg [D] 56 F2
Wildenburg [D] 58 C3
Wildenrath [D] 42 C3
Wildenstein [D] 70 D3
Wildenstein [D] 70 F2
Wildenstein Wasserfall [A]
   120 A2
Wildeshausen [D] 30 F3
Wildhaus [CH] 70 F4
Wildkirchli [CH] 70 F4
Wildon [A] 120 C2
Wilfersdorf [A] 74 D2
Wilga [PL] 48 F2
Wilhelmsburg [A] 74 C3
Wilhelmsh [D] 44 B3
Wilhelmshaven [D] 30 F2

Wilhelmsthal [D] 44 B3
Wilhering [A] 74 A2
Wilków [PL] 48 E3
Wilków [PL] 62 F2
Wilkowo [PL] 46 D2
Willebroek [B] 40 E3
Willemstad [NL] 30 A4
Willingen [D] 42 E3
Willisau [CH] 70 D4
Willsbach [D] 58 C4
Wilnsdorf [D] 42 E4
Wilsin [NL] 30 B3
Wilster [D] 32 B2
Wilsum [D] 30 D3
Wilton [GB] 26 F3
Wiltz [L] 56 D2
Wimborne Minster [GB] 26 F3
Wimereux [F] 40 A3
Wincanton [GB] 26 E3
Winchester [GB] 28 B3
Windeck [D] 42 D4
Windermere [GB] 20 D4
Windisch [D] 60 B3
Windischgarsten [A] 74 A3
Windsbach [D] 58 E4
Wingen–sur–Moder [F] 56 E4
Winklern [A] 118 E1
Winnica [PL] 48 F1
Winnigstedt [D] 44 C2
Winnweiler [D] 56 F3
Winschoten [NL] 30 E2
Winsen [D] 32 B4
Winsen [D] 32 C3
Wińsko [PL] 46 E3
Winsum [NL] 30 D2
Winterberg [D] 42 E3
Winterfeld [D] 32 D4
Wintermoor [D] 32 B3
Winterstein [D] 44 C4
Winterswijk [NL] 30 D4
Winterthur [CH] 70 E3
Wipperfürth [D] 42 D3
Wippra [D] 44 D3
Wiry [PL] 62 B1
Wisbech [GB] 28 D1
Wischhafen [D] 32 B2
Wisełka [PL] 34 D2
Wiskitki [PL] 48 E2
Wisła [PL] 62 E3
Wiślica [PL] 64 B2
Wismar [D] 32 D2
Wiśniewo Ełckie [PL] 38 B2
Wiśniowa [PL] 62 F3
Wiśniowa [PL] 64 C3
Wissant [F] 28 E4
Wissembourg [F] 56 F4
Wissen [D] 42 D4
Wisznice [PL] 50 C2
Witham [GB] 28 D2
Withernsea [GB] 24 E2
Witków [PL] 64 F1
Witkowice [PL] 62 E1
Witkowo [PL] 48 B2
Witney [GB] 28 B2
Witnica [PL] 34 D4
Witnica [PL] 46 D1
Witostowice [PL] 62 C2
Witowo [PL] 48 C1
Wittdün [D] 178 A3
Witten [D] 42 D3
Wittenberge [D] 32 E4
Wittenborn [D] 32 C2
Wittenburg [D] 32 D3
Wittgenstein [D] 58 A3
Wittichenau [D] 46 C3
Wittingen [D] 32 C4
Wittislingen [D] 72 B2
Wittlich [D] 56 E2
Wittmund [D] 30 E1
Wittstock [D] 32 F3
Witzenhausen [D] 44 B3
Wiżajny [PL] 38 C1

Wizna [PL] 38 B3
Władysławowo [PL] 36 C1
Wleń [PL] 46 D4
Włocławek [PL] 48 C1
Włodawa [PL] 50 D3
Włoszczowa [PL] 62 F1
Włoszczowice [PL] 64 B2
Wodzisław [PL] 62 F2
Wodzisław Śląski [PL] 62 D3
Woerden [NL] 30 B4
Woerth [F] 56 F4
Woesten [B] 40 C3
Wohlen [CH] 70 E3
Wohra [D] 42 F4
Woijtowice [PL] 62 C2
Wojcieszków [PL] 50 B2
Wojcieszów [PL] 60 F1
Wójcin [PL] 48 C2
Wojnicz [PL] 64 B3
Wojsławice [PL] 50 D4
Wojtokiemie [PL] 38 C1
Woking [GB] 28 C3
Wola Idzikowska [PL] 50 C4
Wola Klasztorna [PL] 50 B3
Wola Obszańska [PL] 64 D2
Wola Rakowa [PL] 48 D3
Wola Uhruska [PL] 50 D3
Wola Wierzbowska [PL] 36 F4
Wolbórz [PL] 48 D3
Wolbrom [PL] 62 F2
Wołczyn [PL] 48 B4
Woldegk [D] 34 A3
Wolenice [PL] 48 B3
Wolfach [D] 70 E2
Wolfegg [D] 72 A3
Wolfen [D] 44 E3
Wolfenbüttel [D] 44 C2
Wolfhagen [D] 42 F3
Wolframs–Eschenbach [D]
   58 E4
Wolfratshausen [D] 72 C3
Wolfsberg [A] 120 B2
Wolfsburg [D] 44 D2
Wolfstein [D] 56 F3
Wolgast [D] 34 C2
Wolhusen [CH] 70 D4
Wolibórz [PL] 62 B2
Wolica [PL] 64 A2
Wolin [PL] 34 D2
Wolin [PL] 34 D2
Wólka [PL] 48 E4
Wólka Dobryńska [PL] 50 D2
Wólka Łabuńska [PL] 64 E1
Wolkenstein [D] 60 C2
Wolkenstein in Gröden / Selva
   di Val Gardena [I] 118 C2
Wolkersdorf [A] 74 D2
Wollenberg [D] 46 C1
Wöllersdorf [A] 74 D3
Wollin [D] 44 E2
Wolmirstedt [D] 44 E2
Wolnzach [D] 72 C2
Wołomin [PL] 48 F2
Wołosate [PL] 64 D4
Wołow [PL] 46 F4
Wolsingham [GB] 20 E3
Wolsztyn [PL] 46 E2
Wolvega [NL] 30 C2
Wolverhampton [GB] 22 F4
Woodbridge [GB] 28 E2
Woodford [IRL] 10 D2
Wooler [GB] 20 E2
Wootton Bassett [GB] 26 F2
Worb [CH] 70 D4
Worbis [D] 44 C3
Worcester [GB] 26 F1
Worden–Sankt Andra [A] 74 D2
Wörgl [A] 72 D4
Workington [GB] 20 C3
Worksop [GB] 24 C3
Workum [NL] 30 C2
Wörlitz [D] 44 E3

Wormerveer [NL] 30 B3
Wormhout [F] 40 B3
Worms [D] 58 B3
Wörnitz [D] 58 D4
Worpswede [D] 32 A3
Wörrstadt [D] 58 B2
Wörth [A] 72 E4
Wörth [D] 58 B4
Wörth [D] 58 C3
Wörth [D] 72 D1
Wörth [D] 72 D2
Worthing [GB] 28 C4
Wozławki [PL] 36 F2
Woźniki [PL] 62 E2
Wożuczyn [PL] 64 E2
Wragby [GB] 24 D3
Wręczyca Wielka [PL] 62 E1
Wredenhagen [D] 32 E3
Wrexham [GB] 22 E3
Wriezen [D] 46 C1
Wróblew [PL] 48 C3
Wróblewo [PL] 46 E1
Wrocki [PL] 36 D4
Wrocław [PL] 46 F4
Wroniniec [PL] 46 E1
Wronki [PL] 38 B2
Wronki [PL] 46 E1
Wrząca Wielka [PL] 48 C2
Września [PL] 48 B2
Wschowa [PL] 46 E3
Wulfen [D] 42 D2
Wulkau [D] 32 E4
Wullersdorf [A] 74 C2
Wullowitz [A] 74 A2
Wünnenberg [D] 42 F3
Wunsiedel [D] 60 B3
Wunstorf [D] 44 B1
Wuppertal [D] 42 D3
Würgau [D] 58 E3
Wurmlinger Kapelle [D] 70 F2
Wurzbach [D] 58 F2
Würzbrunnen [CH] 70 D4
Würzburg [D] 58 D3
Wurzen [D] 44 F3
Wust [D] 44 E1
Wusterhausen [D] 32 E4
Wüstermarke [D] 46 B3
Wustrow [D] 32 E2
Wustrow [D] 32 F3
Wuustwezel [B] 40 E2
Wybcz [PL] 36 C4
Wydminy [PL] 38 B2
Wygoda [PL] 64 C3
Wyk [D] 178 A3
Wymondham [GB] 28 E1
Wyrzysk [PL] 36 B4
Wyśmierzyce [PL] 48 F3
Wysoka [PL] 36 B4
Wysokie [PL] 50 C4
Wysokie Mazowieckie [PL]
   38 B3
Wysowa [PL] 64 C4
Wyszanów [PL] 48 B4
Wyszki [PL] 38 C3
Wyszków [PL] 38 A4
Wyszogród [PL] 48 E2
Wyszyna [PL] 48 C2

X

Xàbia [E] 108 C2
Xàbia / Jávea [E] 108 C2
Xabier / Javier [E] 88 B3
Xanten [D] 42 C2
Xánthi [GR] 156 D4
Xanthos [TR] 176 E1
Xàtiva [E] 102 C2
Xeraco [E] 102 D4
Xeresa [E] 102 D4
Xert [E] 96 A4

Xerta [E] 96 B3
Xertigny [F] 70 C2
Xesta, Puerto de la– [E] 82 D2
Xhoffraix [B] 56 D1
Xilopároiko [GR] 160 D4
Xinzo de Limia / Ginzo de Limia [E] 82 C4
Xirokámpi [GR] 172 D3
Xirókampos [GR] 170 B4
Xivert, Castell de– [E] 102 E2
Xixón / Gijón [E] 82 F2
Xixona / Jijona [E] 106 F1
Xodos / Chodos [E] 102 E2
Xove [E] 82 D1
Xubia [E] 82 C1
Xunqueira de Ambia [E] 82 C4
Xunqueira de Espadanedo [E] 82 C3
Xylaganí [GR] 156 E4
Xylofagou [CY] 176 E3
Xylókastro [GR] 166 E4
Xylópoli [GR] 156 B4
Xyniás [GR] 162 A4
Xynó Neró [GR] 160 D2

Y

Yablanitsa [BG] 148 E4
Yablanovo [BG] 150 C4
Yablonovka [RUS] 200 F2
Yacimiento de Botorrita [E] 94 D3
Yacimientos de Icnitas [E] 94 C1
Yağcilar [TR] 164 D3
Yağcılı [TR] 164 C3
Yağlılar [TR] 164 C3
Yagoda [BG] 156 E1
Yahotyn [UA] 242 E4
Yaiza [E] 114 E3
Yakimovo [BG] 148 D3
Yakkima [RUS] 210 F3
Yakoruda [BG] 156 B2
Yalakdere [TR] 158 F4
Yalıkavak [TR] 170 B4
Yalıköy [TR] 158 D2
Yalova [TR] 158 E4
Yaman [TR] 170 E2
Yambol [BG] 156 F1
Yamm [RUS] 232 E3
Yampil' [UA] 242 E2
Yampil' [UA] 244 D1
Yampil' [UA] 244 E2
Yanciklar [TR] 158 B2
Yanguas [E] 94 C1
Yanjukalns [LLV] 236 C3
Yaras [TR] 170 D4
Yarbasan [TR] 164 E3
Yarema [BG] 156 B1
Yarımca [TR] 158 F3
Yariş [TR] 164 F3
Yarm [GB] 20 E4
Yarmolyntsi [UA] 244 E2
Yarmouth [GB] 26 F4
Yaroslavchi [UA] 50 F4
Yartsevo [RUS] 240 D4
Yasen [BG] 148 F3
Yasna Polyana [BG] 158 C1
Yasnoe [RUS] 238 B3
Yassıören [TR] 158 D3
Yassıören [TR] 164 E2
Yatağan [TR] 170 C4
Yavorets [BG] 150 B4
Yavoriv [UA] 64 E3
Yaylabayır [TR] 164 D3
Yayladamı [TR] 164 C3
Yaylaköy [TR] 170 F3
Yazhelbitsy [RUS] 240 C2
Yazıkent [TR] 170 D3
Yazıköv [TR] 176 B1
Yazır [TR] 170 F3

Yazır [TR] 176 F1
Yazırköy [TR] 170 D3
Ybbs an der Donau [A] 74 B3
Ybbsitz [A] 74 B3
Ychoux [F] 78 B4
Yderby [DK] 178 D1
Ydra [GR] 168 A4
Ydrefors [S] 184 E2
Yecla [E] 106 E1
Yecla de Yeltes [E] 84 D4
Yeleğen [TR] 170 D2
Yelizavetino [RUS] 200 F4
Yel'na [RUS] 240 D4
Yel'nya [RUS] 240 D4
Yelo [E] 94 B3
Yel'tsy [RUS] 240 D3
Yelverton [GB] 26 C3
Yemel'yanovka [RUS] 216 F3
Yemikaraağac [TR] 164 D1
Yemişendere [TR] 170 D4
Yemişli [TR] 164 E3
Yenibogaziçi (Ay. Seryios) [CY] 176 E3
Yenice [TR] 156 F4
Yenice [TR] 158 C2
Yenice [TR] 164 C2
Yenice [TR] 164 D1
Yenice [TR] 170 D3
Yenicekent [TR] 170 D2
Yeniçiftlik [TR] 158 C3
Yenicöy [TR] 164 C4
Yenidoğan [TR] 170 B3
Yenierenköy (Aigialoúsa) [CY] 176 E2
Yenifoça [TR] 164 B4
Yenihisar [TR] 170 B4
Yeni Karpuzlu [TR] 158 A4
Yeniköy [TR] 158 C4
Yeniköy [TR] 158 E3
Yeniköy [TR] 158 E4
Yeniköy [TR] 158 F3
Yeniköy [TR] 162 F2
Yeniköy [TR] 164 D4
Yeniköy [TR] 164 D2
Yeniköy [TR] 164 F2
Yeniköy [TR] 164 F3
Yeniköy [TR] 176 E2
Yenipazar [TR] 170 C3
Yenişakran [TR] 164 C4
Yenisarıbey [TR] 164 D1
Yenişehir [TR] 158 F4
Yenişehir [TR] 164 E4
Yenişehir [TR] 164 E4
Yenne [F] 80 E3
Yeovil [GB] 26 E3
Yerkesik [TR] 170 D4
Yershi [RUS] 240 E4
Yerville [F] 54 C1
Yesa / Esa [E] 88 B3
Yeşilçay / Ağva [TR] 158 F3
Yeşilköy [TR] 158 D3
Yesilköy [TR] 164 E3
Yesılköy [TR] 176 E2
Yeşiller [TR] 164 E2
Yeşilova [TR] 164 D2
Yeşilova [TR] 170 F3
Yeşilvadi [TR] 158 E3
Yeşilyurt [TR] 170 D2
Yeşilyurt [TR] 170 D4
Yeşilyuva [TR] 170 E3
Yeste [E] 106 C1
Yevpatoria [UA] 246 F4
Yezyaryshcha [BY] 240 C4
Yiğitler [TR] 164 B2
Yılmazköy (Skylloura) [CY] 176 D3
Yılmazlı [TR] 170 F4
Yitteräng [S] 204 D1
Ylakiai [LT] 234 D4
Ylä–Kuona [FIN] 210 D3
Ylä–Luosta [FIN] 210 C1
Ylämaa [FIN] 200 D2

Ylämylly [FIN] 210 D2
Yläne [FIN] 198 C2
Ylihärmä [FIN] 208 C2
Yli–Ii [FIN] 216 B1
Yli–Kärppä [FIN] 222 C4
Ylikiiminki [FIN] 216 B2
Yliklä [FIN] 198 C3
Ylikylä [FIN] 208 B3
Ylikylä [FIN] 208 C1
Ylikylä [FIN] 208 D1
Yli–Lesti [FIN] 208 E1
Ylimarkku / Övermark [FIN] 208 B3
Yli–Nampa [FIN] 222 C2
Yli–Olhava [FIN] 216 B1
Ylistaro [FIN] 208 C2
Ylitornio / Övertorneå [FIN] 222 B3
Ylivieska [FIN] 216 A3
Ylläsjärvi [FIN] 222 B1
Ylöjärvi [FIN] 198 D1
Ylönkylä [FIN] 198 D3
Yngsjö [S] 180 D2
Yoğuntas [TR] 158 B2
Yolağzı [TR] 164 A1
Yolüstü [TR] 170 D3
Yordankino [BG] 156 B1
York [GB] 24 C2
Youghal [IRL] 10 D4
Ypéria [GR] 166 E2
Yport [F] 54 C1
Yppäri [FIN] 216 A3
Ypres (Ieper) [B] 40 C3
Ypso [GR] 160 B4
Ypsoús [GR] 172 D2
Yquem, Château– [F] 78 C4
Yrittäperä [FIN] 216 D2
Yrkje [N] 186 B1
Yrouerre [F] 68 D2
Yset [N] 204 B3
Ysjö [S] 206 C1
Yssandon, Puy d'– [F] 78 E3
Yssingeaux [F] 80 C3
Ystad [S] 180 D2
Ystebrød [N] 186 B3
Ytre Arna [N] 192 B3
Ytre Enebakk [N] 188 B1
Ytre Kjæs [N] 228 C2
Ytre Snillfjord [N] 202 F2
Ytterån [S] 204 E2
Ytterås [N] 204 C2
Ytterträsk [S] 214 D3
Ytterberg [S] 194 F1
Ytterboda [S] 194 F3
Ytterby [S] 182 F1
Ytterhogdal [S] 204 F4
Ytterjeppo [FIN] 208 C1
Yttermalung [S] 194 E3
Ytterselö [S] 190 D2
Ytterturingen [S] 204 F4
Yttervik [S] 212 F2
Yukarıkızılca [TR] 170 B2
Yukhavichy [BY] 236 F4
Yukhnov [RUS] 240 E4
Yuminda [EST] 230 D1
Yuncos [E] 100 E1
Yundola [BG] 156 C2
Yunquera [E] 104 D3
Yunquera de Henares [E] 92 F3
Yuntdağ [TR] 164 C4
Yunuseli [TR] 164 E1
Yuratsishki [BY] 38 F1
Yüreğil [TR] 164 D3
Yürücekler [TR] 164 E2
Yuste, Monasterio de– [E] 92 B4
Yusufça [TR] 170 F3
Yuvacık [TR] 176 C1
Yuzhnoukrains'k [UA] 246 D2
Yverdon–les–Bains [CH] 70 C4
Yvetot [F] 54 C1
Yvoir [B] 40 E4

Yvoire [F] 116 A2
Yxnerum [S] 190 C4
Yxsjö [S] 214 B3

Zaandam [NL] 30 B3
Zabalats' [BY] 38 E1
Žabalj [SRB] 122 C4
Žabari [SRB] 146 F3
Žabice [PL] 46 E4
Zabierzów [PL] 62 F3
Zabki [PL] 48 F2
Ząbkowice Śląskie [PL] 62 B2
Zablaće [HR] 144 D4
Žabljak [MNE] 152 E2
Zabłudów [PL] 38 C3
Žabno [PL] 64 B2
Zabok [HR] 120 C3
Zabolottia [UA] 50 E3
Zabór [PL] 46 D3
Zábřani [RO] 122 E3
Zábřeh [CZ] 62 B3
Zabrodzie [PL] 38 A4
Zabrze [PL] 62 E2
Zabrzeż [PL] 64 B3
Zabzun [AL] 160 B1
Zacháro [GR] 172 C2
Zachloroú [GR] 166 E4
Zadar [HR] 144 C3
Zadni Chodov [CZ] 60 B3
Zadvarje [HR] 152 B1
Zadzyezhzha [BY] 236 E4
Zafferana Etnea [I] 138 C4
Zafirovo [BG] 150 D2
Zafra [E] 98 E2
Žaga [SLO] 118 E2
Żagań [PL] 46 D3
Zagare [LT] 234 E4
Zagklivéri [GR] 162 B1
Zaglav [HR] 144 C3
Zaglavak [SRB] 146 D3
Zagorá [GR] 162 B3
Zagorje [HR] 120 C4
Zagorje [SLO] 120 B3
Zagórów [PL] 48 B2
Zagórz [PL] 64 D3
Zagórzany [PL] 64 B3
Zagoska [RUS] 232 F3
Zagreb [HR] 120 C3
Žagubica [SRB] 148 B2
Zagvozd [HR] 152 B1
Zagwiździe [PL] 62 D1
Zagyvapálfalva [H] 76 C3
Zahara [E] 104 C2
Zahara de los Atunes [E] 104 D3
Zahinos [E] 98 E2
Zahna [D] 44 E3
Zahody [RUS] 232 E3
Záhony [H] 76 E2
Záhoří [CZ] 60 D4
Záhorská Ves [SK] 74 D2
Zahrádky [CZ] 60 D2
Zaiceva [LV] 230 F4
Zaidin [E] 94 F3
Zaisenhausen [D] 58 B4
Zajas [MK] 154 C4
Zaječar [SRB] 148 C3
Zákas [GR] 160 D3
Zakliczyn [PL] 64 B3
Zaklików [PL] 64 C1
Zakopane [PL] 62 F4
Zakroczym [PL] 48 F2
Zakrós [GR] 174 F4
Zakrós [GR] 174 F4
Zakrzewo [PL] 48 C1

Zakrzówek [PL] 50 A3
Zákupy [CZ] 60 E2
Zákynthos [GR] 172 B2
Zalaapáti [H] 120 E2
Zalabaksa [H] 120 D2
Zalabér [H] 120 E1
Zalaegerszeg [H] 120 D2
Zalakaros [H] 120 E2
Zalakomár [H] 120 E2
Zalaksáni [H] 120 E2
Zalalövő [H] 120 D2
Zalamea de la Serena [E] 100 B3
Zalamea la Real [E] 98 E3
Zalaszabar [H] 120 E2
Zalaszántó [H] 120 E2
Zalaszentbalázs [H] 120 E2
Zalaszentgrót [H] 120 E1
Zalău [RO] 244 C3
Žalec [SLO] 120 B3
Zalewo [PL] 36 D2
Załeże [PL] 36 F3
Zalishchyky [UA] 244 D2
Zalivnoye [RUS] 238 A3
Zalla [E] 86 D3
Zaltbommel [NL] 30 B4
Załuski [PL] 48 E2
Załuż [PL] 64 D3
Zalužnica [HR] 144 C2
Zamárdi [H] 120 F2
Zamarte [PL] 36 B3
Žamberk [CZ] 62 B3
Zambrana [E] 86 D4
Zambrów [PL] 38 B3
Zambujal [P] 90 B4
Zambujeira do Mar [P] 98 B3
Zamora [E] 84 E3
Zamość [PL] 38 A3
Zamość [PL] 38 B3
Zamość [PL] 50 D4
Zamostne [PL] 36 C1
Zandhoven [B] 40 E3
Zandvoort [NL] 30 B3
Zangoza / Sangüesa [E] 88 A3
Zaniemyśl [PL] 46 F2
Zánka [H] 120 E2
Zan'kovo [RUS] 232 E4
Zante [LV] 234 E3
Zaorejas [E] 94 B4
Zaostrog [HR] 152 C2
Zaostrov'ye [RUS] 200 C3
Zapadnaja Dvina [RUS] 240 D3
Zapadnaya Dvina [RUS] 240 D3
Zapałów [PL] 64 D2
Zapfendorf [D] 58 E2
Zaplyus'ye [RUS] 232 F2
Zapole [PL] 48 C3
Zapolyarnyy [RUS] 226 F1
Zapol'ye [RUS] 232 F2
Zaporizhzhia [UA] 246 F2
Zaporozhskoye [RUS] 200 F2
Záppeio [GR] 160 F4
Zapponeta [I] 134 F2
Zaprešić [HR] 120 C3
Zaprudy [BY] 38 E4
Zapyškis [LT] 238 C3
Zapytiv [UA] 64 F3
Zaragoza [E] 94 D3
Zárakes [GR] 168 B2
Zărand [RO] 122 E2
Zarańsko [PL] 34 F3
Zarasai [LT] 238 F2
Zarautz [E] 86 F3
Zarcilla de los Ramons [E] 106 D2
Zaręby–Warchoły [PL] 38 B4
Zarech'e [RUS] 232 F4
Zarechnyy [RUS] 216 F2
Zarenthien [D] 32 D4
Zarichchia [UA] 50 E3
Żarki [PL] 62 E2
Zárkos [GR] 160 E4

Zărneşti [RO] 248 D3
Žarnovica [SK] 76 A2
Żarnów [PL] 48 E4
Żarnowiec [PL] 62 F2
Zarós [GR] 174 D4
Žarošice [CZ] 74 E1
Żarów [PL] 62 B1
Zarrentin [D] 32 D3
Żarska Wieś [PL] 46 D4
Zarszyn [PL] 64 D3
Zaruch'e [RUS] 232 E2
Żary [PL] 46 D3
Zarza–Capilla [E] 100 B3
Zarza de Alange [E] 98 F2
Zarzadilla de Totana [E] 106 D2
Zarza la Mayor [E] 90 E2
Zarzecze [PL] 50 B3
Zarzecze [PL] 64 D2
Zás [E] 82 B2
Zasa [LV] 236 C4
Zasieki [PI] 46 C3
Žatec [CZ] 60 C2
Zatom [PL] 34 F4
Zator [PL] 62 E3
Zătreni [RO] 148 E1
Zaube [LV] 236 C3
Zauchwitz [D] 44 F2
Zavala [BIH] 152 D2
Zavet [BG] 150 C2
Zăvideni [RO] 148 E1
Zavidovići [BIH] 146 B2
Zavlaka [SRB] 146 C2
Zavoya [BG] 156 E3
Zavrc [SLO] 120 C2
Zawada [PL] 46 D2
Zawada [PL] 62 D2
Zawady [PL] 48 C4
Zawadzkie [PL] 62 D2
Zawichost [PL] 50 B4
Zawidów [PL] 46 D4
Zawiercie [PL] 62 E2
Zawoja [PL] 62 F3
Zawonia [PL] 46 F4
Zawroty [PL] 36 E2
Zayan'ye [RUS] 232 E2
Zaytsevo [RUS] 200 E2
Žažina [HR] 120 D4
Zázriva [SK] 62 E4
Zbąszyń [PL] 46 E2
Zbąszynek [PL] 46 E2
Zblewo [PL] 36 C2
Zboj [SK] 64 D4
Zbojno [PL] 36 D4
Zborište [BIH] 144 D1
Zborov [SK] 64 C4
Zborowice [PL] 64 B3
Zbrachlin [PL] 36 C3
Zbraslav [CZ] 60 D3
Zbraslavice [CZ] 60 E3
Zbrašovske Aragonitové
  Jeskyně [CZ] 62 C3
Zbucz [PL] 38 D4
Zbuczyn Poduchowny [PL]
  50 C2
Zdala [HR] 120 E3
Žďár [CZ] 60 C3
Žďár nad Sázavou [CZ] 60 F3
Zdenci [HR] 120 F4
Zdenska Vas [SLO] 120 B3
Zdiby [CZ] 60 D2
Zdice [CZ] 60 D3
Žďírec nad Doubrava [CZ]
  60 F3
Zdounky [CZ] 62 C4
Zdunje [MK] 154 C4
Zduńska Wola [PL] 48 C3
Zduny [PL] 48 B3
Zduny [PL] 48 D2
Zdziechowice [PL] 50 B4
Zdzieszowice [PL] 62 D2
Žebrák [CZ] 60 D3
Zebreira [P] 90 E2

Zebrzydowa [PL] 46 D4
Zeddiani [I] 142 B4
Žednik [SRB] 122 C3
Zeebrugge [B] 40 C2
Zeewolde [NL] 30 C3
Zefyría [GR] 174 C1
Żegiestów–Zdrój [PL] 64 B4
Zegorje [RUS] 232 E1
Zehdenick [D] 34 C4
Zeil [D] 72 A3
Zeist [NL] 30 B4
Zeitz [D] 44 E4
Żelazna [PL] 36 C1
Żelazna Góra [PL] 36 E2
Żelechów [PL] 50 B2
Zelená Hora [CZ] 60 C4
Zelena morava [BG] 150 C3
Zelenika [MNE] 152 E3
Zelenogorsk [RUS] 200 E3
Želetava [CZ] 60 F4
Žcolczná [CZ] 60 B3
Żelezná Ruda [CZ] 60 C4
Železnik [SRB] 146 D2
Železniki [SLO] 118 F3
Železný Brod [CZ] 60 E2
Zelhem [NL] 30 C4
Želiezovce [SK] 76 A3
Želin [SLO] 118 F3
Zelina [HR] 120 D3
Zélio [GR] 166 F3
Želiv [CZ] 60 E4
Želizna [PL] 50 C2
Żelkowo [PL] 36 B1
Zell [A] 72 F2
Zell [D] 56 F2
Zell [D] 70 D3
Zella [D] 44 C3
Zella–Mehlis [D] 58 E1
Zell am See [A] 72 E4
Zell am Ziller [A] 72 C4
Železnava [CZ] 72 F2
Zelów [PL] 48 D3
Zeltini [LV] 232 D4
Zeltweg [A] 120 B1
Želva [LT] 238 E2
Zelwa [B] 38 C1
Zelzate [B] 40 D3
Žemaičiu Naumiestis [LT]
  238 B2
Žemberovce [SK] 76 A2
Zemblak [AL] 160 C2
Zeme [I] 116 D4
Zemen [BG] 154 F2
Zemite [LV] 234 E3
Zemmer [D] 56 F2
Zemplínske Jastrabie [SK]
  76 E2
Zemplíriská Teplica [SK] 76 E2
Zemun [SRB] 146 D2
Zenica [BIH] 146 A3
Žepa [BIH] 146 C3
Zepče [BIH] 146 A3
Zerbst [D] 44 E2
Žerczyce [PL] 38 C4
Zerevna [BG] 150 C4
Zerf [D] 56 E3
Zeri [I] 126 F2
Zerind [RO] 122 E2
Zermatt [CH] 116 C2
Zernez [CH] 116 F2
Zernien [D] 32 D4
Żerniki [PL] 46 F4
Zerqan [AL] 154 B4
Zestoa / Cestona [E] 86 E3
Žetale [SLO] 120 C3
Zetel [D] 30 F2
Zeulenroda [D] 60 B1
Zeven [D] 32 B3
Zevenaar [NL] 30 C4
Zevenergen [NL] 40 E2
Zevgaráki [GR] 166 D3
Zeybekçayırı [TR] 164 B2

Zeytinbaği [TR] 158 E4
Zeytindağ [TR] 164 C4
Zeytinli [TR] 164 B2
Zgierz [PL] 48 D3
Zg. Jezersko [SLO] 120 A2
Zgniłocha [PL] 36 F3
Zgórsko [PL] 64 C2
Zgorzelec [PL] 46 D4
Zg. Polskava [SLO] 120 C2
Zg. Polskava [SLO] 120 C2
Zhabinka [BY] 50 D2
Zhaludok [BY] 38 E2
Zhashkiv [UA] 244 F1
Zhedricy [RUS] 232 F4
Zhelezna [BG] 148 D3
Zheleznitsa [BG] 156 B1
Zheleznodorozhnyj [RUS]
  38 A1
Zheleznogorsk [RUS] 242 F2
Zheleznya [RUS] 240 F4
Zhilentsi [BG] 154 E3
Zhilino [RUS] 238 B3
Zhitnica [BG] 156 D1
Zhitom i Madh [AL] 160 B2
Zhitosvyat [BG] 158 B1
Zhlobin [BY] 242 C2
Zhmerynka [UA] 244 E2
Zhodzina [BY] 242 C2
Zhoř [CZ] 60 C3
Zhovkva [UA] 64 F2
Zhovten' [UA] 246 D3
Zhovtneve [UA] 50 E4
Zhuprany [BY] 238 F3
Zhvtkavichy [BY] 242 C3
Zhydachiv [UA] 64 F3
Zhytomyr [UA] 244 E1
Žiar nad Hronom [SK] 76 A2
Zicavo [F] 130 B3
Zickhusen [D] 32 D2
Zidani Most [SLO] 120 B3
Ziddorf [D] 32 E3
Ziębice [PL] 62 C2
Ziegenrück [D] 58 F2
Zieleniec Duzy [PL] 36 F3
Zielona Chocina [PL] 36 B2
Zielona Góra [PL] 46 D3
Zielonczyn [PL] 34 D3
Zielonka [PL] 48 F2
Zieluń [PL] 36 E4
Ziemupe [LV] 234 D3
Zierenberg [D] 42 F3
Zierikzee [NL] 40 D2
Ziersdorf [A] 74 C2
Zierzow [D] 32 E3
Ziesar [D] 44 E2
Ziethen [D] 34 C2
Žiežmariai [LT] 238 D3
Žiguri [LV] 236 E2
Zijpe [NL] 30 A4
Zilina [SK] 62 E4
Ziliz [H] 76 D2
Zilupe [LV] 236 E3
Zimandu Nou [RO] 122 E2
Zimna Woda [PL] 36 F3
Zimnicea [RO] 150 B3
Zimnitsa [BG] 150 D4
Zinal [CH] 116 C2
Zingst [D] 32 F1
Zinnowitz [D] 34 D2
Zinnwald–Georgenfeld [D]
  60 D1
Zinzulusa, Grotta– [I] 136 F3
Zipári [GR] 176 A1
Zirc [H] 74 F4
Zirchow [D] 34 D2
Žiri [SLO] 118 F3
Zirl [A] 72 C4
Ziros [GR] 174 E4
Žirovnice [CZ] 60 E4
Zistersdorf [A] 74 D2
Žitište [SRB] 122 D4

Žitkovac [SRB] 148 B3
Žitni Potok [SRB] 148 B4
Žitomislići [BIH] 152 C2
Žitoradja [SRB] 148 B4
Žitsa [GR] 160 C4
Zittau [D] 60 E1
Živaja [HR] 144 E1
Živinice [BIH] 146 B2
Živogošće [HR] 152 C2
Ziyamet (Leonarisso) [CY]
  176 E2
Zizers [CH] 116 F1
Zlata [SRB] 148 B4
Zlatá Baňa [SK] 76 D1
Zlatá Koruna [CZ] 74 A1
Zlatar [BG] 150 D3
Zlatar Bistrica [HR] 120 C3
Zlatarevo [BG] 154 F4
Zlatari [SRB] 146 F4
Zlaté Hory [CZ] 62 C2
Zlaté Klasy [SK] 74 E3
Zlaté Moravce [SK] 76 A2
Zlatitsa [BG] 156 C1
Zlati voyvoda [BG] 156 F1
Zlatná na Ostrove [SK] 74 F3
Zlatna Panega [BG] 148 E4
Zlatni Pyasŭtsi [BG] 150 E3
Zlatograd [BG] 156 D3
Žleby [CZ] 60 E3
Zliechov [SK] 76 A1
Zlín [CZ] 62 C4
Žljebovi [BIH] 146 B3
Złocieniec [PL] 34 F3
Złoczew [PL] 48 D3
Zlogoš [BG] 154 E2
Zlonice [CZ] 60 D2
Zlot [SRB] 148 B2
Złotniki Kujawskie [PL] 36 C4
Złotoryja [PL] 46 E4
Złotów [PL] 36 B3
Zlotska Pećina [SRB] 148 B2
Złoty Stok [PL] 62 B2
Žlutice [CZ] 60 C2
Zmajevac [HR] 122 B3
Żmigród [PL] 46 F3
Žminj [HR] 144 A1
Zmysłowo [PL] 46 F3
Znamenka [RUS] 232 E3
Znamensk [RUS] 36 F1
Znamianka [UA] 246 E1
Zniev [SK] 76 A1
Žnin [PL] 48 B1
Znojmo [CZ] 74 C2
Zoetermeer [NL] 30 A3
Zoeterwoude [NL] 30 A3
Zofingen [CH] 70 D4
Zogaj [AL] 154 B3
Zolder [D] 40 F3
Żółkiewka–Osada [PL] 50 C4
Żółkow [D] 32 E3
Zollchow [D] 34 C3
Żółtki [PL] 38 C3
Zomba [H] 122 A2
Zonhoven [B] 40 F3
Zóni [GR] 156 F3
Zonza [F] 130 B3
Zoo Svatý Kopeček [CZ] 62 C3
Zörbig [D] 44 E3
Zorge [D] 44 C3
Zorita [E] 100 B2
Zorneding [D] 72 C3
Zornitsa [BG] 158 B1
Żory [PL] 62 D3
Zossen [D] 46 B2
Zoutkamp [NL] 30 D2
Zoutleeuw [B] 40 E3
Zoúzouli [GR] 160 C2
Zovka [RUS] 232 E2
Zreče [SLO] 120 C2
Zrenjanin [SRB] 122 D4

Zrinski Topolovac [HR]
  120 D3
Zrmanja [HR] 144 D3
Zrnovci [MK] 154 E3
Zruč nad Sázavou [CZ] 60 E3
Zrze [KS] 154 C3
Zsadány [H] 122 E1
Zsámbék [H] 76 A4
Zsana [H] 122 C2
Zschopau [D] 60 C1
Zsurk [H] 76 F2
Zuani [F] 130 B2
Zuberec [SK] 62 F4
Zubin Potok [KS] 154 C2
Zubiri [E] 88 A3
Zubné [SK] 64 D4
Zubřič [CZ] 62 C4
Zubrzyca Górna [PL] 62 F3
Zubtsov [RUS] 240 E3
Zudar [D] 34 C2
Zuera [E] 94 D4
Zug [CH] 70 E4
Zuidhorn [NL] 30 D2
Zuidlaren [NL] 30 D2
Zújar [E] 106 B2
Żukow [PL] 50 D3
Żukowo [PL] 36 C2
Žulová [CZ] 62 C2
Zülpich [D] 42 C4
Zumaia / Zumaya [E] 86 D3
Zumarraga [E] 86 E3
Zumaya / Zumaia [E] 86 E3
Žumberk [CZ] 74 B2
Zundert [NL] 40 E2
Zuoz [CH] 116 F2
Żupanja [HR] 146 B1
Žur [KS] 154 C3
Żurawica [PL] 64 D3
Zürich [CH] 70 E3
Żuromin [PL] 36 E4
Żurrieq [M] 140 C4
Zürs [A] 72 A4
Zurzach [CH] 70 E3
Zusmarshausen [D] 72 B2
Züsow [D] 32 E2
Züssow [D] 34 C2
Žuta Lokva [HR] 144 C2
Zutphen [NL] 30 C4
Zuyevo [RUS] 240 C1
Žužemberk [SLO] 120 B3
Zvarisht [AL] 160 C2
Zvečka [SRB] 146 D2
Zvenimir [BG] 150 D2
Zvenyhorodka [UA] 246 D1
Zverevo [RUS] 200 E2
Zvěřínek [CZ] 60 D3
Zvezdel [BG] 156 E3
Zvezdets [BG] 158 B2
Zvíkov [CZ] 60 D4
Zvolen [SK] 76 B2
Zvonce [SRB] 148 C4
Zvornik [BIH] 146 C3
Zweibrücken [D] 56 F3
Zweisimmen [CH] 116 C1
Zwettl [A] 74 B2
Zwettl an der Rodl [A] 74 A2
Zwickau [D] 60 B1
Zwierzno [PL] 36 D2
Zwierzyniec [PL] 64 D1
Zwiesel [D] 72 E1
Zwijndrecht [NL] 30 B4
Zwingenberg [D] 58 C3
Zwoleń [PL] 50 B3
Zwolle [NL] 30 C3
Żychlin [PL] 48 D2
Życiny [PL] 64 B2
Żydowo [PL] 48 B2
Zyel'va [BY] 38 E3
Zygi [CY] 176 D4
Żyrardów [PL] 48 E2
Żywiec [PL] 62 E3
Żywocice [PL] 62 D2

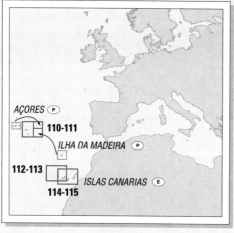

AÇORES (P)
110-111

ILHA DA MADEIRA (P)

112-113

ISLAS CANARIAS (E)

114-115

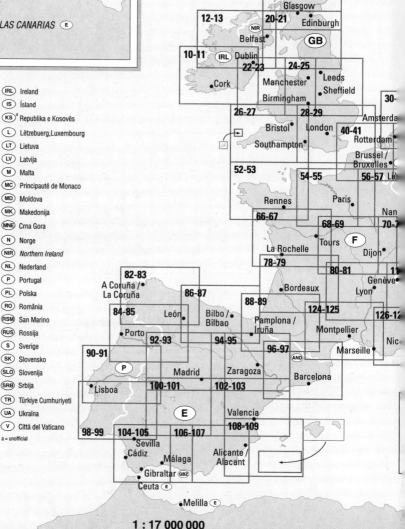

(A) Österreich	(IRL) Ireland
(AL) Shqipëria	(IS) Ísland
(AND) Andorra, Andorre	(KS)ᵃ Republika e Kosovës
(B) België, Belgique	(L) Lëtzebuerg, Luxembourg
(BG) Bălgarija	(LT) Lietuva
(BIH) Bosna i Hercegovina	(LV) Latvija
(BY) Belarus'	(M) Malta
(CH) Schweiz, Suisse, Svizzera	(MC) Principauté de Monaco
(CY) Kýpros, Kıbrıs	(MD) Moldova
(CZ) Česká Republika	(MK) Makedonija
(D) Deutschland	(MNE) Crna Gora
(DK) Danmark	(N) Norge
(E) España	(NIR) Northern Ireland
(EST) Eesti	(NL) Nederland
(F) France	(P) Portugal
(FIN) Suomi, Finland	(PL) Polska
(FL) Fürstentum Liechtenstein	(RO) România
(FR) Føroyar, Færøerne	(RSM) San Marino
(GB) Great Britain	(RUS) Rossija
(GBG) Guernsey, Guernesey	(S) Sverige
(GBJ) Jersey	(SK) Slovensko
(GBM) Isle of Man, Mona	(SLO) Slovenija
(GBZ) Gibraltar	(SRB) Srbija
(GR) Hellas	(TR) Türkiye Cumhuriyeti
(H) Magyarország	(UA) Ukraïna
(HR) Hrvatska	(V) Città del Vaticano
(I) Italia	a = unofficial

1 : 17 000 000

1 cm = 170 km   1 inch = 269.02 miles

0   300   600   900 km

0   250   500 miles